Karl Jaspers

THE PHILOSOPHY

OF

KARL JASPERS

AUGMENTED EDITION
With New Section on Martin Heidegger
in the Philosophical Autobiography

Edited by

PAUL ARTHUR SCHILPP

Southern Illinois University—Carbondale

OPEN COURT PUBLISHING COMPANY
LA SALLE, ILLINOIS 61301

THE PHILOSOPHY OF KARL JASPERS

Printed in the United States of America

ISBN 0-87548-361-5

OC778   10 9 8 7 6 5 4 3 2

The Library of Living Philosophers is published under the sponsorship of Southern Illinois University—Carbondale.

GENERAL INTRODUCTION *
TO
"THE LIBRARY OF LIVING PHILOSOPHERS"

ACCORDING to the late F. C. S. Schiller, the greatest obstacle
to fruitful discussion in philosophy is "the curious etiquette
which apparently taboos the asking of questions about a philosopher's meaning while he is alive." The "interminable controversies which fill the histories of philosophy," he goes on to say, "could
have been ended at once by asking the living philosophers a few
searching questions."

The confident optimism of this last remark undoubtedly goes
too far. Living thinkers have often been asked "a few searching
questions," but their answers have not stopped "interminable controversies" about their real meaning. It is none the less true that
there would be far greater clarity of understanding than is now
often the case, if more such searching questions had been directed
to great thinkers while they were still alive.

This, at any rate, is the basic thought behind the present undertaking. The volumes of *The Library of Living Philosophers* can in
no sense take the place of the major writings of great and original
thinkers. Students who would know the philosophies of such men
as John Dewey, George Santayana, Alfred North Whitehead, Bene-
detto Croce, G. E. Moore, Bertrand Russell, Ernst Cassirer, Karl
Jaspers, *et al.*, will still need to read the writings of these men.
There is no substitute for first-hand contact with the original
thought of the philosopher himself. Least of all does this *Library*
pretend to be such a substitute. The *Library* in fact will spare
neither effort nor expense in offering to the student the best possible guide to the published writings of a given thinker. We shall
attempt to meet this aim by providing at the end of each volume in
our series a complete bibliography of the published work of the
philosopher in question. Nor should one overlook the fact that the
essays in each volume cannot but finally lead to this same goal.
The interpretative and critical discussions of the various phases of

* This *General Introduction*, setting forth the underlying conception of this
Library, is purposely reprinted in each volume (with only very minor changes).

a greater thinker's work and, most of all, the reply of the thinker himself, are bound to lead the reader to the works of the philosopher himself.

At the same time, there is no denying the fact that different experts find different ideas in the writings of the same philosopher. This is as true of the appreciative interpreter and grateful disciple as it is of the critical opponent. Nor can it be denied that such differences of reading and of interpretation on the part of other experts often leave the neophyte aghast before the whole maze of widely varying and even opposing interpretations. Who is right and whose interpretation shall he accept? When the doctors disagree among themselves, what is the poor student to do? If, finally, in desperation, he decides that all of the interpreters are probably wrong and that the only thing for him to do is to go back to the original writings of the philosopher himself and then make his own decision—uninfluenced (as if this were possible) by the interpretation of any one else—the result is not that he has actually come to the meaning of the original philosopher himself, but rather that he has set up one more interpretation, which may differ to a greater or lesser degree from the interpretations already existing. It is clear that in this direction lies chaos, just the kind of chaos which Schiller has so graphically and inimitably described.[1]

It is curious that until now no way of escaping this difficulty has been seriously considered. It has not occurred to students of philosophy that one effective way of meeting the problem at least partially is to put these varying interpretations and critiques before the philosopher while he is still alive and to ask him to act at one and the same time as both defendant and judge. If the world's great living philosophers can be induced to co-operate in an enterprise whereby their own work can, at least to some extent, be saved from becoming merely "dessicated lecture-fodder," which on the one hand "provides innocuous sustenance for ruminant professors," and, on the other hand, gives an opportunity to such ruminants and their understudies to "speculate safely, endlessly, and fruitlessly, about what a philosopher must have meant" (Schiller), they will have taken a long step toward making their intentions clearly comprehensible.

With this in mind, *The Library of Living Philosophers* expects to publish at more or less regular intervals a volume on each of the greater among the world's living philosophers. In each case it will

[1] In his essay on "Must Philosophers Disagree?" in the volume by the same title (Macmillan, London, 1934), from which the above quotations were taken.

be the purpose of the editor of *The Library* to bring together in the volume the interpretations and criticisms of a wide range of that particular thinker's scholarly contemporaries, each of whom will be given a free hand to discuss the specific phase of the thinker's work which has been assigned to him. All contributed essays will finally be submitted to the philosopher with whose work and thought they are concerned, for his careful perusal and reply. And, although it would be expecting too much to imagine that the philosopher's reply will be able to stop all differences of interpretation and of critique, this should at least serve the purpose of stopping certain of the grosser and more general kinds of misinterpretations. If no further gain than this were to come from the present and projected volumes of this *Library*, it would seem to be fully justified.

In carrying out this principal purpose of the *Library*, the editor announces that (in so far as humanly possible) each volume will conform to the following pattern:

First, a series of expository and critical articles written by the leading exponents and opponents of the philosopher's thought;
Second, the reply to the critics and commentators by the philosopher himself;
Third, an intellectual autobiography of the thinker whenever this can be secured; in any case an authoritative and authorized biography; and
Fourth, a bibliography of the writings of the philosopher to provide a ready instrument to give access to his writings and thought.

The editor has deemed it desirable to secure the services of an Advisory Board of philosophers to aid him in the selection of the subjects of future volumes. The names of the six prominent American philosophers who have consented to serve appear below. To each of them the editor expresses his sincere gratitude.

Future volumes in this series will appear in as rapid succession as is feasible in view of the scholarly nature of this *Library*. The next four volumes in this series should be those of C. D. Broad, Rudolf Carnap, Martin Buber, and C. I. Lewis.

The entire project of *The Library of Living Philosophers* still is not on a sound financial foundation, owing to the lack of necessary funds. The *Library* would be deeply grateful, therefore, for gifts and donations. Moreover, since November 6th, 1947, any gifts of donations made to The Library of Living Philosophers, Inc., are deductible by the donors in arriving at their taxable net income in conformity with the Internal Revenue Code of the Treasury Department of the United States of America.

P. A. S.
Editor

DEPARTMENT OF PHILOSOPHY
NORTHWESTERN UNIVERSITY
EVANSTON, ILLINOIS

ADVISORY BOARD

TABLE OF CONTENTS

PREFACE

A VOLUME on the great German philosopher, Karl Jaspers, in our LIBRARY has long been inevitable. Although only a relatively small part of his writings have thus far appeared in English translations, Jaspers' work and ideas are influencing the thinking of philosophers around the world. He is indubitably one of the most seminal minds in the philosophy of the twentieth century.

Yet, there is a sense in which the very title of this book is a misnomer. For, by his own insistence, Jaspers neither has nor espouses a philosophy — he *philosophizes*. For him this distinction is so basic that to speak of "*a* philosophy" is already to have missed the essence of philosophizing. Philosophizing is an activity in which a philosophically inclined mind engages; it is *not* a position he holds, defends, or teaches.

This very insistence already distinguishes Jaspers' type of philosophizing from those of most other philosophers. The uniqueness of Jaspers' procedure comes out, moreover, in his style of writing and in the use of a terminology which is peculiarly Jaspersian. This fact has led to difficulties of translation (into English) which, at times, have seemed almost (if not actually) insuperable.

The reader's attention is called to the Glossary of typical Jaspersian terms, which will be found at the beginning of this volume. It is not too much to say that any reader who fails to use the Glossary and translation (and references to definitions) of Jaspersian terms continuously, will not merely misunderstand much in this book, but is bound to misinterpret much of Jaspers', after all, precise meanings and intent.

The reasons for this are at least two-fold. In the first place, there are a number of terms which either are found only in Jaspers' own use of language or which are given a peculiar meaning by him. Secondly, the translation of some of these peculiarly Jaspersian terms into meaningful and idiomatic English was, in many cases, neither easy nor obvious. In fact, some of these terms were trans-

lated differently by other translators of some of Jaspers' works —
as, for example, *Achsenzeit* (sometimes translated as 'axial period,'
for which we have used 'pivotal age') and *Grenzsituation* (often
translated as either 'border-situation' or 'limiting situation,' which
we have translated by 'ultimate situation'), etc. The difficulties
encountered in translating some of these terms may be seen by the
fact that other translators of Jaspers' works do not agree among
themselves in their respective translations.

The Glossary, we believe, will not merely give the reader the
best possible English terms for those peculiarly Jaspersian ideas,
but gives the best rendering of the actual philosophical meaning
and thought of Jaspers. It will enable the professional philosopher
to check our English terms not merely with Jaspers' own original
(German) words, but will also give him a *definition* of the term,
in most instances in Jaspers' own words.

Two-thirds of the essays in this book reached the editor in
languages other than English. Translating any *one* of them into
both readable and meaningful English proved (— because of the
difficulties and intricacies of Jaspers' philosophical terminology
already mentioned —) to be no simple undertaking. But, to bring
all of the essays at least reasonably into line with each other — so
that the same terms were translated by the same words throughout
the volume —, this turned out to be an almost endless, not to say
insuperable, task. It has, in fact, been one which has literally
stretched out over years of labor and effort. Sometimes we have
found that supposedly identical quotations from Jaspers' works
have, in different essays herein, differed from each other; inasmuch
as each translation was made by a different writer.

All of these difficulties have been multiplied by a fact of which
most German readers of Jaspers' works are well aware, but which
constitutes an unusual — not to say trying — situation, to say the
least. The original German editions of Jaspers' works have appeared — often almost simultaneously — in Germany, in Holland,
and in Switzerland, and sometimes in changed (revised or even
enlarged) editions later on. Although the actual text of many of
those editions was more often than not identical, the pagination
differs. Inasmuch as the editor could not possibly have access to
all of those various editions, the locating of specific quotations has
sometimes been made next to (and even actually) impossible.
Quotations from Jaspers' works are, consequently, in each instance, cited by the pagination of the particular text or edition
which the essayist himself used (except wherever English trans-

lations were already available, in which case we have tried to cite the pagination — and text — of the official English text) .

Inasmuch, however, as we have tried to hold, as much as possible, to a consistent use of our (English) terms of Jaspers' terminology, we have sometimes chosen to render quotations from Jaspers in our translation even when the respective work was already available in English translation. In such instances the reader may find the reference given either to the English translation (as revised by us) or to the German original.

At the beginning of the volume the reader will also find a List of Abbreviations used for all of Jaspers' major works. These abbreviations have been used throughout the book.

The editor's gratitude in getting this volume before the public is due to a large number of persons (to many more, in fact, than can here be mentioned) . First and foremost among these is, of course, Professor Jaspers himself, who, with unfailing courtesy and helpfulness, has co-operated in the production of this book. His straight-forward and honest Autobiography constitutes literally a landmark of such writing, which is bound to create widespread interest. And his "Reply to My Critics" is positively exemplary. This all the more so because he does not shrink back from replying to sharp criticism in equally as sharp a fashion. Such a lucid exchange of ideas should aid greatly in clarifying issues and meanings, and constitutes in itself the *raison d'être* for the very existence of this LIBRARY.

The willingness of the twenty-four contributors to this volume to give of their valuable time and effort to write and compose their essays is, obviously, just as deeply appreciated. Without their kind, courteous and helpful co-operation, this volume could not have come into existence. To each of them we express here our sincere gratitude and profound appreciation.

Our sincere gratitude is due also to Dr. Kurt Rossmann, Heidelberg, for his great kindness in making available for our use the Bibliography of the Writings of Karl Jaspers, which he had prepared for the *Festschrift* to Jaspers' 70th birthday in 1953, and which, in addition, he was so kind as to bring up to date for the present volume. The adaptation of this Bibliography for our English readers was prepared by Dr. Ludwig B. Lefebre.

This brings me to the mentioning of a debt of gratitude which is difficult to pay. Without the helpful co-operation, generous aid, and first-hand knowledge of Jaspers' ways of thinking of Dr. Ludwig B. Lefebre of San Francisco, California, this volume would, I suppose, have seen the light of publication some day, but it could never have been what it now is. The task of correlating different contributors' (and translators') translations of Jaspersian technical terms had — as has already been mentioned — become an endless and practically insuperable one until Dr. Lefebre, most kindly and generously, came to the editor's aid and relief. He not merely checked all essays against each other and against Jaspers' own terminology, but he even undertook to re-translate some of the essays all over again. In addition, he carefully checked and revised the editor's own translations of Jaspers' Autobiography and "Reply." Almost single-handedly he is responsible for the Glossary, an undertaking, by itself, of no mean proportions. During the last eighteen months of the work on this volume, Dr. Lefebre proved to be more nearly the Associate Editor than merely the editor's assistant. Everyone who reads and profits from this volume owes Dr. Lefebre a debt of gratitude which can neither be paid for nor fully expressed in words.

* * * * * *

The order in which the contributed essays appear, in Part II, was worked out on the basis of the following scheme. At the outset there appear seven essays (cc. 1-7) which treat some specific and basic concepts in Jaspers' philosophizing — concepts, without a clear understanding of which no real comprehension of Jaspers' philosophizing is possible. These are followed by three essays (cc. 8-10) which concern themselves with Jaspers' relation to other thinkers. In the third group the reader will find four essays (cc. 11-14) which discuss Jaspers as psychopathologist and as philosophical anthropologist. The fourth group consists of four essays (cc. 15-18) dealing with Jaspers' thought in the areas of political science and of the philosophy of history. In the fifth group will be found four essays (cc. 19-22) which treat of Jaspers' ideas in religion and concerning religious movements. The concluding group consists of two essays (cc. 23-24) which discuss Jaspers' relation to art, to poetry, and to literary criticism.

* * * * * *

The editor also wishes to express his sincere gratitude to the Graduate Research Council of Northwestern University for a small grant-in-aid to help defray some of the costs of translations in this volume.

The editorial work on Vols. X and XI of this LIBRARY is nearing completion. They will deal with *The Philosophy of C. D. Broad* and *The Philosophy of Rudolf Carnap,* respectively. Besides these, two additional volumes are in various stages of prep aration.

The editor dare not let this opportunity pass to express publicly his very great personal regret that two volumes, which were supposed to have dealt with the philosophies of Jacques Maritain and Étienne Gilson respectively, — and which had previously been promised and been announced —, have had to be cancelled. In both instances this was due to the fact that Messrs. Maritain and Gilson — after having previously agreed to co-operate with us in the production of a volume on their respective philosophy — found it necessary to withdraw their previous acceptance of the editor's invitation. The philosophical world will be the poorer for these negative decisions.

PAUL ARTHUR SCHILPP
Editor

"ROCKRIDGE," CABIN IN
THE SIERRA NEVADA
CALIFORNIA, JULY 26, 1956

PREFACE TO THE NEW EDITION

This augmented edition of our *Jaspers* volume includes an exceedingly important *new* section in Jaspers' "Philosophical Autobiography" — Section X/I, titled "Heidegger."

Professor Jaspers had written the autobiography specifically for the original (1957) edition of this volume. When I first read Jaspers' manuscript in Basel on September 18, 1953, the "Heidegger" section *was* part of it. But the next day Jaspers told me that he would probably omit this section, at least until after Heidegger's death. And indeed he did withdraw it.

Jaspers died in 1969 and Heidegger in 1976. In 1977 Jaspers' literary executor, Dr. Hans Saner (Basel), in agreement with Jaspers' instructions, edited the autobiography and published it as a separate book in German, retaining the original title *(Philosophische Autobiographie)* and including for the first time in print the section on Heidegger. The volume was published by R. Piper and Co. Verlag, München.

Through the kindness and cooperation of Dr. Saner, who granted permission for the translation and English publication of the "Heidegger" section, we are now able to present the complete, unexpurgated edition of the autobiography. My esteemed colleague Professor Hans H. Rudnick of Southern Illinois University at Carbondale was kind enough to translate the new section, and I was pleased to go over it with him.

Any student of either Jaspers or Heidegger will undoubtedly be much interested in the "Heidegger" section, a revealing and moving story of the relations between these two great German philosophers from 1913 to 1953. I think this segment says almost as much about Jaspers as it does about Heidegger. In any case, it is a document of such historical value that it warrants the publication of this new edition.

PAUL ARTHUR SCHILPP
Editor

DEPARTMENT OF PHILOSOPHY
SOUTHERN ILLINOIS UNIVERSITY AT CARBONDALE
JANUARY 1981

GLOSSARY

TRANSLATIONS and DEFINITIONS
of terms used by JASPERS

Prepared by Ludwig B. Lefebre

Note: Some of the terms listed below (e.g., "anguish") are included not because their translation represents a problem, but because we consider it helpful to define the specific meaning of the term in Jaspers' work. Wherever possible we are quoting definitions from Jaspers' own works, including the essays "Philosophical Autobiography" and "Reply to my Critics" which appear in this volume. Where a name appears after a definition (in place of the title of a book) it refers to an author and his essay in the present volume.

ENGLISH	GERMAN	DEFINITION
absolute consciousness	absolutes Bewusstsein	... the *signum* for the consciousness of *Existenz* ...

		The consciousness of authentic Being out of unconditional origin. *Philosophie*, 515
anguish Note: This translation of "Angst" was chosen, in preference to "dread," in order to distinguish Jaspers' concept from that of Sartre. Cf.: Thyssen, 329 (Ed.'s note).	Angst	. . . the dizziness and shudder of freedom confronting the necessity of making a choice. *Philosophie, 522*
athwart of time	quer zur Zeit	. . . (outside) the limited temporality of the historical moment. Thyssen, (301f)
Being Note: "Being" is capitalized if it refers to "transcendental" Being, of which all other being is appearance, or for which it is cipher. Cf.: Transcendence and cipher.	Sein	Being can not, according to Jaspers, be defined unequivocally. Being is not produced by us; it is not mere interpretation . . . Rather, by its own impetus, it causes us to interpret and will not permit our interpretation ever to be satisfied. *Wahrheit,* 84 Authentic reality. Latzel, (180) The One and Only, the Unconditional — Infinite, and, as such, the all-encompassing and all-transcending primal source. Pfeiffer, (716)
being as freedom	Sein als Freiheit	The mode of my being as *Existenz*. In this sense I am origin: not the origin of Being as such, but origin for myself in existence *(Dasein)*. *Philosophie,* 15
being as status	Sein als Bestand	Being which must be ack-

nowledged is directly there as a thing. I can grasp it directly, do something with it: technically with the things, argumentatively with myself and with other consciousness . . . Everywhere it is an objectively being given. *Philosophie,* 15

boundary (Cf.: ultimate situation)	Grenze	
cipher	Chiffer or Chiffre	Metaphysical objectivity is called cipher, because it is not itself Transcendence, but the language of Transcendence. *Philosophie,* 786
communication	Kommunikation	. . . the process . . . in which the self . . . becomes itself . . . in its relation with the other self . . . (It) obtains only from man to man in mutual reciprocity. "Reply," (785)
consciousness-as-such	Bewusstsein überhaupt	One of the four modes of the *Being that we are.* Cf.: Existence, spirit and *Existenz.* . . . The comprehensive consciousness in which everything that is can be known, recognized, intended as an object. *Scope,* 12, 13
encipherment	Chifferwerden	Transmutation of the world into a mediation between us and the unique God is its transmutation into cipher. *Wahrheit,* 1051
Encompassing, the	Umgreifende, das	. . . either the *Being in itself* that surrounds us (Cf.: world and Transcendence) or the *Being that we are* (Cf.: existence, consciousness-as-such, spirit and *Existenz*). *Scope,* 12

		What is neither object nor act-of-thinking (subject), but contains both within itself. "Autobiography," (73) . . . that within which every particular horizon is enclosed as in something absolutely comprehensive which is no longer visible as a horizon at all. *Reason*, 52
'exist', *to* (italicized only if used as the verb of *Existenz;* cf.: *Existenz*)	existieren	Life *sub specie aeternitatis.* Löwenstein, (650)
existence (when the term applies to man)	Dasein	One of the four modes of the *Being that we are.* Cf.: consciousness-as-such, spirit and *Existenz.* . . . is the finding of itself on the part of Being . . . expressed (in such sayings) as: 'I am here,' 'we are here.' *Wahrheit, 53* The concrete physio-psychological individual. Thyssen, (299f)
'existential' (italicized only if used as the adjective of *Existenz;* cf.: *Existenz*) Note: "Existential," whenever it occurs in this volume *not* in *italics* or single quotes, has the ordinary meaning found in dictionaries.	existentiell	The adjectival use of *Existenz.* Cf.: *Existenz.*
Existenz	Existenz	One of the four modes of the *Being that we are.* Cf.: consciousness-as-such, existence and spirit.

		. . . is being a self suspended between itself and Transcendence from which it derives its being and on which it is based. *Existenz,* 17
		. . . is what never becomes object, the origin from which issues my thinking and acting . . . *Philosophie,* I, 15
Existenz, illumination of	Existenzerhellung	. . . The *ascertainment in thought* (of) breaking through worldly existence . . . *Philosophie,* 301
		Clarification of the potentialities open to man by appealing to them. Earle, (525)
explanation (when used as a p s y c h o l o g i c a l term)	Erklären	The recognition of objective causal relationships which are always observed from the outside only . . . *Allgemeine,* 24
		Viewing of psychological data in terms of a cause and effect relationship. Lefebre, (475f)
		Cf.: *Verstehen*
foundering	Scheitern	. . . signifies the fruitlessness of all endeavors to reach, from a finite basis such as consciousness-as-such or even from self-sufficient *Existenz,* a satisfactory access to Being, i.e., to arrive at the absolute. Thyssen, (312)
law of the day	Gesetz des Tages	The *law of the day* orders our existence, demands clarity, consistence and loyalty, binds us to reason and idea, to the One and to ourselves. It demands actualization in the world, that we build within time,

		that we complete our existence on an endless road. *Philosophie,* 762 The principle of order, clarity and loyalty ... Hoffman, (107) Cf.: Passion for the night.
leap from anguish to calm	Sprung von Angst zur Ruhe	The leap which reveals reality. *Philosophie,* III, 235ff
limit (Cf.: ultimate situation)	Grenze	
naught	Nichts, das	. . . (has) two opposite meanings: (it) . . . is, for one thing, *actually nothing* . . . (it) . . . also is *authentic Being as the non-Being of everything definite. Philosophie,* 712
passion for the night	Leidenschaft zur Nacht	The *passion for the night* breaks through every order . . . it is the urge to ruin oneself in the world in order to complete oneself in the depth of worldlessness. *Philosophie* 763 Antithesis to reason. Thyssen, (317) The irrational urge to darkness, to the earth, to the mother, to the race, to ruin and the end of all order. Hoffman, (107) Cf.: Law of the day
phenomenology	Phänomenologie	Illustrative representation of individual experience; an empirical method designed to define experienced mental states. *Allgemeine,* 47
philosophical faith Note: At times "belief" is used as translation for "Glaube."	philosophischer Glaube	(A) faith which communicates itself in the thinking of reason. "Reply," (777)

pivotal age	Achsenzeit	(An age where) man, as we know him today, came into being . . . (the) period around 500 B.C. . . . (lasting from 800 to 200 B.C. approximately). *Origin*, 1
reality	Wirklichkeit	Eternity in time. "Reply," (832)
reason	Vernunft	. . . what goes beyond all limits, the omnipresent demand of thought that not only grasps what is universally valid and is an *ens rationis* in the sense of being a law or principle of order of some process, but also brings to light the Other, stands before the absolutely counter-rational, touching it and bringing it, too, into being. *Reason*, 65
self-awareness	Innesein	A philosophical act which aims at attaining clarity regarding itself, which wants to communicate and which strives, for this reason, to become comprehensible and to retain self-control even at its extreme limits. Knauss, (150f)
spirit	**Geist**	One of the four modes of the *Being that we are*. Cf.: existence, consciousness-as-such and *Existenz*. . . . the Encompassing which we are as beings who, in the movement of understanding and being understood, realize totality. *Wahrheit*, 71
Transcendence	Transzendenz	One of two modes of the *Being that surrounds us*. Cf.: World. The source and the goal,

		both of which lie in God and out of whose depths alone we really become authentically human. *Rechenschaft,* 264
		. . . in the real sense (is) . . the Encompassing as such, the Encompassing of every Encompassing . . . Compared with general Transcendence belonging to each mode of the Encompassing, this Transcendence is the Transcendence of all Transcendence. *Wahrheit,* 109
transcending	Transzendieren	. . . going beyond (in thought) . . . a specific objectivity to become aware of its Encompassing. *Wahrheit,* 109
transparent, become	transparent werden	This concept expresses Jaspers' view that empirical being is capable of letting Transcendence "shine through." Thyssen, (306)
ultimate situation Note: "Grenze" means "boundary" or "limit" in German. Although it is felt that "ultimate situation" captures Jaspers' meaning best, the other meanings should be kept in mind.	Grenzsituation	Situations such as the fact that I am always in situations, that I cannot live without conflict and suffering, that I unavoidably incur guilt, that I must die . . . *Philosophie,* 469
Verstehen	Verstehen	Perception of mental phenomena from within . . . *Allgemeine,* 24 Knowledge based on the intuitional comprehension of "understandable" processes. Manasse, (372) Comprehension of mean-

		ingful psychological relations demonstrating an "inner causality" as opposed to the "outer (genuine) causality" discovered by explanation. Lefebre, (476) Cf.: Explanation
Weltanschauung	Weltanschauung	. . . ideas, what is ultimate and complete in man, both subjectively as experience, power and conviction, and objectively as the formed world of objects. *Psychologie,* 1
world	Welt	One of two modes of the *Being that surrounds us.* Cf.: Transcendence . . . the being of which one aspect of our essence constitutes an infinitesimal part, if the world as a whole be considered as something that is not ourselves and in which we are immersed . . . *Scope,* 12
world-orientation	Weltorientierung	Knowledge of existing objects. *Philosophie,* 25 Philosophy on the level of existence. Hoffman, (97)

ABBREVIATIONS for those of Jaspers' works which are frequently quoted by contributors to this volume. Those of Jaspers' works which are available in both English-language and German-language editions appear twice in the list below.

TITLE	ABBREVIATION USED
ALLGEMEINE PSYCHOPATHOLOGIE	*Allgemeine*
DESCARTES UND DIE PHILOSOPHIE	*Descartes*
EINFÜHRUNG IN DIE PHILOSOPHIE	*Einführung*
(WAY TO WISDOM)	*(Wisdom)*
EXISTENTIALISM AND HUMANISM*	*Humanism*
EXISTENZPHILOSOPHIE	*Existenz*
GEISTIGE SITUATION DER ZEIT, DIE	
(MAN IN THE MODERN AGE)	*Situation (Age)*
IDEE DER UNIVERSITÄT, DIE (1923)	*Universität (I)*
IDEE DER UNIVERSITÄT, DIE (1946; not identical	
with above)	*Universität (II)*
MAN IN THE MODERN AGE (GEISTIGE SITUA-	
TION DER ZEIT, DIE)	*Age (Situation)*
MAX WEBER (II)	*Monograph*
NIETZSCHE, EINFÜHRUNG IN DAS VERSTÄNDNIS	
SEINES PHILOSOPHIERENS	*Nietzsche*
NIETZSCHE UND DAS CHRISTENTUM	*Christentum*
ORIGIN AND GOAL OF HISTORY, THE	
(URSPRUNG UND ZIEL DER	
GESCHICHTE, VOM)	*Origin (Ursprung)*
PERENNIAL SCOPE OF PHILOSOPHY, THE	
(DER PHILOSOPHISCHE GLAUBE)	*Scope (Glaube)*
PHILOSOPHICAL AUTOBIOGRAPHY	*Autobiography*
PHILOSOPHIE	*Philosophie*
PHILOSOPHISCHE GLAUBE, DER (THE	
PERENNIAL SCOPE OF PHILOSOPHY)	*Glaube (Scope)*
PSYCHOLOGIE DER WELTANSCHAUUNGEN	*Psychologie*
QUESTION OF GERMAN GUILT, THE (DIE	
SCHULDFRAGE)	*Question (Schuld)*

*Contains three essays originally published in German periodicals. If authors quote any of these essays, footnotes will refer to *Humanism*.

REASON AND ANTI-REASON IN OUR TIME
   (VERNUNFT UND WIDERVERNUNFT IN   *Anti-reason*
   UNSERER ZEIT)   *(Widervernunft)*
REASON AND EXISTENZ (VERNUNFT UND
   EXISTENZ)   *Reason (Vernunft)*
RECHENSCHAFT UND AUSBLICK**   *Rechenschaft*
REPLY TO MY CRITICS   *Reply*
SCHULDFRAGE, DIE (QUESTION OF GERMAN
   GUILT, THE)   *Schuld (Question)*
STRINDBERG UND VAN GOGH   *Strindberg*
TRAGEDY IS NOT ENOUGH (excerpt from VON
   DER WAHRHEIT)   *Tragedy*
URSPRUNG UND ZIEL DER GESCHICHTE, VOM
   (ORIGIN AND GOAL OF HISTORY, THE)   *Ursprung (Origin)*
VERNUNFT UND EXISTENZ (REASON AND
   EXISTENZ)   *Vernunft (Reason)*
VERNUNFT UND WIDERVERNUNFT IN UNSERER
   ZEIT (REASON AND ANTI-REASON IN OUR   *Widervernunft*
   TIME)   *(Anti-reason)*
VON DER WAHRHEIT (excerpt: TRAGEDY IS NOT
   ENOUGH)   *Wahrheit*
WAY TO WISDOM (EINFÜHRUNG IN DIE   *Wisdom*
   PHILOSOPHIE)   *(Einführung)*

**Contains twenty-two not readily available essays. Quotes will be
   handled as described above (*).

Karl Jaspers

PHILOSOPHICAL AUTOBIOGRAPHY

Karl Jaspers

PHILOSOPHICAL AUTOBIOGRAPHY

SYNOPSIS

FACSIMILE REPRODUCTION OF KARL JASPERS' HANDWRITING – FROM HIS "REPLY"

Karl Jaspers

PHILOSOPHICAL AUTOBIOGRAPHY *

P ROFESSOR Schilpp has asked me for an account which
would show how my life experiences led me to philosophize,
what I was looking for on this road, and how my writings came
about. The task seemed appropriate to me, at any rate, for a person of my age. For, all philosophy — because it is an activity of
the human spirit — is, in its themes as well as its causes, intimately
connected with the life of the person who is philosophizing.

This connection is present even if this life, like my own, was
simple and secluded and is devoid of any happenings that could
make it universally interesting or, at any rate, could arouse only
that interest which each human life may have for other persons.

Although there is nothing in the actuality of everyday life that
would not, in some way, be related to philosophy, I shall confine
my report to those facts which became directly significant for my
writings; and even in regard to them I shall make a restricted
selection. Thus I shall speak of only a few of the experiences which
were described or reflected in my writings. And as to the people
to whom I owe so much, I shall not speak of those whose very
being was disclosed to me in our friendship, but I shall only discuss those whose thinking as such had a direct influence on my
work.

Furthermore, I shall not render a comprehensive account of the
ideas expressed in my writings and even less argue their factual
justification. They will be mentioned in part only, but will nowhere be discussed in detail. They will be interpreted as reactions to life situations, but always with the aim in mind to make
their timeless meaning felt.

I. CHILDHOOD AND YOUTH

I was born on February 23, 1883, in Oldenburg, close to the
coast of the North Sea. My father (1850-1940) was descended
from a family of merchants and farmers who had been living for

* From the original German manuscript, written expressly for this volume,
translated by Paul Arthur Schilpp and Ludwig B. Lefebre.

generations in the district of Jever; he became a jurist, high con-
stable of the district, and director of a bank. He discharged his
duties meticulously and with devotion. His favorite pursuits,
however, were painting and hunting. He reared me — by his example as well as in decisive moments, by his judgment — in a
spirit of reason, reliability, and faithfulness. My mother (1862-
1941) descended from a family of farmers, who since time immemorial had been established in Butjadingen. It was her infinite
love which made my childhood and that of my brother and sister
sunny and our later years exceedingly happy. Her boundless
vigor and spirit filled us with courage and determination; her
deep understanding of our aims and ideals, which far transcended
all conventionality, stimulated our enthusiasm; her wisdom gave
us warmth and the assurance of security.

At the humanistic *Gymnasium,* which I attended, I got into
trouble with the principal. I refused to obey blindly certain regulations which seemed to me unreasonable. My father had brought
me up in such a way that, at a very early age already, I expected
to receive an answer from him to every question I would ask and,
furthermore, not to be compelled ever to do anything the meaning of which was not clear to me — be it even out of a sense of
reverence for the traditional which as such would have the power
of persuasion. Thus instructed by my father, I upheld the principle that there was a difference between the necessary order in a
classroom and that of military discipline, which was being introduced into school life without any justification. Such an attitude
betrays a spirit of rebellion, I was one day solemnly told by the
principal. He was aware, he said, that it was rampant in my family.
He most emphatically rejected such a spirit. Our disagreement
reached its climax when I refused to join one of the three school
fraternities — patterned after university-students' fraternities —
which had been approved by the principal. The reasons I stated to
account for my refusal to enter such a "fraternity" were that these
groups made distinctions on the basis of the social status and
occupation of the parents and not on that of personal friendship.
I found myself completely alone in my point of view. My fellow-
students, having originally shown a sympathetic understanding,
later actually rejected my attitude. When a friend of mine had
accompanied me on a week's hiking trip in the mountains, his
fraternity threatened to expel him unless he discontinued his
friendly association with me. When he spoke to me about this
matter, I gave him the advice to stay in the fraternity. This he did.
But the principal made it clear to me that my teachers would keep

a watchful eye on me. My father tried to compensate me for what I had lost. He leased large hunting grounds. Now I could spend my spare time in a great diversity of magnificently beautiful scenery, according to my heart's desire.

The external data of my further life are quickly told. After my graduation (*Abiturium*) from the *Gymnasium* I was matriculated for three semesters as a student of jurisprudence. Then I enrolled as a student of medicine, passed, in 1908, the medical state examination, and received the degree of Doctor of Medicine in 1909. I now started to work as a (voluntary) assistant in the psychiatric hospital of the University of Heidelberg. In 1913 I habilitated myself as *Privatdozent* in psychology in the Philosophical Faculty. In 1921 I became a full professor of philosophy there, after I had declined offers of positions from the universities of Greifswald and Kiel. In 1928 I declined a call to the University of Bonn. In 1937 the National-Socialist regime deprived me of my professional status; but in 1945 I was again re-instated in my office with the consent of the American occupation authorities. In 1948 I accepted a call to the University of Basel, where I am teaching at present.

The course of my inner (intellectual and spiritual) development during my youth deserves at least a few brief pointers. At the age of seventeen I read Spinoza. He became my philosopher. But I had no intention whatsoever of making philosophy my major subject of study or my occupation. On the contrary, I studied law for three semesters, with the purpose of later making the practice of law my life's work. However, the abstractions which were used to refer to social life — a life still entirely unknown to me — proved so disappointing that I occupied myself instead with poetry, art, graphology, and the theatre, always turning to something else. Though unhappy in this state of dispersion, I was happy in particular experiences of greatness, especially in art.

I was discontent with myself and with the state of society, with the false beliefs prevalent in public life. My fundamental reaction was: something is radically wrong not merely with humanity, but also with myself; at the same time, however, I felt the magnificence of that other world, namely, of nature, of art, of poetry, and of science. I retained a basic faith in life — an elemental confidence which preceded everything else — which was inspired by my beloved parents, in whose solicitude I found a sense of security. My choice of a walk of life was my own private decision.

How magnificent the solitude in nature untouched! I enjoyed it in Sils-Maria (Engadin) and on the shores of the North Sea.

How enrapturing the contemplation of beauty in Italy! On journeys I was swept off my feet.

But solitude always became painful after I had indulged it a
while. I felt drawn to people. What should I do? Life had to find
a foundation; for however marvelous specific experiences, scatter-
ing one's attention among them had a devastating effect. It became necessary to enter upon a concrete path of leading one's own
life; above all my university studies now had to have a (definite)
goal. I wanted to discover what knowledge is possible; medicine
seemed to me to open the widest vista, having all of the natural
sciences and man himself as its object of investigation. As a
physician I could find my justification in society.

I made this decision, in 1902, while at Sils-Maria. In a memorandum which I prepared for my parents and in which I asked for
their consent to my change of study from jurisprudence to medicine, I wrote in my clumsy way of writing at that time: "My plan
is the following: I shall take my medical state examination after
the prescribed number of semesters. If then I still believe — as I
do now — to possess the necessary talent for it, I shall transfer to
psychiatry and psychology. After that I shall first of all start practicing as a physician in a mental hospital. Eventually I might enter
upon an academic career as a psychologist, as for example Kraepelin in Heidelberg — something which I would not, however, care
to express because of the uncertainty and of its being dependent
upon my capacities. . . . Therefore, I had best state it this way:
I am going to study medicine in order to become a physician in
a health resort or a specialist, e.g., a doctor for the mentally ill.
To myself I add: the rest will come if and when. And finally, once
I have got that far, and then should not have the courage nor believe myself to possess the necessary qualifications to enter upon
an academic career, I shall not at all be dissatisfied."

In my choice of medicine what was of greatest importance to me
was to learn to know actuality. I strove to achieve this aim by
every means at my disposal. In my studies I was diligent and I
enjoyed to the full the numerous possibilities of acquiring knowledge. In my travels I sought to accomplish whatever was possible
in the way of gaining firsthand acquaintance with various regions,
historical cities, and of works of art.

In all this, however, the basic question, viz., how one ought to
live, remained unsolved. The pursuit of my studies was something preliminary. It was at the same time useful as a preparation
for a profession. But that is not life itself. Without reading the
philosophers, using all my time to study the concrete subjects of my

field, I was nevertheless continually philosophizing, even though unsystematically (unmethodically). Philosophy courses in the University I soon dropped. Against philosophy professors I had an antipathy because they did not treat what really mattered most to me. As persons they appeared arrogant and opinionated. As a personality only Theodor Lipps in Munich made an impression on me. However, the content of his lectures scarcely interested me — with the exception of the geometro-optical illusions, to the knowledge of which he had contributed in an ingenious fashion. That, however, was only one specialized problem in the field of psychology.

All of life's decisions were partially conditioned for me by a basic fact of my existence. From childhood I had been organically ill (bronchiectasis with cardiac decompensation). While hunting I sat many times bitterly crying somewhere in the seclusion of the forest, as the strength of my body failed me. Not until I was eighteen years of age did Albert Fraenkel in Badenweiler make the correct diagnosis. Until then I suffered frequent attacks of fever as a result of the false treatment of my ailment. Now I learned to arrange my life on the basis of the conditions imposed on me by this disease. I read an essay by R. Virchow which described my illness in every detail and made the following prognosis: "Those afflicted with this disease will die of pyemia in their thirties at the latest." I realized what really mattered in treating it. Gradually I acquired the methods of treatment which in part I invented myself. It was impossible to carry them out correctly if I followed the manner of life of normally healthy people. If I want to get any work done, I shall have to risk doing what is harmful to my health; on the other hand, if I want to stay alive, I shall have to apply the strictest discipline by avoiding everything harmful. Between these two poles my life has had to be run. It was often inevitable to sink beneath one's own level by allowing fatigue and poisoning of the body to set in; and it became necessary constantly to recover from such a state. The illness was not to become the chief concern of life by constantly worrying about it. The task was to treat it, almost without being aware of it, correctly and to work as if the illness did not exist. Everything had to conform to it, without becoming victimized by it. Again and again I made mistakes. The requirements which resulted from my illness encroached on every hour and on all my plans. I shall omit here an elaborate account of the concrete course of my illness, something I should like to do at another time.

As a consequence of my illness I was unable to participate in the joyful diversions of youth. Hiking became completely impossible for me as early as in my student days. I was likewise unable to go horseback riding, swimming, or dancing. The illness kept me from bodily excesses. Furthermore, it made military service impossible and with it soldier's death in wartime. "One must be sick in order to get old," says a Chinese proverb. It is astonishing how strong a love of good health can develop in a chronic, stationary disease. The degree of health kept becomes all the more conscious, affords the more happiness, and becomes perhaps even more healthy than any normal state of good health.

Another consequence of my illness was a certain inner attitude which determined my manner of working. Because of constant interruptions, life had to become more concentrated, if one wanted to lead a meaningful life at all. I had to rely on a relaxed manner of doing my studies, on grasping the essentials, on suddenness of inspiration and on speed of making outlines at some favorable moment. My chance lay in tenacious endeavor to seize every good moment and continue working under all circumstances.

Still another consequence of my illness was that I could make appearances in public only as long as certain careful precautions were taken and the appearance was brief. Only in very exceptional cases, of great importance, did I venture to travel to give lectures and to participate in public discussions, and always at the price of upsetting the normal state of my health.

Finally I was dependent, in all my social life, upon the kind attitude of those who would permit me to disregard the forms of social etiquette, who would come to me and be satisfied with a brief visit of from one to two hours. Often I was not understood. People would interpret as pride and aloofness what actually was bitter necessity.

The clarity of my thinking was scarcely blurred by the inhibitions and conditions which resulted from my illness. My character, however, was indeed veiled by this enforced loneliness in spite of the fact that I came to know many people and in spite of the friend I had in the person of Fritz zur Loye. Frequently I was overcome by melancholy. In such moments I thought that everything would soon be at an end anyway. But still more frequently I was literally lifted by a sense of marvelous expectancy of what might still possibly be accomplished.

My friend Fritz zur Loye, who died at an early age, came from my own province and was very much like myself; so that, during our first years of university study, we were intimate associates. Our studies constituted the real bond between us. Together we worked at the microscope and did our experiments. The mood existing between us was sober. I felt his frankness with which he dealt with me in my illness — without any pitying silence — as beneficent. Rather he accepted it as a factor which had to be taken into account in every undertaking. "I am going dancing today at Mariaspring. You can't go along, it would be too strenuous for you . . ." Or just before a field trip of the class in botany: "That'll take too long; you would not be able to endure it . . ." In such fashion he dealt with the sacrifices I was compelled to make. To make up for it, he would report to me in brief descriptions whatever he had seen or experienced. A dependable affection united us. We were students together in Munich, Berlin, and Göttingen, took a course in graphology with Klages, attended the theatre. He liked my industry despite my affliction. A loving irony placed everything in the proper light and perspective. In Göttingen we attended the lectures of a physicist, Riecke, whom we respected but otherwise did not particularly like. He had written a two volume textbook. "What Riecke is able to do," my friend said to me, "you can do too. You will be writing textbooks some day and become a professor."

My reserve in the presence of people had the appearance of cool indifference. This was part of my heritage which I owed to my native region. It was founded, moreover, on the fact that I did not expect too much from people, and it was intensified by occasional disappointments. But this reserve was actually a painful restraint; in my soul there was something altogether different.

Loneliness, melancholy, self-consciousness, all that changed when I, at the age of twenty-four, met Gertrud Mayer. Unforgettable when, accompanied by her brother, I first entered her room! She sat at a large desk, arose, with her back still towards the visitor, she slowly closed a book and turned toward us. I followed each of her movements, which, in her quiet clarity, without artificiality or conventionality, unconsciously seemed to express the essence of purity, the nobility of her soul in her (very) appearance. It was as if self-evident that the conversation soon turned to the basic questions of life, as if we had already known each other for a long time. From the very first hour there was between us an inconceivable harmony, something never expected to be possible.

Yet, the difference between our respective dispositions was extraordinarily great. Gertrud's spirit had been darkened by severe blows of fate, which she could not take with her into a life which was supposed to take its course unquestioningly. Her only sister was a victim of a lingering uncanny mental disease, which made

her constant confinement in an institution necessary. A philosophically minded friend of Gertrud's, the poet Walter Calé, had
taken his own life.

In contrast to me, who was suffering only from my own illness,
the very foundations of things had been torn asunder for her, leading to insoluble questions. In her I saw the reality of a soul which
refused to live by illusions. She was capable of infinite endurance
in silence.

In her my own affirmation of life encountered the spirit who
from now on would prevent any premature acquiescence on my
part. Now philosophy began, in a new way, to become a serious
concern for me. We found ourselves united in its pursuit, but had
not reached the goal. Thus it has remained until to-day throughout a long life together.

The gloom and consciousness of constant danger induced an
inescapable seriousness in her. But, out of this soil grew the infinite
happiness of her immediate presence. I experienced the deep satisfaction of love which has been able to give meaning to each day
even until now.

Gertrud comes from a pious Jewish family, which since the 17th
century has been living in the Province of Brandenburg. When
we met in 1907, Gertrude was in the midst of preparing for the
Abiturium, which she planned to take as an extern, in order to
pursue graduate university studies. Her goal was philosophy. The
experience she had gained as a psychiatric nurse had not been
able to keep her interested in this profession. She now was daily
studying Greek and Latin. When, in 1910, we had been married,
a cordial, mutual affection and complete confidence bound me to
my parents-in-law. The father had gotten over his (initial) antipathy against the marriage of his daughter to a non-Jew, and the
mother had found her pious expectations as to her daughter's love
confirmed.

During the years of National-Socialism we were confronted by
catastrophies in our proximity as well as in our wider environment, which again and again we considered inescapable even for
ourselves; yet we never entirely gave up hope. We seemed to be
miraculously protected as we were spared the worst fate. Being thus
spared, yet, in view of our own survival, having a sense of shared
guilt, we felt increasingly challenged to live right and to work to
the very limits of our capacity.

II. "Psychopathologie"

From 1908 until 1915 I was working in the psychiatric hospital in Heidelberg, in the beginning, right after my State Examination, as an intern, later — after half a year's interruption, during which time I received some training in the department of neurology of the hospital for internal medicine — as a voluntary research assistant. These years are the only ones of my life which, in association with scholars, I spent dealing with the daily practical tasks. The moving realities were not only of a medical, but also of a sociological, juridical, and therapeutic nature.

Head of the hospital was Nissl. He was an excellent research man, a brain histologist who, — together with Alzheimer — discovered the histopathology of the cerebral cortex in paralytics. But I was mostly impressed by his self criticism. It is true, he carried on his work with bold expectations as to what was scientifically possible in getting knowledge of the mentally ill; but he was incorruptible in his awareness of whatever did not coincide with his expectation. Although it surprised him, he insisted on emphasizing, even more sharply than his critics, that there existed, e.g., no correlation between the severity of senile dementia and the size of the abnormal area in the cerebral cortex. He took his departure from the principle which had been prevalent since Griesinger: mental illnesses are diseases of the brain. While he made important discoveries on the basis of this presupposition, he undermined at the same time the general validity of this proposition. While he analyzed his findings methodically, he recognized the limits of their significance. When he became the director of the hospital, he was a specialist in histology, but was by no means at home in clinical psychiatry. He demonstrated that anyone who proceeds really scientifically in any field and has done scientifically fruitful research is capable of quickly grasping what is scientifically essential in all fields. Nissl's clinical lectures, which were originally largely based on Kraepelin's textbook, became from year to year more independent and original. He learned from his assistants; and yet was perhaps superior to all of us in the integrity of his humane way of viewing realities. The discussions with his assistants took place with an attitude of radical unaffectation without any distinction as to rank, etc. Even though the discussion might become impassioned, it never passed the bounds of propriety. Nissl's authority was invulnerable because of the character of his personality, not merely because of his official position. This scholar possessed an exceedingly great amount of kindness towards his patients and his assistants; he was externally harsh, temperamentally easily moved to anger, and in his actions extraordinarily conscientious and cautious. A warm and benevolent atmosphere radiated from him. As a person he was infinitely modest, a man who suffered profoundly, and was convinced of the state of decay of man.

A number of distinguished physicians worked with him in the hospital. If on occasion and by mistake an assistant had been accepted who did not fit into this group and who would violate the unwritten principles of this spiritual community, he would after some time disappear without anyone having been arrogant in his treatment of him. The leading authorities were: my teacher Wilmanns, the deputy chief; then above all, Gruhle, who kept everything moving by his critique, his versatility, and spontaneity; furthermore, the infinitely conscientious Wetzel, greatly gifted with empathy; the humane Homburger, an untiringly active brain histologist; the still very youthful Ranke, whose mind was open toward all scientific possibilities; and finally, Mayer-Gross. These physicians translated into reality a spiritual way of living with each other which had been made possible by Nissl. Gruhle's initiative saw to the regularity of our meetings. For the entire staff of all physicians in the hospital there were first of all the staff meetings, the demonstrations with patients, and discussions of expert reports. There were, furthermore, scientific evenings, spent with Nissl, on which occasions recent papers on specific themes were reported on and discussed. And finally, there were private gatherings at night in a smaller circle, without Nissl, in Gruhle's room, where we discussed, with the greatest freedom and ardor, whatever scientific interest lay closest to the heart of each individual. These talks were continued during our work the next day. Wherever one met, going up the stairs or coming down, there was an exchange of opinions. It was a remarkable life of universal spontaneity, permeated by the generally shared consciousness that we were furthering a magnificent realm of knowledge, with all the arrogance of knowing too much, it is true, but at the same time also with the kind of radical criticism which could tear apart every position. Whoever wanted to get any work done had to take care not to waste his time and energy in conversation. The "spirit of a house" had grown up, belonging to no one individual, but to the combined activity of all, each single one of whom, nevertheless, stubbornly pursued his own course. The form of one of the finest traditions of German academic life was once again realized in this hospital.

My position in this group was peculiar (abnormal). I was only a voluntary assistant. My illness made it impossible for me to become a regular staff assistant. I did not live in the hospital, did not take my meals with the other physicians, and I felt sad about this fact. But I had the permission to collaborate with them in their research. I found the director and the physicians kindly disposed towards me, was present at all the various kinds of gatherings for scientific discussions, took an active part in them, and participated in the ward rounds.

I was allowed to select my own cases for more detailed study. Wilmanns placed a special room at my disposal, in which I conducted intelligence and other tests, which at that time were just coming into use. I examined blood pressure with Recklinghausen's new apparatus, which for the first time made it possible to read off easily and continuously the minimum and maximum of blood pressure and thus permitted observation on what was taking place during psychic changes. However, I never published my results. Occasionally I was asked to make a report in court and to render expert affidavits in regard to accident insurance. Once, during Homburger's illness, I substituted for him at the policlinic. I became examining physician for nervous and mental diseases of the students' health insurance. Without being engaged in the regular daily routine duties of an assistant, the whole experience of a psychiatrist was in this way made accessible to me. The disadvantage of my position became an advantage. I could see and investigate everything without having my time occupied by routine duties. Besides carrying on my own investigations — I did not have a single patient from whose case I did not learn and remember something. I watched what my colleagues were doing, reflected on their procedures and my own, raised them to a higher level of conscious awareness, criticized them and pushed on to methodically pure procedures and formulations.

The common conceptual framework of the hospital was Kraepelin's psychiatry together with deviations from it, resulting in points of view and ideas for which no one person could claim original authorship. Thus, e.g., the polarity of the two broad spheres of dementia praecox (later called Schizophrenia) and of the manic-depressive illnesses was considered valid. The idea of the clinical entity was being discussed, our observations were continuously related to this idea, but without really knowing what it actually was. We distinguished the development of a personality which undergoes natural and understandable changes in the various phases of life, i.e., "biographical" changes, from "processes" which, in a violent break, cause a radical change, for reasons which, without knowing their nature, were held to be organic.

At that time, around 1910, somatic medicine was still prevalent in psychiatry. The influence of Freud was limited to small circles. Psychological efforts were considered subjective and fruitless, not scientific. An exception were the psychological experiments introduced by Kraepelin on the basis of Wundt's psychology, especially those concerning the "work curve" (fatigue and recovery), the investigations concerning the psychological effect of drugs, of alcohol, tea, etc. However, these experiments were unsuited for the investigation of mental patients. The experiments themselves came quickly to an end and did not produce further results 'til, somewhat later, investigations with mescalin produced a few new results.

The realization that scientific investigation and therapy were in a state of stagnation was widespread in German psychiatric clinics at that time. The large institutions for the mentally ill were built constantly more hygienic and more magnificent. The lives of the unfortunate inmates, which could not be changed essentially, were controlled. The best that was possible consisted in shaping their lives as naturally as possible as, e.g., by successful work therapy as long as such therapy remained a humane and reasonable link in the entire organization of the patient's life. In view of the exceedingly small amount of knowledge and technical knowhow, intelligent, yet unproductive psychiatrists, such as Hoche, took recourse to a skeptical attitude and to elegant sounding phrases of gentlemanly superiority.

In Nissl's hospital too, therapeutic resignation was dominant. In therapeutics we were basically without hope, but we were humane and kind and prevented, in so far as possible, any calamity which might unnecessarily result from the condition of the mentally ill. Our attitude towards the patients was humane without being pathetic, it was cheerful and tolerant. The psychiatrist's "gentleness" was held to be the self-evident attitude not only towards patients, but also with regard to life as such. We took a great interest in questions of a sociological and juridical nature. Tramps, e.g., were successfully investigated by Wilmanns. A Forensic-psychiatric Society in Heidelberg brought jurists and physicians together for regular lectures and discussions.

I found all this on my arrival. Deeply affected by all factual data and by every method, I aimed to appropriate whatever there was. The inordinarily voluminous literature in psychiatry of more than a century proved to be largely just so much unfounded chatter. Nevertheless, pearls were discovered therein when on occasion an author actually communicated real insights in a conceptually clear and precisely recognizable fashion. Frequently, the same things were being discussed in different terms, in most cases in a very obscure manner. Several schools had each its own terminology. It seemed as if several languages were being spoken, with deviations to the extent of special jargons at the individual hospitals. There seemed to be no such thing as a common scientific psychiatry uniting all those engaged in psychiatric research. During the regular demonstrations of patients and the discussions among physicians I sometimes had the impression as if we were always beginning all over again; then again that we merely subsumed the particular facts under a few miserable generic types; whereas at other times it would seem to me that what had already been said was constantly being forgotten. As often as I was pleased with what I had learned, just as often it seemed to me that no progress was being made. I felt as if I were living in a world of an insurveyable variety of ways of looking at things, which were at our disposal in chaotic disorder, yet each one of which individually was of an intolerable simplicity. Psychiatrists must learn to think, I once opined in a group of physicians. "Jaspers ought to be spanked," Ranke remarked with a friendly smile.

It now occurred to me that a cause of the intellectual confusion lay in the very nature of the subject itself. For the object of psychiatry was man, not merely his body, perhaps his body even least of all, but rather his mind, his personality, he himself. I read not merely the somatic domga: mental diseases are diseases of the brain (Griesinger) , but also the tenet: mental diseases are diseases of personality (Schüle) . What we were dealing with was likewise the subject of the social and cultural sciences. They had the same concept, only far more subtle, more developed, more lucid. Once when we were recording verbal expressions of patients, in states of confusion and of those exhibiting paranoid chatter, I said to Nissl: we must learn from the philologists. I began to look around for what philosophy and psychology might perhaps have to offer.

In this situation, in 1911, I received Wilmanns' and the publisher Ferdinand Springer's invitation to write a text on general psychopathology. I had already published a series of articles on "Homesickness and Crime," on intelligence tests, on hallucinations, on delusional ideas, on the course of diseases: all illustrated by detailed case histories. These writings made those men feel that a certain confidence in me was justifiable. I was startled; but at the same time I was seized by enthusiasm and buoyancy (and felt challenged) to bring order at least into the factual data and to further the methodical consciousness as much as possible. I wanted to do this the more as I felt myself supported by the spirit of the hospital and the knowledge we all shared. In this circle it was not too difficult to write a general psychopathology. Furthermore, it was high time to carry out this task. I was commissioned to undertake it.

My own investigations as well as my reflection about what was being said and done in psychiatry had led me on tracks which were new at that time. Philosophers gave me the impetus for two essential steps. As method I adopted Husserl's phenomenology, which, in its beginnings, he called descriptive psychology; I retained it although I rejected its further development to insight into essences *(Wesensschau)*. It proved to be possible and fruitful to describe the inner experiences of patients as phenomena of consciousness. Not only hallucinations, but also delusions, modes of ego-consciousness, and emotions could, on the basis of the patients' own descriptions, be described so clearly that they became recognizable with certainty in other cases. Phenomenology became a method for research.

Over against the psychology of theoretical explanation, Dilthey had put another, "descriptive and analytical psychology." I adopted this approach, called it a *"verstehende Psychologie"* and worked out the already practiced procedures — which had actually been applied by Freud in a peculiar fashion — by means of which, in contrast to the directly experienced phenomenon, one is able to comprehend the genetic connections within mental life, as well as meaningful relations and motives. I searched for the methodological justification and a systematic organization of these procedures. An abundance of known but unorganized psychological approaches, together with a description of the facts, seemed to me thus to find their rightful place.

I shall not report on the conceptually clear formulations of the psychology of performance (as compared with phenomenology and *"verstehende Psychologie"*), not on the separation of the phenomena of expression — whose meaning is understandable — from the non-meaningful somatic phenomena accompanying mental processes, not on the remaining methodological elucidations of the factually existing insights. I should like to point out only one thing. Everywhere I fought against mere talk without real knowledge, especially against the "theories" which played such a big rôle in psychiatric language. I pointed out that the psychological theories had been developed in analogy to those of the natural sciences, to be sure; but that they never acquired the character of scientific theories. For them there could never be a continuously advancing development of knowledge about a basic process dominating all mental phenomena. Proof and refutation based on experience, coupled with continuous search for counter-indications, could not be obtained by co-operative research. For in this field it was indeed only a matter of analogies, which at best seemed only to have a certain degree of plausibility, but which were possible in various ways, which never agreed, never could be checked radically. They were mistakenly transformed into factually present basic processes. I tried, however, to find in every idea, thus also in this type of theoretical thought, that factor which had a positive value for science. Thus I presented, in my *Psychopathology*, a systematic arrangement of theories, i.e., of the means to describe, by way of analogy, what otherwise would remain outside of the horizon of cognition. What mattered was to survey all possible pictures without lapsing into any. At that time the theories of Wernicke and Freud were held to be valid above all others. Both are now forgotten; Freud's theory is no longer considered as universally valid even by psychoanalysts today, since it is to a considerable degree regarded as being dated.

The belief that it was possible to develop methods which would enable us to comprehend man as a whole (as to constitution, character, body-type, and disease-entity) persisted, in ever new guises. Despite the fact that, within limits, all of them were fruitful, the supposed totality every time proved to be a totality within the one comprehensive totality of being human, never this totality itself. For the totality of man lies way beyond any conceivable objectifiability. He is incompletable both as a being-for-himself and as an object of cognition. He remains, so to speak, "open." Man is always more than what he knows, or can know, about himself.

The scientific urge for the systematic treatment of the entire field stood behind my desire to bring all of these points of view together. In my psychopathology the object was to bring to conceptually clear consciousness what one knows, how one knows it, and what one does not know. The basic critical idea was to gain insight into the problem of the ways by which an investigable objective comes to be perceived.

To ask such questions lay early in my nature. When, in my final pre-clinical examination (the *Physikum*), I was asked about the structure of the spinal cord, I replied by enumerating the methods of investigation and of what became evident by their use. The anatomist (Merkel in Göttingen) was astonished and praised me, which in turn was a surprise to me.

The systematic treatment demanded that no method, which had

a principle of its own, should be omitted even if only a minimum of knowledge was obtained by it. Every approach to reality was to be kept open by bringing it to conscious awareness. Yet at the same time the presuppositions and limitations of each were to be made distinct.

For this reason I was from the beginning opposed to any schools of thought in so far as they excluded anything, and went along with them in so far as they turned up something real. The greatest possible open-mindedness of scientific opinion was to be attempted in psychopathology.

The guiding principle of my book on psychopathology, therefore, was and remained this: to develop and order knowledge guided by the methods through which it is gained — to learn to know the process of knowing and thereby to clarify the material.

That meant at the same time, however: methodological investigations in themselves do not really matter so long as the methods do not lead to factual knowledge. According to the old saying, progress is not made when one just talks about swimming while standing on the shore, one must jump into the water. I set up the following as my goal, therefore: in my book on psychopathology there shall not occur any purely abstract logical discussions. They are to be reported on only when their meaning is demonstrated on evident data. Every method has value only through a body of real content, i.e., through whatever becomes observable by means of it. The basic empirical attitude of the book demanded that perceptibility and factuality remain prerequisites for anything to be recognized as knowledge in the field of psychopathology. At the same time, however, the heterogeneity of the factual itself was to come to the fore. The facts and observations do not lie upon an identical level. Rather, they prove themselves to be essentially different by the manifoldness of the ways by means of which one reaches them. Therefore the reader of the book was to become acquainted not merely with the subject material, but was to learn to think about the question in what way and within what limits this material might be factually valid. The principle of my presentation was: nothing was to be said that was not verified in the book by example from experience and observation.

This principle of methodological reflection and discipline appeared the more important as the object of investigation in psychiatry is man himself. He is distinguished from all other things in the world by the fact that in his entirety he can no more become an object of inquiry than can the world in its entirety. Whenever he becomes known, something of his appearance becomes known, not he himself. Every knowledge of man as a whole proves to be a deception which arises from the fact that one way of inquiry is elevated to the rank of being the only one, one method is made a universal one.

The principle of ascertaining the manner of knowing by means of becoming aware of the specific method in question, liberates man again from the pretention to being known *in toto*. It was the physician's task to preserve the humanitarian approach by not losing his consciousness of the infinity of each individual human being. Only thereby is any humane physician capable of maintaining the necessary reverence for each person, even if the latter be mentally ill. Man, and every individual, is to be saved for the consciousness of the physician and investigator. Never can the balance, so to speak, be struck by scientific means. Every sick person is, like any other person, inexhaustible. Never does knowledge reach a point where the personality with its hidden mysteriousness can not at least be sensed — be it even as mere possibility, as still reflected in wondrous leftovers (of the original personality).

A book thus conceived could very well turn out, in its first draft, to be a surprise; but it was also bound to be defective. In later editions I have tried to refine and to sharpen the structure, to grasp the facts in a wider perspective. For decades, the book remained important to me as distinctly my own. Later, occupied by new tasks and living away from the clinic, I no longer undertook independent psychopathological investigations, aside from a few pathographies *(Strindberg und Van Gogh* in comparison with Swedenborg and Hölderlin, 1920; and about Nietzsche's illness in the pertinent chapter in my book on *Nietzsche,* 1936).

In the clinic my work on the book from the very beginning encountered sharp criticism, both friendly and hostile. Both were an aid to my work.

The sharpest critic was Gruhle. He seemed to grant the validity of nothing whenever I reported on anything in our meetings. I became greatly excited. His criticism was a fertile stimulus. One evening I had reported on the contents of a short article dealing with the phenomenological method of research in psychiatry, i.e., about my experiments and plans. Gruhle, it seemed, was tearing everything to bits. Only then, certain now to be on the right track, I wrote the article in a very few days, formulated everything more clearly, and submitted my manuscript to Gruhle. To my great surprise and joy he now agreed.

Other criticism was hostile. An assistant of my own age offered a reproach which, in many different forms, I encountered again

and again, even later on with reference to my philosophizing. I
was accused of wanting to dissolve the dogmatism-of-being in favor
of a critical elucidation of all possibilities of research; by so doing
all theories were put into the unstable position of mere analogies.
He retorted: "You have no conviction at all. One cannot do research in such fashion. There is no science without a continuous
theory. Only by way of theory does it become a science. You are a
relativist. You destroy the firmness of the physician's point of
view. You are a dangerous nihilist."

The greatest and unforgettable impression, however, was made
by Nissl's critical and helpful attitude towards my work. He was
so greatly satisfied with my dissertation, "Homesickness and
Crime," that he gave me the best grade on it and agreed to my
desire to work in his hospital. The first conversation we had, when
I told him my desire, was brief. He replied to my request: "Gladly,
what do you wish to work on?" Whereupon I said: "During the
first few weeks I want to orient myself in the library to find out
what is there." He looked at me in astonishment and said rather
brusquely: "Well, if you want to do that sort of monkey-business,
go ahead!" I was depressed by this reply, angrily wanted to give
up my entire work in the hospital, but reflected: "I must pardon
this venerable scholar for venting his anger on a young man; the
hospital is unique, in Germany I would not find another one like
it; it is my career which is at stake, I must not be proud." Thus I
began my work. Nissl let me have complete freedom, listened to
lectures I gave, and expressed himself to an assistant: "Too bad
about Jaspers, such an intelligent fellow and engages in such
monkey-business." Once when, because of the precarious condition
of my health, I was late for a visit, he greeted me: "But Mr.
Jaspers, how pale you look! You do too much philosophy, and the
red blood corpuscles can't stand that." One day, after having
known me for years and after the publication of my article on the
phenomenological method of research, he came to me into the
outpatient clinic asking whether he might listen in while I was
engaged in phenomenological exploration. I was lucky with a case
of initial schizophrenia. Nissl expressed his great satisfaction, saying that there was some merit in it after all. When later I received
the proofs of my book on psychopathology, I thought it proper to
show them to him both as my chief and as the man to whom I
owed my chance to carry on my work. For days I saw him carrying
the proofs around with him in the pocket of his (white) physician's gown. To me he said never a word. But I was told by Wetzel
that he had said to him concerning the book: "Magnificent. It

leaves Kraepelin way behind!" After approximately three weeks, he asked me to visit him in his home in the afternoon. On this occasion he declared: "I consider your book good; surely you intend to habilitate yourself, don't you? Unfortunately, I have already accepted too many people for habilitation. The faculty won't admit any more. You would have to wait until one of them receives a call or leaves for one of the clinics. Therefore I have made inquiries: Kraepelin in Munich and Alzheimer in Breslau are both ready to habilitate you immediately. The choice is yours." I replied that I liked it in Heidelberg so much that I preferred to remain here and to wait. But perhaps I could habilitate myself in the psychology department of the philosophical faculty. "We initiate a sort of colony there, and later I can return to the hospital." "Excellent!" Nissl said and gave me recommendations as did Max Weber and Külpe (Munich). In 1913 I habilitated myself for psychology in the philosophical faculty under Windelband.

At that time I was not aware of the fact that this habilitation would result in my transfer from the world of medicine into that of philosophy in the university. I had forgotten the memorandum I had sent to my parents from Sils-Maria. Now I was teaching psychology, sad that I had to do it outside of the hospital. There was no psychological institute, but I saw to it that I could illustrate my lectures by means of many plates, with simple experiments.

That in the years to come I did not return to psychiatry seemed, at the outset, to be due to the compulsion of an external fact: the state of my health. During the first World War, the then dean of the faculty, Professor Gottlieb, asked me whether I would accept a call as successor to Nissl, who had gone to the research institute in Munich. I asked for a few days time to think it over. With my wife I reflected whether it might not be possible if we received an apartment in the hospital itself, and if I were to a considerable extent relieved of practical obligations. We reached the conclusion that it was physically quite impossible. I could not take upon myself the responsibility involved in the expert direction of a hospital. At that time it was difficult for me to desist. To maintain the spirit of a hospital in co-operation with like-minded colleagues, along the lines already undertaken and to develop that spirit in research as well as in the physician's activity, this seemed most attractive to me. It seemed to be so much more (enticing) than, with mere books and manuscripts, and within the limited area of accidental experience and on occasional journeys, to be restricted to an academic teaching career.

In looking back it all seems remarkable. What at that time was enforced by my illness and was done reluctantly, viz., the definitive choice of the philosophical faculty, was indeed leading me to the road for which I was destined. From early youth on I had been philosophizing. Actually I had taken up medicine and psychopathology from philosophical motives. Only shyness in view of the greatness of the task kept me from making philosophy my life's career. Even at that time I still did not consider doing that. My aim was the teaching of psychology while occupying a chair for philosophy; a chair which, however, existed for philosophy in name only, but actually was psychology. Submission on my part, however painful at the moment in view of the necessary renunciation, in truth meant the good fortune to open up the area of what lay within my possibilities. In the years to follow this became philosophy. I remained loyal to the pursuits of my youth. My *Psychopathology* never became a matter of indifference to me. For decades I worked earnestly and in ever new endeavor on the preparation of new editions of the book.

The memory of the intellectual fellowship of our hospital in Heidelberg has accompanied me throughout my entire life. My later work was quite independent and was undertaken at my own risk, sustained by the affirmative and co-operative attitude of my beloved wife, and encouraged by a friend, but without contact with any professional group. The comparison enabled me to measure how diffused, artificial, and unreal is the professional association of teachers of philosophy, no matter how often its representatives may meet each other in congresses or express themselves in journals and books.

III. "Psychologie der Weltanschauungen"

After my habilitation in the fall of 1913, it was my task to give lectures on psychology. I began, in the summer of 1914, to lecture on the subject: psychology of character-types and of ability, and in the following semesters lectures on empirical psychology: the psychology of sense perceptions, psychology of memory, investigations in the area of fatigue. Furthermore, I gave a pathographic course dealing with numerous sick personalities in history.

Decisive, however, for the further course of my thinking was the fact that, based on Aristotle's remark that, "The soul is, so to speak, everything,"I began to occupy myself in good conscience, under the name of psychology, with everything it is possible to know. For there exists nothing whatever that does not have a psychological aspect in this wide sense. I did not at all accept the delimitation of psychology as formulated by Windelband and Rickert, which at that time prevailed in Heidelberg circles. What I had begun under the title of *"verstehende Psychologie"* in psychopathology now became identical with the great tradition of intellectual and philosophical understanding. Thus I gazed on the wide expanse of the world of history and into the depth of what is understandable in man. I lectured on *"verstehende* psychology," more specifically on social — and ethno — psychology, psychology of religion, the psychology of morals. Among these lectures there was one which became the most important to me. Under the title, *Psychologie der Weltanschauungen* I developed them into a book and published it in 1919. This book became my approach to philosophy, but without my being aware of it at the time. A number of motives became intertwined in the book. They are the following:

Even during the period of work in the hospital I had a startling experience. In the conflict among scientific points of view and the living personalities it was not merely what was empirically and logically equally correct for everyone which played a rôle. The difficult task, for the fulfillment of which Nissl was a model, proved to be: to work out what is thus compellingly valid. In our discussion almost always another factor was noticeable. What was interesting in this was not our need for self-assertion, not our desire to be right, but rather a something which seemed somehow beyond our grasp, although in the discussion it was determinative and appeared to erect barriers among us.

In the personalities of the research psychiatrists, who were giving public lectures, this factor, which, quite independent of scientific accuracy, produced either a feeling of affinity or else of hostility. Thus Freud and Hoche, whom I never met personally and who, compared with each other, were quite heterogeneous, were at that time for me representatives of forces to which I did not turn a deaf ear, scholars whose writings I felt compelled to study. I resisted them, however, inwardly with thoughts and impulses that went far beyond the contents of their discussions. They accompanied my youth, so to speak, as my enemies, who were determined to effect something by way of our science which is not science at all; and they did this in an attitude which I felt to be reprehensible and against which a point of view needed to be clarified and asserted, which came from a totally different source. The nature of this point of view I wished to bring out and get clearly before us, no longer by following their example, but in view of history and of human beings as such.

At the very moment when the question concerning the original *Weltanschauungen* arose, the magnificent tradition of the thinkers who had developed this kind of psychology, sometimes not at all under the name of psychology, came to light. Hegel's *Phenomenology of Mind,* then above all Kierkegaard, whom I had been studying since 1914, and secondly Nietzsche, struck me as revelations. They were able to make communicable a universal and at the same time quite concrete insight into every corner of the human soul and to its very deepest sources. In my book I placed Kierkegaard and Nietzsche side by side, despite their apparent foreignness (to each other) (Christian and atheist). Today their close connection has become so self-evident that the name of the one recalls that of the other.

In my book, *Psychologie der Weltanschauungen,* a tension prevails. It is expressly stated: the book does not intend to be philosophy; philosophy, in the highest sense of the word, is prophetic philosophy; psychology understands all the possibilities of philosophic points of view by looking at them; philosophy itself provides us with a *Weltanschauung.* "Whoever wants a direct answer to the question how he should live, will, in this book, look for it in vain." The essential things are the concrete decisions of personal destiny. In the book, however, only elucidations and possibilities for self-reflection were given. By offering means of orientation, it appealed to the unflagging responsibility of the individuals, but it did not attempt to teach people how to live.

What I was at that time doing made two points clear to me later on: firstly the task of a philosophy which is philosophy in essence and yet not prophetic nor proclamatory philosophy; secondly the demarcation of that type of psychology which one may call scientific psychology from that psychology which itself is already philosophy.

Firstly: what I intended at that time with the distinction between psychology and a prophetic philosophy has remained the intent of my philosophizing until today. To be sure, this philosophizing is by no means merely contemplative. Even the *Psychologie der Weltanschauungen* had not been just that, without my being aware of it at that time. However, with all its appeals, its conjurations, its representations, philosophy does not want to infringe upon the freedom of the other person, who must find himself in his philosophizing: philosophy in its completeness and as a totality of ideas is unable to relieve him of that task. Neither Plato nor Kant are creators of prophetic philosophies in that sense of the word which I had in mind when, at that time, I spoke of prophetic philosophy, looking at it from a distance. Prophetic philosophy would be a substitute for religion. However, what this type of philosophy is and what it can accomplish, later on became for me the big problem. In my *Psychologie der Weltanschauungen* I was, naively, engaged already in philosophizing without knowing clearly as yet what I was doing.

Secondly, the name "psychology" could not be kept for these attempts. My way from psychology by way of *verstehender* psychology to existentialist philosophy caused the old task to become urgent in a new form: the demarcation of a scientific psychology and the methodological knowledge concerning its possibilities and its limits. Subsequently, I have carried out this demarcation along the lines of my *Psychopathology*. In this scientific situation *verstehende* psychology has an ambiguous character. Consequently the question concerning scientific psychology must be formulated quite sharply, to be sure; but the answer which is universally valid, effected, and accepted by all scholars, is not yet given.

The purpose of unobligatory consideration expressed in my *Psychologie der Weltanschauungen* and the factual obligation which becomes noticeable to the reader in trying to think with the author has unfavorably influenced the opinion about the book. One saw in it a gallery of *Weltanschauungen,* from which people were free to choose. Actually, however, it is the ascertainment of all possibilities as one's own and the elucidation of the largest possible realm in which the '*existential*' decisions occur which no thought, no system, no knowledge anticipates. Everything which in the book is displayed in graphic thought contains tensions, because of which there is truth everywhere and error also. My interest was no longer exclusively the psychological one in types of *Weltanschauungen,* but the philosophical interest in the truth of various philosophic points of view. I outlined an organism of the possibilities in their movement, recognizing myself in, and at the same time rebounding from all of them. It was a philosophy not yet conscious of itself. My present attitude towards this book is, therefore, one of affirmation as to its content and its tendency, but one of dissatisfaction with its form.

My authorization to lecture at the university was expressly for psychology with exclusion of philosophy. I did not feel this, at the time, as a restraint, but rather as relief from the necessity of teaching philosophy, a pretense to which appeared to me enormous. Nevertheless, my philosophical impulse impelled me, under the cloak of psychology, towards a consideration of totality. I did not aim at a prophetic philosophy and had no conception as yet of that other philosophy— although secretly I was already groping for it — which, neither in the form of the pseudo-scientific nullities of an alleged technical philosophy nor in that of presumptuous pronouncements of the now definitively grasped truth, had been able to appeal to me. The compulsion necessitated by my academic situation to teach psychology released pertinent necessities which, without that compulsion, would scarcely have become clear to me. Inasmuch as I was philosophizing without being aware of it, I could later on comprehend this factual procedure in such a way that it appeared to me as a fulfillment of the task of philosophy which I then believed to recognize in all great historical philosophy.

The foundations of my *Psychologie der Weltanschauungen* logically can be subject to questioning. They represent a lack of clarity, which, at that time, was fortunate for me because fruitful. I did, at that time, not really see through the methods which I was using, although I spoke about them in the book and although I had insisted so intensively on methodological clarification in my work on psychopathology.

Knowing what I was about, I threw myself into the abundance of possibilities in order to find, through this process of understanding, direction and impetus in my own being. Unforgettable those years in which — under the pressure of the first world war, in the midst of hardships which we, at that time, shared with all other citizens — I found with my wife the happiness of thinking in this manner, in which we philosophized and, more clearly than before, found the way to ourselves. Unforgettable, too, the never-to-be-repeated inner buoyancy of those years, which would scarcely have been possible in a pure, objectively scientific type of knowing. This intellectual and human fulfillment of our co-operative work flourished at that time very quietly, not exposed to negative criticism, unnoticed, shared from afar by a few listeners who were fascinated and some of whom remained attached to us by bonds of friendship, for the most part women, as is natural in wartime. When, in 1921, I learned that Geheimrat Professor Martius in Kiel had said, during consultations concerning his successor, that in the reading of my book he had had the feeling that once more a new spring was budding in German philosophy, it came as quite a surprise. The judgment was an exaggeration; but it did do justice to the mood in which the book had ripened for us.

My book on the *Psychologie der Weltanschauungen* appears, in historical retrospect, as the earliest writing in the later so-called modern Existentialism. Decisive was the interest in man, the concern with himself on the part of the thinker, an attempted radical integrity. Present are nearly all the fundamental questions which later on occurred in lucid consciousness and in broad expansiveness: about the world, what it is for man; about the situation of man and about his ultimate situations from which there is no escape (death, suffering, chance, guilt, struggle) ; about time and the multi-dimensional nature of its meaning; about the movement of freedom in the process of creating one's self; about *Existenz;* about nihilism and about shells*; about love; about the disclosure of the real and the true; about the way of mysticism and the way of the idea; etc. All of it, however, was, so to speak, comprehended in a quick grasp, and had not been worked out systematically. The mood of the entire work was more encompassing than what I succeeded in saying. This mood became the foundation of my further thinking.

One motive of my work was to bring into view the greatness of men, without deception, i.e., not in the veilings of bad myths and not by unmasking — as in a false nihilistic psychology — but in the clarity of realistic observation. The actual nature even of the inimical forces could become more evident, not in personalities of lower rank, but in superior personalities who are strong in thought, creative and of inner consistency.

Among my contemporaries, the actuality of human greatness, the standard for men historically distant, became embodied for me, in a singular, marvelous fashion, in the person of Max Weber. I got to know him in 1909 through Gruhle. Weber died in 1920. His thought as well as his nature became as essential for my philosophy, even 'til today, as no other thinker. I gave public testimony of this fact in my memorial address of 1920 and in a small book of 1932. Not until after his death I became increasingly conscious of what he had meant: in my philosophical writings he often is present. Throughout my life I have confronted the task of trying to understand his reality. Even in those years he had already influenced the draft of my *Psychopathologie,* and still more so that of my *Psychologie der Weltanschauungen,* in the introduction to which I emphasized the meaning which his constructions of ideal types in the sociology of religion had had for my work. At the time this book appeared, in October 1919, Max Weber went to Munich. Only once more I talked with him during a longer visit which he paid us while passing through Heidelberg. On that occasion, mentioning the book only in the hour of departure, he said, in his forceful warmth: "I thank you; it was very much worth-

* Editor's Note: For an explanation of this term, "shells," consult footnote 46 in the essay by Dr. Ludwig B. Lefebre (this volume).

while; I wish you further productivity." Those were his last words to me.

IV. RICKERT

After Windelband's death, Heinrich Rickert, in 1916, was called to Heidelberg as head of the department of philosophy. I was to teach with him for many years, until 1936, first as a *Privatdozent*, from 1921 on as a colleague in the same university. When he came, I was *Privatdozent* in psychology. He enjoyed conversing with the young man. We met frequently and discussed unreservedly. I had so to speak a "fool's freedom" *(Narrenfreiheit)* with him. After all, I belonged to a different sphere, to psychopathology and psychology, and had, according to the absolute separation between philosophy and psychology, insisted upon by the Windelband-Rickert school, nothing to do with his field. "What are you after?" he said at our very first meeting. "You sat down between two chairs, you have given up psychiatry and yet are not a philosopher?" To which I replied: "I am going to get an academic chair in philosophy; what I shall do with that, will be my affair according to the freedom of the teacher, in view of the indefinite structure of what, in a university, is called philosophy." Rickert laughed heartily at this impertinence.

He disagreed with my *Psychologie der Weltanschauungen* of 1919. I had given him the proofs to read. He advised me strongly to strike out one note in which, side by side, I had quoted as delineations of "systems of value" Münsterberg, Scheler, and Rickert: "Not on my account, but for your sake, since you would expose yourself through such a misunderstanding of my philosophy." I gladly acceded to his wish, in view of the insignificance of that note. After its publication he wrote in *Logos* what, in view of his philosophical standpoint, had to be a devastating critique, but one which was still done in a friendly spirit that did not result in a complete break with me. For, his reprimand concluded with an affirmation: "We gladly greet this (philosopher) in his embryonic state."

In my many conversations with Rickert throughout the years until 1922, one question above all others was important for the development of my thinking. Rickert claimed universal and compelling validity for scientific philosophy; I doubted this claim. In the discussion with him what had previously been surging darkly within me became clear.

From an early age scientific insight had been an indispensable element in my life. I never would tire of finding out what can be known and how one gains and proves this knowledge. That concern remained alive in me throughout the years even though, in my later years, it was gratified only by the reading of scientific treatises in all fields of research.

But this did not suffice. Scientific knowing *par excellence* was critical knowledge which knows about its limits. Since I had read Spinoza I was reflecting in a manner which, scientifically, was not tenable. On one occasion, when Nissl ran into me in the hospital and, as was his custom, inquired about any results of my work, it came to me as quick as a flash — inasmuch as I had just been engaged in dreamy cogitation — that there is such a thing as meaningful thinking without results. But this insight had at that time no consequences for my work; I was a psychiatrist and a psychologist and had no thought of making philosophy my profession.

This became the ever recurring topic of discussion between Rickert and myself: I attacked his philosophy relative to its claim to be a science; (my argument was that) what he was advancing was by no means compelling for everyone, least of all as stated in his value-theory. I tried to demonstrate this on specific theses. And, on the whole, I stressed the point that his philosophy — as, for that matter, any other — had never found universal concurrence, which, after all, is accorded to scientific knowledge. In saying this, I developed an idea of philosophy as something altogether different from science. It was to do justice to a claim to truth of a sort which science does not know, resting on a responsibility which is quite alien to science. It would perform something unobtainable by any science. On this basis, I declared against his type of thinking, saying that in reality he himself was no philosopher at all, but was doing philosophy like a physicist. The difference was merely that he was producing cunning logical analyses which, in their entirety, (actually) were soap bubbles, whereas the physicist was gaining factual knowledge whenever he realistically proved his speculations. Rickert was amused by all this, (treating it) as the idle chatter of a young man who had strayed from the proper path of academic work, who might scarcely entertain any hopes for a university career. Once when, as he advanced a point of view, I referred to him on the spur of the moment as a philosopher, he called in amusement to his wife who was just entering the room: "Wifie, Jaspers has just declared me to be a philosopher."

Rickert was a keen thinker, a greatly devoted disciple of Goethe, a gifted author, a superior personality in the faculty, a friend of Max Weber. As long as Max Weber was alive, Rickert and I remained on friendly terms in spite of the *Psychologie der Weltan-schauungen*. The presence of Max Weber was like a protection of all good possibilities and (constituted) at the same time the limitation of Rickert's self-confidence. At a Sunday gathering in Max Weber's home, when Rickert was talking about his system, the six areas of value, and of one of the areas — the "erotic" —as "philosophy of the completed values of the present" and started philosophizing about love, Max Weber suddenly interrupted full of anger: "Now stop talking in this *'Gartenlauben'* style; this is all nonsense!" This is what a soft pathetic attitude was called at the time, after a sentimental, small bourgeoisie magazine, *viz.,* the *Gartenlaube.*

Max Weber had recognized part of his own methodological insights, which he had gained as a historian, an economist, and a sociologist, in Rickert's book, *Grenzen der naturwissenschaftlichen Begriffsbildung.* Max Weber, in his magnificent immoderation, was so grateful that, in such logical questions, he always referred to Rickert and permitted many of his own expositions to appear as a mere consequence and application of Rickert's thought.

When Max Weber died in 1920, it was for me as though the world had changed. The great man, who had justified its existence to my consciousness and had given it a soul (and meaning), was no longer with us. It seemed as if that last resort had disappeared where, in rational discussion, the absolutely dependable, though directly not expressable guidance had resided; that resort from whose deep foundation there came broadest perspectives, the possible insight into the momentary situation and the judgment of actions, events, and asserted knowledge. Max Weber was the authority who never proclaimed, never relieved you of responsibility, but who encouraged whatever had secured his approval in the severity and clarity of his humane thinking.

After Max Weber's death I hesitated to go to Rickert for fear that he might use inappropriate words in the face of this event, which cut so unforseeably deep into our intellectual as well as into our German existence. Not until the fifth day did I decide to see him. At first we exchanged a few words of deep emotion which set me at ease. But then Rickert began to speak of Max Weber as of his disciple; to be sure, he paid tribute to the eminent personality, association with whom he had found congenial; but he also emphasized the tragic wrecking of his work and the slight chance of any influence of his insights. Now the disaster had occurred. I became angry and went so far as to say: "If you think that you and your philosophy will be known at all in the future, you may perhaps be right, but only because your name is mentioned in a footnote in one of Max Weber's works as the man to whom Max Weber expresses his gratitude for certain logical insights."

Since that time the relationship between Rickert and myself was disturbed. Those moments had demonstrated an earnestness which barred him from granting me a "fool's freedom" any longer. When, a few weeks later, I had given my commemorative address on Max Weber before the student body of the University of Heidelberg, at their invitation (the Senate of the university had declined an official university commemoration) and when Rickert had read it, he angrily addressed me as I entered to call on him: "That you construct a philosophy out of Max Weber may be your rightful privilege, but to call him a philosopher is absurd." From then on Rickert was my enemy.

In 1921 the second chair for philosophy was vacated because of Heinrich Maier's leaving for Berlin. I, for my part, had had calls to Greifswald and Kiel, but wanted to remain in Heidelberg, that unique town, intellectually so spirited, and through memories so dear. At first Rickert did everything to prevent this. As early as 1920, when opportunities to receive calls seemed to exist for me because of chairs that had become vacant, he said to me that he considered my appointment very improbable. For I was no philosopher (he said) and I stood, after all, outside of the fields for which appointments were to be had. I answered proudly: "I don't believe this, for that would be a disgrace for the German universities." Now he accounted for my disqualification by saying that in consequence of my background and my temperament I was dominated by the mode of thought of natural science. However, Rickert was wrong. Those calls actually came to me, even though effectuated by (other) faculties and the government against (the wishes of) the representatives of philosophy. In Heidelberg too, Rickert's argumentation against me did not succeed; his own candidates proved to be unconvincing. Both the appointment committee and the faculty enforced my call, to which Rickert on his part finally gave his consent.

Rickert's rejection was an expression of a more universal one. Within the circle of professional philosophers I was rated as an outsider. Already my habilitation in 1913 met with the indignation of the young people who had studied philosophy and were thinking on their part of habilitating themselves. I was not even the possessor of a Ph. D. degree, I was an M. D. I lacked the traditional philosophical education. Thus I remained an outsider even after I had become a full professor. Rickert and other instructors in philosophy tried to build up the notion that I was only a romanticist, and an untalented one at that; that I was confused and arrogant, and had written only one good book, my *Psychopathologie,* and unfortunately had digressed from the field of my real talent. When, sometime later, Rickert was writing about Heidelberg's philosophic tradition and every young *Privatdozent* was mentioned by name, I was ignored. In spite of all this, Rickert had one pre-eminence which made him stand out above his profession: he had a sense of humor. When I was paying him what was to be my last visit before his sudden unexpected death, he had just read my recently published *Nietzsche* and said: "I thank you. I consider it an excellent book, Herr Jaspers; it is, I hope you don't mind my saying so, a scientific book."

V. "PHILOSOPHIE"

When, on April 1, 1922, I took over the full professorial chair for philosophy in Heidelberg, I was, indeed, by my own standards, not ready. Now I began to undertake the study of philosophy in a new and more thorough manner. Counter to all my former aims and goals, I ventured to make philosophy my life work. My task became clear to me. Max Weber was dead. It seemed to me that the philosophy of the academicians was not really philosophy; instead, with its claim to be a science, it seemed to be entirely a discussion of things which are not essential for the basic questions of our existence. In my own consciousness I myself was not originally a philosopher. But when the intellectual world is empty of philosophy, it becomes the task at least to bear witness to philosophy, to direct the attention to the great philosophers, to try to stop confusion, and to encourage in our youth the interest in real philosophy.

In 1920 I stood at the crossroads. My *Psychologie der Weltanschauungen* had been successful. It was read a great deal at that time. During the years that it took form, manuscripts for university courses in the psychology of religion, in social and ethnic psychology and in the psychology of morals had developed simultaneously. It would have caused no difficulties to complete three new books. A large amount of literature was at hand for use, in order to give a presentation of wide horizon. I could have branched out on the level I had reached, viewing things in a way which probably had content but was philosophically unclear. The temptation was great to publish such a book every year or two, each one supposedly momentarily successful. I resisted that temptation because of my awareness that what was alive in my own inner attitude as well as in my esteem of men and of things could not conceptually become clear by such procedure. Replacing philosophy by an ever so extensive psychological approach and by the use of ever so interesting historical material was, after all, an evasion of the serious task of having to understand oneself, one's own existence. It would have remained an irresponsible occupation with a mere abundance of objects. For the task I set for myself there was needed my own methodical reflection and a thorough inquiry into the few original great philosophical works. I still continued to occupy myself with history and with the realities which come to one from all of the sciences, but now only incidentally, in my more tired hours. My chief concern now became the ascent to the height of philosophy proper. That was a slow process. The sudden intuitive insights into what actually matters acquire firmness and coherence only through a kind of work which now assumed a new character. Not the acquisition and increase of knowledge could create it, but only the forms of thinking and the operational procedures which, exercised in one's contact with great philosophers, really could not be learned. Another level of thinking had to be gained. That meant the decision to make a new start from the beginning.

I was reflecting about this situation at that time. To be occupying the chair of a full professor, I thought, gives me complete freedom. I need no longer to publish anything in order to acquire a professorial appointment. I am drawing my salary, which, according to the established tradition, does not impose upon the professor any conditions, restrictions, or controls, but which means that he devotes his energies, altogether but freely, to his self-set task, and thereby, through his instruction gives youth an insight into this kind of work. I decided that my publications, for the time being should cease. Two writings — one about Strindberg and van Gogh (1922) and one about the idea of the university (1923) — were simply revisions of manuscripts which actually stemmed from the time prior to my appointment as a full professor.

When year after year, until the end of 1931, nothing appeared from my pen, the result was that some of my colleagues, whose attitude towards me was not friendly, said that now that I had become a full professor, I had become an epicure who no longer worked. The longer this lasted the more definitely people became convinced that nothing more could be expected of me. The time of my *Psychologie der Weltanschauungen* was looked upon as a mere straw fire. Rickert openly showed his contempt for my "super-science." It was said that I had sacrificed my competence as a psychopathologist which had established the basis for my scientific reputation. My reputation at the University of Heidelberg sank to the point that I was considered "done for." What seemed strange was that I had so many students. This must have rested upon characteristics of mine which earned me the title "seducer of youth."

My lectures and seminars were by no means perfect. After all, I was engaged in the midst of work which was only in the process of becoming. Compliant students of my departmental colleagues reported that my lectures were uninformed and frivolous, the lecturing of one who had never studied philosophy. Other students were fascinated because, in atmosphere and possibilities, a world was opened before them of which they otherwise scarcely would have become aware. To me my lectures were a way of achieving, they were not the repeating of a finished doctrine.

Following the traditional division these lectures were partly historical, partly systematic. In my lectures on the history of philosophy I presented ideas and images which I had made my own in my studies, the characteristics of the epochs and the meaning of their rational structures and methods. Unsystematically, without binding myself to chronological order, I lectured on all periods of the history of European philosophy. In doing this, I appeared to myself somewhat like the conductor of an orchestra who presents the past in the present.

More difficult, more personal and essential, were the lectures in which I tried to gain the fundamental knowledge which, through my own discernment and personal assimilation, convincingly acquired reality within me. It no longer was a matter of communicating ever so grandiose opinions, but truth itself was the main concern, truth as an individual of today may be able to think it. That was a slow process. In lectures on logic, the theory of catagories, metaphysics, and *'existential'* analysis I, to begin with, expounded what seemed to me essential still in the guise of what I was intent on overcoming, *viz.*, the logically-objective and the psychological. Sudden success alternated with painstaking abstractions. Listeners to my lectures would later, on occasion, reproach me because they missed, in my books which resulted from my lectures, many a concrete illumination which the lectures themselves had contained.

Nothing of what I presented in lectures and seminars became known to the public for a decade. Academically I lived in the world of philosophy professors, a world very strange to me indeed.

Whatever I did intellectually was at one and the same time both cautious and daring, was at times thorough, and at some other times wanton. What the others were doing and what I was trying to do ran parallel without ever touching. I did not combat the others as opponents. Whereas Rickert, in his lectures, often attacked me to the enjoyment, and sometimes to the indignation of the students, I taught as if the other academic philosophers did not exist at all and never attacked my colleagues. On the whole, I felt to be on the right track. Nevertheless doubts assailed me. My isolated position among my colleagues compelled me to find my justification in my own work.

From 1924 on, I had systematically been preparing a work which, in December, 1931, was published in three volumes under the title, *Philosophie*. As yet it had neither shape nor direction. My notes for the work kept expanding. Even while traveling I carried my notebook with me. Often I would put down a sentence. The individual detail preceded the whole. It was not devised from a general principle, but it grew together. The arrangement of the whole was secondary.

Whatever did not necessarily belong to the subject was eliminated. This subject was the question concerning the actual nature of philosophy, within which dimensions it moves; not, however, by merely talking about it, but rather in the unfolding of concrete experiences. Whatever I encountered in my association with people, in faculty meetings, in the newspapers, on the street and on journeys, above all, however, what revealed itself to me in confronting beloved persons and their fate — all that was translated into formulations in which the original point of departure was no longer discernible. Whatever became clear to me in the great (classical) philosophers was appropriated as present truth; but here also in such a manner that the source was often scarcely discernible any more. Modest, seemingly accidental, occasions brought insights. Such work is, to be sure, work which requires planning and direction. It can, however, be successful only if something else is constantly effective: namely, dreaming. Often I gazed out on the scenery, up at the sky, the clouds; often I would sit or recline without doing anything. Only the calmness of meditation in the unconstrained flow of the imagination allows those impulses to become effective without which all work becomes endless, nonessential, and empty. It seems to me that for the man, who does not daily dream a while, his star will grow dark, that star by which all our work and everyday existence may be guided.

My philosophical endeavors proceeded under two presuppositions which — remembering Max Weber — had become clear to me in my discussions with Rickert. First of all: scientific knowledge is an indispensible factor in all philosophizing. Without science no veracity is possible today. The accuracy of knowledge in the sciences is entirely independent of philosophical truth; it is, however, relevant for the latter, yes even indispensible. Science, on the other hand, cannot understand why it itself exists. It does not reveal the meaning of life, provides no guidance. It has limits of which it is itself aware insofar as it is clearly conscious of its methods.

The second presupposition was: There is a type of thinking which, from the point of view of science, is not compelling nor universally valid, which, therefore, yields no results that as such could claim validity as forms of knowability *(Wissbarkeit)*. This type of thinking, which we call philosophic thinking, leads me to my very self; its consequences arise out of the inner activity of its own procedures; it awakens the sources within me which ultimately give meaning even to science itself.

It is important, therefore, to bring the sciences to their greatest possible purity as cogent and universally valid knowledge which is conscious of its own methods and to conceive of their results *as such*. At the same time, however, it is also of importance to (work out) philosophic thinking along equally pure lines — philosophic thinking which is not opposed to science, but always in alliance with it, which is not a super-science, but performs a type of thinking which, in its purport, is radically different. The gravity of responsibility for the purity of science is inseparable from the gravity of the type of philosophic thinking which confronts me with myself.

These two concerns have gone with me through my whole life: a constant interest in science, the insistence upon a basically scientific attitude in a person who claims to be a philosopher, and the assertion of the indispensability of science and of its magnitude; and secondly, an interest in philosophizing, the insistence on the seriousness of thought which transforms, without having factually objective results, the assertion of the dependency of the meaning of science *(not* of its correctness) upon philosophy.

The consequence was that I tried to assert myself against the attitude of contempt for philosophy on the part of too many representatives of the sciences as well as against the contempt for the sciences on the part of fanatical, irrational modes of philosophizing.

Another consequence was this: In contradistinction to the sciences which separate the person engaged in research from the substance of his findings, I consider the person engaged in philosophizing inseparable from his philosophic thoughts. Nothing in philosophy is separable from man. The philosophizing person, his basic experiences, his actions, his world, his everyday conduct, the forces which speak through him, cannot be disregarded when one accompanies him in his thoughts.

The time of our joint labor on my *Philosophie* is for my wife and me a precious memory, especially as her beloved brother and my friend, Ernst Mayer, collaborated with us so intensively (more about this in the next section). We were passing through the first mature stage of our lives. The values of philosophy had made both of us become more conscious of our own selves. Against the backdrop of the sinister threats of life and of the terrors which we had compassionately shared, our labor in translating all this into thought became a kind of wistful happiness. Finalities became the theme — but at a moment, a brief interval — of personal peace of mind, of contemplation which found expression in language. My wife transcribed my manuscripts which others found illegible. She read my notes and noted down her own thoughts which, aside from our conversations, became a sort of correspondence in our home.

Especially during the last year of our work we were untiring. The day after the manuscript had been dispatched to the publisher, in October 1931, we left for Bellagio in order to have a respite before continuing our work. In the pure beauty of Lake Como and its villas, and of the sun, we incredulously enjoyed the antique faith in the here and now.

I do not wish here to report on the contents of my *Philosophie* (published in December 1931 with publication date of 1932). The different ways of doing philosophical thinking are arranged in it according to modes of transcending. As a whole it is not a system. The individual chapters need not be read in the order in which they occur. But each chapter, in its entirety, is a movement of thought which the reader has to engage in at a stretch. The book does not have the title *"Existential* Philosophy." For it was my intention, in our spiritually modest present situation, to find a form of *philosophia perennis* in its total range. For this reason, only the second volume has expressly the title *Existenzerhellung* (illumination of *Existenz),* which I had been using for eight years in my lectures. Metaphysics was not to be rejected, but appropriated.

In my simultaneously appearing *Geistige Situation der Zeit* (English translation has appeared under the title, *Man In the Modern Age)*— for a moment pin-pointing the intent of the whole

under the name of " *'existential'* philosophy" — I formulated the
task as follows:

Existenz-philosophy is the way of thought by means of which man
seeks to become himself; it makes use of expert knowledge while at
the same time going beyond it. This way of thought does not cognise
objects, but elucidates and makes actual the being of the thinker.
Brought into a state of suspense by having transcended the cognitions
of the world (as the adoption of a philosophical attitude towards the
world) that fixate being, it appeals to its own freedom (as the illumination of *Existenz*) and gains space for its own unconditioned activity
through conjuring up Transcendence (as metaphysics). (*Age*, 159)

VI. ERNST MAYER

During the decade of my intentional public silence (1923-31)
my friend, Ernst Mayer (1883-1952) proved to be of irreplaceable
importance for my own work. Ernst and I were united by the
common sharing of one inexhaustible devotion. It actualized itself
in an always ready reciprocity throughout an entire lifetime.

We first got acquainted in the summer of 1907. Both of us were
students of medicine in the same class and of the same age. I was
astonished by the obstinacy with which Ernst seized questions,
even questions which ordinarily would be touched on only incidentally or not at all or merely as an object of curiosity: the
fundamental aspects of medical knowledge, philosophical propositions which occurred in books or in lectures, questions about the
nature of friendship and the worth of women, the personalities of
our teachers and the accidental occurrencies in every-day life. In
so far as the quantity of the content was concerned, our studies
were carried on rather carelessly; but a specific case (for instance)
could very well be thought through penetratingly. Ernst was always looking for the essential and therefore also for the methods
of asking questions and of investigating. He did not care for extensive study of books, but intuitively always seemed to find the
most important passages. This kind of student I had never yet
come to know. None of the sophisticated talk, which at that time
was so widespread, but careful continued questioning and perseverance; all these testified to a seriousness from which I did not
withdraw. "We discuss everything except medicine," I wrote to
my parents concerning my new friend.

By nature I was reserved. It was difficult for me to come close
to others. Since my school years I suffered under loneliness despite
some relationships. To begin with, I was reserved also toward

Ernst Mayer, tried to keep him to whatever was going on in our medical courses and what we heard in the lectures. This did not succeed, however. Ernst's unrestrained approach to me was not without risk, because, measured by conventions, capable of being misunderstood. But he was calm spiritually, unusually tender, and at every moment tactful. How deeply moved Ernst turned towards me from the very beginning his wife told me later. Used to going it alone and to keep away from all others, he is supposed, on my entry into the anatomy class, when he saw me for the first time, to have thought to himself: there comes the first German student! At that time he had reported this to her at once. Touching for me was this open affection for me and the interpretation of my ways. Never yet had I met up with such an affirmation of my essential nature and of my possibilities coming from such depth. My reservation melted without subsequent breach, without any immoderation, without any sentimentality. I responded to this affection astonished and happy. There was not a trace of deification towards me, but rather sharp criticism. As, for example, concerning my manner; in those days, (I tended to be) quickly judging, easily disdainful, simply asserting, without giving reasons: "How can you be so quickly contemptuous of something which for me obviously has great significance!", he countered when I tore to pieces a book by Rickert which he was just studying, without my having paid any attention to the particular connections in terms of which he was interested in it. We could excitedly carry on a controversy against such other; but it was strange: somehow I did not feel myself attacked, but only reminded of my own essential nature.

At the end of summer 1907 we separated. On July 14 I still had become acquainted with his sister, later my wife. Ernst continued his studies at another university. Never again did we live in the same community. We saw each other only on visits, often, however, for days and occasionally for weeks; but then always in that profound understanding which was unshakeable even when in the foreground there were differences of opinions, even in important matters which were discussed unreservedly.

Our discussions had a very variegated character. Dwelling on relevant themes such rational discussions could last for days, productive because of the perseverance with which he defended a position and aimed to convince me. Never in friendship with a man have I experienced such a concern that I might get caught in an error, that I might be unjust in an expression, might remain blind to humaneness. Wonderful too were other discussions resulting from already achieved understanding, with much calm-

ness, and his suddenly clear judgments. Some of his sayings, which
thus arose, were taken over into my *Philosophie:* "I did not create
myself" . . . "but what if I remain away from myself?"

In 1910 Ernst established himself as a physician in Berlin and
remained there until he had to flee in 1938. His being a physician
was most uncommon. I shall try to describe it.

Ernst had to live his life under serious biological limitations.
He was disposed to mental illness by heredity and his youth had
been overshadowed by depressions. But his spirit gained distance
from and prevailed over the uncanny heritage. It was as if a wound
in the root of his constitution had produced this marvelous humaneness in him. Something surrounded him which in all reason
was more than reason, but not something alien and demoniac, but
the limitless becoming clear of what, in essence, he was. Sociologically nowhere reliably adapted, but rather everywhere either
openly or surrepticiously pushed out, he became, in a collapsing
or violent society, man *qua* man. The otherwise firm forms of
deportment, of distance-keeping dignity and of manly pride were
rôles which he still played where it seemed called for, but which
he did not at all find crucial. He could, so to speak, abandon himself, disarmed by his humaneness, and thereby awaken others. No
vitality permitted him to make his place in the world with his
elbows. But it is not to be described how all his unrest died away
in considered calmness, when he knew himself on the right track
and when he was helping the sick.

Such an attitude toward human beings predestined him to be
a physician. Whenever he saw disaster he felt himself called to
intervene, even when not called. He sympathized, as if his own
fate were at stake. He grasped the total situation of the sick person, penetrating him with reason and kindness. Confronted by
the opposition of the vulgar he had to limit himself, it is true, to
material medical help; but, whenever anyone got around to talk,
he helped him beyond everything merely medical. He never acted
as savior. Enchantment did not proceed from him but rather
awakening. The sick person came under an appeal which brought
him to reason. Under all circumstances he wanted to help. He
wanted to recognize no situation in which it was no longer either
possible or sensible to do anything. Alleviation, assistance, momentary silence — none of these may stop, no patient must feel himself forsaken. Aptly he quoted: "Even at the grave he still plants
hope."

Such a person is not the right physician for everyone nor even
for everyone the right friend. It could be most irksome. There-

fore, those who came in contact with him divided. On the one hand, there were those who were engaged by him in their inner-most nature and did then not let anything divert them in their faithfulness to him. Others could not stand him; in the severity of his demands, in the inexorableness of his insight, they misunder-stood his kindness. When he himself saw the terribleness of human failure, he might have exclaimed anxiously: "Too bad about men." Being physician and philosophy in him were united into one. Being physician was his concrete philosophy.

For my philosophizing Ernst had the greatest possible signifi-cance, both by way of his being as well as in terms of what he said. In the working out of my three-volumed *Philosophie* more specifically he was an immediate participant. Without him that work would never have become what it is. In 1927, in his own modest way, Ernst expressed the desire that I might send to him notes for my work, which, after having used them, I would throw into the wastebasket anyway. Upon that I sent him carbon copies of my first connected manuscripts. This started his collaboration, a back and forth of questions and discussions, of suggestions, most-ly in written form, orally continued at each meeting. He was matchless in sacrificial selflessness, in which he treated my task as wholly and completely his own. He did not merely read all of the manuscripts, but wrote critical notations on all. He co-oper-ated to the very point of the construction of the chapters, of the matter of content, as well as that of style. He brought to me not merely the mighty impulse of his participation and of his demands, but also those of his enrichments and improvements in great num-bers. It was his joy when I seemed to succeed in achieving some-thing; it was his pain, greater than my own when something appeared to him as incomplete. He did not find me sufficiently careful, scolded my frivolity both in serious discussions and joking-ly in the case of trivials: if a suit is excellently manufactured and in the end a trouser button is missing, everything is ruined. Many a weekend he spent in a small castle in the vicinity of Berlin in order to work freely on my manuscripts, undisturbed by his prac-tice and by men, in quiet absorption. Even during his practice, he often would go for a while into the Cafe Josty at the Potsdamer Platz in order there to plunge into a particularly difficult passage of my manuscript. In his medicine kit he always carried something of my sketches, in which he would still be reading even while walking. To the very last day before dispatching the manuscript to the publisher he telephoned from Berlin to Heidelberg in order to remove some deficiency.

Our work grew together in such a way that, at the end, it was impossible to separate what had proceeded from the one and what from the other. It had been a collaboration in the development of the work itself not just an improvement after its conclusion.

This could not be repeated. We tried it with my Nietzsche book. Here too Ernst contributed much; but there did not occur once more that marvelous unanimity of the work.

In those days I saw my friend as follows: He did not read much. For the study of larger works he had, in view of his practice, neither time nor inclination. But even one significant sentence would release philosophizing in him. What he grasped — in philosophy, science, poetry, music, art, but also in politics — was of central importance. It was as if out of the depth of an encompassing vision he were able to fathom the very foundations: Just as I myself, his other friends were struck, informed, surprised when, as with a single stroke (and from quite sparse data), he seemed to grasp the most essential points. He himself did not write, however. True, in the twenties he published two papers on questions of medical conduct, rich in content, which carried the stamp of his personality. But he decided to write even those papers only after I had declined, in the existing pressing situation, to speak on their theme. In his modesty he seemed to think the friend could do it better and then, in fact, proved the contrary. He carried out the renunciation which, at that time, he considered self-evident: in view of his extraordinary intuitive talents to possess such little capacity for work; in view of such superior powers of judgment to create no corresponding intellectual work; in view of such great ability to get at the heart of a matter in the sudden grasping of the totality of a situation, of a person, not to let himself be carried by the power to construct a consistent course of thought.

This changed when, by the despotic act of Hitler-Germany, he lost his practice and was himself forced to flee. He got into the terrible situation of the emigrants. In Holland, as an emigré who had crossed the border illegally, he was first committed to a camp, to a monastery where he was soon granted a monk's cell in order to be able to follow his philosophical studies undisturbedly. Released as a result of the intercession of highly placed persons, he was for a short time free, until, after the criminal invasion of Holland, the threat of likely murder forced him and his family to go underground. Three years they lived in concealment, kept by the unforgettable humaneness and sacrificial devotion of a Dutch woman, Maria Van Boven, and attended by a small underground group of Dutch students. There, in seclusion from the world, and in daily danger of his life, his philosophical attitude lifted Ernst above the terrors and the anguish of the situation. His wisdom guided the order of the day in this seclusion, determined the caution of all inmates upon which success depended. In this period of intense attention toward the outside (world) and of complete quietness within, his philosophizing found voice. When the house work, to which he had assigned himself, was done, he would sit many hours of each day at his guard-post behind the draped window, on his knees his manuscript, which grew from year to year, until we saw each other again in freedom.

From 1939 to 1945 we had been completely separated, since 1941 also by the impossibility of correspondence. During this time, without knowing anything of each other, both of us had worked on the foundation of the jointly achieved philosophy and brought to each other, when we met again, the manuscripts of our books; Ernst his *Dialeklik des Nichtwissens* (Verlag für Recht und Gesellschaft, Basel) and I my *Von der Wahrheit* (Piper-Verlag, München) .

Only after his death did I see his contribution to the *Festschrift* dedicated to me by Klaus Piper on the occasion of my seventieth birthday: a simple and yet ever so difficult basic conception of the relation between my book *Von der Wahrheit* and my *Philosophie,* a conception which was clarifying even to myself. Once more I sadly experienced the way of his singular thinking along with me as well as thinking on ahead.

Behind he left an extensive work on nihilism, of which I hope that it will soon be published.

Of the connection of our work, in remembrance of the years 1928-31, I would almost like to say: my works are just as much his, as his are at the same time mine — if this were not saying too much, after all.

VII. University

Twice, immediately after the first and after the second World War, I published an essay on the Idea of the University, both times under the same title, with a view of bringing this idea more clearly to focal consciousness in myself, in the students, as well as in the professors. My 1946 essay is unchanged as to sentiment, but newly written and changed in order to serve the recreation of the German university. Both times, however, my word remained without effect; I am glad nevertheless to have said what I did in the spirit of our great tradition and in the inextinguishable hope for a resurrection of the idea. I shall now report of the experiences and attitudes from which those two essays proceeded.

Ever since my student days the university was the institution to which I felt I belonged. Important teachers I viewed with reverence, all of them, even those of whom I disapproved, with respect for their position. The buildings, the lecture-rooms, the forms of the tradition were objects of reverence for me.

What it really was which lent to all this a still visible lustre I did not yet clearly discern. But the mood in the work of this world, the attitude towards the officials who represented this authority, the memory of the preceding generations brought not only a consciousness of order, but of the great tasks to be fulfilled by the intellectual professions which carried, and were expected to fill with meaning, the entire life of society.

Disappointments came, of course. The majority of the students simply did not come up to the idea. The fraternities and student-corps, as they had now come to be, meant for me an impersonal life alienated from spiritual endeavor, a life of saloons, duels, drilled-in forms of conduct. This life guaranteed to these privileged ones later advantages — based on connections with the alumni —, if one just barely met the average norms of studies, nationalism, and obedience. Among the students, aside from a few, I felt myself a stranger. Nevertheless, they put up with me well enough and occasionally even regarded me with astonished respect, because of the objective interest discernible in my manner. For, I went my way quietly and unobtrusively.

But the fraternities became an exciting problem for me, since they determined the tone of university life and were held in highest esteem. It became a question of the freedom of the students' life and studies. Such freedom demanded the spontaneity of personal friendship and self-consciousness in going one's own intellectual way. These appeared to me threatened by the requirements of a fraternity, which, for trifles, robs time and strength and produces a self-consciousness merely from a sense of belonging, made noticeable by the colored ribbon (across the chest). Instead of living for the pursuit of knowledge, out of intellectual adventure, and one's own responsibility, one gave way to the aims of a privileged social set, and submitted to the imaginary notions of youthful happiness held by the older alumni. Instead of doing one's own thinking, one became stamped by conventional opinions which, in view of one's own inner insecurity, were fanatically expostulated. That these students had no contact with the intellectual movements of the age seemed to confirm my judgment that they were not really students. The experiences of my youth as well as later observations have taught me to see in these organizations a fatal trend of the German universities. None of the spirit, which after the wars of liberation had originally led to the founding of these fraternities, was left in them. No real education took place in them any longer but only the training of a familiar type. And this type itself I hated.

Another problem for the freedom of study came with the rise of study regulations and controls. In the 19th century the German student had actually studied freely. If he did not learn enough, he flunked the exams. As a child I still experienced the difficulty of the situation when pre-legal students, who had not reached their goal, had to accept another, non-academic occupation. In the study of medicine regulations were now introduced, which finally guaranteed a definite passing of the examinations, if need be with a condition, i.e., a second examination in one or another special subject. The problems which arose in view of these situations were now and then being discussed. In Göttingen I lived in a boarding house in which a worthy elderly lady cared for a small group of recommended students in surroundings which were in harmony with professional tradition. I was the youngest. When, on one occasion I spoke concerning studying and the students' life and their complete freedom as a necessary condition for any real intellectual understanding, an elderly medical man replied: "That is all very nice. But you are mistaken. It just doesn't work that way. The average student has to be led." Even today I still feel how confounded I was. My answer was that I wanted only what was possible for every human being. That, I insisted, was not a matter of superior endowment — average endowment was, in general, quite sufficient —, but merely that of urge towards real knowledge, and with that of a venturing and of a conscientious attention to the demands of one's studies. The universities are no mere schools, but institutions for *higher* learning. Kuno Fischer in Heidelberg had said: "The *higher* school is no mere 'high school.'" Even if the university was not intended for everyone, everyone nevertheless had the right to select himself for it, provided he was aware of what renunciations were necessary. Anyone who was studying merely in order to pass an examination or to procure for himself a better position, who, instead of gaining genuine knowledge, wants to have mere examination knowledge poured into him, does not belong in a university at all. In that case, my partner opined, the majority of students does not belong

in a university. It is bad, if you are correct, I replied; for that
would be the end of the university.

The other disappointment were the instructors in the universities. Only a few teachers demonstrated and proved the reality of
the higher learning. Men publicly well known often appeared to
me — altho meritorious, of great ability for work, instructive in
orienting the students in their subjects — nevertheless as if they
were standing apart from the idea of the university and its spirit.
It looked more like "pomp and circumstance," to which must be
added intrigues and propaganda. At the base of the tremendously
hard work of the professors there seemed to lie an *'existential'*
rooflessness and confusion. They claimed the highest pretensions
for their own importance. Masses of students enhanced such masters and in so doing achieved status for themselves. What they
were in reality I experienced later, especially 1918-19, in concrete
situations of fate. They were what, in my parental home, named
after a large German (political) party, used to be designated by
the invective "liberal nationalists," i.e., men without determination and without courage in matters of public affairs.

Ever since I first, ominously, heard about the university in my
childhood, it meant to me an instance of truth as such. Later it
became clear to me that this was the supra-national, occidental
idea (of the university). It was one of the greatest disappointments in 1914 that the universities — in the Anglo-Saxon camp as
well as in the German — became partisans. It was as treason
against the eternal idea of the university. For me the university
had been that which could maintain the truth against national
realities. But what had already become apparent before 1914 now
became complete: everywhere in the world one was obedient to
this national reality and conformed to it, one proceeded to justify
it. "Whose bread I eat, his song I sing"* had become terrible
reality. The very responsibility of the university as a super-political
and supra-national Occidental court of appeal had been lost.

I experienced this more concretely by the necessity for personal
decision in 1919. Because of what were meant to be revolutionary
changes in the constitution of the University, I had, at that time,
as a *Privatdozent*, been elected to the (University-) Senate. On
one occasion the following matter was before us: The Rektor of
the University of Berlin called upon all German universities to
join in a document of protest against the conditions imposed by
the later dictated peace-treaty of Versailles, which had become

* Editor's Note: "You don't bite the hand that feeds you," is the American
equivalent of this German proverb.

known. When it was my turn, I said: It is my advice not to sign this protest. All of us agree on the disaster and injustice of the conditions as they had become known. What each one of us as German citizens should do was not the issue. But the more clearly we, as German citizens, faced extremes (of suffering), the more clearly we should preserve to the very last that realm whose meaning surpasses all nations and peoples. We sit here as representatives of the university. True, just as in the case of the churches, the university exists by virtue of state-taxes. But also as with the church, the university's task is supra-national. As the Senate of the University we are concerned here only with this latter. We are primarily an Occidental, not a German university. Our origin lies in the European Middle Ages, not in the territorial states, which have merely taken us over. We should keep our task pure and not push ourselves into problems which we did not have the power to solve. If, nevertheless, we did mix in these problems, it would be a blot on the realization of our idea. Never had it been more necessary than at this moment to maintain a supra-national status of human community. Moreover, the protest, because not a deed, would be as invalid as the claim to the authority for such a declaration would be unfounded. For the world did not at all acknowledge any such authority on the part of the university.

This expression by the young *Privatdozent* produced astonishment. A few spoke even after I had spoken. Gradenwitz, a teacher of law, a Jew and anti-Semitic, spoke, completely ignoring what I had said, to show that a *Privatdozent* has no business to have an opinion in this (august) body. Dibelius, the well known theologian, expressed himself by careful consideration of my statement, declined my comparison with the churches, and concluded: it would be no blot on the university, if we made the protest our own. By unanimous vote, with one abstention, my motion was turned down. It was Ernst, a pathologist, a Swiss citizen, who had abstained from voting. On the way home he told me warmly that I was right and that he had abstained only because he was Swiss, and, as such, had no business to participate in this matter. But, I replied, this was a matter not of the Swiss nor of the Germans nor of the Allies, but of the Occidental idea of the university. To which Ernst opined that perhaps this ought to be so, but in reality it is, unfortunately but certainly, not so.

That the intellectual freedom of the university was being threatened even then became clear to me in an event of 1924 which kept the university in commotion for years. A *Privatdozent* of statistics, Gumbel, recognized because of his scientific works, went before the public with passionate political interest. His brochures with blood-dripping covers disclosed the existence of a secret military establishment, the so-called "black Reichswehr." They also attacked the re-establishment of the German military at that time. In public speeches Gumbel as a pacifist addressed the people. He used the words: ". . . the men who — I would not say fell on the field of dishonor, but — lost their lives in an awful fashion." The wrath of nationalistic professors, which had awakened long ago anyway, picked on this sentence: Gumbel has insulted the honor of the fallen German soldiers; this is unbearable; he is a disgrace to the University, his right to teach must be withdrawn. Disciplinary proceedings were instituted with the aim of denying him the right to teach. I was one of the members of the board of inquiry, which consisted of a member of the law faculty, a representative of the not full professors and of myself as representative of the full professors of the philosophical faculty. The sentence had to be passed by the faculty on the recommendation of this board of inquiry, but for its legal validity required confirmation by the Ministry of Education.

From the first moment it was clear to me: what is at stake is academic freedom. This is destroyed in its very roots if the faculty member's opinions may be examined. I had long been well informed on the history of our university and knew the constitution of 1803, which had been composed in the spirit of our classical period. At that time one still knew what a university is and what dangers threaten it. It contained the regulation which was omitted from the newer constitutions of the 19th century: the right to teach may be cancelled only for actions which are condemned by a court of criminal law. This meant that one could not be deprived of the right to teach on the basis of one's *Weltanschauung,* nor on that of tactlessness; and still less because of one's political conviction.

In our board of inquiry I called attention immediately to these real conditions of our freedom. If today, because of political pacifist convictions and because of actions disclosing a political breach of treaty (even if that breach be that of the Versailles dictate of peace) an instructor can be reprimanded under the guise of an insult to national honor which carefully veils those facts, then tomorrow another one (may suffer this same fate) because of his atheism and day after tomorrow still another because of his nonconformity to the existing regime of the state. But the old regulation (of the University) was no longer in force.

Now the accusation was: Gumbel's words were said to have

offended the sense of honor of the German people, especially of
the ex-servicemen. In doing this one boasted of democracy. Without adopting this thesis as my own, I agreed to that. But I demanded that the factuality of the offense would have to be confirmed by the deposition of witnesses. Those who had heard Gumbel at that particular lecture, all of them ex-servicemen, would be
the legitimate witnesses. Thus a considerable number of men were
interrogated. Surprisingly it turned out that almost all of them
were not at all offended, but actually agreed with Gumbel.

The result of the investigation was an opinion drawn up by
the three members of the board, in which it was proposed that the
right to teach should not be taken from Gumbel. However, before
this opinion reached the faculty, it became known among the
professors. A storm of indignation arose. The theologian came
even before 8 in the morning to the legal member of the board
in order to inform him (of this storm) and to aid and abet it by
a few strong remarks.

Thereupon both of my colleagues on the board requested me to
agree to annul our already given signature on the opinion and to
compose another opinion. I told both that I was agreeable to the
annulling of *their* signatures. But the present opinion was to go
to the faculty as my own. They might compose a new one on their
own responsibility without me. This was done.

After a session which lasted four hours, the faculty decided —
with all votes opposed to mine — that Gumbel's right to teach
was to be withdrawn. This motion had to be referred to the Ministry (of Education). According to custom, the faculty loyally
left to me the right to submit to the government a separate opinion, opposing the resolution of the faculty. This I waived. For, I
said to myself, the Socialist government, which, after all, we knew
from its statements as well as actions, would, for party reasons and
in support of the similar-minded Gumbel, reject the motion of the
faculty in any case, but not in any sense in behalf of the academic
freedom of the university. My concern was not for Gumbel, but
for academic freedom. If the entire faculty was unable to see its
being endangered by the faculty's own action, then the rejection
of the motion by the government might, it is true, save Gumbel,
but not academic freedom.

When I returned home from this session, full of despair I said
to my wife: the freedom of the university is done for; no one
knows any longer what it is; I give up the battle and shall only do
philosophy. — What, she replied apprehensively and challenging,
you surely are not going to lose your wings!

I shall not relate what happened through the years. Gumbel remained *Dozent,* and made renewed provocative remarks. Once more there were disciplinary proceedings (against him). Because of a complicated situation and as the result of a fascinating speech on academic freedom by Dean Ludwig Curtius, the faculty now reversed itself, decided to keep Gumbel in his position. But the faculty was not grateful to its dean for having brought it to a right resolution. Several colleagues felt they had been taken in. It was a grotesque confusion. Those years saw the beginnings of those motives and of that thoughtlessness at the University, which unsuspectingly and against one's own will brought National Socialism to power, which then, by trumping all such battles as trifles, with one stroke extinguished the university as the actuality of the free spirit.

The idea of the university lives decisively in the individual students and professors, and only secondarily in the forms of the institution. If that life would become obliterated, the institution can not possibly save it. That life must, however, be awakened from person to person and must be encouraged to become conscious of itself and be more effective by new publications which are appropriate to the existing situation. The student is on the look-out for the idea, is ready for it, but is really helpless, if he does not encounter it coming from his professors. In that case he must actualize the idea himself.

Within the university the idea of the professor of philosophy became the justification for my own empirical existence. So long as there is such a thing as the freedom of the Occidental university, the realization of that idea depends entirely upon the individual who comprehends it and is entrusted with its realization. As professor of philosophy he is master within the four walls of the area of his teaching activity. He may arrange this area to suit himself. He must prove himself to a youth which in harmony with its nature has as yet more regard for truth than do more advanced ages. It is his task to point up the great philosophers and to see to it that they are not confused with the minor ones. Thus the perennial basic ideas become known in their greatest figures. He must awaken an openness for everything knowable, for the meaning of the sciences and for the actuality of life. All of this he must encompass and penetrate by the basic operations of thinking which cause us to soar. He is to live in the idea of the university and in doing so acknowledge his responsibility for productive, constructive, creative activity. He must not cover up the ultimate limits, but instruct in the ways of moderation.

What I myself owe to the Occidental idea of the university and to its, however blurred, reality in Germany is really quite extraordinary. Complete freedom in our era is like a fairytale; so is the modest empirical existence with just one occupation: to think; and — the necessary calm for this.

The temptations of the institution are great, but not compelling: the scatter-brainedness — the emptiness whenever administration occupied one for a time to the exclusion of everything else — the busy idleness. The freedom of the professor, which may never submit to any kind of control, may, it is true, seduce a specific individual to laziness; but it is also the freedom to dream, to that apparent do-nothing of which no one knows what actually occurs. Here lies the source of everything essential. Whoever is not willing to put up with failure of some individuals, would have to destroy with freedom at the same time the productivity and with that the spirit of the university.

VIII. POLITICAL IDEAS

For want of one's own realization a content of philosophizing may accrue from even the slightest contact with this reality on the part of others. Paradoxically that content gets nourishment and passion from what had to be foregone. I felt this especially in the area of politics. It would be too exacting to say that I had put thinking in the place of action. But, on a modest level, something analogous to that happened to me.

Since my childhood I had heard about politics. My grandfather, father, and two brothers of my mother were state-representatives in Oldenburg, and at the same time liberal, democratic, and conservative. For decades my father was president of the Oldenburg City Council. In those days the Council was concerned entirely with administrative tasks, schools, buildings, streets, canals, railroads, etc. Great commotion arose when a secretary of cabinet rank had not done well; his errors were held up to him and yet the Grandduke did not dismiss him. But this was an exception. Almost always it was possible, by common deliberation, to reach the goal in a reasonable manner. My father enjoyed doing this. One day, however, as a personality respected in city and country, he was supposed to be elected to the *Reichstag* (Congress) by the combined efforts of several who, ordinarily, could not get together on anything. This he declined, however; he had (he said) something better to do in Oldenburg than to run around in Berlin, make speeches and listen to speeches without being able to accomplish anything;—this empty façade of an apparent *Reichs-tag* did not at all attract him. My father was indignant over the invasion of Prussian attitudes in Oldenburg, of Prussian manners (the bearing of assessors and lieutenants), of Prussian militarism since 1866, growing enormously since 1870. Yet, with all his opposition, he had real affection for the old Grandduke, as a worthy, cultivated, decent person. In the new German empire he did not feel at home. Once, in the nineties, on a walk on the Weser-dyke near Porake, he said to me, the lad: Too bad that Holland does not reach to the Weser (as if to say: that Oldenburg is not a part of Holland). In the army my father was an excellent officer in the reserves, but inwardly he was quite reluctant. When, at age 45, at a "love-feast," he learned from the regimental commander that he had been recommended for a captaincy (in those days a very uncommon honor for a civilian), my father opined that nothing would likely come of that. To the urging commander he declared he would not serve one day beyond his legal obligations; that he had found military service barely endurable, that there was something in him which made him look on any superior as a personal enemy. Thus alien was my father to the German political situation, and he became constantly more so. The limited area of Oldenburg with its sensible administration he loved — as one cultivates a garden — as long as possible. But he saw the growing ruin which he could not prevent; he went hunting, painted watercolors, and carried out the duties of his profession. When, for his eightieth birthday (1930), the city offered to name a street after him, he declined with a friendly letter of thanks (glad that he had been asked before publication) and said within the confines of the family: I certainly am not going to have a street named after me by governments which constantly change, acknowledge no tradition and will, after a few years, rename the street!

Altogether different the youngest brother of my mother, Theodor Tantzen. He was only six years older than I, and grew up in my parental home because he went to school in Oldenburg. Already, at the age of eighteen he began as a public speaker in the liberal party of Eugen Richter. He had the qualities of a demagogue, practical efficiency and a robust ability to make decisions. In 1919 he became prime minister (until 1924), and again in 1945, this time appointed by the British. During the period of National Socialism he visited us regularly in Heidelberg to discuss the situation with us. Repeatedly he was arrested by the Gestapo, the last time immediately after July 20th, 1944. By his skill, through friends who had made common cause with National So-

cialism, and by sheer luck he succeeded each time to gain his freedom. He died a few days before the powers of occupation made
the province Oldenburg a part of Lower Saxony and transferred
the seat of government to Hannover.

I myself participated in all these things merely as an onlooker,
although sometimes I did take a lively part in discussions within
the family. Until 1914 my basic attitude was strictly non-political.
Everything seemed to be definitive. Our anguish concerned a much
later future, which we did not believe we would live to see. At
that time I thought more along aesthetic lines: How are we ever
going to get rid of those ridiculous princes (the young Grandduke
was an object of contempt), as for example the Kaiser with his
pompous bombast of words and his provocative actions. Kaiser,
governments, existing situations occasionally were objects of sneer-
ing, the *Simplicissimus* the proper magazine. I turned entirely to
intellectual tasks. For that there was freedom which we took to
be self-evident. Everything else we had to accept without being
too much pinched by it.

With the outbreak of the war in 1914 (I was thirty-one at the
time) things became different. The historical earth trembled.
Everything which seemed long to have been secure with one
stroke appeared threatened. We felt that we had gotten into an
irresistible, opaque process. Only since then do our generations
know themselves thrown into the stream of catastrophic events.
Since 1914 these have not stopped. They keep going in a frantic
tempo. This our human fate I sought from then on to comprehend,
not as the knowable necessity of a dark supernatural process of
history, but as a situation whose results — on the basis of what is
properly knowable, which is always something specific — are decisively determined by our human freedom.

What I have thought since the outbreak of the war in 1914 has
stood under the influence of Max Weber. Through him my political attitude underwent a change. Until then the national idea had
been foreign to me. Through Max Weber I learned to think in
national terms and took that type of thinking to heart. The world
situation places upon a people, which through its government has
become a world power, a responsibility, which it cannot escape.
Posterity will hold responsible, not the small state of the Swiss,
whose existence had a different, highly desirable meaning (the
freedom of individuals in a small state and not the responsibility
of power), but us, if the world will be divided between the Russian whip and Anglo-Saxon convention. It is our task and opportunity to salvage between those two this third: The spirit of radical

liberalism, the freedom and manifoldness of personal life, the magnitude of the Occidental tradition. This was Max Weber's attitude which I now shared.

This calls for politics on a grand scale, i.e., a politics of sure and measured judgment, of self limitation and of reliable carrying out of pledges, a politics which is oriented toward the totality of human events and which so acts, thinks and speaks that the world turns to it in confidence.

This is why Max Weber stood against the political actuality of William the Second's empire, against the obscurity of political thought, against the veiling in a pseudo-constitutionalism, against the braggadocio conduct of the Kaiser in foreign affairs, against the arbitrary, constantly changing intervention. Before 1914 he suffered immeasurably politically, while his illness prevented any kind of activity, even that of his academic duties as a professor. He saw: we are losing the confidence of the entire world. Political stupidity, not the war-mongering of the Kaiser and of his creatures, will lead to war, which is the most terrible fate for Europe. When, in 1913, my wife happened to meet Max Weber on a train, he had just read the papers, was in great agitation and almost screamed: that hysteric will yet drive us into war.

Since 1917 Max Weber — slowly recuperating from his illness — burst forth with political writings. He still wanted to hope that the Germans might yet get there by way of a genuine democracy as over against the unbearable type of Ludendorff who wanted to stamp over all of Europe, against the selfishness of the large land holders, against the political provincialism of big industry, against the political narrowness of the socialists of the unions and of the labor leaders who, without comprehension of the immensity of politics, do not see what is at stake but, full of illusions, want to carry out their ruinous plans. But upon what did Max Weber count, for what powers did he hope? For something which did not yet exist in Germany, although it seemed to be the most natural, the most reasonable, and the most self-evident.

His specific demands during the war corresponded to this: From the very beginnings, all the way through, and at the very height of German victories he declared: No expansion of our borders, no annexation of a single square mile; for Germany it is sufficient to have stood its ground; if it demonstrated that it desires absolutely no conquest and that it has the power to assert itself against a world, then it is fulfilling its great-world-historical task, to salvage the "Between." For this reason he was at all times in favor of a peace of arbitration without claims on either side, so to say for the combined recognition of the error of having gotten into this internecine war at all. He put forth the following thesis: even in case of an occupation by the British and the French we would not lose our essential nature, because they would neither want to nor could they destroy it. Under Russian domination, on the other hand, we would cease to remain Germans, just as all other peoples could not remain themselves under such a regime. For this reason, Max Weber saw the only really great achievement of Germany in the First World War in having stopped the power of Russia at least for this once.

Max Weber was the last genuine national German; genuine, because he represented the spirit of Baron von Stein, of Gneisenau, of Mommsen, not the will to power for one's own empire — at any price and above all others —, but the will to realize a spiritual and moral existence which holds its ground by power but also places this power itself under its own conditions. Max Weber, who very early saw the tremendous danger into which the Germans came due to the course of the empire of William, knew that there is a limit which means ruin, after which the survivors continue, but in a vegetative state which is without political meaning and therefore without common greatness. Politics can exist only in freedom. Where this is destroyed there only remains private life insofar as this is suffered to exist. When, in January 1919, I asked Max Weber what could be done if the communists came to power, his reply was: then I am no longer interested in the matter.

This meant resignation before the reality of brutal might against which the individual is no longer able to do anything. This insight corresponds to the fact that Germany could not be freed of National Socialism from within itself, but only from the outside, that no totalitarianism can be overcome from within but at best can only be transformed into another kind (of totalitarianism) by bloody revolutions. The end of genuine politics suspends the interest for politics; but real politics is possible only if the result is effectuated through the persuasion of others by discourse pro and con, in which the education of public consciousness takes place by means of a free combat of minds.

Completely outside of the horizon of Max Weber, and of everything which he developed in predictions concerning future possibilities, remained such actualities as the murder of millions of Jews by Hitler-Germany, the unrestricted transformation of man carried out by way of terrorism, and man's annihilation into mere function in the SS-state of the concentration camps.

Max Weber's political thought coined my own. Perhaps in basic attitude I may never have been in complete agreement with him. I lacked the consciousness of the greatness of Prussia and of Bismarck, which I recognized only theoretically and, at heart, with aversion. I lacked the military spirit. I was able to admire it, but could not actually verify it myself. I lacked the heroic inclination, the grandeur of boundlessness, which nevertheless I liked in Max Weber. But Max Weber's basic insights I simply learned and took over. The following were the political experiences which were relevant and essential for me.

As early as 1908, when, on the occasion of the first round-flight of the (dirigible) Zeppelin an intoxication went through the entire German population, I was unable to participate, despite my admiration for the technical achievement and my delight with it. The form of the intoxication terrified me. This repeated itself in 1914 at the beginning of the war: the war enthusiasm, a mixture of exaltation and sense of destiny, which carried everything before it (very soon, when trouble arose, this intoxication proved to be a mere straw fire) was alien and uncanny to me. I was happy when I met individuals who did not participate, as for example a young peasant from Oldenburg who disliked a speech of the Kaiser on "War for the German Culture:" "nonsense," he said, "German culture — the others are no barbarians either — we are attacked and stand our man, that is all." This mass movement was there again in 1918, when the revolutionary intoxication of the collapse led to the self-confident expectation of now creating glorious human conditions. And then this intoxication returned grotesquely once more in 1933 with all the symptoms of a mass delusion. Constantly more questionable for me became the saying: *Vox populi vox dei,* insofar as the voice of a people is supposed to speak through its masses. I was unable to restrain myself from inwardly despising everyone who participated in such states of intoxication.

During the first war a political club came into existence consisting of professors of all the faculties in Heidelberg. A club which met often — during the semesters sometimes weekly — to talk about the political and military events, to listen to lectures by its members, and to discuss. When the club constituted itself, almost all prominent professors, altho in a select minority, belonged. Alfred Weber was in combat and therefore was not a member. Max Weber, the only truly political, intellectually superior and universally informed man, was not invited. They called him a calamity howler; they asserted that he dominated the discussion; they were afraid of his immoderation. Indeed, no superior personality was wanted in this circle of mutual admiration and high self-esteem.

Max Weber was pained by the exclusion, for, isolated as he was by illness, he was by nature social and not at all proud.

After some time I was invited to membership, despite the fact that I was only an unsalaried lecturer *(Privatdozent)*. From 1915 until 1923 I attended the meetings. There I came to know the political thinking of our academic world on its best possible level. It was not at all uniform. Very passionate discussions took place. The freedom of expression was almost unlimited. I could take the liberty to express my own points of view unreservedly as they changed, without incurring personal dislike. For example: In spite of the veiled news reports it became clear, in July 1918, that the so-called Ludendorff offensive had not merely miscarried but had been superceded by a mighty counter attack of the Allies. I developed the idea: our defeat is certain. But it might still take a long time. There had been mutinies in the French army, not in ours. The offer of peace on our part would at this moment be just still possible. We should make some radical renunciations; for in that case what would be safe would still be tremendous as over against what would remain after a real defeat. Therefore, even giving up of Alsace-Lorraine would now be necessary, as well as acknowledging the injustice of violating the borders of Belgium in 1914 and therefore restitution to Belgium. Beyond this no benefits but a reconstitution of the old border in the East, despite our present occupation of Russia; and, finally, the introduction of a genuine parliamentary democracy in Germany. Such views at that time in Germany were like treason and were possible to be expressed only in this humanly decent circle. Oncken, the excellent historian, replied in his noble fashion: in his view my conception was to be rejected, but it was nevertheless very noteworthy that such a conception was today possible at all.

Neither in the first World War nor afterwards did I speak in my lectures or in my writings on political matters. I was a bit shy, because I had not been a soldier. For, politics is concerned with the seriousness of power which is based on staking one's life. I lacked this legitimation. The shyness diminished as I became older. Most of all, in the twenties I saw the obvious political failure of the military attitude. I recognized in it the false political claim. My anger was aroused by the then appearing books of Ernst Jünger, the fascinating author and bearer of the order *pour le mérite*. They seemed to me to be a moral-political disaster. In this irresponsible romantic and adventurous squandering away of life there manifested itself the very opposite of the high seriousness of a politics grounded in the very stake of life itself.

That I got on the road of speaking in public on political matters came about through a task I was assigned. I was commissioned to write the one-thousandth volume in the little Göschen-Series. The theme I was given was: the spiritual movements of our age. I changed the theme immediately to: *Die geistige Situation der Zeit* (English translation of 1933: *Man In the Modern Age*). By it I meant to say: I do not perceive the movements, I do not know what happens overall. I can only show the situation and its aspects. I can engross the reader, call to his attention, teach him to see, but I cannot give him an historical survey of the present.

The theme attracted me for various reasons. I could speak of politics grounded upon the total moral-spiritual situation of our age. Out of my work, *Philosophie,* which was in process, I could now eliminate everything which concerned the present (just as I had already taken out all excursions into the philosophy of history for a later work). As I gathered up the sheets, there still was need for bringing in some order and for many additions; but in principle the book was there when I accepted the commission in 1929. The little book was completed in September 1930, just as the elections to the *Reichstag,* which for the first time were successful for National Socialism, became known. At the time I wrote the book I knew very little of fascism and of National Socialism, whose madness I still held to be impossible in Germany. I left the manuscript lying in my desk. After so long an interval in my publications I wanted to come before the public with my *Philosophie* and not with a little volume which, in any case, needed the *Philosophie* as its foundation. Thus I saw to it that the *Geistige Situation der Zeit* appeared only a year later, in the beginning of October 1931, and, immediately thereafter, in December, my *Philosophie.*

Since 1933 unexpected experiences became unavoidable. The extent of man's capacity for monstrous deeds, of the intellectually gifted for delusions, of apparently good citizens for perfidy, of the seemingly decent person for malice, what is possible to the mob in the way of thoughtlessness, of selfish short-sighted passivity, all this became real to an extent that the knowledge of man had to undergo a change. In brief, what formerly was not even so much as considered was now not merely possible but actual. History seemed to have received a jolt. A subsequent consideration of the entirety of world history made it become clear, however, that these impossibilities were not at all new in their roots, but merely in their (particular) appearance, that the prejudices of an age had clouded our view in spite of the intellectual range of its consciousness.

At the same time, however, the unswervability of specific individuals, the faithfulness of loving persons, the power of helping, of daring, of lavish self-giving, the prudence and caution in the midst of helplessness with its hidden lustre of mutual understanding became visible. All of this became, so to say, as never before a guarantee of the undestructibility of what it really means to be human. Heroic ventures occurred — too late, inefficient, not equal to the situation, and therefore ambiguous — which, though they were not representative of any communal consciousness, became nevertheless a great question for us.

In spite of the devilishly enforced anonymity of innumerable ones whose death no mouth reported, one heard occasionally of men who were able to die in the humiliating indignity of torment, of tortures, starved and poisoned to the very point of being unable to resist. Among the murdered Jews were those of whom it was told that they, denuded, delivered to destruction, like vermin, remained pious and certain of God, to the utmost, that they — like the forty soldiers of the Roman legion touchingly depicted on a Byzantine ivory tablet — went to their death nude, amidst simple attestation of their mutual love. And there were others among those who resisted the regime, among those sent to concentration camps because of a careless word, among the executed and the hanged, among the displaced and murdered from the ravished nations, who died no less piously.

Indeed, for those who kept on living the world was so greatly changed, that it was not yet possible to grasp what really had happened, and what the present situation meant. The prophecies, especially those of Nietzsche, were like non-committal visions which now paled because no nihilistic actuality had yet corresponded to them and because precisely what was now happening had not been foreseen. Something immutable in our origin, something whose meaning could not be changed by any historical catastrophe, might uphold us. But this (presently) changeable had to be seen and grasped anew from the (vantage point of the) immutable.

Before this task one stood questioning, listening, not knowing, waiting, while the disaster threatened everyone.

Inwardly my wife and I experienced this threat to corporeal existence without being able to defend ourselves through long years. Outwardly no harm was done to us. We learned from the police by the usual indiscreet round-about way, that it was planned to ship us off on April 14, 1945. Other transports had already taken place in the preceding weeks. On April 1, Heidelberg was occupied by the Americans. A German cannot forget that he owes his and his wife's life to Americans against Germans who in the name of the National Socialist German State wanted to destroy him.

My experiences from 1933 to 1945 I need not here report in detail. From 1933 on I was excluded from any co-operation in the administration of the University, from 1937 robbed of my professorship, from 1938 no longer allowed to publish. The basic experience was the loss of the guarantee of judicial rights among one's own people and within one's own country. The real abandonment could not be balanced by the friendly attitude of specific individuals who did not give up their intercourse with us, not by the friends all of whom, with a single exception, remained faithful, not by merchants and workmen who helpfully stood by my wife, not by the inner closeness of those nearest to us. All of this felt good. It preserved the community with the Germans and the consciousness of belonging, even though it was certain that these Germans, who now became the genuine Germans to us, were a small minority. The situation compelled this reluctant reversal of the exclusion from the German character which the Nationalists and the National Socialists had carried out against this minority and against us by word, print, and deed. I permitted the attempted, even though ineffective, personal help on the part of a few National Socialists, whenever I, by appeal to an unwritten judicial claim, turned to official authorities. In several cases, however, I quietly gave up, as when one of the National Socialist professors answered me: The procedures against the Jews were in principle correct, but he would try to see whether he could accomplish anything in behalf of my wife; or when another inquired of me whether my wife had not done anything blameworthy.

In this situation, and with increasing danger we watched powerlessly, for twelve years, thoughtfully careful and cautious, heedful of the Gestapo and the Nazi authorities, determined to commit no act and to utter no word which we could not justify. Fortune was with us. I did not tempt it by any imprudence.

It was a time for reflection; all the more so because the hygienic conditions of life remained good. According to the "mechanics of the statutes" I did not merely receive a pension, but also was provided with food and fuel. True, there was no concrete hope of surviving the tyranny or for an 'afterwards.' But no one could know this. When, in 1938, a young friend said to me: Why are you writing, it can never be published anyway, and one day all of your manuscripts will be burned, I replied playfully: One never knows, I enjoy writing; what I am thinking, becomes clearer in the process; and finally, in case the overthrow should occur someday, I do not wish to stand there with empty hands.

Until the spring of 1939, I had the good fortune of friendship with Heinrich Zimmer, the Indologist, who, under the pressure of those days, had to emigrate with his family, first to England, and afterwards to the USA. Those were the last broadly-conceived and penetrating intellectual conversations I had with a man in Heidelberg. He gave me much from his immense knowledge, wanted to care for me, brought me much literature and translations from the Chinese and Indian world.

But those twelve years meant an incision into life of a very peculiar kind. On the one hand, there took place the inner gaining of distance from Germany as a political structure. With almost no exceptions, all Germans, even old friends, desired a German victory; whereas I, in the exaltation of victories, despairingly looked about for signs of a possible change, encouraged by Churchill's attitude and speeches in September, 1940. As early as 1936 I had hoped for the entry of the Allies, which I had been desiring since 1933. Now all hope turned on the defeat and annihilation of Hitler-Germany; in order that the surviving Germans might be enabled to recreate their existence from their roots, anew and decently.

The consciousness of being German became a question. What does it mean to be a German? Other peoples accuse us of always meditating on being German, of wanting to be German, and of making what is natural into something artificial and forced. This consequence was not necessary. But for the German the question is, unfortunately, unavoidable, especially since, on the part of his countrymen, the word German is everlastingly being boomed into his ear.

The natural unquestioned being-German, in which I lived, was language, home, heritage, was the great intellectual tradition in which I participated from an early age. Not power as such, power in the service of the moral-political idea was the task. Never would Max Weber have sold the soul of the German for power, as did the majority of the population of the German territories in 1933.

Therefore our despair of the German of 1933 and of all the following years. What is German? Who is German? When, in 1933, my wife, who, as a German Jewess, was betrayed by Germany, rejected Germany which she loved more perhaps than I did myself, I replied definitely and insolently — in order to bring her back to affirmation —: Think me to be Germany.

Nevertheless, my gaining full perspective on the German empire since 1933 brought to my consciousness how completely and unavoidably my wife and I are Germans. The resulting questions remained insoluble.

To the few, among whom I was one, it was since 1933 probable and since 1939 certain, that the events in Germany meant the end of Germany. *Finis Germaniae:* The word passed quietly from mouth to mouth whether Hitler-Germany would win or lose (that it would lose became certain to us in the autumn of 1941), in any case there would no longer be a Germany. But so many German persons, speaking German, partakers in the events, originating in the lost German state, would survive. What shall they do, what gives their existence value, do they remain Germans and in what sense, do they have any task? — such questions were bound to force a German to come to his senses. The very sense of having lost the being-German — transmitted to us by generations — had to turn memory back to the origins, if one wished again to become truthful and worthy of one's forbears. The question has even today not yet been answered, the coming to senses not been carried out. Yet it burns in the soul of every genuine German.

Since 1933 one thing became the self-evident basis of my German self-consciousness. Political Germany — founded as Little-Germany on the basis of the trends of 1848 by Bismarck, out of fateful untruthfulness clothed in the idea of empire (an idea which came from the Middle Ages), as Second Empire spiritually as deceitfully founded as the railroad depots which, in those days were built in Gothic style, — (this Germany) is not Germany as such, but, viewed from the standpoint of world history, merely a short-time political episode. Germany — that has for a thousand years, been something entirely different, something much more full of content. The glorious Occidental idea of empire perished already in the thirteenth century. What is German is held together only by the German language and by the spiritual life which manifests itself in it, the religious and moral reality which communicates itself in it. This Germany is extra-ordinarily many-sided. The political aspect of it is only one dimension, and an unhappy one at that, a history which proceeds from one catastrophe to another. What is German lives in the great spiritual realm, spiritually creating and battling, need not call itself German, has neither German intentions nor German pride, but lives spiritually of the things, of the ideas of world-wide communication.

That there is possible in this something durable and truly political was apparent in the Middle Ages in the freedom spread abroad in the Occident. In progress and transformation of the Middle Ages this is even today still present in Holland and in Switzerland. In the Prussian-German territory it has been lost since the seventeenth century.

The word German has two meanings, therefore. One is the one which, on the basis of the empire founded by Bismarck, is meant by the Germans of this territory and all the rest of the world, namely, the national existence of the so-called German unity. The other meaning is that intended by Burckhardt, when, at the beginning of the forties, he wrote that he considered it to be his task to show the Swiss that they are Germans (a sentence which Burckhardt never repeated, when, even before 1848, he saw that Germany did not move in the direction of federal freedom of a conservative type, but rather toward that of a state of centralized power, of a technical-rational character). The meaning intended by Burckhardt nobody understands any longer today. It is, however, the last refuge in which alone can be found what would again make it possible to develop a decent political existence in the former German imperial territory of Bismarck. When, in 1914, foreign propaganda wanted to split Germany into Weimar and Potsdam, I resisted. In the then existing situation the self-determination of a state was to be weakened. "Weimar" this was by no means that total, great, spiritual-political Germany of a thousand years, in which it was, after all, only an important link. Potsdam had a bad name, even among us, but it was not, after all, identical with the Germany that fought at that time. That today, however, — in the essential interest of the Germans themselves, not in that of foreign desire to weaken us — Germany must be taken in two senses, this fact should not be confused with the superficial antithesis of Weimar versus Potsdam. Such a separation today means: Germany's political existence can no longer be grounded either morally or spiritually upon restoration tendencies, nor upon the memories of the last century and a half. After the shocking inner and outer catastrophes it must rather be created anew from its depths in the new situation with a view to the world situation and to her co-responsibility in it. This depth is laid bare by the illumination and critical analysis of the historical episode that led into catastrophe.

While I dwelled upon such thoughts there grew in me at the same time the drive toward world citizenship. To be, first of all, a man and then, out of this background to belong to a nation, this seemed to me to be the essential matter. How longingly I sought a court of last resort above the nations, a law which legally can aid the individual who is lawlessly being ravished by his state! When there is inhuman injustice, there ought to be a safeguard against the state which commits the crime. The solidarity of all states could constitute this supra-national court. The principle of non-interference in the internal affairs of a state is the cloak for the admission of injustice. The claim to absolute sovereignty is the claim also to be allowed to act criminally according to one's own sovereign will. For, an old principle asserts that the king (now the state or the dictator) stands outside the law, that he is not himself subject to the law. Against such sovereignty stands the responsibility of all states not to tolerate inhumanity and lawlessness in any state without action, because in the long run everyone is threatened whenever such a crime happens, no matter where.

Such reflections occurred to me first when, in 1933, the Vatican concluded a Concordat with Hitler and thereby not only increased his prestige tremendously, but first accorded to his regime actual international recognition as a treaty-making power. They came to me with increased strength during the 1936 Olympics in Berlin when the Hitler regime was supported by the participation of the countries of the entire world. They came to me once again when the result of the International Congress in Evian in 1938, where possibilities for relocation of Jews fleeing from Germany were to be decided, was that the possibilities for relocation of German Jews the world over were actually much worse than before.

When on April 1, 1945, the Americans had occupied Heidelberg, and I seemed to be living in a fairytale, where the world can change overnight — when at the city hall I read the first legal decrees and detected in them for the first time again a decent Occidental note which was now again to be standard among us, I felt great hopes. Within three days I was already one of a commission of thirteen professors, chosen upon my suggestion, for preparing the re-opening of the provisionally-closed university. The CIC, a police institution still unknown to me, represented at the time by two lively, educated, and well-intentioned young men, gave us written permission for meetings and we went to work at once. The university was my own concern. Here I felt I could say and propose something. A few colleagues granted me their affection and their confidence in unforgettable fashion. Without being able to become dean or rektor, I let myself in for something, by way of work, speeches, and proposals which I could not really carry out with my (limited) strength.

Now confronted by these new questions, my wife and I found Hannah Arendt-Blücher, whose longtime affection had not waned through the decades, very helpful. Her philosophical solidarity remains among the most beautiful experiences of those years. She came from the younger generation to us older ones and brought us what she experienced.

Emigrated since 1913 and having wandered over the world, high-spirited under infinite difficulties, she was thoroughly acquainted with the violent terror of our existence, when such existence, torn from the country of its origin, is at anybody's mercy without any rights. She had tried to find a foothold, always had a foothold, but could not be bound by any of them in such a way as to set them up as absolute without criticism — with the exception of the historicity of her love and of whatever tasks she had at that time undertaken. Her inner independence made her a citizen of the world. Her faith in the unique power of the American Constitution (and in the political principle which had held its ground as the relatively best) made her a citizen of the United States. Better than I had ever been able before, I learned from her to see this world of the greatest attempts at political freedom and, on the other hand, the structures of totalitarianism: now and then slightly hesitating, but only because she had not yet familiarized herself with the categories, methods of research, and insights of Max Weber. Since 1948 she visited us repeatedly for intensive discussions and in order to make sure of a unanimity which could not be rationally defined. With her I was able to discuss once again in a fashion which I had desired all my life, but had from my youth on — with the exception of those closest to me, who shared my fate — really experienced only with a few men: In (an atmosphere of) complete unreservedness which allows of no mental reservations — in abandon because one knows that one can overshoot the mark, that such overshooting would be corrected and that it demonstrates in itself something worthwhile, viz., the tension of perhaps deep-seated differences which yet are encompassed by such trust that to differ does not mean a lessening of affection, — (in such an atmosphere to realize) the radical and mutual letting-free of the other, where abstract demands cease because they are extinguished in factual fidelity.

Since 1945 I could actively participate in politics even less than in the university. Many an American came to me in those days in order to inform himself and to get my opinions. At that time, when the Americans were still appointing the temporary governments, they asked me if I wished to become Secretary of Culture. The proposal could not go beyond mere conversation. A painful renunciation for me. Asked my opinions, during the always informal talks with those men — some of them outstanding —, who were the first to come to Germany, I heard and said much, alternating between the verve of envisaged possibilities and hopelessness in the face of the realities.

Political pondering became particularly penetrating when the transformation of the initial administration of Germany occurred. In the beginning German personalities had been appointed by the occupation authorities; now a party government, on the basis of general elections, was supposed to replace the former as a responsible democratic German regime. At that time I said to an American: "You are pursuing a path which is disastrous for Germany. For the best who could be found in Germany old party members are being substituted, people who proved their incapacity before 1933. Not good, but politically-corrupt Germans will rule. In reality it will remain as it is now: the occupation authorities will exercise factual sovereignty in ultimate decisions. But this truth is being veiled by an apparent independence. You ought to administer this Germany quite openly under your own responsibility by using the best, the most reasonable, and the most patriotic Germans. In that case the educational process which history has denied us will be able to begin from the bottom with at least a certain German independence. This does not happen by way of good advice, nor by lectures or writings, nor by means of the pathetic of 'glorious democracy,' but by practice. This latter, however, can only start in the communities. Look at this example: they complain just now about the much too high prices of potatoes in Heidelberg, whereas the farmers are complaining that they are getting much too little (I seem to recall that the farmer was getting three marks per hundred weight, whereas the city consumer paid twelve marks). What happens? Everybody demands governmental regulations. Correct, however, would be this: that farm communities through elective representatives come to an understanding with Heidelberg in order to achieve the goal rationally, by reasonable methods and on their own responsibility. Through concern with concrete questions one learns how to do things, and that everyone shares in responsibility. Whereas with us we still find obedience on the one hand and administrative bureaucracy on the other. Let the communities get practice in ordering their own affairs to an ever-increasing extent. Only thus can men develop who are able to think politically. From among them will then come, in public discussion, the men who, when new parties will be founded, will make an impression and gain confidence. How all of this is to take place in detail I do not know. But not before the expiration of twenty years can Germany be ruled by men who are freely elected. The loosening of the powers and responsibilities of the occupying authorities should take place step by step. Until the power of reasonable men — who exist in Germany and, I believe, in good measure — has matured. Now, when the presupposition is lacking in the mood of the population, when the overwhelming majority of Germans does not yet know at all what is genuinely real or what they want or what or whom they shall elect, to force party-democracy upon them is nothing else than to substitute for the authority of the Germans selected by you the authority of party hacks, party bureaucrats, and their dictators."

The American replied: "Perhaps you are right, I even think so. But it just won't do. In the first place, our American people wish no colonial administration. What you suggest looks like one. Secondly, we cannot do it because of the Russians. We dare not give them an example of dictatorial administration which would serve at the same time as a justification for doing the same thing only with a totally different purpose and in worse fashion."

In the area of such experiences and possibilities I have given many an address. In 1946 I published *The Question of German Guilt,* taken from my lectures on Germany during the winter semester, 1945-46.

Inasmuch as cooperation in active politics was denied me, I could only reflect, write, speak. This reflection led to the fundamental questions of history, to the question concerning world history and concerning our own situation in it. (*The Origin and Goal of History,* 1949.)

Philosophically there remained the task to clarify for myself the moral presuppositions and the real conditions of politics; and secondly: to orient my political thinking on the anticipatory standpoint of the world citizen.

Wherever in the world I felt the grand breath of the kind of political thinking which recognizes responsibility for humanity, i.e., for the freedom of man and human rights, where therein I felt at the same time strength and courage to sacrifice and the total pledge to the one unique grand idea, there I have listened and gained hope. Helpless myself, I had the urge at least to think and repeat whatever could be helpful on this road to political consciousness.

The decisive (point) is this: there is no law of nature and no law of history which determines the way of things as a whole. The future depends upon the responsibility of the decisions and deeds of men and, in the last analysis, of each individual among the billions of men.

It depends upon each individual. By his way of life, by his daily small deeds, by his great decisions, the individual testifies to himself as to what is possible. By this, his present actuality, he contributes unknowingly toward the future. In doing this, he dare not think of himself as unimportant, just as he dare not do so in elections where his is just one among millions of votes.

During this decade the insight, which for thousands of years had been self-evident and which had been forgotten for a short time only, became dominant in me too: philosophy is not without politics nor without political consequences. I was surprised to see this connection, which is so apparent in the entire history of philosophy. No great philosophy is without political thought, not even that of the great metaphysicians, not that of Plotinus, not at all that of Spinoza, who even went so far as to take an active, spiritually-effective rôle. From Plato to Kant, to Hegel, to Kierkegaard and Nietzsche goes the grand politics of the philosophers. What a philosophy is, it shows in its political appearance. This is nothing incidental, but of central significance. It was no accident that National Socialism, as well as Bolshevism, saw in philosophy a deadly spiritual enemy.

It seemed to me that only after I became deeply stirred by politics did my philosophy become fully conscious of its very basis, including its metaphysics.

Since then I inquire of each philosopher concerning his political thinking and action and see the magnificent, honorable and effective line of this kind of thinking in the history of the genuinely philosophical spirit.

IX. "PHILOSOPHICAL LOGIC"

When I grasped that philosophy is not science in the sense of a compelling and universally valid knowledge, this was by no means to imply that philosophy is abandoned to arbitrariness, whim, or the subjectivity of taste. On the contrary, as over against scientific correctness, which as concerns method is universally valid, the truth of philosophy is unconditional truth, in whose consciousness potential *Existenz* achieves historical reality. Scientific truth can be stated in propositions which are unequivocal for the intellect. Philosophical truth can be communicated only in indirect thought-movements and cannot adequately be captured in any proposition.

Now the problem is to think and state philosophical truth not merely factually, but to gain insight into the ways of its communicability. Only thus does philosophical thought become pure in reflection and is disciplined by its own conscious methods.

To become conscious of the methods of thought and therein of those of philosophical thinking, this I had prepared long ago. As early as 1921 I delivered a four-hours lecture-course on "philosophical systematics." Still within the horizon of the universal psychological conception of my youth, those lectures were aimed at a deepening of that conception. Even then I devised a scheme of categories, although external ones, ordering them like a botanist. I already reflected on the methods of all cognition, proceeding from the basic contrast between *Verstehen* and explanation, but aiming at the question of the specifically philosophical kind of thinking. A few pages in my *Psychologie der Weltanschauungen* marked the beginnings of this. In my *Philosophie* the matter is discussed at many points. In the winter-semester 1931/32, after the publication of my *Philosophie,* I developed the concept of the 'Encompassing,' which is basic to my philosophical logic, and discussed it in public first in my Groningen lectures, *Reason and Existenz* (1935). The material for the theme had multiplied in the course of the years. In my last series of lectures (before my dismissal in 1937) I delivered it in a four-hours series under the title, "Truth and Science." What was at stake was to find the very ancient, factually practiced methods of philosophizing. For me it was almost as if I were re-discovering the world of philosophic thinking in its self-consciousness. In my *Philosophical Logic* I sought to depict the entire matter in its systematic connections. I went to work forming the many pages, notes, and manuscripts into a single (coherent) whole.

This work was taking shape in the years of our most bitter agony, during the period of National Socialism and of its war. At a time when we had to negate the state in which we lived as a criminal state and had to desire its ruin at any price, we found peace in working out this seemingly most abstract and world-detached theme. In those years of distress, which we did not share — as we had done in the first world-war — with all Germans, but with those persecuted, tortured and murdered by Germany as our real fellow-sufferers, the work on the philosophical logic was one of the forms of self-assertion. As always before, my wife read my manuscripts and made notes on them for me. Both of us found in it the firm guide of daily work. It took place under a shadow which hung over every day; not in the youthful buoyancy of the time of our *Psychologie der Weltanschauungen,* nor in the confident height of life at the time of our *Philosophie.* We were surrounded by the silence of concealment in the situation of being forced to endure and of sudden terror. We hardly thought of readers. We wrote for ourselves — unless the improbability of survival should again bring us together with our old friends.

Many parts of the manuscript in those days were read by Maria Salditt. She accompanied our labors with her sympathy, and encouraged us in our forsakenness by the very fact that she found our work important, one among few unforgettable others. Over decades she permitted me to participate in the problems of her vocation as a teacher. I saw her stand her ground in her instruction during the Nazi period, quietly supported by an excellent principal. I see her stand her ground in the spiritual chaos of Germany's present, unswervingly passing on to youth the glories of tradition, arousing truthfulness, suffering the forces of regimentation without being destroyed by them. The philosophical transformation of her heritage of pious Catholic faith, enabled her to accomplish a naturalness in metaphysical thinking, which not merely pleased me, but brought me into pleasant contact with the contents of Catholic depth. Mechthild von Magdeburg was one of her favored personalities. Her knowledge of my way of thinking became so extensive and reliable that I owe her precious indices to my *Psychopathologie, Philosophie* and *Philosophical Logic,* which can be of extraordinary help to the reader in the disclosure of the work as a whole.

The spiritual mood in which the "philosophical logic" grew, on the foundation of thinking performed throughout an entire life, was the tendency to see in the abstraction of basic knowledge the genuinely concrete which obtains under all circumstances. True, in logic only the ascertainment of the realms in which truth and Being are given to us could be gained; however, the content of tradition, which speaks in these realms, co-operated in this ascertainment.

The book was written with regard to the disaster of untruth, of distorted truth, of evil. I wanted to secure one's own decision in the clarity of the decisive either-or, where there is only warding off, and no longer appropriation. But, at the same time, I wanted to increase the readiness understandingly to enter into every possibility of a truth even in untruth itself. The questionablenesses of every truth which expresses itself in self-assured universal validity, the arrogance of possessing truth, was to become just as clear as the reliability of a basis which eludes direct objectification.

Were I to emphasize a few themes in this work, I would name the following:

1. The situation of philosophy is as follows: the one truth in totality is not to be had; rather: manifold truth is met in historical

form. The community of all men is not possible, therefore, by means of a universal acknowledgment of any one and only truth, but only by the common medium of communication. To make this medium conscious, available, and reliable is the task of philosophical logic. It recognizes, on the one hand, the conditions of the realization of the unconditional will to communication, and, on the other, the forms of the rupture of communication and the significance and consequences of such rupture.

2. Communication demands the self-consciousness of reason, i.e., knowledge of the forms and methods by which thinking takes place, of the orientation in the task of thinking to the very point of ascertaining its origins. To the degree that the becoming self-conscious of reason succeeds, the superiority of thought over itself is gained; one who thinks philosophically becomes master of his thoughts, instead of unconsciously being bound to trains and forms of thought.

3. In order to get into the realm of origins a type of thinking has to be performed which seems impossible. We think in objects which we intend. The fundamental philosophical operation at all times is, more or less consciously, to transcend towards that out of which the objective as well as the thinking of the subject intending the objective arises. What is neither object nor act of thinking (subject), but contains both within itself, I have called the Encompassing. This latter does not speak for itself either through the object or through the subject, but through both in one as that which is the Transcendence at one and the same time of consciousness as well as of Being. This fundamental thought, although difficult to perform, itself first clarifies the process of philosophizing and makes that process itself only really possible; and yet, once grasped, it is, at the same time, extraordinarily simple, yes altogether self-evident.

True, with the unfolding of this fundamental thought in philosophical logic, a scientifically compelling basic position is not acquired; but while there is gained the idea of the widest possible realm of content, there is still no commitment to a specific truth-content. It is an attempt to gain the medium of communication in the widest imaginable sense.

4. If it is the paradox of philosophizing that in the objective it does not yet possess an object, what, then, is philosophical thinking? If we call objectified thinking rational, then any thinking which, guided by the objective, goes beyond this is itself no longer rational, although at each step bound to rational acts.

That such a kind of thinking is grounded in itself can be actualized only by itself. That it is necessary, can rationally be comprehended at the boundary of rationality. Philosophical logic must, therefore, in the first place, point to the self-enclosure of the rational, as it has long since been known, by the statement of its formal principles (the principle of contradiction, of the excluded middle, of the sufficient reason, of the invalidity of tautologies and circles). As a philosophically essential kind of knowledge, philosophical logic is interested in the insoluble problems which turn up within the rational itself: in the possibility of necessary foundering of rationality on itself, if it places its confidence in itself alone, absolutizes itself, comes in contact with infinity.

Philosophical logic must demonstrate, moreover, how the insufficiency of the rational for grasping the fundamental philosophical questions leads to the point of disclosing a type of thinking which violates the principles of the rational, moves in contradictions, tautologies, and circles — not, however, in order to violate them arbitrarily or at will, but out of another type of order which becomes methodically transparent.

Universal communicability in such anti-logical and a-logical forms is not possible in the same fashion as it is in the forms of the sciences. The philosophical content which desires to communicate itself in such operations is dependent upon being met by others. Whereas scientific knowledge is achieved by perception in the forms of rationality open to everyone, the achievement of philosophical thoughts is given in historical reality and in the possibility of the *Existenz* of one's fellowman. Propositions and sentence-sequences, which for the one remain always just so much empty, "object-less" talk, are for the other the medium of the presence of profoundest truth.

Philosophical logic can bring all of this to consciousness, without bringing it to acceptance as cogently certain. In this realm it only opens possibilities which may appear sensible or senseless to the listener.

5. Philosophical thinking brings about a break-through through rationality, which latter would like to raise itself to an absolute; but the break-through itself is accomplished by rational means. Philosophical thinking goes beyond the intellect without losing the intellect. The medium of thinking reached thereby has, since time immemorial, been called reason in contradistinction to intelligence.

The break-through itself must not again be made into a new conclusion in an objectified structure which, so to speak, as a tremendous circle of circles, again captures in knowledge what can, after all, be presented in totality only as something uncaptured. The purity of metaphysics becomes methodically possible only by discarding all objective knowledge supposedly grasped by it; it can move without deceiving.

These hints must suffice here. Work on these tasks has wondrous consequences. One is moved by the power of the matter, which in the objective sense, vanishes at the same time. In the formal ascertainment already there develops a calm in the openness for the pure confrontation with Being which speaks to us in all modes of the Encompassing.

For working out the *Philosophical Logic* I devised a scheme for myself:

The foundation (Volume I) was to illumine the meaning of truth from all sides. The widest realm of the potential was to be trodden, arranged in realms of different origin, all referring to the One which nowhere is to be grasped as such, the one Center, the one All-Encompassing.

In the thus achieved realm there was to be executed the entire range of the categories (Volume II) by means of which thinking proceeds, as well as the methods (Volume III), by which the thought-operations are in motion carried out: all of these were to be shown in their principles and to be developed to an indeterminate limit. On the strength of the Encompassing, which leads the way, the technique of the thought-forms and thought-movements was to become known and thereby to become recognizable again in factual thinking.

Finally, it was my intention to show the world of the factual sciences as well as of factual philosophy in their fundamental forms and transformations: in a theory of the sciences (Volume IV).

Only the first volume, *Von der Wahrheit,* is finished. In 1945, in the joy of the beginning of a new life, I gave it into print. The theory of the categories and the theory of methods — though sketched in broad areas — are far from ready for the press and are, for the moment, discontinued, in the hope to find time for them sometime in the future. The theory of the sciences has not yet really been begun. Only scattered notes indicate a start.

X / I. HEIDEGGER

What I heard of Heidegger at the end of the first World War gave me hope that he would become a philosopher with originality among the academics. Seven years my junior, one of Husserl's assistants, a *Privatdozent,* he was hardly known to the public, yet it was clear that fame awaited him. I had by now come to public notice through my *Psychopathology* and *Psychology of World Views.* I was eager to establish contact with him.

Our [first] meeting meant surprise for Heidegger and encouragement for me. The younger colleague's obvious commitment to philosophy impressed me. His resolve to follow a philosophical calling was carried out in the style of great decisions made by those who are prepared to face risks and sacrifices when they choose their course of life. In the philosophers' guild of the time, Heidegger was the only one who appeared to me to be of essential significance. This impression still holds true. I have good relations with several other philosophers, I am learning from them, I respect their accomplishments, but as philosophers they are not saying or doing anything about what matters in the sanctuary of philosophy. Heidegger alone addressed himself to complexes of questions that appeared to be the most profound.

During spring 1920 my wife and I spent a few days in Freiburg, and we took the opportunity to visit Husserl and Heidegger. Husserl's birthday was being celebrated. A relatively large number of people were seated around the coffee table. Mrs. Husserl called Heidegger the "phenomenological child." I mentioned that Afra Geiger, a first-rate student of mine, had come to Freiburg in order to study under Husserl. But Husserl had rejected her because of the admission practices of his seminar. Consequently, through academic bureaucracy, both he and the student were deprived of a good opportunity, because he had failed to take the person herself into account. Heidegger enthusiastically joined the conversation and took my side. It was as if we two younger men were in solidarity against the authority of abstract rules. Husserl spoke without embarrassment. I no longer saw in him the vanity that had bothered me so much in 1913 at Göttingen. He was speaking of philosophical subjects that mattered to him. These subjects, he said in a friendly way without conceit and without insult, would not interest me. He asked me about my own, presumably different, pursuits.

Heidegger was in an unpleasant mood. The atmosphere that

afternoon was not good. I sensed something *petit bourgeois* about it, a feeling of narrowness, which hindered free access to the other person and made for a lack of *esprit* and of a sense of *noblesse*. Husserl's friendliness had an air of warmth but was without vigor and generosity. He gave the impression that he felt contented in such an atmosphere. I probably kept myself inwardly a bit distanced, because I was spoiled by the freedom that was for me the natural atmosphere in my father's house *(meiner Heimat)* and at Heidelberg. Only Heidegger struck me as different [from the others]. I visited him, sat alone with him in his study, noticed that he was studying Luther, observed the intensity of his work, was in sympathy with his penetrating, concise way of speaking.

I never returned to Freiburg, although this was not intentional. I invited Heidegger instead. He was kind enough to come to me, as it was easier for him to do the traveling. Thanks to his frequent visits with us in Heidelberg, a lively intellectual exchange developed between us over the years. Nevertheless, it remained a strangely isolated relationship. I did not introduce Heidegger to my friends (except to those who happened to be in the house), and Heidegger did not introduce his to me. In neither case was this deliberate. Yet it was a sign of a defect, as if neither of us wanted the other to enter his own substantial world.

When Heidegger was visiting us, we both used to work. During the course of the day we met several times for conversation. Even our first talks inspired me. One can scarcely imagine the satisfaction I felt in having at least one person in the philosophers' guild with whom I could talk at all seriously. But what did we have in common? If we thought for a short time that we were on the same road, such thinking was, in retrospect, perhaps a mistake. But for me it was, nevertheless, the truth, which I cannot deny to this day. Clearly, we were both opposed to the traditional philosophizing of academics. Less clearly, but somewhere deep down, we felt a vague certainty that something like a reversal was needed in the field of professorial philosophy, which we both were entering with the will to teach and be heard. We both felt the call not so much of renewing philosophy but rather of renewing the *Gestalt* of philosophy as it was then being taught at the universities. We shared an admiration for Kierkegaard.

During our conversations I did most of the talking. The difference in our temperaments was considerable. Heidegger's tendency to remain silent occasionally made me talk more than necessary.

Events provided me with philosophical inspiration. As at that time, in the mid-twenties, I had long been a psychiatrist and was now holding a chair of philosophy at the University of Heidelberg, the rector's office used to turn over to me curious letters that the bureaucracy was unable to answer. One day the letter of a maid-servant from Frankfurt was delivered to me by the porter, who said: "Somebody wants to know what less than nothing is." In the letter, which was full of misspellings and grammatical errors, exalted science was fearfully asked whether there really was something called nothing. It was an imploring letter, written out of fear. The writer was probably in the first stages of schizophrenia and apparently asked the question with regard to death. The sentences were striking because of the use of abstract terminology. I imme-diately told Heidegger about this letter, as he happened to be visit-ing at the time. No colleague except Heidegger would have taken a letter of this kind as seriously as I did. We were in unspoken agreement that the ironical words of the porter were symbolic of the simple-mindedness of the world.

Right from the start, during the first years of our encounters, I failed in one essential respect. When we began to know each other, my *Psychology of World Views* had just been published. The book was read by many, but it was rejected by the Guild of Fellow Philosophers. Rickert criticized my book from points of view that were foreign to its intentions. Heidegger therefore studied the book with extra care and asserted to me that it meant a new beginning for philosophy. But, at the same time, in an unpub-lished* critique he questioned its statements with much less mercy than all the other critics together. He gave me the manuscript of this critique. I felt it was unjust and merely scanned it because it contained nothing fruitful for me. I had taken a direction different from the one Heidegger was suggesting. Besides, I had no desire to involve myself with this critique, to argue about it, and to enter into a discussion for the sake of clarification, which was what the foreignness of Heidegger's wishes, questions, and demands called for. Such a discussion would not have been easy for me in those days, when my philosophical endeavors were still in their *status nascendi,* when I was instinctively distancing them from those influences that could give them no nourishment. Consequently,

---

*Editor's Note: This Heidegger review of Jaspers' *Psychology of World Views* was published in Hans Saner's 1973 book, *Karl Jaspers in der Diskussion* (Piper Verlag, München), pp. 70-100.

I probably disappointed Heidegger. And yet, the fact that Heidegger exposed himself to the contents and points of view of my book — to a lesser degree in his critique than in our conversations — was something so positive to me that I felt encouraged.

I profited from the demand for clarity of abstract thought (*Begrifflichkeit*). I was familiar, certainly, with disciplined work on philosophical thinking through Lask and Rickert. But to me that seemed an artificial and unrealistic endeavor. Ever since about 1910, when I had come to know Husserl, I had been struck by such work. This impression of the Husserlian school, a school recognizable by its manner of speaking and its attitude, was revived for me by Heidegger, and with even more intensity than before. In Heidegger I saw a contemporary who had something that otherwise existed only in the past and that was indispensable to philosophical thinking. Even though the thinking of none of my contemporaries, not even Heidegger's, became the measure for my work, it served to orient me so that I could find on my own, in an exchange with the ancients, at least that form of sufficient and appropriate argument that would make it possible for me to express what had moved me so profoundly since my youth.

It was through Heidegger that I became acquainted with the Christian, particularly the Catholic, tradition of thought, though that was not the first time I had encountered it. He had the unusual freshness of a person who was deeply rooted in this tradition but who at the same time overcame it. Many of the unique expressions, stories, and hints scattered throughout my work are gifts from him. I remember how he spoke of St. Augustine, Aquinas, and Luther. He recognized the power that was at work in them. He told me about useful literature and directed my attention to certain passages.

Certainly, during those days when we were together, and probably far beyond those days, there was a feeling of solidarity. We talked to each other with a beautiful ruthlessness that did not exclude outspokenness about our observations. "By the way, when do you work?" he could ask, probably because he had noticed how late I was getting up, how often I was in a pensive mood, and how much time I spent lying on the sofa. He criticized my style, my lack of discipline, my overlong sentences. In 1924 I was studying Schelling. From the perspective of the Husserlian atmosphere of scientific philosophy he expressed his contempt: "That one is only a man of letters." And yet, Heidegger did not want to reprimand me; he granted me the freedom of my way. We did not refrain from mutual expressions of respect, made in a restrained and unimposing manner.

Our inclinations, mutual stimulation, and shared interests in no way corresponded to an accord regarding practical value judgments, in which what exists for us is self-evident and motivates and guides us. That remained involuntarily unregistered by my consciousness even though, prompted by occasional remarks and judgments, I already had feelings of astonishing aversion during the first year [of our meetings]. From the very beginning, our relationship was devoid of enthusiasm. It was not a friendship grounded in the depths of our nature. In behavior and language, something distancing seemed to be mixed into the atmosphere [of our meetings]. Consequently, the understanding between us was not unreserved; only for a few hours at beautiful moments during our conversations did the atmosphere become clear and unrestrained.

Events occurred that made me think twice. In 1923 I published a short essay, *The Idea of the University*. Someone from Freiburg informed me that Heidegger had said that my booklet was the most irrelevant of all the irrelevancies of the time. During the next visit I referred to his remark. Our relationship, I said, was of a kind that required mutual openness. I would in no way forbid him to utter such judgments. But before we said something like that to others, the code of honor demanded that we first tell each other directly. Heidegger declared emphatically that he had said nothing of the kind. I replied: "Then the matter does not exist for me anymore and is closed." Heidegger was surprised by my reaction. "A thing like this has never happened to me before" was his puzzling answer. The strange fact is that such information reached me repeatedly. Thus in 1923 he made another switch: "Jaspers and I can never be fighters for a common cause." Something was disturbing the atmosphere, something unreal yet not quite to be rejected, though in no way acceptable. Since 1933 I myself had begun to talk about and judge Heidegger without giving him advance notice.

From the outset, without paying attention to it or reflecting on it at all, I had noticed at times what seemed to me the absence of ordinary good manners, and I kept hearing false-sounding notes. Perhaps he experienced the same with me. I felt close to him because, along with me, he could see through the veils of convention the sufferings, the extremes, and the limitations, and yet he immediately seemed far removed in the way he experienced them. I saw his profundity but could hardly tolerate something else, something undefinable. He appeared to be a friend who betrayed you when you were absent, but who was unforgettably close at moments that, as such, remained without further effect. Sometimes it was as if a demon had crept into him; consequently, out of a tendency to seek the essential in him, I told myself to disregard his *faux pas*. During the decade the tension increased between sympathy and alienation, between admiration for his abilities and rejection of his incomprehensible folly, between the sense of one ground of philosophizing on which we agreed and at the same time the sense of another ground totally remote from my attitude.

In the later years the atmosphere during the visits seemed to change. Earlier, Heidegger had come with uncomplicated sympathy, which was reciprocated at first. Now, upon arrival, he seemed to be in an unfriendly mood, even hostile. Within one or two days this would completely disappear. There was again that familiar atmosphere of an open, unrestrained, and participatory discourse, as I saw it then and still see it now. It was as if a previous discomfort had dissipated during the togetherness, because we had something in common. It was as if something frozen had melted.

The publication of Heidegger's *Being and Time* (1927) led, without my actually noticing it, to no deepening of our relation, but to superficiality. I reacted [to the book] by not being particularly interested, as I had years ago reacted to his criticism of my *Psychology of World Views*. As early as 1922 Heidegger had read to me a few pages from an early manuscript. They were unintelligible to me. I pleaded for a natural way of expression. Later, on some other occasion, Heidegger said that he had made considerable progress, that what he had written had now been revised and was promising. I had not been familiarized with the contents of the 1927 book. What I saw now was a work that left an immediate impression because of the intensity of composition, the constructiveness of conceptions, and the accuracy of an often illuminating new usage of words. However, in spite of the brilliance of its powerful analysis, the book appeared to me unproductive for what I sought philosophically. I rejoiced in the achievement of a man with whom I was associated but did not have much desire to read it. I soon got stuck because the style, contents, and way of thinking did not appeal to me. I also perceived that this was not a book against which I would have to mobilize my thoughts and take a position. This book, in contrast to the conversations with Heidegger, did not stimulate me at all.

Heidegger must have been disappointed. I, who was his senior and was fully engaged in my own philosophical work, had not granted him the service of a careful reading and criticism as he, my junior, had done for my *Psychology of World Views* by constantly contrasting his thinking with mine. Understandably, he in turn showed no real interest in any of my later publications. If there has been a genuine relationship between human beings in those matters that precede the *oeuvre* and the achievement, the propensity for wanting to know what has been created is sometimes weaker than the power of that which occurs in reciprocal actions. It is as though one already knows the other and need no longer read carefully and completely. But it was not this alone between Heidegger and me. Rather, the writings of both of us seemed to reveal a hidden discrepancy *(Fremdheit)*.

My attitude toward the book and its author was a continuation of the tension or ambiguity that had existed from the beginning. Because I had sensed a feeling of companionship during the preceding years, I expected to find in the book stations that lay on the way that I also was taking. This did not happen, but I did not reveal my expectations. I was quite discontented with the mood of the book. At times I expressed my concern in questions to Heidegger like these: "What has happened inside you because of the thinking of this book? Is it the sum of insights concerning factual relations or is it an expression of an impulse of *Existenz*? What will the study of your book do to the reader?" I well remember asking these questions in the little attic of my apartment, but I do not remember Heidegger responding.

On some other occasion, in referring to our frequently identical opinions about our colleagues, I said I found it strange that he was quoting professors as though his problems were not completely different from theirs. The dedication of his first book to Rickert and of his second to Husserl emphasized a relationship to persons of whom he had spoken to me with contempt. He was putting himself into a world of tradition that we had opposed. He replied: "You, with your fact-related philosophy, are just as traditional."

For me the decisive questions were, and remain, these: In which direction does a certain thinking lead? What motives does it arouse in the reader? For what actions does it encourage and strengthen him? And what could it cause to disappear and be forgotten? Without being aware of it, I did not answer these questions with regard to Heidegger's book. I disregarded what did not benefit me and continued working on my essays.

This attitude toward Heidegger of continuously suspended judgment regarding him and his thought, my willingness to overlook his *faux pas*, my laxity in refraining from and postponing genuine criticism — all this I could no longer continue when, in 1933, the existence of all of us totally changed, demanding to this day an answer from everybody and, along with it, clarity about what one thinks and the purpose for which one is willing to work.

The last time Heidegger paid us a lengthy visit was at the end of March 1933. Although the National Socialists had been victorious during the March elections, we conversed as we always had. We listened to a record of Gregorian church music that he had purchased for me. Heidegger left earlier than originally planned. "One has to join in," he remarked regarding the rapid development of the National Socialist reality. I was surprised but did not question.

He was briefly with us for the last time in May on the occasion of a lecture that he — now rector of the University of Freiburg — gave for students and professors at Heidelberg. Scheel, chairman of the Heidelberg Student Organization, introduced him as "*Kamerad* Heidegger." It was a masterly lecture as to form; as to content it was a program for the National Socialist renewal of the universities. He demanded a total transformation of the intellectual institutions. The majority of the professors still holding office would be unable to meet the new challenge. A new generation of able lecturers would be educated within ten years. We would then turn our duties over to them. Until that time we would be in a transitional phase. Heidegger expressed anger about many facets of university life, even about the high salaries. He was given a tremendous ovation by the students and by a few professors. I was sitting at one end of the first row, with my legs completely stretched out, my hands in my pockets; I did not budge.

After that, for my part, conversations with him were indirect *(unoffen)*. I told him that he was expected to stand up for the university and its great tradition. No answer. I referred to the problem of the Jews *(Judenfrage)* and the malicious nonsense about the sages of Zion. He replied: "There really is a dangerous international fraternity of Jews." At the dinner-table he said, in a slightly angered tone, that it was foolish to have so many professors of philosophy; one should keep only two or three in the whole of Germany. "Which ones, then?" I inquired. No answer. "How shall a person as uneducated as Hitler rule Germany?" "Education," he replied, "does not matter. You should just see his wonderful hands!"

Heidegger himself seemed to have changed. Already from the time of his arrival, a mood separated us. National Socialism had grown rampant among the population. To extend my welcome, I visited Heidegger in his room upstairs. "It's like 1914 . . . ," I began and wanted to continue by saying, "Again we have this treacherous mass-hysteria," but as Heidegger was beamingly in agreement with my first words, the rest of them stuck fast in my throat. This radical rupture [between us] gave me extraordinary concern. I had not experienced the like with anybody else. It was all the more upsetting because Heidegger seemed completely unaware of it. Yet he revealed himself by never visiting me again after 1933 and by not writing when I was removed from office in 1937. But I heard still in 1935 that during a lecture he had spoken of his "friend Jaspers." I doubt whether he grasps even today that rupture in our relationship.

I was at a loss. Heidegger had told me nothing before 1933 about his leanings toward National Socialism. I should have spoken about it on my own. During the last years before 1933 his visits had become infrequent. Now it was too late. I had failed with regard to Heidegger, who himself had been seized by an intoxication. I had not told him that he had chosen the wrong road. I did not trust his changed nature at all anymore. I myself felt the threat exerted by the power in which Heidegger now participated, and I thought, as at times before in my life, of Spinoza's cautiousness.

Had I been deceived by all that had been positive between us? Was I myself to blame for not, because of all that positiveness, seeking a radical confrontation with him? Had this been determined before 1933 through my own fault of considering the entire National Socialist movement too harmless, so that I did not see the dangers in time, even though Hannah Arendt had already told me clearly enough in 1932 where it would all lead?

In May 1933 Heidegger said good-bye for the last time. We have not seen each other again. During the National Socialist years my thoughts frequently returned to the intellectual reality that is for me tied to Heidegger's name. Against my expectations he had become my intellectual enemy through his public activities as a

National Socialist. He appeared not to notice it, although he provided proof by never visiting me again after 1933. His past image stood vividly before my eyes and to this day it remains unforgettable. What has happened between us since then in letters, concerning, for example, an opinion about him in 1945 and other things, I do not yet want to talk about. I am writing only about how I have thought of him since then.

When I think of Heidegger, I see two separate, independent aspects: Heidegger's actual relationship with me and the public's opinion of Heidegger. The latter aspect reflects the first. The public, Heidegger's road to fame, the reverberation that has sometimes compared us and has often mentioned our names together — all force, so to speak, access to our own encounter. Perhaps the invasion of this public into our mutual perspectives has brought something lopsided into ourselves that was not there before. Both of us, without knowledge of each other's action, refused such an encounter at the same time, about 1937, by writing to Jean Wahl's forum of discussion in Paris. The public creates its phantoms; today it is the phantom of existentialism, with the public taking Sartre's achievement as the measure for judging all others who speak of *Existenz* and have some relation to Kierkegaard. The provocativeness of such a phantom is so great that instructors of philosophy are writing books about subjects that they claim to see as a whole, that they claim to have surveyed historically, and whose development they think they can follow through the centuries. I am thoroughly fed up with this, as apparently Heidegger is too. Something alien is forced upon one's own consciousness.

When speaking of Heidegger, I must ignore this. I did have a personal philosophical relation with him. This has little to do with those discussions that compared us and our works.

A friendship can gain a solidarity that can weather the adverse influence of the public only if it is free from secrecy and hidden reservations, if it is governed by a trust in the simple things of right and wrong, and if loyalty expresses itself in words, thoughts, and deeds. For the fact that such a friendship has not grown between us, neither of us can reproach the other. In consequence, we have the suspension and ambiguity of the potential.

That what had happened to Heidegger in 1933 could happen to him at all raised new questions. We had become adversaries, not because of books but because of actions. The philosophical thoughts had to be understood in relation to the behavior of the thinker.

I now had to ask myself the question I had never before asked, namely, whether there was something at work in Heidegger's thought that must appear to me as the enemy of the truth as far as it had revealed itself to me. Even if in earlier times I had not allied myself with him in principle, I still thought that we were on related routes. Because of the inseparability of thought from the practice of thinking, I now had to expect that his philosophy also would be running counter to what I was trying to do. But that was not clear. The questions, rather, became burning questions, yet they remained unanswered: Can there be philosophy that is true as a work, while its function is untrue in the facticity of the thinker? What is the relation of thought to praxis? Who is Heidegger and what does he really do?

Instead of answering such questions and attempting a critique of Heidegger's philosophy, which would be out of place here anyway, I shall report only on the attitude I have taken up to now.

Heidegger's *Being and Time* was, if I remember correctly, twice the subject of a short discussion in my writings. Neither passage is important. The rift was much too deep for critical remarks about the facts of the case and about intellectual projections to remain relevant. What did take shape for me was rather the incredible opposition that I have noticed in other realities all my life: an impalpable and evasive opposition that does not know itself as such, does not acknowledge or show itself, but that astonishingly enough treats itself as nonexistent. Yet in a concrete situation an attitude appears that offers the choice of either not taking it [the opposition] seriously or being forced into a contest with a being that one somehow senses as not coming from the same grounds as oneself. I did not act toward Heidegger in either of the two ways. From year to year I delayed doing so. To this day I have preserved an inner readiness because of moments experiencd during the 1920s. Convinced of the permanence of the substance I once perceived, I cannot say no when once I have said yes to a human being. But I also cannot gloss over something essential out of conventional friendliness toward fellow humans; I cannot at one stroke forget something that happened in the past (unless mutual clarification has made reconciliation possible down to the fundamentals). That would not do justice to Heidegger's rank and would betray what once existed.

I must counter a misunderstanding that sometimes occurs. In my writings there are many anonymous characterizations. They are actually based on the experiences of contemporary events that I did not name when the ideal and typical characterization did not correspond to the reality of its point of departure, as for instance, the George Circle, National Socialism, magic in medicine, and anthroposophy. At times such characterizations have been interpreted as having been aimed at Heidegger. But that is incorrect, inasmuch as Heidegger is not suited to the intellectual nobility of the George-world, the vileness of National Socialism, or the humbug of medical doctrines of salvation. And again the question arises whether something is at work in him that causes such misidentification by critics of my writings.

Significantly, while I was writing my book *On Truth,* I sometimes thought of Heidegger. It was different from the 1920s, when I was writing my *Philosophy*. In those days I felt somehow related to him, even though this was vague and I did not think about his philosophizing at all while working out my own. Now he had become the obvious and substantial adversary in the reality of my life and conduct, in that reality in which communicative and bookish philosophizing is only a function. Yet I did not arrive at a critique of Heidegger, essentially because I was particularly occupied with philosophy and because I lived in seclusion, having been excluded from the public.

To attempt, therefore, a critique of Heidegger as a representative of an influential intellectual fact among the contemporaries belongs merely to my plans, whose realization I cannot foresee. The precondition of such an attempt, however, is clarity about the possibilities of philosophical criticism per se. This is one of the extraordinary and most exciting problems of philosophy in its search for communication. It is the question of a sensible discourse on philosophy that, it seems to me, has not been posed clearly enough to this day, let alone been answered. I shall circumscribe the problem with a few statements:

1. The question is whether essential criticism and polemics are at all possible in actual philosophy, or whether there remains only the attitude of silent acceptance, as is the case with poetry. Poetry may be aesthetically analyzed, may be measured according to aesthetic norms, and may be explained through interpretation; but no dispute is called for, unless it be a dispute about the substance according to the measure of whether the poetry be true and good because it furthers the progress of man or whether it be false and destructive because it makes him regress and sink. Philosophy

would then merit questions like "Does it rouse a possible *Existenz* for entry into reality? Is it a seduction for the evasion of reality? Does it demonstrate a compulsory truth? Is it a mode of thought that remains 'existentially' inconsequential?"

Philosophy is not yet a knowledge of something; it is not already produced in a work of art consisting of thought. Rather, it lies in the thought process itself as an act of the thinker's nature, an act that generates itself by touching upon something else — namely, Transcendence.

2. Forces, so to speak, are in effect in such fundamental thought or internal action serving as the fountain of philosophical communication. We would love to see such forces, which gain speech in philosophy, which recognize themselves again therein, which attract and repel each other, and which permit misunderstanding and seduction. But that is not possible. With every step taken by our thinking, we are standing in the center of these forces, never outside. We ourselves are serving such forces without being able to survey even one world of those forces. The "world of forces" is only a simile pointing toward what counts in the actual criticism within a work's philosophical reality.

If we direct our attention toward the forces themselves, we are no longer looking at a potential object. Rather, the invitation to pay attention means merely to search for the path leading beyond the objects toward the source from which the objects are being thought about and being perceived within these forces. It is, then, a process with a limited radius of action if one means to grasp already the forces themselves in the shape of communicated insights. Insights always remain only foregrounds. If I take these insights, which are the ultimate as far as they can be formulated directly as the absolutely ultimate, I am draping a veil over the essential. What counts is to become aware, in the formulated insights, of that which is not entirely visible. How, then, can criticism and agreement be accomplished, if we are not dealing with palpable objects and object-relations, but with philosophy itself as the language of the forces?

3. When we are speaking to one another, we are making a tacit but delusive assumption of a common subject. We are assuming, so to speak, the concern of philosophical activity, an objective philosophical world of truth in which everybody — whoever he may be or whatever he may think — collaborates. Then we turn toward the object-relations and, in the form of scientific discussion, attack statements and sequences of thought. That indeed makes sense, but

the sense is limited to rational objectivity. Because rational objectivity is the inevitable medium of all communication, such criticism, although superficial, is adequate with regard to the means through which the more profound forces manifest themselves. But how is it possible to trace and question those forces not merely by arguments, not merely by discussing an object, not merely by agreeing with the forms of scientific discussion? How is it possible to demonstrate the consequences not only of thought but also of the inner state for those who affirmatively follow this path? How can it be revealed in what way thoughts are a preparation for something else?

Discussion of the foregrounds can turn into unnoticed defeat. One allows oneself to be drawn to the level of scientific discussion under the assumption of a common scientific philosophy. Then one runs into banality. Distracted from what matters, one has unknowingly already accepted the opponent's substance as being true.

This discussion among the foregrounds is inevitable. But it becomes philosophically significant only if it is integrated into that more profound discussion of the forces as their mode of expression.

Now, the nature of public philosophical discussion is peculiar. In many cases a critic is apparently tied to his opponent, all the more so if the critic is a creative philosopher who, without being aware of it, has allowed himself to have been drawn into the ways of thinking of the person he is criticizing. This has frequently been the case with critiques of Hegel by Hegelians and anti-Hegelians. As interesting as it may be to intellectual history, such criticism is in itself of no importance because it has no real opponent. It moves against its will, unknowingly fettered, along the same road as the foe-apparent, shackled by him and caught in his web of thinking. Then in a mock discussion, accompanied by the most vehement rejections, the proper discussion has not yet even begun. Struggling, so to speak, the prisoner wants to free himself from his fetters, but in vain.

4. The more profound, the real philosophical power, this something that one senses or does not sense and that one cannot force upon any intellectual insight, this something that is the actual effective in the intellect and that is appealing as such, brings forth the question "Does it exist at all or does it not exist?" That is, "Is there something or is it magic?" And the next question is: "What kind of force or forces are surfacing there?" A final answer will never be found. One will perhaps be able to characterize a

force; one might touch it with rejection or agreement. To come close to it, face to face, so to speak, and not to subsume it under a notion of genre or type, that is the task.

A dispute of this kind makes sense only if it asks questions that go to the roots and if it searches for the appropriate thoughts deriving from related original motives. Then the evidence of the facts, as conceived by the opponent, will teach one to see something that of itself has no significance but is only the sign, symptom, or symbol of a philosophical will toward the essential.

It is impossible to achieve such a cognition of general validity. In whatever way one might circle around that which one is seeking and in whatever way one may be talking about it, what has been critically thought is itself again biased, because it arises from its own source. This bias finds expression in the way of thinking, which is, however, itself again subject to the thought process and to the question.

A struggle of the forces appears in the life of philosophical thought. But it must not be forgotten that nobody can control this world, this organism, so to speak, of the struggling original forces of truth. And nobody can recognize within a final general knowledge all their differences as to the powers of falsity or evil that even destroy *Dasein,* possible *Existenz,* reason, and reality. Such a totality is an image for that in which we are standing and out of which we cannot step forward because we cannot really assess it from the outside.

5. If we glance at the original forces, we are dealing with something incarnate not only in the act of thought but also in the contents of what has been thought. What one, so questioning, seeks is something general within the most personal.

In philosophizing, therefore, the living human being himself in his facticity becomes involved when it is a matter of a critique. This is unavoidable, because the contents of philosophy can no longer be treated as a scientifically researchable process of cognition *(Erkanntsein)* that increases progressively over the years through discoveries and evidence. But at the same time, thereby, the limit and measure of criticism constitute an awareness that cannot be strongly enough remembered and not resolutely enough retained: As little as any human being as a whole can be understood and known, just as little can the philosophical thinker be understood by his work. One may be able to penetrate but not understand. One may question, but one cannot strike something like a balance.

In the attempt at a philosophical criticism that penetrates to the sources, when such criticism appears to reach the limit of almost forcible convictions (a limit it can never, in fact, reach), one objection is possible that can suddenly void the entire critical attempt. The objection is actually valid only with regard to contemporaries and only potentially valid with regard to the dead. The objection goes like this: It would be impossible to expect one's opponent to jump over his own shadow; it would be impossible to expect an attitude from him which would paralyze his characteristic creativity. Goethe once said that one should not subject oneself to conditions that run counter to one's own existence. Against the objection, one could argue: Such an objection holds true only for philosophy, and that is its magnificence. For it is the philosopher who craves every possible insight. For him the mind and its productivity are only tools, not ends in themselves. He will always learn that this tool works the better, the more decisively he is seized by the vitality of truth. That is precisely why the philosopher strives to seek the most extreme criticism.

The approach to Heidegger's thinking with such questions, which have here been sketched in only a general way, is not an incidental approach, one that satisfies itself with arguments by referring to mere reason. Rather, the attempt at a criticism has been directed at the contemporary by analogy with our constant behavior expressing itself in only a one-sided relationship with the former philosopher. I have not even begun my criticisms in this philosophical autobiography. I have only hinted at remembrances spanning decades, remembrances that do not hinge on Heidegger's work but on what occurred, what was thought, and what was done between us. Perhaps there is something here that might be of value in the criticism arising from the attempt to understand his work. Philosophical criticism that up to now has only covertly been in progress in my occasional notes would, if successful, make sense if the partner were to respond. As long as we live, there remain possibilities that we can sense. What has happened since 1933 and what is happening today appear to me open as far as Heidegger and I are concerned. I cannot lock the door.

X. Theology and Philosophical Faith

When I began to philosophize, it never occurred to me that I could ever become interested in theology. When I lectured on the psychology of religion (1916), it is true, I came also upon theology and, for my information, even studied a dogmatics by Martensen (especially because he was the great opponent of Kierkegaard) , but without any (real) participation on my part.

In my childhood I had little connection with ecclesiastical religion. In school there was religious instruction, Biblical history, catechism, and church history. Involuntarily ideas were deposited in the mind of the child which, although without particular momentary effect, were nevertheless not forgotten. When it was time for confirmation, this took place as something which was part of the mores, without religious emphasis, with a holiday which brought purely worldly presents. The instruction given to those to be confirmed was a joke to us and ridiculous (the pastor gave the geography of hell, told with grotesque phantasy that the Pope goes daily into the Castle of Angels in order to touch the heaped-up gold, asserted that the fact that the stars did not collide proved God's guidance, that we would be saved by the fact that Christ was nailed to the cross, etc.). My parents ignored the ecclesiastical world. I characterize the atmosphere here:

In my last year in the Gymnasium — confirmation was already a few years behind me — I came upon the idea that, for the sake of veracity, I would have to leave the church. When I disclosed my intention to my father, he said something like this: My boy, you may, of course, do as you please. But, in your own mind you are not yet clear about what you mean to do. You are not alone in the world. Co-responsibility requires that the individual should not simply go his own way. We can only live together with our fellowmen, if we conform to the regulations. Religion is one of the regulative forces. If we destroy it, unforeseeable evil will break through. That much lying is connected with the church as, indeed, with all human institutions, in this I agree with you. The situation will be different, perhaps, once you are seventy years of age. Before death, when we are no longer active in the world, we may clear the deck by leaving the church.

When my father was past seventy he did, indeed, leave the church. In the respective office he asked that the matter be treated confidentially. After a few days the pastor came. My father: "Reverend Sir, it would be better for both of us, if we did not discuss the matter. My reasons might offend you. My decision is final." The minister kept insisting. Thereupon my father: "I am old and, before my death, arrange my affairs. What the church teaches and does I have rarely approved. Just one example: A few years ago a young man committed suicide. The church publicized a condemnation of suicide, a clergyman refused to conduct the funeral. I thought: what empowers the church to such condemnation? And how can you, unable to reach the dead any longer, so torture his relatives! You, Reverend Sir, will understand why I did not wish my leaving the church to become unnecessarily public. It will mean nothing to others." — To us my father said he had heard so much tactlessness on the part of clergymen at graves that, at his own burial, he wanted to spare his relatives that sort of thing.

When my father lay dying, in his 90th year, and was taking leave, he opined to his pious woman physician, who had been close to him: Faith, love, hope, it says — of faith I do not think highly.

Even after the first world-war I had still no interest in theology. Insofar as it was not a matter of scientific historical research, which as such might very well belong to the philosophical faculty, theology appeared to me so brittle that it might very well interest me as a symptom of the age, but not as such. And yet, to pay no attention to theology proved, in the long run, to be impossible. Its factuality made itself noticeable everywhere. One day I actually became conscious of the fact that I was talking about matters which theology claimed for itself. After a lecture-course in metaphysics (1927/28) at the end of the semester a Catholic priest came to me in order to express his gratitude as one of my hearers and to express his agreement: "I have only one objection to offer, that most of what you have lectured on is, according to our point of view, theology." These words of the intelligent and impressive young man took me aback. It was obvious: I was discussing matters — as a non-theologian — which others considered to be theology; yet I was philosophizing. This had to be clarified.

The reality of the church and of theology dare not be neglected in philosophizing. We do our thinking from an independent basis which the churches do not recognize and which as such has no connection with the churches. The consciousness of the independent power of philosophy, down through the millenia, long before as well as outside of Christianity, became constantly more decisive for me. I do not take my stand against the church and theology as enlightener in order to negate them, but as the servant of that great independent truth. True, I wanted to be a member of a congregation corresponding to my historical heritage in view of the great regulative forces of the Occident. However, I had to assert the life-giving meaning of philosophy, which cannot be forced upon anyone nor be pronounced as universally valid, but which should show itself to everyone who is born to it and who seeks it with a pure mind.

First of all, then, in my lectures on history of philosophy, theology was touched upon as unavoidable. But afterwards I came to speak of something with which I had not grown up, but to which I came only in the process of philosophizing later on, with the astonishment, deep emotion and respect which this tremendous phenomenon extorts the more closely one comes to know it. Throughout I lacked — and therefore never had to get over — any specific ecclesiastical confessional faith. If Kierkegaard, to the query, why he believed, replied: "Because my father told me to," then my father told me something quite different. Only quite late did I become entirely conscious of philosophical faith. No one taught me to pray. But my parents reared us strictly in reverence of the leading ideas of truthfulness and fidelity, in constantly meaningful activity, in free turning to the magnificence of nature and to the contents of spiritual creations. They allowed us to grow up in a full world.

When, at the age of 18, I began my studies, I attended philosophical lectures. I was disappointed, because I did not find anything like what the ground had been laid for in my parental home. With the greatest respect for the far-away philosophy, which had become perceptible to me in Spinoza and which yet I did not know, not permitting that philosophy should be confounded with these mere theories of the (lecture-) desk, I turned to reality in the study of medicine. When, step by step, I then came to philosophy, so to speak returned to it, and finally to theology — even though I may have touched it only from the outside —, it is possible that this made possible for me a freshness of conception precisely because I was not from the beginning a part of it. I lacked the self-evident ground which seemed to carry the others. It is another, for my consciousness deeper, foundation from which I came to the traditions of the historical foundation of the Occident.

A mighty impulse to the question concerning faith came to me from my wife. Quite early, and without any actual break and in substantial fidelity to her heritage, she had transformed the orthodox Jewish faith in herself into Biblically grounded philosophizing. Her life was permeated by religious reverence. Wherever she met with the religious, she had respect. Since Gertrude has come to us, my father said once, Christmas becomes each year more Christian. This life without dogma and without law, from childhood on touched by the breath of the Jewish prophets, was guided by an unshakable moral unconditionality. I felt myself wondrously related to her and became encouraged to bring into the focus of consciousness what, under the veil of the intellect had been, it is true, effective but hidden.

The growth of philosophy into an original power of faith, not merely for one's self (where it had always been self-evident), but for the public teaching of philosophy, did not always seem proper to me. An exorbitant claim, which is not represented by any community. To the *"Recontres internationales,"* the conversations on humanism in Geneva in 1949, representatives of Communism, of Catholic and Protestant Theology, and of philosophy had been invited. I experienced that all those others could speak as representatives of mighty sociological powers standing behind them, from which they derived their basis as well as their self-assurance; whereas a representative of philosophy has nothing behind him aside from an intellectually, it is true, uniquely magnificent but sociologically not at all existing history of philosophy. While I had to stand there, so to speak, all alone, the question which I had long ago felt became mighty real: Are we representatives of philosophy, in our helpless weakness, not doing something absurd, something illusory, while all the time we are so clearly convinced?

The self-consciousness in this situation rehabilitates itself, first, by pertinent reflection on the principles of philosophy, and, secondly, by bringing back into our consciousness the university as the institution of independent philosophical truth.

First: From an early age there never was anything in my mood of the type which sees philosophy as a science which, arched over by ecclesiastical faith, led and limited by such faith, becomes expanded by it into the world of faith which transcends all science. Just as little was there ever in me the mood — only seemingly contradictory to the former — which sees in philosophy a "scientific *Weltanschauung.*" For both, for philosophy as the *praeambula fidei* and as scientific *Weltanschauung,* philosophy is a kind of knowing in the sense of the learning of universally valid facts, something which, like other sciences, is a matter for investigation and research.

Increasingly full of content, increasingly real, genuine philosophy showed itself to me, philosophy which has gone through the millenia and which, at its high points — Plato and Kant — was conscious of itself in just this sense. The essence in it are the philosophical thoughts in the meaning of their own origin, undeducible from anything else. They are forces of life-realization. Nowhere does philosophy render results as means for the planned making of the world. But it does bring the basis of consciousness into clear focus, which alone gives limit and meaning to the results of science and the possibilities of planned creativity.

The composing of philosophizing in written works always seeks the communication for the philosophical faith in the historical form of its author, who thinks of it in its relationship to tradition. In this kind of communication indirectness cannot be overcome in contrast to the directness in all the sciences. It succeeds aided by the will for maximal directness, is lost in that total directness in which the object becomes absolute and therewith philosophically empty. The indirect communication of Kierkegaard, though as intent rejected by us, has, as methodical consciousness, nevertheless brought to clarity this inescapability of philosophical communication.

Secondly: The self-consciousness of philosophy was won back for me as the purpose and idea of the university. In its modern form this institution is the transformation of theologically guided knowledge into an independent will to knowledge, which has its meaning not in the domination of any specific philosophy, but in the living permeation of the whole by philosophizing.

The university as such is no longer Christian and still less sectarian. It would not lose its significance, it would rather enlarge it, if the theological department had several sections, which would teach the Biblical (Catholic, Protestant, and Jewish) and the Buddhist forms of faith through faithful believers.

The guidance of the discerning person by way of faith can be effected either by the theologically communicating religions in their respective historical forms, or else, with a view to those other, alien, orthodoxy-bound possibilities, it can take place as original philosophizing. The polarity, religion — philosophy, belongs to the university.

What, as philosophy, stands as complementary to, not necessarily opposing, religion, is, for the majority of students, at the same time the potential justification of their life. Today one must reckon with the great mass of ecclesiastically non-believing youth. Whether one deplores this or not, for this youth philosophy is the only possible illumination of their faith and (the only way of) thinking, in which this youth can become conscious of its unconditionally recognized ties.

This philosophical guidance may be clarified. It has a character very different from that of the dogmatic theologies. In philosophy the following applies: everyone is referred to himself; — there are no such things as human guides analogous to the priest; — doctrine furnishes impulse, but offers no certainty; — there are no holy writings, but only the great philosophical tradition of millenia in the Occident, in India and China.

Science in the narrower sense is for philosophy as for theology a means and a field. But its relation to philosophy is closer. For, only philosophy understands and desires the unlimited and many-sided sciences. Philosophy has always been ready to justify and protect modern science against anti-scientific forces.

To be sure, philosophy has often misunderstood itself and identified itself with modern science, or through the centuries, has claimed to be "another science." To bring it out of this lapse and back to itself, to purify and clarify it, is a present task.

The philosopher is not a prophet. He does not set himself up as a model. But he does represent the being-human even in its often faulty aspects. He wants to remind, hand down, conjure, appeal. He makes no claim to discipleship; but, if successful, provides the occasion for the other's coming to himself. He is not in possession of truth, but, within time, he lives in the earnestness of the search (for truth).

The philosophical university is the realm of cognition which knows no limits in its endeavor. Out of a multiplicity of faith there meet in it the various presuppositions of thinking in mutual observation: in order to question and to doubt each other. At the base there is an encompassing faith, which no one can call his own in any definite form: faith in the way of truth, on which all can meet each other who search sincerely. They remain open in their thinking; they do not isolate themselves. Other forms of faith are not excluded; to do so is held to be the distinguishing mark of untrue faith. This realm of the university contains every possibility of specialized scientific research. Its spiritual life, over-arching and penetrating, goes on in the tension between theology and philosophy.

Since my *Philosophie* (1931) I have publicly advocated philosophic faith as the meaning of the philosophic doctrine. In the book, *Der Philosophische Glaube* [inaccurately translated in the English edition as *The Perennial Scope of Philosophy,* Ed.] (1947), I have formulated it explicitly.

XI. The Idea of a World-History of Philosophy

Since 1922, I have given lectures on the history of philosophy, without any over-all program and without any specific plan of the order in which I wanted to take up the various periods or report on the great thinkers. Consequently I have lectured on: Modern Philosophy. From Kant to the present. Kant and Kierkegaard. Nietzsche. From Augustine to Thomas. From Thomas to Luther.

Greek Philosophy. Plato. Chinese Philosophy. Indian Philosophy (the latter two only after 1945). I published some specific historical works: *Nietzsche* (1936). *Descartes* (1937). History was important to me as an appropriation for the sake of philosophizing, not for its own sake.

As a result of the terrors of National-Socialism and the experience of being excluded within one's own state, my historical interest underwent a transformation. Philosophical logic was by no means my only work at that time. Since 1937 I have acquired new information about the world by reading. Spiritually I gladly tarried in China, feeling there a common origin of being-human as over against the barbarism of my own surroundings. I turned in loving admiration toward Chinese humaneness. Of evenings my wife used to read to me in those years, according to our mood, Shakespeare and Aeschylus, as well as books on English history and Chinese novels.

A much more rigid examination of minds set in for the entire Occidental history. The question arose, in which sense they were the creators and protectors of the spirit which was able to resist terror, and in which sense they actually became the guideposts towards making such terror possible. Discriminating the truly great, the indispensable and essential had been close to my heart throughout my life. Now this inclination to greatness achieved an intensification with a much clearer view.

At the same time, however, my interest was in humanity as a whole, where the foundation as well as the standard was to become perceptible in order to hold its own in today's world. Totalitarianism meant the most radical rupture of communication from person to person and therewith, at the same time, the end of man's being himself. It became clear that the rupture of communication in favor of violent wilfulness is always not merely a threat to personal existence and the real danger of losing oneself, but that this alternative finds its expression in the great powers of history.

As over against that, to philosophize means: we are working on the presuppositions for the possibility of universal communication. We must clearly elucidate these presuppositions. That in which men are able to find themselves is, on the one hand, what is indeed elaborated in philosophical logic, but which is already realized in every genuine conversation. On the other hand, it is the knowledge of a common history, which concerns all of us reciprocally. The realization of a world history of philosophy can today become the framework for universal communication. It is the presupposition for a maximal illumination of self-consciousness in the discussion with one's fellowman, both in what concerns me as well as in the detachment of reflection.

As soon as this is understood the desire to achieve a conscious view of the totality of the philosophy of mankind becomes urgent. We human beings on this globe share a great spiritual history. But this is not in the first instance, based on factual community. Rather, the mutual contacts in history up till now have been transitory or failed entirely. Isolated developments, side by side, forgetting one's own past — this was frequent, both in world history at large as within any specific limited history. There was no factual continuity of the whole, only partial continuity. To increase communication and continuity, this is the great human concern, especially in philosophy, which latter is response to as well as preparation for life.

In 1937 I conceived the design of a world history of philosophy, which was to be promoted alongside of and together with the philosophical logic. It was, it is true, clear to me that an undertaking of such dimensions is impossible for a single mind, if the entire material was to be historically known and treated. But the necessity for this task was just as clear to me. Because the conception of its entire history is indispensable for philosophizing itself and can be performed only by a single mind, the impossible will have to be attempted.

In contradistinction to the great encyclopedias as collections of materials, which are achieved by the teamwork of many and which certainly are indispensable and meritorious, — an over-all view, attempted by the philosophizing of a single person, must set its task quite differently: not to know everything, not to give completeness of material, but a concise description of the fundamental modes of the historical conception, constantly illustrated by significant examples; — to arouse the mind to a sense of historical wholeness, of hierarchical order and of greatness, and of the few singularly great men; — to find orientation in what is essential in a given period, in a given problem, in the forces that effect the thinking; — to gain intuitive insight into the great historical independent origins in China, India, in Asia Minor and in the Occident; — to make perceptible the historical itself in distinction from the abstractly universal.

The work on the world history of philosophy, with which I am at present occupied, intensified the consciousness which, since my occupation with Chinese philosophy in the 'thirties, had become self-evident, but which formulated itself only later: we are on the road from the evening-glow of European philosophy to the dawn of world philosophy. On this road all of us individuals will be left. But it will go on into a future which, in addition to the most terrible, also shows the brightest possibilities.

XII. Concerning My Writings as a Whole

If I look upon my whole spiritual development, I seem to see something which has remained the same from my childhood on. The basic disposition of youth has clarified itself in the course of life, enriched in content by knowledge of the world; but there have never taken place any changes of conviction, no breaks, no crisis, no regeneration. The only great turning-point in my life was the union which my wife and I concluded with each other. In this union what had been there before was not merely strengthened but infinitely expanded. I lived out of the heritage of the parental home. With all later insight I could always let the light fall there in order to bring it to full consciousness.

Another turning-point in our life came by way of the transformation of our sense of existence by the continuous threat on the part of the National-Socialist criminal-state, which could make our personal future appear as hopeless. To whomever his life in the course of events appears as already forfeited and lost, to him it is, after survival of the danger, as if it had been granted to him once again. But no world catastrophe was able to touch or recast the innermost. With renewed shocks it only brought new verification and new examples in which what already was became clear.

What this is, I can say only through the totality of my writings. In how far the foundation lies in the conceivable experiences of childhood, this cannot be estimated: in having to stand outside already as a pupil; in the illness, which denied most of the natural, blossoming life; in the happy presence of a reasonably thinking family, permeated by love and reliability; in the trusting life-affirmation of the parents; in the community of attitude shared with the beloved sister, which held true throughout a long life; in the conservative-liberal, oppositional attitude of the families on both sides of the house, which inclined towards democracy by way of aristocracy.

a.   I shall sketch two major interests in my writings:

The essence of man becomes conscious of itself only in ultimate situations. For this reason, even from the days of my youth, I tried not to veil the most extreme from myself. This was one of the motives which caused me to choose medicine and psychiatry: to come

to know the limits of human potentialities, to grasp the significance of what in public is readily veiled and unnoticed.

As far as I can think back I was moved by the experience of
understanding and of failure to understand one's fellowmen. Even
as a pupil I suffered when, after a quarrel, a good mood was supposed to be reconstituted by way of conventional friendliness. I
was the impetuous, struggling one, because I drove towards clarity. If the clarification was forbidden by, say, the authority of a
teacher, and the matter ended by a word of command, I felt tormented. However, I wanted still more: in spite of beloved parents
and sister, in spite of friends, I was consumed by a yearning for a
kind of communication which would go beyond every kind of
misunderstanding, beyond everything temporary, beyond every
boundary of the all too self-evident. Man comes to himself only
together with the other man, never by mere knowledge alone. We
become our selves only to the degree to which the other one becomes himself, become free only in so far as the other one becomes
free. For this reason, the problem of communication between man
and man was for me first of all the practical (from the time I went
to school), and later on, the philosophically thought-out fundamental question of our life. In the final analysis all thoughts could
be judged by this touchstone question, do they aid or hinder communication. Truth itself could be measured by this standard:
truth is what really unites us, and under this claim: to measure
the kind of truth on the truth of the union which becomes possible through it. Only with the beloved wife did I come upon the
path of the loving struggle, upon the path of life-long, never completed, unreserved and therefore inexhaustible communication.

In both of these directions (of the experience of ultimate situations and of the illumination of communication) I have reached
no end.

b. The consciousness of being on the road and of achieving
any success in our temporal existence only in the form of incom-
pletion and of the new "further," brought me — by the good fortune of professorial existence, which assures unlimited freedom of
work — to the study of the great dead (over a period of many
years). Systematically I proceeded to appropriate the tradition
wherever I thought to understand something. Antiquity and
Bible — mediated to the child, but for many years held in the
background — were only now consciously taken seriously as the
foundation of our Occidental historical life, not as authorities, but
as the task to listen to them and to translate them into the present.

From very early my longing went towards greatness. I felt reverence for great men and for great philosophers, who are irrecoverable for all of us, from whom we get our standards and whom we yet do not deify. For, each man is supposed to become himself even as over against the greatest. Authority is true, but not absolute. Defiance of the great is pernicious untruth; whereas inpendent patient experience in study is the true form of appropriation.

The first among the philosophers who lent me wings was Spinoza. At the university I read Fechner, Wundt and Schopenhauer occasionally, but did not yet understand Kant. The significance of these authors for my thinking was small. I had immersed myself completely in the sciences.

When, at the age of 24, I came to know my wife, she directed me to Plato. We read parts of a few dialogues together. In so far as time and strength permitted, I then began to study Kant in occasional seminars — alongside my psychiatric work. I understood his Theory of Ideas (*Ideenlehre*). I got to know Aristotle and Descartes a little.

During World-War I we studied Plotinus more thoroughly, but above all there was the illumination through Kierkegaard. To Kierkegaard I owe the concept of *Existenz*, which, since 1916, has become standard for me in order to understand that for which I had, until then, exerted myself uneasily. But of equal power was the concept and claim of reason, which, through Kant, now became constantly clearer.

I sought the grandeur of thinking in philosophy. The fluent levelling in textbooks and lectures was unbearable. I developed a conscience against the confusion of ranks. The philosophical authors whom I had read as a student turned out to be unimportant. There was a real connection between the rank of a philosopher and the truth of his thought. Their truth could not be got in the form of results and doctrines.

c.   In my own philosophical work I had meant to proceed on the path I had felt in my youth and which I had now seen more clearly, the path which had been trod through millenia by at least a few: the path of a fundamental knowledge of man, which makes room for all possibilities and is able to unite men despite the manifoldness of their faith and of their life.

I desired that kind of philosophizing which can be accessible and convincing to man as man; not, however, as the esoteric affair of a few aristocrats. Rather, I would like, so to say, speak as a man-on-the-street to the man-on-the street. Not as if everyone, just because he happens to be a certain way, could derive therefrom an absolute claim to be the way he supposedly is. But because to everyone is given the possibility, by reverent gaze upon the great, to come to himself under the unconditional guidance of love and reason within the framework of eternal order.

d.   Desirable to me was the common thought, which is not the one universally valid knowledge, but the making possible of communication; a κοινή, which is not a watering down, but the consciously approached realm in which we all can meet each other.

I sought this realm, in which the true contents become audible as truths even when they confront each other in opposition. I sought those contents even where I am not participating in them in my own reality. This kind of philosophizing was to make possible every free absorption of those contents; but it was also to result in the recognition that no man is everything, not even the greatest, and that I, when I become decisively real and know where I stand, am the more decisively in need of others.

Yet, from an early age I confronted the boundary which denies this harmony in reality: total demolition of communication, absolute self-will, evil. A philosophy which sees in this world, in the reality of the given present, everything basically in good order, appeared to be plainly untrue.

True enough, in philosophizing I too am searching for the point where all opposites are extinguished. But, inasmuch as I am not there but here, what I thus think must show itself in its consequences for my life and conduct in this world. In it I must know where I stand. In brief: the world as a whole cannot be understood as rational, but I can decide in it, side with reason.

What I wanted to realize in philosophizing, therefore, is what in connection with the word "reason" — recapturing its meaning from Kant and Lessing —, I have thoroughly discussed. The One which is intended may be circumscribed by some such formulas among others, as these: the will to reason out of reason, which nevertheless must steadily be borne by another, namely by *Existenz;* — the consciousness of origins which themselves cannot be proven; — the basic will to let one's self be filled in action by the genuinely given present through which eternity speaks; — etc. This kind of reason gives itself an objectification in the existence of an historical reality and in thinking its order.

e.   To know where one stands and what one wants causes one to look upon one's own age within the horizon of history. My reflections as a student, to the effect that, for the duration of our life, things would remain as they then were, meant not to be concerned with one's age. It was only of incidental interest. Life did not have

meaning primarily for this particular age. The meaning was timeless. Only since the eruption of the war of 1914 did what happens
today, what the age is, become a permanent question for me too.
What got at me, what I participated in, this, from now on, I reflected upon and judged according to its motives and consequences
in this age.

It would be in vain to want to understand one's age first in
order to find out thereby what correspondingly would be the task
of philosophy. One cannot figure out what the age demands, what
the age is, and then proceed systematically to do justice to that demand. Every man, by originally living as he is, is already a moment
of his age. But, in retrospect one may become conscious of the situation in one's own age and examine critically in which sense one
has appropriately thought of this situation as one sees it now, and
what one really wants in this age. Even then, however, the meaning of philosophizing remains something which surpasses every
age and all time.

Looking upon history one seems able to distinguish periods of
originality, of classical perfection, of crisis, as well as periods of
preparation and periods of preservation. It is only one viewpoint
which permits such distinctions. If one entrusts himself to it for a
moment, our own age may offer the following aspect:

This is not the age of the great unique works, like those of
Laotse, of the pre-Socratics, of a few Platonic dialogues, of a few
Bible-texts. The age is more nearly analogous to the world philosophy of late antiquity, to the type of thinking of the Stoics, of Plotinus, of Boethius, a type of thinking which was common in large
circles.

The intent of creating complete works seems in vain today. In
opposition to indolence, to watering down, to chaos, the temptation today is — instead of finding and realizing life out of its origin — to create disciplined works of art in poetry, in philosophy,
and in art, works which actually possess a peculiar sort of finish,
through which there speaks a discipline, a finding of simplicity, a
seamless construction, a well-developed language — but which become questionable in view of their claim to the independence of
a mere work. The resistance to the formlessness of present-day
nullities is good; good, therefore, is also what happens here, because it reminds and warns. But it becomes false whenever the intent of this sort of thing wants to place itself alongside the intent
of the great old masterpieces or whenever there occurs in the contents an artificial, insincere and in one's own life not realized fulfillment.

Today the way to truth seems to be another one. The new for

philosophizing (today) is the unique reality of modern science, together with its misconception of itself in an absolute technic and the consequences of both for our entire existence. Every philosophical effort today, which by-passes or rejects this reality, which does not allow it to become the cornerstone in the structure of encompassing basic knowledge, comes off the loser and becomes untrue. The cheap and untrue accusation of science and of technic is of no help. Of no help is the recipe which suggests that the defective can be brought in order by recourse to an over-all plan (while the energy of thinking meaningfully labors on plans and on the delimitation of the plans for the difficult tasks of the existing order of our age). Nor is it of any help to turn the gaze aside upon a supposedly envisioned metaphysical total process, which, in the false consciousness of a (supposed) necessity, paralyzes factual cognition as well as effective action. The great metaphysicians of the past furnish us irreplaceable means of thought, but not in such fashion that, in penetrating the present situation, we could apply them as a cure. The most marvellous philosophy may seduce to evasion.

f.   In all science, however, there remains, in the nature of the case, the old philosophical task: from greatest universality to arrive at the simple, fundamental knowledge on which the communal spirit of a period rests.

If an unfriendly observer were to view the totality of my writings, he could say contemptuously: All-knower. Whereas, if a philosophically thinking person views them, he will recognize the nature of the case: namely, the necessity of having to become universal in philosophizing.

This universality is precisely not the way to the impossible know-it-all, but to the all-uniting, — relating — basic knowledge, which, as an encompassing consciousness, would like to make itself philosophically communicable.

The breaking down of human affairs into departments is inhuman only when the individual sees everything from his own specialty, from his own point of view. It is human to live in the consciousness of the encompassing Totality by working his own field in his profession in such fashion that it can become like an echo of the Totality. Everyone must prove himself in his own specialty, but no one needs to waive the encompassing consciousness. This is something surpassing, which yet cannot realize itself in an imaginary realm above all, but always only in the form of persons. Philosophizing stands against the decay of the real spirit, against the dissipation of men. It demands concentration.

It is perhaps foolhardy to set one's self the task to work on this all-encompassing and concentrating consciousness as a communicable one. It is not likely that anyone who has not himself been active as a specialist will do it successfully. The history of philosophy shows this specialization on the part of most of the modern great philosophers. But then there is this, for the individual dangerous leap of stepping out of one's specialty into the encompassing totality, not merely as everyone is supposed to do it, but with the intention of co-operating on the encompassing consciosuness by communicable work in the profession of philosophizing. Now this leap demands indeed a participation in every possible intellectual endeavor and in the understanding of all realities, and therefore does tend to seduce one upon the confusing path of knowing-it-all.

But philosophy proves itself precisely by not letting itself be pushed into any 'knowing-it-all,' by not permitting itself to be captivated by all the interesting items which lie on the side of the road; but rather to stop the very moment that the fundamental — that which unites everything with the encompassing general consciousness — seems to have become clear.

The philosopher ventures upon something which advances only with the few great men of original genius, an advance which in each instance is marked by their name. We others, throughout all ages, labor on the realization, the appropriation, the expansion of what has been created, and do so in each respective world-reality and world-orientation. This work is necessary; it wants that to become universally human which, in the great ones, has a hiddenness difficult of approach.

It is a fundamental demand of being human that each individual participate understandingly in the totality of life, while, in his profession, he achieves excellence by way of his specialization. If all were only specialists, humanity would be delivered up as prey to him who, by violence, forces this entire mass under his will. He can do this only if the specialist does not know, with heart and head, upon what everything depends and upon which even his specialization in its development is ultimately dependent.

Philosophy has been called the specialty of the general. That is a paradox. But philosophy has to work with those forms of knowledge in which what is essential for the apprehension of things can become the mode of thought of everyone. In that case the consciousness of the world and of Transcendence, the freedom of being one's self, a universal consciousness would all realize themselves as the spirit of the public, in simplicity, in truth and in depth.

Once upon a time the Occident constituted this public consciousness. Today it is dominated by a sense of the decline of this consciousness into shallowness and into an aggregate of unrelated performances. What is demanded is a "synthesis" of knowledge; but sensibly one does not mean by this an encyclopedic digest of the results of all sciences, but the kind of basic knowledge which carries and permeates all sciences and all practical thinking.

It seems to me that those men who, having come from specialization, venture to work thoughtfully on such basic knowledge, are summoned to concern themselves with everything which is essential in human existence. Whether, by doing so, they produce something which serves the public mind, or scatter themselves in multiplicity, this should not in advance be decided by prejudice. One should observe whether, in thinking along with others, one feels that it is worth while. Let it happen. Do not reject our type of labor as an impossibility. Let's not make a program from the outside for what is here to be accomplished. Let's at the very least listen to the great philosophers of the past and let us, by our present philosophizing, facilitate and deepen our understanding of them.

g. It is improbable that, for the basic knowledge which unites itself into our world, we shall already be able to find the systematic which, as a whole, could last. Rather, the following should be considered:

A system which closes itself has become nonsense. There can be systematic only:

If, in the unfolding of thoughts, in bringing the scattered together, there is a growing satisfaction in the consciousness of agreement in such a way that new observations operate like confirmations or like the occurrence of what was still missing, then such an experience may have many different meanings.

Such designs, as for example, that of a world-vision, may appear like a delusional system of the mentally ill. But if the system, precisely thought through, stands before one's eyes like a revelation of the way things really are, the anxiety which consumed the patient stops.

Or, such designs are merely an ascertainment of the present givenness of one's own thinking, of its possibilities and limits, of its forms and of the worlds open to it. Thus it was in grand style in Kant. He had delimited his task to the self-assurance of reason. How, in the process of his methodical illumination, he is led to new points and how everything fits together — in its totality precisely confirms everything specific and each specific is comprehended as belonging to the whole — this became for him the great philosophic calm. True, he did not know what the world, God, or immortality are; but he did know how these were to be thought, which origins, what meaning and what significance these thoughts have.

Perhaps I have experienced something of this Kantian joy, even if much more restrained. The potentialities of the systematic of reason within the modes of the Encompassing, in which we are and in which we find ourselves, this too has remained in suspense and unfinishable for me. But the systematic, which became a multiple one, in its peculiar ways has brought together what was scattered, has seen in relationships what was isolated. There arose the form of a type of philosophical thinking rich in relationships, in which the one is supplemented and proved by the other, without rounding itself out unequivocally as a thought-form in the system; but in such fashion that each systematic remained in an encompassing realm which, in its totality unperceivable, was in the process of transcending, touched but not paced.

Already in my *Psychopathologie* this kind of systematic was present, viz., the organization according to methods of research. In my *Philosophie* there are, correspondingly, the methods of transcending in world-orientation, illumination of *Existenz* and metaphysics, in *Von der Wahrheit* the modes of the Encompassing, in which we are and which we are ourselves. The meaning of the One unites with the manifoldness of the figures of thought. The clarity of the differentiations points to a foundation and to a goal, where the differentiations are surpassed and lose their absoluteness.

The unity of my thinking, if it exists, consists in its reference to the simple, encompassing basic knowledge, which, nonetheless, can find no final form, and in the fundamental will to communication. Yet there is in my work no such thing as a comprehensive unity of the whole, but a series of unities in an open field, which in the infinite One has both center and circumference; and, although our thinking can reach neither, it is true to the degree that it refers to them and is illuminated by them.

h. A philosophical work is also characterized by its mode of writing. Writing essays in school cost me effort. I was reproached for heavy-handed writing, fussiness, and writing at too great length. A classmate once consoled me: You may have no flourish of abundant words, but you are, on occasion, at least serious in what you are writing about.

My earlier works, the *Psychopathologie* and the *Psychologie der Weltanschauungen*, I wrote without much correcting afterwards. With my *Philosophie* and *Man in the Modern Age* there began a working over of what I had written. This was tied in with the effort to philosophize methodically and above all with the continuous critical demands of my friend, Ernst Mayer. Since then I have published nothing without having worked over the first transcribed text.

Without exception, my works arose from a mass of separate notes, that had been collected. One day these were brought under an ordering point of view, items eliminated, and a coherent reproduction made by filling in the gaps. Whenever an idea objectified itself into an orderly scheme, nothing would be deduced, but rather already existing notes were used. The most comprehensive thoughts of order in my books are the least important, because they are rational thoughts, used only for grouping.

In style my writings differ according to the nature of the subject-matter. Where I had scientifically something to say, I wrote objectively on the matter; where I philosophized, I wrote from the standpoint of the Encompassing.

Because there has been, in my philosophizing, the will to reason in the idea of possible communication, my effort has been directed more at 'existential' clearness than at logical clarity (though I esteem this very highly and strongly strive after it), more at the obligation of an intended thought than at the beauty of poetic expression.

i. In my writings which, without exception, were written in calm impartiality, there lives a will to effectiveness: to do whatever possible in order to however tiny a degree to further reason in the world. To do this by way of creating disquiet in the reader by provoking him to his potential Existenz, to encourage him in becoming himself, to conjure up in him the possible meaning of Being, and to let his thought founder on the uncomprehended. It is a tendency in which I stand, for which and in which I think, to which I would like to encourage others.

In these writings there is no presupposition to the effect that somehow truth will assert itself or that the world, from its inception, is guided by reason. The experience both of history as well as in the present bears witness rather to the contrary, in so far as we take our measurement on humanly accessible reason — and only this can we call reason.

This is why so much depends upon what the individual is willing to live and work for. He must know where he stands. His own essence and the turn of events depends upon his finding important even his tiniest decisions. He is of eternal significance in the face of that Transcendence, which makes him really become himself if he gives himself to it, where he is no longer threatened either by success or by foundering. He is of temporal significance by his deeds in the world. The world does not pursue its path of itself obeying definite inexorable laws — on the analogy with natural laws; rather, what becomes depends upon each individual human being to a degree which, on the whole, is quite incalculable.

What I have written I have, for the most part, previously lectured on as an academic teacher. Were I to speak of a pedagogical will, such was, in my case, never planned. Real education has always seemed to me to be self-education. It is a matter for the individual. Yet, in teaching one cherishes the hope, by calling attention, by thinking ahead, by acting ahead, and by the communication of modes of comprehension, to encourage in youth what keeps pushing towards the light. I have not tried to interfere with the individual, but have let him feel the stringency of the eternal order. It dare not become soft. In complete tolerance there hides the strictest claim. This claim is heard by the individual. That it may be heard more clearly, more decisively, this can be furthered by a philosophizing which communicates itself.

XIII. Age.

A retrospect into one's own life, especially when one is older, leads to an ambiguous mood. It is as if one were concluding something which is still going on.

It is within the nature of philosophy that the truer it becomes the less it is able to round out or to complete itself.

Having become aged the thinker feels himself less than ever at the end. Kant said: when we are precisely so far along that we can truly begin, then we must withdraw and leave the matter again in the hands of the beginner.

One's consciousness is agitated by the fact that one has not yet said the essential thing, not yet found what announces itself.

For this reason a philosophical retrospect becomes a better plan for future work. The expansive power of reason is not enclosed in the biological circle of life. One may get into the mood — paradoxical for old age — that, by virtue of one's spiritual experiences, the vision opens to new distances.

Karl Jaspers

DESCRIPTIVE

AND CRITICAL ESSAYS ON THE

PHILOSOPHY OF KARL JASPERS

1

Kurt Hoffman

THE BASIC CONCEPTS OF JASPERS' PHILOSOPHY

The Premises.   The title of this essay takes us into the midst of one of the problems inherent in the thought of Karl Jaspers and it makes necessary two reservations: From the two "great exceptions," Kierkegaard and Nietzsche, Jaspers takes over the stress upon the contingent existence of the individual and the deep conviction that philosophy must always remain an expression of the individual personality. The thought and the writings of both Kierkegaard and Nietzsche were personal in this sense; both lived in constant opposition to conceptual systems of philosophy, and they attempted to express their deepest thoughts "indirectly" in the form of aphorisms, allegories, or metaphors. The strength as well as the weakness of the philosophy of Jaspers lies in his attempt to integrate, in the tradition of Kierkegaard and Nietzsche, what is by nature unsystematic and mythical in character and thus opposes the form of the concept, into a system of conceptual philosophy, a "system," to be sure, if we understand the word in the specifically unsystematic sense, which Jaspers gives the term. For philosophical thought "can neither be true in a closed system nor in an aggregate of aphorisms."[1] Jaspers terms his philosophical work not a system, but rather a systematically connected, but open structure, an *"offenhaltende Systematik."* The first reservation must thus concern the special place and the unique meaning of the concept in the philosophy of Jaspers.

But further: Jaspers' philosophy is characterized by a peculiar inner tension, by a movement which resists conceptual analysis or to which, at least, such an analysis, which separates static concepts from the dynamic flow of thought, cannot do justice. The peculiar climate of his philosophy, its inner development, its interior connections, are of necessity lost in an expository treatment of the concepts involved, for this philosophy, as few philosophies, must be taken as one integral whole, rounded within itself, as a structure in which each element plays its organic part. This must be

[1] *Wahrheit,* 26.

95

the second reservation. It is based upon Jaspers' enmity to what he terms "premature terminology:" a terminology "at the beginning," and not, as it should be, arrived at as a result of the insights won. Jaspers is always concerned with still indefinite, pregnant, and growing concepts. He wishes to avoid by all means the use of schematizing, exterior, "predetermined" concepts that do not have their origin in the problem itself. Since knowledge for him is always a quest which arrives only at intermediary stations, never at the end, fully determinate concepts are often dispensed with in his philosophy and hence, quite purposely, the sharp clarity of a system that uses determinate concepts and a strictly univocal terminology is not aimed at: "Since every philosophical thought is true only in a movement, and since this movement must be assimilated authentically and its repetition must be alive in order to remain true, a primacy of terminology . . . is catastrophic. . . . The domination of terminology turns philosophizing into that academic pedantry in which philosophy itself has vanished."[2]

For Jaspers philosophy is essentially and primarily metaphysics; it is a search for Being, which is more than ephemeral. But it matters, for this philosophy, *who* asks the question as to the nature of this Being: man's concrete historical situation enters into the question and into the answer. In each individual, in all his insecurity and disquiet, philosophy must make a new start; hence it is always in process and always in suspension, it is never complete and final and can never be set forth in the form of a universally and eternally valid doctrine. Philosophy, for Jaspers, seems to bear two dimensions: that of objective truth, of self-consistence, of consistence with verifiable facts, and that of depth, profundity, of the intensity and authenticity of the personal assimilation of this truth. These two dimensions, corresponding to the concepts of "reason" *(Vernunft)* and *"Existenz,"* are inseparable, and philosophy as a whole, therefore, remains always unfinished, remains a perpetual task. Philosophy must use logic and the instrument of the formal concept; yet it is unable, by these means, to reach Being, which presents itself to man as broken, as a series of ruptures. A premature conceptual restoration of the Whole, such as Hegel's, must ultimately fail, since the reality of Being escapes and recedes and can be grasped only *'existentially.'* Transcendent Being is never "given" as an object, but is rather experienced directly in the very failure of discursive reason to reach it. *Existenz* itself can be made transparent only in what Jaspers calls "illumination of *Existenz*" *(Existenzerhellung)*; whereas every attempt at a conceptual ex-

2 *Wahrheit,* 428.

pression of *Existenz* remains ambiguous and paradoxical at best. A clear definition would make *Existenz* precisely into that which it can never become: an object of thought.

The World.   The task which Jaspers sets himself is, on this basis, to integrate into a connected and continuous whole, concepts which are "soft" and by definition unstable, indeed non-conceptual. Jaspers distinguishes three formal and general concepts of being: being-an-object *(Objektsein)*, being-a-self *(Ichsein* — or in analogy to Hegel: *Für-sich-selbst-sein)* and Being-in-itself *(Ansichsein)*. Only the first of these three can become an object of thought: the objects in space and time, things and persons, tools, even thoughts and ideal objects, such as expressed in mathematics. This kind of being Jaspers calls "existence" *(Dasein)*; it constitutes the "world." World-orientation *(Weltorientierung)* is philosophy on the level of existence. It is never sufficient to itself, since the empirical world of the sciences is not absolute, but presupposes a higher reality beyond. For this reason also world-orientation is not an encyclopedic collection of verifiable facts, but must seek out the limits of the sciences in order to determine the points of transcendence. But the fuller and richer the theoretical understanding and the practical experience of the world are, the clearer will be the recognition of the necessity for the transcending leap. A philosophical orientation in the world must draw and recognize the absolute *(prinzipielle)* limitations of science and distinguish these from the actual *(jeweilige)* limits, which are constantly being displaced. The positivistic picture of the world confuses these two limits and for this reason cannot allow for a transcendence beyond the empirical world.

Although reason by nature seeks incessantly to arrive at the world as a whole and to make it into an object of thought, it is driven by the philosophic impulse beyond the limits of compelling facts and laws and thus runs up against the contradictions at the fringes of the empirical world, — against the Kantian antinomies. The mind is not presented with a unified view of the world, but instead with separate spheres of reality which, in spite of their interdependence, remain separate and demand a separate logic for each.

Jaspers distinguishes four such spheres, each of which presupposes the lower one: anorganic nature, organic life, the soul as inner experience, and at the apex, spirit *(Geist)*, the rational soul of traditional philosophy. In distinction to Samuel Alexander's theory of an emergent evolution, the qualities of the lower levels are, for Jaspers, not contained in the higher ones; the four spheres are discontinuous with each other. Each has its own specific reality: the laws that apply to matter, for instance, need not apply to life, just as again spirit is different in kind from life. Whereas for Alexander the categories of space and time apply even to the sphere of the spirit, for Jaspers this is not the case: each sphere has its own specific categories. Closer, perhaps, is the connection between Jaspers' theory and Nicolai Hartmann's *Seinsstufen,* inasmuch as Jaspers implicity recognizes the law of the autonomy of the higher level in respect to the lower, and allows only for analogous relationships between the various steps. But Jaspers' primary concern is to resist the tendency of making one of the spheres absolute and to subject the others to its logic and its laws. Philosophy must avoid the pitfalls of materialism and biologism as well as those of pan-psychism and radical existentialism. Physics, biology, psychology and the humanities have no common criterion and cannot be ordered according to any one standard. Each order fails, if it pretends to be the one true order. The totality of the universe is neither a possible object of a universal science, nor can it become unified by systematic philosophy. In breaking up the One in order to make it an object of knowledge, Jaspers proceeds in a new direction, different from traditional philosophy, which has always sought to arrive at universals under which all reality could then be subsumed.

Whichever direction we pursue in our quest for Being, it becomes clear that Being is not of one kind and that, as a corollary, the relation of thought to Being is not univocal. Being is grasped by the mind in the multiplicity of its appearances. It is evident that Jaspers must reject every monistic philosophy, every system which, under the presumption of knowing the One, closes of the approaches to the authentic One of *Existenz* and Transcendence. If we assumed, however, that Jaspers, in rejecting monism, embraced some sort of pluralism, a conclusion for which the uninitiated reader would find many indications, we would be far from right: Pluralism makes the dogmatic assertion that there is no One, that the Many are unconnected — and thus, paradoxically, affirms, in the eyes of Jaspers, the very connection which it denies, if its assertion is to be meaningful. Jaspers must reject from these premises similarly the two kinds of systems which attempt to present a "closed" world order: Positivism, which generalizes mechanistic thought and empirical fact, takes the methodologically false step from the particular to the general, from the part to the whole; Idealism, on the other hand, either materializes the ideas or else reduces them to mere validities. Both subjugate the unique and particular to the whole and the general, both leave human reality out of account and make the concrete individual into an empirical object or an empty idea; both pretend, unjustifiably, that Being is something that is essentially knowable in a *Totalwissen,* to use Jaspers' term.

Existenz. For Jaspers human existence can never become an object of knowledge in the sense in which the world does. The individual self has a psycho-physical side, which is empirical in nature and part of the world; this Jaspers calls existence *(Dasein).* As consciousness-as-such *(Bewusstsein überhaupt)* the self is identical in structure with other selves. But the self is also more; it is the possible ground for freedom of thought and action, it can determine its own being. In this sense the self is — potentially at least — *Existenz.* '*Existential*' reality cannot be grasped conceptually since it expresses itself only in its own freedom, in relation to itself and in relation to Transcendence. Illumination of *Existenz* therefore must follow its own peculiar method. The place of the categories is taken by the *signa,* which do not have the power of determining objects. These *signa* — freedom, choice, decision, faith — are ultimately indefinable, because their true content can never adequately be expressed by means of a universal. The very essence of *Existenz* lies in an intentional tending to something else: to Transcendence; to the other self, with whom I am in '*existential*' communication; and, in a reflexive movement, to its own being. Inasmuch as *Existenz* is never achieved once and for all, but remains the *possible* ground of insights, Jaspers often speaks of "potential *Existenz*" *(mögliche Existenz),* which he describes as "that which never becomes object, the origin of my thoughts and actions . . . ," as "that which is always in relation to its own self and thus also to its Transcendence"[3] or again as "that which is individual in the historical particularity, understood under universal categories which are limited by the fact that the individual in the endlessness of his concretion is inexhaustible and thus ultimately indeterminate."[4] And once more: "Being-a-self is called *Existenz.* As such I can become in no manner the object of my own speculation, I cannot know myself, but have only the alternative of either reaching self-realization, or else of losing myself . . ." *Existenz* is, as it were, "the axis around which all I am, and all that can become truly meaningful for me in the world turns."[5] *Existenz,* in distinction to consciousness-as-such is the "hiddenness of the ground" to which Transcendence reveals itself; in distinction to spirit, which is essentially a drive to unity,

3 *Philosophie,* 13.   4 *Ibid.,* 298.   5 *Wahrheit,* 76.

it is a drive to authenticity. Whereas spirit has as its corollary that
which is intelligible, transparent, universal and whole, *Existenz*
is unintelligible conceptually, is the "dark ground" at the root of
all knowledge, is the unique and authentic being in time which
is capable of giving itself in surrender to Transcendence.

The reader will by now have realized that the term *Existenz*
cannot simply be translated by "existence," unless this be done
under certain reservations. The term *"Existenz"* must be understood in the historical implications which have attached to it ever
since it has been used in German philosophy by Hamann and
Jacobi in their attack on the rationalism of the Enlightenment
and in their fight against Kantian Idealism. Ranke and Schelling
opposed *Existenz* to the Hegelian concepts of Reason and of the
Idea. But above all it is Søren Kierkegaard from whom Jaspers
consciously derives the specific content of the term: "The word
is, to begin with, only one of those which denote being. . . . In
philosophy there was from the dark beginnings of history only a
presentiment of that which later, through Kierkegaard, gave the
word its historically binding meaning for us."[6] Kierkegaard, taking over from Schelling the distinction between Idea and *Existenz,*
lifts the *existing* individual out from every determination by the
Hegelian Idea, and sees him face to face with an equally indeterminate and indeterminable Godhead.

Since *Existenz* thus cannot be defined, but only be circumscribed, Jaspers resorts to a set of *'existential'* categories, vaguely
analogous to Heidegger's *Existenziale,* and derived from the Kantian categories, over against which they stand. Whereas objective
reality is thus determined by the laws of causality, *'existential'*
reality is determined by the central categories of historicity and
freedom. To the causality of the substances corresponds on the
side of *Existenz* what Jaspers calls *'existential'* communication, to
objectively determinable size or greatness corresponds the rank,
value or depth of *Existenz,* to endless mathematical time the fulfilled time of the moment.

Existenz and freedom are interchangeable concepts for Jaspers.
But what does Jaspers understand by freedom? If freedom and
Existenz are two sides of the same thing, one must be as indefinable as the other. "Only on the basis of the possibility of my own
freedom can I raise the question as to what freedom is. Thus freedom exists either not at all, or else it is already presupposed in
the very question concerning it." All proofs for the freedom of the
will presuppose the very object of their proof: "Freedom wills

6 *Philosophie,* 13n.

itself, because it already possesses a grasp of its possibility."[7] Freedom is not the same as indeterminism, which is a category pertaining to the empirical world and does not touch 'existential' freedom, since the latter is neither "objective," nor possibly subject to proof or disproof. Although knowledge, arbitrary willing and law are the conditions for freedom, they do not constitute or exhaust it. For Jaspers an analysis of the freedom of the will, such as we find it in Scholastic philosophy, must remain hypothetical, since freedom can be revealed only in the concrete and temporal decisions of the individual. For this reason also Hegel's absolute freedom, separated materially from empirical reality, in resolving for the sake of absoluteness and totality subject as well as object, becomes an "empty" concept for Jaspers. Indeed, the paradox of *Existenz* finds expression in the radical inadequacy of this concept, which contains insurmountable contradictions.

The limitations of 'existential' freedom, which are the basis of unavoidable 'existential' guilt, the fact that man cannot live without struggle and without suffering and that he is faced by death and nothingness, constitute what Jaspers terms the ultimate situations *(Grenzsituationen)*. They are unchangeable, necessary, final and absolute situations. On their rocks we suffer shipwreck. The ultimate situations take their origin in the fact that I am always bound and restricted to specifically determined, historical, and contingent situations, which I am not free to change at will.

Historicity. What Jaspers calls historicity *(Geschichtlichkeit)*, a concept bearing certain analogies to Heidegger's concepts of *Jemeinigkeit* and *Geworfenheit*, expresses more than any other concept his deviation from traditional philosophy. The word 'historicity' derives in part from the philosophy of Wilhelm Dilthey, whose guiding principle was the Scholastic postulate *Omne individuum est ineffabile*. For Dilthey, as for Jaspers, man is an exclusively historical being, unique and concrete, finite and temporal: "The finitude of every historical appearance, the relativity of every human conception is the last word in the historical view of man."[8] The term carries in the German language a resonance based upon the entire tradition of German philosophy of history, and presupposes also an essentially metaphysical view of history, different from the Anglo-Saxon view of history as a precise and sober science; Jaspers speaks of a "metaphysical extension of history." Historicity expresses at once the limitation and the dimension of depth which attaches to man's being-in-time; it stands for

[7] *Ibid.*, 446.

[8] Wilhelm Dilthey, *Gesammelte Schriften*, Vol. V, 9.

the unity of the individual, for personal human existence within the empirical world.

Existenz, as we have noted, is not thinkable conceptually by means of clear and distinct ideas. While discursive thought separates *Existenz* from its proper situation, this situation is in fact the mode of appearance of *Existenz.* Freedom becomes real only in its bond with the body and with the world, while the empirical order in turn dips into subjectivity through its link with freedom. The union of body and soul, one of the timeless problems of philosophy, is for Jaspers a paradox, which at the same time acts as a source and origin of radical novelty. But historicity stands also for the synthesis of freedom and necessity, for the meeting of unbounded possibility with unchangeable fact, and further for the union of time and eternity: "In historical consciousness I become aware of myself in communication with other historical selves; I am, as a self, bound to time — to the flow of my own unique situations and events."[9] *Existenz* is on the one hand a record of changing circumstances, hopes and fears, while on the other hand, it reaches beyond the limits of the empirical world and of time. Its historicity is eternity embodied in time or history at the limits of eternity.

History, which records the passing of events in time, is the condition of historicity, insofar as it is the prerequisite for a historical consciousness, which can yet reach beyond history. The paradox unity of time and eternity finds its proper expression in the high and exalted moment in which we, so to speak, transcend our own existence. This moment, the authentic instance, the instance of decision, of intense communication, of transfiguration, this grain of eternity, as Kierkegaard has already pointed out, must be opposed to the passing moment. Between the two, and subsuming both, historicity mediates, standing, as it does, for the unity of an ephemeral and diaphanous precariousness with the substantial density of the transcendent moment. Historicity is for Jaspers the essential characteristic of all that is concrete, that is not timeless, not abstract, not universal. In this sense it involves an irrational element, as Jaspers concedes. But this kind of irrationality must not be taken as a negative value:

Irrational is not only what is beyond the limits of the general, but there are non-rational generalities as well, such as the validity of character types in poetry and art. Historicity . . . has as its medium that which is rational, as well as the irrational that has taken on form. It is superrational, rather than irrational.[10]

9 *Philosophie*, 398.   10 *Ibid.*, 408.

The concept of historicity recalls in a sense the neo-Hegelian notion of the concrete universal, as well as the *infima species* of the
philosophia perennis. That which can never be reached by logical
deductions or abstract sequences, that which can only be pointed
at by limiting concepts, is the core of *Existenz,* and is thus embodied concretely in the world. "Historical" for Jaspers is what
eludes fixation by universal maxims and any integration into a
system. "Historical" is also every manifestation of transcendent
reality, which in its very nature cannot be understood by means
of universally valid dogma nor be integrated into a system of
revelations.

We have seen so far that the concept of historicity in the philosophy of Jaspers denotes a certain fullness and sumptuousness of
concrete being, which is unique, incomparable, and irreducible
to a conceptual scheme. The necessity for our opening reservation
will thus perhaps have become clearer. The crucial import of the
concept of historicity in the thought of Jaspers is evident, if we
consider that its sway extends not only over anthropology, but
over epistemology, metaphysics and ethics as well. We have seen
that historicity attaches at the outset to individual existence. Jaspers uses the concept, however, so that it becomes applicable to
all empirical reality, insofar as the concrete situation of the individual conditions or includes that reality. Thus the world is
historical in the sense that it is precisely *this* world and not some
other, just as I, in my historicity, am what I am, and not someone
else. The historicity of the world is founded upon its contingency.
The thought of another possible world is vain and empty, just as
was Leibniz's attempt to derive this world from a system of possible worlds. The world is as unique as the individual, as temporal
and as concrete.

A further and most problematic aspect of the concept of historicity presents itself with Jaspers' assertion of the historicity of
truth itself, as opposed to every pretension of its universality,
timelessness or totality. If, for Jaspers, a thought is philosophically
true to the degree to which its thinking furthers communication,
it must be clear that for him discursive thought can never arrive
at a universally valid concept of Being, but only at *one* view of
Being among others. The historicity of truth stands for an epistemological limitation, as well as for a personal dimension in the
acquisition of knowledge. The truth of a thought is, for Jaspers,
inseparable from the thinker, whose temporal situation and biography will determine the intensity and profundity of his insight
into Being. The temporal condition of man is the principal limi-

tation upon the achievement of truth. Man is not a pure Cartesian spirit who thinks in clear and distinct ideas; but he must conquer truth, embedded as it is in the non-intelligible. Striving and
failures, crises and new beginnings, daring and effort are inherent
in the human quest for truth. Absolute truth appears only in the
"becoming" of truth in the individual. Truth without process and
without struggle is thinkable for Jaspers only as existing in transcendent reality, but never as existing for man: it is a limiting
concept. Jaspers is entirely aware of the proximity this theory bears
to relativism and perspectivism. But every attempt at achieving a
premature harmony or at reconciling 'existential' contradictions
conceptually must seem to him to betray the 'existential' condition of man.

The Encompassing. The thoughts which Jaspers expressed in
his *Philosophie* are given a new variation, a new and, in Jaspers'
own words, equally tentative formulation in the philosophy of the
Encompassing *("Das Umgreifende")* which is first announced and
outlined in *Vernunft and Existenz* (1935), systematically developed in *Existenzphilosophie* (1937), and which forms the
proper subject of the *Philosophische Logik,* the first volume of
which, *Von der Wahrheit* (1947), contains a full elaboration of
this thought. Point of departure of this philosophy is the thought
that whatever becomes object for my thinking is only *one* determinate kind of being among others, one mode of being. We cannot reach the horizon, the standpoint from which we can view
the closed Whole of Being, which no longer points to a beyond.
Being remains unclosed for us and draws us into the *apeiron* on
all sides.

We always live and think within a horizon. But the very fact that
it is a horizon indicates something further which again surrounds the
given horizon. From this situation arises the question about the Encompassing. The Encompassing is not a horizon within which every
determinate mode of Being and truth emerges for us, but rather that
within which every particular horizon is enclosed as in something
absolutely comprehensive which is no longer visible as a horizon at
all.[11]

This thought constitutes for Jaspers a basic philosophic operation *(philosophische Grundoperation).* The end of this operation
is the "liberation" of our consciousness of Being *(Seinsbewusst-
sein)* from any specific knowing. The difficulty of the thought lies
in the fact that, as soon as we want to think the Encompassing, it
becomes one specific kind of being, such as the being of the world

---

11 *Reason,* 52; *Existenz,* 13; *Wahrheit,* 38.

or of the mind. Thus every statement concerning the Encompassing, which intends Being itself rather than any determinate kind of being, is in a sense contradictory. Furthermore, we are always faced by the danger of arriving at a false assertion concerning the whole of the Encompassing, if each statement is taken literally.

The one Encompassing, as soon as it is thought, is split into its "modes." If we understand the Kantian antinomies, if we conceive the world as an Idea, not as an object, if we follow Kant, with Jaspers, in subsuming every object under the condition of thinking consciousness, then we can distinguish two modes: the Encompassing, in which external being appears: the world; and the Encompassing which I am: consciousness-as-such. The latter is only a partial category, however: I am also as existence, which carries consciousness. What Jaspers terms existence is my concrete and temporal existence, which has a beginning and an end, which suffers and rejoices, which lives in anguish and in hope. Furthermore I am also spirit, which receives in its ideal constructions everything that is thought by consciousness and concretely experienced by existence. The third step is taken with a leap out of immanence, which is twofold: from the world to the Godhead, and from existence to *Existenz*.

To recapitulate: the first step resulted in a positing of the two modes of the Encompassing into that which we are and into that which (external) being itself is. The second step further split the first category into the three modes of our own being. The third step led from immanence to Transcendence. In the fourth step, which is added in the structural elaboration set forth in *Von der Wahrheit*, reason (*Vernunft*) is introduced as the bond of the modes of the Encompassing and their appearances, as the means whereby unity is restored to their manifoldness.

The term Encompassing becomes meaningful only through the manner in which Jaspers uses it, just as it was Kierkegaard's use of the term *"Existenz,"* from which the latter derives its specific content. The concept itself, in its very elusiveness and ambiguity, in its resistance to a fixation by definition, is the ideal instrument which Jaspers has shaped himself for his purposes. If we understood Jaspers correctly, this concept appeals to the insight of *Existenz* more than to analytical reason. The Encompassing is that by which the things become more than they are on the surface,—it is that added quality by which they assume their peculiar transparency, their depth.

But how is the rich texture of the Encompassing properly

known? Knowledge is, for Jaspers, basically unable to reach Being as such, but is primarily directed at the appearances. Whatever is to be known, therefore, must automatically be reduced to a determinate object of knowledge. Being thus eludes our thought: the moment in which we believe to grasp it conceptually, we have already falsified it by making it into that which it is, by definition, not: into a determinate content *(bestimmter Daseinsinhalt)*. The problematic of Jaspers' conception of Being lies in the fact that it cannot be contemplated as a Platonic Idea.

Yet there is a mode of knowledge proper to encompassing Being: we become directly "aware" of it. This becoming aware *(Innewerden)* is a bridge through which something by nature non-objective *(ungegenständlich)* is thought in the form of an objective entity, which, however, acts merely as a catalyst. Thus we become aware of the Encompassing in a reflexive thought, not comparable to objective knowledge, in which Being becomes lucid and transparent for us, announcing itself, but never taking on a determinate form.

It seems that Jaspers here calls attention again to the forgotten fact that, at the root of all thought and as the basis for all knowledge, there must be a direct pre-rational givenness of Being. Were it not for this primal awareness, the particular could not be rationally surpassed and metaphysics would thus be impossible. But awareness is inseparable from knowledge: Knowledge must be rooted in awareness and awareness in turn must be imbedded in knowledge; for without a deeper, intuitive awareness of Being all knowledge remains but a superficial collection of data, a *Scheinwissen*. Everything that is known objectively becomes pregnant with meaning only if it is melted into an awareness of Being, and the contents of knowledge then assume a new perspective and are seen in new relationships. But such an awareness of Being can only be reached indirectly; knowledge remains its necessary prerequisite.

The Cipher. From this it is evident that for Jaspers metaphysics, which has as its proper object the realm of Transcendence, can only deal with symbols. Conceptual thought breaks down in view of the really real. Myth, theology, and philosophy —in the specific interpretation of Jaspers — are three separate, possible ways that point to Transcendence.

But what is the manner of this pointing? A formal transcending directed at Being itself must cope with the difficulty that the object is a Being that must be thought as a Person remaining, however, forever hidden — a *deus absconditus*. By means of the less direct manner of the *'existential'* relationship, Transcendence is seen in suspension: at the very moment that it becomes an object it disappears, it dissolves. The relationship of *Existence* to Transcendence is never stable, but forever in process, in continuous flux. Jaspers' analysis of this relationship is one of the strongest points in his philosophy and touches on the deepest problems of philosophical anthropology.

In the ultimate situations we are confronted by the question as to why Being *is* and why there is not rather nothing, and also why it is such as it is. I can "reject" this givenness in a Promethean defiance, or else I can accept it in an act of religious surrender and confidence in the ground of Being. An *'existential'* neutrality is impossible in regard to Transcendence. *Existenz* directed at Transcendence is lifted up, otherwise it declines. The possibility of leading a blind, vegetative, merely "vital" existence is not a real *'existential'* possibility. *Existenz* is perpetually in suspension between two magnetic poles: the "Law of the Day," the principle of order, clarity, and loyalty, and the "Passion of the Night," the irrational urge to darkness, to the earth, to the mother, to the race, to ruin and the end of all order. A final decision for the one or for the other does not take place in *Existenz;* a synthesis of the two is equally impossible. The suspension remains unresolved.

We have said that for Jaspers philosophy is essentially metaphysics; metaphysics in turn is the reading of the ciphers of Transcendence: it concerns itself with a universe of objects which are by nature ephemeral and unstable, disappearing as soon as they have spoken to *Existenz*. What experience is for consciousness-as-such, namely the link between object and subject, the cipher is for *Existenz* — the link to Transcendence. The concept of the cipher *(Chiffre; Chifferschrift)* presupposes that reason cannot know the nature of the world directly, but that reality must be "read" in the secret language of the appearances. In this sense Kant already spoke of "the ciphers by means of which Nature speaks to us;" Goethe referred to the "alphabet of the *Weltgeist;*" Novalis and the German Romantics expressed themselves similarly. For Jaspers the ciphers are not identical with the appearances, but are the language spoken through them by Transcendence, not to consciousness-as-such, but to *Existenz*. The direct language of Transcendence is not a language that is universally intelligible. The incompleteness of the empirical world points above and beyond every rational certitude; this pointing has the immediacy of the metaphysical experience. It does not follow a method; it is adventitious, as it were, a gift, and its realization can be forced by no plan and no will. In this sense metaphysics does not constitute an extension of knowledge, but is the process by which reality becomes transparent in time. Transcendence speaks to *Existenz* through the appearances in a process in which these are transformed, losing the nature of objects, and thereby their permanence and consistency. Being, never objectively determined, is given only in its appearances, namely in the world and in *'existential'* freedom. Transcendence is the substance of the world and of *Existenz;* they in turn are the appearances of Being.

Do cipher and symbol, then, stand for one and the same thing? In a sense they do, if we distinguish with Jaspers two kinds of symbols: those, which can be interpreted *(deutbare Symbole),* and those that can only be intuited *(schaubare Symbole).* The first kind refer to a *signatum* in the world. A symbol may become a cipher, however, only if there is no determined *signatum* to which it refers, but, instead a reality different in kind. The *signum* points in this case to a *signatum,* which is not an object and can never become one. While the world speaks in its empirical dimension to consciousness-as-such, it assumes for *Existenz* the character of the symbol. In this sense the *signum is not separable* from the *signatum;* a deciphering or an analysis is no longer possible. Jaspers speaks of the reading of Transcendence in the physiognomy of the things: as through the face of an individual, with whom I am in *'existential'* communication, I penetrate to the non-objective ground of freedom at the core of *Existenz,* I penetrate through world and *Existenz* to Being. What is thus given is not capable of further hermeneutic interpretation — every interpretation must in the last analysis go back to the original language, namely to the immediate givenness of Transcendence, and thus become in turn a cipher of the second order.

When Jaspers speaks of the historicity of the ciphers, he refers to their instability, their constant disappearance and regeneration. While the world presents itself to consciousness-as-such as a stable and consistent entity, capable of empirical exploration, it reveals itself at the same time as a cipher to *Existenz* in its very instability and unintelligibility. Thus the grasp of Being through the ciphers is never achieved once and for all, but is a constant movement, an incessant conquest and recurrent loss. The "truth" of the cipher is not universal, but as unique as the person who beholds this "truth." Its lack of clarity is not one which can be resolved by a perfection of the means at our disposal. Each of the infinite number of ciphers can be read in infinitely many ways and each reading may in turn become a cipher; their endless ambiguity is their very essence.

Philosophy. What is ineffable and inexpressible in the immediate language of Being becomes, in a certain sense, universal — and thus the possible object of philosophic discourse — in the myths and religions on the one hand and in the ontological systems on the other. The language of Transcendence is taken up into the empirical world as a second universe of objects. The theory of the ciphers thus posits two opposite movements: One from the original cipher, the primal language of Transcendence, to the embodiment of these ciphers in the myths and philosophies, which Jaspers calls the language of man; and the second from the myths and philosophies to Being, which is revealed in them. The original experience of Transcendence takes place, historically and concretely, in the first language, whereas metaphysical reality realized in thought and symbols forms a second original language. The connection of the two languages takes place in the union of Transcendence and immanence, as well as of *Existenz* and reason, which enlightens and makes intelligible the message transmitted.

The language of the myths and religions mediates between the original cipher and reason; in the third, speculative language, the language of the classical ontological systems, the reading of the ciphers becomes metaphysical thought. This language is spoken to the philosopher by the philosophers of the past and by him to those of the future. The task of philosophy is, for Jaspers, to carry the original cipher, to lead back to the immediate language of Being.

Is it, in view of this theory, possible to regard the philosophy of Karl Jaspers as one would regard the philosophy of Plato, of Kant, of Hegel, in short, in line with the other philosophers which have found such a magnificent interpreter and reawakener in Jaspers? What is new and characteristic in the philosophy of Jaspers is this: that whereas other thinkers in the great philosophical tradition of the West, in propounding their ideas, believed somehow in their universal validity and, in spite of an awareness of the limitation imposed on human knowledge, in their truth, and whereas they refuted other, contradictory systems in order to establish their own, Jaspers at once accepts the core of truth, the "cipher," in all of the great philosophies with an unequalled openness and critical penetration, while at the same time rejecting their claim to universality. Jaspers' philosophy is, if we may say so, a philosophy of philosophy. With Jaspers philosophy has reached self-consciousness. That Jaspers would consistently regard his own thought as one philosophical metaphor among others is both his weakness and his strength.

For Jaspers the world is the proper object of consciousness and at the same time, through its very unintelligibility, a cipher for *Existenz*. Only by virtue of its historicity is *Existenz* able to grasp Being intuitively in the continuous flux of its appearances. Hence certitude in regard to Transcendence must be forever reconquered and re-established. In the eyes of Jaspers the systematic coherence of a dialectic philosophy cannot serve as an instrument for the understanding of a language which appeals to the historicity of *Existenz*. A philosophical system may be viewed as a cipher, but no *one* system can claim, for Jaspers, to grasp the meaning of the ciphers.

Jaspers' philosophy is an attempt to come closer to an understanding of the universal human possibilities through an investigation of the unique, exceptional and historical individual. His philosophy is neither an abstract universal system nor does it take the form of personal confessions; yet it bears certain resemblances to both: it is, in the truest sense, a philosophy, yet its basis is highly personal. This orientation on two poles makes for the peculiarly dynamic tension of Jaspers' philosophy. Jaspers is primarily concerned with two questions: That of the relation of Being to truth, and that of the connection between *Existenz* and Being. The first question is largely an epistemological one with an anthropological coloring; the second is a metaphysical one. The subjectivistic stress in regard to the first question is countermanded by the metaphysical purport of the second. Although Jaspers insists on the one hand that truth is personal and historical, he speaks on the other hand of Being as adventitious, as a "gift," a presence which reveals itself to me as that which I am not, as something not entirely different from Gabriel Marcel's *mystère ontologique*. Thus *Existenz* is in the last analysis not the source, but the witness of Being.

Jaspers' accent on the temporality and historicity of truth has been interpreted by some critics as constituting a complete lack of objective standards, as "an exasperated individualism,"[12] as "justifying exactly everything."[13] It is true: Every philosophical interpretation of reality must, according to Jaspers, ultimately go back to the individual; no system of essences and universals, which does not take into account the uniqueness of the exception, may be called truly "philosophical." The infinite regression into which a purely subjectivistic philosophy would fall, is broken through, however, by Jaspers' assertion of a certitude of Being which acts as the foundation of a new objectivity.

12 Jean Wahl, in *Revue de Metaphysique et de Morale*, 1934, 442, n.2.

13 J. de Tonquedec, *L'Existence d'après K. Jaspers*, Paris, 1945, 133.

How does this new objectivity break into the circle of immanence? My own "truth" becomes shallow and absurd in view of the chasm revealed by the ultimate situations. I am *aus mir*, as Jaspers says, but not *durch mich:* the origin of my thinking and acting is immanent, but the ultimate ground of my being lies outside. I am conscious not only of my own being, but of a Being, as well, which is adventitious, speaking through its appearances to him who will hear.

Being and *Existenz* are the two polar concepts of Jaspers' philosophy. They are not connected systematically but loosely in the form of an *Eros* acting in both directions. *Existenz*, through the *élan vital* of the metaphysical urge, is directed to Transcendence, which surpasses the individuality of *Existenz* and of thought, appearing only where the empirical and the intelligible orders fail. It is in this sense that Jaspers' assertion must be understood that foundering is the ultimate reality of human existence and at the same time the central cipher of Transcendence. Being encloses *Existenz*, which is aware of it and participates in it. Thus, for Jaspers, individual historical truth is included in and enveloped by the truth of Being and its subjectivity resolves itself in the affirmation of a transcendent reality. The absoluteness of *Existenz* gives way in view of an ultimate non-subjective Being.

World, *Existenz* and Transcendence are the three irreducible realms of Being. They are irreducible, it is true, yet ultimately bridged by the concept of historicity, which connects the world and the self: the world as the ground for the freedom of the self, and the self as accepting and assimilating the world. The concept of the "cipher" leads similarly from the world through its appearances to Transcendence. But Jaspers, the cool and impartial diagnostician of reality, resists the temptation of restoring to Being an ultimate unity, which does not take into account, in his eyes, the symptoms for the rupture in its different spheres. The reading of the primal cipher does not offer a sufficient ground for a permanent conciliation.

*   *   *   *   *

We have tried to make explicit some of the basic concepts in the thought of Karl Jaspers; this necessitated an examination of the place of the concept of that philosophy and of Jaspers' conception of philosophy itself. "Each philosophy creates its own concept; it has no higher criterion outside. To know, what philosophy truly is, I must live in it; I do not know it by a definition."[14] From this

14 *Philosophie*, 206.

it follows that, for Jaspers, philosophical truth does not lie in valid assertions with a claim to universality, but in an *'existential'* assimilation of Being through its appearances, resulting in an inner change, a turning-about in the sense of Plato's Allegory of the Cave. The aim of philosophy, for Jaspers, is not to arrive at a self-consistent closed system, but is rather an incessant drive to set free, to prepare for new modes of knowledge, to make felt the boundless space in which free thought can move. Thus philosophy itself is the Socratic thorn which drives on to wake hidden origins, to bring to realization what has been dormant, to penetrate into the profoundest depths of Being. Jaspers consciously leaves open all concrete decisions, but strives instead to raise the issues to the highest level of discussion, to shed light on them from all angles, to substitute for impersonal "truths" contents that carry the cipher of reality and meet in Transcendence, as parallel lines meet in infinity.

It is evident that Jaspers must reject the question as to his point of view, that the philosopher for him must, as it were, seek out *all* points of view, occupying and leaving each in turn. For him the fact that there is no direct path to Being demands from the philosopher a constant mobility from one point of view to another. To take a position is for Jaspers an expression of an intellectual will to power. Each position can be disproved rationally and becomes unphilosophical in the very moment in which it substitutes a philosophical "knowing" for an *'existential'* philosophizing. Every philosophical doctrine is but *one* interpretation. Each contains a grain of truth, but none represents *the* truth. The world is capable of infinite interpretations; all lead somehow and in some measure to an awareness of Being. Hence philosophy is based on the decision "not to seek reassurance in a satisfying *Seinswissen,* but to listen, in the open, horizonless space, which encloses all horizons, to all that speaks to me, to perceive the light-signals that point a direction, that warn, that entice — and perhaps also announce that, which is . . ."[15]

Thus, what some critics would level against Jaspers as a criticism, he accepts as an integral part of his philosophy: the charge of not taking a position. "At the end we have no firm ground under us, no principle to hold on to, but a suspension of thought in infinite space — without shelter in conceptual systems, without refuge in firm knowledge or faith. And even this suspended, floating structure of thought is only one metaphor of Being among others . . ."[16]

[15] *Wahrheit,* 187f.   [16] *Ibid.,* 185f.

The question remains: what are the limits of relativism, to what extent, if at all, is it necessary for a philosophy to take a definite position in order to be meaningful. Is it possible, in other words, to see all philosophies as ciphers, including the philosophy of the ciphers? The infinite regression must yield at some point to the firm ground from which alone a philosophizing is possible. Jaspers is aware of the problem: "The making relative, by which philosophical speculation frees itself again from its own results, is endless; it may decline to arbitrariness and assume the emptiness of a purely negating relativism. However, relativizing constitutes a meaningful movement only out of something positive, out of the one truth. But to make this one truth philosophically objective (*philosophisch gegenständlich*) cannot be a meaningful aim. Philosophy seeks its enlightenment in thoughts which are themselves always still relative. The one truth is the truth of *Existenz* which moves in the ideas and finds its ground in Transcendence . . ."[17]

If the ultimate justification of a philosophy is seen to lie in the establishment of a logical or rational unity, then Jaspers' philosophy founders — but it founders consciously and purposely by humbling itself, through a humiliation of reason which must give way to a "philosophical faith" in the ground of Being.

KURT HOFFMAN

MÜNCHEN
GERMANY

17 *Ibid.*, 736f.

2

James Collins

JASPERS ON SCIENCE AND PHILOSOPHY

THERE are several highways leading to the heart of Karl Jaspers' thought. One illuminating access to his mind is gained through a study of his distinction between science and philosophy. This central problem holds a prominent place in the two major statements of his doctrine: *Philosophie* and *Von der Wahrheit*. Jaspers is also careful to mention it in most of the popular summaries of his philosophy, written during the last few years. Hence an analysis of this doctrine is indispensable for appreciating his characteristic approach to philosophical issues. The present paper deals with four main points: the relation between philosophy and our age of science, the attitudes of Descartes and Nietzsche toward science, Jaspers' philosophical interpretation of the nature of science, and the relation between science and philosophy. In the final section, a brief critical comparison is made between Jaspers and the philosophies of naturalism and Thomism.

I. PHILOSOPHIZING IN THE AGE OF SCIENCE

One often comes away from a reading of Jaspers with the impression that he is not quite sure, in his own mind, concerning the precise relationship between science and philosophy.[1] For, at one moment, he defends the possibility of a separation of philosophy from the special sciences. He points to the profoundly philosophical remarks that emanate from a child, looking at the world in a pre-scientific way. At another time, Jaspers stresses the indissoluble bond uniting science and philosophy, such that the former provides a necessary preparation for the latter. Again, he seems to waver between praise for the pre-Socratic fusion of the two standpoints and a plea for their rigid, systematic differentiation. Thus, we are led to inquire whether or not there can be genuine philosophizing apart from a scientific formation of the

---

[1] Cf., for instance, *Existenz*, 10f; *Wisdom* (New Haven, 1951) 8ff, 74ff, 168f; *Reason*, 30ff.

mind, and whether it is desirable to make a formal distinction between the scientific and philosophical approaches.

This apparent indecision on so crucial a question can be removed, as soon as we attend to Jaspers' unobtrusive but highly significant use of the temporal qualifier: "today." He admits that, in primitive epochs, philosophical inquiries preceded scientific investigations, and that there are still transient gleams of pre-scientific philosophical insight on the part of children in our own time. But as far as the mature mind of today is concerned, philosophical inquiry cannot be carried on successfully, unless the methodology and meaning of the sciences are grasped, at least in their principal features. Similarly, it was quite possible for the early Greek thinkers to merge science and philosophy in a single vision of nature, and for the tradition of a "natural philosophy" (coalescing philosophy and the sciences in a single whole) to flourish throughout the classical and medieval periods. Yet these conditions were only possible because science, in its typically modern articulations, had not yet developed. Now that this historical development of the sciences has transpired, however, we cannot close our eyes to it. In our era, the philosopher must recognize explicitly that his method and aim are quite distinct from those of the various modern sciences.

As a rough anticipation of his more detailed distinction between the two, Jaspers proposes that philosophy seeks the meaning of Being as such and of the world as a whole, whereas the modern sciences concern themselves about the particular objects and special aspects within the world. Why is it impossible today to ignore this basic contrast or to elaborate a philosophy, without formally attending to it? The fundamental answer is that philosophy is essentially a mode of praxis, an affair of inner activity, a deed in the form of thought.[2] That is why Jaspers prefers to speak of his work as an active *philosophizing*, rather than a static, finished body of doctrine or *a philosophy*. Every practical activity or vital operation is bound up with the concrete conditions of life. In man's case, this means that the work of thought or philosophizing is inextricably associated with, and deeply affected by, the prevailing historical situation. One of Jaspers' chief doctrines is that human existence and all its modes are involved in various situations. He applies this doctrine of situational existence to philosophical thinking, which is a supreme mode of existence and practical human operation. A man cannot engage in this activity,

[2] *Philosophie* (second ed., Berlin and Heidelberg, 1948), 279ff; *Rechenschaft* (Munich, 1951), 342.

in complete abstraction from the situations of his temporal existence. Man's total involvement in situational being would be called in question, were present-day philosophizing detachable from the historical conditions of modern life.

In both of his extended accounts of the modern age — *Man in the Modern Age* and *The Origin and Goal of History* — Jaspers signalizes the paramount rôle of the sciences in the formation of post-Renaissance society.[3] He calls the scientific and technological achievements since the seventeenth century the "simply new" factor, injected into the mainstream of history. It is their presence which sets off the modern Western world, in a radical way, from previous Western civilization and from the entire Oriental development. The most general description of our historical situation is: the age of science and technology. Hence philosophers cannot divorce themselves from this concrete scientific setting for all activity, and cannot evade the task of interpreting the scientific enterprise and differentiating it from their own. This supposes, however, that the philosopher has at his disposal a precise account of the characteristics of the modern scientific spirit.

As a preliminary contribution toward such a description, Jaspers proposes a distinction between the broad, neutral meaning of "science," and one that is sufficiently limited to convey the distinctive features of the modern approach to nature and man. In the wider sense, scientific thinking is regulated by empirical respect for facts and a concern for rational communication of findings. The scientific mind proceeds in a deliberate, methodical way, and is fully aware both of the method being used and of its limitations. Constant questioning, fresh consultation of new situations in experience, and openness to criticism, are hallmarks of the scientific attitude. Philosophy qualifies as scientific thought in this broad meaning. It welcomes searching questions and criticisms; it roots itself firmly in the soil of existence *(Dasein)*, to which it must always return; it employs a methodic manner of investigation, and is fully aware of its methodological principles and their confines; it organizes its truths in the light of a unifying principle, so that rational communication among men will be promoted. To this extent, then, philosophy is scientific, without thereby being aggregated among the sciences.[4]

A profound *caesura* opens up, however, between the specifically modern, Western approach in the sciences and the outlooks of the previous ages. There are several unique traits, marking off

[3] *Age* (new impression of English translation, London, 1951), 133ff; *Origin*, 83ff.
[4] *Existenz*, 9; *Reason*, 146f; *Scope*, 29f.

this new conception of science.[5] (1) Scientific research is animated by the will to know all that is knowable. Consequently, there is nothing too insignificant for careful study, nothing unworthy of investigation. Modern science recognizes no limits to its activity. Every real thing and every sort of possibility provide proper materials for analysis. A drive toward novelty and discovery impels scientific inquiry to explore all the corners of the universe. (2) Correlative to the unrestricted content of science is its unrestricted interrogation of all previous convictions. No belief is too sacred or too firmly established to forbid a radical questioning of its soundness. (3) There is something provisional about all scientific theories themselves. They must submit to the test of fresh experience and experiment, and hence must be prepared for constant revision and even replacement. The scientific attitude includes a willingness to test new hypotheses, even those that seem to contradict facts or outstrip our sensuous intuition of the world. Hence the sciences are essentially incomplete and subject to the law of linear progress, in which each succeeding generation takes a measurable step beyond the position of its predecessors.

(4) Nevertheless, the scientific movement aims at a certainty that is coercive and indubitable. The ideal of mathematical knowledge has exercised a strong attraction over scientific minds, buoying them up with the hope that all fields of scientific work can be impenetrated with mathematical clarity and certainty. The aim of scientific inquiry in the several fields is to bring the objective evidence to a clear condition, where it imposes itself upon the impartial mind, with compelling force. (5) This purpose is promoted by the rigorous way in which scientific methods and categories are applied. A sustained effort is made to universalize the method and categories of a given science, in order to test their scope and cast new light upon familiar situations. Universally valid knowledge is the lodestone guiding every construction of a scientific world of discourse. (6) Viewpoints are not proliferated for their own sake, however, since scientific explanation is also regulated by the requirements of economy and simplicity of means. In regarding an object from every side and with the help of all the scientific perspectives, the investigator intends to bring out its systematic connections with the rest of the universe. Even though the object can never be located definitively in respect to all its relations in the cosmos of being, still its position in the cosmos of interrelated sciences can be ascertained. Although the sciences do not achieve a total unity, grounded in a comprehensive

5 These characteristics are conveniently enumerated in *Origin. loc.cit.*

knowledge of all reality, they do tend toward a systematic inter-connection of methods and categories.

(7) Jaspers defends the speculative character of scientific knowledge. Whatever other ends it may serve, its primary function is to satisfy the will to know all that is knowable. This does not mean, however, that scientific knowledge is cut off from the practical control of nature, but only that such control depends upon the speculative soundness of the knowledge. Indeed, the practical orientation of knowledge is one of the indigenous features of the modern scientific outlook. There is no historical parallel to the success with which modern science has satisfied human needs. In subjecting so many aspects of nature to human dominion, scientific technology has not only changed the face of the world around us but also profoundly modified the inner life of man himself. Our relation with the natural world has been made more remote in one respect (due to the regimen of machines and the demands of industrial production schedules), and yet in another respect it has been made more intimate (due to increased leisure and perfection of the means of communication and instruments of observation). The tremendous potentialities of technological control over mass societies, for good and for evil, set off our way of human living in a scientific epoch.

II. The Historical Lesson of Descartes and Nietzsche

The impact of science and technology has been felt just as strongly in philosophy as in the other areas of human life. In several autobiographical sketches, Jaspers has outlined the condition of philosophical instruction at Heidelberg and other German universities, around the turn of the present century.[6] Philosophy courses were generally confined to epistemology, psychology and history of philosophy. The latter discipline tended to be a sheerly "objective" recital of what had been taught by thinkers in the past, with no hint that the philosophical tradition was still living and relevant for the problems of modern life. The doctrinal courses were made as "scientific" as possible, in the hope of appropriating to philosophy some of the great prestige of the sciences. Evidence, methods and proofs were tailored according to the model of the mathematical or biological sciences. Professors vied with each other in presenting philosophy as one science along with all the others or, at the very most, as the summation of the other sciences. For, unless philosophy were shown to be the meth-

6 *Existenz*, 2ff; *Rechenschaft*, 170ff, 325f.

odology of the sciences or their highest generalization, it could achieve no respectable standing in the university community.

Jaspers himself remained unconvinced by the scientific pretences of the reigning philosophies, especially positivism and idealism. In the latter part of the nineteenth century, idealists like Lotze attempted to deal in a scientifically stringent way with the problems of God, the soul, freedom and moral responsibility. The shaky results of this effort to ape the sciences led many people to deny the spiritual nature of man and his freedom, simply because these latter were not susceptible of becoming objects of scientific demonstration. Positivism profited by this disillusionment with idealism by suggesting that the limits of real being coincide precisely with the limits of scientific thinking. The practical advice was that man should not bother himself about such issues as God, the spiritual soul and freedom, since they lie beyond the possibility of confirmation or rejection through scientific method, and hence can be presumed to be mere fictions of the mind. Both idealism and positivism accepted a common platform: that all philosophical problems can be settled through use of the scientific method. Even Edmund Husserl allowed this fundamental presupposition to go unchallenged.[7] In announcing that phenomenology provides a way of transforming philosophy into a strict science, he simply begged the question of the appropriateness of such a transformation. Jaspers' admiration for Husserl was qualified by the belief that philosophy loses its distinctive approach to reality just as effectively when its main task is to supply the foundations of scientific knowledge as when it is treated as the systematic summary of the other sciences.

Jaspers reports that he wrote his work, *Descartes und die Philosophie,* mainly to bring out into the open the historical source of the modern confusion between science and philosophy. Whereas Husserl's *Méditations Cartésiennes* tried to execute the Cartesian project in a more rigorous and radical way, Jaspers' book casts doubt upon the way in which Descartes and Husserl conceive philosophical method and truth. Descartes was so impressed by the success of his analytic geometry, that he tried to reconstruct philosophy along the lines of a *mathesis universalis.* Although he distinguished between ordinary mathematics and philosophy, he retained in philosophy the mathematical conception of evidence and certainty. To this extent, he absolutized one scientific method, so that he might revamp philosophy in the form of modern science. Having capitulated to the imperialism of scientism, Descartes was

---

[7] For Jaspers' estimate of Husserl, cf. *Rechenschaft,* 327f.

thereafter unable to do justice either to the sciences or to philosophy. Both were eventually the losers by the Cartesian adventure in interbreeding.

Within a half-century after Descartes' death, most practising scientists had abandoned Cartesian physics. For, even though he recognized in advance most of the salient features of modern scientific research, Descartes perverted their meaning, due to his methodological prejudices.[8] For instance, he hailed the trend toward realizing the unity of science. But, at the same time, he artificially imposed the ideal of a systematic deduction of all scientific truths from a few principles, instead of acknowledging that the idea of unity can be realized in different ways, in different sciences. Although Descartes accorded a definite rôle to experience and experiment in his theory of method, his actual construction of physics was excessively deductive and divorced from a direct testing of facts. The arbitrary results of his physical deductions were a steep price to pay for vindicating his monism of method and knowledge. Another unfortunate consequence was his lack of insight into the nature of historical knowledge. He was obliged to depreciate the humanities as constituting merely inexact bodies of opinion, since it was difficult to conform them to his mathematical notion of certitude.

Although the consequences of Cartesianism for philosophy were less palpable, they were just as disastrous. In order to obtain clear and compelling evidence in philosophy, Descartes had to reduce the human self and God to the status of objects for scientific understanding. The self or thinking thing was treated only in so far as it served as a counterpart of the body or extended thing. Despite Descartes' high respect for freedom, the latter was definitely endangered through his correlation between mind and body. Spinoza drew the inference that, if bodily states are strictly determined, then mental states are subject to an equally rigid determinism. Universal determinism is the condition under which alone both mind and body can become the objects of clear and cogent mathematical demonstration. If philosophy can deal with man's inner life only from the standpoint of what indifferently is evident to all observers, then there must be a methodic elimination of freedom and '*existential*' content from the thinking self. Descartes could not rescue freedom and *Existenz* by an apppeal to the self's relation to God, even though he made a strenuous effort to do so. For he admitted God into philosophy only in the degree that He supported a mathematically dominated body of knowledge. The

8 *Descartes* (second ed., Berlin, 1948), 56ff; *Rechenschaft*, 364.

Cartesian God was no longer the giver of *Existenz* but the guarantor of the criterion of clear and distinct knowledge. This systematic adaptation of the doctrine on God to the exigencies of
the unity of science undermined belief in His Transcendence and
thus paved the way for subsequent theories of pantheistic immanence.

In Jaspers' view, then, Descartes was the main source of the
typically modern over-evaluation of science. Jaspers refers to this
scientism as the "superstition of science." It consists in a theoretical absolutizing of some area of scientific knowledge, which is
confused with philosophy, and in a practical tendency to expect
everything from science.[9] Since scientific research can pursue an
endless course among objects in the world, the inference is made
that there are no boundaries whatsoever to scientific knowledge,
and that there can be a total scientific world-picture comprehending all reality. On this basis, science is asked to ascertain all values,
to decide upon what ought to be done in moral conduct, and to
set the ultimate goals for human life. Within this scientistic perspective, philosophy has no distinctive office of determining the
norms and ends of our existence: the latter are exclusively immanent and relative ones, which fall completely within the range of
the sciences. The only rôle allotted to philosophy is to supply the
general logic of scientific method and of valuational judgments.
Individual interpretation and free choice are no longer to be
centrally important in either ethical theory or moral practice.
Impersonal scientific inquiry and public evidence are to be the
sole determinants of the hierarchy of values and actual conduct.

Nietzsche's passionate attack upon the ideal of scientific truth
can only be understood against the background of this modern
surrender of philosophical functions to the superstition of science.
Jaspers does not regard Nietzsche as an enemy of science itself
but rather as a resolute foe of modern scientism. Science contains
one mode of truth but it is not *the* truth, in an unconditional way.
Behind our scientific inquiries lies the passion for knowledge, a
drive that can be properly assessed only on philosophical grounds.
Because the will to truth rests upon a non-scientific basis, science
cannot pretend to attain to any absolute truth. Both the ends of
scientific work and all its other valuational aspects stem from
philosophical commitments, whose justification cannot be undertaken by the scientific method itself. The meaning of science cannot be fully apprehended from within the universe of science
itself.

[9] *Origin,* 93f. Since scientism eliminates the dimension of Transcendence, Jaspers
also regards the absolutizing of the finite world as a form of unbelief; cf. *Scope,* 119.

Jaspers gives a metaphysical interpretation of Nietzsche's critique of science.[10] Nietzsche detected something more stirring at the heart of scientific investigation than the scientific mind is aware of: a search after the meaning of Being as a whole. There is an essential incommensurability between the dynamism of the search for truth and the actual results obtainable through the scientific method. Science alone cannot quench the deep human thirst for metaphysical and absolute truth, which animates the scientific will to knowledge. Scientific method can yield an amount of certainty, within a limited sphere, but it can never bring to man an utter personal security, such as will eliminate the risk of interpretation and decision. Even were the scientific description of the world a complete one, man would still be faced with the question of what attitude he is to take toward a world so described. Even though he may desire to do so, man cannot transfer to an impersonal scientific process the responsibility for making a philosophical interpretation of the total meaning of being, and for determining his own individual relation to being.

Yet Jaspers' ironical criticism is that Nietzsche himself is guilty of absolutizing one zone of scientific knowledge into a philosophical whole.[11] Nietzsche has an elusive conception of philosophical truth. Fundamentally, however, he teaches that the scale of human values is to be determined by the relative ability of goals to heighten life itself. The increase of life means an increase in the vigor of the will to power. Jaspers stigmatizes this will to power as a will to illusion, and sets it in essential opposition to the will to truth. Nietzsche associates the will to power with his theory that the universe consists in a grand circle of becoming, which is incompatible with any stable order of transcendent being. But these metaphysical overtones derive from an identification of biological categories with the meaning of Being as such. Nietzsche has his own unacknowledged absolute, although it is a totally immanent one. He himself falls victim to scientism, when he converts the biological view of process into an unconditioned account of the world, and when he states that sovereign becoming is man's substitute for the permanence of Being.

Jaspers extends his analysis of the overevaluation of science into a study of contemporary tendencies. When the sciences are cut off from any unifying philosophical principle, they lack a guiding idea that can establish order and hierarchy among them. Consequently, each separate science tries to absolutize itself and impose

10 *Nietzsche* (third ed., Berlin, 1950), 176-84. In the present paper, the historical accuracy of Jaspers' portraits of Descartes and Nietzsche is not discussed.

11 *Wahrheit*, 595f.

its perspective upon the other sciences. Jaspers singles out anthropology, psychoanalysis and Marxism as prime examples of scientistic imperialism.[12] The aberrations of racism in Nazi Germany are attributable to the false intermixture of science and philosophy, at the level of biology and anthropology. Unconditioned truth was claimed for the concept of a pure race, running in the face of both the empirical evidence and the essential boundaries of scientific generalization. Similarly, Freud and Marx mistook their own considerable scientific discoveries for total philosophical explanations. Hence they drew an unbalanced picture of man, as being determined ultimately by unconscious impulses or relations of economic production. On a purely scientific basis, there is no principle of integration which can take account of the findings of psychoanalytic and Marxist research, without erecting them into complete descriptions of the ultimate determinants ·of human existence. Human freedom and the goals of human life are at stake in the discussion about the relations between science and philosophy.

III. A PHILOSOPHICAL INTERPRETATION OF THE MEANING OF SCIENCE

Jaspers does not believe that a cultural description of our scientific age and an immanent critique of the sciences are sufficient to establish the proper meaning and scope of science. For the sciences themselves are incapable of seizing upon the fundamental significance of their own form of thought. This is a task performable only by philosophy. The latter is sufficiently close to the sciences to be well-informed about their methods and contents, and yet sufficiently independent of them to take a comprehensive view of them.

Unlike Nietzsche, Jaspers does not regard the will to knowledge as a variation of the will to power. Rather, the speculative quest of knowledge is an authentic and original impulse of human nature. Yet it does suppose the validity of the proposition that the world is knowable. This proposition can be taken in two ways: (1) objects in the world are knowable, or (2) the world as a single whole of being is knowable.[13] Jaspers agrees with the first

12 For typical treatments of these three standpoints, cf. *Age*, 149-58; *Reason*, 8-37. See also Jaspers' warning against the social consequences of resurgent scientism, in his address at the reopening of the School of Medicine in Heidelberg University: "The Rededication of German Scholarship," *The American Scholar*, XV (1946), 180-88.

13 *Wahrheit*, 96.

statement, but denies that the second one is true. The perversion of science into a substitute for philosophy is due precisely to a confusion between these two ways of interpreting the knowability of the world. Because the objects in the world are knowable through the scientific method, the conclusion is drawn that the truth about the world as such is also available to scientific understanding. From here, it is only a short step to the further assertion that the real is coextensive with the totality of objects in the world and that, therefore, the only philosophical truth open to man is that supplied by the scientific method.

(1) Jaspers construes in a strictly Kantian way the proposition that objects in the world are knowable.[14] Science *(Wissen-schaft)* is concerned only with knowledge *(Wissen, Erkenntnis)* or what is knowable *(wissbar)*. "Knowledge" is not an indeterminate general term, covering every relation between the mind and things. Instead, it connotes one definite sort of thought: that in which a polar relation is set up between the subject and the phenomenal object. An object of knowledge is not being simply as such, but is some particular, empirical mode or appearance of being. Hence knowledge cannot extend to the being of things and must remain content with their objective appearances. Furthermore, knowledge always involves a presentation of the object to the subject. Knowing transpires within the context of the subject-object relationship. This dichotomy governs what can be known about the subject, as well as the object. Knowledge embraces the subject only in so far as it is correlated with the object. It is only the mind as an empirical subject or appearance that enters into the field of knowledge. Just as knowledge is limited to the objective appearances of things in the world, so is it limited to the objective papearances of the knowing subject itself. The latter can be held at arm's length from itself, as it were, and can thus become an object of knowledge for itself. But what is known, here as elsewhere, is nothing more than the objective appearance. Knowledge reaches to the object-being but not to being in an unqualified way, whether it be the being of our self or the being of the world.

These general conditions of knowledge apply strictly to scientific investigation. Although every sort of empirical consciousness is faced with its object or counterpart *(Gegenstand)*, the scientific mind lays down certain standards for reliable knowledge. The scientific interest is to secure the maximum clarity, logical neces-

---

14 A summary of the Kantian basis of Jaspers' theory of knowledge is given in *Scope*, 8-9, 25-26. On the subject-object relationship, cf. *Psychologie* (third ed., Berlin, 1925), 21-28.

sity, universality and communicability in its determinate object (*Objekt*).[15] Scientific inquiry is guided by the ideal of rational objectivity, guaranteed by evidence that is universally valid and compelling in an impersonal way. Yet even the rational objectivity of scientific knowledge conforms to the general requirements of objects of knowledge. The categories and methods employed by the sciences to bring the empirical materials to the condition of reliable objects, known with indubitable certitude, can operate only within the sphere of the knowable. Consequently, they yield knowledge only of the appearances or object-being of things. Within this realm, scientific understanding can obtain some necessary and universal truths, along with many probable and statistical statements. Jaspers intends to show, however, that objectivity is not the sole mode of being and that scientific findings cannot, therefore, be taken as exhaustive of reality.

(2) No limits can be assigned for scientific research, within the field of objects in the world. Endless progress can be made in the more precise and comprehensive knowledge of these objects. Yet there is a capital difference between progressively coming to know more about objects *in* the world and coming to know the world as such. There are no restraints or limits (*Schranken*) placed upon scientific research at the intramundane level, but there are essential boundaries (*Grenze*) which it cannot trespass.[16] Although it is customary to speak about the scientific view of the world, Jaspers denies that science can furnish an image or system of the world as a whole. The latter is what Kant called a regulative idea, stimulating scientific investigations but never itself becoming an object of scientific knowledge. Because the world cannot present itself to our mind in the form of an object, it falls outside the region of the knowable and thus lies beyond scientific inquiry.

If science can know things in the world and laws about the world, but never the total being of the world as such, then the unity of science cannot be realized through a single scientific method and body of doctrine. Jaspers offers several special arguments in favor of his thesis that the positivistic conception of the unity of science is impossible of fulfillment.[17] (a) From the fact that scientific thought is a mode of knowledge, it cannot avoid the bifurcation of subject and object. The cleavage between consciousness and its empirical objects cannot be overcome by means

15 *Philosophie*, 4-5, 74-75.

16 On this Kantian distinction, see *Wahrheit*, 96; *Origin*, 94.

17 *Philosophie*, 73-110; *Wahrheit*, 96-103; *Descartes*, 47-48; *Anti-Reason*, 27-30; *Wisdom*, 75-76.

of scientific knowledge, which is unable to embrace the two poles within a higher unity. There is a scientifically unresolvable tension between the private world of the knowing subject and the public world of objects. The empirical knower may himself become an object of knowledge and thus be included within the objective world studied by the scientific method, but this world still retains its otherness from consciousness-as-such. Even the maximum conceivable objective unification fails to bring all the factors in the world to a total unity of knowledge. This is not merely a factual limitation but an essential boundary of all scientific thought.

(b) Jaspers regards scientific knowledge as something more than a pure methodology. Methods can be taken in isolation, but only for purposes of more exact and orderly analysis. At some point, this isolated consideration must give way, and methods must be restored to the concrete setting of the contents and objects of scientific inquiry. Method is not cultivated in and for itself alone, but always for the more adequate exploration of the objective structure and laws of empirical being. But objects are not homogeneous in their mode of being. Jaspers distinguishes four different domains of object-being in the world: matter, life, soul or consciousness, and spirit. Scientific knowledge is intentional, in the sense that it is directed necessarily toward these spheres of objective being, each one of which constitutes an irreducible world of its own. Because of the intentional character of scientific thought and the basic differences among the four objective orders to which it refers, scientific knowledge can never reach perfectly homogeneous unity, either in content or in method. Furthermore, there is something endless about scientific research into opaque matter and into the richness of the organism and consciousness. Since only the finite can be expressed in an objective concept, the scientific view remains essentially incomplete and open. The progressive nature of scientific research would be violated, if its findings and methodological innovations could be expressed in a rounded-off image of the world. Such images are due to the desire to convert a science into a philosophical explanation.

(c) Because the several realms of objects are mutually irreducible, there must also be internal and irreducible differentiations in the methods fitted to study them. Inorganic matter, the organism, inner consciousness and the rational spirit call for different scientific approaches. Each science assumes its own perspective on the world and develops its own proportionate method. Although the method proper to one science gives some insight into the structure of another domain of objects, there remains a need for a method specially fitted to examine the latter domain in its characteristic features. The psychiatric method is not rendered superfluous, for instance, by the physiological study of states of the brain which affect our mental states. Instead of following the tradition of Leibniz and the evolutionist in respect to the continuity between the various objective spheres and scientific methods, Jaspers emphasizes the discontinuities and the need for a leap from one method to the next. Although he recognizes certain generic traits, common to all the sciences (the broader meaning of "science"), he points out that actual scientific work requires several specific scientific methods. There is an analogy between the various levels of meaning in the world, but intrinsic methodological adjustments must be made to pass from one to the other.

The pluralism of scientific methods explains why a given scientific explanation can be universally valid and yet relative, rather than absolute. A proposition may be universally valid and correct within the perspective of a certain science, but its truth is limited to this determinate sphere. Hence it is relative to the method and objective standpoint of the science in question. Thus, while the general constructs of mathematical physics determine something about the structure of all material things, they do not yield an exhaustive account of the nature of organic functions. Mathematical physics neither displaces nor assimilates Goethe's report on the world of immediate sensuous perception. And from his own experience in psychiatry, Jaspers is aware of the need to keep the study of mental disorders free from the "nothing-but" arguments of philosophical scientism, which seeks to explain these disorders in terms of constructs drawn from other sciences.

(d) The absolutization of any one scientific standpoint also breaks down in the face of the distinction in kind between the natural sciences and the humanities. This distinction is not abrogated by observing that the methods of the natural sciences apply to man. The fact of their application is undeniable, but equally undeniable is their limited competence in dealing with human nature. Following Dilthey, Weber and Simmel, Jaspers underlines the differences between the explanatory and the *Verstehen* approaches in psychology and psychiatry. The explanatory method seeks causal reasons and objective connections, based upon the constant operation of universal laws of cerebral and mental action. The attention of the method of *Verstehen* is focussed upon the genesis of subjective states of mind and connections of meaning, rather than causality. The natural sciences use the explanatory approach, whereas the humane sciences use *Verstehen*. The latter is historically orientated. It calls attention to those ideal aspects of human development which cannot be stated in objective, universal causal laws. The humane disciplines pay special attention to the unique correlations of meaning and the unrepeatable sequences of events which actually shape individual and cultural growth.

Yet these arguments do not add up to the conclusion that the various sciences are totally discrete and unrelated to each other. It can only be concluded that the sciences are not united through a single method and mode of knowledge, and hence do not yield a total conception of the being of the world. In Jaspers' terminology, they fail to constitute a *system* of world-knowledge, even though they can be organized into a unified *systematic* of knowledge.[18] Whereas a system bases the unity of science upon the unity of the world as a given object and upon a single scientific method, a systematic appeals to the non-objective idea of the world and a multiplicity of methods in scientific research. The Cartesian ideal of the unity of science is legitimate, as long as it recognizes that, in our world, the pathos of unity needs to be reconciled with the actual multiplicity of scientific methods and determinate spheres of objectivity. The principle of unity for a systematic of knowledge is drawn from scientific understanding itself, rather than from its methods and objects. The understanding employs its categories universally and compares the meanings disclosed at various levels of knowability. Because it is regulated by the idea of the world. Although the world as a whole is never forthcoming as an objectively determined appearance, the idea of grasping its total reality provides a ceaseless stimulation to scientific research. An unending conflict exists between the understanding's demand for total unity of explanation and the pluralizing effect of actual research methods and findings. From this fruitful tension springs not only the drive toward further scientific inquiry but also the desire to gain a fuller acquaintance with the world's reality than the sciences can supply.

There are two false routes by which the human mind seeks to fulfill the need for a deeper grasp on being. One is the way of scientism, which refuses to recognize the essential boundaries of scientific thought. The other is an appeal to sheer feeling and pur-

---

18 *Philosophie*, 144, 128ff, 232-40; *Rechenschaft*, 364-65. On the general conditions for a systematic of the sciences, cf. *Psychologie*, 17-20. The problem of a systematic of the sciences or total views dealing with man is examined in *Allgemeine* (fifth ed., Berlin and Heidelberg, 1948), 625-28.

ported irrational sources of insight. Jaspers is just as strenuously opposed to the latter alternative as to the former. He grants that there are irrational and idiosyncratic aspects of empirical being, which the sciences overlook and which are added proof of the impossibility of a complete scientific system of the world. But he denies that these aspects must be approached philosophically by means that are also irrational or purely sentimental. Reason is not only the heart of scientific understanding but also the proper medium of all philosophical insight. Philosophy moves beyond the sciences, but it does not abandon reason (at least in its Kantian meanings) as its principle of discovery.

IV. The Relation between Science and Philosophy

Scientism and irrationalism bear witness that the human mind seeks to apprehend more about being than the sciences can provide. Truth is wider than the truth about being as such. To know objects is not the same as, and is something less than, to grasp being. But from Jaspers' critique of science, it is evident that our grasp on being cannot be an instance of knowledge, since the latter is confined to the region of objects. We cannot *know* being as such, even though we may be able to use reason to apprehend it in some non-objective and non-knowing way. Jaspers must now present some evidence to bear out his contention that being is wider than object-being and that truth embraces something more than scientific knowledge.

To do this, he returns once more to a salient point in the previous analysis of knowledge: the dualism between subject and object. The two members of this polarity are not placed indifferently upon the same plane. Descartes' mistake was precisely to think that the self which is correlated with the material thing and with the requirements of scientific objectivity, is the total self. This is the source of the naturalistic fallacy, which argues from the fact that man is one object along with others in the world, to the unwarranted conclusion that he is nothing else than such an object. But human reality displays itself as a ground of *Existenz* and freedom, as well as an instance of empirical being or objective appearance. Free, '*existential*' decision does not lie within the range of objective universality, necessity and certainty. It opens up a vein of being that is determined through the unique and free activity of the individual, who is confronted with moral conflict and uncertainty. Here is a dimension of reality that is present in the world, and yet is something other than the objective appearances of the world.

We have some experience of the inner reality of freedom and human *Existenz*. Jaspers refers to this experience as an awareness of the being which man is. Whereas science provides *knowledge* of objects in the world, philosophy rests on an *awareness* of the being of man and the being of the world as a whole.[19] Since this awareness is a form of non-objective and non-knowing thought, it is not subject to the split between the objective and subjective factors in knowledge. Philosophical awareness synthesizes both factors within a single whole of being. We also recognize that man's freedom is not satisfied by a purely immanent union with the being of the world. It seeks to transcend the world and even the human self, in its search after the unconditioned being or the One. Human existence is oriented not only toward immanent contacts with being but also toward Transcendence. Thus, we gradually become aware of being as the Encompassing *(Das Umgreifende)*. Philosophical thought is a non-knowing awareness of the Encompassing, considered as the being of the world, the being of man's inner activity, and the being of Transcendence or God.

Since scientific thought remains wholly objective and finite, it cannot attain to the encompassing whole of Being. This accounts for the distinction in kind between science and philosophy, a distinction which scientific progress is incapable of removing or attenuating. Philosophy draws its vital strength and truth from inner awareness rather than from any sort of knowledge. Hence philosophy has an origin that is intrinsically independent of science. For philosophy to return to its origins does not mean to return to scientific thinking as its source. The wellsprings of philosophizing lie deep within the individual man, in so far as he is a free existent, straining toward Transcendence.

Scientific and philosophic progress do not have the same import.[20]. The former entails a displacement of previous views, in favor of ever more adequate explanations, whereas the latter leads to a renewal of the continuous tradition of perennial philosophy.

---

[19] On inner awareness of *Innewerden*, see *Existenz*, 18-24; *Wahrheit*, 155, 346-47. The contrast between man as a scientific object and as a free, existing subject is developed in: *Scope*, 54-62; *Wisdom*, 63-65; *Existentialism*, 68-69. One of the major epistemological questions raised by Jaspers' philosophy concerns the way in which "thought" and "reason" can serve as common foundations for both scientific knowledge and *'existential'* awareness.

[20] *Scope*, 174-76; *Wisdom*, 140-41. Because of the sharp contrast, Jaspers sometimes denies that progress applies in any way to philosophy. Philosophical reflection on the origins of Being is the heart of the ideal of a *philosophia perennis*.

Gabriel Marcel expresses the difference as that between solving a problem and contemplating a mystery, and Jaspers would accept this as an apt contrast. There is no question about the improvement of modern physics over its Greek antecedents, which are now studied merely in the spirit of curiosity and historical exactness. But the Greek philosophers are still our masters, and we are privileged to enter into a living dialogue with them and share in their abiding wisdom. Philosophical inquiry does move from point to point, but tries deliberately to capture the meaning of the source of freedom within us and the tendency of that freedom toward Transcendence. Every man, in every age, is capable of becoming aware of the Encompassing and thus of exploring the meaning of being in a philosophical spirit. Philosophizing aims at penetrating the origin of being within us and beyond us, rather than moving from one scientific construct to another.

Once having vindicated the essential independence of philosophy, Jaspers is then required to harmonize it with his previous view concerning the practical character of philosophizing. Since the latter is a practical deed, it is indissolubly bound up with concrete historical situations. Granted that our historical era is dominated by the sciences and their practical consequences in technology, philosophy cannot now be dissociated from these dominant factors. Although he does not express himself with all desirable clarity on this issue, Jaspers is advancing a dual affirmation. In its abiding origin, philosophy is independent of science; nevertheless, in our historical situation, philosophy is closely connected with the sciences and even uses them as instruments of its own thought. There is no contradiction in maintaining both that philosophy has an autonomous origin within man's existence, and that it requires science today as its indispensable tool and condition of development. Jaspers complicates the discussion sometimes, however, by stating that philosophy *is* science.[21] The precise sense in which this proposition is meant, must first be clarified, before considering both the dependence and the independence of philosophy in respect to science.

As we have already established, philosophy can rightly be called "scientific," in the broader usage of that term, without confusing philosophy with any of the sciences. Given Jaspers' account of the nature of scientific thought, however, it is now possible to find an even more intimate connection between philosophy and science. Even when "science" is taken in the restricted sense of the scien-

[21] For a concise statement of Jaspers' position, see his essay on "Philosophy and Science," included in *Wisdom*, 147-67.

tific methods and objects of knowledge, philosophy can be said to be present in scientific thinking. The scientist, as a human individual, shares in the human spirit and reason. Hence his investigations bear definite traces of the influence of spirit: they seek not only to reach the scientific goal of universal and cogent knowledge, but also to convey something more. This additional purpose is to obtain a total grasp upon being, and only philosophy can satisfy this tendency. Although the search for the One and for the totality of Being is a properly philosophical impulse, it finds expression in the work of the scientist and thus lends plausibility to the claims of scientism. Because of the presence of a philosophical aim, the sciences respond to the rational idea of the world as a whole and lend themselves to exploitation by scientistic minds. Science cannot fully clarify its own significance, because part of its import is to be an outlet for the philosophical quest itself.

Philosophy and science are distinct but indispensable for each other, especially within our historical era.[22] The greatest service rendered by philosophy to science is a clarification of the latter's structure, its limitations and its distinction from the philosophical enterprise. Nothing is thereby contributed by philosophy to the particular content of the sciences or to the correctness of scientific propositions. But science is enabled to carry on the work of self-criticism, and is saved from making futile inquiries into problems beyond its competence. With philosophy's help, science can restrain the tendency toward absolutizing scientific knowledge and giving the hegemony to some one scientific approach. Jaspers criticizes the view that science is *wertfrei* or indifferent to values. It is *wertfrei*, indeed, in the sense that it cannot set the ultimate goals of moral life and cannot supply the norms for moral obligation. Still, science is not *wertlos* or completely devoid of valuational factors. For, scientific work is sustained by the will to gain knowledge for its own sake. And in a negative way, its progress depends upon a resolute refusal to follow the path of a scientistic absolutization of knowledge. In both respects, philosophy co-operates by strengthening the will of the scientist, so that he may pursue speculative knowledge and avoid scientistic superstition.

Nevertheless, the contribution of philosophy is not wholly disinterested. For, philosophy itself stands to profit by the purification of the scientific attitude. There is a definite sense in which science is the condition and tool of philosophizing, even though the

22. On their mutual service, cf. *Philosophie*, 272-82; *Existenz*, 7-10; *Allgemeine*, 641-44; *Wahrheit*, 156-57; *Rechenschaft*, 348-50. The question of whether science is *wertlos*, as well as *wertfrei*, is dealt with in *Wahrheit*, 322-23.

source of philosophizing is autonomous. To appreciate the reciprocal benefit conferred by science upon philosophy, however, something further must be said about the philosophical search after
Transcendence and the meaning of Being as a whole. Although
this search characterizes philosophical thought, it can never wholly
succeed in its purpose. When metaphysics tries to express the
meaning of Transcendence and the Encompassing (*Das Umgreifende*) in the form of thought, it inevitably becomes entangled in
antinomies. For, it becomes confronted with the decisive difference
between *being* an existing center of freedom and *being* ordained
toward transcendence, on the one hand, and *expressing* these conditions in human thought, on the other. The realities of *Existenz*,
freedom and Transcendence are of a non-objective nature, whereas every attempt to give expression, in thought, to our experience
of these modes of being must submit to the conditions of objectivity. Indeed, the various modes of the Encompassing do not seem
to be real, as far as the human mind is concerned, unless they are
related to the concrete milieu of empirical being or the world of
objective appearances.

Hence philosophical transcendence must be accomplished within the world of objective, empirical being rather than by a withdrawal from it. If the reference to empirical being must be retained in our philosophizing, then the interests of philosophy are
promoted by the advance of scientific knowledge of the objective
world. This accounts for the close alliance between philosophy
and science. Philosophical thought cannot avoid using the categories of objective understanding, so that it may communicate
philosophical truth in a clear, universal and rational way. Hence
the conditions of objectivity are fundamentally insurmountable
for philosophy, which must avail itself of the most highly developed forms of the scientific categories and methods.

Jaspers has a favorite formula for bringing out the mutual distinction and dependence of philosophy and science.[23] Although
scientific knowledge is universally valid, it is also relative to some
determinate sphere of objectivity; conversely, philosophical awareness is absolute in its origin but relative in its objective expression
in thought. Scientific knowledge is not absolute, since it does not
convey the total meaning of being and does not fill our lives with
an unconditional value, for which we should be ready to die. On
the other hand, philosophical awareness is not universally valid
and coercive knowledge, since it does not belong intrinsically to
the sphere of knowledge. Whereas scientific truths can be demon-

23 *Wahrheit*, 733-38; *Scope*, 90-92.

strated and used as principles of deduction, philosophical truths can only be elucidated or evoked in consciousness. The reality of the Encompassing cannot be demonstrated or deduced from something else, since it signifies the origins of being and hence has nothing prior to it. Moreover, the reality of the Encompassing cannot be employed as a premise from which any necessary deductions can be made: it provides no blueprint for the conduct of our lives. Freedom, uncertainty and risk remain the indelible marks of philosophizing.

Given this contrast between coercive, objective, non-absolute, scientific knowledge and free, non-objective, absolute, philosophical reflection, it follows that the philosophical use of scientific categories cannot consist in a direct and positive expression of philosophical truths through that medium. Jaspers' paradoxical view of metaphysics now comes into play, in order to determine the ultimate sense in which science benefits philosophy.[24] As scientific knowledge becomes more perfect, we can see more clearly that the systematic of the sciences cannot actually attain to a complete system of knowledge. This failure of the sciences to achieve a total system of the being of the world provides philosophy with a most significant clue, since it serves as a warning against any identification between object-being and Being as such. Out of his experience of the essential boundaries of scientific thought, the philosopher is led to cultivate a form of unknowing or non-knowledge: the inner awareness of Being or the Encompassing. Simultaneously, he recognizes the fate to which he must submit. He cannot express his philosophical awareness of Being, apart from the objective conditions of thought. Philosophizing is an objectification of a non-objectifiable reality! This is the paradoxical situation of the philosopher. He must use objectifying thought and knowledge, in order to express that which surpasses all objectivity and knowledge: *Existenz*, Transcendence and freedom. Hence he cannot treat the objects in the world and the systematic of the sciences as direct means of expressing his awareness. From the philosophical viewpoint, the world and its objects are so many signs and ciphers, which *are not* the Encompassing and yet which *are* our only context and instruments for thinking the Encompassing as real being, and for communicating our insight in a rational way.

In sum, science and philosophy are engaged in a friendly

---

[24] The entire third book of *Philosophie* (675ff.) is devoted to a study of metaphysical thinking, as an effort to express Transcendence within the sphere of empirical being.

struggle between different but interwoven ways of thinking. Their conflict is not that between enemies but between brethren, who are engaged in an edifying contest to uncover the truth. Philosophy assists science to remain loyal to the truth about objects known in the world; science helps philosophy to concentrate upon the truth of Being, and the deliverances of our awareness. The philosopher maintains a threefold freedom, in respect to science.[25] He must have freedom for the unrestricted study of scientific methods and findings. He must also secure his freedom from scientism and every plan to substitute an absolutized brand of scientific knowledge for philosophy. And above all, the philosopher has to maintain his freedom to contemplate the being of the world, of free human existence, and of Transcendence. Although he can never bring his awareness of these modes of being to perfect conceptual formulation, he can give it his complete, absolute belief, and can freely shape his life in response to its demands.

V. A COMPARATIVE APPRAISAL

One way of evaluating Jaspers' position is to compare it, on a few scores, with the views of American naturalism and Thomism. Jaspers' own thought can profit by such a comparison with other doctrines; it can also make valuable contributions of its own to the common themes of discussion. Perhaps an intensive study of Jaspers will help to break down barriers and initiate a much-needed dialogue between Kantianism, naturalism and Thomism.

Jaspers and the naturalists give different descriptions of scientific knowledge. Jaspers' account fits in well with Newtonian physics and the Kantian philosophy of science. But it does not pay sufficient attention to other theories of science, based upon more recent developments in physics. Thus, whereas Jaspers highlights the ideal of cogent, certain and universally valid propositions, the naturalists stress the importance of probability and the use of statistical averages. Jaspers regards the latter as a failure to attain the scientific standard of knowledge, whereas the naturalists tend to revise the standard account itself, in the light of what can actually be attained by the human mind in this field. Again, Jaspers defends the basically speculative character of scientific knowledge, even though he grants that its practical consequences in technology have shaped the world we live in. From an operationalist standpoint, however, practice is something more than a con-

[25] *Wahrheit*, 104-05; *Rechenschaft*, 349.

sequence of scientific knowledge. The very meaning of the scientific concept or theory is located in the practical directions and operations to which the concept leads the investigator. Mutual benefit would result, if Jaspers paid more attention to the characteristic procedures of post-classical physics, and if the naturalists agreed to reconsider the question of the relation between speculation and control.

Naturalism does not distinguish as sharply between science and philosophy, as does Jaspers.[26] This is in line with the Hegelian parentage of naturalistic thought, since Hegel claimed to overcome the Kantian distinction between science and philosophy, knowledge and faith or interior awareness. Hegel achieved this unification, however, only by universalizing his conception of a single scientific method. Although the naturalists take an empirical and non-dialectical view of scientific thinking, they do retain the Hegelian thesis of a single scientific method. Hence a head-on clash between Jaspers and the naturalists over this issue is unavoidable. Even when the naturalists employ Comte's distinction between the one method and the several techniques or procedures of science, they fall far short of Jaspers' sharp differentiation of methods among the sciences. His vision is directed toward the concretely different ways in which chemists, psychiatrists and sociologists deal with the same empirical materials, whereas the naturalists look to a general logic of the sciences for confirmation of their monism of method. Jaspers presents a definite challenge to the naturalistic position, since he argues that the distinction between a broad, general meaning for scientific method and the more restricted meanings is no warrant for concluding to the singleness of the scientific method. He believes that the differentiations required by research in the various sciences affect scientific method itself in an intrinsic way, and cannot be relegated to the region of subordinate techniques and procedures. The questions he raises for naturalism are: whether there is a sufficiently definite and significant content in the broad meaning of scientific method, and whether the procedures of the several sciences involve intrinsic differentiation of method itself.

Jaspers, in turn, could profit by a serious consideration of the naturalistic program of combining a monism of method with an anti-reductionism of content. He has not made this study, because of his definition of naturalism as the identification of being with the object-being studied by the sciences — an identification en-

26 The naturalistic program was set forth in the symposium, *Naturalism and the Human Spirit*, edited by Y. H. Krikorian (New York, 1944).

tailing a most radical sort of reductionism. There is a conflict here between opposing views of what actually constitutes a reductionist standpoint. Naturalism claims that reductionism is successfully avoided as long as one admits the emergence of new values and fuller realizations of natural traits, without resolving these emergents entirely into their genetic conditions and causes. But Jaspers lays down more stringent requirements for an anti-reductionist philosophy. It is one that refrains both from equating the real with the field of scientific objects and from holding a total evolutionary development of life, consciousness and spirit from matter. Naturalism would be unable to meet these conditions of anti-reductionism. For, it is suspicious of any claim that a zone of reality exists which is not accessible (at least in principle) to scientific inquiry, and which can be approached only in some interior and non-objective way. If the real is that which is accessible in principle to the scientific method, then the distinction between being and scientific object-being is broken down. Furthermore, naturalism regards mind as an evolutionary emergent from matter. It attempts to avoid reductionism on this score, by castigating vulgar materialism in a very severe way. On the positive side, however, naturalism does little more than endow matter with a vague dynamism for bringing forth whatever has to be brought forth. It also points to the progress already made in giving a scientific description of religious, esthetic and moral states. Jaspers' contention is that successful description in terms of another science does not establish causal derivation of the reality under description from the purely material mode of being.

Another area for mutual exploration centers around the problem of values. Naturalists have done considerable work toward establishing a positive relationship between scientific inquiry and the realm of values. They have attempted to reduce normative to factual statements, as well as to furnish a purely naturalistic account of moral obligation. Jaspers seems to be content with repeating the Kantian dichotomy between what is and what ought to be, since this accords neatly with his distinction between scientific objects and modes of being that are grasped through philosophical awareness. In this respect, naturalism comes closer to the approach of metaphysical realism to the basis of moral obligation. There is pressing need for a synthesis between the naturalistic emphasis upon the reference of moral choice to factual situations, subject to scientific ascertainment, and Jaspers' equally valuable defense of the free individual, as the focal center of actual moral life.

Contemporary Thomists will find Jaspers' distinction between

science and philosophy quite instructive. His way of distinguishing them bears some resemblance to Maritain's distinction between the empiriological and the ontological analysis of nature.[27]
For both thinkers, the crucial issue is whether or not the discipline
is formally directed toward a grasp of being. Maritain maintains
that the empiriological sciences deal with sensible being, but only
in so far as it is observable and measurable; Jaspers allows that
the sciences attain to object-being but refuses them any access to
being as such and as a whole. Maritain's conception of empiriological science is more operational and less speculative than Jaspers' view of scientific knowledge. Furthermore, Maritain regards
the ontological approach to the world, self and God as capable of
yielding genuine knowledge, not merely experiential awareness.
But the question presents itself of whether the contrast between
the empiriological and the ontological studies of nature can be
rigorously established, apart from the Kantian distinction between
appearances and the thing-in-itself. The decisive feature of Jaspers' theory is that the difference in attitude between the scientist
and the philosopher is regulated by a difference between objective
appearances and the being of the world.

There are two strains of thought discernible in Jaspers' speculations on this problem. One is the orthodox Kantian correlation
between knowledge and phenomenal objects. But there is also a
tendency to give a more metaphysical interpretation of the object
of knowledge. Jaspers refers to the latter both as an appearance
and as a mode of being. Yet, granted that what we know in the
world is a determinate mode of being and not Being as such or in
its fullness, there is no evident need to equate determinateness or
particularity with phenomenality. From the fact that our initial
knowledge is particularized, it does not follow that it must also be
phenomenal and in no way manifestive of being. A *determinate*
mode of being is still a mode of *being* and gives knowledge of
being, under some particular aspect, and not merely knowledge
of appearance. Such knowledge is not formally metaphysical, but
it can provide a basis for the metaphysical judgment that separates
being-as-such from any of its particular, sensible modes. Such
knowledge is also not fully exhaustive of the reality of the actual
thing, which contains unsounded depths that are not conveyed by
our concept of the object or even by our existential judgment
about it. Metaphysics is grounded, however, not in a pretended
insight into reality as a whole but in the human mind's ability to

[27] Jacques Maritain, *Philosophy of Nature* (New York, 1951), 73-88.

recognize that the existent thing is indeed an instance of being.[28]

Thomists can make constructive use of several features in Jaspers' notion of metaphysics. Thus, his remark about the indissoluble bond between metaphysical thinking and the context of empirical being need not issue in a doctrine of paradoxical assertions about the Encompassing. It can serve as a realistic reminder that metaphysics never ceases to be a human discipline, and hence never ceases to bear a vital reference to our experience of sensible things in the world. This is re-enforced by Jaspers' own observation that metaphysical transcendence does not abandon the world but occurs within the world. For Jaspers himself, this reference of metaphysical speculation to the world of objects leads to endless antinomies, since he phenomenalizes the object of knowledge. Yet, if the being of existent things is firmly retained, then the split between science and philosophy, knowledge and awareness, can be healed. Our grasp on being is not an instance of non-knowledge but an instance of knowledge, in which we recognize the act of being exercised by the sensible thing and also the presence of this act in nonsensible modes of being. The levels of analogical meaning of knowledge extend farther than Jaspers' phenomenalism will allow. They reach from our particular sense experiences and the scientific knowledge of things to the metaphysical knowledge about being-as-such and its causes and principles.

JAMES COLLINS

DEPARTMENT OF PHILOSOPHY
SAINT LOUIS UNIVERSITY

[28] For a more detailed Thomistic analysis of Jaspers' thought, cf. James Collins, *The Existentialists: A Critical Study* (Chicago, 1952), 80-114.

3

Gerhard Knauss

THE CONCEPT OF THE 'ENCOMPASSING' IN JASPERS' PHILOSOPHY *

Sketch of the Previous History of the Concept

A DEVELOPMENT of the previous history of the concept of the Encompassing *(das Umgreifende)* will not be attempted here. For such purpose a separate study would be required. Such a study would, indeed, contribute much interesting material, but very little new for an inner understanding of Jaspers' philosophy. It would amount primarily to a comparison between latent meanings of the concept and Jaspers' use of it. This would lead into the thicket of problems of historical interpretation. For, in an historical approach, we would first have to distinguish between a history (or, more narrowly, a word history) and an actual anticipation of the essential hypothesis of the concept of the Encompassing. In this case interest would center on whether the concept appears in a relevant connection or whether it arises from an alien, accidental use of language.

If, moreover, one considers all philosophizing as philosophizing from the Encompassing, as Jaspers does, then a historical representation of the Encompassing would necessarily have to remain sketchy, lest it become a total history of philosophy. For, where everything is thinking out of the Encompassing, the only meaningful approach would be to portray those formulations in which the thought achieves new lucidity. We shall, therefore, limit ourselves to indicate the most important earlier stages of the conception, especially in view of the fact that a special study of the problem is already available.[1]

Philosophizing is a thinking from out of totality. We speak of philosophy only where there is the intent to penetrate unity and totality. The teachings of the great Greek natural philosophers

---

* Translated from the German by Matthew Cohen, as revised by Ludwig B. Lefebre.

1 Cf. Mader, H. K.: *Problemgeschichtliche Studie zur Periechontologie Karl Jaspers'*, Dissertation, Vienna 1952.

begin that way: Everything is; water, air, fire, spirit, etc. That is
to say, thinking begins with the operation of embracing, of locating in totality. This actually constitutes the beginning of philosophizing, by comparison to which the further interpretations of
this "everything" appear accidental and optional, and very much
bound to some particular time. In order for Being to be thought
of as fire or water, everything must previously be thought of under
the concept of Being. Thus, the beginning of philosophizing does
not really lie in the first fragments which have been handed down
to us, but in the thinking which preceded them. More detailed
qualification of Being signifies, conversely, almost a decline in
thinking. Only by means of its own reflection could thinking be
led out of these limitations, into which, in its naïvete, it had
necessarily fallen. Perhaps there is something similar to this in
Anaximander. Thought, with him, acquires a meaning related to
Jaspers' conception, which may justify our introducing a short
quotation here. In Anaximander we encounter the concept of *Apeiron,* in connection with the formulation καὶ περιέχειν ἄπαντα
καὶ παντα κυβερνᾶν (which has, to be sure, been contested
strongly recently). Notwithstanding the difficulty of whether the
Apeiron is to be understood as infinite or as undetermined, this
much seems certain: Anaximander thought of it in the manner
of an Encompassing of all the elemental materials contained in
it; and not, indeed, as a mere summation of all things, but as
something that penetrates, rules and regulates everything. Being,
therefore, is really thought of as Being and not as a mere heap of
all existing things.

When thought, after its first, great beginnings, began to split
up, Plato re-united it once more and gave it its final unity in the
concept of the Idea. This unity was no longer cosmological, but
ideal, not one to be found directly in nature, but one still to be
formed. The Ideas are not reality but belong to what we, since that
time, have been calling ideality. This ideality is an encompassing
unity of the perceivable. This was necessary because out of the
multiplicity of the sensory emerged nothingness. By means of the
Idea thinking, and thereby Being, were protected from the schisms
of the Sophists. And the concept of the Idea has held our thinking together ever since. But thinking in Ideas stood, for Plato,
again under an Encompassing: the highest Idea of the One and
the Good. This Idea of the Ideas is, to a certain extent, also an
Encompassing of all Encompassings. To how great an extent the
concept of the Encompassing is embedded in Platonic philosophy
is shown not only by the frequent appearance of the concept of

periechon, but also by the fact that this word, in Greek, signifies not only an encompassing but also a superiority of the encompassing over the encompassed. The concept, therefore, implies not only a quantitative encompassing, but a qualitative gradation, which finally binds the Ideas, as in a hierarchy, to a highest.

The concept of the Idea received such dignity through Plato that it became a fundamental idea of all later thinking, either in acceptance of the concept or in analysis and critical rejection of it. The history of the Idea in Western thought is, at the same time, a history of the idea of the Encompassing, which accompanies it. The two main stations on this road are Kant and Kierkegaard. These two are also, biographically speaking, the most important stations in the development of Jaspers' thought. Kant was his starting-point, and this explains his conscious emphasis on the significance of ideas in the whole of Kant's philosophy, as opposed to a Kant interpretation limiting itself to its categorical aspects (cf. the essay on Kant's theory of Ideas in the appendix to the *Psychologie*). Plato and the Pre-Socratics became only late, and only after Jaspers' own views had matured, the subject of years of systematic study. Thus, those beginnings, which might be recalled by the concept of periechontology in logic, were fragments of alien thought, in which the thinker recognized himself.

The document in which Jaspers discusses this Kantian point of departure is the parenthetically mentioned work on the theory of Ideas. In this work the ruling principle of the formation of Ideas is expounded: to make the unconditional, or totality, the guide. Totality and non-limitation are the essence of the Idea. Totality and non limitation are reciprocal ideas. The Idea is the unconditional among the given conditions. The unconditional embraces within itself the totality of the developing conditions. As such a totality the Idea is simultaneously subjective and objective. The subject-object division, which forms the essence of intellect, has no absolute significance for the Idea. Ideas go beyond intellect, by embracing its boundaries together with intellect itself.[2] The Idea undergoes a subject-object division only to the extent that it operates methodologically in the medium of the intellect.[3] The Idea, therefore, is the final Encompassing of subject and object. Seen thus, the Idea forms the highest point in Kant's thought, and this significance of the Idea is stressed by Jaspers, expressly against the interpretation of Kant common at that time, in which Kant was limited to the Transcendental deduction and the problems of

[2] Cf. *Psychologie*, (2nd and 3rd ed.), 477.

[3] *Ibid.*, 484.

the categories. Over against this, Jaspers pointed out, — to be sure without much resonance at the time, — that the distinctive feature of Kantian thought consists in the union and unity of all the faculties of man's nature. He found in Kant's theory of Ideas the representative achievement of this basic intention. Kant's concept of the Idea has remained representative for Jaspers to this very day, and it is the encompassing aspect of the Idea which Jaspers stresses from the beginning. The Encompassing is understood as a mutual encompassing even as early as the Kant essay. Thus: the intuitive *(das Anschauliche)*, as something irrational, goes beyond the intellect, but is encompassed by concepts. Ideas go beyond the intellect by encompassing it.[4] The relationship of the Idea to the concrete individual reality is described by Jaspers as a surpassing *(Uebergreifen)*.[5] His later philosophy, therefore, is already prepared, even to the point of the choice of words.[*] The basic Kantian conception of the subject-object division, his deduction of the basic unity of nature and freedom beyond all possibility of knowledge (at the beginning of Kant's *Critique of Judgment*), and his discourse regarding the common root of sensibility and intellect almost naturally call forth the concept of the Encompassing. Thus it is, perhaps, permissible to say that Jaspers' philosophy, after all the deviations from and misinterpretations of Kant, is the natural development of Kantian thought under contemporary conditions. What distinguishes the Idea in the Kantian sense from the concept of the Encompassing is the change which meanwhile has taken place in subjective consciousness. For Kant philosophy has the character of a possible science and its concepts (the Ideas, too, therefore) claim scientific exactitude. They are not achieved in the basic experience of transcending. Transcending does not become thematic in Kant's philosophy, although carried out by him at decisive points. The reduction of conceptuality, occurring by means of transcending, is, therefore, not recognized. The possible significance of a symbolically pregnant language (the "cipher," as Jaspers later calls it, using one of Kant's own terms) is always misjudged by a philosophy with "scientific" claims.

This break with the scientific claim took place in Kierkegaard. He blasted the concept of philosophy as a rigidly organized discipline as perhaps no one before him; but, in the final analysis, not *against* philosophy, but in its behalf. For philosophy experienced, in Kierkegaard, an equally unique enrichment. What Plato

4 *Ibid.*, 477.   5 *Ibid.*, 460.

* Translator's Note: We translate the German "umgreifend" by encompassing, and the German "übergreifend" by surpassing.

had accomplished for objective consciousness with the concept of the Idea, Kierkegaard did for subjectivity with his concept of *Existenz*. Against the decline of the inwardness, — once so characteristic of the Christian relationship to God and of Christianity's concept of the human soul, but now disintegrating into psychological, sociological and metaphysical fragments, he set his own *'existential'* thinking. Although Kierkegaard still regarded it as Christian, this kind of thinking is actually a form of philosophizing and, as such, separable from Christianity.

Kierkegaard made up for the blasting of the traditional structure of philosophy by making this deed the theme of his philosophizing. Through him occurs the thematization of the basic experience of the limits of human *Existenz*, without which experience all modern philosophizing acquires the character of a mere antiquarianism. Since Kierkegaard our thinking has, so to say, acquired a reverse side, which is able to give the lie to the front. He carried out the experiment, using himself as the object, of pursuing thought, out of its objectification in the Idea, back to its *status nascendi*, i.e., to the thinking person. With Kierkegaard, and, in a different sense, with Nietzsche, thought went back to before Plato in whom it had experienced its initial ideal objectification. The manner of existence in the Platonic Socrates was, for Kierkegaard, the first problem of philosophy (the predilection of modern thought for the pre-Socratics has its origin here). The Encompassing of thought, in which we have lived since Plato, in spite of the inroads of Christianity, has become problematic since Kierkegaard. The Encompassing must be achieved anew, but now no longer once and for all, uniformly binding for all people, but in the subjective adoption by each individual. And the consciousness that the truth of our subjective existence determines the truth of our objective thinking necessarily forced a new, more original understanding of truth. Just as the naive truth of physiologists became untrue when they discovered the spirit qua *logos*, so can objective truth become untrue as soon as thinking is confronted with its own existing. There are truths which can be untrue for me. Since Kierkegaard this is to be understood as follows: Truth is tied to our origins. From now on one can speak of truth only in an encompassing sense, in which is contained both the subjective and the objective. In the conception of the origin of truth the philosophy of the Encompassing remains tied to the thought of Kierkegaard.

It can only be of biographical interest to know at which point in Jaspers' works the Encompassing is spoken of for the first time and mentioned expressly. The word is used occasionally in his *Philosophie* of 1931, but without his making any systematic use of it. But the university lectures of the following years were already based on the concept of the Encompassing, under the title of *Philosophical Systematics*. It was a new onset of thought, after the first complete presentation of his philosophy. *Reason and Existenz,* a series of lectures, originally delivered at Groningen, was the first publication using the new concept. The lectures were taken over, partly verbatim, into his *Von der Wahrheit (Philosophische Logik,* vol. I). The concept was fully developed already at its beginning. Between these two books are the small *Existenzphilosophie* of 1938,*The Perennial Scope of Philosophy* (German edition 1948, American edition 1949), — in which the concept is presented under the aspect of its relationship to revealed religion—, and the historico-philosophical work, *The Origin and Goal of History* (German ed. in 1949, American edition 1953), which introduces the idea of the Encompassing into historical thought.

II. THE SUBJECT-OBJECT DIVISION AND ITS TRANSCENDING

One basic thought commands every great and genuine philosophy. That thought forms the secret guide which thinking, on all its paths, obeys and which, whether strong or weak, sooner or later, aims at a few underlying concepts. Such a basic idea, however, is not the property of one individual thinker. True ideas are the ideas of their time. They determine the thinking of their time. They agree, therefore, with the thinking of contemporaries. Thus, if one were to seek agreement between Jaspers and the early Heidegger, for example, one could, — making allowance for their different inferences, — formulate it thus: the philosophizing of both thinkers revolves around the difference between 'Being-in-itself' *(Sein an sich) and* 'what is' *(things)* [*Seiendes (Dinge)*]. What Heidegger designates 'ontic-ontological difference' is — as far as the difference is concerned, not the further interpretation of Being, but — the difference between Being-in-itself and the manner in which Being becomes an object to us. In this underlying thought, arising, perhaps, out of a mutual conviction as to the finitude of man, both philosophers find themselves together in opposing the idealistic attempt at an infinite extension of thought. The experience of the difference and the systematic formulation of this experience, however, lead them into different directions. They develop the two basic possibilities which can present themselves in such a fundamental situation: a premature anticipation of Being by a renunciation of all objective being, or a philosophy of the Encompassing, which does not desire to pass over the objective world. In Heidegger we have a philosophy which loses patience and which, counter to its own trend, conjuringly tries to grasp Being. In Jaspers we have a philosophy of the "longer way," as Plato terms it, which utilizes knowledge in order to make faith, in the end, believable. Heidegger strides thereby on the paths of classical Western ontology; Jaspers has before him the great examples of Plato and Kant, in a venture similar to theirs: in a situation where knowledge becomes too plentiful, to return to the simple basic possibilities of knowledge and, opposing both meaningless multiplicity and the surrender to one — presumably absolute — mode of knowledge, to point the way towards philosophizing in possibilities. The basic idea of the philosophy of the Encompassing is: always to hold all possibilities open as ways to possible truth, without losing the consciousness of the unity of Being. Jaspers himself has presented this basic concept in various ways. I shall attempt here to render one of them.

All philosophy looks toward a totality of Being and makes basic divisions. Systematic philosophizing consists of the maintenance of one fundamental concept in all of the ramifications of these fundamental relationships.

One of these fundamental divisions is that Being always appears to us divided into subject and object. Since Kant this idea has a permanent place in philosophy. Whenever we think we think *something,* and, indeed, something definite. Every intentional act has an intended object. The phenomenology of Brentano and Husserl, reaching back to medieval concepts, made the concept of intentionality the *leitmotif* of its thought. Every intentional act is a specific one and, therefore, a partial one. Thus we always know that there are many other objects besides this particular one. Our recognition of objects occurs always within an objective horizon. Thinking without an horizon would be infinite thinking. Horizons, however, depend on the position of the observer and are able to shift and broaden if this position changes. Thus, a horizon presents only the extent of all objects known to us from one point of view. But all objects together do not make up everything. There is something which we can never find among all objects and yet it is absolutely certain. It is we ourselves. It is the subject. But "subject" is merely a name for it which deceives us and leads us to believe that the subject is a nameable object like the rest of them. It is the basic insight of the Kantian transcendental philosophy that the subject can never become an object. What becomes an object is a detachment *(Ablösung)*, behind which the actual subject withdraws further. That which thinks is never thought of, for everything that is thought of is thought of as an object. Everything which is to exist for us must somehow become an object for us. For the subject "being" is always being-object. This "being for us" *(für uns sein)* of Being is what Kant terms "appearing" *(erscheinen)*. This concept, since Kant, signifies a revolution in the consciousness of Being. Kant illuminates this consciousness in a new way, by leading us back from the things to which we were at first completely and blindly attached, to the consciousness of these things; from the representations *(Vorstellungen)* to the possibility of representations. We become aware that the things are imagined things (we imagine the things the way they appear to us), and that everything which appears to us as a thing is enclosed in transcendental forms of appearance, which are identical with the "basic faculties of our mind." In knowing them we take hold of the things and thus, as perceiving subjects, we become free to know, because we recognize that we determine the form in which the things come to us. Behind the things we look for the conditions of their being things. We become conscious of our knowledge; that is, in a real sense, we are just beginning to know. To be conscious of the subject-object division already signifies that we think from the Encompassing of both; for the concept drives at once beyond itself. We experience an insufficiency of the possibilities of being as they reach us in the subject-object division. Thought awakens within us the consciousness that precisely the essential, because of which we exist, cannot be grasped in this division, but that it precedes or follows the division. Thereby thought frees us for the second revolution in consciousness. A further insight leads to this.

Whatever we perceive is for us always in the form of an object. But all object-being is not yet the totality of Being. The object is just one side of it. The insight that objects are there only for a subject makes possible, at times, the return to the subject. But the subject withdraws from customary thinking. If, now, Being is more than object, and if, in philosophizing, we always keep Being in mind as a totality, then the thinking of the Encompassing of subject and object can no longer be a thought with a definite object. If the turn from object to subject signifies a transformation of our direct consciousness, then the manner of our thinking must also be transformed. The way in which we think of the Encompassing can no longer be the way in which we think of specific objects as objects. Thinking must acquire a new dimension, it must become movement, become dialectic. It must rise up against itself, contradict itself, and thereby revoke itself in its definiteness.

The thinking which occurs in the reversal is termed "transcending thinking" by Jaspers. All philosophical thinking is, according to Jaspers, basically transcending thinking. What is termed philosophical speculation is any leap from obvious facts and immediate convictions into the encompassing horizons of thought. This leap from the reality of the given does not signify the abandonment of finiteness; for the leaper falls back again and again to his point of departure. The flight into infinity is, in itself, a finite act. This means, for example, that in the attempt to grasp the Encompassing conceptually, we necessarily degenerate into false symbolization. It is the task of philosophy to illuminate the necessity of these falsifications which arise from the nature of our consciousness and, thereby, to bring about the unique transformation of consciousners of thinking. Transcending from the objective to the Encompassing: even in the process of falling to perceive the fall, and by conscious logical operations to follow the tracks which we leave behind in the motion of transcending.

What, in transcending to the Encompassing, occurs on the part of the thinker is an equivalent transcending of all customary manners of thinking. Transcending from the objective to the Encompassing demands from the thinker a corresponding transcending of his intentionality.

Customary thinking is discursive-progressive, because it portrays. It portrays something momentarily unknown, which is to become known, in terms of something already known. We gradually approach the object to be recognized by taking every single step leading to it. We bring the criterion for the truth of something new always with us from something already known. Because our thinking is always conditional, it always takes the direction from a condition to something conditioned.

However, Being, the absolute as opposed to everything that is finite and relative, can no longer be conditioned by our thinking. It cannot rely on something outside itself for the principle of its truth and of its proof. It must contain, simultaneously, the truth and the criterion of truth. It must be the object of knowledge and the criterion of knowledge at the same time: the old Spinozistic concept of *causa sui*. In the thinking of the encompassing Being, thought itself would have to become encompassing. It would have to outstrip, in one leap, all the steps of the discursive development. This would mean, however, that thinking would no longer have any actual movement, no approach to Being. On the contrary, the chain of discursivity must be broken — where the Encompassing is concerned — in order to attain an opening of consciousness for the Encompassing. Therefore, in transcending takes place really less of a movement of thinking than a countermovement of Being, through which Being reveals itself.

Jaspers has various terms for this openness of consciousness. He calls it "fundamental knowledge" (Grundwissen), "philosophical faith" (philosophischer Glaube), and "self-awareness" (Innesein).

Philosophical faith, to be sure, is to be distinguished from the religious faith in revelation; but the two have this in common:

the faith, by which I am convinced, and the content of faith, which I adopt, — fides qua creditur and fides quae creditur —, are inseparable. The subjective and objective aspects of faith constitute a whole. Were I to take only the subjective side, then faith would be something like credulity, a faith without an object of faith, which believes only itself, so to speak. . . . If I take the objective side alone, all that remains is the objective content of faith, a "stock" of tenets and dogmas, something that, in a sense, is dead.

For this reason one can neither say that faith is an objective truth, which is not determined by believing, nor that faith is a subjective truth, which is not determined by the object. Faith is one even in what we separate as subject and object, as faith *from* which and *in* which we believe.

Faith is, therefore, a manner in which we conduct ourselves toward an Encompassing of subject and object. What is thus inherent in the structure of faith can become, as philosophical faith, the actual philosophical manner of conduct. Faith does not bind us to a content as an object, nor does it allow us purely subjective arbitrariness. As a believer one can say neither what, nor whether one believes, nor does it depend simply on my will whether I want to believe. Faith, rather, is a simultaneous presence in these polarities of subject-being and object-being.

This presence Jaspers also designates self-awareness. For, we do not realize the Encompassing by the outer way of knowledge, but rather by an inner transformation of thinking, by means of which we do not move toward another object but toward the actual origin. But this way inward is to be distinguished from what is meant by the introspection (= Verinnerlichung) of the mystics. The mystic abandons, therewith, the realm of communicability. His language becomes obscure and incomprehensible and at last breaks off when the final stage is reached. Self-awareness, on the other hand, is to be understood as a philosophic act which aims at attaining clarity regarding itself, which wants to communicate and which strives, for this reason, to become comprehensible and to retain self-control even at its extreme limits. It does not wish to fuse with the other which, in submersion, is experienced as the godhead, but wants with an intensified consciousness to regain itself. In self-awareness I become one with the Encompassing of myself also, with myself as I actually am. I experience my origin or ground because I am freed, by the awareness of the Encompassing, from the attachments to the definite being, which always places us under conditions and demands a definite countenance from us. Self-awareness, therefore, does not communicate itself by trying to convince, but by reminding us of our own ground, of the "pre-knowledge," as it were, which, as a secret unrest, protects us from all the trivialities of philosophizing. Jaspers himself reminds us of Schelling's tenet of the "secret co-knowledge with creation" *(geheime Mitwisserschaft mit der Schöpfung)*, which refers to the knowledge of Being, already basically present, that can be philosophically awakened, — or of Plato's theory, that we can recall what we saw in our pre-earthly existence. Awareness communicates itself also as an appeal to the freedom, which everyone is, even against his own will, and which, — in its unconditionality, which it knows has been granted to it by Transcendence, — can become the pointer to this Transcendence. In all these ways of philosophizing and communicating we are concerned with keeping our own basis attuned to the grounds of Being.

For this reason Jaspers calls transcending consciousness also philosophical fundamental knowledge. Where I, in faith, realize the Encompassing, I know of it from my very foundations. This foundation is the basis of our being human. The certainty of our fundamental knowledge is not a scientific one, therefore, but an assurance. Its success involves the entire nature of man. It is the encompassing knowledge of knowing, before all particularized knowledge. This fundamental knowledge can therefore constitute a "secret guide for our thought, transforming the multitude of single, dispersed items of cognition into a knowledge of the basic general possibilities of being." It is a knowledge which directs us in all further ramifications of our thinking and willing. What we know basically in this way determines in what way we know everything else, what it means for us, what becomes essential to us and what remains merely secondary. From this basis of our knowledge no specific knowledge can be deduced, even as it, in itself, is not deducible. But it implies an advance decision from the consequences of which we cannot escape.

As fundamental knowledge it forms, in its simplicity, a connecting link. For, by becoming basically like oneself, one becomes like everyone else. It is that which "basically" we always know, and have always known, philosophically, not something newly acquired. What, to a consciousness trapped in objects, appears as an impossible concept, appears later as profoundly self-evident. Self-evident; yet in such a way that this knowledge, once awakened in man, demands new realizations, greater clarity, and new manners of self-representation. Thus Jaspers can designate his *Philosophische Logik* as a study in fundamental knowledge, for which he attempts to delineate possible and, in our present historical situation, practicable ways.

III. The Seven Manners of the Encompassing

The basic structure of the Encompassing is the simultaneity of subject-being and object-being. However we understand Being, it cannot be merely the subject or merely the object. To reach for Being always means to progress to the Encompassing from the limitation of one of the poles.

If by Encompassing we mean what we call Being-in-itself, then there can be only one Encompassing. There cannot exist another Encompassing next to the Encompassing. For, in the change-over to the Encompassing we abandon precisely this multiplicity of objects. In transcending object-being we suspend the possibility of separation and variation. But from the manner of the transcending movement there arise *for us* various manners of the Encompassing. These manners are not the Encompassing itself, but the expression of our finite approach to the Encompassing. For finite thinking the One again and again assumes finite perspectives.

Thus the Encompassing is, for us, in one sense the being that we are ourselves and, secondly, Being as Being-in-itself. From this basic formulation Jaspers develops a system of seven modes of the Encompassing *(Weisen des Umgreifenden)*. These seven modes are:

Existenz; Transcendence; existence *(Dasein);* consciousness-as-such *(Bewusstsein überhaupt);* spirit; world; reason.

Jaspers has retained this seven-fold division since he first presented it in *Vernunft und Existenz;* but, in the course of time, the systematics of the inner relationships have changed. We shall attempt, in our presentation, to limit ourselves to what has remained constant as underlying thought through all the various transformations, and of which all deviations may be considered extensions.

The being which embraces us is called "world" and "Transcendence." The being which we are is called "existence," "consciousness-as-such," "spirit," and *"Existenz."* The common medium of their realization is "reason." That we exist as existence, consciousness-as-such, spirit, and *Existenz* signifies that in them we become conscious of our being.

We are existence. Like everything living, we are bound to our corporeal existence by our vital functions. We live with our bodies in environment, into which we reach by means of tools, forms of social intercourse, language, and our total conduct, thereby objectifying ourselves. The forms of our existential realizations become, when objectified, objects of scientific research, as physiological functions, psychological experiences and sociological manners of conduct. But what becomes, in this way, the subject of research, — such as matter, life, soul or consciousness —, is no longer the Encompassing of existence itself. We are conceived of as a type of being among other types, but not yet as actually human. For, as humans, we always find ourselves encompassed by a vital existential mood, supported by an obscure basis, — from out of which the conscious psychic occurrence arises only as a brief reflex —, and embedded in a general behavior pattern, in which we exist as functioning parts of the body of humanity. Objectified from this Encompassing we become the world for ourselves, we encounter ourselves as objects in the world, objects which possess material and temporal existence and which appear to a living, feeling and observing subject with whom we, objectifyingly, identify ourselves.

Everything which exists for us must also become, in some sense, existentially real: as, for instance, the influences working on my body and the changes occurring in it constitute the manner in which I am conscious of it. Of everything which is not existence we know only insofar as we encounter it in the shell of corporeal existence.

We are consciousness-as-such. All life other than that of man is merely an existence in an environment. Human existence, on the other hand, appears so full and rich because the following modes of the Encompassing enter into it. Whereas as mere consciousness of existence we are a dull and undifferentiated part of our environment, as consciousness-as-such we achieve a clarity of reflection, in which everything appears in the subject-object division. Only what enters this division becomes for us unequivocal, objective, fixed being. Consciousness-as-such is, so to speak, the receiving apparatus which in its categories provides for every objectivity a means for becoming objective. In this way everything that exists must manifest itself in an objective manner and, by means of this fixation, attain communicability. For only what is in an identical fashion valid for two consciousnesses is communicable. As living, individual existences we share a, more or less, similar consciousness. But, by entering into the unequivocation of reflection, we are, above and beyond this, consciousness-as-such. In consciousness-as-such we think of ourselves as aiming at Being not only along similar lines but in an identical manner. As compared to empirical consciousness, this forms the encompassing validity of consciousness-as-such, which, being true, can only be one. We penetrate our mere environment and break through to the idea of the one world, to which . . . environments belong. And, beyond the worldly being, we have before us the timeless meaning of one truth for all people throughout all time.

Spirit is the third mode of the Encompassing. As spirit we participate in the world of the spirit which becomes, for us, the practical impulse of our empirico-temporal existence or of the theoretical directives of our research. Ideas are totalities of meaning which establish a context of understanding. We seek such totalities as objective ideas in reality. We examine reality by means of the guiding ideas of world, soul, life, etc. We seek unity and relationships before any experience and beyond all possible experience. And from out of the world something always meets us halfway which corresponds to our subjective ideas. We cannot prove this, but we have the totality of our increasing understanding and the dovetailing of new perceptions into old conceptions, i.e., the ability to secure, by comprehensive designs, something still unknown in basic possibilities, and this seems to confirm us. We do not investigate mere emptiness. We do not outline our practical plans blindly or without hope for success. We expect and receive answers which confirm or condemn us. The "idealist" is not the lost dreamer but the far-sighted planner.

As spirits we participate in the "realm of the spirit." We take part in everything that has ever taken place in history, in lasting experiences, human wisdom, unique revelations, artistic visions, political destinies. Spirit is, therefore, a temporal occurrence, in contrast to the timeless abstraction of consciousness-as-such. Spirit is bound to contents, where it appears as the totality of comprehensible relationships. It intends something temporal, occurring here and now and something manifest, even though elevated to reflection by knowing it. Nature, even in its power and sublimity, is "spiritless" because what it is is not again contained in a knowledge of itself. Spirit is, to a certain extent, a second nature: nature elevated to reflection. We look at ourselves as natural beings, from without; we make ourselves explicable objects of investigation. As spirits we are in conscious relation with everything that is understandable to us. We transform the world and ourselves into comprehensible totalities. "From within ourselves we understand ourselves as all-encompassing being, to whom everything is spirit and spirit only."

Existence, consciousness-as-such, and spirit are ways in which we find ourselves participating in the world, if we illuminate our being. What we are, and as what we objectively encounter ourselves in these modes of participation, we call, at the same time, world. But in this worldly being not all our possibilities are exhausted. This being is only what we are "in reality." But we are not merely reality but also potentiality. What we actually are as such potentiality Jaspers calls *Existenz*. We are never *Existenz* in the mode of reality but only in the mode of potentiality. *Existenz* is our basis. It is always ahead of us because of the factuality of our existence, but we can catch up with it by attaining our authentic being. As *Existenz* we never become objects to ourselves, in contrast to the other modes of the Encompassing. *Existenz* does not become appearance. What appears, appears as reality. For this reason *Existenz*, for the kind of thinking which only knows reality, is as much as nothing, a fabricated illusion. Compared to all worldly being *Existenz* always remains unsettled, without clarity, without visible effect. It never advances to the side of the object. It is, in a sense, the absolute possibility of being subject. I understand myself it it, where I am I, completely as myself. Such modes of understanding, philosophically reflected as "illumination of *Existenz*," come to light in a consciousness of the unconditional, wherever it enters into life as absolute validity; wherever a total and unconditional decision is demanded; wherever our existence, our knowledge, our spiritual world, seem insufficient to us and a final dissatisfaction arises with everything worldly; in the consciousness of immortality as a timeless security in eternity.

But inquiry into Being does not stop even with the return to the basis of our own *Existenz*. The Encompassing, which I am and which I know as existence, as consciousness-as-such, and as spirit, cannot be understood out of itself but points to something else. The Encompassing that we are is not yet Being itself, but appearance in the Encompassing of Being.

The Encompassing, which we are, has its boundary, first of all, in actuality, in the fact. Even though we "produce" everything we perceive, as far as its form is concerned (since it must enter into the ways in which it becomes objectified for us), we do not produce the slightest speck as far as its existence is concerned. Thus Being is that which, though there are no limits to the investigability of its *appearance,* continually retreats as *itself;* it shows itself only indirectly, whether encountered in the guise of the definitely existing or in the lawfulness of occurrences. This we call the world.

World, therefore, is the Encompassing which we are not, although we participate in it. For the fact that there is a world is not identical with the fact that we exist. World is always more than we are, in the factuality of its existence (which is independent of us), as well as by being, as an idea, always more than emanates to us from it as appearance. It is never an object, but the totality in which we encounter objects. Just the same the world is never the "entirely different" for us. This, the "different," is the second boundary we meet in being ourselves. Though the world in its existence is independent of us, it is still not the cause of our existence. It is the boundary we meet when transcending outward. If we transcend inward with the question as to our own cause, then we strike the "entirely different" of Transcendence. It is the fundamental experience of our finite nature that we are not here because of ourselves. In our empirical existence we are limited to a narrow temporal dimension. Where we, in consciousness of our freedom, experience ourselves as acting unconditionally and timelessly, we know that precisely this freedom does not originate in ourselves. We cannot want to be free, just as we cannot want to be unfree. In certain "ultimate situations" freedom can become lost. "We can stay away from ourselves," as Jaspers says. The paradox is that, in our freedom, we are given to ourselves. Where we most deeply experience ourselves as ourselves, we experience our origin from something else. This "else" Jaspers terms "Transcendence." Theologically speaking this Transcendence is the concealment of God, the consciousness of dependence, the concept of being created as a creature in the act of creation.

Existenz never becomes producible objectivity for us, and Transcendence can never be mistaken for our own subject-being. The consciousness of origin and the yearning — which never leaves us in spite of worldly security — for security in the transcendent, is simultaneously always consciousness of the state of separation. Where this consciousness is lost, there arises self-deification or fanaticism; where Transcendence is absorbed in the world, there arises Pantheism; where the separation itself is denied, a pure cosmism.

But Transcendence becomes just as empty when there is no return to the basis of *Existenz*. It becomes an "indifferent unknowable whose being, in its immanent insignificance, is as much as nothing." Or it becomes a rationally constructed greatness, an *"être suprème,"* to which one can ascend on a conceptual stepladder. In these errors Transcendence is always misunderstood and, as a consequence, one's own being is brought into disorder. This always seems to occur out of an obstinacy, which claims to rely on itself and denies recognition; or because one forgets himself and throws himself away, as the result of unadmitted despair and of an unreadiness to settle accounts with oneself. In both there is a lack of frankness, of honesty, of readiness for criticism which talks about everything and knows no reservation. It is, all in all, a lack of reason.

Reason enters consciousness-as-such as intellect; it is also the capacity to extricate oneself, by reflection, from the narrow confines of the intellect. It is the "faculty of the ideas," as Kant termed it, and, thereby, the way out of the particular into the general. Reason will not let us forget the totality and the essential. It governs existence in the form of a reasonable attitude, which guides the physical-material organization of our life; it protects us from uncontrolled actions; maintains us between excess and asceticism; lends our actions continuity in the totality of our lives by way of reasonable goals; balances the day and night sides of our nature; regulates our co-existence with others in a reasonable manner. It touches us, as love, at the very foundation of our *Existenz* and thereby becomes the language in which God speaks.

Without reason *Existenz*, which rests upon feeling, experience, unquestioning impulsiveness, instinct and arbitrariness, would become wilful self-assertion, distance from the world and reserve in confronting Transcendence. Without reason Transcendence becomes demonic superiority, which attacks us as if from an ambush *(aus einer Hinterwelt)*; faith becomes superstition; love becomes fear. The world becomes a chaos in which there are only isolated spots of clarity. Existence falls into disorder, loses its humanity, goes astray in asocial perversions. Spirit degenerates into ridiculous hypostasies, unworthy of belief. What had been living spirit becomes dead materialization. There arises the picture of beautiful harmony, to be speculated about but not to be lived. Without reason consciousness-as-such is a mechanical thinking device, on which we practice the large multiplication table of the world.

In all of these manifestations reason is more of a negative thing, something which regulates and maintains order. It is most itself when it brings the other to itself. It is unrest where stagnation threatens, a forward drive where there is a standstill. Reason is: becoming transparent and causing to be transparent. It prevents popular and obvious absolutizations of one mode of the Encompassing by demonstrating the significance of every mode in the totality of meaning. It makes every single mode of the Encompassing true, because it bears in mind the totality of all the modes. It knows that truth lies only in the whole. It is everywhere on guard, wherever anyone believes he is able to have a private rendezvous with truth. Reason is always insufficient when it is enclosed definitely in specific forms; it is always too much when it appears as its own substance.

If we consider these seven modes of the Encompassing in a unifying survey, questions arise as to their systematic relationship and their order. As long as we are concerned with objects in the world, our knowledge always takes place by our seeking relationships. We attempt to derive things from each other. Our thinking always deals with conditions and the conditioned. We grasp relationships by understanding the circumstances of conditions. The fundamental idea of the Encompassing, however, is that it does not occur as an object in the world and, therefore, cannot be derived from other objects. Especially, the Encompassing cannot be derived from one of its own parts. We do, indeed, transcend from the particular to the Encompassing, but transcending is not deriving. We utilize special paths of thought to soar up to the Encompassing. We seek, in ultimate situations, to extend our experience of being to the Encompassing. But we still cannot demonstrate the Encompassing thereby. For, we cannot derive thought itself from what is being thought. From something which is *for* us we cannot derive *our* being. From the many existing things we cannot derive Being.

What happens in transcending is not that thought becomes convinced, but that we become consciously aware of something which we had previously only obscurely divined. It is not so much that thought is compelled by conclusive evidence; what happens is more a liberation from thought and an entering into a new kind of consciousness.

It is equally impossible, however, to derive a specific being from the Encompassing. It is the old dream of philosophy to let everything else emerge from a highest being, step by step, by emanation, development, or causality. Even in modern scientific cosmologies this thought is dominant. But such attempts see reality always as a model, the step by step reconstruction of which they then carry out. They are therefore inadequate for everything which does not fit that model. The symbol of the inconceivable in the idea of creation corresponds to the thought model of such attempts; man is, as if he were created in the image of God; the world is, as if it had emerged from a reasonable and order-creating will.

There are attempts to derive all the categories of the conceivable from one highest principle of consciousness-as-such. But, such procedures gradually introduce, with the principle of derivation, precisely what is to be derived. For, before we derive the categories, we already use them in the derivation. At the root of all these attempts lies the misconception of regarding Being itself as something conceivable, from the implications of which one can develop everything else. One confuses the Encompassing with objective being and commits the philosophical sin which perverts all philosophizing at its roots. For this reason philosophizing, which remains in the mode of transcending, does not derive the objective from itself but learns to see it correctly, in its place, and with its particular significance in the whole. Such philosophizing constructs no systems but opens up possibilities, it creates elbow room for deductions in particular sciences.

Nor can the modes of the Encompassing ever be derived from each other. They do, indeed, refer to each other, but in each mode the Encompassing has its own origin. Their relationship is not one of mutual conditioning or of homogeneous, reciprocal effect, but of supplementation and intensification. There is no one Encompassing from which we recognize all the others. Rather do we become conscious of the modes of the Encompassing by pursuing, further and further, the inquiry into Being. In every mode the question, whether the totality of Being has already been grasped, arises anew. Thus, the relationship between the modes of the Encompassing cannot be one which emerges from a single one of them, nor can it be a logical relationship of condition and conditioned, of cause and effect, of higher and lower, etc. Moreover, the relationship becomes apparent only if all the modes are visualized. It is, therefore, an interdependence with reference to one truth which, however, is never completely attainable. The system remains, therefore, provisional and experimental.

The Encompassing is, in every form, a polarity of subject and object.

I am as existence: Inner world and environment.

I am as consciousness-as-such: Consciousness and object.

I am as spirit: The idea within me and the objective idea approaching me from the things.

I am as *Existenz: Existenz* and Transcendence.

The Encompassing that I am encompasses simultaneously the Encompassing which is Being itself, and is at the same time encompassed by it.

Existenz and Transcendence form the two extreme poles of the seven modes. They are quasi the equivalent of subject and object of the Encompassing itself: *Existenz* as that which I am in those of my possibilities which I realize; Transcendence as the absolutely different and the other-worldly. And just as it is true for objective relationships, that there is no subject without object, it is equally true that there is no *Existenz* without Transcendence. Between these two poles lies that being which includes our being and that being, which we are not. The world is, as existence, consciousness-as-such, and spirit, our own being and is, at the same time, as pure world-being, something else, in which we do not participate. The common, unifying bond of all the modes is reason. It must be present in all the modes before we can speak of them.

If *Existenz* and Transcendence form the poles of Being itself, then there exists between *Existenz* and reason a polarity in that being, which we ourselves are. Reason has substance only through *Existenz. Existenz* is illuminated only through reason. Reason depends on something else. Without substance it would be mere intellect, hollow and groundless. *"Existenz* really comes into its own under the sting of the inquiry of reason." "Without reason it is inactive and dormant, as though not there." Thus reason and *Existenz* do not constitute mutually exclusive forces within the Encompassing. The decision is not to be made between rationality and inwardliness, as for instance in the form of a choice between idealism and vitalism. These simple alternatives are equally simple untruths. Truth is neither solely in the clarity of reason, nor in the inwardliness of *Existenz*. Either extreme would amount to a denial of man's potentialities and thus would deny the truth of Being.

To what extent Jaspers places the accent of his philosophizing on these two poles is evident from his first systematic presentation of the philosophy of the Encompassing, which bears the title *Reason and Existenz*. If one were to proceed further, it could be pointed out that, biographically, all of his philosophizing has taken place in this tension. It began as the philosophy of *Existenz* and wants to be understood today as the philosophy of reason. It once stressed the 'existential,' out of opposition to the situation as it existed at that time, and now stresses the connection with the tradition of reason, out of a situation, which, in the meantime, has changed.

What appears here as the conditioning of the situation of the thinker, is valid for the philosophy of the Encompassing generally. In an existence, temporal in its innermost essence, there can be no rest. Repose in the truth signifies a completed truth. No temporally finite being can ever attain completion. As long as we live, that is, as long as we have a future before us, there are advances and revisions, improvements and criticism. Each moment can reveal new truths to us, and, just as permanently, there threatens the danger of falling prey to untruths. In the thinking of temporal existence, therefore, the modes of the Encompassing have always to be run through anew in an endless circle.

IV

The Encompassing In The World, In History, And In Logic.

The Encompassing As World.

In our everyday intercourse with worldly things we recognize that we are already placed in a large context, which determines the possible ways of our relations to these things. Always we already know meaning and purpose, and we adjust our actions accordingly. It is possible for us to name the things because we can determine their places in the system of co-ordinates of the concepts previously known to us. In our scientific penetration into the relationships of the world we are always led by previously accepted ideas. With them we ascertain the extreme possibilities which we could encounter. The fact that we look for continuity and totality is not a result of experience, because experience itself is only possible on the basis of continuity and totality. We bring these ideas with us when we begin to assemble scientific experiences.

If, however, we attempt theoretically to achieve a unified picture of all available experience, we realize that we do not yet know all the possible data of experience and that our theory is only capable of giving us a temporary picture. A new experience may, at any time, prove the incompleteness of the theory. Precisely because the formation of our experience is guided by the idea of continuity, we know that there can be no point, from which no further experience would be possible. Experience, therefore, can never confront us as something complete. If we designate the totality of possible experiences as "world," we can say that the world can never be the object of a closed and complete experience. The world is, therefore, never an object of our research, although, in all our research, we aim at it as the epitome of all experience. We say then that the world is an idea and that our experience always occurs within this horizon of the idea of world. If we think of the spatial cosmos, we shall always find ourselves *within* a spatial dimension. A cosmos limited in any way is inconceivable to us. Space is thus the horizon of all spatial experience. But, in the idea of world we overstep even space as such, for our idea of world is not limited to space. We ask: everything is in space, but what is space in? We know, since Kant, of the dependence of our representation of space on the peculiar make-up of the human consciousness. In pondering this question we seek to transcend this dependency. In a certain sense, this question is senseless, i.e., if, in using the words "what in," we are only inquiring after a new spatial dimension. But the question assumes a deeper meaning if it signifies our intention to soar, beyond all spatial limitations, into an Encompassing, which is no longer bound to our manner of representation. If we mean the world in this Encompassing, it is then no longer an object, because we are no longer capable of conceiving it. It is object and subject, because we ourselves are included in what we mean by it. It is not a goal of research to be determined qualitatively. The world is not *what* we investigate but *that* we investigate. It is possible that there are things and qualities for us because we refer to them from out of the relationship of an encompassing world. Objects without a world to which they belong could not become a valid experience for us, for then we could not bring them into relationship with our remaining experiences. This is the meaning of the idea of world as the unity of our experience.

THE ENCOMPASSING IN HISTORY

When we think of the world as cosmos, time appears to us always in spatial form. We project time onto a spatial dimension. Time becomes a dimension which can, for instance, appear as a fourth dimension in a space-time continuum. In this mathematical form time has lost its particular character as a condition belonging to the essence of man. In history we seek this time as the temporality of man. For, in whichever way we understand history, it is always essentially human history, no matter how much we are concerned with the non-human conditions of historical occurrences. What is of primary interest to us is the form in which man appears in history at different times. The unrepeatable, unique manifestations of his desires and feelings form the contours of history — not what remains the same or develops according to laws. In history we search for freedom, where it breaks through nature and its lawfulness. Wherever we encounter an action out of free conviction we face something that is inconceivable in terms of nature. Freedom, as one of man's temporal possibilities, opens up a dimension which remains hidden from us as long as we consider the world merely as cosmos. It is a new, the "historical," world which opens itself to us here.

But, if we seek freedom in history, we realize that we can only find its manifestations. We find the tracks and the effects of what has occurred out of freedom, but not freedom itself. Whenever we are touched by the free nature of man in another era we know that we have already transcended history beyond the present. If we descend all the way into time we attain simultaneity. Wherever man becomes most real he becomes timeless in time. We aim at an Encompassing of all of man's temporal forms of appearance, because we are ultimately seeking man in history. We find freedom to be the same throughout the millenia. But this is not the sameness of a natural law but the binding force of human nature, true to itself. We have a common history because man is man and is able to remain true to himself under the most extreme conditions. That there is one picture of man, in terms of which we can see everything, permits us to understand even his last deviations — his decline into the animal and his ascent into the apparently superhuman — as possibilities belonging to him. There is no history of geniuses and of subhumans alongside that of man, analogous to a possible history of plants and animals for example.

Thus it is from the one idea of man that the concept of history arises. But we do not in history seek only man as he is. We search for what he ought to be, how he yearns to see himself, how he understands himself, that is, we seek meaning in history. In contrast to everything else in nature, man is not simply what he is. He is, in a more eminent sense, what he is not. Man is not a *factum* but a *faciendum*. His measure is not his reality but his potentiality; not the normal but the exceptional.

Freedom is the way in which one is to conduct himself in view of his potentialities. Wherever man thinks and acts from freedom he indicates what he would like to be. What decisions he makes, as a free man, also means what he wants to be in the future. The future, in the final analysis, means his end; the end, as he sees it as the end of human history. Proceeding from this end, as the goal of human history, we give ourselves to understand what we take to be the meaning of our temporal existence.

But our present actions decide not only our future but also our past. What I do today can transform the meaning of my entire life to date. In everything I do I make my past necessary. What was pure possibility becomes highest necessity, for I understand myself from my past as necessarily bound up with it. Although I am free in the direction of the future, I appear to myself bound to everything I have already been. That there is such a thing as "fate" is always true only for the past, not for the future.

The question concerning man's origin is thus an unavoidable challenge because of his ending — if being human is to have meaning. For this reason one always finds at the beginning of history the question concerning the origin of man. For what man is to be is determined by what he is capable of being. What he is capable of being is determined by the way he is constituted originally. Therefore history attempts to find an encompassing bond in its inquiry into origin and goal, for the meaning of history is at the same time the meaning of man. But the actual sphere of history is, thereby, again transcended, for origin and goal themselves do not belong to history (the beginnings are already set, the goal is still ahead of us). Yet it is out of history that the demand arises to reach beyond it into the Encompassing. Purely historical knowledge remains always unsatisfying; it is never the end. History is encompassed by a horizon in which the temporal blends into the eternal and the relative is consummated in the absolute.

The transcending of history takes place as a thinking to the end of historical perspectives. For history is incomplete in either direction. It flows from the infinite to the infinite. From this fact arises the dissatisfaction with purely historical knowledge. Nor do we have any point of Archimedes outside of history. For this reason all flights into the Encompassing become delusions when they place themselves outside of history. "It remains the basic paradox that only *in* the world can we live *beyond* the world." In his philosophy of history Jaspers indicates the directions of such transcending.

The unhistorical-eternal speaks to us through the great and enduring works of man as he stands in history. In art there appears something in time which is more than time. The historical past becomes contemporary in everything great and absolute, something which is beyond all times.

In the steady change of history we begin to ask for its meaning. for the unity of origin and goal. This unity, in itself, is no longer history. It never becomes present. The meaning of history always remains open until the end. But in history we always aim at this meaning, whenever we attempt to give meaning to our lives. As individuals acting in history we overstep it in the unconditionality of our decisions, in the absoluteness of human ties. The transitoriness of what is produced by action points back to a Being — athwart of time —, founded on freedom, in which we participate by being free.

In everything the Encompassing of history remains man, who makes history and who attempts, through reason, to ascribe to himself a meaning in history. But there is something beyond man. Something in man's origin, which is not historically derivable, points to Transcendence. He knows himself created by Transcendence, not as far as his mere existence is concerned, but in his human dignity.

THE ENCOMPASSING IN LOGIC

If history opens up a new dimension as compared with all natural occurrences, logic appears to be unlimited in its objective realm — insofar as it is concerned with the pure possibilities of thought. If we consider only the possibilities of thought and disregard the possible actual existence of what is thought, the utmost breadth seems to have been reached. Logic could be considered *the* universal science. But this universality of logic is only apparent. Precisely where it pushes toward the boundary of the Encompassing it demonstrates its subjection to particular conditions. What logic thinks demands an Encompassing, but it is not yet the Encompassing.

The most fundamental operation of logic is the disjunction. It is concerned only with the simplest differentiation of objects. By means of a complete disjunction it must be possible to assign an unequivocable place to every conceivable object: the object must be able to be confirmed or denied. This is the minimum of determinateness that must be expected from an object of logic. Without this minimum it would escape from the grasp of logic, the first function of which always is determinateness in the direction of unequivocality. If one were to attempt to overstep this boundary an object would encompass both sides of the disjunction; both confirmation and denial would be applicable to it. If logic is concerned with possibilities, we would here confront the presence of an impossibility. Such an object would logically be an impossible object. It would overstep the possibilities of logic in so far as there would no longer be any rules to determine its logical treatment. Such "objects" have appeared in logic since antiquity, wherever there has been talk, in the proper sense, of logical paradoxes. The fundamental pattern of all paradoxes consists of there being two correct answers to an alternative question, i.e., a thing fulfills both possibilities of a disjunction, thereby encompassing the basic scheme of logic. If the minimum for a logical object lies in the condition of its disjunctive determinateness, then this Encompassing must be unconditionally, i.e., absolutely, valid. Wherever our thinking normally separates into discursive members, such as the condition and the conditioned of a syllogism, the extent and content of a concept, etc., there, in the paradox, the members fall together and are not to be differentiated. The movement of thinking suddenly gives way to an unstable condition of suspension. Thrown back upon itself it senses its own limit in that which lies beyond all determinateness.

By analysis, it is possible to show how, in all known paradoxes, the absolute and unconditional appear, at some hidden point: as the quantity of *all* quantities; as unconditional truth without stating a criterion of truth (Epimenides) ; as absolute condition, in which condition and conditioned fall together (Euathlus) ; as absolute concept, in which extent and content are no longer distinguished (heterological) , etc.

What, in antiquity, was discovered, almost accidentally, and became an odd sport, and what has appeared as a boundary problem in modern mathematics, becomes, in philosophical logic, a conscious operation of transcending. Jaspers calls it "formal transcending," in distinction to all contentual overstepping of boundaries in the reading of the immanent cipher-script of Transcendence. The distinguishing feature of this formal transcending is the fact that it is possible here, to some extent, to overstep logic by means of logic. All genuine speculation has, according to Jaspers, been such a formal transcending, in which thought, under extreme stress, found itself in an "ultimate situation in logic," and where, at the last moment in the speculative flight, it (thought) was discarded as an instrument which had become useless. All pure and reflective speculation is conscious that it thus attempts, in a final exertion, a leap into an Encompassing where logic fails. Plato, Nicolaus von Cues and Schelling are the great stations of this Occidental speculation. But long before them the Rig-Veda knew such a way of thinking in questions concerning the origin of Being, and in Zen Buddhism the paradoxical questions of Koan belong to the methodical training as preparation for meditating submersion.

V. The Significance of the Philosophy of the Encompassing in Our Contemporary Situation

Jaspers' philosophizing, too, originates in and aims at Being. The introductory chapter of his *Philosophie* states this expressly. No philosophy can get going without it. But, just as every form of philosophizing determines its nature in advance by the way it asks this question, so it is also true of Jaspers that his thinking in the Encompassing arises from the way in which he inquires into Being. All genuine ontology asks: What is Being? It expects a straightforward answer in which an attempt is made to say what Being is in any given case. By asking "what," we ask for what can be said concerning certain things. The "what" asks for the concept of things. The presupposition of such asking is, however, — whether the questioner consciously realizes it or not —, the already definite pre-givenness of the things, of their being. To ask, "what is this?," presupposes that it is already known *how* this thing is, what it is, in order to be able to be spoken of as such. If, then, the "what" (asking for the concept) always already presupposes the "how" of being, it is obviously not in a position to ask for being. "What" does not ask for the mode of being but for the distinguishing nature of a thing, i.e., not for existence but for essence. But if the "what" question cannot even ask for the being of things, it can even less ask for Being itself.

We inquire into the mode of the being of things by asking "how?" For, the "how" asks for the "is," and the question appropriate to being can only be that which first and foremost goes by the fact that it is *How* a thing is what it is, constitutes its mode of being.

It is precisely this latter question which is asked by Jaspers. Starting with the basic thought of Kantian philosophy, — the separation of the thing-in-itself from appearance —, his question always is how Being, as Being-in-itself, can become appearance for us. How Being is *for us* is, then, Jaspers' basic question. Beyond asking: "What is Being?," he asks: "How can we and how must we think Being if we want to speak of Being?"

The fundamental difference, thus, between "periechontology" and the ordinary form of ontology is that the former does not assert directly what Being is, but how Being could be for us. Whereas all ontologies are destined, from their very beginnings, to assume the form of a particular science, thinking in the Encompassing intends a new basic orientation, affecting all possible relations with what is. Where the early *Philosophie* began with a "world orientation," that is with a survey and ordering of the ways of our knowledge in and about the world, thinking in the Encompassing unfolds as a comprehensive orientation in being. We are no longer concerned with the methodical ascertainment of scientific world investigation, but with the ways in which we can encounter what is. Not *what* it is can become object for us, but *that* it is is the original starting point from which arises the systematic form of the seven modes of the Encompassing. For the same identical Being is encountered differently in the various modes; and in the quest for them we are spurred on by the question of how Being can appear to us in yet another manner.

By knowing of the forms of appearance of the one Being, we are prevented from considering the various individual points of view, which the giant ferriswheel of the world presents to us as the only real ones in any given case. As soon as we know that we are turning, we believe that heaven and earth are standing still.

No new knowledge is to be attained by thinking in the Encompassing, no higher, no metaphysical knowledge. No rear-world or super-world is to be unlocked, and, finally, there is to be no peeking, by means of some logical trick, around the corner behind which Being is (supposed to be) hidden. Instead of all this a transformation in the consciousness of the thinker is to be brought about, by means of which he is to come into a different relationship to Being. What we are here concerned with is not to know Being but to know *of* Being, what we can know of it in its forms of appearance, and why we can know only this. If, in the consciousness of one who presses for knowledge, this not-knowing leaves a disappointing emptiness, then his consciousness attains, through the transformation, the strength to transform this emptiness into fullness in view of the knowledge that not-knowing is the correct relationship to Being. For the logical operation of transcending leads us reliably to a point where it is clear that Being is of a "kind" which is not knowable. As concerns all worldly objects, it would be unsatisfying to remain in ignorance of them; but Being permits us to find rest in the fact that it remains unrecognizable. Only the inconceivable is a true *non plus ultra* for thought.

The new relation to Being also takes in scientific cognition. Whereas every real ontology degrades the value of the specific sciences or even makes them superfluous (because it considers their discoveries either as derivatives of its own principles or as emanating from a false understanding of Being), such philosophizing as Jaspers advocates utilizes scientific thinking as a necessary transitory stage. Without exact knowledge the Encompassing would become a mystical eccentricity, the systematic form of the seven modes a mere game. For, transcending, as the immanent approach to the Encompassing, always starts from a firm foundation, upon which one treads towards both the inner and the outer horizon.

Today there is a conflict between a certain form of philosophy and a certain conception of the sciences, reminiscent of the scandal in which, according to Kant, philosophy found itself as long as it was unable to prove the existence of the material outer world. For, in the struggle between positivism, as a purely scientific world-view, and a meta-scientific existential ontology, nothing more or less than a reciprocal denial of the opposite type of thinking is at stake. It concerns the meaning and significance of Western science, which is misunderstood, absolutized or damned by both sides. Kant, in his time, considered it to be the urgent mission of philosophy to put an end to the scandal by means of a compelling proof of the reality of the outer world. To do this it was necessary to clarify what could be meant by the concept of reality. The distinction between the "thing-in-itself" and "appearance" was the means by which the different meanings of reality, — for a human and for an absolute consciousness —, were explained. What is real in an empirical sense is not yet real in a transcendental sense. A similar distinction seems to be necessary in the present quarrel over the reality of scientific truth. The manners of thinking do not seem differentiated enough to do justice to the matter. Serious philosophy today must feel no less called upon to clarify a situation, in which, in a special sense, the very reality of what we consider valid reality, is at stake. For, to have doubt in the objective validity of the sciences, is basically to doubt the objectivity of the objects of those sciences.

It is in the very nature of quarrels among *Weltanschauungen* that the various conceptions become progressively more sidetracked in the pursuit of their own paths, and that a clarification becomes possible only when the problems are transferred to another level. It is to Jaspers' credit that he has opened up an encompassing perspective which can assign to the embattled positions their actual places in the order. In his own evolution from medicine to philosophy he outgrew the sober confines of the sciences and entered into the open expanse of all possibilities of thought. This outer evolution indicates that, biographically, he went through an inner struggle similar to that going on between positivism and metaphysics today. What was first indicated in his

world orientation — an orientation about the realm of scientific
world investigation —, grew into final formulation in the concept
of the Encompassing. But, from this encompassing expanse his
thinking today admonishingly points back to the indispensable
condition of scientific research.

The relationship between science and philosophy has become
an ever more important issue for Jaspers, and he is one of the few
who attempt to endure the tension between the two. The Encompassing is the guiding idea under which both are to be united.
Without the Encompassing philosophy would remain, as a science,
one-eyed, incapable of looking into the dimension of depth. But,
on the other hand, man does not have to overthrow science in
order to save his being human. If some quarters desire a new
"saving knowledge" alongside the pure "ordering knowledge" of
science, we must reply that no truth can bypass the truth of science. For the evil consists precisely in the divisions of our modern
consciousness and in the co-existence of truths. The task, rather,
is to transform the scientific consciousness by a new ascertainment
of Being.

By means of the concept of the Encompassing Jaspers is able to
revive all the old, great contents of philosophy. With this concept
the history of Western metaphysics acquires meaning even under
the conditions of our critical and historical knowledge. True, this
history is not completed; but it begins to become comprehensible
in a new, and authentic, sense. For, the coming to consciousness
of the basic modes of the Encompassing brings us complete freedom of thought by indicating the directions which lead out of the
dead-end streets of rigid interpretations of Being. In the reversal
thus consummated the limited meaning and value of all finite
things is clarified by orientation on the encompassing totalities
to which they belong. The logic of the Encompassing as the
organon of Jaspers' philosophy is the attempted integration of
our disintegrating consciousness of Being. Its idea is the union of
all ways of knowledge on the basis of the limitless illumination of
the sciences and of the integration of the basic experiences of all
human history, — from China and India to the Occident of the
present —, in order to achieve a new, encompassing consciousness
of Being. It is, in a sense, the logic of an era of beginning planet-
ary integration. It is an attempt which may provide a starting
point, from which the logical consciousness of the present may
continuously be developed. Completely new approaches to the
Encompassing may be opened up precisely in the present state of
analysis of scientific problems, such as in formalistic logic. To

work on their development seems to be one of the fundamental concerns of present-day philosophizing.

Kierkegaard saw his mission in reminding man of the simple, basic conditions of *Existenz*. Perhaps today's task is to appeal to the simple, basic possibilites of our being. That these possibilities long for realization makes of philosophy an "inner action," by which we practice our own possibilities of being. Jaspers understands his philosophical logic as such a "practice in basic knowledge," "whose seven liberal arts" are the seven modes of the Encompassing. This thinking, as Jaspers understands it himself,[6] is "the necessary and natural conclusion of Western thought to date, the unprejudiced synthesis by virtue of a principle which can absorb, because of its breadth, everything which is true in any way." And it is "the point of departure for future thought, . . . for, far from being the final word, it opens realms where research and life, *Existenz* and history may enter without limitation."

VI. CRITIQUE

My criticism is not directed against the basic concept of the Encompassing, but against the systematic representation it is given by Jaspers. As concerns the basic concept of the subject-object division, which indeed finally calls forth the concept of the Encompassing, Jaspers is able to refer to the tradition of Kantian thought. In this respect the philosophy of the Encompassing appears to be assured and secure for our future philosophical consciousness. One may also agree with Jaspers that his philosophy is the natural and necessary conclusion of Western thought to date. But the "origins," as he terms it, out of which he thinks of the Encompassing in the systematics of his seven modes, can no longer refer to such a tradition, even if Jaspers remarks occasionally that the Encompassing has repeatedly been conceived from certain standpoints.[7] This seems to be a risky backward projection of his own thought. Nor can the connection between the seven modes claim to be really systematic. Although I have attempted, in this presentation, to put in, on my part, several additional systematic points of view, I still cannot help but feel that the seven modes were taken up with a certain arbitrariness.

Indeed, the number "7" seems very strange and recalls no previous philosophizing, neither the 4 of Plato, nor the 10 of Aristotle, nor the 4 and 12 of Kant. The asymmetry of the 7 corre-

---

6 *Wahrheit*, 192.   7 Cf. *Reason*, 54.

sponds to the lack of equivalence of the individual modes. Transcendence, for example, is a mode distinguished from the others. In a certain sense it is the only genuine Encompassing, the Encompassing of all Encompassings. On the other hand, *Existenz* corresponds very poorly to the concept of an Encompassing. There are many *Existenzen,* but just one Transcendence. And there is likewise only one spirit, one consciousness-as-such, one world — but many existences. And when Jaspers, in his *The Perennial Scope of Philosophy,*[8] in describing the polarities in modes of the Encompassing, designates *Existenz* as an Encompassing of *Existenz* and Transcendence, he is using risky phraseology and cannot intend this to mean the same thing as the being encompassed of subject and object in consciousness-as-such. Systematics and conceptualization are really opposed to each other here.

In general, there is Encompassing which we are and Encompassing which we are not and Encompassing which simultaneously we are and are not. In making this division, however, the basic idea of an Encompassing of subject and object is almost invalidated again. As a consequence thereof, the world appears twice within the system: As existence, consciousness-as-such, and spirit, and again as world. This "objective" world, would actually have to be understood, however, as the thing-in-itself, and therefore as Transcendence, if one accepts the basic Kantian postulate of the subject-object division, and of the phenomenal character of the world. Here comes to light a twofold understanding of the world: as Kantian subjective idea and as an objective, actual world (cosmos).

Whereas *Existenz* and existence do not actually fit into the systematics of the Encompassing, one misses the presence of other concepts, or, at least, a reference to them, e.g., space and time, or better, spatiality and temporality. Occasionally there is, quasi experimentally, mention of other modes: Life, the idea, thinking.[9] Or, certain subdivisions are used: Matter, living body, and soul,[10] in connection, to be sure, with the idea of stratification. Final appraisal depends, of course, on Jaspers' doctrines of categories and methods, still to be published. But, in general, it may be said that the system, as it stands, does not establish the relationship of the modes. From a systematic point of view several modes might be missing and others could be accepted. The idea thus arises that the systematics of the seven modes is based on something presupposed and undiscussed. Whatever this ground is on which Jaspers finds himself in the first place when he asks concerning the nature of Being, remains yet to be examined. For Being, as Being

8 *Scope,* 15.   9 *Reason,* 69 ff.   10 *Reason,* 54.

itself, is already thought of in a certain way (the concept of God); the Being which we are is already interpreted in a certain way (the idea of man); the nature of logic has already been decided in a pre-concept, if the inquiry into Being leads to such systematics. The concept of God and the picture of man are not developed in Jaspers' philosophy (perhaps, indeed, in no philosophy at all), but are brought into it and then, perhaps, clarified. That we have and when we have a consciousness of actual Being, that we understand, and how we understand the upsoaring to Being as our own truth, is already anticipated if, out of it, the origins are experienced as modes of transcending.

Regarding the original inquiry into Being and its first turn, a second turn-around is really necessary now: as what must Being be pre-understood in order that it may be recognized in such forms of appearance? The answer would enable us to decide what among that which we encounter is to be understood as an appearance of Being.

Some will be deterred from agreeing with the philosophy of the Encompassing, beyond its initial thoughts, because the modes of Being are contentual interpretations from the start. There can be no argument regarding contents. One can deny that everything that exists has the character of being. One can deny that the objective spirit is more than a "flourish, which existence sometimes allows itself." Whether thinking is more than argumentation, whether to think contradicts the nature of man, depends on the logic which asserts this contradiction.

Thus, our criticism seems to concentrate on the question of the valid logic of this kind of thinking. But the philosophy of the Encompassing recognizes no encompassing logic! Its idea of truth is that there is truth in every mode of the Encompassing and that no mode can replace another. Its concept of truth is always bound to content, and only one of these contents is the so-called formal logical one. The contentuality of this thinking indicates that, in the final analysis, it refers to basic experiences, which enter philosophizing as contents. I don't believe I misunderstand the philosophy of the Encompassing when I believe that the question concerning the basis for the justification of this kind of thinking would be answered by reference to final, basic experiences. It is part of the idea of philosophy that these experiences are reflectingly accepted into philosophizing and that philosophizing itself presses toward such experiences of Being. But, perhaps, they are a limitation in their factuality. Where they are lacking in the other, agreement is impossible.

The demand for an encompassing, no longer contentual, logic

signifies, within Jaspers' thinking, a gain in the importance of consciousness-as-such in all modes of the Encompassing. It is perhaps a just criticism that Jaspers remains unclear at this point. For, the presence of the subject-object division in all of the modes really means that consciousness-as-such has validity for every kind of truth. Thus Jaspers states that the "structure of our thinking, as (part of) consciousness-as-such, includes everything within itself."[11] But when this thought is not maintained, and consciousness-as-such is considered merely one mode among others, the reason lies, in my opinion, in the contentual understanding of this thinking.

On the basis of Kantian philosophy, it really would have to be accepted that, in thinking, we always execute only formal structures, but that the contents must be given to us in some other way. We do think contents, but we do not think contentually. There can be thoughtful agreement only about the formal aspects of thinking. Contents seem historically to come and go. What brings us together in them seems like an incomprehensible fate.

It is obvious that the question of the relationship of consciousness-as-such to the other modes of the Encompassing becomes decisive for every form of presentation. For in every presentation we subject ourselves to the conditions of a general consciousness in so far as we demand communicability. What cannot become universally valid can not become presentation. Criticism from this side would, therefore, have to demand elimination of everything contentual from the presentation. But, on the other hand, we always refer to contents. Indeed, everything formal aims, in the final analysis, at contents. Therefore, the contentual would have to be linked together in such a way as to remain the permanent contour of thought. The presentation would have to aim toward a certain empty form, in which the basic idea of the Encompassing and the forms of transcending are described. One can appeal to contents only by pointing to history and to the philosophical tradition.

Jaspers' criticism of objectification would thereby become still more pointed. For, where thinking objectifies, it solidifies certain contents. In a certain sense the seven modes are still too objective, because they are too contentual. The remaining reproach is that, in Jaspers' logic, the criticism of objectification does not become a systematic operation. In its essence it remains (a form of) self-correction, which practically has to be done again and again.

The objectlessness of the Encompassing does not yet neces-

11 *Wahrheit*, 244.

sarily signify a lack of systematics. Excluded by the systematics are the contentual interpretations.

For the "derivation" of the modes of the Encompassing this criticism means that they may not be drawn from experience nor from historical self-interpretation but, rather, from a formal system, which then would in itself have to be suspended again. Only thus would every objectivity be removed from the conception of the Encompassing. (The Platonic Parmenides seems to me to be a model of this.) Carrying the formalization further would also have to be extended to the concept of transcending. Of all the ways of transcending, Jaspers himself considers only the formal to be an actual philosophical consummation. Where Transcendence appears, in the ciphers of world-being and in the symbols of art, it is only in so far as it is translated into the structures of thinking. The silent language of the symbols always remains, as such, non-committal. It is restricted to content.

That the formalization is going to be carried further and further would seem to be unavoidable. But this does not mean that the contents will be lost. For the contents do not come from philosophy. Philosophy cannot, therefore, invalidate them. It is my conviction, moreover, that any further thinking through of the idea of the Encompassing also aims at its formalization; for the path to ever further formalization seems to be the path of thinking itself.

GERHARD KNAUSS

SENDAI
JAPAN

4

Edwin Latzel

THE CONCEPT OF 'ULTIMATE SITUATION' IN JASPERS' PHILOSOPHY *

"The meaning of philosophizing lies in a single thought, which as such is inexpressible: the *awareness of Being* in itself; each chapter of this work should make it accessible; each should represent the whole in smaller form, but at any given time one chapter leaves dark what will be illuminated only by the rest."
(Karl Jaspers in the Foreword to his *Philosophie*)

THE PHILOSOPHIZING of Karl Jaspers has as its goal the disclosure of the place of the *authentically* real. It is not concerned exclusively with the authentic being of *man,* although the latter is, of course, always kept in view. For, self-realization is regarded as a prerequisite to our catching sight of the authentically real. "Catching sight of" is perhaps not quite the correct expression. I cannot catch sight of authentic reality — either of that which I myself am capable of being in my better hours, the afterglow of which lights up the reality of my every day, or of that which I myself am not — in the way that I can catch sight of the things of the world.

The latter stand over against me in objective clarity. They include objects which I make use of every day — e.g., clothing, household utensils — as well as objects which, although they do not directly affect my everyday reality, arouse my impulse to know, and are rendered investigable and knowable in the various sciences.

My everyday world and the multifariously articulated world of science are not the whole of reality; indeed, they are not authentically real. I feel lost in mere everyday activities; the everyday world tastes flat and dull. Science provides me with universally valid knowledge about things in the world, and this knowledge lifts me up. I am no longer lost in my everyday activities. However, I cannot really know any one thing completely. In the world which science discloses everything is related to everything else: every solution of a problem raises new problems. The more penetrating

* Translated from the German manuscript by George L. Kline.

177

my scientific orientation in the world, the more profound are the enigmas which confront me. I should have to know the world as a whole in order to know any single thing completely. But the world as a whole is not an object of science; it is not given to me objectively. Rather, it is that *within which* all scientifically investigable objects are given.

The world as the encompassing whole *(umgreifendes Ganzes)*[1] thus evades the grasp of the investigator, moving farther and farther away from him as he advances. The more exhaustive and intensive his investigation, the clearer and more articulated the objective world as it constitutes itself in his investigation, an investigation guided by more or less conscious leading ideas — the more forcibly is it brought home to him that the world of science possesses only an intermediate kind of reality and is not authentic reality.

The human beings with whom I come into contact are also a part of the environment which is disclosed to me in my everyday existence *(Dasein)*. Such everyday human relationships can take on many forms, starting with indifferent co-existence, moving through relentless struggle for existence, to co-operative activity in the service of a common idea, e.g., that of an occupation or organization. To be part of such an idea-oriented community serves to discipline and stabilize my everyday existence — which would otherwise readily fall into fragments. However, this common world, defined by ideas, is still not authentic reality.

Thus, neither the world of everyday existence,[2] nor the world of science, represents authentic reality; indeed: "The reality of existence and the objective world of science are dependent upon each other for their being."[3] They are related to one another. We shall attempt to clarify this point by means of an example from Jaspers himself:[4]

As a living existence, I live at any given time in a landscape, in which I am embedded and firmly rooted. But I can free myself from it, set it over against me, in order to know it scientifically. What happens in this process?

The landscape and I do not both remain the same. Previously

---

1 Cf. *Wahrheit,* 85ff.   2 *Ibid.,* 53ff.   4 *Ibid.,* 64f.

3 *Philosophie,* 2nd ed. (Berlin, Göttingen, Heidelberg, 1948), 64. *(Page numbers without any other indication* will be used in the sequel to refer to this second edition of Jaspers' *Philosophie.* It is to be regretted that this new edition, which exactly reproduces the text of the three-volume first edition of 1932, does not give the page numbers of the first edition. Dr. Maria Salditt is to be heartedly thanked for providing a subject index to this new and technically more convenient one-volume edition.)

I was firmly rooted in *my* landscape; no one else could have had exactly the same relationship to it. But now, if I want to know it scientifically — and thus not as it is for me alone, but as it is "in itself" and for everyone else — I must suspend all merely personal or private relationships. I must leave behind my unique, concrete existence, with its fullness of life, and my personal consciousness and become mere "consciousness-as-such"[5] which can be the same in every human being.

What I, as consciousness-as-such, know — and this can, in principle, be known in the same way by everyone else — is no longer *my* landscape, but *"nature* in its determinateness. It is no longer animated as a landscape; it does not respond as the 'totality different' (from myself) but stands there as a mere object."

This world of nature, which constitutes itself in consciousness-as-such, becomes accessible to and usable by me, when, having returned into my existence to my "full, irreplaceable life in space and time,"[6] I relate it to my needs and purposes.

All the other concepts of the world (the worlds of technology, society, economics, etc.) — like that of the world of nature — accrue to me "out of the realities of my existence. I place these realities over against myself, removing them to the objective world as something other, without being able to cease to live in them as existence."[7]

Where, then, is authentic reality to be found, if neither the world as "the immediate whole of existence,"[8] nor the objective world of science — of consciousness-as-such — represents such reality?

I cannot grasp the authentically real in the objective categories of consciousness-as-such; I can only grasp it in *living experience,* in the depths of my concentrating nature, through the process of self-realization.

If authentic reality cannot be grasped in the concepts of consciousness-as-such, since my every attempt to communicate with my fellowmen is bound up with these concepts, how can I communicate my experience of authentic reality to others? How is philosophy as such possible, since philosophy has but one purpose — to disclose the place of the authentically real?

This question is of decisive importance for all of Jaspers' philosophizing. It must be clearly comprehended, for any correct understanding of Jaspers' total philosophical work depends upon it. When this question is answered, the paradox — that, in a philosophy which, both in its final intention and in fact, is concerned

5 Cf. *Wahrheit,* 64ff.　6 *Philosophie,* 317.　7 *Ibid.,* 64.　8 *Ibid.,* 57.

with the authentic reality of Being itself, and not of any particular kind of being, there is a great deal of discussion about the *being* of *man* — is resolved.

If man cannot know authentic being through the objective categories of consciousness-as-such; if he can only experience this being in his own high moments — moments in which he is more than mere existence, more even than a mind guided by ideas,[9] then the philosopher, too, who has himself experienced this being, cannot express it directly. He cannot absolve others from the experience of being, he cannot have this experience *for* others and then say directly to them: this is what being is like. Authentic reality, Being itself, must be experienced directly by every individual; the philosopher can only attempt to assist others in attaining their own experience of Being.

For man, self-realization and the experience of Being coincide. When we philosophize we are seeking authentic being, by breaking a trail toward self-realization for ourselves and for others, using philosophy as a means of communication. But fundamental difficulties immediately present themselves:

1)   If I make self-realization my *direct* goal, I shall be most certain to fail to reach it.

2)   The inner performance in which I become my own authentic self are not objectively comprehensible, and hence cannot be directly communicated.

3)   These inner performances constitute what is most personal in me. In them I attempt to become *myself,* not a self as such. Quite apart from the question of communicability, then, how can anyone else help me in my self-realization, since I am not attempting to become *himself,* nor yet a *self as such,* but precisely *myself?*

Let us examine this problem in greater detail.

1)   I cannot directly undertake to become myself, or, what amounts to the same thing, aim directly at authentic being, either in me or outside of me. "I cannot will what I *really* want."[10] We can express this as follows: my becoming *authentic* is related to my becoming *whole.* But what does it mean to say I "become whole"?

It does not mean that I realize everything which inheres in me, not even all of my positive potentialities. My finiteness forbids this: the span of my life is too short. But I cannot neglect any of the basic possibilities of my being as a man (Jaspers carefully distinguishes the three forms of this being — existence, consciousness-as-such, and spirit). I must entrust myself to the Encompassing,

---

[9] Cf. *Wahrheit,* 71ff.   [10] *Ibid.,* 180 (italics mine).

"to encompassing life — out of the affirmative strength of my existence — to correctness as such, and to ideas of the spirit."[11] None of these basic possibilities should be permitted to become autarchic. As mere existence, I would be confined to the biological realm. I would not be essentially human. As mere consciousness-as-such, I should be replaceable at will, and wholly without individual reality. As mere spirit, I should be "rarified;" I would deny my finiteness and thus become false. Each of these kinds of being requires the other two, if their expression is to be pure. Only as a whole man, a human being who continually lives all three of these kinds of being — all of which reciprocally condition, support, and enhance one another — can I become authentically myself.[12]

2) I can turn not only things, but myself and other human beings into objects of investigation. And just as the world as a whole, as encompassing Being, eludes the apprehension of consciousness-as-such, so I, as consciousness-as-such, am able to grasp neither myself, nor the encompassing aspect of my full being as a man. I can experience myself concretely in the process of living as existence, as consciousness-as-such, as spirit. But I myself am always infinitely more than I can objectively know about myself. What I can objectively know about myself and about other human beings is no longer the encompassing aspect of our existence or of our being as spirit; it stands over against me, objectively, like the investigable things of the being of the world. Indeed, it belongs to this world itself. "World" is to be taken here not in the sense of an encompassing being, but rather as the objective world to which I am related as consciousness-as-such. (It is important to keep these two meanings of "world" distinct in Jaspers.[13])

Since only in *becoming* my encompassing existence or my encompassing spirit I can experience them, i.e., since, then, I cannot know objectively; and since, therefore, I cannot communicate this becoming directly to others in the categories of consciousness-as-such, becoming my authentic being — myself must be even less communicable.

3) Even if the philosopher could in some way communicate to

11 *Ibid.*, 181. "Correctness" means the truth of consciousness-as-such. Cf. *ibid.*, 67.

12 Cf. *ibid.*, 130ff.

13 Cf. *ibid.*, 141ff., for a diagram of the structure of being, and an interpretation of the diagram. — I myself become a part of the *objective world*, which is there for consciousness-as-such, when I am objectified in the categories of this consciousness. But as encompassing existence, as encompassing spirit, and as the encompassing aspect of consciousness-as-such, I am not part of the *World as encompassing Being*, but am an autonomous Encompassing.

us this experience of his own being himself, he would have to call upon us not to follow him. For, if our authentic self is what is deepest and most original in us, we should become false to the core, if each of us, instead of soaring upwards from his own origin toward authentic reality, should attempt to live from alien sources.

Is a philosophy, then, which communicates itself in written works, meaningfully possible? First, we must clarify the problem of communicability, which is the basic presupposition of such possibility; and then we must ask what meaning such communication could have, assuming that it is possible. This is the problem of the *appropriation,* or assimilation, of a philosophy by other human beings.

Now that we are aware of the goal of Jaspers' philosophy, we are in a position to exhibit the fundamental complex of problems which necessarily inheres in such philosophizing: these problems follow from his basic presuppositions. We do not wish to develop abstractly the answer to the question of the communicability, or the possible methods, of philosophizing, thus understood; or the second question — whether such a philosophy is wholly bound up with the personality of the individual who philosophizes, or whether it can be meaningfully appropriated by others. Rather, we shall examine the philosophizing of Jaspers as it lies before us, and see how he philosophizes concretely; we shall follow the way in which he communicates a self-consistent train of thought. In the Foreword to his *Philosophie,* Jaspers writes:

The meaning of philosophizing lies in a single thought, which as such is inexpressible; the *awareness of Being* in itself; each chapter of this work should make it accessible; each should represent the whole in smaller form, but at any given time one chapter leaves dark what will be illuminated only by the rest.

We shall select from the second volume of the *Philosophie,* entitled "Illumination of *Existenz,*" the chapter which deals with "ultimate situations" *(Grenzsituationen).* But, before we examine Jaspers' method and achievement, we shall atttempt to sketch the history and the significance of the concept of ultimate situations in Jaspers' work as a whole, and thus at the same time justify our choice of this particular chapter.

*   *   *   *

The concept of *ultimate situation,* like that of "foundering" *(Scheitern),* has entered into the vocabulary of a broad public, and, though it has often been re-interpreted and misinterpreted, it defines the general public's image of Jaspers' philosophy as a whole. If we examine Jaspers' philosophic work up to now, we find that this concept is today neither the most central nor the most profound; but perhaps it is still the most characteristic for the "climate," the whole atmosphere of this kind of philosophizing. It represents, so to speak, the original philosophical intuition of the young Jaspers, which retains its fruitfulness even in his most recently published works. This concept thus permits us to view Jaspers' entire philosophic production in perspective.

In 1919, Jaspers, who was then a Professor of Psychology at Heidelberg, published his *Psychologie der Weltanschauungen*. In 1941 he was to call this book "a rash work of my youth." However, he still acknowledged its content as his own, although he considered its form unsatisfactory. Even in 1919, Jaspers' psychology had, without his being aware of it, taken on the character of what he was later to call an "illumination of *Existenz*."[14]

The *Psychologie der Weltanschauungen* was intended as a work of *verstehende* psychology. In reality it is already the work of Jaspers the *philosopher* — not only in the section on ultimate situations, but also in its entire substance. Moreover, his later philosophical works are only a systematic development of what is substantially present in the *Psychologie,* but which was developed, clarified, deepened, and at the same time brought to ever higher consciousness only in the greater tranquility of the subsequent great works. Anyone who has carefully studied Jaspers' chief philosophic works, works which were shaped with ever more conscious discipline[15] — the *Philosophie* (1932), and *Von der Wahrheit* (the first volume of the *Philosophische Logik,* 1948) — and admired their masterly architectonic, must have become increasingly fond of the unruly philosophical fledgling of 1919 and the powerful *élan* of its spirited attack.

We have called the concept of the ultimate situation Jaspers' original philosophical intuition. It provides him, in the *Psychologie,* with the leading points of view for his characterization and classification of psychological types, and hence serves the purpose of the book as a whole. Let us recall the construction of this concept.

"When we speak of *Weltanschauungen,* we mean ideas, what is ultimate and complete in man, both subjectively, as experience, power, and conviction, and objectively as the formed world of objects."[16] Chapter I, which is called "Attitudes," considers various *Weltanschauungen* from the standpoint of the subject; Chapter

14 *Rechenschaft,* 362, 334f.   15 Cf. *ibid.,* 363.
16 *Psychologie,* 2nd rev. ed (Berlin, 1922), 1.

II, called "World-views," illuminates them from the objective standpoint. Chapter III carries out the synthesis; it inquires into the living totalities of the spiritual types. These types surpass the attitudes and world-views which in themselves are abstractions.

The discussion of the phenomenon of ultimate situations, a phenomenon "whose fundamental significance goes beyond any psychology of 'attitudes' or 'world-views' " (as Martin Heidegger noted in 1927[17]), is to be found in the Introduction to Chapter III. Of course, Jaspers was aware, in working out this section, that he was not speaking as a psychologist; he asserted that this exposition "is not yet psychology."[18] Even here, in the *Psychologie*, where Jaspers examines the phenomenon of ultimate situations for the first time, this phenomenon is so profoundly grasped and systematically thought out that the "systematic exposition of ultimate situations" in his *Philosophie* of 1932 — although it represents a new arrangement of the material — introduces no substantial modifications. But of this later. Here it is sufficient to reproduce the "definition" of ultimate situations from the *Psychologie*, and to make clear the function of this concept in that early work.

The concept of ultimate situations is introduced in the context of general considerations concerning valuations, tables of values, and value-collisions, formulated in the immediately preceding section.[19] The infinitely multifarious, concrete, particular situations in which man experiences the destruction of values and the constraint upon value-formation

do not appear to the individual at first glance as absolutely necessary; they could have been otherwise. No matter how true this may seem to the acting human being, he stands beyond all particular situations in certain decisive, essential situations, which are related to man's being as such, a being which is unavoidably given with finite existence; situations beyond which his vision does not carry, since his gaze is directed upon objective things within the subject-object dichotomy. These situations, which are felt, experienced, conceived, everywhere at the limits of our existence, we call "ultimate situations." What they have in common is that — within the objective world as dichotomized into subject and object — there is nothing *firm or stable,* no indubitable absolute, no enduring support for experience and thought. Everything is in flux, in the restless movement of question and answer; everything is relative, finite, split into opposites — nothing is whole, absolute, essential.[20]

[17] Martin Heidegger, *Sein und Zeit,* first half, 6th ed. (Tübingen, 1949), 249.

[18] *Psychologie,* 232.   [19] *Ibid.,* 220ff.   [20] *Ibid.,* 229.

The antinomian structure of existence, suffering, struggle, death, chance, guilt, are discussed in detail as ultimate situations.

The concept of ultimate situations functions in Chapter III as "a vehicle of construction and systematic exposition . . . , when we attempt to pass from an intuitive grasp to a conceptual fixation of spiritual types."[21] "If we inquire as to the spiritual type, we ask from where man may receive his support."[22]

There are, of course, people who lack any conscious experience of ultimate situations. They live in the unquestioning security of a traditional world-order, recognizing no form of life except their own. For them, "a *Weltanschauung* is no longer a specific process in an individual human being" and "a consideration of this kind of *Weltanschauungen* is possible . . . only at the level of social psychology."[23] Jaspers does not discuss them further.

However, where ultimate situations become consciously experienced, a "vital process"[24] is released:

The conscious experience of ultimate situations, situations which previously had been covered over with the hard shells of objectively self-evident forms of life, world-views, beliefs and ideas; and the movement of limitless reflection, of dialectic, initiate a process which ends with the dissolution of what was previously a self-evident shell.[25]

But man cannot live entirely without "shells" — "any more than can a mussel from which the shell has been removed." "Thus in the life-process one shell is dissolved only to make room for a new one."[26]

The process of living thus includes both a dissolution and a formation of shells. Without dissolution rigidity would set in; but without shells there would be destruction. Both dissolution and shells can, however, be detached, in a sense, from the living whole; the result is, on the one hand, nihilistic processes and, on the other, an ultimate crawling into one's shell.[27]

Thus we see in advance the organization of the chapter of spiritual types: after a consideration of the processes of dissolution ("Skepticism and Nihilism"[28]) comes the discussion of shells ("Support by Limitation: Shells"[29]). "With this we grasp aspects of the process whose core is life in its infinity; we shall describe this [process] in the third Section" ("Support in the Infinite"[30]).

The *Psychologie der Weltanschauungen* thus provides the basis for an understanding and classification of spiritual types by dis-

21 *Ibid.*, 220.

22 *Ibid.*, 229.

23 *Ibid.*, 281.

24 *Ibid.*, 280ff.

25 *Ibid.*, 281.

26 *Ibid.*, 281f.

27 *Ibid.*, 283.

28 *Ibid.*, 285ff.

29 *Ibid.*, 304ff.

30 *Ibid.*, 325ff.

cussing ultimate situations and the "vital process" which is initiated by the experience of these situations; hence they are both of fundamental significance.

The chapter on ultimate situations in the second volume of Jaspers' *Philosophie* is only one among eleven others, each of which is intended to represent the "whole in smaller form," making us aware of authentic reality. The idea of ultimate situations is here deepened and rendered fruitful in new ways; but one would fail to recognize the "pathos" of the work of 1932 if one were to examine it solely with respect to this chapter. This chapter is indispensable in the general plan of the *Philosophie,* but it is not the decisive chapter. Jaspers' early prototypal intuition of ultimate situations is here overshadowed by the fundamental experience of his mature philosophizing — the experience of " *'existential'* communication." This was foreshadowed as early as in the *Psychologie;*[31] but it was the complete break-through of this fundamental experience which finally changed Jaspers from a psychologist of *Weltanschauungen* to a philosopher — a philosopher who had become aware of his true mission.

In his *Way to Wisdom,* An Introduction to Philosophy (1949), Jaspers sees in the experience of ultimate situations (for example, in the Stoics) , together with the experience of wonder (Plato, Aristotle) and doubt (Descartes) one of the sources of traditional philosophizing. "But for us perhaps none of these is the most fundamental, absolute source": ". . . wonder, doubt, the experience of ultimate situations, are indeed sources of philosophy, but the ultimate source is the will to authentic communication, which embraces all the rest."[32] "To experience ultimate situations," he writes in the *Philosophie,* "and to *exist* is one and the same thing."[33] And again: "Our most luminous moments spring from communication; and the result of communication is the weightiness of life."

*   *   *   *   *

We have given an introductory sketch of the complex of problems inherent in Jaspers' philosophizing: this complex of problems comes to a focus, on the one hand, in the question of the communicability or method of such philosophizing, and, on the

[31] Cf. *Psychologie,* 125ff: "a loving struggle of souls with one another." And in the chapter on ultimate situations in the *Philosophie,* 502ff: "a loving struggle for *Existenz.*"

[32] *Wisdom,* 19-27. For Jaspers the consciousness of ultimate situations is a deeper source than either wonder or doubt.

[33] *Philosophie,* 469.

other hand, in the question as to whether this philosophy must remain wholly bound up in the personality of its creator. We shall now attempt to clarify these questions by reference to the way in which Jaspers works out the chapter on ultimate situations in his *Philosophie*.

Jaspers takes as his point of departure the concrete reality of existence. The first section, entitled "Situation," offers us universally valid knowledge, in the form in which it must appear to everyone, namely, in consciousness-as-such. "Every assertion which I encounter," he writes, "is . . . either testable by intellectual methods and hence is a cognitive assertion, proper to the investigatory world-orientation, and laying claim to universal validity, or else it is a philosophical assertion."[34] But this still leaves us outside the realm of authentic philosophizing. We must take account of the situation-bound character of human existence.

"A situation is not merely something which conforms to natural law; it is a *meaningful reality* which is neither psychic nor physical, but, as a concrete reality, is both together, and this reality means advantage or harm, opportunity or limitation for my existence." A whole series of sciences are concerned with this reality, investigating either universal, typical situations or historically determined, non-recurrent situations.

As existence I am so completely interfused with the situation in which I now find myself, in which "I act or let myself be acted upon,"[35] that I can never know more than a few of its aspects. Only a person who stands outside of this situation — someone else or I myself in retrospect — can survey it more fully, though never, of course, in all of its possibilities. In retrospect I might recognize which possibilities I missed because I was not, in general, aware of them. But, at the moment when I recognized them, the situation — as a result of this knowledge — would already have become different. On the basis of my knowledge of these possibilities I could have entered actively into the situation, thus modifying it.

"Situations exist insofar as they *change*."[36] But, although I can change the given situation, and can calculatingly introduce desired situations, I cannot "leave one situation without entering into another." Existence is a "being in situations."[37]

The second section, entitled "Situation and Ultimate Situation," leads to the limit of what I and, in principle, everyone else as consciousness-as-such, can know; it completes a "philosophical

---

[34] Concerning the relationship of "science and philosophy" in Jaspers, see the references in the subject-index of the *Philosophie*.

[35] *Ibid.*, 468.   [36] *Ibid.*, 468.   [37] *Ibid.*, 469.

world-orientation." Here "the *limits* are sought beyond which there does not have to be any further world, nor yet a nothingness."[38]

Situations such as the fact that I am always in situations, that I cannot live without conflict and suffering, that I unavoidably incur guilt, that I must die — these I call ultimate situations. They do not change, except in their appearance; with respect to our existence they are ultimate. They are not surveyable; in our existence we see nothing else behind them. They are like a wall, we come up against, and upon which we founder. They can not be changed by us, only brought to clarity — without our being able to explain or deduce them from anything else. They are a part of existence itself.[39]

"The word 'limit'* expresses the idea that there is something else, but at the same time that this something else is beyond the reach of consciousness in existence." Thus as a consciousness-as-such I am in principle unable to grasp the specific limiting character of ultimate situations; I can only state as an objective fact, like any other, that I am always in situations, that there is death, struggle, suffering, guilt. This is all part of human existence: man lives and, like all other living creatures, is subject to death. He experiences joy and sorrow. Human existence in its everyday reality attempts to avoid those situations which it experiences as an encroachment upon its life-impulse; but it does not dare to admit that it cannot escape them, even though it sees itself in fact constantly delivered up to them.

Authentic reality, the dual aspect of ultimate situations, becomes palpable to me only when I am no longer mere existence, which experiences this reality only negatively, as a boundary, and hence as a source of suffering; nor yet a consciousness-as-such, which merely registers it externally — but a *potential Existenz*.

Just as situations are a part of consciousness-as-such, so "ultimate situation and *Existenz*" — the title of Jaspers' third section — belong together: "to experience ultimate situations and to '*exist*' is one and the same thing."[40]

In the first and second sections, to which we have just referred, Jaspers leads us step by step to a limit beyond which "there does not have to be any further world, nor yet a nothingness." *Situations* are a reality which can be grasped by consciousness-as-such, and hence can be scientifically investigated from multifarious points of view. *Ultimate situations* as a reality *sui generis* can not exist for the mere intellectual understanding of consciousness-as-

[38] *Ibid.*, 46.   [39] *Ibid.*, 469.   [40] *Ibid.*, 469.

* Editor's Note: cf. glossary.

such. Here intellect comes up against an absolute limit. For ultimate situations are not a mere sub-species of situations in general.
In introducing the term "ultimate situation" — and the related
term *"Existenz"* — Jaspers goes beyond the realm of the objectively knowable. "To experience ultimate situations and to *exist*
is one and the same thing;" not only is this proposition not provable in any universally valid way; it is, for the pure intellect,
wholly without meaning. "Ultimate situation" is not an intellectual concept, nor an objective category, but rather, as Jaspers calls
it, a *signum*, a mere index, which points to the fact that given
situations can attain a particular depth for me, a depth which is
conceptually not exhaustible. The depth which slumbers in ultimate situations becomes palpable only to the depth which is inherent in me as the potentiality for becoming authentically myself, or — to use Kierkegaard's expression — authentically to *'exist.'*

Existence attempts to avoid ultimate situations; but in such
situations self-being can become aware of authentic being by a
leap. "Stages of the Leap taken in the Ultimate Situations in Becoming *Existenz*" is the title of the fourth section. "But how does
Existenz realize itself in ultimate situations?" Jaspers asks in this
section. The answer is: In ultimate situations I accomplish in
three stages — by a conscious inner act — the leap from existence
to *Existenz,* and hence the birth of my authentic self.[41] What I
have to do — by acting purposively in my existence — to avoid
where possible ultimate situations, is something that I can make
clear to everyone. Here intellect speaks to intellect, as in the case
where a physician gives advice for saving human life. But the activity with which I react in authentic significance to ultimate
situations — situations in which I, as existence, must in the end
founder — is quite different, in that I release the profound *'existential'* fruitfulness of this activity. And when Jaspers attempts to
describe this inner *'existential'* action to us, he can no longer appeal merely to our intellectual understanding: the authentic reality of these inner fulfillments in which I realize myself remains
inaccessible to this mere intellect and to all mere psychology. Here
I understand only what I myself have the potentiality of being.

Here, as elsewhere in *'existential'* philosophizing, mere intellect
no longer speaks to mere intellect, but *potential Existenz* speaks
to *potential Existenz,* through the medium of the concepts of the
intellect — for these concepts can not be avoided. Where authentic human *Existenz* is involved psychology becomes an *"illumination of Existenz."* Long passages in the second volume of Jaspers'

41 *Ibid.,* 472.

Philosophie — which bears this title — including the chapter on ultimate situations, can be read as psychology. However, to conceive them as psychology, as giving objective knowledge about man, is to misunderstand them in a radical way. They are not intended to provide definitive factual information as to what man is. In such seemingly psychological discussions one should listen closely for the *'existential'* undertones; these undertones — or, to express the point somewhat too sharply, what stands between the lines and cannot be said directly, because it cannot be captured in our concepts — represent the real essence.

I understand only that which I myself have the potentiality of being,[42] that which finds an answering echo in me. The illumination of *Existenz* sets strings vibrating in me, strings which rigorously objective thought cannot touch; it speaks to potentialities in me which might otherwise have remained hidden from me, but which may be decisive for my authentic being as human. Illumination of *Existenz* attempts to arouse and sharpen my sensitivity for what is essential, for what is genuine and what is false. It attempts to sensitize me to what is relevant in making my life a truly human life.

Let us consider the three forms of the leap in which *Existenz* realizes itself in ultimate situations.

If, in ultimate situations, I have touched upon the fragmentariness and doubtfulness of my existence and of that of the world in general, I can attempt to release myself from all ties, to set myself over against everything, including my own existence, to be only a disinterested and incorruptible eye: I wish to see and to know what may be the matter with the world and with my own existence. The knowledge which I am able to obtain as a disinterested observer serves as my only secure point of anchorage: "I look imperturbably upon the positive which I validly know, secure in this knowledge of my being." The first form of the leap leads "from world-existence in view of the doubtfulness of everything, to the substantial solitude of the universal knower."[43]

But only for fleeting moments can I be a mere eye which wants to see only what is. I remain embedded in my existence; my existence "contains the germ of my *Existenz*,"[44] which enabled me already to complete the first leap. And as potential *Existenz* I surpass the knowledge which I have gained in the solitary pointlikeness of consciousness-as-such.

[42] Thus I cannot understand God, nor can I understand an animal. All that I can authentically understand is the reality of man, and everything else only insofar as it enters into human reality.

[43] *Ibid.*, 472.   [44] *Ibid.*, 472.

The world cannot remain as a merely indifferent object of knowledge; my own being is involved in it. The experience of foundering in ultimate situations had disturbed me; I had attempted to entrench myself in consciousness-as-such as in an impregnable fortress. The surging atmosphere of the world around me had begun to divide itself up for me, as a consciousness-as-such, and had become surveyable realm by realm. As potential *Existenz*, which is concerned with becoming real, I seize this knowledge, without which I would remain entangled in the obscurity of world-existence; but it offers me no satisfaction. I sense that what authentically concerns me speaks to me only at the limits of what is objectively knowable in the being of the world. "Here being-world separates itself from *Existenz* for me; the former I can knowingly leave as a specific dimension of being. But I cannot escape from the latter by considering it; I can only either be it or not be it."[45] And the ultimate situations, from which I previously separated myself in my attempt as situationless knowledge as a disinterested observer, now become of decisive importance for me. I catch a glimpse of their depth, and grasp the fact that they compel me to decide whether I dare expose myself to their authentic reality and in so doing to realize myself. Ultimate situations become an object for my consideration. As potential *Existenz*, I examine them for their hidden potentialities. I cannot analyze them from a cool distance in a way which is universally valid for consciousness-as-such. I know that I myself am affected by these potentialities and I attempt to make them clear to myself by "illuminating consideration." The second form of the leap thus leads "from a consideration of things in view of my necessary participation in the world of foundering, to an illumination of potential *Existenz*."[46] By reference to potential *Existenz*, I illuminate for myself the possibility of my becoming authentically real, of *existing* in ultimate situations.

No matter how deeply I, as potential *Existenz*, must become involved in order to complete this "illuminating consideration" — "I am not yet what I know in philosophizing."[47] It is only the third and decisive leap that leads me "from existence as potential *Existenz* to *real Existenz* in ultimate situations."[48] "What I know paves the way for what I can become."[49] But *Existenz* which really stands in an ultimate situation no longer philosophizes.

Here we must pause. Our consideration of the first section of

45 *Ibid.*, 471. 46 *Ibid.*, 472. 47 *Ibid.*, 471. 48 *Ibid.*, 472.

49 The three forms of the leap are bound up with one another, they are genuine only when they remain related to one another. 472f.

the introduction to the chapter on ultimate situations has carried us far enough into Jaspers' complex of themes that we can now attempt to clarify the questions and difficulties which were raised at the beginning. Let us review them briefly:

Jaspers is attempting in his philosophizing to reveal to us the place of the authentically real as such. Authentic reality is something which I can grasp only in the living experience of self-realization. That authentic reality which I can myself become has, since Kierkegaard, been called *"Existenz."* However, if I aim directly at such *'existential'* becoming, I am most certain to fail to achieve it. In addition to this difficulty, which is present even for the person who does the original philosophizing, two further difficulties appear: How can the original philosopher tell others about the inner fulfillments in which he realizes himself, if they can not be grasped in the objective thought of consciousness-as-such? And: How can *his* self-realization be of any help to others in *their* self-realization?

1) *The Philosopher cannot aim directly at his own self-realization.*

According to the philosophy of ultimate situations, to be in ultimate situations and to *exist* is the same thing. Hence, if I should set up *'existential'* becoming as my direct goal, I should have to *seek out* ultimate situations for my existence to founder in, in order that I might at the same time realize myself. I should have to *want* to founder. Jaspers never tires of protesting against this fundamental misunderstanding. It is so important to become clear on this point that we shall quote at least one passage *in extenso:*

> To will this foundering directly would be to admit a perversion in which being itself would be wholly darkened into nothingness. We do not find genuine revelatory foundering in just *any* shipwreck, nor in *every* annihilation, self-surrender, renunciation, or refusal. The cipher of immortalization in foundering becomes clear only when I do not *will* to founder and yet *dare* to founder. I cannot plan the reading of this cipher of foundering. I can plan only that which provides permanence and stability. The cipher does not reveal itself when I will it, but only when I do everything to avoid its reality; it reveals itself in the *amor fati.* But fatalism would be false, if it gave in too early and hence failed to founder.[50]

Only if I do *not* seek out ultimate situations, if I do *not* attempt to founder, if I do everything to avoid this, can the inevitable foundering of my existence become a gateway to my authentic

being as a man. And I *need* not at all will to founder. The ultimate situations in which I inevitably find myself, continually
confront me with the reality of necessary foundering and compel
me to decide whether I dare, by actively suffering ultimate situations, to "transform ruin into a function of *Existenz*."[51]

Hence in philosophizing I cannot aim directly at my own self-
realization. But I may well *arm* myself for what Jaspers calls
"genuine foundering," by reconnoitering and anticipating in
thought, as potential *Existenz,* the potentialities of ultimate situations, which remain for my active mastery of this necessary
foundering. But the question remains as to whether this anticipatory insight into the necessity of foundering necessarily prejudices
the originality and spontaneity of my active struggle against this
foundering. And the danger of appropriating or assimilating Jaspers' philosophy is that, in this process, philosophizing about ultimate situations, in complete opposition to his intention, could
be turned into a kind of "shell," a covering which would hinder
a really genuine, original, and spontaneous foundering.[52]

Authentic self-being "cannot be forced."[53] Man's situation as
potential *Existenz* is paradoxical: *he must will the impossible:
only by so doing can he attain the possible, which he cannot will
directly.* Even as potential *Existenz* he must will to become whole
in the world. He cannot overleap the reality of his existence. "In
existence I am as a *will to become whole (Ganzwerdenwollen).*"[54]
The philosopher, according to Jaspers, "hungers for the world;
he seeks to know it as nature and in the breadth of its historical
objectivity, to experience it in the factual, historical concreteness
of his own existence."[55] The philosopher's "incessant impulse
presses forward as a will to become whole; nowhere does it find
lasting rest."[56] In its attacks upon the reality of existence, the will
to become whole is constantly being brought up short by the resistance of ultimate situations. In these situations it becomes clear
that the goal has been placed too high ever to be attainable: man
as a finite creature can never round out the reality of his existence
into an encompassing and harmonious whole. He cannot become
really whole. But he must repeatedly will the impossible, in order
to achieve the possible, which "is not to be planned and becomes
meaningless when it is desired, namely, to experience Being in
foundering."[57] The ultimate situations constitute "a barricade of
restraints for potential *Existenz,*" in its "drive against them comes

[51] *Wahrheit,* 885.   [52] See note 108 below.   [53] *Ibid.,* 865.
[54] *Ibid.,* 751.   [55] *Ibid.,* 280.   [56] *Ibid.,* 648.
[57] *Ibid.,* 879. (concluding sentence of the *Philosophie.*)

to itself in existence."[58] Without the will to become whole there is no authentic experience of my finiteness in ultimate situations, which hurl me back upon myself, no genuine foundering, and hence no becoming authentic.

Jaspers' philosophy of ultimate situations illuminates in detail the necessity of foundering; but Jaspers is just as keenly aware of the necessity of the will to become whole as a presupposition of genuine foundering. He does not discuss the latter at equal length, but for Jaspers the impulse to become whole is, perhaps for that very reason, such a spontaneous, powerful and self-evident presupposition — indeed, it supports his whole life's work[59] — that in the creator of the philosophy of foundering there is no danger of any premature resignation.

2) *The Problem of Communication.* The significance of this problem for Jaspers becomes evident from the fact that for large stretches his philosophy becomes a philosophizing about philosophizing, about its potentialities and its method.

The way in which Jaspers introduces the idea of ultimate situation is characteristic for his procedure. His point of departure is the concrete reality of my existence. As consciousness-as-such I separate myself from this reality and analyze it from changing points of view. But in so doing I never grasp the whole of my existence: Existence as the Encompassing evades objective knowledge; this knowledge is brought up short against ultimate limits. As potential *Existenz* I sense that it is precisely here, at the limits of the objectively knowable, that authentic reality awaits me.

How does Jaspers succeed in communicating what is not objectively conceivable? Let us now examine the further construction and elaboration of his chapter on ultimate situations.

The three principal parts of this chapter complete the "illumination of *Existenz*" in the sense already mentioned. Jaspers thus reaches the point where he must be able to take the reader with him to the *second* leap, which leads from existence to potential *Existenz*. His desire to implicate the reader in this leap is probably the chief reason why Jaspers rearranges the grouping of the ultimate situations in the *Philosophie,* as compared to the *Psychologie der Weltanschauungen.*

The *Psychologie* presents the following outline:

[58] *Ibid.,* 510.

[59] Cf. *Rechenschaft,* 326: "a plan of life." This autobiographical sketch which impresses one by the parsimony of its tone, will soon be recognized as a classic (323ff). Concerning ultimate situations as the source of Jaspers' philosophizing, from the very beginning, cf. 330.

THE CONCEPT OF 'ULTIMATE SITUATION'   195

I. The Antinomian Structure of Being
II. Suffering
III. Particular Ultimate Situations:
    1. Struggle
    2. Death
    3. Chance
    4. Guilt

In the work of 1919 Jaspers, who is still, in intent, a purely descriptive psychologist, finds it convenient to start from what is most general, from the antinomian structure of being. "If this structure is a limit of the objective world-view, the suffering which is bound up with every life is its subjective correlate."[60] Struggle, death, chance, guilt are "only special cases of something more general."

The chapter in the *Philosophie* begins, on the contrary, with my fully concrete human existence. The fact that I am a man or woman; that I live in this time and in these surroundings, that I belong to this nation, this family; in short that I am not a "man in general," with *all* the potentialities of being as man, but am bound to the non-recurrent, concrete reality of my existence, and that as existence I always find myself in a specific situation: this discussion of the "ultimate situation of the historical determinateness of *Existenz*," as the first ultimate situation, follows naturally upon the introductory sections of the chapter, in which the ultimate situations are contrasted with *situationality* as such. It introduces the reader, who already knows something about the three leaps of self-realizing *Existenz*, to the fulfillment of the illumination of *Existenz*.

This is carried further in the illumination of "particular ultimate situations" which "confront everyone as a general feature of his otherwise specific historicity."[61] "Death" and "suffering" are ultimate situations to which I am exposed without any effort on my part; but I actively and inevitably help to give rise to "struggle" and "guilt" as ultimate situations.

All of these ultimate situations point toward the fragmentariness and contradictoriness, not only of *my* existence, but of the total reality of the world. Thus, the illumination of the "universal ultimate situation of all existence," as the most general and relatively most abstract ultimate situation, includes everything hitherto said and concludes the chapter on ultimate situations, a chapter whose systematic construction may be indicated in the following way:

60 *Psychologie*, 232.   61 *Philosophie*, 474.

    I. The ultimate situation of the historical determinateness of *Existenz.*

   II. Particular ultimate situations:
1. Death
2. Suffering
3. Struggle
4. Guilt

  III. The ultimate situation of the doubtfulness of all existence and the historicity of the real as such.

Suffering is now treated, from a different point of view, as a particular ultimate situation. All of the ultimate situations which were introduced in the work of 1919 recur here, partly under different names.

Philosophie		*Psychologie der Weltanschauungen*
I	=	III, 3
II, 1	=	III, 2
II, 2	=	II
II, 3	=	III, 1
II, 4	=	III, 4
III	=	I

This entire chapter is impressively constructed and closely reasoned: the illumination of particular ultimate situations is placed in a framework of illumination of the historicity of my human existence, and the illumination of the historicity of the reality of existence as such. This powerful equilibration is, however, only a "bonus," which is found, to be sure, in all of Jaspers' works. The organization of this chapter, however, is — like that of the entire *Philosophie,* in which sensitivity and constructive power are held in a remarkable balance, — not primarily determined by aesthetic considerations. Its sole and deliberate intention is to force the reader into a real fulfillment of 'existential' philosophizing.

We have already made it clear that 'existential' philosophizing cannot be confined to intellectual operations alone. It is, however, evident from the chapter which we are discussing that 'existential' philosophizing does not proceed *illogically,* but implies a more than formal logic; that it is not "*irrational*" but *super-rational;* that in Jaspers it is not *unsystematic,* but rather contains the most rigorous system conceivable.

The systematic rigor with which Jaspers has thought through the chapter on ultimate situations becomes evident when one attempts to lift out its pervasive fundamental ideas. The leading points of view which recur in the illumination of every particular ultimate situation include the following:

1) It is *existentially* disastrous to seek out the ultimate situation directly.
2) I inevitably find myself in ultimate situations.
3) Every ultimate situation has a dual aspect: a negative character with respect to my existence, and a potentially positive character for me as potential *Existenz*.
4) In the ultimate situation I achieve myself as *Existenz*.
5) I can illuminate for myself the '*existential*' necessity of the ultimate situation.

We shall spell this out in detail, thus obtaining a vista of all three parts of the chapter:

1) *The senselessness of a direct seeking of the ultimate situation:*

I. The ultimate situation of the historical determinateness of *Existenz:*

This limits my freedom of action, and represents a restraint upon and a resistance to the development of my existence. "Although this resistance may in part be overcome . . . by rationally purposive activity, it is when the possibility of such action is grasped with all of one's strength, *and only then,* that the insurmountable ground of resistance reveals the ultimate situation."[62]

II. Particular ultimate situations:

1) Death:

"Death can have depth only if there is no flight toward it; it cannot be willed directly or externally."[63]

2) Suffering:

The struggle with suffering is a condition of human existence: "Everyone takes some part in the struggle and demands of himself the highest effort in this struggle — so long as he is honest and sees the situation clearly — making use of every rational and empirically meaningful means."[64]

3) Struggle:

If one should want to produce struggle and war in any form whatever, "they would be robbed of their essence as a possible appearance of Transcendence to *Existenz.* All planning and willing must aspire to exclude them."[65]

[62] *Ibid.,* 478. *(Italics added.)*   [63] *Ibid.,* 491.   [64] *Ibid.,* 492.   [65] *Ibid.,* 616.

4) Guilt:

"Avoidable guilt should really be avoided in order to reach authentic, profound, unavoidable guilt — but here, too, without finding any rest."[66]

III. The universal ultimate situation of all existence:

We must "do everything possible to avoid and to improve upon that which, if it remains and overpowers us against our will not only may lead to annihilation but may also contain within itself a potential revelation of authentic Being."[67]

2) *The unavoidability of the ultimate situation:*

I. The ultimate situation of the historical determinateness of *Existenz:*

"My inevitable dependence upon natural forces and upon the disposition of the will of others is a confining aspect of the ultimate situation."[68]

II. Particular ultimate situations:

1) Death:

"I must experience the end; but (as mere existence) I live by forgetting the inevitability of death and the end of everything."[69]

2) Suffering:

"There are the greatest differences in the kind of suffering and in the degree of torment. But in the end the same thing may confront all men and everyone has his part to bear; no one is spared."[70]

3) Struggle:

"If I want to live I must be a usufructuary of some application of violence; and I must therefore, suffer violence myself at some time or other."[71] "If I wish never to live at the expense of other life, I must renounce life."[72]

4) Guilt:

"By actively participating in life, I take . . . (something) from others."[73] "Every action has consequences in the world which the agent did not anticipate."[74] "Whether I act or refuse to act, there will be consequences, and in either case I incur unavoidable guilt."[75]

[66] *Ibid.,* 508.

[67] *Ibid.,* 511.

[68] *Ibid.,* 477f.

[69] *Ibid.,* 483.

[70] *Ibid.,* 492.

[71] *Ibid.,* 501.

[72] *Ibid.,* 499.

[73] *Ibid.,* 507.

[74] *Ibid.,* 506.

[75] *Ibid.,* 507.

III. The Universal ultimate situation of all existence:

"In this ultimate situation value is seen to be bound up with conditions which are themselves value-negating. Something undesirable must be accepted with every transaction."[76] "The doubtfulness of all existence indicates the impossibility of finding rest in it as such."[77]

3) *The dual aspect of the ultimate situation.*

I. The ultimate situation of the historical determinateness of *Existenz:*

"Determinateness, which seemed only resistance and constriction, assumes the impenetrable depth of the appearance of *Existenz* itself, when comprehended as an ultimate situation."[78] My origin, "as an ultimate situation, is that which at the same time limits and fulfills me."[79] I feel myself a plaything of contingencies, and I experience myself "as at one with the chance which I have seized as my *own*."[80] I experience "Being *'existentially'* in what is objectively a limitation."[81]

II. Particular ultimate situations:

1) Death:

"Suffering, at the end, brings an awareness of *Existenz*."[82] "Neither longing for death nor fear of death, but the disappearance of (outward) appearance as the presence of *Existenz*, becomes the truth."[83]

2) Suffering:

Suffering annihilates factual being; but "the truth of happiness rises upon a foundation of foundering."[84]

3) Struggle:

"Struggle and warfare, whatever form they may take, are equally dreadful in their consequences. . . . These occurrences . . . are a potential appearance of transcendent Being for the *Existenz* which reveals itself in danger and foundering."[85]

4) Guilt:

"Exploitative usufruct obligates us to make some contribution. Impurity becomes the claim to will only in the most luminous reality, in order to bring the original volition to clear expression."[86]

76 *Ibid.,* 509.

77 *Ibid.,* 508.

78 *Ibid.,* 478.

79 *Ibid.,* 479.

80 *Ibid.,* 481.

81 *Ibid.,* 482.

82 *Ibid.,* 483.

83 *Ibid.,* 484.

84 *Ibid.,* 493.

85 *Ibid.,* 615.

86 *Ibid.,* 508.

III. The universal ultimate situation of all existence:

"Historicity, as an incessantly self-destructive creation, is the only phenomenon in which I become aware of myself and of transcendence."[87]

4) *The awakening of Existenz in the ultimate situation:*

I. The ultimate situation of the historical determinateness of *Existenz*.

Potential *Existenz* arises "in those moments in which the particular and accidental — that which could also be otherwise — is freely taken over by me as belonging to me, or where the possibility of taking over this reality is rejected because of the danger of an eternal mulilation of my own being in this guilt."[88]

II. Particular ultimate situations:

1) Death:

"Whatever remains essential in the face of death has been *'existentially'* fixed: whatever falls away is mere existence." Death is not an ultimate situation for potential *Existenz* if it "does not serve to awaken its potential depth, but merely serves to make everything meaningless."[89]

2) Suffering:

"If all of existence were happiness, potential *Existenz* would remain dormant." "Only when *Existenz* has reached the stage which is required if it is to remain itself in happiness does happiness become the phenomenon of Being, before which suffering, as stimulant, retreats."[90]

3) Struggle:

Struggle is "a factor which helps to create man and leaves its mark upon him."[91]

4) Guilt:

"Responsibility is the readiness to take guilt upon one's self. Because of it *Existenz* appears to stand under a pressure which is not to be abrogated."[92]

III. The universal ultimate situation of all existence:

The ultimate situation of the antinomian structure of existence, constitutes a "barricade of restraints for potential *Existenz;*" in its "drive against them *Existenz* comes to itself in existence."[93]

87 *Ibid.*, 512.   90 *Ibid.*, 493.   93 *Ibid.*, 510.
88 *Ibid.*, 478f.   91 *Ibid.*, 615.
89 *Ibid.*, 486.   92 *Ibid.*, 507.

5) *The 'existential' necessity of the ultimate situation:*

  I. The ultimate situation of the historical determinateness of *Existenz:*

> "Only out of a *historically* determined origin in the ultimate situation is satisfaction a fulfillment, time a phenomenal realization, in which the soul marvels at its profound harmony with itself."[94]

 II. Particular ultimate situations:

  1) Death:

> "If there were no passing away, I would be an infinite duration as existence and so would not *exist.*"[95]

  2) Suffering:

> "It is curious that pure happiness appears empty." "If all of existence were happiness, potential *Existenz* would remain dormant."[96]

  3) Struggle:

> "Absence of struggle . . . would produce an *'existential'* void together, perhaps, with manifold relations of existence with existence."[97]

  4) Guilt:

> ". . . Guilt shatters most radically every trace of self-righteousness of *Existenz* which is in the process of realizing itself."[98] Jaspers here refers to the unavoidable, objectively incomprehensible guilt, ignored by rational morality, which consists in the fact that I can realize *'existential'* communication with a few persons only. I cannot *'existentially'* do justice to everyone I meet.[99]

III. The universal ultimate situation of all existence:

> "Since true Being is experienced either in the ultimate situation or not at all, a world without antinomies, in which enduring absolute truth would be something objectively present, would be a world in which *Existenz* would cease to be, and with it that being in existence, to which Transcendence can become palpable."[100]

In what precedes we have laid bare the framework which underlies the construction of the chapter on ultimate situations. After this it would have been relatively easy to transcribe the entire

---

94 *Ibid.,* 479.   96 *Ibid.,* 493.   98 *Ibid.,* 507.

95 *Ibid.,* 484.   97 *Ibid.,* 505.   99 Cf. *ibid.,* 347.

100 *Ibid.,* 511. We were able to take almost all of the quotations used in our systematic outline (notes 62ff.) from the chapter on ultimate situations; we have cited another chapter several times (notes 65, 85, 91) only in the cases of the ultimate situation of struggle.

chapter so as to provide an outline of the complete, self-enclosed, and rigorous *system* of a philosophy of ultimate situations. But, it is precisely this which Jaspers did *not* wish to provide: he would see in any such attempt a fundamental falsification of the meaning of his philosophizing. Philosophizing, as he understands it, cannot result in any fixed or coherent system of knowledge. It wants to be something more, and more difficult, than that: the question is not one of increasing, ordering, and rounding off the area of my *knowledge,* but of modifying my whole *conscious attitude.* And our attempt to lay bare the systematic skeleton of the chapter was intended only to show concretely that it is not any lack of logic or system-building power which prevents Jaspers from producing a system.

Logical clarity is an indispensable presupposition for the illumination of *Existenz;* but by itself it is insufficient. Indeed, by itself it is deceptive; for, where thought deals with authentic, *'existential'* reality, it "cannot demonstrate itself by giving reasons, but can only try to convince by a [non-logical] appeal." "Arguments do not run in a linear series, with truth standing as the result at the end."[101] This proposition also applies to the illumination of particular ultimate situations in Jaspers; hence, no systematic outline can in any way replace a study of the original text.

Jaspers himself, in his discussion of the methods of the illumination of *Existenz,*[102] formulates the supra-logical ordering-principle which lies at the basis of his work: "The ordering of questions, thought and perceptions is such that the spark of self-being, which cannot be directly communicated since everyone either lights it in himself or not at all, may be struck in the co-thinker." In his foreword to a book by M. Dufrenne and P. Ricoeur, entitled *Karl Jaspers et la philosophie de l'existence,*[103] Jaspers repeats what he had already said in the foreword to his *Philosophie:* that each chapter of the *Philosophie* was planned as a self-contained whole. Each chapter, he now adds, should be read at one sitting. Its truth does not reside in any single assertion; this truth can become manifest only in the *movement* which takes place in the reader who is inwardly swept along, compressing the whole into a single thought.

In the philosophizing of the illumination of *Existenz* potential *Existenz* wants to speak to potential *Existenz.* The illumination of *Existenz,* as expressed in a written work, is therefore *an analogue of what Jaspers calls 'existential' communication:* "In the expression of the universal, as the form of thought which illumi-

101 *Ibid.,* 305.   102 *Ibid.,* 302ff.   103 Paris, 1947.

nates *Existenz,* potential *Existenz* appeals both to itself and to others, in order to become fully itself in both."[104] The "formulations which carry [this thought] constitute the unifying grip of the philosopher's potential *Existenz,* with its impulse to communication."[105]

The threefold function of universality[106] and objectivity, with which thought that enlightens *Existenz* — like all thought — remains bound up at every step, may also be shown in this chapter:

1) Moving to the limit (or boundary): We recall Jaspers' sharp distinction between ultimate situations and situations in general.

2) Objectification in psychological, logical, and metaphysical language: here we shall merely point once more to the possibility of misinterpreting thought which illuminates *Existenz* as mere psychology. Although it is true that *Existenz* cannot be understood psychologically, it is equally true that *Existenz* becomes clear to itself only in what is understandable, and realizes its own non-understandability only in a maximum of understandability.[107] On the other hand, all *inadequate* reactions to ultimate situations are psychologically comprehensible. And here in particular, in his inexorable exposure of "apparent solutions," "deviations," "false concealments," and "possibilities of escape," in *all* ultimate situations, Jaspers reveals himself as a master of the "psychology of unmasking." Indeed, in our systematic presentation of this chapter we might very well have indicated the danger of false reactions as a sixth pervasive leading idea.

3) The invention of a specific universal for the illumination of *Existenz:* words like *"Existenz"* and "ultimate situation," are *signa,* indices, which do not point directly to the reality of existence (although as words they are derived from the latter), but point, on the basis of this reality, to *'existential'* reality, and hence, like the psychological categories employed in language which illuminates *Existenz,* they can be understood only by a potential *Existenz.* Only in the latter do they find an answering echo and "a wholly personal fulfillment."

Thus the forms of the universal, which are used as media by any illumination of *Existenz* at every stage of thought, can be exhibited. However, we cannot indicate how, by a combination of single steps, the philosopher can *'existentially'* "charge" a self-contained train of thought so as to generate an *'existential'* "potential," from which a spark may leap into the soul of the adequately prepared reader. At most we can indicate certain specific pre-

---

[104] *Philosophie,* 303.   [105] *Ibid.,* 303f. On *'existential'* communication see 338ff.
[106] *Ibid.,* 304.   [107] *Ibid.,* 305.

requisites on the part of the philosopher: a steady gaze, a sensitive ear for the reader who is his potential partner in the illumination of *Existenz,* and whose possible mode of reaction must be sensed, as well as an unusual awareness and the most rigorous discipline, combined with uncommonly pliable and elastic thought. Furthermore — indeed, above all — he must have his own spontaneous originality.[108]

3) *The Problem of the Appropriation of Jaspers' Illumination of Existenz*

Here we may be brief. We are not concerned once more to point out possible misunderstandings. Our question was formulated at the very beginning: How can anyone else help me in my self-realization, since I do not wish to become *himself,* nor yet a *self-as-such,* but precisely *myself?*

The co-enactment on the part of the reader of trains of thought which illuminate *Existenz* is merely an *analogue* of *'existential'* communication. As in the case of the latter when it is successful, it is the case here too that two persons do not become a self as such *together,* but each one becomes *himself.* And here we see that the dependence of thought which illuminates *Existenz* upon a universal, objective language has its *positive* aspect as well.

The person who does the original philosophizing cannot force the primordially personal process of becoming himself upon another directly. He must *translate* the *'existential'* event which is

108 This explains why it is so difficult, if not impossible, to imitate Jaspers' performance of thought as an illumination of *Existenz* — difficult even to re-enact this thought in a genuine way, especially in the case of the illumination of ultimate situations. Awareness can interfere with the *'existential'* experience as well as intensify it, and the danger of interference is much greater here than in the case of the original illumination. Anyone who re-enacts the illumination of ultimate situations must ask himself, at every moment, whether he still has the "right to philosophize" of which Jaspers speaks in *Von der Wahrheit* (1046): whether his (anticipatory) insight into the fragmentariness of all existence does not after all merely intensify his impulse toward unconditional realization in this same existence. He will have to be sensitive to the danger of premature anticipations as well as to that of going beyond himself; he will have to take heart what Jaspers says *(Philosophie,* 415ff) about everyday activities as a "preparation for and broadening of *historical Existenz."* The mere re-enactment of trains of thought which illuminate *Existenz* becomes authentically fruitful only when what has been read has long been *"creatively forgotten,"* that is, so deeply transformed into my own essence that I find my way in the concrete situation by means of my own original and spontaneous philosophizing. The task of "illumination of *Existenz"* would be complete only "after it had made itself superflous; when everything that it teaches had been 'creatively forgotten' again, that is, when one no longer *talked* about *Existenz,* but simply *existed* in a straightforward and self-evident way." (E. Latzel, "Bemerkungen zum Umgang mit Existenzphilosophie," *Zeitschrift für philos. Forschung,* VI, 410). Concerning "creative forgetting" cf. W. Metzger, *Die Grundlagen der Erziehung zu schöpferischer Freiheit* (Frankfurt am Main, 1949), and G. Pfahler, *Der Mensch und seine Vergangenheit* (Stuttgart, 1950).

taking place in him into a universal language, if he is to make himself universally intelligible. In this universal language, if it is successful, what is most personal in the philosopher literally vibrates along. The reader, on his part, must *retranslate* this universal language into the primordially personal process of becoming himself

Thus, where there is a genuine illumination of *Existenz,* the potential *Existenz* of the philosopher may kindle the potential *Existenz* of the one who thinks with him, transmitting to the latter the impulse to become himself. But the distance between them remains. That which is primordially personal is not touched, precisely because no human being can simply transfer his inmost experience to another, but can only appeal to the other's own primordial *'existential'* potentialities. Illumination of *Existenz* cannot create or transfer life; it works as a catalyst, arousing, releasing, enlivening, setting in motion my inherent *'existential'* potentialities.

Jaspers himself says that his thought which illuminates *Existenz* is universally intelligible, but only for potential *Existenz*.[109] This statement must be further qualified if it is to be understood correctly.

Only human beings "who share the same potentialities of fulfillment of being are able to say to one another what could not anywhere else be heard."[110] At just this point, where the historical restriction of philosophizing itself is discussed, we see the limitation, but, at the same time also the strength of Jaspers' philosophy of the illumination of *Existenz,* which is aware of this limitation and affirms it.

Not all human beings have the same potentiality for fulfillment of being. In the first volume of his *Philosophische Logik (Von der Wahrheit),* Jaspers describes a fundamental human attitude for which there is *no* ultimate situation. In this passage Jaspers' language regains the plastic power of direct portrayal which we admire in his *Psychologie der Weltanschauungen.* These passages are so important for us, who are hearing Jaspers say so much about the *'existential'* fruitfulness, indeed, the *'existential'* necessity of ultimate situations, that we may be permitted to reproduce them here.

Out of our experience of ultimate situations — in the shatteredness of being — we are seized from time to time by a longing for the tranquility of man in a world that protects him. The failure to see ultimate

109 *Ibid.,* 308.   110 *Philosophie,* VI (foreword)

situations does not appear to us in such moments as a lack; it seems rather like a heavenly happiness which we have lost. What for us would be an escape into untruthfulness was at one time truth beyond question.

It is evident that the world is an enduring order; this order is eternal Being, and this Being is the corporeal presence of heaven and earth, and of man within them. Man knows himself to be safe within this order. Violations of this order are isolated and transient disturbances which can be restored to order again. Guilt, being avoidable and expiable, calls forth only a temporary and limited disorder. There is no despair. Man lives solidly in a solid and substantial reality. The world is not distinct from Transcendence. The divine is present, and what is present is divine. Order is both sensory and supersensory. Indeed, such distinctions are not yet made, since the tensions of a different fundamental experience, which might generate them, are lacking.

The human being who appears in such an unquestioning state has a dignity of his own. He attains the high realization of a formed existence, of beautiful bearing of an ardent life. The turbulence of the instincts is disorderly, but it is still natural. Of course, uninhibited individuals, who destroy the order, occasionally appear, but even they remain bound, in the general view, to this order. The individual, from his place of safety in this encompassing order, is capable of heroic courage. He is able to die calmly, to develop a pure, childlike, unaffected humanity. His lament, though moving, is innocent of accusation. Although he is without experience of the all-shattering ultimate situations, he can suffer deeply. But even in his lament there is an endurance of suffering which is contented and tranquil. His innermost oneness with the course of things, a course which is eternally and basically ordered and moves in endless cycles, holds his affirmation of being upright.

This fundamental attitude is closely approximated by life in pre-Buddhist China, the records of which give us a glimpse of the incomparable magic of a life without tragedy. A happiness which is not at all superficial speaks to us from this world, a world which was as full as any other of actual suffering.[111]

Our long quotation is a testimony to the inner breadth of Jaspers' thought — a breadth which has been increasing since the *Psychologie* — and to the impartiality and profound sympathy with which he approaches even what is inwardly remote from him. He sees in it, not his own truth, but another truth. At the same time, this passage is evidence of the extreme honesty of Jaspers' self-awareness, which is perhaps his greatest strength.

We shall leave the question open as to whether a true and full life is possible today without a complete experience of ultimate

---

111 *Wahrheit*, 879f.

situations. But even after experiencing ultimate situations, not everyone will recognize himself in the same way in *Existenz*-illuminating thought.

Everyone will have to relate his own experiences to such thought. And, he will appropriate it in himself in accordance with his own human substance and his achieved inner maturity.[112] Much he will not begin to see clearly until very late and much, perhaps, never. Perhaps he will inwardly oppose many of these things — and their particular formulations — in a decisive way. He may think that there is too much talk of "awakening:" "philosophy as a means of arousing people"! Perhaps he will forbid himself any repeated reading of particular passages, fearing for his own impartiality. In the chapter on ultimate situations there are particular passages which seem questionable when re-enacted by the reader. Perhaps many people will accept this kind of thought once, in order later to assert their own independent position over against it. And, perhaps, that in itself is the decisive test of the inner truth of this thought, the decisive test even for those who re-enact it: whether this *Existenz*-illuminating kind of think--ing succeeds in placing the reader at a critical distance *even from itself.*

Each chapter of Karl Jaspers' *Philosophie* is intended to represent "the whole in smaller form, but at any given time one chapter leaves dark what will be illuminated only by the rest." We have attempted to understand one chapter, in its planned inner unity, and on its own merits,[113] and thus to exhibit the meaning and method of thought as the illumination of *Existenz.*

EDWIN LATZEL

THE LIBRARY
UNIVERSITÄT BAMBERG
BAMBERG, BAVARIA, GERMANY

112 Cf. note 108.

113 We have deliberately refrained from expanding our treatment of ultimate situations to include other works (the subject indices of *Philosophie* and *Von der Wahrheit* provide convenient references to the relevant passages) — but cf. footnote 100. This restriction seemed reasonable. Many expositors and critics of Jaspers' philosophy are weak because they are not conscious of *missing* the point of his philosophizing when they bring together all the discussions of a given subject without regard for the special *function* of the particular discussions in their special contexts. Let us state emphatically that the idea of ultimate situation first demonstrates its full depth and fruitfulness in the third book of the *Philosophie* — the *Metaphysics.* This idea was first disclosed to us through our appropriation, that is, real re-enactment, of Chapter III ("Existential Relations to Transcendence," 736ff) and the fourth (and last) part of Ch. IV of the *Metaphysics* ("The Passing away of Existence and *Existenz* as a Decisive Cipher of Transcendence," 863ff). The first volume

of the *Philosophische Logik (Von der Wahrheit)* justifies the result of the illumination of reality negatively, by reference to ultimate situations. "Only through the latter is there movement, in which that which originally inspired me, the affirmation of being, may perhaps finally appear as free of deception." (872) The original intuition of the young Jaspers becomes fruitful once again, in a new way, in his interpretation of the tragic *(Tragedy,* 23f).

The literature on our theme has grown to almost unmanageable proportions; we shall single out only four works:

Gabriel Marcel: "Situation fondamentale et situation-limite chez Karl Jaspers." In: *Du Refus a l'Invocation.* (Paris, 1948)

M. Dufrenne et P. Ricoeur: *Karl Jaspers et la Philosophie de l'existence* (Paris, 1947), (see especially: "Situations-limites et historicité," 173ff).

P. Ricoeur: *Gabriel Marcel et Karl Jaspers* (Paris, 1948), (see especially: "Les situations-limites" 122ff).

B. Welte: "Der philosophische Glaube bei Karl Jaspers und die Möglichkeit seiner Deutung durch die thomistische Philosophie." In a symposium, *Jb.f. Philos.* Bd.2. (Freiburg i.Br. 1949).

5

Fritz Kaufmann

KARL JASPERS AND A PHILOSOPHY OF COMMUNICATION

SYNOPSIS

210

KARL JASPERS AND A PHILOSOPHY OF COMMUNICATION

A. Report

I

THE PROBLEM of communication towers over Jaspers' philosophy, because it has stamped its mark on his own past life, and because the future of mankind will depend on its effective solution.

The historical timeliness of the problem needs no discussion. In a world interdependent as it never was, and torn by strife as never before, the "absolute will to communication," including the honest and patient negotiation of even the most rending differences, has become a question of life or death. "In today's misery we have learned to recognize the crucial claim which communication has upon us." This is the note on which *The Perennial Scope of Philosophy* concludes.

But the central position of this problem in Jaspers' work bears witness not only to his sense of historical responsibility as a thinker; it is also the expression of an urge which pressed upon him since his youth.

"Having its source in the solitude of self-communication, the search for truth pushes toward communication with others."[1] This is, on Jaspers' part, not merely an objective statement. It is the formulation of an inmost experience. It has both philosophical and autobiographical relevance. It marks one of those points where private matter issues in the realm of the personal, and the personal becomes the soul of philosophical theory.

Existentialist and particularly *'existential'* philosophy[2] suggests more than others do this type of intimate relation between a man's doings and his writings and makes their discrepancy a particularly

---

[1] *Wahrheit*, 644.

[2] Jaspers' philosophy is both — or, rather, it is prior to either alternative: an analysis of existence which is, at the same time, an *'existential'* expression. It repudiates, therefore, an ontology which abstracts from the ontic ties and fetters of human life.

grievous event. On the other hand (and much as this fact has been sinned against, for instance in the Kierkegaard interpretation), no philosophy can be understood in its positive meaning and not only in its shortcomings, and in the treatment of its problems as well as in their selection, by mere reference to the private predicaments of its author.

This does not exclude the mood in which a question is asked in life from being reflected by the tenor in which the philosophical answer appears. The very fact that communication is introduced by Jaspers as a break-through of individual solitude echoes a longing for it which actually haunted him even as a high-school boy and gave him early that experience of human finitude and of the cleavage of Being that was to pervade his whole philosophy.[3]

It was an authentic experience of lonely limitation — different from the knowledge of the factual finiteness of life in time (Locke), from the recognition of the finite intellect's dependence on the world of the things-in-themselves and their affection (Kant), etc. Although Jaspers is inclined to see in it a result of and reaction to the unauthentic and conforming life of the middle classes in the German empire around 1900, it will not be awry to attribute this incommunicado attitude also to the Northern and German temper within and around him — to inhibitions such as those of the North German figures in Thomas Mann. Conversely, this temper serves as the sounding-board for the single voices to which he himself can respond in the polyphony of human life. He selects as his peers, above all, writers such as Plato, Kant, Kierkegaard, Nietzsche and, in his own Heidelberg, Max Weber. Max Weber was to Jaspers "*the* philosopher," the paragon of "human greatness." He — and he almost alone — "faced the agony of our time, diagnosed it on the strength of his comprehensive knowledge and, in a decaying world, rooted himself in his own ground."[4]

He rooted himself in himself. The miracle and blessing of human communication is so great an event just because it is bound up with the process of personal emancipation and is, thus, in its climactic mood a beckoning from peak to peak of existence:

> massed around us arise
> the summits of time;
> and, neighbors, dwell, yet exhausted the dear ones
> on the most separate peaks.[5]

For Jaspers the truest, most intimate communication has this para-

3 Cf. *Rechenschaft*, 323f; *Wahrheit*, 387f; *Scope*, 62f.

4 *Rechenschaft*, 329f, 340; *Philosophie* I, viiif.

5 From Hoelderlin's ode *Patmos*.

doxical feature about it: that it respects, emphasizes and intensifies the differences between one existence and the other, instead of dwarfing, slurring and hiding them, as is the rule in the anonymity of average life. Hence, *'existential'* contact is an unforeseeable occurrence and, as it were, a gift of grace. Its experience seems contingent to us who know the whole of Being only in its divisions, and to whom a true community of persons rests on the insularity of Selves. There is no genuine solidarity in the mode of the "We" except to those who are entitled to say "I," to endure the harshness of selfhood, subscribe to the *principium individuationis* and respect the distance of even the closest friend. Such contact in which each Self holds, reveals and cultivates its own ground — such contact is always the delicate child of the favorable moment—the καιρός; it is always meeting and encounter at once—a "loving struggle" between Self and Self and for their mutual manifestation, in contrast with, and transfiguration of, the selfish struggle and competition in the flatlands of 'common' life.

Conversely, since our God, being God, is also the God of our enemies, there ought to prevail — just as in the *Bhagavadgītā* — even in the *hostile* struggle of fated antagonists, the recognition of the common ground from which all existences originate. Such tragic conflict should be fought out in a spirit which does not exclude all possibility of a positive contact and communication at some time later[6] — a postulate which echoes articles in the *political* philosophies of Grotius, Kant, *et al.*

All genuine communication is in a kind of restless Heraclitean flux. Each moment is unique, not to be arrested and not repeatable. It is the fleeting contact of two poles whose polarity cannot be eradicated without annihilating the very possibility of communication. It takes place between Selves

> which move toward each other out of their solitude, although it is just on account of their communication that they know of their solitude. . . . In all suspense of solitude by virtue of communication, there grows a new solitude which cannot disappear without my ceasing to exist as a condition of such communication.[7]

There is no *'existential'* relationship without duality of the related partners; and no duality without some degree of dualism between two Selves either one of whom realizes and validates his

---

6 *Wahrheit*, 318f, 667, 977f.

7 *Philosophie* II,61. It must be added, however, that the delicacy of *'existential'* relationships does not exclude either the continuity of a life in which a Self has chosen itself together with the other, or the solidarity of an interplay in which either partner can live faithful to the other just because he lives faithful to himself.

own individual selfhood in this process of communication. To be sure, all communication points and strives beyond itself toward a perfect union in "sublime moments" which have the quality of the eternal; but they do not last, or else they prove illusory in time.[8]

The ultimate solitude of the Self is thus confirmed rather than suspended in the solitariness of the "festive night of communion" *(die hohe Nacht. . . , die einsam war, obwohl die Nacht des Bunds.)*[9] All this preserves and synthesizes the decisive experiences of Jaspers' youth.[10]

It countenances the absolute will to communication in unity with, and as the very action of, achieving selfhood. "The possibilities of communication (thus) become the principal question of man as he makes his way toward himself."[11]

II

Social contact, not contract. A pressureless touch of ardent, yet restrained powers,[12] a drawing of *Existenz* toward *Existenz* rather than a being together and sharing life in life's outer institutions and expressions. True co-*Existenz* in the consummation of face-to-face relationships is no less intensive and forceful for being unobtrusive, a model of non-violence.

This is the spiritual intensity of an *'existential'* dialogue such as pictured in the penetrating look by which, for instance, the apostles and prophets on the chancel walls of the Bamberg cathedral are interlocked in their mighty disputations; as it occurs at the height of a discussion about mankind's great objectives, man's ultimate concern in Shakespeare's *Measure for Measure* and in Dostoevski's and Thomas Mann's philosophical novels, or (to choose just one factual example from recent intellectual history) as it was alive in the highly charged controversy between Eugen Rosenstock and Franz Rosenzweig in 1913 and '16; "much to their own surprise the two partners found themselves reluctantly put under the compulsion to face up to one another in a struggle with no quarter to be given or asked for." "For only in this last extremity of a soul

8 *Wahrheit,* 380.

9 R. M. Rilke, *Briefwechsel in Gedichten mit Erika Mitterer,* 43.

10 Hence the autobiographical flavor of such analyses as in *Philosophie* II, 59,73, *et passim.*

11 *Rechenschaft,* 256.

12 Cf. R. M. Rilke, the last section of the second of the *Elegies of Duino.*

in self-defense is there hope to realize the truth in the questions of life."[13]

Whereas the face-to-face relationship will not always be of this nearly convulsive tension, it will always need a vigorous impulse to break through the conventionalities of appearance and overcome the inhibitions that work against one's baring his soul to himself as well as to others. Beyond the tragedies of passion and disillusion, the human drama may thus reach an elevation and a composure which allow men to meet freely as members of a great family. Not similar as particular samples of human types, but related as free and individual partners in the interplay of mankind, they may celebrate a holy day, as it were, of human brotherhood. This is what happens in Lessing's philosophical play, *Nathan the Wise*, which to Jaspers is full of God in its "unfathomable sadness and its smiling calm."[14]

This pure fulfillment of true interpersonal *Existenz* hovers over the abysses of human life — over all the deviations from truth by way of appearances and affectations, all the necessary and lazy compromises, all the handicaps and breakdowns of *'existential'* intercourse which are due to the general and individual limitations of language, to callousness or timidity, bad conscience and bad will, suspicion and prejudice, egotism and disappointment, over all the excommunications due to tribal hatred, but also over all the perversions of communication in idle talk, trickery and lie, all the pseudo-communication in the medium of sentimental and diluted ideologies — such as the protestations of love for humanity where there is no love for one's neighbor.[15]

The positive and deficient modes of communicative life — on the levels of mere existence *(Dasein)*, consciousness-as-such, spirit in the medium and order of ideas, *Existenz* in the realization of the Self — these modes are carefully listed and examined in Jaspers' works. He acts with the eagerness of the *'existential'* thinker, attentive to the possibilities, painfully aware of the dangers and restrictions of man, *every* man; with the mild and circumspect knowledge of a physician of the soul; with that uncanny refinement that penetrates into the most hidden secrets and all the different strata, structures and powers of the inner man — with a perspicacity that has grown in the school of Kierkegaard and Nietzsche.

[13] Eugen Rosenstock in the Introductions to this correspondence, Franz Rosenzweig, *Briefe*, 638. Cf. *Philosophie* II, 66, 116; *Wahrheit*, 48.

[14] Cf. *Wahrheit*, 951, *Tragedy*, 86.

[15] Cf., e.g., *Philosophie* I,16; II, 59f, 81ff; *Wahrheit*, 428f, 543ff, 566ff, 661ff, 983ff; *Rechenschaft*, 350.

It must be confessed that, to the reader, this method has its dark as well as its bright sides. The patient way in which Jaspers accumulates a superabundance of observations, the way he surveys at each point each and every possibility, sometimes taxes the patience of the reader who loses sight of the woods for the trees. Jaspers' force, but also his apparent weakness, is in a mosaic style of agglomerating marvelous details in an often superb phrasing, full of a mellowed wisdom which is quite beyond compare in today's literature. Yet he proceeds without the artistic *mise en scene* which contributes to making Kierkegaard a breath-taking experience, and without the dramatic and aggressive verve of the baroque yet forceful diction of a Heidegger — so much his inferior not in intensity, but in prudence, originality, and true unity of thought.

The lack of stirring effects is the price Jaspers chose to pay for speaking from the depth of incommensurable *Existenz* to the depth of free *Existenz* in his readers, appealing to their self-concern rather than to their compliance with the author. To his whole philosophy, to philosophical communication as he understands and wills it, applies what he says with regard to a specific issue and to the objection that its treatment leaves the reader without anything to hold on to: "This form of discussion cannot be avoided if one wants to reach what is at stake in philosophy. Such discussions shall not result in obtaining and securing objective knowledge about a phenomenon, but rather help to open our soul more widely to the possible." The possible is in this case the possibility of the Kierkegaardian "exception." The very exception to the rule shows "what man can be," omnipresent as it is in all possible *Existenz*. It is no object of unambiguous appearance and knowledge. Still, "if I were to renounce this *docta ignorantia,* I would evacuate a domain of truth in which all other truth has still to present itself for me to verify itself in its true substance."[16]

III

We must stop at this point for some needed elaboration. To be sure, such an exposition cannot be complete. Within the scope of this particular essay, we cannot reproduce the whole network of communicative relations, their extent and their limits and, thus, practically the articulation of Jaspers' philosophy of *Existenz*. The problem of communication brings out, indeed, the problematic nature of human life as such, both in its defaults and in its essential limitations. It is the mainspring of Jaspers' anxious inquiry.

16 *Wahrheit,* 758ff.

"The experience of the shortcomings of communication engenders the mood of the philosophical enterprise."[17]

Communication thus becomes the cornerstone as well as the stumbling block of this type of existentialism. It is a necessary problem — *not-wendig*, 'meeting a need' in the sense of 'necessary' which Nietzsche liked to play with; even where a problem cannot be solved without a remainder, we are helped by facing and recognizing it in its inevitability.

I restrict myself now to this insoluble aspect of the problem. It is caused by the non-objective status of the two correlative, yet antipodean, terms: *'Existenz'* in Kierkegaard's nomenclature and *'Transcendence'* proper in Jaspers' sense.[18] In this strict and ultimate sense 'Transcendence' combines the meaning of the Kantian concept — 'that which is beyond the scope of human knowledge' — with the religious overtones and the forbidding ring of the *totaliter aliter* of dialectical theology: that tremendous mystery of the one ground of Being which defies the grasp of "intentional consciousness"; that rock of absolute Being which gives no direct answer to our questions, but is like the voice of silence itself; the fixed star of Being in the night of *Existenz*.[19]

Transcendence speaks in its very silence. But it speaks only to *Existenz*[20], to the free and attentive listening on the part of reason, i.e., the unobstructed *Vernehmen der Vernunft* (to employ the German expression in which, following the supranatural sensualism of Hamann, Herder and Jacobi, Jaspers profits from the peculiar wisdom of his native language).[21] Transcendence "speaks" in a not really and truly communicable way to absolute consciousness. It uses the cipher of some particular phenomenon in its overwhelming presence — such as the spreading of the heron's white wings against the blue sky in the decisive youth experience that is reported of Ramakrishna.

But this example is not taken from Jaspers and the sphere of personal co-*Existenz*, which he prefers. To him, revelation, the

---

17 *Rechenschaft*, 351.   18 Cf. *Wahrheit*, 108ff.

19 All these metaphors are used to circumscribe an experience which cannot be communicated directly. Besides using Jaspers' own evocative language, they borrow from certain significant passages in Thomas Mann's writings. This is done to show the free convergence between the metaphysician and the artist as mouthpieces of the, perhaps, most intense experience of their generation. (Cp. *Philosophie* III, 219ff, with *Joseph der Ernährer*, 382, and *Doktor Faustus*, 285, 745). The same could be done with reference to R. M. Rilke where the Angels symbolize a similar transcendence; cf. also Rilke, III, 399: *"Nichts ist so stumm / wie eines Gottes Mund"* ("nothing as mute / as of a god the mouth.")

20 Cf. *Wahrheit*, 110.   21 Cf., e.g., *Wahrheit*, 115.

incomprehensible and, therefore, ineffable presence of Transcendence, is a unique event which happens to a man in a single hour of human history and historical awareness.[22] Human language communicates but an echo of this absolute experience in the mythical accounts of religion and art and the speculative accounts of metaphysics.[23]

What really happens to *Existenz* in these experiences is the Icarus flight of reason into the sun of ultimate reality — the assurance and recognition of that unfathomable unity which transcends the unifying efforts of reason just as reason itself transcends the data and spheres of particular objects. Yet death is swallowed up in victory. Facing the eminent presence of the transcendent One and surrendering to it, man is granted in return that freedom of *Existenz* in which he grows beyond the conditions of his natural and historical worlds.[24]

It is, nevertheless, within the medium of his world that he grows beyond it, fulfills his mission and delivers his message. Although his work in the world is, on the one hand, nothing but the daily new fee he cannot help paying to the needs and claims of life in the flesh, it is also sanctioned as the avenue of communication in the co-*Existenz* of man with man, Self with Self.[25]

But, as the world ceases to be man's ultimate concern, as he ceases to cling to it and his position in it, it loses the pressure of its weighing on him and is reduced to appearance, seen as it were from afar and studied like a cryptogram. To use the favorite term Jaspers may have adopted from J. G. Hamann: man sees in the books of nature and history the "ciphers" of Being, whose presence they announce, but whose nature they do not disclose — incommunicative as it is in this very communication. Or rather — in a way such as followed out in Talmud-discussions and lately by Kafka in the analysis of his own parables — infinite meanings suggest themselves since no definite reading of the ciphers can be established. One reading leads to the other, and one confirms the other insofar as the truth of the cipher does not lie in anything

---

[22] *Wahrheit*, 693.   [23] Cf. *Philosophie*, III, 129ff.   [24] Cf. *Wahrheit*, 104ff.

[25] The emphasis on the ultimate validity of *Existenz* and co-*Existenz* of individual Selves constitutes the decisive difference between Jaspers' teachings and those of śaṁkara as well as the *Bhagavadgītā*. Jaspers' way of having reality transfigured into the appearance of Transcendence is often reminiscent of the Hindu doctrine. But, whereas Jaspers confesses to the unity of absolute Transcendence (what the Hindus may call the nirguna Brahman), he sticks to the plurality of Selves (instead of the oneness of Atman). Hence he cannot fully subscribe to the identity between Brahman and Atman. Even though everything may originate from the same common ground, the individual Self is more than the role which the person plays on the stage of this world — and, still, it is not, ultimately, the Absolute 'in person.'

apart from it but rather in the unambiguous, absolute presence which asserts itself in each attempt to penetrate into its nature. The manifest mystery of Transcendence is there — not to be dispelled, but to be enhanced in the spirit of devotion and full absorption. The cipher *is* the presence of the transcendent and the transcendence of the present.[26]

"Transcendence is not an object of (rational) proof, but one of witness."[27] It is both infinitely close to *Existenz* and infinitely distant from it. True *Existenz* is defined by its orientation toward Being *qua* Transcendence, the intimate awareness of its distance. This is done as early as in Plato — "left to herself the soul strives toward and reaches contact with true Being" — and has found its Christian sanction and version in the Augustinian tradition and recently, above all, in Kierkegaard. Still, there is a century and, literally, a *'world'* between Kierkegaard's thesis: "The measure" (not of *man,* as in Plato, but) "of the *Self* is God" and Jaspers' saying: "The depth of my Self has its measure in the Transcendence before which I stand."[28]

It belongs to Jaspers' Christian heritage that this stand will differ with each individual. No Self is exchangeable, none expendable in the economy of the whole. Each has to stand its own ground as it approaches and is approached by the All-Encompassing. Since there is no common platform on which the different Selves communicate — apart from the unity of Transcendence by which they are encompassed, their communication will be both needful and painful. Even the absolute will to communicate cannot but recognize the radical differences amongst the various modes of being and the still more profound separation of one Self from the other in the very act of communicating which frees each Self for itself.

In his interpretation of the Abraham-Isaac story, Kierkegaard emphasizes the impossibility of communicating in general and rational terms what is said to the 'single one,' to each individual one in a singular way. Hence each *individuum est ineffabile:* no

26 Cf. *Philosophie* III, 144ff; *Wahrheit,* 896, 1030ff.

27 *Philosophie* III, 204: *"Die Transzendenz wird nicht bewiesen, sondern von ihr wird gezeugt."*

28 Cf. Plato, *Phaedo,* 65f, 79D; Kierkegaard, *The Sickness unto Death* (transl. by W. Lowrie), 126ff: "Gradations in the consciousness of the Self (The Qualification "before God")." Cf. *op. cit.* also: "By relating itself to its own self and by willing to be itself, the self is grounded transparently in the Power which constituted it." A note in Kierkegaard's *Journal* of 1854 — E.P. IX, p. 240 — makes no sense in Dru's translation, p. 532. It should read: "The *Existenz* of a Christian is contact with Being." As to Jaspers, see *Philosophie* II, 49; also *Wahrheit,* 541ff, 49, 104ff, 175, 631ff, 639ff, 677, 1054 *et passim; Scope,* 17, 64f, 70ff.

objective statement can ever convey the full truth about it and its calling.[29] This fact *cannot* be reduced to the incompleteness of all knowledge in the continuity of the process of scientific experience. It belongs to a different dimension of problems: *Existenz* is no object of objective determination; *'existential'* revelation of the Self, however incomplete, is qualitatively different from, and superior to, any appearance; and *'existential'* truth is not a discovery of independent facts, but part and parcel of truthful *Existenz,* its recovery and performance. Hence the Self may be compared — *cum grano salis* — with Kant's intelligible Ego which is alive as the source of free actions although we *know* only of the appearances it makes on the stage of time and space.

The Self has its original being, its true actuality, only in what cannot be stated as an objective event: in acts which cannot be accounted for in a causal way, but in which it accounts for itself — responsive and responsible acts in which the Self is actualized by choosing both itself and the Thou which it addresses, and whose claims it fulfills in its own way, in a devotion in which it finds its own fulfillment.[30]

The language of such productive and mutual communication is more eloquent than words may ever be. Communication may be *crowned* by silence just as well as it can *die* in it.[31] But it is never a communication which is objectively secured like that of two vessels through which the same water is channeled. Even in the case of the most intimate relationship and the most reliable solidarity it resembles less such a lasting status than the flashing of sparks from one pole of a battery to the other.[32]

The precariousness of this relationship on the level of growing selfhood — not in the gregariousness of animal life or in the common fronts of the objective mind and in the fight for common causes — this lasting discontinuity between I and Thou in the midst of their impassioned struggle for one another, may tempt men to discontinue their relations altogether in a mood of despair or defiance.[33]

But such tendencies are counteracted not only by the pathological longing for close community, but above all by the resoluteness of the will to total communication — a will to unity in co-*Existenz,* pervaded, sustained and directed, perhaps, by the unity of the all-encompassing Being.[34] Even in the case of what, with Kierkegaard

---

[29] Cf. already *Psychologie*, 358ff.   [30] Cf., e.g., *Philosophie* II, 19ff., 182f.
[31] Cf. *Philosophie* II, 74ff; *Wahrheit*, 416, 982.
[32] Cf., e.g., *Philosophie* II, 62.   [33] Cf. *Philosophie* II, 81ff; *Wahrheit*, 983f.
[34] Cf. *Philosophie* III, 122ff; *Wahrheit*, 114ff, 321, 378, 971ff; *Scope*, 44ff.

and Nietzsche, Jaspers calls "the exception" — i.e., the man in whom singularity and loneliness have become so intensive as to exclude him from all others and effect a sort of ex-communication, even in the case of the man who writes 'white papers' in "invisible ink" — even there the enforced silence is interrupted again and again by outbreaks from solitary confinement, by passionate outcries to God and man or by the more artful contrivances of indirect communication.[35]

But even under the most favorable conditions, my meeting and community with other Selves, above all with my 'predestined' *alter ego*,[36] is as it were a gift of grace (a *gratia cooperans*) and constitutes the secret of an invisible church. There is a realm of the spirit. But "the idea of a realm of *Existenzen* as a *totality*, with me as one of its accredited members, is unfounded, if this idea pretends to be objective knowledge."[37]

Co-*Existenz* has its enactment and actuality not in terms of the world, not in a re-public of life interests, activities and institutions, in a cosmos of the objective mind, in any universal organization. It is not manifest in any embodiment as such. This does not free us from our social obligations in this world. '*Existential*' community is not a matter of management.[38] Still, the right growth of the social body may prove indispensable to true co-*Existenz* as the work of the soul, to the realization of Selves in historical community and the consolidation of the "absolute will to communication" amongst men of all classes and races.[39]

The realm of communication is thus the middle realm that stretches between *Existenz* and Transcendence. It is the human 'world' of '*existential*' relations. In it communication — boundless communication — appears as a postulate and perennial task. This claim is endorsed by an absolute will to communicate; and it is validated both by the common ground in which all *Existenzen* are rooted and by their common direction toward truth — the one truth in its different realizations, in the different ciphers and cipher-readings through which it speaks to and through different human beings.[40]

---

[35] *Wahrheit*, 748ff.   [36] Cf. *Philosophie* II, 70ff.

[37] *Philosophie* II, 420. Cf. *Origin*, 228; *Wahrheit*, 741; *Age*, 222ff.

[38] Jaspers' religious individualism is liable to overdo the objections to world organization and total planning and join ranks with 'liberals' who may have become the mouthpiece of powers with which he would hardly sympathize: cf. *Philosophie* II, 366; *Age, passim.; Origin*, 180ff, 281ff.

[39] Cf. *Philosophie* II, 69, 91ff, 426ff; *Wahrheit*, 615f, 965f; *Origin*, 269f.

[40] Cf., e.g., *Philosophie* II, 417ff, 427, 434; *Wahrheit*, 951; *Tragedy*, 87.

It must be added, however, that the scope of communication does not reach any farther than the need for it, i.e., not beyond the realm of existence and *Existenz*. "Communication presupposes the partition" (of the One) "into the many."[41] The One may serve as the ultimate warrant and locus of communication, but it does not enter it as a partner. It is not a unit of being which transcends towards others; it is unity and transcendence as such, all-encompassing, rounded off in itself and self-sufficient — not in need of the approach of communication, whose necessity marks in itself a defect. Whereas Transcendence proper rests in itself, all other transcendence, every going beyond the particular, is ultimately transcendence toward the One which may direct our intentions and is thus intimately present, but can never be reached and is thus infinitely far away. "Communication is the organ through which in time we turn back toward the One."[42]

Our place is within the schism of being; our end is unity, but our way is union. It is unification through reason as the executive of the absolute will to communication. Reason *is* not unity, it is the restless search for the One in which everything comes to rest.[43] The movement of the *logos,* therefore, the synthesis of communication, is stilled in and by that unity of Being toward which we strive. Reason itself, *logos* as rational account, is an upward way, a process of synthesis rather than a finished system. "It is a delight for each spirit continuously to ascend toward the principle of life, however inaccessible it may prove. . . . Hence it comes to pass that the inaccessibility or incomprehensibility of the infinitude of His life is the most highly desired comprehension."[44]

All transcendental use of the logical categories, all attempts to submit Transcendence to the judgment of the finite are overstepping the bounds of rational communication. To Jaspers, even the sublime tautology of the *Eheye asher Eheye,* the *Sum qui Sum* ("I am that I am") is, in the use of the first person, as inadequate an expression of the All-Encompassing as is the *Est quod Est* (the Being *qua* Being) in the Greek tradition from Parmenides to Plotinus. The categories creep even into this final tautology,

---

41 *Wahrheit,* 380.   42 *Wahrheit,* 381; cf. 387.   43 Cf. *Wahrheit,* 114ff, 118.

44 Nicolaus Cusanus, *Idiota de Sapientia,* liber I: in Nicolaus von Cues, *Philosophische Schriften* I (Stuttgart, 1949), 304f. Cf. *Philosophie* III, 125f: "The despair at the nothingness of human life dissolves in the ascent. This that the Being of the One actually *is,* that is enough. What I am — I, whose being vanishes without remainder, — that is of little account, if only I persist in the ascent as long as I live." In the tenor and teaching of "learned ignorance," in the theory of the "complication in God" as the incomprehensible Encompassing, etc., Nicolaus is one of Jaspers' most important spiritual ancestors.

whether it is pronounced in the mode of being an object ("it") or in that of a subject ("I")[45] — whereas Transcendence proper thrones above the difference and the contrast between subject and object and, is, thus, beyond the grasp of human understanding, not to be couched in the terms of human language and communication. God is Being itself (*ipsum esse*) without any subjective admixture by way of human apprehension. That is why he is the *Being that is* when man fades away."[46]

But whereas in the literal sense there is no 'communication' between divine Transcendence and human *Existenz*, which would explicitly let us know God and secure his assistance, we are assured of his presence in the act of our personal ascent: by the spur and directive power in our absolute will to communicate with our neighbors.[47] "The One is like an attractive force that works from an inaccessible distance, yet is present through reason and overcomes all separation."[48] It overcomes also the distraction within ourselves. The flight of time is stopped in our inner concentration, in the concreteness of the *'existential'* moment, in the free and resolute fulfillment of its present claims. In this 'present-mindedness' the eternal, the metahistorical finds its historical realization.[49] In an *'existential'* sense, eternal history is made wherever two people meet in this absolute spirit. In other words, wherever they meet in the spirit of unconditional presence for one another, there is the Absolute present in their midst.

Man's love for God has its proper actuality only in this loving communication with his actual Thou in a concrete situation of human life. Although this love evaporates if squandered in unworldly reverie, it becomes substantial and productive in the absolute seriousness of the partnership between man and man, as sustained appeal to one another's self-hood. Such co-*Existenz* is, within the medium of this world, a kind of holy communion and divine service. To speak with Franz Kafka: "The relationship to our neighbor is the relation of prayer." Being founded in actuality proper and by it, being oriented by and towards its unity, all true communication has its locus *in* God — is an *amare in Deo* (a loving in God) — even though there seems to be no communication

---

45 *Philosophie* III, 67.

46 *Wahrheit*, 702. Cf. my discussion of the problem in section XIV *infra*.

47 *Philosophie* III, 123. *Wahrheit*, 987ff.   48 *Wahrheit*, 118.

49 Cf., e.g., *Philosophie* II, 127; *Wahrheit*, 969f; *Origin*, 275. It is a characteristic tendency of Existentialism to enhance historicity to a point where the sense for the metahistorical content of the moment breaks through.

with Him.[50] "Love in the communication amongst men who have become Selves is the highest possibility there is within this life."[51]

IV

Truth and verification belong together, not only in the objective truth of the scientific method, but also in the personal truth of truthful *Existenz*. According to Jaspers, this truth has to be produced and authenticated as it frees our Selves in the decisions—even the fatal decisions — of genuine life. It is the truth, the ἀ-λήθεια, the revelation *of* (not only *about*) life — a life which may come true even and precisely in its death. It is the truth of an individual Self which posits itself on its own ground — but not in a selfish way. On the contrary, man can bare himself altogether only in an act of love in which he communicates with his *alter ego*. Our fellow being is our companion as partner in a common love for Being as such — for Being as Transcendence proper. Transcendence is the ground — not merely the sum total — of all phenomena, the "common depth"[52] which is not our habitation, and in which, nevertheless, we live, move and have our particular being; it is the "other side of nature";[53] and it is the only locus in which two lines of personal life, surpassing this world and independent in their original spring, can ultimately meet.[54] A philosophical thought is true as far as its actualization both needs and promotes communication and community — without losing, however, its root in individual *Existenz*.[55]

'*Existential*' truth is alive only in this triadic relation — *Existenz*, co-*Existenz* and Transcendence. Its realization is, therefore, at the same time the realization and manifestation of the individual Self. Anchored in and individuated by this Self, it owes to the latter's authenticity and personal rootedness in its own ground that radical and absolute character which, in philosophical thought, takes the place of the universal validity of objective knowledge. Kierkegaard's famous dictum that "subjectivity is the truth" is thus renewed in the sense that '*existential*' truth is individual. It

---

[50] Cf. *Philosophie* III, 123; 164ff; *Wahrheit*, 380f; 897 — ideas which can be considered as Jaspers' personal synthesis of Platonic and Kantian thoughts with thoughts of Max Scheler.

[51] *Wahrheit*, 1010. I have dealt with the never satisfied longing of *Existenz* for co-*Existenz* through communication in the model case of Anne Frank, *The Diary of a Young Girl*, (*Judaism*, I, 4; October 1952).

[52] Cf. Rilke, *Sonnette an Orpheus* II, XIV.   [53] Cf. Rilke, *W.W.* IV, 281.

[54] Cf., e.g., *Philosophie* II, 50ff; *Wahrheit*, 1001ff; *Origin*, 156f.

[55] *Philosophie* II, 62, 70f, 110, 116; *Scope*, 45f; *Wahrheit*, 370ff, 546f, 587ff, 973ff.

is a truth which has its concrete meaning as the truth of the individual subject. It is animated, not conditioned by personal appropriation and propulsion. The individual truth, as the truth of the individual, causes neither indifferentism nor relativism. The truth of the second person concerns me deeply just as I am deeply concerned with and for this person himself. Such personal truth is not subjective and relative in the sense that it is a matter of taste which one, out of a medley of propositions, I select and embrace. The truths of others have neither the same claim nor the same effect on us as has the one which "makes us free" because, in standing for it, we gain and stand our own ground.

By sympathizing with others and their truths, i.e., the ways in which truth presents itself to them, I encourage them to be themselves and may help their possibilities to 'come' actually 'true.' But, for all this, there is no import trade of personal truths: they do not become factors of my actual life; I do not witness them myself nor do I bear witness to them by my life. They express points of view which, to me, are grouped around the one and somehow unique point which I hold and may have to keep; they are not central to me, though — from my viewpoint — I can understand their centrality and vital meaning for others. The truth of others which I 'appresent,' recognize and respect can never take the place of the truth which presents itself to me and whose born representative I 'happen' to be.

This concept of personal truth is the existentialist version of a phenomenological fact which has been set forth by Husserl within the framework of his "transcendental reduction." Husserl, too, starts from the sovereignty of an ego which can never be properly accounted for as part of its world. Its consciousness had its own kind of comprehensiveness, different from that of the world. Hence, all the other egos appear within the world of my consciousness. But they appear there as subjects of consciousness in their own right. Even so, as far as I am concerned, they are just as little co-ordinated with my own ego as they are merely objects and constituta of my mind.

The incompatibility of the co-existence with me of the other ego within the world of my primordial consciousness vanishes when I see that my primordial ego apperceives of the other ego as another one in an appresentation which, in its own nature, can never be transmuted into, and verified by way of, authentic presentation.

"I must first explicate what pertains to myself in order, then, to understand that, within this egological sphere, existential sense can accrue also to what does not properly belong to me and is present only by way of analogical appresentation," i.e., as a being, a subject, a personal agent like me, but always kept in a constitutive orientation toward me as the primordial ego of transcendental reduction.[56]

The *'existentially'* irreversible relation of the *ego* to the *alter ego* leads to a communication in which the other person is both respected and challenged, wooed and questioned in its otherness.[57] As the truth of the one evokes and encounters the truth of the other, one *Existenz* depends on the other for its realization (and its experience of reality) through support, complementation and resistance.

An *'existential'* truth, common to all, one in which the original schism amongst *Existenzen* did not assert itself as both the spur to communication and the ferment of individual thought, would be without the salt of life; it would belie our deepest experience.

Obviously, this applies to Jaspers' own philosophy — and he knows it. In the succession of Nietzsche, he speaks of the *'existential'* postulate: "Don't take after me; take to thyself. Selfhood awakes selfhood."[58] And, heeding this warning, he tries not to lead us into temptation by presenting us with a rigid homogeneous system whose alleged objective validity leaves no room for personal experiences and decisions. Hence his philosophizing is intended to be an eye-opener rather than a systematization of impersonal data. It describes the different modes and dimensions of human life, but leaves and keeps this space open for the changing contents of personal historical experience. Following Kierkegaard, it draws attention to the possibilities of original *Existenz* and co-*Existenz;* it conjures up transcendence and appeals to the absolute will of communication.[59]

---

[56] Cp. *Philosophie* II, 416ff; *Reason*, 100f, with E. Husserl, *Cartesianische Meditationen und Pariser Vorträge* (1950), 148, 176 *et passim; Wahrheit*, 741f. It deserves to be noticed that the translation above of German *"Seinssinn"* by "existential sense" follows the example set by *"sens existentiel"* in the French edition of the *Meditations* (1931), p. 128. This comparison does not deny the radical differences between Husserl's and Jaspers' positions. Husserl identifies the Absolute with the sphere of transcendental intersubjectivity. To Jaspers, Transcendence proper has a special relation to *Existenz* as the ground and tie of all modes of comprehension; but, as all-encompassing, it is beyond both world and consciousness as two specific and overcrossing modes of comprehensiveness.

[57] The ambivalence of this dynamics has its analogy in an ever recurrent theme of Thomas Mann's novels, though in Mann the "loving struggle" takes place not between *Existenz* and *Existenz,* but between spiritual existence and naïve life.

[58] *Philosophie* II, 437. Cf. *Reason*, 41.

[59] Cf *Philosophie* II, 117; *Wahrheit*, 5ff; *Rechenschaft*, 123, 290ff.

He thus summons man to see for himself and take his own stand on his own ground: "no man can help the other in the essential issues of life";[60] nobody can make up the other fellow's mind in those decisions in which freedom and selfhood come into being. Even so, Jaspers' own philosophy cannot but plead its own cause. As far as it is true to itself, it cannot be presuppositionless. It does not leave "everything in suspense," as the saying goes. It rests (or it ought to rest) on a primary and ultimate decision. And it cannot help inviting us to make an analogous decision — and even in the same spirit, in the spirit of self-responsibility *qua* responsibility for the making of our Selves.

To Jaspers each Self is rooted *au fond* in the will to be itself. Jaspers' thought thus embodies the Greek ethos of self-realization together with the Jewish-Christian concept of the Self — and, hence, with all the structural changes which have turned the classical ethos into Christian self-concern (though without the obsession by the idea of salvation as the *unum necessarium* of the individual soul).

B. DISCUSSION

V

It is now time for a somewhat different *'existential'* emphasis to assert and vindicate itself in a cautious and modest attempt to re-arrange some of the lines in Jaspers' great design. I shall try to restate his position in such a way that certain ideas can evolve in reply. In their tentativeness these proposals are certainly no match to what has actually been done in his life-work; they are, however, the only way in which I am able to thank him for his work.

If taken as a criticism, this will be a sufficiently immanent critique not to run the risk of subjecting Jaspers' philosophy to a measurement by quite incommensurate standards. On the other hand, it ought not to be restricted to problems of mere logical consistency — a consistency which is never seriously impaired in a thinker of Jaspers' rank, resoluteness and strength of vision. The discussion which follows ought to penetrate into the dimension of the original impulses of his thought and *Existenz*. It is here — and here only — that minds can meet in productive concurrence and conflict.

The questions I am going to ask do not challenge the right of

60 *Wahrheit*, 846.

a philosophy such as Jaspers' to declare against a definite and unified system of ontology. If Being, as it represents itself to us, is
not of a piece, but divided into heterogeneous modes of being,
how could it be adequately represented in thought by such a system? The transcendent whole within which these forms of being
and transcendence are supposed to appear and figure may provide
a firm ground for faith (*pistis, emunah*), but its *recognition* (in a
"Periechontology"[61]) cannot be implemented by systematic *cognition*. It is Jaspers' contention that the desideratum of communication results from the multiplicity and even disunion of the utterances of the transcendent unity of Being. The state of affairs with
which we are thus confronted is "borne out in ever other and still
analogous ways by logical elucidation as well as practical and philosophical orientation within this world, and by the processes of the
illumination of *Existenz* as well as by those of a metaphysical
transcending" toward the One of Being.[62] Clearly, it would be
meaningless to discuss a philosophy without some share in its basic
experiences — in Jaspers' case without a sympathetic understanding of the motives which make a strictly systematic account of
Being impossible. Still, we may venture a few suggestions to give
'communication' a broader and even more positive sense than it
has in Jaspers and to move in this way a few steps closer — if not to
a system, then at least to a *syndesmos,* a *b'rith,* a covenant of Being.

This will be expressed in terms of a guarded dialectic which
goes somewhat beyond Jaspers' listing of the mutual references
and relations amongst the modes of being, beyond his recognition
of an interplay, through animation and incarnation, immersion
and convergence, of tendencies within and between the world and
ourselves.[63]

VI

Jaspers' vision of Being shows it as both internally torn and interrelated in its modes (*"eine in sich bezogene Zerrissenheit"*). His
method is, therefore, to move cautiously in the open realm of human thought, between the extremes of absolute monism on the
one hand and absolute pluralism on the other.[64] The original
schism lies in the difference of origin (i.e., origination) of the
heterogeneous modes of being and transcendence.

The German language allows us to interpret these differences
of *Ur-sprung* (1) as a *breaking forth* from the ground in different

[61] *Wahrheit,* 158ff.   [62] *Wahrheit,* 261.
[63] Cf., e.g., *ibid.,* 130ff.   [64] *Ibid.,* 261.

directions, caused (2) by a *break*, a cleavage *(Sprung)*, by such a rending of the globe of Being into continents that no continuous way, but only (3) a *leap (Sprung* in this sense) can lead from one to the other.[65]

The irreducibility to one another of the encompassing modes of being — the being which we are, that which the world is and that which is absolute in absolute *Transcendence* — reminds us of the essential irreducibility of the three primeval elements in Franz Rosenzweig's existential philosophy — "the mythical Greek God, the statuesque Greek world, and man as the tragic Greek hero."[66]

In Rosenzweig these potencies are separate as far as their ideas are concerned; and they remain separate in the paganism of the past, but are drawn into a circuit of universal communication in the epoch of actuality proper — the Jewish-Christian age: in the historical egress of the elements from their solitude; their concrescence in the manifest works of *Creation, Revelation* and in that configuration of the "Star of *Redemption*" which becomes, in the end, the shining forth of the face divine.

Jaspers' "philosophical faith," however, does not admit of any such absolute communion. Despite its evocative character, its 'music of abstraction,' it never belies its indebtedness to Kant's sober and critical thought. Transcendence remains to him, as to Kant an *a-logon*, both ineffable and incommunicative, — the strictly unknown and silent God, the *Ain Soph* of Jewish mysticism. Its presence may be experienced; but it cannot be personally addressed and revered in its 'proper name'.[67] And to this silence corresponds, at the bottom of the scale, even in the dark recesses of our own animal lives, the muteness of nature. Nature's physiognomic expression, eloquent and fascinating as it may prove, is not communicative language, it is not empirically controllable and neither responsive nor responsible in itself.[68]

Communication as such may also serve as expression and symbol of *Being;* it may do so even unintentionally: each of our utterances can be considered a symptom and symbol of our own being, of our historical situation, etc. But not *vice versa:* a symbol — such as the swastika — is not necessarily communicative, does not bring true selves together, even where it serves as tie or is made the idol

---

[65] Cf., e.g., *Wahrheit*, 124ff, 163ff, 217f. The idea of the "leap," presupposing as it does a chasm between the Finite and the Infinite may have its origin in Tertullian's *De Praescriptionibus,* and from there found its way to Lessing, and, through him to F. H. Jacobi, Schelling, Kierkegaard and their successors.

[66] F. Rosenzweig, *Der Stern der Erlösung*, I, 109.

[67] Cf., e.g., *Wahrheit*, 643f.   [68] Cf. *Philosophie* III, 142ff; also 643f, 897f.

of a community — or rather of a *Bund*. In this case it becomes the *signum* of a blind, fanatic exclusiveness which claims the monopoly of an absolute status for its blatant historical particularity[69] and chokes the actualization of selfhood as well as of personal co-*Existenz* in the only true *Bund* in the all-comprehensive One.

The imminent triumph in 1932 of a fetishistic cult of racial symbols may have contributed to Jaspers' insistence on the qualitative differences between one mode of language and the other. But it was only a reminder of the early and fundamental experience: the radical contrast between animal growth in gregarious life and self-making in co-*Existenz* — a contrast within the contrast between the being that we are and the being which we are not. Here is the source of his strict opposition to a naturalism of continuous evolution.

Hence the term "communication" proper is restricted to the human realm — a realm that, in a way and despite its specific comprehensiveness, is only an enclave within the universe of Being. Communication is the distinctive and "universal condition of man's being. It is so much his comprehensive essence that both what man is and what is for him are in some sense bound up with communication."[70] He communicates communicability to them. They are actually present in the meaning which they have in his world and which is expressed in terms of his language, in the meaning of words. "The Encompassing which *we are* is, in every form, communication; the Encompassing which is Being *itself*" (i.e., Being in the modes of the world and Transcendence) exists for us only insofar as it achieves *communicability* by becoming speech or becoming utterable."[71] Since, having the *logos,* man is communicative, things become communicable through him.

Again, although there are many "communicative situations," communication in its truest sense takes place only in *Existenz* and co-*Existenz,* in the free and full expression of Selves who "selve themselves" (in the language of Gerard M. Hopkins) in the process of their mutual self-revelation. Notwithstanding their original "otherness and ultimate solitariness," they "mean" to one another what no thing can mean to them, they owe one another impulses that no thing can convey. The single Self communicates *with* the other single Self by communicating *to* it an incentive to selfhood. The evocative power of this appeal from Self to Self creates *in* the world a community of inwardly grounded Selves that is not *of* this world — the existentialist counterpart to Husserl's "transcen-

69 *Philosophie* III, 25: a warning (1932 !) against totalitarian rites.
70 *Reason*, 79.   71 *Ibid*.

dental intersubjectivity" or "community of monads."[72] Although they remain apart as individuals, none of them appears to the other merely as a mute and distant image; in all such communication men speed one another in their different ways toward the One of Transcendence in which alone they find and love each other in truth [73]

It bears repeating that, while being restricted to the human sphere and grounded in the relation between I and Thou, true communication aims at an expansion beyond any historical limits. Its horizon is kept open, by the absolute will to communication, to a universum of mankind. And the idea of this historical universality is historically authorized by the fact that the historical birth of man as we know him now — man who sees himself, his chances and his limitations within the universe of Being — that this birth took place more or less independently in China, India and Greece at approximately the same time: the "pivotal age" of universal history about 500 B.C.[74] The origin and end, retrospect and prospect of history belong together. The possibility of 'existential' selfhood is not the prerogative of any particular tradition. This means an appeal to each of us to verify a common historical possibility by realizing it *in* ourselves and *through* ourselves, entering human communication and working for a human community which may never become all-inclusive, but excludes all exclusiveness.

On the other hand, communication, according to Jaspers, has its legitimate place in the human realm as such. We have seen that it does not extend upward to God or downward to nature. Whenever the tendencies of the German language tempt and lead him to trespass beyond the boundaries, he is anxious to stress the merely figurative sense of these expressions. His philosophical criticism shows not only in a metaphysics which declares the doom of all human striving, its being wrecked on the rock towards which it cannot but steer; it shows also in the way he discredits a *"Sprachdenken"* which is highly favored in contemporary German philosophy. I.e., he warns against relying so much on the wisdom of language as guide to the mysteries of life that, under this dictate, philosophy may forsake the directives and responsibilities of thought.[75]

In this combination of bold metaphysical synopsis and cautious criticism, he gives the word 'language' itself a universal sweep, while emphasizing the merely metaphorical character of this broader use. Language proper, human language is, with him, dis-

[72] Cf. E. Husserl, *Cartesianische Meditationen*, §§55f.

[73] Cf., e.g., *Philosophie* II, 109; *Wahrheit*, 979.

[74] Cf. *Origin*, 1ff.

[75] Cf. *Wahrheit*, 434ff.

tinguished by the specific difference "communicative" — it is communicative language.[76] As will be seen later on (especially in section X), I shall deviate from this terminology by giving the specific difference the status of the genus. This will make a real difference in interpretation, because it may allow us to point out the *fundamentum in re* of Jaspers' figurative speech and sketch the outlines of a philosophy of communication in which a philosophy of human language will have its proper place.

VII

Jaspers' restriction of the meaning of 'communication' is, of course, more than a philosophical expediency. It is the outcome of a philosophical decision made on the strength of that most deep-seated experience of his early life, from which the present essay takes its bearings. Whether or not the light in which Jaspers sees his youth now is quite the same as that in which once he saw himself, there is no doubt that his interpretation is authentic as regards the inner growth and motivating power of those childhood impressions. They actually were to set the mood of his life and thought. Hence the problem of communication was and remained for him (and in more than one sense) an exclusively personal and interpersonal problem. Such a communication with and within nature as we sense and enjoy through the senses as organs of our communication with the sensory world early became questionable to him for *'existential'* reasons, i.e., in view of the obligations of personal and interpersonal *Existenz*. "All intimacy with nature in a lovely world became problematic to me if it does not lead back to human community and serves this community as background and medium of expression."[77]

Inasmuch as human reason *(Vernunft)*, the distinctive gift of human beings, has its proper fulfilment and climax in the practical reason of the conscientious and responsible Self, listening to the voice of conscience may deafen man's ears to the *Vernehmen* of nature, to the listening to what may appear as mere siren song.

It must be granted that, similar to Rilke, Jaspers deplores the modern displacement of pure and primitive nature by nature as material for managerial contrivances.[78] Occasionally he conjures

[76] Cf. *Philosophie* III, 142ff.

[77] *Rechenschaft*, 351f. Cf. *Philosophie* III, 180ff. Led as they are by a specific interest and purpose, the following thoughts cannot pretend to do full justice to the richly faceted concept of nature in the section "Nature" in *Philosophie* III, 173-186.

[78] Cf. *Age*, 57; cf. Rilke, *Sonette an Orpheus*, I, 18, 22, 23, 24; II, 10.

up in passionate words the passionate mood of the elements raging over his native country, the land bordering the German Ocean; here he has an experience of infinity, which connects him with the very mainspring of things — a lasting ground on which to stay.[79]

More often, however, he speaks as a conscientious trustee of selfhood, enhancing its status of responsibility over against the "nuggatory character of mere natural events." Where nature is loved, it is actually God who is loved in her.[80] More often than not, nature appears as mere "empirical matter,"

being there to be dominated and moulded, or as an object of loving contemplation, yet without responsibility on our part and without response on hers, or to be destroyed in those of her appearances that prove annoying and confining, and without proper significance even where she succeeds in getting the upper hand.[81]

Utterances like these cannot but evoke an attitude somewhat derogatory to nature and that 'cosmic piety' which I consider as an aspect of religion that cannot be despised and is not to be reduced to admiration of nature as God's handiwork. Similarly, the message of art — at least as communication to the second power, i.e., communication of a communication with nature — becomes truly significant to him not for what it says, but only for what it does not really say, not as *creation* as such, but as the creation of ciphers for Transcendence, i.e., only insofar as it speaks to us *qua* Selves.[82]

Consequently, the enthusiastic — not necessarily mystic — experience of a union with nature in which we "lose ourselves" is under the verdict of being somehow unsubstantial, distracting and detracting as it may prove from the realization of selfhood. In any case, says Jaspers, the immediate awareness of the life of nature through the natural life within us, this "mysticism of a union with nature is known today only in dim reflection — as, for instance, in the mood of being married to the landscape around us."[83]

It may be possible to give a somewhat more positive account of what happens to man here (and not only as a vanishing mode of

[79] *Wahrheit,* 897. The same experience has been stressed by Thomas Mann.

[80] *Wahrheit,* 112f; *per contra,* 271: the world is not only cipher; it has its own "depth and width."

[81] *Wahrheit,* 743; cf. 78, 88; but cf. 146f, where it remains an open question "whether there is from nature a friendly advance in which the spirit may recognize itself."

[82] Cf. *Philosophie* III, 192ff.   [83] *Wahrheit,* 1006.

experience) and of the productivity that rises from this communication with nature. It may also be asked whether Jaspers' appraisal of this experience gives nature its proper due with regard to *Existenz*. Although in Jaspers' *Existenz* is not unworldly, it is 'unnatural' in the sense that, in its personal decisions and activities, *Ex-sistenz* proper 'stands outside' of the course of natural events — an alien to the natural order. This alienation of the Self from nature is in line with Christian dualism such as is still alive in the extreme conclusions drawn by Jaspers' intellectual ancestors, Kant as well as Kierkegaard — Kant who removes intelligible, moral existence from the life and world of the senses, and Kierkegaard, who even in his own personal equipment feels "in almost every physical respect deprived of the conditions for being a whole man," of the "animal side of humanity."[84]

VIII

It is not my intention to deny the qualitative differences in the dynamics of nature, conscious life as such, spirit and *Existenz*, but to plead for a qualification of the "transcendental contrast" between two main modes of being and representation — a contrast which has been almost a German Credo from Kant to Jaspers and from Schiller to Mann.[85]

This is the German version of a European movement to which both Greek Idealism and Christian contempt of the world have contributed. It proves man's superiority to the outer world not in unworldly asceticism but in the technique of mastering and exploiting nature in a reckless way. It seems to me that here for once Jaspers fails to check or, at least, to keep in check the peculiar assumptions of the technical civilization of our Western world. To declare nature in itself as "essentially foreign and impenetrable to us,"[86] something that becomes my world only through my work,

[84] Kierkegaard, *Journals,* etc., quoted from *Reason,* 41.

[85] Just as in Jaspers man is subject to both the "law of the day" (*Gesetz des Tages*) and the "passion for the night" (*Leidenschaft zur Nacht*) and, thus, pays tribute to two modes of Being between which no synthesis can be achieved, so does Thomas Mann's Hans Castorp decide for life while keeping faith to death; and his Joseph — a Gilgamesh nature — *lives* in the City of the *Dead:* his is a sympathy in which veneration for death and friendliness to life meet without being synthesized. Since Kierkegaard, the wretched conditions of life have led men to see a mere euphemism in all dialectical synthesis à la Hegel. With regard to modern sciences as such and the contribution of Biblical religion to its growth, a different and complementary aspect has to be acknowledged — the loving, yet realistic interest in God's creation: cf. *Origin,* 90f.

[86] *Wahrheit,* 88; cf. *Philosophie* III, 173.

runs counter to an experience of nature which is not restricted to
children and so-called primitive peoples, but is enhanced, above
all, by the high cultures of the East. The Stoic teaching of universal sympathy, the Confucian doctrine of the consonance between
the orders of Heaven and Earth, moral design and physical nature,
are experiences of faith which are not a monopoly of the creature
to the exclusion of the Self (even though the concept of the Self
differs from that of the Augustinian tradition) . The Chinese "unbroken love for the world,"[87] the deep Eastern feeling of unity
with the "aesthetic continuum" (Northrop) , with nature in the
delicacy and unreduced richness of her qualitative features and
changes, a "nature that is ours" and with which we are in tune,
has its own right and truth. When we read the *I-Ching,* it does not
seem to us that "the cipher of nature as such ceases to be the real
thing when *Existenz* steps forth."[88] An inner awareness and careful
control of nature's situational changes seems here to convey to
personal action their own touch of responsiveness and responsibility. They provide cautious tact and serene composure in communication with men and things. The underlying mood can be
given a sort of phenomenological justification in the wake of philosophies such as Whitehead's.

Jaspers accentuates communication as an action of human life
and ultimately an act of *Existenz* proper, as the drama of self-
realization in the dialogue between Selves who struggle together
to free themselves in and for themselves. In this emphasis on interpersonal communication the communication with *nature* is
somehow discarded. According to Jaspers, nature as such is below
communication, just as Transcendence is above it.[89] Whereas *impersonal life* does not really and freely communicate with nature,
but may be absorbed in a loving union with the life of the whole
in which the individual is drowned, *personal Existenz* appears
often as estranged from nature.[90]

Yet, is it entirely true even for modern man that he knows the
"marriage with nature" only as a faint echo of former days?[91] If so,
the art of a Cézanne would be an atavism of merely romantic and

[87] *Wahrheit,* 112.   [88] *Philosophie* III, 182.   [89] Cf. *Philosophie* III, 181.

[90] In view of Jaspers' native country, it may not be wrong to point to Rilke's
three poems on an island in the North Sea, whose inhabitants are silent and lonely,
since there can be no communication between them and the vast space around
them: *"nah ist nur Innres; alles andre fern":* "near is but what is inside; far away
the rest." *(Werke,* III, 93ff).

[91] It would not be fair to point to this passage *(Wahrheit,* 1006) once more without acknowledging, even in the same work, passages of a much more positive tenor:
cf., e.g., 91, 897, 1037. Also *Philosophie* III, 176f, 179f, 196f.

sentimental interest, not the presentation of a new truth and a new and more intensive presence of Being. In the loving struggle with his motif, Cézanne feels how he penetrates to the roots of things, how he germinates with their seeds and comes to light again in their growth. In performing his own marriage with the landscape (such an intimate union that he fears his eyes may bleed when he tears them away from it) he feels empowered to fulfill the inmost longing and secret of nature for a perfection of her appearance in the marriage he performs between color and color.[92] Nature becomes "more truly being" in this union in which both the artist and nature are one — as visions. The face of the universe (its "Gesicht") and the face and sight of the artist (his Gesicht) coincide with one another like the hands of a clock in the midnight hour.[93]

Highly imaginative as the artist's account of his experience is likely to be, dependent on certain philosophical prefigurations as it is in cases such as in Flaubert's, Cézanne's, Claudel's or Proust's — it is not merely imaginary and derivative. It is an adequate and authentic expression which communicates a communion. It breathes the mood of what, with the artist himself, the philosopher ought to recognize as a real communication with nature, a fundamental mode and consummate fulfilment of human prehension — a *perfectio cognitionis sensitivae quae talis*.[94] This is so because the artist acts somehow as the executor of intentions that are inherent in sensory perception.[95] They are recognized in phenomenological analysis, but remain mostly undeveloped or suppressed in practical life and are methodically suspended for scientific purposes. Wherever perception reaches a state of immanent perfection and fruition, a mutual osmosis and concentration takes place: our whole being is absorbed and as it were colored by a qualitative content — which, on its part, seems to achieve a new, condensed and deeper presence from the depths in which it is received.

I point to these facts, not to blame Jaspers for not sufficiently acknowledging the function and significance of *aisthesis* (sense-impression) and aesthetic experience, but to extend to them the recognition as organs of 'communication' in a somewhat broader sense: as a circulation of energies and the transfer of a 'telling' mood in the circuit from nature to the artist and the spectator.

---

[92] Cf. Joachim Gasquet, *Cézanne*, 61, 83, 101.

[93] Cf. R. M. Rilke, "Der Tod des Dichters," "Der Magier" (*Gesammelte Werke*, (1927) III 30, 431). Cf. also Jaspers himself, *Wahrheit*, 917; *Origin*, 275.

[94] Alexander Gottlieb Baumgarten, *Aesthetica* I, p. 14.

[95] See below, p. 41.

Since he reserves 'communication' to the sphere of human life and, above all, personal co-*Existenz*, Jaspers himself is inclined to see in beauty only a more or less spectacular surface phenomenon presenting itself to the living creature for its enjoyment and the celebration of its festivals.[96] And art is given real significance and (not quite convincingly) even an indispensable rôle as a mediator between mere life and personal *Existenz* — and, hence, in orientation toward the latter. According to Jaspers, artistic expression achieves a contact with potential *Existenzen* other than the artist's in their search for Being as such. It discloses the space of authentic possibilities — to aesthetic contemplation. But to see new possibilities of *Existenz* has not yet the resoluteness of an *'existential'* reply to them. Contemplation does not transform possibilities into actualities of our personal life. Even so, experienced in its true greatness, the great work of art is something "like" (!) communication: it speaks and, perhaps, appeals to us in the language of another *Existenz*;[97] and through the concentration and intensity of its appearance it objects to the distractedness and deformity of our present state: *"Da ist keine Stelle,/ die dich nicht sieht. Du musst dein Leben ändern."* ("There is no spot that does not spot thee. Thou must change thy life.") [98]

It may be possible, however, to see in this appeal the highest but not the only function of art. It may be possible to assign to art an even fuller meaning in what it does for the totality of our human being. The work of art may co-ordinate, in a symbol, the antagonistic factors which Jaspers calls "law of the day" and "passion for the night,"[99] the passionate lure of the abyss; i.e., roughly, the rational working for the One of Transcendence and the irrational, intoxicated headlong fall into it — *la morale de se perdre et même de se laisser dépérir*.[100]

However, art as communication may imply even more than a likeness of actual communication with the positive or negative form of other *Existenz*. In fact, the title "passion for the night" seems to stand for many irrational phenomena of entirely different nature and origin. The irrationality of the demonic mode of existence or of the Kierkegaardian 'exception' is the polar opposite

[96] Cf. *Philosophie* III, 110.   [97] Cf. *Philosophie* III, 192ff.

[98] R. M. Rilke, "Archaischer Torso Apollos," *Werke*, III, 117.

[99] Cf., above all, *Philosophie* III, 102ff.

[100] I quote from the carnival scene in Thomas Mann's *Magic Mountain*, just before Hans Castorp's 'fall,' when he forsakes Settembrini's "order of the day" and succumbs to the "passion for the night." Jaspers' section on these two forms of *Existenz* is as it were a philosophical commentary to Thomas Mann. See below, n. 250.

to the irrational of mere and pure elemental passion. That does not mean that the extremes cannot meet. They do in all the Luciferic existences which show man riding a bare-backed beast. But the elemental can have its own depth, consummation and bliss. It need not serve as symbol for the *'existential'* intercourse between the soul and her bridegroom, as in the medieval interpretations of the Song of Songs. The flesh is its own mystery. And without any spiritual allegorization, art may just embody in its medium the dynamics of bare organic and even inorganic nature. It may initiate us (as, in its way, surrealism wanted to do) to the secrets of our own animal and subliminal being and have only the creature, not the person in us, as its sounding board. Or all this could go together — and in the truly classical works of art does go together. The artistic mood *("Stimmung")* in this sense would be a "tuning" and stirring of both our lower and higher powers of 'representation'[101] — a fugue in which they all may have a voice.

Within the realm and by virtue of imagination, art may anticipate the fulfilment of an infinite task — that of the integration of human being in actual life. This is part of art's 'blessing.' The periodical rhythms of organic life may co-operate toward a total impression in their conflux with the free rhythms of personal *Existenz*. In the straits of active and competitive life a pointed and even one-sided response to the challenge of a situation may prove necessary. And, in fact, the individual artist cannot help reverberating the particular needs and tendencies of his age. It is however, the privilege of great, magnanimous art — and a token of its greatness — to be a symphony of nature and of historical life, but so that the personal tone of the artist himself vibrates through the chorus intoned by his class and age and that of many ages and generations.[102] Art thus discloses — if not the sum total, so at least — the complex structure and dynamics of our natural as well as personal, historical being. It provides a broadened, sympathetic understanding of the pluriverse of nature, man and men.[103]

The mood *("Stimmung")* of artistic communication thus has different dimensions of meaning: and just as in this experience we

[101] This is Kant's concept of the artistic mood *(Stimmung):* cf. *Critique of Judgement* § 21 *et passim.* Jaspers, too, refers to this experience and its Kantian interpretation by qualifying it as a playful prefigurement or reminiscence of actual, but actually never perfect, unity: cf. *Wahrheit*, 701.

[102] See also below, footnote 117.

[103] In this function art may serve a purpose not dissimilar to that of Jaspers' philosophy: as a panorama of human possibilities the latter, too, makes us ready to recognize and respect otherness and to co-exist with others in the communication of 'heterogeneous' selfhood.

are tuned to things, give them an ear and a voice, so, according to Kant, things seem strangely tuned to us as they chime in "with the free play of our cognitive faculties in apprehending and judging nature's appearance."[104] This is the aesthetic variety of that ontological movement in which the mind functions as a final cause rather than as an efficient cause (in an idealistic sense). It is as if nature had aimed at man and communication with and through him.

In artistic communication we have a traffic with things that yields returns to either party.[105] "Grateful to nature, who brought him into being, the artist renders her a second nature — but a felt one, a thought one, a nature perfected by the work of man."[106] The ontological function of art in creating a new mode of presence bears out art's androgynous nature, the unity of receptivity and productivity in the artistic process. But the artist acts here only as a representative and mouthpiece of man. He continues and brings to a specific consummation a movement of consciousness in general and of aesthetic consciousness in particular. It is not only the artist, it is man who experiences with Rilke how "all these things . . . strangely concern us."[107] The entreaty to which the artist responds in his medium has its (moral and) religious representation in the feeling that, somehow, we are counted upon, that "the earnest expectation of the creature waiteth for the manifestation of the sons of God," "the delivery from the bondage of corruption."[108] (A unison of the artistic and religious versions of this experience is in Cézanne's longing to become in his painting the redeemer of the vacillating universe.[109]) The message of things and the mission of man belong together. This overcoming of mere juxtaposition, this universal communication of things and with them will be intensified by that communication which Jaspers emphasizes above all: the communication amongst Selves in the boundless concern for personal *Existenz* and co-*Existenz*.[110]

104 Kant, *Critique of Judgement*, Bernard tr., § 67 (286).

105 *Mutatis mutandis*, this applies to non-representational as well as representational arts. "Traffic with things" means here each contact with Being.

106 Goethe, Note to "Diderots Versuch über die Malerei."

107 Rilke, *Duineser Elegien*, Ninth Elegy, *Gesammelte Werke*, 297. The German words are: *"Alles das Hiesige,... das seltsam uns angeht."* In a profound ambiguity *"angeht"* implies three things: "all this affects, concerns and entreats us." Our concern *with* things becomes our concern *for* them, our heeding of their demand.

108 Epistle to the Romans, 8:19, 21.

109 Cf. J. Gasquet, *Cezanne*, 82, 93. In Rilke's poems, cf., e.g., *Sonnette an Orpheus* I, xi and II, xxviii — the complementation of the natural order by the human one. We shall meet a similar conviction in Paul Claudel (see below, 61f).

110 Cf. *Wahrheit*, e.g., 114f, 134, 978, 979. Every thing with which we are concerned has its true significance with regard to life and *Existenz* in human community: cf. *op. cit.*, 378. Cf. also *Origin*, 218f.

The artist thus does not embark on a new and strange enterprise of his own, and the experience he undergoes and creates is not unrelated to human experience as such. Even in his own line he brings to perfection only what is in *statu nascendi* in all perception. It is his privilege to show the indefiniteness and transitoriness of phenomena in the glory of a definite and lasting expression. But the artistic figure has its prefiguration in the perceptions of average life. Perception is as it were an interplay of question and answer, a sort of primitive communication between man and the outer world. Merleau-Ponty defines "sensation as co-existence or communion," as a real give and take. A sense-datum becomes a definite color only through my co-operation. I must give it the right reception in the right bodily attitude[111] for it to adopt the character, e.g., of a sky-blue which gathers in the space I provide for it. "The sense-datum presents to my body a sort of confused problem. And I must find the right comportment which will enable it to determine and declare itself as blue; I must find the right answer to a badly formulated question."[112]

In its way, perception has a defining power analogous to that of conception. Certainly, not each perception has the idiomatic strength of artistic expression; but each contains potentially what is actualized in the style of a work of art; each can be the germ-cell of such a definition of style as the famous *homo additus rebus*. The power of perception has found nowhere a more eloquent and subtle formulation than in Rilke. I quote (in translation) a few striking lines from a posthumous poem (though this is not the place to bring out all of its profound implications):

> We live translating things which we transcend.
> To give a tree true presence we extend
> Space from within to it and let it be —
> Surrounded by surrender. Our abstention
> Defines the measure of its full extension.
> We are the land. Within us grows the tree.[113]

IX

Psychological analysis and artistic wisdom thus confirm one an-

---

111 Cf. the general problem of "Einstellung" in phenomenological analysis. Greek ἐπίστασθαι may have meant originally: "to place oneself in the attitude required for . . . "

112 M. Merleau-Ponty, *Phénoménologie de la Perception*, 274f. Reference is made to gestalt-psychological investigations, particularly by Heinz Werner. What is said here about vision applies equally to other spheres of sensation.

113 R. M. Rilke, *Späte Gedichte*, 150; cf. 84.

other in considering perception and even sensation a co-operative process between man and nature in their communication and communion. The same holds from the point of view of epistemology in its classical pattern as well as in some of its modern scientific forms. We can still subscribe to Thomas' saying that "all that is received in another medium is received in accordance with the nature of the receiver."[114] That "truth superadds something to Being"[115] thus applies already to the "manifestative and declarative being" of the object of perception.

Similarly, the universe of modern science appears as the product of a co-operation of subject and object in an electro-magnetic field wherein they communicate. And, looking down from the conceptual plane of statistical mechanics, the physicists may be inclined to consider the *Gestalten* of conscious perception as being based (to speak with Leibniz) on *petites perceptiones* — discrete units which sensory apprehension integrates to bring about the homogeneity and continuity of our visible world.[116]

It may be profitable to extend the reference to Thomistic metaphysics and epistemology from the discussion of the phenomenon of perception to that of conception. This does not imply a complete identification with Thomism. Nor does it deny an element of the metaphorical in the Thomistic analyses of the process of knowledge. But to see them in this light will not detract from their merit; the farther we go both in abstraction itself and in its description, the more must we move in a realm of figures, and the question is only how striking they are as reminders of 'the real thing.' In our context — unable as we are to write here a whole theory of knowledge — the Thomistic doctrine will help to focus attention on our central point, that of communication. This is, however, no mere pragmatic advantage. The Thomistic theory is perhaps the most thorough-going in classical philosophy. And it has the additional value of pointing to depths of experience of which we must take some soundings for the purpose of this paper. This is ground which, in our days, has born fruit again in French writers such as Paul Claudel and Gabriel Marcel and in that German synthesis of Phenomenological and Thomistic Existentialism

114 Thomas Aquinas, *Commentarius in 1. de Anima II,* lect. 24: Similarly Jaspers, *Wahrheit,* 124: It is so that in the process of comprehensive awareness "each sphere of comprehension reveals as it were its peculiar light, its color, its main character."

115 Acquinas. *Quaestiones Disputatiae de Veritate.* Qu. I, a.l. ad resp.: "Truth is superadded to Being."

116 Cf. e.g., Hermann Weyl, *Philosophie der Mathematik und Naturwissenschaft,* 154.

for which Hedwig Conrad-Martius has paved the way and Edith
Stein found a clear and impressive formulation.[117] In spite of his
personal decision against the absolute systems of thought of an
Aristotle, Thomas, and Hegel,[118] Jaspers is so close to what is here
at stake that the following remarks will not be out of place.

We have seen that in the communication between senses and
sensory things our receptivity defines but does not create the sense
in which sense-data appear. We do not make the blue come 'from
the blue,' rather we follow out suggestions that are offered to us
by way of affection. It is the same way with cognition: things 'make
sense' both *to* us and *through* us; *Sinngebung* and *Sinnfindung,*
the founding and finding of sense in the understanding go hand in
hand; cognition is always re-cognition of what we owe to things
(to "think" and to "thank" belong together). Disclosure on the
part of things and discovery on our part, penetration into their
secrets and opening of our mind to their manifestations, intu-ition
and at-tribution, ex-plication and de-termination are complementary aspects of each process of knowledge, even though sometimes
one, sometimes the other aspect may prevail. As the very word indicates, there is an element of receptivity in conception just as
there is an element of productivity in perception. Knowledge — I
shall come back to that — is a refined way of consciousness, and
consciousness *(con-scientia)* an apprehensive way of 'co-existence'
(not merely in Jaspers' sense) and communication in a *commer-
cium* of give and take.[119]

In his Psychology, Aristotle has described the growth of human
life as it reaches higher and higher levels of assimilation and
appropriation. We can consider knowledge as appropriation on
the intellectual level — appropriation of the present we receive
through the self-presentation of things to our senses. Compresence
is of the nature of the subject as well as of the object of consciousness.[120] Just as intentionality (objective reference) belongs to con-

[117] Cf. my review of Edith Stein's *Endliches und Ewiges Sein,* in *Philosophy and
Phenomenological Research,* XII, 4.

[118] Cf. *Wahrheit,* 965 — these names represent a kind of triad in Jaspers' mind
and appear repeatedly in this conjunction.

[119] Even where we are givers in establishing new meaning and relations, this may
be felt as a gift that is granted to us. That is just what happens in the most 'inspired' moments of human life, so that *Sinngebung,* founding of new sense, would
seem an absolute process which goes on *through* us rather than *by* us. (There was
something of this religious ethos in Husserl's speaking of *noesis* in absolute consciousness.) See also below, p. 294.

[120] Although the whole of the present essay ought to give some plausibility to
this thesis, I must forego, at this point, its detailed systematic and historical discussion — its comparison, for instance, with Samuel Alexander's epistemology.

sciousness, so *realitas objectiva* (its position as an object of representation and hence, a reference to the subject) belongs to the *realitas formalis* (the substantive status which a thing has in itself). The transformation of one mode of being (of *realitas*) into the other takes place through the in-formation of the mind: the mental concept bears out the re-spect in which the mind receives the intellectual a-spect of the thing, the intelligible species.

The study of this connubium between things and man may lend some higher precision to earlier statements (pp. 230f). Perhaps, it is not so that it is up to human communication to provide for the communicability of things and convey meaning to them. But the mind grasps specific meanings by abstracting them from particular phenomena. The contribution of the mind would be, above all, in its liberating function: it frees and defines the obtuse meaning of things. The contribution of things, on the other hand, is in the potentialities of the communicable forms which they embody. The views of Parmenides and Plato complement one another: Reason, says Parmenides, is pronounced in the rationality of Being.[121] But it is also as Plato's *Phaedo* has it: the *eidos* shows in the explicitness of the *logos*. The meaning of things is their manifest essence; i.e., this essence as it comes to the fore in the meaning of words and in their definition.

The communication *(symbiosis)* with things thus leads to the promulgation of their essence by the communication of their meaning. The classical tradition tries, however, to deepen the meaning of communication itself by rounding off a golden chain of communication which has its beginning in God and leads back toward him. It leads toward him: the language of abstraction returns to the ideas the status beyond matter and (maybe) the universality which they originally enjoyed in God; it 're-presents' them to him.[122] And communication has also its beginning in God who

---

121 *Parmenides,* fr. 8, 35 (Diels).

122 That this conception of the work of thought and language is no mere religious philosophism but rather the outgrowth of a general and basic experience becomes probable by artistic parallels such as the following lines from Rilke's *Stundenbuch.* They show God coming again into his own by the return of his songs through the mouth of man:

Er möchte sich wiedergewinnen	"He wants himself back as he spent
aus seinen Melodien.	himself in his melodies.
Da komm ich zu seinen Knien.	So I come to nest at his knees.
Und seine Lieder rinnen	And his songs return in the end,
rauschend zurück in ihn.	ringing and rich, to his peace."

Similar ideas may be found from the time of the Bible to the novels of Mann and Joyce.

communicates to all things that share in being which is apportioned to them.

It is not for me to endorse the literal truth of these statements. But I recognize in them the thoughtful expression of two deeprooted experiences. First of all, they bear witness to man's trusteeship in the economy of the universe — they are, thus, a particular version of the responsible trust which gives human life its, perhaps, greatest strength and deepest significance: that we are counted upon, and that our accomplishment or failure will be of universal consequence. Secondly, this metaphysical doctrine bears out what is implied in the nature of finite and temporal being: it is always out of hand as it always passes away in the passage of time. Temporal being is balanced precariously on the needle-point of the one present, yet vanishing moment.[123] *Vita mancipio nulli datur.* As far as we have part in Being, it seems given, communicated to us — and by whom else (so man asks) if not by the One who has Being actually at his disposal and can dispose of it as he pleases. This is the *Possest* of Cusanus, the "Lord of Being" — of his and therewith all Being — in Schelling.[124] In its analysis of Being, philosophy may redeem the simple wisdom of Job: "the *Lord* gave, and the *Lord* hath taken away; blessed be the name of the *Lord.*"

The ideas of creation and perpetual re-creation have their origin in the experience of being as something communicated to us; all particular being is felt to spring from a creative source; it is, in one way or the other, enjoyed as long as the communication with this source lasts.[125] "God is the place of the world, but the world is not his place," this adage is the theistic counterpart of the idea of Transcendence in Jaspers — the Transcendence which is present to absolute consciousness, and to which we owe the gift of our true Selves, since this consciousness frees us from slavery to the world.[126]

To take a few more steps in this way of thought: the *actus essendi* (the act of being, being in its actuality), in which things originate, communicates to them both their *Quod,* the facticity of their being, and their *Quid,* the specific nature which is their part — and hence, the peculiar rôle they play, the place they occupy in relation to other things. The space of Being is, as it were, parceled

[123] For a profound phenomenological evaluation of this aspect of time, cf. H. Conrad-Martius, "Die Zeit" *(Philosophischer Anzeiger,* 1927/28). This does not exclude other, seemingly contradictory, characters to appear on other levels of consideration of this most puzzling of all phenomena — time.

[124] Schelling, *Werke,* I, x, 260; II, iii, 295.   [125] More details below, 287ff.

[126] Cf., e.g., *Wahrheit,* 173; cf. also *ibid.,* 109, 594, 677, 988, 1036; *Philosophie* III, 192ff.

out to all the particular beings which represent the whole in a limited and qualified manner. They restrict and define each other in the How and What of this representation, in the qualities and functions which they enact and exhibit.[127] Each of them is *aliquid* (something), i.e., an *aliud quid* (something different), a being holding its own ground in its own way. And each substantive being (in difference from a mere phantasm) is what it is in the distributive unity of the whole — in actualizing its both specific and individual essence. None of these entities is self-contained, none can be defined apart from the system of forms and things with which it communicates.[128] This applies first of all to the dialectical system of ideal forms, the community of ideas (the Platonic *eidos* already is considered a *meros,* a part subsumed under the all-surpassing One). But it applies also to the space-time field of actuality in which each point is virtually the whole field. Each is endowed with a power of communication and is, thus, absorbed in an all-pervasive community of being in which a principle of the 'all-together' *(omnia in omnibus)* prevails and 'simple location' proves a fallacy.

The reference to Whitehead's term is intended to give some justification to the language of the preceding paragraph which sounds too peremptory partly because, within the present essay, it has to be allusive and cannot fully justify itself. In fact, if it has any truth, it is only that of a first approximation. The picture it gives has still too much the character of an objective survey of a total configuration and seems, therefore, more adequate as a description of an ideal structure or of objective events than of personal decisions and actions. As it stands, it would seem to neglect the historicity of all being, the peculiar historicity of ours and of our position and the limitations of our finite knowledge. But it may appear even more dogmatic than it is, if measured by the standards of Kant's metaphysics of scientific experience. (The ghost of Kant rises here because actually we are moving now within a realm of Kantian transcendent 'ideas' rather than of Kantian objects of knowledge.[129])

[127] This conception might account for a religious experience of man's being on earth — the feeling that he is installed in his office, given a place in the order of being, not only — as Heidegger had it — thrown into the whirl of this world: cp. Heidegger, *Sein und Zeit,* 175ff, with my *Philosophie des Grafen Paul Yorck von Wartenburg,* 94.

[128] Cf. Paul Claudel, *Art Poetique,* 101: "I am as far as I am limited by the objects that surround me, as far as I experience this limitation and am informed by it."

[129] More specifically — we move in the orbit of problems discussed in Kant's ingenious chapter on the "Transcendental Ideal:" Kant, *Critique of Pure Reason,*

My excuse is twofold. First, the scientific situation has shifted
since Kant's time to a point where certain metaphysical assertions
which would have been anathema to Kant have become meaningful again and represent, at least, a fair risk. I take this risk because
— and this is the second excuse — I try to envisage "communication" as a point of affinity between scientific, religious and artistic
experiences. To be sure, this is an imaginary center from which no
system of metaphysical propositions can be derived. The unity of
experience exists only in its variations. But as variations they point
back to a plastic substrate or, rather, to a fundamental, yet changing dynamics whose change we see reflected in that of the meaning
of "communication." In these dialectical turns "communication"
seems not deprived of each and every identity; it is not degraded
to a mere homonym. It will show a similar controllable ambiguity
as Leibniz's — otherwise antipodean — term "representation" or
"expression," which undergoes significant variations of meaning
in its application to the different levels of the monadic scale.

X

In all these considerations and, indeed, in my whole approach to
philosophical problems, I am guided by an interest in a *general
metaphysics,* that does not deny the difference and even discrepancy between *our* being — above all *Existenz* in Jaspers' sense — and
worldly being, but that would like to have this difference vaulted
over by slightly more positive determinations than the reference to
mighty, yet evasive Transcendence. I do not belittle — indeed, I
emphasize — Jaspers' distinction between the *"mute language of
being",* (such as the physiognomic expression of nature) on the one
hand, and — on the other — "communicative human language,"
the more or less true and honest *("redliche")* intercourse amongst
— *idealiter* — responsive and responsible human beings.[130] But I
want to 'formalize' the idea of communication so much that the
affinity between both languages comes out, and that even the Biblical concept of the Universe as a vast responsory may find a certain
'response.' (The objective determination of things is for instance
in Genesis 1 the outgrowth of their personal designation, their be-

B599ff. Jaspers' own characterization of Transcendence as the "ground of all actuality" *(Wahrheit,* 90, 92, 107, etc.) looks very much like a metamorphosis of Kant's
description of the Transcendental Ideal as "underlying all things as their ground
and not their sum total:" *op. cit.,* 607.

130 Cf. *Philosophie* III, 142ff; and — somewhat modified — *Wahrheit,* 546ff.

ing both *called* into being and given a specific *calling* to which they respond.)

No doubt, we modify the meaning of the word when we first use it simply the way one speaks of two vessels which 'communicate,' then — with regard to their content — declare that they communicate it *to* one another, and when we finally deal with the 'communication' *with* and *amongst* people about a certain issue. But the second communication is made possible by the first one — the establishment of some contact; and the two latter ones are connected as modes of exchange: the second — communication to others — gives them a share in something, just as the third — communication *qua Mit-teilung* — makes others participants in our knowledge and personal understanding of things and lets them take part in our life in the light of this understanding.

This unification of life in the communion of men will not blind us to the complementary fact of polarization in personal co-*Existenz*. Here communication is no longer mere flux from one vessel to the other. No positivistic import-theory will ever do justice to the polar relationship between I and Thou in which intimacy and tension are one. Here is nothing transferred that is not received and assimilated. (There are, of course, mass epidemics of public opinion, etc.; but they are just forfeitures of personal status and value.)

Jaspers is perfectly right in stressing the inner independence of either partner in personal communication and relationship. This independence is a constituent of true personal correlation; it adds to the latter's intensity rather than weakening it. It has one of its expressions in that (not impersonal, but impartial) *objectivity* only man can afford — in every regard. First 'with regard to' the world (which thus — and thus only — will be thrown into relief and appear as a self-contained context of being). The same holds true with regard to my fellow-being (who will be closer to me in due distance, i.e., when I release and respect him in the otherness of an *alter ego*); and finally even with regard to myself (who can thus become an object of my own concern and a product of my own making) .[131]

This character of correlation is maintained and enhanced in the covenant of Biblical religion, where both distance and intimacy are given their maximum values.[132] The paradoxical independence

[131] In contemporary German philosophy, these features of *Existenz* and co-*Existenz* have been delineated not only by Jaspers, but also by writers such as Max Scheler — and particularly Martin Buber from *Ich und Du* on to his more recent booklet *Urdistanz und Beziehung* (1951).

[132] This point has been made first, perhaps, by Adolf Reinach and then by Kurt

of finite man face to face with infinite God is brought out for instance in Abraham's pleading for Sodom and Gomorrah and the post-Biblical commentaries that extol Abraham for walking *before God,* not merely *with* him as Noah did.

There are, thus, different shades of meaning, and qualitative leaps involved in the use of the word 'communication' as we ascend from nature to the personal level. But the inner connection of these different meanings can also be seen in religious experience. A genetic relation may prevail between interpersonal communication in the intensity of *'existential'* partnership, in the covenant between I and Thou, and that prestage or remnant of personal relationship that may appear as cosmic piety, most eloquently in William James:

> We with our lives are like islands in the sea, or like trees in the forest. The maple and the pine may whisper to each other with their *leaves* and Conanicut and Newport hear each other's fog horns. But the trees also commingle their *roots* in the dark underground, and the islands also hang together through the ocean's bottom. Just so there is a continuum of cosmic consciousness, against which our individuality builds but accidental fences, and into which our several minds plunge as into a mother-sea or reservoir.[133]

Is it only our natural being — as Jaspers has it[134] — that communicates quasi bodily with nature at large and is — by *Einsfühlung*[135] connected with the very ground of all things? Is it here not often our *whole* being, including our personal one, that enjoys a peace beyond understanding, because it realizes a ground beneath the ramification and divergency of our modes of life — beneath the opposition of creaturely life in the shelter of nature, and personal *Existenz* in the exposure to the unfounded freedom of decision? In and through the enjoyment of nature, in the communication of aesthetic and artistic experience we feel a quasi heavenly bliss — not exclusively that of the children and favorites of nature. Here even a naturalist such as Dewey speaks in a tone of higher comfort than that of an organism however well-adjusted to its environ-

---

Stavenhagen, two pioneers of a phenomenology of religion. Cf. Adolf Reinach, *Gesammelte Schriften,* xviiiff; and K. Stavenhagen, *Absolute Stellungnahmen* (1925).

133 James, "Final Impressions of a Psychical Researcher" (1909), *Memories and Studies,* (1911), 204.

134 Cf. *Wahrheit,* 1006, 897.

135 The term *'Einsfühlung'* means 'feeling one with' and is contrasted with *'Einfühlung,'* (empathy, feeling oneself into another person or thing) by Max Scheler in his *Wesen und Formen der Sympathie, 16ff.*

ment: "Through the phases of perturbation and conflict, there abides the deep-seated memory of an underlying harmony, the sense of which haunts life like the sense of being founded on a rock."[136] And it is not merely Chinese conformity with nature or aesthetic gourmandise that is expressed in Kuo-Jo Hsü's (around 1075 B.C.) account of how he enjoys the paintings of his collection "in a quiet communion, blissfully unaware of the extent of Heaven and Earth and all the myriad complications of existence."[137]

The system of knowledge is an outgrowth of the real context of forms and things and men in their mutual 'definition' and delimitation. Our intellection is an *inter-legere* or (as Thomas has it) an *intus legere* trying to penetrate into things toward their essence *(usque ad essentiam rei)*: it is or was, at least, intended to be an "intimate penetration of truth," in some aspect or other.[138] Its system is an ectypal, a synthetic and tentative reconstruction of the original (archetypal) structure. I.e., it is not, as in Neo-Kantianism, a pure construction in its own autonomous style, but even in the boldest, most abstract ventures of constructive imagination it remains somehow guided and is certainly controlled by the nature of things, is confronted with their objections, supported by their concurrence, and exploits a previous familiarity with them. Altogether, that "free engagement" of ours of which Sartre speaks is preceded by a rootedness in being which he denies; I *find* myself engaged owing to what Marcel calls "an anterior encompassment of myself on the part of Being." (In Marcel, *'engagement'* — the word and the idea — has an overtone of religious betrothal.[139])

At this point, i.e., in the account of the nature of knowledge, the lines which I try to draw converge again with those of Jaspers. Whereas he reserves the word 'communication,' German *'Mitteilung,'* to information in the medium and tradition of language, and uses *'Teilnahme'* for that participation in being which takes place in knowledge, his description of knowledge comes very close to that presented with the help of my formalized concept of communication:

In the simile of participation is stated that the subject takes in, as it were, something of the object — not, to be sure, its material reality, but its essence. Whereas in the outer world things and organisms af-

136 John Dewey, *Art as Experience*, 17.

137 Kuo Jo-Hsü, *Experiences in Painting*, 1; cf. 127, n. 180.

138 Thomas Acquinas, *Summa Theologica*, 2-2ae, VIII, 1, c; XLIX, 5, 3m.

139 Cf. G. Marcel, e.g., *Etre et Avoir*, 13, 16, 56, 60ff, 159, 203f, 254; *Du Refus à l'Invocation*, 44, 94.

fect, touch, destroy, devour each other, knowledge represents the entirely different relation . . . of a boundless expansion of the thinking subject without being *eo ipso* an extension of its power over things. Participation is the simile for compresence, assimilation — . . . this puzzling phenomenon of being together with all things of this world and, at the same time, transcend them as a thinking being.[140]

There is *religio* in Jaspers' acknowledging — not only, as the Marxists and other sociologists do, the *Seinsgebundenheit* of all thought, i.e., its conditionedness by being, but above all, — the *Seinsverbundenheit* of true thought, its connection with and obligation to Being.[141] Here I am in full and grateful agreement with Jaspers. Indeed, knowledge grows from communication with Being and beings; it is a superior form of it, able both to utilize and to deepen this relationship.

XI

In this sense knowledge is "recollection" and is acknowledged as such by Jaspers himself. Platonic teaching and Goethian sentiment blend when he speaks of the high moments in which we seem to be let into the secret and to enjoy the knowledge of bystanders of the creation itself — a *Mitwissenschaft mit der Schöpfung* — a mood "as if *au fond* we had been witnesses to the origination of all things, and as if this knowledge had been veiled to and forgotten by us in the narrowness of our world."[142]

It is thus in the profoundest depth of myself that I feel at one with the ground of this world. This happens in the absorption by philosophical meditation and speculation as well as when I am surrounded by the spectacle of nature.

"When the soul of the landscape speaks, that is nothing in objective terms; as an experience, however, it is the bodily presence of something (!) known to a Rembrandt and Shakespeare. It is something like (!) a revelation of Being . . . Something (!) emanates from there that makes me independent (of the world of appearances) because it keeps me in contact and communication *(Verbindung)* with the ground of things."

Without actually being a believer, I thus become a brother to those who enjoy this connection with the Infinite in the holy communion, in the reception of the Eucharist.[143]

---

140 *Wahrheit*, 238.   141 *Ibid.*, 262ff, 314.

142 The phrase "*Mitwissenschaft mit der Schöpfung*" is taken from Schelling; cf., e.g., *Werke*, II, III, 303. It is a favorite term with Jaspers: see, e.g., *Philosophie* III, 209; *Scope*, 15. *Wahrheit*, 104, 112, 175f, 217, 1046. The quotation is from pp. 175f.

143 *Wahrheit*, 698, 897. (The exclamation marks are mine.)

Passages like this have their own *'existential'* significance in the way they *express* experiences of such significance: they have it because they are no precise objective statements, but, by all sorts of 'if' and 'quasi,' protected from being mistaken for definite assertions of an impersonal truth. This guardedness shows Jaspers' honesty and his critical sobermindedness prevailing even in the transcendent flight of "absolute consciousness," the Icarus-flights in which the Infinite is ascertained by its imperviousness to the finite. But this attitude is also the result of Jaspers' primal experience which is, of necessity, the Alpha and Omega of our discussion — the partition of the modes of being and the ultimate solitude of the Self. Although the Self may relate itself to the transcendent One, though it may exist on the strength of faith in it, it will never enjoy a perfect union or grasp the absolute unity. We understand only manifoldness within a unity we do not understand.

That is why man's will to communication can never be fully satisfied, and why the feeling of communication between the ground within us and the ground of the world — the *Mitwissenschaft mit der Schöpfung* — remains in the state of an "as if" or, at best, a matter of indistinct divination, merging in silence.

Jaspers, the moralist and critic, moves but warily toward a position such as is confidently held and proclaimed by the poet, Paul Claudel. Claudel's famous plays on the words *"connaissance"* and *"co-naissance"* (cognition and recognition), *"connaissance* and *reconnaissance,"* genesis and gnosis, *causer* (to cause) and *causer* (to converse), etc., are the result of artistic introspection as well as metaphysical thought and the linguistic musings of a master of language and have added significance due to this co-operation. Co-existence is *co-naissance* because to exist together means "to be born together," to originate from the same source (though according to specific intentions — intentions and forms that complement each other in the one act of creation). All things conspire thanks to the unity of the creative spirit.

This universal sympathy and correspondence has only a more discerning expression in human con-sciousness and con-science, in human knowledge and communication, in philosophy, science and art. Just as Leibniz speaks of universal representation, Whitehead of universal prehension as the organ of universal nexus ("actual entities involve each other by reason of their prehensions of each other") [144], so does Claudel assume a mutual knowledge amongst all things: "Nature knows by way of its oceans and mountains, its mines and volcanoes, and by the minute points of its leaves of

[144] A. N. Whitehead, *Process and Reality*, 28.

grass, just as we know by way of equation, theorem, syllogism and metaphor."[145]

The particular artistic ingredient in Claudel's account consists in the conviction that the knowledge which is communicated *to* us, in our co-existence and cognation, is in return communicated *by* us through the creative word. This word is, so to speak, the final procreation of the creative word in the beginning; a product of the synergism of the human poet with the *poeta mundi:* the presentation of an eternal presence, in the form of the word, to things which pass and, therefore, need to be represented.[146]

Proférant de chaque chose le nom,
Comme un père tu l'appelles mystérieusement dans son principe, et selon que jadis
Tu participas à sa création, tu coopères à son existence.[147]

The artist realizes, intensifies and communicates a communication which is founded in the configuration of things; he consolidates the "liquid tie" amongst all creatures, including himself:

Je connais toutes choses, et toutes choses se connaissent en moi.
J'apporte à toute chose sa délivrance.
Par moi
Aucune chose ne reste plus seule mais je l'associe à une autre dans mon coeur.[148]

Calling things to universal consecration,[149] the artist does not cause but restores the engagement and performs the marriage of things.[150] That is, at least, what he feels in heeding his mission.

[145] P. Claudel, *Art Poétique*, 65 *(Mercure de France).*

[146] P. Claudel, *op. cit.,* 150.

[147] P. Claudel, *Les Muses*, 24: "Stating of each thing its name, like a father you call it mysteriously according to its principle and, just as of yore you participated in its creation, you now co-operate in its existence" — the same motif which we met before in Cézanne, Rilke and other artists. Cf. also Claudel, *La Ville,* 425.

[148] Paul Claudel, *Cinq Odes, (L'esprit et l'eau):* "I know all things and all things know themselves in me./ I come to every thing's rescue./ Through me/ No thing remains lonely any longer. No, I connect it with another one in my heart."
I must refrain from accumulating evidence by extended quotations from Rilke's poetry in confirmation of Claudel's experience. I restrict myself now to referring to pp. 237 and 243 above, and to such poems as Rilke, *Ausgewählte Werke* I, 404; *Späte Gedichte,* 23, 84; *Aus Tagebüchern und Merkblättern,* 25. — There is, however a difference which should not be overlooked: the profound resignation, both modest and full of loving pride, in which the later Rilke restricts the realm of the poet to the human realm. This may be compared with Jaspers' emphasis on the limitations of 'existential' communion.

[149] Goethe, *Faust*, v. 148.

[150] Cf. Gasquet, *Cézanne,* 80, 93; Paul Claudel, *Connaissance de l'Est,* 163.

XII

The purpose of the preceding section has not been to subscribe to the words of the poetic account of the artist's function, but to substantiate Jaspers' allusion to a *Mitwissenschaft mit der Schöpfung* by reference to the testimony of some who know creative communication better than most of us, because they participate in it more actively.[151] To take this evidence seriously seems to me one of the main demands on a philosophy which is not an *ancilla scientiarum* but in the ramifications of experience tries to show their origin in, and 'working out' of, a common ground.

For this reason, and without detracting from the qualitative differences of the modes of being on which Jaspers insists, I am inclined to use "co-existence," "community," and "communication" in the universal sense to which the artists confess as "the real thing." This means to ground the objective and measurable external relations amongst phenomena — the residue of methodical abstraction on the part of the scientist — in internal relationships such as they are experienced and set forth by, e.g., the artist.

Such a philosophical account will be necessarily couched in somewhat personalistic terms. But we should not be overly afraid of the bogy of anthropomorphism. As, so to speak, a penultimate, the heterogeneity of natural and personal being is not to be questioned. Still, general metaphysics cannot describe certain universal features of being without using, in a formalized and neutral sense, terms which are psychological when applied to the realm of human consciousness. In other words: we do not indulge in *Einfühlung* (empathy) in Theodor Lipps' sense, we do not project ourselves into things when assigning to certain data of outer experience names that have a specific meaning and familiar ring in and through inner experience.

We had already occasion to point to such indispensable metaphysical categories as the practically equivalent "expression," "representation" or "prehension." Other instances would be *orexis* and *mimesis* in Aristotle, which mean "desire" and "imitation" proper only in their application to the animal realm. There is also the *conatus* concept of Hobbes and Spinoza who certainly cannot be accused of confusing the "order of things" and the "order of ideas:" in Spinoza *conatus* as such, as a neutral term, means "impulse;" it

---

151 This will not blind us to the fact that, from the point of view of inter-personal life, the artist and artistic communication have their own problems and shortcomings.

means "will" with regard to the mind and "appetite" with regard
to the whole of mind and body.[152]

We treat "communication" and "relationship" in a similar way,
i.e., without imputing consciousness to all things that communicate with and are turned toward each other. The only implications
are those of actual intercourse in a shared existence and of a
positive or negative attitude toward one another, both pull and
tension in a universe of forces. It is in this dynamic sense (not
in the well-worn of merely objective relation and reference) that
Rilke uses for the fugue of being the word *"Bezug"* — a noun
which derives from *"ziehen,"* ("to draw," "to pull.") [153] There is
tension in this draw and draw in this tension.[154] *"Bezug"* implies
"intention" and, therefore, "tension" between two that "mean"
one another, tend toward one another (in German *meinen* — to
mean — and *minnen* — to love — have the same root) —and, nevertheless are not one.[155] This tendency which draws things together,
towards the *unerhörte Mitte* — toward the fabulous center — appears thus as *inclination:*

> *Inclination:* word abundant with truthful meaning!
> Young one — the one of the heart that still silently pines;
> no less the bent of the hill whose softest leaning
> toward the lawn which receives it inclines,
> let it also be ours to add to our essence;
> or let the bird's overflowing flight
> draw the space of our heart, displace future by presence.[156]

There are 'intentions' that are alive in a landscape as a whole
of experience, not merely a sum of objects. But it is only in man

---

[152] Spinoza, *Ethics,* Part III, propositions 7 and 9, *schol.*

[153] Rilke uses the term in many linguistic combinations. Cf. *Werke,* III, 324,
356, 386, 417, 453, 454, 463; *Aus dem Nachlass* II, 49; III, 5, 22; *Briefe an seinen
Verleger,* 393; *Briefe aus Muzot,* 196. Cf. also M. Heidegger, *Holzwege,* 260ff; O. F.
Bollnow, *Rilke,* 190ff.

[154] Rilke, *Werke,* III, 324; *Aus dem Nachlass,* III, 25.

[155] Cf. Rilke, *Werke,* III, 365, 366.

[156] Rilke, *Nachlass* III, 67.
NEIGUNG: *wahrhaftes Wort! Dass wir* JEDE *empfänden,
nicht nur die neuste, die uns ein Herz noch verschweigt;
wo sich ein Hügel langsam, mit sanften Geländen
zu der empfänglichen Wiese neigt,
sei es nicht weniger unser, sei uns vermehrlich;
oder des Vogels reichlicher Flug
schenke uns Herzraum, mache uns Zukunft entbehrlich.*

that these intents of nature are realized in the new presence they acquire through the 'intentionality' of consciousness.[157]

That this approach to things is not merely the outcome of poetic sentimentalism on the part of unthinking dilettantes, can be shown, for instance, by reference to metaphysicians of the last hundred years from Fechner to Bergson and Whitehead. I quote from the latter and his characterization of "physical purposes:" "The subjective forms of these physical purposes are either 'adversions' or 'aversions.' The subjective forms of physical purpose do not involve consciousness unless these feelings acquire integration with conscious perceptions or intuitive judgments."[158]

Above all, however, considerations like these are not at all foreign to Jaspers' own thought. They give them only some more assertive weight and a slightly stronger 'monistic' tenor. We saw that Rilke's *"Bezug"* meant partnership in uni-versal communication and communion, compliance with the pull toward the center of gravitation. This may be compared with the significant passages in which Jaspers speaks in a quite similar vein of "infinite relatedness" and the One of Transcendence: "This One — present as it is, by virtue of reason, as if from inaccessible distance — is the attraction which overcomes all schism."[159]

XIII

"On this principle, then," to speak with Aristotle, "depend the heavens and the world of nature." As giving direction to all striving, Transcendence is, thus, both an ideal limit, infinitely remote — and an immediate presence, the inmost stimulant and guide of reason and love. Its function resembles that of Aristotle's Unmoved Mover, "who produces motion just by being loved."

---

157 The universalization of the concept of intentionality would, in my opinion, establish the proper frame of reference in which Husserl's claim of the absoluteness of intentional consciousness could be endorsed. Cf. my article, "Art and Phenomenology" in *Philosophical Essays in Memory of Edmund Husserl* (edited by Marvin Farber).

158 A. N. Whitehead, *Process and Reality,* 406; cf., e.g., 124; 173: "The datum" — says Whitehead in criticism of Kant — "includes its own interconnections, and the first stage of the process of feeling is the reception into the responsive conformity of feeling whereby the datum, which is mere potentiality, becomes the individualized basis for a complex unity of realization."

159 *Wahrheit,* one of the references to *"Zugkraft"* on 118; cf. 109; 681: "It is always the One which moves us to produce the unity which insinuates itself to us." We feel the *"infinite relatedness"* of all things and "experience the One as the all-pervasive attraction which, from the realm of Transcendence, keeps together what to us is scattered and threatens to slip into chaos." *(My italics!)*

Whereas, in Jaspers, reason is not the One itself, but a reflection of its splendor, the "bond" of all unity, the organ of loving union and communication, — the One 'in person' is unity pure and simple and, therefore, beyond reason, beyond love and truth. It is beyond all the restlessness of our actions which only shows the vanity of our projects, the nothingness of our 'achievements,' the fragmentariness of this life, the discordances and contradictions of this world through which we needs must go to fulfill ourselves and recognize, at the depth of all struggle, the lasting peace of the One — and acquiesce in it.[160]

Transcendence is not really the *truth* which will set us free, according to Jaspers. "To speak of truth with regard to it, would mean to apply to it possibilities of immanent (i.e., worldly) being and imply the possibility of falsity. We can speak of it in this way only figuratively, confounded as we are when all questions come to an end."[161]

According to Jaspers, Transcendence is not itself the love which animates our will to communication, though, as the Infinite, it may be the locus where the parallel developments of all Selves can meet. "In the beloved one I love the lover: I love in him what we love in common: Being itself."[162] "Although it is through love that God can be felt, God is not love." It is only by way of an edifying symbol that I can speak of Him as "love." Taken in a strict sense, such language would "impute to Deity that movement, imperfection and striving that inhere in the nature of man."[163]

It is obvious that this (Aristotelian) one-way conception of love which removes God from correlation, correspondence, and communication with man, abrogates the idea of the covenant —

---

[160] Cf. *Wahrheit*, 328. The Beyond seems here even more radical than in Bradley's Absolute — that harmonious system in which all the contradictions of the phenomena are transmuted and absolved. Obviously, the difference between the being of Transcendence and that of the world (like the Greek distinction between Being and Non-Being, etc.) is largely a difference of value. The reality of things and the world as their transcendent unity is not denied. They are rated as appearances (not as phantoms) because, in their transitoriness, etc., they point beyond themselves to the integral being of Transcendence. *"Le monde existe, . . . il est, puisqu'il est ce qui n'est pas. . . . Dieu seul est cela qui est."* ("The world exists; it is since it is just that which is not . . . God alone is the Being that is", (Claudel, *L'Art Poétique (Mercure de France)*, 145.) This interpretation of the *Eheye* accords, by the way, with Hermann Cohen's interpretation of the unity of God as his uniqueness.

[161] *Wahrheit*, 638; cf. 981.

[162] *Wahrheit*, 1001. This idea, which originates in Plato's *Symposium*, has found its classical Christian expression in Augustine's *ipse amor amatur*, "it is love itself that is loved" (*Civitas Dei*, XI, 28).

[163] Cf., e.g., *Origin*, 242; *Wahrheit*, 1012.

just as Spinoza did, though not in Spinoza's way. Jaspers' idea of love is moulded after the demon Eros in the *Symposium* rather than in the image of Jewish *zedakah, hesed* and *ahawah,* of Greek *agape* and Latin *caritas*. Whereas the latter terms apply to both God and man, whereas in the New Testament as well as in the Old, God's antecedent love encourages finite man to lift his eyes up to Him in the gratitude of responsive love — "we love Him, because He first loved us"[164] —, Jaspers sees in *love* only the human striving for union in God through communication with man, hence in the need for communication a mark of our finiteness, of the particularity which, in the return to the One, we try to overcome. And he has little respect for *charity,* which he does not take in the sense of the foremost of the theological virtues, but preponderantly in the degraded sense of a social expediency. It is to him not the condescendence in God's love for needy man and man's imitation of God in compassionate love for the poor.

Since this terminology is not accidental, a detour will prove necessary to show its symptomatic meaning as to the relations between man and man as well as between God and man. For it is well to remember that "all modes of love are interrelated: each one has its actuality and consummation only in and through the other."[165] The depreciation of charity will reflect upon social as well as religious community. "God is present to us only through man, man through God. Man and God are lost to us only one with the other;"[166] and an attenuation in one way of relationship will be indicative of an estrangement in the other.

Charity is to Jaspers mostly the condescendent attitude of man toward man — incompatible with true love, which is a noble love among peers, a mutual summons to truthful selfhood. Charity, on the other hand, is to him a mere compensation, on the part of the State or the Church, for the most dangerous inequalities in the economic order, "without neighborhood of one's own self to that of the other. It goes together with the maintenance of class-levels and lacks the unconditionedness" of free communication.[167]

The emphasis on the neighborhood of free Selves on the peaks

---

164 I John, 4:19. As to the Jewish teaching, cf., e.g., Franz Rosenzweig, *Kleinere Schriften,* 364f.

165 *Wahrheit,* 1003.   166 *Wahrheit,* 1002.

167 *Philosophie* II, 383. A milder expression 278f: "There is love in charitative assistance; yet in its decline it becomes self-gratification in indiscriminate compassion." Cf. also *Age, passim* — this harsh aristocratic document of 1931 — with too little productive sympathy for man in the gigantic struggle and experiment of modern life.

of *Existenz* prevents Jaspers from fully realizing the power of compassionate love in which men meet "in the valleys of human needs, in those extremities in which we all are naked and poor," in which we " 'render the deeds of mercy' for which we pray," that "disillusioned yet not discouraged love" in which we bear with one another and show that patience without which human community is doomed, but with whose help we may be able to do something to heal the wounds caused in our time by impatience and passions.[168]

What is in question here, are not only the *dehors* of social manners, the inevitable compromises and appeasements in the external organization of life on the biological level. As an *'existential'* motor, social conscience enters and surpasses all "security administration of the outer life of the masses *(Massenordnung in Daseinsfürsorge)* that provides for the satisfaction of their needs."[169] Social equity is a holy task before it becomes a matter of expediency. Social care would not work, and the wheels of social legislation would not turn, were it not for the prophetic passion and compassion of those without whom all social politics would be soulless indeed. It is not enough to put in control of the apparatus of social organization "a metaphysically founded basic attitude revealed in ethos that guides the organizational plans,"[170] if this is the exclusive ethos of self-realization. What is needed is less a policing of social and socialist activities by an ethos that is alien to them than their inspiration by a trustworthy and congenial moral faith.[171]

Jaspers' ethics of self-realization through self-communication is not quite of this type. Certainly, only a quack could offer a panacea for all the sufferings of our time. And an ideal of life is not discredited by the fact that it appeals only to an aristocratic minority among men.[172] A philosophy has a right to be esoteric. It is courageous and honest to stand, without compromise, against the falsification of ultimate human truth, against a much propagandized progress — toward the abyss. But it seems an objection

---

[168] Cf. my *Geschichtsphilosophie der Gegenwart* (1931), 41f; and my paper, "Reality and Truth in History," *Perspectives in Philosophy* (Ohio State University, 1953), 43-54.

[169] *Situation,* 27 (my own translation above, because the translation in *Age,* 33, completely fails to render the telling phrase, *Massenordnung in Daseinsfürsorge);* cf. still the more cautious version in *Origin,* 172ff (with the partly justified warning against a "total planning" at the price of totalitarianism).

[170] *Origin,* 192.   [171] See below, 283f.

[172] Cf., e.g., *Age,* 220ff. The problems of that little book are treated in a somewhat more academic fashion in *Philosophie* II, 363ff.

to a social philosophy — as responsible social action — , if it helps
to undo what little can be done, and, after 1918, could be done
for human communication even under the most adverse circumstances; and if it helps to bring about the very opposite to its
professed (and sincere) purpose.[173] It is sadly ironical that Jaspers
admired no one more highly than Max Weber, the democrat —
and had no faith in democracy.[174] And it is tragic that his plea in
1931 — to *"save,"* in the time of the revolution of the masses,
"the efficiency of the best who are the fewest"[175] — had its direct
reply in the overthrow of social democracy by national socialism,
the most vicious blend of tyranny and ochlocracy.[176]

This much had to be said — though *sotto voce* and in grief,
not to rub salt into the wounds of the past nor to detract from
the respect for one of the few sages of our time; but because it
may help us to go to the root of this problem — which is not only
the problem of an individual philosophy.

XIV

Why this lack of sympathy, i.e., of compassion for the 'masses'?
Why this undervaluation of charity, which — over against compassion — had been endorsed even by the Stoics? Why the almost
exclusive concern with and for the "happy few," the Self and
the Selves?

The answer cannot be as simple as to see the cause in a mere

---

173 If this was the effect of *Age,* — highly advertised and widely read as volume
1000 of the *Göschen Library* — it must be remembered that in 1931 the democratic
process was at a low ebb in national and international affairs, and that even its most
ardent defenders could not but almost despair of its workability. Even then Jaspers
spoke out against the pseudo-authority that prevailed in the totalitarian movements
of both Fascism and Bolshevism: *op. cit.,* 100f.

174 *Age,* 106f. It may be conjectured that it was just Weber's failure to win a
candidacy in the Democratic party that added to Jaspers' skepticism as to the
chances of democratic government. *Cum grano salis,* his case can be compared with
that of a Plato who was a deadly foe of tyranny while despairing of a republic in
which a Socrates was doomed.

175 *Age,* 221 (Jaspers' *italics* in the German edition only).

176 In fairness to Jaspers, it ought to be stated (1) that, obviously, his advocacy
of the best, the καλλοὶ κ' ἀγαθοί, had nothing to do with a defense of privileged
classes; (2) that the problems of *Führer,* nobility and mass were no longer political
problems to him. He did not want for his 'noblemen' any distinctive position on
the political scale. He did not believe in the possibility or desirability of a minority
rule; he wanted for them only elbow space for their self-realization as anonymous
workers in the order of the whole, the inevitable "mass order"; and he saw in them
the torch-bearers who could carry the light of selfhood through the dark of our
decaying world into the world of the future: cf. *Age,* 227, 229f.

intoxication by the idea of the Self. Nor can it be given on strictly Christian ground, viz. that 'after all,' at the 'last judgment,' it is the individual self that counts and will have to account for itself. To Jaspers, this would be only the mythical garb of the *'existential'* truth.

It is of the nature, at least, of Jaspers' philosophy that the first root and the final reason is to be found in a very personal sentiment — in his thirst for and insistence on a truly personal communication with truly personal Selves, i.e., with men who were not products of circumstances and parrots of conventional phrases, but makers of themselves and free to communicate the genuine truth of authentic experience. This longing for free communion in a covenant of personal greatness is not likely to find quick and frequent response and was more likely to find it in the dialogue with his brothers in destiny, his 'contemporaries' in the past than in the converse with people on today's mainstreet. The following sentence has a strong autobiographical coloring:

> If practically everybody whom the individual now encounters in life seems to lack value and distinction, if disillusionment is heaped upon disillusionment, then it becomes the measure of man's own stature how far he succeeds in breaking through, in finding indications for his path amid the dispersed embers of the true, and in becoming certain where it is that man really is man.[177]

'The individual against the masses' will become the watchword particularly in a mass-civilization like ours, which represents a menace to the independence of the Self and the spiritual dignity of life. It is on the way of this reaction that Jaspers has found succor first in Nietzsche and his critique of our time — to some degree even in his concept of the "superman" (though not as the "blond beast") — and, since 1913, in Kierkegaard and his fight for the "individual" as the "exception," against the tyranny of "the masses, the numbers, the public."[178]

"And yet, to be the Exception under polemical conditions . . . is in one sense so frightful, almost deadly. Not only is it the greatest possible, almost superhuman exertion; but the attitude of opposition to others, and such a degree of opposition, is deadly to all human sympathy."[179] It must be asked, however, whether

---

[177] *Age*, 217 (in a slightly revised translation).

[178] *The Journals of Søren Kierkegaard* (translated by Alexander Dru), 207.

[179] Kierkegaard, *op. cit.*, 517. Jaspers, too, recognizes in the unconditioned Self a *"quasi-unnatural* severity . . . and violence" — but, strangely enough, only "against itself," *Age*, 219.

this position is as unavoidably Christian as it appeared to Kierkegaard. Christianity preaches, after all, the brotherhood of men
and not only the neighborhood of a few individual Selves in
their diaspora in the world[180] (a phenomenon whose value I
certainly do not want to underrate). But even the bearer of
Christian election and predestination cannot be equated with
(somewhat maliciously phrased) 'the exceptional Self.'

Still, there must be in the Protestant tradition, from which
Jaspers as well as Kierkegaard and Nietzsche rose, an element
which favored their extreme reaction to the time. I see it in the
inwardness of the Protestant man, a deep and absorptive self-
concern, in comparison to which all social concern, concern for
the outer welfare of man, is liable to appear shallow and second-
rate. It is this attitude which prompted Luther's stand in the
Peasant's War, determines Nietzsche's understanding of religion
("a religious man thinks only of himself") [181] and has an echo
throughout Thomas Mann's work, first of all in his *Reflections of
an Unpolitical Man*. Despite his disowning of Christian unworld-
liness and his strong sense of social justice, there seems a residue
of this feeling in Karl Jaspers.

Although religious and theological problems enter this paper
only as far as they involve, and are involved in, the problem of
communication, it is pertinent to point to the contrast between
Protestantism of the type mentioned and Judaism in the question
of social ethics and religion. The Jewish God is, emphatically,
the God of the needy, the stranger, the widow, the orphan and
the poor. And there is — Kierkegaard's stirring interpretation of
the *Akedah* (the Abraham-Isaac story) notwithstanding — no
such thing in Judaism as the "teleological suspension of the
ethical" by virtue of the religious. To the Jews, the covenant
between God and man is itself a moral contract binding on either
partner: they are defined by their positions on it. God is the God
of the covenant and, thus, the God of man, just as man is — not the
animal rationale or the *homo faber*, but — the man of God. 'Zedakah' (justice seasoned by charity) of both God and man means
their standing the test in a common trial, in a correlation *(b'rith)*
of mutual responsiveness and responsibility.

That to the Jews correspondence in co-operation belongs to
the very nature of God as well as man is to be emphasized over
against the Augustinian Neo-Platonism in the interpretation of
God's name in Exodus 3:12ff, the translation of *Eheye asher*

180 *Age*, 222f.
181 Nietzsche, *Werke* (Kröners Taschenausgabe) vol. 77, 281.

Eheye by the *Sum qui Sum*. It is no overstatement on Gilson's part to call this formula the very cornerstone of Christian philosophy.[182] One feels the trembling of Augustine's heart in the exclamation: "Behold! This is the great Is, the great Is."[183] And we have quoted (pp. 222f, 228f) reverberations of this Christian Leitmotif in Jaspers' own thought. It is not possible at this place[184] to analyze in detail what has happened to the holy name by assimilation into the medium of hellenistic and scholastic philosophy. Suffice it to say that the promise that is implied in the name: "I shall be with you the way I shall decide to be with you whenever you seek me in your need" has completely disappeared in Philo as well as in its Latin version and, therefore, also in the English "I am that I am." The phrase is rendered into Latin not only in the tense of the eternal present to designate the Immutable Being *(Esse est nomen incommutabilitatis)*; it is also said to denote the self-sufficiency, self-containedness, the inner absoluteness of Being as such, apart from any relations: "I am that I am — this is the name I own as my proper name; that I am the God of Abraham, the God of Isaac and the God of Jacob — this is what you may own," since "it is both true and comprehensible to you."[185]

Seen in this way, God is no longer essentially the God of the Covenant. In Jaspers, *"Bezug"* — the being drawn of things toward one another and, thus, toward the ultimate ground[186] — may have its reward, but it has no authorization, has no response and is none. In responsible action, we may answer for ourselves by answering the claims of our fellow beings; but 'in this respect,' i.e., in our respect for them, we do not answer a question of which they are the carriers rather than the authors. The irreversibility of a relation which is no mutual and personal relationship gives it the character of Schleiermacher's "absolute dependence" on the Ab-solute which, as such, is under no personal com-mitment to us.[187]

---

[182] E. Gilson, *L'Esprit de la Philosophie Médiévale* 2, 51.

[183] Augustinus, *Enarrationes in Psalmos* 101:8.

[184] This will be done in an article *"Eheye asher Eheye vs. Sum qui Sum."*

[185] Augustinus, *Enarrationes in Psalmos,* 134:6.

[186] See above, pp. 253f.

[187] Jaspers' conception of divine Transcendence has much in common with Schleiermacher's idea of God as the absolute One, the living yet impersonal and transcendent ground which excludes all contradictions just as the world in its transcendence includes them all; and which in contrast with worldly transcendence, cannot be approximated as the *terminus ad quem* of progressive knowledge. Cf. particularly Schleiermacher's *Dialektik,* § 218-227; also Appendix B (Jonas), pp. 152ff; D 475; E, 525ff. Bradley's concept of the Absolute is also of this type.

This is, indeed, what seems to follow from the *"Sum qui Sum."* But it has dangerous implications. It threatens both the personal and creative nature of Deity. A person belongs into a social context. In the social grammar it is a first, second or third person. "Personality," says Jaspers, "is that mode of being oneself which, in its very nature, cannot be alone; it is something related, must have something else apart from it: persons and nature." As person, "Deity would be in need of man for the sake of communication."[188] But this would be a violation of divine majesty. It is only consistent with this consideration that Jaspers substitutes an incommunicado Transcendence for God *qua* person, God in loving communication with his creatures. At the same time, he points at the idea of Trinity only as a way of Theism to extricate itself from the dilemma brought about by the 'needless' insistence on a personal God: the communication amongst the three persons is supposed to place God's personal being beyond the dependence on beings outside.[189]

Yet is it not obvious that, in this way of arguing, personal relatedness, which seems not unworthy of an infinite Being, is reduced to mere relativity and objective conditionedness, which is, indeed, contradictory to the very idea of the Absolute? Somehow Jaspers is still committed to the original Greek idea of the true and supreme Being as unmoved and immutable (for what should cause it to move and to act? "The circumstances of action would appear trivial and unworthy of the Divine."[190]) Under the present aspect, at least, this appears the reason for his exempting Deity from all relation and giving it the status of anonymous, absolute Transcendence.

But the absoluteness of the Divine need not be interpreted literally as unrelatedness. Nor is monotheism compelled to give way to the monism of an "all-encompassing" substance which cannot tolerate any substance besides itself without being limited and, therefore, deprived of its boundless infinite. The Absolute would not be mediatized nor would any status of being be compromised by free relations with other beings. The substantiality

---

[188] *Philosophie* III, 166.

[189] A similar reflection, but in faithful adherence and justification of the Catholic dogma, appears in Edith Stein's *Endliches und Ewiges Sein*, 324: eternal creation, the circle of creative love within Deity is necessary because the mere correlation of love between Creator and creature would make God in his love dependent on the creatures and their love. (This circle of eternal creation within God is as it were, the Christian counterpart of the *noësis noëseōs* — the thinking on thinking — in the God of Aristotle.).

[190] Aristotle, *Nicomachean Ethics*, X, 8, 1178 b 17f.

of a being would even be enhanced wherever it entertains a relation that implies an element of the creative, i.e., wherever it posits another being — either altogether or by giving it an entirely new rôle and status. A person, for instance, would not be its true Self, did it not give and were it not given recognition as a fellow being. Thanks to this relation it is not merely another subject or object. As to God, there is no competition of things with divine Transcendence since, in the ontological order, Transcendence would not be at par with the beings with which it deigns to communicate. They are not founded in and by themselves, but taken to owe their actuality to an act of communication of being, their nature to their calling in the distribution of parts within the whole, and even their freedom, perhaps, to a sort of divine self-restraint which entrusts the creature with an active and responsible function in the process of creation.[191] Divine excellence would not be impaired by this relation to beings that depend with all they are on God — not, indeed, as a first cause but as a ruling and creative power — in this sense on divine authorship, so that the primary initiative and ultimate merit would remain his.

Is it not enough, then, to secure for God that position of absolute sovereignty which makes him, for instance in Augustine, the "Lord of the Soul?" *"Est Deus in nobis"* — "God is within us," declares Kant in his *Opus Postumum,* "not as an eternal substance, but as a moral relation within me;" i.e., the Absolute is present in my unconditional respect for the moral law and, therefore, my recognition of the moral agent in my fellow beings. The Holy is here revered as the spirit that creates true human community and rules in it: "where two or three are gathered in my name, there am I in the midst of them."[192]

From a more universal point of view (from which the difference of the moral and the natural orders does not disappear, but seems somehow provided for in the ordinance of the whole and vaulted over by it), God would be the power of powers, the binding and ordering power, which gives things a hold in their own concrete-

---

[191] In German 'to relate oneself' *(sich verhalten)* has a meaningful ambiguity which has been exploited by Rilke and is relevant in this context. The relationship to others is here maintained by containing oneself *(sich verhalten qua* restraint) and setting them free. (See above, the poem on p. 240.) The Self-containedness of God would thus be an act of supreme resignation rather than a spurning of all relations by virtue of absolute transcendence. In one of its aspects, his Transcendence would be a product of this abdication so that he appears absent thanks to the discretion of his presence and is present in the terror of his absence.

[192] Matthew, 18:20.

ness and in the concrete universe of subservient powers to which
they belong and in which they have a chance to establish themselves for a time.[193] It is this conception — that of the power of
powers — which, according to the tradition, underlies such names
of God as *Elohim* and *Shaddai*. A monotheism of this type includes, therefore, rather than excludes a host of subaltern powers
— the gods and goddesses of polytheism. That is to say, it can
recognize the spirits of the different spheres and outlooks of life,
but adds the faith in a unity of the spirit which relates them all
with one another as constituents of the concrete unity of the
world and of all mankind.

Newton's famous scholium to the *Principles* lodges the nature
of Deity in precisely this relation (not relativity) of Lordship.
'God' is to Newton a *vox relativa: Deitas est dominatio Dei*. And
Schelling has most eloquently commented on this concept of
God as, at once, "the Lord of Being" and the Lord of the Cove-
nant:

> one could say: God is actually nothing in himself. He is nothing
> but relation, pure relation. For he is nothing but the Lord. What-
> ever we attribute to him over and above this, makes him mere
> substance. . . . Just because he is not concerned with and for him-
> self, but *sui securus* (secured in and not burdened by his existence),
> He can be engrossed in the care for other things. He is, so to speak,
> altogether ecstatic, hence free from self-concern and devoted to the
> liberation of everything else.[194]

It is true that Schelling himself did not stop at the idea of God
as the creator of the world nor even at that of the intimate rapport of man and Deity. In this rapport man is God's paramount
concern, since man is the vinculum of divine unity and realizes
the unity of the divine aspects (just as, in Jaspers, man's reason
is the tie of all modes of transcendence). God's absoluteness is
not properly accounted for, according to Schelling as well as
Jaspers, by a concept which still contains — as creation does —
the correlation with something *extra Deum,* or at least, *praeter
Deum.* Creation — it seems to Schelling, though we would question two of these equations — creation is causality, causality is
correlation, correlation is relativity. Hence, he moves towards
that *Absolute Voluntarism* in which the divine Will ceases to
appear "transitive and to move a Being apart from itself: it is
an immanent Will that moves nothing besides itself."[195]

193 Cf., e.g., Plato, *Philebus*, 27A.
194 Schelling, *Werke*, I, X, 260.
195 Schelling, *op. cit.*, 277.

The detailed reference to Schelling has been necessary because this *Absolute Voluntarism,* characteristic as it is of the German philosophical tradition, finds a new and most radical representation in contemporary Existentialism, above all in Heidegger's *Holzwege.* But, thanks to the early and close relationship to Schelling, the common inheritance from Nietzsche, this tendency, though less conspicuous, may still have its sway even in Jaspers' thought.

In reformulating Nietzsche's will to power, Heidegger insists on that immanent Will that wills but itself. "The substance of Being is Will." The Will is the immanent nature of every one thing as each thing gathers and collects itself in itself. In this concretion each has its being as a self-willed entity. This — and not the love of Christian faith — is taken to be the actual and active principle of the present world.[196]

Jasper's agnosticism as to the inner nature of ultimate Transcendence does not allow him to indulge in any such outright statement. He even denounces the dogmatism of Nietzsche's principle of the Will to Power as "the ultimate substrate and substance of everything."[197] And there are decisive differences between him and Heidegger — indicated, for instance, in Jaspers' enthusiastic praise of both reason (the archvillain in Heidegger's show) and love. But, for all this, reason is to Jaspers but the will to unification,[198] not transcendental unity itself; and love in its highest sense is restricted to the never secured, distinctly human sphere of co-*Existenz.* All correlation and, therefore, all love is banished from the icy heights of pure Transcendence.

Under these circumstances, what can it mean to call Transcendence "the power through which I am myself," the One "that attracts us and gives us hold?"[199] What is it actually that gives reason the confidence to disclose the substance of Being? According to Jaspers, the substance of thought is will. What, then, is the inmost nature of that one actuality which is illustrated by each true, i.e., well-founded act of thought? Is it also will — but the absolute, absolutely self-assertive Will (not the wilfulness of the selfish individual nor the particularity of a will which still lives in the never satisfied intention of union with the One)? Is the unifying power of reason — this reflected splendor of primeval Unity —, is reason's will to total communication, after all, but the Absolute Will itself, whose light, broken in the manifoldness of human *Existenzen,* converges again towards its original

---

196 Cf. Heidegger, *Holzwege,* 216, 234, 256f. This does not mean that Heidegger identifies himself with this conception of the Will.

197 *Wahrheit,* 272.   198 Cf. *ibid.,* 701.   199 *Ibid.,* 79, 111.

source? If so, this may, to some extent, hold of all modes of true thought. Indeed, says Jaspers, "the identity of Being and thinking has, perhaps, to be sought eventually in the identity between the actuality of the Will as it prevails in thought, on the one hand, and of pure Being, on the other."[200]

Somewhat wary hints like this one seem few and far between in Jaspers' writings. But they may help to explain the 'existential' analogue to the stoic amor fati concept, for instance in the last pages of Philosophie. Our love in God would be the community we find in the acceptance of common historical destiny. Instead of both dreading and enjoying the correlation and communication with the Divine, we would freely join in the free surge of the Absolute Will which may throw us high and throw us away without husbanding care. To become Selves before Transcendence would include becoming free from the fear for our particularity, free and ready for the great venture and sacrifice of Existenz; it would mean to obtain composure in the active suffering of our nothingness, to be able to fulfill ourselves in the very shipwreck of our intentions, in which Being proves its Transcendence to finite man.

This is, I suppose, a fair résumé of the famous concluding lines of Philosophie, but given in a tenor which slightly accentuates the dynamics of those pages so as to give them a more deliberate slant toward absolute voluntarism. Read this way, Jaspers would insist on a bold 'going with' natura naturans,[201] with the creative will in which ours is absorbed and carried beyond itself. We would have a heroic variety to the Bible's "not what I will, but what thou wilt" — heroic, because man would not be supported by confidence in a power of love as the ruler of that movement to which he is to confide his life.

The recognition of such an undercurrent in Jasper's thought, of a metaphysics of the Will that wills itself would go far in explaining the self-containedness and all-encompassing, even — from the human perspective — the recklessness of Transcendence, in which correlation and communication are left behind. In German tradition, the denial — not of God, but — of a God "to hear our lamentations" goes back to the Spinozism of Goethe's youthful storm and stress poem "Prometheus." And the cruel harshness of the world regime to which we have been subject during our lifetime cannot but lend strength to such a philosophical faith.

200 Ibid., 310f.

201 This is the way Heidegger interpreted (Holzwege, 255ff) Rilke's poem, "Wie die Natur. . . . ," Späte Gedichte, 90. Cf., e.g., Wahrheit, 997.

There is, weirdly familiar to us, something demoniacal in the absoluteness of such an irresponsive and irresponsible Will, whether our own wills are sparks from it or not, whether — enthroned in silence — its unity transcends the unifying efforts of our reason altogether, or reason tries to draw us back into the current and dynamics of an absolute, absolutely self-willed movement. In any case, and in tune with the original mood of Jaspers' thought, the unity in question would be beyond duality as well as dualism. It would seem to be an absolute, monolithic unity rather than the unity of the spirit in an absolute relation. But it may be submitted that, in the long run, an interpretation of Deity in terms of — *sit venia verbo* — a more constitutional monarchy will not only be milder, but may be farther-seeing and do better, and may thus carry the day — even if only the day after next.

XV

In fact, there are in Jaspers himself strong, though carefully qualified indications of a more parliamentary procedure, of a dialogue of life that does not leave out even the Highest. The main trend of Jaspers' philosophy and, on the whole, his concept of Transcendence run actually counter to an excessive voluntarism. The mystery of Transcendence cannot be simply equated with the incomprehensibility of an absolute, absolutely uncommitted Will. Jaspers is loath to read into Transcendence the dynamics of human life. To the "eternal peace which all struggling and striving find *in* God, the Lord"[202] corresponds — to be even, somewhat ambiguously, identified with it — the "stillness *of* pure Being itself."[203]

Similarly ambiguous as the "calm in God" seems, at first, the "guidance" granted by Transcendence to *Existenz* and faith.[204] To clarify the sense it has in Jaspers will help to determine the proper locus of his theory of Transcendence in comparison with monotheism. Now, "guidance" partly means, in voluntaristic terms, that the Absolute Will guides ours just as one movement takes the other in tow, or as in a machine the particular motion is regulated by the working principles of the whole — with the difference, however, that we freely entrust ourselves to the order of the One. Aware of it in an ultimate certitude *(Grundgewiss-*

---

202 *Wahrheit,* 328 (a quotation from Goethe). My *italics.*

203 *Ibid., my italics.* Cf. *op. cit.,* 180f.   204 Cf., e.g., *Scope,* 17.

heit) and contact, we are in a kind of "permanent dialogue (!) with Transcendence." But there are no certainties in this certitude. There are no clear-cut prescriptions to be gained from this "dialogue," but only challenges to try and risk and to leap into an opaque situation. It is only owing to this resoluteness on our part that the "hints and signs awaken" to the significance they can have for us.[205] Hence, the "guidance" which Transcendence gives, means often not more than this: that our trust in it sets us free — free from identifying ourselves with our worldly projects and with the state and course of worldly affairs.

In any case, the *Zugkraft* (attraction) of Transcendence, to which Jaspers frequently refers, seems the attractive force which draws reason in us toward the center of unity rather than the tractive power which draws us along.[206] As the "fountainhead of strength," Transcendence is the independent value in its relation to *Existenz,* as the dependent one — dependent even and just when the Self realizes and asserts itself: "The 'I am' combines the weight of my being *irreplaceable* and *unique* with the defect of existing only owing to, and in view of, Transcendence which gives me to myself; I thus experience the most radical dependence in the most authentic act of being my Self."[207]

While thus maintaining its superiority, Transcendence seems turned toward us in a way which gives to its "guidance," after all, much of the flavor of personal correlation in what Jaspers himself compared with a personal "dialogue." Not only *Existenz* is oriented towards Transcendence; Transcendence is also oriented towards *Existenz.* "Without *Existenz* the meaning of Transcendence would fall away."[208] However qualified this correlation proves to be — Transcendence is present only *to Existenz,* whereas *Existenz* is altogether *due to* Transcendence — still, it seems as if we were counted upon and can count on Transcendence: "It is only to Transcendence that I can surrender unconditionally."[209] It is on its guidance that I can rely. Love transcends everything in a move toward Being itself. "There is working within us from our depth something that fills us with longing and hope. It is the ground of confidence that it will speak whenever we are in need. It connects us with Being prior to creation, with fathomless *(abgründige)* Transcendence."[210]

Utterances like these — and there are many — are animated by a personal warmth such as seems adequate only in communica-

205 *Wahrheit,* 698f.

206 Cf., e.g., *ibid.,* 111.

207 *Ibid.,* 621; cf., e.g. 110, 164.

208 *Ibid.,* 79.

209 *Ibid.,* 110.

210 *Ibid.,* 991.

tion with a personal element in Transcendence: "as far as we are personally affected as individuals, as far as we enter *qua* persons a relation to Transcendence *qua* person, we call it God."[211] 'God' is a name that is not merely "sound and smoke" as the vague sentimentalism of the young Goethe called it,[212] but it does not cover the whole of Transcendence either. God may be said to be personal, but *qua* Transcendence, he is no person — no-body to communicate with. Communication is and remains "what makes men human."[213] Being in its fullness, the being of an *intellectus archetypus* for instance *(seinsursprüngliches Denken)*, is beyond the schisms of subject and subject as well as subject and object, with no need for bridging the gap between them through *Meinen und Beziehung*, i.e., intentions and intentionalities of will and perception, through any contrivances of communicative language or other means of communion.[214]

Hence — *finitum incapax infiniti* (the finite cannot grasp the infinite) — Transcendence, according to Jaspers, cannot be grasped in the categories of either subject or object. But does the *Sum qui Sum* for this reason have no preferential status at all over the *Est quod Est?*[215] If not, how could Transcendence affect us, as person to person? How could it assume the rôle of a guide? How could reason appear as "the reflected splendor of the One?"[216] Does not Jaspers' own analysis suggest that Transcendence lies beyond both subject and object, but — perhaps as absolute Will — in the direction of the former rather than the latter? (Just as, for instance, Descartes' creative substance, although being above *res cogitans* as well as *res extensa,* is more closely related to the former and its freedom.) And, if we may come back to our expanded use of 'communication,' would it not be possible to speak of communication on three levels — the impersonal one, that of things, the inter-personal one between man and man, and the suprapersonal as the way in which — being superpersonal itself — Transcendence speaks to us? The transition from the first to the second level would consist in our giving a hearing to the entreaty and a voice to the meaning of things.[217] The transition from the second to the third would be our listening to what, in an ascending scale, may be called the 'voice' of reason, conscience, the Super-Ego, God; and also that communication in which we lay ourselves

---

211 *Ibid.*, 111.

212 Goethe, *Faust*, v. 3457.

213 *Wahrheit*, 6f; cf. *Scope*, 79f.

214 *Wahrheit*, 387.

215 See above, pp. 222f.

216 *Wahrheit*, 185.

217 See above, sect. VIII.

open (whether in prayer or not) to powers which strengthen us
to make up for our failures.

These suggestions are tentative. They are not simply true or
false. They are more or less adequate interpretations of what
we would like to call 'uncurtailed' experience. They represent
a mode of "absolute Empiricism." They are *existential* proposals, not demonstrable propositions. Still, they have a sort of
pragmatic verification in what they can do for us. They may
give us a deepened feeling of life and seem to illumine the world's
depth in their own, slightly magic way — as reminders in which
something like that *Mitwissenschaft mit der Schöpfung,* that
original familiarity with the creation, wakes up of which Schelling and Jaspers speak. I am not tempted to overrate the strict
validity of these interpretive formulas. But they have their value
in the inner concentration and the meditative mood from which
they spring, and which they may create — an intellectual atmosphere which keeps the avenues open for new experiences and
their account, or for the renewal of old ones which we forgot —
or, finally, for decisions which philosophy may bring into sight,
but which it cannot make on anybody's behalf. This attitude
certainly does not go against the grain of Jaspers' own philosophizing. It is also a "faith in communication," wider (though, perhaps, less firm) than Jaspers' "philosophical faith."[218]

XVI

Although not quite satisfied with Jaspers' account of incommunicable[219] and incommunicative Transcendence, I do appreciate his reasons. His position may be partly clarified by a brief
comparison with a significant passage in Husserl's *Ideas concerning a pure Phenomenology and Phenomenological Philosophy.*
Husserl speaks there of the stream of pure consciousness and the
transcendence, with regard to it, of God, of the Ego and of the
world. But transcendence means something different in each
case. God's absolute Transcendence would be, as it were, "the
polar opposite" to the merely relative transcendence of the world.
And it would also differ from the status of every ego of pure
consciousness: my ego shares in the absoluteness of consciousness
and transcends it only in the sense of being not a part of the fleet-

218 Cf. *Scope,* 45f.

219 Cf., e.g., *Philosophie* I, 58: "*Existenz* is related to what it is not — the other
which appears incommunicable in its decisive presence and always garbled in philosophical expression."

ing experiences through which I live. It is the subjective pole flanking consciousness on one side, whereas the object of intentional experience flanks consciousness on the other.[220]

Although at this point he is Husserl's equal in the cautiousness of his distinctions, Jaspers has the merit of locating Transcendence more precisely by characterizing it in two ways. First, he correlates it to *Existenz,* whereas the world is the correlate, "the other," to *consciousness-as-such.*[221] Secondly, the Divine does not only *have* to him a transcendence that differs from those of the subject as well as the object; it *is* Transcendence pure and simple. Hence, being absolutely unlike any object, it can never become an object of knowledge; falling not under the specific category of 'subject,' it cannot be of the nature of a person, an individual Self. It plays no part in that communication which constitutes interpersonal life; and its presence is not communicable in positive terms, but only by the *neti, neti* of negative theology. Everything has its being from and toward it: but — being all-comprehensive — Transcendence is not comprehensible in itself.[222]

XVII

These formal arguments, somewhat in the style of the Neo-Kantian school with which Jaspers was familiar through its representatives at Heidelberg, carry enough weight with the philosopher Jaspers not to be neglected in the statement of his position. Yet he did not reach this position because of them.

We have traced the sources of his philosophical faith in the decisive experiences of his life, including the productive intercourse with those thinkers who helped him to understand himself and articulate his ideas. His way through Kierkegaard in reacting to the general 'intellectual situation of the time' explains his opposition to the positivistic as well as dialectical schemata of evolution. As concerns the problem of Transcendence, this way leads to a marked affinity of his thought with that of the 'theology of crisis.' They are contemporaries in position and opposition — despite all the differences between his struggling for *'existential'* truth (increasingly under such auspices as Lessing's[223]) and the reliance on revealed truth in the sophisticated 'fundamentalism' of the Barthians.

220 Cf. E. Husserl, *Ideen zu einer reinen Phänomenologie und phänomenologischen Philosophie,* §§ 51 and 58.

221 *Wahrheit,* 79.   222 Cf., e.g., *ibid.,* 1050.

223 Cf., e.g., *Wahrheit,* 119, 853, 918, 949ff; *Tragedy,* 83ff.

In the paradoxical union between intimate closeness and infinite distance of the Divine — this *signum* of the religious phenomenon — Jaspers stresses the numinous character of Transcendence, though not to such an extent that the immensity of the mystery overshadows the confidence felt in the presence of the One. This is not a short-range confidence and security. The ruling of the One is revered in the very wreckage of our projects. Self-realization confronting Transcendence may need (and triumph in) the freedom of self-abdication for the sake of possibilities which are not ours, and the freedom of self-sacrifice which knows of "infinite hope even though not for us" (Franz Kafka). In the shipwreck of their own world, in the face of nothingness, men may still be able to endorse the claims incumbent on man for a world yet to be.[224]

Communication with the past is thus complemented by the communication with the future, the reverent devotion to the former by sacrificial devotion to the latter. The inner freedom of this historical attitude rests on a religious ground which — *mutatis mutandis* — may still be the ground of the religion of our fathers — though it is no child's faith.

It is equally far from panicky fright of the unknown as from naïve familiarity with it. Precisely in exploring things and extending the realm of comprehension and communication we may learn to revere the One in silence. Transcendence is strictly a dimension of its own. For Jaspers to deny it the status and attributes of a person and urge restraint in 'thouing' God is, however, not only to assert, as a *metaphysical* recognition, the absolute disparity between God and man; nor is it, so to speak, a mere postulate of 'taste' — in tune with a time which brings this otherness home to us, a time of agony, a time full of incomprehensible suffering on the part of millions of innocent people; it seems to him also a postulate of the *moral* life. "Communication with the Deity tends to obstruct communication amongst men . . . Communication from Self to Self as the true actuality in which Transcendence can have a voice, will be crippled by a direct and obtrusive approach to Transcendence as a Thou."[225]

It must be said, however, that this last point which concerns us here particularly is not beyond doubt. There is, on the one hand, a *non sequitur* in the contention that to love God first will stand in the way of loving our fellow man. Christian doctrine —

---

224 *Age,* 230. A somewhat similar ethos of religious rather than heroic resignation in Hermann Hesse.

225 *Philosophie* III, 166f; cf. II, 272f.

such as we have it in Bernard of Clairvaux's "Sermon on the Song of Songs" or in Luther's *The Liberty of the Christian Man* — has it that the *filiatio* from God engenders the *imitatio* of God in the love for his children: "from the love for God flows a free, willing, cheerful life of gratuitous service to man."[226] From the human point of view, this order of love has the great advantage of giving the imperative of love a universal scope. It cannot be narrowed down by racial definitions or class distinctions as to which men have a title to my love — or even as to which of God's children I may consider my fellow beings. Is Jaspers' position equally well protected against the creeping in of dangerous discriminations?

It could be, if it were on equal ground with the Jewish teaching for instance of a Hermann Cohen: "The correlation between man and God can become an actuality only through the correlation which it implies — that between man and man."[227] In the Bible, this latter love is kindled by compassion — compassion which is so little in evidence in Jaspers' writings (even as it is fought in those of Nietzsche). There is, however, compassion in all human love, since there is suffering in all human beings. It is through compassion, according to Cohen, that the 'other' being becomes my 'fellow' being with whom I bear and for whom I live. This is religious socialism which is not contrary, but complementary, to religious individualism. Co-*Existenz* is here largely communication in suffering with and for my fellow creatures.

It is noticeable that amongst the *'existentials'* of Heidegger as well as of Jaspers, the 'living with' — also co-*Existenz* in the literal sense — has a conspicuous place, whereas the 'living for' is somehow discredited. The care for the other — Heidegger argues — tends to put him under tutelage instead of helping him to become free to care for himself, for his Self. Exemplary exsistence *(Vorausspringen)*, not compassionate as-sistance *(Einspringen)* is the watch-word.[228]

In the same vein, and for the same reasons, Jaspers had to deny that anybody can help the other in the essentials of *Existenz*.[229] The essential thing is self-realization, not devotion. Nobody can 'leap' for the other. Communication with others is, after all, only a means for self-realization, the relation to others only a means for that relation to oneself which is one half of *Existenz*

---

226 Luther, *Von der Freiheit eines Christenmenschen*, 36 *W*; cf., e.g., 38 *W*.
227 Hermann Cohen, *Religion der Vernunft aus den Quellen des Judentums*, 133.
228 Cf. M. Heidegger, *Sein und Zeit*, I, 122.
229 *Wahrheit*, 846.

(in Kierkegaard's definition) , and which — as faithfulness to one's demon, angel, entelechy — I do not wish to deny, as Buber does.[230] The contact with others elicits selfhood. As the vehicle of this appeal communication is indispensable to concrete *Existenz*. Indubitable as this may be, it is more emphatically asserted than convincingly shown.[231] Communication "seems (!) to produce . . . that which is communicating: independent selves." Hence, my freedom is not without that of the other, my Thou.[232] No argument is needed where decisive experience speaks — once more, the experience of Jaspers' youth: the insufficiency of the lonely individual, a life without adequate response, in this sense an 'ex-communicated' and frustrated existence. Finite existence is in search of co-*Existenz*. ("It is not good that man should be alone.") *E contrario,* the Infinite, the self-sufficient Being, seems beyond the need of communication.[233]

The way toward my Self thus goes through my Thou. The absolute will to communication is for Jaspers an *'existential'* imperative. But, whereas this will make us ready to welcome or, rather, to re-cognize the friend when he comes, he may fail to do so. His appearance is a *datum,* a gift — not a *factum,* an achievement.[234] And, inasmuch as love in communication with free Selves — "personal love — is the first and original one in which all love for Being finds its consummation,"[235] there remains an element of metaphysical chance in our Self-realization as well as in our love for God in whom the lines of love meet and the union between Self and Self is performed. When philosophy has said all it can, there remains for the individual thinker the possibility of Atheism which the philosopher, faithful to his ground, may reject but whose menace he cannot ignore as the human being he is.[236] Life is never exclusively true or untrue, faithful or faithless.

[230] M. Buber, *Between Man and Man,* 167. As to the different angles of the problem of self-realization, see below, section xix.

[231] "The questions: 'why is communication?', 'Why am I not alone?' can be just as little answered in a positive understanding as the question about selfhood:" *Philosophie* II, 50.

[232] *Reason,* 92; *Philosophie* II, 57; cf. *Origin,* 154f.

[233] This corresponds to the Greek idea of the Good as the Self-Sufficient; hence the Aristotelian praise of the self-sufficient contemplative life. It is in adaptation to this concept that one of the Hebrew names for God — *El Shaddai* — has occasionally been interpreted as "The Self-Sufficient Being." It will be better to translate *El Shaddai,* in accordance with the original meaning of *Eheye asher Eheye,* as "the Power of Powers," "the almighty power that suffices to satisfy all needs," "sufficient to bring into being and keep alive" whatever it wants: cf. Maimonides, *More Nebukhim,* Book I, ch. 61.

[234] Cf. *Philosophie* II, 59, 71.   [235] *Wahrheit,* 1002.   [236] Cf. *Reason,* 137ff.

Jaspers takes exception to the worldlessness of Kierkegaard's Christianity. Yet, however excruciating Kierkegaard's solitary existence may have proved to be, his worldlessness, his failure to communicate with others as the 'exception' he was, was compensated for by the fact that, 'after all,' he was not threatened by godlessness; the one communication with the divine Thou seemed always open to him: "It costs exertion! But how blessed to be so near to the source as I am. If thou, O God, art like the source, I am the man at the source. No one can help me, and in a sense I understand no one. But I have the source so near, oh, so near."[237]

This exacting comfort may not be ours. I for one am siding with Jaspers in seeking a way through the world toward a God who often seems so far away that the most we can do seems to expect (and expect in vain) his message like that in Kafka's parable — "a message from a dead man. But you sit at your window when evening falls and dream it to yourself."[238]

Or is it no death message, after all? The correlation of *Existenz* and Transcendence implies (in personal terms) that God is alive if he is alive in us and our living faith, even in our struggle for faith.[239] That he is dead does not mean that he does not exist (such an objective statement has no place in the syntax of religious experience). It may mean that our soul has become dumb, and that the circulation between *Existenz* and God has ceased to function. "For who will give thanks ere he receives, and answer ere he has heard the calling?"[240] The very term 'Transcendence' which Jaspers uses seems to indicate for God a state pending, as it were, between life and death. A correlation with strict 'Transcendence' as one of its partners is not only paradoxical — like the covenant between the Infinite and the Finite — but paralytic. Yet, is all silence that of death? Perhaps, the Nietzschean news of the death of Great Pan was not altogether verified by the fact that nobody seemed to care: maybe, some people did not care because they knew it was not altogether true. Transcendence is absence in presence. And one of its forms may correlate to the state of expectancy of a presence which we do not, or do no longer, enjoy and the feeling of a void and a need which is not, or is no longer, satisfied. Transcendence is like the other half, the dark half, of the

237 Kierkegaard, *Journals*, 521.

238 Franz Kafka, "An Imperial Message," in *Parables*.

239 "Faith" — says Kierkegaard — "is an infinite anxiety as to whether one has faith — and, behold, just that anxiety is faith": cf. *Journals*, 243.

240 From Hölderlin, *"Der Mutter Erde"*: "Wer will auch danken, eh' er empfängt. Und Antwort geben, eh' er gehört hat?"

moon, which is nevertheless there for us — there as the complement of the one we see; or, to speak with Rilke,[241] it is like the
"other opposite" of the swing — the half circle which we cannot
'swing,' and which is familiar to us as that which, in turning us
down, directs our ascent.

XVIII

But the way of this ascent, the rise to Transcendence may be —
if not less steep, then at least — less narrow than it appears under
Jaspers' presuppositions: it need not lead exclusively through
self-realization; and, above all, this realization itself will not be
restricted to communication with our peers and the loving struggle with our predestined Thou. To argue this point will help us
to recapitulate some of the principal issues of the present paper;
and, again, it may be helped by looking, in the following sections,
at man — to use expedient terms — as creature, as creator, and
as both.

It is the creaturely feeling which prevails in the 'cosmic piety'
not only of primitive religions but of most of the pagan creeds,
and — in combination with social piety — for instance in the
teaching of a Kungfutse. Cosmic piety can be found even in the
naïvete achieved by sceptics such as Montaigne — the feeling
that, through our whole bodily being, we are in contact and
communication with the life-giving powers of 'mother' nature,
on a much broader front and in a greater depth than in the
pointed way of our juvenile intellect: "the simplest way of giving
oneself up to nature is the wisest way of doing it."[242] From this
half indulged and half affected ignorance the faith of a naturalist
may branch out in many directions, for instance in that of a
scientific naturalism such as Spinoza's. The element of the crea-
tural is retained here in the subordination of man to the universal
order, the rejection of his claims to a privileged status within the
whole. The religious reverence consists here of the feeling that
we are rooted in a deeper ground than that of *natura naturata,*
the phenomenal world; we confess to a nature which we cannot
understand in the infinitude of its infinite attributes. The "face
of the whole physical universe" gives not the full expression of
natura naturans. In the "union of the mind with the whole of
nature" we have the fruition of the One *sui communicabile,* i.e.,
the One which, thanks to its own goodness, communicates to us

241 Rilke, "Schaukel des Herzens," in *Neue Literarische Welt,* January 10, 1952.
242 Montaigne, *"De l'Expérience."*

its eternity of joy, and which kindles in our souls the desire to communicate to others and share with them the same happiness.[243]

I refer to this well known example of scientific ethos for two reasons. First, it shows the making of a Self which does not take place directly within the medium of co-*Existenz*. (*'Existential'* communication appears here as a result rather than as a means of self-realization.) Moreover, it represents devotion to a ground of being in which man and world, and, again, the series of things and that of ideas, the Encompassing which we are and that which we are not, are grounded as different expressions of the same order and do not form a transcendental contrast. But, whereas the peace in God-Nature may still seem immanentism to a Kierkegaardian Self in its confrontation with divine Transcendence, I submit that this *Deus sive Natura* has become both an abstract part and a necessary aspect of every image in which Deity may appear to us today.[244]

The second reason is that the philosophical ethos of an *amor intellectualis,* in which nature is embraced rather than mastered, is kindred, on the one hand, to the love of *Existenz* for Transcendence ("he who loves God, cannot attempt to make God love him in return"[245]). And it is akin, on the other hand, to that ethos of the artist which, in the rehabilitation of Spinozism, was extolled by Herder and K. Ph. Moritz and incarnated in Goethe. It is noteworthy that from Spinoza Goethe derived, together with the unselfishness of devotion to the order of Being, an idea of art which sees art as congenial to nature in the inner necessity and purposelessness of communication which distinguish both. Goethe's gratuitous spending to men of his art as a gift of nature was thus to be kept apart from the complementary handling of things in practical life and in the service of human ends.[246]

It has been said of Goethe that he made himself, "out of a dark product of nature a clear product of himself."[247] He thus verified the incorrect, yet revealing etymological definition of person as *per se una.* But he did it in three media: not only as

---

[243] Spinoza, *Tractatus de Intellectus Emendatione,* Opera, ed. Gebhardt, II, 5ff.

[244] In other words: whereas Jaspers leans toward a negative theology, in which the categories of the personal and the impersonal are equally inapplicable, I see in Transcendence a Beyond in which the personal and the impersonal are both eminently actual and far (but not equally far) surpassed.

[245] Spinoza's *Ethics,* V, 19.

[246] Cf. Goethe, *Dichtung und Wahrheit,* Books XIV and XVI. Also Herder, *Gott,* especially 3rd Dialogue, and K. Ph. Moritz, *Von der bildenden Nachahmung des Schönen.*

[247] F. W. Riemer, *Mitteilungen über Goethe* (ed. Pollmer, 135).

persona dramatis, as an actor and agent on the stage of inter-
personal relations, but also, and above all, through the study of
nature and in the concentration, integration and composure his
life gained in the medium of art, the composition of his work.
Art was the center-piece, the outcome of empathy, communication
and communion with nature (including man). It was the fruit
ripened in this communication — to be communicated again to
the reader and spectator and to convey to them a similar freedom
of unbiased, impartial outlook, a similar *katharsis* from the passions. Art was thus believed to be a service to nature,[248] but also
one to man. And, indeed, its human mission should not be
slighted for being indirect, through the mediation of the work,
not in personal intercourse of immediate action and reaction
within a concrete situation. *Suum cuique.*

While being a child of productive solitude, the making of the
Self in the work of art may thus provide for new possibilities
of communication amongst Selves in their self-constitution, co-
Existenz and relationship. Conversely, communication in life as
well as through art may not be less intensive and, in a way, profound, for being not altogether, nor even predominantly, on the
level of proper selfhood.

Nature, also nature in man, has its own heights and depths —
which, in fact, Jaspers does not overlook.[249] He is also eager to
point out, over against the tornness of Being, the interrelations
and even the interpenetration of every mode of being and comprehension with every other. Still, *Existenz* always enjoys a preferential status. The orientation toward it is responsible for the
unilinear hierarchy of these modes which seems to prevent Jaspers
from doing always full justice to forms of intercourse different
from communication amongst Selves.

For this reason, I take the liberty of using another reference to
Goethe — to *The Elective Affinities* and the ruling there, within
the human sphere and in competition with the moral order, of
an analogue to the natural law of gravitation. The attraction is
not simply toward the other sex, but it is just as little that which
elicits communication between one Self and its Thou — it is a
blessed and fatal being drawn and "flowing out" of one being
towards the other, for them to enjoy perfect peace in "purely
being together," "without need for either glance or word or
gesture or touch." Edward and Ottilie have their beings concentrated in a relationship whose speechless happiness is not
that of eloquent silence beyond communication, i.e., in view of

---

[248] See above, 239ff.   [249] Cf., e.g., *Wahrheit,* 271.

the ineffable, but an effortless and delightful calm in one another's presence. It is like the fitting together of two halves of one lovely fruit.[250] This is a perfection such as cannot be found in the unending struggle of personal life, and gives a glance into mysteries of Nature and the dynamics of universal rapports, — a glance which adds to indications we found in previous sections (XI, XII) under the titles of *co-naissance,* in-tention, in-clination, ad-version, etc., — there from the point of view of cognition and a general metaphysics.

XIX

Let us now move from a self-realization whose organ is not directly inter-personal communication, and from a communication which is not properly an organ for the realization of personal selfhood, to self-realization by way of communication among individual Selves. This leads to the problem of the ethical status of the two factors — self-realization and communication — in relation to one another. For reasons which should be evident from previous statements (sections XIV-XVII) I give preference — though both are inseparable — to an ethics of free devotion, an ethics of self-giving over against one of self-realization. That means, in a way, a conversion of the means-end relation in question. From the moral — and, perhaps, the metaphysical — viewpoint, self-realization would become a factor in the order of communication, communion and community among free Selves. An indispensable factor — since the individual Self would be a constituent of this order; and since, without being somebody myself, I cannot possibly be anything to anybody. Even so, the shift of emphasis will make a practical difference.[251]

250 Jaspers himself deals with these problems in discussing what he considers two types of *Existenz* "the law of the day and the passion for the night." Relevant are particularly the thoughtful though enigmatically phrased paragraphs on eroticism in *Philosophie* III, 105f, 187ff. But with him the profundity and transparence of the erotic depends on its becoming a human cipher to *Existenz:* "Eroticism becomes a cipher in the sensualization of the intercourse of human beings in the state of absolute communications" (189). But is this the key to the mystery of a love such as Romeo's and Juliet's?

251 Here, as so often, it is important to distinguish between the axiological, ethical and metaphysical perspectives. *Axiologically* — in objective evaluation — there may be no act superior to the making of the Self by itself. But this making will not normally be the *moral* objective. It seems an offshoot rather than the aim of human striving. The moral spirit is one of loving respect for man; moral action is to be a contribution to an order of life in which this spirit prevails — and as an action of love and respect it is devoted to my fellow being and true fellowship rather than to

It will make me less dependent on meeting my predestined Thou, together with my peers and contemporaries of all ages — the supreme challenge which may yield me the supreme profit of gaining myself. Freed from the preoccupation by paramount religious self-concern, I ought to be ready to recognize my Thou in everybody with whom and for whom I can do the works of love, who, in his sufferings, is the object of brotherly charity — for we, too, have been in 'the land of bondage' —, and who as a free personal agent commands our respect and is our ally in establishing a 'kingdom of ends.' It is true that the concrete situation will exercise a selective function as to who can actually figure in this rôle of the present Thou. But this Thou will then step forth from a space of Thouhood, i.e., as an individual representative of an order to which I belong as a person and constitutive member.[252] This order is alive in my responsible response to the claims which the Thou presents, and which I have to recognize in attending and making myself available to whatever or whoever speaks to me and lays hold of me through them. As human claims, they have a holy right and place me confronting the Holy, even though they may be arbitrary and illegitimate as to their special contents and objectives. This openness and present-mindedness, both in respect *to* and respect *for* the other human being as my fellow being in the personal realm, recognizes the other as both second person and *alter ego,* an agent like me, and in his own right. And this rootedness in common ground and readiness for communion and 'community service' is the best guarantee of that unqualified will to total (i.e., complete) and boundless (i.e., universal) communication which, in Jaspers, is *Vernunft* itself as the gift of *Vernehmen,* reason as attention to the voice of the One in the claims of the many.

The need for such a warrant, for a representative of universality, has been acknowledged by Jaspers himself. This is evidenced

---

myself (even though, in fact, it adds to my growth). And *metaphysically* the Holy, the Absolute, may be experienced in just this sacramental spirit, as the highest expression of that unity *in actu,* i.e., that power of unification through which the universe is permanently renewed. It transcends, it seems to me, the unifying power of reason in us not as a sort of monolithic unity in static perfection; it transcends it only in the sense that our reason respects and tries to join it in its universal sweep in which we are given a distinguished co-operative part.

252 Over against the nihilism of a 'love' for everything and nothing — a mere and empty declamation, the warmth of *humanitas,* philanthropy (just as that of the love for nature) has its own right and is not to be disposed of as condescendingly (as in *Philosophie* II, 279) as mere "extenuation" of true and ardent love. Cf. also Max Scheler, *Wesen und Formen der Sympathie* (1923), 115ff — in contradistinction to Scheler's earlier writings.

by the fact that (1) the introduction and rehabilitation of reason as a major term, (2) its intimate connection with *Existenz* and (3) the decree, as it were, which equates reason with the will to absolute communication date only from 1935. They appear in the lectures on *Reason and Existenz,* given at the University of Groningen two years after the appeal *of* reason and *to* it and the will to such communication had been abrogated by Adolph Hitler.[253] Hence the change of terminology is somewhat of a conversion; it is, at least, of more than terminological relevance. Although communication remains even now a vehicle of self-realization, "the historical narrowness of communication" is no longer played off, as an inescapable guilt, against a superficial and "imaginary universal possibility" of doing justice to all others. And it seems now left to reason to give the secure confidence that intensive communication in small circles will lead into the "historical width of a possible unity with all mankind."[254]

What I would call the formal equality of men as personal agents, which vaults over the material differences of the individuals,[255] is thus intensified to kinship by reason. In this way, reason now serves in Jaspers once more to define man — not, however, as a rational animal, but rather in his existence as a unique personal Self, living with other Selves in unique historical communication, in relations of his and their own making.

XX

The authorship and authenticity of man in these inter-personal relationships shows communication in our sense on the distinctive human level of personal response and responsibility. It is by way of communication of all sorts — social and political, artistic and philosophical — that man realizes himself as a "second maker."

253 A pre-stage of the recognition of the quasi superrational function of reason can be seen in the Appendix on "Kant's Theory of Ideas" to the *Psychologie der Weltanschauungen* (cf. also *Reason,* 49f). The three volumes of *Philosophie* (1932), however, fail to assign reason a distinctive and a distinguished rôle. They speak, e.g., (II, 116) with regard to objective and empirical knowledge of 'the rationality of mere life,' of 'reasonable consciousness-as-such' — two functions which are heterogeneous, according to *Wahrheit:* only a leap can lead from the comprehensiveness of "consciousness-as-such" to reason as the bond of all modes of comprehension.

254 *Philosophie* II, 60; III, 123, in contrast with *Wahrheit,* 837: "In the genesis of man by way of reason, the One of Transcendence is felt by the One of actual historical *Existenz:* the unity of *Existenz* appears together with the emergence of the unity of all history."

255 "Our respect is due to the human being as such and has no degrees" (Simone Weil, *L'Enracinement,* 20).

Die Mitwissenschaft um die Schöpfung, the recollection in which he proves privy to creation, is translated into life and 'worked out' in the creation of social, moral, political order and community, in education and in all communications *via* language and art. In all these realms not only Being as such seems communicated to us from the source of all being, but also — and in particular — creative being, that spark of creativity which Jaspers calls reason. The image is Plato's: the spark seems transmitted to us from an ever turning "wheel of fire," the creative spirit that animates the whole.[256] Don't we thus partake in that "formation, transformation" in which "the eternal meaning is eternally entertained?"[257]

But (reads the counter-question) are these not merely highsounding phrases, rejected not only by the cynicism of our age, but contrary to any sober appraisal of our condition? They will have to be qualified indeed. They appear completely meaningless, however, only to a life which has lost its meaning completely.

It was not mere hybris on Michelangelo's part to represent, in the Sistine Chapel, the Creator in the image of the artist himself. It is through his own creativity that man becomes aware of the creativity in which he participates. The narcissism in contemporary art, a *poiesis poieseos* which adores itself in its own mirror, is caused by the mechanization of an age in which the creative impulses have atrophied in most other realms. This accounts for art's functioning today often as a religious substitute, a remnant of fuller religious experience: "The relation of art to life," says Wallace Stevens, "is of the first importance in a sceptical age since, in the absence of a belief in God, the mind turns to its own creations and examines them, not alone from the aesthetic point of view, but from what they reveal, for what they validate and invalidate, for the support they give."[258]

But — to repeat an earlier quotation — "man and God are lost to us only one with the other."[259] To the average estrangement from God correspond self-alienation and man's alienation from man. That is why "alienation" has become so important a philo-

256 Something of this Platonic feeling and Christian Neo-Platonism is still alive in Jaspers' descriptions of reason as deriving from and working toward the One of Transcendence: cf., e.g., *Wahrheit,* 116ff.

257 "Gestaltung, Umgestaltung, / Des ewigen Sinnes ewige Unterhaltung" . . . Goethe, *Faust* II, vv. 6287f.

258 Quoted from William Van O'Connor, *The Shaping Spirit: A Study on Wallace Stevens,* 58.

259 *Wahrheit,* 1003.

sophical category — particularly, but not only in Hegelianism and
Marxism.

'Self-alienation' — that means, first of all, with regard to the
individual Self a lack of true individuality and authenticity, a
lack of rootedness in his own ground: and it is against this robot
existence that thinkers like Kierkegaard and Nietzsche as well
as Jaspers remonstrate. Jaspers' zealous insistence on the need
for roots *(enracinement)* is not a completely timeless demand.
In its urgency it is to him, just as for instance to Simone Weil, a
countermovement to the growing uprootedness of the masses.
"Misery is deracination"[260] — as an, at once, personal and social
phenomenon.

As a matter of fact and — paradoxical as it is — almost as a
matter of course, Jaspers has not only been antagonistic to this
state of estrangement, but was also subjected to it as its child
and, at one time, its victim.

Jaspers could not fail to see this alienation of man from man
and that between man and world as a product of the inhuman
conditions of human life in the factory world of the 19th century
— a world in which man became an object among objects to be
employed and exploited instead of being respected as speaker and
hearer in interpersonal communication. But he may have resigned too easily to this state of affairs as the ultimate fate of
modern man. He felt and feels the obligation to stand for *Existenz*
and the community of free selves — metaphysically destined as
they are for one another — against the technique and routine of
mere existence *(Dasein),* society and mass civilization.[261] German
social philosophy ran along the lines of these alternatives between
community and society, culture and civilization; and people like
Tönnies and Spengler seemed to be vindicated by the social and
technical developments all around. In view of all this, Jaspers'
deep concern for the inner freedom and the culture of the soul
could not but paralyze the zeal for reform and deepen the feeling
of the abyss between the two ways of life.[262]

260 Simone Weil, *L'Attente de Dieu,* 181.

261 The new technical age of mass civilization has led not only to a decline of
inter-personal communication proportionate to the growing shallowness of personal
life and to a — partial — disruption of direct communication with nature; it has not
only invented new means of social intercourse; it has even created mechanical substitutes for social communication — robots which behave more and more like persons, whilst persons behave more and more like robots. This technical development
confronts a philosophy of communication today with problems that lie outside of
the range of the present paper.

262 The lasting difference between an inter-personal community of love and a
more or less impersonal organization of society in the management of individual in-

It is only in his reaction to Hitler, i.e., in his more recent writings — especially in *The Origin and Goal of History* — that, in spite of the old dualisms, the will to an order of existence worthy of human beings, the will to a social democracy has asserted itself more strongly. It has issued in constructive proposals which try to liquidate the phenomenon of the masses rather than to perpetuate it in a spirit of aristocratic despair. Higher liberal education and responsible partnership in the social and political enterprise are to free the potential Self in all men and make democracy a working concern rather than a form on paper.[263]

But this order of inner political freedom will do away with the strict separation of outer and inner life. This order will be an *ordre du coeur* in which the interest of our whole existence is engaged and alive — it is not only an organization of selfish interests and powers or, neutral in itself, a mere protective shell for the "high goods of inner liberty, of faith, and of the spirit."[264] True democratic politics is more than a "lower plane of humanity," more than a *conditio sine qua non* for the free existence of the Self.[265] Justice can be the sword of love. And, although the institutional separation of Church and State will prove desirable,[266] Jaspers may agree that the energies — though not the tenets — of faith ought to contribute to an earthly city after the dream and in humble imitation of a City of God. Our deviations and shortcomings will always provide material for the distinction between loving community and organization of bodily interests, but it may be a less thorough dichotomy than it appears in Jaspers even now. The uniqueness of the Self will remain a matter of deepest concern and respect. It shall not be sacrificed on the altar of the body politic. In the attempt to bring both sides closer together, I may find a common denominator with Jaspers in this sentence by Martin Buber: "True community and a true commonwealth will be actualized only to the extent to which those Single Ones will be actually present out of whose responsive and responsible existence the *res publica* is renewed."[267]

---

terests, class interests, etc., is not to be denied. The question is only whether nothing can be done to diminish their distance and tension and turn hostility into mutual aid. To accept lovelessness as the inescapable law of social organization may be grist for the mill of a theology which surrenders sinful man to God and his love and mercy; yet it is almost suicidal in a philosophy in which divine Transcendence speaks only to individual *Existenz* — but not even to it in the voice of *love*.

263 Cf. *Origin*, 129f, 151ff.   265 *Ibid.*

264 *Ibid.*, 164.   266 *Ibid.*

267 Martin Buber, *Dialogisches Leben*, 255.

XXI

What applies to man's relation to himself and his fellow-beings, applies *a fortiori* to his relation to God. We consider it partly an outcome of the torn conditions of modern life, of its decline into mechanical dependencies, of its estrangement from the creative source of life that, with 20th century theology, Jaspers stresses more God's distance from man than God's proximity to him. He speaks of God rather in the anonymous term of Transcendence than in the personal confession to God the Father.

And yet, however remote the Deity my appear to our *intellectus quaerens fidem,* to an intellect in search of faith — in the process of what Jaspers calls "formal transcending"[268] — God does not cease to be intimately close to us, according to Jaspers, in the *guidance, support* and *security* we experience in that free adventure which is at once the making of a Self and the ascent toward Transcendence. (And, let me add, we may feel this presence also in an encounter with stern *objection* when we deviate from personal truth.)

There is, then, a creative element which sustains the surge of man's self-realization and self-renewal — to speak with Leibniz, the 'monadizing' of the monad. And of the same or a similar order are the creations of the State, of a work of art, but also a philosophical authorship which "consists in working back from the intellectual and social plane to a point in the soul from which there springs an imperative demand for creation."[269] We move almost in a circuit of mutual demand and supply, in which we are granted powers which we need and use not only for ourselves. This is the basic religious experience of which we spoke before — the feeling of being counted upon for co-operation with the Divine, for continuing the work of creation and translating it into a new language on a new level of being. Even the machine and its products can serve to exhibit the purity and beauty of an order which has been latent before in the products of nature,[270] and can thus become an inspiration to modern art. Hence creation may well appear to the philosopher "as God undertaking to create creators" and, thus, "join to himself beings worthy of his love."[271]

Strong and vague as it is, the deep-seated feeling of such a congeniality and communication with creative impulses that are at

268 *Philosophie* III, 36ff.

269 H. Bergson, *The Two Sources of Morality and Religion,* 242.

270 Cf. *Origin,* 116f.   271 H. Bergson, *op. cit,* 243.

work in the universe would tend to reveal this world as their fabric. It gives nature somehow the transparency of creation and justifies to some extent the anthropomorphism of speaking of Transcendence as God *qua poeta mundi, in* whose likeness and *to* whose likeness we *are* made — and make *ourselves* as far as we free the creative *élan* in our souls and others. Conversely, in a technical age, which may still be inventive, but in which creative inspiration is on the point of expiring, "Transcendence" will be just as taboo and obsolete a term as the name of God. [272] And nature will appear mute, a mere material to be moulded and managed. It will be left to the 'quixotism' of the philosopher and the 'old-fashioned romanticism' of the poet to entertain a thou-like intercourse with kindred powers in nature. Only "to him who in the love of Nature holds Communion with her visible forms, she speaks a various language."[273] Even now, however, this language is not dead. Although it is not the language of modern technology (or is not always audible in it), it has remained familiar to us in our life with things or is murmured to us in mysterious words when we bend over the fountains of this earth:

"Still we know the enchantment of Being. Creation
still wells up in a hundred springs. A play of pure forces
none can touch but who kneels in profound admiration."[274]

In its scientific aspects, ours is a "disenchanted world" of objects, leveled down and classified as mere specimens of species and genera, easy substitutes for one another — just as even individual man has become an easily replaceable and expendable commodity. But things as factors of our personal world are no mere manufactures, identical samples of the same make. To speak with Peirce, everyone of them has its "Firstness."[275] Even without individual selfhood, they are individual creatures — to be told from each other the way the shepherd can tell his sheep apart. If the Leibnizian *omne individuum sua tota entitate individuatur*

---

[272] It will be understood that my own doubts, as far as the terminology is concerned, do not apply to the transcendence of God but to God as Transcendence. I agree with Jaspers, above all, in the contention that, in his own nature, God is always more than my God and our God — namely, God.

[273] W. C. Bryant, *Thanatopsis.*

[274] Aber noch ist uns das Dasein verzaubert; an hundert
Stellen ist es noch Ursprung. Ein Spielen von reinen
Kräften, die keiner berührt, der nicht kniet und bewundert.

Rilke, *Sonette an Orpheus* II, 10. A similar, more strictly Christian, statement in Simone Weil, *L'Attente de Dieu,* 181: "Each human being has his roots here below thanks to a certain terrestrial poetry, this reflection of celestial light which is his link, more or less consciously, with his universal fatherland."

[275] Cf. Charles S. Peirce, *Collected Papers* I, 303ff. Similarly William James.

("each individual is individuated through its own whole nature") is true — as I think it is — it would be so as the product of a unique art and a unique 'principle' through which it has its 'beginning' — "in the beginning was the Word,"[276] — and through which it is endowed with its entelechy, the individual law of its being. Now, this is just what we understand by 'creation.' It has its religious expression in such a saying as that of the Talmud: "Man coins with one and the same mold many similar coins. God's creation consists in the fact that each of his coins, each of his creatures is produced in a mold which is new and different for each of them." This is the lasting distinction between God as creator and man as worker.[277]

To speak of man as a second maker is not to deify him: it only attests to man's peculiar communication with the ground of all particular being and individuality. I have tried to show the actuality of this experience somehow in the spirit of Bergson. And I have followed his method even more extensively than he did, prolonging the lines of all sorts of prehension and pursuing them all toward the point of their eventual intersection. (As is well known, Bergson had concentrated on giving *scientific* knowledge a meaning through which it confirms, and is confirmed by, the claim of *mystic* intuition — the claim to lead beyond a community of tradition and learning to a direct getting "into touch with a transcendent principle,"[278] *l'amor ehe move il sole e l'altre stelle*.

But even in the highest moments of productive communion man participates in creation only as both creature and creator. To enter into communication with Transcendence and partake in the work of creation is, therefore, an elating and *strengthening* experience, but also an *humbling* one. It elates us by making us co-workers with the Deity: we try to be 'on God's side' in our small section of universal history, to follow the dictate of reason such as is audible in the historical moment, and to empower Deity in this world by furthering, on our part and under the particular conditions of our lives, the life-giving powers of the whole. Thus

[276] To speak of the "word of God" need not — and, e.g., in Augustine, does not — show that anthropomorphic naïvete which Jaspers attributes to prophetic religion and tries to overcome in his own philosophical faith: cf. *Scope*, 81.

[277] The above quotation — from *Seder Elijahu Rabba* II — is given in the version of Leo Baeck's admirable essay "Individuum Ineffabile" in *Eranos Jahrbuch* (1947), p. 387.

[278] Bergson, *op. cit.*, 236.

only do we become, in our finite way, 'creative mirrors' of the Infinite as the source of all creation.[279]

(Co-operation with God and men thus becomes the primary directive of human *Existenz* and co-*Existenz*. And it may be said in parenthesis that, to the present writer, co-operation seems a worthier and more promising procedure especially in *economic* life than the free play in the competition of individuals of which Jaspers makes the most[280] — a strange and dubious parallel, in the sphere of business life, to the 'loving struggle' in the communication of free Selves on the way to themselves and on the level of *Existenz*.)

We are strengthened by this communication. It gives us the confidence of drawing, in our own creative attempts, from eternal and inexhaustible resources for the formation of ourselves as well as our works.[281] It is a sobering thought, however, that the power of self-productivity and productive communication is not at our sovereign disposal: it is communicated to and can be withdrawn from us. Through concentration or distraction, devotion or selfishness, we can open or close the floodgates to the waters of life: but we cannot smite the rock and cause water to come out of it. The productive spirit feels in need of the grace of 'inspiration.'[282] The poet is not altogether, as the stage-director in *Faust* wants him to be, in command of his poetry.

And as to the making and remaking of ourselves — it seems only the personal form of what had been organic communication of ever new life in the creaturely world: that re-covery and re-creation which represents an ever recurrent phase in the universal periods of "Die and Rise." Goethe's *Faust* shows the unique concreteness of his experience in this regard also.

All the spheres of being are passed through as we are led, in a sequence of resurrections, from the revival of nature in the rhythms of day and night and of the seasons to the rebirth and re-

---

279 These words may be reminiscent of Max Scheler; but they could also be used as a rendition of the main tenets in the historical philosophy of religion of Ernst Troeltsch — another former member of the University of Heidelberg with whom Jaspers is connected in various ways. Cf., e.g., *Scope*, 72.

280 This does not mean that Jaspers indulges in the ideas of liberalistic *laisser-aller* politics. With detailed references to writers such as Walter Lippmann, F. H. Hayek and J. Wilhelm Röpke, he defends a very liberal socialism in *Origin*, 172ff, 281ff.

281 Just as in Hebrew *boro*, "to create," originally means "to cut out of a whole; to clear a wood," so German "*schaffen*" ("create") is originally the same as "schöpf-en" ("draw"): a fact which has been sagaciously exploited by Paul Natorp in his *Praktische Philosophie* (1925).

282 See also above, 242.

juvenation of man. The revival at Easter in the *imitatio Christi*
has something like a hellish travesty in Faust's being restored to
youth in the kitchen of the witch and a sort of pagan counterpart
in his re-awakening in the morning glory of a new day after a
night of despair: the powers of life are renewed in the dance of
the hours and through the refreshing balsam of nature's spirits.
And there follows, for instance, the renaissance of a past historical
world — Helena's union with Faust — and finally his redemption
from the grave thanks to the victory of divine love.

This example is intended to illustrate what accrues to man's
whole being through wholesome communication with all the
formae formantes of his world. But even on the strictly personal
level of *Existenz* and co-*Existenz* I am inclined to give communication still more credit than Jaspers does. To him, personal
intercourse seems to be, above all, of the nature of an evocation
— a challenge for each partner, to realize, perhaps to transform,
his own Self in the face of the other and in loving struggle with
him. But does it not also belong to the mission of such relationships to be a transmission of historical possibilities which are not
originally ours, even though the capacity of receiving such a
message, of appropriating such a communication, must be presupposed? (The universality of such communication is — not actually,
but basically — secured, first of all, by the community of human
pathos, i.e., by the same raw material of basic experiences, the
exposure to the same elemental powers, in all of us.) In this
growth and plasticity of our own being, in this enrichment of
our own historical heritage by foreign tradition, lies what hope
there is for the formation of the One World without which man
is lost, but which cannot be enforced by arms or bought by money.
The fundamental possibility of such a personal exchange is less
evident in the relative homogeneity of the German people among
whom Jaspers spent most of his life. But should it not have presented itself more convincingly now from the Swiss perspective
— just as we see it, in all its precariousness, more clearly in the
British Commonwealth and the United States?

The fact that the process of self-realization takes place in an
inter-personal medium does not detract from its uniqueness as
a not negotiable task for each individual person. In this regard,
there is no bartering down of Jaspers' terms. There is no voting
by proxy in the choice of our *Existenz*. But this *birth* of the Self
in the crucial decisions of life, and his always possible and even
necessary *rebirth* in backing, renewing, revising and even over-
throwing them — this permanent *status nascendi* of selfhood shows

how the Self is always in suspense between being and non-being, never fully and definitely realized in the acts of its self-creation. Our finitude as individual Selves appears precisely in our falling short of perfect and definite selfhood; and our need of a Thou shows our need of his loving faith in us.[283] In this faith and love he holds up to us a mirror to see ourselves in our true being, our native possibilities which belie our actual status. He confirms and goads us on in this truth and restores our confidence in and respect for ourselves.[284]

The urge for self-realization grows precisely from the feeling of tension that we are not in fact what we properly are, and are in fact what we are not in proper truth. The love and faith of others may help us to bring and keep ourselves on the right way. But *we* only can go this way. There may be a wider range for men to help one another than Jaspers and Heidegger admit. But there are, indeed, limits to human assistance as there are limits to the intimate communication between two Selves:

"Can ever on earth a man be as much ours
As longing has him be?"[285]

Hence, there will also be limits to the purity of the image in which we are seen by our next friend. Although we enjoy the benefit of true communication and learn to 'know us as we are known' by the eyes of human love, we may still yearn for the grace of that perfect knowledge which no man can have or bestow. And we try to convince ourselves (I dare not speak in more positive terms) that this longing cannot be in vain. The religious feeling that we are counted upon seems to imply that, in order really to count, we must really be known.

The demand for self-realization through self-renewal appeals from the creature to the creator in us. It is the *humble* status of the creature — given to inertia, endangered by staleness, distractedness and inauthenticity of life — and it is the *corrupt* state of

283 In so far, Jaspers is justified in attributing the necessity of communication to a defect (*Wahrheit,* 380, 387). Only the finite being is in need of communication and discussion in order to make itself understood and to understand itself. But this does not exclude a completely free communication on the part of Transcendence — and were it only to provide for our needs. Only the *Sum qui Sum* is, by definition, incommunicative.

284 Cf. *Wahrheit,* 372ff. — The tension between my Self and its realization has its moral expression in Kant's Categorical Imperative: it elates us through its content — the respect which it demands for humanity in man; and it humiliates us in its imperative form, which is an objection to the *status quo* of human life.

285 *"Kann auch ein Mensch des andern auf der Erde
     Ganz wie er möchte, sein?"*
Eduard Mörike, *"Neue Liebe."*

narrow selfishness in lieu of communicative selfhood which make
renewal *necessary*. On the other hand, it is the creative spark in
man, his personal power of re-collection and re-integration which
make renewal *possible* as an honorable charge. Like the demon
Eros of the *Symposium,* man has his being in the perennial
counterworking of opposite trends and their unstable and uneasy
equilibrium. Integral selfhood in unswerving, unrelaxing devotion to the One is for us within hail (otherwise reason could
not respond to its claim), but it seems beyond our reach, an unattainable goal.

This constitutive weakness, which delays us on our way to
ourselves and to our brothers, is felt as the default of our being —
none of us is all right *(dans le vrai)* — as the sin of estrangement
from our Selves, from others, from the creative ground of all
being.[286] Heaven is the state of gracious communication; Hell is,
to quote Dostoevski, the condemnation to lovelessness. Sin is
isolation of the selfish individual; at-onement is communication
of the individual Self. The turning, returning toward the One
is the orientation man can give himself in the hour of crisis, the
Ent-scheidung, i.e, decisions between an old and a new way of
life: this is the belief, at least, behind the Hebrew *teshuvah*
("turning" — less of a spectacular break than "conversion," more
of a total and wholesome human movement than a too subjective
"repentance"). But the strength of persevering in this ascent
and overcoming all that draws us down must be given to us by
the sustaining grace which is alive in true communication as
such.[287] Biblical wisdom[288] knows of either part of life's renewal —
one in God's appeal and summons to man, one in man's appeal
to God: "Return ye . . . and make you a new heart and a new
spirit."[289] But also: "Create me a clean heart, O God; and renew

[286] Cf. *Wahrheit, e.g.,* 531f, 667.

[287] The complementary aspect of this religious experience is the consciousness of
man's responsibility as a partner in a universal enterprise. The importance of his
rôle in this co-operation seems by far greater than what little energy he can invest
in it. Conversely, the failure of his mission would appear to be more than a minor
accident in some corner of the universe. Properly understood, i.e., from the angle of
religious conscience and consciousness, it would assume universal proportions. See
above, 244.

[288] Obviously, I have recourse only to this profound *human* wisdom of the Bible,
not to any miraculous revelation of which philosophy does not and cannot know.
My references to religious experience and expression are in keeping with the phenomenological principle which I followed before, e.g., in taking examples from philosophical poetry: without committing ourselves unconditionally to any particular
approach, we try to profit from each type of experience, i.e., to respect its peculiar
evidence and relate it to insights won from other and complementary aspects.

[289] Ezekiel 18: 30f.

a steadfast (!) spirit within me."[290] Such prayer is answered by
the divine assurance that man's stony heart shall be enlivened
and his spirit grow strong in the vigor and strength of this communication: "A new heart will I give you, and a new spirit will
I put within you , . . and cause you to walk in my statutes, and
ye shall keep my ordinances and do them."[291] And finally, the
concise expression of reciprocity, but in recognition of the divine
precedence; man responds to God's claim and his coming to our
rescue: "Turn me, O Lord, that I may turn."[292]

"To all that draw near to me I draw near"[293]: the phenomenon
of turning and renewal is another instance of the power of correlation and correspondence experienced in the responsory of
communicative existence.[294] But in our context this example may
serve still a second purpose — to open up another vista in which
the heterogeneousness of animal life and personal existence loses
the character of an ultimate. The self-renewal of man in communication with the transcendent power meant that a sparklet
from the ground of absolute creativity has been communicated
to man and is kept alive and grows if this communication with
the ground is revived again and again. Now, this renewal of
man in which God co-operates appears as only one phase in the
permanent recreation of the world in which man has his tiny,
but unique part. This holds true if the idea of perpetual creation
has any *fundamentum in re* — as it actually seems to be founded
in the experience that finite and temporal things are not *per se;*
their being is somehow communicated to them, and they are
kept above the abyss of non-being as they pass from one passing
moment to the other.[295] The prayer to God to "renew our days
as of old" is not a sentimental longing for the good old days;
it is rooted in that faithful conviction in which God is praised
for "renewing . . . continuously each day the work of the beginning."

In this way, renewal appears as not only a human possibility
but as a universal fact. It is more than mechanical re-currence,
it is re-petition in a new key, rebirth from a creative ground
and, therefore, in a new and individual occurrence. From this

290 Psalms 51:12.   291 Ezekiel 36: 26f.

292 Lamentations 5:21.

293 Isaiah 57:19 (in a midrashic reading). Conversely, our turning away from God
and men is reciprocated by their estrangement from us: God is dead to us when our
approach to the Thou has died away in the exploitation of the It.

294 This point has been stressed, e.g., by Will Herberg, *Judaism and Modern
Man,* 121ff.

295 See above, 244f.

point of view, the articulation of Being[296] (though not caught in an all-encompassing system of understanding) tends to prevail over the opposite aspect — the disruption of being, which has haunted Jaspers from his youth. The opposition between nature and history (and, therefore, the necessary difference between the methods of natural and historical sciences) appears subdued in the recognition of the course of nature as (broadly) a historical process and the process of history as part of that creation which — in a different, unreflected form — goes on in nature. The rivers of creation flow asunder, but come from the same mountain; it is from the same source that their waters are supplied and renewed. "I shall be who I shall be, that is — it was my compassion in which I created the world, am sustaining and guiding it now, and in which someday I shall renew it again."[297]

Before the creator we are all equally creatures. We feel something like this in the equanimity of the great works of art where the natural and the personal trends of life are interwoven in a perfect texture,[298] and where, in a way, we have the same sympathy for Iago as for Othello: as Shakespeare's creations they are there all right: it is his blood that is communicated to them all and runs in all of them.

'Existentially,' there is tension between the two main forms of being — creaturely being and selfhood — a difference which is decisive because it calls for decision. Anthropologically, there is complementation and even pervasion between them — Existenz will be incarnated, vitality may overflow to serve Existenz.[299] I refer, once more, to the similar allurement for one another of the opposites in Thomas Mann's novels. But they remain opposites in life. Art, metaphysics, and religion, however, may lead to a divination, at least, of that "Holy of Holies" to which they are all drawn, and "where in eternal and original unity burns as it were in one flame what is separate in nature and history, and what in life and action as well as in thought cannot but perennially flee each other."[300]

[296] As I acknowledged before, this aspect is by no means neglected by Jaspers (cf., e.g., Wahrheit, 127ff, 672ff); but it is not the dominant one from his 'existential' viewpoint and experience.

[297] Quoted from the Talmud by Adolf Jellinek, Bet ha Midrash III, 25. This is another confirmation of the true nature of the Eheye asher Eheye, not as self-contained, loveless Transcendence, but as the communicative and compassionate love of the God of the covenant.

[298] See above, 237ff. [299] Cf. Wahrheit, 123ff, 672ff, 704ff.

[300] Schelling, System des Transzendentalen Idealismus (Werke, III, 628). This is no doubt in the spirit of Jaspers' own thought, e.g., in Wahrheit, 695; and elsewhere.

I, too, have yielded to this attraction by the center toward which everything gravitates, because it is the spring of *all* communication in the still growing community of being in which we believe — I have yielded to it in *this* communication which I would like to consider a *dialogo d'amore,* a struggle of love in Jaspers' sense: out of different origin, but in search of the One,

FRITZ KAUFMANN

DEPARTMENT OF PHILOSOPHY
UNIVERSITY OF BUFFALO

6

Johannes Thyssen

THE CONCEPT OF 'FOUNDERING' IN JASPERS' PHILOSOPHY

O N ACCOUNT of the many difficulties — which will perhaps be realized more easily towards the end — it is with some hesitation that I have undertaken to write this essay. Jaspers' treatment of the subject of "foundering" *(Scheitern)* forms the climax of his *Philosophie,* a work in three volumes and 1000 pages.[1] Owing to the closely knit fabric of this existentialist system, the concept of foundering cannot be dealt with in isolation but must be interpreted in the light of the whole. Even the basic concepts of *"Existenz"* and "Transcendence" present such difficulties to the reader that it would be impossible to interpret them adequately within the limited scope of an essay such as this. Due to the close relationship between our concept and Jaspers' over-all philosophy, foundering inevitably appears frequently throughout the work. There would be little point in collating philologically all the passages where Jaspers speaks of foundering, in order to "distill" a clear-cut concept. Foundering is in no way a mere concept; it represents an ultimately irrational *experience.* So we can only try and understand the emergence of this complex of problems in relation to the whole body of Jaspers' philosophy. In order to do this we shall restrict ourselves to his main work, *Philosophie.* Before embarking on the (apparently) modest task of interpreting the final section, it will be necessary to review the major presuppositions. The basic concepts of *"Existenz"* and "Transcendence" and a few other indispensable elements will be dealt with briefly in Part I. Inasmuch as foundering is regarded as a symbol or "cipher" *(Chiffre)* of Transcendence and as Jaspers' metaphysics reaches its climax in the deciphering or "reading" of such ciphers, these will form the topic of Part II. Finally we can devote ourselves to our subject proper in Part III.

I called the present interpretation an "apparently" modest task: its object permits of conceptual elucidation only to a limited

---

[1] I quote from the three volume edition published in 1932.

degree, on grounds of principle. There is a danger of over-rationalization which we must try and avoid. Nobody, surely, can interpret except by using *thought,* and all we can do is to put in a reminder here and there that for Jaspers himself his philosophical account means a rationalization of what is in essence irrational. There are additional difficulties for those who — like the author of this essay — start from different assumptions. We can only follow the text closely and do our best to come to an understanding. The significance of such an attempt will be touched upon at the conclusion of the essay.

I. *Existenz* and Transcendence

As is natural, we look for an initiation into the basic notions in the introduction to the main work. It is typical for this type of philosophy that we "take our own situation as a starting point of inquiry." The great philosophical problem is the quest for Being. Jaspers does not take this up in an abstract way, like the usual ontology, but by inquiring after Being in our own situation. Our own situation will never surrender to a complete and objective survey. I do not know the whence and the whither of my existence — either my origin or my ultimate destination. It becomes apparent also that my situation involves anguish *(Angst),* an anguish about the future in which I might not be, or in which death threatens me. Thus we look for a more complete and profound Being than is dealt with in ontology in the form of abstract reasoning. To allay my quest for Being, "I want an answer which gives me support," which frees me from that anguish; I require a Being "which is not elusive."[2] Evidently, the quest for Being takes on a certain value aspect here. Being, about which otherwise ontological statements of general validity might be made, is deflected towards myself and my particular situation, and a peculiar solution comes into sight: I can find the Being I am seeking only by seizing it, i.e., by freely deciding and by acting. "I find myself searching for Being, and this I do by doing something in the world of events."[3] This is, at first sight, quite unintelligible. It becomes somewhat clearer if, borrowing from the next section, the close relationship to Kantian philosophy is realized. In searching for Being I search, of course, for Being-in-itself, not for an apparential being. In the Kantian division of appearance and thing-in-itself all appearances have an un-

2 *Philosophie* I, 2.   3 *Ibid.,* 3.

knowable thing-in-itself behind them. Only in one instance we come closer to it, viz., in ourselves (in our "intelligible egos"). The idea is that this final unknowable Being is in our grip in so far as we decide for free action. This may be sufficient here to indicate that ultimate Being in its profundity is sought in myself. It cannot be known, but may be effected (getan). Obviously, this is the place that will be assigned to *Existenz*. It should be emphasized at once, however, that Being, as that which provides security or support for me, has its place not only within me. I have not created myself but have been thrown into the world (to use Heidegger's term *"geworfen"*), so that the transcendent being within me has the closest connection with Transcendence-as-such, with Being as such. This close connection between *Existenz* and Transcendence is a major point. First, however, let us try and obtain a somewhat clearer idea of the difficult concept of *Existenz*.

For Jaspers, too, cognition gives only appearance. The in-itself of an object "is not accessible to me because, in seizing it, I would objectify it and thus make it an appearance, a 'being for me'."[4] Because I can make myself an object of consciousness — psychologists do this systematically — the following is true: "If I objectify myself as empirical existence I am then not what 'I' am myself *(was "Ich" an sich selbst ist)*. Inasmuch as I am an object to myself I do not know what I am in myself."[5] In the next sentence, this leads on to the idea of an 'I' that can not be objectified, *Existenz*. Jaspers continues: "I should be capable of a self-awareness *(Innesein)* which is no cognitive knowing."[6] Here the problem of the two following paragraphs comes into view: the idea of a basic dichotomy within the 'I' and correspondingly a dichotomy of self-awareness. On the one hand we have empirical consciousness (comprising a number of phenomena), on the other there stands *Existenz*, connected with Transcendence in a special way which will concern us later.

On the first issue, empirical consciousness, only a few remarks, indispensable to our present purpose, can be made here.[7] The concrete physio-psychological individual is called "existence" *(Dasein)*; as to its type of consciousness, the emphasis is mainly on feeling and instincts — I say "mainly" because within an empirical individual another important subject factor, closely con-

---

[4] *Ibid.,* 5.   [5] *Ibid.*   [6] *Ibid.*

[7] In his much later work, *Von der Wahrheit* (1947), Jaspers has developed a properly systematization of the different modes of Being, postulating seven modes of the Encompassing *(das Umgreifende)*. When I speak subsequently of Jaspers' "system," I do not want to imply a "closed system" in a sense deprecated by Jaspers but simply mean an orderly, organized sequence of ideas.

nected with the cognitive function, is discernible, viz., "conscious-ness-as-such" *(Bewusstsein überhaupt)*. This is not a metaphysical absolute ego in Fichte's or Hegel's sense, but the vehicle — homogeneous throughout all individual egos — of universally valid knowledge and meanings.[8] Precisely with reference to our problem it is important to realize that Jaspers' relativism — to what extent such exists will become clear later — is not universal. The entire volume I of the main work is set apart for the subject of "world-orientation" *(Weltorientierung)* — finding your way about the world — which rests on consciousness-as-such; more particularly, there are sciences of universal validity, among them psychology, etc.

Opposed to these modes of consciousness stands *Existenz*. It is essential to realize that *Existenz* is no objective status of being *(Bestand)* but rather potential being effecting itself in freedom. (Being as status and being as freedom is an important distinction of Jaspers).[9] That depth of my own being which I cannot discern in cognition comes to light when I prehend myself in action. I acquire the certainty that this particular action is not a wilful and accidental choice of mine but is in fact an — already conscious — expression of that depth of my personality which is not strictly capable of consciousness.

Existenz is naturally "just mine" in the same way as my 'I' is just mine. It is, so to speak, the depth of my empirical I. It would not be correct to see the main feature of existentialist philosophy (not only Jaspers') in the emphasis placed on the singleness and individuality of [any specific] man as opposed to general human qualities shared by all. Of importance rather is the dimension of depth which Heidegger has very impressively contrasted with "the everyman" *(das Man)* or inauthenticity, constituting something like a surface-ego. On the other hand, as to "contents" also, *my Existenz* in fact does not coincide with that of other human beings. My being comes to light only in freedom, and another *Existenz* might very well assume actions contrary to mine (cf. Jaspers on the nature of "exceptions" and the "passion for the night:" *Leidenschaft zur Nacht).*

Before we contemplate the "totally different" other side of *Existenz*, i.e., Transcendence, a few features may be discussed

---

8 The problems connected with consciousness-as-such — as far as the historical and Jaspers' use of the term are concerned — cannot be analyzed here. According to *Von der Wahrheit*, this mode of consciousness is an Encompassing, with its own origin but without a content of its own. (The "prehension" of generalities is naturally dependent on the contents of individual perceptions, etc.)

9 *Philosophie* I, 18.

which are essential to Jaspers' system. In spite of their differences and their unknowable essences, the individual *Existenzen* are not barred from all relationships: they can understand and disclose their "contents" *(Gehalt)* to each other. This, for Jaspers' philosophy fundamental relationship between *Existenzen* is called "communication." In the same way as I can experience somebody else's essence in a non-objectifying approach, historical phenomena can also be understood and appreciated. A good illustration is the fact that somebody may not only *know* about a metaphysical view held in the past but may make it a part of himself and "seize" it as his own "possibility." But *Existenz* is historical not only in this particular sense, it is historical as such. The fact that its essence is freedom, i.e., future formation, does not mean that it decides willfully, disconnected from its past. It means rather that I decide as someone who has developed into a particular person and who lives in a specific environment and situation. And Jaspers discloses here one of the most peculiar tenets of his teaching: namely, that "within time, decisions are made for eternity."[10] This does not mean that Jaspers is talking of a life to come where my actions earn their reward and punishment respectively. Nor does eternity mean "abstract timelessness" as assigned to mathematical entities. It means that "I, within time, stand above it, though not outside of it."[11] The *'existential'* reaching out into the future and past is understandable as a point of departure for Jaspers, but it is peculiar that eternity is introduced here at all: eternity is said to come into play inasmuch as I "act *unconditionally* in time, love unconditionally."[12]

It is such absoluteness which makes Jaspers speak of eternity here. He is wise to state at once that my understanding cannot grasp this and that it is at best in short glimpses that the mystery is illuminated. In this view, eternity is neither timelessness nor everlasting duration but "the depth correlated to time as the historical form of *Existenz*."[13] What Jaspers means here can perhaps be made somewhat clearer if one remembers that for Kant time is a subjective form of intuition behind which lies that "depth" where a free decision originates, timelessly or — to use Jaspers' term — "athwart of time" *(in Querstellung zur Zeit)*. For Kant too, such a decision will become manifest empirically in certain conscious experiences. Jaspers' 'historical being' — which may, e.g., mean my being determined by a traditional *Weltanschauung* — is also "appearance" for consciousness. In Kant's view, however, temporal-historical existence rests on the

[10] *Ibid.*, 16. [11] *Ibid.*   [12] *Ibid.*, 17.   [13] *Ibid.*

time-less (the noumenal ego decides freely). For Jaspers (on the other hand) the strictly "historical" aspect of *Existenz* is timeless and "eternal" in the depth of *'existential'* deciding. Doubtlessly there is an historical relation to Kant's timeless freedom (we shall return to this point below). Toward an understanding — a limited understanding only, to be sure, as Jaspers expressly states — of what Jaspers means here, however, an earlier thought may contribute more, viz., that the "unconditional" refers to that Being which contains no "negation," no limit, which would mean in this case: it doesn't contain the limited temporality of the historical moment in which the unconditional is claimed to show itself.

Contrary to Kant this "certainty," which involves unconditionality, is not one of knowing but one of experiencing *(Erleben)*.[14] Similarly the "eternity" of the moment is experienced though not understood. (Jaspers notes the parallelism with the "eternal now" of the mystics; we will have to return to this theme later.)

Let us now consider that other difficult concept which is a prerequisite for the understanding of Jaspers' metaphysics and also of this essay: the concept of Transcendence. As with the previous concepts, I want to introduce it in concurrence with Jaspers' own account in Vol. I of *Philosophie*. I shall also draw on the Introduction to Vol. III. In the latter passages Transcendence is on the one hand bound up with *Existenz,* on the other it is its opposite pole, so that the emergence of "foundering" is foreshadowed.

In Jaspers we find three levels of transcending: (1) the step from the world of objects as they appear to us towards Being-in-itself of which they are appearances. It is possible only as a negative awareness of the boundary reached. In a way it would correspond to the Kantian transcensus from the world of appearances to that which renders them possible, granting that objects are to be considered mere appearances. (In Vol. I Jaspers turns against the belief of science and certain philosophical doctrines in [the possibility of] final and total attainment of knowledge about the world.) (2) Transcending belongs to *Existenz,* i.e., to that *Existenz* which is mine alone. Transcendence is included in the essential definition of *Existenz:* "*Existenz* is what never be-

---

14 We use "experience" in the usual contradistinction to "knowing." It is to be noted, however, that for Jaspers not all *'existential'* experience is fully conscious experience. For the act of "touching on Transcendence" *(Berührung der Transzendenz)* he uses the term *Erfahren,* whereas *Erleben* takes the meaning of conscious empirical experience. We use "experience" in the following without this differentiation, though we do not want to imply that "transcending" in its *entire* content is a conscious act.

comes object, the origin from which issues my thinking and acting, that whereof I speak in ideas which discern nothing; *Existenz*
is what has reference to itself and thus also to its Transcendence."[15] This means: my experiencing of *Existenz* does not simply
"give" me Transcendence; rather is Transcendence the deepest
basis within me to which I have reference in this experience.
Transcendence "inheres" in the performance of the experience,
so to say. If we remember that we have access to Being-in-itself
only in the I — although no cognitive account is possible —, it
becomes clear that Transcendence is this deepest I (or the unfathomable depth within it) to which I have reference when I
make a decision, etc. But Jaspers claims immediately afterwards
that — and this brings us to (3) — it would be wrong to limit
Transcendence to this depth in the I.

Existenz is indeed not the only thing; just as basic is the fact
that the I confronts objects. "Because we cannot in any sense
derive the world from *Existenz*, *Existenz* cannot be all there is
of Being, Being as such."[16] We then have two kinds of appearances: *Existenz* as experiencer, as which it can be observed psychologically, is appearance of the depth behind itself *qua* appearance. Then again, along with the principle discussed earlier, objects are also appearances. If we realize this, the following passage,
which introduces Transcendence as something other than *Existenz*, will be sufficiently clear:

We think of all being under the category of appearance . . . precisely
when we search for *the* Being. But Being, as far as it appears, retains—
irreconcilable with temporal existence — a duplicity, viz., the inaccessible Being-in-itself of Transcendence which cannot be rationalized as
the objective basis, and the self-present being of *Existenz* which is not
identical with consciousness of existence. *Existenz* and Transcendence
are heterogeneous but have reference to each other. Their relationship
appears in existence too.[17]

We saw under (2) that Transcendence belongs to *Existenz*
as its own unfathomable depth. This can now be seen to agree
with the last passage quoted in that this ultimate reach within
the I has in turn to be assigned to inaccessible transcendent
Being-in-itself. But, for Jaspers, to assert this would already constitute an overconceptualization. In *my* transcendence [in the
sense of (2)] a contact with absolute Transcendence [in the sense
of (3)] is supposed to take place. We shall have to clarify Tran-

---

15 *Philosophie* I, 15. As far as I can see this is the passage in Jaspers' main work
where the concept of Transcendence is introduced for the first time.

16 *Ibid.*, 26.   17 *Ibid.*, 20.

scendence in this latter sense, and also the resulting relationship between *Existenz* and Transcendence, from the material of Vol. III.[18]

Before we turn to this volume which bears the name *Metaphysik*, it should be noted that we must pass over all of Vol. II, called *Existenzerhellung* (illumination of *Existenz*). We thus miss details of doctrine we can hardly do without. We are thinking particularly of Jaspers' account of "ultimate situations" *(Grenzsituationen)* and of "absolute consciousness." All we can do here is to give some indication of what is meant.*

If *Existenz* is, as it were, the locus of contact with the absolute which is at the root of all appearances, of all objects in causal order and of any objects as such, then it is decisive, in order that man's attention be caught and this depth made accessible, that he should come up against the limits of his empirical existence "as against a wall:" he must suffer death, must contract guilt and suffering. In general, man finds himself always in situations, entangled in irremovable restrictions (as, for example, to be man or woman). This mysterious "That," called fate or the like, cannot be accounted for within the realm of the visible and controllable; it is its limit. An heroic decision in the face of death, coming from deep down within me, may contain an experience of absolute certainty transcending the knowable and may constitute a contact with non-temporal Being. Such are the modes of "absolute consciousness." Without embarking here on an analysis of the many different modes described in Vol. II, we note that *'existential'* freedom with its experiences of absoluteness is not restricted to so-called decisions in choosing a certain action. It operates in any self-determination of man, especially in basic and "fulfilling" ways of conduct such as love and faith.

To be trapped in ultimate situations, to search for *the* Being from within the isolation and scatteredness of worldly existence, and lastly, to touch the in no way scattered absolute, i.e., Transcendence, in absolute consciousness, all this belongs intimately together and constitutes different sides or aspects of *Existenz*. And the "wall" *Existenz* comes up against is Transcendence, the absolute which surpasses the I's own transcendent depth.

Let us call attention to two points in the opening paragraphs

18 In the rigorously systematic work, *Von der Wahrheit*, the multiplicity of meaning of Transcendence is made explicit to such a point that to signify the *one* Being (3) Jaspers speaks of the "Transcendent of the Transcendent." It will be remembered that the transition from existence to *Existenz* (2) also discloses "a" transcendent aspect.

* Ed.'s Note: Cf. Latzel's essay for a detailed discussion of these.

of Vol. III which have a significant bearing on *Existenz* and Transcendence. Here will be found the most rational, i.e., comprehensible account of absolute Transcendence, that "wall" or fate we have been speaking about. Prefacing it here will also shed some light on the notion of freedom with which we want to deal later.

It is asked, "what is the reality of the incalculable, if it cannot be known?"[19] This question leads to the quasi-ontological analysis which concerns us here. All events can be traced to their causes. The natural laws indicate potentialities which materialize in events. Through such laws future events can be predicted as potentialities and, if not predictable, they are at least known to be possible. In quite a different sense I, *qua Existenz,* am potentiality too: I am the potential prehension of a particular decision. In contingency or accident, however, I find out that, in spite of all conformity to natural laws the actual occurrence of events, *hic* and *nunc,* cannot be concluded from a law. Here I encounter "absolute reality." This idea now serves to define Jaspers' notion of Transcendence. All empirical realities are particular and, as it were, retranslatable into potentialities given in natural laws or, in my own case, into the possibilities I face before my decision is taken. In the encounter with chance, however, we become aware of a reality devoid of potentiality, we encounter a reality which is not retranslatable into potentiality, i.e., "absolute reality," Transcendence.

The reality of Transcendence is inaccessible to retranslation into potentiality; therefore it is non-empirical. It lacks potentiality — which would make it real and comprehensible to us [by furnishing the *terminus a quo*] — not because of a deficiency but because the separation of potentiality and reality is constitutive of empirical reality, a reality requiring something outside itself. Nor is the reality of Transcendence identical with *Existenz:* it lacks the possibility of deciding, not because of a deficiency but, on the contrary, because the possibility of deciding is an expression of the deficiency of *Existenz* due to its temporal existence. Wherever I encounter reality and it is not transformed into potentiality I meet Transcendence.[20]

Here we are clearly in closest proximity to the ontological idea of God: that Being to whose essence belongs *Existenz* or which can be thought of only as existing, but not merely as potential. Jaspers, of course, knows of this historical parallel; but for him all rationalizations like this proof of God's existence are forbidden solidifications. But the, so to say ontological, account of metaphysical objectivity given in our passage is indicative of

[19] *Philosophie* III, 8.   [20] *Ibid.,* 9.

the aim of the whole doctrine, as we already know it: Transcendence is conceived of as *ens realissimum,* the One which is not split up into juxtaposed entities; which is this *and* that, A *and* B in conjunction. It is to be noted at once that this philosophical elaboration — as we shall show in greater detail — claims to be no more than an "illumination," i.e., a rational paraphrase. It only wants to express in abstract terms what in *'existential'* experience, barred from knowledge and proof, is supposed to become evident. In the present version this experience is so far objectified that astonishment at the absolute contingency of the empirical world becomes, by reaction as it were, possible. The empirical world becomes "transparent."

"Becoming transparent" is a well-known concept of Jaspers. It implies the view that empirical being can let Transcendence "shine through," as a screen transmits rays, so that individual entities turn into code entities, ciphers for Being. Let us for a moment ignore the endowment of Transcendence with particular contents and dwell on the mere "That" of Transcendence.

I have started with the quasi-ontological characterization of the "That" in order to prepare for the second important point I am to deal with now. The freedom of *Existenz* pushes through to a depth where it ceases to be *my* freedom and *my* decision; where, though still freedom, it knows itself "granted" *(geschenkt)* by that surpassing Transcendence which is neither freedom nor compulsion.[21] From the point of view of this absolute "That" even my freedom is "fate." The fact that in my freedom I am given possibilities originates within that sphere which is no longer potentiality but absolute reality and where *'existential'* freedom touches my own freedom.

Let us consider more closely how Jaspers comments on this profound connection between *Existenz* and Transcendence. It becomes more noticeable that *Existenz,* which was often enough described as "origin" and "self-creative," is, in the end, not self-sufficient. Actually this is already known from what has gone before. If *Existenz* had created itself it would be God; it is creativity but at the same time it is given, is "historical" or, in Heidegger's term, "thrown" into the world. Jaspers declares that *Existenz* would have to fall into "despair" if it were left to rely entirely on itself and that it can be true *Existenz* only if it knows itself grounded in some other, in Transcendence.

To rely on itself entirely is certainly the truth of the absoluteness

21 *Ibid.,* 5.

amid temporality of *Existenz,* but it also brings about its despair. [*Existenz*] is aware that as an absolutely self-sufficient entity it would fall into the void. If it is to become real it must depend on something that meets it halfway and fulfils it. Whenever it fails in its realization it is not itself; it takes itself as if it were granted to itself. It proves its potentiality only if it knows itself grounded in Transcendence. It loses its openness for its own becoming if it takes itself for authentic Being.[22]

In this "dissolution of potential self-sufficiency" can "lie final fulfilment in temporal existence," precisely in that I, as empirical consciousness and as *Existenz,* am doomed to "founder."

This final stage, this "letting Transcendence be granted to us," involves for Jaspers yet another factor which we will have to take into account before reaching our more specialized subject. We are not left with naked Transcendence, with the mere certainty of contact with it; it "speaks" to us, if only in symbols or ciphers. This means that the bare "That" takes on material content. This is our next problem.

II. Interpretation of the Ciphers of Transcendence

If empirical consciousness and its world are, so to speak, the surface of the one Transcendence, then it is truly omnipresent. Jaspers holds accordingly that this presence of Transcendence in different entities can be experienced as their background. Psychologically speaking, what Jaspers has in mind are experiences like sensing the sublimity of the sea through its immensity or, e.g., the fact that in looking at a landscape by Van Gogh[23] we do not only pass from the mere color and formal arrangement to a realization of beauty values, but that these seem to express something deeper and impalpable. Such an intuitive perception of what lies beneath signifies for Jaspers a becoming transparent of the empirical; the landscape, e.g., admits the shining through of the underlying absolute Being. This is thus not always tangible in the same way, but may become so in infinite ways, depending on the reality expressing it. But, on the other hand, it must be noted that none of the empirical realities expresses Transcendence as it is in itself — this would mean that objects or appearances coincide with non-objectifiable, unknowable Being-in-itself. All appearance is simply a code-entity, a cipher. A cipher in this sense does

22 *Ibid.,* 4.

23 Both illustrations occur in Jaspers' work. Van Gogh had attracted the attention of Jaspers, the psychopathologist, at an early date. Cf. *Strindberg.*

not work like a mathematical sign: for that it would have to refer to some intentional content which eventually could be isolated or deduced. The cipher, however, leaves us merely with the experience that this or that individual entity is more than itself, that it is transparent for Transcendence.

If I say we are left with mere experience this is not an adequate statement. As it stands it only indicates the essential difference from any cognitive grip on Transcendence. We have to add now — following Vol. III, ch. 4 — that we do not stop with the mere experience of absolute consciousness, but that this presence of Transcendence, originally only in some way "perceptible" to individual *Existenz,* finds a more universal "language." This "immediate language of Transcendence" is made communicable to other *Existenzen* through illustrative symbols, e.g., myths, a religious revelation of a world to come, or a mythical reality (such as transmitted in a landscape by Van Gogh) .[24] In addition, philosophical or speculative thought produces a rational account, interpreting Transcendence "as if" it were empirically existing like myself and the world. Such interpretation will never attain a true knowledge of Transcendence, but constitutes in itself another cipher-script *(Chiffreschrift).* All forms of cipher-reading gain their weight and — though undemonstrable — certainty only from that unmediated presence which animates every cipher experienced by absolute consciousness. Ciphers in general constitute that type of reality which "brings Transcendence into presence."[25] This unmediated experience is the foundation on which, in turn, rests the reading of it in terms of the "second language," that of myths, etc., and, eventually, the speculative reading. (The language of art is yet another level of ciphers, placed between the mythical and the speculative. It cannot be dealt with here) .*

Inasmuch as, without a deeper understanding of the essence of ciphers, we cannot continue to the cipher of foundering, I want to portray Jaspers' views on the matter and their outspoken paradox in two ways, which are closely linked with each other.

1. Since transcendent Being is always experienced through ciphers, and since *Existenz* is always an historical individuality, not every cipher is intelligible to every *Existenz.* The myths of the aborigines, e.g., may — for the members of such a society — be genuine ciphers, experienced by each *'existentially;'* but this will not be so for members of a higher civilization. Similarly, dogmas and also metaphysical systems are only historical ciphers.

---

24 *Ibid.,* 133.   25 *Ibid.,* 137.

* Ed.'s Note: This subject is treated in the essay by Johannes Pfeiffer.

In one word: Ciphers do not only give no knowledge of Transcendence but the experience of Transcendence through ciphers varies along with the historical habitat of a given *Existenz*. ("Historical habitat" is used here in a wide sense. Thus, e.g., it certainly depends also on the intellectual gifts and the education of a given person whether, say, a painting by Van Gogh achieves metaphysical significance as a symbol of Transcendence.)

The significance of the "definition," that Transcendence is reality without potentiality, emerges here again: It is claimed that the impulse of fundamental metaphysical experience is exactly to reach this point beyond the isolated experiences of potentialities, viz., Transcendence, the nothing but real which is Being as such.[26] It is significant that this quasi-ontological account of Transcendence appears here, where the concept of the "direct language of Transcendence" is introduced. This is apparently the content of Transcendence which is common to all ciphers, which belongs to their essence. (Their amazing variety is treated in a second part of *Philosophie*, Vol. III, chapter 4: The World of Ciphers.) The following question could now be asked: is Transcedence, thus qualified, not already touched upon in 'existential' decisions or in absolute consciousness? Why then ciphers? The answer is that, beyond the experience of finality, there is in, and because of, 'existential' experience a "presence" of Transcendence, something that corresponds to objectivity: the transparency of the world of objects, i.e., the ciphers. Transcendence, as it were, does not remain hidden, as in the experience of finality, but assumes "perceptible language" in ciphers. Expounding Jaspers one might say: *Existenz* constitutes the depth of the total empirical I and it can live its part only in the form of empirical consciousness and within an empirical world. The necessary condition of *Existenz:* to be here — one might also say, the essential characteristic of consciousness: to partake in the cleavage between subject and object as co-extensive with intentionality (in Husserl's sense) — requires that Transcendence be represented in quasi-objective form, if there is to occur an authentic experience of Transcendence going beyond the impalpable experience of finality. I say "quasi-objective" because Transcendence can, of course, not take on an object character (which would only mean appearance over again). The idea is rather that empirical objects may become symbols of Transcendence in the way indicated. This happens only in 'existential' conduct. Here Transcendence can, beyond the experience of finality, manifest itself in the different mode of

[26] *Ibid.*, 131.

the empirically given, as its transcendent background as it were, and this manifestation is quasi-objective. (We have omitted the intermediate chapter 3: *'Existential'* relationships to Transcendence, which connects the notion of *Existenz* as such with the reading of ciphers by *Existenz*. We shall return to this chapter briefly in another context.)

2. Another question suggests itself: Is the difference between individual ciphers due to the empirical element in them, so that their divergent contents do not infringe upon the unity of the *one* Being conceived along the lines of the quasi-ontological analysis of Transcendence? This is not Jaspers' view. "A bare 'beyond' would be empty and might just as well not exist."[27] Paradoxically, "there is totality and unity in every symbol *qua* appearances of Transcendence," "every symbol remains one individual aspect of Transcendence."[28]* One is reminded of the *coincidentia oppositorum* of Nicolaus Cusanus. While existence "is constituted in relationships between itself and others" — by mutual implication as it were — this antithetical relationship does not hold for the different aspects of the one Transcendence: the One is at the same time manifold. There is one point, however, which distinguishes Jaspers from such a *coincidentia oppositorum:* Transcendence in its aspects is not separable from the *Existenz* experiencing it; Transcendence is only accessible in the "obviously paradoxical" form of "immanent Transcendence." The access to Transcendence is not separable from the character of a particular *Existenz*.[29] This non-Cusanian element, the inclusion of a *subject,* suggests the idea that the differences or even contradictions of the ciphers among each other might all be explained by the different subjects experiencing them. But this is not Jaspers' view. Precisely this separability of *Existenz* and Transcendence is rejected, and the differences cannot therefore be attributed solely to the different *Existenzen* but belong also to Transcendence itself, even though it is the *One*.

We have arrived at a main manifestation of Jaspers' irrationalism. In the last resort it is to safeguard this inseparability, to formulate it and to bring it into relief, that the great later work, *Von der Wahrheit,* was written.[30]

---

[27] *Ibid.,* 136.   [28] *Ibid.,* 138.

* Ed.'s Note: Jaspers uses the terms "symbol" and "cipher" interchangeably here. Cf. Kurt Hoffman's essay in this volume.

[29] *Ibid.,* 136.

[30] I have given a short analysis of this work, together with a criticism of its main epistemological problem in an article, "Karl Jaspers' Buch *Von der Wahrheit*," *Archiv für Philosophie,* Vol. V, Nr. 2 (1954), 170ff.

The unity of Transcendence becomes eloquent in true, though occasionally contradictory, aspects which are experienced *'existentially'* and which are expressed symbolically in the quasi-objective language of ciphers.

"The standard to apply is no longer that of scientific and methodical inquiry aiming at a final result; the issue is: *'existentially'* true and *'existentially'* ruinous symbolism. What broke down in its cognitive claim remains as a symbol for a mode in which self-being knew its Transcendence."[31]

We are left with the ambiguity of ciphers in the sense that different *Existenzen* will adopt the one Transcendence in a number of ways. Any interpretation will be unequivocal for a particular *Existenz* precisely at the moment of adoption; the interpretation will "at the moment of historical presence become unambiguous for *Existenz,* unexchangeably and unknowably so [even] for itself" ("unknowable" because speculative interpretation gains its certainty only from the "direct language" of Transcendence).[32] Not only the individual *Existenz* but also "the Transcendence giving fulfilment to this particular *Existenz*" is "non-interchangeable" and only in this sense unambiguous. It is even possible that the same person will, at different "high moments" of his life, experience as true different symbols and speculative interpretations, even new symbols. In this sense ambiguity belongs to the essence of ciphers. If any one cipher would be "final" — it is argued — "perfection," absoluteness would enter the realm of finite being, i.e., the realm of the existence of *Existenz*. If one wanted to outtheorize Jaspers and separate the factors involved, one might say that the ambiguity of ciphers is due to finiteness; conclusiveness and absence of ambiguity, in turn, is due to the — in each case historical — attainment of Transcendence. Both factors are, for Jaspers, inseparably one in the reading of ciphers. (It is characteristic of the ambiguity in question that a mutually elucidating exchange among all ciphers, including the mythical ones, is possible.[33])

In view of the ambiguity of ciphers it will be well to look back to our starting-point. The unifying factor which reduces ambiguity at every historical jucture to conclusiveness is the One, Transcendence, which is experienced as reality without potentiality. In this sense Jaspers will say "it is sufficient that Transcendence is;" but this Transcendence will, perceptible through its particular cipher-language, be "granted" to individual *Existenz*

---

31 *Ibid.,* 148.   32 *Ibid.*   33 *Ibid.,* 150.

in its transcending experience of certainty and yet, at the same time, according to what we said above, be prehended in freedom.

III. The Cipher of Foundering

In the context of Jaspers' main work the concept of "foundering" comes as the last great theme, unifying the whole in a new climax. It would have been of little value to discuss foundering in isolation; our main task was rather to outline Jaspers' whole account of Being which finds a precise expression in this concept. It is not true, however, that an understanding of foundering is derived automatically from the views stated previously. It involves a new element.

Foundering signifies the fruitlessness of all endeavors to reach, from a finite basis such as consciousness-as-such or even from self-sufficient *Existenz,* a satisfactory access to Being, i.e., to arrive at the absolute. More will have to be said about this presently. For the moment it may suffice to say that in Jaspers' explicit treatment of foundering towards the end of the work it takes on another sense or function: foundering itself comes to be a cipher, a cipher determining all other ciphers. Therefore it was unavoidable to speak not only about the basic concepts of *Existenz* and Transcendence but also to deal with the idea of ciphers of Transcendence. In spite of the limitations of this essay, we had to look into this particular language of metaphysics.

Let us consider the explicit treatment of foundering in Vol. III, ch. 4, part 4. We find a division: Factual foundering *(faktisches Scheitern)* is, as it were, simply the consequence of all fruitless endeavors to reach ultimate Being. Turning his attention to this failure, Jaspers then asks in what way foundering itself is interpretable, in what way it can be a cipher for something and have a referential character: factual foundering is *understood 'existentially'* as a cipher.

This dichotomy reflects the division of the above-mentioned passage. A peculiar thing happens to the latter alternative, i.e., the interpretation of foundering as a cipher: Foundering admits of interpretation, of reading it as a cipher, but there are also remainders — so to say — of foundering, remainders encountered in the world, in regard to which not even that kind of an interpretation is meaningfully possible. This is then the actual difficulty: foundering may remain an uninterpretable cipher. One may ask (with Jaspers) if this whole system of metaphysics is not thus doomed to founder. In what sense this is not supposed to be the case will be our final problem.

Let us first remember clearly that for Jaspers foundering does not emerge only at this juncture, but that for him all the various ways of transitoriness and all vain attempts to remodel them cognitively or actively into "enduring being as such" *(Sein schlecht-hin als Bestand)*[34] are types of human foundering. Naturally, therefore, the concept of foundering occurs already in early passages of the work; as a matter of fact, on the very first page where Jaspers reflects on the breakdown of any attempt to obtain, by way of ontology, durable Being as something objective, independent of my situation.[35] Similarly, the concept occurs in the introduction to Vol. III, the "Metaphysics," not as related to consciousness-as-such (which is the vehicle of universally valid knowledge and also of ontology), but as related to *Existenz*.[36] The occurrence in passages acting as preludes either to the work as a whole or to Vol. III may be an indication of the paramount significance of foundering. In accordance with the dimensions of the work, it is small wonder that the concept is made to cover the different factual forms of foundering as they occur. There would be little use in making a list of all these; because something may be a case of foundering even if the term has not been used (e.g., in a number of descriptive analyses where Jaspers declares that it is impossible for positivism as well as for idealism to arrive at a comprehensive conception of the world). Nevertheless we may hint at two uses of the term which are of particular importance to the concluding section and thus have a significance for Jaspers' views as a whole.

What I have in mind is, first of all, so-called "formal transcending" which, in demonstrating the contradictions of ontological reasoning and the absurdity of any claim to understand God, Being, naught, etc., keeps the way open for the positive *'existential'* metaphysics of ciphers.[37] It became apparent, in Vol. I, that philosophical "world-orientation" cannot arrive at an all-embracing, closed system like those of Aristotle, Hegel, positivism or idealism. In Vol. III, where we concentrate on Transcendence and the divine, the dialectic of foundering in thought appears: It is already a case of "transcending" if human speculative thought (which is never superfluous but always an inevitable attempt to comprehend the transcendent) tries and concentrates on its own antinomies and contradictions, viz. on the attempt to objectify and contemplate what is non-objective, Transcendence. Through this failure of

[34] *Ibid.*, 222.   [35] Cf. also I, 58.   [36] III, 3.   [37] *Ibid.*, ch. 2.

consciousness-as-such with regard to a rational comprehension of Transcendence, philosophy comes to realize the limits of its *thinking*. If this means that fundamentally the way is cleared for a non-objective *contact* with Transcendence, then even this merely "formal" transcending indicates something positive: to touch on a boundary means to touch on something else beyond that boundary. "Contemplating the non-absolute I touch indirectly on absolute Being."[38] And again: "Philosophical thinking of God which gains certainty in the foundering of thought prehends thus the 'that' not the 'what' of the godhead."[39]

If foundering is a metaphor for thwarted endeavor, then the ontological attempt — mentioned at the beginning of the work — to arrive at a conclusive account of Being by way of thinking or of consciousness-as-such is *the* thwarted endeavor. As in III, 43 and 54, foundering serves, here too, to characterize the rejection of the traditional, ever-repeated approaches of metaphysics; thus the way for the existentialist approach is cleared. Foundering is to become the great symbol for *all* endeavors — not only those in terms of thought — bent on Transcendence. It is not by accident, however, that the notion comes into prominence in connection with the rejection of what used to be the *via regia* to Transcendence: thought and reasoning. But it is significant that foundering is not restricted to a negative function but appears here in the positive one intimated by the last two quotations. The simile of "coming up against a wall" makes this even clearer.

It would be tempting to pursue the ways of formal transcending which exemplify foundering in the sense indicated above. Within the scope of this essay, however, I can only say that Jaspers' analysis of the great antinomies of being is meaningful also for a metaphysics more sceptical than his. He who does not "believe" in Jaspers' fulfillment (of which we shall talk at once) will probably stop short of the discovery of such worldly contradictions, because they are the last stage metaphysics can reach. But this is only a marginal comment from outside of Jaspers' system.

We must go on to the second important aspect of foundering. We can deal with it briefly because in this connection foundering is treated in line with the previous idea that foundering on a barrier makes me aware of just this barrier. It is here that the simile of "coming up against a wall" reveals the true meaning of foun-

---

[38] *Ibid.*, 37.

[39] *Ibid.*, 39; I refer readers to a helpful passage from Jaspers' *Von der Wahrheit*, 136: "The result of such 'somersaulting' thinking *(sich überschlagenden Denken)* is not a stable knowledge of God; but: that we can and must think in this manner is a pointer towards Transcendence."

dering.[40] We do not mean the failure of speculative thought to solve the *rational* antinomies, but the fact that *Existenz* symptomatically finds itself in ultimate situations in which it fails. To experience ultimate situations and to *exist* are in fact called one and the same thing. They exhibit, in a certain parallelism with the antinomies of thought, the antinomical structure of our total being, as *Existenz* — not consciousness-as-such — experiences it. To the few details given above (p. 305) I can add here but little from part 3 of the chapter on ultimate situations, e.g., the idea that "the valuable is tied up everywhere with conditions which are, as such, of negative value."[41] Life is tied up with death, freedom goes with compulsion to choose only a limited possibility, etc.; a state of affairs which, following Heidegger, is labeled "guilt."[42] Before we turn to the concluding section of Jaspers' work let us simply note that in the part of Vol. II which deals with ultimate situations Jaspers has succeeded in giving descriptions which convey a very clear picture of the concept of foundering, in its double meaning of "coming up against a wall" and of "transcending the wall existentially." I particularly want to point out here the *'existential'* conquest of death — as contrasted to all the "faulty proofs of immortality." We may, e.g., see such mastery in heroic courage in the face of death, where it would manifest itself as certainty of super-apparitional Being.[43]

Now we come at last to the passages in the final chapter which deal explicitly with foundering. It has been mentioned before that Jaspers begins with modes of actual foundering. The heading reads "The multiple meaning of actual foundering," and we find first (1) an enumeration of these different modes, (2) subsequently the multiplicity of meaning of these different modes is commented upon.[44]

The first point, the enumeration of modes of foundering, subdivides into the above-mentioned dichotomy of failure of thought and failure of *Existenz*. Here we should note the following: The "World-Orientation" demonstrated already the foundering of all life in death, that of history in progress (down to the menacing annihilation as a result of new weapons). The attempt to escape into thought, into the world of timeless validity of values and standards, and of absolute truth, fails too. These topics point to important tenets within the system as a whole with which we could not deal. We saw, while discussing ciphers, that there can be world-immanent objective truth, but that the ultimate truth is one of

40 *Ibid.*, II, 203.   41 *Ibid.*, 250.

42 *Ibid.*, 247.   43 *Ibid.*, 220ff.   44 *Ibid.*, III, 219ff.

Existenz, not one of universal validity (therefore formulations such a "failure of logic in relativity," "emergence of non-rational truth as surpassing knowledge").[45] Quite generally, timeless objectivity, i.e., universally valid standards and ideas, such as ethical values, are regarded as "not only unreal but void."[46] Jaspers confronts such timelessness — which he calls duration — with *'existential'* reality which has access to eternity in quite another way: eternity is athwart of time (cf. above, pp. 301f).

Next in the enumeration of modes of foundering follows the discussion of foundering of *Existenz:* "the in-itself of *Existenz*" fails; "wherever I am authentically myself, I am not only myself."[47] Finally there is a mode of foundering where *Existenz* has express reference to Transcendence and yet founders: foundering in the face of Transcendence. In the passage under discussion it is illustrated briefly in this way: "In the face of Transcendence thought fails because of the passion for the night."[48] On the basis of what we have said so far about Jaspers' system this passage cannot be understood. We have to add that the "Metaphysics" has three parts: between the chapter entitled "Formal Transcending" and the one called "Reading of the Cipher-Script" stands one called *"Existential* Relationships to Transcendence;" ['passion for the night' is one of these relationships]. In the whole chapter on "relationships" the attitude of *Existenz* before Transcendence is treated in its subjective aspects, so to say; its — likewise antinomical — structure is revealed and interpreted as "defiance and surrender," "uplift," etc. The level of discussion lies beyond illumination of *Existenz* and thus metaphysical and religious attempts at solutions begin to appear, e.g., the attempt at a theodicy, or the different God-concepts. Cipher-reading is here "search" for Transcendence through certain antithetic *'existential'* attitudes. Volume III (apart from the disposition and Introduction) is divided into three parts: (1) *Formal Transcending;* it "keeps the way open" for (2) the *quest for Transcendence* (the *'existential'* relationships), and for (3) the only form of *finding* Transcendence, viz., the reading of the ciphers in which Transcendence attains "presence." Here, then, is mentioned the third among four antithetic relationships to Transcendence: the "passion for the night." It is impossible to give an account here of this profound paragraph. Just to comment on the suggestive title: We would mistake Jaspers' intentions if we claimed that he rejects order in the human domain as brought

---

45 *Ibid.,* 220.   46 *Ibid.,* 222.

47 *Ibid.,* 220; to be interpreted in the sense of what we discussed on pp. 302ff.

48 *Ibid.*

about by reasonable rules and conceptions.[49] Without reasonable order, without the 'law of the day' *(Gesetz des Tages)*, man, who is not only *Existenz* but necessarily existence also, could not live. The 'passion for the night' appears as the antithesis to reason (which Jaspers tends to emphasize strongly in *Von der Wahrheit)*; it is, so to speak, an ultimate and insurmountable experience, not assimilable to order, though justified as "exception" in the eyes of *Existenz*. It appears in a variety of ways: as passion for death, with its well-known connection with Eros,[50] but also as unavoidable "inhumanity" such as that which forced itself on the mind of a statesman like Cromwell.[51] A mythological interpretation of these opposite worlds is the belief in a good and a bad world-power (e.g., in the ancient Persian religion). But in reality every attempt at a "synthesis of both worlds" fails.[52]

This may be sufficient to indicate what, in our enumeration of forms of foundering, may be the meaning of foundering in the face of Transcendence. It is foundering of *Existenz* inasmuch as *Existenz* has express reference to Transcendence (this is why it comes under metaphysics and not under illumination of *Existenz)*; it is foundering because a compromise or adjustment between the opposing orientations, each of them experienced and justified by *Existenz,* cannot be obtained. We will have to ask in what respect there could be another form of foundering before Transcendence.

After the enumeration of the forms of foundering we now turn to the second point: the multiple *meaning* of foundering (we shall return to the previous discussion presently and we shall also have more to say on the foundering of *Existenz)*. Jaspers considers it necessary to discuss the multiple meaning of foundering because the variety of forms of foundering is "confusing" if the meaning of foundering in each of them is left undifferentiated. Jaspers starts by saying that foundering happens only to man, not to animals, being a response to the "ambiguous" or "equivocal" *(nicht Eindeutiges)*. After the above-mentioned antithesis of failure of thought and failure of *Existenz* we should expect these two kinds to appear as the main varieties of meaning. This is quite

[49] Cf. especially the chapter on "Subjectivity and Objectivity" in vol. II, where Jaspers demands participation in the state and its rational order which, however, constitutes an inexorable "tension" in relation to *Existenz*, the ultimate court of decision. In the more recent *Origin and Goal of History* Jaspers goes so far as to acknowledge principles of natural law. As an example of foundering we might mention that the attempt to establish an everlasting world-order in terms of unlimited progress betrays in a significant way the failure of consciousness-as-such, the faculty of order. Cf. the references mentioned above.

[50] *Philosophie* III, 105.   [51] *Ibid.,* 107.   [52] *Ibid.,* 113.

true. But we are surprised to find that failure in ultimate situations and even failure in the *'existential'* relations to Transcendence are grouped together with the first of these kinds. All these forms of foundering are supposed to have a meaning similar to that of foundering in consciousness-as-such and the whole group is contrasted with foundering "on a different plane," i.e., foundering of *Existenz,* which exhibits the second main variety. That means obviously that also in the experience of the antinomic structure of ultimate situations and in those futile attempts at a "synthesis" of the *'existential'* responses to Transcendence, rational compromise is being sought. This group, therefore, comprises the ways by which man, *qua* existence, "unavoidably" tries to win the upper hand over those "real" antinomies through *thinking.* It is indeed a fact that man lives not merely as *Existenz,* but that he exists also and that, even in his *'existing,'* he also thinks; he even thinks in reading ciphers. This then, viz., thinkability, is the aspect under which foundering in the *'existential'* relations to Transcendence is to be understood first of all: Those kinds of *'existential'* experience which cannot be mastered in thought, i.e., foundering of *'existential'* experience itself, cannot be understood in this fashion and thus form a natural contrast to those which can. Here come now the other forms of foundering set out above: the experience of freedom in which *Existenz* learns that it cannot absolutely rely on itself; the *'existential'* "guilt" of having to choose; furthermore the realization that truth is in the last resort not demonstrably valid for everybody, but is variable in relation to *Existenz,* as we discovered when discussing ciphers — an observation which applies equally to the field of ethics (here used in a wide sense) where truth is supposed to surpass all attempts at general validity.

Here we might mention that, in accordance with his style — which is actually not our concern — Jaspers does not, as might appear from our account, give a complete list of all forms of foundering and then divide them carefully according to their meanings. He does make a distinction between mere enumeration (or "representation" as he has it) and elucidation of the meaning, but his way of handling the problems is more labile; the differences between the individual phenomena are not clearly marked. I mention this with an eye both to the preceding part of this essay and to what is to follow. In an important concluding passage Jaspers introduces a new aspect which brings the previous forms of foundering into a new light.

It may look like an exacerbation of a, by now familiar, idea when we hear that *Existenz,* as it fails in its craving for self-sufficiency, comes up against its limits and thus becomes open to Transcendence. This would mean the "success" both of *Existenz* (which is said to be authentic only in its reference to Transcendence) and of its contact with Transcendence. A new feature, however, now comes to light: The authentic self as well as Transcendence may remain in abeyance *(sich ausbleiben)* and, since to force the issue is impossible, I will not know to what extent I am to blame. This leads to the most astonishing formulation of foundering: "Even if all honesty and readiness seem to be there, I may fail, with neither philosophical confidence, nor God's word, nor religious security being of any use to me."[53] This puts into negative language the familiar idea that *Existenz,* in spite of its freedom, "is granted to itself" inasmuch as it is rooted in Transcendence. We can detect here a somewhat new meaning which calls for our attention. The idea of *Existenz* as something bestowed does not only mean that it is not *causa sui,* but also that *Existenz* may be denied, in spite of all good will, to become *Existenz* in a full sense, i.e., to experience itself in relation to Transcendence. We should note that this does not refer to a lasting state of affairs, as if there were a predestination of those who might never be called to authentic *Existenz.* What is meant is that the depth of experiencing may vary: what I am being granted now may be withheld at some other time. — This consideration will be of importance when we come to deal with the notion of "ultimate foundering."

The note of potential ultimate foundering has been struck and the section now under review[54] continues with the question which seems to lead from an account of actual (or mere, non symbolic) foundering to its *interpretation.* Is foundering really annihilation or can "Being be revealed" through it; can foundering be coincident with eternalization? This section is called *"Scheitern und Verewigen"* (foundering and eternalization), therefore. Inasmuch as the second section following thereafter has the title, *"Deutung der Notwendigkeit des Scheiterns"* (interpretation of the necessity of foundering),[55] one might wonder if the section preceding it does not in fact contain an "interpretation," or if the above division is wrong. We should recall that Jaspers has a peculiar vagueness in contrast to our, necessarily systematic, interpretation. In the present section, "Foundering and Eternalization" foundering is claimed to be a cipher,[56] where we are no longer dealing with

53 *Ibid.,* 221.   54 *Ibid.,* 221ff.

55 *Ibid.,* 227.   56 *Ibid.,* 223.

actual foundering in isolation but with foundering as transparent for something, introducing us to something.[57]

Turning now to foundering as access to eternity, the theoretical elements are already known to us. If "foundering is the end" — this is the result of the previous considerations — and if the escape into the realm of timeless validities leads into the void, the only authentic being we are left with, following the earlier argument, is "the concrete and present reality of the being-itself of *Existenz*."[58] And here lies a positive answer to the above question whether foundering is coincident with eternalization. I have picked out two views which, brought together, give this result. First, the essence of *Existenz* is freedom, and ruin and destruction can therefore also freely be taken on — in contrast to mere accidental transitoriness and subjection to it we can, so to speak, "adopt" foundering; the corresponding cipher is *"amor fati."* Secondly, in the free prehending of foundering we are supposed to experience or, past all conscious experiencing, have access to that timelessness which is eternity within time, "athwart of time." In it Transcendence, which is not tied to our *apparential* time, will shine through.

It would be a mistake to see in this free adoption a will to fail. It is a feature of man as a unity comprising existence not to will his foundering but to promote, say, reasonable order. The positive attitude towards foundering which Jaspers has in mind is "daring," courage to take foundering upon myself. If I do what is in my power, regardless of the possibility or eventual necessity of foundering, I live in a certainty of action surpassing the temporal and actual. After such daring "activity" I may well fail.

Penetrating more deeply, there is a difficulty in these words: The cipher of foundering becomes "manifest" *(offenbar)* to "*Existenz* which, perishing *qua* existence, produces it [this meaningful cipher] *qua* freedom; which founders *qua Existenz* and thus finds its ground in Transcendence."[59] One could be led to think that *Existenz* fails only in its apparential component, namely as existence only. Here, however, *Existenz* itself founders. The difference is that with the word "foundering" *(Zerschellen)* is linked a positive feature: foundering on the rock of Transcendence.* *Existenz*, whose "body" is its realization in existence, experiences

---

[57] On the other hand, let us realize that the subsequent section does not read "Interpretation of Foundering" but "Interpretation of the Necessity of Foundering." We have, so it appears, levels or aspects of interpretations and, on the whole, our main division seems to be justified.

[58] *Philosophie* III, 222.   [59] *Ibid.*, 223.

* Ed.'s Note: Here Jaspers uses *Zerschellen* — the literal translation of "foundering" in the narrow, nautical sense — as a metaphor.

the shipwreck of this reality. *Existenz* possesses, however, a non-apparential depth, its root in Transcendence, and from there will come the echo that it dared rightly. The free daring of *Existenz* has Transcendence for its basis, and even in its ultimate foundering it can assure itself of that. *Existenz* can read this assurance in a cipher which it "produces while undergoing annihilation *qua* existence." "The cipher of eternalization in foundering appears only if I do not want to founder but dare to."[60] Judging merely from appearance, the "contradiction" involved will stand — but foundering becomes a cipher with regard to Transcendence. In genuine foundering *Existenz* touches Transcendence and therein lies eternalization. In this sense foundering itself is cipher.

It will be clear from this that Jaspers' foundering is far removed from any mystical "other-worldliness," if this should have any quietistic significance. The following section can be taken as an appeal for action irrespective of inevitable failure. I cannot dwell here on all the important points of this section, *"Verwirklichen und Nichtverwirklichen"* (realization and non-realization). Let me mention only one which could have been listed among the forms of actual foundering. In passing we remarked on page 301 that for Jaspers communication between individual *Existenzen* belongs to the *'existential'* essence of man, whereas universal validity is only a matter of consciousness-as-such. E.g., I cannot possess truth in isolation, but only through exchange with others can I be sure of my truth. Similarly, in the part I play in modelling the world, I must allow for the freedom of others and exercise consideration. But — and this brings us to the kind of foundering we want to outline here — in communication with others, too, I will eventually fail, and yet in doing so "Being will be revealed."[61]

We come now to what I have called another level of interpretation, the "Interpretation of the Necessity of Foundering."[62] Here we expect an answer to the question whether there must be foundering. We might say we are dealing with something like a theodicy of foundering. Such an interpretation would mean, of course, the creation of a new cipher in terms of existentialist philosophy. Before dealing with that, however, we must mention that, at the end of these justifications for foundering, appears something new, an ultimate level of cipher-reading: the uninterpretable. It leads to the point where interpretation passes into silence, i.e., it leads to what may be called Jaspers' mysticism.

In the following section[63] the basic elements are arranged in

[60] *Ibid.*   [61] *Ibid.*, 226.   [62] *Ibid.*, 227ff.   [63] *Ibid.*

antitheses in such a way that foundering appears as a necessary consequence. (1) The timelessness of "ideal being" (universal truths, etc.) and the duration of everything factual are lumped together as a kind of inert permanence, whereas, in comparison, profound transcendent Being is accessible only in those moments when that entirely different eternity, athwart of time, is perceptible. Inert eternity is set against a, quasi living, eternity which freedom can prehend for an instant at a time. There is no way in which freedom can aspire to Transcendence, unless it fails in its obedience to those inert kinds of eternity; that is, unless their claim for totality is broken. (2) The second antithesis is that between freedom and "nature;" they cannot be reconciled without foundering. Freedom can find realization only in the world, in nature. *Existenz* is real only in the form of existence, not as pure *Existenz;* it can realize itself only against the resistance of nature. Nature, however, on its part, is not only resistance to be mastered by *Existenz,* but is itself rooted in the quite other realm of Transcendence, and it "revolts" therefore against that mastery which is *Existenz'* task. This is why Jaspers speaks of an "antinomy of freedom." "To become one with nature" (not trying to master it but submitting to it as to being-as-such) "brings about the annihilation of *Existenz qua* freedom; to offend against it precipitates its breakdown *qua* existence." It holds, therefore, also for this second antithesis that foundering is a necessary corollary to freedom. (3) *Existenz* must fail because it exists and realizes itself only as finite existence, and yet it must by its essence "surpass, in its absoluteness, the bounds of finiteness." The world of existence, in this view, is constituted as a world of restrictions, of compromises, etc. *Existenz* in its boundlessness offends against this stability by disturbing it. For this "guilt of absoluteness *Existenz* must do penance and founder. It founders because it aspires to things infinite," because it wants to impose its unconditional absoluteness on the conditional world of existence.

This offense against the constitution of the world is seen on one hand as an "exception"[64] — cf. Jaspers' illustration of Cromwell — on the other hand, however, this offending and consequent foundering is considered essential to *Existenz* as such, a consequence of its true being. This is one of those "oscillations" which seem to belong to Jaspers' style. A similar one is noticeable in

---

[64] We should note in passing that this is a particularly relevant passage about Jaspers' ethics: The two types of ethics, that of universally valid standards and that of the unconditional *'existential'* "exception" stand in opposition to each other, thus each relativizing the other.

the following point (4). What I have in mind is this: under points (2) and (3) we were dealing with that sort of foundering which *Existenz* incurs through its realization in nature and in the world of history, i.e., *qua* its alliance with existence. It was to such finiteness that absolute *Existenz* stood in opposition. Now finiteness is claimed not only for *Existenz qua* thrown into nature and the world, without its consent, but — and this is the new point (4) — finiteness holds also for *Existenz qua* individual. Contrary to Schopenhauer, the multiplicity of individuals cannot, for Jaspers, be a matter of appearance only; *Existenzen* are always just this or that *Existenz*. This squares with Kant's assumption of numerous intelligible egos. One might therefore ask if, irrespective of its necessary failure *qua* existence each *Existenz* will fail, purely by itself, as such. This cannot be, inasmuch as *Existenz* lives only in the form of existence, is not "here" *(da)* by itself. Nevertheless, we find here a philosophical motif which could be called the idea of "primordial foundering:" to become finite, to separate from comprehensive Being, is seen as a kind of apostasy, a kind of primordial guilt.[65]

Jaspers calls this a "mythical conception;" but we know that such a conception is a cipher also and may contain truth, though it will not be true in the sense of objective, unequivocal knowledge. The primordial guilt of finiteness (as I would like to call it) cannot strictly be experienced as such by *Existenz*. *Existenz* finds itself allied to an antecedent will to survive as existence. *Existenz* can master this blind force (e.g., in a heroic attitude towards death) and surpass the bounds of finiteness [in the sense of (3)]. "Only then, at this absolute level, is unavoidable guilt realized." If "guilt" refers here to that mythical conception above — viz., that finiteness or individuation, though unavoidable, constitute an apostasy — we have, strictly speaking, an oscillation. According to (3) there was an experienceable "guilt" of foundering at the world-order of existence, and then, secondly, there is that primordial "guilt" which is experienced in foundering: the metaphysical apostasy incidental to individuation is the basis for (1) the guilt that can be experienced in existence, and (2) for foundering in the world of existence.[66]

The following paragraph[67] refers back to foundering in exist-

65 Cf. Anaximander's *gnomon* about the penance the things have to do in atonement for their separate existence, lately revived by Heidegger in his *Holzwege*.

66 I remind readers of "original Nothingness" *(Ur-Nicht)* in Heidegger's conception of guilt (cf. *Sein und Zeit*), which is claimed to be the basis of all guilt in the customary sense. Cf. also the theological antithesis of original sin and factual sins.

67 *Philosophie* III, 230.

ence: "In existence Being is not only veiled but reversed." As *Existenz* is compelled to realize itself, to "create" itself in the world, it looks as if existence is the only thing there is. This is the "fundamental fallacy with regard to Being, to believe that it is identical with existence." Only through the experience of foundering can this fallacy be resolved. With this statement Jaspers returns to the main trend of thought, that of a justification for foundering. He continues to the concept of ultimate, i.e., uninterpretable foundering.

With point (5) of the present section (Interpretation of the Necessity of Foundering) we reach the turning point: There are conditions where this interpretation of ciphers breaks down, too, because thought is no longer met by a "matching content." Foundering becomes uninterpretable. Jaspers mentions three varieties: (a) Ruinous destruction as opposed to constructive annihilation (the prototype is mental disease which, unlike annihilation in death, cannot be prehended by my freedom). (b) Premature destruction of potentialities already apparent. I will pass over the loving description of human beings living in the "lonely torment" of non-realization in "unknown heroism." Such persons may win a kind of new "substantiality" which will again admit of meaningful interpretation. Over and above such non-realization of embryonic potentialities, claim is made for cases where "potentiality as such is ruined" and all that remains is "uninterpretable Nothingness." (c) Jaspers considers the possibility of the annihilation of historical continuity through the loss of documents and of all evidence telling of valuable human activity. This would be "the ruin of oblivion" which also defies meaningful interpretation.

We have now arrived at the concluding and most difficult section of Jaspers' work, *"Die Chiffre des Seins im Scheitern"* (foundering as cipher for Being). It occupies a key position of such nature that, admittedly, with its acceptance or rejection the whole system will stand or fall. The uninterpretable annihilation of which we have just spoken is such that not only "will all existence fail us," but "foundering itself is only the presence of Nothingness, not a cipher any longer."[68] Through ciphers Transcendence was to be made present; intuition or thought were to find a (though merely symbolical) content. Here now such a content is no more available and all transcending, therefore, so far confident to gain a "hold in Being," is "like a delusion." "To live without transcending, however, is to live in radical despair, with

68 *Ibid.*, 231.

only Nothingness left." Therefore we must ask if this ultimate uninterpretable foundering might not, beyond all interpretation, become a "potential cipher." If at this stage foundering is to be considered a cipher — in apparent contradiction to the previously stated collapse of any cipher-reading — it will have to be in a sense quite different from the ordinary conception of cipher reading.

Before we go into detail, let us try and give a provisional answer to the last question. It is not in a quasi-objective understanding but only in a peculiar experience that this ultimate uninterpretable foundering can win a hold in Being. In Jaspers' description, an "incomprehensible leap" from anguish in the face of Nothingness to calm is possible, establishing contact with Transcendence without meaningful interpretation. Since without interpretation "no determinable content" is given, such an experience must be simply "silence." We can here talk of a cipher only in the sense that this muteness becomes in turn an "ultimate cipher" which is "no longer definable;" "it remains open, therefore it is silent."

This is a preliminary sketch of Jaspers' most important views which lead from quasi-objective experience in cipher-reading to that pure non-objective experience parallel to the *unio* of the mystics, where similarly all objectifying understanding ceases. We will realize that this is the climax of Jaspers' irrationalistic doctrine. It is so important that we must look more closely.

Before we study Jaspers' account of the problem we must direct our attention to another oscillation in the passage on the "uninterpretable cipher."[69] First, a merely "contemplative" approach to foundering is set over against genuine foundering *as an experience,* without which we would "fall back into finite existence." This means, if we performed the foregoing analyses with their justification only as rational analyses, we would make of them a complete system of speculative knowledge about the world. *Interpretable* foundering, too, will establish contact with transcendent Being only if it is experienced as foundering. Then, however, Jaspers returns to the discussion of *non-interpretable* foundering to which no contemplation can do justice. Jaspers gives short comments on the three varieties of uninterpretable foundering which we mentioned in the preceding paragraph.[70] The transition from ordinary foundering to such "ultimate foundering" is not facilitated but rather blurred by a passage inserted before the reference to these three ultimate varieties, not really referring to them but to another example of cipher-reading: "No one can

69 *Ibid.,* 233.   70 *Ibid.*

know why the world exists; perhaps it can be experienced in foundering, but it cannot be told." For this famous problem there are certainly legitimate ciphers, take e.g., the theological analogy of God's creative will, for one. It is true, if one tries to transform a cipher into objective knowledge, a statement, a "telling" of its content will certainly be impossible. But this limitation is not identical with that silence to which the next sentence reverts; the silence before that which lies beyond interpretation, which has no meaningful cipher.

We shall turn to this oscillation (or, if one prefers, contradiction) presently. In any case, the following remarks refer to that silence which results when we are face to face with the uninterpretable. Above we have explained in what sense it is "silence." We will now have to see in what way something can be asserted about it. Let us bear in mind, too, that many religions accept the concept of a "holy silence."[71]

He who wants to give an answer (or a meaning) to this silence can merely "speak without saying anything." "Face to face with meaningless ruin" (that first type of ultimate foundering) "an answer may be the plain awareness of Being," the "conceptually empty," simple "it is." It is interesting that Jaspers compares Being with matter here. "In all the transitoriness of world-patterns matter remains the downright other, but indifferent, being." The likeness lies in the indeterminacy of both, transcendent Being and matter. Being, however, is not indifferent: "... it is intrinsic Being in whose dark meaning essence shines." This basic essence is inaccessible, incomprehensible in its meaning; but this obscurity to which no clarifying determination can do justice is an indication of the indeterminate One which shines through it. This indeterminate obscurity is not a nothing, it is lit, as it were, by the great positivity of Being.[72]

If matter in this comparison is also "one," *qua* indeterminate, transcendent Being on the other hand, contrary to the indifference of matter, is the essence, the supporting basis of all determinate, apparential being, it is *the* Being.

This point, which Jaspers just hints at, I have enlarged on a little. It lies in the direction of negative theology. We should, however, remember that such considerations differ from those of negative theology in that they may not be taken as accomplished knowledge but only as symbolic circumlocutions of what will

---

[71] Cf. G. Mensching: *Das heilige Schweigen* (1926).

[72] In *Von der Wahrheit* the idea of the one "Encompassing" is brought into prominence.

remain: even in the face of ruin, Being, transcendent to ruin, will be experienced.

In the light of this inaccessible Being, the two other varieties of ultimate uninterpretable foundering — the unexploited potentialities and the ruin of oblivion — can also refer to temporal being only; only within temporal being are potentialities wasted and achievements forgotten. They do not infringe on transcendent Being which is not subject to temporality. All three are varieties of the same empty formula, called "being."

Next, before we reach the leap from anguish to calm,[73] follows quite a different reflection. In it, unexpectedly, this uninterpretable silence is raised to universal significance in that all previous ciphers are made dependent on it for their meaning. Foundering comes to be the encircling foundation (umspannender Grund) of all ciphers. What does this mean? If worldly existence or individual Existenz were self-sufficient and did not, as in ultimate situations, come up against the wall of Transcendence, there would not occur that "presence" of Transcendence which the ciphers effect. Our passage does not emphasize so much the aspect of the diversified quasi-objective contents to be accorded to the ciphers, as that of contact with Transcendence which gives such contents meaning and life. Foundering, with its twofold function, the positive: to connect with Transcendence, the negative: to precipitate destruction, is this contact.

All ciphers consisting of an interpretation of the different forms of foundering are "called in question" from the standpoint of this uninterpretable foundering. If foundering in its purest form, incapable of any meaningful interpretation of symbolic content, cannot be accounted for satisfactorily, are not all the other, richer experiences of foundering untenable? In this sense our attitude towards that universal foundering decides the validity of all ciphers. From here they derive their "resonance," their confirmation. The uninterpretable itself becomes an "ultimate cipher," not filled with content but "open," inconclusive.[74]

Truly we have here the fulcrum of Jaspers' metaphysical doctrine as he himself admits. The question is: can this doctrine assimilate ultimate foundering, come to terms with it? What has been said on it in the way of assertions was only "empty" speaking about what is intrinsically silence. In fact, on this central point

[73] Philosophie III, 234.

[74] The transition from uninterpretable to universal foundering resonant in all ciphers (and the dependence of the former on the latter) may supply the solution of the oscillation referred to on pp. 325f, above.

it is difficult to say more than what has been said above. The answer lies in the leap from anguish to calm which is the "most enormous," "the most difficult and incomprehensible" step man can succeed in making. It is not to be explained or expressed in concepts, it can only be experienced. Jaspers, however, does say a number of things about the *"a quo"* and the *"ad quem"* of this leap from anguish to calm, and also on the totality of this experience and its effects on the life of man in the world. So we must try and bring out a few points.

As is well known, anguish *(Angst)* has a prominent place in existentialist philosophy, beginning as early as Kierkegaard. Its significance — open to criticism which we shall here not undertake to make — is to reveal man intrinsically. This would be a large subject on its own account, which we could not raise here even if we restricted the discussion to Jaspers.* Anguish is experienced in ultimate situations (e.g., anguish before death); in them *Existenz* comes up against the limits on which it founders. So much for a brief account of anguish. But where we speak of uninterpretable foundering, anguish is carried to extremes: "ultimate anguish" corresponds to "ultimate foundering;" "intrinsic anguish ... considers itself ultimate and there is no way out of it." In this anguish we realize we cannot leap over the abyss and yet, incomprehensibly, this leap into calm can succeed.

This leap presupposes dread before the abyss, fear of sinking into Nothingness; but it does not presuppose such anguish as a cause. Causal inference is a matter of objective knowledge about the world. The leap that is meant here is unknowable spontaneity. Existentialist freedom occurs here in Jaspers in an extreme and incomprehensible form, as a leap over the abyss revealed through anguish. If we take a glimpse at other existentialists, "dread before freedom" signifies the response to the fact that I have to choose, spontaneously, in a leap as it were, one and only one of my possibilities. "Nothing," e.g., will keep me from jumping down a real precipice.[75] In any case, dread in this connection seems to signify something of a more general nature than the anguish of which our passage speaks, viz., anguish before Nothingness in the experience of uninterpretable foundering, "ultimate an-

* Ed.'s Note: Cf. on this the definition and reference given in the Glossary at the beginning of this book.

[75] This formulation refers to Sartre. In Part I of *L'être et le néant* dread *(angoisse)* before a real precipice is used as a central illustration for the essence of freedom. For Heidegger, too, dread and Nothingness are, however differently, yoked together — a central feature of his "system." Cf. particularly his *Sein und Zeit* and *Was ist Metaphysik?*

guish."* Bearing in mind what has been said on the resonance the ciphers derive from universal foundering, this ultimate anguish should not be taken in a too limited sense: it is foundation, it constitutes, together with our leap into calm, "the basic fact of our *Existenz* in existence." Down to the last pages of Jaspers' work it is emphasized that anguish is a "most mysterious turning-point" where "even the language of Transcendence can be dispensed with." But then again its general significance is visible in the fact that the ultimate experience of a leap from anguish to calm is a prerequisite for "facing the real world unflinchingly."

This is subsequently elaborated. "Mere anguish" without venturing the leap "conceals from itself its own nature by clinging to pieces of knowledge that put it at rest." Empirical existence is thus made to believe that it can grasp its own nature completely and shape it accordingly. This would be "mere" calm, fallacious because it endeavors to overlook the fact that existence is not the whole. (A problem is touched here which, in my view, has found no satisfactory answer either in Sartre or Heidegger: How can anguish keep itself at bay, how can it avoid being experienced all the time? How can it have a central significance if it is such a rare phenomenon?) Both, mere anguish and mere calm "conceal" the "real world" which is disclosed, so to say, only on the basis of *that* being which belongs to it. It is through venturing the leap that the world will become visible on this foil. The leap does not, like "mere" anguish, blur the issue of foundering, but, with "authentic" anguish at its root, it is coincident with foundering, made possible by it. Ultimate anguish plunges the whole finite world into the light of Nothingness; the leap, however, which, in a way, reaches the firm ground of Transcendence, returns a positive meaning to the finite world; it does not let it fall into Nothingness but re-attaches it to *the* reality.

This process in which "self-being is bound up with utmost proximity to reality" is never complete. A final (irrevocable) reality would founder no more (would no longer be called into question by foundering), and thus would be incompatible with the finiteness of man and *Existenz*. The leap is, so it appears, reserved to "high moments." To bridge this gap, as it were in psychological terms, Jaspers introduces another attitude or re-

* Ed.'s Note: To distinguish the two interpretations, "anguish," in preference to "dread," was chosen as translation of *Angst*. Usually *Angst* and *angoisse* are translated with "dread." Cf. *Existence and Being*, excerpts from Heidegger's works, with an introduction by W. Brock, Chicago, 1949; and *Existential Psychoanalysis*, J. P. Sartre, N.Y., 1953.

sponse, that of endurance *(Dulden)*, as "the way preceding accomplished calm." He constrasts "passive endurance," a mere letting-things-be or non-resistance, to "active endurance," endurance in the realization of foundering. There will not always be enough strength to realize foundering; which is the same as saying that active endurance will not always fulfill its function of precipitating calm through foundering. But, once foundering has resulted in a leap, that kind of endurance is possible of which Jaspers says: "Endurance will hold on to Being in spite of foundering in which the cipher remained in abeyance." (Here "cipher" comprises the uninterpretable cipher which can, like the others, be lost sight of; even then, however, endurance, patience, equanimity are possible.) This incongruity, not always to be able to perform the leap, produces that great virtue of the mystics, equanimity.

Dependent on the experience of the leap — which is also decisive for all elevation through thought and interpretation — endurance, with its varying power to bring about contact with Transcendence, is seen as a kind of permanent attitude which determines the relationship of man towards himself and his world. But this is perhaps saying too much in view of the following paragraph.

The assurance of Transcendence gives, even if the "language" of cipher-reading breaks down, a security, a hold, an infallible calm in the midst of existence. But "this certainty, dependent on the presence of *Existenz,* cannot in time be constituted as an objective guarantee, but must disappear again and again. However, when it is present, nothing can prevail against it. It is sufficient that there is Being."[76] It may be well not to link this passage too closely with the reflections on endurance. As the work draws to a close, in two final paragraphs the emphasis is on those "active" experiences of Transcendence which are possible at the turning-point of uninterpretable foundering. If a permanent possession of certainty is not possible, this need not exclude that there is, based on the experience of certainty, permanent equanimity, distinct from the "objective guarantee" which is rejected — a frame of mind for which "it is sufficient that there is Being." "Truth is where foundering *Existenz* is capable of translating the ambiguous language of Transcendence into the plainest certainty of being." We know that the wealth of interpretative ciphers have their significance and value in making Transcendence "present" and we realize that they are ambiguous. Even if, as in ultimate

[76] *Philosophie* III, 236.

foundering, no significant cipher is left, there may still remain that leap into calm which, in itself silent, purports "Being" and has its hold in transcendent Being that surpasses the world.

We come to the concluding paragraphs which survey, as from a summit, the whole work. Only if the world of existence becomes transparent (for the underlying Transcendence), that is, only through the adoption of foundering can *Existenz* be truly world-open: "The world becomes unspeakably beautiful in its abundance rooted in Transcendence." This realization leads to investigation (world-orientation) and an active contribution towards the shaping of the world. This absolute calm may "afford in fleeting moments a vision of perfection;" but it is only a "vision" with the significance of a cipher (e.g., it would be fallacious to cherish the idea of a perfect world-wide welfare state as a concrete aim). The world with all its beauty and

with its co-existent terror [remains] a question which, for temporal existence, will never be conclusively answered once and for all, even though individuals have the power to endure [it] with a clear mind and [are able to] find rest . . . Not through intoxication with perfection but following the ways of suffering, with our eyes fixed on the inexorable face of worldly existence, in absoluteness of self-being and of communication, *Existenz* may achieve that which cannot be planned and whose meaning is perverted if it is desired: in foundering to experience Being. (End of volume III.)

In connection with these last pages of Jaspers' metaphysics, one more thing may be added: in his analysis of the incomprehensible leap from anguish to calm, we may detect a kind of "argument" for the existence of God. It is not objective proof; but like all other metaphysical assertions, it falls into the realm of speculative ciphers. I need but quote one sentence to give an idea of the kind of "argument:" That man succeeds in the "enormous leap must have its reason beyond the existence of the self; his faith connects him indeterminably with the being of Transcendence"[77] (similarly two paragraphs further on). Not proof but faith is the link with Transcendence. The "proof argument" just cited and its "must" I take to be a reflection on the immediate experience of the leap. The reflection is not intended as proof with a claim to universal validity, but as an elucidation of the immediate experience of the leap. It belongs to this experience in the same way as the innermost core of *Existenz*, as given in *'existential'* consciousness, always has an admixture of reflection.[78]

[77] *Ibid.*, 235.   [78] Stated expressly, e.g., in the later *Way to Wisdom*, 56.

It would be a new problem to go into Jaspers' concept of faith and to investigate the "doctrinal faith" which he gave in his book, *The Perennial Scope of Philosophy*. Essential to it are the dichotomy and yet the intimate unity of immediate experience and cipher-reading, of which we have spoken. In our case the unity is one of leap, "proof argument," and faith. The proof argument is a covering cipher, an interpretation of the leap, it is "philosophical faith," elucidating immediate experience.

Regarding the interpretive reflection, it is certainly as a philosopher that Jaspers tries to elucidate an experience which cannot be self-evident in its import; but it is not as a philosopher working with scientific methods in search of universally valid truths, but as one who derives faith from his *Existenz*. His experience of faith is offered to other human beings in communication, wondering if they, too, have this experience and can believe this way. Such philosophy is in its entirety illumination and indirect communication of immediate experience, it is not psychological objectifying of such experience or argument for God's existence. Indirect in Kierkegaard's sense: everybody must himself make the experience, a direct transmission of the experience or of the accompanying belief is impossible.

*   *   *   *

With this comment we find ourselves plunged into a concluding appreciation which cannot altogether avoid striking a critical note. If we survey the complex network which we have tried to present and interpret, the relationship between *Existenz* and Transcendence is twofold: (1) the immediate experience of contact with Transcendence and (2) the "language" of Transcendence, the ciphers. What separates Jaspers from myths or dogmatic convictions of religion as well as from the speculative systems of Hegel and others is this: The latter take all their assertions to be objectively true, i.e., as reflecting existing facts correctly, independent of man, and with a claim to universal validity. Jaspers, on the other hand, takes the same assertions to be merely ciphers. Objective knowledge exists for him only in the realm of empirical existence. Now that another approach to superempirical Being, i.e., the immediate experience of Transcendence, exists (or rather, can be achieved by *Existenz* again and again), those assertions become, if not for everybody in the same way, symbolic representations of this immediate relationship reflecting Transcendence, however divergent, or contradictory, the symbols may turn out to be. We dealt with this aspect on page

310 above. Here we must point out something else: The security afforded by the objective claim of the old teachings is, in Jaspers, replaced by the virtual opposite, foundering. The very fact that all quest for perfection and security in the realm of finite things is doomed to failure gives the certainty that "there is" Transcendence.

We shall not repeat here the individual stages of foundering and their interpretation but merely suggest the following: foundering becomes the new great cipher for the philosophical experience of Transcendence. But it is not only a cipher. Rather is it the *experience* of foundering which is fundamental. This became particularly apparent when we spoke of ultimate foundering before the abyss of Nothingness.

What separates Jaspers from the old teachings is, thus, not the opinion that genuine contact with Transcendence cannot be established through the medium of their dogmas — they may very well be the expression of genuine experience — but (1) the emphasis is placed on the experience of foundering as a key experience (the experience of foundering occurs, of course, elsewhere also, especially in Christianity) ; (2) the reduction of all objectifying assertions to mere ciphers. From the key experience of foundering is obtained the new key cipher of foundering, first that of interpretable (meaningful, significant) foundering, and eventually that of uninterpretable, mute, complete foundering.

After this reminder, the points most liable to criticism can be stated. (1) Will all these experiences really establish contact with Transcendence? In view of the facts it will, for example, not be denied that there is something like a leap from anguish to calm — this must have been one of Jaspers' basic experiences. But will Transcendence, divine Being, really be "touched" in this leap? Much could be said about this point,[79] particularly in comparison with mysticism. If Jaspers did see in the contact with Transcendence an ecstasy, a union of man with God, and an extinction of everything finite, we would be treading on old paths. The contact with Transcendence, however, keeps the distinction between the individual *Existenz* and the one Transcendence intact[80] but

[79] I have attempted a detailed analysis of this contact with Transcendence in an article mentioned above. Cf. fn 30.

[80] It is interesting to note that Jaspers, in *Von der Wahrheit,* places the *unio mystica* as another kind of transcending beside the existentialist ones already known to us. As far as I can see, Jaspers himself has not accomplished the change-over to mysticism (he retains the non-dissolution of individual *Existenz*), but has recognized the "approach of mysticism" as something "the experience of which cannot be denied." *(Wahrheit,* 137; cf. 111 and 187).

at the same time denies it, because such clear-cut opposites belong, for Jaspers, exclusively to the world of objects. This would be a *coincidentia oppositorum,* in which a merging not only of aspects of God, but of God and man is envisaged (cf. above, page 310). From this follows (2): If we add to our misgivings about the consequences of the experience of contact [with Transcendence] our doubts about the idea of the *coincidentia oppositorum,* our criticism will have to start right at the beginning of Jaspers' system, at his epistemology. We must raise the question whether objective knowledge will give objects only in relation to an experiencing subject, or whether it could also lay hold of what is in itself. In this respect Jaspers is closely connected with Neo-Kantianism, but differs from it in assuming an accessible in-itself, the transcendent of Transcendence. Incidentally, the hostility towards objective knowledge (if we may put it that way), a basic character of irrationality, is not only a feature of Jaspers, but is shared generally by existentialism and other current trends. We cannot here enlarge on this problem and its current-day aspects.

Let us formulate briefly the following misgivings: (1) Does foundering involve coming up against a wall of Transcendence which is thus experienced as existing with certainty? (2) If so, will I not, at one with my *Existenz,* experience a genuine non-I, the surpassing Transcendence, i.e., something opposite me, other than I? Or is the difference of I and non-I a characteristic of "object knowledge" in Jaspers' sense, so that it belongs exclusively to the empirical world?

For all who — like the author of this essay — cannot agree with Jaspers on these questions, his metaphysics is an interpretation of experiences of conviction which owe their character, as connectives between *Existenz* and Transcendence, only to philosophical thinking. To take these interpretations for more, for ultimate truth, is indeed a matter of faith. To give reasons why philosophers who, like myself, do not share Jaspers' views, nevertheless follow him with keen interest, would take too long. It is better, in conclusion, to restrict ourselves to a few remarks. In an age which has largely lost its belief in the Christian dogmas, and which in its uncertainty and anxiety in the face of the future looks out for a new "hold," such a hold in divine Being is offered here in a doctrine that retrieves the basic religious values without a *sacrificium intellectus.* In this sense Jaspers practices a far-reaching "demythologizing" (Cf. Bultmann's *Entmythologisierung*) and he says with regard to myths and revelations that his philosophy tries to retain their contents, though their claim to validity cannot stand.[81] This endeavor, the sincerity and difficulty of which we have witnessed, is in fact an appeal to all who seek a spiritual hold and have access to philosophy. It leads the way to undogmatic religion by means of philosophy (in some respects comparable to the young Schleiermacher). We have attempted to reach an understanding of this way in its relationship to the key-note of the doctrine, foundering. So we have at least complied with Jaspers' demand for "communication." Whether it will be possible really to go this way and seize this "hold on Being" through experience and philosophy, is another question.

JOHANNES THYSSEN

PHILOSOPHISCHE FAKULTÄT
UNIVERSITÄT BONN

[81] *Philosophie* III, 71.

7

Eduard Baumgarten

RADICAL EVIL: PRO AND CON*

JASPERS tells what often happens to him when engaged with the history of philosophy: for a time he is charmed by the radiant clarity of the Greeks. Yet it is impossible to tarry with them: inevitably he feels himself drawn away from them to the profundity of St. Augustine. But there again, when the radicalism of conscience finally threatens to obscure and do violence to the intellect, the urbane brilliance of Athens beckons anew. As against this, it is noteworthy that, in an area some centuries closer to us, Jaspers no longer permits himself the same freedom of happy alternation — I refer to the contrast between Goethe and Kant. True enough: the respective contrasts are hardly comparable; and yet, Kant and Goethe seem also to represent two worlds in juxtaposition, each complete in itself. To the reader Jaspers' inclination and capacity of alternately attending to each appears positively immense. Yet, philosophical duty demands a return from so superficial a pleasure — which would indulge itself equally joyfully and persistently in both worlds — to concentration on "the one thing needful." At times one thinks to have struck a central point in Jaspers' philosophy by asserting that one of its essential convictions is the necessity of coming to a decisive choice between Kant and Goethe. If one persists on this path, the highest possible reach for truth reveals itself, indeed, to be connected with such a decision — and it then appears *compulsory* to cast the decisive vote in favor of *Kant*. One has the feeling that this philosophy, which rejects the external form of a system, here congeals into an internal system of its own; that all the wide-open vistas beyond the horizons — together with these horizons themselves on which they depend — actually revolve around a hidden, yet fixed center.

Jaspers' decision in favor of Kant and against Goethe stems

* Translated from the original German by Stanley Hubbard and Paul A. Schilpp

337

from a deep-seated point of experience and reflection: from the experience of Evil and from the inquiry into its nature.

* * * *

"On the basis of long experience and of fundamental conviction I have come to the conclusion that only by testing one's own, supposedly 'ultimate' attitude against his conduct in the face of sharply put and entirely concrete problems, can the individual's real desire become clear to him." This statement of Max Weber might well occur to anyone who believes he has come to a genuine understanding of Jaspers' basic philosophy by letting himself be lured by its conspicuous 'attitude' towards so sharply put a problem as that of 'Evil' to an examination aimed at investigating no more than precisely *this* attitude. But, is 'Evil' (or: 'Radical' Evil), in that case, really such an 'entirely concrete' problem, in the sense of the passage cited from Max Weber's letter?[1] Is it not, rather, highly abstract? Or is the relation perhaps reversed in philosophy, so that what is the most abstract conceivable (Evil) would then be, for it, the most concrete? In Jaspers' view, 'Philosophy' — philosophy-as-such — serves virtually as a definition of man *as* man; and, of it I believe he would say (although only under certain conditions) that in reality and in essence it lives from this inversion: what to the common man is most abstract, for philosophy is the most concrete, i.e., what is originally given to its type of experience.

As over against this, however, Max Weber seems to insist upon the everyday sense of this statement — and he seems to do this, not as an advocate of 'common sense,' but rather by virtue of that philosophical potency which Jaspers has taught us to see in Max Weber's life and work. Weber's statement retains its naïve sting. In circumambulating Evil — Radical Evil — philosophically, Jaspers finds himself obliged, as it were in the name of 'philosophy,' to decide against Goethe, and proclaims this decision to be a philosophically unconditional or necessary one — by no means as an 'objective' philosophical truth, to be sure, but nevertheless as the indispensable condition for the very possibility of primal philosophical truthfulness. This rather looks like an 'ultimate' position. Max Weber's statement diverts our attention from such ultimate positions to the superficies, where differences of concrete behavior expose motivations of choice which, insofar as he is right, are also still effective even in 'supposedly ultimate' positions. It is not philosophy-as-such which, for the sake of some

1 Max Weber, *Political Writings* (Correspondence Appendix), 474.

possible highest and *only* truthfulness, constrains us to decide between Kant and Goethe; rather, a concrete and specific philosophy has made its decision between the two in terms of acts of genuine, i.e., personal choice. Max Weber demanded that such personal choices declare themselves in science (and, for that matter, in philosophy too, I suppose) by way of a discussion of the objective possibilities of those various modes of conduct, from among which the acting subject (in our case, Jaspers) sacrifices the one by choosing the other. According to Max Weber's conviction and claim, such an impartially comparative "discussion of values" would mean, in complete transparency, to assume responsibility, both in behalf of one's self and of others, for the hidden emotions of him who makes the sacrifice, for the hidden struggle inhering in the choice, as well as for the hidden pathos of the evaluations and devaluations effected thereby.

In his philosophical view of Radical Evil we find a definite, deeply rooted aspect of Jaspers' philosophy ending up at a distance from and in tension with Max Weber's philosophy, both in method and in content.

Regarding Method:

In order that, in dealing with the problem of Evil, he may advance straightway to the philosophically ultimate, Jaspers skips the 'discussion of value' between the positions which Kant and Goethe had taken in the matter. Within limits there is indeed an extremely fine weighing of positions, but no fully carried out discussion of values in Max Weber's sense. To the extent that such a discussion takes place, it leads to a view of opposed possibilities of human conduct; to choose between them is an affair of the person philosophizing, no longer one of philosophy as it appears in Jaspers.

Regarding Content:

Max Weber's philosophy was interested in the ethical consequences which religious experience and fantasy have in the behavior of the respective believers in their everyday or extraordinary, inner situations. He traced, so to speak, the *return*-flight of ideas: the landing operations of religious and philosophical speculation on the fields of mundane (everyday-practical) existence. Proceeding with his inquiry in the exact opposite direction, Jaspers seizes on Kant's view Radical Evil. In approximation to the Kierkegaardian hierarchy and order of rank as it rises from the aesthetic by way of the ethical to religious existence, Jaspers

shows that the Kantian ethic — which, he is convinced, under·
stood the essential depth of Evil — possesses infinite religious
significance precisely insofar as its practical value (as a regulatory
instrument of human conduct) is trifling, is, indeed, rendered
available, as it were, only by way of misunderstanding its philosophical import. Here Jaspers' philosophizing deviates not merely
from Max Weber's trend of interest, but deviates, to some degree
at least, also from Kant himself whom he interprets. In the course
of this interpretation, Radical Evil takes on a significance quite
surpassing in extent and import its significance in Kant. On the
strength of Kierkegaard's belief in human *Existenz* from an
absolute origin, Jaspers inflates the already highly demanding
claims of Kant's ethics. Such a central idea, which illustrates this
most clearly, is, for example, determined by the very points
where, in Jaspers' agreement with Kant's concept of Radical Evil
— surpassing that of Kant — one sees the appropriation of Kierkegaard's thought and belief shining through. Here the "integrity
of philosophizing," which Jaspers perceived in Kierkegaard's life
and works, emerges as a controlling factor, which also played its
part in his agreement with and surpassing of Kant. For Max
Weber "integrity" (as 'intellectual honesty') was epitomized
chiefly by the pathos of Nietzschean unmasking analyses (in himself this pathos persevered even less prejudiced, less masked than
in Nietzsche). But, Nietzsche distrusted every kind of belief and
thought which encompasses and contains the concept of Radical
Evil: he *fought* this concept — out of "integrity." And, as it seems
to me, Max Weber, in order to clarify matters of fact in question,
again demands a recognition and investigation of this hidden
struggle between Nietsche's and Kierkegaard's [use of] integrity
(using his technical language, he again demands a "discussion of
values"). For the sake of the unity of ultimate philosophical
truth, Jaspers was inclined to let the differences in content between Kierkegaard's and Nietzsche's modes of belief cancel each
other out; he was of the opinion that the radical integrity *common* to both was the medium in which a deeper "resolution" of
their comparatively non-essential differences could be seen to be
effected. Did this inclination perhaps lead him to overlook the
fact that the radical differences in the attitudes of both to "sharply
put, entirely concrete problems" was so great that they broke
through the form of a "general" integrity (common to both) , —
that they led to an integrity in the one totally different from that
in the other? At this point Jaspers — by his taking the thought and
existence of the two as "exception" — was evidently diverted from

kindling a discussion of values in Max Weber's sense. The probable result of such a discussion would have been the revealing of an irreconcilable, natural and substantial (subjective and objective) conflict between Nietzsche and Kierkegaard, affecting even the essential differences of form.

In Jaspers' eyes, for anyone who thinks and philosophizes as an "exception," the content which could easily be distinguished (and is worthy of being distinguished) and learned is not important, but rather the appealing form, which precisely puts *totally* — and thus, so to speak, without making distinctions — in question what is established in all assumptions which relate to content. To his general concept of the *exception* (as over against "authority" in life and philosophizing) Jaspers has given a specific stamp by attaching it to the lodestar of Kierkegaard's self-interpretation. For Kierkegaard, being exceptional meant *existing* in the eminent sense. However, *existing* in the eminent sense signified to him martyrdom, suffering, the perishing of happiness. Nietzsche, on the other hand, decisively refused to be exceptional in this sense or to "exist eminently" in this sense, just as he also "disenchanted" and "unmasked" suffering, martyrdom and perishing (once again, in sharpest contrast to Kierkegaard). And at this point too we now see Max Weber following Nietzsche in *substance* as well. Indeed, at *all* the intimated points in question: Radical Evil, suffering, exception, integrity, I see Max Weber siding substantially with Nietzsche and, at the same time, — together with Nietzsche — siding with Goethe against Kant and Kierkegaard. If, then, Jaspers 'opts' in favor of Kant's concept of Radical Evil and thus at heart in favor of Kierkegaard, and if — moreover — he expresses and articulates his option everywhere as a carrying out of the choice in Weber's sense, the extent of the sacrifice involved in this option must reveal itself forthwith: by dint of it there is sacrificed not merely a great part of Goethe but also of Nietzsche and, above all, important (and, as I believe, decisive) aspects of the views, thought, and philosophizing of Max Weber.

I.

In his famed and so extremely well nuanced lecture on Goethe (in Frankfurt, 1947), Jaspers spoke, among other things, of Goethe's limitations, as was certainly most appropriate in view of the German habitual penchant for blind idolatry *(Führerverehrung)*. Even though Jaspers himself would never formulate it thus, except conditionally and even then only by using explicit remonstrations — one might simplify it by saying that Goethe's limitations are revealed, for example, in a near angry or even outspokenly angry rejection — in the figure of Newton — of modern natural science as a method of procedure. They are revealed too, perhaps, where there has been talk — for the most part unjust and of a moralizing nature — of Goethe's [so-called] 'fickleness in love.' Revealed, finally, where, in view of the tragedy or of the frightfulness of world history, he either averts it or withdraws behind mollifying interpretations. This last point concerns our theme. Jaspers probes this limitation of Goethe also with greatest caution.

Goethe mastered his horror of world-events not by self-deception but by aloofness. He sees and touches the terrible. But the closer he comes to this unfathomable, the more hesitant his words become. In the end he hides behind silence. But, on his way there, he now and then utters desperate phrases. On the other hand, he rejects it whenever the cleft in existence is, with philosophical decisiveness, openly maintained by a thinker. Thus he indignantly rejects Kant's knowledge of Radical Evil.

A passage from one of Goethe's letters is cited as evidence of the 'indignation' with which Goethe repulsed Kant's (conclusive) "knowledge" in the matter in question: Kant had "slobbered his philosopher's gown" with his doctrine of Radical Evil. But that Goethe did not remain 'aloof' to Kant's alleged 'knowledge,' but, on the contrary, reacted with plain aggressive anger and felt it to be a 'sacrilege' — this fact does not appear in the passage quoted, nor does it appear later in Jaspers' further discussion of their differences.[2]

At the end of his lecture Jaspers sums up:

Although we ourselves are infinitely less than Goethe — it is precisely Goethe's limitations that we have pierced . . . . In breathing his atmosphere, we must not let ourselves be prevented from doing what he himself concealed: looking into the abysses. In Goethe we find, as it were, recovery and encouragement, but not release from the burden placed upon us, nor guidance through the world that is ours and which Goethe did not know.

[2] In the letter cited, Goethe had written to Herder and his wife (from the encampment at Marienborn near Mainz, June 7, 1793): Kant too, "after having employed an entire lifetime in cleaning sundry nasty prejudices from his philosopher's gown, has sacrilegiously slobbered it with the stain of Radical Evil in order that Christians, too, might be enticed into kissing the hem." In Jaspers' address on "Kant's Radical Evil," this passage is *fully* cited, i.e., inclusive of the 'sacrilegiously,' and is even supplemented by reference to Schiller's similar indignation. This appears characteristic of Jasper's sense of justice: in the address on Goethe, Kant, as

What is this incredibly new kind of a world which Goethe did not know but which Kant, on the other hand, in his philosophical insight, is supposed to have anticipated and seen through? What kind of *knowledge* is it which Goethe blindly rebuked and blasphemed? Was it really "knowledge?" Or were these, perhaps, merely Kantian interpretations, comprising his choices within them? But how, then, could Jaspers accept — and impart — them as "conclusive?" Let's see. What was it that caught Goethe's eye when he received the April 1792 issue of the *Berliner Monatsschrift* with Kant's article "On Radical Evil?" Kant begins with statements and then develops his interpretation. He states that Evil manifests itself in man on three levels of his nature:

1. In his predisposition to animality, i.e., in the realms of self-preservation, reproduction, and natural sociality: three areas which man has in common with the beast.

2. In his predisposition to humanity, i.e., on the level of the exercise of his intellect and in the realm of man's ability to think of himself as "I," an ability which elevates him infinitely above all other living beings on earth.

3. In his predisposition to personality, i.e., in the realm of the fact that man can experience himself as free, subject only to the law of his own reason.

1. In the predisposition to animality, in the realm of the instincts of self-preservation, reproduction and gregariousness, Evil appears in the form of the vice of *bestiality:* in the brutality of the struggle for existence, in the ravages of lust, in "negative association," i.e., wild lawlessness towards others. Here Kant scarcely offers interpretation; he simply states the general experience of natural drives in their evil effects, i.e., the manner in which they are generally felt to be so by the doers as well as by

---

the opponent, is given preponderance. In the recital of Kant's views, *his* opponents express themselves, conversely, by the more forceful quotations. Nevertheless, even here the impartiality, at the decisive point, does not prevail. Their words are not taken up, receive no weight in the issue itself, which is subsequently treated without their participation. In Jaspers' opinion, their argument cannot be valid in the matter: they portray Evil — it is summarily maintained — in an "aesthetic grandeur" which as such affords no real access to it but rather "veils" it, since it does not lend itself to direct presentation. — On the theme of poetic "veiling," Thornton Wilder, on the other side of the Atlantic, proposed his counterpoint to Jaspers' German Goethe lecture: he sees Goethe, in contrast to Kierkegaard, Nietzsche, Carlyle, Emerson and Browning, as "proof against anxiety." "Goethe was not afraid. One may almost say that Goethe gained his confidence by having deep insight into the very things which caused consternation in others." (Our translation from Thornton Wilder's "Eine Rede während der Goethetagung in Aspern, Colorado, 1949," in *Perspektiven* #1, Frankfurt, 1952).

those affected. Nowhere did Goethe object to this knowledge. Anyone may check and see that the strange lack of perceptivity in Kant's oddly telling, brief and dry enumerations is, at each of the points mentioned thus far, in full concreteness verified in Goethe's poems, reflections and maxims, not merely incidentally but with the full power of his soul. Thus the horrors of the French Revolution — the savage struggle for existence, the perverted lust, the gregarious frenzy of the abasement and annihilation of fellowmen — affected Goethe more directly and far more violently than they did Kant; because Kant's immediate feelings were sheltered and toned down by his will to believe (his belief in the idea of freedom, which he thought he recognized in the Revolution) , with which we are all familiar. Goethe, not Kant, was capable of suffering much as we suffer from the "cleft" in existence of which Jaspers speaks, at least where naked evil is concerned, a sphere which is indeed decisive for "our" experience and world. If, as Jaspers believes, our world were actually severed as if by a total abyss from that world which had no knowledge of what has "caused us, in terrible anxiety, to lay aside all books, even Aeschylus, Shakespeare and the Bible," then our world would seem to be more radically severed from Kant than from Goethe.[3]

2. Within the predisposition to humanity, Kant ascertained that evil appears in the form of the vice of intellect, whenever man uses his intellect as a means of comparing, with evil zeal, his own 'I' with the 'I' of others. Envy, jealousy and ingratitude crop up. Kant calls them vices of culture. Goethe liked to quote these Kantian statements and concepts, agreed completely with them, and offered detailed illustrations of them. Unlike Kant, who from a certain architectonic love for his classifications tended to stop

---

[3] It is known that Goethe was extremely vulnerable to terror. In such a situation he experienced that not only could he not read books, but also that he no longer could *talk* with *anyone.*

Concerning his experience of the French Revolution, cf. Goethe's "scheme" for the 2nd and 3rd parts of his trilogy, "The Natural Daughter:"

I. ...Absolute despotism, without any actual sovereign. Fear of nothing. Intrigue and violence. Rage for pleasure. Dispersal downwards.

II. Subordinate despotism. Fear of higher ranks. Ganglia governments by proxy.

III. Obscure, dawning situation. Fomentation from below. The lawyer's trick. Aspiring soldiers. Bestiality practiced everywhere.

IV. ...Loosened bonds of the last form.
   The mass becomes absolute.
   Banishes those who falter.
   Quashes those who resist.
   Debases what is high, elevates what is low in order to debase it again.

Cotta Anniversary Ed'n, 12, 366.

short of their boundaries, Goethe remarked that what is penetratingly 'wicked' originates above all when the vice of egocentric comparing fuses with the vices of brutality to produce a total effect sometimes merely bizarre, but sometimes also dreadful in character, Omitting the many bizarre ('malicious') aspects of the matter,[4] I shall cite only one example of the dreadful type. Once, when someone accused him of being a pagan, Goethe replied: "I, pagan? But I permitted Gretchen to be executed and Ottilie to starve to death; isn't that Christian enough for the people?" The cruelty of man as a Christian which Goethe had in mind here is, to be sure, too complex a phenomenon to admit of adequate comprehension in terms of the predispositions to animality and humanity, even when these are considered together. This cruelty is practiced in the name of higher perspectives transcending both animality *and* humanity. With this we reach the point, however, where Kant and Goethe part company; because here no longer mere assertions and 'knowledge,' but interpretations and variously pointed evaluations come into play.

3. In the realm of man's predisposition to *personality*, Kant sees Evil as consisting in man's infidelity to his destination for freedom. The vice of personality is one and only one. It consists in the partial or entire and voluntary surrender of the performance of duty for the sake of duty alone (an act which is free from all natural impulses) in favor of an act performed from natural inclinations and for worldly purposes. This vice has three aspects: frailty, insincerity, and wickedness. Man is incapable of adequately meeting the claim of pure duty in any act, he relapses into his inclinations and natural purposes: frailty. Unintentionally or furtively he mingles natural propensities with his pretended pure motives: insincerity. He offers defiance in the name of his pretended right to guidance by aims promising happiness and frankly orients his actions towards these; he deliberately spurns the duty which bids him make respect for the law of pure reason the sole impetus of his actions: wickedness.

Kant interprets Biblical passages as follows: "Love God above all" — that is, do your duty for the sake of duty alone.

"All that does not stem from this belief" (from the belief in the possibility of pure duty) "is sin."

But inasmuch as, where the fulfillment of duty is concerned, "every man has his price" (as a candid Englishman admitted in Parliament), "for which he sells himself" (to mundane goals, market values, and inclinations), what the Apostle says may be

4 For examples cf. Cotta Anniversary Ed'n, 22, 77.

generally true of man: "There is no difference here, they are all sinners — there is none that doeth good (in the spirit of the law), no, not one." (Cf. Rom. 3, 12)

For Kant *this* is the rotten stain of mankind: this is "Radical Evil." This Kantian interpretation of primal Evil was what aroused Goethe's ire and what he emphatically rejected (not merely in 1794, but throughout his life). On the publication of the *Critique of Practical Reason* and of all writings pertaining to it, Goethe had deemed Kant's foundation of ethics upon universally valid and binding principles to be a salutary procedure as over against the coddling of men by the customary enlightened ethics oriented on narrow or even on shabby *calculations* of happiness. However, the positing and utilization of strict principles ought, in his opinion, to serve only as means — to a loftier choice of the natural and for the disciplining and elevation of the sensory and spiritual impulses, not as a goal for transcending nature as such nor as any elimination of natural propensities and worldly intentions from the range of dutiful motives.

To his annoyance Goethe saw that destructive sacrifice and self-sacrifice — which occasionally may occur and may even be requisite (which then automatically achieves equilibrium again) — was raised by Kant to an *absolute* canon and thereby spoiled.

As if nature were not so arranged that the individual's aims do not conflict with the whole, yes, even serve his preservation; as if anything could happen without (vital and interested) motives, and as if these motives could lie outside the acting being and not, on the contrary, in his innermost self; yes, as if I could promote the welfare of the other person without its reacting on me, by no means to my loss or to my sacrifice, which is not always required and which can occur only in certain cases.[5]

If one inquires into the decisive key points of the agreement, as far as it goes, and of the contrast which presently arises, as they obtain from Goethe to Kant, one will instinctively look for them at the point where Goethe showed himself most shocked: e.g., in his tragedy, "The Natural Daughter." And, indeed, here we find everything we need. There are *two* pivotal points: The first, of a severity comparable to Kant's:

> " 'tis base to live beneath the yoke of lust,
> The noble man aspires to higher laws."[6]

[5] In a letter to Riemer, February 3, 1807.

[6] "Nach seinem Sinne leben ist gemein,
Der Edle strebt nach Sitte und Gesetz."

But the second [furnishes] a diametrically opposed justification and interpretation thereof:

"Life's pledge is life, reposing solely on
Itself, its own last guarantor and instance."[7]

Kant's ethics and his interpretation of Radical Evil were incompatible with Goethe's fundamental views. The Kantian acknowledgement of duty within the framework of an unworldly autonomy of the merely inner person (reduced to pure reason), seemed to Goethe a specific instance of the misconstrued, "Know Thyself." In the radical turn of the Kantian ethics toward pure inwardness and transcendence, Goethe detected a piece of inverted priestliness, "confusing man with unattainable demands and diverting him inwards." Goethe declares: "Man knows himself only in knowing the world, of which he becomes aware only in himself and of himself only in it." In the domain of ethics Kant averred exactly the opposite: in order to know his duty one need know nothing of the world. *"Quod petis in te est ne tu quaesiveris extra."*[8] Or the Lutheran saying: "Watch o'er thy heart with all diligence, for from it stems life." From experience and on principle Goethe distrusted all protestations [upholding] the blessings of a onesidedly cultivated inwardness.

Kant and Goethe are so diametrically opposed at this point that, where Goethe finds the origin of profound confusion in the principle of *absolute* duty, i.e., one directed against nature, Kant finds the source of *all* possible human freedom and purity. Goethe felt that "confusion" to be directed against all rules of his own life. (In Goethe's opinion,) no sooner had Kant peremptorily denatured duty than he proceeded to his concept of Evil which, if he were right, would condemn all channels by which Goethe fashioned and confined freedom and personality to be examples of "insincerity," if not flatly illustrations of "intrinsic wickedness," in short, of the "rotten stain of humanity."

It appears certain that Goethe detected the shocking result which this publication of Kant's old age had for his own life and work. His indignation, therefore, ranged from his current existence down to the most obscure memories — for, despite his alert, open and grim eye for the dimensions of potential cruelty in the power-structure and world-set-up of the Christian tradition, there was hidden in him a vulnerable Christian faith all his own. Simple attitudes in him were on terms too faithfully friendly with the

---

[7] "Das Leben ist des Lebens Pfand, es ruht
Nur auf sich selbst und muss sich selbst verbürgen."

[8] Inscription under his silhouette in Kant's own handwriting.

truth of Christianity — with the Gospel — to react otherwise than in anger against the Kantian identification of that truth with an ethics which declared its (supernatural) autonomy *vis-à-vis* God's love and mercy on earth.[9]

* * * * *

In his *second* Goethe-speech, in the movingly beautiful 1949 address, delivered in Basel's Minster, on "Goethe's Humaneness," Jaspers closely portrays Goethe's "Philosophy of Evil." Almost everything we have, in the foregoing, thrown into sharp relief, he himself there touches upon lightly or distinctly. Other, equally important, data he adds. He points up Goethe's severe judgment on Faust: Faust's course of conduct was (even for Goethe) to the very end restlessly ruinous. "Unconditioned activity, of whatever kind it may be, finally leads to bankruptcy." Despite this, Goethe is finally placed in that line of thinkers — Plotinus, Nicolaus of Cues, Spinoza and Hegel — "for whom Evil amounted to Naught." In Goethe and in all these men "Evil loses its acuteness;" "it possesses no independent power." In support of this Jaspers cites Goethe's utterances: "The world is an organ whose bellows are being tread by the devil." "The demonic is to be considered as the instrument of a higher government of the world." But, does the spacious portrayal of Goethe in this address really make it credible

[9] Unfortunately, there is no space here for details. Under what specific circumstances had Goethe been so startled by Kant against Kant? It was between 1788 and 1794, a particularly critical period of his artistic career and human development. The turmoil passed; the antagonism against Kant lost much of its emphasis and fighting edge. But the principles arrived at during that period quietly remained with him even when "Kantianism" now entered his life most intimately in the form of his friendship with Schiller.

At least this much of Goethe's Christian indignation against Kant must be noted here:

One may, in this matter, entertain some doubt about Goethe's "Christianity." One might ask what Goethe could, in seriousness, have meant when he said that, although he was a "decided non-Christian" in matters of scientific research, philosophy and curiosity about the world, he was nonetheless "perhaps the only true Christian in the way Christ meant it." (*Conversations*, IV, 261.) From the many possible examples [one might choose] in answer to this question, we select one which may well serve to conclude the present discussion of this dispute, all the more since it simultaneously abandons it. In 1816, in retrospect on the two preceding years, Goethe wrote to Zelter: "I shall not deny that I realize that, during those few summers along the Rhein and the Main, I labored well; for, after all, I merely preached John's Gospel: 'Children, love one another, and if that won't do, at least tolerate one another.'" *This* piece of Christian freedom designates an area where Goethe and Kant soon approach each other again. Kant's second Categorical Imperative (respect for the other person), Goethe admiringly, always and unqualifiedly held in high esteem.

that for him Evil "amounts to naught" — say, in the statements just cited, or even more so in this one: "Pure humaneness atones for all our human frailties"?

For Jaspers, too, the "thrust into Evil is the goad to the flight" into pure Being — hence Evil is not an ultimate but a turning point. The divergence of views appears by no means to lie in a greater or lesser degree of realism or measure of spiritual courage towards Evil, but in the *goal* to which the horror of Evil drives us, and in the *means* of flight away from it. Only at *this* point choice confronts choice. So heartfelt and passionate was Goethe's faith in and sensitivity to man's unbroken relationship to God and to all God's creatures, that, in the "unconditional" imputation of "pure" attitudes (meaning, for him, in the Kantian context: "extra-natural"), he could only see a gratuitous and useless over-exertion on the part of man — in wanton offense to his human nature, indeed, in arrogant presumption above God's will. Instinctively Goethe tendered the Kantian moral law a high degree of respect insofar as it remains comprehensible and applicable as a beneficently stern "regulative principle in empirical use." But, in raising it to the rank of a "constitutive principle" of the "one true Good" in the world and of an exclusive human dignity, he felt, not the splendor of freedom radically thought through, but the sacrilege of detached philosophical reasoning which soars ruinously beyond "what is godly and what is human, as these are revealed in the truth of religion and of poetry."

As Kant had done, Jaspers places man's "purity" in the absolute and unconditioned. By so doing he chose differently from Goethe and has, accordingly, made many different evaluations. Jaspers takes this option not as a *choice* liable to be called to account, but rather as the mandatory assumption of the one and only possible freedom. In Goethe's parry against Kant, Jaspers sees an "aesthetic escape" rather than a peer's opposition. Nowhere does he see or show the real acuteness of Goethe's counter-position. He fails to see (or does not take seriously) that Goethe rebelled with "fiendish malice" (in the precise Kantian sense) against Pure Reason and against its kind of freedom as *principles:* —against them *as such.* In the strict sense of the Augustinian and Kantian "perversion," —which we shall presently discuss—, Goethe "reversed" the Categorical Imperative into a principle from which the "gravity of the Either-Or" is deliberately excluded, because it is a misguided and misguiding gravity. God's designs can be fulfilled only "if we, in being obliged on the one hand to realize ourselves, do not fail on the other hand to cast loose from ourselves in regular pulsations."[10] "Radical Evil," the reversal of the subsumptive relationship of nature to reason, is here commended as a "turning and re-turning" which is "good," basically and because of God.

II

Jaspers' philosophical determination to use the experience of absolute Evil not so much as an ethical-practical stimulus as for the flight into pure Transcendence and for therein gaining one's selfhood (as a person), is brought to insurpassably sharp expression in his 1935 lecture, "On the Radical Evil in Kant."

What does "radical" mean? Evil is radical is supposed to mean that it is absurd and impossible to attempt to disclose a causal genealogy of Evil by psychological or sociological, historical or biological-phylogenetic research; rather, we must investigate its "origin." And, "origin" is a transcendental-philosophical category. True, as Jaspers uses the term, it has many meanings (compare, for example, *Reason and Existenz*, 27ff), designates, however, above all, in Jaspers as in Kant, the presupposition of a phenomenon that must be thought if it is to be possible in its fully experienced sense. Impelled by this method, Jaspers flatly declares: "for psychological experience there is no such thing as Evil." That Evil is "radical" means: it has its origin in the psychologically unanalyzable ideas of freedom and reason.

Man has two incentives: because of his origin in reason — which Kant calls intelligible — he obeys the law; because of his origin in time, as a psychologically knowable natural being, he obeys his inclinations and passions, desires his happiness (or what he takes to be such) in the world.

The incentive by way of the moral law, which irresistibly forces itself upon his predisposition to reason (his intelligible nature), would govern him, if no other incentive would counteract it; he would be morally good without a struggle. The incentive by way of his inclinations is his natural disposition (his empirical nature); this he would obey without a struggle and, like the animals, would not be evil, if the other incentive were not at work in him.[11]

10 Cotta, *op. cit.*, 23, 167.

11 It is not clear whether Jaspers is merely reporting this statement, or whether he also considers it correct. In any case, there is no criticism whatsoever of it. But this statement is based on a simply erroneous assumption, namely, that the configuration of impulses (allegedly) devoid of conflict and struggle, in a merely animal volition is, in human beings analogously considered, correlative to the "infallibility" of animal instincts. On the fiction of an "infallible instinct of animals" Kant erected his renowned argument: for the regulation of his activity man does not require rea-

Inasmuch as man admits both incentives (the one by way of the moral law, and the other in his craving for happiness) into the formation of his will, and since, furthermore, he would find each, taken by itself, sufficient for its formation, he would simultaneously be both good and evil, — the one by virtue of the one incentive, and the other by virtue of the other , if the state of being good or evil lay in the incentives as such. Such a contradictory simultaneity is, however, impossible. Man is confronted by the question of being good or evil. Simultaneity would extinguish both. The gravity would have disappeared: the Either — Or. Good and evil, therefore, does not lie in the difference of the incentives, but in the manner of their subordination to one another.

That will is good which makes obedience to the law the condition for the fulfillment of the craving for happiness. But the will turns evil, when it makes the satisfaction of his craving for happiness "the condition for obedience to the law."

To choose the one or the other order (of subordination) is a voluntary act within the province of reason. Evil is the freely chosen inversion of the right order and subordination; it is the will to be good (to follow the law of reason) only on condition of being happy. This inversion is the primal act of evil, i.e., an act which has its origin in the nature of human freedom.

Radical Evil lies indeed in a depth of my Reason which first spawns all specific sorts of Evil, but itself cannot once and for all be known with objective certainty. The decisively basic characteristic of Radical Evil is that I cannot envision it as an object before my eyes.

In support of this Jaspers cites the following sentence of Kant's: We can no more account for the fact that "Evil corrupted in us

---

son; a dozen animal instincts would serve the purpose better. Nietzsche's insights already *rectified* these and other equally erroneous Kantian presuppositions; more recently even: William James, John Dewey, Max Weber; on the biological side today above all Konrad Lorenz and N. Tinbergen (author of *Social Behavior in Animals; Die Instinktlehre);* also Gehlen on speech and human drive-structures in *Der Mensch;* further, "Der Gegenwärtige Stand der anthropologischen Forschung," *Merkur,* 1951/54. — Just as I do not understand the statement, "for psychological experience there is no such thing as Evil," so I cannot believe that it is possible thus neatly and absolutely to divorce causal research from inquiry into origins that the one may remain indifferent to whatever the other has learned in the meantime, and *vice versa.* Nowhere and at no time has Jaspers ever declared this to be admissible. Rather, he teaches again and again that, where "correct and false" are concerned, philosophy may never act as if it were independent of science. If this is so, do Kant and modern adaptations of Kant enjoy immunity at this point? For, in the immediately following passage of the above text, the fiction we have mentioned continues to operate undiminished, while at the same time all that follows rests precisely on this section of key importance.

precisely the supreme principle, although this deed is our very own, that we can [account] for any basic characteristic belonging to our nature."

* * * *

Jaspers compares the voluntary corruption of the supreme principle, the reversal of inversion of the proper order of nature and reason as Kant sees it, with the *perversio* as St. Augustine, the Christian, sees it: there love of God *(frui Deo)* constitutes man's nobility of faith and being. In that case the inversion consists of making God the means and the world the end. "All human perversion, also called vice, consists in wanting to use what is there for enjoyment and wanting to enjoy what is meant for use."[12]

Liberation from Evil, then, is return or re-inversion. The will to this [return], which does not imply a reform in detailed specifics but rather, in the Kantian sense, a "revolution of the heart" and "immutable decision," allows man to penetrate to bedrock, beyond which nothing more exists for him, by which he can become his true self. The rigor, the seriousness with which we then realize our existence and find our happiness — on condition, namely, that we at all times obey the law of lawfulness of our behavior, out of respect for the law for its own sake — is identical with the rise of this tireless reversal, which as effort is always at once questionable, imperilled or fragile, in which we experience ourselves as our selves.

There is a difference, however, between Christian conversion and the Kantian revolution of the heart from the ground of Evil back to Reason. The Christian is dependent on grace and on God's help. As one who is redeemed he may rejoice in and be sure of God, but not really in (and of) himself. For Kant, a person cannot have done good without having wanted it *purely* (for the sake of its sheer lawfulness) and thus deliberately. In the Christian view, however, knowing one's own purity would precisely be corruption: *superbia*. "No good deed remains intact if I love myself in it." For Kant, on the other hand, an analogue to the divine joy in purity is possible. There can never be certainty that one's own will was or is pure. Yet there can be the joy over an increasing independence from inclinations and requirements. There remains a genuine similarity to the Christian position, after all: that "immutable decision" can be maintained only if there is no fixation on an over-all knowledge.

---

12 Omnis itaque humana perversio est, quod etiam vitium vocatur, fruendis uti velle, atque utendis frui.

At this juncture there appears a discrepancy between Kant's opinion and Jaspers' exposition. The fact that nescience holds sway at the beginning of our reversion is for Jaspers the source of the steady movement of our possible rising or falling. As evidence Jaspers cites the statement: "The depth of the heart (the subjective primary basis of his "maxims") is always impenetrable to man's scrutiny." But, for Kant this statement does not have the Jaspersian import of a foundering [faculty of] reason. In no case does the statement mean that the law to which man rises is imperceptible to him. It only means that, in judging any particular action of his, man is always uncertain as to whether respect for the pure law was actually the primary basis of his "maxims" (i.e., of his objectively statable motives for acting) , or whether there was not, after all, possibly some hidden inclination or substantial interest, etc., also mixed in with pure respect for the law. What reason demands is not enigmatic for Kant; enigmatic (in the simple sense of "uncertain") is merely what man really desires or has desired at any given time — not, however, what he ought to desire. The Ought is completely translucent in the application of the reasoning power of the Categorical Imperative: Can you wish —what you wish — purely?, that is, in such a way that it can be objectified into an universal law without contradicting or abrogating itself? Whatever you can thus wish, you *ought* to wish; that you may, unequivocally, regard as your duty. But: who has ever been capable of purifying his true maxims (motivations) to such a strict, transparent degree of the nature of law? The *heart* of man is too deep, not his reason too enigmatic or too opaque.

Jaspers is of the opinion that the directive force of Kant's teachings concerning human behavior is disappointing to anyone who, here and now, expects *practical* guidance in his everyday conduct. Jaspers does not care to see purification from Evil in the direction of practical unequivocalness (towards which Kant's intention definitely seems to point) ; but rather in its significance for "inner conduct:" in the transformation of non-knowledge into a soaring flight in the encompassing of a riddle. The inadequacy of Reason, as revealed in Radical Evil, invites him to entrust himself exclusively to that Reason, in order that, at its limits, he may become aware of the Encompassing.

This is already an important discrepancy. Kant sees Reason foundering on the resistance of the heart's depth; Jaspers has the heart foundering on the incomprehensibility of Reason and, at the same time, Reason foundering on itself. It matters very much to Jaspers that the instances which drive towards the leap into the absolutely unknowable of Transcendence shall be enhanced. This, finally, reveals itself in that still sharper differentiation from Kant which arises from the gradation of steps by which Jaspers lets the Encompassing arise out of Kant's doctrines concerning Radical Evil.

In this connection Jaspers sees the Encompassing emerging in three dimensions:

1) His world and its content always reveal themselves to man as phenomenal only (as what is able to appear to his finite constitution). Thus the thought is offered (though expressly mentioned by neither Kant nor Jaspers) : that the insoluble discrepancy, inhering in the contention that man can desire either his happiness *or* the good, is no ultimate reality, but only appearance; that the above described reversion, his Radical Evil, — where man adheres to his desire for the good only on condition of his personal happiness —, is only an evil phenomenon, not any evil reality subsisting of and for itself.

2) An Encompassing is disclosed as the idea of the highest good: the postulate of God, who, in the future, will lead man's pure will — which here can and dare produce only an inconsequential *worthiness* to happiness but no claim on *actual* happiness — to the realization of happiness after all, and thus, finally and justly, will grant to man what must (and should) seem evil to him here below if he himself desires it. In Kant this marks the necessary transition from philosophy to religion. But, whereas in Kant this idea of the highest good and the postulate of God stands as the last — wondrously reconciling — word on the problem of Radical Evil, Jaspers assigns it an only subordinate and dispensable significance. Instead, what is for Kant the human penultimate Jaspers elevates to the ultimate and highest.

3) The Encompassing shows itself in the actual thrust at the irrepealable Radical Evil itself. For Jaspers this constitutes Kant's proximity to Christianity: "to the incurable rupture with the world." It is this rupture and cleft which, encompassingly, affects us as an absolute enigma. By contrast Kant's God-postulate is only more like a "reservation" — a tempering of the necessary thrust into an absolute enigma. It would seem that the greater severity would have to be turned against this reservation in Kant himself, a severity which Jaspers expresses as follows: Wherever in clearest conduct there still is any kind of reservation (any desire for happiness, any anxiety concerning existence, any striving for worth or power-interest), there "what is decidedly moral

becomes, by this surreptitious inversion, sophistical and radically evil."[13]

This thrust into Radical Evil is, for Jaspers, the genuine 'Kantian goad,' rousing in me the innermost motive by which I will and which yet I can not will: to want, that is, *not something*, but to be myself.

In Jaspers' eyes the Kantian formalism of the Categorical Imperative is either degraded to a mere regulatory function, or else it is understood *only* and exclusively as the illumination of this enigmatic origin; only in this case can it be 'constitutive' for the reversion to the good: "Everything good, all love springs from the counter-movement which the goad of Radical Evil releases — this scarcely surpassable demand on man's inwardness."

In the portrayal of this third Encompassing one seems almost at once to sense Kierkegaard's influence:

1. It is as if Kierkegaard finally impelled Jaspers to proceed more like Kant than Kant himself, unless we are mistaken in taking the sentence concerning "the reservation of any sort of desire for happiness" to be directed against Kant. But, how otherwise should one understand it? Insofar as the Kantian God-postulate does in fact permit "still one last" regard for the idea of happiness, the consequences for Jaspers — provided he takes Kierkegaard's Either-Or seriously — must be the subsumption of this consideration under the concepts of "sophistry" and "Radical Evil."[14]

[13] This sentence would, indeed, seem to have to count against Kant.

[14] That Jaspers must assume this attitude towards Kant's God-postulate lies (as our text will presently demonstrate) in his final and central (religious) position. Superficially considered, one might find this attitude to be quite in accord with the stream of German philosophy since Fichte, in which it has been customary to act condescendingly towards enlighteners and free-thinkers. Thomas Jefferson, that apostle of the Enlightenment, promised the world in 1776 that Americans intended, in the future Constitutional regulation of their community life, to proceed from the assumption that, — as regards a three-fold craving — all men are equal: (1) they want to *live*; (2) as individuals they want to assure to their life ample scope for *freedom*; (3) and they want to live life in such a way that, individually and collectively, they may deem it a *happy* one. Germans (by contrast) seem always to have striven to be an *exception* to the third instance of this "equality of all men." In the manifold directions this attempt has taken, there have not merely resulted forms of self-deception; but there was achieved so much loyalty to work, dutiful obedience, uprightness and calm inwardness of attitude that even Nietzsche finally — conscious of this mastery — uttered that aggressively vehement word which declared the exception to be the rule and the rule the exception: "Man does not desire happiness; only the Englishman does that." To this John Dewey gave the answer which Nietzsche himself could very well have given to some third party (meaning Nietzscheans) who might have tried to pin him down to the one-sided and incidental *caprice* of that remark: "When Nietzsche says: 'Man does not desire happiness; only the Englishman does that,' we smile at the fair thrust. But persons who profess no regard for

2. Kant had often and expressly given voice to his pleasure over the fact that the principle of the Categorical Imperative discovered by him could, by virtue of the purity of its formal quality as a law, act constitutively for [producing] a good will, and was at the same time capable of *proving* this constitutive power in concrete behavior — by dint of its fitness as a regulative and orienting instrument.[15] Jaspers, on the other hand, holds that the Kantian attempt, as concerns precisely this practical-moral aspect,

---

happiness as a test of conduct have an unfortunate way of living up to their principle by making others unhappy. I should entertain some suspicion of the complete sincerity of those who profess disregard for their own happiness, but I should be quite certain of their sincerity when it comes to a question of *my* happiness." *(German Philosophy and Politics, 1915)* By the same token one might take Jaspers' deprecatory classification of Kant's postulates of happiness and of God as part and parcel of this German tradition. But, however motivated, Jaspers' above noted reading of the Kantian text, though apparently altering it only slightly, had a two-fold effect: 1) the traditional German prejudice had, in any case, no longer any reason to speak of Kant's compliance with the commonness of the craving for happiness; 2) but — more significantly — that there is no longer any transition from philosophy to religion. Philosophy now has the last word. — But, was it really 'compliance' in Kant on which Jaspers has improved? Or was it not rather humble and generous philosophical candor? Humility in confronting that "innate equality of all men" — and candor with reference to the cardinal thesis and deepest basis of his own philosophy. He had pronounced his word in this matter to be a penultimate one only. He carried out the "necessary transition to religion" by means of the God-postulate, who guaranteed, after all, the very happiness he, Kant, had chided. The evil Kant had imputed to the human aspiration to happiness (whenever it gives itself priority or delegates to itself the rôle of judge and commander) God lifts again from his creatures insofar as (according to Kant) God in the end transforms what unfortunately must be 'evil' in them into the good of his grace and mercy towards them. — In Jaspers' interpretation this Kantian inversion loses its force as a result of the above mentioned arrangement of the stages of the Encompassing which Jaspers introduced into his presentation: here the last, decisive stage is what Kant took to be only a provisional one, to be compensated for by religion. Thus deprived of its philosophical force, the happiness- and God-postulate as Jaspers takes it, can scarcely function any longer as the stimulus for effecting an *immanent* rectification and critique which the Kantian *God* exercised on the Kantian concept of happiness — i.e., an express and direct criticism of Kant himself —, directed above all against the inadequacy of Kant's discussion of the foundering conceits of the aspiration to happiness. In fact, Jaspers now appropriates these discussions for his own use — even exaggerating them against Kant. Instead of explaining that the modes of foundering of *any* concept or phenomenon (here that of 'happiness') can furnish no serious argument against the properly understood truth of the same (proper: that is, within its natural limits), he welcomes them all alike as justification for the *'salto mortale'* from the "nothingness of happiness" into the "purity of the law."

[15] Cf., for example, this footnote in Kant's Preface to his *Critique of Practical Reason:* "A reviewer who wanted to find some fault with this work has hit the truth better, perhaps, than he thought, when he says that no new principle of morality is set forth in it, but only a *new formula. . . .* But whoever knows of what importance to a mathematician a *formula* is, which defines accurately what is to be done to work a problem, will not think that a formula is insignificant and useless which does the same for all duty in general." (p. 93 of 6th 1923 ed'n of Abbott's translation of Second *Critique).*

is emphatically doomed to foundering. Yet, in this foundering Jaspers sees the purity of the Kantian law actually enhanced and transformed into the purity of pure *spirit*. Accordingly, the ethical disjunction happiness : duty becomes the religious disjunction 'natural life' : 'existing in the spirit.' Thus Jaspers anticipates Kierkegaard in Kant. Not, in the first instance, the Kierkegaardian Either-Or, but rather the Kantian disjunction reveals already the rupture between the spirit and the world to be incurable. Kierkegaard's definition applies already to Kant (as Jaspers understands Kant) : "What is spirit? (and Christ is indeed spirit, his religion that of the spirit). Spirit is: to live as thought dead (in the process of passing away) ."[16]

3. By "happiness" Kant in the last analysis always meant only the sum of all inclinations insofar as they may be thought of as reaching their goal, but which, in their character as natural inclinations, must, taken all together, also be thought of as "barriers to morality" (to "duty") .[17] Analogously, but altered and radicalized, Kierkegaard linked "happiness" (and "unhappiness") with the merely "aesthetic" attitude to life and pitted against this kind of "happiness" the *"existential* pathos" of the religious life: suffering.[18] Suffering means to die to all happiness and at the same time to love for the love of God. This, evidently, is the pathos of that almost incomparable and practically unheard-of final sentence in Jaspers, which we quoted from his paper on "The Radical Evil in Kant": that " . . . all love springs from the counteraction which the goad of Radical Evil releases." True enough, for man's "good will" (as the only unqualified good in the world) Kant had as-

---

[16] Kierkegaard's *Journals,* Haecker ed'n, II, 405.

Despite the submersion of the Kantian ethics in this depth of transcendence, Jaspers nevertheless (or now more than ever serving as a reminder from somewhere) kept some recollection of the worldly (practice-regulatory) intent of the Kantian Imperative: the possibility of orienting everybody's conduct on a law capable of being valid for everyone. As concerns this unforgettable point, however, Kierkegaard's life of the spirit does not seem adaptable to the Kantian intention. It appears to the reader, therefore, that Jaspers accepted and fully articulated the passionate self-interpretation, which Kierkegaard himself gave of his spiritual *Existenz*, also in order to fit it into the unity of the Kantian world of ideas: Jaspers did this by placing Kierkegaard's doing and thinking as "exception" side by side with Kant's universal law. For, to be an "exception" in Kierkegaard's sense does not, after all, imply mere wilfulness, it is not an empty, merely obstinate rebellion against universal standards; but it is, rather, a suffering from these, it is correction, illumination, and finally (indirect) confirmation of the universal. Only law and exception *together* constitute the "truth" of the law. Only Kant and Kierkegaard *together* (one could almost say) constitute for Jaspers the *whole* truth of the Kantian philosophy.

[17] Cf., for example, *Critique of Pure Reason,* A 808f.

[18] Cf., for example, his *Concluding Unscientific Postscript,* II, 112ff.

sumed a pure "origin in freedom;" but never and nowhere did he think of vindicating "all of man's *love*" in such an origin in freedom. It remained for Kierkegaard to do this. A few days before his death, Kierkegaard, talking with his friend Boesen, uttered a sentence, euphorically exalted to be sure, yet showing, nonetheless, in the image he used that Kierkegaard, too, throughout his entire conscious life conceived of love as originating not in nature, but in something opposed to nature: as a *"counteraction to the whole of Evil."* The aim of his *Existenz* as an exception, he said, was to be as if "put away," but then finally to sing the "Hallelujah" engendered in suffering; "everything else is evil. I don't mean that what I said (against 'Christians' or Christendom, against bishop and brother) was evil; but I said it in order to clear Evil away, and then to attain to the Hallelujah."[19]

III

The "integrity of philosophy" against "philosophy as system" and against philosophy as "reasonable reconciliation" (as a substitute for the Christian-theological story of redemption) was the general war-cry of Feuerbach, Bauer and the left-wing Hegelians against Hegel and against the Hegelians of the right. Kierkegaard as well as Nietzsche wanted to radicalize this integrity to the last degree. However, in both this spiritual exertion and task ran, as it were, on tracks which certain childhood impressions seemed to have etched upon their respective modes of thinking. As children both had the profound experience of a Christian atmosphere — but in radically different ways. To the child Kierkegaard his father, who was a guilt-conscious sinner and "penitent," said: "You *must* be Christian, i.e., 'believe.' (You dare not curse God as I once did as a child.) " The child Nietzsche was taught in unbroken and simple Christian faith: "In life's difficulties you cannot rely on people, but only on God."

This is why Kierkegaard, later on, put the question of integrity thus: How can I be a Christian in a *conscientious* way? (For, a *Christian* he *ought* and *had to* be.)

Nietzsche, on the other hand, later on put the question: Is the belief that God is trustworthy a *sincere* belief?

Kierkegaard with *his* question, in the last analysis, prohibited any expression of scepticism in religion. He assigned to scepticism an *existentially* subordinate place. He demanded obedience and

[19] Quoted by Chr. Schrempf, *Sören Kierkegaard*, II, 327.

subjugation to the "paradox" of (an historically and dogmatically fixed) faith. The degree of integrity he perceived in the degree of rigor of both the prohibition and the command.[20]

In exactly the opposite way, Nietzsche, out of integrity, set his scepticism — especially the scepticism with reference to historically transmitted theology and dogma, but also with reference to God himself — no bounds at all, except the limit of the native, naïve, and still uninitiated pious souls. Here he asked: is scepticism as a mode of behavior finally beneficial to life — i.e., is it *trustworthy?*

These two kinds of integrity in questioning and of the [overall] attitudes they entail lead — among other things — to two totally different kinds of *readiness to suffer.*[21]

For Kierkegaard, suffering as subjection was connected with the idea of *absolute obedience* — it was, thus, goal and end in itself.

For Nietzsche, suffering was worthy of affirmation only insofar as it enhanced life, insofar as it was beneficial to the *whole* of life (encompassing both vitality and spirituality) .[22]

[20] Kierkegaard writes: "Savonarola says somewhere that the genuine convert does not care what people say of him, but takes courage and says: thus I desire that one should live in my house. — This reminds me of the words with which my father used to cut off other people's objections to his way of living: 'such is the custom in my house'." (*Journals*, II, 250.)

(Nietzsche, out of regard for hierarchy and for the power to command — and, on the other hand, also for discipline and obedience —, would have approved of these sentences as being 'sincere.' But the ones we have already quoted must be taken together with the following, which are, for Kierkegaard, the really essential ones:)

"They would have us believe that objections to Christianity arise from doubt. This is entirely mistaken. Objections to Christianity arise from insubordination, from aversion to obedience, from rebellion against any authority. This is why thus far they have been fighting windmills with objections, because they have fought doubt intellectually, whereas rebellion must be fought ethically." (*Book of the Judge*, 128.)

Summarizing: Man should in absolute obedience — meaning: in unconditional and absolutely valid *suffering* — proceed to "perish" (viz., die) to his scepticism as well as to his reason: at least insofar as he wants to be a sincere Christian. (Such a will Nietzsche rejected as being both humanly and philosophically dishonest [insincere].)

[21] It is probable that this statement could just as well be reversed, perhaps even *must* be reversed: innate or early "impregnated" differences in the fighting instinct, in the instinct to flee or to attack with reference to suffering, resulted, on the part of the two, in their working over their childhood impressions into the above named, diametrically opposed forms of intellectual interrogation.

[22] Nietzsche oriented his attitude towards suffering and consciously disciplined it on the model of *Emerson*. For almost all of Nietzsche's vital existential attitudes, his 'magnificent' Emerson was, in every decisive epoch of his life, his companion, and encouraging and guiding 'friend' and lode-star — so also in the way he mastered and interpreted grief and suffering. In Emerson's essay, "Compensation," Nietzsche ran across the following passage (in the poor Fabricius translation which he read):

Statements by Kierkegaard and by Nietzsche, supporting now one and now the other thesis, are to be found everywhere in their thought and output. Here I shall offer only a tiny selection (chosen without intentional bias) :

1. Kierkegaard writes: "Between man and the truth lies dying."[23] *Not* to suffer, not to want to perish, is for Kierkegaard the all-embracing — i.e., absolute and final — negative token. It says that:

a) a person is "evil" (see p. .... above) , and

b) inextricably, therefore, he is "untrue."[24]

Evil is *essentially* — or "originally" — evil as a cleaving to existence, so far as existence partly hems in and partly dissipates the

---

"The indignation which arms itself with secret forces does not awaken until we are pricked and stung and sorely assailed. . . . When (a great man) is pushed, tormented, defeated, he has a chance to learn something; he has been put on his wits, on his manhood; he has gained facts; learns his ignorance; is cured of the insanity of conceit; has got moderation and real skill. The wise man throws himself on the side of his assailants. It is more his interest than it is theirs to find his weak point. The wound cicatrizes and falls off from him like a dead skin, and when they would triumph, lo! he has passed on invulnerable. . . . Every lash inflicted is a tongue of fame; every prison, a more illustrious abode; every burned book or house enlightens the world; every surpressed or expunged word reverberates through the earth from side to side. . . . In general, every evil to which we do not succumb is a benefactor." (Modern Library ed'n of *The Complete Works . . . of R. W. Emerson*, 184f.)

This — and other — passages Nietzsche condensed for his own (following) reflection, penned on the fly-leaf of his copy of the *Essays:*

"The capacity for pain is an excellent preserver, a sort of insurance on life; and this is what has *preserved pain:* it is just as useful as pleasure — to put it mildly. I laugh at those enumerations of pain and misery by which pessimism would prove itself — Hamlet and Schopenhauer and Voltaire and Leopardi and Byron. Life — all of you say — is something that ought not to be if this is the only way it can maintain itself. I laugh at this 'ought' and take a position to life in order to help, in order that from pain life may emerge as mature as possible; — security, caution, patience, wisdom, variety — all its bright and sombre colors, bitter and sweet — in everything we are suffering's debtor, and a whole canon of beauty . . . is possible only in a world of deep and changing and various sorrows. What prompts you to pass judgment on life can not be justice — for justice would know that pain and evil are our friends. We must multiply pain in the world if we wish to increase art and wisdom." (Only this last, outrageous imperative is to be charged against Nietzsche; in Emerson there is no thought of such a thing.)

It would seem possible to assert the thesis that the depth and tension effective in the difference between the thought and *Existenz* of Nietzsche and the thought and *Existenz* of Kierkegaard could be measured by the resp. content of Emerson's philosophy: "Nietzsche a absorbé la pensée (d'Emerson) jusqu'à ne plus toujours la distinguer de la sienne" (Charles Andler, *Nietzsche, sa vie et sa pensée*, Vol. I, les precurseurs, 340.) Kierkegaard, on the other hand, could never have followed Emerson, even at a great distance: of necessity he would have denounced Emerson's literary work as the ruinous doings of a 'free-thinker' and child of the world lost to Christianity.

23 *Journals*, II, 197.

24 Throughout the section on *Evil* of his work, *Von der Wahrheit*, Jaspers makes an assumption which at first astounds the reader: Evil is viewed as a source and

breadth or the unity of truth. Kierkegaard writes: "The difference between whether the unconditional concord is in me or not, I recognize at once in this," whether I "have let go of the here and the there, of the particular" or not.[25] To carry this thought radically, inexorably and uncompromisingly to its consequences seems to have been the condition on which the integrity of Kierkegaard's life and thought depended.

The integrity of the Nietzschean radicalism, on the other hand, lay — utterly disregarding idealistic convictions (which he unmasked as "habits of thought" and "prejudices") — in raising the attachment to life (in the sense of life's *intensification* through its own nature and strength) to the status of "duty;" duty born of innate honor and the honesty of those who "turned out well" (well-bred). Thus Nietzsche writes: "It is probable that in . . . well-bred people the most sensuous functions are ultimately transfigured by a symbolical intoxication of the highest spirituality; they sense in themselves a kind of deification of the body and are farthest removed from the ascetic philosophy of the saying, 'God is Spirit.' It thus becomes clear that it is the ascetic who is the 'ill-bred man,' who calls a some*thing* in himself — and precisely the judging and condemning some*thing* — *good* and calls it 'God'."[26]

Inasmuch, however, as Nietzsche too probably knew that life and body die, how did his integrity measure up to a specific (surviving) honor of the spirit? As if to the Kierkegaard in himself — to the radical honesty and honor of suffering, understood perhaps as the voluntary and sovereign anticipation of death — he declared: quite understandable and worthy of esteem is the pride which the human 'spirit' may take in anticipating death. But, because in the final analysis it remains empty, he refuses to recognize in this capacity the real function, honor and truth of

---

kind of untruth — but not the other way around, untruth as a source and kind of evil (this latter would terminate in Pragmatism). A comparison with the text above shows that this is the assumption which Kierkegaard makes also. — The logical dubiousness of the category of 'origin' (or of 'source'), which also, almost constantly disquiets the reader of the work mentioned, is revealed in the case of 'Evil' in this way: despite the continual suggestion of an antecedent-and-consequence relationship (from Evil to untruth), which, for the train of thought and its presentation in the chapter under consideration, is essential (here it appears, moreover, as an *irreversible* relationship), both appear again as being *equally* original, and then the "origin" of both — of Evil as well as of untruth — is defined in exactly the same way: as the discrepancy (inability-to-be-one) of the modes of the Encompassing within the whole.

25 *Journals*, II, 181.

26 Nietzsche, *The Will to Power*, Aphorism 1051.

philosophizing. He declares that men are, in any case, inclined enough to unite in a "brotherhood of death." He praises men that *en masse* they nevertheless manage to avoid such a union. *Even* as a philosopher he recommends, as over against the brotherhood of death, the far more exacting brotherhood of life: "It fills me with happiness to see that men do not at all want to think thoughts about death. I should like to do something to make thinking about life a hundred times more worthy for them to think about."[27]

2. Kierkegaard writes: " . . . the unconditional obedience to being trampled on, as if one had accomplished nothing, surely is and remains the highest." This is Jaspers' thought-form of "foundering" in its entirely severe and extreme Kierkegaardian original form. There is no need to introduce evidences for the fact that, against the Christian attitude exemplified by this statement of Kierkegaard's, Nietzsche directed his integrity to the two-sided effort: 1) to demonstrate the innately masochistic or (caste-determined) servile origin of this faith; and 2) to concede its "value for life" in the sense of breeding a more cunning and interesting (Christian-priestly) type of man.

At this point we break off arbitrarily. Meaning and direction of Kierkegaard's and Nietzsche's "integrity" appear to be incompatible. It is not possible that both simultaneously "open our eyes to the plain truth" *("uns die Augen öffnen und den Star stechen"* — Jaspers). One can become genuinely "seeing" according to the bent of the one or of the other only if one shares their pathos, their faith. Whoever sees through the eyes of the one, offends those of the other. Methodologically, this is Max Weber's *'ceterum censeo.'*

As far as content goes, I believe that Max Weber's substantial and personal pathos aimed in the direction in which Nietzsche tried to open Kierkegaard's eyes — not, however, *vice versa*. For this latter he would have had to be a devout Christian (or, in a related sense, "religio-musical").[28]

---

[27] Nietzsche, *The Gay Science,* Book 4: Sanctus Januarius, 278.

This Nietzsche-passage is of some interest for the history of philosophy; and this not merely because of its divergence from Schopenhauer. Heidegger too, for instance — with probably explicit reference to this passage, to which he at first had promised adherence — cast his option (1923-25) in favor of *"conscience"* as a "Being to death" *(Sein zum Tode),* amassing its forces by way of concentrating in this direction towards "Nothing."

[28] In his *Psychologie der Weltanschauungen* (c. "Ultimate Situations," sc. "Suffering"), the book of his young manhood, Jaspers had sharply emphasized the antagonism between Nietzsche and Kierkegaard: "From Kierkegaard's standpoint,

In *Reason and Existenz* Jaspers characterized Kierkegaard's "being exceptional" by the following phrases: "Nobody actually loved him;" "a shattered existence in the abandonment of one's age;" "standing helplessly in nothingness;" "pure mentality;" "indifference of all worldliness."[29]

In connection with his criticism of Kant (the vehemence of which increased with the increasing liveliness of his extolling of Goethe and praise of the high capacities for happiness in Goethe's life), Nietzsche attempted a number of trenchant analyses and definitions of happiness.[30] One of them runs: "For ascending life happiness is instinct." Nietzsche certainly would not have wanted to see this sentence applied to the interpretation of Kierkegaard's "ascent" to religious *Existenz* and exception — on the contrary, he would have interpreted this process as "decadence." Meanwhile, we may (for our purpose) appropriately pass over this Nietzschean "prejudice" and place Jaspers' description

---

Nietzsche is a-religious. From Nietzsche's standpoint, Kierkegaard is hostile to life. In any case, Kierkegaard professes to be a Christian, Nietzsche an anti-Christian."

In a certain way these sentences represent the point of greatest methodical proximity of Jaspers to Max Weber. Were one to look for a sentence — later on: *after* the accomplished transformation from the psychologist of many *Weltanschauungen* to the philosopher of the one and only Occidental philosophy and to the announcer of the one philosophical truth — which would be similarly representative of the greatest *distance* from Max Weber, the following one might well be the most impressive: "I see in my thinking the natural and necessary conclusion of Occidental thought up till now, the ingenuous synthesis by virtue of a principle, which in its breadth is capable of taking in everything which is, in any sense of the word, true." (*Wahrheit*, 192) —

— As concerns this exciting, immeasurably rich philosophical relationship to Max Weber, it seems to the author that Jaspers behaved towards Max Weber just as Nietzsche desired of a genuinely philosophical disciple: "You go East: then I shall go West — without this sensibility every friendship, every discipleship, every pupilship at some time or other becomes hypocrisy." The author of these pages desires nothing more than that Mr. Jaspers would respond to this 'attack' on him in such a way that he would show why and in how far he was forced, in the progress of his philosophizing, to depart from Max Weber's positions. As, for example: (for the sake of 'Truth') to replace Weber's discussion of value — aiming at the clarification of the struggle among irreconcilable gods (i.e., ultimate spiritual possibilities) — by the construction of a much more peaceful Pantheon. — With such a critique of Max Weber, Jaspers would help the author and many others in their own attempt to love the great man with that kind of complete freedom which at one time was his own gift to us.

[29] Compared with the portrayal of Kierkegaard in *Reason and Existenz* (1935), the presentation in *Rechenschaft und Ausblick* (1951) seems very different, much simpler and more human. In this latter the category of "exception" does not even occur.

[30] The vehemence of Nietzsche's attacks on Kant (in his later works) shows a surprising structure. One catches in it the formal aspect of a *process*, intensified and precipitated as if pathologically. But, if one traces this increase in irritability from beginning to end, the process is seen to be enmeshed with a calm, even maximal

of Kierkegaard's just mentioned "exceptional existence" under the light of this definition of "happiness" — just as Nietzsche on his part explained and bore the courage and high significance of his own life (as an exception) from the point of view of this same concept of happiness. If we carry out this attempt, if we interpret Kierkegaard's 'being exceptional' by Nietzschean standards, *every one* of Jaspers' characterizations quoted above is at once shown to be no longer cogent. Kierkegaard the "exception" is now revealed to be animated by certainty of instinct and by happiness. A plethora of information (above all from his *Journals)* is available to show the powerful *support* which Kierkegaard had: 1) in his innate (emotional) *modes of movement* (flight: attack; leading : following; rivalry as a "fight for rank" and as "fight for territory" (meaning field of competence), etc.) ; 2) in the masterpieces of his many-faceted endowments; 3) in his ability to transform melancholy almost *ad libitum* into conversation and thus abolish it; 4) in his inner "clock:" in the tension of reserving himself and the course of his life for an (at least to himself) incontestably "authentic deed" (which was to be more than merely "interesting") ; and thus 5) to die in the harness of his "exceptional existence" (but, at the same time, in the hospital, while confessing — thus returning home to the "universal") .

---

steadiness of substantial motivation. Even in the very last climaxes of vehemence, the *substance* of these attacks on Kant is still the *same* as the content of Nietzsche's Kant-criticism in his youth and in his "middle phase" *(Dawn; Gay Science).*

During the time of his Schopenhauer veneration, Nietzsche educated and schooled himself philosophically in Kant; he studied Kant with particular philological thoroughness (in contrast to other philosophers, whom he often did not know in detail). His criticism, unvarying in content, began already at the time of his enthusiastic veneration of Kant. The substantial motives of his Kant-criticism develop into definite points of view, always adhered to and always present, which are *central* and fundamental to all the constancy that may be found in his own philosophy:

(1) Against Kant's "poor concept" of happiness, Nietzsche achieves recognition and philosophical respectability for the idea of happiness — stemming from Goethe.

(2) Nietzsche criticizes the validity of the "Categorical Imperative" for *everyone* from a (religiously unembarrassed) concept of "exception," which every individual deserving of the name 'individual' represents.

(3) Nietzsche contrasts Kant's ethics and metaphysics, on the one hand with perceptions of Goethe's, and, on the other, with Darwin's viewpoints. Partly influenced by Goethe and partly by Darwin, he criticizes above all the wilful conceptions of "origins" out of "freedom," and conceives as over against it the idea of a "natural history of morality."

(4) (Even very early, but later on with increasing fervor) Nietzsche sees in Kant the "great retarder" of psychological analysis and of the unwarped view of *'homo natura'* in all its wealth of phenomena — and (later), the retarder of "intellectual integrity" as such.

(5) In Kant's confusion of *every* kind of "egoism" with "Evil," Nietzsche sees an utmost contrast to Goethe's "far truer knowledge." He takes Goethe and Kant to be *the* great "antagonists of the German spirit."

Which interpretation of Kierkegaard's exceptional being carries the greater truth: Kierkegaard's self-interpretation (which is also Jaspers'), or the interpretation seen through Nietzsche's eyes?[31]

Once again — methodologically —, Max Weber would insist on demonstrating, in the struggle of these interpretations with each other, their irreconcilable nature. And again we see him inclining, substantially, towards the Nietzschean interpretations (and causal analyses) as against the Kierkegaardian—Jaspersian (idealistic) interpretations (concerned with "origin").

* * * * *

Let us return to our theme at its point of departure; viz., to the Jaspers-Kierkegaardian convictions concerning Evil's origin in freedom — as well as the origin of the good and of love in the freedom of a counteraction to Evil. We think that — together with Nietzsche — Max Weber is here, for numerous reasons, in agreement with Goethe in Goethe's rejection of this doctrine concerning the origin of Evil and good (insofar as he encountered it in its Kantian form), as being an ungrateful or impious speculation contrary to the nature of the world and of man.[32]

In his old age (1824), Goethe partly retracted his harsh judgment of Kant's idea of a Radical Evil in man. Since his friendship with Schiller he had remained inclined to call himself a "Kant-

---

[31] Socrates, the third great historical "exception" placed by Jaspers alongside Kierkegaard and Nietzsche, could be properly understood by *neither* of the two interpretations. In the Introduction to his chapter on Socrates, in his *History of Philosophy*, II, Hegel discusses him in a magnificent way. Also in the chapter on the "Doctrine of Law," in his *Nürnberger Propadeutik* (par. 77) he writes: "The goodness of God consists therein that single individuals even as single epochs may cultivate their one-sided viewpoints to arrive at their own consciousness of justice and, at the same time, participate in the *universal* (higher and progressive) Righteousness through the honor of being *guilty* before it and of falling *victim* to it." In sharp contrast to the magnificence of these Hegelian portrayals stands the profoundly differing Section, entitled, "*Ausnahme*," in Jaspers' work, *Von der Wahrheit* (745-766), as the magnificent counter-pole.

[32] The sad upshot thus seems to be that of devoutness scolding devoutness. Representative of *Kantian* devoutness is Kierkegaard's statement: "Authentic earnestness reposes solely in the thought that God is looking upon men." (*Works*, VIII, 63); and this other one: " 'But he that is spiritual judgeth all things, yet he himself is judged of no man.' (I Cor. 2:15) In other words, the spiritual man has the power and the key with which to explain all lower forms of existence. To that extent he can be judged by no one except by whatever is *higher* than he." (*Journals*, II, 95)

Against all that, Goethe's devoutness in this single remarkable sentence: "To subordinate oneself is no achievement at all to be marvelled at — but: in downward movement, in descent, to recognize as above oneself something which stands beneath one."

ian." Only the following still seemed "blasphemous" to him in that [Kantian] thought (and we would have liked to have avoided the severity of that earlier word) : that Kant had fixed the experience of Evil in such a way that, as *absolute* Evil, it could be resolved only by a leap into a state of pure redemption — only by the acquisition of citizenship in a completely different (intelligible) world; and, furthermore, as follows from the foregoing, that Kant, at the same time, gave us to believe that Evil in man is a more radical phenomenon than is the good in him, such that, by dint of this negative constitution of man, morality and ethics are for ever justified in their proceeding in categorical opposition to man's nature, instead of proceeding, according to both possibility and the ideal, in co-operation with it.

The aging Goethe made it his concern to mediate between Kant and himself, and thus to remove the necessity of a choice, of an Either-Or, between himself and Kant. He wrote:

Piety, until now a virginally chaste word in German, since our purifiers have rejected it and put it aside, fortunately, as being foreign. *'Pietas gravissimum et sanctissimum nomen,'* says a noble forebear and concedes to it that it is the *fundamentum omnium virtutum.* Time and place preclude our digressing on it now; let only this much be briefly said, therefore:

If certain aspects of human nature, looked at from the viewpoint of morality, require us to ascribe to it a kind of Radical Evil, an *original sin,* other manifestations of human nature require us likewise to admit an *original virtue* in it — an innate goodness, uprightness, and especially an inclination to reverence. This fountainhead, insofar as it is cultivated in man, insofar as it becomes active and reaches life and public opinion, we call *piety,* as did the ancients.

It shows itself powerfully from parents to children, somewhat more weakly from children to parents. It diffuses its beneficent influences from brothers and sisters to relatives by blood, clan, and nation. It proves effective with princes, benefactors, teachers, patrons, friends, protégés, servants, menials, beasts and consequently with land and soil, with country and state. It encompasses everything and, since the world is its province, it bestows its last and best on heaven. It alone holds the wiles of selfishness in check. If, by some miracle, it were to appear instantaneously in all men, it would cure the earth of all those evils from which she presently and perhaps incurably suffers. But — we have already said too much and yet would, even with the greatest fulness of details, always still be saying too little . . . .[33]

[33] Goethe in his review of *Don Alonzo, ou l'Espagne,* in *Cotta Anniversary* ed'n, 37, 283.

Postscript.

An expert on Max Weber and the modern world-quarrels may well ask in astonishment: How can one write a discourse on evil (where, of all things, emphasis and guidance are placed in Max Weber's hands), without — as concerns the subject-matter — entering into *politics,* and without — as concerns persons — mentioning *Marx.* Indeed: the problem would really have only begun to interest Max Weber — being the impassioned politician of his nation and time that he was — at the point where we stopped. And rightly: in the debate over good and evil in this his own peculiar field, he could exclaim against *all* the classics, from Kant to Kierkegaard, from Goethe to Nietzsche: "Into the corner with that old trash!" — with one exception: Marx. However, the author wanted to save a discussion of the mechanics of evil in politics and of Max Weber and Marx for some later occasion.

EDUARD BAUMGARTEN

GEORGE WASHINGTON INSTITUTE
INSTITUTE OF TECHNOLOGY
STUTTGART, GERMANY

8

Ernst Moritz Manasse

JASPERS' RELATION TO MAX WEBER

WHAT MAX WEBER means to Jaspers is rooted in the communication which existed between the two. Communication designates an *'existential'* relation and therefore cannot be the object of a cogent rational analysis. But some light may be thrown upon it if one uses a dialectical approach. The following discussion is to be understood as an attempt in this method. It will be centered about the thesis that the communication with Max Weber has been the living spring from which Jaspers' thinking has taken its origin. But the truth of the thesis is counterbalanced by the possible truth of an opposite thesis. This opposite thesis or antithesis says that everything which is here traced back to Jaspers' communication with Max Weber can also be explained differently. The antagonism of the antithesis will be particularly felt in the second section of this paper, where the communication with Max Weber is interpreted as the *'existential'* basis of Jaspers' relation to Kant, Kierkegaard and Nietzsche. But, although the second section is more dialectical than the first one, it is still written from the point of view of the thesis.

In a dialectical discussion of this sort the antithesis does not have the function of canceling the truth of the thesis. Neither is it to be assumed that both are surpassed by the truth of a synthesis. Rather it ought to be understood that the truth of the thesis is not final and has to be defended against the antithesis in a never ending debate. The following discussion, therefore, presents only the first half of an argument, the second part of which (that is, the actual debate against the antithesis) is always to be felt as present even though it remains unwritten.

I. The Idea of Max Weber's Philosophical Existence in Jaspers' Work

For Jaspers Max Weber was like Socrates.

In the monograph, *Max Weber*,[1] first published in 1932, Jaspers

[1] *Max Weber, Monograph*, 3rd ed., 1948.

compares the spiritual situation of our time with that of declining Antiquity. At that time the Stoic philosophy offered spiritual support to the single individual whose fate was an ever growing isolation. Stoicism was prepared to furnish such support, because it was inspired by the example of Socrates who "as a real person had been, had done, and had suffered what philosophy tried to comprehend for centuries afterwards."[2] Ours is a time again, Jaspers believes, when individuals who are concerned about spiritual truth may turn to philosophy. This does not mean that they ought to become the partisans of any of the philosophical schools of the day. But the true flame of philosophy may be kindled in them through the "manifest mystery"[3] of an extraordinary man. The appearance of Max Weber is a challenge to the present generation as the appearance of Socrates was a challenge to the Ancients.

The first who tried to comprehend the philosophical meaning of Socrates' existence were his pupils, foremost among whom was Plato. Jaspers does not compare his relation to Max Weber to Plato's relation to Socrates. Perhaps this is due both to his modesty (Jaspers has repeatedly asserted that he does not consider himself as the originator of a new philosophy but rather as a renewer and preserver of the *philosophia perennis)*[4] and to be a certain distance which he has felt towards Plato. It may be necessary to state this in order to escape misunderstandings. On the other hand, the comparison of the relations of the two ancient and the two modern thinkers is so suggestive that to omit it would mean to deprive the interpretation of a unique instrument. It will be used in the following pages, therefore, whenever it appears helpful to clarify the issues.[5]

For Plato Socrates was a puzzle and a paradox. In Socrates' appearance Plato perceived a combination of obvious simplicity with unfathomable depth. Whatever Socrates expressed seemed to be down to earth, simple and precise. When, in an attempt to solve a problem, he ran into intricacies, he often confessed his ignorance and left the problem unsolved. Yet there was something in the admission of his ignorance which carried the spell of mystery. One spoke of Socrates' irony. But Socrates tried neither to hide anything nor did he want to mystify his partners. At any rate, Plato was convinced that this irony had another meaning. For Plato, Socrates' ignorance was not something merely negative

---

[2] *Monograph,* 57.   [3] *Ibid.*   [4] Cf., for instance, *Wahrheit,* 192.

[5] The same comparison was made by Julius Stenzel in his review of Jaspers' *Philosophie;* cf. *Logos,* vol. 22 (1933), 85ff.

but a *docta ignorantia*. Instead of pointing to the pure nothing (and even less to a nothing clad with the garment of mystery), it seemed to point to a reality of a different order. On the level of discussion, this reality remained ineffable (ἄρρητον). Perhaps it was something inherent in the speaker's person. Plato could not evoke it, for a long time, except by portraying Socrates. Little by little, he found other ways of expressing it. It would be one-sided, but probably not altogether wrong, were one to maintain that the theory of Ideas and the dialectics of the later dialogues were Plato's final attempt of unfolding the mystery which had appeared to him in Socrates' person.

Max Weber's words are distinguished by a similar directness and lack of pretense as Socrates'. To be sure, in the scientific age philosophy cannot appear in the simple forms of a conversation in which it had come to ancient Athens. Socrates needed not to acknowledge any certainties other than those at which he could arrive any moment by agreement with his partners. A modern dialectician is at once confronted by a vast amount of scientific knowledge which has been ascertained by methodical research. But this difference does not exclude the possibility of a basic similarity.

As Plato saw it, Socrates emphasized the limits of non-dialectical thinking in order to make room for the *docta ignorantia* which is the beginning of true philosophy. As Jaspers sees it, Max Weber pointed out the limits of empirical science in order to protect the '*existential*' freedom of the individual from the encroachments of the cogent. Weber's negations, as do Socrates', have a positive aim. Instead of stopping the flight of the spirit they are to stimulate it. Weber's determined separation of the scientifically knowable from what belongs to the realm of personal evaluation aims at more than the contrast between the rational and the irrational which leaves the latter without light and responsibility. On the contrary, Weber's whole energies were directed at narrowing the sphere of the irrational. In a gigantic effort he attempted to gather all the light which reason provides and to focus it on the secret sources of our choices and decisions. Thus he pointed to the true freedom while engaging his whole strength in the service of the un-ending rational analysis. Weber's example, like Socrates', inspired those who were susceptible to the greatness of such an undertaking. In no one did it produce a more profound effect than in Jaspers. Just as Plato's philosophy could be interpreted as his attempt to say what he had experienced through Socrates, so it is possible to consider Jaspers' thinking as his way of expressing what he had experienced through Max Weber.

On two occasions Jaspers tried to evoke Max Weber's personality directly. In the immediate grief over Weber's death he addressed the students of the University of Heidelberg in a commemorative assembly.[6] What he had then said he later re-interpreted and expanded in a little monograph. The occasion for this second publication was the rise of National Socialism in Germany. Reminding his readers of the man whom he considered as the greatest among the contemporaries, he spoke against the rising confusion.[7] But Address and Monograph are only the two most explicit references to Max Weber within Jaspers' work. One may say without exaggeration that Max Weber's personality appears in each of Jaspers' major publications. A reader who has become sensitive to Jaspers' enthusiasm and who is familiar with his style may discover silent references to Weber even within his most abstract discussions. I shall refer to some of the more obvious ones.

Through many years Max Weber accompanied his sociological investigations with studies on the logical and methodological foundations of the social sciences. One of the central problems which he discussed concerns the meaning of *Verstehen* as it is used by both sociologists and historians. Jaspers, who started his career as a psychiatrist, was deeply impressed by Weber's analysis of this concept. It helped him to distinguish in psychopathological theory the kind of knowledge which is based on the intuitive comprehension of "understandable" processes from that which "explains" non-understandable causal relations in the manner of the natural sciences, that is, by external observation and inference. In Jaspers' terminology, there is a *verstehende* psychologie and an "explaining" psychology.[8] Weber himself welcomed Jaspers' continuation of his own analyses and in turn referred to Jaspers when he later characterized his own approach as *"verstehende sociology."*[9]

It might be possible to interpret the development of Jaspers'

6 Cf. *Rechenschaft*, 9ff.

7 Cf. *Monograph*, Preface to the Second and Third Editions, (Heidelberg, Oct. 1946).

8 "Kausale und verständliche Zusammenhänge zwischen Schicksal und Dementia Praecox," *Zeitschrift für die gesamte Neurologie und Psychiatrie* XIV, 850ff (1912); *Allgemeine*, Introduction to the Second Part.

9 Max Weber, "Ueber einige Kategorien der verstehenden Soziologie" in *Gesammelte Aufsätze zur Wissenschaftslehre* (1922), 403ff; *Wirtschaft und Gesellschaft* (1922), 1.

·thinking by showing how, through the continued analysis of "understanding," he was led to his most characteristic philosophical intuitions. A *verstehende* psychology, as Jaspers was soon to discover, has its limit where *Existenz* is involved. The limit points to the need of an '*existential*' analysis and of a new philosophical logic. It is significant that in the fourth edition of the *Allgemeine Psychopathologie,* Jaspers added several paragraphs on '*existential*' and metaphysical understanding to the general section on the *verstehende* psychology.[10] The additions prove that there is a direct connection between those problems to which Jaspers had been introduced by Max Weber and the "philosophy of *Existenz.*" But such a construction would be misleading. The mere logical analysis of the concept of *Verstehen* would, by itself, never lead to a comprehension of *Existenz,* unless it were based on immediate '*existential*' experience. Jaspers had made such an experience, so it appears, when he was enchanted by the "manifest mystery" of Max Weber's personality. The most direct expression of this experience, in addition to the two essays titled, *Max Weber,* is the *Psychologie der Weltanschauungen,* the first edition of which appeared one year before Weber's death.

The theme of this book as well as the way in which Jaspers approaches it give evidence to his closeness to Weber. Jaspers has always felt that psychology and sociology are related sciences: both are dependent on *Verstehen;* both occupy a middle ground between the natural sciences (which seek to discover general "laws") and the historical disciplines (which interpret individual events) ; both make use of ideal types to clarify structures with which they are occupied. But both of these sciences are also exposed to a common danger. There is always a tendency in psychology and sociology to transcend the limits of empirical knowledge and to pass into psychological or sociological pseudo-philosophies. This danger is especially great when it is attempted in these sciences to analyze the presuppositions and consequences of religious and non-religious *Weltanschauungen.* There are but a few scientists who, under such circumstances, have withstood the danger. Max Weber had given an admirable example of a genuine scientific analysis in his investigations in the sociology of religion. In his *Psychologie der Weltanschauungen* Jaspers may be expected to have faced a similar task, and such an assumption seems to be confirmed by the Preface to the first edition. In sentences clearly reminiscent of similar propositions by Max Weber, Jaspers emphasizes that his book aims merely at the

10 *Allgemeine,* 4th ed. (1946), 246ff.

clarification and the pointing out of possibilities of *Weltan-schauungen*, not at the solution of the problem how one has to live. "The actual *Weltanschauung* remains a matter of (the individual's) life."[11]

Does this mean that Jaspers actually refrains from all evaluations and offers an "objective" psychological typology? It is not easy to answer this question. To be sure, Jaspers is faithful to the promise of the preface that he will only talk about possibilities. But the meaning of "possibility" seems to change in the course of the book. In the end it discusses possibilities which are not, as one might infer from the Preface, the psychological possibilities of ideal types but which reveal themselves as *'existential'* potentialities. With this Jaspers does not lapse into a psychological pseudo-philosophy which derives the "right" *Weltanschauung* from a supposedly objective psychology. But he makes it evident that there can be no self-contained psychology of *Weltanschauungen* and that it needs the framework of a genuine philosophy for its own truth.

Max Weber had stressed that the selection of a scientific theme is dependent on the author's interests and preferences, in other words, that the selection itself is not "value-free." Jaspers may seem to be interpreting Weber's words when he states, in his *Philosophie:* "Psychology and sociology are held together by an *'existential'* interest which seeks orientation in the world because it looks for existence as a whole *(das Dasein als Ganzes)* in its relevance for *Existenz*. What is thus found as the truth calls for rejection or attachment."[12] But this *'existential'* interest does not only concern the results of Jasper's psychology, it also determines the whole process of his investigations. In the "Introduction" to the *Psychologie der Weltanschauungen* Jaspers declares that the formulations of this book "are not self-sufficient and complete but somehow dependent on an extra-logical factor."[13] Jaspers is not satisfied with the isolation which a purely objective treatment would impose on the subject matter. He also wants to express its relations to something pre-scientific which encompasses it.

The "encompassing" which thus plays a rôle in the *Psychologie der Weltanschauungen* is the same which was soon to become the central theme of Jaspers' philosophy: it is the Encompassing *qua Existenz*. One opines that the "*'existential'* interest" does not

---

11 *Psychologie*, 3rd ed. (1925), v. All references in this article are to the third edition of this work.

12 *Philosophie* I, 201.   13 *Psychologie*, 12.

permit the author merely to practice scientific psychology but urges him to include what bursts through the framework of pure science and to turn back upon itself. This is especially evident in the analyses of the "enthusiastic attitude," of the "demonic person," of the "ultimate situations," and generally of the whole section on the "life of the spirit" which aims to point out the possibility of an "hold on the infinite" and destroys the deceptive alternative of the flight into a "shell" and the despair of nihilism. All these analyses have one thing in common: they all discuss possibilities which Jaspers, in one way or another, attempts to see in connection with the personality of Max Weber. For Jaspers Max Weber represents a new type.[14] But this is not a psychological type but an *existential* possibility. Whoever analyzes the structure of the *Psychologie* will discover that this book is so composed that it centers about the elucidation of this type. The book which is so much indebted to Max Weber for what he said is even more so for what he left unsaid: the ἄρρητον of his philosophical existence.

The *Philosophie*, which appeared thirteen years after the first edition of the *Psychologie*, tries to express in a new and more direct language what had already been the secret motive of the earlier work. This time the concept of *Existenz* is clearly recognized as the center of the author's thinking. The systematic analysis of this concept provides Jaspers with the main categories of his philosophy.

As early as in the Commemorative Address, Jaspers had stated that through Max Weber, "the philosophical *Existenz* became 'visible to others'."[15] One may infer from this that "the idea of this philosophical *Existenz*"[16] is the lasting inspiration of Jaspers' "philosophy of *Existenz*," and this conclusion is confirmed by the new work. Indeed, each of the three volumes of the *Philosophie* contains evidence of the presence of that idea. In the first volume ("Philosophical World Orientation") it is felt in the emphasis on the dignity as well as on the limits of science and in the referring to *Existenz* and Transcendence as the non-scientific sources of the will to know. In the second volume ("Illumination of *Existenz*") the idea of Max Weber's philosophical *Existenz* seems to be present as the secret standard by which all *'existential'* possibilities are being judged. Finally, since *Existenz* cannot be without Transcendence, the idea which inspires the whole work work includes the necessity to explore the ways in which *Existenz*

14 Cf. Marianne Weber, *Max Weber: Ein Lebensbild* (1926), 580.
15 *Rechenschaft*, 17.   16 *Ibid.*, 25.

approaches the absolute. The third volume ("Metaphysics"), which is dedicated to this task, shows the idea fo Max Weber's *Existenz* in new and previously unheard perspectives. In order to recognize them in their full significance it is perhaps necessary to compare the "Metaphysics" with Jaspers' Monograph on Max Weber which appeared the same year.

In the Monograph Jaspers points out that Weber's appearance was full of contradictions. There was something "antinomical" in Weber's personality as well as in his thinking. Jaspers enumerates several pairs of contrasts which especially struck him. The last of these pairs sounds quite mysterious. Weber combined, it says, "the unconditional fulfilment of the moral demand as the Law of the Day and the clear-sighted openness for the demons of the Night."[17] In the "Metaphysics" there is a section which carries the title: "The Law of the Day and the Passion for the Night."[18] The glance into the Night is the acknowledgment of the possible truth which remains in the ultimate negation of reason, life and light. The existence of this possibility is one of the most disquieting and tormenting insights of Jaspers' work. It is an almost unbelievable and yet a consoling thought that even on this path Jaspers is still accompanied by the idea of Max Weber's philosophical *Existenz*.

"The Day is tied to the Night, because the day *is* only, if it ultimately and truthfully founders."[19] The contrast of Day and Night is as indissoluble as the foundering is inescapable. The *Philosophie* as well as the Monograph culminate in a discussion of the meaning of foundering. In the Monograph, Jaspers comprehends Max Weber's fate as "genuine" foundering which appears to be symbolic and "like the return to the origin"[20] (from which *Existenz* and Being have descended). Symbolic of what? The answer is found in the last chapter of the "Metaphysics," where foundering is recognized as "the decisive cipher of Transcendence."[21] Max Weber's foundering is symbolic of the manner in which all philosophy comes to an end.

The completion of the *Philosophie* and of the Monograph represent the climax of that phase in Jaspers' development in which the explication of the idea of Max Weber's philosophical *Existenz* caused him to think through the problems of a philosophy of *Existenz*. This accomplished, his thinking turned more and more to a problem which is designated by him by the names of "the Encompassing" *(das Umgreifende)* and "the origins" *(die*

17 *Monograph*, 46.   18 *Philosophie* III, 102ff.   19 *Ibid.*, 110.
20 *Monograph*, 56.   21 *Philosophie* III, 219ff.

Ursprünge).[22] Both expressions refer to what is prior to reason
and yet the source of all knowing, all being, all truth. The first
publication in which this new turn in Jaspers' thinking is evident
are the five lectures which appeared under the title *Reason and
Existenz*. The book begins with the statement: "The rational is
not thinkable without its other, the non-rational, and it never
appears in reality without it."[23] There is a new tone in this statement and this new tone is echoed throughout the five lectures.
And yet: is not this first new sentence related to a number of
propositions which he had issued earlier? Does it not remind
of the antinomy of Day and Night and of the inevitableness of
foundering? To be sure, there is this difference: What was
formerly taken as the ultimate realization of truth is now recognized as the origin and the very foundation of truth. But even this
thought seems to have been anticipated by the remark in the
Monograph that Max Weber's foundering was "like the return
to the origin."[24] It thus appears that the idea of Max Weber's
philosophical *Existenz* has remained Jaspers' point of departure
even in this latest phase of his production, and that only its radi-
ation has penetrated farther and farther.

Plato's thinking which was inspired by the idea of Socrates'
philosophical *Existenz* seems to have taken a similar development.
In some of Plato's later works his thought has moved so far away
from his origin that he chose others in place of Socrates as the
representatives of his judgments. But it is hardly a coincidence
that even then Plato wanted the discussion to go on in Socrates'
presence. If one takes the words in a dialectical and not in a trivial
sense, one might say that in those dialogues Plato was still interpreting what Socrates had been with the modification that henceforth the discussion of what Socrates had been included that which
he had *not* been. In the same sense Jaspers' later works may be
said to deal with Max Weber, both with that as which he had
existed and with what he could not be since it is being of a non-
'existential' nature. A few examples may illustrate this continued
presence of the idea of Max Weber's philosophical *Existenz* in
Jaspers' more recent publications.

(a) In *The Origin and Goal of History,* Jaspers attempts the
construction of the whole of man's history, something from
which Max Weber, in spite of his comprehensive knowledge, had
always shrunk. But this construction is not presented as factual
knowledge. Origin and goal remain unknown. They are ideas by
which *Existenz* is directed toward the Encompassing in which it

22 Cf. *Wahrheit*, 28.   23 *Reason*, 19.   24 Cf. note 20.

is rooted. The point of departure of this philosophy of history seems to be indicated in the Monograph, where Jaspers describes Weber's interest in any kind of empirical causality together with his awareness of the relative importance of each. For it so happens, Jaspers observes, that "Max Weber, in his empirical research, arrives all the more decisively at the sources from which, as uncomprehended presuppositions, he has to proceed."[25]

(b) In *The Perennial Scope of Philosophy*, Jaspers declares: "Faith is life out [of the source] of the Encompassing, it is guidance and fulfillment through the Encompassing."[26] Philosophical faith is one of the permanent themes of Jaspers' thinking. In the work with this title the relation to the Encompassing may seem to indicate a new horizon. Yet this, too, was already anticipated in a chapter of the *Psychologie*, which unmistakably suggests the nearness of the idea of Max Weber's philosophical *Existenz*. Faith there is said to be "the all-embracing *(das Umfassende)*; not something particular — neither a merely isolated content nor something specifically religious — but the ultimate power of the spirit."[27] Such a faith has a twofold character just as does its counterpart, the ideas. "It is subjective power as much as objective content."[28] In the Monograph the relation of philosophical faith to Max Weber's *Existenz* is made explicit. Weber, Jaspers says,

remained in the process of experiencing, seeking and distinguishing. Yet each distinction was superseded by a unity of which he himself was not aware, since it was anchored in the truthfulness of his being himself. The content of this faith was nothing that could be expressed in a permanently valid formula; but it was imperturbably present as the substance in everything that he experienced and thought.[29]

(c) In *Von der Wahrheit* Jaspers quotes Max Weber's last words "The True is the Truth" *(Das Wahre ist die Wahrheit)* and takes them as a cipher of absolute truth itself. "Absolute truth," Jaspers declares,

can only be where falsehood is no longer possible, that is, in Transcendence. There, however, the 'truth for us' ends also together with falsehood, and there remains only the pure light which is indicated by the mysterious sentence of the dying Max Weber: 'The True is the

---

25 *Monograph*, 38.

26 *Scope*, 17. (Ed's. Note: *Das Umgreifende* has here been translated in harmony with its general translation throughout this vol.)

27 *Psychologie*, 337.　　　　　　28 *Ibid.*, 338; cf. *Philosophie* II, 279ff.

29 *Monograph*, 53.

Truth.' These words are meaningless for us [only] in so far as we are finite beings.[30]

The mystery of Max Weber's last words never ceased to occupy Jaspers' mind. One may be inclined to take them for the very seeds of his book, *Von der Wahrheit:* So one reaches this same conclusion when one reads Jaspers' comment in the Monograph. "For us this is not a tautology but like the magic expression of an *Existenz.* Its truth is the acknowledgment that even the ways of knowing as empirical knowledge are but functions in a responsible process the origin and goal of which are uncertain and yet approved."[31]

II. Max Weber's Philosophical *Existenz* as 'Repetition'

In the foregoing, Jaspers' philosophy has been construed as an interpretation of the idea of Max Weber's philosophical *Existenz.* It may be objected that this is a distortion. Jaspers himself has declared that he owes his basic insights to an ancient tradition in philosophy and, in the Preface to his *Philosophie,* he named ten philosophers to whom he feels especially indebted. Also, it has been assumed that the center of Jaspers' thought is the "philosophy of *Existenz.*" Now it is a well known fact and attested by Jaspers' own words that the spiritual ancestors of this philosophy were Kierkegaard and Nietzsche. One may argue that this cannot be reconciled with the contention of the unique importance of Max Weber for Jaspers' philosophical development.

These objections have to be met; yet the problem can be limited without prejudice to the relevant facts. Looking at the names of the ten philosophers who are mentioned in the Preface to the *Philosophie,* one may or may not feel able to determine what Jaspers owes to each of them. But one will hardly conclude that each of them was equally important for the formation of his thought. Besides Weber, there are only three whose impact can be traced through all phases of Jaspers' philosophizing. These three are Kant, Kierkegaard and Nietzsche. Jaspers recognizes them together with Max Weber as his predecessors in the *Psychologie der Weltanschauungen,*[32] and in *Reason and Existenz* he mentions these same ones as those thinkers who have paved the way to his *Philosophie.*[33] I think this will justify it, if, in the

---

[30] *Wahrheit,* 597. [31] *Monograph,* 53. [32] *Psychologie,* 12ff.

[33] *Reason,* 155f. The only other philosopher whose importance for Jaspers comes near to that of these four is Hegel. But with all his admiration for Hegel, Jaspers

following, I shall deal only with Jaspers' relations to Kant, Kierkegaard and Nietzsche. If it can be shown that the idea of Max
Weber's philosophical *Existenz* played an important part in the
shaping of these relations, one may infer that either the same
is true for his relations to the other thinkers he has mentioned;
or else that these relations concern less central areas of his
philosophy.

Max Weber was not a philosopher in the technical sense, and
Jaspers received from Kant and Kierkegaard and, to a lesser
extent, from Nietzsche, the conceptual tools which he needed in
order to analyze what he had experienced through Weber. But
this would not have been possible unless Jaspers had felt that
there was an *'existential'* relationship between those three thinkers
and Weber. Since Jaspers has given no name to this relationship,
I shall call it "repetition." The *'existential'* potentialities of this
term have been recognized by Kierkegaard and have since been
re-interpreted by Heidegger. It is to be noted, however, that
"repetition" here is used to describe a structure which is not
identical with those analyzed by Kierkegaard or Heidegger. "Repetition" here does *not* mean the *conscious* re-collection of former
'existential' possibilities. If the present interpretation is correct,
the consciousness of the repetition has to be sought in the observer (Jaspers) and not in the repeating individual (Weber).
"Observer" is of course also to be taken in an *'existential'* sense
and means an *Existenz* which in the enthusiasm of the communication discovers new horizons. To summarize: Repetition here
means that by communication with Max Weber Jaspers experienced that Weber's being, doing and suffering was intimately
related to the being, doing and suffering of Kant, Kierkegaard
and Nietzsche. It is as though the enthusiasm of Jaspers' communication with Max Weber had been transformed and led to
new forms of an "indirect" communication.

Here it is, however, necessary to make a distinction. Kierkegaard's and Nietzsche's significance, as Jaspers sees it, lies in the
fact that both were "exceptions." Kant cannot be called an exception in the same sense (though perhaps in a modified one).
Repetition therefore does not designate a single pattern. If an
"exception" can be "repeated" at all, this implies the existence of
a very special mode of repetition. In the interest of method it

---

has always considered Hegel's metaphysics as the opposite pole of his own thinking. Like Kierkegaard, Jaspers arrives at his own truth by distancing himself from
Hegel.

will be best to start with the simpler case, that is, the "repetition" of Kant.

A. The 'Repetition' of Kant's Philosophical *Existenz*
(The Prototype of the Demonic Person)

Kant's importance for Jaspers has scarcely been recognized to its full extent, although Jaspers' comprehension of Kant surpasses in depth that of most of the so-called Kantians.[34] In the Preface to the *Philosophie,* Jaspers calls Kant "the prototype of a philosopher" *(den Philosophen schlechthin).*[35] He thinks that possibly only a small number of German readers have grasped the true meaning of Kant's philosophy (as only a few Greeks may have grasped the true meaning of Plato's philosophy).[36] Kant's originality appears to him as great as that of the pre-Socratics.

According to Jaspers, Kant means the end of all objective metaphysics, and no one who has recognized the importance of Kant's achievement will seek refuge in a new 'shell'. Kant's thinking is infinite movement. It cannot come to rest because it is in continuous transition from the "antinomial structure of the world" to the ideas and *vice versa.* The antinomies reveal the dependent nature of reality as it appears to the human understanding and prohibit a calm contemplation of it. Yet, although they threaten to upset the spirit which is longing for order, they point the way to the ideas. Because of Kant's insistence on the difference between rational empirical knowledge and the pseudo-rationality of an objective metaphysics, the Kantian ideas are not to be understood as given "objects" of another reality. Kant's "theory of ideas," in a unique manner, elucidates the process of transcending without lapsing into a new sort of pseudo-objectivity.

Like Kant, Max Weber was struck by the "antinomial structure of the world." Sociological studies and political experience convinced him that each individual runs into rationally insuperable antinomies whenever he tries to analyze his own evaluations and principles of action. There is a never ending "battle of the gods" which baffles all efforts of trying to deduce what is right. Every single attempt to realize a particular set of values leads to inevitable conflicts. The realization of almost any chosen value presupposes preliminary acts (means) or produces unintended

---

[34] Even the plan of the present volume foresees articles on Jaspers' relations to Kierkegaard and to Nietzsche, but none on his relation to Kant.

[35] *Philosophie* I, viii.   [36] *Origin,* 250.

consequences which run counter to the chosen end. Just as Kant was confronted by the limits of a rational comprehension of the physical world, so Weber faces the limits which prohibit a rational deduction of moral principles. As Kant insisted on the separation of metaphysical concepts from those of empirical science, so Weber insists on the separation of moral and metaphysical evaluations from sociological and related investigations. There seems to be but one important difference. Whereas Kant meets the metaphysical needs of the human mind by pointing to the non-objective "objects" of the pure reason, that is, the ideas, Weber's final word on metaphysics seems to be negative.

Jaspers, who repeatedly points out the similarities, must have felt this as the crucial point. If he had had to believe that Weber's negativism was real and not merely apparent, the comparison could not have meant much to him. But, from his communication with Weber Jaspers gained the conviction that, against all appearances, Weber possessed a powerful equivalent for Kant's apperception of the ideas. This equivalent was Weber's faith. Jaspers describes it as a "simple unknowing faith which again and again said 'yes' from the deepest spring (of his *Existenz*); which sought and found what remains lovable in the midst of general ruin, even still in what was altogether foreign to him."[37] For Jaspers, faith and ideas are reciprocal terms;[38] the thinker who lives by faith is the same who also is inspired by ideas.

Although all this corroborates the fact that Jaspers is aware of a basic affinity between Kant's and Weber's philosophical attitudes, it may not seem sufficient to justify the assertion that he considers this affinity a "repetition." One may demand a token which calls more directly for such an interpretation.I believe that such a token is presented in the identity of style in which Jaspers refers to both Weber and Kant. Not only does he occasionally use the same terms to characterize Kant's and Weber's thinking,[39] but there are entire passages in his work with mute but unmistakable references to an *Existenz* which seems to be Kant's as well as Max Weber's. An example from the *Psychologie* may illustrate this.

In order to overcome the lame contrast between a narrow rationalism and a directionless irrationalism, Jaspers points out that one has to distinguish among *three* basic types. Besides the

---

[37] *Monograph,* 52.   [38] Cf. above with notes 27 and 28.

[39] For example, Jaspers praises in Kant "the purity and depth of his *infinitely moving* spirit" *(Philosophie* I, viii); and he says of Weber: "he united in himself opposites in *infinite movement.*" *(Rechenschaft,* 15).

rationalistic rigorists and the "chaotic" irrationalists, there are also those whom Jaspers calls "demonic."[40] A 'demonic' person is characterized by an "antinomial synthesis"[41] his thinking is said to move in the following "circular" pattern: as his creative forces demand articulation, he cannot avoid constructing 'shells' (*Gehäuse); but these 'shells' will not satisfy his reason; being aware of the antinomies which no shell is able to eliminate, he will destroy the structure he has erected and free his energies for higher realizations.

In a demonic person

the ardor of the living process reaches its highest intensity. As soon as he feels the (threat of the) torpidity inherent in everything finite, he senses the antinomies which limit it. Whenever his words and deeds are taken as program or as model, he dreads such lifeless fixation and disowns his own past. It is a continuous process of 'surmounting' and thereby in direct contrast to the thrust toward chaos.[42]

The work of the demonic person,

sometimes carried out with rapid speed, seems not to serve the construction of a shell in which he would have trust as in something final; it seems to be but a stepping stone for his next move toward the infinite. . . . His actions grow out of the totality of a situation and can but inadequately be comprehended by formulas or rational calculations.[43]

In spite of this, demonic persons are animated by the highest sense of responsibility. "They are never able to know in advance where their path is leading them. They are representatives of entire successions of generations — unless one actually considers them as the very image of man."[44]

"The demonic spirit realizes itself . . . in fragments . . . . The fragmentary character of his realizations is increased by a relentless urge which carries him from attempt to attempt, from work to work: scarcely has he completed one when a new one becomes important to him." A demonic person may seek realization in politics, in the sciences, in the arts. If he has chosen the sciences, "he is profound, decisive, a turning point in the history of ideas and yet: without a system, without a school, without successors."[45] A demonic person who avails himself of the medium of rational thought can, of course, not avoid to express fixed positions and evaluations. In such a case he strives toward a maximum of consistency as passionately as a rigorist. Pursuing every thought to

40 *Psychologie,* 354.   41 *Ibid.,* 353.   42 *Ibid.,* 355.
43 *Ibid.*   44 *Ibid.,* 356.   45 *Ibid.,* 357.

its most remote consequences, he causes the critical re-examination of the very foundations of the sciences.[46]

The demonic person realizes most profoundly that he does not understand himself and others; and that others, in the final analysis, do not understand him. Yet to understand and to be understood is his most ardent desire. As soon, on the other hand, as the demonic impulse grows weary, men creep into shells and are satisfied by the feeling of mutual understanding. They become masters and leaders, pick up disciples and successors instead of going on with the infinite process of intellectual communication, growth and clarification. The demonic person abhors such rôles of master and apostle; [for he feels that] they petrify and arrest the spirit and threaten to impose a fixed pattern to motion itself. The demonic person does not attract but repels others who desire to devote and to subject their individuality to his own. Instead of passing out the slogans to a flock of idolizers, he is suspicious of every fixed formula. To be sure, he himself invents formulas all the time, but he immediately disavows them again [i.e., when they have served their purpose].[47]

With this analysis of the 'demonic' person one has to compare what Jaspers says about Max Weber. "This man," he declares in the Commemorative Address, "who was never at a standstill but always demonically driven on, did not want to set forth a perfect system or work; had he done so, it would have oppressed, deceived, blinded him."[48] Elsewhere in the Address and again in the Monograph, Jaspers speaks of the "infinite mobility" of Weber's mind (the result of his gigantic effort to synthesize opposite forces) ; his bursting of any shell and his surmounting of any stage which he had reached; the fragmentary character of his work, caused by his constant attempts to extend his views farther and farther; his passion for consistency together with his readiness to re-examine his choices in the light of actual situations; his rejection of the rôle of the charismatic leader and his insistence on meeting every one as an equal. True, Jaspers asserts that the *Psychologie* describes types, not personalities. Yet, one can hardly escape the notion that the image of the demonic man is less the result of an abstraction than the reflection of an immediate intuition: the intuition, one readily concludes, of the idea of Max Weber's philosophical *Existenz*.

There is, however, an objection to this conclusion. Although several names are mentioned in order to illustrate features of the demonic type, Max Weber's name is not among them. Those nominated include Socrates, Kant, Kierkegaard and Nietzsche.

<hr>

[46] *Ibid.*, 358.   [47] *Ibid.*, 373.   [48] *Rechenschaft*, 17.

The references to Kant are of special significance. There is, for instance, an extraordinary exposition of the fragmentary nature of Kant's work. Kant's writings, Jaspers says, "are gigantic fragments and at the same time an entire world full of contradictions, the source of heterogeneous possibilities; their power to generate is infinite . . . their power to instruct is small."[49] Only the discerning eye of enthusiasm could reach such insight. One may be inclined to suppose that, if it had not been done by Max Weber, the image of the demonic person would have been furnished to Jaspers by Kant. Another statement in the *Psychologie* leads, however, still further. According to this book, the "life of the spirit" climaxes in what Jaspers calls mysticism, that is, in the overcoming of the split which tears reality apart into subject and object. To overcome this split is not the exclusive prerogative of those mystics who reach their goal in ecstatic flights. There is another type of mystic who attains the same end in a different manner. These are the "demonic" philosophers who transcend reality in the direction of the ideas. In this connection Jaspers hails Kant as the prototype of the demonic philosopher: "On the basis of Plotinus' example," he says, "one has to approve the mystic (that is, the ecstatic) type; on the basis of Kant's example one has to approve the demonic type with its direction toward ideas."[50]

Does this mean that it is Kant and not Weber who inspired Jaspers to his conception of the demonic type? Not at all. The presence of Weber's spirit in these analyses is as indubitable as is Kant's. The omission of Weber's name may be due to the fact that Weber was still alive when the first edition of the *Psychologie* appeared. In no case can it do away with the evidence that Weber like Kant represented (for Jaspers) the prototype of the 'demonic' person. But is it possible that there are two prototypes of one type? I believe this possibility must be admitted. Its explanation is contained in the concept of "repetition."

B. The 'Repetition' of the Philosophical *Existenz* of Kierkegaard and Nietzsche (The Exception and the Sacrifice)

The assumption of the possibility that there are philosophical prototypes and that there is repetition seems to stand in conflict with the notion that every philosopher is an exception. "Wherever philosophy appears originally and in personal form, it is a stranger in the world."[51] To live philosophically means to live as an ex-

---

[49] *Psychologie*, 358.   [50] *Ibid.*, 448.   [51] *Wahrheit*, 765.

ception. In this sense the 'demonic' Kant was an exception, even though he may have been a prototype. Yet the meaning of 'exception' is ambiguous. Jaspers found the term in Kierkegaard, who comprehended his own existence as that of an 'exception.' But Kierkegaard as well as his counterpart, Nietzsche, were exceptions in still another sense than Kant.

> ... everything great is unique, and can never be repeated identically. But there is something essentially different in our relation to this uniqueness: and this whether we live through them, and, by making them our own, revive them, or see them through the distance of an orientation which changes us but makes them more remote.[52]

Kierkegaard's and Nietzsche's uniqueness is of the latter sort: "Nobody has accepted their answers; they are not ours. It is for us to see what will become of us through ourselves as we look upon them."[53] With Kant it is different. Through Kant we might gain ourselves back, because he is both 'exception' and prototype.

The contrast between a philosophical *Existenz* which is both 'exception' and prototype and that which is an "absolute" exception can be characterized by the contrast between belief and unbelief. The nature of philosophical faith is symbolized by Kant's theory of ideas. Kant's faith in ideas is both philosophical and imperturbable: it is careful not to mistake itself for knowledge and yet is guided by reason. Compared with Kant, Kierkegaard and Nietzsche appear like the heroes of unbelief. True enough, Kierkegaard struggled to be a Christian and staked his *Existenz* on the outcome of this struggle. Nevertheless, Kierkegaard's efforts may appear "like the peculiar art of perhaps a non-believer, forcing himself to believe."[54] In spite of his radical Christianity, Kierkegaard's spirit seems to be related to that of the unbelieving Nietzsche more than to that of anyone else. If it is true that genuine belief always stands in a dialectical relation to unbelief,[55] there remains this difference: that the faithful lives by his faith, whereas Kierkegaard, as it appears, lived just as much by his negations. His negating faith, like Nietzsche's unbelief, mark the very edge of nihilism.

Faith permits repetition in the mode of succession. If, as has been suggested, Max Weber's philosophical *Existenz* can be understood as a repetition of Kant's philosophical *Existenz*, this relation illustrates what succession means. The faith that lived in Kant seems to have come to a new life in a succeeding thinker

[52] *Reason*, 46f.   [53] *Ibid.*, 48.   [54] *Ibid.*, 36.
[55] Cf. *Philosophie* I, 246ff; *Scope*, 19.

and to have radiated once more. Because of this faith, Weber is, like Kant, both 'exception' and prototype. In spite of his warnings against regarding Weber as a charismatic leader, Jaspers sees in him "the man who in a unique manner spread confidence; since every one may and ought to go the way Max Weber went."[56]

In contrast to Kant and Weber (who had such faith), Kierkegaard and Nietzsche (who lacked it) appear like "absolute" exceptions. Their paths we cannot go. But, because of them, "the question is: how those of us shall live who are no exceptions but who are seeking our inner way in the light of these exceptions."[57] This is no easy task, and it may sometimes appear to be altogether impossible. Yet,

we are in that cultural situation where the application of this knowledge already contains the kernel of dishonesty. It is as though through them we were forced out of a certain thoughtlessness, which without them would have remained even in the study of great philosophers. [Because of the example set by Kierkegaard and Nietzsche] we can no longer tranquilly proceed in the continuity of a traditional, intellectual education.[58]

Was Max Weber aware of this situation? Did he live with his eyes fixed on the exception? I do not recall that Weber ever referred to Kierkegaard in his writings, although I assume that he knew of him, through Jaspers if not otherwise. As for Nietzsche, there are several references in Weber's writings which prove that he had read him. Weber seems to have been especially interested in Nietzsche's theory of the rôle of resentment in the world's history. One wonders whether Weber was not also impressed by Nietzsche's discussion of the potentialities of asceticism. Nevertheless, Weber's interest in certain problems Nietzsche discussed does not imply that he was affected by the phenomenon, Nietzsche. Jaspers, who occasionally mentions Weber's admiration for Kant,[59] says nothing about Weber's attitude towards Nietzsche. In spite of this, Jaspers feels that Weber and Nietzsche represent the same humanity and that both belong to the same tradition. "The [type of] man who was born in the world of Homer and of the Jewish prophets has not yet disappeared with Nietzsche. Thus far he had his last great representative in Max Weber."[60]

But Jaspers sees Weber not only in the tradition which connects Nietzsche with classical and Biblical Antiquity. He also sees in

---

[56] *Monograph*, 48.   [57] *Reason*, 47.   [58] *Ibid.*

[59] Cf. *Rechenschaft*, 24.   [60] *Monograph*, 56.

Weber the marks which make him akin to the *Exceptions,* Nietzsche and Kierkegaard. His statement that in Weber there was both "the unconditional fulfilment of the moral Law of the Day and the visionary openness for the demons of the Night"[61] permit, perhaps, the interpretation that Weber repeated *'existential'* potentialities of Kierkegaard and Nietzsche as well as of Kant. But, whereas Weber's relation to Kant has been understood as a repetition in the mode of succession, the idea of Kierkegaard's and of Nietzsche's *Existenz* can only be repeated in the mode of exception.

One is an exception in that one founders. Since every *Existenz* is bound to founder, every *Existenz* is a potential exception. It constitutes the character of the absolute exception that it faces its foundering with an active consent. The foundering of the absolute exception means sacrifice. The life of the absolute exception (like Kierkegaard and Nietzsche) appears like a continuous sacrifice.

The concluding paragraph of Jaspers' *Monograph* on Weber deals with Max Weber's foundering. Fate had denied to Weber an adequate employment of his political talents, the objectivation of his knowledge in a definitive, and comprehensive work, the realization of his humanity in a representative deed. Yet

there was about him an atmosphere of foundering in a more profound sense. His foundering is no more to be identified with what he could not do than his accomplishments could be identified with what he achieved. His foundering was a suffering which is like an active will: the true foundering of a man in the historical situation into which he had been placed.[62]

Weber's attitude toward his own foundering makes it appear like a sacrifice.

The actual sacrifice is the choosing of one's own ruin. It constitutes the potential greatness of man that he can accept with his active will what he must suffer. It is the truth of the exception that it becomes conscious of this with increasing clearness. Man really becomes man only because he can sacrifice himself: life for life's sake is, on the whole, not worth living for him.[63]

Sacrifice is man's opportunity in so far as he is a potential exception. A sacrifice cannot be repeated in the same manner in which faith can be awakened to new life. Each sacrifice is a new sacrifice. Because the actual sacrifice means foundering, it causes the end of all communication. There is only communication in

---

[61] Cf. above, n. 17.   [62] *Monograph,* 55.   [63] *Wahrheit,* 884.

the "readiness for sacrifice."[64] By actual sacrifice the loose ends of communication are impelled to the openness of Transcendence.

In the communication with Max Weber, Jaspers experienced that "atmosphere of foundering" which seems to have been the *'existential'* origin of his comprehension of foundering, exception, sacrifice. Kierkegaard and Nietzsche, the "absolute" exceptions, offered the "great sacrifice." Without seeking immediate death, "they lived as though they were dead."[65] They are like beacons which show how far the boundaries of humanity can be extended. In Max Weber Jaspers sensed the thrust toward the same boundaries.

Several circumstances in Weber's fate suggest that he was heading towards a fate very much like Kierkegaard's or Nietzsche's. Like the latter Weber early was forced to interrupt an academic career because of a nervous illness. A new phase of production followed (and was perhaps furthered by) the disease.[66] However, in contrast to Nietzsche, Weber recovered and years later returned to his academic profession. Instead of loosening every tie of love and friendship, he remained in communication with his wife and friends. Jaspers was early aware of this ambiguity. In 1916 Marianne Weber reported to her husband in a letter that Jaspers considered him as "a new type who, in spite of a complete lack of illusions, has the strength of holding together and surmounting the huge tensions of his inner self and the contradictions of the life outside; a type which can even afford to be sick and to expose himself to ridicule."[67] What Jaspers here stresses are the marks of an exception; still, he claims them as the signs of a new type.

The idea of Max Weber's philosophical *Existenz* is the point of departure of Jaspers' own philosophy as well as of his understanding of Kant, Kierkegaard and Nietzsche. Through these three philosophers that idea became articulate. In their works and lives Jaspers discovered the presence of a complex *'existential'* dialectic which is like the anticipation of the possibilities which Max Weber was going to repeat both as a prototype and as a sacrifice.

Conclusion: The Dialectics of Communication

Jaspers' philosophy is rooted in his communication with Max

---

[64] *Ibid.*, 885.   [65] *Ibid.*, 887.

[66] For the new phase in Weber's production, cf. Marianne Weber, *Max Weber,* 318ff.

[67] *Ibid.*, 580.

Weber. This means that one cannot speak of an influence of Max Weber on Jaspers as of an element which could be separated from the rest of Jaspers' thinking. Communication means an *'existential'* relation, means loving communion in search of truth.

Communication as an *'existential'* relation is not an objective fact which can be ascertained by scientific methods. Everything that is said to illuminate it points to a *potential* truth. At the same time it may happen that deception creeps into the discussion, even though there is no proof of an error. In the introductory remarks of this paper it was stated that the present approach is to be understood as dialectical. It may be useful once more to call attention to this statement.

In the Monograph Jaspers mentions a certain type of criticism which was brought up against Weber and which, if it were true, would contradict his intuition.[68] Against those who denied Weber's fitness for political leadership and charged him with self-righteousness Jaspers declared:

Weber's personal qualities could be perceived in this manner only by one who did not love him because he had no trust in reason or conscience and did not dare to meet him in combat; otherwise, he would have experienced how Weber's passionate temperament was at once kindled and checked in the communication in which men who 'remain themselves' meet, understand, trust, and agree with each other.[69]

It is Jaspers' ultimate answer to this antithesis that, in order to know Weber one has to love him.

The idea of Max Weber's philosophical *Existenz* is alive today because of Jaspers: through his philosophy as well as through his direct evocations of Weber's personality. Even those who study Weber's works in order to reach that idea are usually dependent on Jaspers, whether directly or indirectly. To be sure, there are other sources to which we owe information about Weber's person.[70] But to them applies what applies to Xenophon's writings on Socrates. They complete the picture Plato had drawn, confirm it and add question marks to it. But what Socrates means to philosophy is known only through Plato. Even those who have tried to play Socrates against Plato (like Kierkegaard and Nietzsche) gained their conception of Socrates through Plato.[71]

---

[68] Cf. *Monograph,* 20f, 39f, 56.　　　　　　　　[69] *Ibid.,* 21.

[70] Marianne Weber's biography of her husband must here be named in the first place. Cf. note 14.

[71] There is, however, one document which stands on the same level with Jaspers' words. This is the poem, "Max Weber," by Friedrich Gundolf. Cf. Gundolf, *Gedichte* (1930), 23f.

Weber is a philosophical power today because he is the spirit of Jaspers' philosophy. Occasionally the question has been asked what Max Weber would have thought of the "philosophy of *Existenz*," with the implied idea that Weber would scarcely have approved of it. There is no way of finding out. But one ought to realize that the question is of the same sort as if one asked what the historical Socrates would have thought of Plato's theory of Ideas.

Does this mean that Jaspers created a Weber myth? Not at all, if "myth" designates a picture which is but loosely connected with historical fact and which passes for authoritative because of its aesthetic attractiveness. Jaspers never ceases to refer his readers to Weber's own writings. His scrupulous respect for historical fact is beyond doubt. Nor does he invite to the tranquil contemplation of an aesthetically satisfying picture. Speaking of Weber, he confronts his audience with disquieting antinomies and tries to provoke his listeners into philosophical self-activity.

Plato found that the enthusiasm which Socrates had aroused did not cease until it was transformed into philosophy. Jaspers has had a similar experience. He too was enchanted by a 'demonic' man and, since he wanted to speak of him, he had to talk philosophy.

ERNST MORITZ MANASSE

DEPARTMENT OF PHILOSOPHY
NORTH CAROLINA COLLEGE AT DURHAM

9

Jean Wahl

NOTES ON SOME RELATIONS OF JASPERS
TO KIERKEGAARD AND HEIDEGGER*

I. JASPERS, KIERKEGAARD, AND *Existenz.*

TAKING Jaspers' *Von der Wahrheit*[1] as our point of departure, it is not too difficult to see some of the principal points
of Jaspers' philosophy which have felt the influence of Kierkegaard's thought. Jaspers tells us that, following the moments in
which one has insisted on an objective knowledge of being, there
occurs a kind of impulsion towards subjectivity.[2] This reaction
against objectivity explains precisely the rôle of the notion of
existence in Kierkegaard. It was Kierkegaard who gave to the
ancient term "Existing" a new meaning. He termed "existential
thinking" that manner of thinking which is most essentially
linked to being and which is most decisive for man.[3] By means of

* Translated from the original French manuscript by Forrest W. Williams.

[1] Passages of earlier works by Jaspers which corroborate *Von der Wahrheit* are
separately discussed or cited in the footnotes to Part I of this essay.

[2] Cf. *Wahrheit,* 1024.

[3] "The contemporary philosophical situation is determined by the fact that two
philosophers, Kierkegaard and Nietzsche, who did not count in their times and,
for a long time, remained without influence in the history of philosophy, have continually grown in significance. Philosophers after Hegel have increasingly returned
to face them and they stand today unquestioned as the authentically great thinkers
of their age." *Reason,* 23f.

"Both Kierkegaard and Nietzsche questioned reason from the depths of *Existenz.*"
(Cf. *ibid.,* 25.)

Kierkegaard, wrote Jaspers in *Reason and Existenz,* elevated the word *"Existenz"*
to a new sphere and deepened it in a manner unprecedented in other philosophers.
(Cf. *ibid.,* 49.)

Jaspers sets himself the problem whether it was not a kind of failing on the
part of Kierkegaard to place so much value on the thought of *Existenz.* "Here
finally is the question, the paradoxical question: Is not the state of anxiety of the
existent regarding *Existenz,* in Nietzsche and in Kierkegaard, *'existentially'* a failing?"

Are not both of them essentially isolated, scarcely fitted for society or communication? Can not one say the same of Strindberg and Van Gogh? It is by ailing
geniuses that humanity advances toward the sources of experience. In the dramatic
and problematic condition of humanity, its fundamental revelations are due to
men who were not normal men.

this notion he has enabled us to approach the concrete, a concrete impossible to describe.[4] We can say at least that the self is a relation which is self-relating. Man is the relation of freedom and necessity, of time and the eternal, of the finite and the infinite. He is a self because he is the consciousness of this relationship and thus relates himself to himself.[5] This relationship is always becoming: it is something which must emerge, which has to emerge, rather than anything which, strictly speaking, is.[6]

The existent presents itself as an exception; and we know that Jaspers represents himself as philosophizing in the light of those two exceptions who were Kierkegaard and Nietzsche.[7]

The exception occurs in a century which looks flourishing but which is actually falling into ruin. The exception opposes his century on the matter of the depth of the totality and on the matter of profoundly historical, all-enveloping truth. The excep-

---

[4] Cf. *Wahrheit*, 543. "The being of *Existenz* cannot be expressed by a definable concept; for that would presuppose an object-being of some sort. The *word* is, to begin with, only one of those which designate being. From obscure beginnings this reality has emerged into history; but in philosophical thought it was no more than an adumbration until Kierkegaard gave it an historically compelling expression." (*Philosophie*, 13 note 1.)

[5] Cf. *Wahrheit*, 541. To the idea of *Existenz* may be connected, on the one hand, that of sin, and on the other hand, that of faith and freedom.

For Kierkegaard as for Jaspers sin is unthinkable: it is the inconceivable, the secret of the world, the irrational; and before our sinful *Existenz* we undergo a kind of penetrating anguish. The existent will feel infinitely distant from God because of his consciousness of sin. But it is by this distance from God that he will finally be able to approach Him. It is through sin that he will conceive and feel the category of "for God." And through sin is revealed the sphere of *Existenz*, of freedom, of faith.

As for freedom, we cannot define it satisfactorily. It is a unity of free will and necessity. For Jaspers as for Kierkegaard it is linked to the notion of a return to the origin (*Ursprung*).

As for faith, Jaspers like Kierkegaard opposes his immediacy to the mediation of knowledge. Faith is that in which I am authentically, in which I love and live, in which there are no more "whys."

The existent will be beyond good and evil. "Jesus stands beyond good and evil. Kierkegaard recognizes the absolute truth in the religious, by which one can undertake what he calls the suspension of the ethical. And Nietzsche too is at times oriented toward that authentic yonder which moves us to transcend good and evil." (*Wahrheit*, 599.)

[6] Cf. *Wahrheit*, 542.

[7] Here we detect a paradox. Jaspers himself is not an exception. Professor of philosophy, he philosophizes in the light of those two exceptions who were Kierkegaard and Nietzsche.

We may consider the philosophy of Jaspers as a sort of reflection on the case of Kierkegaard, a generalization, — in certain respects a profound generalization — of Kierkegaard, that is, in so far as he stands aside, in so far as he feels himself to be an exception, and in so far as he attains by his very narrowness more depth than other philosophers. Meditation on the case of Kierkegaard led Jaspers to the notion that the depth of a doctrine comes from its limitation, and meditation on

tion exhibits the impossibility of true classifications in the century in which he installs himself.[8]

For Kierkegaard it was a matter of taking upon oneself the fact of being an exception in its radical ambiguity, in that impossibility which it raises of locating oneself or of becoming a whole truth. The exception cannot accomplish what he must accomplish. There is a "closed-ness" about the exception which prevents him from bringing the general to expression. But his renunciation before the general, his action against the general, enables him to understand all the more clearly the exigencies of the general.[9] Like Nietzsche, Kierkegaard is the exception at the service of truth. His very particularity moves us to feel the universal. The unique situation, he tells us, becomes the illumination for the universal by means of the reality of the non-universal.[10] No rest is possible here. This is the abnormal, sickness, the thorn in the flesh which is to be the sign of his vocation. But the exception cannot know this, at least not with any scientific certitude. He may believe that he hears God, and go to a psychiatrist. He may simultaneously have a sense of his election and a sense of his perdition. "I do not know," said Kierkegaard, "whether there is a justified exception; but if there is one, he cannot himself have any assurance of his justification."[11] The exception cannot justify himself as exception. He must bend beneath the general which bruises or breaks him. He cannot justify himself, for one can justify himself only by means of the general.[12]

---

sin, doubtless also derived in part from reflection on Kierkegaard, leads him to say that limitation is sin. To deepen oneself by passionately limiting oneself, and to deepen oneself by becoming conscious of sin, are almost the same truth expressed in different ways. They are the two essential teachings which Jaspers derived from Kierkegaard and which he was skillful enough to fuse into a single idea.

Two philosophers, Kierkegaard and Nietzsche, gave us, at the close of the nineteenth century, a new conception of philosophy. In place of the peace offered by a Parmenides or a Spinoza, they have left us anguish. Both aspects must be preserved: the security of Spinoza as well as the anguish of Kierkegaard.

Objectively, says Jaspers, the exception is a deviation from the norm. 'Existentially' the exception is that which is closest to Being. Thus the exception isolates himself in order to unite with Transcendence.

The exception is not a *case*, strictly speaking, for it occurs only once. A Socrates, a Kierkegaard, stands outside the continuity of what is general. But by placing themselves outside the general, they represent reality better than many ordinary human beings. Kierkegaard knows himself to be outside the human community, and yet presents himself as the example of man in man's profound reality. Going further, one would see that every human being is at once the exception and the general. The exception only carries to the limit what is in each of us. It was Kierkegaard who said that it is equally true that every man represents the human in general and every man is an exception.

[8] Cf. *Wahrheit*, 764.   [9] Cf. *ibid.*, 754.   [10] Cf. *ibid.*, 753.

[11] Quoted by Jaspers, *ibid.*, 755.   [12] Cf. *ibid.*, 755.

We are in the realm which is without guarantees.[13] On the road of philosophy no *Existenz* in the world can have the last word.

The function of the exception, if one can speak of him as possessing a function, is to alert us. But in his desire to address others, the exception can only address indirectly; for direct expression would first of all run the risk of vanity, and secondly would deprive us of some of our freedom.

And yet, if we ask ourselves: Who is the exception? — we must reply: Not only Socrates, Kierkegaard, or Nietzsche, but the universal presence of every possible *Existenz (das Allgegenwärtige jeder möglichen Existenz)*.[14] Thus, the exception is not merely that rare event which occurs as a limit.[15]

And when the general finally expresses itself directly from the very bosom of the exception (see Kierkegaard at the end of his life) it has the force and the intensity — of an exception — wrought from the tension between the different and the same; for the exception feels himself infinitely different from others and infinitely like others.[16]

Kierkegaard insists on the notion of self-revelation, on '*existential*' manifestation, or rather '*existential*' open-ness. This is what opens up my possibilities for me. To be oneself, and to be open, are one and the same thing. The self is openness to itself.

Both Jaspers and Kierkegaard maintain that the evil man is self-enclosed, a prisoner of himself held captive by his melancholy and his despair. The path of the good is also the path of communication.[17] But there is an immurement in oneself which is legitimate and may be beneficial: that of Socrates. This self-enclosure is in part the explanation of indirect communication.

At the same time as he relates himself to himself,[18] the self relates himself to Transcendence. The self grasps himself as given

---

[13] Cf. *ibid.*, 965.   [14] Cf. *ibid.*, 759.   [15] Cf. ibid.

[16] Cf. ibid., 761.   [17] Cf. ibid., 544.

[18] And the more will there is, the more self there is. The self creates itself.

But one must also remember that the self is always in situation. Here again his meditation on Kierkegaard has oriented the thought of Jaspers. Do not all the Kierkegaardian concepts originate in a lived experience, the triple experience of his relation to his father, his relation to Regina, and his relation to God?

Jaspers finds in Kierkegaard not only the concept of situation, but also the reality of those ultimate situations which lead us toward Transcendence. In such situations, I accomplish unconditional and absolute actions, and in so far as I act unconditionally and love unconditionally, eternity is there, eternity is in time.

Existenz is always directed toward Transcendence. "Its authentic being consists in the search for Transcendence." And what is Transcendence? "There is Transcendence only by virtue of the reality of my unconditionality," says Jaspers. (*Wahrheit*, 632) This is certainly a thought which transmits one of Kierkegaard's

to himself, as flooded with himself, so to speak.[19] One could go from this idea to the realization that the self may have a grasp of eternity.[20] Finally, we would discover that Transcendence speaks by means of an existent like Kierkegaard.[21] And just as we have finished saying that the self increases with his self-consciousness, so now we can deepen this proposition by saying that the greater the accord with God, that is to say, with Transcendence, the greater the self.

Kierkegaard, like Nietzsche, is a tragic philosopher. This is to say that like everything tragic: — like the Greeks caught tragically between myth and a philosophy of enlightenment, like Eckhart between the Church and the freedom of the spirit, like German idealism between Christianity and Atheism, — both Kierkegaard and Nietzsche are the manifestations of a turning-point which achieves self-consciousness at the moment when an immense and terrible novelty begins to dawn upon it.[22]

There are philosophies of sublime austerity. They offer us absolute choices. The mediate is for them evil seduction, corruption, debilitation. They offer us alternatives, those of being and nothingness as in Parmenides, those of the God Creator and the world as in the severe view of primitive Judeo-Christianity, those of being and illusion as in Hindu philosophy. They show us the absolute decisions of totality, as in Kierkegaard. But their defect is that they are manifestations of the extreme. They cannot be incarnated in concrete life. They soar sublimely in the vacuous air. They are like lighthouses for all philosophical thought, helping us to find the truth, without being the goal. In philosophies of vaster design, the mean, the mediate, the mediator does not disappear: he is the path toward the truth. The alternatives remain, the extreme oppositions persist. The mediate does not destroy them, and he is open to them: he is the way. And even in Kierkegaard, there is a dialectical value to the mean, a speculative value to the mediator.

We spoke of the exception. Opposed to exception is authority. And yet we must see the deep associations between the exception and the authority, both grounded in Transcendence, both failing to achieve fulfillment, both profoundly historical, both eluding objectification. Neither exception nor authority can furnish the last

---

most profound conceptions. Transcendence is by virtue of my relation to it, yet in my relation to Transcendence I affirm that it is other than this relation. Such is the paradox of Transcendence.

[19] Cf. *Wahrheit*, 542.   [20] *Ibid.*   [21] Cf. *ibid.*, 754.

[22] Cf. *ibid.*, 905, 919.

word. The problem becomes even more acute when authority
takes on the guise which Jaspers calls "catholicity." He tells us
himself that he does not understand by this notion anything
essentially related to the Catholic Church, but only something
which can be perceived there, as elsewhere in various other
spiritual manifestations. Catholicity is essentially the affirmation
of an exclusive truth of revelation. This sense of catholicity is
incompatible with reason. From the standpoint of reason, catholicity must be maintained in the world; otherwise, there would no
longer be historicity, nor obstacle to act as a contrast and a stimulant to reason. Nevertheless, there is a contradiction between
catholicity and reason: one must choose in a "concrete collision."[23]
Since catholicity always has the better chance of dominating the
world and reason always threatens to disappear, the best course
is to give reason an opportunity to survive in each individual.
But it remains true that the absolute opposition between catholicity and reason is one of the fundamental contradictions which
show us the contradictory essence of all appearance in time. We
must not permit either alternative to disappear, even though we
must protect ourselves, that is, protect one of the alternatives,
reason, against catholicity.

Jaspers does not believe that there is the same contradiction
between authority and reason that he finds between catholicity
and reason. "To think authority by means of reason makes possible obedience for him who philosophizes."[24] Philosophy wishes
to preserve authority wherever it finds a content to authority.
There is no life without an authority for all. Even for the philosopher, authority must have an insuperable privilege: "Authority
must persist as the unsuperable source of confidence."[25] Truth is
said to have an "authoritative" ground.[26] In the last analysis, it
is no longer a question of an authority without catholicity, but
of a relative catholicity.[27]

There remain questions which might be posed to Jaspers:
What are the "authoritative" grounds of truth? What is a relative
catholicity? Is not the notion contradictory? No doubt Jaspers
would reply in terms analogous to these: "At this limit of the
mysterious openness we stand as if on the shore of that sea which
is Being itself, either prepared to take haven in port, or impelled
to sail toward the high seas where lies the homeland of our
essence, the source of all being."[28]

This discussion enables us to broach the question of the rela-

23 *Ibid.*, 865.   24 Ibid.   25 *Ibid.*, 866.
26 *Ibid.*   27 Cf. *ibid.*, 868.   28 Ibid., 748.

tionship between Jaspers and Christianity, in so far as Christianity is implied in the message of Kierkegaard. There is a difference, at least in appearance, between the philosopher Jaspers and that source of philosophy who is Kierkegaard. For the latter has a model, Jesus and an authority, the Scriptures. He has a revelation historically granted. But is not this difference superficial, compared to the resemblances? Only subjectivity can say. Who gives authority to the authority? Who is to say that it is God who speaks? Kierkegaard, Abraham? There is a self-examination by the subject. There is a responsibility assumed by the subject in his solitude and anguish. There is risk, risk infinite.[29]

If Jaspers avows himself against any Christianity of dogmatic content, his disagreement with Kierkegaard, he tells us, is only apparent: "Despite Kierkegaard's powerful auto-destructive faith in Christ, analogous to his other negative decisions and fundamentally anti-ecclesiastical, Kierkegaard was indeed the first to overcome the Christianity of dogmatic content."[30] "It was the merit or the destiny of Kierkegaard to have dispelled the lack of clarity which surrounds the faith of whoever thinks himself a Christian."[31]

Kierkegaard drew from Christianity its negative consequences: the idea of martyrdom, the negative decision not to adapt himself to reality in a career and marriage, the decision to destroy understanding. But, inquires Jaspers, is this negative interpretation satisfactory? Christianity has, after all, been a "mundane" development.[32] Jaspers finds it necessary to go even further. This Christianity which has endured through the centuries is not founded on Jesus, but on a faith which refers itself to Jesus as a source of catholicity, which refers itself to Christ as to God, but not to the imitation of Jesus as a man.

I may see dishonesty in the adaptation of Christianity to the world, in the accord between Christianity and culture, in the accommodation of religious faith to philosophy by means of Christian theology, I may see all that as the inevitable consequence of the founding of a cathol-

---

[29] Cf. *ibid.*, 965.   [30] *Ibid.*, 853.   [31] *Ibid.*, 854.

[32] Kierkegaard appeals to the founder of the Church's authority, Jesus. But thus he abstracts deliberately from the succession of the centuries and from the Church itself. He does not take account of the fact that Christianity is a relation to God across the centuries, and he wants to make us contemporaries of Jesus over and above the centuries in which the Church evolved, thus adopting again the point of view of the exception.

Theory of *Existenz* and faith in the God-man can be linked in Kierkegaard. If he is able to connect these notions, it is by virtue of his theory of paradox. And the consequence of establishing this link was an abandonment by Kierkegaard of what he called "Christendom" and the Church. (Cf. *Philosophie*, 271f).

icity on an impossibility. But it does not follow that I do not see the great achievements, that I do not myself live in terms of these achievements, which developed in the soil of a radical inconsistency in an infinite torment of impossibility.[33]

This is to say that the unconditioned unity cannot be attained in this world, and can only be based on an *'existential'* irruption.

The transformation of the God-man into myth — a transformation which properly speaking was not completely accomplished by Jesus: "Why do you call me Good? No one is good outside of the one God" — is the destruction of the truth which was manifested.[34]

These considerations must be completed, moreover, by views of other religions in which the sacred is grasped in other ways. "Christianity ushered in the most deeply grounded catholicity, the grandest in appearance, but catholicity is everywhere."[35] We should ask whether this last assertion can have meaning for a given individual, since the essence of catholicity is to present itself as not being everywhere. Jaspers strives to direct us toward a flexible catholicity which would manifest itself in various expressions and modes of life, and which would be, each time, the manifestation of unity. But is this supple catholicity possible?

We have compared Kierkegaard and Nietzsche, in following Jaspers, on numerous points. But one should also compare Kierkegaard and Marx; for, like Marx, Kierkegaard turns the gaze of man toward action. The one, however, directs man toward social action, the other directs him toward the *Existenz* of the individual and toward the internal deed.[36] We shall best understand Kierkegaard by taking different perspectives, by aligning him now with Nietzsche, now with Marx, now with Plato, now with Kant. And we shall thus conform to the universal maxim, that the one God, as well as the one Kierkegaard, cannot be reached by a single path.

The drive toward unity can only be realized in the totality, on the basis of historical depth, in the apprehension of all that can be thought and all that can be experienced.[37]

Philosophy arouses, makes vigilant, indicates paths, guides for awhile, readies, makes ripe, that we may experience the extreme.[38]

---

[33] *Wahrheit*, 855.   [34] *Ibid.*   [35] *Ibid.*, 856-866.
[36] Cf. *ibid.*, 312.   [37] *Ibid.*, 1053.

[38] *Ibid.*, 1054. Philosophies of *Existenz* retained from Kierkegaard's philosophy the ideas of solitude, of anguish, of subjectivity, of abandonment, of care, and of death. There is not a single idea of existentialist philosophy whose origin could not be traced to Kierkegaardian thought. Jaspers develops, annotates, sometimes deepens the thought of the union of *Existenz* and Transcendence, the will to go to the origin, to the source *(Ursprung)*. When Jaspers says that the particular is above the general, when he speaks of the unconditionality of the decisive instant,

II. JASPERS, HEIDEGGER, AND BEING.

We shall now attempt to show that certain thoughts of Heidegger in *Holzwege*[39] concur with many ideas delineated or predelineated by Karl Jaspers in his *Philosophie*.[40] In two of the most important ventures in contemporary ontology, we find ourselves in the presence of closely related problems and very similar solutions.

We have more in mind than certain important ideas regarding truth which these philosophers have in common. It is true that both believe the classical theories mistaken in seeing truth as belonging essentially to the domain of judgement, and both look for truth in something prior to judgement which is Being itself. For both philosophers this theory of ontological truth is connected with a theory of *'existential'* truth. Since truth is prior to understanding, truth may involve the presence, at times even the pre-eminence, of feeling.[41] We have more in mind, also, than simply

when he tells us that no one can put himself in our place, when he presents *Existenz* as deciding its eternity in time, when he sees in *Existenz* the paradox of a unity of temporality and eternity, when he defines faith as the immediacy of *Existenz*, when he shows us that in the most *'existential'* moments we have the double feeling of a passivity with respect to a superior force and at the same time a sense of extreme activity, and that we have a third feeling which tells us that all our activity is as nothing compared to this superior force — these are all affirmations which remind us of Kierkegaard. It is man as Kierkegaard describes him which nourishes the thought of Jaspers, man as the solitary existent who, confronting Transcendence, ceaselessly has first the feeling of sin, then the feeling of redemption from sin.

In Kierkegaard and Nietzsche, Jaspers tells us, the modern world becomes conscious of its failure. In them modernity denies itself and wishes to return, in Kierkegaard, to the primitive Christian vision, in Nietzsche, to a pre-Socratic ideal. This is the modern world's way of getting rid of itself and rediscovering being.

Kierkegaard is an example of the failure of *Existenz*. To measured ethics he opposes the demand of unconditionality. We want the impossible, we want finiteness: hence the failure.

But this downfall is not the last word. No doubt we witness the ruination of everything supreme. An infinite anguish arises. But the course of Jaspers' thought again follows that of Kierkegaard. If anguish settled into itself, it would become something static and would lose its authenticity. Therefore, one must make the leap which goes from anguish to *calm* and which enables us to see the transfigured reality of the world.

Jaspers believes that the thought of Kierkegaard, and even that of Nietzsche, must be taken less as something given and static than as a sign of that which infinitely surpasses us. Each liberates us without setting us to any narrowly defined tasks. They are educators; not educators in any doctrine which they expound or impose, but educators within our own becoming, within our very being. Through them we can nourish and develop in ourselves the passion of thought, the passion of interrogation, and, at the same time, affirm the unthinkable.

[39] Frankfurt a/Main (1950).   [40] Berlin (1948, 2nd unrev. ed.).

[41] I take the liberty of calling attention on this point to my *La Pensee de l'Existence* (Paris, 1952), 241-243. (Henceforth abbreviated: *PE*).

a theory of the world. Each finds behind the world, as it is conceived by science, an idea, or more precisely a universal feeling of the world which would be the world felt, the world in its entirety; or, even better, not the world, but its ground. Nor do we have in mind only that sense of the incalculable, as Heidegger would say, of the unpredictable, in Jaspers' way of speaking, whose meaning is associated by Jaspers with the just mentioned idea of the world. The felt world alluded to is, according to Jaspers, the other in its unpredictability.[42] This notion of the other recurs several times in Jaspers. The being of Transcendence is not only being, but being and its other. The other is obscurity, ground, matter, nothingness.[43] We could pass, then, to Jaspers' notion of an irreducible ground of nothingness on which existence irrupts, to his notion of "the passion for the night," and to his idea of Nothingness, and thus establish additional possibilities of comparison between Jaspers and Heidegger. The theory of truth leads of its own accord to a theory of being: Being is not produced by us; Being is not simply an interpretation; rather Being is in a certain sense that which produces our interpretation or our judgement by its impact. Judgements have meaning and content only by virtue of the action of that other by which they fill themselves, from which they come, and toward which they proceed.[44] On the other hand, I know that being is not given to me; rather I am given to me. Grasping in myself the other, in so far as I am given to myself, in so far as clarity arises from an obscure depth and "choices" arise from an invincible given, and grasping the other above me in so far as I orient myself toward Transcendence, I am always in a relation to being.[45] *Existenz* exists only by opposition to Transcendence and, at the same time, by its relation to it. And Transcendence is Being: We come to the view, therefore, that *Existenz* exists only by its separation from Being and by its union with Being.

Let us first note the separation. "*Existenz* is the reality which essentially maintains its distance and . . . rejects identification with Transcendence . . . . Here, in radical nearness is revealed most clearly the absolutely remote."[46]

Now let us observe their union. We should say a word here on the theory of existence (*Dasein*). However different may be the *Dasein* (existence) of Jaspers and the *Dasein* of Heidegger, for both philosophers the *Dasein* is the luminous point at which the universe opens. If it is self-clarification, this is because the

42 Cf. *PE*, 247.   43 Cf. *ibid.*, 211.   44 Cf. *ibid.*, 243.
45 Cf. *ibid.*, 212.   46 *Philosophie*, 730.

Dasein (existence) is a luminous point in which the obscurity of a bottomless doubt brings itself to itself and thereby also makes the world appear.[47] The *Dasein* becomes the fact, the revelation that "it is there," and the cipher of absolute presence and absolute historicity.[48] But just as the *Dasein* discloses being, so it hides being. The fact discloses itself, yet veils itself mysteriously. *Existenz* is indeed linked to being, according to Jaspers and Heidegger, but the being which it seeks can only be a being lost.

What has been said from the standpoint of *Existenz,* could be said even more cogently from the standpoint of being, to whatever extent we can dimly make out the point of view of being. We said that we maintain our distance from being; but when in greatest proximity it is the unique divinity that maintains its absolute distance. The solution is not an object of cognition; it lies in the Being which remains hidden. That Being gazes at him who, at his own risk, approaches.[49] If Being is lost, therefore, Being must itself have willed to be lost. We said that the *Dasein* hides Being; but it is in some manner by the will to being that *Dasein* hides Being.

Transcendence is mirrored by irreducibly diverse *Existenzen,* ricochets off them. If true Being is one, but in such a way that knowledge of this One falsifies, then as a temporal being here and now true Being can only appear to shine forth from (existence) *Dasein* to *Dasein* (existence).[50] We shall have occasion to say a few words on the difference between historicity, particularly the historicity of philosophy, as conceived by Jaspers, and historicity as it is conceived by Heidegger; but we may observe that for both there is a donation of being itself to every existence — *Dasein* (or to the *Dasein*). We are faced here with one of the ultimate problems of the philosophy of Jaspers. Transcendence lacks the generality which pertains to the truths which are thought by consciousness-as-such. Transcendence is the particular-general, the unthinkable unity of the particular and the general.[51] "The paradox of Transcendence is that it can only be *grasped historically,* but cannot be adequately conceived as *being itself historical.*"[52] Transcendence lacks the historicity which belongs to truths thought by consciousness-as-such; nor is Transcendence the concrete universal of Hegelianism. However much beyond the historicity which characterizes *Existenz,* Transcendence unquestionably seems, to us in Heidegger's language, to give itself historically to *Existenz.*[53] Thus, we never see Transcendence except in its contradictory and vanish-

47 Cf. *PE.,* 245.   48 Cf. *ibid.,* 231.   49 Cf. *ibid.*
50 Cf. *ibid.,* 120.   51 Cf. *Philosophie,* 694.   52 *Ibid.*
53 Cf. *PE.,* 221.

ing traces which scarcely can make their mark in space to endure in time.[54] The One must not be sought where the idealists and the positivists seek it, for it will not reveal itself in the guise of a unique world or unique truth.[55] Transcendence is something more general than *Existenz*. Transcendence is something absolutely historic, in which the historical achieves its supreme degree of historicity. There is an unthinkable union of uniqueness and generality which expresses itself in irreconcilable and opposed forms.[56] One cannot help but compare these ideas of Jaspers to Heidegger's conception of the history of philosophy, according to which each of the phases reveals an aspect of the One. But, whereas for Heidegger these various aspects depend above all on the phase of thought in which they take place and are always, even from the beginning, stages of decline to the point today of complete decadence and nihilism — perhaps auguring a new dawn —, these aspects depend, according to Jaspers, on existing personalities and sometimes unite us with the absolute, the Transcendent itself. (But it should be observed regarding this last point that for Heidegger too an identity appears through this variety of phases, and that in a sense Leibniz and Hegel — or to choose extreme examples, Anaximander and Nietzsche — acknowledge a similar reality.) The problem of the One and the many cannot be resolved in intellectual terms. Behind the differences we detect feelings of an identity, and *Existenz* remains always the same behind its numerous masks. Though its forms are infinitely various, the truths of *Existenz* are not multiple. One encounters an unthinkable unity. "The absolute unattainability of the distant Unity," says Jaspers, "forces us to seek communication in things most distant from each other."[57] The flame of my *Existenz* flares up in contact with other *Existenzen*.

In both philosophers we are again faced with a like problem. Are not the *Dasein* of Heidegger and the *Existenz* of Jaspers on the verge of becoming absorbed in *Sein,* and vice versa? Do we not end in a kind of pantheistic monism? Are not *Existenz* and Transcendence in Jaspers more closely united than Jaspers sometimes seems to say? Finally the distinctions drawn between them seem almost to vanish, though without leading for all that to a total disappearance of the notion that *Existenz* is oriented toward its other.[58] What being is, abstracted from its existence *(Dasein),* cannot be grasped by us. Thus we go beyond *Existenz* — without surpassing it, however — because there is no Transcendence except for *Existenz*.[59] Let us recall also that Transcendence, however

54 Cf. *ibid.,* 222.   55 Cf. *Philosophie,* 778; also *PE,* 215.   56 Cf. *PE,* 219.
57 Cf. *ibid.,* 215.   58 Cf. *PE.,* 215.   59 Cf. *ibid.,* 258.

much an absolute separated absolutely from everything else, is an absolute which envelops everything else.[60] Moreover, Transcendence is that which is itself apart from an other, but at the same time we must not ask what Transcendence, God, may be apart from God.[61]

All this is: *thinking*, in Heidegger's sense of the term, but also in Jaspers' sense. We must not invoke reason here.[62] This is a thinking by which one strives to think the unthinkable, a non-thinking thought by which I make contact with the other.[63] It is a thinking, adds Jaspers, which is filled by non-thought[64] (an emendation which Heidegger would not make).

This parallelism of ideas passes over into a parallelism of feelings, whether with regard to modesty,[65] the clairvoyance of patience,[66] or a "seductive terror" before the completely hostile, before the utterly foreign element which can transform itself into the most intimate.[67] And beyond all these feelings we find the feeling of mystery, the "it is thus."[68] Jaspers no less than Heidegger is inspired by meditation on Van Gogh and on Nietzsche. Then future and past meet. I sense a being which as past comes to me from the future, or a being which I recall by anticipation. For Jaspers there is a grasp of the future through memory, as there is for Heidegger when he discusses Hölderlin.[69]

No doubt defeat is everywhere, the defeat of the cipher, essentially ambiguous,[70] the defeat of the various ontologies (and, like Heidegger, Jaspers is particularly severe with Descartes), and of ontology itself. We are faced with an ontology which is, so to speak, seriously disabled, a dysontology. This explains Jaspers' tendency to replace it with what he calls a theory of the Encompassing *(das Umgreifende)*, or "periechontology,"[71] though perhaps with no greater success; for the interrelationships of the various Encompassings and their relation to the whole eludes us and must elude us.

But it is in this very defeat that truth opens itself before us. In disaster we experience Being.

We have already drawn attention to the principal differences which cannot be overcome, e.g., Heidegger's distinctions between the phases of the history of philosophy and Jaspers' conception of

60 Cf. *ibid.*, 277.
61 Cf. *Philosophie*, 816.
62 Cf. *PE.*, 218.
63 Cf. *Philosophie*, 520, 707.
64 Cf. *PE.*, 217.
65 Cf. *ibid.*, 216.

66 Cf. *ibid.*, 229.
67 Cf. *ibid.*, 216.
68 Cf. *ibid.*, 218.
69 Cf. *ibid.*, 230.
70 Cf. *ibid.*, 228.
71 Cf. *Wahrheit*, 158-161.

the various ways of grasping being by certain *'existential'* personalities. (Although even here one could find analogies beneath the differences.)

The idea of *Existenz* offers Jaspers a solution which Heidegger does not permit himself. For both, the One as limit, the transcendent unity, is the One which I am not at all; for both, it is at the same time the being by which I am. But for Jaspers it is the being in relation to which I stand when I stand in relation to my self as identical self *(Existenz)*. Each individual attains Transcendence only by immersing himself in that which is most specific in his vision of the world.[72] "In transcendence I attain only that which I myself become."[73] Thus, *Existenz* and Transcendence tend to be more closely identified by Jaspers than by Heidegger. But the *Dasein* of Heidegger, we should add, is not entirely separated from *Sein;* it is rather the case that the union in Heidegger is more ontological than *'existential.'*

We have endeavored to cast into relief certain similarities between Jaspers and Heidegger. Has there not been something arbitrary about our undertaking? In order to effect these comparisons, we have sometimes violently separated certain affirmations from their contexts. It remains to be seen whether we have fulfilled our hope of respecting the essence of each of these two philosophies. We leave that decision to the judgment of others.

JEAN WAHL

UNIVERSITY OP PARIS

[72] Cf. *PE.*, 214-216.   [73] *Ibid.*, 223.

10

Walter Kaufmann

JASPERS' RELATION TO NIETZSCHE

J ASPERS' conception of Nietzsche is of unusual interest for a
number of reasons, apart from the fact that Jaspers himself
has suggested the topic. Most obviously, it throws light on the
philosophy of Jaspers, who has always closely related his own work
to Nietzsche's, besides devoting two whole books to him, including
a comprehensive 400 page study. Then, Jaspers' *Nietzsche* is unquestionably one of the most competent and suggestive interpretations; hence the discussion should also throw light on Nietzsche,
and a critique of Jaspers' view requires some discussion of Nietzsche's historical significance. Finally, any reflection on these two
German-born Basel professors will focus some of the development
of modern German thought. *Of the Use and Disadvantage of History,* published after the Franco-Prussian War, in 1874, and *The
Origin and Goal of History,* published after the second World
War, in 1949, frame an epoch; and we shall give attention to at
least some characteristic facets of the broader cultural context of
Jaspers' relation to Nietzsche. Germany's military and political
fortunes during this time are better known than her philosophic
career, but both agree in encountering less and less understanding
and sympathy abroad. Jaspers is surely far removed from recent
nationalistic aspirations and outrages, yet his work is less European, less international than Nietzsche's. This is not a function of
his intentions any more than of his stature; more nearly of his
style. Against his will, his work seems another manifestation of
Germany's withdrawal from the West, her departure from traditions once shared with France and Britain.

1. *Jaspers' General Attitude toward Nietzsche — and Kant.*

Recently, Jaspers has characterized his relation to Nietzsche as
follows:

Kant became for me, and remained for me, the philosopher *par excel-*

lence. . . . Nietzsche became important to me only late — as the magnificent revelation of nihilism and of the task of going beyond nihilism.[1]

An epigram will oversimplify and yet elucidate: for Jaspers, Nietzsche's philosophy is the handmaiden of Kant's postulational theology; or if not the *ancilla,* the revelation of the realm beyond which one encounters Kant.

As an admirer of the philosophy of the categorical imperative, Jaspers naturally respects Nietzsche, the man, not as a means only but also as an end. Yet the passage just quoted proceeds: "In my youth I had avoided him, repelled by the extreme, by the frenzy, and by his multiplicity." Nietzsche's Dionysian philosophy has never been accepted by Jaspers as an end: he values it as a means, as a steppingstone toward his own existentialism. Failure to recognize this bars any adequate understanding of Jaspers' *Existenzphilosophie.* In the search for precursors, he has too often been pictured as the spiritual progeny of Kierkegaard and Nietzsche. Actually, Jaspers might be called one of the most original of the neo-Kantians, albeit widely separated from the school associated with that label, not only by virtue of his general impatience with philosophic schools and the philosophy taught at universities (he calls it "professors' philosophy"), but also because his point of departure is not the *Critique of Pure Reason,* nor even that of *Judgment,* but decidedly the *Critique of Practical Reason.*

Jaspers' concern has always been less with theory of knowledge or aesthetics than with the "practical" in Kant's sense — the realm of decision, freedom, and faith. And even as Kant "had to do away with knowledge to make room for faith," Jaspers values Nietzsche in large measure because he did away with knowledge — probably

---

1 "Über meine Philosophie" (1941) in *Rechenschaft* (1951), 339. Since the present contribution was first written in 1952, a complete translation of Jaspers' essay has appeared in *Existentialism from Dostoevsky to Sartre,* edited, with an introduction, prefaces, and notes, by Walter Kaufmann (Meridian Books 1956).

All translations in the present essay are my own. A few of them have appeared previously in my *Nietzsche: Philosopher, Psychologist, Antichrist* (Princeton University Press 1950; rev. ed, Meridian Books 1956) and in *The Portable Nietzsche,* selected and translated, with an introduction, prefaces, and notes, by Walter Kaufmann (The Viking Press 1954).

A list of some essays in which I have further developed my conception of Nietzsche may be found in the Meridian edition of my *Nietzsche,* p. 363. Cf. also my article on Nietzsche in the new edition of *Encyclopaedia Britannica.*

A detailed comparison of Jaspers' *Nietzsche* and mine has appeared in *Les Temps Modernes,* May 1951, pp. 1921-1954: "Nietzsche aujourd'hui" by J. Vuillemin. His account of my intentions is very good, but he overlooks Jaspers' debt to Kant and mistakes Jaspers' faith for a "resurrection of Christianity." In fact, Jaspers' religion is not oriented toward Christ; and in his philosophy of history, too, Jaspers does not find the "pivot" of history in the Incarnation but in the age of the Hebrew prophets, the Greek philosophers, Confucius, Lao-tse, and the Buddha.

more radically, and certainly more obviously and unacademically, than Kant had done — thus making room for Jaspers' "philosophic faith."

This diagnosis implies that Jaspers' conception of Nietzsche is an integral part of Jaspers' philosophy, not an external accretion. But it also means that Nietzsche's philosophy is accepted only as an antechamber. Would Nietzsche have been happy with this approach? Of course, he fancied himself as a Socrates who exhorted his pupils to go beyond him, creating their own philosophies: "One repays a teacher badly, if one always remains a pupil only." (Zarathustra) Even so, it would undoubtedly have struck him as a preposterous irony, had he seen his thought reduced to a doormat for the edifice of Kantianism — or to a labyrinth which one enters only to become convinced that there is no way out except Kant's Indian rope-trick. For Kant throws his postulates of practical reason into the air and uses them to climb out of sight into the transcendent realm, to God, while most of the onlookers rub their eyes, incapable of explaining how the feat was performed, and wondering, perhaps, whether it was a matter of hypnotic suggestion — a trick protected by Kant's unique prestige.

Nietzsche saw himself as a "herald and precursor" of the "philosophers of the future" (Beyond Good and Evil) — not of Kant's postulates of God, freedom, and immortality. In fact, just this "practical philosophy" was what he could not forgive Kant and what he never tired of deriding.

I bear the Germans a grudge for having made such a mistake about Kant and his "backdoor philosophy," as I call it — for that was not the type of intellectual integrity.[2]

All these great enthusiasts and prodigies behave like our little females: they consider "beautiful sentiments" adequate arguments, regard a heaving bosom as the bellows of the deity, and conviction a criterion of truth. In the end, Kant tried, with "German" innocence, to give this corruption, this lack of any intellectual conscience, scientific status with his notion of "practical reason;" he invented a special kind of reason for cases in which one need not bother about reason — that is, when morality, when the sublime command "thou shalt," raises its voice. When we consider that among almost all peoples the philosopher is merely the next development of the priestly type, then this legacy of the priest, self-deceiving counterfeit, ceases to be surprising.[3]

2 Götzen-Dämmerung, IX 16. I am citing Nietzsche according to the numbers of the aphorisms or sections, not of the pages which differ from one edition to another.

3 Antichrist, 12.

And in the immediately preceding aphorism, Nietzsche even writes: "Kant became an idiot."

Jaspers has criticized Nietzsche for lacking respect for greatness, and cited his outbursts against Kant. Yet it should be noted that Nietzsche often expressed his respect for Kant. What enraged him was that Kant should have followed up his first *Kritik* with the second: the "invention" of "the transcendent world."[4] How, then, would he have felt about Jaspers' suggestion that it is Nietzsche's great value to prepare us for the necessity of a Kantian faith?[5]

So far, we have rather oversimplified Jaspers' relation to Nietzsche, and somewhat exaggerated his debt to Kant. In a general preamble that may be pardonable, but we must now proceed to a more detailed account. We shall begin with Jaspers' *Psychologie der Weltanschauungen* (1919) which is more Nietzschean, and less Kantian, than his later work.

2. *Psychologie der Weltanschauungen.*

This books deals with a fascinating but little explored topic. Where one would usually raise questions of truth and falsity, it is the psychological background of different outlooks which is probed here: "psychology" in Nietzsche's sense. Even more crucial is the precedent set by Nietzsche in offering descriptive analyses which are simultaneously appeals to the reader: a type is depicted in such a manner that we should recognize some of its features in ourselves and either renounce them with indignant disgust or develop a burning aspiration to realize them more fully. This kind of psychology wants to implant, or strengthen, a deep dissatisfaction with our present state of being. It aims to pierce the soul as an "arrow of longing." *(Zarathustra)*

Jaspers himself seems to have become fully conscious of this only at a much later date. Thus he writes in 1941, in his essay "Über meine Philosophie:"

> In *Psychologie der Weltanschauungen* . . . I believed that I let pass in pure contemplation what occurs; yet, as a matter of fact, I projected the one truth of human existence which was peculiarly mine . . . and

4 *Wille zur Macht,* 578.

5 The Kantianism of Jaspers' "philosophic faith" is well expressed at the beginning of the chapter on "Faith and Englightenment" in *Einführung in die Philosophie:* "We have pronounced principles of philosophic faith: God is; there is the unconditional demand . . . Not one of these five principles is provable like finite knowledge of objects in the world. . . . They are not valid as something professed, but remain, in spite of the strength of being believed, in the suspension of that which is not known." *Wisdom,* 85.

everywhere I showed the current of that which falls off from, empties of content, or perverts this norm. It was hidden philosophy which here misunderstood itself as objectively descriptive psychology.[6]

In the same paragraph, Jaspers calls the book "an overbearing work of youth, whose contents, indeed, I still recognize as mine, but whose form was inadequate." But did Jaspers later find a more adequate form, when he moved away from psychology to straight-forward philosophy? Is his subsequent *Existenzerhellung* (1932) a more satisfactory mode of illuminating possibilities of human existence? To point out that his later efforts are thinner, because lacking in the wealth of concrete illustrations, does not answer this question. But perhaps it was wrong in principle for Jaspers, who had started as a psychiatrist and first published *Allgemeine Psychopathologie* (1913), to renounce psychology more and more, moving gradually from Nietzsche's psychologically penetrating philosophy to Kant's. For all his greatness, Kant is open to attack precisely for his sweeping disregard of psychology and his pointed-ly unempirical approach to the human mind. To throw light on human potentialities and to fashion an arrow of longing, Nietz-sche's example might have served Jaspers far better. Not to speak of Nietzsche's style.

Even *Psychologie der Weltanschauungen* culminates in an "Ap-pendix: Kant's Doctrine of Ideas," and is, of course, much less "overbearing" than Nietzsche's psychological etchings with their bold, sharply defined lines. Those, however, who consider it main-ly a progeny of Dilthey's psychologizing overlook the central call to the reader: the work does not want merely to add to our in-formation; it wants to change us. And what it leads toward is not the Christianity of Kierkegaard, who occasionally attempted some-thing similar, but a state of being which is, no less than the method employed, very close to the spirit of Nietzsche.

Beyond all this, the book abounds in important parallels to Nietzsche. At the very outset, for example, there is a distinction which comes straight out of Nietzsche:

> Philosophers have not only been calm, irresponsible contemplators, but movers and shapers of the world. This philosophy we call *pro-phetic philosophy*. It confronts universal contemplation as something essentially different because it *gives Weltanschauung*, shows sense and meaning, and sets up tables of values as norms, as valid. This philoso-phy alone would deserve the name of philosophy, if the name were to retain its noble, powerful ring. (p. 2)

[6] *Op. cit.*, 362.

This recalls *Beyond Good and Evil,* 211, which culminates in the claim: "The philosophers, properly, however, are commanders and legislators." Even Jaspers' subsequent complaint that "today there is no longer any prophetic philosophy" can be found in Nietzsche's aphorism; only Nietzsche is still more resigned and questions whether any philosopher has ever perfectly represented the prophetic type: "Are there such philosophers today? Have there been such philosophers yet? *Must* there not be such philosophers?"

As a second parallel, take Jaspers' use of Nietzsche's psychology of the will to power and of his conception of *ressentiment:*

Our present psychological task is precisely to abstract, as far as possible, from the mass appearance of that which is not genuine, while giving the relatively genuine forms of *Weltanschauung* psychological clarity and formulation. The genuine forms are those from which all those which are not genuine have also borrowed their spirit. When one sees the genuine, one needs only to know the universal mechanisms of those processes which lead to the not genuine, in order to survey the multiplicity of actual human existence. These processes . . . are, for example, the utilization of doctrines for self-justification and for one's justification in the eyes of others. Principles are thus made to serve for an apology, *ex post facto,* for something which originated from quite different sources. Among the oppressed, such an apology employs the doctrines of *ressentiment* which, by a revaluation, change the weak and bad into the stronger and better. Among dominant types, it employs the legitimistic doctrines of race, history, and superior ability to gain recognition for their power and their exercise of force as something that is right, and to permit themselves to experience it as right. These processes have as their ultimate source some drive for power which can appropriate any contents of any *Weltanschauung* in quite different ways, too, to win out, as the case may be, through *esprit,* profundity, or dialectical superiority. Thus all contents of the spirit are, as it were, a mere arsenal of arms to give oneself significance. (p. 37)

This is surely straight Nietzsche, and the absence of any express acknowledgment is probably motivated by the feeling that the debt is obvious enough to render specific references overly pedantic: words like *Ressentiment, Umwertung,* and *Macht* automatically remind the German reader of Nietzsche.

A sweeping acknowledgment to Nietzsche may serve as our third example. At the beginning of the section on "Types of Philosophic Thinking" Jaspers writes:

The psychologically significant directions of thinking could, of course, be made evident with reference to any thinking whatever. We choose the pre-Socratics on account of their relative simplicity, on account of their greatness, and above all on account of Nietzsche's example; for he used them to demonstrate the types of philosophic personalities. (p. 204)

And in a footnote on the next page:

The following account rests chiefly on the following sources: Diels, *Fragmente der Vorsokratiker,* and Nietzsche, *Die Philosophie im tragischen Zeitalter der Griechen.*

In other words, the account is based "chiefly" on the fragments themselves and on Nietzsche's interpretations. Of the following ten pages which cover Greek philosophy from Thales to Aristotle, four pages are devoted to Heraclitus, and Jaspers' intense admiration for him is even more obvious than Nietzsche's.

Jaspers' view of Aristotle is no less striking. It is as negative as a popular misconception pictures Nietzsche's. Actually, it recalls Nietzsche's jibes at later Alexandrian erudition. Jaspers finds Aristotle "without original, creative vision" and merely "the eternal type of the great scholar." And the chapter ends: "Jacob Burckhardt had a contempt for Aristotle." There is, to put it mildly, no indication that Jaspers differs from Burckhardt. Nor has he changed his mind since. In one of his most recent works, we encounter an eloquent omission of Aristotle's name. Jaspers enumerates the world historical contributions of the Greeks during the period from 800 B. C. to 200 B. C.: "Greece saw Homer; the philosophers, Parmenides, Heraclitus, Plato; the tragedians; Thucydides and Archimedes."[7] Later in the same volume (p. 147), Jaspers concedes: "From Aristotle one learns the categories which dominate all occidental thinking since. He has determined the language (the terminology) of philosophizing—" but Jaspers adds significantly: "whether one thinks with him, or against him, or in such a manner that one overcomes this whole plain of philosophizing." Here Jaspers suggests clearly that he is breaking with the main stream of Western philosophy, although he himself may consider it a "falling off" from, or a "perversion" of, the true line which leads from Heraclitus and Plato to Kierkegaard and Nietzsche. But the view of Plato and Nietzsche implicit in this conception is open to question; and we shall try to show later how Nietzsche is really much more in the tradition from which Jaspers would dissociate him.

In the next section of *Psychologie der Weltanschauungen,* the

[7] *Einführung* (1950), 96. (Cf. *Wisdom,* 100.)

very title, at least in German, at once brings Nietzsche to mind:
"Valuations and Tables of Values." So does the discussion in which
Nietzsche is soon mentioned explicitly. Again, the descriptive account is heavy with valuational overtones which further strengthen
the association with Nietzsche. Thus the four cardinal virtues are
traced from Plato, via Cicero, to Christianity, until the knowledge
of God becomes

> conditional upon grace and at the same time, in its contents, unfree
> and churchly. . . . The width and freedom of Plato is replaced by a
> narrow otherworldliness; Plato's integration of everything, by suppres-
> sion and elimination of drives and of what is worldly. (p. 223)

A page later, we hear "how Aristotle already had shallowed the
conception of measure into that of a mean between two extremes."
Then "the doctrine that happiness is the highest good" is depicted
— from Nietzsche's, rather than Kant's, point of view — as "a doctrine to renounce enthusiasm, to affirm mere existence *(Dasein)*,
while undercutting life as a process; everything is to remain as it
is." (p. 227) We are thus urged to reject this view, not because it
is incompatible with sheer respect for duty, but because it is said
to lead to a Stoic acceptance of the *status quo* and is hence considered incompatible with the desire to raise one's state of being.
Kant, as a matter of fact, is specifically commended here — but for
rather Nietzschean reasons.

As the final instance from this section, consider Jaspers' characterization of a type with which he clearly identifies himself: "He
does not crawl off into the shell *(Gehäuse)* of a determinate value
hierarchy." (p. 228) The conception of the shell is one of the key
ideas of the book, and the phrase quoted leaves little doubt concerning Jaspers' opinion of those who, unlike Nietzsche, make
their home in such a construct.

Next, let us consider two contrasts which closely parallel Nietzschean suggestions. Jaspers introduces his section on "Skepticism
and Nihilism" with the declaration: "The first and the very last
question concerning *Weltanschauung* is whether one says Yes or
No to life as a whole." (p. 285) Nietzsche's name is encountered
only a page later; but this dichotomy runs through his entire philosophy, from his first book to his last. Thus he contends in *The
Birth of Tragedy* that the ancient Greeks, confronted with "the
dreadful destructive turmoil of so-called world history as well as
. . . the cruelty of nature," did not have recourse to "a Buddhistic
negation of the will," but with their tragedies said Yes to life as
a whole with all its agonies. Later, Nietzsche came to denounce

Christianity as saying No to life, and his last work, *Ecce Homo,* ends: "Dionysus versus the Crucified." If a brief commentary is wanted, one may turn to *The Will to Power* (401): "Why has there been no philosophy which said *Yes,* no religion which said *Yes?* ... Dionysus versus the 'Crucified'." Dionysus, to Nietzsche, stands for the exuberant affirmation of life, for the creative employment of the instincts as opposed to the allegedly Christian doctrine of their abnegation; for this-worldliness as opposed to all other-worldliness. In another note in *The Will to Power* (1041), Nietzsche explains:

> Such an *experimental philosophy* as I live it anticipates experimentally even the possibilities of thorough nihilism. But this does not mean that it remains a negation, a No, a will to a No. Rather it wants to get through to the opposite — to a *Dionysian saying Yes* to the world as it is, without subtraction, exception, and selection.

What distinguishes this Dionysian affirmation from the Stoics' acceptance of the world is that Nietzsche's enthusiastic Yes embraces all the extremes of joy and suffering, whereas the Stoic would minimize both;[8] and Nietzsche further ridicules the Stoic notion of living "according to nature" by claiming that life is "the very will to be otherwise than ... nature" — a perpetual self-overcoming, a ceaseless aspiration for a higher state of being.[9]

Another contrast in Jaspers' book which echoes Nietzsche is that of the "chaotic" and the "demonic" man. (pp. 345ff.) This recalls Nietzsche's juxtaposition of the "romantic" and the "Dionysian" type.[10] "Romantic" became as much of an opprobrium for Nietzsche as "chaotic" is for Jaspers, and the final flight to the authority of the Church is one of the features emphasized by both men. Jaspers also speaks of *"die chaotische Romantik"* and uses Nietzsche as one of his models for the description of the "demonic" type.

Later on, the "demonic" type is broken down into three subtypes, the demonic realist, the demonic romantic, and the saint, and Nietzsche — certainly no realist or saint — is understood as a "demonic romantic." This is quite consistent with an earlier passage in the book (p. 13) where Jaspers says of Kierkegaard and Nietzsche:

> Both are romantics in their inner movement; yet both are passion-

---

[8] *Fröhliche Wissenschaft,* 2.   [9] *Jenseits von Gut und Böse,* 9.

[10] *Fröhliche Wissenschaft,* 370 and, in draft form, *Der Wille zur Macht,* 846. For a discussion, cf. my *Nietzsche,* 327-334; also my juxtaposition of Friedrich Schlegel and Nietzsche, *ibid.,* and 102, 113-17, 129.

ately anti-romantic because the actual representatives of that which
has been called romanticism have almost always been lacking in seriousness, arty, epicurean, or unfree —

in short, "chaotic" types. In the later characterization of the "demonic romantic" no names are mentioned, but such phrases as
"here is the genesis of the great original psychologist" and "in the
form of aphorisms and fragments" point in Nietzsche's direction.
And the following passage apparently presents what was Jaspers'
conception of Nietzsche in 1919:

> The torrent of overcharged life, which melts down all it creates,
> leaves behind as something objective only this tremendous pile of ruins
> to bear witness to the wealth of his genius. Every whole, whether a
> work of systematic thought or poetry, remains uncompleted and is in
> its very disposition a fragment, a great aphorism. In action, in love,
> and in friendship it is the same: the most tremendous enhancement
> of the moment, the utmost deepening, yet the incapacity for holding
> on, for giving final form, or for shaping into a whole. The onrushing
> torrent of the demonic drives to new dominant destinies and experi-
> ences. All this romanticism is somehow meteoric. (p. 437)

In essentials, Jaspers' picture of Nietzsche has never changed. He
still envisages him very much like this in his recent work. We shall
see later that this interpretation can be traced back to the poet,
Stefan George —and that it is highly questionable.

To conclude these reflections on Jaspers' *Psychologie der Weltanschauungen,* let us cite another instance of Jaspers' evaluations,
of the manner in which his psychology is not merely descriptive,
but a vehicle for an appeal to the reader.

> This is a psychological contemplation of man and his possibilities.
> We try to resist the temptation of drawing any conclusions in the
> direction of a *Weltanschauung* of our own: we are conscious only of
> contemplation. If our instinctive valuations always react, nevertheless,
> and, perhaps all by themselves, draw the conclusion of everywhere
> affirming "life" and the demonic type as the summit, we must remem-
> ber: this valuational attitude is not yet *Weltanschauung,* only an
> empty intention. We do not yet have a *Weltanschauung* when we can
> contemplate and comprehend all the forms of the spirit — which is
> what we are trying to do here — nor do we have it when we direct our
> affirmative intention toward types which we call "life;" we have it
> only when we actually exist in a type or — insofar as a rare human
> being has been elected for a life in the demonic sense — when this life
> creates forms and shapes in action, in the conduct of life, in works of
> art, or finally in prophetic philosophy. (p. 373)

Thus the early Jaspers "directed his affirmative intention" toward Nietzsche whom he considered one of the "elect." Nietzsche was one of his "educators" in the specific sense which Nietzsche himself associated with that term when he wrote on "Schopenhauer as Educator."

Yet it would be a mistake to think of even the early Jaspers as a follower of Nietzsche or a Nietzschean. He is surely speaking of himself when he writes: "Personalities like Socrates, Kant, Kierkegaard, and Nietzsche give him the strongest impetus; heads like Hegel, the richest education." (p. 379) In a general way, the influence of Hegel's *Phenomenology* on Jaspers' *Psychologie der Weltanschauungen* is quite obvious; in detail, it is discussed by Jaspers himself in the latter work. (364-379) The impetus he received from Socrates and Kierkegaard is similar to that from Nietzsche: the attempt to live one's philosophy, the effort to raise oneself to a higher state of being, and to help others do likewise. In some ways, Jaspers is closer to Nietzsche than to Kierkegaard: he recognizes no theological framework nor any commitment at all to a particular religious tradition. Beyond that, many specific parallels have been adduced above. Even so, there was always one philosopher whom Jaspers revered at least as much, probably more: Kant.

3. *Jaspers' Nietzsche and the George Circle's.*

In 1912, Jaspers attended an exhibition in Cologne. Ten years later, in a study of *Strindberg und Van Gogh,* he wrote up some of the ideas which had occurred to him on this occasion, and remarked with a rare flash of humor:

In Cologne at this exhibition in 1912, where the wonderful Van Goghs were surrounded by expressionist art from all over Europe in queer monotony, I sometimes had a feeling as if Van Gogh were the sublime and only case of one "mad" against his will among so many who want to be mad but are only too healthy.[11]

This certainly does not sound romantic, but consider Jaspers' judgment of Van Gogh:

His works, taken in isolation, would probably stand very far beneath the great creations of art in the last five hundred years; yet the *Existenz* taken as a whole — which, however, would never be clear without the works of art and expresses itself clearly above all in these works — this is of unique stature.[12]

11 *Strindberg* (Bremen, 1949), 182. (First published in 1922.)
12 *Ibid.,* 157.

This sentence might serve equally well as the motto of Jaspers' *Nietzsche*.

An almost perfect parallel to this approach can be found in Friedrich Schlegel's view of Lessing, the greatest literary exponent of the German Enlightenment: "He himself was worth more than all his talents. In his individuality [Jaspers might say, *Existenz*] lay his greatness."[13] Schlegel, as guiding spirit of the original romantic movement, had no use for Lessing's enlightened views, but admired his restless, searching mind. It was similar with the German romantics' attitude toward Goethe: admiration for his Protean development, coupled with either neglect of, or outright opposition to, his professed views.[14] Kierkegaard's attitude toward Lessing was the same: enthusiasm for the man who had preferred the way to the goal, but a lack of interest in his ideas. Stefan George, finally, adopted the same attitude toward Nietzsche and, through the members of the George Circle, influenced the Nietzsche picture of a generation of German writers, including Jaspers.

George's apostrophe of Nietzsche, on the occasion of the philosopher's death in 1900, creates the picture later elaborated by Jaspers:

> Didst thou create gods but to overthrow them,
> Never enjoying rest or what thou built?
> Thou hast destroyed what in thyself was closest
> To tremble after it with new desire
> And to cry out in pain of solitude.[15]

First, Bertram, one of George's lesser minions, propagated this view in his *Nietzsche: Attempt at a Mythology* (1918): what made the philosopher so remarkable, was not his philosophy, which Bertram all but ignores; it was his heroic, yet aimless, self-laceration. Then the rest of the George Circle took up the cry. Ernst Gundolf, for example, relying on the master's intuition and on "the most perfect instruction" of "Bertram's brilliant book" rather than on any solid knowledge of Nietzsche's work, produces this picture of Nietzsche:

> He followed his law and his fatality: to sit in judgment over all that existed, to move the goal beyond all that had been achieved into the

[13] *Friedrich Schlegel 1794-1802: Seine Prosaischen Jugendschriften*, ed. J. Minor (2nd ed. 1906), II, 151. Cf. my *Nietzsche*, 113-117.

[14] Cf. my *Nietzsche*, 129f.

[15] For a translation of more of George's "Nietzsche" from *Der Siebente Ring* and for the discussion and quotations in this paragraph, cf. the "Prologue" of my *Nietzsche*.

unachievable, and to strive for the infinite out of a finitude which he could not bear any more.

It is a fundamentally similar conception of Nietzsche which Jaspers expresses fifteen years later: "Out of every position one may have adopted, i.e., out of every finitude we are expelled; we are set *whirling*."[16]

Nietzsche is thus envisaged as a thinker who proudly refused to seek refuge in the confinement of any 'shell'; but, whereas Jaspers agrees with the George Circle up to this point, his evaluation differs sharply. For George's disciples pitied the poor philosopher: the poet had called him "most unblessed" and his followers outdid each other in patronizing expressions of sympathy; for they had found refuge in their master's 'shell.' In fact, they were so blinded by their authoritarian worship of George that the relatively greatest Nietzsche scholar among them, Kurt Hildebrandt, who wrote four books on Nietzsche, could offer this explanation for Nietzsche's allegedly endless dissatisfaction: "Only George *is* what Nietzsche convulsively coveted to be."[17]

Jaspers' judgment has never been clouded by adherence to any party line or by prostration of his critical faculties before a human oracle. He values Nietzsche's alleged explosion of every finite position, not as the best that was possible before Stefan George was given to us, but as the proper function of philosophic reason — as opposed to philosophic faith. In Kantian terms, this is the best that pure theoretical reason can do; but practical reason is another matter.

Jaspers' agreement with the George Circle is, however, far-reaching. He accepts their judgment that Nietzsche's doctrine of the eternal recurrence of the same events is a "deceptively mocking mystery of delusion"[18] and that his other conclusions, too, are — to cite Jaspers himself — "a pile of absurdities and vacuities."[19] The conception of the superman is arbitrarily emptied of its rich psychological content and written off as a symbol of the unachievable; the eternal recurrence is misunderstood as a religious myth; the idea of the will to power is marked off as a dead end street; and the conception of sublimation, which links the will to power with the superman, is all but ignored. One need not agree with Nietzsche to realize that his central ideas are neither empty nor absurd. Yet elsewhere, too, Jaspers gives us this same picture:

Nietzsche: endless reflection, sounding out and questioning every-

---

[16] *Christentum* (n.d.), 71.   [17] *Nietzsche als Richter unserer Zeit* (1923), 102.
[18] Bertram, *Nietzsche* (1918), 12.   [19] *Christentum*, 71.

thing, digging without reaching a new foundation, except in new absurdities.[20]

Surely, this is George's and Bertram's conception over again.

To this over-all continuity, one may add at least one more specific link: Bertram, who later defended the Nazis' suppression of free speech under the motto, "the most genuine freedom is a holy imprisonment of the heart,"[21] proposed to understand Nietzsche as "the typically ambiguous one."[22] Surely, an instance of self-projection — unfortunate, because Bertram so little resembled Nietzsche, and because he was unimpeded by any scholarly conscience in "finding" ambiguities. Yet, although Jaspers justly criticized Bertram for ignoring the context of Nietzsche's ideas and the process of his thinking,[23] Jaspers himself developed this theme, and "ambiguity" is one of the key conceptions of his *Nietzsche*, too.

Students of Nietzsche are apt to take this for a corroboration of Bertram's very unscholarly thesis — unless they know Jaspers well enough to realize that "ambiguity" is one of the central terms in his philosophy, no less than in Sartre's or Simone de Beauvoir's. Thus, although the notion of Nietzsche's ambiguity links Jaspers' interpretation closely with Bertram's, Jaspers employs the term to designate Nietzsche's profundity, not to criticize him. The assumption is that truth actually is "ambiguous," i.e., irreducible to any set of propositions.

The concrete examples which Jaspers gives of Nietzsche's ambiguity are very questionable. Let us here, consider

the example which exhibits *in concreto* the most extreme reversal possible: Nietzsche's attitude toward Jesus. We recall how Nietzsche envisaged Jesus with respect to the honesty of this way of life, yet at the same time with rejection of the type of decadence which finds expression in this way of life.[24]

So far, of course, there is no ambiguity or reversal at all. One can reject a position without questioning its honesty, and one may respect a type one considers decadent. Nietzsche pictured Jesus in

---

[20] *Einführung*, 155. (cf. *Wisdom*, 188.)

[21] *Von der Freiheit des Wortes*, Inselbücherei, n. d.

[22] Bertram, *Nietzsche*, 8.

[23] I take it that this is what Jaspers means when he says of the symbols in terms of which Bertram discusses Nietzsche: "they oversimplify, cancel the movement, reduce Nietzsche to rigid being . . . instead of going after him in his actuality." *Nietzsche*, 5.

[24] *Christentum*, 71.

the image of Prince Myshkin in Dostoyevsky's *The Idiot*;[25] and the attitude here under consideration is presumably that of most readers toward Myshkin.

Jaspers' next point is that, according to Nietzsche, Jesus was psychologically incapable of resistance (like Myshkin) and no hero; yet Nietzsche says, in *Ecce Homo*, that he himself is also a type sharply distinguished from the heroic. The wording in both passages is similar and seems to Jaspers proof of "self-identification with the opponent." This conclusion, too, is unwarranted: two types can differ from the heroic without being identical; Myshkin and Goethe can agree in lacking any passion for seeking out obstacles or for changing the world, and still be quite different from each other. And it is with Goethe and Socrates rather than Myshkin and Jesus that Nietzsche seeks to link himself in the hyperboles of *Ecce Homo*.

The same considerations apply to Jaspers' other points: Nietzsche's claim that Jesus (again like Myshkin) represented spontaneity of action, and was thus in a sense opposed to morality with its rigid prescriptions, is no proof of self-identification with Jesus any more than Nietzsche's belief that Jesus experienced blessedness as present in his heart. Jaspers' failure or refusal to examine Nietzsche's psychological conceptions of Jesus, and of such approximations of the superman as Socrates or Goethe, bars him from understanding Nietzsche's quite unambiguous position. Nietzsche's pictures are neither absurd nor vacuous, though he is probably mistaken about the historical Jesus. The vacuity is a function of Jaspers' approach which empties vivid conceptions of their empirical content; and the absurdity is due to an interpretation which plays off these hollow symbols against each other.

The section on "self-identification with the opponent" begins:

> This ambiguous attitude toward Jesus — once fighting against him, then identifying himself with him; once negating him, then affirming him — is itself only an example of an occurrence which is universal in Nietzsche.

On the contrary, we assert that the method of interpretation which leads to this false result, is an example of an occurrence which is universal in Jaspers' discussions of Nietzsche.

The section just quoted ends:

> One finds in Nietzsche the most amazing attempts to bring together

25 Cf. my *Nietzsche*, 296-299, where Nietzsche's conception of Jesus is discussed, without reference to Jaspers, and distinguished from his attitude toward the Christ of the creeds.

again into a higher unity what he has first separated and opposed to
each other. The most extreme case is again the manner of his affirmation of Jesus. Nietzsche imagines — without any power of vision and
unrealizable — the synthesis of the ultimate opposition . . . ". . . the
Roman Caesar with Christ's soul."[26]

Yet this is not a convulsive attempt at synthesizing two symbols
which exclude each other by definition, no conceptual jugglery
which defies imagination, but the very heart of Nietzsche's vision
of the superman. Being capable of both sympathy and hardness,
of loving and ruling, not using claws though having them, and
creating out of an overflow and a superabundance: that is Nietzsche's ideal and norm by which he judges both the Roman Cae-
sars and Jesus. The idea is not unattainable but historically represented, to Nietzsche's mind, in varying degrees of perfection by
Socrates and Julius Caesar, Frederick II of Hohenstauffen, Leonardo, and Goethe.

The two sections from *Nietzsche und das Christentum* which
we have been quoting here are preceded by, and supply the evidence for, a section entitled: "The Failure of All Positions and
the Whirl." It is in this section that we find the previously cited
dictum: "Out of every position one may have adopted, i.e., out of
every finitude we are expelled; we are set whirling." We now see
that this is false as a characterization of "Nietzsche's New Philosophy" (the name of the chapter containing these sections), and true
only of Jaspers' moving, but methodologically untenable, interpretation — which here echoes Bertram's.

Among Jaspers' differences from the Nietzsche picture of Stefan
George and his Circle, one of the most decisive has already been
suggested. George's disciples not only accepted the master's whims
as dogma, but set a preposterous precedent by writing history to
order. Even the most gifted among them, Friedrich Gundolf, in
his three volumes on Shakespeare — one specifically devoted to
Shakespeare und der deutsche Geist — is not content to tell us that
he disapproves of Count Baudissin's versions of thirteen Shake-
spearean plays in the famous so-called Schlegel-Tieck translation,
but reads the poor man out of history by not deigning to mention
him. It is surely one of the great merits of Jaspers' *Nietzsche* that
he gives due emphasis to Nietzsche's radical anti-authoritarianism.
And Jaspers has consistently followed Nietzsche in rejecting the
master-disciple relationship and in teaching independence.

Where George had considered Nietzsche his own precursor,
Jaspers' takes him for a precursor of *Existenzphilosophie*. But,

26 The quotation is from *Wille zur Macht*, 983.

whereas George's conception of himself — tirelessly echoed by his adulators — lacked all sense of proportion and bordered on the pathological, Jaspers is not at all like the wren who soared above the clouds on an eagle's wings, unnoticed by him, and then flew up another ten feet, boasting that he could fly higher than the eagle. Jaspers is no wren, nor claims to be an eagle. Certainly, he does not, like George, consider Nietzsche his own personal John the Baptist. A sense of modesty, even diffidence, is the very basis of his decision to teach philosophy:

When I became convinced that at the time there was no real philosophy to be found at any of the universities, I believed that now, confronted with this vacuum, even the weak, though unable to produce a philosophy of his own, has yet the right to bear witness to philosophy, saying what it has been and what it could be. Only then, close to 40 years old, I made philosophy my life's task.[27]

Such modesty and candor offer a stark contrast indeed with the pomp and self-congratulation of the Stefan George cult.

Even so, Jaspers agrees with the *George Kreis* in discounting Nietzsche's philosophy. And this disregard is quite intentional and expressly announced in the subtitle of Jaspers' *Nietzsche: Einführung in das Verständnis seines Philosophierens,* Introduction to an Understanding of his Philosophizing. Jaspers is interested, and sees Nietzsche's historic significance, in what he considers Nietzsche's way of philosophizing, not in his philosophy. This is clear throughout the book; it is equally unmistakable in Jaspers' subsequent smaller study, *Nietzsche und das Christentum;* and he has recently restated this point in a discussion of "Nietzsche's Importance in the History of Philosophy:"

One must know what it means to be concerned with Nietzsche, and how this concern leads to no conclusion. For Nietzsche leads into realms of philosophizing which still lie this side of clear conceptualization, but press toward it. . . . Nietzsche is interpreted in two ways. One interpretation finds his importance in an achievement he completed. He becomes the founder of a philosophy . . . the philosophy of the will to power, the eternal recurrence, the Dionysian grasp of life. For quite another interpretation, which we profess, Nietzsche's importance lies in his loosening function. His exciting force, which leads the human being to the authentic problems and to himself, does not instruct the reader, but awakens him.[28]

27 "Über Meine Philosophie," *op. cit.,* 335.

28 "Zu Nietzsche's Bedeutung in der Geschichte der Philosophie," first published in *Die Neue Rundschau,* and then in two different English translations in *The Hibbert Journal,* April 1951, and in *Partisan Review,* January 1952. The above translation is my own.

There is certainly much truth in this; and yet such phrases as "leads to no conclusion" and "this side of clear conceptualization" are stunning when one recalls Nietzsche's acid clarity, his uniquely vivid concepts, and his often violent conclusions. In view of Jaspers' own relative vagueness and inconclusiveness, one is tempted to sarcasm: is this merely another wearisome instance of an interpreter's reading himself into Nietzsche?

Jaspers says: "The procedure in understanding texts is a simile for all comprehension of being."[29] May we not conclude that Jaspers' interpretation of Nietzsche reflects Jaspers' general philosophy? And when Jaspers tells us that concern with Nietzsche "leads to no conclusion," is not this because Jaspers is concerned with Nietzsche as a means of *Existenzerhellung* (illumination of existence) — and *"Existenzerhellung* leads . . . to no result"?[30] Or consider the following discussion of "all true philosophizing." Nietzsche is not mentioned at all, but the phrases used are the very same which Jaspers employs elsewhere when he characterizes Nietzsche — an association which is still further strengthened by the use of the masculine pronoun, *"er,"* he, where an English translation must say, "it."

It loosens us from the fetters of determinate thinking, not by abandoning such thinking, but by pushing it to its limits. . . . It forces us to return out of every dead end rigidity. . . . The loss of the absoluteness of things and of the epistemology of things is called nihilism by those who thus lose their footing. . . . Our philosophic thinking passes through this nihilism which is really the liberation for true being. . . . The plunge from the rigidities which were deceptive after all, turns into the ability to stay in suspense; what seemed abyss becomes the space of freedom — the seeming nothing turns into that from which true being speaks to us.[31]

One recalls Jaspers' declaration, cited at the beginning of this essay, that Kant is for him "the philosopher *par excellence,"* and Nietzsche only "the magnificent revelation of nihilism and of the task of going beyond nihilism." We have also seen that for Nietzsche himself "nihilism" was something to pass through to a Dionysian affirmation, whereas Jaspers simply discounts Nietzsche's positive conclusions as "absurdities" and thus reduces him to a labyrinth which one enters only to become convinced that there is no way out except Kant's Indian rope-trick. Or to vary the metaphor, we go to Nietzsche to be set whirling, to be forced to plunge

[29] *Einführung,* 74. (cf. *Wisdom,* 77.)					[30] *Situation* (1931), 147.

[31] *Einführung,* 36f. (cf. *Wisdom,* 37f.)

— that the angels of Kantianism may then come to our rescue and keep us suspended in mid-air.

Martin Luther declared that "the commandments" of all sorts of good works in Scripture "were ordained solely that man might thus realize his incapacity for good and learn to despair of himself."[32] As a preacher of grace and salvation through faith alone, Luther boldly interpreted all Biblical demands to do good as demands to realize that we cannot do good. Similarly, Jaspers understands Nietzsche's challenging conclusions as demonstrations that no conclusions are possible and that "philosophic faith" is needed. Such interpretations are less helpful for those who would gain an understanding of the Bible or of Nietzsche than for students of Luther's thought or Jaspers'.

Sarcasm, however, would be utterly out of place in an examination of Jaspers' *Nietzsche:* Jaspers' stature is sufficient, and his philosophy important enough in its own right, to command respect; and seen in its historical setting, his *Nietzsche* was an act of courage, whatever its connection may have been with the fact that the Nazis suspended the author as a university professor within a year of its publication.

4. *Jaspers' Nietzsche versus the Nazis.*

At a time when such self-styled Nietzscheans as Richard Oehler at the Nietzsche-Archiv and Alfred Bäumler at the University of Berlin were loudly proclaiming Nietzsche as a proto-Nazi — when Bertram, the author of the most influential pre-Nazi interpretation, had aligned himself with the party, while Klages, who had written the perhaps most brilliant monograph, was carrying irrationalism and anti-Semitism to such extremes that, at that time, even the Nazis would not follow him — the appearance of this new Nietzsche book by a widely respected Heidelberg professor was eloquent indeed. Here was a solid study which presented Nietzsche as not having been a Nazi. Seen in this historical perspective, the section entitled "Nietzsche wants no believers" (19f.) takes on a new signficance; and the end of the long Introduction appears as a protest:

The task is to become oneself as one appropriates Nietzsche. Instead of yielding to the seduction of accepting doctrines and laws in their apparent univocality as something universally valid, it is his challenge to produce the [highest] possible rank of one's own character.

[32] *Sämtliche Schriften*, ed. Walch, St. Louis, 1881-1910, XIX, 992.

In Germany, in 1936, these words were a slap not only at the prevalent Nietzsche picture, but also at Nazi education generally.

Even more outspoken is a later passage:

Nietzsche can be used by all the powers which he fought: he can serve . . . the violence which mistakes the idea of the will to power as an order of rank for a justification of any brutality. (p. 391)

But to Jaspers' catalogue of such misinterpretations one might well add his own attempt to use Nietzsche to lead us back to Kant's faith.

Jaspers' *Nietzsche*, although not improvised as a political polemic, but the kind of interpretation Jaspers might have written in any event, was the antithesis of Bäumler's Nazi version of Nietzsche. Where Bäumler and his followers saw Nietzsche as a metaphysician with a system, who wrote "as one having authority," Jaspers extolled the lonely seeker after truth, the great challenger not only of all authority but even of his own ideas, the dialectician who can — and this is where Jaspers goes too far — always be cited in contradiction to himself.

Of course, Nietzsche can always be cited as contradicting the views the Nazis found in him; so — as long as one does not question that Nietzsche *also* maintained these Nazistic tenets — it follows that he always contradicted himself. Yet it would be superficial to assume that Jaspers merely could not, at the time, say outright that Nietzsche never held the views ascribed to him by Bäumler. Like other Existentialists, Jaspers too is deeply impressed by the puzzling character of all existence and by its confounding irreducibility to any one set of principles; and when he tells us at the outset of his *Nietzsche* (p. 8) never to be satisfied, when reading Nietzsche, until we have *"also* found the contradiction," he is not casting aspersions on Nietzsche, but describing Nietzsche's greatest value: he sets us whirling. And Jaspers himself goes on to say that we should "experience these contradictions in their necessity."

Jaspers could have written his *Nietzsche* independently of any Nazi provocation, though the time of its publication makes the book even more remarkable. Jaspers read himself into Nietzsche; but, since he has stature, his Nietzsche does, too. What is tragic, however, is that this courageous interpretation by a penetrating philosopher should have helped unwittingly to mute a singularly unambiguous message to Germany. In the whole history of German letters no other voice has spoken out with such prophetic vigor and withering sarcasm against the very forces which culminated in National Socialism; neither Lessing and Schiller nor Goethe and Heine approximated Nietzsche's brilliant indignation or the sustained wit of his scorn of nationalism and state idolatry, anti-Semitism, militarism, and cultural barbarism, and all the other festering vices to which he opposed his ideal of the Good European.

To be sure, no German could have made his interpretation the vehicle for such a message in 1936. But why not in 1926? Why did the German Republic's attempt to link itself with Weimar remain such a feeble, ineffective gesture? Was it not in part because the writers and scholars of Germany failed to show how much of the great German cultural tradition pointed toward the ideal of the Good European? Was it not tragic that they let the rightist opposition spread the utterly mendacious myth that all the great Germans had been rightists and nationalists? Lessing's enlightened ideas were ignored, as if he had been nothing but a restless seeker and a brilliant literary critic. Kant's vision of a League of Nations and of eternal peace and his insistence on never reducing a human being to a mere means was ignored, while his insistence on "duty" was perverted into a sanction for blind obedience to authorities, as if the autonomy of the rational person were not the core of his ethic. Schiller, who had celebrated the striving for liberty and equality in drama after drama, from *Don Carlos'* "Sir, grant liberty of thought" to *Wilhelm Tell's* tyrannicide, was brazenly claimed as a German nationalist, although not one of his major dramas was set in Germany, unless one wants to count his first effort, *The Robbers.* The rich heritage of the Enlightenment in Fichte and Hegel, Mozart and Beethoven was ignored, while Fichte's later nationalism and Hegel's glorification of "the State" were emphasized out of context and out of all proportion. This was surely one of the most preposterous and fateful falsifications of history ever perpetrated.

Nietzsche's thunderbolts might perhaps have penetrated this miasma and cleared the air. His flashes might have exposed the rot and corruption. The shower of his questions, punctuated by the thunder of his denunciations might have purged the intellectual filth in which Nazism was breeding. Yet Nietzsche himself was partly responsible for not getting his message across. Seduced by the beauty of the language, by suggestive phrases and bewitching metaphors, he had often written in a manner which invited misunderstanding. He had tried to counteract such misapprehensions by the most scathing denunciations elsewhere and knew that if not the immediate context, certainly his work taken as a whole showed his views to be quite unequivocal. Yet the beauty of the language attracted an unforeseen host of readers, and the words and parables which had intoxicated Nietzsche soon intoxicated other, lesser minds as well. Zarathustra's apes — to use an appropriate Nietzschean phrase — had no mind to consider flamboyant passages in context or to ponder their relation to the author's earlier and later works; and they still had some of Nietzsche's phrases on their lips when, like the monkey hordes in Kipling's *Junglebook,* they were dancing, hypnotized, to the tune of the great snake.

Nietzsche's fault here is a tragic function of his personality, a chapter in the long saga of the relation of philosophy and poetry. But it is no less tragic that not a single German interpreter of stature should have liberated Nietzsche's timely, sorely needed, message from the irridescent webs of myth and metaphor, that not one should have mastered his abandoned bow to drive his well fashioned arrows into the unworthy suitors of his people. It is tragic that even Jaspers should not have risen above the conception of "ambiguity" which, although certainly at odds with Nazi versions, could scarcely become a rallying point of any opposition, nor do justice to Nietzsche.

This criticism may appear to be reducible to a mere difference of opinion between Jaspers and his critic. In that case, it could lead at best to an intellectual duel, apt to prove just as little as any other duel. I reject his Nietzsche, he mine. If the reader has sufficient imagination, he may well reject both. And some will suggest: everybody is entitled to his own Nietzsche. But the question here is not one of one interpretation versus another: the charge — which will be discussed further later on — is that Jaspers' *method* is indefensible.

This is a serious criticism, but great philosophers have rarely been disinterested guides to the thought of their predecessors. One would hardly gather from Plato how close some of the Sophists had come to many facets of modern democratic thought; Aristotle's portrait of Plato, in turn, is a fine instance of partiality; and Nietzsche himself excelled in aphoristic caricatures with pedagogical intent. Today, there are Santayana's and Russell's often uninformed distortions, especially of German philosophy since Kant. So viewed, Jaspers' *Nietzsche* appears highly distinguished: Jaspers is exceedingly well informed; unlike Aristotle, he is beyond the very suspicion of envy; and unlike Plato, he is not using great names as foils, or to prevail in a historic contest by eternalizing his opponent's name in infamy.

It is thus the very excellence of Jaspers' book which makes its faults important. He does not claim the poetic license of the architect of dialogues or sculptor of aphorisms, but presents us with a wonderfully learned full-length study and offers more direct quotations per page than any previous Nietzsche interpreter, invariably giving the page references, too. Use of an illicit method in such a superior work is doubly serious.

Finally, it adds to the historical momentum of the charge against Jaspers, although it is morally an extenuating circumstance, that previous German interpretations had almost entirely ignored the whole heritage of the Enlightenment in Nietzsche, and indeed that whole aspect of his philosophy which might conceivably have given German history a turn for the better. Jaspers' failure here is clearly not due to any lack of courage, but to lack of vision.

5.   *Jaspers contra Freud.*

It may be revealing that the same oversight, even blindness, occurs where Jaspers is confronted with the man who is likely the greatest among Nietzsche's heirs, a man who followed in the footsteps of Goethe, Heine, and Nietzsche by attempting to deepen and enrich the attitudes of the Enlightenment with the insights of romanticism. For Freud tried to bridge the gap between the German romantics' profound preoccupation with the irrational, on the one hand, and the Western faith in liberty, equality, and fraternity, and in science as an instrument to their realization, on the other. But, instead of recognizing in Freud a Good European and a great prose stylist who, like Nietzsche and Heine, wrote clearly, lucidly, and powerfully enough to be read outside of Germany, Jaspers completely overlooks Freud's radical individualism and links psychoanalysis with Marxism and racism as presenting "brutalizing demands."[33]

Jaspers even denies outright that Freud is in any important sense carrying forward Nietzsche's work:

The self-reflection of the human being of integrity, which . . . had culminated in Kierkegaard and Nietzsche, has here degenerated into the uncovering of sexual desires and typical childhood experiences; it is the covering up of genuine, dangerous self-reflection by a mere re-discoverey of already known types.[34]

If this is a half-truth, the following claim seems almost entirely wrong:

[33] *Situation* (1931), 143.   [34] *Ibid.,* 139.

Psychoanalysis, though this may not meet the eye, leads to the consequence of not thinking up, but of making one feel, the ideal that man return out of all schism and violence through which he might find the way to himself — return back to nature which no longer requires him to be human.[35]

It is easy to counter such allegations with direct quotations from Freud — and it is relevant here to do so, because Jaspers' position depends on attitudes which also mar his understanding of Nietzsche. Here, then, are three brief quotations from Freud's *Introduction to Psychoanalysis:*

By raising the unconscious into consciousness, we overcome the repressions, abolish the conditions for symptom formation, and change the pathogenetic conflict into a normal conflict which must somehow find a resolution.

Where there is no repression to be overcome, nor any analogous psychical process, there our therapeutics has no business.

We hold that whoever has passed successfully through an education for truthfulness toward himself, will thereby be protected permanently against the danger of immorality, even if his standard of morality should somehow differ from social conventions.[36]

Here Freud speaks as the heir of Nietzsche, and Jaspers' failure to see this is as revealing concerning his relation to Nietzsche as it is regarding his conception of Freud.

In 1950, Jaspers published a book on *Reason and Anti-Reason in Our Time* and, five years after Hitler's defeat, used Marxism and psychoanalysis as the two examples of anti-reason. The fact that most of his strictures against psychoanalysis are extremely well taken does not allay the apprehension that he shows a lack of historical perspective. Jaspers, of course, would not agree with the German reviewer who recently said of a collection of essays published in 1952 that they point to many wounds, but not to the main wound, the immoralization through psychoanalysis. Jaspers stays this side of the incredible. But he fails to recognize Freud's central intention: to help those who have lost their freedom to find it by teaching them to be honest with themselves, facing their problems instead of running away from them. Jaspers notes all the bad features which so often attend the formation of schools or sects, but does not see how Freud has both given new meaning to the ancient conception of human equality, regardless of race, culture, or creed, and lent new impetus to the longing for a higher,

35 *Ibid.*, 139.

36 *Vorlesungen zur Einführung in die Psychoanalyse* (Taschenausgabe, 1926), 460f.

but *attainable,* state of being. It seems fair to add that, had Jaspers recognized Nietzsche's central intentions, he would have understood Freud's too. But following in the footsteps of Schlegel, Kierkegaard, and George and his *Kreis,* Jaspers has romanticized Nietzsche: self-projection takes the place of understanding; basic purposes are disregarded; and positively stated conceptions are discounted as absurdities or as utterly empty, or again as "symbols" of which Jaspers says frankly:

Only via detours and with effort can one summon a significant content out of these symbols, by interpretation.[37]

Thus Jaspers' critique of Nietzsche's conception of the superman, in *Nietzsche und das Christentum* (p. 54) , presupposes the untenable interpretation of the George Circle, who had considered this ideal essentially *unattainable,* and completely overlooks the empirical, psychological content of the idea or its relation to "sublimation" — a key concept of Nietzsche's philosophy to which Jaspers, in his *Nietzsche,* devotes exactly half a page.

6. *Summary of Criticisms.*

My criticisms of Jaspers' interpretation of Nietzsche might be summarized as follows. First, Jaspers admittedly discounts Nietzsche's philosophy as opposed to his "philosophizing;" he refuses to take seriously superman and recurrence, will to power and sublimation, or any other definite concept.

Second, Jaspers fails, his intention notwithstanding, to introduce us to Nietzsche's philosophizing because he employs an untenable method. He makes no distinction, either in his references or in his evaluation, between Nietzsche's finished works and his fragments and notebook scribblings; and generally he makes no distinction either between early and late passages, but disregards the dates and thus necessarily also Nietzsche's intellectual development. He uses Nietzsche as a means to arouse us and to introduce us to *Jaspers'* philosophizing, not Nietzsche's. If we spread out Kant's writings, pre-critical, critical, and *Opus postumum,* we could also find one statement after another challenged by some statement elsewhere; and it would be little different with Plato. It may be a stimulating exercise, or even a deeply disturbing and shocking experience, to consider contradictory statements, one after the other; it may, as Jaspers says, make us aware of "authentic problems" and have the power of "loosening" the mind;[38] but all this should be sharply

---

[37] *Reason,* 30f.   [38] See note 28 above.

distinguished from an introduction to Nietzsche's own philosophizing. Jaspers' claim that concern with Nietzsche "leads to no conclusion," but only arouses the reader, is clearly a function of Jaspers' approach. If we studied Kant in this manner, the result would be the same, except insofar as Nietzsche's problems are of more obvious concern to laymen.

Third, Jaspers' frequent references to Nietzsche's "ambiguity" are misleading. He is taking up one of the central notions of Bertram's "Attempt at a Mythology," though he justly repudiates this latter work. Nor does this seeming partial agreement amount to any mutual corroboration. Jaspers uses the term "ambiguity" in three different senses,[39] of which none corresponds entirely with the usual meaning of the word, equivocality. Rather "ambiguity" is one of Jaspers' favorite words in his other works, too — even as it is a favorite with Sartre and Simone de Beauvoir, whose book on *The Ethic of Ambiguity* is a good case in point. What is meant is the irreducibility of existence to any single system, and Nietzsche's alleged ambiguity is thus the very virtue which Jaspers projects into Nietzsche by means of the illicit method just described. To cite Jaspers' *Nietzsche* (p. 407): "education by Nietzsche is like a *first training in ambiguity.*"

Fourth, Jaspers' interpretation of Nietzsche as "ambiguous" does not only fail to do justice both to Nietzsche's philosophy and to his philosophizing; it is also a chapter in a major historical tragedy. It contributed to the muting of a message which was sorely needed. It helped to reduce to relative ineffectiveness a philosophy which was unalterably opposed to the forces which have determined recent German history.

Fifth, from a more strictly philosophic point of view, it is regrettable that Jaspers dissolves all the more limited problems which Nietzsche posed and occasionally advanced toward a solution. Nietzsche's philosophy of power, for example, is certainly open to criticism, but can be made the point of departure for fruitful and precise philosophic reflection which may lead to definite results. Jaspers dictum, "but power is ambiguous"[40] is not incorrect, but admittedly aimed to lead us away from precise conceptual thinking, instead of making us think more rigorously than Nietzsche did.

All these criticisms are, in a way, condensed into a single sentence in Jaspers' own essay, "Über meine Philosophie:"

[39] Cf. my *Nietzsche*, 54, where the three senses are distinguished.

[40] *Nietzsche*, 267.

Through my *Nietzsche* I wanted to introduce the reader into that loosening up of thought out of which *Existenzphilosophie* must grow.[41]

Nietzsche is used to introduce us to Jaspers. And it remains for us to consider Jaspers *vis-à-vis* Nietzsche.

7. *Jaspers versus Nietzsche.*

First, there is the matter of style. Kant set a fateful and wholly unfortunate precedent when he departed from the lucidity of his magnificent essays to write his main works in a thoroughly graceless and often hopelessly obscure German. Fichte, obsessed with the desire to outdo Kant, naturally had to "better the instruction" in his *Wissenschaftslehre,* although he showed elsewhere how movingly he could write. Hegel, convinced that Fichte's pseudo-scientific rigor represented the only alternative to the romantics' raving lack of discipline, all but spoiled his grandiose *Phenomenology of the Spirit* by forcing it again and again into the spurious mold of "deduction." By then, a tradition had been created. Nietzsche, who loved to crack conventions, exploded this tradition, too, and showed that there is nothing about the German language which prevents it from being used brilliantly to illuminate the most obscure problems. In his *Zarathustra,* however, he went to the opposite extreme and created so dazzling a medium that it distracted from the ideas he sought to express. Elsewhere, too, his aphoristic style and often extreme emotional pitch introduce difficulties, but these are never in the tradition of sedate opaqueness established by Kant and frequently approximated by Jaspers. Almost every sentence in Nietzsche's works is crystal clear; his style is European. Jaspers, on the other hand, is often vague; and his sentences, frequently all but untranslatable. Here, too, he is closer to Kant than to Nietzsche.

Of course, comparing Jaspers' style with Nietzsche's is like juxtaposing contemporary painters with Van Gogh: one is reminded of Plato's saying, in the *Phaedrus* (245): "the sane man disappears and is nowhere when he enters into rivalry with the madman." Yet in philosophy much is to be said for sanity, and still more against madness. What makes an evaluation so difficult in this case is that what Nietzsche celebrated with such brilliant madness was precisely sanity — not the sobriety of the Philistine, but that of Socrates who could outdrink his companions at the symposion and yet go after his day's business. In Nietzsche's analyses the weak-

41 *Op. cit.,* 364.

nesses of debauchery and abstinence alike stand revealed, while he points to the power of the passionate man who is the master of his passions. But his readers have been more struck with his own lack of control, his frantic gestures, and the pitch of his voice.

In Jaspers' work we find the opposite disharmony. Gravely, he describes the demonic type and, without raising his voice, speaks of those elected to live in this way. His style of reporting is often deceptively drab, even when he reports contradictions which to him indicate basic antinomies, the limits of reason, and the whirling rapids into which we are carried inevitably if we try to follow rational thought. And when he speaks of the realm beyond the rapids — the "Encompassing" or "the space of possible *Existenz* which grows wider and brighter" — his style becomes, not prophetic but involved and obscure.

Where Nietzsche, even under the spell of inspiration, denied himself the transport of the flight beyond reason, Jaspers, speaking more like a lecturer than a prophet, soars to God. He formulates his faith in brief assertions, but tells us quietly that these are not to be accepted as a piece of knowledge, but as goals towards which we may direct ourselves. With seeming assurance, he speaks of ultimate mysteries or defines the significance of the great thinkers of the past in a single sentence each, but adds that his assertions are inadequate. Jaspers versus Nietzsche: didactic mysticism versus Dionysian enlightenment.

In his intense preoccupation with the individual and his *Existenz*, Jaspers is closer to Nietzsche than to Kant; yet it would be misleading to say that he follows Nietzsche. For Jaspers is more exclusively concerned with the individual and his state of being than European philosophy has ever been before; only a few thinkers who were religious writers first and philosophers second — such as Augustine, Pascal, and Kierkegaard — even approximate this exclusiveness. In Plato, on the other hand, this preoccupation is accompanied by an equally intense interest in theoretical problems as such; and this is also true of Nietzsche. When Jaspers speaks of overcoming the whole plain of philosophizing which characterizes Aristotle's work,[42] he also dissociates himself, even if unknowingly, from Plato, Kant, and Nietzsche, not to speak of most French, British, and American philosophy.

Jaspers' concern with the limits set to us by "old age, sickness, and death"[43] — which reminds us of the Buddha — and his repeated discussions of ultimate situations *(Grenzsituationen)*, such as death, accident, guilt, and the unreliability of the world, are

42 See note 7 above.   43 *Wisdom*, 21.

all closer to religion and literature than to *most* Western philosophy, but they are certainly compatible with the dominant philosophic tradition and characteristic precisely of some of the greatest minds. What separates Jaspers from such partly *'existential'* thinkers as Plato and Spinoza, and also from Nietzsche who still stands in this tradition, is the exclusiveness of this concern and his resignation concerning precise conceptual thinking.

Such critical reflections, however, should be balanced by an emphatic acknowledgement of Jaspers' strength. If he shares some of Kant's shortcomings, he has also forwarded the best elements in Kant's heritage. He has repeatedly spoken out for the good elements in the Enlightenment — an unpopular cause in Germany — and whenever he has expressly discussed it at all, he has unequivocally denounced the recent German animus against scientific procedures and critical thinking. The presence of elements in his own philosophy which seem to run parallel with this animus cannot cancel such merits. And recently he has gone far beyond Nietzsche in also insisting on the political and moral conditions under which alone free scientific inquiry can flourish. His consistent championship of humane attitudes and of respect for every human being as such, certainly dwarfs many of the objections voiced above.

Then Jaspers' *Nietzsche,* too, has made a contribution insufficiently suggested by the words of acknowledgment scattered through this essay. Reading it is a profound experience which has the very effect at which the author aims: we find every assumption we make dislodged; we are led to question what seemed certain; we are constantly forced to think. Beyond that, the author's mastery of the relevant factual material — for example, that pertaining to Nietzsche's biography — and his references to various sources of information make the book most helpful for any student of Nietzsche. Finally, the book brings to the reader's attention a wealth of enticing quotations from Nietzsche which do not fit previous interpretations and attract to further study. Many of us are deeply indebted to the book for this. Altogether I know of no other German interpretation which is as well informed or suggestive.

Above all, Jaspers possesses an honesty of which Nietzsche, for all his celebrations of intellectual integrity, would have been quite incapable. Where Nietzsche resorted to the sarcastic hyperboles of *Ecce Homo,* Jaspers can judge himself with calm and simple candor:

In my last two years at school, I stood alone. . . . That I behaved honestly but not heroically was the earliest shock. The consciousness of the limits of my self precluded the pride of defiant isolation. My character was penetrated by resignation which, in the form of knowledge of finitude and of the guilt of the free man, runs through my later philosophizing.

At that time, my attitude was for the first time as it later remained peculiar to me, only partially justified by the lack of strength of my never healthy body. In the years of National Socialism, it remained the same. I have remained internally free and did not yield to any pressure by committing a bad act or saying a false word in public, but I did nothing in the fight against this crime. I omitted to do what my heart told me to do, while caution advised against it. In 1945, therefore, confronted with false tales on the radio and in the press which glorified my alleged deeds as exemplary, I had to publish a correction with the conclusion: I am no hero and do not want to be considered one.[44]

The man who speaks of himself like this may be no Nietzschean firebrand, and we may on many issues disagree with him; but we cannot deny him our respect and affection.

WALTER KAUFMANN

DEPARTMENT OF PHILOSOPHY
PRINCETON UNIVERSITY

[44] "Mein Weg zur Philosophie," (1951) in *Rechenschaft,* 323f.

11

Kurt Kolle

KARL JASPERS AS PSYCHOPATHOLOGIST*

MANY psychiatrists pricked up their ears, when, in 1910, at the age of twenty-seven, Karl Jaspers published his paper on "Paranoia — a Contribution to the Problem: Development of a Personality or Process?"[1] At the time Jaspers was assistant at the Psychiatric Clinic in Heidelberg, which was under the direction of the famous neuro-pathologist Franz Nissl, successor to Emil Kraepelin. Why did this paper,[2] in which Jaspers gave an unusually vivid and detailed description of several cases of paranoic patients, receive such wide attention among his psychiatric colleagues? For one thing the *method* of presentation was remarkable: Jaspers related life histories at considerable length, with many particulars from the patient's life prior to hospitalization and with an exhaustive description of their mental condition during clinical observation. With this mode of presentation Jaspers introduced the *biographical method* into psychiatry: a summons to regard a patient's illness always as part of his life history. From the carefully carried out analysis of his cases Jaspers deduces — and this was the new element he introduced into psychiatry — conceptual differentiations which have remained controversial topics among psychiatrists until now. With a realistic psychology, always using the concrete psychopathological material, Jaspers arrives at new concepts[3] and thus approximates a provisional and heuristically valuable solution of the question posed in the subtitle: Development of a Personality or Process? Already in this first major psychopathological paper we are struck by the unusually critical attitude of the author. After Jaspers has differentiated between the understandable development of the inner life of an individual

---

* Translated from the original German manuscript by Elizabeth Mayer.

[1] *Zeitschrift für die gesamte Neurologie und Psychiatrie*, Bd. 1. (1910).

[2] Already in 1909 Jaspers had published his dissertation "Heimweh und Verbrechen," in the *Archiv für Kriminal-Anthropologie und Kriminalistik*, Bd. 35.

[3] Jaspers differentiates: 1. Development of a personality (e.g., a querulous reaction of the type of Michael Kohlhaas). 2. Mental process (e.g., paranoia of the type of the mass murderer Wagner, described by Gaupp). 3. Somatic-psychotic process (e.g., schizophrenia of the type of Hoelderlin).

and the biological series of happenings at the onset of a psychosis, and has explained the difference precisely, he continues:

It always seems a great advantage to differentiate in some way between phenomena. Although, in most cases, these differences can be better felt then explained, we should attempt to describe them in the form of concepts in spite of possible objections whose validity could only be considered within a completely developed system of psychopathology and despite the fact that all concepts of this kind are always merely provisional, always 'wrong.' If they stimulate analysis and lead to finer distinctions they have served their purpose.

In this paper Jaspers reveals also his infallible, keen eye for psychopathological detail. Thus he is struck by the hypomanic behavior of his first two patients, an observation which could later be corroborated by extensive case-materials.[4] Jaspers' research in paranoid jealousy has stimulated not only psychiatric science but also psychiatric practice. In many cases of mental illness a conscientious psychiatrist, even today, is confronted with the question: development or process? (Decisions full of responsibility frequently depend on the answer to this question.) Psychopathological speculation, aroused by this paper of the young Jaspers, has not come to rest since then: a fortunate indication that Jaspers had touched the very roots of our psychiatric knowledge.

To proceed now chronologically: The young assistant at the Heidelberg clinic develops an astonishing productivity. The paper just mentioned is followed in the same year by another important one "The Methods of Intelligence Tests and The Concept of Dementia."[5] Reading this classical report today one finds that almost nothing is outdated. After critically reviewing all existent intelligence-tests, Jaspers continues: "The selection of questions for each individual case in order to demonstrate its peculiarities, shows the particular intuitive gift of the psychiatrist, a gift which at present is, unfortunately, still more successful than all specific 'methods'." This situation also still prevails today, although in the meantime many new tests have been devised.

With his first papers Jaspers had already made valuable *phenomenological*[6] contributions to psychopathology. In those that followed[7] he proved convincingly, by means of well selected case

4 Kolle, K.: *Die primaere Verruecktheit*. Leipzig 1931 and: *Ueber Querulanten*, Berlin 1931.

5 *Zeitschrift f.d. gesamte Neurologie und Psychiatrie*, Referatenteil, Bd. 1, 1910.

6 *Vide* his paper "Die phaenomenologische Forschungsrichtung in der Psychiatrie," *Zeitschrift f.d. gesamte Neurologie und Psychiatrie*. Bd. 9, 1912.

7 "Zur Analyse der Trugwahrnehmungen (Leibhaftigkeit und Realitaetsurteil)".

materials, that phenomenology helps us to discover "what patients *really experience.*"

The last paper[8] published before giving up psychiatry, already indicates the basic structure of his *General Psychopathology* (at that time already far advanced). Jaspers describes in great detail two schizophrenic patients (the clinical records cover 24 and 29 pages in small print!) "in terms of phenomenology, causality and genetic understanding." Although Jaspers' main object is "the exposition of the connection between destiny and acute psychosis, i.e., reactivity," he emphasizes in his concluding words that "no general conclusions can be drawn" from these two cases. His principal concern has been to achieve through "a collection of material of appropriate cases with extremely detailed records . . . lucidity of method and differentiation of viewpoints."

The *General Psychopathology* was published in 1913. It was a daring venture. After only four years of psychiatric experience, the young author, barely 30, surveys in one bold sweep the totality of psychiatric knowledge. The subtleness of his thought, trained in the history of nature and of ideas, is conspicuous in his scientifically exact and at the same time excitingly vivid draft of a psychopathological system of methods which gives psychiatry, for the first time in its history, a firm foundation. The author, at present still at the height of his creative power, will forgive an unreserved value judgment:[9] a book of sovereign conception, a unique and magnificent achievement which occupies a place of epoch-making importance in psychiatry.[10]

In order to understand how this was possible, we should, briefly, contemplate *the situation in psychiatry* in the years before the first world war. Scientific psychiatry did not exist until the middle of the 19th century. (Practical psychiatry, i.e., the recognition that mentally disturbed people are sick people and should, therefore, be treated in special hospitals, made slow progress only after the close of the 18th century.) This change of opinion and the subse-

---

Zeitschrift f.d. gesamte Neurologie und Psychiatrie, Bd. 6, 1911 and "Die Trugwahrnehmungen," *Zeitschrift f.d. gesamte Neurologie und Psychiatrie,* Referatenteil, Bd. 4, 1912.

8 "Kausale und verstaendliche Zusammenhaenge zwischen Schicksal und Psychose bei der Dementia praecox. (Schizophrenie.)" *Zeitschrift f.d. gesamte Neurologie und Psychiatrie,* Bd. 14, 1913.

9 Jaspers himself is not exactly chary of value judgments both of the positive and negative kind; he has often been reproached for this unusually candid attitude.

10 Bumke wrote in his review of the first edition *(Zeitschrift f.d. gesamte Neurologie und Psychiatrie,* Referatenteil, Bd. 9, 1914): "A very unusual book which at once wins for itself and its author an enduring place in the history of our science."

quent incorporation of psychiatry into medicine was brought about by a book, published in 1845,[11] by the German psychiatrist Griesinger. He made the significant statement which was later rightly disputed: "Mental diseases are diseases of the brain." As a result of Griesinger's postulate, psychiatry became associated with natural science. Brain pathology became an important basis of psychiatry. The main problems of psychiatry — the mental disturbances proper (so-called endogenous psychoses, abnormal mental developments and reactions) — were, however, hardly touched by these investigations of the brain. The scientific papers were more or less limited to meticulous descriptions of symptoms. The French, in particular, developed this symptomatological approach into a fine art, although the practice of psychiatry profited little from these investigations. Emil Kraepelin brought this era to a close when he, with the vision of genius for the essential, singled out large groups of diseases like 'dementia praecox' and 'manic-depressive psychosis' as nosological entities, which were soon universally acknowledged. The system drawn up by Kraepelin (later deepened and extended mainly by Bonhoeffer to include the exogenous psychoses) still constitutes the relatively secure foundation of psychiatry. But the idea of Kraepelin was — as is frequently the case with great ideas — too simple. The disciples who took over the doctrine of the master were far too quickly satisfied with classifying the individual 'case' according to the Kraepelinian recipe. The empirical system, passionately and painstakingly advanced by Kraepelin, threatened to degenerate into pure formalism. The most powerful attack on the structure of Kraepelin's — by now classical — doctrine, the *psychoanalysis* of Sigmund Freud, received scant attention by psychiatry. The Zürich group alone, headed by the great Eugen Bleuler, opened itself to the new impulses emanating from Vienna. Bleuler, with his *Dementia Praecox or the Group of Schizophrenias*,[12] presented a work that — as Jaspers writes pertinently — "at last knows again how to use *'verstehende'* psychology* in the analysis of these psychoses." Under the influence of Freud and Bleuler, Gaupp was the first who attempted to make paranoia understandable by tracing it back to character, environment and experience (a later formulation by his pupil Kretschmer). At the same time increasing efforts were made to elicit the causes of mental disturbances by using the procedures of natural

[11] *Pathologie und Therapie der psychischen Krankheiten*. 4th ed. Braunschweig, 1876.

[12] Vienna, 1911.

* Editor's Note: Cf. Lefebre's essay for a discussion of *"Verstehen."*

science. Ruedin, a pupil of Kraepelin, demonstrated with exact methods the significance of hereditary predisposition for the genesis of schizophrenia. Histopathology received a fresh impetus when the staining methods, suggested by Ehrlich and Weigert, were used by Nissl and Alzheimer for the investigation of the nervous system. The study of fibrous connective tissue in the nervous system, inaugurated by Flechsig, Oscar Vogt and Brodmann, promised new insight into the relations between the brain and mental activity. The discovery of the spirochete as the causative agent of syphilis, and the Wasserman reaction furthered the knowledge about syphilitic brain diseases enormously.

Soon the situation was as follows: Anatomical, physiological, genetical, neurological, psychological and clinical methods of research were carried on side by side, for the most part peacefully, but without correlation. Rarely were they fused harmoniously in one clinic, still more rarely in one investigator. Psychiatry, rapidly growing after the disappearance of external obstacles, was completely under the spell of the advance of the natural sciences, but it still lacked a firm methodical framework. Evidently, natural science alone could not carry the heavy burden. At this time Jaspers began the construction of a psychiatric system of methods. Even then he showed his philosophical penetration which later led him to philosophy altogether. He made it clear that psychiatry is neither brain anatomy, physiology of the nervous system, experimental psychology, nor clinical assembling and classifying of data, but all of these together and yet each of them by itself within this whole. Jaspers assigned to psychiatry, which like any other science has to find its own methodology, its place in the history of ideas; a place which psychiatry, being a discipline comprising the whole man, has to know exactly. The impression that the Freudian doctrine was a foreign and confusing encroachment could be created only because psychiatry had no connection with the history of thought. All that the great philosophers of all times have thought about man, psychiatry had now to acquire anew, starting from the firm basis of the reality of clinical experience. If Jaspers, whose book unfortunately never had a far-reaching effect, had been better understood, a striving for meticulous analysis and synthesis of methods would have begun much earlier.

We shall now give an outline of the formal arrangement of the material in Jaspers' epoch-making work. The Introduction, dealing with: "Delimitation and Task of General Psychopathology," "Prejudices in Psychopathology," "Fundamental Concepts and Methods," is followed by eight chapters, as follows:

I. The subjective manifestations of mental illness (phenomenology).
II. The objective symptoms and performances of mental life (objective psychopathology).
III. The connections of mental life: 1. Connections discovered by *'Verstehen' (Verstehende* psychopathology).
IV. The connections of mental life: 2. Causal connections (Explanatory psychopathology).
V. Theories.
VI. The totality of mental life: intelligence and personality.
VII. The synthesis of the syndromes.
VIII. The sociological relations of abnormal mental life.

The book closes with an Appendix, containing the following sections: "On the examination of patients;" "On therapeutic tasks;" "Prognosis;" and "Historical Matter."

After a repeated reading at the present time, two closely connected questions force themselves into one's mind:

First: Why did this book create such a sensation in psychiatry immediately after its publication?

Second: Why did it take effect so slowly in the domain of psychiatric science and practice?

To begin with: Jaspers presents an inventory of the existing stock of assured psychopathological knowledge in an astonishing completeness. He had not overlooked any even of the obscure or neglected lines of research, whether it be graphology as a method of the psychology of expression, or the study of effects of the time of day, the seasons, the weather and the climate on mental life. With an almost disconcerting impartiality the author tries to do justice to all trends. The results of brain pathology or of the aphasia theory, valuable for psychopathology, are presented in the same unbiased fashion as psychopathological biography or the phenomena of hypnotic suggestion. He displays an equally profound knowledge when he writes about general psychology or about psychiatry proper. Reading the chapter "The synthesis of the syndromes," the uninitiated might suspect the author to be a venerable clinician with long clinical experience. The section, outlining the therapeutic tasks, i.e., the work of the psychiatric practitioner, does not show the uncritical optimism of the beginner but the mature wisdom of one who has weathered the storms of life. His judgment of Freud, whom he later opposed with all the fervor of his philosophical faith, is here still prudent and moderate. After having demonstrated the principles of psychoanalysis in a positive sense, Jaspers says:

In his writings Freud emerges as a personality of noble reserve in contrast to the noisy exaggeration and tasteless caricature of some of his pupils. . . . But he does not disavow these pupils and is therefore partly responsible for them. Compared with them he is temperate, however surprising and bold his theses may be. His writings show — with a few exceptions — a taste unusual for a psychiatrist; his presentation is elegant, occasionally fascinating. He avoids the philosophical appeal, never poses as a prophet, and yet has in fact been able everywhere to arouse an interest in *Weltanschauung*. (646 of 5th ed'n)

These are samples only, taken at random from the wealth of the book which captivates the reader not only by its wide range but also by its daring style, which shies away from neither blame nor praise.

The *General Psychopathology* aroused a lively discussion among the author's professional colleagues. Today, forty-three years after the publication of the book, the debate is still going on. The differentiation between *verstehende* and explanatory psychopathology, on which Jaspers had already touched briefly in his paper on "Paranoia," received its conclusive definition in this book. At the outset Jaspers gives the following formulations:

1. "Through *empathy* we understand *genetically*, how one mental process evolves from another.[13]
2. By *objectively* connecting several elements into regularities on the basis of repeated observations, we explain *causally*."

Proceeding from the basis of the normal range Jaspers then attempts to verify these two theses in the realms of abnormal phenomena and mechanisms (again with an astonishing scholarly knowledge, unusual in a man of his age). A proof of the lasting impression which Jaspers' profound thoughts have made is the fact that, e.g., an old, experienced psychiatrist[14] has recently felt compelled to re-examine thoroughly the concepts introduced by Jaspers.

Secondly: With his characteristic probing seriousness Jaspers also deals with the "ultimate and most difficult problems" (as Bumke said in the review we mentioned in fn. 10). Not everybody who has chosen the psychiatric profession as his life work matches him here. As in any other professional group, we find only a minority of psychiatrists who are open to the breadth and depth of true psychiatric cognition.

It was to be expected therefore, that only a few were sufficiently

13 This definition of "genetic" differs from the psychoanalytical one where it means: developmental-biographical.

14 Kehrer, F. A.: *Das Verstehen und Begreifen in der Psychiatrie.* Stuttgart, 1951.

open-minded to risk with Jaspers the leap into the Unknown. Nevertheless, it is surprising that such a stirring work has not found a larger following. A leading German psychiatrist,[15] writing a very positive appreciation of the book, confesses: ". . . that the leading psychiatric text books, e.g., have hardly and in any case insufficiently, utilized Jaspers' (ideas), and that, in general, psychiatrists have, unfortunately, learned very little from his methodological discipline and self-reflection." One can certainly agree with Kurt Schneider, that "clean, methodical thinking and the endeavor to clarify concepts is rarely an attribute of the medical practitioner." But this seems hardly sufficient reason to explain why Jaspers' work has all too generally been ignored. His critique, schooled in philosophy and more particularly in Kant, was (and is) highly uncomfortable for the positivistic majority of psychiatrists. ". . . to know what one knows and what one does not know, and in what sense and within what limits one knows something, by what means this knowledge was attained and can be proved" (Jaspers' words in his Preface to the third edition) — this basic attitude of the author deterred many from reading his book. The average physician, whether psychiatrist or surgeon, has a practical orientation. A work whose methodological character has been repeatedly stressed by the author himself, does not, unfortunately, attract the majority of physicians (despite the fact that Hippocrates already had maintained that ἰατρός φιλόσοφος ἰσόδρος). Especially in the Appendix to his book Jaspers makes it clear that such philosophical self-reflection is indispensable to the young profession of psychiatry, and that it is essentially the practitioner who will benefit from it. "Without this foundation (namely, the knowledge of somatic medicine and psychopathology) the psychiatrist can be nothing but a quack," is Jaspers' dictum. Even for a simple job like writing case records Jaspers prescribes, apart from practice, "one approach only: the all-around study of scientific psychopathology." The author states precisely and unmistakably what attitude the psychiatrist (I may add: every physician) must adopt when he examines patients:

When examining patients one can take a wrong course in two opposite directions. Two apparent opposites have to be united: it is necessary to yield to the *individuality* of the patients and allow their peculiarities to express themselves; but, on the other hand, one must carry out the examination with firm viewpoints and must be guided by goals. Neglecting the latter, means becoming entangled in an infinite

[15] Schneider, Kurt: "25 Jahre *Allgemeine Psychopathologie* von Karl Jaspers," *Nervenarzt*, 11, 1938.

chaos of details; neglecting the former, means placing the cases into a few petrified pigeonholes, no longer noticing anything new and doing violence to the cases. The ideal examiner is one who combines a wealth of firm viewpoints with great adaptability with reference to the individual case. *(Allgemeine,* 4th ed., 687)

Jaspers' characterization of the psychiatrist and his therapeutic possibilities is magnificent and permanently valid. The good, the ideal psychiatrist constantly looks at the patient in terms of body, mind and spirit; he must take the unity of these three in all seriousness. But though he has to bear in mind, constantly and consciously, this totality of the individual, he should not forget "the profound difference between *somatic* and *mental* therapy." The goal of the first is clear: "recovery in the biological sense." "As soon as we wish to exert our influence on the patient's mind, however, the goal is no longer clear." The concept of mental health is questionable; Jaspers had already expounded this insight in his "Excursus on the concepts of Health and Disease," which is, as yet, unsurpassed. What Jaspers says, in a few words, on *Psychotherapy* is also still valid today, in spite of an enormous, steadily increasing, literature on this subject and a continuous rise in therapeutic practice. Jaspers distinguishes three possibilities: suggestive therapy, psychoanalysis (which is here evaluated very reasonably as an empirical method); and appeal to the (human) personality. Whether a psychotherapist is successful or not in his endeavor "to help man to an increasing awareness of himself[16] . . . depends on his own view of life, on the goal he would instinctively like to attain, but also on the pressure which the *nature of his patients* constantly and unnoticeably brings to bear on him." Jaspers' profound insight into the character of the relations between physician and patient is astounding.[17] He knows about the struggle between them, and even in those early days he ranks the "struggle for clarity" highest. He anticipates his concept of communication (later the core of his philosophy), when he writes that "every really deep elucidation is possible only . . . in reciprocity, so that the physician has to illuminate himself as well as the patient."

As one reads all these wise and profound words, one would think that Jaspers' own vocation would have been that of a psychiatrist "who combines scientific scepticism with the strength of an effective personality and with consciously employed diplomatic skill."

16 Already here we find delineated what Jaspers later carried out in his philosophy as illumination of *Existenz.*

17 This reviewer, e.g., has to confess that he himself would have been able to formulate his experiences only after decades of psychiatric practice.

However, paths of destiny, unknown to us, led Jaspers very soon after the publication of his remarkable book away from psychiatry; henceforth he dedicated his life exclusively to philosophy.

The second edition of the *General Psychopathology* (1920) does not differ much from the first in its basic conception; but it does contain some new observations by the author. The objections which had been raised against giving this kind of a book to the student are refuted. Jaspers "stands firmly by [his] conviction that a science can be comprehended either as a whole, i.e., including its central problems, or not at all."

Before the publication of the third edition, Jaspers takes up his pen once more to treat a problem of importance for psychopathology. He publishes a psychopathological analysis of *Strindberg und van Gogh* (together with comparisons with Swedenborg and Hölderlin).[18] These four notable personalities — two poets, a thinker and a painter — developed a serious mental disease, classified by modern psychiatry as 'schizophrenia.' Only the diagnosis of van Gogh is open to controversy. With this work Jaspers originates a new style for the biography of creative personalities who became mentally ill. He does not concentrate exclusively on the disease; he does not attempt value judgments of their work based on its creator's illness. Not at all; the disease "is a determinative *existential* factor . . . and should, therefore, be clearly described." He presents the life histories with his usual masterly skill, and with critical utilization of the extensive literature. The analysis of Strindberg, whose work offers a wealth of autobiographical material, is exemplary presentation of a psychopathological case. As handled by Jaspers, the medical histories of these great artists have become model cases for psychopathological research. Jaspers' most urgent concern is the constant striving toward a unified view of disease and life, even in the case of the simplest patient. But the value of the book is not exhausted in this psychiatric demand alone. The study caused a sensation and aroused opposition on account of the two concluding chapters, "On the relation between schizophrenia and schizophrenic creations," and even more so on account of "Schizophrenia and modern culture." As might be expected, Jaspers is not content with mere summary judgments, but divides his questing into subtle sub-questions. Then he pushes dauntlessly ahead toward the fundamental issue. Is there not something "unique" in these works of schizophrenic personalities, something that ". . . has a specific character with a defined place in the cosmos of spirituality, but which materializes in reality only

18 *Strindberg und van Gogh.* 1st ed., Bern, 1922; 3rd ed'n, Bremen, 1950.

if and when the conditions are created by the process of the disease?" Jaspers seems to be inclined to give an affirmative answer:

The philistine habit of using the concept 'ill' in a disparaging sense or of considering its entering into cognitive connections as pedestrian, makes one blind to a reality which until now, we are not able to grasp otherwise than through case-material, and which we are not at all capable of interpreting. Even its formulation offers difficulties, probably because we are enmeshed in limited categories of evaluation and in a conceptual framework which still captivates us, although we are aware that it is dissolving in favor of a more comprehensive, freer, and more flexible one. (173)

The author, however, does not make a decision. How could he? As in the domain of philosophy, Jaspers remains in psychopathology also the 'Great Inquirer,' who pushes his persistent questioning to ultimate decisions, but eventually dismisses man into his own freedom. It is quite obvious that it is not easy for Jaspers to make his closing statement:

It is not only increased productivity — precipitated perhaps by the excited condition — which, among other things, leads to the discovery of new (artistic) tools and thus to an enrichment of the artist's language; but new forces also emerge which in their turn objectify themselves, forces which are spiritual, i.e., neither sick nor healthy, but which thrive in the soil of disease. (177)

In his brief concluding summary Jaspers touches upon the grave question whether the schizophrenic style might not possibly be typical for our cultural epoch. It is, he states, "a striking fact that today some outstanding personalities who became schizophrenic exert an influence through works dating from their schizophrenic period." (179) In contrast to this, he states, "[he] knows of no personality of rank in past civilizations, where there was any reason to suspect schizophrenia." (180) On the other hand, Jaspers draws attention to the great *rôle of hysteria* in earlier times, while he disclaims knowledge of any prominent contemporary hysterics. Particularly in the case of van Gogh he had had the feeling of catching a fleeting glimpse of "the ultimate source of *Existenz*," "as if the hidden foundations of all existence were becoming directly manifest." (181) Further on Jaspers formulates his question once more in the following way: "May schizophrenia be the condition of authenticity in such periods, which in previous times could be experienced and portrayed without schizophrenia?" (182)

The third edition (1925) of the *General Psychopathology* shows the same basic scheme as the earlier editions, but it has an addition: the "Excursus comparing the extant descriptions of a general psychopathology" (at the end of paragraph 3: "Basic concepts and methods"). Jaspers briefly reviews the earlier descriptions by Emminghaus (1878) and Stoerring (1900) and then turns to two more recent works, published after the second edition of his own book. First he discusses the *Medical Psychology* by Kretschmer (1922)[19] and examines minutely this book of an author, who even at that time was already famous for his brilliant studies.[20] In the introduction Jaspers blames the book "for the speed with which it has been written." He then briefly characterizes the genetic theory of the mind, on which it is based, and Kretschmer's postulate of basic biological mechanisms. He censures the author with extreme severity:

Kretschmer furnishes another example of *verstehende* psychology which would like to disguise itself as natural science — in conformity with the mental climate of the medical faculty — but which is successful (in this) only because he has little inclination towards exact natural science and its methods. In another context Kretschmer himself expresses the attitude responsible for his 'simplifications' pertinently: 'In order to enliven the dry material I have, at times, used unusual expressions and pointed formulations.' Such theoretical simplifications and seeming mastery of abundant material betray a basic conception of the world [in all psychologies basic attitudes come to the fore in one way or other], that is — conceding intuitive understanding of parts — a sort of knowing it all which itemizes with surprising speed and naively applies classifying concepts to expressionism or to historical personalities, and is animated by the enormous delusion — from the point of view of the history of ideas — of some psychiatrists that 'the psychology of neuroses is the psychology of the human heart as such. . . . He who knows about neuroses, knows *eo ipso* about human nature.' It is characteristic that the style [of Kretschmer] has a literary flavor. There is no indication of respect for the infinity of each single individual and no amazement in the presence of the infinite problems of the mind. Instead, he [Kretschmer] provides easily adoptable slogans, the use of which enable one to achieve a self-satisfying consciousness of a penetrating knowledge of human nature. . . . But . . . with this procedure Kretschmer does not succeed in outlining a real design of the totality of mental life; rather he stops with a selection of problems. His language is more picturesque than conceptually precise; the dash of his diction is more evident than any idea. (35)[21]

[19] 10th edition, Stuttgart, 1951.

[20] *Der sensitive Beziehungswahn*, Berlin, 1918. *Körperbau und Charakter*, Berlin, 1921.

[21] Cf.: the recent criticism by W. Wagner, in: *Der Nervenarzt*, 22 (1951).

Before we start commenting on Jaspers' verdict which was, of course, resented, we shall quote his attitude toward the book by Gruhle,[22] his former co-assistant at the Heidelberg clinic. In "complete contrast to Kretschmer" the book by Gruhle "impresses, even superficially, by its carefulness and sober style." But Jaspers is not satisfied with Gruhle either who, "foregoing creative construction [of his subject-matter] . . . does not get beyond the rich factual material. Without discriminating between important and unimportant data (a discrimination based, as we know, on inspiration and not on formal classifications), he misses the real substance of the problems." *(ibid.)*

Jaspers confronts these attempts of others with his own in order to accentuate the specific character of his scheme. "My book," [on the other hand,] would like to help the reader to acquire a true psychopathological education *(Bildung)*. It is much simpler, of course, to memorize a scheme, and thus, with the use of a few slogans, to appear equipped for everything. Education *(Bildung)* comes from the knowledge of the *limitations* of systematic knowledge and from such mental skill as is able to move in every direction. Psychiatric education consists in personal acquaintance with the existing fund of knowledge coupled with wide experience, always at one's disposal — something no book can provide — and then in conceptual versatility coupled with penetration, in clarity coupled with flexibility of comprehension. This latter my book would like to further. . . . Generally speaking, my book has been, from the outset, an enemy of all fanaticisms, which are so strongly inclined to claim absolute value for *one* idea, *one* interpretation, motivated by the human will to power and prestige. (44 in 5th edition).

The chapter "Psychology of Expression" was re-written (it is independent now) for the third edition. In an extensive footnote (comprising several pages) Jaspers criticizes Kretschmer's recently published book, *Physique and Character*. He misses a "synthesis of the methods" and reproaches Kretschmer with "lack of (methodical) discrimination" *(Vermischung)*. The line taken by Kretschmer — a combination of good physiognomical and characterological ideas with anthropometry — drapes his investigation with a "pseudo-exact, scientific cloak" and creates general confusion. Jaspers' scepticism goes still further:

No case can refute this doctrine; if this is so, it cannot be proved by reality either. There is a 'plausibility' in the fusion of genetics, so-

[22] *Psychologie der Abnormen,* München, 1922.

matic typology, psychopathology and characterology, which nowhere is anchored in empirically unassailable facts, but always allows the noncommittal interpretation of an intuitively derived picture in scientific sounding terms.

Jaspers detects the "enthusiasm (which colors Kretschmer's book) also in several recent studies by other authors, a mood as if everything were shaken, as if a brand new psychiatry (were) in the making and a deeper penetration of the ultimate dynamic factors (had been) accomplished." Jaspers contemplates these new currents in research with extreme reserve:

If we see the meager results of these investigations . . . , we are forced to conclude that what is best about them is not the empirical comprehension of dynamic factors at all, but an intuitive grasp of mental manifestations. The rest, however, is mainly empty talk about possibilities. We are reminded of the old natural philosophers who thought they could recognize the essence of nature. When one of them reproached Kepler for recognizing the surface of nature only, the latter replied: 'I grasp, as you say, reality by its tail, but I hold it firmly in my hand; you may go on trying to grasp its head, but I fear it will only happen in your dreams!'

This, unquestionably severe, criticism of Kretschmer and of other authors was deeply resented. We are not inclined to accuse Jaspers of philosophical arrogance, since his principal concern is, undeniably, the clean definition of concepts and clarification of methods. It should certainly be acknowledged as a mitigating factor that Jaspers applies to an eminently productive author like Kretschmer a standard in keeping with the high position of this scholar. Jaspers praises the "high intuition" of Kretschmer who, he admits, accomplished "the most" among the new group of workers. He acknowledges the "new creation of the pyknic-syntonic type, which can be immediately visualized and confirmed by one's own experience." The profound scholar and philosophical thinker should, therefore, not be blamed for declaring: "I consider the whole doctrine untenable (though not essentially senseless) and (I consider it) a naïve, self-assured anticipation of a knowledge about ultimate biological factors under which each separate individual — whose case as such is clear now — is subsumed."[23]

[23] In the fourth edition Jaspers' criticism is as strong as previously but modified, because he had at that time "been mistaken about the fruitfulness of the approach and about the meaning of the constitution-idea . . . ," and had also not foreseen its impact. This writer wishes to comment that Jaspers here overrated the stimulus which the book by Kretschmer briefly gave to psychiatric research. In a practical

With the publication of the third edition of his *General Psychopathology* in 1923 Jaspers seems definitively to have turned his back on psychiatry and psychopathology. On the whole, quiet settles around the famous author, his latest — already more philosophical — work *Psychologie der Weltanschauungen*, appeared first in 1919, the second edition in 1922. This book is, in general, extremely important for psychopathology, because it reveals the wide range of true *"verstehende"* psychology. For the thoughtful psychiatrist who studies the book carefully, it will be a safeguard against forming rash value judgments derived from his psychopathology with its meagre stock of provisional concepts. Every individual who consults us — full of confidence but often also slightly suspicious — should be seen by us with Jaspers' words in our mind (from the Preface to his book): "This book has meaning only for those who begin to wonder, who reflect on themselves and who see the contradictions attending life; and also only for those who experience life as a personal, irrational responsibility from which there is no release." (p. v.)

Inasmuch, however, as the scope of my task in this book is limited to the portrayal of Jaspers as a psychopathologist, I shall limit myself to two comments

First: In the brief section, "Absolute nihilism in psychoses," Jaspers vividly describes nihilism as a symptom of mental illness or, in other words, as a manifestation of ultimate situations in which a human being can find himself in depressions and schizophrenias. Whereas the psychiatrist, constantly subject to practical considerations, sees primarily the destructive forces at work in the psychoses, Jaspers — probably for the first time in the history of psychopathology — takes the decisive turn to *anthropology*. The illness with all its concomitant despair and its novel experiences, is a necessary transitional stage for man who now has experiences, which he would not have encountered without the crisis of the illness, (without) unspeakable suffering. (Even at that time Jaspers was probably already deeply impressed by Nietzsche.) Consequently Jaspers argues: "Nihilism is psychologically inevitable as a step toward the attainment of self-consciousness." One of my patients who, going through menopause, recently relapsed into serious depression, said to me: My illness does not now return by accident;

---

sense psychiatry has not benefited at all by Kretschmer's investigation; theoretically it has never produced fruitful discussions. The only generous attempt, by Conrad, to view the doctrine of his teacher Kretschmer in larger biological connections, has been completely ignored by Kretschmer himself. (Cf. Klaus Conrad, in: *Studium Generale*, 4, 1951).

it challenges me to work out for myself a new pattern of life. And, only today, another patient told me, right after I had written these lines, that each time, after she had gone through a depression, she had felt a special creative urge. These examples show that Jaspers, even where he is primarily concerned with philosophizing, never does so from an ivory tower. Thus his *philosophical* logic is not suspended in mid-air either; it is firmly attached to the empirical existence of the living individual. "Hence logical knowledge, though based on science as the clearest objective discipline, is just as much grounded in everyday thinking, in any kind of experience, in empirical actions and decisions, in all human contents." (3f., *Wahrheit.*)

Second: In the Appendix to the *Psychologie* Jaspers gives (in barely twenty pages!) an interpretation of Kantian Idealism, exemplary in its brevity and lucidity. By this study he shows that it is possible to keep philosophy alive in transmitting it. Many psychopathologists and other scholars for whom a reading of Kant may conceivably offer difficulties, should at least peruse this Appendix by Jaspers. A great deal of muddled thinking, perceiving and imagining could thereby be avoided.

Many outsiders may worriedly have asked themselves, whether Jaspers might not be one of those prodigies whose productivity exhausts itself prematurely.[24] This fear is unfounded. In 1932 Jaspers published his *Philosophie,* which placed him at once among European thinkers of first magnitude.[25] A smaller book, *Man in the Modern Age,*[26] published shortly before, had, of course, already proved that Jaspers was not 'dead.' But now external events intervene: Hitler comes to power in Germany. An independent thinker like Jaspers, married besides to a wife of Jewish extraction, was a dangerous man in the eyes of the National Socialists.

[24] A personal note may be permitted here. The author of this essay has enjoyed the privilege of occasional private conversations with Jaspers in his house in Heidelberg. It may have been in the year 1926 or 27, when Jaspers for the first time mentioned his *Philosophie* to me. He told me that he had finished the book, but that he was not satisfied with its form. For that reason he had set about rewriting the book (3 volumes) completely. This little anecdote characterizes Jaspers' working methods better than any long-winded explanations.

[25] Ludwig Binswanger ("Karl Jaspers und die Psychiatrie," *Schweizer Archiv für Neurologie und Psychiatrie,* 51, 1943) is right in stating that "the paragraph on medical therapy in the first volume of *Philosophie* (121ff.) belongs to the best and profoundest (statements) ever written on the 'relationship between physician and patient.' Binswanger also points out other paragraphs of *Philosophie,* where Jaspers, despite his recent detachment from practical psychiatry, evidences his rank as a mature psychopathologist. (The paragraph "Gliederung der Wirklichkeitswissenschaften," I, 185ff. or III "Sein im Scheitern," 219ff.).

[26] London, 1931; new ed., 1951.

The fact, however, that Jaspers was already internationally famous probably prevented the men in power from dismissing him at once from his office; this happened later, in 1937. Jaspers, passionately dedicated to his work and suffering terribly under the perversion of the German mind, rejects any form of escape; he does not emigrate but neither does he allow himself to be caught up in hate and resentment against the country of his birth. He carries on his work. At first he is still permitted to publicize: hence the publication, in 1935 (though by a Dutch publisher) of his Groningen Lectures *Reason and Existenz;* and, in 1936, of his *Nietzsche, Introduction to the understanding of his philosophizing.* In this book Jaspers has drawn upon the rich fund of his psychopathological experiences and presents an objectively true, formally brilliant description of the disease to which Nietzsche eventually had fallen victim. Even Jaspers admits his inability to answer the ultimate medical questions; a big question mark remains. Equally, the problem — in Nietzsche's case of particular urgency — of the relation between disease and work cannot be solved completely. Nevertheless Jaspers presents an authentic psychopathological biography with a grasp far beyond his earlier attempt *(Strindberg und van Gogh):* "Nietzsche's illness not only cut off his life ruinously, but in its gradual progress it belonged to him in such manner that without the disease we could scarcely imagine him either in his life or in his work." (100)

After this book the general public no longer hears from Jaspers. Only his close friends know that he carries on his work untiringly. There is, first of all, the great philosophical work *Philosophical Logic* (Volume 1, *Von der Wahrheit).* In this work, too, gigantic as regards both size and contents, significant statements of importance to the psychiatrist can be found. Under the general heading "Truth and Falsehood" Jaspers analyzes the relationship of "Physician and Patient" as an example for the discussion of "untruth" (557). On p. 825 the reader comes upon some extremely critical, almost unforgivingly severe judgments on psychotherapy. If these remarks were not connected with an unprecedented endeavor to help human beings in a loving and understanding fashion in their *'existential'* misery, one might turn away radically from Jaspers or at least ask him reproachfully, whether, in his clinical practice, despite its brevity, he had never had the wonderful experience of genuine contact with his patients. But our critical judgment proves wrong as soon as we turn some pages and come upon such magnificent phrases as those on "Sexual Love" (994ff.) or even earlier (993) "On Vital Existence:" "The encompassing vitality is dimly realized as (the) strength and flowering of the body; and also as (the body's) being-one with nature in which and with which it exists. The glory and splendor of the world reveal themselves to him who exults in life."

It is, then, impossible to hold a serious grudge against Jaspers. But a thoughtful and experienced physician, who himself is well on in years, may, in all due modesty, point out to him: completely dedicated to his work in a secular asceticism, engrossed in his wonderful idea of man guided by reason, rooted in love, sustained by communication, Jaspers overrates the average man. Although we do not intend to accuse Jaspers of a relapse into philosophical idealism, we must state that he idealizes man in an inadmissible way. A good many human beings, primitive or complex, stupid or intelligent, are, by reason of their God-given simplicity, incapable of interpreting their existence transcendentally or their being-in-the-world in relation to the Encompassing. Thus they cannot really [in Jaspers' sense] become themselves. Unfortunately — the author vouches for this — philosophical faith animates only those few who are capable of orienting themselves in their world and who are able to elucidate their existence in order to gain metaphysical orientation. The mass of the people, including the dull ones, the philistines and many intellectuals as well, are in need of the little remedies among which we reckon psychotherapy also. To help these human beings, who may be poor in spirit but who are frequently well equipped with excellent faculties for feeling and reasoning; to assist them in a kind, i.e., humane or Christian spirit, is, and will always be, the task of those very physicians who elevate their thoughts and acts above the material world, animated by their philosophical faith.

I can well imagine Jaspers' answer; for only recently I had a most fruitful conversation with him on this very subject. Jaspers said: "Yes, you, as a psychotherapist, must be extremely tolerant; but I, as a philosopher, must be intolerant. The idea of man has to remain pure, must not be falsified." We reflect on this attitude philosophically and respect it. But, even if we partake of it ourselves, we can transfer it to our patients only to a small degree. In our unpretentious work, however, we refuse to be regarded as outsiders, as if we had nothing else to offer to human beings but communication clothed in dubious truth. Certainly, we should always keep our minds open and live in constant readiness for the rare encounters with great individuals whom we dare face only as we authentically are. But we should also have the grace of approaching, in a way appropriate to him, the ordinary man who, despite his deficiencies, is often animated by the divine spark. In these cases the end, indeed, does justify the means.

Once more Jaspers returns to psychopathology: He accepts the suggestion of his former publisher, Ferdinand Springer, to revise the *General Psychopathology*.[27] This book could not be printed, however, until 1946, after the collapse of Germany. Jaspers, "inspired by the task, (decided) to make a new draft of the whole book instead of merely revising it." In this he succeeded, as the response from psychiatric circles has proved. The author's intention that his book (enlarged by 300 additional pages) would like to satisfy the desire for "universal knowledge ... [and] be of service to physicians and to all those whose theme is man," makes this new edition even more difficult reading than the previous ones. For this reason, Gruhle,[28] just as Bumke had done on the occasion of the first edition, feels justified to express a warning that the book "should be kept away from the beginner." Even to the experienced or to the humanist (for whom, according to Gruhle, the book is particularly suitable) "much which was formerly clear will become obscure."[29]

What then, is the new book like? After the Introduction the new book is divided into the following sections: Separate facts and phenomena of mental life; *Verstehende* connections of mental life; the causal connections of mental life; conceiving mind in terms of wholes; the abnormal mind in human society and history; the totality of man's being. This is again followed by the Appendix. We see that the framework is basically the same as before. Many sections have been revised, others extended. New chapters have been added. With unremitting zeal and with the critical penetration characteristic of the author, nearly all the important

27 Again I may be permitted a personal remark. For his work Jaspers needed the use of the library of the psychiatric clinic which was under the direction of a psychiatrist who actively participated in the so-called euthanasia program. Jaspers had no scruples about visiting this man and about asking his support for his work by granting him the privilege to use the library. The director of the clinic (by the way a man of a great scientific talent) engaged him in a long conversation. Jaspers was very upset by this talk and shocked that a capable and thoughtful psychiatrist could be at the same time a convinced follower of a dictatorial government.

28 *Nervenarzt*, 18, 1947.

29 This reviewer does not share the view of Bumke and Gruhle. With Jaspers I am "firmly convinced that a science can be comprehended either as a whole, i.e., in its central problems too, or not at all." Gruhle admits that the reader will eventually "obtain clarity on a higher level, though only the clarity of a very complicated, somewhat disappointing, universal relativity." Exactly this is, in my opinion, the extraordinary merit of the book which should actually be made the criterion by which the qualification for psychiatry is tested.

contributions to the literature,* published in, unfortunately, cata-
clysmic numbers since the year of the third edition, are taken into
consideration. But this profusion of material is not the distinguishing feature of the fourth edition. Its novel character cannot easily
be defined. A new spirit pervades the whole book. It bears the
imprint of the new philosophical positions which the author has
meanwhile made his own. The "philosophical faith" of the scholar
who, at the time he wrote the book, was almost sixty, has taken
more definite form; the empirical psychopathologist sees his subject inevitably integrated into the conception of the world which
he, in his philosophy, has in the meantime painstakingly worked
out for himself. Jaspers may not be satisfied with this interpretation of his work, since he wants to be in this book merely a psychiatric scientist, who, acutely conscious of the limits of science, wants
to demonstrate where science as empiricism comes to an end and
where the scholar is no longer guided by an experience but by an
idea. In the new edition, too, Jaspers remains the critical scholar
who pays due tribute to empiricism. But his philosophical position
is more in the foreground than he may himself be aware of.

The essence of the fourth edition is most strikingly expressed
in the sixth section: The Totality of Man's Being. This section is
divided into the following paragraphs: I. Psychopathology in Retrospect; II. The Problem of the Essence of Man; III. Psychiatry
and Philosophy; IV. The Concepts of Health and Disease; V. The
Meaning of (psychiatric) Practice. Jaspers himself formulates
"arguments against the outline of my psychopathology," but refutes them convincingly. He concludes:

> The pregnant question for us is: did we succeed in preventing any
> confusion in retaining, on the whole, our awareness of the multidi-
> mensionality of scientific striving and of man himself? That conscious-
> ness of being, which is accessible only to philosophical illumination,
> is the tacit reason for a methodical attitude instead of becoming the
> acme of a purely dogmatic total knowledge. (624f.)

As scholarly psychopathologists we can only attain particular insights, even though we are guided by the idea of wholeness. A
methodological reflection, carried through to the ultimate positions of reason clearly reveals to us the limits of our striving. *"In
order, however, to reach this limit, we must be at home beyond
the limit."*[30]

* Ed's. Note: This refers primarily to German language publications.
[30] *Allgemeine*, 625; *italics* mine.

Jaspers firmly turns against any confusing of science with philosophy. Man can only be "accessible to scientific investigation . . . insofar as he can be investigated objectively." "Philosophy creates the realm wherein all knowledge takes place, in which it attains measure and limit and the basis on which it can sustain itself. . . ." The importance of the ontology of Martin Heidegger and of the "analysis of existence" of Ludwig Binswanger, which is based on it, is minimized by Jaspers. He also judges with skeptical reserve the intentions expressed in the papers of V. E. v. Gebsattel and W. v. Weizsäcker. The 'Meaning of Practice' demonstrates that knowledge and action are correlated. Philosophical self-illumination prevents medical practice from slipping into empty activity and quackery. Active work, directed toward reality, safeguards the physician against persisting in fatalistic reflection and also against regarding experimentation as an end in itself which ranks higher than the misery of human existence. Psychotherapy, the "attempt to help the patient through communication to plumb the very depths of his inner life in order to find the rudiments for a guidance on the road to health," proves distinctly that "the physician is inevitably a philosopher." Here it will become apparent whether he has become transparent to himself or whether he is bogged down in dogmas, schemata and theories which he only wishes to see corroborated by the person he faces. If this methodical self-reflection, which distinguishes the philosophizing physician, is claimed as an ideal, Jaspers' thesis that "physicians, to the degree that they are psychotherapists, are equal to their total task," is not presumptuous.

If we try to give our *provisional summarising* judgment on Jaspers' book in its new shape, the following can be said:[31] many psychiatrists who have experience as practitioners and are active in research, will feel compelled to raise objections to numerous details. (For instance: to the rigorous condemnation of any kind of eugenic measures; Jaspers denies that 'degeneration' is an 'inescapable process.' The present writer believes that Jaspers does not sufficiently take into account the total rise of the population which carries with it the danger of the suppression of valuable minorities, the increase of inferiors and the gradual dying out of the white races — to his over-sceptical attitude towards psychotherapy — to his comments on psychoanalysis and on the existential analysis of L. Binswanger.)

[31] I am here making use of earlier formulations in my *Psychiatry*, 3rd ed., Berlin and München, 1949, 4th ed., 1956.

But it seems to us of greater importance to ask what the book has to offer to any scholar who has to deal with human beings. Besides the stimulating profusion of single observations, drawn from his own and other people's experience, which Jaspers has carefully fitted into the right places, the book presents a unique survey of the patterns of the human mind. Thereby he addresses every human being, every scholar, in particular every physician who is willing to discard the blinkers of natural science. Jaspers does not restrict himself to a characterization of the "attitude of natural science as not sufficient though indispensable." In an arrangement of the knowable facts encompassing the whole of human existence, the roads are indicated which assure an approach to the human being in particular and in general. But only in philosophizing are the limits of the knowable, the comprehensible, the explicable made evident. There the totality of man is refuted as being unattainable, and the enigma of man manifests itself. Jaspers pushes his analysis to a degree where the whole frequently threatens to get blurred. His critical judgments often seem to be so devastating that we are shocked, almost paralyzed. A reader who is not sure of himself might be overwhelmed and endangered by a feeling of resignation, when he constantly encounters statements such as "one does not know anything," "one cannot know anything," "all striving is senseless," "there is nothing but existential communication." To us it seems to be a positive quality that Jaspers questions everything, unsparingly exposes the lacunae in our knowledge and barrenness of empty concepts, and that he points out philosophical prejudices. The book is one single challenge to the freedom of being human *(Menschsein)* which is not abrogated by the fact that man is a creature of nature. Jaspers' words carry weight, because — both as a philosopher and as a physician, and like almost no one before him — he has penetratingly paced the realm of human existence and has, in his philosophizing, illuminated it for himself and others.

We have tried to demonstrate to all who are not, or only insufficiently, acquainted with psychiatry and psychopathology, the importance of Jaspers, as a psychopathologist, for the world of today, i.e., his achievement as an empirical scholar and as the philosophizing interpreter of man's ultimate situations. This, certainly very rough and sketchy, picture would, however, be incomplete if we did not mention his lifelong battle against the psychoanalysis of Sigmund Freud.

In the first three editions of his *General Psychopathology* Jaspers restricted himself in the main to reviewing the basic princi-

ples of psychoanalysis. There are only a few critical comments. Even in the third edition we still read:[32]
"It will be advisable to suspend one's final judgment." But the disciples, whose "writings . . . are unbearably boring in their simple-mindedness" are already being flogged.

Jaspers takes a more decisive position, for the first time, in his small book, *Man in the Modern Age*. In the chapter, "Our present conception of human existence" Jaspers briefly characterizes psychoanalysis as a typical phenomenon of the world of today. He first criticizes the fact that until now psychoanalysis has not produced any adequate or convincing record of cases. Man as the "puppet of his Unconscious" provokes his disgust.

The self-examination of a sincere thinker, which after the long-lasting Christian interlude attained its climax in Kierkegaard and Nietzsche, is in psychoanalysis degraded into the discovery of sexual longings and typical experiences of childhood; it is the masking of genuine but hazardous self-examination by the mere rediscovery of familiar types in a realm of reputed necessity wherein the lower levels of human life are regarded as having an absolute validity.[33]

Thus Jaspers forms his judgment that psychoanalysis tacitly leads to the consequence that an ideal should not be thought out but felt. Man, freed "from the cleavage and the coercion through which he may come to himself, is to return to that nature in which he no longer needs to be man." (154) In further reflections Jaspers arrives at the conviction that psychoanalysis belongs into the same category of theories as Marxism and Racism; all of these theories have ruinous qualities since they "tend to destroy what has been of worth to man." (157) Marxism, Racism and psychoanalysis "turn against anyone who has faith of whatever kind; and they will 'unveil' him in their sense of the term." (158)

Most recently Jaspers has taken up the same subject[34] once more: his battle against psychoanalysis, insofar as it claims to represent an idea of man, is of fundamental concern to him. Jaspers hates Freud, not as a person (whom he respects as an independent, free personality); nor as a scholar (whose intuitive insights he evaluates with justice) — but as a philosopher who created a theory which degrades man. In the first place Jaspers rejects "the claim

[32] Already here the essential arguments against the concept-formation and the theory of psychoanalysis are cautiously formulated, even if not yet fashioned into the determined, well-founded criticism of the later works.

[33] *Age*, 153.

[34] In *Reason and Anti-Reason in our Time*. New Haven, 1952, and in "Zur Kritik der Psychoanalyse," *Nervenarzt*, 21, 1950.

of an absolute knowledge of man" which psychoanalysis promises. "Pseudo-faith," not revealed as such, but disguised as science, promises man "an illusory liberation which is as untrue as the humanity of which it is the reflection." *(Anti-Reason, 26).* In Jaspers' opinion, psychoanalysis is

an enormous process of self-deception conditioned by the age we live in, which bewitches its victims, who find in it the satisfaction of their lives. But the source of the process is so false that it is bound to confuse hopelessly not only the knowledge of those who are swept into it but their whole being. *(Ibid., 27)*

Jaspers rejects *a priori* such a conception of man. His position rests solidly on his empirical occupation with man and on his "methodological reflection" which "leads to a separation of the various modes of scientific enquiry from the methods of philosophical thought." *(Ibid.)*

What, then, is the basis of his scathing indictment which claims that psychoanalysis is false at its roots? The "errors are (to be found) in the field of medical science" is Jaspers' dictum. This is, of course, right from the historical point of view, since Freud was a medical man. But was Freud's rôle really just that of a scientific physician when he established his theory? He *was* insofar as his doctrine unmistakably bore the stamp of the scientific mental climate predominant at the close of the nineteenth century. He was *not,* insofar as the claim to achieve a total knowledge of man, a claim, rightly censured by Jaspers, was rather remote from the thinking of the competent physicians of that epoch. We know almost nothing about the humanistic *(geistesgeschichtliche)* background of Freud during the years when he laid the cornerstone of his theory. But we may suppose that Freud, the born theorist, was motivated not only by experiences, but also by ideas which rose from the depths of his existence *(Menschsein)* and were moulded with the aid of his discursive reason. Apart from all these reservations it should be admitted that the accusation raised by Jaspers against medical science can be supported by the evidence. Jaspers propounds the following arguments:

1. Understanding of meaning *(Sinnverstehen)* is confused with causal explanation. . . .
2. The therapeutic agent is not clearly understood. . . .
3. What is called 'neurosis' is not characterized by the intelligible contents of phenomena but the mechanism of transmuting spiritual into physical processes, by turning sensible into senseless physical occurrences. Only a tiny percentage of human beings suffer from

this mechanism, this gift or fate, by which they encounter their own spiritual and intellectual processes *(Vollzüge),* the acts of their own free will transposed into physical phenomena, as something foreign to themselves and beyond their control. Most people repress, forget, leave unsettled, suffer and endure the worst without transforming it into physical symptoms. *(Ibid.,* 22f.)

Most psychiatrists will agree, more or less, with the first two points of Jaspers' accusation; the critical psychotherapist, too, will thoughtfully ponder Jaspers' theses, even though he may at times be inclined to opposition. The third point is not as ripe an accusation as Jaspers' plea would indicate. Medicine defends itself through myself as the 'humble counsel for the defense' of such a big cause in the following way: Neurosis (a 'concept' from the vocabulary of de-humanized man) is, by no means, characterized only by somatic processes, alienated from meaning, which originate in the repression of not, or insufficiently, worked-out experiences. Many human beings who are in conflict with themselves — whose 'being-in-the-world' is impaired[35] — do not at all repress into the body, as Jaspers has correctly stated. The inhibited, the despairing human being, enmeshed in his antinomies, may also escape into spiritual and mental derangement. Depression, anxiety neurosis, marital crisis, the emotional crises of puberty and change of life — all these are repressions, too: man shuns decision, but certainly not of his own free will, not in full, clear consciousness. Psychoanalysis has helped us to understand these patients better in their crises, and has thus enabled us to treat them more effectively. In his criticism of the concrete errors of psychoanalysis, insofar as it is medical theory and therapeutic technique, Jaspers goes too far. But it would not be Jaspers — who always fanatically takes up the cudgels against dogma of any kind —, if he did not acknowledge that psychoanalysis "is like a beacon, challenging the physician to examine himself, a self-examination not to be taken lightly." Jaspers merely attacks the abuses of psychoanalysis which he sees exclusively — and one-sidedly — as a sectarian movement. The revered author finds kind words for the "independent psychotherapists who love man and want to help him;" and who, in each case, as individuals, are doing their best, "using psychoanalytical methods without becoming their slaves." *(Ibid.,* 21.)

Jaspers also opposes categorically, even vehemently, the requirement that every psychotherapist should submit to a training analysis. On the other hand, Jaspers demands that "the psychotherapist should make himself the object of his psychology, to at least the

[35] Jaspers will forgive my trespassing into the idiom of Heidegger.

same extent and with the same profundity which he exercises in the treatment of his patients." A very small elite only would seem capable of this self-illumination. Jaspers has misgivings because "the *'existential'* process of self-illumination and self-realization of our inner acts, of freedom itself, is not possible in seriousness in the presence of another human being, is possible only in the *'existential'* communication of a life time. . . ." This statement does not, we feel, do justice to the realities of day by day medical work. Single individuals (among them Freud, who never went through an analysis himself) will time and again find this path. But the great masses of the present age are in need of many competent psychiatrists who, being themselves part of the masses, do not belong to the chosen few. They are confronted with a task to which they will be equal only after having taken at least a few steps on the road to their true self, under the guidance of an expert. A training analysis will answer this purpose remarkably well. The leading psychiatrists ought to do their part by heeding Jaspers' warning, taking care that the training analysis is kept within limits. Closing the subject of psychoanalysis, we feel that there is reason to be grateful to Jaspers for his criticism of the empirical basis and the methods of psychotherapy. Psychopathological education sharpened by methodological reflection is an urgent necessity for physicians who devote themselves to psychotherapy. If all physicians and psychologists who are, in practice and theory, engaged in psychotherapy, were psychiatrically trained and familiar with the psychopathology of Jaspers, the unpleasant and unfruitful controversies, which at present are again prevalent in the field of (medical) literature, would come to an end.[36]

Concluding, we shall attempt to outline in summary fashion the place of Jaspers as a psychopathologist in the present situation of psychiatry and its border-sciences. The *General Psychopathology* by Jaspers is an unparalleled achievement, if we consider the wealth of new insights which have been gained by the natural sciences during the first half of the twentieth century. Only in conjunction with an unusually broad and profound education in the history of thought *(Geistesgeschichte)* could the attempt have been made to separate the theoretically ascertained and practically usable elements from the accumulating material, to combine it

[36] Physicians who are experienced psychotherapists, unless they are dogmatically rigid, i.e., pure proselytes, come very quickly to an understanding, though they may diverge in their basic philosophical views. Proof of this are, e.g., the Lindau meetings of psychotherapists where, owing to the meritorious initiative of Speer, the most heterogeneous representatives of psychotherapy are collaborating quite harmoniously.

into a survey of the symptoms and problems of abnormal mental life, and, simultaneously, to demonstrate the variety and varying validity of the sources and methods of the knowledge gained. *As long as there is a science of mental illness Jaspers' book will remain a basic work and as a beacon.*

Jaspers is a clear mind. His extremely concise language, more and more personal in its expression, has led many readers, particularly those who are not used to thinking, to conclude erroneously that Jaspers is difficult to understand. True, Jaspers does not write for the general public. Even the Bible, the popular book of faithful Christians, does not satisfy this ideal demand. Any sampling of the shorter works, however, e.g., of *The Perennial Scope of Philosophy,* will convince the reader that Jaspers is accessible to any person of average intelligence who does not shun the time or the effort to re-think Jaspers, and who is, therefore, capable of following his ideas. The difficulty of making the inquiry and philosophy of Jaspers one's own, is to be sought not in the author but in the reader. The average contemporary is used to being handed something ready-made. He is expected to subscribe to a theory or idea which has been appetizingly prepared, or to a palatable program or organization. Jaspers makes no concessions to today's bureaucratized society, without which [concessions] the great masses of the world can, apparently, no longer be controlled. He addresses himself exclusively to the single individual whom he wishes "to force," by the power of the word, to attain clarity about himself and his world. Conjuringly he appeals to human Reason, this tool which God gave to Man and to Man only, a tool which enables Man to orient himself in his world, to illuminate his *Existenz* and to satisfy his metaphysical needs. As a psychopathologist Jaspers summons the individual psychiatrist ceaselessly to look on his patient as a human being instead of a case. The single individual who, in distress, in suffering, is looking for help and submits to medical treatment (or is entrusted to the care of a physician) can never, or only in rare exceptional cases, be comprehended in a way which the totality and singularity of his being would demand. Dismayed by our incapacity to meet the single individual as a primal entity *(urtümliche Wesenheit)* (unless it be in loving communication) we dare, nevertheless, not despair or withdraw in resignation. Even though we are resigned to an understanding of the single patient, now in terms of neurology, or brain pathology, now in those of "explanatory" psychopathology or *"verstehende"* psychotherapy, i.e., even though we submit the single human individual to the concepts formed by our intelligence, we still must not forgo a comprehension of him as an individual in terms of the Encompassing of his world-design *(Weltentwurf)*. The road to this goal is full of agony. Jaspers tries to make our task easier by showing us how we can attempt cautiously to encircle the individual patient — despite our incapacity of grasping him as a whole.

Jaspers' basic thesis is that there is no total knowledge of Man, only partial insights. Such partial knowledge (frequently intuitive in origin) must be corroborated empirically, proved logically, and, thus given immediate living demonstration. It must not, however, be forgotten that Jaspers, the keen analyst, as a philosopher, scholar and person, is obsessed by the idea of portraying man as a whole in his once and for all uniqueness *(je einmaligem Wesen)*. This intention stands out not only in his early psychopathological studies, his biographical studies, his *Psychologie der Weltanschauungen,* but, above all, in his philosophical works.

Yet Jaspers considers it fatal to give absolute value to an intuition or an idea of man. As a conscientious scholar he insists on differentiating between what is knowable and can, therefore, be proved by rational processes, and of what I become conscious by philosophizing out of the Encompassing. I am then able to grasp both by virtue of my reason; but the process is a different one in each instance. As a scholar I must, in strict self-discipline, remember that only clear distinction of methods can promote authentic scientific knowledge. As a philosopher I am free to indulge in the flow of my brainstorms, of my ideas.

To return to psychopathology: the disease-entity, the localization of mental occurrences in definite areas of the brain, the genesis of neurosis from the repressed unconscious, — these are fruitful working hypotheses, which originated — often in a flash of genius — in the mind of scholars. Such 'ideas' can become subjects of scientific psychopathology only to the extent to which quite specific methods, appropriate to the relevant matter of investigation, are indicated, methods that is, which make clinical, experimental or psychological approaches and tests possible. Moreover, many empirically established facts of psychopathology can be successfully viewed from different angles and treated by different methods. A psychopathologist who does not subject himself to this methodological self-reflection — which Jaspers was the first clearly and emphatically to insist upon — is constantly in danger of slipping into fanaticisms (e.g., the sex-Theory of Freud), or into mythology (e.g., the localization doctrine).

That Jaspers, despite his strict analytical demands, does not favor an atomistic approach, remaining stuck in a hollow methodology, — purposely neglects the synthesis whose aim is the comprehension of totalities, of personalities, of human destinies, is particularly evident in his psychopathological biographies. In the cases of Van Gogh, Hölderlin and Nietzsche, Jaspers, unlike anyone before him, endeavors to view the disease and the work, and the disease and the life as one. It is true, that Jaspers — if we criticize his position strictly — even then still remains within the limits of his idea of the unconditional distinction between *verstehende* and explanatory psychology. As an experienced psychopathologist, he clearly recognizes the destructive influence of the disease; yet he does not make the terrible mistake (if viewed in the light of the *history of thought*) of classifying the works of these men of genius, who had fallen victims to a mental disease, from the psychiatric viewpoint alone. On the other hand, his judgment as a scientist prevents him from ignoring the disease as a matter of perhaps incidental importance. On the contrary, tracing back the subtle relations which connect a being of flesh and blood with his spiritual achievement, he painfully wrestles with the full reality revealed in the individual's life and work.

Nevertheless, does Jaspers not perhaps overlook the fact that the disease is a necessary constituent of the sustaining basis of each of these individual lives? Does Jaspers' synthesis of the functional and biographical conceptions *(Schau)*[37] of *verstehende* and explaining psychology, exemplary though it is, suffice to exhaust the meaning and content of the existences of individual patients? Should the attempt (made by L. Binswanger in his 'Analysis of Existence,' modelled on Heidegger),[38] not be permissible to divest the disease of its meaningless *(sinnfremd)* character by viewing it as a particular mode of being-in-the-world; as a predetermined world-design *(vorgegebener Weltentwurf)?* These are real questions, momentous questions. However, is not Jaspers' searching and philosophizing one single quest?

Indeed, it seems to us that the keen and intent questioning, incessantly disquieting to the listener, forms the core of Jaspers' life work. The concepts of health and disease, heredity, disposition, physiognomy, psycho-somatic unity, the understanding of the meaning of biographic material, psychoanalysis, the possibilties of true mental aid (psychotherapy) — all this he has called in ques-

---

[37] Making use of the concepts introduced by L. Binswanger.

[38] Cf. the principal work by Binswanger: *Grundformen und Erkenntnis menschlichen Daseins,* (Zürich, 1942), and his "Daseinsanalytik und Psychiatrie," in *Nervenarzt,* 22, 1951.

tion. As in his philosophical works, he also dismisses the inquiring psychopathologist, who turns to him for advice, into his own freedom. But should we scold Jaspers for not providing us with ready made recipes (though he is particularly qualified to do so in virtue of his wide range of culture, his profound knowledge of man), but guiding the psychiatrist to his own decision instead?

We should not want to expect more from a scholar than he himself has promised. Jaspers did keep the promise made in the first edition of his *General Psychopathology:* that psychiatrists should learn "to observe psychopathologically, to question psychopathologically, to analyze psychopathologically, to think psychopathologically." He is with us as a great teacher, a voice of warning, reminding and questioning us, and as such he will enter into the history of psychiatry. Our grief that Jaspers left psychiatry is alleviated only by his philosophical work which illuminates our modest actions with a belated but never fading splendor.

KURT KOLLE

PSYCHIATRIC AND NEUROLOGICAL CLINIC
UNIVERSITÄT MÜNCHEN
GERMANY

12

Ludwig B. Lefebre

THE PSYCHOLOGY OF KARL JASPERS

S Y N O P S I S

INTRODUCTION
A. *JASPERS' CONTRIBUTIONS TO GENERAL*
   PSYCHOLOGY
   I. JASPERS' ARRANGEMENT OF GENERAL
      PSYCHOLOGY
   II. THE PHENOMENOLOGICAL METHOD
   III. THE CLARIFICATION OF THE CONDITIONS OF
        GENERAL PSYCHOLOGY
       a. Results of Jaspers' analysis of the *modes of cognition* in
          the psychological realm and his inferences therefrom
          1. Explanation
          2. *Verstehen*
          3. *Verstehen* and Explanation
          4. Introducing the psychologist into psychology
       b. Results of Jaspers' analysis of the *limits of cognition* in
          the psychological realm
          1. Critique of psychological thinking
          2. Critique of theories
          3. Critique of methods in general
          4. Arrangement according to methods
          5. The new foundation of psychological thinking
   IV. THE CHANGE OF LOCALE OF PSYCHOLOGY AND
       ITS CONSEQUENCES
       1. The meaning of right and wrong
       2. The validity of objectively correct statements
       3. The psychological center
       4. The psychologist's conception of the mind
       5. The unification of psychology
       6. Undogmatic psychology

467

B. *JASPERS' CONTRIBUTION TO THE PSYCHOLOGY
   OF THE INDIVIDUAL:*
   DIE PSYCHOLOGIE DER WELTANSCHAUUNGEN
C. *CRITIQUE*
     I. THE SUBJECT-OBJECT CLEAVAGE
    II. EXPERIENCE AND BEHAVIOR
   III. LINEAR THINKING AND SYNCRETIC
        EXPERIENCE
D. *THE RELATIONS BETWEEN JASPERS' PSYCHOLOGY
   AND HIS FUNDAMENTAL CONVICTIONS*

THE PSYCHOLOGY OF KARL JASPERS*

Introduction

THE SUBJECT of psychology is mind — but only the *mani-festations* of mind can be experienced. This fact not only gives psychology as a whole a peculiarly disunited character; it also leaves — more or less — to the individual psychologist the task of defining his subject. Thus various types of psychologists produce various types of psychologies, all of which leave something to be desired. The "natural science" type of psychologist, for example, treats with disdain everything that is not tangible and that cannot objectively be shown to exist — but he usually ends up with a psychology without psyche; the "visionary" type gives the impression of having complete insight into the workings of the "soul," but manages at the most to transmit to others faint glimpses of what he seems to perceive; the "theorist" constructs causing confusion — and creatings sects. In spite of these unfavor-grandiose conceptions of the regions of the mind; but these, though they prove their author's inventive ability, add little to psychological knowledge. These three types, however extreme, are to be preferred to a fourth, the "eclectic" type whose contri-bution to psychology more often than not consists of a conceptual conglomeration, mixing mental content and mental structure, reality and thoughts about reality, facts and speculation, thereby able conditions, psychology has developed as a science, due, in the main, to the efforts of a fifth type of psychologist who con-centrates on research, does not cling too dogmatically to one of the extreme points of view and is satisfied with finding out as much as possible about mind with the means available to him.

Because of the disunited character of psychology and the dif-ferent types of psychologists, every really new psychological dis-

* All translations from the German appearing in this article are mine. In all cases where I believe no adequate translation of a term or phrase is possible I either use the German term or the closest translation known to me plus the German orig-inal in parenthesis.

covery leads — almost automatically — to new theoretical conceptions and eventually to mutually exclusive psychologies. Thus different psychological "parties" result from almost every psychological discovery of importance. These express themselves with the help of a steadily growing variety of theoretical conceptions, although, in the final analysis, they all talk about the same thing. It is therefore necessary from time to time to redetermine what psychology is all about and to redefine its aims. Since the great progress of psychology during recent years makes such a reexamination of its basic concepts and methods highly desirable even now, it is fortunate that at least part of this important task has already been accomplished. Karl Jaspers has analyzed the problem: what is psychology? As a result of his deliberations he has pointed the way to a unified view of all psychologies. More than that: he has traced the fundamentals of a new — potentially encompassing — psychology, the *psychology of the real, existing man.*

From the point of view of the psychologist it is to be regretted that, early in his career, Jaspers turned from psychopathology and psychology to philosophy and, maybe for that reason, completed only parts of his psychology. Who if not he, whose thinking centers on the living existing man, would have been able to create this kind of psychology as contrasted with the psychology of "man as a conceptual object" (Kunz)? But, on the other hand, the incompleteness of the psychology of Jaspers may also be regarded as a challenge to contemporary psychology, one, moreover, which it can ill afford to overlook. For the new approach that is manifest throughout Jaspers' work is the beginning of a psychology that may well answer some of the questions which are specifically puzzling to psychologists at the present time.

A. *Jaspers' Contributions to General Psychology*

When Jaspers' first publications appeared during the first decade of this century most psychologists, although differing in other respects, started from the tacit, positivistic conviction that in principle everything can be known; and that man, or even the mental region of man, is no exception to this rule. The assumption that with proper methods and sufficient endurance everything would eventually be understood, had produced excellent results in the natural sciences, so that most scientists, including psychologists, saw no reason to question this assumption. Although the representatives of psychology — at the time a comparatively young science — realized that most of the riddles of the mind remained unsolved, the majority of them seemingly did not doubt that they could be solved in principle and would be solved eventually. Nor did the way by which solutions would be found seem to pose too much of a problem. Experiments, controlled according to the criteria valid in the natural sciences, were looked upon as the most important method of psychology; they revealed the physiological and psychological conditions as well as the causes of mental phenomena, and it was thought that this sufficed. Causal explanation and scientific understanding were considered to be practically synonymous.

As over against this Jaspers declared: 1. Man cannot be known; 2. cognition and causal explanation are not identical; 3. there are essential aspects of mind which cannot be rendered accessible by experimental methods. If these were merely philosophical or epistemological statements they would be of limited interest to the psychologist; inasmuch, however, as they are among the basic principles of a new and fertile psychological theory of method, it is necessary for the psychologist to probe their validity.[1]

I. Jaspers' Arrangement of General Psychology

In order to give an initial idea of Jaspers' fundamentally new approach to psychology the following scheme, which shows his division of the subject matter of psychology, is reproduced. It ap-

[1] This article is based on *Allgemeine Psychopathologie* (General Psychopathology), 5th ed., Berlin & Heidelberg 1948. *Allgemeine* is the most important of those works of Jaspers which deal — directly or indirectly — with psychology. It contains all his new ideas concerning psychology but, owing to the purpose of the book, formulated in most cases in terms of psychopathology. For this reason access to the psychology of Jaspers is made difficult for the psychologist. This applies particularly to the American psychologist because he must, in addition, cope with the difficulties of a foreign language. For these reasons I assume that the readers of this article will, in most cases, not be acquainted with Jaspers' psychology and I will therefore stress the portrayal of his more important ideas, not their discussion, in my treatment of the subject. It is my opinion that Jaspers' contribution to psychology consists above all in his critique of its basic conditions and of the innovations introduced as a result of this critique. These will therefore be stressed most. Accordingly, the theoretical psychologist Jaspers will be in the foreground of my presentation. In a sense this amounts to a distortion, inasmuch as Jaspers is also an accomplished practical psychologist. As such he appears, for example, in his profound analyses of Strindberg and Van Gogh (*Strindberg*, 3rd ed., Bremen 1949) and in *Psychologie*, 3rd ed., Berlin 1925.

My article may also create the impression that *Allgemeine Psychopathologie* deals primarily with purely theoretical reflections and with a critique of psychological methods. This is not the case; it deals predominantly with empirically observed facts. It contains a wealth of vivid descriptions of mental phenomena and of extracts from case records. Cf. Kolle's essay, this volume.

proximates the one which forms the basis of his *Allgemeine Psychopathologie.*[2]

I. Mind viewed in terms of separate empirical data
   a) subjective (experienced) data
      1) separate phenomena (i.e., "object-consciousness," "space- and time-experience," etc.)
      2) The momentary whole (the state of consciousness) [3]
   b) objective data
      1) performances
      2) somatic findings
      3) meaningful objective data: expression, behavior, creations of the mind

II. Mind viewed in terms of connections
   a) connections dicovered by *Verstehen*[4]
   b) causal connections

III. Mind viewed in terms of wholes
   a) the individual
   b) constitution
   c) biography, etc.[5]

I shall try to clarify some of the principles on which this division of the subject matter of psychology is based. By so doing I hope to point up some of the most important ideas of Jaspers as far as they pertain to psychology. First, however, I shall refer briefly to the article which established Jaspers' reputation both as a psychopathologist and as a psychologist.

2 Cf. *Allgemeine,* 39f. Differences between this scheme of division and that of *Allgemeine* are mainly due to the fact that I have omitted or changed all specific references to psychopathology in the scheme of the division of *Allgemeine Psychopathologie,* because I am dealing in my article exclusively with Jaspers' contribution to psychology.

3 It can be seen that the "empirical data" are dealt with individually (under "separate phenomena") and in their entirety (under "the momentary whole") as well.

4 *Verstehen* is one of the basic concepts of Jaspers' psychology. Unfortunately it is practically impossible to translate it into English. Its meaning conveys something between "comprehension," "understanding" and "intuition," all of which, however, fail to convey correctly the meaning of the word in Jaspers' usage (which again differs from Spranger's use of the term). For this reason I decided to use the German word throughout. The real meaning of *Verstehen* will — it is hoped — be increasingly clarified in the following paragraphs. Cf. also G. W. Allport's discussion of *Verstehen* in *Personality* (New York 1937), 539ff. Allport's definition differs from mine because he bases it mainly on Spranger's use of the term.

5 #I is subdivided according to the material with which the psychologist is actually confronted in practice; #II and III according to the concepts he uses in dealing with this material.

II. The Phenomenological Method

In 1912 there existed a number of methods for the investigation of the *objective phenomena* of the mind as they appear in somatopsychology, performance-psychology, etc., such as memory-experiments and threshold-experiments; but there was no clearly circumscribed method for the description of *subjective experiences*, although their firm establishment is a necessity for every kind of psychology. There were, it is true, those who considered the investigation of experienced phenomena of prime importance. Husserl in particular, being the first in modern psychology, had already started a "descriptive psychology of the phenomena of consciousness" and had also introduced the term "phenomenology" (hitherto customary in philosophy only) for this branch of psychology;[6] in the Würzburg school of psychology too, under the guidance of Külpe, phenomenological research was in progress. It was left to Jaspers, however, to present the first comprehensive description of the phenomenological method — and at the same time to introduce phenomenology into psychiatry —, with the publication of his article "Die phänomenologische Forschungsrichtung in der Psychopathologie" (the phenomenological method of research in psychopathology).[7]

In Jaspers' usage "phenomenology" means: illustrative representation of individual experience *(anschauliche Vergegenwärtigung individuellen seelischen Erlebens)*; it is an empirical method designed to define experienced mental states — i.e., subjective mental phenomena — within the narrowest possible confines; to distinguish between them; and to separate them terminologically. Phenomenology accomplishes all this, "depending on the individual case, by the enumeration of a number of outward characteristics of the mental state, of the conditions under which it occurs, through vivid, illustrative comparisons and symbolizations, through a kind of suggestive representation" which is based on empathy and which is supposed to enable the reader of a phenomenological description empathically to perceive the phenomenon described.[8] It ranks with and is complementary to the various procedures which make evident the objective phenomena of mental life.

6 In Husserl's later writings "phenomenology" stands for "perception of essence" *(Wesensschau)*. In Jaspers' work the term always carries the narrower meaning mentioned. Cf. *Allgemeine,* 47f.

7 In *Zeitschrift für die gesamte Neurologie und Psychiatrie,* No. 9, 1912, 391ff.

8 *Allgemeine,* 47.

Phenomenology is the *static* version of *Verstehen* (only the other — genetic — version though is meant whenever Jaspers uses this term) ; it comprehends individual mental states by *treating them as if they were static*. In contrast, the *genetic* comprehension which characterizes *Verstehen* in the narrow sense of the word, tries "to grasp the restlessness of the mind, (i.e.) motion, connections, intrinsic developments."[9] Phenomenology is the condition upon which those methods depend which make their results objectively available and accessible to everybody in the form of graphs or statistics, measurements on mechanical appliances, etc.; in a sense it localizes phenomena whereas other methods take them for granted.

It is obvious that this psychological method is different from the descriptions common in the natural sciences: the object is not in itself visible to our eyes; the experience is merely one of mental visualization. But the logical principle is not different. Apart from systematic categories, describing requires successful formulations and contrasting comparisons, the demonstration of relationships among different phenomena of their arrangement in series, or of their occurrence in disconnected leaps.[10]

The ideal of phenomenology is an infinite array of irreducible mental qualities, arranged in a surveyable order.[11]

III. The Clarification of the Conditions of General Psychology

a. Results of Jaspers' analysis of the *Modes of cognition* in the psychological realm and his inferences therefrom

The introduction of a new psychological method — phenomenology — into psychopathology grew out of Jaspers' search for an answer to the question: What are the conditions determining cognition in the psychological realm? Phenomenology is one of his first contributions to the attempted control of these conditions. Soon the problem of the basic conditions of psychology presents itself to him in another form. Is, he asks, our understanding of psychological occurrences really based on explanation alone, as seems to be generally assumed? Jaspers denies that this is so. He finds that explanation is limited to "the recognition of *objective*

---

9 *Ibid.*, 23.   10 *Ibid.*, 47.

11 To read "Die phänomenologische . . ." today, is still profitable for the psychologist. Among other things the article contains valuable instructions for protocolling interviews with patients; these instructions are equally valid for protocols of subjects' statements in experiments.

causal relationships" and that in this manner of recognizing the observed is "always observed *from the outside only (italics* mine)". Explanation therefore is adequate for the psychophysical sectors of psychology and — on the whole — for all "outside" views of mind. But neither is it the only way to comprehend mind nor, in the narrower psychological sense, an adequate one. **Our real** understanding of mental life is derived from a different source: from that "perception of mental phenomena *from within (italics* mine)" which Jaspers calls *Verstehen.*[12] In psychology this *Verstehen* represents an ultimate source of experience analogous to sensory perception in the natural sciences. Consequently Jaspers claims that all psychologists actually use two kinds of cognition: explanation and *Verstehen;* but, he points out, they consider only one of these — explanation — to be scientifically sound. This erroneous opinion he refutes by showing some of those realms in psychology which are accessible to *Verstehen* alone: "reactions to experiences, the development of passions, the origin of error, . . . the contents of dreams and delusions, . . . the effects of suggestion, . . . the individual structure of an abnormal personality, . . ." etc.[13] (Jaspers does not overlook the fact that — in principle — these, too, are subject to causal explanation.) [14]

1. Explanation

A short characterization of explanation will further the understanding of the difference between explanation and *Verstehen.*

Jaspers uses the term "explanation" always in the sense of "causal" explanation.[15] If this kind of explanation is applied in the realm of psychology, it means that connections between different psychological data, because of repeated experiences, are recognized as regular or even necessary and seen in a "cause and effect" relationship. For example: recognition of a connection between the

---

12 *Allgemeine,* 24.   13 *Ibid.,* 251.

14 Cf. *ibid.,* 253; Jaspers is not the first psychologist to introduce *Verstehen* into psychology. His most important predecessors were Dilthey and Spranger. Dilthey distinguishes between "descriptive" and "dissecting" psychology as Jaspers distinguishes between *Verstehen* and explanation in psychology. Spranger uses the term *geisteswissenschaftliche* psychology to designate approximately what Jaspers calls the psychology of *Verstehen.* I might mention here that Jaspers' importance — even though he is one of the first phenomenologists, among the earliest to depart from elemental psychology, etc. — does not lie in the introduction of specific innovations, but in his altogether new approach.

15 The possible objection that Jaspers first arbitrarily limits the meaning of "explanation" and then shows the shortcomings of this kind of explanation is not valid. Jaspers can show that only this kind of explanation is being used to explain psychological phenomena, regardless of the fact that the term as such carries a much broader meaning which includes *Verstehen.*

deterioration of performance on one hand, and fatigue on the other, is an explanation in the Jaspersian sense. Thus 'explanation' may be said to mean: *ascertainment of empirically existing cause and effect relationships which in themselves cannot be understood but are recognized as necessary.*

2. *Verstehen*

Verstehen, too, is a form of explanation. But it is a psychological, not a causal mode of explanation. The relations uncovered by *Verstehen* — whether they are relations between coexisting phenomena or whether they have the structure: one phenomenon follows another — are *meaningful* relations whose evidence is final. If, for example, the psychotherapist grasps the meaning of a patient's symptom by viewing it in connection with certain of the patient's biographical data, he is practicing *Verstehen*.[16] Jaspers says: "One has sometimes called the relations comprehended by *Verstehen* '*inner causality*' and thus pointed to the unbridgable gap between these relations, which can be called causal only by analogy, and the genuine causal relations, (i.e.) outer causality."[17] The juxtaposition of these two kinds of causality is basic to the psychology of Jaspers.

3. *Verstehen* and explanation

In his phenomenology Jaspers had developed a method which made it possible to portray subjective experiences accurately by describing their formal characteristics. In his analysis of *Verstehen* he creates the foundation for the interpretation of the material thus gathered. With *Verstehen* he adds a new region to scientific psychological research, one that before him was accessible solely to the "intuitive" way of understanding, whose chief characteristic it is that it cannot be objectified. But, because of its hermeneutic character, *Verstehen* can never be the only source of psychological knowledge; *Verstehen* and explanation must supplement each other just as phenomenology and the "objective" methods do, "Where *Verstehen* ends, causal questioning begins."[18]
With

Verstehen (we) . . . soon (reach) *limits*. Something new emerges in the mind in a completely incomprehensible manner. . . . The stages

---

[16] Accordingly psychoanalysis could be called a psychology of *Verstehen*. Jaspers, however, believes that psychoanalysts do not use real but "quasi"-*Verstehen*, among other reasons, because they misconstrue the material they uncover by means of *Verstehen* by thinking of it in terms of casual relations. Jaspers demands that each psychologist use both modes of cognition, but that he keep them apart. Cf. *Allgemeine*, 254f.

[18] *Ibid.*, 444.   [17] *Allgemeine*, 250.

of normal mental development, the phases and periods of mental disorders, belong to such successions in time which cannot be understood. The historical aspect of the mind cannot even approximately be grasped in its entirety by genetic *Verstehen;* it also needs to be explained causally, . . . just like the objects of natural-scientific research.[19]

The obvious supposition that the mind is the realm of *Verstehen* and the physical region that of causal explanation is wrong. There is no actual occurrence, be it of a physical or mental nature, that is not, in principle, subject to causal explanation; the happenings of the mind can be made the subject of causal explanation too. . . . *Verstehen, however, finds limits everywhere.* The existence of the distinct mental predispositions, the laws that pertain to the acquisition or loss of memory-traces, the mental condition as a whole at different age levels and everything else that falls under the heading 'substructure of the mind,' puts up a barrier to . . . *Verstehen.* Every limit of *Verstehen* provides a new impulse for causal questioning.[20]

Jaspers describes the procedure of the psychologist of *Verstehen* as follows:

He starts out from an intuitive overall conception. This he dissects, clarifying successively: expression, contents and phenomena on the one hand, nonconscious mechanisms on the other; there is an awareness of *Existenz*, the fundamental factor that cannot empirically be explored. Finally an enriched understanding of the whole is reconstructed, based on the facts and possible meanings thus displayed. In every concrete case, whatever result has been achieved is questioned; the procedure is repeated and intensified through the collection of objective data, new conceptions of the whole alternating with renewed dissection.[21]

---

19 *Ibid.*, 24.   20 *Ibid.*, 253.

21 *Ibid.*, 259. It should be noted that the term *Existenz* is found among the concepts which serve as points of orientation for the psychologist of *Verstehen* (which does not mean that *Existenz* in the Jaspersian sense could or should become an object of psychological research). To the purist psychologist the introduction of a philosophical concept in a psychological context may mean that Jaspers' psychology is a metaphysics in disguise and scientifically unsound. The opposite is true. The scientific soundness of any psychology is maintained only when philosophical concepts are introduced at the appropriate place, i.e., at the limits of psychology. Jaspers says that man is existence, consciousness-as-such, spirit and potential *Existenz*. As existence, consciousness-as-such and spirit he is an object of biological, psychological, sociological and humanistic research; as *Existenz* object of philosophical reflection *(Scope,* 12f.). One might take issue with Jaspers' categorization of man; but it is impossible to overlook the fact that man can be viewed under the aspects he mentions and others as well. No psychology is conceivable, which does not take notice of the biological, sociological, humanistic as well as other aspects of man. Similarly a psychology which overlooks the fact that man is essentially "potential *Existenz*" remains incomplete. This should not be taken to mean that the psychologist should use philosophical concepts, such as *Existenz*, in his psycho-

4. Introducing the psychologist into psychology

Through the separation of *Verstehen* and explanation Jaspers focuses attention on those sources of knowledge which are at the disposal of the psychologist *within himself*. He no longer asks: "What can I, the psychologist, know?", but: "What can I, the psychologist, know when viewing my object through *Verstehen?*", or: "What can I know when viewing it through explanation?" This new approach is important for two reasons: 1) it ranks *Verstehen* equal with explanation and thus legitimizes an additional dimension of cognition; 2) it implies the demand that the psychologist should include in his contemplation of psychological data the way in which he mentally perceives them. The fact that the psychologist as such is one of the essential factors determining the conditions of psychology is thus given its proper importance. We shall see later, when discussing the question of the limits of cognition, that the seemingly self-evident postulate of including the manner of cognition in the consideration of psychological data — we call it *"introducing the psychologist into psychology"* — has far-reaching consequences in psychological practice; it may well be considered the beginning of a new kind of psychology.

It can even now be discerned in what respect Jaspers differs fundamentally from all the other psychologists who started new psychologies in the years immediately preceding the first world war. Then Wertheimer, in his interpretation of experiments on the perception of motion, first formulated opinions which prepared the way for the replacement of elemental psychology (primarily of associationism) by *Gestalt* psychology. At about the same time Watson, with his "behaviorism," began his fight against the introspective methods then customary and proclaimed the belief that psychologically relevant knowledge could solely be acquired through the study of objectively observable behavior; and Freud was replacing the static view of the mind with a dynamic one by building his theory around the central concept of "drives." I can only mention — not discuss — here other contemporaries of Jaspers such as Klages, Köhler, McDougall, Thorndike, etc., whose contributions are equally essential to modern psychology. It must suffice to point out in what respect Jaspers differs from all of them. The psychologists mentioned either replace, consciously or unconsciously, an existing theory, a familiar conception of man or mind, with a new one and thus disclose new perspectives of psychology;

logical practice. It does mean that he must realize that one of the limits of psychological understanding is precisely that fundamental characteristic of man called *Existenz*.

or they open up hitherto inaccessible regions to psychological research.[22] They do not, however, "relativize" their findings, as does Jaspers, by including the manner of cognition in their systems. This is not intended as negative criticism of the scientists mentioned. On the contrary: most of them deal with material which does not necessarily require this step; they could hardly be criticized, therefore, for not taking it. Introducing the psychologist into psychology is stressed here solely because I consider it to be one of the symptoms indicating the fundamental change made possible and started by Jaspers in psychology. Other manifestations of this change will become apparent in the following paragraphs.

b. Results of Jaspers' analysis of the *limits of cognition* in the psychological realm

Jaspers progresses from the clarification of the bases of cognition present in the person of the psychologist to the analysis of the limits of any possible psychology. Soon, further consequenes of his "relativizing" point of view become apparent. He follows Kant in recognizing in human cognition a barrier to knowledge.

In the process of cognition being *(Sein)* is available to us . . . only as an object of our consciousness. . . . In empirical reality we therefore grasp being only through the way we encounter it in the categories of consciousness, through the way it appears in the manifold modes of experience, explicability, comprehensibleness.[23]

A further limitation of cognition is contained in the impossibility to grasp fully in thought certain empirically given wholes such as the world and man.

Wherever I try to grasp the whole, be it the world or man, the object escapes me since the intended meaning is an idea (a task for never-ending research), not a distinct and complete finiteness. What I recognize is never the world but something within the world; the world is not an object but an idea. . . . In the case of man it is no different. . . . As soon as he has become an object to me — which he always becomes in a certain way and under certain points of view — I no longer have all of him.[24]

The impossibility of possessing man in his entirety as an object of knowledge means that psychology must take into account not only those limitations which are valid for all sciences but also the special

22 I am aware of the fact that these remarks do not begin to do justice to the contents of the different new psychologies mentioned. But we are concerned here not with differences of content but with those of approach.

23 *Allgemeine*, 632.   24 *Ibid.*, 468.

one originating in the above-mentioned character of its "object."

Jaspers surmounts both barriers to knowledge — those contained in the psychologist himself, and those presented by the object of psychology — with a systematic *critique of psychological thinking,* particularly of theories and methods, and with the *arrangement of all psychological knowledge according to theories and methods.* With these two steps he actually starts the systematic introduction of the psychologist into psychology.[25]

1. Critique of psychological thinking

Jaspers claims that the act of thinking, because of the categorial limitations of all thinking, introduces errors into psychology (as well as into other sciences). He argues as follows: The object of the psychologist appears to his thought solely in the concepts used. These in turn are based on theories or, at least, on working-hypotheses. Since every theoretical construction necessarily arranges a given material according to certain points of view, it must inevitably disregard possible others. It follows that even the most encompassing theory leaves out a number of mental phenomena. Therefore the psychologist's thinking, which is oriented on theories, always includes a specific and limiting way of grasping the data reflected upon. Considered from this angle every observation in psychology and even more so every theory, presents a kind of falsification.

But on the other hand a scientific psychology —as every other science — is only possible if observations and contemplations eventually crystallize into theoretical constructions. To neutralize the falsification which they introduce into psychology, constant criticism is necessary. Jaspers therefore considers a systematic critique of psychological thinking and of the methods used in psychology, such as statistics, experiments and tests, to be an indispensable part of psychology. "That which in every finding has been presupposed . . . (must) be consciously realized, that 'trace of theory contained in every fact.' Thus we learn to perceive realities and to know at the same time that they are never reality as such, complete reality."[26] The conceptual apparatus — the concepts, categories, theories and methods — with which the psychologist views

---

[25] The introduction of phenomenology into psychology also represented a more than hitherto customary inclusion of the psychologist in psychology. It is possible to regard it as an attempt to counter the ever-present danger of using concepts in psychology which are removed from actual experience and devoid of meaning. By installing phenomenology as the basic psychological method Jaspers pushes the psychologist in the direction of what concretely exists, by forcing him to make sure that a phenomenon is the basis of his reflections.

[26] *Allgemeine,* 15.

his object must be checked continually, just as the mechanical appliances he uses in his experiments.

2. Critique of theories

Jaspers himself carries out the critique he considers to be a fundamental requirement of psychology. I quote, as an example, an excerpt from his analysis of psychological theories since the views expressed therein determine to a large extent the character of his psychology.

To Jaspers theories are no more than ideas through which psychological thinking orientates itself. In this they differ from theories in the natural sciences.

Firstly the difference is noticeable in the manner of verification and falsification. In psychology theories are outlines, in which known facts are arranged, for which facts, which may fit, are sought and in which room is made for facts which may possibly become known in the future, but in every respect without the systematic method which aims at a general regard for all facts and is continually in search of those which are in opposition. It is a grouping under the analogon of a theory, the theory is not a tool of research. *Secondly* succeeding theories are not based one upon another, there is no transformation during which they become increasingly unified and more adjusted to reality. On the contrary a theory is completed and afterwards forgotten as a whole. *Thirdly* there is a multitude of separate theories which exist next to one another without being connected.

It is therefore possible to say: *in psychology there are no genuine theories as in natural science (italics* mine) . They fail; they are deceptive speculations about a presumed reality *(Sein)* which appear in forms that are analogous to theories in natural science but which in most cases lack a clear logical method.[27]

3. Critique of methods in general

In addition to the definition of the meaning of "theory" in psychology, Jaspers makes a critical analysis of all psychological methods, concepts and theories known to him. This amounts to a critique of all of psychology. The subjects he deals with range from statistics and experiments in psychology, on the one hand, to typologies, psychoanalysis, theories about constitution, etc., on the other. Jaspers points out the intrinsic limits of every psychological method and theory he discusses, thereby establishing their possible value to cognition, and underlining equally their merits and their drawbacks. He discloses the premises on which every method and

---

27 *Ibid.*, 459; I have replaced the term "psychopathology" of the original text with "psychology" throughout; what is meant is as applicable to the one as to the other.

concept-construction is based, and thus makes it possible, even where one does not accept his conclusions, to view whatever problem he happens to deal with in a new light. At the same time he causes the reader to think over the problems for himself. Furthermore, since to him all theories are limited, he is more open than more dogmatic writers to the heuristic value of even those theories which he thinks are false.[28] Altogether he succeeds in ascertaining the realm of applicability of theories and methods in general and that of specific theories and methods in particular. After reading Jaspers, the psychologist is in a position to know what a given theory or method will do, and also what it cannot do.

4. Arrangement according to methods

The critique of theories and methods is only one of the two major measures taken by Jaspers to allow for the limits of the psychologist's cognition. Equally important is the other one, viz.: the arrangement of psychological knowledge according to methods.

It is necessary for the psychologist to form the knowledge he acquires into a cohesive whole in order to achieve a synthesis. Here a new problem arises. Each theoretical arrangement of psychological knowledge would necessarily be an arrangement according to a specific and therefore limited theory — i.e., to a specific way of regarding psychology or a psychological subject. But we have seen that man cannot be caught within the net of any one particular theory, however comprehensive. It is therefore a mistake to arrange psychological knowledge according to a specific theory. For this reason Jaspers designs an arrangement which he characterizes as an "arrangement according to methods," i.e., an "unfolding of . . . the basic modes of . . . perception, of . . . thinking and its categories."[29] In this "methodological" order *every theory has a place as one particular method among others*. It is "not like the map of a continent, but like a map showing the means of travel within it."[30]

With this innovation the "lack of cohesion" of man as an object of research[31] is made the regulating principle of all psychological knowledge. In several respects the overall psychological method is

---

[28] Jaspers' critique of Kretschmer's constitution-theory (*Allgemeine*, 540ff.) is a good example of his critical method. Among other things it contains his basic objections to all pseudo-exact methods. The following extract from his critique of a theory by Conrad (*Allgemeine*, 550) shows how tolerant he can be, even where theories he considers to be false are concerned. "I suspect that all his genetic hypotheses are false but this does not keep them from being of greatest interest as a new 'set of ideas.' Magnificent questions arise even if a provable answer is lacking."

[29] *Allgemeine*, 625.   [30] *Ibid.*, 626.   [31] *Ibid.*, 633.

now adjusted to the object of psychology. *First* of all, the subject
matter of psychology can now be arranged according to logical
principles without doing it violence. *Secondly,* the new arrangement permits the addition of new methods, the replacement of
no longer useful ones by new ones or a reordering at all times.
It cannot be thrown out of focus by the discovery of new facts
which are incompatible with the theoretical assumptions of a
particular theory. *Thirdly,* the psychologist who arranges his
knowledge in this manner remains alert to those unexpected
phenomena which are easily overlooked by theory-centered psychologists.

5. The new foundation of psychological thinking

But since the firm basis of one encompassing conception of the
mind no longer exists, a new foundation is necessary. This, Jaspers
claims, can legitimately consist only of the phenomena, facts and
data — i.e., the *empirical realities of psychology* — themselves. As
a result, these occupy in the new psychology the place held by
theories in others. They serve as the point of orientation for the
psychologist.

Empirical realities are "there" for the psychologist only if he
practices psychology, i.e., if he actually carries out psychological
procedures. Jaspers can therefore not be content with acquisition
of conceptualized knowledge, but must insist on the actual carry-
ing-out, in thought and in practice, of all procedures which make
psychological knowledge possible.[32] The psychologist must become
"aware of all manners of comprehension, forms of perception,
thought patterns, methods of research and basic attitudes of cogni
tion and *practice them (italics* mine) in connection with the empirical material to which they belong."[33] We can see that as soon
as the barrier between psychologist and psychological facts, represented by rigid conceptions of the mind, has been eliminated, the
real existing psychologist — the place in which psychology actually "happens" — assumes an importance he did not have before. He
who structures the empirical data now becomes the center around
which psychology is grouped.

IV. The Change of Locale of Psychology and Its Consequences

With the "arrangement according to methods" Jaspers has located psychology one step "beyond" the place where psychologists

[32] "The method is creative only when used, not in the reflection about it"
(*Allgemeine,* 37).

[33] *Allgemeine,* 37.

had been accustomed to locate it, just as he had gone a step "beyond" the customary methods with the introduction of phenomenology. By returning — by way of the object thought of — to the subject who thinks of the object, he anchors psychology in the psychologist. *The way in which a psychologist considers a psychological datum becomes the basic element of psychology.*

In all other psychologies the basic elements are concepts, assumed to characterize various aspects of the mind. If we examine some fundamental concepts of the more familiar psychologies we find that this is what they all have in common — in spite of other, profound, differences of approach. In associationism, for example, all contents of consciousness are combinations of "elements," such as sensations and ideas; in functionalism *(Aktpsychologie)* the fundamental factor of each perception is the "act of registering" an object; in psychoanalysis "libido," in Gestaltpsychology *"Gestalt,"* "field," etc. are basic concepts. Obviously all of these refer to something that is present in the mind in some form or other. In this connection it does not matter that "mind" and the "being-present" are pictured very differently by the various psychologies mentioned. Important is that all of them take it for granted that characteristic aspects of *mind itself* are revealed by their concepts. This is as much as to say that the locale of these psychologies is *outside* the psychologist.

Contrary to the conception that psychological concepts refer to mind itself, it is Jaspers' belief that sensation and idea, act and libido, Gestalt and field along with all other basic concepts of any psychology, along with even the most encompassing theories, are merely *frames in which the psychologist thinks* of the mind. This means that the locale of Jaspers' psychology differs from that of all others. His psychology has its place *inside* the psychologist. Consequently only the *product* of the thinking of the psychologist in the Jaspersian sense is at all comparable to the "object" of other psychologies.

Why does Jaspers change the locale of psychology? In the last analysis because of philosophical considerations. These are highly relevant to psychology. Jaspers asks: Should I view man as a creature characterized by the fact that in principle any unforeseeable change is possible to him at any given moment, i.e., as "potentiality incarnate"? Or should I think of him as a sharply definable, causally determined being? Just because it is possible to work successfully with both conceptions it is necessary for every psychologist to decide the question for himself. Jaspers' own answer is: man *is* potentiality incarnate; but, in order to arrive at objectively correct statements about him, *I must think of him as a sharply definable, causally determined being*. Jaspers thus reduces the latter view to one of the modes of contemplating man: that mode by which objectively correct knowledge about him can be gained. Since that kind of man only exists in the thought of the psychologist, Jaspers arranges his whole psychology in such a way that the psychologist must be constantly aware of the fact that his thinking and reality do not run parallel. The localization of psychology in the thought of the psychologist, i.e., the change of locale of psychology, is the method chosen to anchor this awareness firmly in the psychologist's mind. The most astonishing feature of this innovation is its simplicity; after it had been introduced it is difficult to realize that nobody thought of it before.

The change of locale makes it possible to view all psychological problems in a new light, because it moves all lines of demarcation between the different psychological regions. It separates everything the psychologist *thinks* 1) from the data which are the subject of psychological observation and reflection, i.e., from the manifestations of the mind; 2) from what is assumed to be the basis of these manifestations, i.e., from the mental apparatus. This separation is the basic reason why Jaspers demands of the individual psychologist: 1) unceasing control of his thinking, i.e., continuous criticism of the concepts, categories, etc., he uses, beyond all their precise definitions (accordingly, the *Allgemeine Psychopathologie* is full of such definitions);[34] 2) in each particular case, at each step of psychological activity — in order to avoid the ever-present danger of slipping into speculation — repeated ascertainment as to whether he is dealing with something actually existing or with something merely imagined, i.e., confirmation of conceptual constructions by observation and in general constant *orientation of psychological thought towards demonstrable facts*.

The change of locale of psychology has far-reaching consequences. I shall mention some of the most important.

1. The meaning of right and wrong

Since in Jaspers' psychology theories are merely grouping expedients, they cannot be right or wrong in an objective sense. The

[34] Excerpts from Jaspers' definition of "species" and of "type" may serve as an example. ". . . A (given) case belongs to a species or it does not. To a type . . . a case corresponds more or less. Species is a concept referring to a really existing, limitable kind. Type is a fictitious creation, corresponding to a reality with flexible borders, on which a particular case is measured but under which it is not classified. . . . Species exist or they do not. Types prove to be valuable for the comprehension of specific . . . cases or they do not. Through species real limits are recognized, whereas by means of types merely a structure is given to a fluid variety" (*Allgemeine*, 469).

realm of possible objectively correct statements about mind is therefore limited to regularities of a lawful nature in the mental region and thus made more precise than customary. An example of such regularities would be Ebbinghaus' law.

2. The validity of objectively correct statements

In the narrow sense of the term "objectively correct" psychological statements do not refer to an individual of the species "man," but to a conceptual, devitalized object, be it "man," "mind," or parts thereof. I can make statements of that kind only about something static and completely determined by causality, i.e., about something non-living, about the *object* "man" or the *object* "mind," both of which only exist in my thought. ". . . If we conceive a living person in terms of his appearing before our eyes in his entirety it is an act of inhumanity which disrupts any real intercourse with him. It is like drawing a line under (him), . . . as if burying him while he is still living . . ."[35] An actually existing individual is always more than the sum-total of possible knowledge about him. He cannot be grasped as a whole, either momentarily or historically. Caution is necessary when applying objectively correct psychological knowledge to the individual case, and in making "objectively correct" psychological statements about an individual.

3. The psychological center

By transferring psychology into the psychologist Jaspers creates a psychological center. There now exists a general system of reference in which there is room for every possible psychology as long as it makes sense. Not only all theories but also all psychologies are now revealed as particular ways of grouping psychological material or psychological knowledge. This is not equivalent to their devaluation; rather does it mean that every psychology is allotted a place in overall psychological knowledge. This means in practice: every method and theory of every possible psychology may be used, the only criterion being that it produces results in the form of objectively correct knowledge; on the other hand, it would be an error to try to prove the correctness of a theory by the fact that it produces results. The critique of methods takes care that the toleration — in principle — of all theories does not degenerate into uncritical equalization of all psychological opinions; among other things it develops criteria for the comparative value of different systems of thought.

4. The psychologist's conception of the mind

The psychologist collects the results of his cogitation and re-

[35] *Allgemeine,* 564.

search in himself. Although he uses these to complete his personal conception of the mind — on which he orientates his thinking —, he does not mistake it to be an objectively correct "being-so" of the mind. The psychologist, in his capacity as psychological center has, of course, a definite idea of the totality of the mind; but it remains his personal, unobjectifiable, idea which, although it grew out of the sum-total of his psychological knowledge, differs from it in principle because it is a whole. This idea keeps changing constantly with the progress of the psychologist's knowledge; it is a basic principle of Jaspers' psychology that it should be questioned again and again.

5. The unification of psychology

The superficial observer might think that Jaspers has dissolved psychology into many disconnected parts. On the contrary: Jaspers is the first to have made possible a really unified psychology. By grouping psychological knowledge from the point of view of and around the psychologist who uses it, he has established a stable relation between psychology and psychologist.

6. Undogmatic psychology

The psychologist who works according to the principles set up by Jaspers is free to choose, in every particular case, the manner of approach, theory or method most suitable for the region, problem or case at hand; he never has to subordinate a given problem or phenomenon to a specific theory. Jaspers frees all of psychology from its almost obligatory dependence on dogmas in the guise of theories — and from the dogma of avoiding theories. Obviously Jaspers' psychology represents a supplement, not an alternative, to other psychologies. Because it systematically clarifies the usability and validity of psychological concepts, procedures and methods, it can be of great value also to those who do not agree with it.[36]

The characteristics of Jaspers' psychology and its importance for psychological practice could only be hinted at here. I hope that this short exposé of some of his most important innovations, although it could mention only a very limited segment of them, will have suggested the extraordinary unity, the logical and psychologi-

[36] The problems Jaspers tries to solve by the change of locale of psychology have been known for a long time and have been discussed frequently, usually as problems in the theory of knowledge. New in Jaspers' work are not so much the problems as his solutions. Instead of lamenting the limits of human cognition and regarding the subjectivity of man, etc., merely as obstacles, he transforms them into tools of cognition. By establishing first what he considers to be unknowable in principle and by putting this at the beginning of his psychology, he clears the horizon for what is knowable.

cal consistency, and particularly the extremely simple design of his psychology. This simplicity is by no means accidental but a direct result of the fact that all innovations introduced by Jaspers serve the same purpose: they are intended to guide the psychologist in finding answers to psychological questions without losing sight of the two fundamental ones: 1) the question concerning the object of psychology: "How do I take into consideration the true nature of man who is essentially potentiality incarnate"? This question Jaspers solves through showing the zone in which the point of view of causal determinism, with all its consequences, is applicable; through the introduction of an "acausal" method — phenomenology —; and through installation of equally "acausal" *Verstehen* on the same level with explanation.[37]

2) The question concerning the *psychologist:* "How do I overcome the barriers to cognition presented by the cleavage between subject and object (the term used by Jaspers to summarize the categorial limitations of human knowledge)"? Jaspers answers this question by showing — in the critique of theories and methods — how it is possible to define the object of the psychologist in any given case in spite of the fact that mind itself cannot be grasped; and by changing the locale of psychology in order to prevent confusion of the psychologist's thoughts with the object of psychology.

With "cleavage between subject and object" we encounter a problem which plays an important part in the thinking of Jaspers. One of its manifestations we saw in the scheme on which the arrangement of his psychology was based (p. 472 above). There it served as one of several ordinal principles. The subject-object relation becomes the central theme in *Psychologie der Weltanschauungen,* the book which represents Jaspers' main contribution to the psychology of the individual and which can be regarded as a practical application of his psychological method.[38]

B. *Jaspers' Contribution to the Psychology of the Individual:* Die Psychologie der Weltanschauungen

In *Psychologie der Weltanschauungen* Jaspers attempts to por-

---

[37] The acausal point of view noticeable here follows from Jaspers' conception of man as not essentially subject to causal determination.

[38] The term *Weltanschauung* is ambiguous because it may mean both "general view of life" and "conception of the world," depending on whether the philosophical or the conceptual aspect of the word is stressed. Jaspers' usage tends towards the former meaning (for the latter he uses the term *Weltbild;* comp. footnote 41, below); but he complicates the matter because he — purposely — uses *Weltan-*

tray the possibilities of individual human existence. In this sense the book is a counterpart to *Allgemeine Psychopathologie*. In the latter Jaspers had tried to give a relatively complete picture of psychology by a delineation of the roads to psychological knowledge; in *Psychologie der Weltanschauungen* he tries, by the design of possible *Weltanschauungen*, to depict the sphere in which the mental life of individuals is possible. In *Allgemeine Psychopathologie* Jaspers had described the methods by which psychological knowledge is acquired and which determine its structure; in *Psychologie der Weltanschauungen* he describes the various frames in which the mental life of the individual takes place and which determine the formal characteristics of his mental manifestations. These frames he calls *Weltanschauung*. They represent "what is ultimate and complete in man, both subjectively as experience, power and conviction, and objectively as the formed world of objects."[39]

In *Psychologie der Weltanschauungen* Jaspers is guided by the basic conception of the "manifold relations between subject and object and the many meanings which (these terms) . . . can acquire."[40] In practice this principle results in a double approach to the problem of *Weltanschauung*, one from the side of the subject — *Weltanschauung* being "attitude" *(Einstellung)* in this case, the other from the side of the object — *Weltanschauung* now appearing as "world-view" *(Weltbild)*.[41] Both attitudes and world-views are to be thought of as dispositions. They are the relatively abstract, quasi "static," elements of *Weltanschauung*. Attitudes are patterns in which the individual world is experienced, be it actively or contemplatively, rationally or esthetically, sensualistically or ascetically, etc.; they are general modes of behavior, formal possibilities of mental existence.[42] World-views on the other hand are "the whole of the objective mental content an individual pos-

---

schauung to designate both individual attitudes and philosophical or religious systems. Again, as was the case with *Verstehen*, I find it less confusing to use the German word than to give different translations of the same word in different places.

39 *Psychologie*, 1.

40 *Ibid.*, 21. Examples of such relations: mind — world, ego — subject, experience — content, personality — thing, psychophysical individual — surrounding space, etc. For further consequences of this basic principle of order, cf. *Psychologie*, 20ff.

41 I have chosen this translation in order to distinguish *Weltbild* from Binswanger's *Weltentwurf* (Cf. footnote 50, below). Otherwise "world-design" would have been equally good.

42 "Attitudes" are the psychological analoga to the "transcendental forms" of Kant.

sesses."[43] They are conditions as well as results of mental existence.

Attitudes must be thought of as part of an individual's innate or early acquired structure; they are mental factors and subject to psychological investigation. With them man takes hold of the objectively given. The totality of contents thus created are world-views.

Jaspers mentions many different types of world-views, among them that of natural history, the technical, the mythological-demoniacal and the philosophical. These terms show clearly that world-views are nothing mental, although they result from the filling of attitudes — which are mental — with content and are, in this sense, products of the mind.

Each of the different varieties of attitudes and world-views can be looked upon as a basic pattern of human existence, as a characteristic psychological "type." In the two first chapters of *Psychologie der Weltanschauungen* Jaspers develops types of this kind. They are ideal-types (Weber),[44] intended to serve as standards for concrete cases; designs, not abstractions from mass-investigations. But the varieties of human existence described in these types are not yet what Jaspers calls *Weltanschauung*. These can only be visualized if the enveloping forces which contain attitudes and world-views within themselves are taken into consideration; those spiritual forces which cannot be realized directly like their elements (attitudes and world-views) because they are processes of motion, totalities based on a moving force. Nihilism, scepticism, authoritarianism, freedom, romanticism, autonomism, the demonic, the rigoristic are forces of that kind. When we talk of them, "we have proceeded from the static (region) of elements to the dynamic (one) of forces, from the unmoved to the moved, from the isolated to the whole, from the appearance to the core, from the fleeting to the personal, total."[45]

Jaspers devotes the third and last chapter of *Psychologie der Weltanschauungen* — entitled "The life of the spirit" — to the portrayal of these spiritual types *(Geistestypen)*. There he discusses values and ultimate situations *(Grenzsituationen)*, shell-

---

[43] *Psychologie,* 141.

[44] Ideal-types result from the following mental procedure: starting from given premises all consequences are developed consistently either through causal construction or through psychological *Verstehen*. This means that ideal-types are not deduced from experience. They are conceptual constructions which portray what would be possible if all possibilities of a given set of conditions were completely carried out. Cf. *Allgemeine,* 469.

[45] *Psychologie,* 43.

building,[46] chaos and form, etc.; what he has to say on these subjects shows him throughout to be a psychologist who not only knows how to present his ideas lucidly, but who also possesses the rare talent of being able to sense that which is psychologically relevant. Here we get to know him as a practical psychologist who uses his psychological gift to advantage in the description of the different psychological types. But, perhaps for this reason, *Psychologie der Weltanschauungen* is, on the whole, not so much a psychological discussion but a philosophical one, based on psychological insight. Jaspers seems to hold a similar view of this work today. In a recent publication he said of *Psychologie der Weltanschauungen* that "in it he had (written) a latent philosophy which . . . misconceived itself as an objectively confirming psychology."[47]

Altogether *Psychologie der Weltanschauungen* has less to offer to the practicing psychologist than *Allgemeine Psychopathologie*. The types drawn up by Jaspers offer insight into possibilities of human existence; but they are not suitable — as, for example, the types of Jung, Jaensch, Kretschmer or Sheldon — as guides for daily psychological practice (e.g., for use as diagnostic aids in psychological testing). Jaspers did not develop them for that purpose. He aimed rather at a systematic portrayal of the possibilities of human nature. What he actually accomplished, however, was an extremely stimulating, but in the last analysis personal, design of such.[48]

C. *Critique*

My critique of Jaspers' psychology will be limited to pointing out gaps in it. This form of criticism seems justified here because the design of a new psychology which Jaspers developed and which is mainly concerned with determining the possibilities of psychology, does not, in my opinion, contain any fundamental errors. It would therefore be of little value to criticize comparatively unimportant discrepancies which do not affect the design as a whole. Pointing out the gaps seems much more important to me. This all

[46] "Shells" are petrified world-views. The latter develop into shells either if one's own way of experiencing the world is mistaken to be the world-as-such, i.e., if it is made absolute and regarded as universally valid and necessary; or, if a specific world-view which is complete in itself, such as the Epicurean or the Stoic, is taken over as a whole by an individual.

[47] *Rechenschaft*, 362.

[48] Samples of Jaspers' manner of psychological analysis: the description of the Epicurean (103ff) and the opportunist (374) in *Psychologie;* of the sophist in *Age*, new ed., London, 1951, 165ff.

the more so because I am under the impression that the gaps could be filled in comparatively easily.

I. The Subject-Object Cleavage

It would be a natural counterpart to the change of locale of psychology to change the place of the psychologist by transferring him — in thought — into his object. This could be accomplished by furnishing the psychologist with a system of concepts which disregard the subject-object cleavage. Jaspers did not take this step, although he has tried something similar in *Psychologie der Weltanschauungen;* the "attitudes" were described from an assumed place within the object. But the attitudes mentioned in *Psychologie der Weltanschauungen* are abstracts from behavior patterns; in the framework of Jaspers' psychology better results would have been achieved had he drawn them from experienced phenomena. It is possible — and has, to a certain extent, already been done — to describe the experience-structure of an individual from an assumed place within the individual. Only then is it possible to surmount the " 'cancer' of all psychology . . . [the] doctrine of the subject-object division of the 'world' . . .," as Binswanger has put it pointedly.[49] For the experiencing subject no cleavage between subject (his experience) and object (the outer or inner world) exists; "to experience" is identical with "to experience the world" (in one form or other). If the design of individual worlds is made the focus of psychological investigations, the subject-object cleavage is eliminated from the thought of the psychologist and thereby from psychology.

For Jaspers' psychology, which puts so much stress on the singularity of the individual who is totally different from all others, the investigation of individual "world-designs" (Binswanger)[50] — made possible by the elimination of the subject-object cleavage — would be most important. In this manner of approach "inner" factors are stressed (which is not the same as the neglect of outer ones) and the differences in the "worlds" of different individuals constitute the center of interest. The accent is on: possible patterns of individual human existence instead of on average ones; the best possible realization of individual world-designs instead of adaptation to more or less arbitrary standards of the outside world; reactions

49 Ludwig Binswanger: *Ausgewählte Vorträge und Aufsätze,* Bern 1947, 193.

50 Binswanger's term is *Weltentwurf;* he means the specific (modifiable) experience-structure of an individual.

of individual world-designs to outside influences instead of trau-
mata as prime determinants of the final form of mental structures
assumed to be fundamentally alike in all individuals.[51] It may
seem paradoxical to maintain that Jaspers' psychology, which
sharply distinguishes subject from object throughout, should of
necessity require an annulment — if only in thought — of this distinction to round it out. Nevertheless, this is my impression. I am
further of the opinion that Jaspers has in general identified himself too much with the concept of subject-object cleavage in his
psychology. Possibly this is one of the reasons why it has not been
as successful as it might have been otherwise, particularly in that
sector of psychology for which it seems to be predestined — in
psychotherapy.[52]

II. Experience and Behavior

Jaspers' psychology, which consistently distinguishes within
from without, subject from object, etc., and which aims to get as
undistorted a view of real, existing man as possible, also should
distinguish throughout between experience and behavior. Jaspers
naturally takes this basic distinction into consideration; it even
figures prominently in the scheme of division of *Allgemeine Psychopathologie*. But Jaspers does not give it the central place it
would occupy if the basic principles of his psychology were really
consistently adhered to. For example: we have seen in the preceding paragraph that he does not make the distinction at a point
where to do so would result in a very important supplementation

51 The beginnings of a psychology which centers on the psychological conditions
of experience are contained in the works of those psychologists and psychiatrists
who have been fundamentally influenced by Heidegger's analysis of existence
(Daseinsanalytik), i.e., Binswanger, Boss, V. Gebsattel, Kunz, et al. This psychology
is, in my opinion, the only one now existing to form a complement to Jaspers'
psychology. Jaspers' opinion of the works which have so far been produced by these
writers has been negative in the main, possibly because he feels that here, too, a
process has set in which will eventually lead to an identification or confusion of
thought and reality. It is too early to judge whether his objections are valid or not.
But even if they were, this would not speak against the method used by these
psychiatrists and psychologists. Above all it is their manner of conceptualization
which would be quite compatible with a psychology such as Jaspers visualizes, even
if the actual concepts formed thus far would prove to be inadequate.

52 Jaspers has had a decisive influence on many psychologists, psychiatrists and
psychotherapists of rank. It is mainly the phenomenologist Jaspers, however, who
has made this great impression, not the psychologist of *Verstehen*. What has been
produced by the psychology of *Verstehen* outside of Jaspers' own works contains
primarily vague discussions of "meaning" which do not contribute much in the way
of psychological enlightenment. It is possible that the lack of resonance of this part
of his psychology is due to its present incomplete form.

of his psychology. It is clear that experience, the essentially subjective, "inner," factor in man, does not have the importance in Jaspers' psychology one would expect it to have in so subject-centered a psychology.

Jaspers' psychology owes much of its clarity to the careful distinctions it consistently carries out. There are the constantly repeated — actual or implied — distinctions between psychology and psychologist, facts and thoughts about facts, the observed and statements about it, psychological concepts and psychological reality, etc.[53] These distinctions make it possible to pierce the tangle of multivalent concepts — so frequently encountered in psychology — at all times, so that the intended meaning becomes clear. This is why I think it would have been better if Jaspers had not only distinguished between experience and behavior in principle, but had elevated this distinction, along with that between subject and object and with the arrangement according to methods, to the position of a general principle of order.[54]

III. Linear Thinking and Syncretic Experience

We have seen that Jaspers holds the experience of the psychologist to be the basic factor of psychology. His psychology should therefore include a more thorough analysis of experience than it does. The act of thinking as such should have been included in Jaspers' investigations. I am not thinking of logical inquiries, but of investigations with the aim of linking *Verstehen* and explanation unmistakably to modes of experience. It seems to me that this would be the only way to provide a firm foundation for this very important part of Jaspers' psychology. A counterpart to the analysis of *Verstehen* and explanation is required with the goal of examining the instruments which perform *Verstehen* and explanation. Jaspers' classic analysis of the phenomena of consciousness[55] does not suffice for this purpose, because in it he does not make a very important distinction, one which seems as necessary a complement of his psychology as the annulment — in thought — of the subject-object cleavage: he does not distinguish between "linear

---

[53] "Cognition comes through discrimination" (*Allgemeine*, 33).

[54] Neither does Jaspers differentiate, as Lewin does, between vector psychology and topological psychology (*Principles of Topological Psychology*, New York and London, 1936). Lewin's postulate of two psychologies geared to each other seems of similar importance to me as Jaspers' postulate of two modes of cognition which complement each other.

[55] *Allgemeine*, 51ff.

thinking" and "syncretic experience" (Werner) or *phantasieren* (Jung) (I am aware that, from the point of view of the phenomenologist, the separation of the two modes of experience is artificial). In Jaspers' psychological work a clear delineation of the demonstrable differences between linear thinking and syncretic experience is lacking.

The relations between linear thinking and explanation do not require an investigation as much as do those between syncretic experience and *Verstehen*. The connections there are obvious; furthermore, explanation, the generally accepted source of knowledge, needs no support by a mode of experience. Conditions are different where *Verstehen* is concerned. I consider syncretic experience to be the condition for *Verstehen* and believe that an understanding of its structure may shed light on the process of *Verstehen*. A thorough analysis of syncretic experience — particularly as it appears in child psychology — could probably contribute much to the clarification of *Verstehen* and of the psychology of *Verstehen* for which it forms the basis. *Verstehen*, in spite of Jaspers' efforts, remains difficult to pin down conceptually. It seems to me that it will not be firmly established as a useful and methodically unobjectionable source of psychological knowledge until it is linked conclusively to a mode of experience common to all.

D. *The Relations Between Jaspers' Psychology and His Fundamental Convictions*

In summing up I shall try to show that Jaspers has, with rare consistency, followed through certain basic ideas in his psychological works. His psychology may be characterized as an attempt, imposing both in the width of its conception and in the thoroughness of its execution, to make allowance, in theory and in practice — up to and including every single action of the psychologist — for the "X" in man; the "X" representing the *being-alive* of real, existing man. With every means at his disposal he tries to counter the reification which every act of the psychologist, especially every psychological statement, invariably includes. It is as if Jaspers wanted to leave untouched the object of psychology — whose subjectivity is its essence — by using the device of retracing every psychological action to the psychologist who performs it.[56] The means

56 It may be pertinent to point out the basic difference of Jaspers' point of view from that of other psychologists who also stress the unmistakeable individuality of the human subject. W. Stern and G. W. Allport, for example, introduce the concept of "personality" in order to make due allowance for the factor of individuality.

he uses I summed up under the headings "introducing the psychologist into psychology" and "change of locale of psychology." It is clear that they are meant constantly to remind the psychologist that the way in which he thinks of a human being is never identical with the object of his thought, insofar as this object is a real, existing person. This person has the possibility to decide this or that way, to act in one way or another; he is *free*. This freedom is meant when Jaspers talks of man as being "potentiality incarnate."

Jaspers' view of man as "potentiality incarnate" is by no means accidental. On the contrary, it is the result of a conscious decision to see man in this light. And this decision again is synonymous with a decision against causal determinism. I have mentioned already (pp. 484f above) that Jaspers knows it not only to be possible but necessary to think of man also in terms of causal determinism, when dealing with him as an object of scientific research. But this carries with it the ever present danger that psychology misunderstands itself and becomes committed to an exclusively deterministic point of view. Hand in hand goes another danger: to want increasingly to manipulate man with the help of the steadily growing knowledge about him. There can be no question that it is possible to prove that man is essentially causally determined and can be manipulated at will. The question is: *should* one prove it?[57] Fundamentally two psychologies are possible at any time: the psychology of historically unique individuals — the *psychology of freedom;* and the psychology of individuals who can be replaced at will — the *psychology of manipulation.* Jaspers has made his decision for the psychology of freedom, and this decision stands behind the accentuation of "potentiality" in his conception of man. Freedom, in contrast to causal determination, cannot be proved.

So far as empirical happenings can be recognized as necessary ac-

---

From Jaspers' point of view this, too, amounts to a reification of "X". The concept presupposes something knowable — personality — whereas Jaspers denies in principle that the factor I have called "X" is ever knowable. This denial he introduces into the basis of psychology. To grasp what is meant here is to hold the key to Jaspers' psychology.

[57] The decision *pro* or *con* determinism may influence everyday tasks of the average psychologist. Supposing I have to work out a diagnosis from a battery of tests. If I think in terms of determinism I will be inclined to stress the being-so of the subject tested. Apart from the questionable validity of statements based on that belief another point needs to be considered. The individual whom the diagnosis concerns may take it to be a factual statement — if he is equally deterministic. Because the diagnosis was made by an expert he may even alter his behavior to fit the statements made — which is exactly the opposite of what a diagnosis is intended to do.

cording to rules, and so far as facts can be shown empirically, there is no freedom. Denial of freedom makes sense empirically, but it applies to the realm of empirically recognizable factual data only. The attempt to prove freedom as a compelling experience arrives at no result and makes freedom itself suspect. Freedom is not an object of investigation. The alternative is not whether I can show it empirically or not, but whether I am willing to assume the responsibility for the theorem 'there is no freedom' and its consequences.[58]

To find out which of the two possible psychologies he wants to practice, each psychologist must come to grips with the philosophical aspect of the question: "What is man?", i.e., with the question of what man is before he appears as an object of any kind of research. Two answers are possible, depending on which of two entirely different attitudes toward himself man takes.

[Man] can observe and *investigate* himself as an existence that happens to be as it is and suffers changes according to recognizable rules; and he can apply standards to himself and *make demands* on himself with whose genuine acceptance he first starts really to become himself. But fundamentally he cannot do one without the other. With absolute separation these attitudes become lame and empty. In their realization, however, a methodical separation is temporarily inescapable. Then the manner of viewing man as existence is called anthropology and psychology, the manner that makes demands of his essence, philosophy. Psychology investigates, establishes facts, predicts. Philosophy appeals, projects possibilities, unlocks the realm of decision. But in all psychology of man there is secretly present the interest in possibilities and the challenge of self-realization. And in all philosophy psychology remains a means of expression, a premise *(Voraussetzung)* without which the challenge of thought would become incorporeal.[59]

To take these ideas of Jaspers seriously means to demand that psychology should be oriented toward philosophy. Since they are proposed by a man whose psychological and philosophical work is characterized by always being close to life, they cannot easily be ignored. On their acceptance or denial may depend how much headway the reification of man is going to make, even in the most "human" of the many sciences which deal with him.

LUDWIG B. LEFEBRE

SAN FRANCISCO
CALIFORNIA

[58] *Allgemeine,* 630f. [59] *Nietzsche,* 2nd ed., Berlin 1947, 125f.

Hans Kunz

CRITIQUE OF JASPERS' CONCEPT
OF TRANSCENDENCE*

THE MEANING of Kant's oft-quoted statement in the preface to the second edition of the *Critique of Pure Reason* — that he must "deny *knowledge,* in order to make room for *faith*" — seems to be unequivocal and clear. "It is evident," he writes, "that even the assumption — as made on behalf of the necessary practical employment of my reason — of *God, freedom,* and *immortality* is not permissible unless at the same time speculative reason be deprived of its pretentions to transcendent insight."[1] It was, therefore, the illusory kind of "knowledge," the kind which hides, and at the same time oversteps, its limitations, — a manifestation of which might be a presumably compelling "proof" of freedom or of the existence of God, — which Kant denied; and this he did with the aim of making room for "faith" in order to "justify" the postulates of the practical reason. Now, it would certainly be erroneous to assert that thus, by a somewhat out-moded terminology, the situation in which the idea of Transcendence and its related concepts are today maintained by Jaspers, would be described *exactly.* The "practical employment" of my reason is not identical with the imperative, '*existential*' relevance of the kind of philosophizing which Jaspers has in mind; but one may say that Kant's formula points in the direction of that relevance. Similarly, there exists merely a certain relationship — no identity — between Kant's "denial of knowledge" and, for example, Jaspers' fundamental denial of the demonstrability of freedom. Nevertheless, disregarding these and analogous differences — in themselves not to be neglected — the basic approach to the question is the same here as there.

For the pattern of philosophizing which Jaspers considers still

---

* Translated from the original German by Mary Feagins, as revised by Ludwig B. Lefebre.

1 The translation quoted here is that of Norman Kemp Smith, *Immanuel Kant's Critique of Pure Reason* (New York, 1950), 29.

possible, meaningful, and necessary in the present historical situation,[2] the modern scientific approach is absolutely obligatory — and this primarily because what can be known methodically and within the framework of definite presuppositions, which are generally valid and intellectually compelling, i.e., what can be known "scientifically," can no longer be, at the same time, the object of a specifically different "philosophical," e.g., speculative, "knowledge." Since the Greek origins of Western thought, when what later divided into "science" and "philosophy" was still one, the scope of what is accessible to scientific research has been steadily widening, while the former foundation of philosophy has been continually crumbling away to a corresponding degree, not vanishing, but becoming the domain of objective knowledge. Occasionally it is difficult to escape the impression that Jaspers is standing, as it were, at the last — perhaps already lost — outpost of the kind of philosophical endeavor which derives its nourishment from sources of its own, and that he is seeking to hold this outpost against the encroaching claims of the empirical sciences (hence the "still" in the first sentence of this paragraph). We cite, as an example, his manner of holding on to a certain concept of science, which indeed raises the question whether it does full justice to all those endeavors which are today understood as "scientific," but which offers the possibility of rejecting certain tendencies within these endeavors as "unscientific," "destructive to science," or as a "superstitious cult of science." Here one is reminded especially of Jaspers' criticism of psychoanalysis.[3] It is debatable whether Jaspers does not adhere to an idea of "scientific method" which, on the one hand — being still too greatly oriented towards exact natural science (whose principles cannot even do justice to the descriptive natural sciences) — remains, and must remain, fundamentally unsuitable to the understanding of both historico-sociological events and human experience and conduct; and which, on the other hand, actually already superseded by research, no longer commands any authority. We merely present this question here and do not assert positively that the situation is thus; for to do so would require an extensive discussion of the presuppositions, potentialities, and import of scientific knowledge.

A second way pursued by Jaspers — with the same goal of securing and "redeeming" for philosophizing a legitimate place along-

2 Cf. especially: *Rechenschaft* (Munich: 1951), 204ff., *Philosophie* (Berlin, 1932), I. 85ff.

3 Cf. *Rechenschaft* 221ff., *Anti-Reason* (New Haven, 1952), 20ff.; *Allgemeine* 4th ed. (Berlin & Heidelberg, 1946), 299ff., 450ff., 646ff., 679ff.

side objective research — leads to the radical rejection of the possibility of a conclusively verifiable ontological knowledge concerning Being itself (or Transcendence)[4] and especially, of the nature of man's being.[5] At this point, he has not only the greater part of Western philosophical tradition against him but there also exists — in Heidegger's "fundamental ontology"[6] — a design, which can hardly be dismissed off-hand as a basic philosophical "aberration." Finally, one might ask whether Jaspers' "illumination of *Existenz*" — for him the only possible form of "philosophical anthropology" — actually has not, after all, a latent, unexpressed "ontology" of human nature as its basis. Jaspers himself says at one point that "the basic characteristics of human nature must have established themselves as hereditary biological traits which are still present today."[7] Why should only the relatively comprehensible "biological traits" be hereditary and not also human nature as such? Not necessarily in the sense that we would thus have at our disposal or could ever achieve a "complete solution" of the problem of man's nature. The nature of man — although its being and ongoing *(Seins- und Geschehenscharakter)** is determined and immutable — could well be such that we are unable to arrive at "definitive" knowledge concerning it. If this be the case the question arises why it is so. What can and is to keep us from seeking an answer, be it ever so provisional? In Jaspers' view man's being possesses "potentialities" which man has the innate freedom to seize and realize, or fail to develop; in other words, potentialities which make possible a transformation of "existence" *(Dasein)* into *"Existenz."* Is freedom endangered if — rather than to leave them in darkness — we attempt to know the specific characteristics of these potentialities, thereby defining the nature of man's being which those potentialities, the realization of *Existenz (Existenzwerden)* and freedom help to constitute? And, granted that this might be the case, should this will to know be rejected from the outset, or even be forbidden, in order to save freedom? That seems to us to be the crucial problem here.

One thing must not be overlooked: Jaspers rejects any sort of

4 Cf. *Philosophie,* III, 31ff., 157ff.   5 *Allgemeine,* 649.

6 Cf. Martin Heidegger: *Sein und Zeit,* 6th ed. (Tuebingen, 1949.)

7 *Ursprung* (Zürich, 1949), 58.

* Tr.'s fn.: Kunz uses the term *Geschehen* to emphasize that *characteristicum* of man's being which the term "being" describes inadequately because of its static nature. The German words *Geschehen, geschehend, Geschehenscharakter,* etc., imply motion without directional, developmental or any other attributes. They will be translated in this text by the terms "ongoing," "occurring," "evolving," "event," "process," "processive," etc., depending on the context.

ontology of man's being because of his concern for the preservation of the "highest potentialities" of this very being, because he
wants to "keep open the horizons of humanity in philosophical
thinking."[8] Therefore, he does not reject Heidegger's analysis of
being-here* (Daseinsanalytik) by arguing directly to the point, but
objects to it on the ground that "instead of leading toward philosophizing, it leads to an over-all knowledge of man's being."
Furthermore, he judges it to be "no aid to the historically authentic Existenz of the individual (for the enhancement and substan-
tiation of his reliable way of life) ", but instead a "means of beclouding — which becomes all the more fateful because, with
propositions having greatest proximity to Existenz, it misses authentic Existenz and can become trifling."[9] Whether this unfortunate consequence follows necessarily from Heidegger's Daseinsanalytik remains open to question. It is, in this connection, merely
supposed to reveal to us the basic question concerning the "existential" relevance of philosophical knowledge: May and should such
knowledge be denied, if it — to suppose the most extreme case —
destroys man's being? But can it, of itself, do any such thing?

If we, first of all, get a clear picture of the actual situation, then
there will be no doubt that wherever cognition is in any way
achieved — be it pre-scientific, scientific, or philosophical — it occurs in a situation which involves more than cognition (in the
sense of "pure" cognition). More precisely expressed, the act of
cognition always involves impulses of a non-cognitive origin, e.g.,
impulses related to self-preservation, possessive ones, and others.
These are present at the beginning of all knowledge and form its
enduring, underlying foundation. Nevertheless, they are not cognition's true source which, however weakly it may exert its influence, has a specific nature of its own. The nature of cognition is
misconstrued in the pragmatic theories and also in several of the
terms — such as "grasping" or "comprehension" — which describe
it, if one takes them literally. Perhaps cognition can most clearly
be conceived of in terms of the functions of that organ which
renders the greatest service to it in man's reactions to his surroundings: the organ of sight. Its great vulnerability keeps it from
coming to grips with things and events; and although it is probably wrong to consider visual perception incapable of any kind of
"activity" and capable only of "receptivity," still its activity does

8 Scope, (New York, 1949), 3.

* Tr.'s note: Heidegger's term Da-sein we are translating with: being-here (in
contradistinction to Jaspers' term Dasein, which is being rendered as: existence).

9 Allgemeine, 649.

not, at any rate, involve any excursion on its part into the realm of objects, or any change of this realm. It is far from our intention to identify the process of cognition with that of seeing; still, the essential moment seems peculiar to both: The non-violent, detached, apperceptive "letting-be" what is (*Sein-lassen des Seienden*). This is in accord with the "emotion" of wonder — which is part of the will to know according to Plato and Aristotle — which, in contrast to most of the other emotions, is characterized by a corresponding "restraint" and "repose." Instead of this brief suggestion, a careful, penetrating analysis would be necessary to demonstrate at all convincingly that the fundamental meaning of all cognition lies in the open reception of what is encountered, just as it presents itself. Certainly, cognition often cannot be achieved — for instance, in experimental research involving the phenomena of life — without some destructive interference with the objects; and there can be no denying that the impulses and motives sustaining cognitive endeavors arise, in the main, outside the pure intention of knowing. Nevertheless, they do violence to its fundamental meaning, to the very nature of which all — and especially destructive — activity is in contrast. The aim of the will to know is: to preserve what is and occurs; this is true even in those cases where it (the will to know) destroys misleading and beclouding illusions. For this reason cognition, in all its forms, can by no means be restricted or rejected on the strength of its allegedly destructive character. If it becomes destructive, it does so always either because of some factor in its realization or because of its misuse by man, and not on account of its actual nature in man.

Thus Jaspers, as well as Kant in his day, makes no attempt to delimit scientifically objective and philosophical cognition as such.[10] For by doing so he would obviously relinquish the freedom of modern research and thought in favor of arbitrary and dogmatic forces, which, in every respect, can only lead to man's ruin. What alone he strenuously opposes are those movements which — in his opinion falsely — think they are, and claim to be, scientific and philosophical ways to knowledge, but which he considers to be *Weltanschauungen*, offering substitutes for religion and which — he feels — are falsifying and destroying the true nature of empirical research and philosophic knowledge. Therefore, Jaspers does not in any way preclude the desire to "prove" or "disprove" the actuality of freedom by means of rational, discerning argument; rather, he shows that neither the one nor the other is possible, because freedom can, in principle, not be encountered or experi-

10 Cf., for example, *Scope*, 7.

enced in the dimension of objective proof and refutability.[11] "Objective redemption" turns freedom "itself into something apparently objective and thus into something heterogeneous to itself."[12] Whereas the situation is clear here, there remains a slight uneasiness in regard to Jaspers' repudiation of psychoanalytical research as genuine research, as well as in regard to his rejection of Heidegger's *Daseinsanalytik* as philosophical aberration, an uneasiness that the motive for his rejection may not be sought solely in his striving for the preservation of his own philosophical intentions. We do not, however, intend to pursue our critical analysis of Jaspers in the manner of a defense of these two — after all completely different — attempts of gaining knowledge. We rather choose for purposes of analysis a problem which is central in Jaspers' philosophy itself: His concept of Transcendence.

Jaspers says: "*Existenz* is either in relation to Transcendence, or not at all;"[13] "I am '*existentially*' myself only in the act of apprehending Transcendence."[14] In statements such as these, and in many others, Jaspers expresses the conviction that the individual human being, who can always only be found in a specific historical situation, can realize the transformation of his mere existence to authentic *Existenz* only in confrontation with the Transcendent or, — in religious terminology, — with the godhead. We shall now attempt to show that it is possible, and why it is possible, to realize Jaspers' "illumination of *Existenz*," as well as the transformation to authentic *Existenz*, without any relation to Transcendence, as interpreted by Jaspers. This means that we have in mind a different "interpretation" of that which Jaspers designates as "Transcendence" — indeed, one which is in part diametrically opposed to his. Transcendence will be "shown" to be an immanent constituent of man's being. However, there is no attempt here to oppose Jaspers' view simply by a contradictory one; rather, we are using a more appropriate interpretation of a fact substantially involved in the illumination of *Existenz* — the fact of death — to carry out an analysis within that general area.

Jaspers subsumes death under the concept of "ultimate situation."[15] The future reality of my own death is thus left out of consideration from the beginning. Now, death possesses no sort of reality as something that happens to human beings except as

---

11 Cf. *Philosophie,* II, 188ff.   12 *Ibid.,* 191.   13 *Ibid.,* III, 6.
14 *Ibid.,* 15.

15 Cf. *Psychologie* (Berlin, 2nd ed., 1922), 259ff; *Philosophie,* II, 220ff; also K. Lehmann, *Der Tod bei Heidegger und Jaspers* (Heidelberg, 1938), 32ff., 56ff., 59ff.; also Latzel's essay, this vol.

the specific death of a specific individual. Whatever it "is," it is only in the form of a future event thought of as vaguely negative or envisaged by means of imagery and ideas, something I thus incorporate by anticipation into the context of my existence, and toward which I develop an attitude. In other words: Not death itself, as a future event, but only *its meaning for me,* can become an *'existentially'* relevant ultimate situation. Thus Jaspers says that death — "a uniformly recurrent event only if it is viewed as an objective fact," — does not cease to be in the ultimate situation; "but it is changeable as to form, according to whatever I happen to be as *Existenz.* It is not conclusively what it is, but it is absorbed in the historicity of my being as it appears to itself."[16] We are not questioning the validity of this view of death as ultimate situation; indeed, it alone gives death the possibility of being *'existentially'* decisive for me. But this is not "actual death." Death as such does not enter into the ultimate situation at all, no more than I am able to experience it as my own, as Jaspers himself confirms.[17] Nevertheless, this does not keep me — once I have reached a certain state of awareness — from knowing about its future arrival with an absolute, singular certainty, which hardly stems from the experience of the dying of others, and which is matched solely by the certainty of my own being. This certainty does not include the essence or non-essence of death — whatever death may be as such — but, exclusively, the factuality of death's happening, uncertain as to its specific 'When', but definite as to its coming at some time. If this is so, it seems to us that the following assertion of Jaspers is wrong: that I cannot "in objective contemplation . . . convincingly apprehend the necessity of death and evanescence,"[18] that "in objective thought . . . the necessity of death's belonging to life [is] incomprehensible" although "this knowledge of [death's] being inseparable from life . . . is nevertheless inextinguishable."[19] Here we are dealing with an objective, verifiable knowledge of the fact of the coming arrival of death and of its necessity in the sense of factual inevitability; the situation is such, however, that at the same time, because of the conceptual emptiness of death, because, that is, of the incomprehensibleness of its nature, the object, as it were, slips away, is submerged into the unfathomable and turns this knowledge into an object-less cognition. This self-sustaining, unshakeable certainty of the knowledge of our own death's approach which, by virtue of the incomprehensibleness of its content, can become beclouded and seemingly questionable, has led us to suppose that, at

16 *Philosophie*, II, 229.   17 Cf., *ibid.*, 222.
18 *Ibid.*, 220.   19 *Ibid.*, 228.

the very source of the act of knowing itself, possible death may manifest itself; that the "pure" act of thinking may be a manifestation of the constant presence within existing man of the potential loss of being. For this reason we speak — in contradistinction to factual, actual, coming death — also of a possible, immanent death which, as an essential constituent of man's being, is not to be mistaken for the "idea" of death or for the more or less concrete "thinking" of it. Actually it is the other way around: It is potential death which first establishes in us the basis for being able to think of death as factual, to visualize it in variegated imagery, to yearn for it or to be afraid of it;[20] and it is also potential death which provides us with the ability to interpret death in different ways, such as, e.g., an ultimate situation.

This is not the place to point out all the reasons which could support the above supposition. This supposition is, and can only be, a hypothesis, because what is maintained by it — the constant presence of potential death at the source of thought as one of the hidden, ongoing foundations of man's being — can never be directly evident.[21] Let us, however, briefly indicate some of its aspects. If factual death brings to an end, at least "earthly," life — the latter as well as the former are "encountered" by us exclusively as the particular life and the particular loss of life of a particular, existing person and the concepts of "life," "death," and "man" are abstractions from this encounter —; and if death thereby brings to an end a process, — bound by time and "producing itself within time" (sich zeitigend) — which gives man's being its ontic character, then one may be permitted to say that a sort of "timelessness" belongs to man because, for one thing, the end of the original, lived, time "is" time-less. However, we would be totally incapable of experiencing, of knowing, or even of thinking of such a thing as timelessness (or other so-called "time-free" phenomena), if the factual ending of finite being would constitute its only realization. If ending occurs, however, not solely in the factual form of the death I must die, but, in addition breaks forth at all times, as a possibility, in the form of immanent death — it being the source of thought within existing man —, then this opens up to man the possibility for realizing the various kinds of "immanent timelessness": The "eternity of the moment," the "transcendency over time" of the contents of thought, the "point-like timelessness" of

---

20 The original, acute anguish of death (Todesangst) is a different phenomenon from the fear in anticipation of death (Furcht vor dem Tode).

21 Cf. H. Kunz: Die anthropologische Bedeutung der Phantasie, (Basel, 1946), II, 86ff.

the act of thinking, etc. The "ongoing immanence" (Hereinstehen) of potential death is, however, at the same time the constant invasion of the "beyond-himself" into man's being, insofar as his end in actual death may be considered as the factuality of the "completely other" or the "beyond" of man and the world. In any case, we see here *man's* only possibility to *question* and to *search out* — enabled and compelled by his awareness of radical dissatisfaction — the Transcendent in its double meaning as the "source" of his Whence and the "goal beyond" of his Whither. This urge to question and to search — Kant has correctly viewed it as established in the nature of reason — does not stem from the subjective choice of philosophizing and believing man; rather, it belongs to his "nature," i.e., to his unchangeable ontic character, because one of the constituents of man's being is the continuous presence of the potential loss of being, i.e., the "incompleteness" which he experiences as dissatisfaction. Driven by external forces or by his own will, man may lose himself in his own being-here, in communal existence, or in encountered objects, and thus may forcibly suppress this urge to question and to search, or he may shut it out from his view; but he can never drive it out of his nature. Finally, immanent death, although we must by no means consider it the only factor responsible for the potential character of man's being, nevertheless is a decisive one and is therewith responsible also for the fact that the individual, in the factuality of his existence, may be able to change his mere existence to *Existenz* in the Jaspersian sense. Not accidentally does thought achieve the highest stage of potentiality, reaching out into the boundless; and not accidentally does it share substantially in that "inner activity," derived from the source of freedom, in which the '*existential*' soarings (*Aufschwünge*) realize themselves. For, on the one hand, the boundlessness of man's potentiality for thought corresponds to the negativity present in him as proof of immanent death; and, on the other, it is the possible loss of being, manifest in immanent death, which the individual uses as a springboard to propel himself into his authentic *Existenz*. Such attainment does not, however, depend solely on voluntary decision; it requires those basic human tendencies which — inaccessible to voluntary control — point in the same direction. "Authentic being-oneself cannot through itself alone sustain itself; it may fail to appear, it cannot force its own realization," says Jaspers.[22] Or, he says elsewhere: "As *Existenz* I am, since I know that I have been given to myself by Transcendence. I am not by virtue of my decision alone. Even my freedom, my being-

[22] *Philosophie*, III, 221.

through-myself *(Durch-mich-sein)* has been given me. I can be absent from myself and no will can then enable me to give myself to myself."[23] Although freedom and the achievement of authentic being based on freedom belong to a special domain, both must be viewed in relation to other involuntary phenomena, as Jaspers himself indicates.[24] To interpret these manifold ongoing phenomena — which are part of the dynamic character of man's being — as strange, anonymous forces, i.e., demonologically, seems only then to be inescapable or, at any rate, plausible, if man mistakenly views his being exclusively — "idealistically" — in the light of his voluntary activity and fails to recognize that he himself has neither created nor can he change the fundamental structure of his being. Having-to-be *(Sein-müssen)* as factuality includes not only human corporeality and its functions, but also such phenomena as willing, thinking, being free and dying, which simultaneously we must and, within limits, we can, engage in; or, in other words, phenomena which have the characteristics of processes and acts. To single out freedom from these phenomena and to interpret its realization — which, partially, I am also able to bring about by my own original efforts — as an indication of a "transcendentally granted" realization of being, seems to me to be, from the point of view outlined above, a last, abstract and purified version of the demonological interpretation of human nature which is heterogeneous to that nature, as are all such interpretations.

The common basis of the illumination of *Existenz* (or the " *'existential'* relations to Transcendence")[25] and of the thesis suggested here is the characteristic 'potentiality' of human nature. Jaspers has not expressly explained this potentiality as such, but, in a sense, makes direct use of it in keeping philosophizing open, finding in freedom and the constantly changing situations in which each man lives out his own history its basic sources. Yet it is self-evident that Jaspers' appeal to *'existential'* potentialities is based on a different conception of potentiality from that intended by the traditional concepts of categorial-modal and logical possibility. Granted the essence of *'existential'* potentialities cannot be revealed by an objective, demonstrable analysis; this does not seem to us to be a cogent argument for depriving ourselves of a more exactly conceived definition — perhaps derived from psychologically perceptible phenomena — of the specific character of potentiality; especially since such a definition by no means entails a fixation of this character in the sense of any loss of potential flexibility and freedom. We venture a step in this direction with our thesis that,

[23] *Scope*, 17.   [24] *Philosophie*, III, 133.   [25] *Ibid.*, 68ff.

potential death presents itself in the very origin of thinking; a thesis which, first of all, was meant to explain the unique certainty of the knowledge of our own coming death — a certainty for which experience apparently cannot account sufficiently. In this knowledge death functions, it is true, as object, for all knowledge and thinking is, by nature, knowledge of, and thinking about, something. However, the significant step consists in treating death as potential death, by moving back objectively known factual death — which moreover partially escapes any objectifying apprehension — into the non-objective dimension which is the source of the act of knowing, and to understand thereby the exceptional certainty of precisely this particular objective knowledge: it attains its elusive object from the objectification of its own origin. Potential death is part of man's being and shares in the constitution of his potential nature, which — among other things — can also be inferred from the experience of the factual mortality of man. It would be worth considering whether the conceptions of non-objective terms — such as *"noumenon,"* "transcendental subject," *"Existenz,"* etc. — would have been at all possible without the presence of immanent death in man's being, which is, so to speak, like something unfathomable within him and the reason why his essence again and again eludes any attempted objectification. Nevertheless, disregarding this, potential death, as well as the knowledge of the prospective, actual having-to-die — grounded in potential death — remain in themselves at the same time both objective and non-objective. Because of this it is unavoidable to use the empirical, objectifiable data of knowledge (biological or psychological, for example) as guides to an explication of the ontic character of man as an active, experiencing and self-understanding being, and not to be content with using this objective knowledge (as e.g., in the case of Jaspers, in the form of *"verstehende"* psychology) *merely* as a medium for the illumination of *Existenz;* that is, for appealing to authentic *Existenz* while leaving it in utter darkness and without questioning its true nature. For, *Existenz* and behaving, experiencing man (as an object of psychological research) are essentially not two isolated provinces, but one single reality — that of the concrete individual living at any given time in definite situations.

The thesis, according to which immanent death is considered a decisive constituent of the ontic and ongoing character of man's being, includes the second proposition that consequently the *" 'existential'* relations to Transcendence" and Transcendence itself may be interpreted, at least in part, as immanent — immanent, that is, in the sense of being restricted to man's nature, including that nature's limit in factual death whose peculiar limiting-character *(Grenzcharakter)* is also apparent in potential death.

This interpretation in terms of immanence we should like now to try out on some of Jaspers' own concepts. It is to be considered as a *possible* interpretation; we by no means claim to give a conclusive or, indeed, the only pertinent one. For that matter, this is not an interpretation or an exposition in the usual sense of making explicit and clarifying the thoughts contained in Jaspers' statements. Rather, we shall attempt to envisage those autonomous facts which the statements intend to convey, and which have not been created by the thoughts expressing them; and we shall approach them from an angle differing from that of Jaspers, with the purpose of discovering something of the nature of these facts as such. The fact that Jaspers' own concepts of transcending and Transcendence are essentially related to the experience of the limits of man's being and man's cognition, offers, to be sure, no guarantee that this critical analysis stays within the area, or at least close to the source, of his philosophizing; but there is, nevertheless, a chance that this may be so. To quote Jaspers: "The place of Transcendence is neither in this world nor beyond, but it is boundary — the boundary, however, at which I confront Transcendence whenever I am my true self."[26] And, again: "The appearance of Transcendence occurs on the boundary between two worlds which are related to each other as being and non-being."[27] Above all: Jaspers claims the disappearance of existence and *Existenz* as the "decisive cipher of Transcendence."[28] A radical restatement of this could well provide the basis for our own interpretation.

In his lecture, "On the Spirit of Europe" (1946), Jaspers says in respect to its possible decline: "When, however, we are overcome by dizziness for lack of a foundation — and the worst seems yet to be ahead of us — the main point is: When all is lost, God remains. It is enough that there is Transcendence."[29] Seemingly in contrast to this is the following: "To founder *(Scheitern)* is the *ultimate;* any unflinchingly realistic orientation shows this. Furthermore, it is the ultimate experience ever to present itself to the thinking mind. . . . The being-in-itself of *Existenz* is shattered in the *illumination of Existenz:* When I am truly my authentic being, I am not just myself. In *Transcendence* thought fails because of the passion for the night."[30] Both of these views — the fact

---

26 *Ibid.,* 13.   27 *Ibid.,* 17.   28 *Ibid.,* 219ff.
29 *Rechenschaft,* 264.   30 *Philosophie,* III, 220.

that one can characterize them as contradictory has no significant bearing on the matter, since for their complete explication "logical" processes remain inadequate anyway — represent perhaps a shift of emphasis, also noticeable elsewhere, in the thought of Jaspers, inasmuch as Transcendence, since the appearance of his *Philosophie,* has taken on a "more positive" character as well as greater certainty. "Faith" — particularly as an attitude opposed to nihilism — has correspondingly been brought to the foreground, although in the form of "philosophical faith" it had always been a fundamental concept. For a mode of thought which finds it necessary to deny a place to Transcendence — whether I become aware of it through revelation or by the experience of foundering — as long as its assertion can be made understandable through an analysis of man, the question forcibly arises whether, within the nature of man's being itself, there might not be evidence of a phenomenon which would be able to fill exactly the role of Transcendence as conceived by Jaspers. Indeed, expected death seems to us to meet these requirements. Of all the possible events to come, it is the only one whose certainty is absolute. With no future event of our own existence, as well as of the world around us, is there identified the same unshakeable, "absolute" certainty of coming to pass. "When all is lost," — if the tradition from which we draw our strength were totally extinguished and all that lives around us completely demolished, — what would remain would be one's own death. Obviously, however, future death implies one presupposition of equal certainty, one without which its future realization would be neither possible nor factual: The present being-here and the certainty of existence of existing man. Since, however, the knowledge of man's disappearance goes together with that of expected death, the "enduring" quality of Transcendence cannot be modeled after a counterpart in finite human existence.

Whence, therefore, is derived the "eternal Being" of the godhead? Here the concept of potential death offers a solution. As such, it manifests itself solely in existing man, thus at once dependent on and pointing to his existing. But this ongoing "pointing-to-being" is grounded solely in the negativity of the potential loss-of-being which offers, as it were, to thought its own, *radically different other side,* i.e., the conceptually empty Being *(Sein)* — which, because of its emptiness, potentially encompasses all that is *(Seiende)*. (Jaspers speaks of a naught which can "suddenly become plenitude and authentic Being.")[31] Since, furthermore, the nature of man as an historical being is in itself limited by time,

31 *Origin,* 219.

and factual death brings about its end and, consequently, time-lessness, it is understandable that and why Being is characterized by "eternity" and "permanence." For the time-lessness in death, at the end of lived time, is immanent as a potentiality in being-here, manifesting itself as "eternity." Eternity, by the way, is capable of being experienced and interpreted in various ways. Just as Being represents the necessary opposite of the naught present in man — necessary, that is, because naught breaks forth in man's being only —, so does it participate in the potential timelessness present in being-here; that is to say: it shares in "eternity." The fact that on the one hand "enduring" Transcendence is relegated to the "other side" of life's boundary, and on the other is already present in life, as an eschatological event, in certain versions of the belief in revelation, can be explained by the twofold nature of potential and factual death. Similarly, this duality manifests itself in the following quotation from Jaspers: Transcending from existence to Being

is neither being-in-the-world nor being-out-of-the-world. The result [of transcending] is that naive being-in-the-world becomes self-conscious, which, in turn, was brought about because a being-out-of-the-world (never actual but nevertheless potential) was experienced and produced a fundamental realization of being-in-the-world. No psychology is capable of describing the experience of this unique being suspended (Schweben) between being-in and being-out-of-the-world. It is an act of freedom arising from absolute consciousness.[32]

The question might arise, indeed, whether this "being suspended" is not experienced in certain so-called mystical states — varying as to content — and whether therefore it could be described in objective psychological terms. However, the essential point would thus be missed. What matters here is the non-objective basis of man's being, the basis which supports and makes possible both the experiential manifestations we mentioned and their objectifying cognition. To be sure: in a strict sense being-out-of-the-world is not experienced at all; in this case an actualization — as distinguished from analogous "ecstatic experiences" — would have to take place, it would have to be actual, not merely potential. But the being-in-the-world of the existing individual includes potential being-out-of-the-world insofar as immanent death is an essential part of it. Thus in being-in-the-world is present — (in the mode of potentiality) —what later (in the mode of factuality) appears as loss-of-the-world in factual death. Of course, we do not know by

[32] Philosophie, I, 43.

experience that being-out-of-the-world will be realized in loss-of-the-world. Furthermore, the situation is probably just the reverse; only on the basis of potential loss-of-the-world in potential death can actual death be mentally conceived and interpreted as "departure" from the world. Jaspers' "being suspended" between being-in- and being-out-of-the-world is — in our interpretation — a manifestation of the constant breaking forth *(aufbrechen)* of worldlessness in potential death and the breaking up *(Einbrechen)* of the ongoing foundation of man's being.

We add here another statement of Jaspers concerning Transcendence. In the quest for Transcendence, as *the* origin, it actually eludes cognition; but, in Jaspers' words: I can "brood, as it were, towards it" by leaping "from the objectified to the non-objectified, from the conceivable to the inconceivable."

The initial origin is not the first link in a chain of existence, nor is it the whole of existence; it does not in fact exist at all. I think of it by way of the incompletability of existence by means of not-thinking *(Nichtdenken)*, which latter I seek by means of, in each case definite, categories, in which I leap to a point where thinking stops. Transcendence, thus revealed, remains indefinable; yet, although it is unknowable and unthinkable, it is present in thought in the sense of [a certainty of] *that* it is, not *what* it is. Concerning this "it is" nothing can be stated other than the formal, redundant assertion, whose potential realization is impenetrable for us: *it is what it is*.[33]

If we reconsider the certainty of coming death, we must admit that, strictly speaking, it refers only to the fact of its actual appearance but leaves undetermined what, essentially, it is. To be sure, it implies the one element of purport which determines *what* death is: namely, the *end* of being-in-the-world. Nevertheless, this essentially negative definiteness grants to thought and imagination, in principle, an unlimited variety of contents as well as possibilities for interpretation, —, as, for example, the interpretation of the end of existence as a passageway into a world "beyond" of "pure spirits," et al., interpretations which amount to relativizations. These interpretations of content participate in the certainty of the coming of future death; and imaginative thought enlarges upon them in its own creative activity, although it obviously perpetrates an illusion thereby. A critical reconsideration then reduces this manifold content to the one Being — devoid of all contents — and its certainty which, in turn, rests solely on the rebound from the certainty of death. If we attribute — we cannot develop this here

[33] *Ibid.*, III, 67.

in further detail — the origin of, both the experience and the concept, of "naught" to immanent death and thus, at the same time, to the origin of thought, then the "dialectic" of Being and naught, developed by Hegel [34] and adopted, with a different intent, by Jaspers,[35] is transformed into a *basic process pervading man's being:* The constant breaking through of potential death within man, as the source of the idea of Being (which is "above all being," i.e., transcends every individual being), reveals at the same time the ever-present abyss of naught, as the potential — and in coming death actual — loss of being. With this, Transcendence is not disdained as "illusion" or held to be the pure Nothing, in the sense of irrelevant nothingness — Frank once called this an "arbitrary construction."[36] Rather is it preserved, because the search for Transcendence is regarded as an essential constituent of human nature, but only as that.

Included in the certainty of being which is based on Transcendence is the *one* being of the *one* godhead. The unity of Being, encompassing all that is and rooted in the Transcendent, follows, first of all, from the formalized, universal applicability of the existential judgment,[37] and, on the other hand, from the existence of each existing individual who, in his certainty of being, is certain of his — so to say naked — being-here, and not of his "subjectivity." Still, the question remains whether from this alone the fascinating power of the nameless One, of the one truth and of the one God, can be understood — an experienced power which Jaspers has so emphatically affirmed.[38] We suppose again that death, as the paradigm of uniqueness, plays a fundamental rôle here. Granted, all that occurs in human history and the world of nature is, as such, singular — at least in a strictly numerical and temporal-spatial sense, but perhaps also in a qualitative one. This is true, although our cognitive interest, as a rule, is directed, especially in regard to happenings in nature, not to their factual uniqueness but to their "lawful recurrence." Still, this cognitive emphasis on the recurring

34 Cf. G. W. F. Hegel, *Sämtliche Werke*, ed. by G. Lasson, III, 66ff. (*Wissenschaft der Logik*, I. Bd., I. Abschn., I, Kap.) Leipzig, 1932.

35 *Philosophie*, III, 17ff., 43ff.; *Wahrheit*, (München, 1947), 880ff.

36 E. Frank, "Die Philosophie von Jaspers," *Theol. Rundschau*, N.F. 5 (1933), 316.

37 Jaspers (*Wahrheit*, 260) says: That which is held in common by all that is — "that it *is* and not *is not*" — "waters down, of course, on the one hand, to the simple assertion: All being is, as assertion, merely the being of the copula. This commonality, however, points, on the other hand, to the unfathomable foundation in which all being is *one* Being." We are not making this foundation, as such, the basis of our study, but are questioning, rather, its origin.

38 Cf. *Philosophie*, III, 116ff.; *Wahrheit*, 162ff., 680ff.

constant in the events, does not nullify the fact that each event happens just once, just as the establishment of "historical laws" does not alter the fact that historical events do not repeat themselves. Since, however, the ordinary usage of language is oriented towards objective, practical and relevant cognition and not towards the essential character of what is, it is not surprising that a misleading ambiguity has become attached to the expression "unique," which carries over even into philosophical terminology. It offends our feeling for language to call the constantly recurring activities within the life of an individual "singular," even though they are just that in a strictly temporal sense, and must be so, if only because of the continual, one-directional, "elapsing" of original — lived — time. We reserve "singularity" either for that which appears to us as especially significant — e.g., for experiences and events which cause a decisive turn of life and which, as such, stand out in relief, as it were, above the average level and thereby acquire an accentuated, "qualitative" singularity; or we reserve it for the experiences of birth and death which, in the strictest sense, are unique experiences, never recurring, not even in a similar manner. And yet even the uniqueness of these experiences is itself qualified when they are placed in relationship to the historical setting encompassing the life of the individual. Nevertheless, the singularity of death, even as compared with that of birth, remains distinctive insofar as, once it has come to pass, the possibility of a recurrence of both similar phenomena and singular events within the history of an individual is radically eliminated. If such be the case, then the essential singularity of factual death must also be revealed in some form in potential death. And, indeed, it seems to be manifested in the up-soaring contemplation of the One, in the search for the one truth, and in the belief in God. In the realm of worldly experience, on the other hand, the infinite variety of what is encountered and a multiplicity of truths and of divinities are vying with each other. Therefore, unless one eliminates the problem by brusquely rejecting the three manifestations of the One as speculative figments, he must search for the origin of this quest for oneness in the unobjective nature of man. And right here death suggests itself, because it is not only an event happening only once to each individual, but also one which belongs uniquely to each individual life. Its essential content remains, as we have seen, to a great extent indefinite, hence, in a certain sense, "empty," and therefore available for other fulfillment. In fact, the One does not manifest itself in the three traditional forms alone; the one person who matters, too, can become, so to speak, bearer of the One which

I affirm without qualification. This does not necessarily mean that the varieties of content of the One are merely "masks" or "veilings" of the one death — present as potentiality and prospective as factuality. We are, however, of the opinion that they derive the absolute, alluring power of the One from the hidden power of immanent death. For although death, both potential and factual, depends on life as a condition of itself, still its appearance wipes out at once this condition: and this loss of conditionality, as a possibility, is the basis of man's capacity to make absolutely unconditional decisions which, as unconditional ones, are always characterized by the extreme "either-or" of — in the last analysis — being or non-being.

It should be demonstrated that man's freedom — the consciousness of freedom leaves no doubt as to the possibility of freedom, whereas any of its actual realizations are always open to doubt — is grounded in immanent death. But that would lead us too far away from our concern with Transcendence in Jaspers. Instead, we turn to one last consideration of Transcendence.

Jaspers speaks of a "calm in reality." The "leap" from anguish to such calm is the

most enormous accomplishment possible to man. That he succeeds in it must depend on something over and above the existence of his own being; his faith links him indefinably to the Being of Transcendence.

It is the basic fact of man's existence that reality, which brings forth annihilating anguish, can be seen as it really is neither without anguish nor without the transition from anguish to calm. That man can at once see reality, exist in reality, and still live without perishing in anguish, decisively ties his being-himself to being close to reality, but in an unfinishable process, in which neither anguish nor calm, nor any form reality takes, are ever final. Because, in order to see reality, it is necessary to experience even the most extreme anguish as one's own, it is through this anguish that the most difficult and the most incomprehensible leap, the leap to calm, where reality remains revealed, becomes possible.

Only in the assurance of Transcendence — felt and sustained in suffering, in spite of foundering — an assurance,

which in the depth of the crisis could even relinquish the language of Transcendence, does man find the support which enables him to reach a calm that is no longer deceptive. Still, this certainty, dependent on the presence of *Existenz,* cannot in time be constituted as an objective guarantee, but must disappear again and again. However, when it is present, nothing can prevail against it.[39]

[39] *Philosophie,* III, 235ff.

The Godhead is origin and goal; it is peace of mind. There is security. It is impossible for man to lose Transcendence, without ceasing to be man.[40]

We shall not discuss anguish here, not because it is meaningless for the experience of naught and Being — although Heidegger was mistaken when he presumed that they were revealed exclusively or, at least, primarily in this way,[41] thereby apparently influencing Jaspers in the same direction. But we believe that Being, as well as naught, are perceived first of all and to the greatest extent in thought, and that their emotional expression in primitive anguish — an expression which, as such, testifies to their essential relation to potential death — breaks through only occasionally. Therefore man attains calm — such as that which is granted to him by faith in God — not only in the "leap" from anguish; nor does anguish alone bring about a vision of reality free from illusion, although the contrast between anguish and calm remains perhaps the most impressive. What, then, is the essence of each?

The most obvious sign which we accept as proof of another man's death is his motionlessness, i.e., the utter loss of that which is accepted as visible proof of life — spontaneous mobility. The simple experience that the dead does not react to any of our actions directed towards him — especially that he no longer responds or otherwise reacts to our words — does not characterize, of course, the condition of death alone; nevertheless, it is not mere chance that among the images which we form of our own death this motionlessness, this incapacity for self-movement — sometimes linked with the thought of absolute, spaceless darkness, — plays a dominant rôle. We are not here concerned with the question of the adequacy or inadequacy of these images regarding the "objective essence" of being dead; and we are just as little interested in their subjective biographical and historical sources. It suffices to state the indisputable fact that the condition of death is characterized, among other things, by factual motionlessness—which we interpret as resulting from the loss of the capacity for motion characteristic of life — and that, presumably, we derive from this also the different images of our own being dead which, however, are essentially insufficient. Corresponding to the perceptible *outer* motionlessness, there is the loss of the inner agitation of feeling, willing, thinking, etc., thus of what constitutes the *inner* manifestations of animation *(Lebendigkeit und Beseeltheit)*. If one tries to imagine what kind of emotional state would correspond to the *potential*

40 *Origin*, 219.
41 For criticism, cf. *Die anthropologische Bedeutung der Phantasie*, II, 66ff.

loss of motion[42] within life, then one is reminded of that peculiar inner calm and quiet which is realized in contemplation, when it is directed towards what is and which perceives, but at the same time restrains, its onslaught. In the field of vocal expression we distinguish between intentional silence, — ambiguous in its motives and aims —, involuntary loss of speech, and the variously caused forms of muteness, one of which is characteristic of death. It seems not to be mere coincidence that meditation is lacking also in inner verbal expression, that it is absorbed for moments in pure contemplation of being, although this is interrupted again and again by active thought. Is it too much or too far fetched to presume that immanent death, the source of thought, for moments fills this meditative quiet, as though it were stepping forth, out of concealment, into the "hiatus" of thought? Is it not here that we find the basis for the leap from the whirl of anguish into calm, which Jaspers attributes to the nature of Transcendence? And is this calm not "calm in reality," because being confronts here the possibility of loss of being and asserts itself, in its very "reality," as the opposite of non-being?

The fact that calm cannot be sustained for any length of time can be understood — apart from the processive character of thought and of existence in general — from the peculiar rôle of potential death: on the one hand I am able to grant it, as the source of freedom, a place in my inner actions[43] and thus can achieve *Existenz*. On the other hand, I am still at its mercy, insofar as it is a constituent of man's ongoing being; and I must suffer its constant presence — which accounts for the limited degree to which *'existential'* up-soaring (the being granted to oneself of *Existenz*) can be brought about actively, and which, in the final analysis, has its basis in having to bear the inevitability of factual death. Thus calm offers to thinking man a support which participates in the certainty of future death, a support characterized by security insofar as death — in the Platonic-Christian interpretation — reveals to him a pathway for the soul's return to its "eternal home." But this support, in itself unshakeable as such, nevertheless slips away again and again, because of the ongoing character of existence and

[42] Following Heidegger, we regard motion as a characteristic of life, not only in a physical, but also in an emotional sense. Linguistic phrases, such as "being moved" (emotionally), and, indeed, the word "emotion" itself, support his view. Thus both motion and emotion are seen as, modally different, concretizations of one identical constituent of man's being.

[43] Here rests the still more extreme possibility of bringing about one's own death by suicide.

the out-standing[44] character *(Ausstehen)* of "eternal calm." Finally, as regards Jaspers' thesis concerning the impossibility of losing Transcendence, we account for it by the nature of man's being, to which belongs the constituent of potential death, the source of creative thought, and, with it, of Transcendence.

We have — as stated in the beginning — attempted an interpretation of some features of Jaspers' concept of Transcendence. This interpretation has been reductive and immanent; that is, we interpreted each of these features as stemming from the immanence of death. If we ask how our interpretation affects the two aspects of Transcendence—as the "source and the goal, both of which lie in God" and out of whose depths alone we "really become authentically human"[45]—we may perhaps say: indeed, we stated, when discussing Transcendence under the aspect of source, that in our opinion immanent death provides the basis for man's possibility to transform himself by inner action into *Existenz*. But the idea of the creation of man by God, which Jaspers seems occasionally to be considering,[46] cannot—on principle—be deduced from immanent death. That it occurs to us, however, to inquire in *this* sense also into the source of our being and of the world is, in any case, essentially human and presumably is likewise grounded in potential death; but obviously potential death cannot provide the answer, which would have to be deduced solely from the realm of objective experience and not from speculative thought. Apart from this, the realm of Jaspers' concept of original source covers, in our attempt at interpretation, only that which, on principle, can be understood as part of man's being, to which belongs the "transcendent immanence" or the "immanent Transcendence" (to use Simmel's terminology) of death: in death the origins of *Existenz* are one with Transcendence, as goal. That communication — a specific and central concept in Jaspers' philosophizing — can play no rôle here is plainly seen from the import of potential and factual death. In both forms it destroys communicative relations. Therefore, Marcel can interpret the acknowledgment of the death of a beloved one as a breach of *'existential'* faith;[47] and Fichte, in his *"Reden an die deutsche Nation,"* once reproached the "basic faith of the aliens," because they believed, "of necessity, in death, as the beginning and the end, the fundamental source of all things and

---

[44] Out-standing in the sense of "outstanding debts." The relationship between eternal calm and ongoing life is characterized by the former's quasi "standing outside" the latter.

[45] *Rechenschaft*, 264.   [46] Cf., for example, *Wahrheit*, 216ff.

[47] Cf. G. Marcel: *Homo Viator*. Tr. into German (Düsseldorf, 1949), 204ff.

therefore of life."[48] From the standpoint of an absolute desire for communication, Marcel's interpretation, especially, is profoundly right; but in the last analysis only this is decisive: whether the denial of death — either our own or that of another — abolishes its factuality or only deceptively veils it.

If Transcendence, as original source and goal, is "deduced" from potential death, then the question arises whether a "nihilism" must not result from this as an inescapable consequence. If one understands the concept in its original sense, historically speaking, as coined by Baader — as a falling asunder of scientific knowledge, especially that of natural science, and of the truth of revelation[49] — then there can be no doubt as to the answer. For neither the natural sciences nor philosophy are concerned with revelation; if they were, they would betray their own basic intention. But "nihilism" is today, above all, characterized as an "absence of faith," which professes to oppose Western tradition and leads to the destruction of those conceptions of man whose realizations are the ideals which serve as our standards. With this in mind, it seems appropriate to use a certain caution and careful reticence in the allegation of nihilistic tendencies. No one can rationally deny that all of us today still live out of the substance of antiquity and Christian faith; but this includes hardly the blind acceptance of all teachings of Greek thought or of all biblical tenets of faith. Their rejection in the name of the sincere, though perhaps painful, striving toward sober truth does not necessarily imply a lack of appreciation for this bountiful tradition. Even Jaspers, in his modified adoption of Biblical content, has taken out an unquestionably central section and discarded it;[50] that the matter ends there is improbable. One must also remember that the very faith which supports life and gives it its direction has not always kept the men inspired by it from doing away with their disliked, dissenting fellowmen. In any case, neither faith, as such, nor lack of faith, on its part, necessarily enforces a humane or inhumane attitude — although the singular worth of each individual soul, discovered by and preserved in the Christian faith, has no doubt actually been more conducive to humane sentiment than have anti-Christian movements. Furthermore, it is not to be inferred as a matter of course that nihilistic activity represents the direct con-

---

48 J. G. Fichte: *Sämtliche Werke*, (Berlin, 1846), VII, 361.

49 Cf. E. Benz: *Westlicher und östlicher Nihilismus in christlicher Sicht*, (Stuttgart, no date).

50 Cf. for example: *Wahrheit*, 850ff.; also: H. Frh v. Campenhausen: "Die philosophische Kritik des Christentums bei Karl Jaspers," *Zschr. f. Theologie und Kirche* 48, 1951, 237f.

sequence of a corresponding theory; the reverse may be the case — that the theory serves, *ex post facto,* as "idealogical justification" of preceding destructive activity; or we may have a reciprocal dependence of the two. Nevertheless, whichever way the intricate problem may be resolved, there remains, untouched by it, the unavoidable, practical and *'existential'* relevance of philosophical interpretations in the present historical situation, even if one is inclined not to overestimate their practical importance. In this regard, we are convinced that the immanent interpretation of human nature, — which rejects Transcendence or interprets it reductively in the manner designated, — leaves room for the realization of both its conserving and destroying potentialities, as does faith in God. If I am convinced of my finiteness and of the extreme evanescence of my own being, and if I will not be led astray, by the conceivability of an eternal Being, to its hypostatization, or to having faith in my own participation or my being grounded in it; if this is so, I can fall into hopeless despair and, relinquishing all reason and human dignity, can thrust myself into the nihilistic intoxication of destruction. However, out of this consciousness of transitoriness I can also experience, with an unutterable intensity, the irreplaceable preciousness of every action and of all being and, on this basis, accept as an authoritative obligation the highest challenge to man: to be, for a while, the guardian of eluding being and therewith of humaneness. We are free to choose either possibility; although it remains open whether the possibility for destruction is not essentially more appropriate to man's nature. It is, however, questionable whether, in the future, faith in Transcendence will have any better control over such a possibility than the attempt, without Transcendence, to realize the task which Jaspers once set for philosophizing: of "rendering mankind aware of itself."[51]

This brief critical discussion of Jaspers' idea of Transcendence rests on a presupposition which, on principle, breaks through the conception of his philosophy insofar as it asserts — concerning the nature of man's ontological constitution — that in man potential death, as origin of thought, "precedes" factual death; and maintains that this assertion is pertinent without being able to "prove" it or even so much as establish it as being evident in itself. With the immanence of death, however, is closely connected the potential character of human nature and therewith its transformability from mere being to *Existenz* in Jaspers' sense. Whereas Jaspers leaves this potential character as such in unilluminated suspension

[51] *Age, (London,* 1951, 2nd ed.) 205.

and does not differentiate it from either pure conceivabilities or from the potentialities, inherent in lifeless entities, we see its true nature decisively determined by immanent death. Hence we try to understand the *'existential'* potentialities of man in part by relating them to potential death. This thesis — since it cannot be demonstrated as indubitable fact — on its part, represents only a possibility. But it gains its importance from the indubitable factuality of actual death, which is what it is, as my own future death, both objectively knowable and incapable of objectification. Just the same, the fixation of this one point in human nature does not paralyze our freedom, which, as Jaspers has claimed, is the case if we know the nature of Transcendence;[52] for this point "is" itself the origin of freedom. And, although, the thesis concerning immanent death is quite contrary to the character of Jaspers' thinking, it still owes it its origin. It is for this reason that we have dared to try its — perhaps illuminating — power in the confrontation with some of the characteristics of Transcendence, sacrificing Transcendence, but not the high potentialities of human nature.

HANS KUNZ

FACULTY OF PHILOSOPHY
UNIVERSITY OF BASEL
BASEL, SWITZERLAND

52 Cf. *Rechenschaft,* 110.

William Earle

ANTHROPOLOGY IN THE PHILOSOPHY OF
KARL JASPERS

THE PROBLEM of man is not, of course, an exclusively modern one. As soon as man learned to express anything, he attempted to express his idea of himself, and the ensuing history of culture reveals a continuous struggle of philosophers, poets, prophets, scientists, and statesmen to arrive at a formulation either of what man is, or of what he ought to be. Periods of culture might be defined in terms of the temporary convictions men arrived at concerning their own essence, just social relationships, their place in nature and history, and their final ends.

Man has been the plaything or cherished darling of the gods, he has been a chance conjunction of atoms or the fulfillment of the hidden desires of nature. He has been a rational, tool-using, laughing, playing, speaking, social, worshipping animal. He has been a stream of passions and sense-data, a substance, two substances, an ego working out transcendental problems, an eternal soul, and a gust of wind. He has been freedom incarnate and a machine of cords and levers; he has been an infinite value and a futile passion. And, corresponding to this almost indefinite number of "definitions" of man, is an equally indefinite number of evaluations of his life varying from hatred and disgust through laughter to worship. This is what man has thought of himself.

Finally the sciences have come in to investigate this curious subject. If philosophy had arrived at no "agreement," perhaps the cause was lack of rigor in method; philosophy, in the eyes of the scientists, was too speculative. It had disdained fact, and the corrective to this is observation. And so the empirical sciences, anthropology, psychology, sociology, etc., have set out to watch man as closely as possible in as many variant situations as could be found or made, hoping to collect a common definition. We have kept company with the monkeys, trying to teach them to become like us, or ourselves to believe we are like them; we have lived with the primitive, the degenerated, the insane, the perverted; we have watched the child, the genius, the mediocre and the fool. The information that has accumulated is greater than anyone can master, and it is mounting daily. But ever and anon the suspicion makes itself felt that instead of knowing man better than the old poets, we know him less. A concept of human nature was to result from these facts, but none has been forthcoming. All the facts are indeed facts: they all say something true about this paradoxical creature; but we have intimations that the center has dropped out. Man himself has disappeared into the multiplicity of his aspects. And so the question recurs in a peculiarly urgent form for us: what *is* man? This question is at the heart of Jaspers' philosophizing.

If, then, speculation was thought to have yieled nothing but polemical disputes, empirical research yielded controlled statements of fact, but not about what we were looking for. The question which Jaspers now raises is a methodological one: may not both rational philosophy and empirical science be inappropriate to their subject-matter? Man, Jaspers insists, is not an object which can be investigated empirically nor one which can be conceived abstractly, for his most authentic being is not objective at all. It is inconceivable, inexhaustible by its appearance or behavior, an *x* which can to some extent be clarified but never known. We can *be* men, but we can not *know* what it is that we are. His name for this properly human existence is *Existenz,* and the clarification of *Existenz* is not science, nor any rationally cogent discipline, but something unique, *Existenzerhellung* — the illumination of *Existenz. Existenzerhellung* is the pivot of Jaspers' whole philosophy.

The sciences have always insisted about this or any other subject-matter that there would always be more to be known. Such constituted the "advance" of science; but for Jaspers there is a peculiarity about man which renders such an advance towards ideal completion impossible. Man is not the sort of being which one can progressively exhaust by knowledge. And worse, what we do not and can not know about man is of such a sort that it calls into question what we think we do know. Man is radically exceptional, exceptional in the order of nature, and exceptional also so far as any supposed positive knowledge or laws of his "nature" are concerned. He has the possibility of being free, and with this freedom all positive conceptions of his nature break down. The indefinite variation in patterns of behavior, modes of life, values, and attitudes testify to an intrinsic freedom hidden at the core. Man is not a fact waiting to be described, but an outbreak of freedom and unforeseeable potentialities. No empirical investigation of choices which are in fact made would touch the source of those choices. *Existenz* is origin *(Ursprung)* and not mere existence *(Dasein)*.

Jaspers' critique of anthropology goes even deeper; not only are the empirical sciences hopelessly inadequate for man, but *no* cognitive or rational discipline whatsoever can touch him. Man is not primarily an *object* at all, and thus can not be *known;* only the objective can be cognized. Man as *Existenz* is radically *individual,* historically situated, unique, and irreplaceable. Knowledge can not touch the unique and irreplaceable, or rather as soon as it does touch it, it evaporates it into the general and abstract.

Existenz, which is the most authentic side of man, is thus inaccessible to cognition as such. Illumination of *Existenz* is not a new science which will fill in the gaps left by the empirical sciences or rational philosophy. But if *Existenz* is not an object to be described, how can it even be clarified? The answer to this question reveals how radical Jaspers' criticism of knowing in general actually is. For illumination of *Existenz,* we read on almost every page of his *magnum opus, Philosophie,* is not a doctrine, and is not even knowledge. What it "clarifies" are the *potentialities* open to man, and the clarification consists in an indirect appeal to the reader to *become* free, to *become* authentic, to *come to* himself. The reader then will not know what *Existenz* is, but will perhaps have *become* himself (or *Existenz*). No cognitive knowledge about man is possible; illumination of *Existenz* would carry us beyond knowledge altogether into non-knowledge, *Unwissen,* i.e., into the *'existential'* consciousness of ourselves and our freedom. This movement, which is not a logical one and which can not be forced by the cogency of argument, must be a *leap* accomplished by the individual reader from a realization of the inadequacy of knowledge to the task of actually becoming himself, as an *'existing'* human being. Illumination of *Existenz* thus is not knowledge about man, is not simply true or false, is not description, but is rather appeal. The "conclusion" of illumination of *Existenz* is not a proposition, but an *'existential'* movement within the reader by which he becomes authentically himself.

Such, in brief outline, is what Jaspers is saying about man and our knowledge of him. It involves explicit theories of man, knowledge, and Being. I shall now proceed to discuss in greater detail the steps of his analysis. To state my criticism of his position at once, I feel that, although Jaspers has made essential contributions to the study of man, his further view that these contributions must be interpreted as appeals designed to awaken the reader to his own *Existenz,* such that illumination of *Existenz* is not a cognitive discipline at all, nor man a proper object of rational knowledge, — such views are wrong, inconsistent with what Jaspers himself says about knowledge, and therefore a dispensable aspect of *Existenzphilosophie*.

The problem concerns more than a word or turn of phrase; it touches eventually the old dispute between rationalism and irrationalism, which has broken out again in our times as a dispute between phenomenology and existentialism. Is there anything which in principle is unknowable? Jaspers insists that there are at least three such subjects, the World as a whole, *Existenz*, and Transcendence (or God). I shall here attempt to argue that, at least on the general grounds Jaspers presents, man is not exempt from cognition, and that a good number of Jaspers' own insights can be absorbed into a rational, cognitive philosophy of man, to which they constitute a major contribution. The problem will be discussed under three heads: 1) the limits of knowledge, 2) *Existenz*, and 3) the interpretation of *'existential'* assertions.

1. *The Limits of Knowledge*

Knowledge, to be knowledge, must have its object; it is about this object, and attempts to discover the properties which the object has. If the object does indeed have these properties, anyone who turns his attention or experience toward that same object will be in a position to discover the same properties, and thus confirm the assertion; objective knowledge thus is accessible in principle to all, and both corrigibility and communication are possible with respect to assertions about that object. Hence, objective knowledge is universal in intent. And if the object should be a unique, unrepeatable instance, then what we would mean by universal validity is that anyone *would* have had the same knowledge, if he had cognized that object. The objectivity of knowledge, its universal validity and verifiability, and its communicability are three interrelated terms. Clearly, the key term in this set is the term, "object."

Jaspers wants to say that there is a mode of "clarification" which is not objective; it is about no object, it has no universal validity nor verifiability, and it is not directly communicable. *Existenzphilosophie* in all its parts is conceived by Jaspers as an attempt to push to the limits of objective knowledge, so that we can "feel" beyond. *Existenz*, the most authentically human, lives in this beyond; to attempt to know it objectively is a radical error for Jaspers; instead we must push to the limits of objective knowledge only to leap into *Existenz* ourselves and *be* what is beyond cognition. Clearly, whether or not this is a tenable or even meaningful theory depends upon a rather exact analysis of what we are to mean by the term, "object."

What does *Jaspers* mean by "object"? I think he alternates between two conceptions, a wider and a narrower, and it is largely due to this indetermination that he can support his thesis that *Existenz* is non-objective. His widest conception of object is found in those places where he is considering knowledge or cognition in general:

> the empirically real in space and time, the dead and the living, things and persons, tools and foreign matter, thoughts which are valid of the actual, cogent constructions of ideal objects like mathematical constructions, contents of the imagination, [are] in one word, objectivity in general. Being which I encounter in a situation is for me object.[1]

And in another place the concept (of object) is taken in its widest possible sense:

> Thus everything that has being for us has a side of objectivity: the thinkable and the unthinkable, the real and the unreal, the true and the false, the intuited and the imagined, the possible and the impossible. Whatever we think is somehow object: numbers and figures, $\sqrt{-1}$ and the class of all classes, atoms and electrons, formulas and similes, angels and centaurs, virtue and right.[2]

From these definitions by enumeration, we can gather the sort of notion Jaspers has in mind: "object" means whatever we can become aware of, whatever has its own properties, what we "encounter," etc., and is by no means to be identified with "object" taken in a narrower sense of "physical thing." Physical things in space and time are, to be sure, possible objects; but so are angels and centaurs, ideal constructions, etc. In *Von der Wahrheit*, Jaspers proceeds further to characterize objects in general: they are all unities of a manifold, and are split into a universal-particular pole.[3] Thought *(Denken)* apprehends their universal aspect, and intuition *(Anschauung)* apprehends them in their particularity. The object itself is a synthesis of both poles.[4]

It becomes clear in the following pages of the same work that neither pure, abstract thought, nor pure intuition without concepts gives us knowledge; *actual* cognition or knowledge is a synthesis of thought *and* intuition in one apprehension. Thus objective knowledge can not be identified with merely thinking some

1 *Philosophie*, 2nd ed., (Berlin, 1948), 4.

2 *Wahrheit*, 231.   3 *Ibid.*, 232.   4 *Ibid.*, 233.

universal character, nor with blindly intuiting a sheer "this," but combines both, such that we apprehend a "this somewhat," a particular characterized in a certain way.

This is the more general characterization of cognition. But, when Jaspers wishes to find limitations in knowledge, I believe he tends to forget the full characterization he has already given, and to emphasize only one abstract side of cognition, in order to show that there is indeed something more, namely, the other side. When he finds that *Existenz,* for example, can not be cognized, the cognition which is supposed to be inadequate is not at all cognition in the full sense of the term, but in a very narrow sense, which would not even be adequate to characterize all of objective knowledge admitted by Jaspers himself. And similarly the term "object," when found inapplicable to *Existenz,* is taken in a sense so narrow that it is inadequate to many sorts of objects previously admitted to be such by Jaspers. This is an argument which can be supported only by extensive quotation. But I shall cite a single passage at length here to stand for them all:

> Were I to try to look at *Existenz* directly, I would not see it. What is clear, is so in the degree to which it is objective. What stands before us visibly in space is the model of all objectivity; "objective thought" means thinking in spatial pictures. To be sure the structure of consciousness no longer has the objectivity of a spatial thing; it has, nevertheless, a derived metaphorical objectivity which makes it a possible object of empirical investigation. Only when we go to *Existenz* do we approach an absolute non-objectivity, whose self-certainty however is the center of our existence, out of which Being is sought, and the essentiality of all objectivity is illuminated.
>
> If something can not in general be an object, it might seem that one can not speak of it; who does speak of it makes it into an object. In fact, every supposedly knowable result of such thought makes *Existenz* into an object, and thus psychologizes. But we can think and speak not only of objects; there are also means by which, in thinking, one can become clear *oneself,* without that giving us any insight into any thing. Becoming clear is a form of existence of a non-objective, possible *Existenz.* Thinking and speaking are also concerned with a non-objective self-certainty, which can be called attitude, clarity, consciousness of Being, or absolute consciousness.
>
> We say: "*Existenz,*" and speak of the being of this reality. But "*Existenz*" is not a concept, but an indicator pointing to a "beyond all objectivity."[5]

Existenz, thus, is regarded as an "absolute non-objectivity;" and

5 *Philosophie,* 22.

the reason is that it can not be apprehended by picture thought! But in the earlier and more general characterization of objects, nothing was said about "spatial pictures" being the model, *Urbild,* of all objectivity, for then it would have been perfectly evident that such objects as $\sqrt{-1}$ can in no wise be reduced to a picture, even in a "derived, metaphorical" sense. If we are to take the view that all objects have spatial pictures as their *Urbild,* we should then have a much more serious problem on our hands than the possible non-objectivity of *Existenz.* We should find ourselves in the classical difficulty of making clear our own cognition of universals, given nothing more than individual Humean sense-impressions.

On the other hand, Professor Jaspers does not really wish to limit objective cognition to spatial pictures. In some places, cognition becomes identified with the sheer universal, the law, the principle; at this point, his objection will be that it is incapable of grasping the true *individuality* of *Existenz.* But before we consider these problems further, we shall attempt to clarify Jaspers' concept or sign, *"Existenz."*

2. *Existenz*

The second volume of Jaspers' *Philosophie* is so rich in insights into the life and predicament of the soul, that I must risk the charge of misrepresentation, if I summarize. Nevertheless, there is a basic pattern of analysis which I shall attempt to elicit, so that the general conclusions and point of view can be discussed. *Existenz* is conceived as hanging between two radically different modes of Being: the world and God. The world is the world of objects, or rather objectivity; it is the physical world, the body, human behavior, *Dasein,* or observable, factual being. *Existenz* expresses itself in this world, but never adequately, or univocally. The existence *(Dasein)* of *Existenz* is inevitably a finite, shrunken appearance. But *Existenz* must appear on pain of being nothing at all. The appearance or expression of *Existenz* is however an expression of *Existenz only to Existenz;* life, decision, communication are not *'existential'* facts; they are seen as possible expressions of human freedom only if interpreted as such by another in *'existential'* relations. Thus Bruno's refusal to renounce his freedom of thought and his martyrdom as a consequence is a series of facts which are, taken in themselves, ambiguous. We can not objectively conclude from the observable facts of the case anything about Bruno's inner decision. There are a plurality of possible interpretations. But this does not imply that Bruno himself was in an ambiguous state of mind. He may have seen his act as expressing a certain *'existential'* choice which for him could not have been otherwise. It is an act that expressed his decision *for him,* and which may recall other *Existenzen* to themselves and their own situations.

Existence thus is always an unsatisfactory, ambiguous, equivocal expression of *Existenz.* But existence alone, according to Jaspers, is objectively investigable. We can only empirically inquire into what appears, and not into what does not appear; thus man, who is most authentically *Existenz* and freedom, is not exhaustively subject to empirical investigation. Not only is his life an inadequate expression of his most inward, authentic being or his possible *Existenz,* but that life will itself only appear as an expression of *Existenz* to a proper "observer," i.e., to another *Existenz* in *'existential'* communication with him. Thus anthropology, psychology, sociology, etc., can never touch the fundamental thing in anyone's life; so long as they restrict themselves to objective, experienceable phenomena, they are dealing with what is merely an inadequate and equivocal expression. The true self in each remains inaccessible for external observation, though not necessarily to a lover, friend, or oneself.

Let us now return to the principal problem of this essay: in which sense now is *Existenz* "absolutely non-objective"? So far, the sense in which it is non-objective is the sense of "object" which means "externally observable behavior," or existence. But this is the narrower sense of object, akin to "picture thinking." I should agree at once that the self is certainly not identical with externally observable behavior, and that it is only equivocally expressible by such. At this point, I think anyone who is not a rank behaviorist would find little to which to object.

But Jaspers would go even further; not only is *Existenz* inadequately expressed in external behavior, but it really can not even cognize itself. Why can I not know myself? Because "the self is always more than all the knowable."[6] When we attempt to know ourselves, according to Jaspers, we apprehend ourselves either as consciousness-as-such, *(Bewusstsein überhaupt)* or in a series of 'I-aspects' *(Ichaspekte),* which are the various rôles I take in life, or as having a character. Of these, two, the first and last are mere abstract universals, whereas the "I-aspects," are too immersed in existence properly to exhaust my inner self. Thus when I objectify myself to myself, I end up with something too limited and particular, or too general and abstract. However, "there arises an

6 *Philosophie,* 323.

indirect knowing *about* me, which is no knowing *me*."[7] This lo-
cates the realm of *'existential'* philosophy. It is an indirect knowledge *about* me, but not a direct knowledge *of* me.

I do not wish to quibble at this point, but I utterly fail to see
how *'existential'* knowledge differs in this respect from many other
forms of objective knowledge. Could we not say the very same
things about my knowledge of this pencil? It is not Pencilness, nor
is it merely pencil-as-writing-implement, plus pencil-as-economic-
exchange-value, plus pencil-as-aesthetic-object; no, it is more than
any of these *Bleistiftaspekte*. Further, it is not to be identified with
its character as capable-of-making-marks, etc. No, *this pencil* is
unknowable, and escapes all objective categories. Its existence is
inexhaustible. We can have indirect knowledge *about* it, but can
never know it in itself. We can only suggest its nature, and call
upon others to feel as we do.

On the other hand, we do perceive this pencil, and we do know
something of it. We have objective knowledge of it which is verifiable. Now, granting that external observations of behavior do
not discover the inner self, still our own intuition of ourselves as
an individual characterized in certain ways has nothing in it that
is not objective. To be sure we do not *exhaust* ourselves in any
series of general predicates, any more than we exhaust *any* individual thus. But we directly intuit that individual self which is not
exhausted, else we should not have the slightest idea that our
universal predicates were inadequate. Such intuition or "feeling"
gives us to ourselves.

Naturally what we then intuit is not to be spoken of in terms
of *pictures*. So in *this* very limited sense of "object," the self which
is intuited by me is "non-objective." But we must forget about
these pictures once and for all. "Object" we had already conceived
in very general terms at the beginning of *Philosophie* as what had
a determinate nature. In this general sense of object, which is the
only one adequate for all that would be recognized as objective
knowledge as such, intuition and consciousness of oneself is as objective as any cognition.

Let the objects and their cognition be as *indirect* as you like, as
much unlike sense-experiences as possible; either they are cognized
somehow or they are not cognized at all. And if they are not cognized at all, then we do not know them either directly or indirectly, and our words become *absolutely meaningless*. But we never
said, in the first place, that all cognition in order to be objective
must be *direct*. For, if we had, again there would have been much

[7] *Ibid.*, 323.

simpler problems on our hands than our cognition of *Existenz*. We should, for example, have had to account for the simplest act of interpreting signs.

Which brings us to Jasper's antinomial method as it is applied to man. *Existenz* is treated in this book from four points of view which, Jaspers says, do not represent any exhaustive schematism, but rather aspects of its total life. These are i) the self in communication and historicity, ii) selfness as freedom, iii) *Existenz* as absoluteness in situation, consciousness, and act, and iv) *Existenz* in subjectivity and objectivity. These are very brilliant chapters which no one can read without extending his insight into the human situation. But how dismaying then to discover that it all is not to be interpreted as objective knowledge, but as appeals to the reader to *become* himself!

The method which Jaspers uses is to pose each '*existential*' situation between two opposites, neither of which, by itself, really exhausts the concrete; since neither is adequate, the synthesis must occur in the actual experience rather than in knowledge. We must push to the limits of the abstractions which represent objective knowledge and then leap into *Existenz* ourselves.

Existenz, for example, tries to communicate with other *Existenzen*; it must try to communicate in order to achieve some measure of rationality and objective being. But then it can never wholly succeed except in some moments and then ambiguously. So it both does and does not communicate; it is always in danger of failing by falling into either empty chatter or truculent silence.

Existenz is rooted in history. But again, only in a certain fashion. It must neither contemplate itself as one more passing event in a series of indifferent events, nor must it flee history altogether and see itself as an abstract, atemporal universal. It both is and is not in time.

It both dies and does not die. It makes an error if it supposes that the final end of its life is a snuffing out in death; similarly it is wrong to suppose that death makes no difference at all. Death must be internalized as my own potentiality.

There are many ways in which Jaspers analyzes the situation of *Existenz* or *Existenz* itself, always poised between two equally meaningless poles, particularity and universality, time and eternity, silence and communication, love and struggle, existence and freedom, etc. Each of these poles *taken by itself* represents a collapse of the properly authentic life of *Existenz*. They must be held together somehow, and Jaspers insists that they can only be held together by actually living the paradox. But I can not see that living a paradox solves the problem. The problem insofar as it is cognitive at all, is a problem *for* reason and cognition; and the synthesis of the paradox must therefore occur on the level of reason and objective cognition.

This reason or cognition is not, of course, either the empty shuffling of pure abstractions, nor the dumb immersion in the "this-here-now." The "paradoxical" synthesis, however, occurs in the very simplest act of cognition, in those acts of cognition which Jaspers himself would insist were indeed objective. And so I conclude that either *all* cognitions are paradoxical to themselves, or that *none* are, and there is no special illumination of *Existenz* which is radically different in kind from other objective cognitions.

The method of approaching a concrete by means of opposing abstractions is, to my way of thinking, a good one. It is in principle the method of Hegel. But, where Hegel finds the thesis-antithesis-synthesis structure everywhere, Jaspers finds it only in a certain range of topics, God, the World, and *Existenz*. And for these three the last word to be said is that our cognition of them ends in antithesis; the synthesis is a paradox for thought.

But how do we *know* of the paradox? Must we not already *know* what these three things are in order to know that the abstractions are inadequate? If I do not know what I am, how can I know that I am not what either empirical anthropology or rational philosophy says I am? If I "feel" what I am, then this feeling is either the intuitive element of cognition, or some mixture of intuition and conception. In any case we have no new or paradoxical view of self-knowledge or illumination of *Existenz*. It is a synthesis of intuitive and conceptual sides, like all cognition. Either there is no objective cognition at all, or illumination of *Existenz* is a species of it.

Let us suppose that we have achieved for a moment some perception into our *'existential'* situation. Let us further grant that in order to achieve such an insight, we must have lived through the limiting experience, that we must have come to consciousness of our historically rooted and situated lives, that we must have striven for honest communication with nothing held back. What do we arrive at? Either a state of being which is unaware of itself, or a state of being which is aware of itself. If it is aware of itself, then we have extended our knowledge, we see more, and more truly. But we *see*. We are then in a position to express what we see, although as always we know in advance that our assertions will be thought either wrong or unintelligible by those who have not honestly looked at their own lives. Too bad; they have not the same object before them, or we have made mistakes. Here there is nothing which in *principle* suggests either *Unwissen* or radical paradoxes, or descriptions which do not describe but arouse. At this point we need to clarify Jaspers' theory of his own mode of communication.

3. *The Interpretation of Existential Propositions*

Thought and expression can not have their proper sense as direct meanings and utterance [in illumination of *Existenz*]. Only indirectly do they touch the 'I myself,' which is out of 'freedom,' in 'communication' as 'historical consciousness,' which comes to itself in 'ultimate situations,' becomes sure of itself in 'unconditional acts' and fulfills itself in 'absolute consciousness.' . . . All of these words again, which are not concepts but *signa* refer to no being which can become object while yet remaining what it is. What is referred to in these thoughts is not to be found through consciousness-as-such. For consciousness-as-such, in whose medium alone they express themselves, they remain unintelligible. . . . Only to the degree that I am myself, do they find trial and echo, aversion and rejection. Where a justification in the world is sought through the universal, illumination of *Existenz* must keep silent. It gives up when one argues with it. It turns to possible *Existenz* from possible (since it would appeal and awaken) and not to consciousness-as-such (since it can not be proven).[8]

That illumination of *Existenz* as thought can not complete itself but must finally transcend thought and pass into act we find everywhere in *Philosophie,* but neatly expressed in the following quotation:

Existenz-illuminating thought *(der existenzerhellende Gedanke)* always leads to the limits from which an appeal is possible to the individual who can make a leap, a leap which is never identical but always is accomplished by the individual in a fashion which can not be generalized. Therefore the generalizing mode of thought is only a way, and its fulfillment never to be anticipated.[9]

In these quotations we see the antinomial mode of Jaspers' thought applied both to the problem of knowledge and the problem of communication. The principal reasons why illumination of *Existenz* must end in appeal and awakening is that its assertions can not be understood as sheer universal assertions, or direct communication, or by the abstract understanding. There are places where Jaspers considers the opposite of the abstract universal, and there we run into existence which reduces itself to sense-pictures and what they are taken to represent. Oscillating between

8 *Ibid.,* 40.   9 *Ibid.,* 47.

these two poles, each taken in isolation and in abstraction from its opposite, it is no wonder that illumination of *Existenz,* to become meaningful, must make a final appeal to its reader to *become* that which can not be said. But is not our paradox here a product of a forgetfulness of what objective knowledge and objective communication were said to be in the first place? When we considered these things explicitly we found that objective, or "scientific" knowledge was itself a "synthesis" of a universal aspect and a particular individual aspect. Universals totally abstracted and separated from any particularity certainly have no rôle in any kind of thought, and it seems probable that no mind can entertain such total abstractions. And similarly, absolute particularity itself is a mere limiting concept, and can only be approached in the vaguest mode of semi-consciousness, in which we are aware only and solely of a "this" which has no "what" in any respect. But neither of these ghosts describes any instance of objective knowledge; even the simplest proposition represents a "synthesis." These syntheses do not constitute a problem, since they are what we *do* know, when we know anything. They would constitute a problem if we tried to arrive at them by the mechanical addition of sheer individuality which has no character and sheer character which is nothing but universality.

Jaspers then finds a radical paradox in the illumination of *Existenz,* namely that it speaks indirectly about "absolute non-objectivities" in a mode which can not defend or justify itself, but must appeal to the free *'existential'* potentialities in the listener, and which ends not in objective cognition, but in what is described both as an "illumination" *(Existenz-erhellung),* and as an *act* (a leap into one's own situation and into oneself). But I see no paradox here, nothing peculiar about illumination of *Existenz* which raises any particular difficulties. Can not the entire situation be stated quite simply? Suppose I, as *Existenzphilosoph,* wish to say something about the self, in its most inward or authentic aspect. I can either talk about myself, in which case I write autobiography, or else I say what is true of all selves in their most inward aspect. But, as *in all discourse,* if my words are to be understood, my reader must have what I am talking about before his inner eye; and this will be himself insofar as he is like me. Now it is granted on all sides, that to know yourself is difficult; but this isn't the question. My reader compares what I say about the self with what he knows, and comes to some agreement or disagreement. He is here using exactly the same concept of truth and falsity as applies to any proposition. He is interpreting what I say "objectively," although quite obviously the object in this case is also subject. He will be hopelessly lost, of course, if he has only colored pictures at his disposal; but he will also be hopelessly lost if he tries interpreting thus *any* proposition about physical things, or certain mathematical abstractions.

But this doesn't satisfy Jaspers. He wants his propositions to be understood not as descriptions, but rather as appeals and arousals. His assertions are therefore hortatory in intent, calling or suggesting to me that I *become* something. This introduces a distinct function in philosophy and language. Notice that it is not that Jaspers wishes to *describe Existenz* as essentially involved in moral ideals and choice; this itself would be a cognitive assertion. But he wishes to induce his readers to become authentic; his assertions are therefore only pseudo-assertions, whose real meaning is indirect, i.e., hortatory in function. Now I have no objection to hortatory speech, and no doubt we can all profit from it; but how can we profit by listening to appeals to become that which can not be said, known, or rationally discussed? *What* would it be that we are exhorted to become? Thus, the hortatory aspect of Jaspers' speech is voided by the same stroke which abolishes its cognitive or objective aspect. With the disappearance of the object, we are left with intense but meaningless words; we are urgently called to unintelligible tasks.

This is what *would* be the case if we were to accept Jaspers' own interpretation of his philosophy. On the other hand, I find his philosophy very perceptive and in places profound. But the perception and profundity I find dependent upon objective, communicable knowledge, of a difficult and subtle sort, to be sure, but cognitive perception nevertheless. And, as I have said, it is cognitive knowledge in the same sense in which any knowledge is objective and cognitive, not in the alternating views of knowledge by which Jaspers is enabled to show that it is not knowledge. For in the alternating senses, there is no knowledge at all; anything could be reduced to paradox and unintelligibility.

I shall finally consider one last proof by which Jaspers wishes to show the radical difference between 'existential' assertions and objective propositions. The argument is that 'existential' assertions are not *cogent* like real assertions, because no one can be *forced* to acknowledge their truth. Now if the 'existential' assertion is to be regarded as "understood" only when one becomes what it urges, then, indeed, these assertions are not cogent in any sense, since they assert nothing, but simply urge. On the other hand, if they do make any assertion, then they are as "cogent" as the most objective proposition. No one can be forced to recognize their truth, Jaspers says; but no one can be forced to recognize any truth, as stubbornness and madness commonly illustrate. The acceptance of any truth requires a free inner acquiescence, whether that truth be objective or 'existential' From this supposed difficulty, Jaspers concludes that his assertions are not "cogent," that no evidence is sufficient to establish them. But there are two matters involved here, which are combined ambiguously in the German term, *zwingend*. *Zwingend* means both *forcing* and *logically cogent*. 'Existential' propositions do not *force* their meanings upon anyone, any more than any proposition forces its meaning or truth upon its hearer. But if *'existential'* propositions are not *logically cogent,* that is, if there is no evidence for them insofar as they are descriptive, then they must be abandoned.

But of course there *is* evidence for them, namely the sort of evidence which Jaspers presents abundantly in *Philosophie,* and which is accessible to us in our own inner observations. To that extent then there is evidence, although it is granted at once that the evidence is not as simple and obvious as it would be for some assertion in chemistry. The evidence is not public, of course, since the propositions are wholly about our inward life, and not about external behavior.

Again, I find *'existential'* propositions — whatever difficulty and subtlety there is in locating their referent and determining their evidence — no different from the most blatantly objective knowledge. They do not require a mixture of exhortation and quasi-descriptive modes of discourse, nor do they float like Mahommet's coffin between the true and the false, the evidential and non-evidential; nor are they about "absolute non-objectivities," for that would mean they are about nothing; nor are they to be proven by feelings of acceptance or rejection without further analysis.

To conclude: It seems to me that a sound phenomenology of the total structure of the inner life and the self could absorb all that is valuable in the illumination of *Existenz,* without becoming involved in paradoxes and appeals. This is not the place even to sketch out such an alternative. But it is the place, perhaps, to signalize again the monumental contributions Jaspers has made toward such a theory, contributions which put every student of man in his debt. I believe he has demonstrated in a definitive fashion that no empirical investigation, limiting itself to external observations of human behavior, can hope to touch the source and center of such behavior; and further, that he has enriched our conception of the self to a point where any philosophical anthro-pology relying on nothing more than Freud, the older introspec-tive psychology, the views of Locke and Hume, or the earlier rationalists, must be considered hopelessly inadequate. My own criticisms of Jaspers' philosophy are not directed at what I con-sider its content; if they are sound, they would do nothing more than reinterpret the meaning of his work, and purge it of exhorta-tion, and paradox; but these aspects seem to be at the heart of what Jaspers considers valuable in his philosophy.

WILLIAM EARLE

DEPARTMENT OF PHILOSOPHY
NORTHWESTERN UNIVERSITY

15

Hannah Arendt

KARL JASPERS: CITIZEN OF THE WORLD

NOBODY can be a citizen of the world as he is the citizen of his country. Jaspers, in his *Vom Ursprung und Ziel der Geschichte* (1949), discusses extensively the implications of a world-state and a world-empire.[1] No matter what form a world-government with centralized power over the whole globe might assume, the very notion of one sovereign force ruling the whole earth, holding the monopoly of all means of violence, unchecked and uncontrolled by other sovereign powers, is not only a forbidding nightmare of tyranny, it would be the end of all political life as we know it. Political concepts are based on plurality, diversity and mutual limitations. A citizen is by definition a citizen among citizens of a country among countries. His rights and duties must be defined and limited, not only by those of his fellow-citizens, but also by the boundaries of a territory. Philosophy may conceive of the earth as the homeland of mankind and of one unwritten law, eternal and valid for all. Politics deals with men, nationals of many countries and heirs to many pasts; its laws are the positively established fences which hedge in, protect and limit the space in which freedom is not a concept, but a living, political reality. The establishment of one sovereign world-state, far from being the prerequisite for world-citizenship, would be the end of all citizenship. It would not be the climax of world politics, but quite literally its end.

To say, however, that a world-state conceived in the image of sovereign nation-states or of a world-empire in the image of the Roman Empire is dangerous (and the dominion of the Roman Empire over the civilized and barbarian parts of the world was bearable only because it stood against the dark and frightening background of unknown parts of the earth), is no solution for our present political problem. Mankind, which for all preceding generations was no more than a concept or an ideal, has become something of an urgent reality. Europe, as Kant foresaw, has prescribed

[1] *Origin*, 193ff.

its laws to all other continents; but the result, the emergence of mankind out of and side by side with the continued existence of many nations, has assumed an altogether different aspect from the one which Kant envisaged when he saw the unifications of mankind "in a far distant future."[2] Mankind owes its existence not to the dreams of the humanists nor to the reasoning of the philosophers and not even, at least not primarily, to political events, but almost exclusively to the technical development of the Western world. When Europe in all earnest began to prescribe its "laws" to all other continents, it so happened that she herself had already lost her belief in them. If anything, in the realm of the spiritual, is as manifest as the fact that technology united the world, then it is the other fact that Europe exported to the four corners of the earth its processes of disintegration (which had started in the Western world with the decline of the traditionally accepted metaphysical and religious beliefs and had accompanied the grandiose development of the natural sciences and the victory of the nation-state over all other forms of government). The same forces which took centuries to undermine the ancient beliefs and political ways of life, and which have their place in the continuous development of the West alone, took only a few decades to break down, by working from without, all beliefs and ways of life in all other parts of the world.

It is true, for the first time in history all peoples on earth have a common present: no event of any importance in the history of one country can remain a marginal accident in the history of any other. Every country on earth has become the immediate neighbor of every other country and every man feels the shock of events which take place at the other side of the globe. But this common factual present is not based on a common past and does not in the least guarantee a common future. Technology, having provided the unity of the world, can just as easily destroy it. It is no mere coincidence that means of global communication were designed side by side with means of possible global destruction. It is difficult to deny that at this moment the most potent symbol of the unity of mankind is the remote possibility that atomic weapons used by one country according to the political wisdom of a few might ultimately come to be the end of all human life on earth. The solidarity of mankind in this respect is entirely negative; it rests, not only on a common interest in an agreement which prohibits the use of atomic weapons, but — since such agreements share with all

---

[2] *Idee zu einer allgemeinen Geschichte in weltbürgerlicher Absicht* (1784).

other agreements the uncertain fate of being based on good faith
— a common desire for a world that is a little less unified.

This negative solidarity, based on the fear of global destruction,
has its correspondence in a less articulate, but no less potent, apprehension that the solidarity of mankind can be meaningful in a
positive sense only if it is coupled with political responsibility. Our
political concepts, according to which we have to assume responsibility for all public affairs within our reach regardless of "guilt,"
because we are held responsible as citizens for everything that our
government does in the name of the country, may lead us into an
intolerable situation of global responsibility. The solidarity of
mankind may well turn out to be an unbearable burden, and it is
not surprising that the common reactions to it are political apathy,
isolationist nationalism, or desperate rebellion against all technology rather than enthusiasm or a desire for a revival of humanism. The idealism of the humanist tradition of enlightenment and
its concept of mankind look like reckless optimism in the light of
present realities. These, on the other hand, insofar as they have
brought us a global present without a common past, threaten to
render all traditions and all particular past histories irrelevant.

It is against this background of political and spiritual realities,
of which Jaspers is more aware than probably any other philosopher of our time, that one must understand his new concept of
mankind and the propositions of his philosophy. Kant once called
upon the historians of his time to write a history *"in weltbürgerlicher Absicht."* One could easily "prove" that Jaspers' whole
philosophical work, from its beginnings in the *Psychologie der
Weltanschauungen* (1919) to the forthcoming world-history of
philosophy, was conceived with a "cosmopolitan intention." If the
solidarity of mankind is to be based on something more solid than
the justified fear of man's demonic capabilities, if the new universal neighborship of all countries is to result in something more
promising than a tremendous increase in mutual hatred and a
somewhat universal irritability of everybody against everybody
else, then a process of mutual understanding and progressing self-
clarification on a gigantic scale must take place. And just as the
prerequisite for world government in Jaspers' opinion is the renunciation of sovereignty for the sake of a world-wide federated
political structure, so the prerequisite for this mutual understanding would be the renunciation, not of one's own tradition and
national past, but of the binding authority and universal validity
which tradition and past have always claimed. It is by such a break,
not with tradition, but with the authority of tradition that Jaspers

entered philosophy. The *Psychologie der Weltanschauungen* denies the absolute character of any doctrine and puts in its stead a universal relativity, in which each specific philosophical content becomes means for individual philosophizing. The shell of traditional authority is forced open and the great contents of the past are freely and "playfully" placed into communication with each other in the test of communicating with a present living philosophizing. In this universal communication, held together by the existential experience of the present philosopher, all dogmatic metaphysical contents are dissolved into processes, walks of thought, which, because of their relevance to my present existing and philosophizing, leave their fixed historical place in the chain of chronology and enter a realm of the spiritual where all are contemporaries. Whatever I think must remain in constant communication with everything that has been thought. Not only because, "in philosophy, novelty is an argument against truth," but because present philosophy cannot be "the natural and necessary conclusion of Western thought up to now, the candid synthesis brought about by a principle large enough to comprehend everything that in a sense is true." The principle itself is communication; truth, which can never be grasped as dogmatic content, emerges as 'existential' substance clarified and articulated by reason, communicating itself and appealing to the reasonable existing of the other, comprehensible and capable of comprehending everything else. "*Existenz* only becomes clear through reason; reason only has content through *Existenz*." [3]

The pertinence of these considerations for a philosophical foundation of the unity of mankind is manifest: "limitless communication,"[4] which at the same time signifies the faith in the comprehensibility of all truths *and* the good will to reveal and to listen as the primary condition for all human being-together, is one, if not the central idea of Jaspers' philosophy. The point is that here for the first time communication is not conceived as "expressing" thoughts and therefore being secondary to thought itself. Truth itself is communicative, it disappears and cannot be conceived outside communication; within the 'existential' realm, truth and communication are the same. "Truth is what binds us together."[5] Only in communication — between contemporaries as well as between the living and the dead — does truth reveal itself.

[3] *Reason*, 67.

[4] "*Grenzenlose Kommunikation*" is a term which appears in almost all of Jaspers' works.

[5] Cf. "Vom lebendigen Geist der Universität" (1946) in: *Rechenschaft*, 185.

A philosophy that conceives of truth and communication as one and the same has left the proverbial ivory tower of mere contemplation. Thinking becomes practical, though not pragmatic; it is a kind of practice between men, not a performance of one individual in his self-chosen solitude. Jaspers is, as far as I know, the first and the only philosopher who ever protested against solitude, to whom solitude appeared "pernicious" and who dared to question "all thoughts, all experiences, all contents" under this one aspect: "What do they signify for communication? Are they such that they may help or such that they will prevent communication? Do they seduce to solitude or arouse to communication?"[6] Philosophy has lost both its humility before theology and its arrogance towards the common life of man. It has become *ancilla vitae*.[7]

This attitude is of special relevance within the German philosophical tradition. Kant, although he was the first to doubt radically the ability of common sense to grasp truth, seems to have been the last great philosopher who was still quite confident of being understood and of being able to dispel misunderstandings. Hegel's remark on his deathbed has become famous: "Nobody has understood me except one; and he did not understand me either." Since then, the growing loneliness of philosophers in a world which did not care about philosophy because it had become entirely fascinated by science, and the curious equivocality of all strictly solitary, uncommunicative thought have conspired together towards a common opinion which almost identifies greatness with not being understood. Jaspers' numerous utterances after the war, his articles, lectures, radio broadcasts, have all been guided by an almost deliberate attempt at popularization, at talking philosophy without using technical terminology, and by the conviction that one can appeal to reason and to the *'existential'* concern in all men. Philosophically this has been possible only because truth and communication are conceived to be the same.

From a philosophical viewpoint, the danger inherent in the new reality of mankind seems to be that this unity, based on the technical means of communication and violence, breaks all na-

---

[6] Cf. "Über meine Philosophie," (1941) *Rechenschaft,* 350, 352.

[7] Jaspers does not use this term. He mentions often that philosophizing is "inner action," practice, etc. The relationship between thinking and living cannot be discussed here. But the following sentence may show in which sense my interpretative use of *ancilla vitae* could be justified: "Was im denkenden Leben getan werden muss, dem soll ein Philosophieren dienen, das erinnernd und vorausgreifend die Wahrheit offenbar macht." *Ibid.,* 356.

tional traditions and buries the authentic origins of all human existence. This destructive process can even be considered a necessary prerequisite for ultimate understanding between men of all cultures, civilizations, races and nations. Its result would be a shallowness that would transform man, as we have known him in five thousand years of recorded history, beyond recognition. It would be more than mere superficiality; it would be as though the whole dimension of depth, without which human thought, even on the mere level of technical invention, could not exist, would simply disappear. This leveling down would be much more radical than the leveling to the lowest common denominator; it would ultimately arrive at a denominator of which we have hardly any notion today.

As long as one conceives of truth as separate and distinct from its expression, as something which by itself is uncommunicative and neither communicates itself to reasoning understanding nor appeals to *existential* experience, it is almost impossible to believe that this destructive process would not come about out of the sheer automatism which made the world one and, in a sense, united mankind. It looks as though the historical pasts of the nations, in their utter diversity and disparity, in their confusing variety and bewildering strangeness for each other, are nothing but obstacles on the road to a horridly shallow unity. This, of course, is a delusion; if the dimension of depth out of which modern science and technology have developed ever were destroyed, the probability is that the new unity of mankind could not even technically survive. Everything then seems to depend upon the possibility to bring the national pasts, in their original disparateness, into communication with each other and thus correspond, or catch up, with the global system of communication which covers the surface of the earth.

It is in the light of such reflections that Jaspers made the great historical discovery which became the cornerstone of his philosophy of history. The idea of the one origin of humanity, as exemplified in the myth of creation in Genesis and of one aim, as exemplified in the Christian doctrine of salvation and final judgment is beyond knowledge and beyond proof. Christian philosophy of history, from Augustine to Hegel, saw in the appearance of Christ the turningpoint and the center of world history. As such, it is valid only for Christian believers; and if it claims authority over all, it is as much in the way of a unity of mankind as any other, more particular belief emanating from some other historical origin.

Against this and similar philosophies of history which harbor a concept of one world history on the basis of the historical experience of one people or one particular part of the world, Jaspers has discovered an empirically given historical axis which gives all nations "a common framework of historical self-understanding. The axis of world history seems to pass through the fifth century B. C., in the midst of the spiritual process between 800 and 200 B. C." — Confucius and Lao-tse in China, the Upaniṣads and Buddha in India, Zarathustra in Persia, the prophets in Palestine, Homer, the philosophers, the tragedians in Greece.[8] It is characteristic of the events which took place during this era that they were completely unconnected, that they became the origins of the great historical world-civilizations, and that these origins, in their very differentiation, had something uniquely in common. This peculiar sameness can be approached and defined in many ways: it is the time when mythologies were being discarded or used for the foundation of the great world religions with their concept of One transcendent God; philosophy makes its appearance everywhere: man discovers Being as a whole and himself as radically different from all other beings: for the first time, man becomes (in the words of Augustine) a question for himself, becomes conscious of consciousness, begins to think about thinking; great personalities appear everywhere who will no longer accept or be accepted as mere members of the respective social structure, but think of themselves as individuals and design new individual ways of life — the life of a wise man, the life of the prophet, the life of the hermit who retreats from all society into an entirely new inwardness and spirituality. All basic categories of our thought and all basic tenets of our beliefs were created during this period. It is as though for the first time mankind discovered the human rational understanding. The historical axis of mankind then is

an era around the middle of the last millenium B.C., for which everything that preceded it would appear to have been a preparation, and to which everything subsequent actually, and often in clear consciousness, relates back. The world history of humanity derives its structure from this period. It is not an axis of which we might assert the permanent absoluteness and uniqueness. But it is the axis of the short world history that has taken place up till now, that which, in the consciousness of all men, might represent the basis of the historical unity they recognize in solidarity. This real axis would then be the

8 *Origin,* 1f.

incarnation of an ideal axis, around which mankind in its movement is drawn together.[9]

In this perspective, the new unity of mankind could acquire a past of its own through a communication-system, so to speak, in which the different origins of mankind would reveal themselves in their very sameness. But this sameness is far from being uniformity; just as man and woman can be the same, namely human, only by being absolutely different from each other, so the national of every country can enter this world-history of humanity only by remaining and clinging stubbornly to what he is. A world citizen, living under the tyranny of a world-empire, and speaking and thinking in a kind of glorified Esperanto, would be no less a monster than a hermaphrodite. The bond between men is, subjectively, the "will to limitless communication" and, objectively, the fact of universal comprehensibility. The unity of mankind and its solidarity cannot consist in a universal agreement upon one religion, or one philosophy, or one form of government, but in the faith that the manifold points to a Oneness which diversity conceals and reveals at the same time.

The pivotal age began the development of the great world civilizations which together constitute what we usually call world-history, and it ended a period which because of this subsequent development we call pre-historic. If we think of our own era in terms of this historical design, then we may well come to the conclusion that the emergence of mankind as a tangible political reality marks the end of that period of world-history which began in the pivotal age. Jaspers, in a way, agrees with the wide-spread feeling that our time somehow has come to an end, but he disagrees with the emphasis of doom that usually accompanies such diagnoses. "We live as though we stand knocking at doors which are still closed to us."[10] What so clearly appears as an end, is better understood as a beginning whose innermost meaning we cannot yet grasp. Our present is emphatically, and not merely logically, the suspense between a no-longer and a not-yet. What begins now, after the end of world history, is the history of mankind. What this will eventually be, we do not know. We can prepare ourselves for it through a philosophy of mankind whose central concept would be Jaspers' concept of communication. This philosophy will not abolish, not even criticize, the great philosophical systems of the past in India, China and the Occident, but will strip them of their dogmatic metaphysical claims,

---

9 *Ibid.*, 262f.   10 "Vom Europäischen Geist" (1946) in *Rechenschaft*, 260.

dissolve them, as it were, into walks of thought which meet and cross each other, communicate with each other and eventually retain only what is universally communicative. A philosophy of mankind is distinguished from a philosophy of man by its insistence on the fact that not Man, talking to himself in the dialogue of solitude, but men talking and communicating with each other, inhabit the earth. Of course, the philosophy of mankind can not prescribe any particular political action, but it may comprehend politics as one of the great human realms of life as against all former philosophies which, since Plato, thought of the *bios politikos* as an inferior way of life and of politics as a necessary evil or, in the words of Madison, "the greatest of all reflections on human nature."[11]

In order to grasp the philosophical relevance of Jaspers' concept of mankind and world-citizenship, it may be well to remember Kant's concept of mankind and Hegel's notion of world-history, since these two are its proper traditional background. Kant viewed mankind as a possible ultimate result of history. History, he says, would be a "disconsolate haphazard" *("trostloses Ungefähr")*[12] if there were not a justified hope that the unconnected and unpredictable actions of men might in the end bring about mankind as a politically united community together with the fully developed humanity of man. The "disconsolate haphazard" of history assumes meaning only if we assume that there exists a "cunning of nature"[13] which works behind the backs of men. It is interesting to note, and characteristic of our tradition of political thought, that it was Kant, not Hegel, who was the first to conceive of a cunning secret force in order to find meaning in political history at all. The experience behind this is no other than Hamlet's: "Our thoughts are ours, their ends none of our own," except that this experience was particularly humiliating for a philosophy whose center was the dignity and the autonomy of man. Mankind, for Kant, was that ideal state in "a far distant future" where the dignity of man would coincide with the human condition of earth. But this ideal state would necessarily put an end to politics and political action as we know it today and whose "disconsolate haphazard" is recorded by history. Kant foresees a far distant future when past history would indeed have become "the education of humanity" in the words of Lessing. Human

11 *The Federalist,* No. 51.

12 In: *Idee zu einer allgemeinen Geschichte in weltbürgerlicher Absicht.*

13 Cf. *Über den Gemeinspruch: Das mag in der Theorie richtig sein, taugt aber nicht für die Praxis.* (1793).

history would then be of no more interest than natural history, where we consider the present state of each species as the *telos* inherent in all previous development, its end in the double sense of aim and conclusion.

Mankind for Hegel manifests itself in the "world-spirit;" in its quintessence it is always there in one of its historical stages of development, but it can never become a political reality. It is also brought about by a secret cunning force; but the cunning of reason is different from Kant's "cunning of nature," insofar as it can be perceived only by the contemplative reason of the philosopher, to whom alone the chain of meaningless and seemingly arbitrary events can make sense. The climax of world-history is not the factual emergence of mankind, but the moments when the world-spirit acquires self-consciousness in a philosophy, when the Absolute finally reveals itself to thought. World-history, world-spirit and mankind have hardly any political connotations in Hegel's work, despite the strong political impulses of the young Hegel. They became immediately, and quite properly, leading ideas in the historical sciences, but remained without notable influence on political science. It was in Marx, who decided to "put Hegel back on his feet," that is, to change the *interpretation* of history into the *making* of history, that these concepts showed their political relevance. And this is an altogether different matter. It is obvious that no matter how far distant or how close at hand the realization of mankind may be, one can be a world-citizen only within the framework of Kant's categories. The best that can happen to any individual in the Hegelian system of historical revelation of the world-spirit is to have the good fortune to be born among the right people at the right historical moment, so that one's birth will coincide with the revelation of world-spirit in this particular period. For Hegel to be a member of historical mankind meant to be a Greek, and not a barbarian, in the fifth century B. C., a Roman citizen and not a Greek in the first centuries of our era, to be a Christian and not a Jew in the Middle Ages, etc.

Compared with Kant, Jaspers' concept of mankind and world-citizenship is historical; compared with Hegel, it is political. It somehow combines the depth of Hegel's historical experience with Kant's great political wisdom. Yet, decisive is what distinguishes Jaspers from both. He believes neither in the "disconsolate haphazard" of political action and recorded history nor in the secret cunning force that manipulates man into wisdom. He has abandoned Kant's concept of a "good will" which, because it is grounded in reason, is incapable of action.[14] He has broken with both the despair and the consolation of German idealism in philosophy. If philosophy is to become *ancilla vitae,* then there is no doubt which function it has to fulfill: in Kant's words, it will rather have to "carry the torch in front of her gracious lady than the train of her dress behind."[15]

The history of mankind which Jaspers foresees is not Hegel's world-history, where the world-spirit uses and consumes country after country, people after people, in the stages of its gradual realization. And the unity of mankind in its present reality is far from being the consolation or recompensation for all past history as Kant hoped it to be. Politically, the new fragile unity brought about by technical mastery over the earth can be guaranteed only within a framework of universal mutual agreements, which eventually would lead into a world-wide federated structure. For this, political philosophy can hardly do more than describe and prescribe the new principle of political action. Just as, according to Kant, nothing should ever happen in war which would make a future peace and reconciliation impossible, so nothing, according to the implications of Jaspers' philosophy, should happen today in politics which would be contrary to the actually existing solidarity of mankind. This in the long run may mean that war must be ruled out of the arsenal of political means, not only because the possibility of an atomic war may endanger the existence of all mankind, but because each war, no matter how limited in the use of means and in territory, immediately and directly affects all mankind. The abolition of war, like the abolishment of a plurality of sovereign states, would harbor its own peculiar dangers; the various armies with their old traditions and more or less respected codes of honor would be replaced by federated police forces, and our experiences with modern police states and totalitarian governments, where the old power of the army is eclipsed by the rising omnipotence of the police, are not apt to make us over-optimistic about this prospect. All this, however, still lies in a far distant future.

HANNAH ARENDT

NEW YORK CITY

---

[14] ". . . the revered, but practically ineffectual general will which is founded in reason." *Zum Ewigen Frieden* (1795), translation quoted from Carl Joachim Friedrich, Modern Library edition, which brings Kant's Essay, *Eternal Peace,* in a new translation.

[15] *Ibid.*

16

Golo Mann

FREEDOM AND THE SOCIAL SCIENCES
IN JASPERS' THOUGHT*

TWO FUNDAMENTAL assumptions have characterized the revolutionary spirit of the West since the late eighteenth century: our age is *unique;* our age is *comprehensible.* It is unique in the sense that in it begins something completely new, something absolutely and finally distinct from the entire past. It is comprehensible in the sense that all the various forces which govern it correspond to general concepts. Whoever recognizes the concepts understands reality and can project the future in terms of its own law.

Perfect comprehensibility logically excludes freedom, that is, choice, or creative decision. If the concept of freedom is nevertheless to be saved, then it is defined as comprehended necessity as Marx has done and, with a different shade of meaning also Oswald Spengler.

These two fundamental assumptions do not always appear together. For example, Karl Jaspers believes he is capable of demonstrating the unique quality of our age in a few, if not in all essential aspects. He does not assume a complete comprehensibility nor the scientific capacity derived from it to project the future. In fact this negation is the nucleus of his philosophy.

At this point we must remember first the theses of Jaspers' doctrine of science which are also the theses of his philosophy since they distinguish science from philosophy and necessity from freedom. Scientific comprehensions are partial; there is no totality for our comprehending. The world "does not rest within itself." If it did rest within itself, if the world were God, then it could be known and could be given a structure by means of a single science. Thus there would be no gaps between various spheres, between matter, life, soul, spirit, between natural science and the humanities, between science and philosophy. There would be no eternal riddles, no contradictions, no antinomies. But the

* Translated from the original German manuscript by Richard J. Doney.

world does not rest within itself. Knowledge is a matter of particulars, not of the world, but of the things in the world. "The whole must be disintegrated in order to become objective."[1] The process of research is without end.

"Universal science" would be science which "observes all things with reference to one medium, without which there is nothing." Logic embraces all thinking, psychology and sociology embrace all human existence. For this very reason they are not genuine sciences; they must ever be individual sciences with a leading idea and a method fitted to the object. Even psychology and sociology have their empirical objects: The phenomena of consciousness, social relationships. But as long as they are limited to these objects, they acquire no relevant comprehension. Psychology cannot be separated from biology, nor from the humanities. Sociology cannot be separated from history, from the philosophy of history, nor from religion. Neither sociology nor psychology can be separated from each other. They do not achieve unity from their object and method, but rather from the creative will of the researcher. At this point the researcher is not "consciousness-as-such" nor does he aim toward pure comprehension, but rather toward his own individual condition, toward his relations with his fellow men, and toward politics. As universal sciences sociology and psychology are closest to philosophy. In this is to be found their fascination and at the same time the danger to which they are continually exposed. Sociology and psychology hover between scientific, that is particular, comprehension and that totality which the philosopher can "illuminate" but not apprehend. They incline to exchange these spheres and the result is bad science and bad philosophy. They believe they have the totality of man in a scientific grasp. That is, they deny freedom, since, where scientific comprehension exists, there is no freedom. Genuine science cannot destroy freedom because it does not presume to apprehend totality. Only false science, mingling philosophy and science, absolutizing particular comprehensions, destroys freedom. This is the error of the followers of Marx and those of Freud. Both groups have achieved scientific comprehensions but have made them absolute. "In every absolute lies a truth which is destroyed only by absolutizing."[2] Science becomes dogma; dogma leads to the formation of sects, to fanaticism, and to an attitude which is equally destructive to science and to philosophy.

Freud and Marx remain for Jaspers the classical examples of

[1] *Philosophie* I, (Berlin, 1932), 201.

[2] *Allgemeine*, 4th ed., (Berlin, 1946), 628.

a degenerated universal science. He has given his criticism of psychoanalysis and of historical materialism in his "Systematics of Science"[3] and has introduced it again and again.[4] Formulated in another fashion this criticism maintains that man is always more than he knows of himself and this "more" is an indication of his freedom. Man can never make the totality of himself the object of empirical research but only partial aspects of himself. Even partial comprehension causes change in the man who achieves it and it is, therefore, not true from the moment in which it is achieved.

Empirical science and "philosophical faith" not only exclude each other, but rather require each other. Freedom, and the sense and totality of our existence are not objectives of science, but matters of philosophical faith. Science neither confirms them or refutes them. In a negative sense, however, freedom appears perhaps through science, that is, through the endlessness of the scientific process, through its inability to obtain fulfillment. There is no freedom in the world (of science), but there are signs which point to it. One of these would be the fact that history can not be scientifically foretold.

The positivist does not believe that he can foretell the future of man, or at least not with complete certainty, because he is still missing a few data. The limits which are set to the exactitude of historical prophecy these days are not determined by the nature of the object but, on the other hand, by the incomplete quality of the methods which still prevail. The meterologist foretells the weather; even when he errs he does not doubt but that everything has taken place according to natural cause and effect. The "political weather," too, is determined causally toward a single interpretation and is, therefore, in principle, foreseeable. And in the social sciences the methods of the mathematicians and statisticians have taken the place of literary dilettantism, intuition and guess-work.[5]

The fact that history cannot be foretold and that every attempt to foretell it changes *ipso facto* the course of that which has been foretold, is, for Jaspers, a sign of that freedom which does not exist objectively. The attempt to determine history in advance is scientifically false and philosophically destructive. It is scientifically false because it moves toward that totality which we our-

[3] *Philosophie*, I, 205.

[4] Cf. particularly: *Anti-Reason, passim.*

[5] Cf. e.g., Hans Reichenbach, *The Rise of Scientific Philosophy.* Berkeley, 1951, 309.

selves are and which science cannot apprehend. It is philosophically destructive because it denies our freedom and responsibility. If we could determine our future in advance by scientific means we would no longer be men. We would be God. Or dead.

* * * * *

Sociological investigations within limited fields of interest can contribute to the illumination of our consciousness of the present day, particularly in fields such as population statistics, nutritional possibilities, economic, social and political structural changes. It is however the investigator who limits these fields of interest. In reality there are no purely economic or purely political processes. What will become of the American economy and of each of America's individual sectors in the near future does not depend upon the laws of the economic mechanism but on total historical development, on the attitude of the American nation and, reciprocally, of all nations. Economics and economic history are one and the same, a fact that no one knew better than Marx and that no one forgot with more fatal consequences. The humanities are, for Jaspers, essentially historical sciences; this turns out to be true even for sociology. Like every historical situation, an economic situation can also be described in terms of its past but not seriously in terms of its future. The impressively confirmed predictions which history knows, were not made by economists or sociologists but by thinkers in the field of universal history. The source of these predictions was intuition, not investigation of the particular.

Sociological research goes astray whenever it does not include freedom, that is, when it does not continually question itself. Sociological research treats of possibilities, not of necessities. It goes even more fundamentally astray when in place of its own abstracted object it demands a primacy above all other fields and informs us that the fate of mankind depends upon and is determined by conditions unavoidably comprehended by itself; the overpopulation of the earth, "the amalgamation into masses" (Vermassung) and the process of bureaucracy, the struggle of the major powers which leads to world dictatorship, the triumph of the worker over the business man, of the manager over the shareholders (J. Burnham), the military over the civilian, or the pilot over anyone who cannot fly (H. G. Wells).

To be conscious of the limits of its own objective knowledge, of freedom, means that there is room for the will to help. We can help only where the issue is uncertain. There, at that point where we are personally concerned, we must want to help. Sociological research, which strictly forbids — at least ostensibly — all personal concern and will, awakens the unhappy suspicion that the author is concerned only with proclaiming to his audience his own knowledge, his preferential knowledge, his improved knowledge. If his predictions are realized, his abilities have been proven; if they are not realized he can count on the public capacity to forget. But matters which are concerned with the fate of mankind are at any time too serious to be used as an opportunity for the mere self-revelation of journalistic insight.

The closed systems which treat present and future as if they were already past, deny the will to help. Only the complete human quality *(das volle menschliche Sein)* of the philosopher, his participation *(Einsatz),* his consuming enterprise can speak for him here. For Jaspers genuine philosophy is never without personal participation and every self-sacrifice derives from the will to help — or otherwise why would the philosopher act in this way? Systems which tell us what cannot be known and what should not be known do not derive from the genuine philosophic spirit.

Quite different are those visions of the future which have their origin not in systematic pseudo-science but rather in the agonized sensitivity, the profound insight, in that knowing hysteria of the philosopher. Nietzsche's predictions are helpful — for anyone who does not succumb to them. Anything that stirs restlessness or consciousness is helpful, even when it appears in the form of a prophecy which admits of no hope.[6]

* * * * *

The fundamental distinctions of Jaspers' philosophy which have been indicated here determine and color what he himself has to say about our present and future. They are negatively effective in his criticism of contemporary philosophers of history and political prognosticators. This latter criticism appears as important as Jaspers' own positive contribution, for this philosophy is, in the tradition of Kant, essentially critical, one that sets limits.

Jaspers' criticism of Marx is directed fittingly against those lesser writers of our day who, in the spirit of Marx if without his genius, set themselves the task of naming the law of our time and predicting the future *sine ira et studio.* Perhaps it is also

[6] Cf. particularly: *Nietzsche,* 70.

directed at James Burnham's *The Managerial Revolution*. His criticism would be just as effective against the insubstantial analogies between physics and history which Henry Adams concocted in an unhappy moment and which recently have again had to furnish the "scientific" basis for a grotesque prophecy of history.[7]

Spengler's prognosis of the future rests on another insubstantial analogy — that between organic life and historical civilizations. This analogy, too, increases the spheres of philosophy and science, confuses meaningful evidence and causality, seizes upon a totality which does not exist, and denies freedom.[8]

In the same connection Jaspers' criticism of the brothers Ernst and Friedrich Georg Jünger deserves to be mentioned. Both writers, impressionists of the greatest sensitivity, have exercised considerable influence on German thought. Both have drawn pictures of the totality of our time and of our age. Ernst Jünger in his vision of "the worker," of the total machine, the work-state and the war-state; F. G. Jünger in his apocalyptic presentation of technology as a demoniacally destructive force, one that enslaves mankind. "In such thinking," writes Jaspers, "there is in all seriousness really nothing true."[9] The aesthetic attitude contrasting to this, which cannot be the object of the aesthetic process, leads, on the one hand, to nothing whatsoever. In this case the discrepancy between the lack of seriousness of the claim and the seriousness of the subject introduces itself in a manner of speaking and is not contested. Or, on the other hand, the aesthetic process leads to fatalism. We can do nothing but fulfill the given picture and to fill out all details. The wildest misdeeds may be justified in that they belong to the ostensibly comprehended picture of the epoch. The aestheticizing attitude contrasting to our own age as an image or *Gestalt* is the same as a denial of freedom, negation of good-will, of creative effort, of personal concern, and of humility.

From false total knowledge arises false total planning or projection of the future; from the one-to-one ratio of philosophy and science arises the total state. He who knows the totality, will set himself to plan and dominate totality according to his knowledge. Through the logic of his position he will be driven to a program of total domination, whether he be a man of action (Lenin, Trotzky) or a giver of poor advice (Spengler, Burnham). Plan and action will be exactly as false as the presumed knowledge. The result is mostly that which had not been planned:

[7] Roderick Seidenberg, *Posthistoric Man. An Inquiry*. Chapel Hill, 1950.
[8] Cf.: *Origin*, 277.   [9] *Ibid.*, 279f.

Unwelcome reactions at home and abroad; tyranny, terror, war, often enough the ignominious fall of the omniscient planner of totalities himself. Out of neglect of the concept of man arises the actual neglect of man.

Man is neither completely understandable by science nor completely perfectable through politics. There exists the idea of man but not the ideal of man. Unreconcilable contradictions will always arise. That which cannot be foretold will always thwart the most hopeful calculations. Utopia is as destructive to the art of government as the grasp toward totality is to science.

*   *   *   *

The above could suggest that Jaspers is an agnostic and mystic: he would recommend that the scholar know nothing, that the statesman plan nothing, do nothing. No more profound misunderstanding could be conceived. The *docta ignorantia* which he defends is actually *docta* founded upon knowledge. By his own accomplishments in the field of psychopathology Jaspers has confirmed his thesis that the philosopher must himself play the rôle of scientist in order to achieve the limits of knowledge. An encyclopedic knowledge of reality lends substance and color to his work. What he attacks is false science and superstitious politics.

To be sure we may know much about our own time, much, but not everything. Knowledge is not supposed to have the purpose of determining in advance what cannot be avoided. Knowledge is to awaken, warn, to reveal possibilities and keep them before the eyes of men.

Knowledge is also to show what is impossible. Jaspers was never a romanticist or an "escapist." It is impossible to return to a fancied past and to withdraw from the fundamental conditions of the age, from technology, from mass civilization, from technical — although not moral or cultural — world unity. These, along with democracy in one form or another, along with the "concern over social welfare" and "planning" are all unavoidable. What remains is the how and the degree.

Jaspers quotes with approval the writers of the so-called "neo-liberal" school, Hayek, W. Roepke, and Walter Lippmann. What connects him with this group is his understanding of the dangers to human freedom, which are inherent in every form of socialism, and his refusal to recognize fatalistically the undivided dominance of certain comprehensible tendencies of development. It seems to me, however, that a significant difference exists between Jaspers and the "Neo-Liberals." The latter simplify the problem in that they maintain it to be soluble. They attribute exclusively to the presumptuous employment of false economic theories what, at least partly, has deep historical causes which can no longer be ignored. Moreover they are themselves fatalistic in that they do not believe that any development can be influenced, once it has been ventured upon. According to them we are free at the first step, but are slaves at the second, third, or hundredth step. Thus they saw in the benevolent and humanitarian measures of the British Labor government the beginnings of the most horrible despotism. On the other hand Jaspers is concerned with separating the objectively existent *(das Vorgegebene)*, the unavoidable, from that which we can do with it in terms of guidance, valuation, and restraint. We are not as free in the choice of our social and economic milieus as the neo-liberals maintain; we are therefore not as un-free as they maintain after having made a choice or having accepted an existent.

In his analysis of the existent Jaspers is no palliating optimist. After the appearance of his first great interpretation of our age, *Die Geistige Situation der Zeit*,[10] he was criticized occasionally for what was actually too cold an objectivity, an almost solipsistic observation of things, as if he were himself standing completely outside the world he was analysing. But Jaspers is concerned with just this objectivity, the objectivity of de Tocqueville, who tried to grasp the inevitable march of events so that the free man might prepare himself and that the *liberté humaine* might be saved. As was the case with de Tocqueville, so also with Jaspers; behind the cold self-control of the scholar one will sense at all times personal emotion, concern, the will to help.

As an additional remark on the content of his observations, it should be said that the last two decades have not produced much that Jaspers had not already anticipated in 1930. His observations were not such as to round out a system, nor were they ostensibly deduced from any system, nor did they exclude the possibility of the unanticipated. Much that would have surpised the philosopher, who in his melancholic, knowing way warned us, has since 1930 unfortunately not occurred. The book can be regarded today as if it were describing the "intellectual situation" not of the first third but rather of the middle of the century.

---

[10] First German edition: 1931; English title: *Man in the Modern Age.*

Jaspers is not an historical thinker in the manner of Leopold Ranke or the English "Whig historian." His interest is not the pleasant understanding of the past for the sake of his own learning. Even less is he interested in those constructions which serve a so-called victorious cause and the kind of history which becomes a congratulatory oration. He has not had to sacrifice in a tragic manner the idea of progress, nor has he had to fight scornfully against it. The idea of progress is foreign to him. He finds it quite understandable that the great thinkers of the past — prophets, founders of religions, philosophers, poets — have known just as much as we have. The universal history of philosophy which he is preparing is supposed to be, I have heard, not a history of progressing knowledge *(Wissenschaft)*, but rather an exposition of timelessly effective possibilities of thought.

To be sure, these will be possibilities of thought which have been realized in time and by individuals. Individuality signifies a limitation in time, mortality, decision, identification with the age. This is "historicity" *(Geschichtlichkeit)* in Jaspers' meaning of the word. Time is not the abstract "now," but the concrete and historical with which the individual spirit must identify itself. When someone complains that he does not belong to his own age, that he should have lived a century before, we certainly know the false aspects or at least the comparative aspects of such talk. He who is at variance with his own age is at variance with himself. He who hates his own age hates himself. 'Had he lived at another time, he would not have been the man he is.' Therefore nothing is more useless than the question of what this or that great man of the past would perhaps do today. The empty form of the "I," consciousness-as-such is the same everywhere and at all times. The real self, the individual destiny is identical with the historical time which is its particular fate, in which it wanders not only by chance. One is not un-free because one lives in this time and in no other.

Nietzsche objects to those biographies whose titles add to the name of the subject 'his life and times.' Nietzsche maintains that one must be one's self, against his own time, independent of that time; one must live in spite of it, not with it. But Nietzsche does not protest against the identity between *Existenz* and the historical now. He believes that one should not be the lackey of the tendencies and fashions of the times, which is a different matter. Nietzsche himself did not escape his own age but was its true prophet, conceivable in all of his creative suffering only in his own historical time and place. Hegel is of the same opinion when he says, "So far as the individual is concerned, each one is a son of his own age. Likewise philosophy is its own age expressed in thoughts." Hegelian figures are often similarly lonely, suffering men, who do not swim with the current. The subsequent age will understand that they belonged to their own age and will understand with what intensity they belonged. In this sense, but only in this sense, Jaspers would approve of the Hegelian statement.

Jaspers' restless feeling for the Now of the twentieth century, his own Now, has led him to historical studies. These are historical observations essentially derived from the present day, serving the understanding of the present day. The study, *Man in the Modern Age* was written before *The Origin and Goal of History*, a work in the philosophy of history. The latter is an expansion of the former. From a survey of the age arose a survey of all ages. Jaspers' historical thinking is in terms of epochs, crises, like that of those masters who have influenced him most profoundly: de Tocqueville, Burckhardt, Max Weber and Nietzsche. "A universal view of history and consciousness of one's present situation mutually sustain one another."[11]

The original contribution which Jaspers has made as an observer of history is the concept of the "pivotal age." Thus he characterizes the period from the end of the ninth century to the beginning of the second century before Christ, a period which had as its middle perhaps the second century before Christ. This period, so Jaspers suggests, is a kind of axis of world history. At that time in China, India, Persia, Israel, Greece, those religious and intellectual works were composed, and the feats of thought accomplished by which mankind everywhere has since lived by recovery and further development. This was the time of the intellectual enlightenment in the consciousness of man, not to be compared with anything that had been before, nor to be compared with anything that later was derived from or added to it. It is characteristic of Jaspers' philosophy that he leaves unanswered the question why this intellectual eruption occurred almost simultaneously among so many people separated from each other by vast distances and knowing almost nothing of each other. The explanation of chance he considers as telling nothing. He discusses with interest and respect more serious considerations which others have attempted; but they all appear insufficient to him. And why should this puzzle be completely answerable? The unity of mankind — of which it is an outward sign — remains

11 *Origin*, 271.

just as much a mystery as the appearance of man, the origin of life, or the origin of the cosmos. These are mysteries for which science should seek and always will seek rational explanations. But so far mankind has not come any nearer to these eternally challenging border-lines.

Jaspers' philosophy stands or falls with the existence of mysteries. His scheme of world history which he has projected with his concept of the "pivotal age," seems much more satisfying to me than perhaps that of Toynbee. His system emphasizes much more than Toynbee's the unity of mankind and movement through time and, again, the specific character of the Western world and the unique quality of the present moment. According to Jaspers we live today in a "second pivotal age," one just as fateful and significant as the first, not comparable to the first in its intellectual accomplishments, but certainly comparable in its unification and shrinking of the world, in science and technology, in its possibilities, dangers, its analytic and destructive effects. The question here is not the simple one of comparison beyond which Toynbee cannot reach if he is to remain true to his system: There have been twenty-one civilizations-cultures; what will happen to the twenty-second? It is rather the more serious question of what will happen to man. Jaspers' view of history does justice to continuity as well as to spontaneity, to free decision based on contemporary facts; it does justice to the possibilities of comparison and to the eternal repetitions of history as well as to the differences and to what is new. It does justice to the radical quality of difference and the newness of our own age.

Thus Jaspers cannot condemn *a limine* the modern solutions — socialism, world federation — as our conservative empiricists do. Where a situation is quite new, obviously the purpose, goals, methods must themselves be new. Jaspers sees this more clearly than, for example, Reinhold Niebuhr is inclined to see it.

But both have much in common.

*　*　*　*　*

Both overcome the contradiction between positivism and idealism. They are positivists in that their scientific curiosity has no limits. There is no scientific knowledge which, for the sake of their theology or philosophy, they would refuse to accept. Niebuhr, the theologian, knows of the animalistic origin of religion; Jaspers has devoted one of his most significant papers to the relationship between the natural course of insanity and artistic productivity. Nature and spirit are separated in principle but not in reality. The intellectual is cradled with the natural, is conditioned and admitted by the natural, and by the natural is destroyed. The history of mankind rests upon the facts of nature and is interpenetrated by these facts. Nature is cruel.

But this does not constitute either for Niebuhr or for Jaspers the real character of history. The cradling of the intellectual in the natural, of the understandable in the mere causally explainable, does not refute the separateness of the spheres, which is a matter of principle. Man, says Niebuhr, should not excuse himself on the basis of nature. Nature is not the source of most of the evil which he encounters, but rather his own freedom which he can use for good and evil. And for Jaspers history is no process of nature. Man denies nature and converts it into blind happenings when he eliminates from it freedom and sense, guilt, merit and hope.

Therefore science is not the solution of the human problem. Science cannot provide us with the purpose which, in turn, is to be made serviceable for science. Niebuhr shows this in his masterly analysis of the inseparablity of self and mind.[12] Selfhood is that which Jaspers calls *Existenz*, mind, "consciousness-as-such." Science is valid for every consciousness-as-such. But even sociology, which is not a real science, obtains unity from the *'existential'* *(vom Existenziellen)*, that is, from will and freedom. What is valid for the social sciences must be all the more valid for their practical applications, for politics. Neither for Niebuhr nor for Jaspers is there such a thing as scientific politics, for a scientific shaping of history.

Both thinkers can regard history seriously as something distinct, without expecting salvation or the millenium from it. For both men history remains for good or for evil in equal fashion to the very end. Both the philosopher and the theologian, prove a realism without illusion, something that professional historians have often missed. They know that neither nature nor man can be trusted and least of all the power that is wielded by man. The just man is destroyed with the unjust.

Jaspers does not possess the sanctified tradition under which Niebuhr takes shelter. This may explain why Jaspers' sense of the unique character of our age is sharper, more concerned, not to mention more nervous. Where Niebuhr is able to appeal to faith, Jaspers appeals to the seriousness, the daring, the good will

12 Cf.: Reinhold Niebuhr, *Faith and History*. New York, 1951; 83.

of the individual and to the community of individuals through communication. This distinction has lost its significance in the course of time. Today, a man of years, Jaspers does not seem to believe any longer that philosophy can provide us with a positive content. Philosophy has come to be to him more and more a mere preparer of the way to the portal of religion. What he calls philosophical faith is substantially — if not formally and dogmatically — the Christian faith. Without this faith, he believes there is no significant observation of history. Niebuhr says the same: A Christian philosophy of history is ultimately a theology of history.

That which is common to both men serves to distinguish them from the other side, from the negation of all philosophy and all theology, that is, from positivism.

*   *   *   *   *

At this point a choice must be made. If we do not make this choice we will be led to those unanswered contradictions, those fluctuations between too great a hope and ultimate dismay. These are the contradictions and the fluctuations which the observations of Bertrand Russell on the contemporary scene continue to depreciate. To make the choice in favor of positivism leads to what is practically absurd. If the world "rests within itself," and if unified science reveals itself as without mystery, then there is no argument against the total planning of history. There is then no more serious charge to bring against bolshevism other than that it is, perhaps, not quite the correct unified science.

Jaspers does not consider freedom to be an object of science, a thing among other things, an institution among other institutions. For this reason freedom is for Jaspers the very highest human concern.

In spite of this fact his philosophy is not particularly appropriate for purposes of political propaganda. It is difficult of access. It forbids the romantic theses which would have a power of penetration and which could be easily summed up. In Jaspers' philosophy is much of that which John Dewey considers unhealthy, not in keeping with the times and un-American in the classical tradition. It is dualistic or antinomian, it is not tragic only because in the face of its serious content the tragic attitude would appear as an aestheticizing untruth. It offers not a whole world but rather a world torn apart, one continually falling apart; it offers a world of philosophy and science, freedom and necessity, meaning

and causality, spirit and nature, theory and practice. Never to
say what can not be answered exactly, to supply every possible
counter-argument in response to what has been said, and to let
everyone decide for himself and thus to consummate his own
philosophy by a long series of negations. From the standpoint of
philosophic artistry all this signifies a difficult renunciation. But
it is a renunciation conditioned by history. "We no longer believe
the great philosophers," Jaspers was accustomed to say in his
seminar. Which is to say, we can no longer believe them in the
face of historical experience, in the face of the facts of scientific
knowledge. But man should never give up. There must be philosophy. What can philosophy be in our time? Jaspers' complete
and imposing life's work is the only answer to this question.

GOLO MANN

KILCHBERG NEAR ZÜRICH
SWITZERLAND

17

John Hennig

KARL JASPERS' ATTITUDE TOWARDS HISTORY

THE DIFFICULTIES which foreign readers have found with German philosophy are largely due to linguistic reasons. To a considerable extent German philosophy has been based on, and evolved from the original meaning of Teutonic words used instead of, or along with, international Graeco-Latin terms. Familiar examples are Kant's distinction between *Vernunft* and *Verstand,* inexplicable without reference to the original meaning of the verbs *nehmen* (seize) and *stehen* (stand), and even more so Hegel's basic conception of the threefold meaning of *aufheben* (elevate, preserve and cancel); we shall see that these two examples have gained in significance through the philosophy of Karl Jaspers.

In our own generation, Heidegger's philosophy is quite incomprehensible without reference to its etymologies. The absence of linguistic considerations in Jaspers' philosophy is remarkable. Speaking of the "universal comprehensibility" established by the "pivotal age of world history" (the cultural systems arising between 800 and 200 B. C. in the Western Mediterranean, India and China) and extended by the "planetarian" traffic-system in our days, Jaspers never refers to linguistic difficulties, which have beset relations in particular between Europe and Asia;[1] we shall see that he implicitly claims universal applicability of the terminology of existentialist philosophy in both time and space. Nowhere, to my knowledge, has Jaspers explained why the word *Dasein* (existence), traditionally at least one of the attempts to render the word *existentia,* has been used by him for the very opposite of what in his philosophy has been termed *Existenz.* In a philosophy clearly limited to the study of man, the common meaning of the expression "having (an) existence" (="making a living," *gagner sa vie, Lebensunterhalt*) denotes as much rock-bottom as does the traditional use of the term *existentia;* and the meteoric rise of the emphatic meaning of the term *Existenz,* which

[1] *Origin,* 24, etc.

has been the outward sign of existential philosophy, can be largely ascribed to the self-evidence of this term from its common meaning. Other key conceptions where, choosing the Latin rather than a corresponding German term, Jaspers preserved essential features in the common use are "communication" (rather than, e.g., Goethe's term *Lebensverhältnis*[2] — the common idea, implying technical realities, emphasized by Jaspers) and "transparence" (rather than *Durchsichtigkeit* — the common meaning implying artistic objectivity) .[3] On the other hand, Jaspers maintained the German word *Geschichte,* using only in a derivative sense the adjective *historisch* and in a clearly inferior sense the noun *Historie.*

In contrast to *historia,* the German word *Geschichte* originally had an objective meaning (from *geschehen,* decisive happening) , developing the subjective meaning (narrative) simultaneously with the evolution of the objective meaning in the derivations of the Latin term, notably in French and English.[4] From the outset it is clear that in the mode of being of history, as understood in Western Europe, the subject-object relationship is closer than in that of nature; only in our terms for the chemical or non-mathematical senses (smell and taste) have we even linguistically the same close relationship, a point rarely considered in the *Critique of Judgment* or in the theory of the humanities.

In Jaspers' philosophy, the term *Geschichte* (history) is secondary to that of *Geschichtlichkeit* (historicity). The German language cannot distinguish between "historic" (significant) and "historical" (past), and the ending *-lich* can denote both property and likeness. Nouns ending in *-keit,* derived from adjectives ending in *-lich,* can denote both the abstract quality and the concretion. Applied as it is in the first instance to present existence, Jaspers' term *geschichtlich* (historical) seems to imply primarily the ideas of significance and of similarity. The word 'historicity' is used by Jaspers only in the singular, i.e., the abstract sense; concretions are denoted by the term *das Geschichtliche.*

These preliminaries are relevant not only to the translations offered in this paper, but to its very subject-matter, which is the

2 Cf. my note on Goethe and Byron in *Modern Language Review,* xliv (1949), 366.

3 See my early studies in the history of this terminology in *Lebensbegriff und Lebenskategorie* (Leipzig 1933), 137.

4 Cf. my paper on the history of the term "history" in *Deutsche Vierteljahrsschrift für Literaturwissenschaft und Geistesgeschichte,* xvi (1936), 511-21.

discussion of Jaspers' philosophy through the determination of the relationship of his term historicity with, and its significance to, the conception of history.*

Based on the definition, given in the preface to Jaspers' *Philosophie*, of philosophy as "the way in which man, *geschichtlich* in his time, seizes being," let us consider one of the passages in which Jaspers describes the transcendence from the empirical or objective to the *'existential'* sphere: "The individual as this individual transcends from his empirical individuality to his being-himself in the intransferable historical concretion of his being in existence *(Dasein)*."[5] The historical force of *'existential'* philosophy cannot be understood without reference to the tradition, now come into the foreground, of the conception of man's being himself.[6] Distinctively modern manifestations of spiritual life are based on the realization of the dependence of objective values upon personal being-oneself translucent in the advocacy or acceptance of such values. What is traditionally described as grace is experienced by modern man in the rare moments when it is given to him to be himself *(Existenz)* and to encounter adequately such being-oneself in others (communication). In view of the difficulties which traditionalist writers have found with existentialist philosophy, these basic facts have to be stated here in the simplest possible way. They are not theories which could be condemned as heresies, but descriptions of what ultimately any modern man in the Western world knows by himself, of facts which may be deplored but which can scarcely be denied.

According to Jaspers, the decisive break-through from the unreality of the objective world (the suffering from which unreality being the inexhaustible theme of modern literature) to the reality of oneself (the all-embracing intention of modern art) is made in "historical concretion," in the ultimate situation (i.e., those exposed situations of life which provoke transcendence from the unreality of the empirical world). That "as existence I am always in a definite situation, never general as the whole of all possibilities"[7] has been described by Jaspers as the basic theme of his work[8] from his early struggle against the self-satisfaction of individual sciences and against finding shelter in a *Weltan-*

5 *Philosophie*, 40.   * Cf. Editor's Note at end of this essay.

6 Cf. my article on Jaspers' *Reason and Existenz* in *Zeitschrift für Theologie und Kirche*, xvii (1936), 46; and my discussion of the apparently contradictory readings of II Cor. 10:12 in *Catholic Biblical Quarterly*, viii (1946), 332ff.; also my note, with reference to Grimmelshausen's *Simplicissimus*, in *Modern Language Review*, xl (1945), 38.

7 *Philosophie*, 474.   8 *Anti-Reason*, 30.

schauung, to the systematic exposition of the conception of *'existential'* truth, infinitely modest in its contents and thus *capax infiniti,* and its defense against various forms of totalitarianism and against the perversion of the experience of *Existenz* in brave or cowardly nihilism. At this point, we do not consider the significance of Jaspers' basic theme to his ideas on historical truth, but we examine what is described as *geschichtlich* in transcending self-realization. Jaspers continues:

I am in this historical period, in this social position, male or female, young or old, led by opportunity and by chance. The border character of my being tied to a unique situation within the narrow limits of my conditions, becomes accentuated by its contrast with the idea of man as such and what accrues to him in all his ways of perfection and completion. Narrowness, however, also leaves room for the possibility remaining in every situation as an indefinite future. In this ultimate situation there is a peculiar restlessness, arising from the realization of the fact that what I am to decide is still to come. In this situation there is therefore the freedom to take my condition upon myself by making it my own as if it were desired.[9]

Death, suffering, struggle and guilt are met with by the individual as his general ultimate situations within the specificity of the historic character of each moment.

It may be said that the fact that we and our thoughts are conditioned in either the strictly historical sense or in the applied historical sense of psychology and sociology, is a common-place almost hackneyed in modern philosophy. From the outset, however, it is clear that for Jaspers

(1) it is not so much the past which conditions us, but our free will to accept what we are presented with as a result of the past (freedom is even more responsibility for the past than it is decision for the future),

(2) our determination concerns the essential form (namely, *Geschichtlichkeit*) rather than material details of our existence, and

(3) this self-determination becomes the basis of the positive unfolding of the highest possibilities of man. Far from leading to the conception of truth as an ideological superstructure of conditions, it brings us to full realization of the personal responsibilities of truth. (In English the expression "I am determined" has both an active and a passive meaning.) "Determined reality as the boundary of empirical reality can be seized in unpredictable

9 *Philosophie,* 474.

chance by potential *Existenz.*"[10] The primary features of historicity *(Geschichtlichkeit)* are, therefore, concreteness and determination, undoubtedly elements also in the traditional conception of history (particularly when history is defined, in contrast to mere past, as the range of freedom), but clearly removed from the idea of past. In fact, the positive turn given to determination as "seizing potential *Existenz*" makes the future at least as important a dimension of historicity as is the past (in responsibility).

In this conception of historicity, the position in time is determined insofar as it is intransferable, but only in a subordinate sense is it determined by its relationship to other historicity earlier or later. Moreover, in this conception of historicity, intransferable and thus determined position in time is only one of the many elements through the realization of which my present situation becomes concrete and determined, whereas in the traditional conception, determined position in the sequence of time is the basic character of history in contrast to mere past. Indeed, in the traditional conception, determined position in the sequence of time is the objective basis of history, because it is prior to memory.

Though Jaspers himself nowhere does so, we may make use of the original meaning of the word "concrete," saying that historicity grows together from the realization of all the determinants of my present situation. We notice already at this stage that, by comparison with the perfect subject-object partnership in the traditional conception of history, the accent has decidedly shifted to what is traditionally known as the subjective side, because the conception of history is approached from this side, namely the historical self-consciousness of the subject. Neither determination nor concreteness exist before realization in the same measure as do, in the traditional conception of history, definite position in, and quickening of, time provoking history-forming memory. Determination implies the idea of positive opening up of possibilities arising from the realization of the *termini*. This positive conception of determination has become the point at which Jaspers' "Existentialism" is most clearly distinguished from Heidegger's, not to speak of Sartre's; but it is rarely recognized that it is of specific importance to the traditional conception of history as the acceptance of the claim of the past to our memory.

By abandoning the arrogance of the belief of possessing in one instance the whole truth, we become open for truth, each time realized as determined in its concretion, in particular through

10 *Ibid.,* 681.

communication. The first fruit of positive determination in
Geschichtlichkeit, communication, is a distinctive element in Jaspers' *'existential'* philosophy. In his conception of communication, Jaspers stands in the tradition of the discovery that interpersonal knowledge is not covered by the subject-object pattern of traditional epistemology; again the recognition of a basic experience of modern man rather than a philosophical theory. However, in *'existential'* consciousness the idea of communication has reached unprecedented acuteness. Communication is in the first instance the realization of each other's historical determination, thus breaking the *'existential'* monadism, movingly expounded by Kierkegaard and Heidegger, and opening the only possible way left to modern man of searching for truth. We shall presently see to what extent this conception of communication has deepened our relationship to history, that is (the testimony of) personal being in the past.

In contrast to historical relativism, Jaspers' idea of historical determination does not lead to sceptical quietism or destructive nihilism, but is the foundation of free activity guided by reason; a point which, from historical experience, has lately been much emphasized by Jaspers. "Historically determined reality can be seized by potential *Existenz,*" because "incapable of completion (or perfection) in time, it restlessly produces antitheses, incessantly demanding change."[11] *Geschichtlichkeit* as ever self-effacing production (the double meaning of "determination") is the only way in which I become certain of myself and of transcendence. At this point we are reminded of the original meaning of the German word *Geschichte* (in contrast to that of *historia,* which is the experience of static facts), and it is clear that Jaspers' conception of history is decidedly Western, being essentially dynamic and voluntarist: "The interpretive contemplation of history becomes a determination of man's will."[12]

Individual consciousness of my present historical character is described as historical consciousness proper (namely *'existential'*) in contrast to improper (or "objective") historical consciousness.[13] The former is termed *geschichtlich,* the latter *historisch,* the foreign term — as usually done in German — being applied in an inferior sense, perhaps also from a memory of the original meanings of the words *Geschichte* (the thing itself) and *historia.* The inferior sense is even more pronounced in Jaspers' use of the term *Historie* (an old-fashioned word used for mere stories or traditions) for the subject of historical sciences. The relationship

11 *Ibid.,* 512.   12 *Origin,* 263.   13 *Philosophie,* 27.

between *Geschichte* and *Historie* is comparable to that between *Existenz* and existence.

Objective historical consciousness or the knowledge of history

is not simply the knowledge of what has happened, as something happens *(geschieht)* all the time and in every place, but the knowledge in which I conceive what has happened as objective condition of my present existence and as something different which, as having been, is in itself unique in time and kind.[14]

If we accept Nietzsche's distinction of the three main attitudes to history, we may say that Jaspers refers to the monumentalist and critical attitudes rather than to the antiquarian attitude (which when properly understood was most purely represented by Ranke). Jaspers does not consider as historical consciousness an attitude confining itself to happenings which, having taken place at a definite point in the sequence of time in the past, are in themselves unique in time and kind, without reference to the present, *my* present. There is no internal connection between the two qualifications by which "some happening" becomes historical (namely "conditioning my present existence" and "unique in time and kind"). We shall see that the fact that I recognize it as different (because past) and unique (because occupying a definite point of time) does not necessarily imply that it remains objective to me. This objective character is rather based on the material relationship established in this historical consciousness between present and past as cause and effect. "Something totally different from it (objective historical consciousness) is historical consciousness proper in which the Self becomes aware of its historical character as which alone the Self is real."[15] The difference between these two historical consciousnesses is clearly reduced to that between objective and *'existential'* thought. "In objective historical consciousness, though relating the objects to ourselves, in our examining them and search for their causes, they remain objects. Reduced to an object, the present is examined as if it were already past."

There is a strict parallelism between Jaspers' use of the sequence *Geschichte — Geschichtlichkeit — Historie* and *historisch* and his use of the sequence *Gegenstand — Gegenständlichkeit — Objekt* and *objektiv*. In the present instance, Jaspers uses the — derogatory — term *Objekt;* his use of the word *objektiv,* in contrast to *existentiell,* is the fundamental subject of the present investigation which tries to establish an *'existential'* conception

14 *Philosophie,* 397f.   15 *Ibid.,* 398.

of what is traditionally known as the objectivity of historical sciences. "(On the other hand), the historical consciousness of *Existenz* [genit. objectiv. and subjectiv.] is originally personal. In it I am conscious of myself in communication with others who are themselves historical (or historically themselves)." From his conception of historical consciousness, Jaspers says that "the historical being [*das geschichtliche Sein* means "historical existence" — in the traditional sense — but should presumably mean "historical character"] of objects, as they are in the intention of my knowledge, is historical only for me," because only by relating them to myself as the causes of my condition do they attain to that "significance" which traditionally marks the difference between mere past and history, whereas I know myself in my historical being as historical for myself.

In this latter part of this sentence, Jaspers uses the word *geschichtlich*, thus making it quite clear that in an attitude objective in the sense of '*existential*' philosophy, history as such fails to become objective in the traditional sense of the word (but remains *Historie*), because it is attributed by the subject. *Geschichtlichkeit*, however, is not attributable but based on self-consciousness, and with regard to other beings, as with regard to myself, '*existential*' philosophy is not speculative interpretation but recognition of facts.

Only in objective thought do we distinguish between historical being *(geschichtliches Sein)* and our knowledge of it; "existentially they are so close *(gleich)* to each other that one cannot be without the other" (the German word *gleich* means both "like" and "identical"). Whereas the word "object" implies the idea of subjection, the German word *Gegenstand* (in this respect related to *Verstand*) implies the ideas of distance and resistance which are characteristic also of what must be termed the existentialist conception of "object" (i.e., existence outside mine). Jaspers' philosophy is personalistic; the word *Ding* (thing, It) does not occur in the indices to his works. The *Gegenstand* in his philosophy is Thou, as is obvious from the short but decisive passage in his *Logic*, speaking of *Sache (res):* "The closer the concept is to being . . . the more it seems to signify, in spite of the remaining separation, the true essence of Being, and the greater the freedom of him who forms this concept with regard to what is conceived: He is entirely in it, and thought and thing *(Sache)* coincide,"[16] clearly the basis of Jaspers' use of 'like' *(gleich)* in the preceding passage. "With regard to what is not conceived or inconceivable

16 *Wahrheit*, 281.

we have no freedom, we are not in it; it is foreign and untransparent as mere difference from us,"[17] that is the way in which objective historical consciousness knows the past as "something different." The word "mere" implies that the perception of difference is opaque and that transparence is brought about by appropriation or assimilation (gleich) to myself. The further implication is that what is opaque is 'existentially' irrelevant. (It will be shown, however, that the past is not "mere" difference but the essential difference from the present and as such 'existentially' relevant) .

In 'existential' self-consciousness, historical knowledge identifies itself as historical with other historical being, and my own historicity thus established is the standard by which objective historical knowledge is measured. Historical knowledge breaks out of monadic confinement in communication (as, in the original meaning, histor, in contrast to the idiotes, is he who, by moving about, establishes that behind yonder mountains there are also people, different people) . In contrast to the self-righteousness and egocentrism of Verstand, Vernunft is the loving acceptance of the determination of my truth by that of other personal beings. Historical being outside my own

is disclosed only to love, and to the power of intuition and clairvoyance that grows in love. Entirely present in love, the single individual becomes endlessly open to the desire for knowledge that is guided by love. It is revealed in phenomena which also become unpredictably different. It is real as an historical individual, and yet to mere knowledge it is, at the same time, non-existent as such.[18]

Defining historical (geschichtlich) as "being oneself united with the origin of all being and in its self-consciousness certain of itself in this ground," Jaspers emphatically denies that historicity can be recognized in objective knowledge. The transition from the conception of historicity (present determination) to historical being is almost imperceptible:

To love of the historical individual, the matrix of Being to which it is attached becomes simultaneously perceptible. In the infinitude of the loved individual, the world becomes manifest. Hence genuine love experiences expansion and intensification through itself, spreads to everything historically existent, becomes love of Being itself in its origin. Thus it becomes manifest to loving intuition how Being, this one single vast individual, is historical in the world. But it is revealed only in the historicity of the love of an individual to an individual.[19]

17 Wahrheit, 281.   18 Origin, 242.   19 Origin, 242.

All this applies to love or communication in the present, and the transition to history (in the traditional sense) is made only in the subsequent passage:

To the Being of history corresponds the particularity of historical cognition. Historical research creates the prerequisites in real [cf. footnote] insight, through which and on the margins of which there may dawn upon us that which is no longer accessible to research itself, but from which research is guided in its choice of themes and in its differentiation between essential and inessential. On the road *via* the always universal object of our cognition, research shows at its margins the irreplaceable individual of history as that which is never universal. To catch a glimpse of this individual links us with it on a plane that lies above and beyond cognition, but is attainable only through cognition.[20]

'Existential' relationship to historical past is an application of communication in present existence rather than *sui generis,* the difference between present and past being immaterial on the *'existential'* plane. The relationship between Jaspers' idea of *'existential'* transcendence and Husserl's[21] idea of phenomenological reduction is striking: So far as the material (or objective) contents are concerned, both aim at establishing "empty forms." The "empty form" established in communication is "being-oneself," i.e., individuality self-conscious in its historical determination, whether past or present. Love is no longer a reaction to values, but active singling out *(di-* or *inter-ligere),* acceptance of the claim of and to determination outside ourselves. (Hatred is levelling down into objective generalities.) Love is determination (in the subject) to determination (in the object), in both instances active and passive. This conception of love again is not a philosophical theory but a description of a truly tremendous change which modern man found in himself long before Existentialism was heard of, and indeed his best and decisive characteristic. The convenient perversion of this discovery is to drag down such determination to the level of orientation in the physical world and to make it there the basis of values. In reality, it is the transparence and ultimate transcendence (the threefold meaning of *aufheben*) of the highest values encountered on the objective plane. The same confusion can be detected in much of contemporary

20 *Ibid.,* 242f. The word *real* is static, in contrast to the corresponding German word, *wirklich.*

21 *Rechenschaft,* 327. "Only by such pure formality, thought has the power of penetrating to my origin." *(Ibid.,* 112).

writing of history, in neglect of fundamental research and in disorderly craving for personal evaluation.

Jaspers' interest in the historical sciences is obviously indirect and legitimately transitory. Objective historical research provides the raw material for communication, arising through it ("transparence") and at its borders. Establishing these borders, objective historical consciousness is the indispensible basis of *'existential'* historical consciousness. Objective historical consciousness in historical research shows itself in consciousness of the historical situation determining choice of subjects and the distinction between what is essential and what not. "History is seen in hierarchies of value, in its origins, in its crucial [where something "happens"] stages. The real is divided up into the essential and the inessential."[22] The traditional definitions of history are based on the term "essential," history being distinguished from mere past as what is "significant" to mankind, society, civilization, nations, the great individual, progress, freedom or the proletariat. Why these things or any of them should be the standard and what is significant in them, is determined by the individual historian (or his party) and presented by him as universal truth. Instead of deriding the lack of consciousness in this arrogant subjectivism, and instead of being led to despondent relativism, Jaspers shows that any such standards of defining history, or even better ones possibly proposed in historical modesty, are fundamentally and ultimately destined to founder in order to make room for historical consciousness proper. All those objective standards are material; the standard adequate to the unlimited possibilities of history must be free of material limitation. It must be the very essence of history, which is not found by wandering about in viewing the past as an object, but in communicating with what appears in the past to correspond to the depth of my own historicity.

Even though he considers it only as of preliminary character, historical science has obtained through Jaspers a conception of its dignity rarely parallelled in depth and acuteness. Its end is to recognize the historical character of personal being in the past as determined individuality. This recognition is not possible in unconcerned objectivity; it requires the whole weight of the historians' historical consciousness and loving communication with the individuality speaking from out of the past. Material standards, which research cannot do without, are pushed aside

22 *Origin*, 262.

at the outset, since they have to be abandoned before true historical being can become transparent.

"Objective historical consciousness reaches its fulfillment in
historical science. It stands confirmed by the panoramic picture
of a world history and in the always limited capacity to interpret
the present out of the past."[23] Whether the second sentence is an
exposition of the purpose of historical science or of its transcendence into philosophy, both sentences seem to refer to objective
attitudes.

Historical science is furthermore concerned with . . . sociological and
political aspects, institutions and customs, works and effects. This
knowledge presents itself to me not as to this individual but as a
specimen of present-day man or even of man in general, accidentally
living today, thus limited in his knowledge of the *contents* of the past
but not limited in the *kind* of knowledge. In this knowledge I am not
myself but consciousness-as-such, separated from the object of my
knowledge ["mere difference"].[24]

That is to say, historical science, according to Jaspers, aims from
the outset at what is general rather than what is individual, at
objective manifestations rather than their creative ground. It
levels individuality by considering it in a causality pattern. It
is indifferent to its object; at most it will admit that its material
knowledge is limited. But it is incapable of even conceiving the
decisive difference in kind between objective and 'existential'
knowledge. At this point, we have clearly the difference between
the three-dimensional conception of truth in 'existential' philosophy (the decisive dimension being that of depth) and the two-
dimensional conception of philosophy in the traditional sense
("hit and miss"). In contrast to emotional and vitalist subjectivism, however, the 'existential' conception of truth is not simply
vertical (depth — or agreeability — being the only dimension that
counts) but three-dimensional, rising from the broad and solid
plain of objectivity.

While historical science supplies 'existential' realization with
this indispensible foundation, it is shallow and flat without 'existential' consciousness: "Without the historicity of *Existenz* there
is no historicity of objectivity of its existence in society, law or
moral order, but only *Historie* of endless relativities."[25] Since
"only *Existenz* recognizes for itself in the objectivity of the external historical object its (this object's) historical presence," it is

---

[23] *Philosophie*, 397.   [24] *Ibid.*, 397f.

[25] *Ibid.*, 633. In this instance the word *Historie* is clearly used in the sense of
"recitation."

clear that "while recognizing universal historicity as the ground receiving and embracing it, *Existenz* is confronted by this ground in individual phenomena of objectivity, seized and animated by its *(Existenz's)* subjectivity. The depth of this ground is history as such which from it (such animated objectivity) meets *Existenz*."[26] The connection, in terminology, imagery and indeed contents, with theological descriptions of *unio mystica* or modern descriptions of inter-personal love is obvious. There is a clear hierarchy in this descent to "the deepest ground:"[27] "In order that *Existenz* can understand *Existenzen* in their common historical ground [common as historical rather than by contents], knowledge of the past is required. This knowledge, methodically and critically examined, as such, is *Historie* as science. Transformed into *'existential'* self-understanding, it is philosophy of history."[28] Philosophy of history is realized in three stages:[29] (1) In orientation in the world, it makes us conscious of the boundaries of history as *Historie,* that is, historicity appearing to us in the objectivity of the past, the conditions and forms of historical knowledge and understanding, and of speculations on the meaning of history as a whole. Thus it supplies what is missing in historical science, namely understanding of the historical limitations of knowledge, not only in its contents but also in its kind, and knowledge of what is beyond the "panoramic picture of a world history," which knowledge again is determination, telling us above all that, however wide and detailed our panorama, it is not universal and does not absolve us from making concrete decision. Philosophy in general prevents history and other sciences from turning into dogmatic theories, "historism" ranking on the same level with "psyschologism" (Jaspers' life-long adversary), "sociologism"[30] and, no doubt, "existentialism." The traditional question of the meaning of history, i.e., a uniform tendency comprehensible or desirable for everyone, everywhere and at any time and expressed in objective contents (freedom, civilization, the greatest good for the greatest number, class-less society, the conversion of mankind, etc.) is clearly reduced to its true rank as a working hypothesis or a cipher, providing a garment to be worn as long as it is fitting, ever ready to be obliterated in *'existential'* transcendence. (2) In illumination of *Existenz*, the objectivity of history (as supplied by historical science) is conceived as the universal region of the communion of my *Existenz* with other

[26] *Ibid.*

[27] Goethe, *Faust*, ii, v. 6283ff.

[28] *Philosophie*, 635.

[29] *Ibid.*, 638.

[30] Cf. the first of Jaspers' lectures in *Anti-Reason* (1952).

personal beings. Such illumination of *Existenz* is purely present, the past being entirely related to the present and the future being planned from this con-cretion. Philosophy of history is the conception of this communion of *Existenz*, not yet its realization in communication. (3) The historical character of this universe is transcended. The picture of an historical universe with beginning and end becomes the basis of a myth which for the present historical moment represents transcendency through the medium of history.

The ultimate dividing-line of history as *Historie*, Jaspers says, is in the methodological sphere.

In matters of the spirit, a fact can only be apprehended through the understanding of meaning. Understanding, however, is by its nature valuation. Though it rests empirically upon an accumulation of separate data, an historical construction never comes into being through these alone. Only through understanding do we arrive at our view . . . and this view involves understanding and valuation at the same time . . .[31]

Should we not say again: They are so close *(gleich),* that one cannot be without the other? The history of the relationship between understanding and evaluating has been the fundamental theme of the history of historical methods, and great historians from Thucydides to Ranke claimed that understanding should be kept free from evaluating. Let us try to clarify Jaspers' terms "understanding" and "evaluating."

The understanding of the meaning of something takes place in mutual communication: causality is foreign to this process and means recognizing something as different and distant. Understanding does not have an effect on things, but leaves the road open to freedom. Causal explanation enables one to intervene to some extent in the process of events. . . . [thus] I am treating [freedom] as an object, as if it were a perceptible object, which is to degrade it.[32]

Dilthey's distinction between understanding (as the method of the humanities) and explaining (in the natural sciences) is here clearly placed parallel to proper and improper historical consciousness. It would therefore appear that, when saying that "historical science is concerned with . . . works and effects, knowledge in which I am separated from the object of my knowledge," Jaspers refers to a perversion of true historical science, as indeed it is.

---

[31] *Origin,* 9f.   [32] *Anti-Reason,* 22.

In the situation of German universities in 1946, Jaspers demanded

devoted study of a thousand years of our German past. Instead of supposed omniscience and historical derivatives absorption in the truly great . . . the Othonic world, Switzerland's and the Low Countries' fight for freedom and the formation of their states, in the shipwreck of the grand projects of von Stein, Gneisenau and Humboldt.[33]

It is from the 'existential' view of truth that such demands must be distinguished from an opportunist treatment of history. Jaspers continues: "A new picture of German history, based on what is good in our tradition and which sees right through the idols, is not gained by convenient reversion to previous [Nazi] evaluations, but must be worked out by research." What is "great" or "good" and what is "idol," is, however, even more difficult to judge than what is "essential." What does historical research have to do with such clearly objective evaluations? Earlier in the same lecture (which, although not strictly philosophical, illustrates Jaspers' attitude to history at a crucial point), Jaspers refers to a practical problem in historical research:

We are able to understand (verstehen) even what we ourselves are not. It has been said: It is possible to understand Caesar without being Caesar. Is it, really? This is the riddle of the humanities: on the one hand, understanding hits something in the understood person of which he himself was not at all aware; did Caesar, perhaps, understand himself, had he become translucent to himself? And, on the other hand, understanding produces a change in the spiritual life of him who has the understanding, since it opens up to him new possibilities of understanding. He enters into the infinite movement of illumination, performed on the material of history.[34]

Are we to take it that the situation is similar to that described by modern physicists: In and through the act of understanding both subject and object undergo changes; they can never be the same? Through understanding they become even more historical (as modern man knows that in love we become even more single). The transition from this conception of understanding of historical character, freed from material objectivity, to applications in concrete historical situations cannot be retraced outside the experience of those situations.

Unless prepared to make such transitions in concrete determination, the historian, as envisaged by Jaspers, tends to make himself "independent of the historical consciousness of Existenz,"

<hr>

[33] Rechenschaft, 177f. [34] Ibid., 164.

thus remaining in a *mere* knowledge situation. Thereby he faces the danger of either losing proper historicity (not the consciousness of it, since historicity itself is the organ of establishing other historicity) to the point of its becoming endless knowledge, or else he makes himself independent of its historicity by claiming to have possession of universally valid truth.[35] The development of this alternative in Jaspers' thought is significant. His "Discussion of the contrast between catholicity and reason" started with a reduction of this contrast to that between "forced and original historicity."

When man becomes conscious of historicity in its objective form, two dangers arise: [Either] what is historically known takes the place of historicity, being accepted as the authentic *(das Eigentliche)* — [(1) historical consciousness proper, (2) history appropriated, (3) being oneself, (4) being myself]. What I know of the past conceals, as myth[36] of what has passed, origin and approach to the whole for me. What does not find a place in knowledge is allowed to be drowned [in oblivion of non-existentiality], whereas what is possibly alien to my self-being is artificially elevated. The desired does violence to my essence. What arose out of historicity and was, as objective structure, particular and relative, mobile and changeable, becomes the historical itself. But, forced clinging to accepted knowledge and having such knowledge forced on one, deprive of historicity. Thus subjected to thought and to what is fabricated, I have, in merely apparent historicity, actually become entangled in confined generality. I myself become thus unhistorical material, abandoned to the Naught in the passing appearance of historicity; a fact which becomes obvious in the moment of the collapse of this appearance by the intervention of external forces.

Or, the knowledge of historicity, in its accidental objective incarnations, robs our life of its absoluteness. The relativity of historical objectivity makes life itself relative. The non-generality distintegrates the absolute validity of my historicity for me. I distrust the historical and embark on the impossible and self-destructive attempt of living in the merely general validity of consciousness-as-such. Thus I lose my bearings in the bottomless.[37]

Between those two perversions there is but one highway:

Historical research in the service of historical consciousness maintains passionately and with radical truthfulness what can be critically explored, but also penetrates through it to what is *Existenz*. The origin of the meaning of historical research is the recognition of *Existenz*

---

[35] Cf. *Philosophie*, 636.

[36] In this instance the word "myth" is used in a derogatory sense, in contrast to the use of this word in the exposition of philosophy of history.

[37] *Wahrheit*, 834.

in every historical phenomenon as being "immediate to God." In historical knowledge, *Existenz* is present as it were invisible, both in him who sees and in him who is seen. There is love of what has been, even in minute detail,[38] as long as *Existenz* is perceptible. There is the awe of what is beyond exploration. There is the presence of our own roots, the sense of that past which, as great for us, belongs to our world, and on the other hand the search for even the remotest fact from which man still speaks to us. By all these internal connections, what can be known and what claims to be conceived with such preparedness, is animated and appropriated.

Since Ranke's lectures before King Louis of Bavaria (to which it alludes), there has been scarcely a more inspiring exposition of the nature of historical science than this passage. Its radiance is so overwhelming that we can hardly conceive that the perversions which, according to Jaspers, are inevitable outside this conception of history are difficult to account for.

The question is whether the alternative between objective and '*existential*' historical consciousness is as clear as suggested by Jaspers or whether traditional objective historical research is not of a more positive relevancy for existentialist philosophy.

In objective historical knowledge we have mere changes or what everywhere is transitory, what is related by causality, infinite ups and downs, an arbitrary variety without beginning or end. In *Existenz*, however, the present as historical is not merely vanishing but listening to the past, thus capable of speaking to a possible future, growing together (concrete) from past and future in a substantial *nunc*. Having become my own in communication, the past is no longer merely the causal condition of my presence, which even when left unknown exercises its influence, but is present reality as ground coming to me in what the past says to me. The relativity of merely historical presence *hebt sich auf* (is raised, preserved and cancelled) in the historical consciousness of *Existenz*, whenever this claim of the past is responded to. For this *Existenz* alone, the *Geschichtlichkeit* of the objectivity embracing it is visible as content in which my *Existenz* meets other *Existenz*, dispersed in time and space, so far as it appears as external in historical records, eternity in temporal appearance in which it is gained.[39]

There can be little doubt that what is here confronted is the description of an obvious perversion and the theory of an ideal. Yet it is by this ideal that Jaspers would have us measure the concretions of his attitude to history in his monographs in the field of history of philosophy, in the guidance given by him in Germany after the war, and in his "plan for a world history."

[38] *Rechenschaft*, 207.   [39] *Philosophie*, 637f.

When, in existentialist philosophy, we leave the sphere of descriptive interpretation, the difficulty presents itself whether it will be possible, in the neutral atmosphere of a paper, to maintain the minimum of communication and to avoid "endless discussion as the play of accidental opinions, the vanity of being in the right and sophistic skills with the mental reservation everywhere in force that everything is, after all, undecided and ultimately nothing is to be taken too seriously,"[40] that perversion with which intellectual life in the West is beset. The present writer has lived through his formative years with Jaspers' philosophy and for more than twenty years has closely followed Jaspers' attitude towards history. The principles of this attitude have guided him in historical research. In fact, due to the vicissitudes of history scattered over a wide range, his work is held together only by the search for the 'existential' significance of historical objectivity.[41]

Jaspers' historical monographs follow a definite pattern, which may be described as the sifting of the 'existential' wheat from the objective chaff. In each of them, Jaspers goes with his object from its origin a certain distance, sometimes even a long stretch, until he reaches what he terms its fixations or ultimate limits, measured by the standards of his philosophy rather than by those of the historical position of the object.[42] Essentially based on conscientious recognition of a spiritual position (namely the cleavage between objective and 'existential' reality) , existentialist philosophy is not only the transcendence of totalitarian claims to the possession of universal truth, but also the reduction of philosophy from theories about what *should be* to description of what *is*. It is the conscience of modern man, because it does not confuse thought and being. It is fundamentally non-controversial, because there is no way of enforcing the recognition of facts. Its conception of communication, as the only responsible way of conveying truth between personal beings, precludes mere arguments. Its preoccupation with death and suffering is of epistemological significance: Concerning both death and suffering we cannot argue, because we know nothing of them outside of them; yet death and suffering are the inevitable themes of philosophy in our age, having rebelled to an unprecedented degree against the

40 *Rechenschaft,* 171.

41 Cf. in particular my studies in the conceptions of time and history underlying the liturgy of the early Irish church, notably in *Speculum,* xxi (1946), 49-66 and in *Medieval Studies* x (1948), 147-161.

42 Cf. my review of Jaspers' *Descartes,* in *Blätter für deutsche Philosophie,* xii (1938) no. 3.

traditional attempts at meliorizing. Communication is spontaneous and unexpected. It is all-embracing. Jaspers has shown us that the vanishing of objective standards in communication is not blind love, but the way to become entirely open to historical individuality.

Where there is fundamental antagonism, as in Goethe's attitude to Newton[43] or in Jaspers' to Descartes,[44] communication is impeded. The consequences of such impeded communication could only be demonstrated in detailed argument, limited in fruitfulness, on the basis of specialized knowledge. A concise and extreme example in Jaspers' monographs of an objective approach to an historical phenomenon is his study on Ezekiel.[45] This is not the place to re-trace Jaspers' progressive preoccupation with what he describes as the limitations in the Biblical and Christian traditions; the following examples must be taken as symptomatic in the field of historical method. "The truth of Biblical religion runs counter to the fixations [such as the conception of Law] that have been effected within it, that were once perhaps historically valid, but are no longer valid for philosophical reflection."[46] Confronted by such apparent fixations, historical consciousness must not remain in the undecided vagueness of suggestion ("perhaps") : As long as there is a possibility of breaking through the appearance of fixation, there is a chance that the historical reality may still be valid. — Segregating in Biblical religion what may still be philosophically maintained and what not, Jaspers inserts the clause: "; no man can be God."[47] While scarcely relating the meaning of the doctrine of the Divinity of Christ, this statement presents a universal truth, embracing even the future, and breaking off communication with at least 1500 years of our spiritual tradition and with a few hundred millions of our fellow-men. This is not a question of belief but of an admission of non-transparence. Learning to make the distinction between

---

[43] Rechenschaft, 34.

[44] Cf. note 42 and Wahrheit, 814.

[45] Rechenschaft, 80f, and Scope, 102. Jaspers knows, of course, that "psychiatric analysis does not affect the material and historical value of intellectual and spiritual contents" (Rechenschaft, 89). Yet, on the basis of such analysis, he rejects these values in detail, against the testimony of Ezekiel and his tradition. The idea that we can penetrate to historicity (by-passing, as it were, its testimony and tradition, by which tradition we nevertheless are determined), is typical of the aristocratic attitude to history. See my studies in liturgical and exegetical traditions in Catholic Biblical Quarterly x (1948), 360 and xiv (1952), 233; Theological Studies, iv (1943), 445 and vii (1946), 126; Irish Theological Quarterly xviii (1951), 187 and xix (1952), 84 and 192, etc.

[46] Scope, 104.   [47] Ibid., 105.

admission of non-transparence and outright rejection is the aim of historical education.

On a more elementary plane of historical consciousness, the statement:

> To die for something in order to bear witness to it is to give an aim to one's death, hence to make it impure. Where martyrs have actually been inspired by a longing to die, perhaps in imitation of Christ, by a death urge which not infrequently darkens the soul with symptoms of hysteria, the impurity is still greater. . . .[48]

is an illustration of the preclusion of historical realization by a psychological theory.

Existentialist philosophy has been essentially aristocratic. Involuntarily it has given a deeper meaning to the definition of the proletarian as the man without *Existenz*. If, however, it was true in Germany in 1945 that "it is our fault that we are still alive,"[49] it is even more true of all of us who still have both time and a mind to devote ourselves to philosophy, that it is our fault that we can still strive for *Existenz*. A conception of communication as the invisible contact between the few scattered throughout the world[50] who aim at "an ascent to high-minded, devoted, penetrating, pure humanity,"[51] hopelessly leaves behind the masses whose spiritual condition has been movingly described. The consciousness of our guilt, social and racial,[52] must not remain metaphysical.

A "vital humanism will have to ally itself with those forces which truly desire to promote the fate and the chances of all,"[53] recognizing that, "in the future even more than in the past, no spiritual reality will remain unless carried by the masses."[54] It must renounce even the last vestiges of a condescending aristocratic attitude:

> Achievement at a high level will, nevertheless, always be a matter for a few individuals, for the elite who educate themselves. Yet, the coming humanism will, while scaling the summits, also have to discover the simplest forms which become approachable and convincing to everyone. An effective humanism would, in principle, have to be a humanism for all. *(Ibid.)*

---

[48] Cf. above Note 45. The quotation is from Jaspers' *Wisdom,* 53.

[49] *Rechenschaft,* 138.   [50] *Ibid.,* 184.   [51] *Origin,* 227.

[52] Whence shall the white man take the courage to ask: "Will the people conscious of liberty, numbering at most a few hundred millions, be able to bring conviction to the spirits of more than two thousand million others, and enter with them into a free, legal world community?" *Origin,* 203.

[53] *Rechenschaft,* 275.   [54] *Ibid.,* 279.

Yet — the greatest humanizing force in world history is severely censured for the "fixations" to which such "simplest forms" invariably lead!

With regard to history, this aristocratic attitude results, methodically, in assigning to the present the right and indeed the duty of evaluating the past, and, materially, in a disregard of the fundamental problem in our existing historical situation, viz., the continuous increase in world population in the face of ever decreasing food production, resulting in ever shrinking chances of communication and in an inevitable increase in pre-occupation with suffering.

Jaspers' derivation of history from historicity is due to his minimizing the differences among present, past and future so far as their mode of being is concerned.[55] Nowhere, so far as I am aware, is the point made, decisive though it is for any conception of history, that — whereas the past is irrevocable, — the present is undecided and the future possible; these being the only features in present, past and future which are indubitable and applicable only to them respectively. We can doubt whether there will be a future, we may even doubt whether there is a present (Descartes' anticipation of Leibniz' question why there is anything at all), but we cannot doubt that there has been a past, although and *because* it is irrevocable. When Jaspers says that "Something endless opens up into the past and into the future,"[56] we cannot forget that the infinity (or extent lost to sight) of the past is given to us in a way quite different from that in which the infinity of the future is given, if given at all. Historical communication differs from communication in the present in that the past can only call on but not respond to us. Anything that appears to us as response is our interpretation of what the past says without specific reference to us.

If "history — into the future in fact, and as the past in interpretation — is an open, infinite world of relationships of meaning,"[57] then the decisive rôle of the historian in the world, both intellectual and material, is to assert the fact that, in spite of its infinite (or considerable) openness to interpretation, the past is irrevocable and that the present is bound to become so. To speak of the future is natural to man; to listen to the past requires the

[55] What is attempted in these last pages is a projection of Jaspers' ideas into a field which was outside his historical choice of subjects. In the field of history it has never been properly attempted "not only to determine the limits of the functions of reason against each other, but even more so to elucidate the limits of reason with regard to what encompasses reason" (*Rechenschaft*, 108).

[56] *Origin*, xiii.   [57] *Ibid.*, 263.

special effort of the *histor*. In personal, national, social and racial experience the irrevocability of the past is the measure of guilt, and the consciousness of guilt is the source of our responsibility, the concretion of determination in every historical moment.

However, the historian prevents breaking off not only our own history but history and the past as such. The past is irrevocable, separated from the present by the unbridgeable chasm of death.[58] Some day, I myself shall be as defenseless as is the past, open to ever new interpretation, mostly mis-interpretation or, even more likely, oblivion. While the realization of our inevitable vanishing into death is negative *(vanitas vanitatum)*,[59] that of vanishing into history creates responsibility. Yet, however deep and acute my historical consciousness of existence, it can never transform the irresponsiveness of the past. Only in the past do we encounter an authority which, — completely free of objective content, based entirely on its irrevocability as past, — has to be listened to whether it becomes transparent to us or not. Historical consciousness is the concretion of conscience which is the realization of what is, *'existentially,'* in an eminent sense, though, objectively, no longer.

Jaspers says, that in history the past "speaks to us," "says something to us," "raises a claim to be responded to." The future does not speak; in fact, as mere possibility, it cannot raise a claim except as self-projection of the present. On the other hand, irrevocable and therefore inaccessible to subjection, the past is the absolute limit of the present. The present can throw itself forward into the future, but it forgets its elementary limitation if it believes that, it can, in any sense, throw itself back into the past.

The past would be a dull negative boundary (as is death), if it were mere vanishing and oblivion. That it is not entirely so is due to the fact that we have history which is testified past. What we know of the past, what speaks to us, lays claim on us, transmits to us historicity, is not the past itself but the testimonies it has raised. So far as I can see, Jaspers refers to this mode of being of history only in one instance, namely when he says that the natural sciences deal "with the thing *(Sache)* itself rather than with residues of reality such as texts, documents, monuments and works of art."[60] Whereas, so far from concealing the thing itself, records are the very substance of history. The "leap from . . . mere happening into history"[61] takes place where, conscious of the inevitability of oblivion, testimony is raised. Historical con-

58 *Ibid.*, 47.   59 *Philosophie*, 485.   60 *Rechenschaft*, 165.
61 *Origin*, 46.

sciousness is the meeting of the will not to permit the falling into oblivion with the will not to forget, across the chasm of death and oblivion, in mutual determination. The will not to permit the falling into oblivion is the concretion of historicity in the past, which is traditionally known as history. We do not encounter historicity of the past directly but through the medium and in virtue of its testimony. Not to permit a falling into oblivion, or positively, memory, is the basis of communication, in the sequence of continuously vanishing time, as the continuity of humanity. In the word "memory," as in the word "history," the subject-object relation is inseparable. What responds to the historical claim of memory is not our historicity as such but its concretion in the specific preparedness of what is traditionally known as historical consciousness, better conscience, namely the preparedness to remember. This preparedness is in itself an 'existential' attitude, historical as determination of the time-bound character of our existence. It is not only today that "there is one great anxiety: The world is pervaded by terrible forgetfulness,"[62] though perhaps in our age for the first time we "shudder at the possibility of terrifying despots wanting to blot out history."[63]

Historical consciousness as unlimited preparedness to listen to the claim of testified past is far from being an aesthetic attitude to history, according to Jaspers.

If, vis-a-vis the endless material of historical knowledge, it is deemed worthwhile recalling everything, simply because it was — in a spirit of detachment that merely ascertains actual facts without end — this unselectiveness arises out of an aesthetic attitude, to which everything can in some way be considered as a means to the stimulation and satisfaction of curiosity: one thing is beautiful and so is the other. This historism devoid of obligations,[64] whether it be scientific or aesthetic, leads to a state of mind in which, after everything has become of equal value, nothing has any longer any value at all. Historical reality is not free of obligations, however. Our true approach to history should be to wrestle with it. History concerns us; that in it which concerns us is continually expanding, which makes it a question of immediate importance to mankind.[65]

---

[62] Rechenschaft, 261. Also: "Pride and selfishness enjoy forgetfulness if it is profitable to forget; they destroy loyalty towards others and towards oneself." Anti-Reason, 49f.

[63] Rechenschaft, 278.

[64] In Anti-Reason (87), Dilthey is described as a typical representative of such 'irresponsible understanding.' A refutation, naturally immature, of this criticism of Dilthey was attempted in my thesis (cf. Note 3 above).

[65] Origin, 269.

Recognizing the peculiar mode of the being of history, irrevocable as past and claiming transparence as testified, the reluctance of historical science with regard to all material standards of selection and evaluation is anything but aesthetic pleasure. It is rather the determination to remain open to the claim of historicity, which is heard the more clearly the less the present talks. It is the traditional failing of philosophical theories of history to assume that the historian interprets the (testimony of the) past. In reality, the historian knows that it is he who is interpreted by the (testimony of the) past. It is a traditional misconception, originating in the aristocratic trend of Western thought, that history requires the activity of the present, selective and critical, to come into its own. Actually, the historian is continuously aware of the inadequacy of his preparedness to understand history's claims. Even more than he fails in his duty to love his neighbor, he fails in his duty to listen to the voice of the dead. If "Reason wants to draw near to everything that is and that must therefore be able to find expression in speech, in order to preserve it and give it a validity of its own,"[66] history is indeed the practice of reason.

In the 'existential' conception of historical understanding, the traditional theories of monumentalism and criticism, aestheticism and ethicism, which looked in history for super-history, appear as attempts to seek shelter from the overwhelming claims of the (testimony of the) past. The traditional fear that unlimited openness to the claims of the past might crush the living, is a theoretical sublimation of what Kierkegaard called the laziness of the human heart. In the pressure of the day, "the works of the past, however great" may appear to us as "rubbish;"[67] their testimonies can never do so. Leonidas will never decide to retreat, and the testimony of Simonides will stand, whether in evaluating it we decide that Leonidas saved Europe or not.

The principles of selection in historical science do not derive from the aristocratic arrogation of a right to select, but from the humble admission of our limitations in openness. Such principles, therefore, are methodical rather than philosophical, and are, therefore, even more destined to be abandoned than any objective contents. Asserting the right of the past to be heard, the historian is the guardian of the conscience of mankind. In everything that has happened and has raised a testimony, the present becomes determined, not by individual objective contents but by history as such which is quickening at certain points in the sequence of

---

[66] *Anti-Reason*, 41.

[67] (Max Weber): *Rechenschaft*, 14.

time and testified to as such,[68] that peculiar reality which as past should be *for*gotten but through its testimony can still be *be*gotten: "And the word was made flesh and dwelt among us; John beareth witness of him." "If I say that all this is a figment of the imagination it means that I do not want it to be a reality."[69]

The elementary attitude of historical love implies that, when failing to establish transparency, we do not blame the past but ourselves. Evaluating what has been in the past by what should be possible in the future (as in Jaspers' comparison between religion and philosophy), the basic difference in the modes of being between past and future, — history to be forgotten and history still to be begotten, — disappears and what remains is the incommensurability of an external objective view and a beloved ideal.[70] Accentuating one historical period at the expense of another, in order to avoid the aesthetic attitude to which one thing is beautiful and something else also, we inevitably shut out rather than open up reality. In Jaspers' accentuation of the pivotal age, the mythical age has become reduced to a period of mental sleep (rather than of the unsurpassed and lasting experience of the superiority of things to all attempts of mental appropriation),[71] while Christ becomes the last of the prophets (against his testimony and that of 1900 years).[72]

The clear distinction between objective and '*existential*' thought was not made before the seventeenth century. It is a feature in the *Weltanschauung* or better the mental state of the *troisième état* and has remained so to this day. It is still unknown outside the Western part of the white race. The evaluation of being one-

---

68 Cf. note 21. In my studies in Irish-Continental hagiography (*Mediaeval Studies* 1945, 21-33, and 1946, 217-244, etc.) investigation of "minuate details" (in both instances the spelling of one word) has made transparent a layer of historicity which, though basic to our own, has almost lapsed from the consciousness of the West. My approach was the same as that of Jaspers in his early anatomical studies (*Rechenschaft*, 327).

69 *Anti-Reason*, 65. In analogy of the Hebrew, the German word *zeugen* means both "testify" and "beget."

70 Also in Jaspers' comparisons between "proper" and "improper" historical consciousness, terminological investigations reveal a fundamental suspicion resulting at the crucial point in descriptions of what is so obviously a perversion that communication cannot seriously be sought with those credited with supporting it. Attitudes burdened with historical responsibility, vast in space and time, are confronted with speculative pictures of possibilities assigned to an elite — the traditional argumentation of sectarianism (*Rechenschaft*, 338). Significantly enough, Jaspers says: "We cannot too often quote Kant's statement that it is plebeian [non-aristocratic] to refer to experience [past] when the object of experience is yet to become real through our freedom" (future). (*Ibid.*, 319).

71 *Origin*, 2f.   72 Cf. notes 45 and 46 above.

self as the highest good and the claim that recognition of a universal truth inevitably means everywhere for everyone and at all
times loss of freedom, are both cause and result,[73] not of the
collapse of Christianity but of that metaphysical consciousness on
which the positive religions have rested. The emphasis laid by
Jaspers on achievement rather than on possession, on *forma*
rather than *materia*, on *potentia* rather than *actus*, on possibility
rather than stability, on freedom rather than submission,[74] on
the future rather than the past, — all these things would at certain
points have to be abandoned not only to future possibilities, but
even more so to historical reality, especially when dealing with
other classes and races than our own.

Ezekiel's conception of the law of God, Aquinas' of truth,
Descartes' of objectivity, Goethe's of fidelity — these must not be
measured by the standards of a philosophy so clearly determined
in its historical application. The *'existential'* potentialities of
historical communication rest on the peculiar fact that the claim
of the past can be heard before *'existential'* transparency is realized,[75] an experience by no means of purely aesthetic interest, but
the very foundation of those who try to live *'existentially'* as
Christians.

In historical communication, the term "communication" itself
undergoes a significant transformation. Our relationship to our
interlocutor is that of the all-embracing love of his historicity;
but it is not a conversation *(Gespräch):* in contrast to a work of
art, the historical testimony has no body. In cor rast to a work
of literature or philosophy, the testimonies of political history
(that sphere where history is really made) often carry almost no
personal weight. Whereas in present communication there is
indeed no truth outside mutual *'existential'* transparency (at
least in our generation and climate) , in historical communication
'existential' transparency is basically not mutual. The claim of
the past is blunt and irresponsive; in this field I must, therefore,
allow myself to be told rather than to tell. Man, however, can
accept responsibility not only *for* the past but *to* the past. It is
his dignity to be faithful to the past, against his natural inclination
to forgetfulness.

One fruit of such historical consciousness is that it makes us

73 "Origin and tool:" *Rechenschaft,* 310.

74 Cf. my review of A. Gehlen's study of freedom in *Kantstudien,* xxxix (1936),
361ff.

75 "What remains foreign and incomprehensible is the boundary (limit) of our
own truth:" *Rechenschaft,* 337.

expect that our interlocutor knows us better than we know ourselves. My intention has been to apply in my field of work what I believe Jaspers has taught me. I expect that I have said nothing he did not either know or perceive. "History will cease to be a mere field of knowledge, and become once again a question of the consciousness of life and of existence; it will cease to be an affair of aesthetic culture, and become the earnestness of hearing and response."[76] It is boldly claimed that from the experience with this philosophy in practical historical work, nothing has been said which did not arise from this idea. If existentialist philosophy is limitless communication, rejection of all self-limitation of knowledge in objectification, and love as the ultimate guide,[77] it will find in historical science an inexhaustible source of inspiration.

JOHN HENNIG

BASEL, SWITZERLAND

[76] *Origin*, 266.   [77] *Rechenschaft*, 263.

Editor's Note: As is explained (on pp. xi-xiii) in our Preface, we have usually cited quotations from those of Jaspers' works which have already appeared in an authorized English translation by quoting from that translation. After this book was already in page-proofs, Dr. Hennig called the editor's attention to Jaspers' distinction between *Historie* and *Geschichte,* a distinction which has become obliterated by the authorized translation of *both* terms by the English word "history." This tends to lead to misunderstandings of and incongruities in some of the points Dr. Hennig has made in this essay. This is unfortunate. Such incongruities, then, are the fault, *not* of the author of this essay, but of the inadequate official translations of some of Professor Jaspers' books. The editor apologizes for the fact that this was not caught till too late to make the necessary changes in the here printed text. *Ed.*

18

Jeanne Hersch

IS JASPERS' CONCEPTION OF TRADITION
ADEQUATE FOR OUR TIMES?*

ONE DAY, when we were speaking of my political involve-
ments and the frequent solicitations to which he is subject,
Karl Jaspers said to me: "You, you are something. I myself am not
anything. I am of air. Like reason." The words were accompanied
by a gesture which made the surrounding space more fluid.

This was in his home in Basle. But it could just as well have
been his home in Heidelberg, before the war. When I am in his
home, I no longer know — is this Basle, or Heidelberg? This
feeling begins immediately, in the street, at the door. Here is the
same high, narrow entrance, in line with the others, effortlessly
attuned to the note of the surroundings, yet indefinably more
silent, more withdrawn. Inside, here is the same sense of order,
of daily ritual; the same books everywhere, as high as the ceiling,
separating the light inside from the daylight outside, behind the
big windows, which is shining on the streetcars, the birds, the
shops; the same chairs, in the dining-room, arranged around the
table to suggest a way of placing oneself and partaking of the
meal as a friendly little ceremony — a summons from the same
past. "I myself am not anything." That is: open, infinitely open,
to infinitely inaccessible truth. Sartre says something very similar:
"I am *nothing*." He is nothing because a nothing separates him
from his past, because he is his past, because he is his past in the
mode of not being his past. Jaspers is not separated from his past.
He is not anything because his past is so entirely his that it does
not burden him, does not fetter him. His past is precisely his
openness. It is a welcoming saturation — in a word, it is tradition.

"I am not anything. I am of air." That is to say: I am that tradition whose fullness does away with all tyranny. I teach nothing. My
books, my courses, though they blacken the page and shake the
silence, originate in the Socratic refusal, in the missing, unwritten
work which presides over the West through tens of centuries

* Translated from the original French manuscript by Forrest W. Williams.

and guards against the din of catchwords. Wherever I seem to have a doctrine may be found my personal imperfection which has arbitrarily clouded the pure transparency of philosophic faith. These opaque marks are everything arbitrary, fortuitous, or deterministic which may affect me. Free, I would be the very presence of tradition. In the face of tradition, everything becomes possible; since Socrates, and since the Bible — ever since God has been beyond our human representations — tradition has been just this: that everything is possible, and nothing excluded. But the possible is none other than truth and fidelity. For what is it to choose, if not to choose that which is and to choose as oneself?

A complex play of arguments and antinomies, all this rational mythology, whereas the act of presence is so uncomplicated; though more difficult, no doubt, and intolerably beyond all possession because contested as soon as achieved, and never secured for the next instant (but the books one writes grace the shelves of the library), and because impervious not only to language, but almost to consciousness itself. (Consciousness distributes it in time, assigns it a past, a present, a future, breaks it down into tradition, freedom, and hope, whereas by itself it fastens onto time with such force that time is pierced through, and a sort of momentary coincidence with eternity is actualized.) And thus we are brought back to silence.

Tradition is one of those many elements of human destiny that should never have been named. This is not an injuction of modesty, nor of a taste for mystery, nor of that cowardly fear or that lack of faith which leads men to tend sentimentally their deepest attachments without daring to bring them before the light of the mind. But to name tradition is to remove it from oneself, to set it *before one*, to make it opaque as any object proposed or imposed. It is to place oneself outside — perhaps even the better to choose it — in exemplary fashion. It is to lose its free presence the better to view its contents — customs, principles, examples, values — displayed in the past. At once, all is different. Tradition appears, among others, as *a* tradition which by chance happens to be mine.

To be in a tradition is not to exclude another, but simply, to use Jaspers' words, to accept an *'ultimate situation,'* a datum like one's birth, epoch, or mortality. To choose a tradition, even that in which one was reared, is, on the contrary, to exclude others. Once labeled, objectified, surrendered to the relativity of history, tradition denies other traditions. No longer tacit, it defends itself, it attacks, it enlists force on its side, it becomes both fragile and aggressive. As it becomes more explicit, it gradually loses its *meaning,* in the vectorial, dynamic sense that indicates the very direction of time from a past to a future. Instead of remaining the welcoming simplicity of the present-past for the future, a way of change and of inventing the newness of the future, tradition then bends back upon itself, takes itself for its object, rejects all else. Tradition dies, a mere flower of rhetoric in speeches and ideologies. It no longer serves life, but keeps others from living.

Henceforth, freedom seeks its salvation, not in tradition, but against tradition, in rebellion. Freedom, excused from the burden of inventing the future, finds the battle against what is sufficient. The past destroyed assumes a futurist value. Destruction is equated with creation. To shatter structures and forms is already to create the society and the manners of tomorrow. Strange faith in the creative virtue of sheer negation. Freedom is so absorbed in its battle against tradition that it finds itself wholly turned toward the past and embedded there. The past imposes on freedom its categories and its laws even as freedom destroys it. Only the inventive life of tradition, tending toward the future, is lost upon this freedom.

This was the situation when Jaspers created his philosophy. Tradition had long been labeled, attacked, justified. So Jaspers spoke of tradition. But for him there was no question either of reducing it to hardened contents bequeathed to history or finding fulfillment in a revolt against tradition. Going against the tide, he undertook to rediscover, behind the traditional figures, the living tradition, in order to replant freedom in its soil of history. His entire achievement may be viewed as a set of "spiritual tasks" in order to return, with the aid of the past, to the living sources, to the lost treasure without which the future is uninventive, arid, and dying — with the aid of a past which, on the other hand, is itself but a heap of sand if it does not serve to invent the future.

What do these spiritual tasks consist of? It is a question of studying the objective elements of tradition, not for their own sake, but for the sake of rediscovering through them the inspiration which nurtured them. Sacred writings, myths, rites, dogmas, principles, values, all are assimilated through a sort of give-and-take in depth which goes beyond their historical peculiarities and unites with what they reveal of the human condition as such. Make no mistake, however; it is not a question of rationalizing them, of substituting for a supposedly "symbolic" cloak of language an abstract interpretation more general and more worthy of the attention of modern man; nor is it a matter of softening their edges to render them more liberal and thus more acceptable to common good sense. Quite the contrary, the "refractory" aspects are often the loci of energy which give to the rest its import and vitality. To be sure, these must be distinguished from any historically conditioned oddity, superstition, vulgarism, and magic. A frequently valuable criterion is that the points of genuine depth, once deciphered, can yield no empirical result, no achievement, no victory, no gain, no power over earthly things, but turn the toiling of the soul upon itself, upon its arbitrary and frivolous desires.

"Cipher-script" is Jaspers' phrase. He who "deciphers" the content of tradition exhausts it in its particularities, and at the point of greatest density he transcends them without losing them, as they come to assume their true meaning or rather their true strength. This method differs from both liberal and dogmatically literal interpretations. It stays close to the letter to elicit from it the human presence, and the result is a more receptive welcome than any universalistic tolerance. At the same time, the letter subsists through the result, as the verbal body of the poem subsists through the poetic experience; for the letter of tradition, like the letter of poetry, is richer than any spiritual accomplishment, and keeps alive inexhaustible potentialities. For the living subject "deciphering" tradition does not stand before a thing in all its irrevocable inertia; he hears, rather, a language which varies with as it transcends history. The variations of this language are not due to any distorting vision of the subject, but to the fact that tradition actually speaks a different language, modifies itself for him, according to the way in which the subject listens, the moment of history in which he is situated (as a person may change to some extent, and often in decisive fashion, according to his interlocutor) . Tradition has no self-sufficient existence from the past. It is, rather, that which lives and ceaselessly transforms itself according to the gaze of the present which falls upon it, and at every time tradition communicates a different past inviting a different present to invent the future.

The "tasks" in question consist of a to-and-fro of the self and the bequests of tradition (dogmas, myths, rites, symbols, doctrines, values, principles) , a to-and-fro whose poles are not the particular and the general, the concrete and the abstract, superstition and enlightenment, but Transcendence and *Existenz*. This means a being so wholly one that it transcends the mystery of the most concrete sign or symbol, and a being so entirely free that all its associations amount to the unpredictable re-creations of returns upon itself.

Such deciphering turns upon an essential paradox which itself assumes a ciphered meaning and therefore demands deciphering. The language of tradition always is — and must be — particular, rooted in a place, an epoch, a level of civilization, in short, in historical conditions. This is not a matter of hard but regrettable facts calling for resignation, but the very mark of authenticity, the sign that deciphering is possible, and that the spiritual task can really be achieved. In fact, this historical dependence, which in some way is to be penetrated and transcended without being lost, is the cipher of the essential character of our human condition: historicity. To speak a language not dependent on history or to treat a language as if this were so is to falsify at the source by putting oneself outside the conditions in which truth is possible for man. But to accept the historical particularity of a traditional element is to install oneself, without losing one's own present, in the present which gave birth to it and to regain communication and interaction with others who, like ourselves, have been historically determined and thus remain at once irremediably different and yet inseparable from our situation and our viewpoint. Clearly, this is a case of history, the passage of time, being abolished by its very intensity. By means of a grasp of irreducible historical differences and of the constant variation of perspectives, all men, all languages, all beliefs become contemporary. A dialogue is heard, through the extreme specificity of epochs, above centuries and millenia.

It is essential to realize how this virtually universal dialogue, above the byways of place and time, differs from the historically equable interpretation of the nineteenth century. The latter aspired to sufficient goodwill, sufficient condescension, with respect to all past tradition to reinstate it and make it live again as it had once been. The interpreter thought of himself above all as a historian. Deeply convinced that progress guaranteed his own superiority, he effaced himself before his object, ridding himself of his own prejudices the better to comprehend. He made a vacuum of himself. His research was morally committed to the sole value of truth, similar to the physicist in the laboratory. But he had equally little moral association with the object of his research as did the man of science. Whereas the dialogue of Jaspers requires that the interpreter, far from being an "impartial observer," commit himself in his research with everything which he is as a human being, with everything he believes, and that, instead of proffering to the past the docile emptiness of a mirror, he debate with the past as an equal, without concessions. From this debate there will issue no summing-up, no eclectic result, no compromise — in fact, no spiritual acquisition which could be formulated and transmitted. The meaning of the debate is in the debate itself, the event which it is, the way in which it involves Transcendence without possessing it, the energy with which it modifies the terms it opposes, the respect and the importance which it displays for the human particularity where truth is refracted.

But to recognize, accept, cherish, undergo historical particularity as the fundamental element of our common human condition, and to establish communication by and through it rather than in spite of it, is simultaneously to grasp and to lose the inner nature of all tradition. We grasp it by consenting to the most profound experience of its historical particularity and committing to it one's inner being. We lose it because an understanding of the necessity and meaning of any particularity is to make this particularity an impossibility *for oneself* in its incomparable uniqueness. It is to place oneself outside all tradition — even if, like Jaspers, one maintains for oneself the tradition of living in a tradition.

In a social body, an effective tradition is one which incarnates itself in sacred writings, in institutions, in examples. It thus imposes at the level of habits its rules and its hierarchies. It establishes an order, limits the permissible, demands whatever is necessary for it, without justifying itself. Because it does not justify itself it is able to exercise sufficient authority over individuals to keep in abeyance the violent appetites and passions, or at least to limit their destructiveness. But, when I say that it exercises authority over individuals, I express myself badly: it constitutes them, it is an integral part of their being. It gives to their essential ways of behaving an air of imperious evidence. The conventional formula of the most undistinguished conformism: "that is done" or "that is not done" has a profound meaning. Justifications come later, and only then does the self-evident seem weak. It is almost as if the transparency of arguments could not do without a density, thick and opaque, in which conduct is rooted.

An Italian friend of mine who spent seventeen years in various prisons of Mussolini described to me his torment of several days when he learned that, to be freed, he needed only to sign a declaration of his submission to the regime. "Do not imagine anything heroic about my not doing so," he said. "I simply couldn't." Thus does tradition function when it is strong and deep. And doubtless my friend, revolutionary and violently non-conformist, would be pained that I consider his behavior an example of purest tradition.

Roderick had to kill the father of Chimene; there was no question about it. For us, today, this is far less obvious. My Italian friend would contest it. Antigone had to throw earth upon the corpse of Polynice. But someone might consider this suicide and hold that her duties toward her living sister should have taken precedence over those to her dead brother. That which renders Phaedra more great than infamous is the fatal, irremediable nature of her passion. But one of my students asked me one day at school: "I don't understand. If she knows that nothing can come of her and Hippolytus, why does she cling to him?" He was placing himself outside a tradition, perhaps a dying one, which valued love as an unjustifiable absolute. But perhaps he was also placing himself outside of any traditional mode of valuing.

Nevertheless, perhaps my Italian friend, Roderick, Antigone, and Phaedra would understand each other notwithstanding the verdict of absurdity which each could pass on the others. They have something in common. They are anchored in the absolute requirement of a tradition. Perhaps they would destroy each other by each pursuing blindly *his* blinding evidence. My student, if he has really emerged from the tragic grotto in which resound absolute demands in order to practice only the technique of adjusting means to vital ends, can no longer understand any of them, nor tragedy in general. Jaspers, however, would understand them all, and each as if he were all, each as each understands himself.

But what would he do? Above all, what would he teach, if he had before him, not students already immersed in such-and-such a tradition — or lost to all tradition — but children, children with eyes enormous and open, expecting everything from him? The answer seems evident: he would bring them up in the tradition which is in his eyes fundamental for the West: the Biblical tradition. This is the tradition that posits the existence of an unique God, transcendent, present, rejected in the world, to whom man is, willingly or not, committed, and by whom the absolute, whether we will it or not, enters the human drama. But what would be the particular visage, the exact demand, of this absolute? One of the visages, one of the demands, of the Biblical tradition (for this tradition is multifarious, and each assists the other to surpass the exclusiveness which would render it opaque to Transcendence) is exclusiveness. Yet exclusiveness as such must be understood and accepted. Here enters that untranslatable little German word: "jeweils." The object of faith (the visage of the absolute) is *jeweils einzig,* that is to say, "each time unique." But how prevent such a thought from actually exceeding these diverse unities and escaping the proper perspective which takes one of these as its point of departure? What is more difficult: how prevent a fruitless escape, since the escaping thought recognizes the ciphered meaning, the ontological necessity of unity, and nothing can further instruct it in this regard? "I am not anything. I am of air."

The child asks if the Bible is an unique book, if only there did God speak to man, if Jesus Christ was God on earth, present only once. For him, if there is only one God, this is the same as to believe in *that* sole God. The forms of the sect, the texts of the prayers, could they be different? And in the moral region, when one teaches him what is permitted, what is forbidden, and what is demanded, can one give him moral cultivation by making him understand that the essential thing is that something be permitted, forbidden, and demanded — the something being, moreover, variable rather than specific? Can one say of the values which one tries to make him love that he may replace them by others so long as he prizes *one* (categorically, not hypothetically) above his own life and above any of his desires?

The child puts simple questions to which he expects a reply of 'Yes' or 'No'. Or rather, every action by an adult constitutes for him a reply more efficacious and more profound than any other kind. In the religious domain, for example, many children in our Western countries find themselves in an ambiguous situation. Their parents, whatever their sect, send them to religious instruction, etc. Eventually they see to it that their children observe the prescriptions of the priests and monitors. But they themselves abstain. They are not hostile to religion; they appreciate its educative powers in the moral domain, sometimes in the poetic or metaphysical domain. They wish their child to benefit by this support in the trials of life. Only, in one way or another, they themselves remain short of or beyond their Church. They scarcely accede at all to its practices any longer. They have ceased to exist on the religious plane, or their religion survives without a Church. The child learns that religious practices are necessary, that to abstain from going to mass on Sunday, for example, is a sin. His parents send him, but, without a word of disrespect or irony, they do not attend. This implicit denial, stripped of any aggressive air, can weigh heavily on the child. It proves that one *can* do without the Church and mass. Here we touch on a point at which the defense of the non-sectarian public school — as apparently so impartial — conceals a sophistry after all: to abstain from any practice or position with regard to religion is to prove *in action,* more convincingly than by a demonstration, that it is possible to do without it, and to make of religion, at least in the sense understood by the Churches, an optional thing, thus denying its very essence. I do not wish to assert in any way that the public school is to be rejected and that we must return to sectarian schools — the problem is extremely complex and involved in all the political, social, economic, and ideological structures of our times. I only wish to underscore that this matter is not so simple as some believe or would have us believe and that the so-called sovereign impartiality of public educational institutions with respect to sects is not experienced to be such by believers.

The child in question can take only two attitudes. He may align the religious practices imposed upon him with the various obligations which mysteriously befall children — whereas grown-ups are free of them. He is in danger of developing the feeling that religion is only good for controlling children — later, he may come to think, to control the people. Or, on the other hand, he may take his religious instruction quite seriously, and the abstention of his parents will assume in his eyes a tragic character, which might give birth to conflicts whose consequences are too remote and ramified to be predictable.

It is also possible that to spare their child such problems, the parents will submit to the same discipline as he does. But I do not believe in the effectiveness of such attempts. No one is more aware than a child of the true or fictitious nature of a situation or attitude. This is, incidentally, the principal difficulty of education in general. Good will, mere will, or virtue, are not enough. Heart, body, and mind must be in harmony. In broken families, for example, the sacrifices agreed upon to keep up appearances before the child do not generally bear the desired fruits: the child does not understand, but he becomes nervous, difficult, gets hay-fever or an inexplicable cough. And it can happen that if, on the contrary, he is tortured by frequent scenes, he will transcend it all, thanks to the very explosiveness of the conflicts around him, because nothing hidden can weigh upon him. This kind of instinct functions in all areas, and in particular in the religious domain. If so many pastors' sons, for example, become militant atheists, it is not simply, as is banally said, "out of reaction to their environment." Rather, they were bound to feel, as children, that the professional obligations of their father obliged him to act as if his inner being were always maintained at the level of fervor and faith, whereas this level, in comparison to the course of a man's life, can be attained only occasionally, at privileged moments. Thus, there had to be days during which the words and the attitudes of the pastor lacked substantial support, inner presence, and there was more in the expressions than in the being who expressed himself. Children, to be sure, understand none of this. But they are extraordinarily sensitive to it. And when that happens, they hate. The same hate, the same imbalance, the same challenge, the same passionate distancing often occurs among the children of writers and, in general, of artists, when they experience that mysterious revulsion before the disparity between the expression and the being. Therefore I do not believe that the parents can resolve the problem by subjecting themselves externally to the ritual and dogmas of the sect in which they rear their children.

Jaspers would doubtless support me on this point. Moreover, what he calls "tradition" in the religious domain is never this or that sect, but the "Biblical tradition" stripped of its particularisms, its shortnesses and its pretensions, recalled to the essential humility of man in the grip of the greatness of God. (And well do I know that this very expression, "religious domain," already rings false to a man of faith, that it emits a note entirely external to what it would stand for, and that in some way so empties it of all substance as to constitute almost a negation.) And doubtless it is possible to practice within the embrace of any sect whatever that very deepening, that deciphering of particularities, of dogmas, of rites, which ends by rejoining none other than that Biblical tradition — that *Biblical religion,* Jaspers frequently says — in its essentials. But then, should the religious education of the child be the discovery and the art of the deciphering of those signs, charged with historical particularity, of the unique Transcendence? Or should such apprenticeship follow upon a "naïve" period of adherence to *a* particular tradition considered as unique — an adhesion whose religious substance would continue then to nourish the adult's more open, more extensive "deciphering?" In the first case, I must say that I have not found in the sects which continue today the Biblical tradition which might provide such a religious formation; and even supposing I found it, I doubt whether inculcated since childhood it could find an adherence either sufficiently rooted in the fiber of being or sufficiently communal to exert a profound practical influence on the lives of individuals and groups. And, in the second case, the crucial problem appears to me to be that of transmission: we are all bathed, willy-nilly, in a social atmosphere saturated with beliefs which are no longer ours, but which were those of our parents or our grandparents. A mere undisputed adherence to such-and-such a religious or moral credo is not very far away in the past. But, from generation to generation — one might say, from year to year — this saturation tends to disappear, leaving a wildness virgin and inaccessible. In the years 1938-39 we all ripened for war. The acceptance of war, the will for war conquered each of us before conquering on the diplomatic and military terrain. In the succeeding years we ripened for the bombardment of open cities and civilian populations. And a people subjected to a different kind of training ripened for torture and crematory ovens. A third of the world is ripening at this moment for a permanent regime of terror, of decreed truth, of forced labor — while the remainder, as a consequence, ripens each day for the atomic bomb. Yet the ten commandments are still taught. It is true that, at the level of history, they apparently have never hindered very much. But those few limitations, those constraints, which, in collective and private life, they have maintained all the same, even if only by imposing the necessity of certain forms, of certain justifications, of certain hypocrisies — who will preserve these, who will transmit these, when no one will be able *sincerely* to teach their literal demands? Despite the commandments, Jesus defended the adulteress. He did not say she had not sinned. "Let him who is without sin throw the first stone." But in the case of Isolde, one no longer knows: did she sin? There was the philter. And perhaps her marriage with King Mark was not a true marriage, perhaps God had not united them? Transcendence remains concealed, unknown, beyond human efforts — so frivolously pious — to make it enter into life. Interpretations begin, symbols, casuistry. The Catholic Church defends itself, proclaims the indisputable, mysterious, yet literal efficacy of the sacrament. But that is no longer a part of Jaspers' "Biblical religion." Perhaps all of us — and more than anyone Jaspers, in whom is incarnated, full, living, and free, a whole tradition — are like the children of rich men who live unknowingly off a still sumptuous inheritance (while we think it already exhausted). Perhaps we are going to leave to our descendents a misery far deeper than we can even imagine.

Considered not in itself but reinstated in our world of today, so strangely attacked from the outside and undermined from the inside, the attitude of Jaspers toward tradition seems to me the only possible one, and at the same time, perhaps the only helpful one, — and perhaps pernicious as well. I have nothing else to suggest and when I cast doubt upon it, when I suspect it, when I sense in it a possible Trojan horse, it is myself whom I suspect, I who could not help opening to this horse the gates of the city.

Let us try to specify as closely as possible one aspect of this menace which hangs over us in order to see better the probable effectiveness — or rather, the *possible* effectiveness — of "tradition" as Jaspers visualizes it.

One might say that all of human life takes place between two poles: the pole of *being,* that is, everything which is given whether outwardly or inwardly, everything which the subject is without having chosen it or made it; and the pole of *doing,* that is, everything which is on the contrary chosen, willed, made by the subject. The subject chooses neither his epoch, nor his natural surroundings, nor his heredity, nor his physical make-up, nor his human condition, nor many other factors decisive for his life here below. Each of these is, in Jaspers' terms, an ultimate situation. On the other hand, each of these givens only really becomes a humanly efficacious factor through activity of the subject himself, by his acceptance, his refusal, his particular valuations, his way of giving meaning to an ultimate situation. To be and to do, substance and freedom, are inextricably interwoven. At every instant in his history the subject finds himself in a *given* situation, in a network of facts and obligations which in part he has produced because of what he is, and which in part he is because he has produced them.

Now the following has taken place among us: the *doing* has bit by bit devoured *being* in our consciousness of ourselves. This does not mean that the subject has actually succeeded in conquering, surpassing, or even abolishing an ultimate situation. But everything which he does not himself create, everything which he does not choose of his own free will, he detaches from himself: it is not himself, it is no longer himself. Everything given by destiny is an accidental garment, rather than the skin, the flesh, the skeleton of his being. He throws into the exterior everything which does not depend on his own decision in order to rediscover his original, even "originary," purity.

Let us look at some examples. Not so long ago a man felt his social or national membership as a constitutive element of his being. He *was* son of a clockmaker, of a peasant, of a philosopher, or of a duke. The son of a clockmaker thought — rightly or wrongly — that he felt at the focus of his gaze, at the tips of his fingers, and all the way into the operations of his mind, the life of an especially precise kind of sensibility. The son of a peasant believed that he had an instinct for the development of living things, a more assured patience, a faculty better rooted to collaborate with the slowness of time and the great laws of nature. The son of the philosopher found within himself a characteristic tendency to dissect the appearances of experience or of reasoning and to discover, beyond them, their meaning. The son of a duke thought that an imperious power was measured out by the very rhythm of his heartbeats and inscribed in the image which God made of his existence on earth. Thus, when the regal state of a king is threatened in Shakespeare, it is the question of to be or not to be that is posed.

To us, a dethroned yet still able king is no longer astonishing. Rank, the trade of the father, the family circle, all that is more or less tossed into zoology, heredity. The same is true of ethnic or national membership. That is all "outside," "the converse of freedom," that which determines human beings in so far as they are not themselves and are content to be what they are rather than to create, that is to say, in Sartre's language, to be what they are not. The essential being of man is not to be, but to *invent himself* by tossing into the "world" and its determinism everything which has been *given* him.

The rejection goes deeper. In the course of his life the subject does not cease, even as he invents, even by the very act of invention, to deposit factors doomed to have determining effects. Take, for example, the special case of a man whose family and economic conditions do not impose on him a certain profession. He chooses of his own free will. But as soon as this profession has become his, it falls back among the data of the external world. At once it ceases to be himself, peeling off him like an old skin. Allow me to refer here to Sartre's analysis of the waiter in *L'Etre et le Néant*.* This figure constantly separates himself from his function, he is a waiter "in the mode of not being a waiter." And this

* Translator's note: cf. 98-100 (Paris: Gallimard, 1943).

is not the case because in Sartre's eyes this profession is for some reason less interesting than others. The analysis remains valid for any social function whatsoever. Moreover, it is valid for anything which, created or chosen in a remote or near past, survives to the present moment.

Bergson was not far from an identification of the being of the subject with the living presence of his entire past. The intuition by which the subject apprehends himself plunges — metaphorically — into an indistinct, entangled, but thick depth of memory. Intuition is a gluttonous faculty, and this basic gluttony of a mode of thought so refined in its language yet substantially imprisoned in its final plunges, doubtless explains in part the increasing attraction which Catholicism came to exert over it.

No one has gone further in the opposite direction than Sartre. The subject brings himself into being by the very act which wrenches him from every given, hence from all the past, by means of that which separates him from everything which *is*, that is to say, by means of that slice of nothingness which isolates him from things, from facts, from traditions, and from all the continuities engendered by his own choices.He constitutes his own being by being none of all that, by creating the nothing that preserves him from being, *by being that nothing*. The ideally free subject is a nothingness of substance, a pure *doing* of nothingness. Oddly enough, by most unexpected pathways we rediscover certain theological notions, but now applied to man, as if man, having ceased to attack God (since "God is dead") took the same paths to his latest victim: man himself. In fact, according to the Judaeo-Christian tradition, God is only God if he creates *ex nihilo*. According to the doctrine of Sartre, man is only man, that is to say, free, if he creates *ex nihilo*.

In speaking thus, I do not think I am falling into an error already too widespread which I am attempting rather to denounce. It is not true that Sartre uses this nothing which separates the past from the present to reduce the subject to an irresponsible point for whom each new instant would secure him a new moral virginity. This interpretation is mistaken. On the contrary, the link between the subject and his past — that specific link which renders the subject his past in the mode of not being it — is never broken, and at the moment of death, when the interstice of nothingness separating the future-present from the past is abolished, it is his entire past which becomes the definitive being of the deceased. Far from facilitating matters or constituting a moral escape-hatch, the "nothingness" which for Sartre guarantees the discontinuity of time serves to corner the subject for a free choice, integral and without benefit of excuse. The past furnishes no alibi, no extenuating circumstance. The responsibility is total, ontological, untouched by any "psychology." It remains nonetheless true that the subject realizes himself only in pure, point-like nothingness, when he withdraws from all memory and all substance by a pure *doing* without substance. It is the inverse of Bergson: here the language seems to embed itself into the very flesh of the concrete, but the sights of this exploration are trained upon a refusal, a fanatic negation, a perfect nothingness. There is a kind of horror of substance: substance is not an inexhaustible plenitude, but a kind of quicklime.

One can see throughout a surprising survival of theological categories applied to man, and of a deep-rooted Cartesianism. We find not only the idea of creation *ex nihilo,* but also that of discontinuous time and ceaselessly renewed creation. Freedom is asserted as an absolute energy which is absolutely unrestrained. It is not without memory, but recollections are necessary only so that one can say: "I am not you." They are a body which is constantly rejected.

Tradition is both internal and external. It stands over the subject as an authority and is at the same time constitutive of his being in an organic, indistinct, dense manner. It is an external given internalized, and what is worse, internalized *as a fact,* which means that its very internalization is something given. The thinking of our times, which doubtless finds one of its extreme articulations in Sartre, necessarily condemns all tradition by rejecting the substance in favor of a pure doing, by setting aside the past in favor of an integral creation. This is indeed a Cartesian development: Descartes, for the sake of pure will and pure thought, ascribed to the spatial machine the entire confused zone of affectivity; our contemporaries, for the sake of pure freedom, ascribe to social determinism the confused zone of tradition and memory. Just as the abstract painter no longer needs to find a resemblance to any object whatsoever, so the man who wishes to be free today no longer needs to adjust his behavior to any traditional morality, but has to invent or create a morality by each of his actions.

All well and good — but there is something wrong. This uncompromising rigor, which is both rationalistic and puritanical, destroys itself. For, though it is quite true that if the subject *is* something, his freedom in some sense cancels itself out and merely follows from his substance (here again, moreover, we find applied to man the theological query concerning the determinations of

God), yet if the subject is not anything — or even, to repeat Sartre's phrase, if the subject *is nothing* — only a functioning, not a freedom, is conceivable in this vacuum. The freedom of a substance is a possibility full of mystery; but the freedom of a nothing is simply an absurdity. Such freedom reduces to the functioning of an electronic brain.

And it is scarcely a matter of chance that the other extreme philosophical expression of our times is Stalinism — a philosophy with which the former extreme, moreover, seeks some affinities and with which it tries, though vainly until now, to communicate. Stalinism stands for a totally functioning system. For Sartre, on the plane of freedom there are only possibilities — never being. For Stalinism there is no being either, and possibilities are once and for all gathered into the unique necessity of the universal and historical machine. Either possibilities for a subject who "is nothing," or the mechanical order for a whole in which there are no persons: such are the alternatives offered us by these contemporary humanists. But if the subject for whom, according to the former hypothesis, possibilities exist, is himself nothing, why not prefer rather the unbroken order of a competent Engineer?

Thus, without too many detours, the lost tradition leaves the subject and his rigorous freedom in the Stalinist dead-end of total immurement.

How locate Jaspers against this background? An absurd question. He cannot be located. He is, through all the snares and temptations of the period, the free movement which approaches them, confronts them, embraces them, knows them, and with a kind of incorruptible sureness, transcends them without rejecting them or losing them. There is only one rejection, and that one is categorical and beyond any possible compromise: the rejection of immurement, closure, which for Jaspers destroys man's relation to his neighbor, to truth, to history, to himself, to Transcendence. The closed — dogma, fanaticism, magical or scientific superstition — is a final call to the free subject for human comprehension, for a last attempt for the sake of the most profound of all traditions, that which teaches man that his fellow contains something precious — something more than precious: something necessary. This final effort is to try to discover the ciphered meaning of the system in which the other is enclosed, to vanquish his apparent literalness, to show him, if possible, his perspective on Transcendence. But further one cannot go.

For totalitarian structures of all leanings there is no more irreducible enemy than this receptive and yet substantial thinking, secured against emptiness by a tradition in which the faith in truth is so unshakable that it rejects all illusion and exposes itself to every risk. It neither ignores nor despises the totalitarian myths (knowing the inevitable and necessary place of myth on the human horizon) , but deciphers them, grants them their share of transparency, reinstates them in history and in tradition, and by giving them their ciphered meaning removes their constraining power and disarms them. The maniacal sleepwalker of an exclusive ideology, now touched, awakens, passes his hand across his forehead, and sees once more the true confusion of things human.

But in a world so greatly menaced and tempted as ours, what can be the *social* effectiveness of a tradition like that which Jaspers tries to revive, a non-particular tradition open to all particularities? If Stalinist thought drives the mind into the dead-end of total enclosure, may we not fear that Jaspers abandons us before mortal dangers in the dead-end of a total openness in which spirits beyond temptation may well breathe, but not huge cities of men?

To be sure, Jaspers' thought is capable of bringing forth, here and there, free beings, or a least beings who will to be free because they prefer truth to a formula, Transcendence to a doctrine. For them and through them are saved, in a certain manner, all human traditions. Nourished by many traditions, concrete and precise traditions, which they seek to replace and to relive in the epoch where they existed in full force, in order thus to rediscover by penetrating history their permanent meaning, they remain associated, nourished, reassured, through all traditions by tradition. And this homeland, this paternal dwelling from which no exile can eject them and in which substance and freedom cease mysteriously to exclude each other, guarantees forever that they will never become fearful vagabonds nostalgic for the shelter of prisons. Open and linked together, open by their very associations, linked to all through space and time by their very openness, they rely on an absolute exigency in which everything is grounded, even the particular exigency of a specific tradition. Thus Socrates, who chose to die under a verdict which he scorned.

But paradoxically Jaspers' thinking, prepared to accept any particularity of tradition to give it its ciphered effectiveness, may be self-condemned to social ineffectiveness. It makes more and more difficult, and ultimately impossible, the allegiance of society to a given tradition, definite and particular. And to learn to decipher the myths of religious or moral tradition is to make impossible for oneself the creation of myths. The life of Jaspers and his teaching still benefit from a background of tradition which was transmitted as well as possible above or rather beneath two world wars; or rather, not so well, but vaguely, diffusely, often in scorn and contempt — yet always giving value and power to certain words, certain images, certain exigencies. I have heard Jaspers speak in the classroom of the precious substance of tradition safeguarded today by the Churches. But to what avail if, on the other hand, to teach the art of deciphering and the non-literalness of all traditions amounts to making impossible collective life within *one* of these traditions? — if it becomes impossible to simply transmit tradition without hypocrisy? And how, then, defend oneself henceforth against that leanness of mere doing, that hemorrhaging of substance which threatens us on all sides? Finally, if the definite precepts of every moral tradition must lose their objective prescriptive rigor to become the ciphers of a transcendent and rigorously personal experience of morality, how resist collectively, in numbers, the appeal of anonymous innocence proffered by totalitarian machinery?

I realize that universal history, by taking place on our globe, beckons and obliges us to go beyond local frames of reference, and only a line of thought like that of Jaspers, no doubt, enables us to conceive of this expansion without a loss of the particular traditions. Thus would that leap be accomplished of which Bergson spoke, by which one goes beyond every social group, however large, to rejoin at one stroke one's person and all of humanity. But does one thus find fullness or emptiness? Neither emptiness, nor fullness, but *possible* fullness. Is this enough to ground and safeguard a society which safeguards it? — to solve the daily problems posed by the education of children, the transmission of the substance of tradition, the maintenance of some rules without which man is lost before he can stop to think? Can a possible plenitude become the foundation of a univeral tradition?

Perhaps Jaspers, who knows the cost and the fragility of the tradition which he incarnates and the violence of the threats which hang over us, will answer these questions.

JEANNE HERSCH

PARIS, FRANCE

19

Paul Ricoeur

THE RELATION OF JASPERS' PHILOSOPHY
TO RELIGION*

KARL JASPERS is today one of those rare philosophers who attempt to maintain a difficult position between positive religions, with their *Credos* and confessional structures, and atheistic humanisms derived from Auguste Comte, Karl Marx, or Nietzsche. His position is the more difficult for appearing at a time in which, on the one hand, Christian devotion is returning to its sources, ruling out all cultural contaminations, and rediscovering in this way how foreign is its heritage to Hellenism and Western culture, and a time in which, on the other hand, the great humanisms inherited from the nineteenth century also are pressing to the outer-most limits of their intentions and their pretensions with the growing awareness of a tragic risk presiding over an existence without God. In short, Jaspers writes at a time when his cross-examination of religion is promoted only by the atheist and his evocation of a divine Transcendence at the root of human existence is corroborated only by the devout.

The task proposed in this essay is to clarify this equivocal situation. Karl Jaspers' opposition to religion will be envisaged first in its dual character of (I) a protest by freedom and by the commitment of *Existenz* to this world, and (II) an emergence of a truly philosophical faith. Reflecting then on this "philosophical faith," we shall see (III) how it appropriates for itself and raises to the rank of "metaphysical speculation" that religious faith over which it has triumphed. Finally, we shall attempt to pose some *personal questions* (IV) regarding Jaspers' conception of religion.

I. *Religion and Freedom*

The type of philosophy exemplified by the thought of Karl Jaspers cannot permit a critique of religion to remain a merely auxiliary part of his reflections. The philosopher *as philosopher*

---

* Translated from the original French manuscript by Forrest W. Williams.

cannot make an abstraction of the position *from which* he addresses religion. Philosophy cannot be neutral. Why? Because wittingly or not every philosophy of *Existenz* stands on the very territory of religious inquiry, more precisely, of Christian inquiry. The existent interrogated by a philosophy of *Existenz* is not the *I think* of Kantian philosophy whose unity is responsible for the possibility of objective representation, nor is he a *form* of reality which, like any *"form,"* cannot be corrupted or lost; rather, he is precisely that being who is always in question, who may lose himself or gain himself, who is in danger, who must "surge forth," and who can "forget himself" in things, in happiness, in politics. The proximity of the *" 'existential'* question" to the "religious question" is such that the rejection of religion is a serious act, a crucial decision of the philosophy of *Existenz* which forces it to discover arduously and single-handedly the path of Transcendence without religion. Despite the considerable differences in philosophical context, Karl Jaspers faces religion from a standpoint and with a feeling similar to Plotinus, Bruno, Spinoza, Kant; that is to say, he is a *religious thinker* fighting for the faith of the devout.

It is quite notable that Karl Jaspers' anti-religious *motivation,* like the wholesale criticism of *all* transendence by atheistic existentialism, originates on the terrain of freedom. Jaspers' principal work, *Philosophie,* was written in 1932, hence prior to Albert Camus' *Mythe de Sisyphe* and Jean-Paul Sartre's *L'Être et le Néant.* Rereading Jaspers after these powerful atheists, one will be struck in hindsight by the parentage common to certain aspects of his criticism, strictly aimed at religion and retaining a philosophy of Transcendence, and their radical critique of all religious and philosophical faith. We shall return to this point in our concluding remarks.

But this protest by free inquiry, or on behalf of the risk attached to the historical adventure of man, does not exhaust his critique; there shines through a conception of Transcendence and of its relation to the world different from the religious conception. This second aspect of the cross-examination of religion is entirely foreign to French existentialism. That which comes to expression during this test of religion is another faith, a purely philosophical faith. This second aspect, already discernible in Jaspers' *Philosophie* of 1932, has become increasingly pronounced in his subsequent works and finds fulfillment in the great work of 1947, *Von der Wahrheit.* Let us consider first the cross-examination of religion in its initial aspect.

Religion as seen by Karl Jaspers turns two faces toward man: the visage of mysticism and the visage of authority. Both "petrify" freedom.

On the one hand, religion presents itself mystically to man, that is to say, as vertical communication, direct and immediate, in which man absorbs himself and loses himself in the Supreme Thou. Between this religious immediacy and the human quality of freedom Jaspers sees no possibility of harmony. Mysticism is charged with being suicidal.[1] It is true that the suicide has its grandeur, a nocturnal grandeur — the grandeur of "the unconditioned" — which reminds us that life is neither the supreme reality nor the supreme value. But suicide, which serves in this case as an "analogon" to mysticism, signifies that the tension of *Existenz* in a world of things and men is broken by suppressing the worldly pole. The mystic, like the suicide, flees: the latter flees nowhere, the former flees beyond, to the other side (*Jenseits*), to a *Hinterwelt* which "doubles" for this world. Mysticism is the "negative decision," the "negation of the world" (*Weltverneinung*).

This elementary process of religion (which is located in Book II of *Philosophie,* devoted to illumination of *Existenz* [*Existenzerhellung*], and not in Book III, devoted to Transcendence) is a warning of what is at stake: the meaning of human existence. Mysticism perverts its being-in-the-world. The world betrayed is above all the world of men; for he who communicates with God as with a Supreme Thou has left the grim game in which we have only the advice of our friends and the debates of "horizontal" communication to illuminate and invigorate our choices. In a way, Transcendence is not another word alongside the word of man, to which we might oppose it. It is not even an immediate inspiration which could relieve us in our choices and would furnish a sort of absolute alibi for our responsibility among men at the heart of man's history.

Confronting mysticism, philosophy asserts itself as *ethics,* if we understand by ethics, broadly speaking, a philosophy of human conduct in the world, a philosophy which renounces religious immediacy. "Every relation to God that does not simultaneously transpire as '*existential*' communication, which alone can give it truth, is not only intrinsically suspect, but also a betrayal of *Existenz*."[2]

In the monumental work of 1947, *Von der Wahrheit,* this opposition between ethics and mysticism is presented once more, in a different fashion, in the framework of the admirable discussion

[1] *Philosophie,* 560ff. [2] *Ibid.,* 528.

devoted to "awareness of the tragic" *(das tragische Wissen)*.[3] The dramatic masterpieces of humanity depict the greatness of misfortune and the greatness of man in misfortune. "At the edge of doom, the tragic heroes act out the pattern of tragic reality."[4] But the tragic is prematurely relieved and surmounted by revealed religion. This is comparable to the apathy of Stoicism, which immerses the tragic in a soothing lucidity of indifference. "Christian salvation opposes tragic knowledge."[5] This is the reason that "no genuinely Christian tragedy can exist"[6] and that "a Christian is bound to misunderstand . . . Shakespeare."[7] No experience is radically tragic for the Christian. The fault becomes the *felix culpa* which makes salvation possible. The calamity of Christ puts an end to the radical tragedy of defeat. Not that the tragic is blind to redemption: rather, there inheres in tragedy a "tragic deliverance"[8] which is opposed to religious salvation. This is not a redemption objectified in a sacred account and guarded by a Church, but a metaphysical depth which saves in the tragic and by the tragic, viz., "in the face of the tragic [authentic] Being is revealed in foundering."[9] This is not the victory of another world over this one. "Tragedy disappears to the degree that an equitable settlement is possible."[10]

In this initial development Karl Jaspers prolongs a Kierkegaardian theme and simultaneously turns it against its author. In Kierkegaard for the first time, communication with God could only be "indirect," remote from union and blessedness. But in Kierkegaard there is precisely a proof, as it were, by the absurd, that the passage from "the ethical stage" to "the religious stage" means suffering, sacrifice, the ruin of existence. "I am in a deep sense a miserable individuality who, since the furthest era, has been nailed to one sorrow or another in an agony which touched on madness."[11] In *Stages on Life's Way,* Kierkegaard consciously places the negative, the religious calamity of the martyr higher than the positive, the ethical accomplishment of marriage. It is true that one could cite numerous passages by Kierkegaard on joy, peace, and infinite happiness. But Kierkegaard moved further and further from the hope that at the crowning moment of faith

---

3 Cf. *Wahrheit,* 917ff. (Ed's. note: This section of *Von der Wahrheit* is available in English under the title *"Tragedy is not enough."* We shall refer to *Tragedy* whenever Ricoeur quotes passages from this part of *Wahrheit.*) *Tragedy,* 27ff.

4 *Tragedy,* 90.　　　　5 *Ibid.,* 38.　　　　6 *Ibid.*　　　　7 *Ibid.,* 39.

8 Cf. *ibid.,* 72ff.　　　　　　　　　9 *Wahrheit,* 947. *(Tragedy,* 80.)

10 Goethe (quoted by Jaspers: *Tragedy,* 86.)

11 Kierkegaard's *Journal* (1846).

God would return Isaac to Abraham, and Regina to Kierkegaard. More and more, for Kierkegaard, the "infinite movement" must be away from this life — with no return, with no hope of "reaffirmation," of Repetition. "I gradually came to know that all those really loved by God suffered in this world."[12]

Karl Jaspers looks from afar at this "negative hero" with the conviction that he sees the inimitable exception (Ausnahme). Likewise, the "absurd" celebrated by Kierkegaard — the absurdity of a man-God — heralds in Jaspers' eyes the bankruptcy of modern Christianity, both Protestant and Catholic. The "subjective thinker" invokes an impossible Christianity completely contemporary with the first apostolic testimony, beyond all justification, all continuity, and all authority. He awakens, but he transmits no thought which one can repeat. "The problem for us," declares Jaspers, "is to philosophize without being exceptions, but with our eyes on the exception."[13] That is why philosophy, here, is the return from the mystical to the ethical.

But Kierkegaard by himself is not religion, precisely because religion is a historical magnitude, stable, continuous, authoritarian. The opposition of philosophy to religion is brutal, like that of autonomy to heteronomy. To understand it one must begin with the sociological wrapping of religion, the cult which makes Transcendence into a sort of real presence. Through the cult Transcendence falls into the circle of objectivity, whose prestige Jaspers sweeps from every stage of philosophical reflection, from the objectivity of positivism, through the authority of the Hegelian State which synthesises the objectivity of the real and of the ideal, to the objectivity of a rational duty, of a ready-made ethics in which freedom would be guarded and bound. Religion is the supreme objectivity. Jaspers is here more severe than Hegel, who did not place religion among the forms of "objective Spirit," but saw in it at least a moment of "Absolute Spirit" gathering into itself an estranged form of "Objective Spirit." If Jaspers is more severe than Hegel, it is because the center of reference of Jaspers' philosophy is not Spirit, but the singular, unique existent in his "originality" (Ursprung). Henceforth, only the moment of choice, of anxious venture, of responsibility without guarantee or security, bears the stamp of authenticity.

The existent puts into question all universal validation and thus puts himself in question. He is the being who risks himself. Hence, Karl Jaspers employs a philosophy of freedom in order to reject the certainty and security of religion.

---

12 Kierkegaard's Journal (1849-1854), II, 319, Haecker.   13 Reason, 129.

All other aspects of religion are measured by the same criterion of freedom espoused and risked.

Thus, the event of revelation, which religion places at the center of the cult, appears essentially as a way of fixing or localising, hence of guaranteeing, a Transcendence which subsequently persists among men by means of authoritarian instruction. The word of God lends authority to certain human words which henceforth release the anguish of decision through an objective commandment, an objective justification, an objective consolation. In contrast to the believer, the philosopher accepts the poverty of a faith without cult, without word of God, without Church, without *objective* Transcendence. He takes freedom into his charge. He is the supreme heretic, taking the part of Galileo, of Bruno, of Spinoza, against the priests. "Whoever lives as a philosopher, without the proviso of a religious certitude, must battle internally with this possibility his whole life long."[14]

Ethics, already contrasted with mysticism, is now opposed to religious obedience. The philosopher opposes conscience to prayer: "Conscience surrenders to another power when it abandons itself to the *life of prayer* in which the godhead speaks directly."[15] Cromwell wrenched from himself, by prayer, the political decision for which his conscience lacked sufficient courage. Let man expect nothing apart from unlimited communication with other men and from the upsurge of the act in modest solitude, and let him never cover his acts with the objective authority of the Transcendence which he calls God. Jaspers' criticism of prayer effectively embodies the converging dual criticism of mystical *immediacy* and religious *authority*. Prayer claims to hear the divine voice directly and at the same time to obey an authority which undertakes responsibility. On this matter Jaspers makes no special concession to the zealot who opposes the word of God as *he* apprehends it to the word transmitted by the Church, for the zealot is no less enclosed in the enchanted circle of authority; perhaps more so, living as he does in the intimacy of an immediate subjective relationship.

The other reproaches which Jaspers directs against religion can be arranged around this dual criticism. First of all, the religious is condemned to insert itself like an enclave in the midst of the secular behavior of man. This unbuttressed condition of cult, sacrament, and prayer is due to a "real-isation" of Transcendence. Religious conduct mixes God into the to-and-fro of human conduct. Consequently, the act of the cult either ruins secular life in the joyous sacrifice of the monk or it intrudes into secular life at

---

14 *Philosophie*, 529.   15 *Ibid.*

the price of a hypocritical uneasiness. Moreover, it is a general characteristic of the miracle to signal the invasion into this world of the beyond, and to remain like an intruder. The Church, too, is a great sociological enclave, in humanity, and the unbeliever is in turn banished from it or absorbed against his will.

If it is true that "the cult is the way to avoid the burden of freedom,"[16] the last word is that of freedom. Philosophy is the herald of this freedom: freedom unauthorised, without institutions, without schools, without authorities, and always in tension like a pure dialogue between two solitudes philosophizing.

But, while this criticism of religion is exalting human freedom in the face of objective authority or of the authoritarian objectivity of cult, prayer, revelation, and church, another theme rises slowly on the horizon of the critique; the theme of a *hidden divinity*. This theme will soon have to be aligned with that of freedom ventured and without guarantee. But first we must observe its emergence in the background of this biting criticism. For, a sort of wounded, shocked piety in view of the believer's familiarity with his God also sounds through these lines. This entire protest, apparently proud and arrogant, is strangely bathed in reverential love for the *hidden Transcendence*. In another passage,[17] Jaspers writes:

Prayer is an importunity which irrupts in the unfathomable: man may dare it at the height of solitude and distress, but if it has to be a daily habit, a custom acquired, it is no more than a suspicious fixation which philosophy must renounce. In the daily security of a divine proximity, relation to God would be robbed of that depth which it retains in doubt; its transcendence of the world would be suppressed at the same time as would be obtained a peace and contentment too easily purchased by *Existenz*. For divine inscrutability seems to require that man torment himself in doubt and distress.

This fine passage indicates rather well the exact inflection of a critique which exalts freedom only to acknowledge from afar a *hidden* divinity, the One who speaks only through *silence*. It is this very silence which entrusts me to myself. The voice of conscience is this very silence of the divinity.

Thus is the critique of religion to be understood as the paradoxical emergence of a *philosophical religion*.

It is "philosophical faith," not the pride of freedom, which rejects "religious faith."

This is understandable from the standpoint of the analysis of tragedy in *Von der Wahrheit*. Religion dispels the tragic. Yet Karl

[16] *Ibid.*, 567.   [17] *Ibid.*, 783.

Jaspers refuses to absolutise the tragic into a *philosophical pan-tragicism*.[18] It would be absurd for the foundation of Being to be tragic. "Tragedy resides only in the phenomena of this world. For through the tragic, something different speaks to us, something that is no longer tragic."[19]

The tragic is in the world. The tragic is man. "Tragic knowledge has its limit: it achieves no comprehensive interpretation of the world."[20] Pan-tragicism suppresses the polarity with the non-tragic and tends toward a frightening aestheticism in which the spectator "lets himself go" to exult in the absurd, in torture, in destruction as such. To philosophize is not to absolutize the tragic, but to read the transcendent being in its symbols, in the ciphered text of reality.

Because unity fails in our temporal existence, it appears to us in the guise of the tragic.

This is, however, tantamount to saying that tragedy is not absolute but belongs in the foreground. Tragedy belongs neither in the realm of Transcendence nor in the basis of all Being, but in the world of sense and time.[21]

This *hidden being* thus provides the vantage point from which must be reread the entire preceding critique of religion, which seemed to be sustained only by a vindication of free, historical *Existenz*.

II. *Religious faith and philosophical faith.*

One would look in vain for anything like a proof from Jaspers of the relation which joins *Existenz* to Transcendence. One does not gain the ideas of the world and of subjectivity in order to carry out afterward a leap from the empirical world and human subjectivity to the hidden being of Transcendence.

On this matter the structure of a book like the *Philosophie* of 1932 must not mislead one. It seems to follow a classic order of ascent: the world (Book I), the self (Book II), God, (Book III). Actually, one stands before a work of a single propulsion whose true articulations are its chapters.

In the work I called *Philosophie,* each chapter — and not the work in its totality — was conceived as a self-contained whole which must be read at one sitting and whose truth resides not in an assertion which

---

[18] Cf. *Tragedy,* 90ff.   [19] *Ibid.,* 94.

[20] *Ibid.,* 99.   [21] *Ibid.,* 104.

could be found at such-and-such a place, but can appear only through the movement of embracing the whole in a single thought.[22]

Indeed, each chapter — and each is in a way a *total part* — contains the essence of the movement which Jaspers calls *Transzendieren*. This transcending movement has the empirical world for its theater, human existence for its conscious sense, and hidden Being for its aim. From the very first pages of *Philosophie,* absolute Being is already present as the goal of philosophy.[23] From one stage to the other there are breaks; but these breaks are discoverable simultaneously, not successively; only an order of exposition displays them in an apparent succession. This is to say that the relationship of *Existenz* to Transcendence is itself preliminary to this exposition in a written work, because it is *originative*.

Our present task has a limited objective: to discern the *specifically religious note* of this movement of *Transzendieren*. To this end we shall proceed more or less in reverse, beginning with the final thesis of the work, the theory of ciphers, which we believe to be the actual religious philosophy of Jaspers. Thence we shall pass gradually to the more inclusive forms of the linkage between Transcendence and *Existenz*.

It is most striking that Book III of *Philosophie* (entitled "Metaphysics") is not oriented toward a solution of that paradox which may well be called Kierkegaardian: how freedom can be the *original upsurge* which I call *myself,* and also a radical gift of grace by the hidden divinity. Curiously enough, it is in Book II (entitled "Illumination of *Existenz*") that one finds some light shed upon this difficulty inherent in every philosophy of double domicile, *Existenz,* and Transcendence.[24] The principal weight of the "Metaphysics" does not bear upon the inner drama of freedom in the grip of what others have called "grace" or "predestination;" rather, the main effort of Jaspers is directed to the discovery of a specifically metaphysical dimension of reality. The living, personal relationships of *Existenz* to Transcendence (which Jaspers calls *Existentielle Bezüge zur Tranzendenz*) constitute a path toward a new "reading" *(Lesen)* of all reality as "a cipher-script of Transcendence" *(Chifferschrift der Transzendenz)*.

---

22 Cf. Preface by Karl Jaspers, in M. Dufrenne & P. Ricoeur, *Karl Jaspers et la Philosophie de l'Existence* (Paris, 1947).

23 "I am always consciousness *(Bewusstsein)* in a situation, confronting objects, and oriented by my search toward Being in itself." *(Philosophie,* 13.) "*Existenz* is that which relates to itself and to its Transcendence." *(Ibid.,* 15.)

24 Cf. *Philosophie,* 465: "There where I was authentically myself. . . ."

The *search* for Transcendence lies in the *'existential'* references to this Transcendence, its *presence* lies in the cipher-script; as for the *space* required by each, formal transcending *(das formale Transzendieren)* must keep it cleared.[25]

Thus *Existenz* itself is only the place from which one reads the manuscript, from which one deciphers the language which Jaspers calls "ciphers."

Von der Wahrheit confirms the overall movement of *Philosophie.* The whole work is oriented toward the problem of "the achievement of true Being."[26] It is this single totality of the true Being which ceaselessly incites us and flees from us; which traverses the *breaks* of reality, situation, and existent; which finds in philosophy its fulfillment even if not in a form that can be rendered comprehensible for all. "Reason" is the name of this movement of thought toward the One. Love is its momentum. "The cipher constitutes the achievement of truth in philosophizing."[27] It is not a new domain of objects which is discovered; on the contrary, the object as such masks the cipher. Ciphers are, rather, the *symbolic* dimensions of every object. Every sensible reality, every thinkable object, every existence, suddenly transparent, becomes the *absent presence* of Transendence. "Originative *(ursprünglich)* philosophical thought is cipher."[28] "Symbols exhibit the ontological presence of the real."[29] Like *Philosophie* in 1932, *Von der Wahrheit* in 1947 concludes in an exegesis of the "cipher-being *(Chiffersein)* of all reality."[30]

By the same token, the wholly Lutheran or Augustinian — or even Kierkegaardian — problem of predestination at the heart of freedom is eclipsed by the less theological and more philosophical problem of the absolute reality of the world as cipher, that is to say, as appearance of Transcendence. To "orient oneself" among the ciphers — such is the supreme philosophical act.[31]

Thus, the religious philosophy of Karl Jaspers is less a different solution to the same problem — the problem of freedom and the Almightiness of the divine — than the emergence of the new problematic area of *the metaphysical dimension of reality.*

This philosophical act of orientation among the ciphers differs essentially, first of all, from the mystic flight, in that it is the very reaffirmation of the world as absolute. The *Ueber die Welt hinaus* is not a *Jenseits der Welt.* It is *this* world which is the synthesis of "appearing" and *trans*cendence into that *trans-appearing* which

---

25 *Ibid.,* 704.   26 Cf. *Wahrheit,* 33f., 869f.   27 *Ibid.,* 871.
28 *Ibid.,* 1038.   29 *Ibid.,* 1041.   30 Cf. *ibid.,* 1033f.
31 Cf. *ibid.,* 1030, 1036, 1038ff; also, *Philosophie,* 821.

Jaspers calls "immanent Transcendence."[32] Whereas, beginning with *Fear and Trembling*, Kierkegaard immures himself in the one-to-one relationship of the individual to his God and considers reaffirmation impossible, Jaspers turns here toward German romanticism and Nietzsche. When he writes, "Metaphysical objectivity is cipher,"[33] he rejoins, by-passing revealed religions, the great current of philosophical lyricism, which, beginning with Hegel and Schelling, Goethe and Hölderlin, passes through the Eternal Return and the *Amor Fati*. Christian Incarnation, Passion, and Resurrection are now radically secularised: from historical events they have become a vast symbolism of reality, a vast symbolism of nature, of history, and of freedom.

Doubtless the reading of ciphers is, like mysticism, an act of faith in the broad sense of the term, in the sense that it is not an act accessible to abstract cognition, to the Kantian *I think*, conceived as the condition of the possibility of objectivity; in short, it is not an act accessible to the cognitive subject. He who reads the ciphers is the very one who is anxious concerning himself, who breaks forth into freedom, who suffers its limits, who holds a dialogue with another: he who reads the ciphers is the existent. Philosophy is faith in this broad but well-defined sense, that one must be more than an universal understanding, that one must be a singular existent, to see Transcendence appear (or "trans-appear") in every appearance. This is why philosophy is faith, not wisdom, system, or ontological science.

But the secret difference between religious and philosophical faith is that the latter does not betray the world. The Kierkegaardian language may well be retained *("In unbelief is belief. . . . In belief is unbelief. . . . The strength of belief* consists in . . . [its] *polarity"*[34]), but the accent and the intention have changed: one might venture to say that Jaspers has attempted to elaborate a Kierkegaardian *equivalent — affected by anguish and subjective trembling — of the third type of knowledge in Spinoza*, which knows nothing new relative to the second type but apprehends everything and itself in God. "The more we know individual things, the more we know God," said Spinoza. Jaspers' metaphysics of ciphers has a similar ring.

It seems to us, therefore, that Jaspers inaugurates on the edge

<hr/>

32 Cf. *Philosophie*, 793: "Immanent Transcendence is *immanence*, but at the same time *evanescence;* it is *Transcendence*, which gained utterance as cipher in existence. . . . Transcendence and immanence were at first thought to be mutually exclusive: but in the cipher understood as immanent Transcendence we must find rather their intimate dialectic, in which Transcendence does not founder."

33 *Ibid.*, 786.   34 *Ibid.*, 217.

of religions a sort of philosophical gnosticism. Kierkegaard and
Nietzsche are mutually comprehended and surpassed by a kind of
superior synthesis by which the faith of the one and the *amor fati*
of the other, the Repetition of the one and the Eternal Return of
the other, would be in some manner superimposed on each other.

Opposed to religion understood as mysticism — that is to say, in
Jaspers' sense, as betrayal of the world — philosophical faith is even
more basically opposed to religion understood as authority. The
ciphers of God are without authority for they are nowhere and
they are everywhere. There is nothing which cannot be cipher.[35]
No sacred book can fix them, no sacred history can contain them,
no sacred Church inherits them. This is the sense in which Jaspers
calls this reading absolutely "historical" *(geschichtlich)*.[36] This
"metaphysical experience" comes to us like a gift, without constraint, without guarantee, as if things suddenly took on a physiognomy: here, the Wholly-Other is present analogically, symbolically, like a total presence at once disguised and unveiled, hidden
and exposed.

Henceforth its truth is incessantly vanishing, unique each time
as *Existenz* is unique.[37]

From this vantage point *Von der Wahrheit* opposes "reason's"
quest for unity to "catholicity's" pretension to unity.[38] The perspective is different enough from that of *Philosophie,* but at bottom the doctrine is the same. The truth here in question is no different from the truth of Being in its ciphers. And "reason," in all
of Jaspers' works, is not the understanding which is identical in
everyone, consciousness-as-such, but the movement of the existent
bringing to bear all his thought upon the Encompassing *(das
Umgreifende)* with all the resources of communication and in a
total openness to the real.[39] Consequently, the opposition between
"reason" and "catholicity" illuminates from a new angle the opposition between "philosophical faith" and "religious faith." The
very term "catholicity" is important, because it does not cover the
notion of "authority." *Von der Wahrheit* makes an ultimate effort
to assign a value to authority. Authority is not in itself a force

35 Cf. *ibid.,* 820.

36 Cf. *ibid.,* 690: Disappearance as the Essence of Historicity.

37 "That Transcendence changes its appearance with *Existenz* is . . . [no] argument against its reality and its truth; rather is change its necessary aspect, if its
appearance is to become its language for *Existenz* in the temporal order. . . . The
necessity for the passing-away of all metaphysical objectivity belongs therefore to
the historicity of *Existenz* in temporal existence." *(Ibid.,* 691).

38 Cf. *Wahrheit,* 832ff.

39 Cf. *ibid.,* 966ff. Also, *Reason,* Lectures 3 & 4.

hostile to the true, but one of its avenues of "penetration" (Durch-bruch). Diametrically opposed to the "exception" which awakens without binding, authority is salvaged by this diametrical polarity, as also by the inner tension between its propulsion and its histori-cal forms. Authority, at the boundary, is the very prestige of the truth of Being, but it speaks only from "the totality of histori-city."[40] It is in motion, it is open. Catholicity is, as it were, closed authority in contrast to open authority.

Moreover, catholicity extends beyond the historical phenome-non of Catholicism. The pretension of such-and-such a philosophi-cal system, Hegelian or otherwise, to be the unique and exclusive truth, corresponds to the same type of truth and existence. But Judeo-Christian or Islamic orthodoxy is the most remarkable il-lustration, and the pages devoted to such orthodoxy are of a vehe-mence rarely found in the work of Jaspers. It is the very principle of the revelation which is scrutinised with a great inner violence: if history is *centered* on an event which gives it meaning, a "his-torical unity" is erected to which reason opposes "the unity of all histories" over and beyond the conflict of revelations. To the authority localised in the space and time of the revelation, reason opposes "the encompassing authority of the historicity of the world as a whole."[41] To the guarantee (Sicherung) of revealed wisdom, reason opposes the unguaranteed, constantly imperiled certainty (Gewissheit) of the original upsurge of *Existenz* before its hidden Transcendence. To the pretension of catholicity to include all truth and to exclude all heresy, reason opposes its unlimited com-munication. This is why the philosopher says Yes to authority as a limiting character of "the all-enveloping truth," and No to catho-licity.

Tightening his grip, Karl Jaspers focuses his severe criticism on the theme of the God-man.[42]

The attack launched against religion had touched it at the pe-riphery. Now it is wedged in the very heart of revelation. A direct and exclusive revelation in the sense claimed by religions can only be the pretension usurped by some men and some groups to render their own historicity universally valid. It is the pride of man which is concealed beneath obedience to the Revelation and which exacts from other men that they bend to its truth in the name of humility.

The key criticism, therefore, enters here: "The God-man is only once,"[43] from which arises the pretension to catholicity at-tached to this unique event. It is not so much the absurdity of the

40 Cf. *Wahrheit,* 784ff.   41 Cf. *ibid.,* 837.
42 Cf. *ibid.,* 850ff.   43 Cf. *ibid.,* 851.

incarnation that reason rejects: "The absurd is a form of the appearance of Transcendence for thought, in every philosophy which
advanced into greater depths." The rub is between two absurdities: one which reveals and another which misleads. The second
absurdity is that of the God-man who by his uniqueness suspends
history, fastens one to a dogma, and at the same time proposes to
the "exception" like Kierkegaard imitation of a disaster foreign
to any realization in the world, in the state, in marriage, or in
culture.

This is why the opposition between "reason" and "catholicity"
does not remain one of polarity, but becomes one of exlusion.[44]

This criticism is completely understandable only in the light of
the last pages of *Von der Wahrheit*. The God-man is the antithesis of the cipher. In both cases there is *mediation* between Transcendence and human existence. The "transmutation of the world
into a mediation between us and the unique God is its transmutation into *cipher*."[45] One must choose between the "encipherment"
(Chifferwerden)[46] *of all things, and the Christian incarnation.*

III. *The annexation of religion by philosophy.*

This is not, however, Jaspers' last word on religion. From this
same theory of ciphers it is possible to initiate a second movement
of thought which compensates for its rejection by an "annexation"
(Aneignung). For the "traces of God" which are His ciphers or
symbols are mute signs that require the specific mediation of a
language. The original primitive ciphers of which we can speak,
in effect, only through the figures of art, myth, religion, and metaphysical systems are, if you like, the "very language of Being." But
they would have remained inaccessible to us if they had not been
"mediated" by the "language" of men.[47] Religion regains its meaning here, no longer in opposition to the cipher, but within the
movement of the historical reading of ciphers.

This second movement is as important as the first. The same
religion which the philosopher rejects as dogma he espouses as
myth. At the same time, the cipher replaces the miracle, contemplation replaces prayer, and communication replaces the Church.

But how appropriate the myths philosophically? The comparative science of religions is not enough, for one does not reach the
essence of the religious by a sociological method which extracts
from the multiplicity of myths a sort of "primal form" *(Urform)*

---

44 Cf. *ibid.*, 833.   45 Cf. *ibid.*, 1051.   46 Cf. *ibid.*
47 Cf. *Philosophie*, 786ff; also, *Tragedy*, 23ff.

which would constitute the religious ground of humanity. The agnosticism which originated in the eighteenth century — as may be seen in Lessing's famous tale of the three rings — rests on such a prejudice. One must, on the contrary, immerse oneself in the multiplicity itself and espouse in some sort the religious rhythm which has no unique religious language. The language of men is shattered. The myth is "historical" in another sense, by virtue of a historicity which is collective rather than individual. I must therefore go beyond that "objective universal" which comparative religious sociology could extract and which is no longer the faith of anyone. I must even go beyond faith in its anonymous, collective form, the "relative universal" of the group's confession of faith, in order to espouse the intimate faith of the individual believer. At this point I descry, insofar as it is possible, the "unique universal" (das Einzigallgemeine).[48]

Only then may the philosopher employ myth to read the cipher at the same time that he effaces the myth in the cipher. Jaspers thus underscores his digression from Kierkegaard, and perpetuates rather the attempt of Spinoza, Schelling, and Hegel to reintegrate religion into philosophy by means of myth.

In this conversion of dogma into myth, authority has become tradition.[49] This change of perspective is of paramount significance. Authority is inimical to freedom. Tradition is the sustenance of freedom. It is to freedom what memory is to the present. It is piety with regard to the past which gives to freedom ground and root. Tradition belongs, to be sure, to the childhood of freedom, but since no one has outgrown childhood in every way, no one can say that he no longer needs authority.

The Church in which I was born, I cannot put aside, for without it I would not have attained freedom. . . . And yet the Church of the theologians who would wish to exclude me is not a Church of truth, but always an empty, frozen distortion.[50]

And yet, in rejecting religion, I say: Yes, and cannot but hope, even for my own sake, that it survives in the world.[51]

But, while Jaspers hopes for the survival of religion as the provocative counterpart of philosophical faith and as a reservoir of myths for philosophical reflection, he continues its dissolution all the more subtly by his conception of the fate of the myth. What, in fact, happens to myths when they return to the original language of being? At one level, the myth represents the divine as a

48 On this entire development, cf. Philosophie, 692ff.

49 Cf. ibid., 267.   50 Ibid.   51 Ibid., 268.

sacred portion of reality, viz., the Greek gods. At a second level, myth recounts the "revelation" of a "yonder;" this is the level of Christian religion and confession. At the third level, nothing less than all of reality becomes "mythical." Jaspers refers us here to the transmutation of all things in the paintings of Van Gogh,[52] thus seeming to proclaim a kind of twilight of the gods in the aesthetic. Certainly the "nostalgia" *(Sehnsucht)* for a plenitude of the truly real in Transcendence would seem to find its native fulfillment in an aesthetic vision of reality. In *Von der Wahrheit* myths figure along with poetry and the plastic arts among "the original spiritual intuitions, deeds, figures . . ." which render truth present.[53] Philosophy gathers them up in their totality and uses them as its instrument in the "achievement of true Being."[54] Myth, poetry, the plastic arts, constitute the unique, vast matrix from which proceeds the infinite movement of reason and love, both turned toward the truth of the cipher. This language of truth is primordially one and entire; it never completely separates as it divides in the three directions of religion, poetry, and art.[55] Thus it is that "to abandon religion would be to stop philosophizing. . . . Even science would eventually founder."[56]

Thus, the critique of myth rather seems to point to a common root of religion, poetry, and the arts. The place of the arts in the "world of ciphers"[57] seem to confirm this interpretation. Art is the mediation of the reading of ciphers in nature, in history, and in man, provided this mediation occurs at the intuitive, not the speculative, level.[58]

The succeeding pages contain yet another episode,[59] the transition from mythical language as a whole (a second language) to the "speculative reading of the manuscript" (a third language). Consequently, the passage from the second language to the third sets a limit to a purely aesthetic interpretation of Jaspers' conception of philosophical faith. This latter interpretation can prevail only at the second level of metaphysics, located *between* immediate ciphers and "speculation" concerning the ciphers (which is metaphysics in the strict sense). But because this intermediate region *(Zwischenreich)*[60] is precisely the one which religion does not surpass, the metamorphosis of cults into art does indeed seem to be the supreme exaltation of religion *at its own level*. Here the myth is no longer a tale told, but mute like the primordial ciphers. And yet, as the work of man, it still belongs to the "language of men."

52 Cf. *ibid.,* 788f.   53 Cf. *Wahrheit,* 871.   54 Cf. *ibid.,* 870.

55 Cf. *ibid.,* 916f.   56 *Ibid.,* 916.   57 *Ibid.,* 917; *Philosophie,* 840ff.

58 *Philosophie,* 840.   59 Cf. *ibid.,* 840ff.   60 Cf. *ibid.*

In "metaphysical art" is realised the very pulsation of the "immanent Transcendence." On the one hand, this art wrenches me
from the prestige of the empirical world and the banality of everyday life, freeing me by "fantasy," by the unreal, and thus preparing me for another dimension of the real; and, on the other hand,
it remains among the visible signs of Transcendence which are
betrayed by mysticism.

Therefore, if the interpretations of religion by myth and of
myth by art suggest a certain "aestheticism,"[61] this is so only to the
degree that Jaspers concomitantly confers on the arts a seriousness
quite opposed to the conception of "art for art's sake." Not that
art has the function of imitating. This puerile conception of the
relationship of art to reality is entirely foreign to Jaspers. More
profoundly than any limitation art discloses a primordial meaning. But, "the empirical world itself is made into a cipher by the
art of immanent Transcendence. Although it seems to imitate
what happens in the world, it renders transparent."[62] Thus, its
function is indeed to raise the ciphers to the dignity of language.
It is because art itself has a metaphysical dimension that it is
worthy to play host to the metamorphosis of gods and cults. If the
example of Van Gogh seems so significant to Jaspers, this is precisely because his art is no longer related to myth through the
representation of gods, as is still the case with Aeschylus, Michelangelo, Shakespeare, Rembrandt; rather, it is the whole of secular
reality which becomes mythical. By strictly limiting himself to the
real and forsaking all myths, Van Gogh made Transcendence
speak (in a way which is) true for our time — although of necessity infinitely humbler.[63]

With the qualifications made, and considering art in its most
metaphysical sense, one may certainly say that in Jaspers art tends
to become *an aesthetic equivalent of revelation.*

But this annexation of religion in the form of myth does not
acquire its full significance until the total triumph of philosophy
under the title of "speculation."[64]

The word "speculation" is not used by Jaspers in a deprecative
sense. It designates a supreme form of cipher in which not sensory
realities become "transparent" but the great metaphysical thoughts
(proofs of the existence of God, the fundamental origin of the

[61] Jaspers speaks very severely of the "aesthetic attitude," its uncommitted character, its predilection for the emotions of a disinterested spectator (cf. *Tragedy*,
87ff).

[62] *Philosophie*, 844.   [63] *Ibid.*

[64] Cf. *ibid.*, 847ff; also, *Wahrheit*, "Thinking and Being," 251ff.

empirical world, reminiscence and eschatology, philosophy of history and of nature, the system of German idealism, etc.)

Thus the reintegration of religion into philosophy is complete. Religion dissolves first into mythical figures. Then the mythical ciphers themselves subserve speculative ciphers. Prayer is definitively reduced into *'existential'* contemplation.[65]

To be sure, philosophy is faith, as all the preceding developments show, and Jaspers might well echo the words of Kant: I criticized knowledge and I established faith. In this respect, the condemnation of *ontology* as a system pretending to universality and objectivity is beyond appeal, for its crime is at least twofold:[66] it extends to *Existenz* and Transcendence a mode of knowledge limited to mathematical and physical objects, and it masks, by logical transitions, the real hiatus between the empirical worldly object and the historically free existent, as well as between the existent and Being-in-itself.

And yet the very expression "philosophical faith" indicates that if philosophy is faith, that is to say, not cognition, faith is philosophy, that is to say, thinking *(Denken),* reflection, and speculation. This last point is important for a proper understanding of the religious import of the philosophy of Jaspers. Neither the mythical interpretation of religion nor even its aesthetic dissolution remain foreign to this impulse to comprehend which finds its first expression in scientific knowing. All of Jaspers' efforts are bent toward the integration of the reading of ciphers to a reflection on Being which would be the equivalent of a rational theology. This reflection proceeds at two levels. On a lower level, it recalls the pattern of *negative theology,* viz., the second chapter of the "Metaphysics" entitled "Formal Transcending." On a higher level this reflection is called "speculation." It completes the theory of ciphers and proceeds in the direction of what we have called a modern philosophical gnosticism.

According to Jaspers, thought is fraught with a twofold urgency: that of "enveloping" and that of "transcending." The first aspect of thought is domination, reduction, inclusion. The elaboration of a scientific universe responds to this exigency of thought, which may also be called "objective," because the relating of all things to rules of consciousness-as-such amounts to establishing objectivity all around me by thought. This objectivity does not constitute an absolute expatriation of consciousness, however. On the contrary, it marks the triumph of the unity of consciousness over the diverse and the indeterminate. This objectivity presup-

[65] Cf. *ibid.,* 806.   [66] Cf. *ibid.,* 232ff.

poses that consciousness is the measure of being, the center of reference for all conceived and comprehended being. In short, objectivity means immanence.

But a second exigency cuts across the first: the meaning of being as Being, as One, as the Whole. This sense of Being is at the bottom of all the uneasiness which attends thought in its triumphant use. This is what flees from me in the *question*. I question because I am seeking Being. And here is Being before me, shattered: shattered between objectivity and the primal origin *(Ursprung)* of the free existent, shattered at the very level of objectivity which explodes into irreducible cycles of reality, into disparate methodologies which touch off the irrational everywhere. Thus the whole critique of knowledge at the very level of objectifying thought is magnetised by the question of Being. This impulsion toward Being *(Trieb zum Sein)* is the cause of the foundering *(Scheitern)* of cognition in its pretension to crown my efforts by its universality, its consistency, its logical constraint, its demand for totality and ultimate unity. If the world were a whole and cognition a totality, immanence would be achieved and there would be neither freedom nor divinity. To transcend would be impossible:

But we must not fail to realise that this entire negative critique is governed from the beginning by the quest for *a new objectivity,* a new sense of *reality,* namely, the cipher of Transcendence, accessible to the free existent in his capacity to effect an original upsurge. In *Existenzphilosophie,*[67] the third and final discourse has "reality" *(Wirklichkeit)* for its theme. It moves from the object of science toward the cipher of Transcendence. The solidity of cognition dissolves before a unity which is not given, but aimed at, in the "trans-appearance" of a "physiognomy."

Thus one can read philosophy "backwards," beginning with the philosophy of ciphers. It is the reading of the ciphers by faith which takes effect in philosophy and which is critically reflected in a difficult disquisition. Conformably, this λέγειν must in turn violate its own consistency, its pretension to know Being, to describe it universally and definitively. In short λέγειν must disallow its own claim to be a λόγος.

This attempt to reflect on reflection itself found its expression in a "philosophical *logic*" which would be homogeneous with "philosophical *faith.*" In the work of 1932, Karl Jaspers had already attempted to display this movement of thought which surmounts and sustains itself (". . . for it is thinkable that there is

[67] *Existenz.*

a non-thinkable . . . ") [68] by a "dialectic of transcending thought." This dialectic concerns the categories insofar as they are *formal* articulations of the thinkable; hence the term, *"formal transcending."* [69]

This essentially *negative* dialectic which utilises in turn the method of absolutizing a category conceived relatively to objectivity, the coincidence of opposites, and the vicious circle, leads thought to sink into the unthinkable and thus prepares the "space" for the encounter with Transcendence.

But that very same reason which thus prepares a "space" for contemplation by this entirely formal process recaptures the original and the mythical ciphers at the level of the highest pretensions of metaphysics — Platonic, neo-Platonic, Cartesian, Idealist — and seeks in the ontological argument itself a symbol of the Being which is. The ontological argument signifies that it is Being itself, the thinking itself, which gives itself as symbol. "Even that which in the eyes of *idealism* was raised to knowledge in the form of system, is now, *as a totality, a possible cipher."* [70]

The power of transforming by ciphers all realities, all beliefs, into "speculative" symbols of Transcendence is thus unlimited. This conception of the cipher enables Jaspers to uncover a transcendent *intention* even in those thoughts whose objective or dogmatic *pretension* seems at first to destroy all Transcendence.

This is not the place to develop for its own sake Jaspers' conception of "reason" and "thinking." It is enough to have perceived the outlines of the structure in which the criticism and the annexation of religion take place. The theory of "speculation" noted in conclusion testifies, in any case, how much closer Jaspers may be to Plotinus, Spinoza, or Hegel, than he thinks, by his subordination of religion to philosophy, despite the immense gaps which, according to Jaspers, distinguish these systems from "the historical reading of the cipher-script of Being."

IV. *Critical remarks.*

It would be futile to elaborate a critique of Jaspers' theory of religion in which argument would be opposed to argument. Such a critique would be sterile by reason of its external character. It is more useful and more suitable to the goal of *communication* — of *"symphilosophieren"* — to bring into focus, at the very foundation of the work of Karl Jaspers, another perspective which reveals a different relation between philosophy and religion.

[68] *Philosophie*, 707.   [69] Cf. *ibid.*, 705ff.   [70] *Ibid.*, 863.

A.

All of the foregoing analysis tends to show that Jaspers' criticisms of religion take shape around the theme of hidden Transcendence and its passing historical ciphers. This is the stumbling-block for the Christ-myth *("Christosmythos")*. For this "myth" is banished by a totally different conception of the "mediation" *(Mitteilung)* of Transcendence and appearance. To this theme of Jaspers is also subordinated the acute problem of authority — or rather, "catholicity," as it is described in *Von der Wahrheit*. If religious mediation is unacceptable because it claims to localise, and then to guarantee, the presence of Transcendence in immanence, this objective and exclusive presence serves Jaspers as foil for the non-coercive, transitory universality of the cipher.

It does not seem to me that Jaspers has sought to progress from this *pretension* of religious mediation to its *intention*. Religion is thrown into a relief in which its own problematic character vanishes. For the primary religious intention is to save freedom from its "vanity," from a specific nothingness which keeps it in bondage; hence, to liberate, to save freedom. That is its true problem. By contrast, the ultimate philosophical question, as Jaspers understands it, is that of absolute reality, that is to say, the question of Being *qua* Being and of the appearing of Being. Jaspers has indeed shown that this problem arises from the subject-object division and that the achievement of a consciousness of Being consists in attaining an objectivity situated beyond that dichotomy. *Religion becomes a philosophical question when its own dialectic of deliverance is transferred to the properly philosophical problem of absolute reality.* The salvation of freedom is then translated into the terms in which the philosopher poses the relation of appearance to Being. It is inevitable that the Incarnation emerge as a pseudo-solution to the problem of absolute reality. The revelation confronts the philosopher as a limited, fixed, authoritarian apparition. What Jaspers recognizes under the name of "catholicity," moreover, is a culpable, violent projection of religion into territory which is foreign to it. (I shall return later to the question of theological culpability and its relation to philosophical culpability.)

If we pass from the pretension of religion to the intention of faith, that is to say, if we refer its preachment to its own problematic area which is not that of the resolution of the speculative problem of reality but the salvation of freedom, we are led to reread the work of Jaspers from the standpoint of the problem of guilt *(Schuld)*. We may now have occasion to find another possible account of philosophical reflection and religion. We have purposely not discussed this possibility, although it is an essential center of reference in Jaspers' work. In *Philosophie* Jaspers returns to the problem of guilt several times: in connection with his theory of character;[71] especially in his theory of ultimate situations, in which guilt stands as one of the four situations of extremity, alongside death, suffering, and struggle;[72] and in connection with defiance and the "passion for the night" *(Leidenschaft zur Nacht)*,[73] which are two specific modes of the link of *Existenz* to Transcendence. In *Von der Wahrheit* Jaspers speaks of guilt in connection with "the sources of untruth," and under the heading of Evil,[74] and returns to it again in his fine study of tragedy.[75]

It is a singular — and revealing — fact that for Jaspers guilt is an ultimate situation *like* death, a test of the empirical failure of *Existenz*. The moral fault lies in the act, the metaphysical fault lies in the very foundation of my being.[76] No *beginning* of my guilt is discoverable, for guilt is radical and inevitable. It is revealed precisely in the murderous effects of good will, in the narrowness of communication, and ultimately it *is* my very character. "That I am thus-and-so *(Sosein)* itself gives me my sense of guilt."[77] Guilt is to choose myself to be thus-and-so. But I can only choose a limitation, if I wish to realize myself in this world. When I accept the limitations of my own character, it is as if I had chosen myself before time, and made mine a choice which I never really made. Guilt thus adheres to the root of freedom.

Thus, in contrast to the whole Christian tradition, which conceives guilt only as *fall*, that is to say, as a debasement with respect to . . . , as a *lost* primordial innocence, Jaspers derives guilt from the primitive, unfathomable, unchosen constitution of existence. Guilt is that very limitation of existence which is espoused by freedom. This confusion of guilt and finitude appears to me to be one of the gravest confusions of contemporary *'existential'* philosophy. Christian philosophy, indeed, never placed guilt on the same plane as the condition of the creature. Finitude as such was an ontological notion, guilt an ethical notion. Finitude was the condition of the creature, guilt "entered the world." Finitude was a state, guilt an event. In modern existentialist philosophy guilt loses its character as a bad *use* of freedom to become the constitu-

---

71 Cf. *ibid.*, 323, 334. 72 Cf. *ibid.*, 506ff. 73 Cf. *ibid.*, 734f.
74 Cf. *Wahrheit*, 531ff. 75 Cf. *Tragedy*. 76 Cf. *Guilt*, 63ff.
77 *Philosophie*, 323.

tional limitation of existence. And since existence becomes deeper only through limitation, freedom and guilt become indistinguishable as soon as freedom attempts to become "real" or "historical." But by becoming inevitable, *guilt tends invincibly to become a misfortune of existing which is absolutely past possibility of pardon and redemption.*[78]

What the believer cannot understand is a doctrine of guilt loosed from a doctrine of forgiveness. For him guilt is known only retrospectively from the depths of a dawning restoration.

A considerable number of characteristics of the philosophy of Jaspers are clarified if we notice this substitution of inevitable guilt for Christian sin. From this guilt without forgiveness one can doubtless understand the whole orientation of the philosophy of Jaspers toward foundering rather than toward "rebirth." It is most striking that the function of the ultimate situation is to make *Existenz disappear* as a final ground, as a pretension to Being. The defeat is inevitable and affects every case of *appearing* with regard to the human being. To become real is to enter into a process of interrogation and doubt which leaves standing no definitive, fulfilled, happy, harmonious, innocent being.

Every existence who would pass for authentic being disintegrates before the interrogation which seeks the absolute. The precariousness of all existence [that is to say, its mutable character which constantly generates further interrogation] signifies the impossibility of finding peace in existence as such. This manner of always appearing as internally discordant in the ultimate situation constitutes the antinomial structure of existence.[79]

Historicity in its totality is ravaged by a disintegrative process whose fantastic progression is shown in the remainder of the work. Disaster is finally the supreme, though silent, cipher of Being. A strange appetite for ruin seems to be the last word of the human being.

... Only in Transcendence can freedom be *suspended.* ... Only then does man become aware of his freedom as a temporal appearance which tends to suspend itself. Freedom has its time. It remains an inferior which wishes to annihilate itself. Yet this thought has no meaning save for a transcendent conception of an end of all days, which will not be in this world.[80]

Thus guilt, insofar as it is an ultimate situation, is referred to

[78] Cf. *Tragedy*, "Delivery within the Tragic," and "Deliverance from the Tragic." 76ff.

[79] *Philosophie*, 508.   [80] *Ibid.*, 466.

Transcendence through disaster which has itself become *cipher*. The fourth and last part of the "Metaphysics" is entitled: "Disappearance of existence and *Existenz* being understood as the decisive cipher of Transcendence (Being in foundering)."[81]

It is remarkable to see how, in the perspective of defeat, the religious problem of guilt is replaced by the philosophical problem of the *appearing* and *disappearing* of Being. The theme of ultimate situations belongs to the philosophical problem of absolute reality under the title of an aspect of the *realization* of possible *Existenz*. "Boundary means: there is something else; but for my consciousness immersed in my time and in my empirical order, that other is not."[82] Guilt no longer makes its appearance to us as the malady of freedom; it is not that vanity which spreads over everything, as in St. Paul. It is an episode in the "realization" of the existent. This episode brings appearance to disappearance, and in this downfall relates appearance to Being.

Freedom in its realization is *never complete;* in its most decisive effort at realization, freedom is, rather, confronted by itself as by the most abysmal lack: I am real, but neither fulfilled, nor close to possible fulfillment. In the process of becoming real, I am already referred, by my failure *(Versagen)* — which, as freedom, is guilt — to my Transcendence.[83]

This interpretation of the theme of sin in Jaspers is confirmed by the fact that it recurs with a new virulence in the analysis of defiance *(Trotz)*,[84] and of the "passion for the night."[85] Defiance, which is at the heart of the will to know, of the "question," goes to the root of freedom, as soon as freedom struggles away from Being and says *No*. It is the *Urschuld* inherent in the *Ursprung* of freedom. This movement cannot be annulled, even in the most total surrender to God, for "the surrender retains its origin in defiance."[86] Thus the inevitable fault attaches to the relation to Transcendence, and maintains the pulsation of defiance and surrender.

The theme of "the night" definitely turns meditation toward defeat. Here, perhaps, Jaspers is furthest from the Christian tradition. All of German romanticism is now related to the quest for Being. For the "passion for the night" is "blind to every task and every purpose; it is the drive to destroy oneself in the world in order to fulfill oneself in the depths of a worldlessness."[87] "Day

---

81 *Ibid.*, 863ff.   82 *Ibid.*, 469.   83 *Ibid.*, 465.
84 Cf. *ibid.*, 733ff.   85 Cf. *ibid.*, 762ff.   86 *Ibid.*, 742f.
87 *Ibid.*, 763.

is tied to night because day is itself only if *in the end it fails completely.*"[88] With the passion for the night, guilt deepens as it darkens. Limitation has become autonomy, and autonomy, defiance. Defiance wants to take form under the sober and reasonable humanism which Jaspers calls "law of the day" *(Gesetz des Tages).*[89] Guilt is then betrayal of the passion for the night, whereas otherwise, in the passion for the night, "guilt is an *original possession.*"[90] And yet, "this subversion of the self, although experienced as guilt, is the deeper truth."[91]

It seems that guilt, propelled by the passion for the night and absorbed into a philosophy of disaster, has become totally estranged from any *redemption.* It is by withdrawing from this latter problem that it enters into the problem of *appearance* and *disappearance,* that is to say, into the philosophical problem of appearing and Being, which Jaspers himself calls *absolute reality in its ciphers.* "Night is the drive of *Existenz* toward its own failure. . . . The lesson of the night: everything that becomes must be ruined."[92]

This is the point at which the believer will begin to wonder. Does not this "inevitable guilt," oriented toward disaster and not toward redemption, cover up the true guilt, that which "Biblical religion," to use Jaspers' language, calls vanity and servitude, and which the Old Testament symbolized by the captivity of Israel in Egypt? Moreover, "Vanity" lies at the heart of the philosophy of Jaspers — as of every philosophy which passionately emphasizes the subjective — though without being plainly recognized by the philosopher. The culpability of philosophy takes refuge in the concern for *Self (Selbst)* which animates all of existentialist philosophy. A strange shriveling-up, a frenzied preoccupation with the self, besets every such philosophy. It is hidden in the proudest pronouncements on choice, which is choice of myself: "The decisive element of choice is that *I* choose[93] . . . I am myself the freedom of this choice[94]. . . . Freedom is the choice of my Self."[95]

Is not this bitter vindication of autonomy a kind of agitation within the enchanted circle of some sort of captivity? Gabriel Marcel wrote in *Journal Metaphysique:*

February 24, 1920. This seems at first surprising: is not to be free, to choose? And when one loves, does one choose to love? But no doubt

88 *Ibid.,* 769.
89 Cf. *ibid.,* 734f; also, *Wahrheit,* 762ff.
90 *Philosophie,* 770.   91 *Ibid.,* 765.   92 *Ibid.,* 769.
93 *Ibid.,* 450.   94 *Ibid.,* 451.   95 *Ibid.*

one must radically dissociate the notions of choice and freedom. To what extent can I say *I?* That is the real problem.[96]

If choice seems to characterize my ultimate freedom, is this not because it is always possible for me to return to the idols, to weaken, to betray, to surrender to the powers of despair? But is there not an asceticism of freedom itself which discloses levels of freedom among which the anguish of choice would be its lowest degree, in the sense that Descartes termed "indifference" the lowest degree of freedom? And is not the highest degree of freedom beyond the freedom of option, in a freedom of adhesion, beyond all risk, in responsive freedom, in a freedom of recollection, and beyond anguish, in a freedom of assent?

Perhaps, in the last analysis, all illumination of *Existenz* remains burdened by the "vanity" of a freedom which is less enamored of Being than of its own power to choose and its own glory. Perhaps it is more important to be torn from oneself and to emit the call of liberation than to be '*aus möglicher Existenz.*' At certain times, the inability to admire, to communicate, bears witness that our freedom may be beyond our own instrumentality and that the Self may be, not the *Ursprung*, but the invisible cordon of our own vanity. Then the question is less to be free than to be liberated, to be freed by a healed freedom. The primary thing is no longer freedom as it relates to the Self, but the articulation of this gift of freedom.[97]

B.

The undermining of the Christian idea of sin by the metaphysical idea of "inevitable guilt" and the consequent absence of a specific mediation of sin through forgiveness seem to us to characterize Jaspers' philosophical faith from the viewpoint of Christian faith. This new reading of Jaspers can be substantiated by regrouping several important aspects of his philosophy around this exegesis of the "inevitable guilt." Numerous breaks, paradoxes, and unresolved oppositions can be attributed to this lack of conciliation.

1. Jaspers speaks of Transcendence as a gift at the very heart of freedom — and he talks about it in admirable terms.

I come to myself like a gift: everything is clear, manifest, decided. . . . How could doubt have lasted so long?[98] . . .Where I am wholly

---

[96] *Journal Metaphysique* (Paris, 1927), 228.
[97] Cf. Gabriel Marcel, 'Don et Liberté,' *Giornale di Metafisica*, #6, 1947.
[98] *Philosophie*, 466.

myself, I am not merely myself[99] . . . I cannot be *through (durch)* myself what I am *in (aus) myself.*[100] . . . Where I was authentically myself in willing, I was at the same time granted to myself in my freedom.[101]

But this gift is not conceived to be a liberation of freedom but, rather, to be a sort of ceremony integral to choice in the sense of Nietzsche's Eternal Return, as if now, always, and again I must choose thus. This gift introduces into the center of freedom a sense of *necessity.*

The transition is exceedingly abrupt from that upsurging philosophy which implies an autonomous creation of the self and which means at least a sort of unconditionality and absoluteness, to a philosophy of donation. The transition transpires through the opposition within choice of the arbitrary to the necessary. There is no question of an external necessity imposed by brute nature, or of a duty, a *Sollen,* but of an intimate and invincible necessity of a *Müssen.* When an act is anchored in the depths of my being "I say: This is where I stand; I cannot do otherwise!"[102] Will thus becomes destiny. Fate is no longer an obstacle against which I collide, a threat which descends upon me. Rather, it is that within which I choose.

When, in my 'I choose,' my consciousness of the decision meets with authentic freedom, this freedom does not prove to reside in any arbitrariness of choice, but in that necessity which expresses itself as an 'I will,' in the sense of an 'I must' *(ich muss).*[103]

Thus, I choose *that which* I am, but I choose *from the depth of what* I am. *Amor Fati.*

This phrase cannot disguise the total paradox of an absolute upsurge, with its incurable guilt, and a Transcendence in which are extinguished all possibility, all temporality, all process, and consequently all freedom. "It may be that its ultimate meaning is to will its own cancellation *(sich aufheben);* that in which it cancels itself is no longer freedom, but Transcendence."[104] These last words tell us that Transcendence is less the Supreme Thou in which freedom could be achieved than the Wholly-Other in which freedom annihilates itself.

2. Even in those phrases whose style is most Kierkegaardian, one can perceive the religious problem of liberation slipping into the philosophical problem of absolute reality. Transcendence is

99 *Ibid.,* 465.   100 *Ibid.,* 466.   101 *Ibid.*
102 *Ibid.,* 463.   103 *Ibid.,* 454.   104 *Ibid.,* 462.

less the deliverer than the reality which extinguishes possibility. "The authentic reality is the Being which can no longer be thought as a possibility."[105] This explains why the principal weight of Jaspers' metaphysics does not bear on the inner drama of freedom, in terms of what Christian theology has called "grace" and "election," but on the discovery of a properly metaphysical dimension of the world. The reading of ciphers is therefore the philosophical analagon of redemption. The Paulist, Augustinian, and Lutheran problem of predestination at the center of freedom is eclipsed by the specifically philosophical problem of the absolute reality, of the transparency of all reality. This overall movement of *Philosophie* and *Von der Wahrheit* marks the true originality of Jaspers relative to Kierkegaard.

But when the doctrine of ciphers and the theory of inevitable failure are brought together, one may ask whether Jaspers has not simply juxtaposed a philosophy of *unreconciled tragedy* and a *lyric philosophy which tends toward a disquieting aestheticism.* The specific resolution of Jaspers' philosophy lies, in effect, in the contemplation of primordial ciphers. The cipher is the mediator between *Existenz* and Transcendence.[106] Freedom is admitted only when it contemplates itself as one cipher among others, like an evanescent apparition, like an apparition whose downfall consists in its disappearing. But if this contemplation exerts no control over the inevitable failure, what is to check it in its own tendency to slide into the aesthetic attitude? We have noted above how forcefully Jaspers contrasts the total commitment of *Existenz* in deciphering to the non-commitment of aestheticism. But the weight of the theory of ciphers carries him down the latter path, for want of a link between contemplation and an experience of liberation in which freedom would be a "re-creation." Aestheticism is the particular danger of his theory of myths, which is connected, as we know, with the theory of ciphers. For is it not the destiny of myths to perish in art? And how can the myth, once unmasked as myth, remain for the philosopher the "unique universal" *(das Einzigallgemeine)* in which is expressed the hidden divinity, if one of these myths does not, in the form of revelation, take them out of their discordant relationships and re-order them through a pronouncement to the philosopher which would simultaneously heal him of his very vanity? Does not the philosopher run the risk of losing the "narrowness" and the "commitment" of *Existenz* when he embraces the *totality* of myths —

105 Cf. *Existenz*, 59ff.
106 Cf. *Wahrheit*, 1051.

those of Greece, those of India, those of Christianity — like a Don Juan courting all the gods?

It is to be feared that tragic comprehension and its incurable guilt, the Nietzschean *amor fati,* the romantic passion for disaster, and the lyricism of contemplativeness all threaten to disintegrate into an absolute incoherence, for lack of the binding, golden thread of religious conciliation.

3. Robbed of its function of restoring freedom, Transcendence threatens to be no longer the "unique divinity" named in the closing pages of *Von der Wahrheit,* but an obscure ground in the self. One sometimes has the impression in reading Jaspers of looking at an incomplete atheism born of an unstable compromise between Kierkegaard and Nietzsche. For Jaspers too the ancient God is dead. It is therefore inevitable that the false proper name of Transcendence — God — betray a final timidity in the eyes of the atheist, a final mystification, and that the "cipher" of Transcendence appear to him as the successor to the mediating Logos. Separated from the context of invocations, the tension between Transcendence and *Existenz* can be resolved into an inner tension between the self who asks and the self who answers, between the hidden depth of my subjectivity and the acts and experiences which give currency in everyday life to those riches which are inaccessible to the spirit of lucidity. A proud ethics could grow out of this final dissociation from religious philosophy, a kind of neo-Stoicism which would balance its sense of tragedy by a lyric sense nourished on the original intuitions of the myths, poems, and works of art of humanity. To be sure, Karl Jaspers struggles with all his strength against such a development. But it is doubtful whether beyond himself his work can resist this degradation if his essential themes are not rephrased by means of meditation of the relationships between *prayer,* the *tragedy* of the *Ursprung* and the *Urschuld,* the assent to inner necessity, and that admiration for the ciphers of Being which does not draw the line at disaster.

Jaspers sees in prayer a direct relationship with the hidden divinity which betrays communication and eases responsibility. But does not prayer contain in abbreviated form all the paradoxes which Jaspers has so lucidly and courageously espoused? The moment in which the self seems to treat God as a second person is the moment in which the self discovers Him as the Transcendence before which he is almost nothing. The moment in which Transcendence seems to render futile his invocation is the moment in which he rises to his full responsibility in the world and among men. For the great men of prayer did not flee, but changed their life and transformed existence around them. Also, prayer is for the praying self the living paradox, but the reconciled paradox, that is to say, the mystery. Who talks *to* God as Thou can talk *of* God as Transcendence, so far as that is fitting for man.

C.

We have attempted to restate the controversy over religion by placing it in its proper context, which is not that of appearance and Being, but that of vanity and of the salvation of freedom. We believe we have thus progressed from the pretension of religion to its intention. At this juncture, one could say that Jaspers' critique remains intact. That is so; and his severe attack on religion is implacably forceful. But perhaps the faithful can grant its essentials relative to its own problematic context.

1. It is useless to disguise the opposition between a unique Revelation, localised in history, and the universal, evanescent symbolism of the ciphers. The most one can say is that this opposition involves *different problem areas:* that of salvation, and that of speculation on Being or on absolute reality.

The conflict arises the moment Revelation takes its stand on the plane of a philosophical dialectic of appearing and Being and that, conversely, the philosophy of ciphers assumes the religious function of a reconciliation of *Existenz* and Transcendence. And this conflict is inevitable the moment that the sermon, passing into cultural activity, enters the field of philosophical problems and imposes its own dogmatic content with the aid of philosophical formulas on reality, on *Existenz*, on essence, and on Being, as may be seen in the great theologies of the Alexandrian and medieval periods. It is impossible for the intention of the sermon not to take on the guise of an unacceptable pretension in the eyes of the philosopher. The most that can be said is that this tension between philosophy and religious faith need not be fatal if it is traced to its origin, that is to say, to the distinction between the primordial problems of salvation and speculation.

2. A consideration of religious intention enables one to distinguish, within the phenomenon of authority or catholicity, where the blame lies. The original authority of the Scriptures and of the Church is none other than the authority of the *witness*. The witness constrains no one. He shows the truth which has authority, but which is not the authority of a group of men. To be sure, this authority conferred on the witness necessarily comes

into conflict with the authority of the truth according to science and according to the philosopher. This conflict is the consequence of the history of the West. Two modes of comprehension confront each other, one based on absolute events, the other based on a universal understanding or a human experience indefinitely open to history and to dialogue. But this polarity does not take on the character of mutual exclusion until clerical violence perverts the non-coercive authority of the Word. Authority is a fundamental phenomenon of the religious sphere. It is its "catholic" pretension (in Jaspers' sense) which is at fault. It is the power of man over man in the ecclesiastical community which maintains this *guilt* of a violent Truth. The clerical passion follows the history of the Church and churches like a shadow. This fundamental problem of clerical authority is the key to an understanding of the pretension of churches to recapitulate truth at all its levels — scientific, philosophical, political, etc. — in an actual system which is at once a doctrine and a civilisation. The affair of Galileo is not a simple accident; it expresses the culpable passion of a clerical alliance.

It was therefore beneficial that the clerical synthesis of truth exploded in the Renaissance. It was natural that the autonomy of science should furnish a privileged place for this rupture. It was necessary that philosophy should be the nerve of the revolt by its power of ceaseless questioning. Through this cruel history, the Christian is invited to rediscover the eschatological sense of the unity of truth. The unity is not a force of history. One must say, rather, what Jaspers said of the suppression of freedom in Transcendence: "This idea has no meaning save for a transcendent representation of an end of all days, not of this world."[107] In the meantime, we do not *know* what it means that there may be at the same time a mathematical truth, a truth of *Weltorientierung*, a truth of *Existenzerhellung*, a truth of *Lesen der Chifferschrift*, and the Truth who was a Person. Eschatology is the cure of clericalism.

3. The culpability of theology signifies also a contrary culpability of philosophy, a *hybris* of great philosophical systems, even (or especially) if these systems are systems of God. The philosophy of *Existenz* does not escape this charge either. We have already alluded to a culpability of '*existential*' philosophy immured in its preoccupation with the Self. "Vanity" has extended to the Self as to everything else. There is no less of a pretension in

107 *Philosophie*, 466.

the *Ursprung* of *'existential'* philosophy than in the *I think* of Kantian philosophy or in the *Spirit* of Hegelian philosophy. The admirable and redoubtable freedom of the Socratic doubt has always to be saved from its subtle bondage.

Perhaps it is because philosophy and theology never face each other openly, but rather behind the masks of their specific bondages — libertarian on the one hand, authoritarian on the other hand — that the contrast between them appears fatally to be "not, polar, but mutually exclusive," as Jaspers said vigorously of the contrast between "reason" and "catholicity."[108]

PAUL RICOEUR

UNIVERSITY OF STRASBOURG

[108] Cf. *Wahrheit,* 833.

20

Julius Izhak Loewenstein

JUDAISM IN JASPERS' THOUGHT*

J ASPERS is one of the few German scholars who did not falter, even for a moment, in the tide of Nazism. He preferred dismissal from his professorship at the university and exposure to danger to making the slightest concession. In his first speech after the collapse of the Nazi regime he designated what had happened to the Jews as "our ineradicable shame and disgrace," and took even upon himself and upon the few, "who, in utter impotence, outraged and despairing, were unable to prevent the crimes," metaphysical, though not political or moral guilt.[1]

One is immediately reminded of this attitude of Jaspers when speaking of the position which Judaism occupies in his thinking. In this study, however, we shall not be concerned with his position concerning contemporary Jewry, but rather with his attitude toward the Judaism of the Bible. For contemporary philosophers, when they consider the origin of the European spirit, the Bible recedes behind Greek philosophy. Jaspers, however, emphasizes its importance, even in the history of non-religious thought and of modern science. But, for Jaspers the Bible does not have merely historic significance, a meaning now superseded by a loftier view of the spirit, an opinion accepted in many quarters today. *The Bible has significance for contemporary thinking.* We must, therefore, consider what Jaspers has to say regarding Judaism in the light of his entire philosophy.

I.

The great philosophers of all ages, regardless of their divergent paths, were all in agreement that, as Kant said, "all the interests of my reason, speculative as well as practical, combine in the questions relating to God, freedom and immortality;"[2] "at the

* Translated from the German manuscript by Matthew Cohen and Ludwig B. Lefebre.

[1] *Question*, 71ff.   [2] I. Kant: *Critique of Pure Reason*, B 826 (Kemp-Smith).

solution of which all the equipments of Metaphysic aim, as their ultimate and unique purpose."[3] Greek philosophy since Parmenides and modern philosophy since Descartes have sought to reach this goal by freeing themselves from the transitory world, the world as it appears to the senses. They wanted to discover the one, true, liberating Being through reason. Idealism as well as materialism are stages of these constantly renewed endeavors. Hegel topped them in an all-embracing rational system, which deduced "the absolute and whole truth."

This philosophy was impeded from two sides, however. Kant showed that we are not able to perceive Being-*in-itself*, but only in time and space.[4] Then, individual thinkers, i.e., Pascal in the time of Descartes, Kierkegaard and Feuerbach in the time of Hegel, Nietzsche and William James a generation later, opposed the victorious rationalistic philosophy. "Even if this [i.e., Descartes' philosophy] were true," said Pascal, "we would not consider the whole philosophy worth one hour's effort." *(Pensées)*. For, what matters is not the mere thinking of truth but its verification in life, not the objective knowledge of the truth but the subjective experience of truth in genuine conversion, as Pascal said, in *Existenz,* as put by Kierkegaard, in love, as Feuerbach said, or, in the enhancement of life, as Nietzsche put it. According to William James the truth has its "cash-value," i.e., "true ideas are those we can assimilate, validate, correlate and verify. False ideas are those we cannot."

Only afterwards do we see what these various thinkers have in common: they are all fighters against the dominant rationalistic philosophy. As long as it ruled they remained outsiders, "exceptions," as Kierkegaard and Nietzsche said of themselves, and they were so little noticed that one hardly knew of the other.[5]

But *existing* — the term which Jaspers adopted, retaining Kierkegaard's meaning — does not mean renunciation of thinking or a call for irrational feeling; rather does it mean that thought arises out of this feeling. Thinking does not deduce the truth from itself but, as Kierkegaard says in connection with the "mid-

---

[3] I. Kant: *Critique of Judgment,* (Bernard tr.), § 91, p. 411.

[4] But Kant did consider possible the deduction, not of Being itself, but of the forms of Being, the categories. This principle of deduction had a fateful effect on idealistic philosophy from Fichte to Hegel.

[5] Feuerbach influenced the Marxist school. But the original meaning of his philosophy was forgotten. It is significant that the Christian, Kierkegaard, found the book *Wesen des Christentums* by the atheist, Feuerbach, "so excellent that it was a pleasure to read it." *(Abschliessende unwissenschaftliche Nachschrift,* German translation by Gottsched, *Werke* VII, 291).

wife method" of Socrates, only brings forth what is already within us, "reminds" us of what we are and what we are able to be.[6]

But if truth is subjectively *'existential'* and not objectively conceivable, how can it be expressed and communicated? For, every statement which is made about truth does have an objective meaning. And how is a truth, which everyone verifies himself, referred to a common denominator? For, there can be only one truth. When Kierkegaard expresses truth in "indirect communication," when Nietzsche conceives of truth as "interpretation," they only raise questions but do not solve them.

These problems receded for Kierkegaard and Nietzsche in the face of the danger which they revealed: that in the concern over intellectual knowledge its verification be forgotten, that over the feeding of the cultured class with rationalistic education only, the process of actual self-education *(Sich-Bilden)* be neglected. Whereas Hegel's successors imagined "to have achieved gloriously much,"[7] they (Kierkegaard, Nietzsche, Feuerbach) saw in the then prevailing kind of education nothing but "hypocrisy;"[8] "revelation of emptiness;"[9] and "bourgois mediocrity, wretchedness and insincerity."[10] Kierkegaard and Nietzsche were shocked by this development and saw in it the warning signals of a mounting nihilism.

But their warning cries were not heeded during their time. When Jaspers began to philosophize, academic philosophers were going their own worn-out paths, with no concern for Kierkegaard or Nietzsche. After the collapse of the Hegelian system, they limited themselves to logical and methodological inquiries and forgot — the Kantians, too — what, for Kant, was the final and sole purpose of philosophy.[11] The confusion was heightened by the fatal effect of their opponents; not their "yes" but their "no" was heard. Thus the religious pragmatism of James in America led to shallow utilitarianism, and Nietzsche's critique led to anti-

6 This is also the original meaning of Feuerbach's statement, which provided the starting point for the young Karl Marx: "The true relationship of thought to Being is this: Being is the subject; thought is the predicate. Thought emanates from Being, but not Being from thought." (Vorläufige Thesen, 1842, in *Sämtliche Werke*, II, 1846, 263).

7 David F. Strauss, in: *Der alte und der neue Glaube*, 1872.

8 Ludwig Feuerbach: *Das Wesen des Christentums*, 1842.

9 S. Kierkegaard: *Kritik der Gegenwart*, German translation, 1922, 57.

10 Nietzsche, in his writings from *Geburt der Tragödie* until *Wille zur Macht*.

11 Cf. Einstein in the Russell volume of the *Library of Living Philosophers*, 289: "Fear of metaphysics . . . has come to be a malady of contemporary empiricistic philosophizing."

rational and amoral sentiment in Germany, facilitating the rise of Nazism.

II.

Is this, then, to be the 'decline of the West,' as many people asked during the crisis following the First World War, and ask again today? No, says Jaspers. "In fact, we are not standing before nothingness, but rather, as always where men are living, before our fundamental bases."[12] True, the empty answers given by philosophy have become meaningless; but there remain the original quest and inquiry of man face to face with death and suffering, the search for salvation from want, the quest for eternal Being in this transitory world. It is precisely this dissatisfaction with old answers which always has urged man on to new inquiries: Dissatisfaction with the traditions of primitive religions drove him to their sublimation; dissatisfaction with mythical answers drove him to ask, with rational consciousness, the philosophical question: what is Being? And today, when the old answers of philosophy no longer suffice, after the old methods have failed, Jaspers undertakes anew, and with new methods, to answer the question concerning Being. The problem of Being is made the central problem of philosophy.[13]

Jaspers' philosophizing will interest us only to the extent that it leads to the faith of the Bible. In the philosophy which originated with Parmenides and, in modern times, with Descartes, there was no room for faith, because these philosophies wanted to conceive of the truth of Being, "the absolute and only truth" (Hegel), through reason alone. For Jaspers, thinking, from its very start, demands its supplementation by faith. He holds fast to Kant's critique on the one hand, and to those of Pascal and Kierkegaard on the other. But he sees in this critique not only the negative, but the positive as well, i.e., not only the statement of not-knowing Being, but the reminder, as well, of Being in this not-knowing.

But, if not through knowledge, how then is Being to be reached? Jaspers answers: by means of a method which originates with the object, — which alone is knowable, — and thinks beyond it to the non-objective, to the no longer knowable. Every object stands in a relationship, in a horizon of our knowledge, as it were. If we

12 *Reason*, 128.

13 *Philosophie* I, 1; 19; III, 206; 233; *Reason*, 32f; *Existenz*, 1; 59; *Wahrheit*, 35; *Scope*, 27f; *Wisdom*, 28.

press on beyond this horizon we never achieve a final horizon, just as in circumnavigation of the globe. Being is beyond every horizon of knowledge. Being is the *Encompassing* which is no longer object. "The Encompassing . . . is that which always only announces itself — in the objectively present and in the horizons — but which never becomes object or horizon. It is that which appears to us not by itself, but in which everything else appears."[14]

Every statement about the Encompassing is a contradiction in itself, because it speaks of the Encompassing in an objective manner — and we cannot but speak objectively — but does not refer to an object. But this transcending from the knowable to the unknowable, to the "pre-logical,"[15] must be attempted in order to shed light on the content of the unknowable Encompassing.[16] This illumination of the Encompassing takes place in two perspectives: as the encompassing being which we ourselves are: the Encompassing of man; and as the encompassing being which is everything and *in* which we are: the Encompassing of the world.

1) In his approach to the Encompassing of man Jaspers first follows Kant. We do not know Being as it is in itself but only as it appears to consciousness-as-such. Consciousness-as-such is the condition for all knowledge. But, what consciousness-as-such actually is, we cannot know. It is not psychological consciousness and it is not empirical subject, but is really a manner of the Encompassing that we are. For anyone who finds it difficult to understand this, it is sufficient to know: as consciousness-as-such we are more than we are able to know about ourselves.

But the Encompassing of man is not fully explored with the elucidation of consciousness-as-such. Here Jaspers goes beyond Kant. The Encompassing of man is also actual existence, which has a beginning and an end and lives in an environment; and it is also spirit, which creates the spiritual worlds of profession, community and performance, all of which have temporal manifestations. By existence and spirit are meant not only the physical, mental and historical processes and accomplishments of man which we can recognize, but rather the Encompassing which remains an unknowable secret, the secret that existence finds itself: at first unreflected, in fear and jubilation, then in becoming con-

---

14 *Wahrheit,* 38.   15 *Ibid.,* 27, 179.

16 Formal logic is a restriction of the original logic. Original logic seeks methodically to know also what is no longer knowable (Socrates and Plato in dialectical conversation; Nicolaus Cusanus in his *docta ignorantia:* that is, in fulfilled notknowing; Kant in the transcendental method which is transcending from knowing to not-knowing).

scious of itself. In this self-finding human existence becomes conscious of its finiteness and is not satisfied with this knowledge. Human existence is distinguished from all other existence in that it is conscious of itself and, precisely through this knowledge, points beyond itself.

2) The Encompassing of the world reveals itself thus: we know only what is *in* the world, but not the world as a whole. In the world we are able only to explain one thing by the next, but not the world by itself. The world is not *causa sui*. But we can neither explain nor deduce the world from something else (as rationalistic philosophy tried to do). The world is appearance, as Kant said, i.e., we know the world as it appears to us, not Being in itself. The world, like man, points beyond itself and this reference beyond itself remains enigmatic.

With the realization of the modes of the Encompassing of man and the world we gain no new knowledge. But the secret which surrounds our entire knowledge of man and the world is revealed. If science, forgetting the limits of its knowledge, nevertheless tries to enclose the whole of man and world in a supposedly scientific system, then correct knowledge of particular processes is combined with a pseudo-scientific contruction of the whole. For example, in systems like that of natural science, which want to explain life as derived from matter; or, in systems like Marxism and psychoanalysis, which want to explain spiritual creativity as originating in economic or drive factors respectively. In these systems a particular sphere of knowledge is erroneously absolutized and universalized. Such "scientific" systems (well understood: as systems of the whole, not as investigations of the particular) are unscientific no less than mythical cosmologies.

III.

The educated person of today who finds satisfaction in scientific knowledge resists the idea of the Encompassing. Let, then, Jaspers' train of thought be illustrated by a statement from Goethe:

The true, which is identical with the divine, never permits itself to be known by us directly; we see it only in reflection, in example, in symbol, in individual and related phenomena; we become aware of it as indescribable life, and yet we cannot renounce the wish to comprehend it. This holds true of all phenomena of the tangible world.[17]

[17] J. W. von Goethe: *Versuch einer Witterungslehre.*

Goethe expresses here the aim of the idea of the Encompassing. Our knowledge is surrounded by a secret which we cannot know. "We become aware of it as indescribable life;" that is, we do recognize the individual life processes, but life as a whole is not conceivable; it is a manner of the Encompassing. "This holds true for all phenomena of the tangible world," for human existence as for the world. They are not comprehensible, are not explicable through themselves, and point beyond themselves to —

To what? To the true, identical with the divine, to the Encompassing of the Encompassing. Thereby are we transcended from the immanent ways of the Encompassing (from the Encompassing of man and the world) to Transcendence. Transcendence, as conceived by philosophy, means Being; as experienced by man it means God. In thought Transcendence withdraws from us; we can never directly know it. But in experience it can approach us quite closely in concrete moments.[18]

The individual who has broken through the immanent world

---

[18] Here is revealed the radical difference between the philosophies of Jaspers and Heidegger. Conversely, a far-reaching similarity to Franz Rosenzweig is noticeable, a philosopher who, unjustly, has hardly been noticed outside of a small Jewish circle. All three agree that reason cannot deduce, or conceive of, Being, as idealistic philosophy wanted it to do. Man and the world are here ahead of all explanations. Jaspers', Heidegger's and Rosenzweig's philosophical efforts are all concerned with the self-finding of human existence. They do not consider the mission of philosophy as knowledge of the nature of the world, as did Greek philosophy; nor of the nature of God, as did the medieval philosophers; nor of the nature of man, as do modern philosophers. Philosophy, rather, should remind man of himself, of his *Existenz*.

But, according to Heidegger, human existence discovers itself in that it "wrests Being from obscurity," and Heidegger wants to do this through the phenomenological method of his fundamental ontology. This method is supposed to reveal concealed Being (i.e., the Being which is forgotten in daily life and in idealistic philosophy), whereas Jaspers and Rosenzweig know that Being withdraws itself from all knowledge. Therefore, Jaspers holds Heidegger's method to be "in principle a philosophical error," which, "with propositions having greatest proximity to *Existenz*, misses *Existenz* and can become trifling." (*Allgemeine*, 649). Being can only be experienced in authentic Transcendence, but cannot be known. (Regarding the contrast between Heidegger's ontology and Jaspers' not-knowing, see Ernst Mayer: *Die Dialektik des Nichtwissens*, Basel, 1950). Like Jaspers, Rosenzweig says: "He (God) conceals Himself while He reveals Himself." (*Der Stern der Erlösung*, 1930, III, 156). The contrast between knowing and not-knowing is simultaneously the contrast between immanence and Transcendence, and between temporality and eternity. Heidegger reveals to man his nothingness in his freedom; man is "thrown" into his being-here and held into Nothingness. In Jaspers, on the contrary, and in Rosenzweig, man experiences himself, in his freedom and in his nothingness, as God-created. To all three every self-reflection is historical. But by "historical" consciousness Heidegger means only that human existence reveals itself as finite temporality, which produces itself within time *(zeitigt sich)*; i.e., runs on ahead toward death. But to Rosenzweig and Jaspers "historical" consciousness means at the same time that the eternal reveals itself to man in the temporal.

relates himself in the world toward that which is not of this world. This self-conduct, life *sub specie aeternitatis*, is called *"existing"* by Jaspers (with reference to Kierkegaard) ; and him who lives in this way Jaspers calls *Existenz*.

The realization of the modes of the Encompassing is only the first step toward philosophy, a step which frees our consciousness of being from the narrow world of appearances in which we live and directs us toward the Encompassing. Our thinking receives a "jolt;" it frees itself from the real, which approaches us at first, and becomes "suspended,"[19] leading us to the abyss where we may experience either God or nothingness: the second step. Philosophy cannot predict whether one will experience God or nothingness in the second step. Each one of us must answer for it himself in his own *Existenz*. Philosophizing is not really abstract thinking about God or nothingness, but the expression of the experiences which the individual thinker has.

If, now, a positivistic scientist were to say to Goethe: Your research of nature is quite proper, but the radiance of the divine which you see in your imagination does not exist in reality, the philosophy of the Encompassing could answer him: Certainly, scientific research knows only the objective world and nothing over and beyond it. Philosophy, however, "can puncture the cataract of our blindness,"[20] the blindness with which our knowledge is cursed if it sticks to the object. If, however, you take the first step, it might happen to you, too, that you will see, in the second step, whereof Goethe and Jaspers are speaking.

IV.

Many thinkers, shaken by the contemporary crisis and desiring to overcome the faithlessness of positivism, are not satisfied with Jaspers' philosophy which, although it gains "insight into the nature of the entire scope of truth" with methodical clarity,[21] does not, for reasons of method, proclaim truth itself.[22] Therefore, two often contested and misunderstood steps of Jaspers may be made clearer by an analogy. For those to whom, because of a stern

---

[19] Goethe says the same of his procedure in art and in natural research, and he distinguishes himself from those "who stick to the real" (*Gespräche mit Eckermann*, December 25, 1825).

[20] *Wahrheit*, 966.   [21] *Rechenschaft*, 217.

[22] At any rate, "speculations of . . . Professor Jaspers are pursued with close attention" by those who are turning away from positivism and who have a "thirst for belief," as the *Times* writes in its special issue, "The Mind of 1951," London, August 24, 1951, 2.

puritanical upbringing, love appears taboo, the ideas of D. H. Lawrence and John Middleton Murry can have a liberating effect, because they overcome "the conflict between *Eros* and *Agape*" and include "fear and shame in their love-making."[23] But even the reference to love and the readiness thereto do not guarantee the actual love experience. In this same way the concept of the Encompassing can operate as release and prepare us for faith. But the actual experience of faith, as of love, happens to a person — or it does not. I cannot desire it. It is "granted" to us as a gift, or else it fails to appear.[24]

Even if man has had the experience of faith, when he has "become aware of the true, identical with the divine," he still cannot grasp it. The believer, just like the lover, can only know — of the experience of which he is certain — what it is *not*. Thus, love is not just sexuality, not merely the rearing of children; but what the intrinsic essence of true love is, the lover cannot directly express. He can speak symbolically, as Goethe does in the following lines:

> "For, in times already lived,
> You were my sister or my wife."

But this verse precisely does not express knowledge — say of a transmigration of souls —, but it expresses the incomprehensible: that in the temporal experience of love something eternal became present to him. Thus the believer becomes aware of the divine: not as a knowable object but as the Encompassing of the Encompassing. The philosophy of the Encompassing is, "on the way of demythologizing our thought, the most far-reaching attempt at liberation to date,"[25] and this liberation "leaves realms open in which God is able to speak,"[26] after the pseudo-scientific world system had closed these realms through pseudo-knowledge.

All objective expressions remain suspended in mid-air. They are ambiguous and leave room for doubt. Only personal experience is not to be doubted. Philosophical faith remains, therefore, in tension between the indecision of expression and the decision of action; between not-knowing and inner certainty. Socrates, the first philosopher who knew that he did not know the absolute, preserved his determination in the face of death. "Against my

23 J. M. Murry, *Adam and Eve* (1944) 118, 132.

24 It is, therefore, a misconception of F. Heinemann to conceive of not-desiring as "fear of decision." (Articles in the periodicals: *Die Neue Rundschau*, winter 1949; *Revue Internationale de Philosophie*, July 1949; *Zeitschrift für Philosophische Forschung*, V/1, 1951).

25 *Wahrheit*, 184.   26 *Ibid.*, 187.

doubt there is no refutation, only action. Transcendence is not to be proved, but to be testified to."[27] The believer can only prove and assure himself in communication with others, but he can prove nothing objectively.

Herein lies the strength as well as the weakness of philosophical faith. It appears as a weakness to him who seeks guaranteed knowledge of Transcendence to which he can cling. But what first appears as weakness is actually strength, because only in not-knowing is human freedom preserved. Were man to know God's will, the only course open to him would be automatic obedience. Together with Socrates, Pascal, Kant and Kierkegaard, Jaspers sees the "unexplorable wisdom by which we exist, not less venerable . . . in that which it denies us as in that of which it allows us to partake."[28]

V.

The vision of divine radiance is, according to Goethe and Jaspers, not a mystical vision. The mystic achieves Being by freeing himself from the world and by blotting out his temporal consciousness. For Jaspers, on the contrary, Transcendence becomes present to man while he remains in the world and comes "to the unthinkable through the development of the thinkable."[29] In a transformation wherein he remains earth-bound, the world appears to him in a light which it never had before. It becomes transparent to him, it becomes "the language of Transcendence."[30] This can also be expressed thus: The world becomes "cipher (Jaspers);" "symbol (Goethe and Jaspers);" or, "Everything transitory is only a parable" (Goethe: end of *Faust*, II); or, man is a creature, the world is created.[31]

That the world is a symbol does not mean, however, that this world signifies another world. And it is no scientific hypothesis of creation to say that the world is created. Rather, these manners

27 *Philosophie*, III, 204. Rosenzweig says the same thing: "Faith and doubt clearly mean: to do Yes and to do No. . . . Doubt is sin, and sin only; theoretical doubt is not doubt at all." *Letters* (1935), 222f.

28 I. Kant: *Critique of Practical Reason*, 266; cited, in agreement, by Jaspers: *Psychologie*, 343, and *Rechenschaft*, 111.

29 *Wahrheit*, 893.

30 *Philosophie*, III, 129; *Wahrheit* and *Scope* in various passages.

31 Max Brod expresses the idea that the world is a cipher or a symbol with the fitting term "immanent miracle *(Diesseitswunder)*." Max Brod: *Heidentum, Christentum, Judentum*, (1921), I, 228ff. For Rosenzweig, too, the world is "the miracle." Franz Rosenzweig: *Stern der Erlösung*, I, 62.

of expression reveal the secret that in this world something is revealed to us which we do not know, and, therefore, cannot objectify as a concept of Transcendence. We cannot know it and cannot form any image of it. In this sense must one understand Jaspers' "being in two worlds;"[32] also Kant's, Goethe's and Kafka's statements that man is a "citizen of two worlds."[33] "That there is cipher at all is identical with the idea that there is Transcendence, because, as existences, we can conceive of Transcendence in no other way than as existence."[34]

If the world achieves this significance, there are consequences for our actions, for our cognition and our creativity. The world for us is no longer a stage for frivolous and senseless bustling, from which we may keep ourselves apart. We want to partake in it, "to inspire and animate it,"[35] and to love it. The world is no longer of no concern to us. First love served us as a comparison; now it turns out to be the action of faith. Again let us refer to Goethe as an example. The infinite importance of the world occasions him (1) "to get to know himself . . . through action" in the world according to the "demands of the day;"[36] (2) to investigate the world through science (therefore his interest in natural science) ; and (3) with "imagination [attuned] to the truth of the actual . . . to perceive the larger in the small"[37] in his art.

The demands of the day are ambiguous, however. According to Goethe and Jaspers, only he does justice to these demands who is imbued with the historical consciousness that "every time is in immediate proximity to God;"[38] that is, he who, in the [passing] moment of time, is conscious of eternity. Whoever follows the demands of the day without this faith, however, degenerates in the dissipating aspects of the day and is lost in senseless activity.[39]

Now, does not the question arise, whether this relationship which Goethe had to the world was possible only in a time which

---

32 *Wahrheit,* 392.

33 J. W. von Goethe: *Gespräche mit Kanzler von Müller,* April 29, 1818; Franz Kafka: *Gesammelte Schriften,* VI, 208.

34 *Philosophie,* III, 206 (852).   35 *Ibid.,* I, 82; II, 141.

36 J. W. von Goethe: *Maximen und Reflexionen.*

37 J. W. von Goethe: *Gespräche mit Eckermann,* Dec. 25, 1825.

38 *Wahrheit,* 914; Jaspers repeats Ranke's phrase here.

39 Pragmatism also evidences this ambiguity. In William James the *Pragma* achieves the meaning of the demands of the day in the way Goethe and Jaspers understand it. The majority of his disciples, on the other hand, understand it only in a utilitarian way.

did not yet know the terribleness of the present? In Max Weber Jaspers saw that man can fulfill the demands of the day even in the present crisis. Max Weber had seen calamity coming already in the sheltered days before the First World War, and yet — or because of it — he reminded us "to go to work and do justice to the demands of the day."[40] He did them justice, for, as Jaspers says of him, "the worse things got, the more his faith grew."[41]

Jaspers' own philosophy was kindled by the flame of Max Weber. He considers the tension between action in the world — to "accomplish what is possible today"[42] — and foundering in the world to be characteristic of Max Weber. This tension between action and foundering is an essential feature of Jaspers' own philosophy. Man is certain of God in the face of the ultimate situations of suffering and death.* In contrast to the Stoic position, which was content in such a situation with passive endurance, "active endurance is capable of experiencing the foundering** of all existence and of still going on, as long as there is any strength left."[43] Jaspers adopts the old phrase: philosophy is learning to die. But he supplements it by adding that knowing how to die is only possible through really "learning to live,"[44] learning to live in order to realize oneself in communication with others and to bring to realization what the hour demands. This faith of Jaspers stood the test throughout the terrible Nazi period.

VI.

We have not yet spoken of Judaism in Jaspers' thinking, and yet we have been speaking of it for some time. For what kind of faith is it which experiences the one God, the God of Whom we cannot form any image or idea? What sort of faith is it which demands of man conversion (metanoia) and love? A faith of active endurance which, in suffering and in failure, hears the voice of God? Which, in the face of calamity, does not despair of the

---

[40] Max Weber: Wissenschaft als Beruf (1919), 37.

[41] Monograph, 72.

[42] Max Weber: Politik als Beruf.

* Editor's Note: Cf. Latzel's essay for a discussion of these.

** Editor's Note: Cf. Thyssen's essay for a discussion of foundering.

[43] Philosophie, III, 236 (878). "To experience Being in foundering (Philosophie, III, 237)" does not mean, as Jaspers is often misunderstood to say, to seek foundering, but rather this: although all realization ends in foundering, still to aim for realization in the world. Man has the strength for this through faith, in everyday life as well as in his great moments.

[44] Wisdom, 126.

world but leads man to activity in it? What sort of faith is it, if not that which finds expression in the Bible?

In fact, in the decisive moments of his thought, Jaspers is conscious of the connection of his thoughts with the Bible. Let us see what he says of this in his various works. In the philosophical transcending to Transcendence he finds expressed what was demanded "of the Old Testament Jew: Not to make unto himself any image or any likeness; and what he has his God say: 'I am that I am':"[45] The one God "is the originally experienced God of the Hebrew prophets."[46] The myth of the fall of man expresses to him the experience of human freedom and guilt.[47] The story of Job is the story of defiance and devotion.[48]

During the terrible period of the Nazi regime the Bible was to Jaspers the "book which was our comfort for those twelve years."[49] The comfort which the Bible gave him one can see in his *The Question of German Guilt,* his first published work after the overthrow of the Nazis. Here he points to the example of Jeremiah who experienced the destruction of everything for which he had worked all his life, and who, in this desperate situation, called to his disciple, Baruch, and said: "The Lord saith thus: Behold; that which I have built will I break down, and that which I have planted I will pluck up, and seekest thou great things for thyself? Seek them not." These words of Jeremiah mean to Jaspers: "That God is, is enough. When all things fade away, God is — that is the only fixed point."[50] Again and again he returns to these words of Jeremiah, in order to show that the person who is certain of God does not despair in the ultimate situation.[51] In this same sense he says: "herein the Jews exemplify Europeanism," in that they experienced the "lostness" of man, but then did not turn away from the world, as did the Stoics, but rather bestrode the path to reconstruction *in* the world. "In this Biblical thought is rooted a basic strength of Western history."[52]

In Jaspers' second systematic work, written during the Nazi period, the references to the Bible increase, beginning with formal transcending up to the experience of the "deepest, absolute

45 *Philosophie,* III, 67 (732).

46 *Ibid.,* 124 (781).   47 *Ibid.,* 73 (737).   48 *Ibid.,* 74 (738).

49 Von der biblischen Religion, in: *Die Wandlung,* I, 407 (1946).

50 *Question,* 122f.

51 *Allgemeine,* 636; *Wahrheit,* 794; *Wisdom,* 39.

52 *Rechenschaft,* 243.

trust" in God.[53] Also in his position regarding the questions of the day does he use the Bible as his point of departure. Thus, he says of the re-education of the Germans that it is only possible through a "metamorphosis," which has the Bible and Greek antiquity as its "source and standard."[54] He finds symbolic expression of the idea of a world order of free states in Isaiah; that the swords shall be beaten into plowshares.[55]

He even sees modern science as conditioned by Biblical religion. True, research is without presuppositions. But precisely this pre-suppositionless research is tied to "the state of mind and the impulses that have their roots in Biblical religion."[56] These motives are: 1) God's demand for truthfulness, which gives cognition its seriousness; 2) the idea of creation, which makes even the most abysmal thing worth knowing, in contrast to Greek science which contented itself with an already closed cosmos; and 3) the Job-like struggle with God in the face of terrible reality, which leads to an illusion-free hazarding of cognition. Jaspers sees a danger that with the elimination of even one of these motives science becomes crippled. For this reason it appears certain to him that, not only for philosophy but for all political and spiritual life as well, "the decision on the future of our Western humanity lies in the relation of our faith to the Biblical religion."[57]

All this does not imply that Jaspers affirms everything contained in the Bible. Rather, it will be seen that other aspects of Biblical religion remain alien to him. He groups together into seven basic elements what is, to him, the "irreplaceable" and "eternal truth" of Biblical religion.[58]

1) *The one God:* Not the thought of Him is what matters, but the transformation which the idea of the one God effects; namely, that this thought induces seriousness toward the One and Unconditional from out of the dissipation in the riches of the world.

2) *The Transcendence of the Creator-God:* It overcomes magic and the demonic, and it brings to consciousness the secret that the world does not consist of itself, — it is created —, and that man experiences himself in his freedom as a gift granted to himself: he is created in the image of God.

3) *The encounter of man with God:* Man can, in prayer, turn

---

53 *Wahrheit,* 692. 54 *Rechenschaft,* 158. 55 *Origin,* 213.
56 *Ibid.,* 91. 57 *Ibid.,* 226.
58 *Scope,* 88 and 109. By "Biblical religion" Jaspers does not understand an abstraction from the individual religions, but the original comprehensive scope out of which all of them once arose. In this sense Jesus, too, belongs to Biblical religion.

to transcendent God as to a person. Pure prayer is unselfish and expresses the trust: Thy will be done.

4) *God's commandments:* All of God's basic truths are expressed in the Ten Commandments and in the exhortation to the love of one's neighbor.

5) *Historical consciousness:* God's guidance is experienced in history. Through the historical consciousness that God is present in temporal occurences, the here and now gains significance.

6) *Suffering:* Whereas man in Greek tragedy remains silent in the face of foundering, Biblical man overcomes tragedy by continuing to operate in foundering.[59] The previously mentioned phrase of Jeremiah, the story of the Deutero-Isaiahan servant of God, and the symbol of the Christian cross express this active suffering.

7) *Candor toward the insolubles:* Job and the writer of *Ecclesiastes* evidence the insoluble of every expressed theodicy, but not in order to end in despair, but to expose belief to extreme verification. Job asks why the innocent is caused to suffer and, although he knows no answer, he believes.

VII.

Even adherents of established religions could be in agreement with what has been said thus far. But they would not yet be satisfied. As for them, a certain something is still missing. Thus, says Kierkegaard, "religiousness B (by which he means Christianity, in contrast to religiousness A, which we call philosophical faith) makes stipulations in such a way that these stipulations ... are a certain something which more closely define eternal salvation."[60] This certain something to which salvation is bound — as seen from the outside: by which it is limited; as seen from the inside: through which it is guaranteed — is, in Christianity, the belief in salvation through the cross, which occurred once and for all at Golgatha; in Judaism it is obedience to the law, which was proclaimed once and for all on Mount Sinai. The particular revelations establish cults and religious communities, — in Christianity the Church, in Judaism the people of the covenant —, and these separate the religions from each other.

[59] Cf. Jaspers' interpretation of tragedy in *Tragedy*, 80ff.

[60] Søren Kierkegaard: *Abschliessende unwissenschaftliche Nachschrift, Werke* VII, 238.

To philosophical faith, which does not isolate itself, this certain something is alien. To the particular religion as well as to philosophical faith the perception of God's voice is essential. But in the physical hearing of God's voice philosophy sees a remnant of pre-scientific, mythical knowledge. It understands the hearing of God's voice or the vision of the divine radiance only in a figurative sense: it expresses the experience of the eternal in temporal existence. Revelation of the eternal, therefore, cannot be definitely known, but can only be perceived indirectly in the world and is indescribable. It cannot have happened once and for all, but it can "at any time be freely and newly grasped."[61]

Thus man, as discussed here, is a believer and a non-believer simultaneously. A non-believer from the point of view of religion, because he does not believe in that certain something; but a believer, nevertheless, in that he is no less certain of the presence of the divine in the transitory. And because, despite his disbelief in the religious tradition, he is still, basically, a believer, he can adopt the content of the religious tradition by demythologizing it. He adopts Christ not as dogma of a God-man,[62] but as "the deepest symbol of foundering in the world . . . knowing, fulfilling, and completing in foundering,"[63] or, as Rosenzweig adopts the Jewish law, not because of the "pseudo-historical theory of its origin, nor because of the pseudo-juridical theory of its power of obligation," but because of its "present meaning."[64]

Jaspers calls this demythologized revelation "historical consciousness" because he knows that God's voice is always perceived historically, in a concrete moment and throughout the course of history. In contrast to religion which proclaims the Messianic or Christian fulfillment of history at a definite moment, and in contrast to the secularization of this pronouncement by Hegel and Marx, — who, with their hybrid reason, imagined a goal as the fulfillment of history —, divine revelation becomes, for Jaspers, perceptible through all of history, but not knowable in the sense that every period is in immediate proximity to God. In the demythologizing of revelation religion sees an attenuation and

---

[61] *Wahrheit*, 788.   [62] *Ibid.*, 853.   [63] *Ibid.*, 925.

[64] Franz Rosenzweig: *Kleinere Schriften*, 1937, 111, 116. Even though Rosenzweig understands the law in its demythologized form, he nevertheless adheres to it as being that element which distinguishes Judaism from the other religions. Herein is his position distinct from that of Jaspers, where previously their similarity has been emphasized. Jaspers wants to penetrate to the original Biblical religion by way of Judaism and Christianity and, as will be shown later, through this Biblical religion, to the one truth which no religion possesses by itself, but of which all partake. For Rosenzweig "mundane truth" remains "split" into Judaism and Christianity. *Ibid.*, 396.

abstraction; philosophy, on the other hand, a "purification and deepening."[65]

Philosophical faith is, by its very nature, tolerant, because it knows that the Absolute appears in historical form. The religions which know that they are in possession of absolute truth need not exclude the recognition of other truths either. The religions of India remain, in fact, always tolerant. In the Biblical world, the Talmud promised the devout of all nations a share in the other world; and Cusanus, too, saw the truth in other religions. *"Una religio in rituum varietate."* But, on the other hand, there arose, now and then, in the Bible and especially in solidified Christianity and Judaism, the claim to the possession of the sole and absolute truth for all. Excommunication, inquisition, burnings at the stake and wars of annihilation against those of other beliefs are the consequences of such a "fatal claim."[66] It continues to operate to this date, in secularized form, in the truth-fanaticism of Communism. The heterogeneity of philosophical faith and religion then turns to enmity. With the same passion which he shows for the truth of the Bible, Jaspers rejects the claim of exclusiveness when it occurs in the Bible, and combats the claim of *"coge intrare."*[67]

But the fruitful times are not those in which the two remain apart, but those in which they penetrate each other. By setting them in opposition we see only what divides them. But precisely in their one-sidedness are they actually dependent on each other. Kierkegaard, who served as our authority for characterizing religion (religiousness B, according to his designation), presupposes for religion also the free relationship to God which characterizes philosophical faith (religiousness A). Biblical religion is distinguished from others in that God is experienced in it as a personal Thou and is addressed as such, but still remains image-less. The basic character of God, of whom no image or likeness is made, is pure, however, only in the momentary experience, and it solidifies into a conception of an image or likeness already in its expression. But, the holding fast to this conception, "the *having* turned into *knowing* by virtue of revelation" is "superstition."[68] In order that faith should not be transformed into superstition both Kierkegaard and Jaspers demand self-examination by means of philosophical reflection.

In thought, conversely, the idea of God grows pale. The philosophical idea of God achieves its fulfillment only in the religious tradition. Philosophy, therefore, needs the solidified tradition of

65 *Wahrheit,* 854; *Scope,* 84.

66 *Scope,* 88.　　　　67 Luke, 14:23.　　　　68 *Wahrheit,* 789.

religion no less than religion needs the self-consciousness of philosophy. Even when philosophers like Nietzsche fight against religion, they are themselves well aware of this. "We immoralists, we Godless ones of today . . . (we too) feel ourselves the heirs . . . to the piety of millenia."[69] Were the religious tradition to disappear, however, in the communities in which the philosophers live, then the sources from which philosophical faith draws its content would run dry.[70]

VIII.

Biblical religion contains both: the free relationship to God and the solidification into cult, national religion, law and dogma. But it is precisely these tensions "which have kept the Western world in motion up to now."[71] Solidification has made tradition possible, but the constantly recurring breakthroughs of direct experience have prevented the solidifications from hardening.

Immediately after the pronouncement that we should not make for ourselves any image of God, the people deserted to an image of God, to the cast golden calf.[72] Desertion and return are interwoven throughout Biblical history from beginning to end. All through the Bible these opposites continue to be found: cult religion versus the prophetic struggle against the cult: "I desired mercy, and not sacrifice;"[73] the religion of law versus the prophetic doubt of the law: "The pen of the scribes is in vain;"[74] national religion versus the abrogation by the prophets of the chosen-people characteristic: "Are ye not as children of the Ethiopians unto me, O children of Israel?";[75] the Christ-God versus the statement of Jesus himself: "There is none good but one, that is, God."[76]

The dialectical movement continues after the close of the Bible. In the word of God, which the prophets knew to be spoken univocally, there remained a remnant of a corporeal presence. They still lacked the critical examination through philosophical

[69] Friedrich Nietzsche: *Morgenröte, Werke* IV, 200.

[70] Cf. *Wahrheit,* 916; *Scope,* 112; *Rechenschaft,* 359.

[71] *Scope,* 107.

[72] In the story of the golden calf, a dance around the gold is not what is meant, but the dance around the "cast and craven object." The people did not aspire to gold; rather, they gave their gold away in order to form a visible God, and in this way they deserted when celebrating "the feast for JHWH." Cf. *Exodus,* 32:5.

[73] *Hosea,* 6:6.   [74] *Jeremiah,* 8:8.   [75] *Amos,* 9:7.

[76] *Mark,* 10:18; I cite the same passages from the prophets which Jaspers used himself. Cf. *Scope,* 98f.

self-consciousness. For that reason the meeting of Biblical monotheism with the monotheism of Greek philosophy was very fruitful. "They interpreted each other."[77] In the new theological-
metaphysical speculation the idea of God was spiritualized and
purified of the remains of mythical personification.

But the drawback of the philosophical idea of God has already
been revealed: in thinking, God is far removed and in knowing
Him, the actual relationship to Him is apt to be forgotten. And
this is precisely what happened. But over and against the Graeco-
Judaic and Graeco-Christian speculation, first of all in the Gnosis,
then in medieval theology and metaphysics, there broke through,
again and again, the "Transcendence as against all metaphysics . . .
a completely free relationship to God, a personal trust instead of
all guarantees," according to the fitting words of Count York.[78]
The same thing happened with Augustine and Luther, then again
with Pascal and Kierkegaard.[79] They are the ones who, from time
to time, renewed the entire spiritual life after it had solidified.[80]

By Christian thinkers from Augustine to Kierkegaard, as well
as by Jewish thinkers like Jehuda Halevi, Biblical and Greek
monotheism was not interpreted in a way wherein the former
receded behind the latter; that is, the actual relationship to God
behind the knowledge of Him, but rather in this way — to use
their own words — that the "God of Abraham," the personally
experienced God, was explained through the "God of Aristotle,"
through the *idea* of one God.[81] They were not only concerned
with thinking and knowing (knowing, in Greek, is: *gignoskein*,
therefore *Gnosis*), but with *existing* and doing.

But, however far-reaching the free relationship to God — instead of all guarantees — may be for them, these thinkers still
retain a remnant of a personified reality which guarantees Transcendence. To Augustine and Pascal the Church, to Luther and
Kierkegaard the Scriptures, were, as formerly the word of God

---

77 *Scope*, 81.

78 Cf. *Briefwechsel zwischen Wilhelm Dilthey und dem Grafen York von Wartenburg* (1923), 144.

79 York speaks only of Augustine and Luther.

80 We purposely say: the entire spiritual life, not only the religious. Even the
origin of the Renaissance resulted less from the renewal of the Greek-classical
motifs than of Biblical-religious ones, as K. Burdach has shown in contrast to prevalent opinion. The influence of Augustine, particularly in the movement of
Joachim of Fiori and Saint Francis of Assisi, was a "main factor in the rise of Humanism and the Renaissance, as well as of the Reformation." Cf. K. Burdach:
Reformation, Renaissance, Humanismus (1918), 214.

81 Cf. Pascal's *Pensées*, Kierkegaard's *Fear and Trembling*, and Jehuda Halevi's
Kuzari.

to the prophets, a remnant of personified reality, although essentially they attacked this kind of reality.[82]

IX.

Basically Jaspers continues their struggle. Only Jaspers succeeds in freeing Transcendence from the last remnants of mythical imagery and intellectual objectivity by means of his basic idea of the Encompassing. Let Jaspers speak for himself:

He [the one God] is the Encompassing of all Encompassing and [He] arouses the deepest, absolute trust. He is *the* power . . . and the greatest closeness which has its place within the inwardness of man. He is providence, not fate; inscrutably He guides in inconceivable judgement.

But whatever is said about Him, is immediately also false. The Godhead's every manner of speaking is not itself in its absolute Transcendence, but is a way in which it seems to speak to people in an appearance. There is no objective guarantee that it is God who is speaking. Rather, everything in the world is expressed ambiguously. Our urge to possess Him just the same, in some form of knowledge, some thought, some concept, is resisted by the sublime, relentless demand of Transcendence, a demand that was recognized in all its depth and relentlessness by the Hebrew prophets: Thou shalt not make unto thee any craven image, or any likeness. What historically referred in the first instance to images, came to include the condition under which genuine Transcendence alone makes itself felt and remains real to people. . . . The consequence is: A free relationship to the one God in His infinite distance is truthful only in the deepest inwardness, in a nearness which is immediately historical — in this destiny, in this situation, in this world and reality.[83]

Jaspers' philosophizing has been followed here from the point of view of the question: what is Being? After the old ontological and metaphysical answers to these questions had collapsed, and after Kant had revealed the limits of our knowledge, Jaspers sought to transcend the knowable to the unknowable, to the modes of the Encompassing and, through them, to Transcendence. But man does not become aware of Transcendence through thinking, — if he finds satisfaction with the knowable content of thought (clings to it, as Goethe says) —, but only if he brings the knowable into suspension and relates himself toward Transcendence. Statements concerning Transcendence are negative and limiting only (since they tell what Transcendence is not) , or

[82] *Scope,* 79ff. esp. 81.   [83] *Wahrheit,* 692f.

ambiguous and suspended (since the statements are made in objective form and yet refer to no object). They do not state what we objectively know but what we inwardly experience.

"Let us never forget," says Kierkegaard, "that the not-knowing of Socrates was a form of fear and service of God; that his not-knowing is the Greek expression of the Jewish 'Fear of God is the beginning of wisdom'."[84] As previously stated, the believer lives, therefore, in the tension between objective not-knowing and subjective certainty, between indecision of expression and decision of doing. Inasmuch as the concept of the encompassing Transcendence has meaning only in respect to personal experience, it does not permit the expression of the experience to harden. Faith is affirmed only in personal relationship to God — or it is not. "[To faith] all formulated and written philosophy is only preparation or recollection, only inspiration or confirmation."[85]

It was thus that Jaspers carried to its [logical] conclusion the struggle of Pascal and Kierkegaard in behalf of the *experience* of God, as over against the mere *knowledge* of God. Out of our own faith-experience we understand again the original faith-experience of the Bible. We rescue it from its fixations. Thus we adopt the Bible transformed. "We philosophize out of Biblical religion."[86]

[84] Søren Kierkegaard: *Die Krankheit zum Tode*, German translation by Bärthold (1905), 122.

[85] *Scope*, 10.

[86] *Scope*, 88; here translated more literally. When Freiherr von Campenhausen, in an otherwise fruitful theological discussion of Jaspers' philosophical faith, sees Jaspers taking a position in favor of Judaism as against Christianity, he misunderstands Jaspers' intentions (Cf. "Die philosophische Kritik des Christentums bei Karl Jaspers," in: *Zeitschrift für Theologie und Kirche*, XLVIII, 238 [1951]). Jaspers does define his position in favor of the original Biblical faith-experience as contrasted to metaphysical knowledge and, to that extent — and only to that extent — in favor of the Jewish element. But, in so doing, he does not oppose Christianity but the Hellenistic-Gnostic element, in the same way as the above-mentioned Christian thinkers who defined their position as being in favor of the experienced God — the God of Abraham — as against the invented God of Greek philosophy. Judaism is the Old Testament *plus* the "verbal law" of the later Talmudic development. This is why the Samaritans, who did not participate in the post-Biblical developments, and the Karaites, who abrogated them, are not counted as belonging to Judaism. *Every* religious separation, Jewish as well as Christian, is alien to Jaspers' philosophical faith. If Judaism is considered in terms of its difference from Christianity, it is understood in its narrower sense. But when, in this essay, we speak of Judaism in Jaspers' thought, it is to be understood in its wider sense: as the original, encompassing realm out of which Talmudic Judaism — Judaism in its narrower sense — *and* Christianity arose, as distinguished from the Greek spirit. Just as the Church Fathers considered Judaism and Christianity together — in contrast, either in similarity or in opposition, to the Greek spirit — when they gave Plato the name of Moses Atticus.

X.

But if, in this way, the source of Jaspers' thinking is shown to be Biblical religion — the purpose of this treatise — it is not implied that the Bible is the only source of his thought. His basic concept of the Encompassing expresses not only the Biblical experience of the image-less God, but also the Greek conception of pure Being. "Every philosophy was, in fact, a philosophy of the Encompassing. . . . My basic concept is . . . only apparently new."[87] Absolute truth appears to us only in historical form. And yet the truth can be only one. But the unity of truth, which the editor of this series — together with F. C. S. Schiller — justifiably raises as the central problem of philosophy, cannot be reached by a general concept which abstracts from all historical particulars, but only by a penetration of all historical forms of truth to its source; to the elevation of man above the sensory world to Transcendence, to the revelation of Being in man. The one truth is not the exclusive property of one religion or of one philosophy, but each has a part in it as the *philosophia perennis,* the invisible religion and the invisible realm of spirits. They meet each other and understand each other in reference to the one God, and they belong to one another.[88]

Philosophy, therefore, is impelled to communication with all truth. It goes beyond Biblical religion and seeks to open itself to the other two sublime religious circles alongside the Bible: The Hindu and the Chinese. Indeed, the particular value of the West becomes even more apparent by contrast; namely, the road to Transcendence through activity in the world and through the unfolding of the conceivable. But, in contrast, our deficiency, too, becomes apparent, "what we lack and what vitally concerns us."[89]

What we hear simultaneously from an Oriental philosopher seems as if in reply to Jaspers' readiness to open his soul to the truth of the East also.

We must be in a position to consider sympathetically the precious heritages of other religions. . . . It is not a question of fusing all religions into one, but enabling each religion to assimilate whatever it can from the truths of other religions. . . . It is the age-old wisdom of the prophet souls of East and West that . . . the many religions are the varied dialects of the one language of the human spirit.[90]

[87] *Wahrheit,* 191f.   [88] Cf. *Philosophie* I, 284; *Wahrheit,* 979; *Origin,* 269ff.
[89] *Origin,* 69.

[90] Sir Sarvepalli Radhakrishnan: "Religion and World Unity," in the *Hibbert Journal* (April 1951), 223ff.

XI.

Since early antiquity, in the story of Adam's fall, thinking has been considered to be a curse, because it destroys our innocence and, along with knowledge, brings pain. Especially in our own intellectualized times, threatened by nihilism, thought is accused of disintegrating traditional faith. Will not the radical Demythologizing contained in Jaspers' philosophy — even if contrary to his intention — only strengthen this nihilistic scepticism?

But thinking is our lot; we can no longer abrogate it. It depends on us whether it is to have a destructive or a liberating effect. Only half-thinking, which sticks to the objectively knowable and to which the perceptible world is everything, leads to disbelief. Conversely, full-thinking "is a weapon against nihilistic scepticism,"[91] because it points out to hybrid thought, — which wants to *know* what faith *believes* —, what its limits are. It renders unto science what is science's, and unto faith what is its due.

But it does not render faith itself. It does not because there is no knowledge of that which encompasses the perceptible world. Such knowledge of the supernatural as characterized naïve mythology would today, after the Enlightenment, be superstition. Yet, every philosophy worthy of its name concerns itself only with God, freedom, and immortality, as we previously quoted Kant as saying. Philosophy pronounces no knowable teachings about these, but it reminds us of them and refers to them. However each individual must become certain of them himself.

A nihilist is not a person who does not know about God, but rather one who does not *exist* with this knowledge, who does not adopt its seriousness to his own life. Regardless of how one interprets Nietzsche's cry "God is dead," whether as "obscurity and eclipse" or as "a new dawn," Nietzsche is in any case right in contending that "the greatest recent occurrence, that God is dead," consists of this: that "an old, deep trust" has disappeared before "even its proclamation [of the occurrence] had arrived."[92] Nihilism, therefore, cannot be overcome by contradicting this occurrence, nor by any other pronouncement, but only by the reversal of the occurrence itself: through the personal conversion of man.

The source of this conversion is the Bible. Hitler, who wanted to establish a nihilistic, bestial empire of blood and power, and who wanted to destroy conscience and the love of man, did not accidentally wage his campaign of annihilation against the Jews.

91 *Wahrheit*, 187.   92 Friedrich Nietzsche: *Morgenröte, Werke*, V, 272.

For, with the keen eye of the hater, he saw conscience as a "Jewish invention."[93] Although conscience is not an invention of Judaism, it is still bound to Biblical religion and to its transmission through Judaism and Christianity. This knowledge is vital in Jaspers' thinking. "Whatever we are, we are through Biblical religion . . . It is in fact thus: without the Bible we would slip into nothingness."[94]

JULIUS IZHAK LOEWENSTEIN

TEL AVIV
ISRAEL

[93] Hermann Rauschning: *Hitler speaks* (1939), 220.
[94] *Rechenschaft,* 260.

21

Søren Holm

JASPERS' PHILOSOPHY OF RELIGION

1. Is Karl Jaspers a Philosopher of Religion?

AN ESSENTIAL part of Karl Jaspers' philosophical "system"
is his *philosophy of religion* — although he has written no
book by that title — and we are entirely within our right in placing
him among the leading philosophers of religion of our time. To
prove this assertion one must, however, realize what is meant
by philosophy of religion, and on this point opinions have differed
greatly. Among theologians it is regarded as an introduction to
systematic theology or as a system of dogmatic principles. But this
view is scarcely tenable, because it overlooks the fact that the
philosophy of religion is by name a *philosophy*. Harald Høffding,
the great Danish philosopher, begins his *Philosophy of Religion*
by inquiring whether philosophy of religion ought to be a method
of thinking, springing from religion, or a method of thinking
treating religion as its subject. In the former case we arrive at
one of the traditional introductions to systematic theology, and
in the latter, preferred by Høffding himself, we arrive at a kind
of positive science of religion, religion becoming a positive subject of study as is the case in the history of religion, the psychology
of religion, etc., Høffding's religious philosophy bears the unmistakable marks of having been formed in the age of positivism.
The book is certainly philosophy, but also to a great extent
religious psychology, and as such it has nothing to do with
philosophy.

The philosophy of religion is a *philosophy*, as the name implies,
and this again indicates a contemplation of the world as a totality,
from a religious point of view. We have to realize, however, that
this is not a question of contemplating life on the basis of any
specific, concrete and positive religion, as for example, Christianity or Buddhism. If this were the case we would arrive at a confessional theology, not at an undogmatic religious philosophy;

and religious philosophy is, after all, philosophy and not theology, it is a philosophical discipline, not a theological one.

In religion we find man's total attitude towards life. The justification of such an attitude in philosophical form is the philosophy of religion. Just as metaphysics is incapable of commenting on the truth or untruth of a definite scientific tenet or law, so the philosophy of religion cannot treat of a tenet or dogma of a given specific religion. It must confine itself to discussing the validity of a religious attitude towards life, if it wishes to remain a philosophy. It must decide on the attitude to adopt with regard to the meaning of life, possible ends, and our personal relation to the totality of life. Is doubt our duty or is belief our right? I do not mean doubt about this or that particular phenomenon, but doubt or belief with respect to life in its totality.

If we use this meaning of the term, Jaspers is undoubtedly to be regarded as a philosopher of religion. His philosophy, taken as a whole, is a view of life rather than a view of the universe. It is not based on any particular picture of the universe, and it does not profess any definite philosophy of nature. In its essence it is rather a personal attitude towards life or, as we might also put it, an *'existential'* decision. Whereas much of the philosophy of the 19th century came into being in a struggle against natural science, the philosophy formed by Jaspers, the naturalist, developed under rather different conditions. His is a philosophy of personality, the creator of which faces an existence which is, in his view, encompassing, and for a man in this position metaphysics, religion, and faith must needs be exalted to their former rank. In this respect, then, Jaspers is a philosopher of religion, and no one could more *decidedly* be a philosopher of religion; though it is probably quite possible to be so on other grounds than these and with other sets of problems in hand.

2. TRANSCENDENCE

Whenever Jaspers expounds the relation between philosophy and religion demonstrating certain points of contrast, he refers to a definite, positive religion, especially to Christianity in its traditional, ecclesiastical form. When a specific religion makes concrete claims to revelation a conflict arises between religion and philosophy, because philosophy, rejecting all presuppositions, wants 'truth for truth's sake;' whereas the concrete revelational contents of any religion may grow into an unyielding dogma obstructing the way for the dynamic and personal quest for truth. But, if we leave religion in its positive, historic form, out of account, philosophy and religion appear to have the same purpose: They both strive to grasp something which lies beyond the pale of the human, outside of immanence. In the Platonic manner Jaspers is of the opinion that philosophy should be a crystallization of the timeless, which thus corresponds to the Platonic "eternal Ideas" or the "eternal" and "changeless Being." But, this being impossible in practice, philosophy can only be the attempt of a certain historical era to conceive Being, which latter is never in itself accessible to man. Then philosophy cannot be an expression of absolute knowledge, as it claims to be in the intellectualistic thinking of Hegel, but must be an expression of *faith,* as Jaspers with particular emphasis has expressed it in his book on *The Perennial Scope of Philosophy.*[1] The kind of faith that is expressed in the philosophical attitude, is, however, a faith without revelation; whereas in Christianity, for example, faith is a faith based on revelation.

In Jaspers' work faith is the expression of an *active* attitude towards life. It is not something which is bestowed on man as a gift of grace, as Luther doubtless opined it to be, however obscurely he may have set forth this view. Whereas faith and revelation may be described by a line pointing "downwards" from God to man, from supra-nature to nature, faith in Jaspers' view becomes a human achievement, which may be described by a line pointing "upwards" from man to Transcendence, and without passing outside the domain of Jaspers' philosophy we may give to this Transcendence the name of God. In traditional theology as well as in the philosophy of Jaspers we then seem to have the same contrasting concepts: On one side man and God, and on the other Transcendence or *supranatura.* It appears that only the directions of the religious relations differ. In theology God is the active, who conveys his grace from *supranatura* downwards to *natura,* whereas according to Jaspers there is a movement in the opposite direction from active man to the Transcendence which man in his religious attitude endeavors to grasp.

This difference is of supreme importance. But it is not the only difference. Being men, we are, empirically, placed in a world which — adopting a term often used in German philosophy — Jaspers calls *"Dasein,"* i.e., the empirical cognizable existence, and from this position man seeks to grasp *"Sein,"* which stands for Transcendence or Being as such. In traditional, protestant

[1] New York, 1949.

theology the grace of God is all-powerful, and man is thus unfree; whereas in the philosophy of Jaspers grace has been replaced by freedom to choose among possibilities. Existentialism constantly demands freedom and thus comes to stand in opposition to grace; whereas inversely, grace is the enemy of freedom, as Luther so emphatically put it in his book *De servo arbitrio* of 1525, in which he protests against Erasmus of Rotterdam's pamphlet *De libero arbitrio* (1524).

Another difference must also be stressed. For Jaspers Transcendence is not identical with the *supranatura* of the old theology and the metaphysics connected with it. According to the old conception of the relation between *natura* and *supranatura,* between immanence and Transcendence, this has always been thought of as being vertical. The words *supra* and *trans* actually tell us that something is placed above something else, which consequently must be below. This vertical position cannot, however, be maintained in our present scientific picture of the universe; it may doubtless be ascribed to some ancient, mythological picture, which is no longer valid. I think Jaspers may be said to have substituted a *horizontal* Transcendence for the vertical one. Transcendence is not so much what is "above" us as what is "around" us, and Jaspers himself has defined a concept which he calls *das Umgreifende:* "the Encompassing." This concept we shall have to examine a little more closely, as it involves some difficulties and is also, I think, marked by some obscurity of exposition.

In Jaspers the Encompassing and Transcendence are related, but not identical, concepts. We always live and think within a horizon; but behind it we find a new and wider horizon, behind which again there is still another, yet wider, horizon, and so forth *ad infinitum.* Thus the concept of the Encompassing comes into being. It is not identical with any one horizon, within which we always find the concretely real and true, but the Encompassing is that within which each horizon is enclosed. It is the absolutely Encompassing, which cannot any longer itself be regarded as horizon. Here Jaspers employs formulations which seem to call our attention to Nicolaus Cusanus' well-known term *coincidentia oppositorum,* which includes all differences and contrasts within its boundless frames — if we may use this paradoxical expression. The Encompassing contains a dialectical feature of uncertainty, being for us both present and disappearing. The Encompassing is either Being itself, which is everything in and by which we are, *or* it is that which we ourselves are and in which a certain form of Being makes itself visible to us. But in either case, both as Being itself and a medium for Being, the Encompassing is not the bare sum of definite and singular forms of Being, which are known to us singly, in parts and relations, but totality in its capacity as the extreme and self-supporting foundation of all Being, whether Being-in-itself *(sein an sich)* or Being-for-us *(Sein für uns)*.

The Encompassing and Transcendence are, as we noticed, not quite identical. Standing in immanence we only reach the Encompassing by transending, i.e., by a movement which passes beyond immanence. Only if the Encompassing finds expression in the world can it become an object of scrutiny, it can never be so in a direct manner. The Encompassing, when understood as ourselves is existence *(Dasein)*, consciousness-as-such, spirit, and is *Existenz*. But, when understood absolutely, it is identical with Transcendence, which may be defined as "The Encompassing of all Encompassing" *(das Umgreifende alles Umgreifenden)*. If we consider Transcendence as that which lies above and behind all forms of the Encompassing it becomes the Transcendence of all Transcendences. In this sense of the word Transcendence cannot be known, as the old metaphysics thought it could. Our relation to it is a practical one, and thus metaphysics and religion are very closely allied in Jaspers. The religious attitude in Jaspers' view is the *'existential'* aiming towards the Encompassing, towards Transcendence, towards God.

3. EXISTENZ AND FREEDOM

If we consider grace in its least personal form, it becomes more or less substantialized as in the Roman doctrine of "infused grace," *gratia infusa*, which works *ex opere operato* and thus cannot be connected with any personal freedom. Grace is a part of "nature," inasmuch as it is *supranatura* projecting itself on *natura* in order to penetrate and recreate it; but in this manner grace becomes a kind of contrast to spirit. Jaspers says, in his work *Psychologie der Weltanschauungen*, that the life of spirit is freedom.

It is true of both freedom and spirit that they are incapable of being totally perceived and known. As to freedom, the reason for this is that it is never, empirically, found anywhere to its full extent. Freedom is only experienced in its initial stage, in its development; in its pure form it is a construction or something towards which life or existence is moving. If freedom were to be known adequately, it would be something static. But it is, on the contrary, something dynamic, something inconceivable and, consequently, it cannot be known — a train of thought this which we also find in Nikolaj Berdyaeff and Paul Tillich. Freedom is at once something real and something paradoxical. To know something implies a setting of limits; but where there are limits there is no freedom, and to the extent that man is knowable, he is not free. Freedom is found subjectively only in the experience of infinity, which, by definition, is limitless. Freedom is nothing concrete and empirical to be demonstrated psychologically, but is always "floating, suspended, in labile equilibrium." Freedom is like the ocean or the starry sky, whereas the world of restriction is like a closed cage. Freedom can never become possession; it is indefinable, because it is not an object, and cannot, therefore, be scrutinized as an empirical object either.

As an individual I can never live in isolation, but must always be in communication with others. But this communicative relation is not something timeless or something of universal validity. It belongs in a definite, historical situation. In this situation I must, in freedom, make a decision with regard to eternity, so that in the midst of time I am raised above it. This is not to be understood in the manner of the mystics: that I am placed outside time in abstract timelessness. The idea is that eternity is drawn downwards into time, whenever I act and love unconditionally in time. The life that I am living here in freedom is a personal life or the being-free of *Existenz,* which forms a contrast to objective being or "the world;" and this contrast cannot be overcome by thought, nor can it be divided by it either. Being as status and being as freedom belong together; but they are so different that they cannot be compared. Object-being and being-as-freedom preclude each other, since the former moves from time into the timeless, whereas the latter moves from time into eternity, which, as mentioned, is not to be understood as the negation or dissolution of time, as the mystics held. What is, or is valid, for all time is objectivity, and what is eternal — although it changes and disappears at any moment — is *Existenz,* says Jaspers. Here he expresses himself in a manner which, obviously, is anything but Platonic.

The reason for this is that Jaspers desires to combine Being and *Existenz. Existenz* is always a sign-pointing towards a being which, it is true, is not objectively conceivable to anyone. But *Existenz* without relation to Transcendence has no meaning; and *Existenz* is defined as "authentic being," which has relation to itself and thus to Transcendence, through which latter it recognizes itself as being passive, and on which it founds itself. For this reason true *Existenz* also presupposes the leap from immanence to Transcendence; this leap is at once double and yet only one. It is the leap from the world to the divinity and from the existence of conscious spirit to *Existenz*. This leap takes place in freedom and always by concrete action in time. *Existenz* is something that is to be realized through freedom; it thus becomes the possibility of individual man in the given historical situation to which he belongs. *Existenz* is "grasping of the extratemporal through the temporal, not through the general concept." Being can never, in its essence, be comprehended or known intellectually or objectively. No consciousness, only a given form of *Existenz,* can be related to this Being. This is the reason why Jaspers' philosophy of this Being is not an ontological one. We never possess Being itself. We only constantly attempt, by way of the *'existential'* attitude or by free choice, to make our way towards this Being. This is the purpose of *'existential'* philosophy. It carries us out of our isolation, out of our want of communication, and it leads the godless to Transcendence. *'Existential'* philosophy is in its essence metaphysics, because it believes in that from which it itself springs. Transcendence is the strongest reality of all, but it is not object, since it cannot be apprehended by our cognition. It is Reality, not just possibility or fiction. "Wherever I come upon Reality without its being converted into possibility, I come upon Transcendence." In actual fact we never come upon it. We only find its vestiges in the "cipher-script" *(Chifferschrift)* and this very cipher-script is the form of Being which makes Transcendence in some sense experienceable without it becoming the direct object of our cognition. The cipher-script is the *vestige Dei,* but it is not God Himself in His hiddenness. It shows us God Himself as the extreme and real Being, but it does not unveil Him.

4. PHILOSOPHY AND RELIGION

Jaspers realizes that the age of myths is past. While philosophy and religion originally had myths for their common vehicle, philosophy has now freed itself from myth and employs reflection instead. Inasmuch as religion has not yet passed through this transformation, a conflict has arisen between the two. In this dispute philosophy is compelled to defend its case with only spiritual weapons and out of consideration for nothing but truth.

Philosophy, however, is not an indisputable quantity which can be employed for passing judgment on religion. The two disciplines are merely the historic garments concealing eternal truth. No one can know anything with any certainty about religious truth, and no one any longer believes in the possibility of a *philosophia perennis,* the validity of which Roman Catholicism has so long maintained. There is no third standpoint outside of religion and philosophy, from which those two might be judged, and we are thus placed in a relation of polarity. Standing on one side we speak of the other without sufficient experience. A philosopher must, therefore, be careful not to speak of religion, unless he is himself engaged in it and possesses religious experience; nor is he to regard religion as an enemy, since religion to a considerable extent appertains to philosophy and keeps the latter in the necessary state of unrest.

Religion differs from philosophy in possessing a myth and a cult, but it is allied to philosophy by its relation to Transcendence, and the Transcendence of religion is something sacred and distinguishable from the profane. Where this is no longer the case, all that is characteristic of religion has disappeared. Philosophy, by contrast, has neither myths nor rites, and it does not have the idea of congregation, because it is always the concern of the individual. Whereas religion expresses itself in concrete terms, philosophy speaks in abstract terms; this is true, too, with regard to the idea of God. To philosophy the religious view of God seems too massive and too seductive to the senses; whereas, inversely, the philosophical view of God appears to religion as being too pale, too remote, and too abstract.

Philosophy should never contend against religion in general, but always only against the untruth of some specific religion. Such an untruth arises when, for example, Transcendence is materialized, in which case religion becomes a mere horror of ghosts, or a fanatical persecution of heretics. Philosophy only contends against religion in order to offer freedom an opportunity to conceive of God in such a manner that he is not dragged into the dust. However, philosophy should not only content against the untruth of concrete religions; it must also search for the core of religion, which is not to be considered as merely a psychological or sociological fact, but also as a possible truth. Even though I personally may not be able to appropriate this truth, I must acknowledge its possibility, inasmuch as I am not everybody. "In the realm of possible *Existenz* the truth of every genuine possibility must be acknowledged." Finally, philosophy must endeavor to define the distinctions between itself and religion with the greatest possible clarity. The exposition of this contrast appeals to the real source of the two factors, and every man must settle the conflict for himself, not by making his choice from a neutral position outside of them, but by realizing that he is already lodged on one side. The meaning of the choice is that either I philosophize or I do not philosophize; in either case I should consistently and decisively take possession of what I already am.

Whereas, as regards religion, this decision is definitive, — although there can always be true possibilities of doubt and uncertainty — in philosophy the decision is ever left open, and the philosopher must remain a seeker. He cannot profess a materialized Transcendence in the form of a *supranatura* and he cannot in his capacity as having *Existenz,* anticipate any result. For *Existenz* is always connected with possibility, and freedom in *Existenz* always denotes that a being is given, the non-being of which is also possible. The question really becomes a question of God, whether God is hidden or revealed; and, since it asserts that God is hidden, philosophy can never become religion. So long as religion confines itself to speaking of the absolute in cipher-script, it is true, and, as such, at one with philosophy. But, whenever it assumes objective forms of expression, so that it becomes a spiritual realm along side of other areas, it becomes untrue to philosophy. True religion as well as true philosophy embrace man in his entirety, since they penetrate all the areas of the world without being areas themselves. It is only by appearing as a particular area in the world that religion becomes the object of attacks by philosophy, and to these attacks it must succumb. Jaspers has thus endeavored to vindicate the autonomy and, finally, the theonomy of the forms of culture as opposed to a religious heteronomy, which confuses the conditional with the unconditional, as Paul Tillich would put it, or confuses the cipher-script with Transcendence itself, to use Jaspers' terminology.

Inasmuch as God is the hidden God, he can only be the object of faith, but can never be reached by thought. We are not led to God by speculation as to His nature or by developing such speculation into a dogmatic cognition, for such procedures make the existence of God only the more problematic. God is uncognized, both when He is conceived as being a limit and as being the One. Moreover, He is not to be confused with various conceptions of God or with the cipher-script — that would be sheer arbitrariness. Jaspers maintains, like many other philosophers of the 20th century, that God is one, though not necessarily numerically one, because in that case other possibilities than the one God would arise. But God cannot be object among other objects either, seeing that He is bound to the true Transcendence, and for that very reason He is the Absolute. In the relation to the world we can neither conceive of the Transcendence of God as an individual being, detached from the world so that God and Transcendence would become identical concepts, nor can we imagine that Transcendence or God should be the essence of all that is at all conceivable. We here face a dialectical dilemma, which is inseparably connected with Transcendence itself. If this problem where solved, Transcendence as such would be eliminated.

The statement, "God is" belongs to the philosophical content of faith as intimately as the statement: "An unconditional demand is given." There is a decisive difference between, on the one hand, viewing the totality of the world as Being-in-itself and calling nature by the name of God, and, on the other hand, considering the totality of the world as something which is not resting in itself, seeking the foundation of the world and myself outside the world. The world is always something inconclusive, and the conception of a conclusive picture of the world is doomed to failure. We always come to face a precipice, and here we either encounter nothingness, or we experience God. But we cannot prove God, and a God proved is no God, as others have declared through the ages. God is rather a kind of *a priori*, though Jaspers does not employ this term, for we can only seek God, if we proceed from Him. There is always behind our philosophizing, and as a basis of this philosophizing, a certainty of God's existence, no matter how faint this certainty may be. But God is never the result of our philosophizing. *That* God is must then be the given condition. But *what* God is we cannot tell, not even by means of the *theologia negativa* of Neo-Platonism. But, for the purpose of keeping the presence of God we may employ metaphors, symbols, and analogies. It is not the nature of God, but the relationship to God that matters. To stand in this relationship is to be independent of the world. But this being independent of the world or this relation to Transcendence only becomes a reality to the man who is active in the world. Thus Jaspers disassociates himself from pietism in the widest sense of that word.

God then is always the object of faith, never the object of knowledge; but this belief* in God is exposed to the assaults of

---

* Editor's Note: The terms "faith" and "belief" are employed interchangeably. "Faith" is, on the whole, a better translation of Jaspers' "*Glaube;*" but its opposite,

doubt. One may doubt as regards the existence of Transcendence; this happens when the consciousness of being is engulfed in mere immanence or blindness.

Against such concrete doubt no logical or philosophical refutation, but only action, is conceivable. The reason for this is that Transcendence cannot be proved, but only witnessed, because the cipher-script through which it reveals itself to me is independent of my action. From dissatisfaction with the present and from love alone does the action spring which is capable of realizing the cipher-script which again is an expression of Transcendence.

There is a difference between belief and unbelief. Only belief which vindicates itself through doubt is real belief. A belief which is not compelled to make a decision or a choice is a potential belief not a real belief. Doubt is in a manner of speaking the medium in which belief and unbelief encounter one another, and they may, therefore, also be said to determine one another. If unbelief disappears altogether, belief is deprived of the stimulus which prevents it from falling asleep. Only that belief which is constantly viewing unbelief as an obvious possibility is real belief. On the other hand, it is also true that the unbelief which has no belief to contend with lapses into a torpor. "Belief and unbelief are the poles of being-oneself." Where the conflict between them is resolved philosophy ceases to exist; it may thus be destroyed either by belief or by unbelief. Under these circumstances it will be the task of philosophers to create a situation in which a conscious decision can be made in belief as to what I am. Unbelief is not unproductive, since it contains another belief in the nature of agressive negativity which negates in order to reach genuine belief. These thoughts remind us of Nietzsche's words about "the great scorners" who are "the great admirers." But they remind us even more of Paul Tillich's warning that God as the primaeval foundation of the world threatens to disappear in the abyss of the world. Jaspers professes here an irrational dialectic of tension, characteristic of so much existentialist philosophy and anti-intellectualism.

5. RELIGION

According to Jaspers, it is belief which establishes the contact between philosophy and religion. In his book, *The Perennial Scope of Philosophy*, he aims to demonstrate that a true philoso-

---

"unfaith" *(Unglaube)* is an awkward term in English.

phy without belief is impossible and that philosophical faith is inconceivable except in union with knowledge. It desires to know what can be known, and to look through and illuminate itself. But belief is not a purely intellectual or personal act, because we cannot distinguish between belief as the act I consummate and that which I grasp through this act. In other words, we cannot distinguish between subject and objects, between *fides qua* and *fides quae creditur,* because the objective and the subjective sides of faith form a whole. If we confine ourselves to the subjective or the *fides quae* alone we possess a lifeless substance of belief or a dogma. Consequently belief is always belief in something, and, being that which is neither pure subject nor pure object, belief comes to be related to Being or the Encompassing, and therefore cannot be expressed in positive, thetical statements. It is "negative" in so far as it cannot become a confession or find philosophical expression in any dogma. Belief will never be anything static, nor will it attain to a definitive form. "It remains the daring venture of radical openness." Belief is dynamic and cannot allege itself as something irrevocable, being always an intentional and 'existential' act.

Belief, therefore, is not to be understood intellectualistically, nor does it depend on any cognition of universal validity. If Jaspers were to express himself in medieval terms, he would not have said *"intelligo ut credam,"* but rather, with Anselm, *"credo ut intelligam."* Belief is not a more or less definite form of knowing, but an act which makes possible and lends significance to the movement towards knowing as a whole. Belief is all-embracing, it is not just a separate force, it is nothing specifically religious, but it also conditions philosophy, and thus it becomes the last force of spirit. Belief is spirit, and belief involves a dialectical uncertainty, despair, and fear, because the nihilistic movements are always an element and a possibility for any life of the spirit. In belief man lives as a being subjectively existing, whereas in knowing he grasps something of objective validity. But, although belief is always associated with the objectively uncertain, and although it lacks proof, it is yet more certain than all proofs, when one is forced to stop and take an attitude towards existence. And whereas knowing always concerns separate elements, and specific relations, belief is always directed towards totality and the Absolute. Unlike cognition, it demands a personality and rapture of the soul in which man realizes the end and the significance; whereas it can never perceive more than the mere means in cognition.

Whenever belief poses as a contrast to knowledge it becomes, to use Søren Kierkegaard's term, absurd or paradoxical; but in no other way can the relation to the absolute be expressed. One of the paradoxical terms although not originally understood as such, is myth. If a belief finds expression in a myth it becomes gnosis. Jaspers has rightly observed that so long as myths are genuine they are concrete and not merely symbolic statements, a category to which so many philosophers of modern times have tried to reduce them in order to preserve them unchanged. The believer learns in his personal existence that the contents of myths are reality. If this belief in myths degenerates into a general "knowing," which looks upon the relation to the absolute as a relation of knowing, then religion has become wholly dialecticized and we arrive at dogmatic (theology). Jaspers refuses, however, to believe in a possible thorough "de-mythologizing" of religion, because real belief also demands a metaphysical picture of the universe, and it is impossible to make general assertions as to how long such a "picture of the universe" can endure before giving way to necessary rational criticism. But this criticism is bound to assert itself when mythical doctrines are supposed to be rationally demonstrable, and when they allege a supranaturalistic revelation. A similar difficulty arises as soon as a religion places itself in relation to a historic personality, in order to find its own contents in him and understands him to be an expression of the absolute — an allusion which is quite unmistakable. In that case the historic takes the place of myth, and revelation is objectified as a historical fact, which causes Transcendence to lose its necessary, symbolic character. It will never be permissible to see more in a historic figure than "a possible language of Transcendence," which is to be appropriated on one's own responsibility and at one's personal risk.

Human existence recognizes truth in belief, but in existence we find not only belief, but also despair. In contrast to both stands the longing for the calm of eternity, in which despair is overcome and faith has been replaced by contemplation — or, as the Greek fathers would have said: *theoria* has replaced *pistis*. By now we have entered the realm of mysticism; and, in Jaspers' view, it is a fact that there arises such a longing towards the mysterious or towards a direct experience of the divine as it is in itself. Just as, inversely, it is also a fact that an urge is felt which leads others away from the mysterious, because they regard it as an expression of sheer fanaticism. The former urge we find in mysticism in the more restricted sense of the word; whereas the latter is met with in all forms of positivism. A synthesis of the two tendencies is also possible, however. Through our thinking, our acting and our creating, our horizon is constantly widened, and, at the end of this process we find the idea, which encompasses all positive, separate acts. Here it is possible to attain to a mystical state of totality. Only this cannot be achieved by escape from reality, as is traditional mysticism, but, on the contrary, on the basis of reality itself. So much value does Karl Jaspers assign to mysticism that he places himself at an intermediary stage between quietism and escape-from-the-world on the one hand, and pure positivism on the other.

Mysticism and positivism, then, are contrasts, and in Jaspers' religious philosophy we find another such pair, namely pantheism and the defiance of God. *Pantheism* is closely associated with mysticism. It considers God as being the totality of existence, but it cannot tell us what God is. As in mysticism the motive is the union with God. Pantheism is thus the opposite of the defiance of God, which latter arises when man himself desires to be totality. Man revolts against God when he seems to experience the injustice of life; he then wants to live on his own responsibility, to be his own totality, which he endeavors to create himself. A man thus defying God is filled with a desire for expansion and power, and Jaspers, using these terms, probably had Nietzsche in mind, whom he has treated so carefully. The godless, God-defying man is not socially inclined. But the religious man sometimes resembles him in this, since he is often, sociologically, an individualist.

The original expression of religion is the cult. But the historical evolution has constantly moved from *cultus* to *ethos*, which latter Jaspers defines as a religious service without cult, but a service in truth and faithfulness, in openness and loving strife. Along this road it is possible to reach the essence of the world, which can be made transparent to man only by action and by the ethical decision of *Existenz*. Besides being Transcendence God is also the "ground," which, after doubt, responds to my good will, and which I meet in my solitude, and, which, yet, is not 'there' — once more the dialectical relation which we have previously observed. In this situation, where the good will resolves in love, I am raised above all realities, capable of completing the communication with other men; and this pure communication is all that God demands. For himself he claims nothing, neither praise nor cult nor propaganda. I am an existing being, living in a world of other existent beings, and in this world I only find my neighbor, but never God directly or personally. In this situation I do not belong to *my* church, but to *the* church, which is the catholic and the only true Church, in which the presence of divinity is not one historic appearance standing forth among others, but the all-embracing universal. Such a religion is far more capable than philosophy of penetrating into reality; although the philosophical faith is "the substance of an individual life," and although I am also able to recognize the reality of Transcendence with the aid of philosophy.

6. Demonology

Against philosophy Karl Jaspers sets un-philosophy, which may in fact just as well be called un-religion. Where thought abandons its descent from faith, philosophy reaches a limit, thus losing its real content. It is this mode of thinking which Jaspers calls un-philosophy. For it conducts itself as if it were philosophy, but in reality it is not, though it is often regarded as such. Fundamentally, however, it is a negation or amplified, cognitive or intellectual, insight, but only on the condition that man is *reborn,* having by reflective deliberation come back to himself. What we are dealing with here is really a practical-religious and not a theoretical-philosophical attitude. The philosophical man must realize his own nature by constantly overcoming the unphilosophy which is always found in him. Unphilosophy arises when man, rejecting Transcendence, chooses to conceive of reality, the world, or existence in a final formula. But it is false philosophy to try to make the world appear as final object, and the belief that it is a final thing is unbelief. Whereas belief is always oriented towards being, unbelief is always a relation to a substitute for Being. It only recognizes immanence, although Transcendence must necessarily attain a certain validity. Unphilosophy and unbelief may assume various forms: they may consider themselves as belief, knowing, or contemplation, and in these three forms they are expressed in practical terms in demonology, the deification of man and nihilism.

Demonology is a view which finds being in powers or demons, and regards the immanent as pertaining to the divine. Passions, powers, vitality, beauty, destruction or cruelty are identified. Transcendence is rejected and the fact that our immanence is not simply mere immanence is left out of account. Immanence is, as Georg Simmel has it, an immanent transcendence. The objects are not conceived as being possible expressions of divinity. Whereas transcendence is held to be a power carrying its effect directly into the world; and this power is furthermore divided into several others. If man gives himself up to these powers, life receives its radiance from the mysterious, which is also the awesome, and man is seized by these powers. A desire or a longing arises for an approach towards the divine and an experience of it as being present in the world. Thus man invents new myths and is led into demonism.

Whereas Socrates, in the *Apology,* maintains that one cannot believe in demonic things without believing in demons also, Jaspers claims that the demonic is a reality in our age, even though the belief in demons has been abandoned. Although the demonic cannot be directly observed, we must imagine it as something real and something efficacious. The demonic cannot be defined as being irrational. It is something entirely unconceived, unwilled, perverted, and accidental, springing from itself and having overpowering effect — a line of thought quite reminiscent of what is found in the Russian emigrant philosopher, Nikolaj Berdyaeff. The demonic is, as it were, without cause, but it is not without effect. It can seize man's will, and it may become the unyielding will to will and to assert one's own contingent self. It becomes a "desperate attempt to be oneself." The demonic will nourishes all the powers which will keep man confined within himself and keep him from being open and communicative in his relation to others. What really distinguishes the demonic — which has withdrawn itself into its own contingent self, which it regards as being absolute — is the fact that it cannot consider anything seriously. Eternity must no longer be seriously contemplated, it must be feared; and fear thinks out innumerable evasions.

Demonology misses Transcendence. Even the highest potential of its own final and limited self never reaches transcendence nor does it attain to grasping God. But without God only idols are left, idols which we ourselves have created. These "gods" have come into being in the world, and consequently they participate in the objectification of the immanent, and are thus dominated by mere nothingness. Jaspers' second objection to demonology is that by it man is lost. Freedom is reduced to a fate which carries man away, it is given supreme value and humanism becomes a human attitude, which enjoins one to be human in certain circumstances; but no reverence is shown for that individual soul which holds eternity by its relation to Transcendence.

Third, demonology lets man lose his relation to the One. "Life with the demons becomes fluid, a disintegration in the indefinite." Everything is defensible, and in spite of all the energy that may be put into each separate moment, no continuity exists, and even the best attempts at self-assertion do not lead to any real concentration of being. Fourth, demonology is bound in nature, which appears to it as the last and all-deciding necessity. Confidence in God is replaced by confidence in nature. But, whenever this confidence in nature encounters obstacles, it can find no real ground to build upon, but degenerates into idolatry, as is shown, through the ages, by all natural cults in the world. Fifth, modern demonology gives expression to a definitely aesthetic attitude towards the world. No real obligation exists. We may be called upon to do good; but the recognition of evil in the tragic may neutralize this decision for good. Ethics and aesthetics are engaged in constant interaction, and it is therefore always possible to leap from the ethics to aesthetics, the former thus losing is primacy. Sixth, and last, we may raise the objection that demonology sets forth a kind of intermediate being between empirical reality and transcendent reality, which is neither God nor the world, but sheer fraud and illusion. All realities may be either God or the world; we can perceive God through the cipher-script, but never directly. But, outside of God there are neither gods nor demons. At the limit of realities I can perceive the trace of God's finger; but whatever may thrust itself between God and the world is materialistic foolishness or ungodly illusion.

The deification of man is also a form of unphilosophy or unbelief. History abounds in examples of it from the heroes of antiquity to the tyrants and movie-stars of our age. It is in a way a kind of demonism. Man in the godless world reaches for the demonic as an imagined transcendence at the same time that he reaches to his concrete fellow men to make them gods. But no man can be made god for us. At best there may be men who, in their free listening to God, are able to show us what is possible for man and give us courage to act in communication with others. The deification of man in reality debases man. It means, by misconceiving the conditions of life, to give us the tangible; though it is man's lot to do without the tangible and to resign himself to the cipher-script of God. Only through these can man, with God's aid, find himself as active *Existenz* in its communication with other *Existenzen*.

7. Nihilism

Demonology and the deification of man are at one in affording a substitute for faith. In contrast to these, nihilism is sheer godlessness presuming to appear directly and without disguise. Nihilism has rejected every doctrine of faith and regards all attempts at world and being-explanation as illusory, because everything, in its view, is conditional and relative. For nihilism there exists no unconditional, no Being-in-itself, no truth, and no moral obligation — everything is permissible. Nihilism builds on the attempt at vitality; its base is a biological desire to live and the will to power — terms again borrowed from Nietzsche. When this will to power is confirmed, nihilism seems to change into a vital faith, and something dialectic in its nature appears. As pure Nihilism it can exist only as a negation of something or as opposed to something; but, in order to find expression it requires a basis of positivity, and the moment this dialectical position is fully realized, nihilism must in fact be resolved. Its method usually consists in rejecting inevitable and approved standards to let everything disappear in a whirlpool of reciprocal negation.

Another important postulate in nihilism holds that there is no God, simply because his existence cannot be proved. This "argumentation" is fallacious, because the question of Transcendence is understood and dealt with very much like the question of ultimate things in the realm of experience and relations, which lies within the sphere of immanence. Second, nihilism holds that these "experiences" are the expression of an illusion as well as a false interpretation of the experiences in question. Nihilism renders absolute our immanent experiences in their empirical and spatio-temporal form, simultaneously with denying the 'existential' experience of freedom. Third, nihilism asserts that there can be no obligation towards God. It will only accept our obligations towards the final forms or relations in the world; and, on this ground, it negates the profound, unconditional and life-sustaining obligation, which is of such a nature that it can never be expressed in easy, simple formulations or in given, concrete laws.

This form of nihilism is really a "positive" nihilism, because it teaches a full and banal cognizability of the world. This cognizability is contrived by an identification of existence *(Dasein)* with Being *(Sein)*, although existence is open to us in immanence, whereas Being is something which can never be definitively grasped in cognition — a distinction this which is particularly conspicuous in the philosophy of Hermann Cohen, the founder of the Marburg School of Neo-Kantianism. "Positive" nihilism thus does not insist that nothing is; it only maintains that, if existence is understood absolutely, it is nothing. This nihilism is a Philistine nihilism which deserves no respect. But we find also another nihilism, which in its origin is sustained by fear and horror of the reality of the world and of human life. When the conception of God as being goodness, love, truth, and omnipotence is made the standard by which reality is measured, both God and the world are rejected. If God really were goodness, love, truth, and omnipotence, He would have made everything much better. Consequently, either He is not God or He is not almighty. Against this background it is then claimed that evil demons have created the world. And the complaint ends in a nihilism which tells us that there are no such things as gods or demons. The world is either what it is or it is mere nothingness.

The three positions, demonology, deification of man, and nihilism are closely allied; but nihilism seems to be the least cogent of them. It cannot be endured in the long run, and therefore it resorts to demonology and the deification of man. But nihilism still remains something that will never entirely disappear. The reason being that in demonology there seems to be a longing for nothingness or a desire to grasp the negating powers. The deification of man is often taken to be a rescue from nihilism. But to all intents, it is itself nihilistic. Jaspers obviously alludes to Hitler; and he maintains that experience will show that men are only men, and that thus, in making of men a cult, one relapses into nihilism.

There is, nevertheless, an element of truth in these three irreligious forms. At the base of demonology there lies the truth which is found in the ciphers of transcendence in this world. In the speculation of mythology, too, we find a truth that possesses something unconquerable, if only it is rightly understood, and if it were lost the soul would be impoverished and a "depletion" of the world would be effected, since the latter would thus be deprived of its contents. If one no longer hears this language of myth he does not seem to be able to love any more; for in the Transcendent, which lies outside the sphere of our senses, there exists no object for love. It is not only because we are finite beings, but also because we love the world as God's creation, that we refrain from seeking a foothold in Transcendence.

The deification of man is, ultimately, based on a truth which holds that man is the only being in the world that exists for man. God made man in His own image, but man has deserted Him and blurred the image of God. Great men may, therefore, serve as models for others; but the free relations among men in mutual communication must never be replaced by one individual slavishly imitating the other. Finally, nihilism, too, is relatively justifiable. Every faith must permanently confront the possibility of its own nothingness; for no faith can arrogate to itself a security of the kind we possess in our cognition of the objective phenomenon of the immanent world of the senses. The security of faith is partly a gift and partly a venture. In either case it is confronted with nihilism in the form of the threat of the arrogance to which faith may become prone, and against which it has often harshly and inexorably fortified itself.

Demonology, the deification of man, and nihilism are all three — though each in its individual way — expressions of a mistake which consists in an attempt by man to comprehend truth in too short a grasp and to hold it firmly in his hands. When it is an indisputable fact that God is, all the mistakes of delusion must needs disperse and vanish. But when we seek to grasp God, concrete and materialized, in the ultimate forms within immanence, the mists will once more descend upon us. Truth can never become accessible and surveyable; and because it is unsurveyable, it always threatens to sink back into nothingness. We can only reach God and truth by the devious route which leads us through the world and its immanent forms. God himself is the remotest of all; He is the Transcendence against which all that is conceived absolutely has been comprehended by far too short a grasp. What God is in Himself as Transcendence cannot, as already mentioned, be told. It can only be adumbrated by negations, but never really comprehended. All the arrogant despising of nihilism is, therefore, unjustified, indeed, revolting. Here again we see how strongly Jaspers protests against heteronomy and professes autonomy, which for him, as for Paul Tillich, in the last resort coincides with theonomy. Jaspers is, moreover, entirely at one with Tillich when he insists that religious relations always intend more than we are able to express, because the unconditional cannot be enclosed in our conditional forms, whether or not these are the separate data of sensuous cognition or Jaspers' symbolic cipherscript.

The relation between philosophy and unphilosophy is, like the relation between belief and unbelief, a dialectical relation. Belief is only acquired when snatched from unbelief; and he who has not acqainted himself with unbelief will not be able to construct a belief which is conscious of its own nature. Like unbelief, unphilosophy is neither superfluous nor accidental; it is always philosophy on the threshold. At the same time it is the transition to philosophy itself and that which is to be rejected when the latter has been reached. Truth is to be found on all roads of philosophy. But if you wander too far along one road it will soon lead you to an untruth.

Here we stand — again — in a dialectical tension, in polarities, and in dialectical movements; but only under such conditions can we give philosophical expression to the contents of life. We are moving in a circle. But it will be to no purpose to replace this circle by a rectilinear movement, in which case we would not merely miss our aim, but also paralyze life itself. We must forever reject unphilosophy, and yet we are forever engaged in it. We dare not simply despise it, but we must confront it for the purpose of knowing ourselves and our situation. We must never be so arrogant as to fancy that we have utterly defeated it, in which case we would be killing life itself.

8. SOME CRITICAL REMARKS

In a system of metaphysics and religious philosophy which, like that of Karl Jaspers, is of an *existential* and practical nature it is not possible to detect "errors." In fact, we can only inquire whether or not the position of problems is tenable, and whether obscurities or contradictions can be pointed out in his metaphysical and religious thinking. To call attention to the fact that oneself would perhaps have treated these problems somewhat differently would only be to arrogate to one's own opinion a significance and a general appeal to which they cannot lay claim, at least not in this context. Once we have established the fact that Karl Jaspers does not regard metaphysics as an extended science nor religious philosophy as a doctrine of *supranatura* — on this point he is undoubtedly right — we only have to inquire whether the religious attitude he assumes is justifiable, and what position religious philosophy has been given within his philosophy as a whole. What remains can only be a matter of details.

Jaspers has not written an independent, separate exposition of religious philosophy. The reason for this being, undoubtedly, that no clear distinction can be made between the religious philosophy and the metaphysics within his philosophy. It would have been convenient to understand the two philosophical branches as, respectively, the theoretical and the practical attitude towards the totality of the world or Transcendence. But, in reality Jaspers' metaphysics is, as we know, in itself a practical attitude, which does not, as metaphysics often does, inquire about the *what* of the world or about its ultimate nature, whether it is spirit or matter or both; whether it is to be monistically, dualistically, or pluralistically interpreted, etc. For Jaspers true philosophy and true religion alike are attitudes towards life, which find expression in a definite intellectual and practical ethos. Religious philosophy thus becomes an organic constituent of philosophy, not just a part of it or a philosophical sub-branch, but, as it were, a something that pervades philosophy in its entire extent and yet cannot be concretely demonstrated anywhere. Jaspers' philosophy *is* in itself religious philosophy, it *has* no religious philosophy. But for this very reason philosophy of religion, in Jaspers' view, cannot be abused as a basis for the doctrine of a positive religion.

When metaphysics is not a science, but a practical attitude of the spirit, one is tempted to inquire into the relation between Jaspers' metaphysics and that of Kant. Kant, as is well known, would reject metaphysics as a theoretical science. While Spinoza had built up his ethics on metaphysics, Kant, inversely, formed his metaphysics with its practical postulates about God and immortality on the basis of his ethics, that is to say, on a purely practical basis. The question is then — as has been much discussed — whether in Kant's ethics we find an ontological metaphysics, as Max Wundt claimed, or pure fictions, as is Hans Vaihinger's view. We could ask the same question with regard to Jaspers' philosophy. Here one may inquire whether Transcendence or God is an expression of the last Being or Reality from which all empirical being emerges, as e.g., the wave rises from the sea, whether to exist (ex-sistere), to possess concrete, perceptible being, means to stand forth from the depth of the great, featureless Being, or whether this Being is not "real," but just intended. Is this "Being" a characteristic of a reality or a value? Must we understand it ontologically or axiologically? To choose an example: Does God exist, or is he just an "idea"? Will the cipherscript and the symbols be the only reality and God himself a fiction? Søren Kierkegaard, to whom Karl Jaspers is in no small degree indebted, holds that God *is,* just as the perennial Platonic ideas, but God does not exist, because existence only pertains to a finite spirit which lives in time. I do not think that Jaspers has exposed the problem thus acutely, and I should imagine that he would reject this alternative — as, perhaps, I might do myself, because I consider the validity of an idea of the mind as being tantamount to its existence, by which, namely, I understand: A Being outside of the categories of time and space.

We are, however, faced with the question once more when we

turn to Transcendence, without being concerned with whether it is God or not. Jaspers' doctrine of Transcendence reminds us, in more respects than one, of the concept which, under the influence of Schelling and Jakob Böhme, Paul Tillich calls the *Urgrund* or *Abgrund* of the world, the abyss from which the cognizable world springs according to William James and Henri Bergson, in whose philosophy we doubtlessly face a metaphysical reality, and not merely an idea or just something axiological. But Jaspers does not seem to agree entirely with this view. For he does not want to "materialize" Transcendence, probably because he regards such materialization as unscientific and unspiritual. If he did, he would also have to materialize or hypostatize the demonic or the forces that work in nihilism. Demonism and nihilism are not, however, the reflection of cosmic powers and forces but of human attitudes or intentions. The nihilistic and demonic forces are not ontological, but dynamic. Consequently demonology and nihilsm do not represent a dualism in Jaspers' philosophy. These forces, on the contrary, contribute to preserving the balance of the world, and the relation between good and evil cannot, therefore, be a contradictory one. The two factors need one another. The relation is a dialectical one. Thus arises a certain kinship between Jaspers on one side and Schelling and Hegel on the other. The term "pole," which is used by many philosophers in the 20th century, belongs in Schelling's philosophy. Whenever unbelief is held relatively justifiable as opposed to belief, and unphilosophy is held relatively justifiable as over against philosophy, etc. we confront Schelling's poles with their identity of tension. When Jaspers says of unphilosophy that it is the transition to philosophy itself as well as that which must be rejected, we distinctly seem to hear Hegel's words about the "stratagem of idea," about suffering or evil, which is the necessary detour enroute towards the higher good. Here we have a dialectical movement, which is Hegelian, just as in Schelling's doctrine of poles we have a doctrine of a more cosmic ring. Jaspers expresses himself in cosmic and noetic, in actual and ideal categories, but it is probably the latter interpretation, the spiritual one, which is his real conception. Jaspers is, like Schelling and Hegel, a monist rather than a dualist, and he is thus in strong opposition to the two great Danish philosophers, Grundtvig and Kierkegaard, who were both professed dualists. Just as Grundtvig at the beginning of the 19th century had protested strongly against Schelling's philosophy of identity, Kierkegaard, towards the middle of the century, attacked Hegel's dialectic "mediation" of contrasts, which latter, in Kierkegaard's own view, can never in all eternity be mediated.

That Jaspers' standpoint is ideal rather than real, and that he does not believe that empiricism can lead us to a full comprehension of the world, is clearly revealed in his doctrine of freedom. Like Kant in the 18th and Nicolaj Berdyaeff in the 20th century, Jaspers maintains that freedom is not a psychic, but a spiritual fact, and in the chapters on *Existenz* and freedom we have seen that Jaspers prefers the spirit to nature. In order to reconstitute our own nature, a spiritual choice in freedom must be made. The change cannot be brought about by a penetration and modification of nature by the supernature. This pointedly anti-Catholic trait in Jaspers is associated with his repudiation of *revelation,* which he only seems to be able to conceive of as being the invasion of nature by supernature, and that, of course, would mean a disruption of the given natural continuity. The conditioned forms cannot hold the unconditioned within their frames. We cannot perceive God or Transcendence itself, in an historic figure, but only possibly a linguistic expression thereof i.e., a cipher. The allusion to the dogma of incarnation in the sense used in Christian theology is evident here.

But at this point I would like to raise an objection. Our religious and philosophical attitude is, as we know, not only an attitude towards Being or Transcendence, but must be — and at least in ethics and religious philosophy — an attitude towards values. Jaspers says that it is the puropse of philosophy to seek to grasp Being; but — and this Jaspers will probably not deny — it is also its purpose to grasp values, and it is these, after all, which in Jaspers' view play the most important part. If we inquire into the origin of values, we are bound to own that they are derived from history, from great men, who, as Jaspers admits, can be models for others. But where can we find the origin of these new thoughts which suddenly occur in history as inspirations of these men? If we will not profess a pure psychologism, sociologism, or historicism, and that, we know, Jaspers will not — we must admit that these thoughts are due to a "revelation," or "inspiration," if one prefers this term. We cannot prove the divine origin of these thoughts. But we can ascertain that they were not there before. Now, suddenly, and in and with this particular man, they are there; and since their derivation is causally inexplicable, we may say that they have come "of themselves." But it is clear that the problem is not so easily solved. For, we feel ourselves to de dependent upon, or responsible towards, these thoughts or ideals.

They are not valid on the strength of a resolution of ours, but they are experienced as being valid, and thus, they may after all be. The easiest solution is to refer to a "revelation." But, as regards the more exact "how" of this revelation, we should remain silent, lest we be guilty of philosophical heteronomy; and neither Jaspers nor I wish to run that risk. In Christianity, however, we find something that has been introduced in the world through an historic man. What he has said we appropriate at our own risk, in other words in faith; but we may also do so without adopting the concomitant mythology. This latter possibility Jaspers seems to question, however.

If Jaspers takes a comparatively unsympathetic, even though not strongly polemic attitude toward Christianity, the reason seems to be that he regards Christianity as myth and cult rather than as ethos and communication. But this view of Christianity seems to me more Catholic than Protestant, despite the fact that many Protestants share it. When Jaspers opposes *my* church to *the* church in the sense of the true and catholic church, it may reasonably be asked whether the church, in the latter sense, is not what Christianity is really aiming at. For the great commandment in the Law concerns the love of neighbor, not love of God in disregard of the neighbor, as the story of the good Samaritan so clearly shows. *The* church is not a separated church or a community of sects, but the Kingdom of God in a universalistic sense. Jaspers has, it seems to me, taken the concepts of Church and Christianity a little too empirically and historically. The church is not necessarily a community based on cult. It can also be taken to include those fellowmen who condition ethical communication. Although Jaspers rightly says that the historical evolution has moved from cult towards ethos within the Church and within Christianity, Christianity must not be judged by the distance this evolution has so far covered, but must rather be evaluated by its idea or intention. And this intention lies much closer to the religion which Jaspers has made his own than he seems to have noticed. The fact that it is sometimes a little difficult to distinguish between reality and symbol in Jaspers' philosophy is probably a consequence of his *'existential'* thinking. I should not call Jaspers' philosophy pure existentialism, as we find it, for example, in the philosophy of Jean Paul Sartre. Jaspers is, after all, too much of a kinsman of Plato, as is also true of Søren Kierkegaard. Existentialism is always "an attitude towards," and is, then, of a practical nature. But this practical quality is always confronted by theoretical difficulties when the question is being asked, towards *what* the above mentioned attitude is taken. In a discussion of Jaspers' philosophy we must inquire whether Transcendence really is a reality, just as in Nicolaj . Berdyaeff, we should ask whether the ground or "abyss" of the world is indeed reality. The establishment of a distinct either-or between reality and symbol, between historic incident and myth, between Transcendence and cipher-script does not seem to be possible in the case of either of the two philosophers. The indistinctness of the dialectical tension is too impenetrable. Only this is certain: the two realms, Transcendence and cipher-script, must not be confused.

SØREN HOLM

DEPARTMENT OF SYSTEMATIC THEOLOGY
UNIVERSITY OF COPENHAGEN
KØBENHAVN, DENMARK

22

A. Lichtigfeld

THE GOD-CONCEPT IN JASPERS' PHILOSOPHY

IN THIS brief paper I want to discuss the critical points which have been raised against Jaspers' concept of God as *the* reality, a reality which can only announce itself but can never become object of thought, because it is impossible to reach the reality which is beyond all phenomenal thought. On Jaspers' premises there remains only the ever to be renewed movement towards Transcendence. This Transcendence is disclosed in the reading of the language of the 'cipher' by which Transcendence is felt in this world, but never made available as an object which can be laid hold of in its actual reality. This is the more significant because the demand for a transcendent supreme reality is justified, — since its absolute character would be lost by descent into human thought — by the objectifying effort of which it would be colored and conditioned. Inasmuch as the realm of Transcendence is inexhaustible, the human mind at its farthest point of progress in knowledge must still see stretching before it as its 'limiting condition' the region of the Unknown — the unfathomable depth of that Being concerning which any figurative or objectifying attempt must be denied in order to keep its transcendent character pure. This is not to suspend the Transcendent in mid-air, as some of Jaspers' critics have assumed. It is rather meant to keep the movement in the direction of Transcendence going, instead of paralyzing it into a possessive inactivity.[1] This is why Jaspers, on

[1] In this connection attention should be called to the following query raised by B. Welte: "Thence *'existential'* philosophical faith questions the message which demands faith in historical revelation. Such faith will be forced to ask: Is it possible to believe in an historical and concrete revelation of God, carried out by specific persons, in deeds and words which are definitive for them — is it possible to believe in this fashion, once I have raised myself to the level of philosophical faith in seriousness and staked my true Self on the outcome? If the authentic relationship to God can only be real and genuine if it grasps the concrete reality of earthly figures and concepts, but at the same time transcends them toward the limitlessness and the inconceivable chasm of Being, how is it possible, then, that it can tie itself again, completely and definitely, to a concrete and therefore finite figure? And, if divine Being itself talks to my Self out of everything that is and in every word, because everything can become a cipher for my Self, how, then, can *one*

a Kantian basis, developed his conception of a God not liable to the dangerous distortions of anthropomorphism, distortions which have been prevalent throughout history. It was not merely that Jaspers found God to be indescribable in human speech but also to transcend the utmost power of human thought. For this reason and on account of the failure of words and symbols — there no longer being anything in our imagination which would correspond to such words or symbols — many thinkers took recourse to a theory of negative attributes of God, according to which all affirmative statements about God are false. This latter theory, however, was found wanting: it came close to emptying belief of all content. Dissatisfied with such a purely negative position, other thinkers, starting from the premise that God's image as the source of all creation must indwell and therefore be discernible in that creation, assumed that we might draw conclusions as to His character at least indirectly, by way of analogy, passing from the finite to the infinite, thus supplementing the theology of negation with an affirmative theology.

In support of such a theory, resting on analogical inference, J. B. Lotz, James Collins, and, along somewhat similar lines, J. N. Hartt and F. J. von Rintelen have challenged Jaspers' position in this respect. In fact, it may be best to reproduce here the main argument as it has been put forth by Lotz, as follows:

It is the Kantian heritage, leading away from analogy, which determines the final cast of "becoming-aware" and of "foundering." Behind Jaspers' concept of "appearance" stands Kant's merely subjective phenomenon, and behind Jaspers' fulness of Being-in-itself threatens Kant's completely unintelligible noumenon or 'thing-in-itself.' Kant's transcendental dialectic is everywhere noticeable: The three basic modes of the Encompassing — world, man, and Transcendence — correspond to the three Ideas: world, soul, and God. These Ideas are incapable of constituting the objects corresponding to them; as unobjective regulative principles they can merely anchor the appearances in ultimate

---

figure, one message, one word claim universal validity and exclusiveness? Must this not be viewed as a relapse into an exalted immanence and finiteness?

"Furthermore: If the authentic voice of Transcendence can be heard only in the commitment and performance of being my Self, how, then, can an authority which approached me from outside gain final significance for my transcendental relation to God? No authority can relieve me of being my Self; do I not forget myself and deceive myself, then, whenever I try, nevertheless, to unload my burden on something outside myself? May one do this if one desires to be entirely truthful to himself and therefore to the holy and inexpressible basis of all Being? Do I not relinquish therewith the indispensable basis of all authentic experience of God in favor of the pseudo-transcendence of a 'craven image'?" Symposium (1949), 189 [Tr. by Ludwig B. Lefebre].

totalities. Thus the Encompassing too, with all its modes, remains likewise an unobjective realm which surrounds and fills the knowledge based on appearances with ultimate meaning. . . . Jaspers, just like Kant, knows of only one avenue of approach to the in-itself or to Being or to the — immanent and transcendent — fullness, and this avenue is called *vision (Schau)*. Where no vision is possible, only unobjective "awareness in foundering," typical for Jaspers, remains. In conclusion we now have to show how "becoming-aware" can be completed in analogy. . . . Real appearance is given only if the content of an appearance reveals some of the content of inner abundance, if the content of both is identical to some — possibly very small — degree. We said that appearance is a segment of inner abundance; this is to say that in the content of an appearance *some* of the content of abundance becomes visible. We therefore recognize in the shading of the appearance how the thing *is* according to its inner abundance (in other words, we are not just confronted with empty appearance which doesn't disclose the Being behind it unequivocally). . . . For, behind and within apparential objectivity a higher 'objectivity of Being' *(seinshafte Gegenständlichkeit)* reveals itself, on the strength of which I can objectify abundance without making it "directly visible," without sinking to the level of its mere bare, empty appearance. . . . With the objective knowledge of abundance or of Being the road to analogy is open.[2] [Tr. by Ludwig B. Lefebre]

In considering what is involved in this principle of analogy, we come to see that it justifies, by its method of arguing from effect to cause, "a discursive ascent from the immediately given to the transcendent, even though such an ascent will give only an imperfect understanding of the term of this movement."[3] In thus advancing to Transcendence, we are not conquering alien territory, but we are reclaiming that ground of reality which, by analogy, is identified with ourselves as created in the image of God. The argument, then, to which these considerations lead, according to Collins, is as follows.

The richness of the object of metaphysics is of two sorts: an immanent secondary kind which coincides with categorial being, and the transcendent richness which is primary and supracategorial. Thus concrete things are included within the order of essences or categories, which are present in, and yet surpass, the individual instances embodying a given perfection. And essences for their own part are included under being and its attributes, without exhausting the resources of being itself. The immanent fullness of categorial essences and concrete finite things supposes a primal reality in which the transcendental per-

2 J. B. Lotz, "Analogie und Chiffre," in *Scholastik* (1940), 40, 53-56; cf. also J. B. Lotz in *Stimmen der Zeit* (1939), 71ff and in *Orientierung* (1948), 121ff.

3 James Collins, "An Approach to Karl Jaspers," in *Thought* (1945), 690.

fections of being are realized absolutely, and in which the reality of essences and things is also found in an eminent way. Along these lines the Scholastic theory of transcendence provides the metaphysical foundation of the doctrine of analogy as understood from the stand-point of the creature. A .critical appreciation of Jaspers' philosophy can be gained through this approach. . . .

We have no immediate or comprehensive knowledge either of cre-ated essences or of God. Both in the immanent and in the transcend-ent order our knowledge must be perspectival: we know substantial essences through their various properties, and God by means of cre-ated things as bearing the sign of their origin. Jaspers turns our awareness of transcendence to a more-than-thought, a thinking by means of categories about what is beyond categories, a thinking which is therefore indirectly transcending. That there is a place for 'aware-ness' in the Scholastic economy is seen from an analysis of particular judgments, e.g. 'Peter is a man,' in which an essence and being itself are affirmed of a directly perceived concrete thing. Although only in-directly intended in these judgments, there is necessarily some refer-ence to the essential structure and ontological status of the particular objects of such judgments. Individual things are taken as 'sections' of the essences and being in which they participate. But the intellect penetrates behind this spatial imagery to see that the essence is inte-grally present in this thing as its immanent plenitude. Similarly, es-sences are not mechanical segments of being, but sustain intimate re-lations with the whole of reality in its transcendental scope. We some-how become aware of these relations, for otherwise judgments would be impossible. The doctrine of analogy clarifies what is meant by 'somehow,' and in so doing, it also specifies the nature of the unity of metaphysics.[4]

The presupposition on which the inquiry rests, according to Lotz, is that analogical knowledge surpasses the realm of the categorial and by so doing establishes, still within the bounds of the rational, the realm of the supra-categorially Rational — a realm which in Jaspers' system is totally cancelled out. In addition, the supra-cate-gorial would give Transcendence a fulness of essence, thus making a concept of God, however incomplete and in suspension, possible. On any other supposition, the act of transcendence, being without content and therefore, empty, could not yield a picture of God and would finally sink to the level of an empty sphere which, al-though all-encompassing, could not develop into an object which would stand over against us. In this connection Lotz points to Jaspers' statement to the effect that "Though God is, however con-cealed, yet all-present as reality," it remains doubtful what reality in fact seems to assert:

4 *Ibid.,* 686f.

The super-categorial conceptuality imparts to the process of transcending a fulfilling inner content; thus it makes possible a view of God which — despite its incompleteness and remaining suspension — is full of content. Where, on the other hand, super-categorial conceptuality is lacking, transcending loses its content and becomes empty, and any image of God becomes impossible. In that case transcendental reality sinks down to the empty, unfulfilled ground which encompasses everything, but it is incapable of concentrating itself into autonomous being, i.e., into an object we encounter. Consequently God is "that which itself does not happen, but in which everything else happens" (14), "that which always only announces itself . . . , but never becomes object" (ibid.). "Instead of knowledge of something" we find "the presence of a peculiarly bright and in each instance inaccessible realm" (18). If, then, on the one hand, it can be said: "God is" "even though concealed, nevertheless present as actuality," it must be said, on the other hand,: "what, however, it (reality) seems to say remains equivocal" (70f), precisely because of the just shown uninterpretability.[5]

In like manner, the cipher, though for philosophy the transcendent reality in the world, can only point to a transcendent reality which is emptied of any content; whereas in the philosophy of analogy God appears as an independent Real, as infinite Spirit, restoring an object of worship and adoration worthy of the human mind. The difference between the two kinds of metaphysics, that of the cipher and that of analogy, or the stages through which knowledge (of Transcendence) passes, is, therefore, defined by Lotz in these terms: "The metaphysics of the 'cipher' is the metaphysics of unfulfilled transcending. The metaphysics of 'analogy' is the metaphysics of fulfilled transcending and with that of the Transcendent."[6] Or, as Collins puts it:

Thus what Lotz calls the explicative or interpretative method of the theory of ciphers is an incomplete process of transcending, reaching only to the immanent depths of the given. It finds its justification and completion only in the metaphysic of analogy, for the analogical method not only completes the transcending process, but also rises by mediate knowledge to a transcendent and subsistent reality.[7]

The standard by which the admissibility of the symbol of the cipher is to be judged must also be given attention, according to Hartt, for

the notion of Symbol, so important for Jaspers' system, is cheated of

[5] J. B. Lotz, in Stimmen der Zeit (1939), 73. The page-numbers given for the quotations cited by Lotz refer to Jaspers' Existenzphilosophie.

[6] J. B. Lotz, in "Analogie und Chiffre," 54.

[7] Collins, op cit., 691.

its full significance and power by the underlying Kantian epistemological perspective, for a very large part of his thought is devoted to
the creation of an ascending scale of intentionality, whereby either
from its last level, i.e., freedom, or from the whole scale, certain positive affirmations concerning the divine nature could be reasonably and
intelligibly formulated. But at the end, and I believe with real violence
following the system as a whole, Jaspers lumps the whole scale together
in a blanket denial that any analogy yields positive knowledge of
God's nature.[8]

Having thus attempted to show in which respects this part of Jaspers' system is inadequate, Hartt concludes:

> For me this remains the most perplexing question of all: does God
> become positively meaningful even then? Or is He left as *Wirklichkeit*
> mysteriously expressing itself through its modes, all of which are 'signs
> and symbols,' including Existenz itself? But how are the symbols to be
> interpreted, unless symbol and reality symbolized are somehow or
> other positively and simultaneously embraced, unless this embracing,
> this primal apprehension can be brought up out of the vagueness and
> mistiness of the 'merely intuitive' into conceptual clarity? This failing
> we are left to ponder God as *Umgreifendes des Umgreifenden*, mani-
> festing itself in mysterious unity and fecundity.[9]

It is noteworthy that F. J. von Rintelen carries this reasoning
still further, pointing out that our awareness of ultimate Being is
intrinsically possessed of cognitive reference to the Transcendent.[10] He asserts that one has to attribute Being, be it in its space-
time reality or in its spiritual expression as cosmos, a trans-subjec-
tive meaning, an essence, an inwardness which in ultimate depth
discloses itself to the inwardness of the individual. This interaction
is, according to von Rintelen, not to be defined as mere appearance. His argument does take into account that Jaspers' difficulty
does not lie in a denial of objective reality, but rather in the fact
that objective reality can not become an object of our thought and
therefore not an object of any proof. Von Rintelen furthermore
draws the conclusion that in our *'existential'* encounter and final
act of decision and intellectual appreciation of what is significantly conclusive, the unconditional is bound to become objectified
content at least insofar as we intend one particular thing rather
than something else. Thus, when the question of moral action is
raised, the appeal is to an act of judgment. Here, again and pre-

---

8 Hartt, in *Review of Metaphysics* (1950), 256.

9 Hartt, *op. cit.*, 254f.

10 F. J. von Rintelen, *Philosophie der Endlichkeit als Spiegel der Gegenwart*,
(1951), 380ff.

eminently, though recognizing the *'existential'* self's historical situation as peculiar to itself only, one has to assume, so von Rintelen argues, that the *'existential'* self seizes a certain and specific content of truth, claiming objectivity.

The entire discussion has but a single point. It aims to show that Transcendence as assumed by Jaspers is endangered by the fact that it cannot become an object of thought. It is argued that it is only through an objective bond which can sustain relation to *'existential'* selves and to their activities that Transcendence can subsist. According to Jaspers, however, once we enter upon this road the time is sure to come when the appropriate object of thought is stripped of all its transcendent character and, by becoming final and self-sufficient, Transcendence will be found to be lost forever. It is one of the ulterior motives of Jaspers' system to make Transcendence — and not merely the ever changing results of the process of thinking about Transcendence — prevail in human experience. Those results, gained in ultimate situations (*Grenzsituationen*) will be saved in Jaspers' system by his theory of communication. In any sense in which objectivity is legitimate boundless communication it is of the essence of life. The capacity of *'existential'* selves to enter into communication and thereby generate further meanings of *Existenz* and Transcendence more profound and far reaching than those from which they sprang, guarantees to human existence what Jaspers' critics seemed eager to deduce from a concept of Transcendence which, on their view, should be available to categories of human thought.

So much for the problem of (fulfilled) Transcendence. We must now examine the claim of the supporters of the doctrine of analogy. What shall we say of the justice of the claims of the critics? Their claims do not, in principle, seem to us to be sound; for the process of analogy also lands us in a dilemma and, indeed, some would say that it creates at least as many problems as it seems to solve. Much as we should like to accept analogical inference, it would be a futile guide in questions dealing with the relationship between the finite and the infinite, where the infinite differs from the finite not merely in degree. For, if we were content to register analogies taken from human life and history, what criterion would we have by which we could decide among the claims of conflicting revelations? Moreover, if we take analogies seriously, we are very likely to fall prey to our anthropomorphic tendencies, making the image of God in the light and likeness of our own predilections. But if, on the other hand, we stress the otherness of Transcendence as a difference in kind, we find ourselves back again in the teachings of negative theology. Jaspers' doctrine of Transcendence offers precisely a way out of this impasse. Here Transcendence is generated by the direct experience of the *'existential'* self's ascent to freedom, which gives rise to positive expression, not (it is true) of the essence of Transcendence — this latter must remain beyond the reach of knowledge —, but of the actions of God in relation to man in their historically determined mode of existence. In fact, it is here that one finds the clue to Jaspers' acceptance of the fundamental principles of the Bible. These principles were disclosed to man in the *ultimate situations* in which he found himself, yielding — as a result of the struggle with the conditions obtaining in a secular order — that insight which was in boundless communication, taken up into a wider movement of thought, never to be arrested and revealing to us the secret of our capacities for good and evil. That process may reflect God's love; but it can never freeze into a fixed substratum of a knowledge of the Transcendent for man which, if it were possible to attain, would rob man of his freedom. In order that freedom — which is the necessary condition for the realization of man's individual destiny — should be preserved, we must refrain from any pretense to a knowledge of Transcendence; for, such knowledge could only have the effect of destroying this most essential link of man with God, namely: freedom. In their zeal to vindicate Transcendence and to assure its permanence in the life of man, those critics — by appealing to the (supposed) analogical character of Transcendence (thus bridging the gulf between the finite and the infinite) — have shut their eyes to the significance of Jaspers' most fundamental presupposition, which, by the way, also constitutes his 'Critique of Transcendence,' namely that "God exists for me in the degree to which I in freedom authentically become myself. He does not exist as a scientific content but only as openness to *Existenz*."[11] And:

Freedom for being does not see the ultimate in the world as such. In the world eternal being and temporal manifestation meet. Yet we do not experience eternal being outside of that which is empirically manifested to us in time. Since that which is for us must be manifested in the temporality of the world, there can be no direct knowledge of God and existence. There can only be faith.[12]

11 Karl Jaspers, in *Wisdom*, 45f.

12 *Ibid.*, 82. In this connection it may be well to refer to another critic of Jaspers. F. Heinemann, in his essay "Was ist Lebendig und Was ist Tot in der Existenzphilosophie?" *(Zeitschrift für philosophische Forschung,* 1951, 1ff and 17ff) maintains that the philosophy of *Existenz*, in the latest works of Jaspers, "completes itself, founders and then conquers itself." It "completes itself" because its purpose is from the start to pave a way (and keep it open) to Transcendence; but,

Thus individual *'existential'* life acquires supreme value, and the significance of human history is to be judged by its relation to spiritual values.

It is this certainty of the ultimate triumph of the free human spirit, this combination of the despair of pessimism (nihilism) with an optimism which not only overcomes it, but also absorbs it as an element into itself, which constitutes the unique character of the philosophy of Karl Jaspers.

A. LICHTIGFELD

JOHANNESBURG
SOUTH AFRICA

---

by so doing, it "founders" as a philosophy of *Existenz*, because it cannot establish any logic or ethics; it finally "conquers itself" by recognizing a metaphysics of the Encompassing, with its acknowledgment of principles of the Biblical religion, thus breaking the chain of the sphere of *Existenz*.

This interpretation, however, merely takes sentences from Jaspers' major work out of their context in order to prove a particular thesis. As over against such procedure, we maintain that there is a harmonious development of Jaspers' thought, reaching a climax in his latest works. Furthermore, against Heinemann — who thinks that a world-spirit guided by Jaspers' ideas could not create anything, since on Jaspers' premises no fixation in the form of any object or thing in nature could be admitted — we must say that such fixation, even on Jaspers' own premises, seems to be possible in the *'existential'* decision; even though it could not be a lasting one because it is continually involved in further progress. Nor can we adopt the standpoint of God and look at things from that divine point of view, as Heinemann attempts to do. Also: ethical demands follow quite naturally from Jaspers' theory of communication, which in fact led Jaspers to the adoption of Biblical principles. Thus the idea of moral demands ('ought') remains unconditional for the *'existential'* self, whose realization alone assures to it (i.e., to the *'existential'* self) its possible freedom to develop into authentic *Existenz* while relating itself to Transcendence.

23

Johannes Pfeiffer

ON KARL JASPERS' INTERPRETATION OF ART*

I N THE WORK of Karl Jaspers we encounter the phenomenon
of art three times: 1) on the level of his *Psychologie der Weltanschauungen;* 2) in the course of his *Philosophie;* and 3) within
the framework of his *Von der Wahrheit.* In the first case the inquiry is spiritual-psychological; in the second *'existential'*-meta-
physical; and in the third universal-logical.[1]

I

"Whatever is experienced, visualized and perceived by man as
authentic reality, and, above all, the decisiveness with which he is
concretely certain of this reality — these things determine man's
essence."[2] Accordingly, the *Psychologie der Weltanschauungen* inquires into the spiritual contents and forces which are active in the
mind. *Mind* is to be understood as the experiencing consciousness;
spirit as the consciousness of meaning, guided by ideas. Although
the spirit, in itself, is not mental *(seelisch),* but is, rather, something objectively meaningful, yet it grows only on a mental foundation; and, although the understanding of spiritual meaning-
contents is not a psychological kind of understanding, yet it becomes intermediate thereto, in so far as the mind is accessible only
to the extent that the contents, in which and for which it lives, are
understood.

---

* Translated from the original German by Matthew Cohen as revised by Ludwig
B. Lefebre.

1 Having to consider here the contribution of Jaspers to the interpretation of
art, a mere report would be as inadequate as a general discussion. Instead of this,
it is of greater importance to examine the insights achieved by Jaspers and — by
assimilating them — to summarize and clarify them. Some repetition and cutting
across lines is unavoidable, since Jaspers thinks in a spiral-like movement which,
at times, circles back into itself on a higher level.

2 *Allgemeine,* 275.

However, psychological understanding of spiritual meaning always shifts to *'existential'* understanding, since, on the one hand, the comprehensible is limited by what is unconscious in our (psychophysical) existence *(Dasein)*, and, on the other hand, by the ungiven-unconditional of potential *Existenz*. In this way, *"verstehende"* psychology inevitably becomes the medium of an illumination of *Existenz*, which — offering man basic attitudinal possibilities — challenges him and brings him to himself. "Through *'verstehende'* psychology, illumination of *Existenz* touches this more-than-understandable, touches authentic reality in the possibility of being-myself, recalling, arousing attention, and revealing."[3] Phrased differently: in the medium of psychological understanding of spiritual meaning the issue is always the illumination of what we accomplish ourselves at any given time, nourished by the impenetrable source of freedom.

1

The *Psychologie der Weltanschauungen* examines, at first, only the subjective, generally human conditions of the phenomenon of art. The "aesthetic" attitude belongs to the possibilities of the "contemplative" attitude; the latter is distinguished from the "active" attitude in that it is concerned only with things as such; detached from all impulsive or voluntary interestedness, we yield to the world of objects, viewing, seeing, gazing, and becoming absorbed in it purely for its own sake.

As a transition from activity to contemplation appears the "playful" attitude. In common with the aesthetic attitude "it interrupts the connections to the whole of *Existenz*."[4] Although we are absorbed in the playful experience at the moment of experiencing we do not participate in its real contents as a total personality, but merely experience its form, its ease and cheerfulness. When the playful attitude absolutizes itself into a way of life, it unites with the aesthetic, and, at the same time, with the "enjoying" attitude. This attitude is characterized by not being concerned with the object, but with the enjoyment of the object; not with the experienced content, but with the experience itself and as such. Instead of surrendering to an object or to a situation, we are, in the enjoying attitude, concerned with and relating to our own ability to experience, over against which all contents finally become indifferent, because they are only gratuitous material. This attitude signifies the end of all naiveté and of all connection with the object.

---

3 *Ibid.*, 256.　　　　　　　　4 *Psychologie*, 57.

Life disintegrates into a multitude of discontinuous stimuli and impressions. Indeed, one disciplines enjoyment by producing richness through contrast and change, in order to overcome boredom. Nowhere, however, is an unconditional claim to take things seriously permitted; rather, all that is experienced must always remain suspended in the balance of the non-committal.

2

In order to clarify the essence of the aesthetic attitude, Jaspers begins with a concrete example: the physician at the sickbed of a dying person. As long as the physician has an active attitude, all perception and thinking remain part of the desire to heal. Conversely, it signifies a leap, if he, in a rational attitude, reflects on what this case could teach him. A second leap, however, leads him beyond discerning observation. Now there is submission to the isolated totality of purely pictorial contemplation. On the subjective as well as on the objective side all relationships and connections are severed. Escaped from the enchainment of our desires, wishes and strivings, we perceive an objectivity, detached and therefore whole.

On the side of the perceived there corresponds to this liberation for an irresponsible distance pictorial wholeness and symbolic depth. For, isolation is at the same time the condition for the appearance of something like supra-aesthetic significance in the aesthetic impression which transforms the impression into a "cosmos of relative totality."[5] As far as the perceived is being formed in the creation of a work of art, its organization is compelling. The artist, in his aesthetic experience, is, on the one hand, without responsibility in regard to the totality of existence; but, in creating he is, on the other hand, filled with the specific responsibility of him who, in the act of creating, obeys a law which indeed is strict and binding, though it cannot be fully and consciously recognized.

If the supra-aesthetic significance is lacking or dwindles, mere technique remains; mere form and impression without meaning to animate it, and, therefore, without symbolic transparence, is left. To this formalistic emptiness there corresponds, as an opposite danger, a characteristic spuriousness. Precisely because great, true art is translucent for a background significance; precisely for that reason can it mislead man into confusing the pictorial design of the possible with the actual transformation of life. Instead of

5 *Ibid.*, 70.

recognizing, either consciously or instinctively, that aesthetic meaning is limited and relative, it is permitted to become a substitute for any responsibility felt toward the reality of *Existenz* as the decisive test of meaning.

3

In which way art is meaningful, is more closely considered by Jaspers by referring to Kant. The appendix about Kant's doctrine of Ideas (in *Psychologie der Weltanschauungen*) explains the "Idea" as both an effective force *in* the subject and as mandatory wholeness, arising from the world of objects, *meeting* the subject. Ideas are an Encompassing, at which we cannot aim, but *in* which we must live, acting, understanding or creating. The Idea contained in a work of art is, for Kant, that which gives it, — beyond its formal perfection, — its spiritual and moral significance. Kant defines the aesthetic Idea more precisely as "that representation of the imagination, which occasions much thought, without, however, any definite thought, i.e., any *concept* being capable of being adequate to it; it consequently cannot be completely compassed and made intelligible by language."[6] Two things act together here: one, that such representations strive after something which lies beyond the bounds of experience; then, that it concerns inner intuition which, precisely as such, remains incommensurable for the conceptual as well as for any direct expression generally. Accordingly, "genius" is the capacity to rise from something given to an Idea, and to express these Ideas in symbolic representation in such a way that the "subjective state of mind" corresponding to them communicates to others.

II.

Scientific knowledge concerns particular objects or object relationships in the world and is, as such, just as coercive as relative. Philosophy ventures the penetration of everything objective into the non-objective depth of *Existenz* as the transcendental beingmyself, and, together with it, into the encompassing and allsurmounting primal source *(Urgrund)*. For, what is existentially understood always stands in need of metaphysical interpretation. Whereas psychological and existential understanding aim at what

6 *Ibid.*, 485f, after Kant's *Critique of Judgement*, #49, 197 (Bernard).

we experience factually, or which we accomplish from freedom, metaphysical understanding attempts to go beyond that and to find in every original experience the meaning it derives from the absolute.[7]

Phrased differently: metaphysical understanding refers to existence as a cipher-script of Being, which (viz., the cipher-script) we encounter athwart of all objectivity. "In cipher-script the separation of symbol from that which is symbolized is impossible. It transforms Transcendence into presence, but it is not explicable.[8] In the becoming transparent of existence we perceive a meaning which does not permit of translation into the form of knowing, because this meaning shines forth only in contemplation. What shines in this manner is simultaneously given and created; given, not in the way of actual objectivity, but as language, which comes to meet us from Being itself; created, not in a fashion which can be deduced from a psychologically understandable subject, but in one which appears only "on the basis of *Existenz*, as the nearness of *Existenz* to Being in intuitive imagination."[9] What reveals itself to us in the cipher is a Being with which, on the basis of origin, we are connected; confronted by the final, anticipating vision of the imagination, world existence and being-as-freedom are no longer separated, but become one in their common basis.

1

In Jaspers' *Philosophie* we first encounter the phenomenon of art where, at the boundary of world-orientation, philosophic thought comes into its own. At one and the same time philosophy stands in conflict and in league with religion and art: as transcending assurance, which perceives authentic Being — in recoil, so to speak — by means of foundering thinking, and which, by means of meaningful not-knowing, indirectly interprets it. For certainty of Being through religion occurs as authoritative proclamation on the basis of positive revelation, whereas to transcend in philosophizing is a voluntary risk of the searching reason, led by faith. Also, assurance of Being through art occurs as formal completion on the basis of symbolic contemplation, whereas the philosophical quest for Being immediately breaks up what has congealed into structured presence.

"That from which all spheres, in their autonomy, get their

<hr>

[7] *Allgemeine*, 257.   [8] *Philosophie*, III, 141.   [9] *Ibid.*, 153.

existence, cannot itself be a sphere."[10] If one understands the beautiful as that which is common to all works of art, in that it makes them valid in form and in quality, then one conceives of art only according to its autonomous medium, not according to the encompassing source. "In its origin art is the illumination of *Existenz* by an assurance which brings Being into the present by intuitive contemplation."[11] Art, therefore, is bound up with Being as representability. As intuitive realization, the assurance of Being occurring through art remains inscrutable for thought. In so far it is just as direct as indirect.

Because art, as a symbolic illumination of *Existenz*, implies an original reference to Being, it becomes non-binding and, therefore, empty whenever, as pure art, as art for art's sake, it detaches itself from this hidden root. Scrutinizing discretion must always differentiate, therefore, between genuine art, which has the meaning and force to bring the hieroglyphics of Being to shine through in the phenomena, and the playful, formalistic art, wherein ever new, gratuitously changing experiences and impressions become the material and the occasion for representation as an end in itself, whereby existence inevitably aestheticizes itself; that is, de-realizes itself to an existence in the isolated moment, an existence without faithfulness and without consequence, with the single criterion of intensity of experience.

To be non-committal is, indeed, a danger which belongs to the essence of art as such. Art is separated from factual daily existence and its strivings by a discontinuous leap; the difference lies in its detachment which brings the totality and depth of life to present completion. In that the world of appearances is rounded and transfigured into a meaningful picture, it is as conserved in the eternal truth of Being. Therein lies the seduction: in artistic creation as in imitation, to lose oneself, in contemplative enjoyment, to a timeless fulfilment in the present. In the perception of the whole, which takes up into itself everything dark and fragile, something akin to salvation from temporal existence is finally anticipated, at the price, however, of an 'existential' de-realization. What is a matter of active attitude, daily renewing itself, becomes a matter of contemplative imagination, which permits the finite to fuse into the infinite. Responsible vigilance demands, therefore, that the detached calm in the symbolic presence of Being always be experienced only as a temporary withdrawal, which remains dependent on the compelling seriousness of the *Existenz* which carries and comprehends it.

10 *Ibid.*, I, 316.   11 *Ibid.*, 331.

The problem returns when we, in the course of *'existential'* understanding, illuminate "absolute consciousness' as the way in which we become aware of authentic Being in existence. As a constitutive moment of absolute consciousness, imagination has an ambiguous position between the possibility of revelation and the possibility of deception. "Through imagination I comprehend Being in the cipher of everything objective as something which cannot become objective, although it is directly present."[12] In the perception of imagination existence becomes as if transparent. In perceptual presentation we become aware of something beyond all perception. Imagination enables us to look into the perfection of Being, where even the terrible and the confused are balanced in the beauty of a transcendent harmony. All this makes imagination's positive meaning for essential life evident: it unlocks the realm of the possible for us. Without it we would remain constrained in the narrowness of the bare reality of existence. But this function is a positive one only on condition that the contemplative fulfilment in beholding the possible remains connected with the actual reality of *Existenz,* and that it is authenticated by the inner actions of the whole person. If, instead of this, contemplation isolates itself, then the pictorially perceived becomes a non-committal appearance, which smooths over, conceals, and diverts from the temporal existence to which we are committed. The consequence is a side by side of self-sufficient soarings and unpenetrated reality of life.

2

Metaphysics of art is not mere thinking "about" art; not a kind of thinking, therefore, which makes art the object; but rather, thinking "in" art and with the help of art, in such a way that we seek to adopt what art communicates, in symbolic perception of the hieroglyphics of the transcendent basis of Being. Thus, if art is to be understood, as Schelling said, as *"organon* of philosophy," then the difficulty is this: that by thought we aspire to penetrate something which is not accessible in any other except symbolic form.

"Man pushes ahead to art in metaphysical thinking."[13] In thought we are concerned with whatever ascertainment of Being occurs in the work of art. The task is to illuminate this inspiring background "by means of, but beyond, formal analysis of works

12 *Ibid.,* II, 282.   13 *Ibid.,* III, 194.

of art, historical narration of their worlds and intellectual cli-
mates, and biographies of their creators."[14] Only in metaphysical
thinking do we perceive and consciously reflect on the decisive
cleavage which divides everything that is called a work of art,
"according to the outward attributes of the man-made:" yonder
the creations which represent a cipher of Transcendence; here
those others, "without basis and depth."

Art, then, in its essential and fulfilled meaning, is intermediate
between the worldly manifold and the unique one, between
finite temporal existence and eternal Being; put in terms of the
subjective act: between 'existential' encounter and mystic submersion. Artistic contemplation remains separate from that which
is the object of its perception: in such a way, however, that the
latter becomes transparent for the world-transcending origin.
Neither factually nor conclusively, but in the suspended anticipation of the possible does artistic intuition raise phenomena to
the consummation of all-encompassing, omnipresent Being. Therefore, the perception of the artistic imagination is at one and the
same time both more and less than the reality of our existence in
time: *more,* if one proceeds from the mere factuality of the dull
cares of existence; *less,* if one looks at authentic *Existenz* in the
concentrated seriousness of its responsible openness. From the
point of view of the former, art is a soaring which liberates; from
that of the latter, a non-committal suspension; but this suspended
self-oblivion is at the same time a condition for the possibility
of authentic self-being: In so far as it frees us from the narrowness
and constraint of our own purpose-circumscribed private existence. Or vice versa: In the world's transfiguring of itself into a
cipher, phenomena gain their beauty in themselves and grant us,
for fleeting moments, the consciousness of time-conquering fulfillment. But if, on the one hand, contemplative imagination is,
so to speak, the eye, without which *Existenz* would remain blind;
then, on the other hand, *Existenz* becomes untrue, if contemplation frees itself as an ideal sphere from the reality of temporal
existence.

3

"In order to be able to express what is read as cipher, the
artist must *imitate* realities."[15] But this imitation refers neither to
empirical facts nor to conceptual constructs, but, rather, to the

14 *Ibid.*   15 *Ibid.*

forces, — reflected in the ideas, — of encountered phenomena. In that such forces are perceived imitatively, art gains the materials for the symbolic formation of the cipher at which it aims. If the basic artistic act demands, on the one hand, creative talent as the capacity for irreplaceable unique expression, then it demands, on the other hand, *Existenz,* as the essence which refers back to its origin, and which speaks to us through the work of art. "Where, however, someone able to get at the foundations of Being, finds it possible to express what is in ciphers, *Existenz* and talent become one in genius."[16]

The cipher occurs differently in the cult-bound and in independent art. Whereas the former evokes visions in mythical symbols which reflect the transcendent primal source, the latter makes the empirical reality as such transparent. "The artist of pure transcendence gives shape to traditional conceptions; the artist of immanent transcendence teaches anew how to read existence as cipher."[17] Where, however, the independent man melts down mythical elements into the picture arising from his own, free experience of being, and thus manages to bring the traditional representations to a transfigured present, there are found the culminating peaks of art to date.

In the separate arts, cipher appears differently in each case. What looms up as cipher-script in music, is "the form of self-being as temporal existence;" in architecture it is organized spatiality and in the plastic arts it is physical compactness. As over against such immediate givenness of the cipher-bearing medium, poetry and painting communicate by way of an illusory world of the imagination. As concerns more particularly poetry, it conjures up the cipher-script of the transcendent primal source "in the representation of everything perceptible and thinkable as such, as language brings it to expression."[18] Precisely this communicability, which rests upon the interposition of something intended and represented, is the stipulation which opens up the allness of appearances, so that "all of being and non-being" becomes accessible. Just as poetry, on the one hand, can deceive "because of the manifoldness of gripping experience," thus, in order to fulfill itself as realized cipher-script, it demands, on the other hand, with the same decisiveness which characterizes music, "the temporally accentuated cooperation" of our "actual momentary self."[19]

16 *Ibid.,* 195.   17 *Ibid.,* 196.

18 *Ibid.,* 197.   19 *Ibid.,* 199.

III.

"The *Philosophie* concerns itself with the *'existential'* consciousness of Being . . . *Von der Wahrheit* deals everywhere with the self-consciousness of encompassing thought, directed toward itself, in all possibilities."[20] If, then, existential-metaphysical understanding, in thoughtful ascertainment, aims at Being, universal-logical understanding comes back to thinking as such: in philosophical logic, there occurs the radical and universal self-examination of the reason, which aims at Being, but which, in so doing, remains latent. Or: the existential-metaphysical type of understanding concerns reality; the universal-logical type aims at truth. As certainly, however, as the different forms and modes of being-true refer back to the one and final truth which is grounded in the transcendent primal source, just as certainly do the two perspectives strive at a synthesis in an encompassing totality.

1

If Jaspers inquires now for a third time after the meaning of art, the question now concerns the manner of its being-true within an all-embracing total language, which continues to operate as a uniform primal source even after it has split into religious proclamation, plastic art, and poetic creation. For the basic artistic occurrence lies not, in the first instance, in its autonomous representation, but, above all, in producing a beauty, which is one with Being as such. Whereas the plastic arts permit us to perceive this being-beautiful through the medium of visibility, poetry accomplishes this through linguistically mediated conception. "Language turns experience into concepts. Within language poetry is the vocabulary which can communicate everything so discovered."[21] For, among all possible modes of meaning, only language is universal, in so far as it includes all other forms of meaning, because it mediates between them and refers to them.

In producing linguistic sound-pictures, we are intentionally directed towards a distanced content. That, however, which we mean in this way, is Being itself, as out of itself it speaks in meaning-characters. "What becomes conscious in language and in its meanings is itself a meaning, which becomes clear therein."[22]

[20] Ernst Mayer: "Philosophie und Philosophische Logik bei Jaspers," in: *Offener Horizont. Festschrift für Karl Jaspers,* (Munich, 1953) 66.

[21] *Tragedy,* 26; (*Wahrheit,* 917).　　　　　[22] *Wahrheit,* 412.

That language, as much all-present as evanescent, — because it is a medium of meaning never adequately to be objectified, — is not only adequate to Being but, beyond that, is related to it: this inscrutable secret finds, in the phrase of the "language" of Being, a metaphorical-transcending expression.

What becomes clear in linguistic meaning remains enveloped by an irremovable darkness: in contrast to the unequivocal sign, — which is definable in its meaning because it is definite, — the genuine word is ambiguous, because its meaning comes out of the Encompassing, and carries with it something of its infinity. Furthermore, whereas the sign is separated from the designated thing, there prevails in the living word the unity of the producing with the produced, of the expression with the remembered or incited performance.

In so far as we interpret Being, which speaks in meaning characters, by means of language, it becomes at the same time communicable. The danger in this is that the linguistic form of communication, instead of remaining the medium of the encounter with Being, may become the aim, and finally its own end. Instead of yielding, in the production or reception of poetry, to something which for fleeting moments issues from the depth of Being, we remain caught in the linguistic form as such, in the preciousness of its sounds and images. Thereby the meaning of poetry is basically falsified: in place of the kind of seriousness, which experiences something akin to an 'existential' metamorphosis, there enters an aesthetisizing, non-committal, enjoying attitude which is concerned in the end only with ornamental stimuli.

2

To remain legitimate, therefore, linguistic-artistic discipline must stand in the service of a vision, which — as an encompassing carrier of meaning — guides creation. All perceptible objects in the world can become carriers of such meaning when they are filled with supra-objective content. "Ciphers are not new objects, but newly filled ones."[23] They are not in addition to actual objects, inasmuch as they are hidden in all objectivity: the object becomes cipher when it is transcended and is thereby made transparent for unfathomable meaning. One cannot distinguish here between appearance and meaning, between what is present and what is added by one's mind: the suspended appearance itself

23 *Ibid.*, 1043.

and as such is the presence of Being; the sensorily given present permits, in vanishing, something to shine forth from the supra-sensory.

That is why ciphers, in order to be perceivable, presuppose an upsoaring of the whole individual: from the phenomenon there speaks to me, at any time, only what I am capable of hearing. "It reveals itself to me according to my attitude."[24] Although the symbols come to us from Being itself and are, therefore, no mere conceptions, but contain reality; their perception, still depends on *'existential'* presuppositions. "It is Eros to whom Being shows itself, in that it simultaneously veils and reveals itself in symbols. The meaning of the symbols is the presence in being of the real."[25]

Next, there appear three types of abuse: Objectification robs the symbols of their suspended transparency; allegorization lowers their essence to mere meaning, when the sensory-actual is absolut-ized to the only reality; and aesthetisizing detaches them from the spiritual-moral basis of life and thereby makes them non-committal. As over against that, the genuine symbol has binding force precisely because in it there occurs an indirect participation in Being: in so far as symbols are true for us, we live through them in the depth of transcendent reality, which is accessible in no other way.

Concretely Jaspers reflects on the being-true of poetry, using the example of the tragic. The tragic is both formed existence and knowing consciousness; what is experienced as a tragic event is at the same time understood in a knowing perception, which basically resists intellectual explanation. "The original tragic vision consists in thoughts and questions experienced in concrete images."[26] Knowledge about the tragic, and the overcoming of the tragic which it contains, is not in the nature of a doctrine, but rather that of an inquiring concern.

What constitutes the tragic first of all is, beyond misery and fright, beyond suffering and transitoriness, the inescapable foun-dering of responsibly-behaving man aiming at perfection; in such a way, however, that, in the experience of the tragic, he also experiences liberation in that, precisely in collapse, the encom-passing primal source opens up to catch the foundering one. In order to perceive the tragic, the spectator has to have that genuine sympathy, by virtue of which he identifies himself with the pre-sented action: participating as ourselves, we are deeply moved and thus experience the soaring which frees us for authentic self-being.

24 *Ibid.,* 1041.   25 *Ibid.*   26 *Tragedy,* 102; *(Wahrheit,* 959).

If, on the other hand, *'existential'* pathos deviates into a non-committal experience, in which we edify ourselves in aesthetic contemplation, then the tragic transforms itself into a mere educational phenomenon, a museum-like experience, without any moulding or liberating power.[27]

Finally the experience of the tragic must not be absolutized: the tragic does not lie in any transcendent origin, but in phenomenal temporal existence. Whoever relocates it in the Absolute itself encroaches on both, the tragic and Transcendence. For it is true that the basis of Being shines through the tragic, but precisely as something else, which in itself is no longer tragic.

3

If, in the genuine symbol, there occurs an indirect participation in Being, one may ask what such participation means in reference to "God" as the All-Encompassing, the One and Only. "The soaring up to the one God pervades the world of appearances. The transformation of the world into a mediation between us and the one God is its transformation into cipher-being."[28] There is no other way to God than this indirect one, in which we experience true reality in the becoming transparent of the actuality of the world. Where a direct and exclusive revelation of God is asserted, it rests upon the fact that one confuses historically conditioned ciphers with the unconditional, absolutely eternal basis of Being. Whether by way of mystical submersion or by absolutizing a particular historical mediation: every direct comprehension of God falls short.

If, therefore, on the one hand, one must avert the deception which believes in the absolutized symbol to possess God himself definitively, one must, on the other hand, avoid getting caught in the ciphers as demonic cosmic forces. What is important, rather, is that beyond all the mediating ciphers we should seek, again and again, the concealed unity of the divine source, which, as the truly Encompassing of pure, absolute Transcendence, supports and limits all other forms of the Encompassing. "The disclosure of the phenomena is not yet that of the source. The former achieves, at any time, its greatest possible fulfillment; the latter, it is true,

[27] Regarding the emptying of the work of art to an object in a museum, compare the remarks of Gerhard Nebel in his treatise: "Das Ereignis des Schönen" in *Offener Horizont. Festschrift für Karl Jaspers* (Munich, 1953), 403-414.

[28] *Wahrheit,* 1051.

occurs through the phenomena, but itself remains encompassing and, thereby, infinite and unfulfillable."[29]

Here, following Kant, we must take a final step, in order to illuminate once more the possible being-true of art as being the meaning which, at the same time, sets its limits. Artistic perception is true in the sense that it opens perspectives into the infinite depth of Being; in such a way, however, that we always remain in the balance of the suspense of a game, which induces all emotive forces to achieve a free accord. What is involved here is a passing perfection at the moment; man becomes "whole" only at the cost of a withdrawal from the totality of his life, which is always still out-standing and pre-ceding, because it is entrusted to his responsibility. The formatively realized perspective remains a metaphor and a memory; and art must thus, from within itself, come upon that boundary, "where what has become form in it is, as such, not the final inwardness at which it aims."[30]

*   *   *   *   *

Let us summarize:

Jaspers understands the "revealing" function of art to be its basic meaning. *How* does art reveal? By conjuring the perceived into form. *What* does art reveal? Being. Here three stages stand out. First of all Being is the sum total of pictorial-phenomenal entities, in which the effective powers of the world and the moving forces of *Existenz* become condensed. Next, Being is that ungiven totality and depth of existence, in which the natural ground of the world would be one with the basic freedom of our supra--sensory destiny. Being is, finally, the One and Only, the Unconditional-Infinite, and, as such, the all-encompassing and all-transcending primal source.

When Goethe says: "Holy poetry, may it strive heavenward," he thereby places the artistic process under precisely this claim: in an ever so temporary and metaphorically reflected mediation to disclose some of the transcendent basis of Being itself. And, indeed, beyond the elementary forces of the reality of appearance and beyond the ungiven identity of the ground of nature and the basis of freedom, it is the dimension of "heaven" which is revealed in artistic perception and creation. The essentialization and transfiguration of world existence occurs against this background of unity; and this in such a way that in its concealed light the relationships of things become transparent. Pointedly expressed:

29 *Ibid.*, 458.   30 *Existenz*, 46.

There occurs in art something like a return of things into the source, and, thereby, a symbolic conquest of finitude.

But instead of "heaven," Jaspers goes beyond that and speaks directly of "God:" is this not founded upon an encroachment of metaphysical speculation, which equates a token anteroom of God with God Himself, in His absolute, supra-earthly as well as supra-heavenly differentness?[31] We could speak of God *qua* God only if He would on His own accord reveal Himself to us, — linked with our inquiring and searching pre-comprehension —, by way of an event which we would understand as a divine revelation through the "proof of the spirit and of power." In devotion to God's loving judgement, de-secularized down to the very ground of our being and life, we would achieve the strength to open ourselves to what at any given time, gets at us with an unforesee-able claim, a claim for which one must be responsible in faithful trust. The tension between perception and faith, and, thereby, between cipher and revelation would remain indissoluble: What we perceive in the mirror of art would always enter into our eschatological relationship to the world as a reflected and, as it were, bracketed, possession.

If, indeed, we want to remain honest, we can and may speak philosophically here always only in "the subjunctive:" autono-mous reason is unable to decide whether, in any revelation handed down by human beings, God Himself truly and actually speaks, and permits us to know him, or whether this is a presumptuous absolutizing, resting on self-deception. But, whether we, in devout awe, leave it undecided, or whether we experience this tension in such a way, that at times a not forethinkable and unavailabe certainty is granted: metaphysical speculation is deprived of God *qua* God.

The occurrence of art is so far from being error or illusion, that, on the contrary, it elevates us heavenward in anticipating upsurge. But no thought, winged by artistic illumination of Being, is able to transcend the border which divides the anteroom from what, in strict and actual sense, is other-worldly and eternal.

JOHANNES PFEIFFER

HAMBURG-VOLKSDORF
GERMANY

31 For a supplementation of the following I may refer to the third edition of my essay: *Existenzphilosophie. Eine Einführung in Heidegger und Jaspers.* Hamburg, 1952, "Nachtrag 1952," III, 3.

24

Helmut Rehder

LITERARY CRITICISM AND THE
EXISTENTIALISM OF JASPERS

I.

MANIFOLD are the relations between literary criticism and the existentialist philosophy of Karl Jaspers. Even the casual observer will not fail to detect "existentialist" criteria in the arguments of contemporary criticism. Difficulties arise when he attempts to describe and define them; for then the absence of any sort of platform or "school" becomes manifest. Although Jaspers has attracted many students, he has had few disciples. However provocative his thinking, its very principles discourage the formation of a school or the idea of an apostolic succession.

Jaspers himself came to philosophy from the natural sciences. Yet his appeal has been strongest among "humanists," that is, among writers, journalists, scholars who are concerned about the future of mankind and who, with this end in view, interpret the written past in the consciousness of an active mission in the present. *Mutatis mutandis,* the history of this appeal may be compared with that of Fichte, whose philosophy inspired the younger generation of romanticists — writers and intellectuals of most heterogeneous intent and scope; it cannot be compared with that of Hegel, whose influence upon subsequent philosophers and scholars was promoted and determined by the tangible formalism of his system. The followers of Hegel may still be labeled Hegelians in spite of doctrinal differences between them; the "followers" of Jaspers lack uniformity of intellectual physiognomy. None of them has gone again the way Jaspers himself went — the way which at times he has seriously recommended: through the exact sciences to an interpretation of the "spirit." As a result, elements of Jaspers' existentialism have found their way into the thinking of those who are accustomed to sociological judgments and political opinions as well as of those who prefer psychological reflection; his ideas have been appropriated by some who espoused the cause of the Third Reich and by others who vigorously opposed it; and the traces of his extraneous influence have ranged from faint reminiscences of his technical terminology to the esoteric language of the anointed. For many who are looking for "meaning" in a bewildering contemporary scene, existentialism offers a tool with which to erect a secure launching platform; for others it is a welcome landing strip. Viewed against the background of the modern age, Jaspers' existentialism, like other intellectual "operations" of the day, is a symptom of the very nihilism which it condemns. Its distinction lies in the fact that it attempts to diagnose and cure this malady, if a remedy can be developed, as it were, "from within."

A comparison between Jaspers and Fichte is both illuminating and misleading. Jaspers, to be sure, is in no way based on Fichte; Fichte's philosophy is demanding and exclusive; Jaspers' is detached and cautioning. Nevertheless, their comparison, merely suggesting a historical parallel rather than a possible affinity, reveals remarkable correspondences. The most striking is their philosophical departure from Kant's transcendentalism; both realize that Kant, by establishing the frontiers of exact knowledge, not only emancipated the sciences from the interference of metaphysics but also freed genuine thinking from the interference of premature scientific conclusions. Similarly striking is their dialectical circling about the problem of the "self," which Fichte pursued through the three stages of "doubt," "knowledge," and "faith,"[1] whereas Jaspers proposes the three stages of philosophical "orientation," "illumination of *Existenz*," and "metaphysics."[2] Furthermore, neither Fichte nor Jaspers is attached to history as such, although both, absorbed in the philosophical task of elucidating and actuating the absolute ego *("Ich überhaupt")* and the personality *("Existenz")*, respectively, are filled with the pathos of the irretrievable significance of the present historical situation into whose idiom the past must be translated. Both agree in the conviction that philosophy is vindicated only by its illuminating, ordering, decisive participation in life. If Fichte, in a period of national desperation, rallied the conscience of his listeners in his *Grundzüge des gegenwärtigen Zeitalters* (1806) and his *Reden an die deutsche Nation* (1808), Jaspers similarly makes the diagnosis and, consequently, the alteration of the present *"geistige Situation der Zeit"* the real concern of philosophy. "The mental situation of our day is pregnant with immense

[1] Cf. J. G. Fichte, *Die Bestimmung des Menschen* (1800).

[2] Jaspers, *Philosophie* (1932).

dangers and immense possibilities; and it is one which, if we are inadequate to the tasks which await us, will herald the failure of mankind."[3] It is this preoccupation with the current, 'existential' mission of philosophy which, in Fichte and Jaspers alike, promotes an unsentimental, objective, and yet intensely personal mode of interpretation, even though their own work is otherwise peculiarly free from interest in literary, that is, secondary criticism of human experience.

Jaspers has dealt significantly with subjects of literary criticism on two occasions; both times the choice of the literary medium seems to indicate no more than an incidental application of his philosophical method. Still these ventures into the literary field, written more than a quarter of a century apart and without any apparent affinity in scope, are related to one another by virtue of the underlying 'existential' theme and by the implied concern about the intellectual tendencies of the times. The first of these two essays appeared when Jaspers had made the transition from science (psychiatry) to philosophy; the second came at a time when his philosophy, already manifest in numerous publications, had become an integral part of these tendencies themselves. Both essays betray the consciousness of a cultural crisis which, anticipated at first with apprehension as an intellectual phenomenon, in the end asserted itself as an inescapable reality.

The early study on *Strindberg und Van Gogh* (1922) was a "pathographic" study with philosophical intent. Methodologically it owed as much to the scientific detachment of a specialized discipline, expressed in Jaspers' *Allgemeine Psychopathologie* (1913), as it did to the systematizing energy of a philosophical perspective, displayed in his imposing *Psychologie der Weltanschauungen* (1919).

But it was also symptomatic of its time. Had such a study been written during the waning of the Middle Ages, it might have resulted in one of the numerous satirical treatises on "folly" — treatises which, relentlessly but with persuasiveness and detachment, unmasked human foibles in an age marked by diminishing faith. In the late Middle Ages, with the signs of crisis and centrifugal tendencies already in the air, such a treatise was still able to relate even extreme vagaries of psychological experience to a basic concept of "wisdom" or "reason" as the common standard of human thought and behavior. The modern psychologist has at his disposal no such common metaphysical standard for judging human affairs; nor is he interested in one. His only standard is

3 *Situation* (1947), 20. *Age,* 27.

that of specific evidence which places his object, man, within a framework of infinite factualities and references, but allows no conclusions with regard to ultimate principles regulating the actual conduct of life.

Yet, a distant parallel between medieval and modern typology of psychological experience cannot be overlooked. In his serialization of "foolish" cases or types — and any individualizing drive was likely to appear abnormal one way or another —, the medieval satirist presented a system of material ethics, culminating in the ideal norm of the "wise man" who knows how to keep himself in proper balance between empirical and transcendental interest and, for the sake of his spiritual existence, knows how to remain aloof from too great an involvement in the things and in himself. Where the medieval satirist "unmasked" his types, presenting them, as it were, in the physiognomy in which they were to appear before their Creator, Jaspers' descriptive analysis of pathological processes seeks to determine those phases of personality that appear "fake" *("unecht")* within the hypothetically "total" structure of a personality. His criteria of truth can no longer lie in such metaphysical systems or articles of faith as supported the medieval critic. If at all, they must be derived from a methodology of understanding *("Verstehen")* itself which recognizes as the "foundation of our ethos" solely the will for clarity, veracity, and corresponding realism.[4] According to Jaspers, the understanding of "fake" in the intellectual and emotional make-up of personality represents one of the central problems of psychology which has by no means been solved nor even sufficiently formulated.[5]

Under these premises the pathographic analysis of Strindberg and Van Gogh, drawing on Swedenborg and Hölderlin for supporting evidence, describes the genesis of insanity in four pathological cases of creative personality; it observes changes in their *Weltanschauung* corresponding to typical "shifts" in the pathological process — which, therefore, cannot have been without influence upon their works; — but it disclaims any intention of explaining or evaluating the literary or artistic aspects of these works.[6] What is said about Strindberg may be said as well about Hölderlin, whose schizophrenia, though of a different type from Strindberg's, brought about marked alterations in the emotional and mental habitus of the poet, — alterations which are distinctly discernible in corresponding changes in the style and content of his works.[7]

4 *Strindberg,* 3rd ed. (1949), 182.   5 *Ibid.,* 183.
6 *Ibid.,* 8.   7 *Ibid.,* 125.

These considerations affect the premises of literary criticism, but on the basis of their philosophical rather than their psychological implications. Works of literature are independent intellectual and aesthetic entities which, comparable to products of nature, can be understood and appreciated only within themselves. On the other hand, they cannot be detached from the pathological frame of reference within which they were produced. For it makes a difference indeed in the understanding of a literary work of art whether the objectivity of a mythical world (e.g., classical antiquity for Hölderlin) remains merely metaphorical and symbolical imagery for the sane or whether it becomes actual reality for the insane; it makes a difference whether a certain obscurity of style may be considered the perfection of artistic profundity or is to be taken verbally.[8]

The critical results of Jaspers' essay represent no particular insights into facts and circumstances surrounding Strindberg's plays or Hölderlin's poems. Rather they lie in the method of philosophical questioning itself which, beyond the demonstration of the complete clinical detail, advances to the *boundaries of the comprehensible*. Through the comparison of contrasting types of disease we become aware of what in itself can no longer be compared and therefore remains the mystery of the genuine, authentic *("eigentlich") Existenz*. Behind the symptoms of the pathological process and behind the "shifts" in *Weltanschauung*, something singular and unique in the personality structure of Strindberg, of Hölderlin, or of Van Gogh becomes visible which can at best be circumscribed because it can no longer be recognized in its entirety.

Jaspers hesitated to imply wider connections between his Strindberg study and the intellectual situation of the time in which it was written. Still the book can scarcely be separated from its historical background, the searching and unstable years following the first World War. With its examination of then fashionable artistic favorites, its interest in the border cases of creative mentality, the book was reminiscent of, though not identifiable with, the literary movement of expressionism and its groping for new standards of literature and life. Factually Jaspers observes that schizophrenia as a pathological phenomenon, in contrast to hysteria, is of rather recent occurrence and frequency in Occidental history. However, to recognize schizophrenic tendencies in the mental physiognomy of modern times is a different matter, and Jaspers is ready to admit the subjective nature of such

8 Cf. *ibid.*, 138.

generalizing reflections. Nevertheless, these reflections indicate
the root of his thinking and the point of departure for a possible
application to literary criticism. If the modern age is characterized
as a time of artificial imitation and of a histrionic mode of experience, as a time in which any form of intellect is institutionalized,
any form of existence becomes consciously manufacturable, and
the mere desire for originality can pass for originality itself,—
then the transition from scientific (psychiatric) observation and
judgment to the prophetic pathos and intent of *'existential'*
philosophizing has become evident. "In such times," Jaspers asks,
"is schizophrenia perhaps the condition of genuineness in spheres
which in times of bondage could be experienced and represented
genuinely without schizophrenia?"[9] It is for this reason that the
detailed and objective study of schizophrenic types and cases
possesses *'existential'* relevance; for they permit a passing glance
into the absolute which is otherwise "always concealed, visible
only in finite figures."[10]

As pointed out, the Strindberg study was a side issue of the
Psychologie der Weltanschauungen and, like this work, has frequently served as a guide for literary criticism in the analysis of
the world-views, attitudes, and creeds of poets and writers. The
Psychologie was inspired by the desire to discern the totality of
possible personal motivations. Its objective was "to see and to
know what, psychologically, has been real and still is possible."[11]
How deeply — even though only defensively — this work was indebted to the spiritual tendencies of the age can be seen from the
prefatorial remarks which restrict the scope of the book to an
objective analysis of "ultimate psychological positions" and refer
anyone in search of new directions to the "concrete decisions of
personal destiny" in practical life. The book was not meant to
furnish new contents but to provide a means by which contents
might be understood. What made it philosophically appealing to
literary critics was precisely the impartial equanimity with which
it penetrated to the limits of the rationally comprehensible in the
description of structure patterns of mental attitudes. For a moment it appeared as if certain types of world-views could become
objectively discernible. As to its own position, the work occupied
a place midway between the History of Ideas *(Geistesgeschichte)*
and structural psychology, deriving from both a framework of
spiritual types *(Geistestypen)* of which some were faintly suggestive of types currently employed in literary criticism (e.g., enlight-

9 Cf. *ibid.*, 182.   10 Cf. *ibid.*, 183.
11 *Psychologie* (1919), 2nd ed. (1922), 4.

enment, romanticism, classicism, etc.) . Others — for example, the "vantage point in the infinite" — seemed to indicate the direction in which future development of existentialist philosophy was possible. The *Psychologie,* fascinating though it still is to many a reader, has since been partially disavowed by its author as mere "latent philosophy;"[12] in spite of its emphasis on method of analysis, it could be interpreted as having its origin in the attitude of relativism and aesthetic contemplation — the attitude of modern nihilism which it sought to overcome.

The existentialist position was clearly defined in 1947 when Jaspers, for a second time, came to deal philosophically with problems of literary criticism. For now it was the concern of philosophy to salvage from the shambles into which totalitarianism had shattered Germany's cultural existence a spiritual heritage that was meaningful, and more than just magnificent abstraction. In 1945 Jaspers had been among the first to answer this need, and his repeated statements of purpose — in dedicating the re-opened Heidelberg University, in frankly raising the question of guilt, and in alerting the minds to the consciousness of a new common cause[13] — testify to his postulate of an active service of philosophy. In all of these statements, and in his introduction to the periodical *Die Wandlung* in particular, his demand for a non-illusory, present-day interpretation of past values had brought him close to the very essence of the literary tradition itself: the Germany he defended against Sigrid Undset's vindictive charges was the "intellectual world of Lessing, Goethe, Kant and the many great whose nobility and truthfulness are inviolable for us, even though we receive them critically and do everything to avoid any form of deification."[14]

It is in keeping with these principles that Jaspers, in accepting the award of the Frankfurt Goethe Prize, presented his famous Goethe lecture, "Unsere Zukunft und Goethe,"[15] which revealed some unusual implications of *'existential'* philosophy for the standards of literary criticism. Taken together with the Basel Goethe address of 1949[16] it represents Jaspers' answer to the question to what extent an historical *Existenz,* a great personality of the past, which is relatively accessible to objective, i.e., "scien-

---

12 Cf. *Rechenschaft* (1951), 362.

13 Cf. "Erneuerung der Universität," "Antwort an Sigrid Undset," "Geleitwort für die Zeitschrift *Die Wandlung*," (1945), all contained in *Rechenschaft*, 137-158. Cf. also *Guilt*, (1947).

14 *Rechenschaft*, 153.   15 *Ibid.*, 26-49.

16 "Goethes Menschlichkeit," *ibid.*, 50-68.

tific" approach, can still be meaningful for the present without becoming the object of mere scholarship, purely aesthetic appreciation, or narrow cult and deification.

In these lectures, Goethe is conceived as a unique realization of human *Existenz* which in such completeness perhaps seeks his equal in history. Like few other figures of the past, Goethe has become accessible through his works, letters, conversations, and numerous other documents so that his presence can still be as real as that of any living person with whom we commune. Still there are limitations. Even if Goethe were conceived as the fulfillment of human possibilities, he still would remain impenetrable as an individual. It is impossible to comprehend him completely. His reality was more than our concepts and different from our image of him. He cannot be captured. When he is seen from a different age and through new eyes, there will always remain the infinite variety of possible interpretations.

That is why Goethe, as a human specimen, cannot become a model to be emulated nor an authority to be heeded. We cannot adopt his views as having the same validity for our times which they possessed for his. Nor can we crystallize from his works an ideology for our use; for, even if that were possible, it would contain an element of untruth because, as an abstraction, it would not be our belief, sanctioned by our experience. "What really matters is that we adopt Goethe's world by translating what was true for him into our own world." But in doing so we find ourselves beset by contradictions; for in Goethe we discover positive qualities offset by apparent limitations. Goethe's humanity, for example, suggests ways to respect every human being in his own right; ways to become clear, realistic, and detached; ways to see the essential, preserve balance, and feel sympathy for all forms of existence. But it also reveals Goethe's unwillingness to accept the modern development toward technological civilization, his distrust of abstraction, his misunderstanding of the most fundamental factors in the emergence of the modern age. His humanity was distinguished by humble reverence for the inscrutable, but also by his refusal to acknowledge the tragic as a foundation of *Existenz* and by his disbelief in the reality of radical evil. Aware of these limits of human existence, Goethe did not seek to escape them by means of aesthetic concealment; nor did he try to probe them and thereby possibly disprove their existence. Rather he recognized them, but he eschewed them. It might be said that Goethe knew about life, and that he also knew the limitations of his knowledge. Philosophically he confessed to no ultimate creed or system, which in its exclusiveness would have resulted in dogma; but he reserved for himself the freedom of many ways of philosophical thinking. Thus he was able to be a pantheist as a student of nature, a polytheist as a poet, a monotheist as an ethical human being. What appears, to the rationalizing observer, to be a shifting of grounds, actually is the inward mobility and activity through which Goethe realized — and maintained — himself.

If Goethe thus embodied a unique realization of possible human *Existenz*, then — Jaspers concludes — any future reception of Goethe, if it is to contribute toward the elucidation and liberation of our own selves, must be free from the inherent danger of idolization. It was the misfortune of post-Goethean German culture that such paths were followed. "So many wanted to be each a little Goethe." To explore the scope of an *'existentially'* relevant and meaningful Goethe image, Jaspers suggests the alternative of two possible positions: on the one hand the "exceptional" personalities who, like Kierkegaard or Nietzsche, became victims of their own effort to judge man unconditionally, — on the other hand Goethe, this one case of human existence manifesting itself as an "ideal norm." The former failed when they identified themselves with the absolute; the latter persisted when, from the deepest crises threatening his inner self, he emerged transformed and ready for continued affirmation of reality. Still the dilemma arises that Goethe, as an historical phenomenon, is totally past and unrepeatable. He can no longer be a universal example. Only the single individual, carrying within himself the imperative of his own self-realization, can be the basis for a genuine, present-day reception of Goethe.

In other words, the problem involved concerns "genuine" adoption without imitation. If Goethe managed to be completely "himself," a much wider gap separates him from our age than separated him from the ages preceding him. For the modern age, which Goethe was unable and unwilling to endorse, has thrown up barriers and distractions which tend to prevent the individual man from being "himself." Goethe managed to keep himself aloof from the "brittle ground of human existence;" but for the modern reader of Goethe the spectacle of Goethean harmony must not conceal the fragile condition of this very foundation itself.

Thus it is the concept of *Existenz* which connects Jaspers' two Goethe addresses with his Strindberg essay; in both instances various "layers" of comprehensible personality features had to be removed before a glance into the possible originality of the human "self" was permitted. But what in the early pathographic study appeared as an heuristic concept has been developed into a compass for philosophical reasoning. In both instances *Existenz* is the center about which the circle of a possible totality of personality is drawn, seen in reference to an only partially penetrable historical situation. Unlike the Strindberg study, however, the Goethe essays no longer claim to make ultimate, and therefore exclusive, positions discernible — as the *Psychologie* had done. They confess to a "belief in the common origin of all human existence."[17] Venturing into the area of literary evaluation, they are the expression of a philosophy that claims to be "the organ for the assimilation of the past, — meager, to be sure, but testifying to present-day life; — modest, to be sure, but endowed with the sensitive conscience of veracity."[18]

With basic assumptions such as these, the two Goethe essays indicate that they are more than an incidental transfer and application to the literary field of certain philosophical precepts. In fact, both literary criticism and 'existential' philosophy have in common the problem of reviving for present-day needs the historical manifestations of the human mind. It is in regard to the method of historical understanding that literary criticism, as a specific discipline, must be ready to consider the implications of 'existential' reasoning; and it is in regard to the historical substance itself which literary criticism, along with other "historical" disciplines, has mined that philosophy is able to apply its analysis of *Existenz*. The wealth of human experience upon which Jaspers' philosophy is built includes the achievements of literature and criticism as it does those of the arts and the sciences. Since poetry seeks truth through illusion, it is accorded an important place in Jaspers' systematic inquiry, *Von der Wahrheit;* indeed, great poetry is akin to philosophy: through both there leads a way toward the perception of reason in reality.[19] Throughout Jaspers' work the reader will find profound respect for the great in literature — the ancient Greeks, Dante, Shakespeare, Goethe; but he will look in vain for extensive analyses of those poets who have been the object of numerous 'existential' appraisals — Kleist, Hölderlin, Stifter, Mörike, Rilke. Only the poetic utterances of Nietzsche are subjected to scrutiny and evaluation, — not for their artistic merit, but on account of the 'existential' struggle for independence which found expression in the outcries of this early representative of modern isolation and nihilism.[20]

The singling out of Nietzsche signifies a thrust against the

[17] *Ibid.,* 149.   [18] *Ibid.,* 46.   [19] *Wahrheit* (1947), 986.
[20] *Nietzsche* (1936).

aesthetic standards of literary criticism. Nietzsche's case typifies the *'existential'* dilemma of the 19th and 20th centuries. He was a creator of myths; in his apocalyptic visions of the "last man" and "superman" he sought to objectify, and to overcome, his own intellectual emergency: he was burdened with the romantic heritage which by and large was responsible for the purely aesthetic evaluation of the absolute and for the unfortunate, though much publicized, alternative between citizen *(Bürger)* and artist *(Künstler)* which has dominated much of the modern literary criticism. As critical categories these two concepts may serve to point up the extraordinary situation of literary interpretation in the late 19th and early 20th centuries: by establishing types of which one could be considered, at the expense of the other, as a desirable though tragic configuration of human existence, literary criticism raised either an aesthetic or a sociological "norm" to the level of an absolute standard of measurement. In doing so, it lost sight of the concept of man himself — a fleeting reality — which had been the main concern of the classical and romantic poets and critics when they made dialectic use of the two possible extremes in the first place. And it is presumably because Goethe, in his studies of nature and art and general conduct of life rather than in the accomplished myths and images of his poetic works, was concerned with the essential nature of man himself that Jaspers could select him as a test case for the possibilities of a "new humanism." It is not without significance that the two Goethe essays, chronologically, coincided with Jaspers' inquiry into the conditions of a new humanism in our times.[21] In order to examine the implications which the *'existential'* approach possesses for literary criticism, it might be well to compare it with the factual tenets of Jaspers' philosophy, and to indicate the directions and limitations which *'existential'* philosophy might impose upon literary criticism.

II.

According to Jaspers, it is a striking though inescapable feature of the present age that the seemingly intensified realism of modern thought, brought on by the growth of the exact sciences, has been accompanied by a deplorable loss of "reality" in personal substance.[22] In the attendant development toward normalization,

[21] "Premises and Possibilities of a New Humanism," in *Humanism*, 65ff.
[22] *Existenz* (1938), 2.

mechanization, and proletarization, individual man appears to have become expendable and replaceable and no longer be able to be "he himself." Attempts to counteract such a development appear to have resulted in reversals: the desire to "live originally" could be perverted into a penchant for primitivity, and the will toward self-realization could be confused with a worship of mere vitality.[23]

Such reversals might have been avoided, had spontaneous and critical self-examination been in operation, that is to say, had the expansion of knowledge been accompanied by an equally clear visualization of the limitations of knowledge. Before offering any "new" or "positive" philosophical doctrine, Jaspers' philosophy of *Existenz* seems to be concerned with just such a visualization. It makes an inventory before it ventures on an expedition of discovery. Its two fundamental steps involve the reassessment of critical thinking within the present historical situation and the self-illumination of man with a view toward his potential freedom. For this purpose both historical and scientific knowledge offer unusual opportunities: for it appears that never before have the substance and tradition of human thought been so readily available as today, and never before have the sciences with their compelling methods and results penetrated further into the mystery of physical and historical reality. Yet this very wealth of knowledge and thinking has placed the world in a state of bewilderment and confusion of tongues.[24] Whereas the technological application of science is enjoyed and handled by many, science itself is controlled by only comparatively few; the mass of people continue to live in pre-scientific attitudes and behavior.[25] Indeed the position of science itself is not entirely beyond dispute; although it is in touch with realities, it is unable to furnish ultimate directives for human behavior. Thus the status of science has wavered between the almost superstitious belief that science is capable of solving all practical human problems, and a similarly superstitious spirit of hostility which considers science a paralyzing factor in the pursuit of a "natural" or "harmonious" life.[26] Over-optimistic confidence in science has been responsible for the creation of new dogmatisms, elevating particular scientific doctrines to the rank of guiding philosophies — e.g., psychoanalysis and Marxism[27] — whereas an over-pessimistic view — and here one is inclined to think of that of Spengler and such "conservative" German writers as Hofmannsthal or George — has found

---

[23] *Ibid.*, 2. [24] *Wahrheit*, 24. [25] *Scope*, 179.
[26] *Existenz*, 5. [27] Cf. *Anti-Reason* (1952).

no other solution of the dilemma than the return to the aesthetic, the romantic, the detachment of contemplation.

The existentialism of Jaspers is distinguished by its critical attitude toward science. Rather than claim for philosophy the character of a science — a step of desperation frequently made to save philosophy's dwindling prestige — Jaspers insists that philosophy redefine its own relationship to the sciences, that is to say, that it become aware of their mutual boundary lines and relative purposes. Scientific knowledge is particular and specific knowledge, dealing with definite objects; it is not concerned with Being, nor with the fundamental philosophical realization that thinking an object presupposes a thinking subject, and vice versa. Scientific knowledge establishes no values, nor is it able to answer the question of its own meaning. But, although it is thus distinct from philosophical inquiry whose domain begins where that of science is terminated, science is essentially indispensable for systematic philosophical reasoning. Without philosophy, science would not understand itself; but without science, philosophy would lack not only the compelling evidence of that which *is,* but also the practical check of a critical method. Philosophy must absorb the scientific attitude, not attempt to duplicate the scientific act. Participating in the sciences, philosophy will dissolve the dogmatism that might rise within them; it thus becomes their best defense against their enemies. "Living philosophically is inseparable from the attitude which accepts science without reservation."[28] Similarly, any future humanism must be contingent upon the sincere effort to acknowledge, adopt, and control technology, "the unbounded field of human struggling."[29]

While science and technology thus seem to be dominating the intellectual scene of modern civilization, they have also clarified the position and function of genuine philosophical thinking, of age-old philosophy, — *philosophia perennis.* Instead of lingering over the "scientific" aspects of philosophy (e.g., epistemology, semantics, theory of knowledge and of values), Jaspers resolutely returns to the root of all philosophical concern, — the question of the nature and meaning of human existence itself. If philosophy is to satisfy any modern thinker, it must be "original" and authentic, must reflect his specific situation and problems, and cannot possibly be found among or appropriated from any of the readily available systems of the past. Besides being able to stand the test of the sciences, philosophy must demand the independence of personal, spontaneous *(ursprünglich)* origin. "From this origin

28 *Existenz,* 9.   29 *Rechenschaft,* 274.

alone can be learned what no science can teach us. — Philosophy demands another kind of thinking, a kind of thinking which, through knowledge, reminds me, awakens me, makes me find myself, and transforms me."[30] Gaining its clarity from communing with the older philosophers (in particular, Kant, Hegel, Schelling, Nicolaus Cusanus, Anselm, Plotinus, Plato), this philosophical thinking must be "original" *(ursprünglich)* and in each age realize itself historically in accordance with the new conditions. In an age of science, therefore, philosophy cannot be "naïve" and still remain "true," if its purpose is to increase the state of consciousness. Thus philosophy seeks to comprehend the reality of Being, but neither as a definite content of knowledge (as in the sciences) nor in mere experience (as in feeling). Philosophy strives to get to the point where thinking might become the experience of reality itself.[31]

Now it is a fundamental condition of our conscious existence that we are inextricably involved in the subject-object relationship of consciousness: whether outwardly or inwardly, we are always confronted with "objects" of our consciousness. Being, on the other hand, is beyond this dichotomy: as totality, it can never be comprehended objectively. Jaspers defines it as the Encompassing *(das Umgreifende)* which can never be conceived either as object or as subject but only as that which becomes apparent in the subject-object relation itself. As the realm of references and relations, the Encompassing does not reveal itself; but it is that in which everything else is revealed. Even though this thought operation leads to no rational, objective result, "it transforms the meaning of the world of objects, by awakening in us a faculty of sensing what authentically *is* in the phenomenon."[32]

For example, in the interpretation of personalities or their works it is a fundamental fallacy to confuse the tangible content of ideas, their definite objects, the sensible character of the existent, — to confuse all these particulars with the Encompassing. It is only with the Encompassing that authentic communication, attraction and repulsion, begin. Everything susceptible to objective statement is on the other hand merely the language of the underlying seeking attitude, and, as mere language, it turns into nothingness when the source from which it arose vanishes. . . .

Philosophical thought grows out of the Encompassing. Pseudo-philosophy stands always on the solid ground of a particularity and objectivity that it chooses at will.[33]

---

[30] *Existenz*, 10.   [31] *Ibid.*, 12.   [32] Cf. *Wisdom*, 29-31.

[33] *Scope*, 154. (The above translation gives *"das Umgreifende"* by the Encompassing.)

The notion of the Encompassing (that which itself cannot be comprehended) gives Jaspers' philosophy its distinctive and characteristic tenor.[34] It is the result of a fundamental philosophical operation: whatever the object of my thinking, it is always a specific *mode* of being, never *Being itself*. Being that is *known* cannot be universal, all-encompassing Being; for any view that we may have of the whole is still *within* the whole, never the whole itself. Just as a motorist driving through a great plain always sees the horizon ahead of himself and never reaches it — although he will reach points that once were on or beyond his horizon — our progressive cognition will comprehend ever new phenomena, while Being itself always seems to recede. The Encompassing, always unrevealed, is nevertheless that in which everything else is revealed. To become aware of it in a moment of spontaneous illumination[35] is an act of consciousness not comparable with and transcending all objective knowledge.

In a transcendental analysis the Encompassing presents itself in several modes of the subject-object dichotomy depending on the level of reflection, namely, whether I, as existence *(Dasein)*, am oriented toward an environment; whether I, as consciousness-as-such *(Bewusstsein überhaupt)*, am oriented toward objectivity as such; or whether I, as *Existenz,* am oriented toward Transcendence (God). Accordingly, as Being itself, the Encompassing is conceived as "world" (environment, objectivity) and as "Transcendence" (God), whereas as Being, which we ourselves are, it is conceived as "existence" (in which form each of us is a particular individual), as "consciousness-as-such" (in which form all of us are identical), and as *Existenz* (in which form we are authentically ourselves in our historical situation).[36] In each of these acts of thinking, the Encompassing is included, as it were, without ever being in itself recognizable. As existence and consciousness-as-such, the individual realizes himself in a framework of references and contingencies. *Existenz,* on the other hand, is the act in which the individual, spontaneously and independently, realizes his origin, in the Encompassing "through the mediation

---

[34] "The philosophy of the Encompassing is the logical foundation of the philosophy of *Existenz.* (It seeks to understand the meaning of all knowledge; it seeks to drive knowledge forward and to comprehend it within its boundaries; it wants to make receptive for 'origins.' It desires to teach how to be 'oneself' in thinking, and how to have Being unfold itself through thinking.) It insists on the extreme objectivity of knowledge and, at the same time, on the extreme subjectivity of self-illuminating *Existenz,* knowing that both are contingent upon each other, and that the one cannot be gained without the other." *Wahrheit,* 209-210.

[35] Cf. *Existenz,* 15f.   [36] Cf. *Wisdom,* 28-33.

of history and thought."[37] On the boundary between the objectivity of the specific and the realm of infinite possibilities there is a momentary act in which the self straddles the gulf between the world and Transcendence and realizes itself as participating in the meaning of all existence. "*Existenz* is being a self suspended between itself and Transcendence from which it derives its being and on which it is based."[38] As *Existenz*, our origin lies beyond empirical and objective reality, beyond the generality of consciousness-as-such, and beyond the practical and theoretical ideas in which human life is generally classified *(Geist)*. This our *Existenz* becomes manifest (1) in the dissatisfaction man experiences with his own life, knowledge, and intellectual world, (2) in the desire to live unconditionally in the face of all traditional dicta and values, (3) in the unceasing urge to attain unity transcending any and all *modes* of the Encompassing, (4) in an unfathomable consciousness of participation in the primordial existence of the world, and (5) in the consciousness of immortality, not conceived as mere self-perpetuation in another form but as a feeling of participation in the evolution of history.[39]

What *Existenz* is, as a content, cannot be put into words; its experience is revealed in an act of transcending. It is no state of consciousness, for consciousness binds man to the sphere of objects; nor is it a value that can be possessed or applied, for man can be deprived of his values without ceasing to be "he himself." *Existenz*, or being a self, lies beyond all specific conditions; indeed, negation of all but Transcendence is one of the fundamental characteristics of its realization. Nevertheless, the experience of a boundary, instilling in the individual the consciousness of infinite possible freedom, provides for the *'existential'* nucleus of man which ceases only upon his physical or spiritual death.[40]

No science is able to furnish a complete and lasting definition of man; no anthropology, no theory of art or of religion can comprehend, or ever present in a knowable formula, the real existence of man, the true reality of art or of religion. He who believes that he knows himself or the nature of man clings to an abstraction which, in view of the historical uniqueness and unrepeatable reality of the present moment — and the infinite number of such moments and reference patterns — is necessarily an illusion. *Existenz* is being a self that discovers reality neither in the world of the senses nor in that of abstract concepts, but in the unconditional momentum of transcending. "Just as the sense organs

[37] *Scope*, 10.   [38] *Existenz*, 17.   [39] *Scope*, 14f.
[40] Cf. O. F. Bollnow, *Existenzphilosophie* (3rd ed., 1949), 23.

must be intact in order to perceive the reality of the world, the selfhood of possible *Existenz* must be prepared and alerted in order to answer the call of Transcendence."[41] Only in facing Transcendence is man — as *Existenz* — independent and responsible for himself; the question is whether, by his inward action, he accepts this challenge and struggles for his participation in Being or whether he resigns himself to being a mere representative of "man." "Thinking philosophically I remain suspended between the effort of realizing my potentiality and my being granted *(Geschenktwerden)* my reality."[42] As a thinking individual, man is constantly tempted and prone to identify himself with a specific *mode* of being, — with the immediate reality of his sensations, with the categories of consciousness, or with some form or classification of intellectual or cultural life. As *Existenz*, he seeks to extricate himself from this tendency of falling back into such generalizations.

I take myself in hand, I experience the decision for which I am responsible; but this process of becoming a self is synonymous with the most sensitive listening to Transcendence without which it would not be taking place. In my actions, in my resistance, success, failure and defeat, and ultimately in my thinking — which comprehends and conditions all of these — I undergo the experience in which I perceive the symbol of Transcendence. Whatever occurs, and whichever way I am involved in it, resembles the relation of question and answer. I am a receiver tuned for that which befalls me in that I am in relation to it. My struggling with myself and with the things is a struggling for Transcendence which appears to me only as a symbol with the immanent world. I project myself into the world of factual experience, into the reality of doing in victory and defeat, because this alone is the realm in which I hear that which is.[43]

The touchstone of *Existenz*, therefore, cannot be any given reality to which a man might attach himself, nor any abstract standard of truth according to which that which he does is either right or wrong; nor can it be the ideal that he would most like to "represent." For rational understanding *(Verstand)* — because it thinks in abstract generalities — *Existenz* remains an enigma. For ever alert reason *(Vernunft)*, which hovers between the prudent ignorance in matters of the whole and the desire for truth, it is an expression of the will for freedom. For *Existenz* is not based on itself but depends on the participation in something else — Transcendence —, and only the degree to which it is able

41 *Philosophie* III ("Metaphysik"), 150.

42 *Ibid.*, 152.   43 *Ibid.*, 151.

to perform this relationship in an act of communication lends it its substance. However, the very performance of this act is beset by the risk of backsliding into objectification and generalization. Thinking and speaking are bound to communicable, i.e., *general* contents. Hence, any statement that aims at the illumination of *Existenz* must be both of general and of quite personal, specific validity. Still, the philosophy of *Existenz* is precisely not concerned with the general, but seeks to transcend it in the search for possible *Existenz*.

'*Existential*' thinking has two sides, one of which, by itself, is untrue (the merely general), whereas the other, by itself, is impossible (speechless *Existenz*); combined as a whole, they form a fortunate coincidence of expression which is beyond the reaches of conscious methodology. — It is, as it were, thinking with two wings which is successful only when both wings beat simultaneously, — thinking in terms of possible *Existenz* and thinking in terms of the general.[44]

Expresssing itself in terms of the general, possible *Existenz* is intent upon itself and others in order to find itself in both. For it appeals to *others,* not to *all,* as scientific thinking does. And it finds confirmation not in *any* other individual, but only in the *one* who recognizes that that which is no longer expressible in general terms belongs to him as the complement of the general element in him.

Existenz, like existence, is realized in the medium of time; but it is distinguished from the objective reality of the world in that it springs into operation in decisive moments, freely and spontaneously; whereas the latter is subject to causality in the time series. Objective reality is persistent in the duration of time; *Existenz* is saltatory and evanescent. Time, as a form of logical consciousness, is objective, measurable, and capable of being experienced by everyone; accordingly, it is a medium of impersonal, unfulfilled permanence and without specific significance and inner relation to the self except that of consciousness-as-such. For *Existenz,* however, time is the present moment in which irrevocable decisions convey the assurance of freedom, for which nothing else can be substituted, or it is the future whose very undecisiveness holds infinite possibilities of choice. Thus, in its particular historical consciousness, *Existenz* has its own (relative) time, and its reality depends on the intensity with which it acts in the present moment as if it were for all time.[45]

It is within the time dimension, then, that '*existential*' philoso-

[44] *Philosophie* II ("Existenzerhellung"), 11.　　　　[45] *Ibid.,* 17-18.

phy seeks to awaken a radical consciousness of man by appealing
to the individual self in an age in which the individual himself,
sociologically and psychologically, is threatened with being swallowed up by mass institutions and mass norms. In contrast to
other prevailing metaphysical conceptions, which are generally
materialistic or pantheistic by nature, 'existential' philosophy
emphasizes the temporal limitations that separate the individual
from the whole and therefore activate its inner mobility and
freedom. However, speaking about *Existenz* is not the same as
speaking about "the individual" as a possible content of knowledge. Philosophical reasoning which aims at certitude through
consciousness of being within the consciousness of self seeks to go
beyond such conceptual abstractions as "the individual." Its
method is discursive and divinatory at the same time; it proceeds
in the circular motion of dialectics and through the leaps of
historical understanding; it seeks to imbue the abstractions of
dialectics with historical content and to validate the historical
with the dialectical laws of reason.

In this perspective *Existenz* may be realized as an infinite variety
of human relationships which, though often logically contradictory, are sanctioned by actual experience. For example,

> while, as an empirical individuality, I may be fully devoted to a spe-
> cific job, I am, as possible *Existenz*, more than this empirical individ-
> uality and more than that objective, impersonal matter-of-factness
> which is required, e.g., of achievements in political, scientific, eco-
> nomic life. Although *Existenz* is realized only through such participa-
> tion in the actual historical process, it is engaged in a struggle against
> the inscrutable principle of the world encroaching upon it; still it is
> through this principle that *Existenz* discovers itself and it is against it
> that *Existenz* strives to maintain itself in the eternity of Being, though
> it may founder in the world.[46]

Touched by the concreteness of the empirical moment, *Existenz*
wills eternity. It dwells in the silence of loneliness and it unfolds
in the discourse of communication. As the will for freedom it
asserts itself most strongly in the bonds of dependence. *Existenz*
knows the gloriousness of life in elevated moments as well as the
fears of mortality. In the mutability of practical life it maintains
loyalty to its own being and to him who partakes of its communication; but this loyalty is silent and does not assume the
form of a repeatable creed. In the face of despair over the unreliability of worldly affairs, *Existenz* maintains trust in the
essential quality of man and faith in a reasonable order of things.

[46] *Ibid.*, 7.

Tempted by the lure of nihilism, it ventures belief in existence.

Most specifically *Existenz* is revealed in the "ultimate situations" of life in which rational consciousness no longer can conceive of a plan of behavior. In fact, mere practical understanding seeks to ignore or evade them. Such ultimate situations are above all the inescapability of struggle and suffering, of guilt and of death.[47] In the course of human civilization these forms of "destiny" have represented the greatest dilemma. Understandably they have led to many modes of public or private disguise or other compensatory forms of adjustment. The fact that ultimate situations are terminal, that they cannot be penetrated, transcended, or reduced to recordable knowledge, and that behind them there is no horizon left, makes their *'existential'* relevance inescapable. Since they are no ordinary situations which might be altered or controlled, rational consciousness is at a loss in facing them. To be sure, in the course of history, rational thinking has achieved a relative degree of individual and collective security through social legislation and control of natural forces; however, it has not eliminated the realities of death, aging, sickness, of guilt or struggle, nor the risks they involve. They must be met individually. Thus individual man shows his *'existential'* substance in the manner in which he rises to meet these boundaries of empirical life, whereas rational consciousness remains this side of them, be it in indifference or escape or helpless dejection. In situations such as these, the individual, as *Existenz,* may become aware of the foundations of all Being and, though not objectively conscious of their significance and content, act in a manner singularly historical and inimitable. "Experiencing ultimate situations and *existing* are one and the same thing."[48] For here it is shown whether a man will return into the shelter of conventions and traditional ideologies and doctrines, or whether he will act in a manner of which he alone is capable. Facing the alternative of Being or Nothingness, *Existenz* discovers itself through a decision transcending all empirical considerations. Here neither idealistic defiance nor romantic surrender, neither materialistic disbelief nor pious devotion will suffice. For the question is whether a man will yield or dodge the issue, or whether he will choose a path that none has walked before him, guided by the truth that, for him, the objective no longer is knowledge but faith.

To the literary critic to whom both idealism and materialism appear as mere ideologies and therefore as equally relative and fallacious, the reflections on philosophical faith represent the

47 *Ibid.,* 201-254.   48 *Ibid.,* 204.

core of Jaspers' existentialism. He will realize at this point that the stern and strenuous dialectic of *'existential'* reasoning is indeed more than subjective speculation and that its target — in spite of all self-illumination or, rather, on account of it — is the ultimate question of reality.[49] It must be remembered that the immediate reality of experience and observation, though a *sine qua non*, is *'existentially'* insufficient, partly because individual factuality is truly endless and inexhaustible, partly because any fact can be interpreted within the frame of countless relationships. *'Existentially'* relevant reality is not identifiable with any given objectivity, nor with any concept of a harmonious whole: the one is merely "factual," the same for all, and as such without latitude for the freedom of possible thinking; the other is in fact an aesthetic, deceptive harmony. Rather, the experience of *'existentially'* relevant reality is transitory, unrepeatable, and contained in the Encompassing. Comprehending such reality "historically" is not the same as knowing it as a historical fact; but it can be experienced by venturing the possibilities which the present moment holds for me. In any such supreme venture, man takes on the challenge of Transcendence itself. "Only through realizing the transitoriness and absoluteness of all being *(Geschichtlichkeit)* do I become aware of Transcendence itself, — only through Transcendence does transitory life assume historical substance."[50] And again: this experience of reality is "like a break-through through phenomenality."[51] *Existenz,* or the highest freedom of man, is experienced in two ways simultaneously — in freedom from the world and in a profound bond with Transcendence.[52] Metaphorically speaking, this experience places man, who is always on his way toward his horizon, into a position in the horizon where he finds himself in immediate relationship with the Encompassing. We reach "the climax and goal of our life at the point at which we ascertain authentic reality, that is, God."[53] This act of *Existenz* in which Transcendence becomes transparent in its reality is the essence of philosophical faith. "Faith is life out of the Encompassing, it is guidance and fulfillment through the Encompassing."[54]

Within his own personal and historical situation and without the need of an intermediary, the individual *(der Einzelne)*, as *Existenz,* is confronted with a supreme and ultimate decision — the decision whether, in the extreme anguish of ultimate situations, he will preserve the faith in reality (God) and in his own selfhood and independence, acting as it were for all time to come

49 *Existenz,* 55. 50 *Ibid.,* 64. 51 *Ibid.,* 68.
52 *Wisdom,* 45. 53 *Ibid.,* 47. 54 *Scope,* 17.

— or whether he will abdicate as a self, offer rational or even "scientific" reasons as excuses and thereby surrender to the faithless, anonymous power of nihilism as an escape.

If thinking philosophically means: learning how to die, it does so not by abandoning the present in fear and with thoughts of death, but by intensifying the present through never ending activity in the light of Transcendence. Hence, Transcendence means nothing to us if everything that is, is merely 'a form of life' for us; and likewise, Transcendence is everything to us if that which is essential to us is so only in relation to Transcendence, or as a symbol of Transcendence.[55]

The first of these conclusions is the conclusion of nihilism which, as a modern attitude, can no longer be ignored. The second is the attitude of existentialism; in fact, 'existential' philosophy received its impetus and meaning by bracing itself against nihilism.[56]

Philosophical faith is seeking to apprehend "truth," not many truths. In this respect it occupies a position between religion and science. Like religion it is "wrestling with God." But is distinguished from religious faith in that it cannot surrender its own will of *Existenz* to the will of God, or dismiss personal reasoning in favor of a dogma. Like science it demands an absoluteness of truth; but it refuses to accept the universal validity of scientific knowledge as an absolute by which to live. The unconditional by which I exist is precisely not universally valid but "historical" and unrepeatable, and, therefore, not true for all. 'Existential' philosophy agrees with Lessing who preferred the search for truth to the possession of truth;[57] and it agrees with Kant who confessed that he had to deny knowledge in order to make room for faith.[58] 'Existential' philosophy is the attempt on the part of the thinking individual to participate in reason; but unlike pantheism which views the things of life as a universal mind ("God") would view them — in their timelessness and intrinsic, unalterable meaning — it conceives of reason only in the historical realization in each individual. In fact, in recent years, presumably when "existentialism" was threatening to become a fashion, Jaspers himself suggested that the name of "philosophy of reason" be substituted for that of " 'existential' philosophy."[59] Reason, as the Encompassing within us and without, is revealed as the age-old desire for truth, centered within individual *Existenz*. Its atmosphere is present within the great works of poetry, pri-

[55] *Existenz*, 71.   [56] *Scope*, 173, 176.   [57] Lessing, *Eine Duplik.*

[58] Kant, *Critique of Pure Reason*, Introduction to 2nd edition. (Smith transl.)

[59] *Anti-Reason*, 63.

marily in the great tragedies,[60] and hence it seems particularly fit for the interpretation of poetry. In brief, "philosophy, always in the form of *individual* effort, strives to realize universality, to preserve men's openness, to distill the simple, to concentrate it and illuminate it in its unfathomable depths."[61]

III.

The philosophical purpose of literary criticism and interpretation, in the light of existentialism, lies beyond the mere "knowledge," the mere "enjoyment," or the mere "understanding" of literary art. Where criticism seeks to discern reason in its widest possible scope, it transcends the level of aesthetic, psychological, or sociological curiosity. This position is exemplified by a casual though not insignificant remark by a poet himself.

In the discussions on the nature of poetry which fill the correspondence of Goethe and Schiller during the summer of 1797, Goethe reflected on the indifference of a metropolitan public in matters of poetry: The constant whirl of gaining and consuming, he observed, does not permit a genuine poetic atmosphere to be produced or communicated; for poetry demands calm and collected spirits, it isolates man against his will, it thrusts itself repeatedly upon him and is therefore as inconvenient as a clinging paramour. — Compared with Goethe's composed irony, Schiller's impassioned plea reveals an injured soul: Through poetry, he wrote, people on the whole cannot be made to feel comfortable but rather uncomfortable, and if a poet cannot achieve the former he must try the latter. "One must inconvenience them, disturb their comfort, one must alarm and perplex them. Poetry must appear before them as one of the two — either as a genius or as a spectre. Thus alone will the public learn to believe in the existence of poetry and acquire respect for the poet."[62]

These observations throw a light on the aims and purposes of existentialist literary criticism. Rather than pursue objective cognition of literature as a purpose in itself, it seeks, through the experience of literature, to intensify the consciousness of human existence. Goethe and Schiller believed in an appeal of poetry through which individual man is drawn from his center of self-possession and integrated into an imagined higher order of

---

[60] *Existenz*, 53; *Wahrheit*, 119.   [61] *Scope*, 117.

[62] Cf. Goethe, *Gedenkausgabe der Werke, Briefe und Gespräche*, ed. Beutler (1950), XX, 387, 398.

reason. For Schiller, freedom through catharsis was a matter of *aesthetic* experience. Convinced that "the higher his purposes, the more will man grow," Schiller strove in his plays "to stir up the deep foundations of man."[63] Existentialism, too, endeavors to arouse the experience of freedom in individual man; but it differs from Schiller's idealism in that the latter views man as complete or perfectible in an abstract universality, whereas existentialism, maintaining that man is of divided nature, seeks to enact radical awareness for Transcendence in the depth of our own origin and historical self.

In view of this difference it might be said that existentialism performs another "Copernican turn:" as criticism, seemingly dealing with given works and authors, it is in reality a critique of our own concept of man. Philosophizing in the spirit of Kant's *Critique,* existentialism does not ignore "objectivity" in a sort of mystical contemplation; to the contrary, it seeks to mobilize a maximum of possible scientific information about literature in order to incite, at the limits of such information, the individual effort to realize universality and to preserve the historical authenticity of human *Existenz.* Though its eyes are trained at a universal, its appeal is directed at the historical self.

The relationship between literary criticism and 'existential' philosophy may therefore be summarized as follows: Criticism is a scientific discipline: we expect its contents and findings to be generally transmissive. 'Existential' thinking, on the other hand, leads to no "results;" it cannot be universally transmitted but must be enacted by each "self" in his own way and according to his own situation. Criticism seeks to establish universally valid standards of judgment; existentialism reminds us that, in doing so, we become aware of man's limitations and being-in-relation with Transcendence. The two do not exclude but complement one another; the shortcomings of the one are balanced by the achievements of the other. As a scientific pursuit, the critical study of literature possesses the advantage of certainty; it may fail whenever, through generalization, the critic himself becomes a victim of his own method. 'Existential' thinking, on the other hand, makes us sensitive to historical origins and authentic relations and thus keeps in check the dangers of abstraction and generalization; it may fail whenever, in the absence of proofs, its intellectual efforts lead to mere dialectical rhetoric. No criticism will ever be final; nor will the mystery of a masterpiece ever be exhausted by any one critical reconstruction. 'Existential' criticism

[63] Schiller, *Wallenstein* (Prologue).

takes its cue from human existence itself: "As an individual, each of us reaches the end of his life without really knowing what it is. He achieves nothing definitive, but remains on a road which merely breaks off and ends in no absolute goal."[64] Held against the disillusioning tenor of this observation, many a masterpiece of literature seems to suggest an answer as being an image of possible perfection. Yet in the moment in which criticism should succeed in pointing at *'existential'* origins, their truth becomes an abstract and universally valid content and ceases to be *'existentially'* "true."

In conclusion, then, these inferences may be drawn: If *'existential'* philosophy is an attempt to arrive at a certitude of the "self," its enactment is personal and cannot be imitated nor transferred. Its method must be systematic, but it offers no system. Its principles are those of independent thought which Kant described as "to think for oneself," "to put ourselves in place of everyone else," and "always to think consistently."[65] Thus philosophy ventures to escape from the prison of conventions, opinions, concealments, and unquestioned traditions into which the run of life has led us. Its sources lie in man's wonderment, his doubt, and in the sense of forsakenness when he begins to inquire into himself.[66] Its possible achievements cannot consist in furnishing new "contents," or in presenting complete or conclusive *Weltanschauungen*. Therefore existentialism meets with distrust the general belief in mere "progress," as long as this belief considers the later and newer to be automatically superior to the older and earlier; but it is genuinely preoccupied with the phenomenon of progress itself, insofar as human achievements, accomplished in periods of transition, may reveal the active forces of authentic *Existenz* in the moment of crisis and change. That would mean that in the medium of time all reality is viewed as being in a process of change and transition,[67] a process which in the medium of thinking is duplicated by that of transcending. Thus, in every aspect and on every level of thought, Jaspers' existentialism proves

---

[64] *Scope*, 156.

[65] Kant, *Critique of Judgement*, Par. 40. (Bernard transl.)

[66] *Wisdom*, 17.

[67] "The great transitional phenomena are merely the highest configurations of what is constantly taking place: all reality, in its pertinent state of transition, everything, even the least exalted, in its uniqueness and authenticity, is at the same time end and perfection. Everything which uniformly endures, everything that has been handed down and can be repeated, is only the medium in which the essential is realized. The traditional makes the historically relevant possible; but it does not persist as what it originally was. It is knowable, discernible, conceivable; but it is no longer present in him who contemplates it and reflects upon it." *Wahrheit*, 905.

to be a dynamic philosophy of *movement* which, with every step, performs an act of transcending possible contents of knowledge until it comes to a halt in Transcendence itself. In philosophical faith it advances toward the horizon to totality, knowing full well that the latter will never be reached.

Doubtless the structure of *'existential'* thinking, its high regard for the idea of truth as totality, owes much to Hegel. With stern consistency, similar to Hegel's, it performs circles of dialectical reasoning in which every result is a new starting point of inquiry. With similar consistency it seeks to guard itself against the dangers of abstraction which, in Hegelianism, imply a loss of this historical substance and of the ethical responsibility of the individual "self." Existentialism is akin to Kant and German Idealism when it purports to restore reason *(Vernunft)* as the genuine vehicle of philosophical thinking, distinguishing it from its strongest adversary — and ally —, objective understanding *(Verstand)*. The relationship between these two powers of the mind and, implicitly, the possible relationship between *'existential'* philosophy and a pragmatic philosophy of experience, appears to have been anticipated in one of Goethe's maxims: "Reason is concerned with Becoming *(das Werdende)*; understanding is concerned with that which has already become *(das Gewordene)*. The former does not inquire: what for? The latter does not ask: where from? Reason delights in the act of developing; understanding desires to retain everything developed in order that it may use it"[68] The implications of this distinction for the evaluation of literature are evident. They signify an almost complete reversal of traditional criticism: they suggest that the "causes" of a literary creation lie beyond the pale of understanding in the "origins" of possible *Existenz;* and they intimate that an explanation in terms of "intent" may fall short of the aim because the "purpose" of genuine art transcends that of limited, practical consideration.

Jaspers' *'existential'* philosophy is distinguished by the seriousness of its purpose and the solemnity of its performance. In view of its ultimate objective — "to remind man of himself" — it would be out of place to look for anything but this consistent earnestness. In regard to literary criticism, therefore, it may be concluded that the existentialist perspective lends itself primarily to the interpretation of high tragedy; that is to say, existentialism will recognize the validity only of such works of literature in which man is shown in defeat when venturing his freedom in the face of Transcendence. (It need not be stressed that the poetic pre-

[68] Goethe, *Gedenkausgabe*, IX, 571.

sentation of this ultimate situation is not necessarily confined to the *dramatic genre*). Consequently the literary critic will not find in Jaspers' work any metaphysical interpretation of humor or comedy, whereas the tragic, as a fundamental mood of *Existenz*, is accorded extensive treatment.[69] This failure to consider humor or any other form of indulgence for human weakness and imperfection has sometimes been felt as a flaw, especially since the presence of the element of humor in life and in literature seems to testify to its importance for the preservation of personal balance and emotional freedom.

The tragic, an image of Being in the medium of time, reveals the fundamental structure of human existence, — its irrefutable finality. Comedy possesses no such ultimate significance unless it is conceived as containing the potentially tragic in pleasurable disguise. In the mood of the comic the individual is being preserved as individual; he neither transcends nor does he perish; instead he is able to return relieved and refreshed to his daily pursuits. With its view toward Transcendence, existentialism recognizes no such freedom and relief as essential. For authentic freedom is enacted in the alternative between the world and Transcendence in a vanishing moment of time, whereas the freedom of comic relief is but an imagined, timeless freedom of aesthetic play which must appear as dubious as soon as we return to reality and the world of change. The tragic is part of reality, the comic is not. Existentialism demands that reality be faced rather than evaded, and that life be lived in a twofold relation to time and temporality — *with* the current of history, toward and in the service of those who come after us, and in the life that cuts *across* the current of history, in personal responsibility to an unrepeatable present and to Transcendence which alone can set man free.[70]

It cannot be denied that the unremitting call for alertness which issues from Jaspers' philosophy in its battle against nihilism is both arousing and stifling. It is arousing in that it derives from genuine love and respect for man; it is stifling because it denies thinking the possibility of recuperative repose. For, in the words of Byron, even "the heart must pause to breathe, and love itself have rest." According to Jaspers, the philosopher is granted no such rest. Not only is he "the heart in the life of time, but he is able to express the time and, by holding up a mirror before it, determine it intellectually."[71] It has been pointed out above that

[69] *Wahrheit*, 915-961. Also in *Tragedy*.

[70] *Scope*, 157.   [71] *Rechenschaft*, 13.

the humanistic mission of existentialism, its concern about the future of man, its appeal to the self, its effort of transcending, possesses a historical parallel in the writers of late medieval satire who never tired holding up the mirror before their times, reminding their readers of the inadequacy of human nature and reason before the reality of time and being, and alerting them to the necessity of faith. In both instances the intensity of eschatological consciousness is fundamental and real; and the warning against nihilism in Jaspers' philosophy is no less urgent than the medieval cautioning against worldliness. In both instances, the searching for truth — *"de Veritate"* — calls for the merciless unmasking of human foibles; but the mercilessness springs from compassion for man as much as it does from love of "wisdom" — *"Philosophia."* For it is age-old wisdom rather than knowledge that judges man in terms of despair or of hope: either as the being which has lost faith in God and himself or as that which exists as a self in being oriented toward Transcendence.

Existentialism demands self-transformation, self-identification, and communication with the entirely alien. As to the specific task of literary criticism, a word of Goethe, who in many respects came peculiarly close to precepts of Jaspers' existentialism, may indicate the direction: "All excellent things oppress us for a moment, because we do not feel equal to them; only if we subsequently assimilate them, joining them to our intellectual and emotional energies, shall we love and value them." Literary criticism, in the sign of *'existential'* philosophy, desires to be impartial, human, and free; still it will always be confronted with particularizing tendencies which will press it into the service of sociological, psychological, theological, aesthetic, and political interests.

HELMUT REHDER

DEPARTMENT OF GERMANIC LANGUAGES
UNIVERSITY OF TEXAS

Karl Jaspers

REPLY TO MY CRITICS

Karl Jaspers

REPLY TO MY CRITICS

SYNOPSIS

REPLY TO MY CRITICS*

1. PLACE AND TASK OF THE REPLY

WHEN an author sees a considerable number of eminent and well meaning critics of his position gathered around himself in a group, it is a strange sensation. If he has listened to all of them together and consequently has them present in his consciousness, he sees himself as if illuminated by many searchlights or as if before mirrors held up before him in this illumination. But the mirrors are not in agreement nor are they flat; they are of various kinds and have a life of their own. In the one the author seems to recognize himself at once, whereas in the other he sees himself transformed in a way which, although quite natural in itself, appears strange to him. This perplexes him, for they are, after all, his own concerns which find their reflexion in those mirrors.

He finds himself challenged to re-examine his position, both in the particular and with a view to the whole. He cannot go into hiding, but must be ready to answer. The situation forces him once again to get an objective view of his own thinking, guided by the threads of the critical points of view. He does not merely have to attend to definitely formulated problems, but he must also trace the motives of his own thinking.

If I reflect in order to find my answer, then I must first of all express my gratitude to the distinguished persons who felt like concerning themselves so thoroughly with my writings. Secondly comes the realization that I shall not be able to express this gratitude sufficiently in my reply. Not merely one's own insufficiency hinders him to do justice to all the ideas which have been advanced, but most of all the available space. It is inevitable that my reply can touch only a portion of the content of these essays. The essays in this volume give an impression of the manifoldness of contemporary thought. What we have long since known cannot remain hidden in this case either: the fact that ways of thought are side by side which often have hardly anything in common and yet view each other and try to meet. Each

* Translated from the original German by Paul Arthur Schilpp and Ludwig B. Lefebre.

within itself seems unshakable, borne as it is by self-evidence, which latter is nonetheless not commonly accepted. We are not certain that we really understand each other. Not only are those self-evident propositions not universally accepted, but often we are ourselves unable to express them in any direct fashion, especially insofar as in each of us they form the almost unconscious and in any case unilluminated foundation. We do not philosophize — to change the metaphor — together in a brightly illumined room of identical horizons or points of view. Rather, we first have to look for that common room. Only the good will to exert ourselves most strenuously in uncovering our self-evidences, our presuppositions, our points of view and our horizons — our own as well as those of others — can bring us together. But no one can survey the whole; that is to say, no one is able to pass a comparative judgment on the totality of the particular types of thinking, which are determined by those presuppositions. For, none of us stands outside; each one of us already stands within his own particular way of thinking and finds himself facing other intellectual forces. Understanding of remote self-evidences does not penetrate to the depth of which only he is aware who lives out of them. The reality seen by the understanding observer is not the same as that which supports him.

In this situation I see the following as the task of my reply:

It would be misleading to attempt to group the essays at hand as a totality, as if it were possible to order their authors in the pigeonholes of a typology.

Uninteresting also would be a reply which would set out pedantically to ascertain which topics in my works have remained unconsidered here. For it is of the very essence of philosophers not to be capable of being broken up into topics, of being exhausted in subjects (or problems), but to be a whole; a whole which [however] gains utterance only in [specific] topics.

That I must often limit myself to categorical assertions will, I trust, be conceded, in view of the sparsity of space. The specific arguments which must be given in thought-movements — and only subordinately in logical conclusions — have been attempted in my writings, to which the reader is implicitly always referred.

Finally, it seems fitting in this reply not to interpret once more my own writings, but rather to think anew on the basis of what is being said to me. I should not defend my writings; all the less so since I have no system to protect. What, self-assertively, I am defending is neither a work nor a confession nor a thesis, but the power of philosophical faith which I serve, but which I did not produce.

Consequently, instead of pretending a false superiority by means of systematics, I want to reply to the remarks of the individual authors and to specific theses, with the intent of letting the origin of my philosophizing become perceptible in the manifoldness of its aspects. The way I start is purely accidental. I begin with particulars.

2. CONCERNING POLITICS

Hannah Arendt seems to me to have written such an excellent report on the present world-situation and on the idea of a world-citizen which emerges from this situation, that I fear that, in the form of reporting my thoughts, she has often presented me with her own.

For my own part I must, first of all, correct a bad mistake which occurred in my discussions of a coming world-federation. Hannah Arendt has corrected it, without underscoring it. In *Origin and Goal of History* (193ff), I wrote that the inclusive sovereignty of a federated legal world-order could be limited to matters of elementary powers — e.g., police and the making of laws — and in this sovereignty all of humanity could participate by way of elections. To that I must add: first of all, any world-order is utopian which is supposed to be realized in its entirety and immediately on the basis of a constructive blueprint. The decisive fact, a confederation of all mankind, will come into being, if at all, only by way of a historically growing structure of treaties. To anticipate this total structure in the form of a plan can only mean intellectually to master all possibilities of the course of events and situations, in order to find in each specific political circumstance the best possible procedure for negotiations and treaties. A world parliament, if by that is meant a transfer of present national parliaments to a world-state, is a naïve conception. Experience has taught us what can briefly be formulated as follows: the absolute sovereignty of a world parliament would, because of the abstract relationship of humanity-wide elections to such a mammoth structure — far removed from the individual person — produce the danger of governmental incapacity, of chaos and dictatorship. This is in contrast to contractually constructed federations and ways of procedure, which develop in history, are constituted by each specific situation, organized as a whole without any particular scheme, and which, therefore, cannot be devised as a whole in advance. Beyond this the demand for a reduction of the military to a police force is to be affirmed; but there must not be a single police force which would be subordinated to a single worldpower; rather, the police force must remain a multiple, in each case locally governed force, united for mutual assistance by international treaties, but not directed from one central point. In this instance already the very first step toward centralisation is to be rejected. For, if the police (which would be identical with the armed forces and have merely been greatly reduced in number) were to receive their orders from a single authority, the rise of a terroristic dictatorship would be almost certain. If armaments were abolished, if there were no longer any atom bombs, poison gas or cannons, mankind would still remain the prey of the remaining weapons, if these succeeded to fall into a single hand. To the rejoinder that, with a multiple police force, new wars would break out, the reply would have to be: rather the danger of a war than the danger of a totalitarianism of the entire world. Rather the danger of war so long as the situation — regardless of what may happen — leaves open the struggle for human freedom. Rather such hazard than the quietude of dictatorship, which, in view of the fact that it would be a world dictatorship, could no longer be broken up from without, and therefore not at all, since there no longer would be any outside.

The statesmen of the future will make people see what they [the people] really want, because they will realize a moral-political order — which as possibility lies ready in man — *with* man and not *against* him or over his head. They will need the creative wisdom of the founders of the U. S. A., but, precisely because of such wisdom, will not be able to repeat the content of what they created. They may get orientation from the existing attempts in history, beyond that of the U. S. A. itself; as concerns large states, from, for example, the gradation of the treaties of the Roman Republic with its allies, from the illogical and yet so effective formations of British self-government; as concerns smaller ones from the federated life of Switzerland, and from the hegemonic structures which occurred in Greek, Hellenistic, and medieval times. Yet none of these phenomena can be their model, none they will dare to imitate, for everywhere they will see not merely the successes but also the deficiencies.

The decisive factor in all this — something which Hannah

Arendt points out — is faith in the honest intent of keeping treaties. Whoever permits his vision to be blurred as concerns the enormous reality of the drive for power, of human independability, of the range of everything which, in spite of the average dependability of a population, is being kept in check by the police, although it seems ever and again to break through on a large scale — whoever does not recognize the still existing incapacity of vast masses of population on this earth for a life treaty-bound in freedom, such a one cannot achieve genuine responsibility in his political action. And whoever, on the other hand, thinks that wars have always existed and always will exist; that the only thing that matters in this world of beasts of prey is to assert oneself as a strong and cunning beast of prey together with such betrayal of the idea of man betrays also every chance [for mankind]. At the turning-points of a population's great decisions such as one will steer it by an appeal to its vulgar and intoxicated instincts, instead of arousing the idea of the moral self-education of a community, an idea which slumbers in all of us. No one perceives the course of possible history. What men can achieve is the concrete orientation concerning present realities, the knowledge of that for which one wants to strive, and faith in opportunities. Whoever, intent on an — always — abstract ideal, wants impatiently to realize that ideal with one blow, actually succeeds in destroying it entirely. This is why, given an uncompromising attitude, in the ideas themselves, the path of patience and of compromise is the only possibility for constructive political activity. This requires the readiness to master brute force when the situations demand it, by the strength of one's own force. No one can in honesty withdraw from political activity and co-operation except by such failure to resist on the part of monks and ascetes ready for death. In spite of all the achieved certainties, everyone must know that what is at stake is still a matter of life and death. Statesman is he who realizes at all times that this uncanny situation constitutes the basis of his responsibility. If he attempts to hide it from himself and from his people, he remains only an irresponsible functionary, thoughtless and a danger for everyone. Napoleon can be defeated only in Napoleonic fashion. But, whoever in battling the dragon becomes a dragon himself, has already lost the battle, even if he wins.

Hannah Arendt compares our present political orientation with that of Kant and Hegel. The greatness of the political ideas of these philosophers can, indeed, not bar us from trying to know better where something quite simple and elementary is concerned.

This applies at least to Hegel. I am in agreement with Hannah Arendt's characterization of him. In the case of Kant, I disagree with her. For no actual future did Kant expect what he outlines in the idea of perpetual peace. The task seen by way of the Idea is placed in time before the infinity of the way of its realization. Kant's undeceivable insight into the realities of our human nature does not regard the oppositions to the Idea as entirely surmountable. But any man who performs the "revolution in thought" (and this is task and possibility for everyone, but becomes no one's secure property) cannot want to do otherwise than work for the Idea. To explicate the Idea schematically in the form of outlines and principles, is, according to Kant, the task of philosophy; but it is not its task to set up a program for what can or should be done here and now. In the spiritual realm of rational philosophical insight this latter emerges only from the responsibility of the acting political person in each specific singular situation. At this point Kant did not continue his thought. He did not grasp actuality nor the meaning of historicity, and therefore also missed the meaning of the ethics of responsibility, which latter Max Weber thought through and delimited so simply and clearly. The derivation of principles from the Idea, as Kant attempts it, is, even if not a statement of recipes, in any case the lighting of torches, which light the way for anyone who sees the concrete situation in their light. To the Kantian principle (nothing should be done in war which would make a later peace impossible) Hannah Arendt convincingly adds this new point: today nothing should be done in the realm of politics that is contrary to the solidarity of mankind, which is still to be realized. No state today is responsible only to itself, but must ask itself what consequences its actions have for the possible free federative unity of mankind — and with this it is already on the road to renouncing its absolute sovereignty. What Kant, in the "melancholy haphazardness" of historical occurrence, expects as "the cunning of nature," I would not, with Hannah Arendt, entirely reject. Kant not merely points to relationships which, although outside of human consciousness, nevertheless factually and, afterwards, recognizably influence human conduct. With his formula he makes the boundary-line perceptible at which all our reason would sink into Nothingness, if nothing came to meet it. Just as Kant, in the moral revolution of each individual, to the extent to which he exerts himself with all his might, expects that he will be aided by something which theologians call grace, so he expects in history something like guidance. But, just as he forbids to count on grace or to know at which point it comes into play, so he forbids to know the "cunning of nature" *in concreto*. What, from the point of view of a philosophy of history, he permits is merely the attempt to write a history in which it is shown in how far and in how far not — measured by the ideal of reason — the events and transformations which occurred were advantageous, and how all this is connected. It seems to me, therefore, that Kant, too, would acknowledge Hannah Arendt's remark about philosophy as the *ancilla vitae*, that is to say, that philosophy should carry the torch before its mistress, not her train behind her. Kant, who used this simile in his interpretation of the ancient view of philosophy as the *ancilla theologiae*, would interpret the new formula thus: Neither life nor theology can help themselves. Rather, he who, in the process of philosophizing carries the torch ahead of those others and seeks justice, knows — in disappointment and in hope — that he is dependent upon what is beyond his knowledge. It is decisive, therefore, that Kant can neither — like Hegel (by changing Kant's "cunning of nature" into the "cunning of the idea") — comprehend, nor, like Marx, politically act in terms of the thus comprehended. For, philosophy cannot furnish a complete knowledge of history, and such knowledge can therefore, also not be used as a means of political activity (as, for example, natural science can be used for technical activity).

*   *   *   *   *

In his moving contribution, Golo Mann avows freedom. He directs attention to the points in my philosophizing which bear witness to it and follow from it. Hegel, too, wrote: the basic concept of philosophy is freedom; but Golo Mann speaks in a way which makes it impossible to mistake Hegel's meaning for our own. It seems to me Mann has looked into the very heart of my philosophizing. This is why I agree so completely, including even his differentiation of our own position from that of the so-called neo-liberals, that there is barely anything left for me to say. If, in some specific formulation, I seem to deviate, this implies less a correction than a continuation of his discussion. Thus, for example, at the point where he seems to think that in the playful scheme of a survey of history, I seem to be speaking of today as a second pivotal age. No, I have merely compared our own technological age with the (to us unknown) Promethean age of the first great inventions of tools, of the making and the use of fire, and I opined that perhaps a second pivotal age might lie ahead of us upon the new material basis, we don't know just when. One might also well continue the discussions about prediction, particularly about the basically different character of possible kinds of predictions: as, for example, those on the basis of natural laws, or those resting on statistical probabilities, or those which depend upon reliance on a friend, or which rest on confidence in a business-partner. In a specific sense, the most dependable prediction is perhaps possible in the sphere of freedom. Still another exploration would be possible into Golo Mann's characterization of my older days as a return to faith. This does not appear to me as it seems to him. He calls the philosophical faith a Christian faith. Historically this may not be incorrect; nevertheless I would prefer to speak of Biblical faith. First and foremost, however, I assert the independent origin of philosophical faith, which derives some of its content also from Biblical faith "within the bounds of mere reason," but which nonetheless stands in a both necessary and desirable polarity to the specifically religious faith. Finally I could wish that Golo Mann were mistaken in his slight hope for the penetrative efficacy of philosophizing in this world. For, the political ideas of freedom may, in the long run, very well have an indissoluble connection with philosophical faith. Despite all instances to the contrary, I venture the power of philosophic insight; it alone is reliable. The Vatican enters into concordats with Hitler and with Franco and thereby lifts them into the saddle of international recognition, thus enabling them to conclude treaties.

3. ABOUT THE QUESTION OF ARISTOCRACY

Two of the men who are favorably disposed towards my way of philosophizing reproach me for my aristocratic attitude (Hennig and Fritz Kaufmann).

Hennig writes: "The concept of an invisible contact with a very few individuals in the world leaves the masses hopelessly behind." Fritz Kaufmann considers it tragic that my conjuring word of 1931, — to save the effectiveness of the best, who are the fewest — found an immediate answer in Germany: the destruction, by the tyranny of national socialism, of the attempt to create a social democracy.

Hennig relates the sentence of a few Germans of the year 1945: "It is our guilt that we are still alive," to a sentence which he claims applies to all of us who still have time and a mind to devote ourselves to philosophy: it is our guilt that we can still wrestle with *Existenz*. For, unintentionally, he claims, existential-ist philosophy gave a profound meaning to the definition of the proletarian as the man without *Existenz*. This consciousness of guilt should not remain metaphysical. Against the aristocratic trait in my philosophizing Hennig cites sentences from my own writings which declare that of the spirit only that remains which is accessible to the masses; that it is the task of the spirit to find for its content the simplest possible forms in order that humanism might become accessible to everyone, accessible to man as man. Fritz Kaufmann misses the power of compassionate love in my democratic and social volition. "The emphasis on the neighbor-hood of free Selves on the peaks of *Existenz* prevents Jaspers from fully realizing the power of compassionate love in which man must meet 'in the valleys of human needs'."[1] Something more, he feels is at stake here than just social welfare, something more than mere compromise and relief. According to my false concep-tion, *caritas* is, in most cases, a condescending attitude towards man which I regard as incompatible with genuine love. My *Geis-tige Situation der Zeit* of 1931 *(Age)* is said to be a harsh aristo-cratic document with too little constructive sympathy for man who finds himself in the gigantic struggles and experiment of modern life.

These reproaches rest, I think, upon confusions which are easily possible when dealing with terms like democracy, aristo-cracy, equality, justice, and love. I shall defend myself against these reproaches. Precisely such confusions I have tried to illum-inate:

The regard for the community of the few, who, in their dis-persion in the world, are always singular and who are united by their recognition of the highest demands, this does not stand in opposition to a regard for the chances and rights of every human being. The regard for the rise of the singular individual is by no means contradictory to a regard for justice in the conditions of life which make such rise possible for everybody. The one regard leads onto the path of philosophizing as the inner activity of the individual; it makes possible his spiritual purification and deep-ening. The other regard leads into politics, to the shaping of the conditions of existence for all.

The opposition between aristocracy and the masses, between the individual and all, is not of the kind which enforces a choice between them. What is being called aristocratic in my thinking

1 His paper, pp. 257f. above.

is never a leaning towards the upper classes, towards the materially privileged, towards those who rule or are successful. Rather, running through all of these, I recognize the difference between freedom which grows into the responsibility of continuous self-elevation and mere accidental being which just lives. The singular individuals of whom I have spoken, the nobility which not just "is" but chooses itself, this luminosity of the soul, this power of love, this veracity and incorruptibility, is to be found in all social strata, whether publicly recognized or not. Such nobility bears no external marks of distinction. It makes no claim upon others, but only on itself. It cannot be found by a selective process. It is rarely — at least so it appears to me — to be found in the upper strata of the educated and the wealthy; but when found there it is likely to be of unique development, depth and clarity. It is more frequent among the so-called simple people, among workers and farmers. It is by no means missing among the specifically so-called nobility, this remainder of a past history. It can perhaps be realized in the calm existence and privileged security of systematic mental endeavor, although deviation towards indulence, towards self-satisfaction, always lies close at hand for the privileged. It is more real, more dependable, and more tried and proved in disaster, where works no longer speak, but the soul itself. But there it is threatened by concealment, as well as by oblivion; there, too, is the danger of physical inability, of perishing by violence and in hopelessness.

The impulse towards justice shows two directions. The one is concerned with the salvation of the effectiveness of the best. Unjust envy, which pulls everyone down to the equality of one's own nothingness, is not permissible. There must remain the interest in the representative activity, creativity and existence of the best, on whom the free man can look with love for improvement. None of us may believe that he can be everything. But everyone has in himself the possibility, by seizing that wherein he is given to himself, by freely choosing himself and by inner activity, to become a being embedded in eternity, whether he becomes only an indestructible grain of sand, a block of granite, or a mountain-range.

The second aspect of justice is concerned with the rights of all men *qua* men. In spite of the abiding factual injustice of nature, which lets us become what we are, and of society, which delimits our opportunities and ever and again also constrains us unbearably, the impulse toward justice wants to conquer both. It is the claim of this justice on a moral-political foundation continuously to improve the order of existence (*Daseinsordnung*) in terms of equalization of opportunity. From it proceeds the demand upon the hidden aristocracy not to seclude itself but to open up and communicate itself, without self-surrender to be concerned for the possibilities of all men. But justice also lays a claim upon everyone to choose himself on the road to aristocracy, which as possibility is denied to no one. The two impulses to justice, the one concerned with saving the effectiveness of the best who are the fewest, and the other concerned with the equalization of opportunity for all, are really inseparable from each other. If they do separate, both become unjust.

It was in my *Man In the Modern Age* that I expressed those observations and exorcized those dangers which made me appear as undemocratic to these critics of that treatise. However, unless I am completely deceiving myself, I did it out of the impulse toward justice itself, which since Plato has been the idea of the moral state. This idea and its democratic consequences — at this point contrary to Plato — I have never denied or even restricted.

Fritz Kaufmann sees something ironical in the fact that I admired Max Weber, who was a democrat, but had no faith in democracy. But this is not a matter of faith, either for Max Weber or for me; it concerns rather the idea of human freedom and justice, which is seeking its way. Only people of good faith can be good democrats, but not by means of faith in democracy. I was and still am a democrat. But I am such in the knowledge that democracy needs to be seen as concrete responsibility within the specific situation; not as an illusion in which the idea itself perishes (as was the case, according to my own observation, in Germany before 1933 and is now again) ; nor as pretext which destroys it (as in the claims of the totalitarianisms to be democracies) . The critique of specific forms, which political reality assumes under the name of democracy, is not rejection of the idea but intellectual labor for it.

F. Kaufmann regrets the absence in me of the warm sense for justice, which originates in love for the masses. I deny, he thinks, the *caritas*, which turns to the masses, to everyone. What appears as love in my philosophy is really only Plato's Eros. My inclination, he intimates, is towards the few lucky ones. My philosophizing he claims to be rooted in personal communication, not in sympathy with everyone. I do not recognize the condescension of God's love for us, which we imitate in our love for the poor.

To this reproach I offer the following defense. (1) I do indeed deny any condescending love, which is still worse when it thinks of itself as an imitation of God. (2) If Kaufmann does, as he claims, have more confidence in communication than I have, optimism in this regard appears to me as little justifiable as pessimism. I trace the possibilities of success and failure and, with Kaufmann, I insist unconditionally upon the road of communication. But I renounce the presupposition of predetermined success. I am convinced that the chances for success are far greater if one is conscious of the dangers which could destroy communication. (3) The alternative between aristocratic love and democratic *caritas* I would like to cancel out in favor of the recognition of the truth of both in their [rightful] place, but in such a way that the one cannot really be effective without the other. (4) It is perhaps really so that I did not let the impulse of justice and of the love for every man as human being speak sufficiently in my writings. If this should be so, I deplore it as a defect. It could improperly have resulted from the fact that I perceived — properly, I think — in the desire for justice of a Karl Marx, after a precise study of his work and life, not, indeed, love nor justice, but the will to power (which itself always becomes unjust) which arose out of the total, and in its origin unjust, indignation of his hatred. The fateful consequences [noticeable] in the feeling and attitude, in the abstractness and incommunicability of his fanatic disciples (in contrast to the thoughts and endeavors of the British Fabian society and of considerable numbers among the German social democrats) were visible to me in many forms through half a century.

4. On the Meaning of History

Hennig bases his essay upon two utterances from my writings: History has again become a live issue instead of a mere problem of knowledge; instead of a matter of aesthetic culture the seriousness of listening and answering — and, secondly, the way to truth is found by boundless communication, by the abolition of the self-limitation of objective knowledge, by love as the final guide. In his own field of historical studies he had applied what he believed to have learned from me. Because of his noble gratitude, however, his helplessness in the presence of the mistaken paths, which, according to his conception, I have come to tread, sounds even shriller by contrast. His attack moves me deeply. Indeed, we are together in so many really essential matters that our parting company at the most essential of all points is painful to

him, and to me a confirmation of my love for him in the seriousness of that which completely occupies him. But here, where we
speak to each other in public, this constitutes only the personal
background against which objective discussions can take place
with a sharpness from which Hennig, in his formulations, does
not shy away and which I shall not avoid in my reply.

What is under consideration is our relation to history. Hennig
reproaches me for not respecting the transparency of historical
reality in the evidence. In the way in which I speak of martyrs
(namely, in the manifold possibilities of reality which afterwards
counts as martyrdom) Hennig sees an example of the exclusion
of historical reality by a psychological theory. In my application
of the sentence, "No man can be God" to Jesus, he sees a denial
of the witness of the apostles and of two thousand years. My
study of the prophet Ezekiel he considers an extreme example of
objective research, which fails to reach the essence of its object,
because I for my part do not carry through the communication
with it. He finds in me a growing bias in my description of the
boundaries of the Biblical and Christian tradition. The *existential* attitude towards history, which, according to Hennig, I assert
and demand incontestably, I myself am supposed to be neglecting
in the most essential directions.

As the foundation of all historical knowledge Hennig demands
the awareness of the transparency of tradition. There is awareness
in piety, there is mystery in obscurity, which in bright splendor
suddenly bursts upon the intuition; there is such a thing as the
substantiality of a spirit which really becomes physically present
in the places, monuments, and documents of history. There is
such a thing as an awareness of the myths which speak to us out
of immemorial ages, the handing down of which continues,
particularly by means of one's own mythical thinking, which
latter is able to see what no [rational] understanding comprehends. This awareness is always uncritical, and it is entirely
certain of itself because of the present givenness of what is understood. There can be no doubt, any notion of 'perhaps' is ruled
out, inasmuch as what is seen is as if bodily present. This is the
view of history which, if I understand correctly, was held by
Bachofen, is held today by Walter Otto and was formerly held
somewhat differently and less strongly by Welcker, a type of view
which, on the basis of their research, is rejected as knowledge by
philologists and historians, as today for example by Nilssen. Such
a view of history was expressed by our great romantic philosophers
and also, e.g., by Grundtvig. The latter says it is impossible to

make this view clear to anyone who regards the spiritual union, which unites all generations of men into One Man and this latter again with God, as folly and chimera.

I myself do not merely follow such a becoming transparent of history, but I consider it as indispensable to entrust oneself to it if one does not wish to lose the fullness of one's own spiritual life nor the clearness of one's own faith. But the decisive point of the difference is this: in which sense do truth and reality become accessible here?

Whatever becomes transparent is present as sensory reality in tradition, texts, deeds, and symbols. Out of these an actuality lays hold upon us which is more than all reality. But this actuality bears another character than any worldly reality. In the first place, the language of this becoming transparent of reality is manifold; this language has no character of universal validity as do the propositions of science concerning reality. True, this language is more deeply grounded for us than all science, but not for our knowledge, but rather for our *'existential'* potentiality.

It has this character not in any universally valid but only in historical form, and for us human beings this latter is varied and objectively not sufficiently surveyable. Faith in this actuality has the greatest historical effectiveness that can be observed in an objectively valid manner. [But] it never reaches all men. Where this has happened, it has become an historically limited reality enforced by ecclesiastical power. It is observable how this has brought about untruth and narrowness. If ever a totalitarianism were to dominate the planet and would enforce a single historical tradition as the only valid authority, the freedom of the language of Transcendence would become ever less audible, seriousness would be replaced by fanaticism or by blind, thoughtless obedience.

In view of the fact that transparency in history is met in varying forms, Hennig, it seems to me, is quite right in regarding it as a goal of historical education to learn to distinguish two things: the admission that a [given] reality may not be transparent for me; and, the complete rejection of this transparency for everyone. Here is an example. In my attempt (following the tradition of Lessing and Kant) to extract philosophical truth from the Bible and to preserve the same for effective (daily) living, I used the sentence: "No man can be God," and applied it to Jesus. To which Hennig replies that this scarcely strikes at the doctrine of the deity of Christ (in which point he may be right, although the senselessness which I intimated remains just the same), and that (by that sentence) I had broken off communication with at least fifteen centuries of our spiritual tradition and with several hundred million men. I contradict this passionately. I concede that the dogma in question is "non-transparent" for me; but this is no reason why I should reject it for others. The fact is, I seek to co-operate with the kind of historical education, demanded by Hennig, which is able to make distinctions.

Often enough in my writings I have pointed out the incompleteness of philosophizing, also with regard to the fact that philosophy has religion as its opposite pole, which philosophy can neither understand nor prove, which it recognizes and does not reject, by which it is perplexed and yet toward which its thinking is directed. But the contradiction sets in at a quite definite point: namely, where religious sources make assertions about things in this world which are subject to proof, and where they make demands as to how I am to behave in this world. Such instances philosophy does not simply accept, but it examines them scientifically and enlightens them philosophically in terms of secular meaning and, on the basis of these, rejects them in numerous instances. This rejection stops before any genuine faith, which shows itself in that it demands neither deception concerning empirical reality nor a *sacrificium intellectus* nor immoral conduct.

As over against all pronounced transparency, against all symbols which serve as the realities of a possible language of transcendental reality, there is, on the one hand, one's own participation, which is filled by the splendor of the super-sensory, and on the other hand, an understanding without participation, or else mere external knowledge and awareness.

For this reason there is, on one side, the danger of the claim, arising out of one's own participation, — this happiness of truth — of demanding that everyone else shall see and believe the same thing. This is fanaticism. On the other side lies the danger of regarding as null and void what is not understood instead of remaining in readiness for the possible. This is intolerance. Both dangers usually appear together. To guard against these dangers language contains the word "perhaps," which is applicable to everyone except the obviously evil or the obviously absurd. This "perhaps" is indispensable for the readiness in everyone of us, in the consciousness of his own limitations, the precise boundary of which he does not know. But this "perhaps" Hennig rejects in

me with the pathetic note; there can be no perhaps here. To this
I object. The "perhaps" is the form of acknowledgment on the
part of one who does not so believe.

Aside from transparency Hennig's second concept important
for historical awareness is that of witness (testimony, *Zeugnis*).
What is transparent is the reality of handed down testimony. But
what is testimony for Hennig? What is not forgotten but begotten
(bezeugt). Example: "And the Word became flesh . . . John was
its witness." If such testimony were to be rejected, according to
Hennig such rejection would itself have to be rejected by a
sentence which I myself have used in another connection: "If I
say, this cannot be, I mean, this dare not be." Hennig uses this
sentence of mine against me. Unjustly; for the sense in which I
"reject" such witness must be clear. I do not reject the assertion
of faith on the part of others, but I recognize it as historical,
which as an insight of faith can not become universally valid. I
own up to a faith in God, a faith which on its part is historical
and as such cannot lay claim to universal validity; from which is
deducible: a human being cannot be God. I reject the witness-
character of that John [the Baptist]. For, witness means both: the
attestation of realities, the same for everyone, which can be
verified by the critical method of comparing the testimonies in
hand — and the confession of faith which I have, but which not
everyone shares or even understands. Confessions of faith are
themselves realities and belong to history. But, whatever it is
to which they bear testimony is no object of historical investigation. What is witnessed to independently of each other by a group
of contemporaries may achieve a very high degree of probability
that it was so, and as such knowledge may endure for ever and
for all. What millions of men through the centuries here testified
to as the content of their faith is for themselves quite certain, not
just probable; but it can never achieve even a minimum of
knowledge about the reality of the historical event, despite the
fact that it had validity for large groups and long ages. The meaning intended by the believer is for him unconditional truth. But
its content (such, for example, as the resurrection of Jesus) is not
historical reality (whereby its weight as symbol need lose nothing
whatsoever), but only the fact that men have believed it and
found it attested to, or that they effected such a meaning of an
idea. Contents of faith are, *qua* contents of an expressible nature,
not universally valid for everyone; they may, therefore, at one
and the same time, be admitted as faith and also put in question

in their claim upon universal validity for all of what has been asserted.

Hennig's reference, however, to the millions of men and the two thousand years of history must be supplemented by the trivial yet striking reference to the many more numerous millions who are non-Christians, and to the division among Christians themselves (even to the point of religious wars) plus the claim of each confession to possess the true faith, starting as it did with the split between East and West within the first thousand years and continuing in the split brought about by Protestantism and beyond that within Protestantism itself. A Catholic Christian church exists only by way of the unjustified claim to catholicity. The idea of catholicity has grandeur, although I myself consider it impossible without spiritual and in consequence thereof finally also material violence. The claim to possess such catholicity impresses all who do not belong to it as arrogance. One must not grow tired of rejecting this claim, therefore. The idea of such catholicity is in principle the principle of totalitarianism.

It is nevertheless true when Hennig says: History is not yet the past in itself, but it exists only by way of the testimonies which it has called forth. Remembrance is the leap from mere happening to history. Testimony testifies to the will not to let it fall into forgetfulness. The historicity of the past we achieve only by the medium of testimony. But the ambiguity of the concept of testimony dare not be forgotten.

I consider true as well as beautiful what Hennig says about the transparency of history. History concerns us in its true essence only when, on the way over everything explorable, we become clearly aware of this transparency. Research is rewarding only if from inception it is guided by transparency, but only in the selection of what is worthy of knowledge, not in the proof of the correctness of any historical reality, which is demonstrable or refutable without any transparency as such.

Furthermore, Hennig's statements about time and history seem to me to be true and beautiful: the past is irrevocable, the present undecided, the future possible. The irrevocability of what is past is for him the source of our responsibility to see it correctly in its reality. Beautiful, too, is the pointer that every kind of communication with the past is bound to be one-sided. We listen, but we get no answer. Every answer is our interpretation.

This irrevocability, he further opines, is inaccessible to subjectivity, which on its part is peculiar to all designs of the future.

History cannot be taught anything by us; rather we have to let it teach us. Because the past is irrevocable, it is said to be authority. We become aware of this irrevocability in the transparency of the past. The elementary limit would be forgotten if we imagined we could, in any sense whatsoever, sink ourselves into the past.

Against this one must ask with all possible determination: Is there only a single history to be heard? Do not men hear it altogether differently and yet is it not, to all of them, meaningful in their own particular way? Do we only hear the victorious, that which has been effective, or also that which has been overcome, violated, extinguished, insofar as from its hiding place it still accidentally speaks to us in parts? Do we, in transparent awareness, see only the history of the *ecclesia militans* and *triumphans,* or do we not also hear, out of a "transparency" which seems to speak to many a one out of greater depth — especially since Gottfried Arnoldt — the history of the heretics as the history of truth?

Furthermore: Is it possible at all to hear history as a whole, as a single substance, or is it not in its very nature full of many meanings, full of possibilities for us? Can not everything in history in its transparency be seen as something which is to be acknowledged? Can not everything in it be justified as authority? Are not the limits of its interpretability infinite?

For, after all, historically we find ourselves in this basic situation: We never know the infinite, impenetrable, inexhaustible whole of history. It is the foundation which we sense only by virtue of the fact that we continue the struggle which has been going on all along. In history itself we are, in the very process of trying to understand it, struggling with the forces that have arisen in it. We appropriate that out of which we live and we ground ourselves in the history which bears us. We revoke what was done and thought wherever it appears to us as a strange force or as untruth. History is irrevocable only in factuality, but not in its meaning or consequences. We acknowledge historical decisions not as decisions for always, but will give battle, too, in the name of the defeated against the victors. Nothing is final except external reality. This is why we can want to cancel — at least in its effect — and to extinguish the results of evil, or continue to keep ourselves within the great polarities which are insuperable. We do not revise the process by viewing it as a whole, but by keeping our place within it and by fulfilling the task to which we believe ourselves destined. We repeat what has been. C. F. Meyer lets the dead say, "All our loving and hating and fighting still beats above in mortal veins . . . We are still seeking human goals," but also: "All earthly paths remain bound to what valid propositions we have found."

We are historical only if we thus stand in history. We then pass judgment, and we neither forget nor do we sugar-coat. History is no uniform, indifferent objectivity of a final nature *(Sosein)*. We dare not hesitate, wanting to know where we are. And in this the judgments must contradict each other. One of these judgments, for example, is this: Eternally cursed be the wars of the Albigensians! Pope Innocent III has shown that it is possible to annihilate an entire culture together with its bearers. What totalitarianism is repeating with equal unconcern and what is menacing us as future possibility, was put up at that time as model for the first time in Occidental history. Worthy of curses the burnings of the heretics, the Inquisition; cursed should be all censorship which is as murderous for the mind as were the former for the body! In radiant splendor stands Giordano Bruno, representative of Occidental freedom, over against the criminals who murdered him, stands Spinoza over against the Synagogue which excommunicated him in a ban which must be read.

No man, no institution, no faith, no knowledge is everything, none is all-embracing. No one can make the claim to be hearing history as the one and only true totality. This is why every total philosophy of history, from St. Augustine to Hegel and Marx, has lapsed into untruth which in principle is the same throughout. It entails at the very least an intellectual violation. We free ourselves from it by listening to the truth in history by means of being open-minded towards every *Existenz*. Since, however, no one hears all truth in history, each one of us ought to acknowledge his limitations. Everyone, and no less every institutional authority, ought to know his limits and keep himself open-minded. The manifoldness of the forms of historical truth is insurpassable. No one can live out of all of them at once — without self-deception. But it is possible in love to acknowledge what one is not himself (without the use of force and without deceiving either one's self or others). If one is at all grounded in truth, it is possible to live with all forms of truth without himself partaking of them. Whoever cannot endure other truth, proves thereby his own untruth.

Again I am in agreement with Hennig when he speaks of responsibility in the face of history: Our historical memory anticipates the demolition not merely of one's own history, but also the demolition of history and of the past as such. The chasm of death is bridged in the preservation [of history], but proves to be unbridgeable because we can only hear what is past but can no longer receive any answer. Communication with history keeps in mind the foundation of the continuity of humanity. Expiring in death is a natural event, but history effects responsibility. The past is defenseless, as I shall be when I have died (Schelling says we have to hope some day to find other defenders, even as we ourselves are responsible for the defense of our ancestors). After my death, says Hennig, I shall be an object of interpretation, mostly misinterpretation, probably of oblivion — but no longer replying.* The historical shows itself to our love, no longer opens itself in conversation. But the past in itself is untouchable, it remains secure in its eternity without us. We do less injury to the past than we do to ourselves when we forget it, misunderstand it, fail to see it in its transparency. The historian is the custodian of the consciousness of mankind. Thus far I follow Hennig with deep emotion.

But now Hennig severely indicts many of my statements about historical appearances. I speak, for example, of the "mythological age" before the "pivotal age" as being in a condition of sleep: Hennig calls this an unkind reduction. I call Jesus the last of the Jewish prophets: Hennig says that I am doing this against Jesus' own witness as well as against that of nineteen-hundred years. I speak of the pivotal period: Hennig considers this a subjective claim; etc.

These grave errors he interprets as the consequence of a single basic error: namely that of my acknowledgment of the principle of selection on the part of the activity of historical interpretation. As over against that he puts his own assertion: The historian knows that it is not he who interprets, but that he himself is being interpreted by the witness of the past. In the same sense we read: The claim of historicity will be heard all the more clearly the less the present speaks. Truth lies in the fulfillment of the overpowering claim of the testimony of the past. The picturing of history in monumental contemplation and critical history, both, he thinks, serve to guard against this claim.

Such references seem to me to be ambiguous. They deny the differentiation between objective, scientific, historical knowledge and the historical view, which is capable, out of 'existential' sources, to be aware of Existenz. This differentiation, which in

---

* Which constitutes the major reason for the existence of THE LIBRARY OF LIVING PHILOSOPHERS. Ed.

methodological discussions is usually spoken of as the differentiation between the determination of facts and evaluation, Hennig
regards as an error of the "third estate" since the 17th century.
This differentiation, he claims, was unknown to all former Occidental as well as to the entire Asiatic interpretation of history.
But it is precisely this differentiation which constitutes the foundation of critical research. It is part of modern science, which is,
indeed, something new and grand in the history of the world.
It does by no means imply that, after the differentiation, what has
been differentiated is not again closely connected; but it does
mean that both (aspects) become pure, clear, and truthful only
on the basis of the distinction. It seems to me that there has
ensued in Hennig's statements a collapse of the modern scientific
consciousness, which (latter) has produced realistic critical research, (and therefore) the science of history. When Ranke remarks he would like to extinguish himself in order that he might
see purely what was historical, there lies in this remark, in the
first place, that principle of critical historical research with its
distinction of the type and validity of testimony; and, secondly,
the aesthetic attitude of looking on, which finds its infinite satisfaction in getting to see the realities of history with your very
eyes. Inasmuch as historical reality is inexhaustible, one must
agree with Hennig that the principles of selection in historical
science do not arise out of any presumption of the right to selection, but out of "the humble admission" of the limitations of our
open-mindedness; the principles of selection are methodical rather
than philosophical. But one must add that, first of all, scientific
historical research and description is entirely conscious of the
fact that all of its points of view are merely attempts; that all
principles of selection require in the final analysis a justification
of their meaning which cannot be found within science as such
(because research may achieve completely correct results which,
however, as merely correct, are of no significance at all). And,
secondly, it must be added that the relation between a view of
history and the actual occurrences in history, between scholar
and object, between the present and the past, is not a one-sided
but a reciprocal one. The activity of the investigator in his
sketches, proceeding as he must from the present reality which
he is, cannot be replaced by an empty point, which latter could
be filled up only from the past. Rather, one who views (things)
historically is comparable to a living mirror, which cannot be
detached from what it mirrors. Criticism is concerned as much
with the mirror as with what is mirrored, as much with the

methods, the subjectivities, and the obligations of the investigator as with the reality of what is past. It is an extraordinarily involved intellectual structure which arises here. The responsibility in it is enormous, but it cannot simply be reduced to the principle of letting oneself be determined by the past.

To this problem discussed by Hennig belongs also an unusually penetrating formulation of a question by Jeanne Hersch. She sketches a picture of the dying of tradition in the life of today. She is in agreement with my tendency to preserve tradition everywhere by means of philosophical faith and by factual participation. But in my attempt — which might just possibly still be successful for us — she actually sees the promotion of the end.

She differentiates: tradition as the factual living in it, led by the unquestionable, without reflection filled with all that has come down to us in pictures, symbols, and doctrines. The other tradition, on the other hand, is as such being known, questioned, restored, intentionally held on to. The consequence of the second (type) is supposed to be the state of the world today. Tradition, having become an object, became just one tradition among others, and thereby became endangered. However, as such known and intended tradition it became aggressive. It applies pressure and force in order to be saved. Actually by doing so it dies, because it loses its meaning. For, its intent was to be living towards the future out of the background of its origins. This is why against the desired tradition there is now in progress a revolution which, on its part, expects salvation from negation alone: deceiving itself about the Void, sees in negation itself already the creation of the future. The portrait of our age, therefore, is as follows. We are living in an atmosphere of forces of belief which are no longer our own. Against them we hear the claim of Nothingness which declares itself in favor of freedom and creativity. The bright atmosphere of freedom, which makes everything possible, becomes the poisoned atmosphere which dissolves everything into nothing. Man as man degenerates, because he believes less and less. His essence seems to be getting ready to become the material of still unrealized terroristic totalitarianisms.

This, then, is a picture of the present, which indubitably contains factual and meaningful movements of thought, which are widely held today. But we must not forget that the indicated connections of ideas, which lead to dissolution, are not necessary natural laws. To understand them already marks the beginning of getting away from them. Moreover, this picture is only one, not *the,* picture of the present. Who knows what forces still are quietly at work, or what is experienced unobtrusively in the communication of individuals, or what, suddenly like a storm, could again pull up human reality!

True, I myself, like so many contemporaries, have, in my writings, spoken about the loss of substance during the last century. So far as the public aspect of works and deeds is concerned, this judgment is not unfounded. Nevertheless, even there I have my doubts; most certainly, however, if this judgment is applied to living men. Should such a judgment ever have been made by me, I would have to retract. The power of love and of self-assertion, the bravery of enduring and of dying, integrity, the being profoundly moved by the ground of being, these, it seems to me, exist no less today than they did in former times. Under the duress of the objective confusion of all validities and total lack of leadership in the world, a few German soldiers in the time of national socialism nevertheless managed to find their way without any mediation by world or church, directly guided by deity, which inspired them to see the truth and to do the right contrary to an oath which was no oath. Lovable men are today no fewer than in former times. They meet face to face, not so easily in the noise of public exhibitionism, but even there. It is no judgment on humanity today that — measured by the criterion of those periods in which such figures arose, valid and effective for all time to come — men of grandeur (by actual work and visible accomplishment) are almost absent today.

Presumably Jeanne Hersch will be in agreement with this limitation placed upon her pessimistic view of the present. But now she views my philosophic enterprise amidst this situation. She assigns an extraordinary place to my philosophizing — something which, for the intent of my work, I am, of course, glad to hear, provided the insufficiency of my realization is not forgotten. She says: "This philosophizing distributes consciousness in time, assigns it a past, a present, a future, breaks it down into tradition, freedom, and hope, whereas by itself it fastens onto time with such force that time is pierced through, and a sort of momentary coincidence with eternity is actualized." She praises my effort to find once again the life of tradition itself by going through and beyond the traditional schemata. She sees in my work a totality of spiritual exercises aimed at finding the return to the lost living sources, to the lost treasure, without which the future can not find itself.

However, for this apparently so happy enterprise Jeanne Hersch lets me pay a terrible price. My attempt to find tradition, as well as seeing this tradition expanded to the history of mankind as a whole, might, she thinks, some day lead to personal success. In general, however, this attempt would actually have to destroy all tradition. It is a case of living from a wealth which, precisely through such a way of life, would be entirely lost to future generations. My attempt appears to her, in today's situation, as the only possible one, but at the same time also as destructive. Why? If I become conscious of my tradition and out of my own tradition proceed to communicate with every other tradition, this means to lay hold of every tradition, by agreement with its experience. But this means at the same time to lose it. For the acknowledgment of each specific tradition makes it impossible to maintain the peculiarity of one's own in its incomparable singularity. To understand and affirm every tradition would basically mean to place oneself outside of all tradition. For, in the original and living tradition lies the Absolute, the unquestionable, that which no longer requires any justification. Where tradition is being justified, says Jeanne Hersch, there it has already become weak.

I reply briefly as follows. As living actuality there is no such thing as a total tradition of all mankind. It is, nevertheless, philosophically possible — out of one's own historicity, which for me, insofar as I stand within it, is indeed something unconditional, something which cannot be overcome by any question, — to gain insight into the historicity of mankind as a whole. Everyone can himself actually be this tradition only in his own specific historicity. But this can, so to say, open itself in loving understanding of the others. Everyone belongs to the one historicity of mankind which as a whole is actually accessible to no one. From every piece of ground on which we stand — and everyone, if he is alive and is not nothing, inevitably and properly stands somewhere — the direction leads to the same, identical center of the earth.

It would indeed be grotesque in one's own life to realize the entire tradition of mankind by incorporating it through a kind of collection [of traditions]. To understand the foreign traditions, lovingly to turn towards them, is not the same thing as living in them. Such understanding itself will presumably succeed only by virtue of the strength granted by living out of one's own historical heritage.

Now, however, I shall attempt to meet Jeanne Hersch's arguments more basically. I participate in her question by searching for the presuppositions on the strength of which that question first becomes possible. It seems to me, those presuppositions are the following:

First presupposition: Truth can exist only as universally valid. The tradition, which I live in truth, appears to me necessarily as universally valid.

Against this I posit: Historical truth is unconditional in the life of *Existenz,* but, in its pictures, symbols, and assertions, it is not universally valid for all men. The lack of universal validity does not rob lived truth of its depth. As historical, truth is infinite; not the particularity of a genus (as it inevitably appears to external historical research), but the actuality of the historical itself. Each truth is the whole, because related to the One, and because, in view of its own infinity, it is not subsumable. Yes, each truth is potentially everything.

Second presupposition: One must try to specify how one is to think and operate at decisive moments and on the whole, in order to find the correct road of history.

Against this I posit: It is impossible to gain a true picture of the whole. This is why rational prognoses always expect either the absolutely ruinous or the illusory paradise to arise from absolute Nothingness. A prognosis of the actual, accomplishing historical path is impossible, because the prediction would be identical with producing and creating.

Third presupposition: One should not be satisfied merely to watch the course of events. Philosophy in its essence has its eye on the whole. If it does that, its truth exists only when philosophy's knowledge of the whole transforms the world as a whole.

Against this I posit: Philosophical insight requires that we be content with what is possible for us. We have to operate within limits wherein realization through us is possible. If we want more than we know and are able to do, our thinking becomes deceptive and ruinous at the same time. Wanting too much becomes the occasion for neglecting the possible. Philosophy permits me to actualize the rational way of thinking, orientation, critical knowing. With such actualization the intellectual climate develops in which, under the control of rational philosophical insight, the concrete setting of aims and plans — meaningful as they are within their limits — are found. But I reject all types of total knowledge and total planning.

If I dispute those three presuppositions, I believe nonetheless to recognize in them a hidden truth. That they are clearly stated is useful. For they turn against any possible self-satisfaction within the necessary limitations and resignations. They keep the consciousness of finiteness awake.

If in the crisis of world history something develops or gets lost which no man can survey or plan, it can only be a matter of knowing in this crisis out of what and for what one is to live and labor. This includes: an intellectual conscience engaged in a continuous examination of what one knows and does not know, of what it is possible to know and not possible to know; — keeping oneself free of every hidden form of totalitarian thinking; — practicing the types of thinking which illuminate what tradition is and which one I grasp as my own, while I would like to become comprehendingly open towards all.

Jeanne Hersch seems to argue as if she were standing outside, viewing the entirety of human things, as if one could see how the world must run, and as if one could know the plan (although one does not yet know it) , to form it correctly as a whole. She speaks of tradition in the same fashion.

However, tradition, as factual living in it, can in no wise be willed, it can only be actualized. With one's own heritage it is found already present and affirmed, but neither rejected nor planned.

Tradition is specific only when it is looked at from outside. It is infinite in the uniqueness of the place where it is being lived. In that case, for example, a landscape is no longer the specific instance of all landscapes, but the representation of the entire world in the inexhaustibleness of its historical nature, which is not undone by the comprehension of its universal aspects. Parents, for example, are not an instance of parenthood as such, but this, always singular, historical actuality.

Rationally considered justification makes as little sense here as does refutation, as if the peculiarity of externals were accounted for. Rather, in philosophizing about tradition the good conscience of being grounded as well as fulfilled in history can be strengthened; at the same time there can be strengthened with it the appreciation of all other genuine historicity in its incomparableness and, therefore, the awe of it. The representation of the idea of a Biblical religion, for example, would be false, if it wanted either to extinguish the specific figures and forms, the confessions of Christianity, of Judaism, or of Islam, or wanted to bring them to a common denominator, or wanted to unite them in a single institution.

In philosophizing we seek to eliminate false ideas; false, because they lead away from the Encompassing and from the center. If tradition and freedom, being and doing, are in mutual exclusion set over against each other, this creates a mood which no longer listens to the language of the basis in the Encompassing. In this case our *Existenz* is thought of only as freedom out of the Nothing, as creation out of Naught (in transposition of the cipher of God's creation of the world out of nothing), as Jeanne Hersch so aptly remarks. Thus there comes into being a treacherous magic of the extreme. This cuts off man's roots and lays upon him a responsibility to which he cannot possibly measure up. If the creation of his freedom out of the Naught is expected of man, only the road into the bottomless nothing is opened to him. Philosophic thoughts gain their truth not by knowledge about something which is thus and so and which is known, but by the creation of a type of thinking which illuminates man's potentialities. What becomes real (whether we love it in its creating and created actuality, whether it unites us with each other in a community which builds its own world, or however otherwise we may formulate this becoming real), only this decides the matter of truth.

Arguments are valid in reference to particulars. But if, on the other hand, I think rationally about the whole, I come — because from the start I am proceeding wrongly — to a view of the world in which everything goes to wreck and ruin. The intellect makes only ruinous prognoses. What, in a total knowledge, I foresee is either the deceptive illusion of magnificent good luck, in behalf of which all sacrifices are justified, or else the disconsolate picture of man losing himself, which even now robs all life of its meaning. Over against this stands the process of philosophizing, which remains in the present and fulfills the possible today. It has an inner connection to the whole of the Encompassing, but is not subjected to a rational picture of the whole. In such procedure no idea is created in order to throw off tradition and to create oneself out of nothing in supposedly complete freedom. Nor will a tradition be crystallized or thoughtless subjection to its authority be demanded. Everywhere universal judgments are fully exposed. From the very center of the present, which is eternity itself, life is being lived in the confidence that its effects will be good if only it itself becomes truly good. Planful particularity is being comprehended *(umgriffen)* and led by an unplanned actuality — but without ever becoming objectively certain in the self-satisfied assurance that one's own conduct is definitively good and right.

In philosophizing we become certain not by a decision between alternatives. As for example: our past is the desired chain which has been laid upon us, a possession in which we may rest; or: it is what is to be shaken off, the mere rôle which has been forced upon us. More such false alternatives: Our freedom lies in the substance of our heritage, or: it lies in the insubstantiality of life out of the Nothing. Everything which is thus formulated in alternatives may very well be real in the distortions which the intellect sees as such. But the rise of the potentiality of our *Existenz* is certainly just as much bound to the depth of our given being as it is to the responsibility of our inner and outer conduct. Freedom remains in the foreground, whenever it chooses rationally among possibilities. A deeper form of freedom is the choice of him who, through his potential *Existenz* — he becoming himself — takes himself over in his heritage, in this body, in this tradition. This taking over of oneself is not the desperate desolation of the "well, this is the way I am," but the free subjection to an unrecognizable Encompassing by coming to myself in transforming this my actuality *(Sosein)*.

This is why it is possible for us today to philosophize against the disastrous spirit of Descartes, who threw off history and wanted to gain himself out of the Nothingness of the "I think;" — as well as against its modern analogies in totalitarianism and existentialism, which go their way without substance, without the modes of the Encompassing. For this path leads him who interprets thus out of the pretended knowledge of the whole into an *Existenz* which is null and void. Such an interpretation, leaving behind a world of destruction, appears to note something in the destruction itself which pleases its triumphant claim.

All of this, it seems to me, Jeanne Hersch sees and thinks and expresses indirectly by letting the intellect make its leaps, which she herself does not quite believe. The only remedy against such duping by the intellect is to educate it so thoroughly that it will recognize its own limitations and perceive its own errors. This negative remedy prepares the ground for philosophizing, which ascertains for us our true capacities and possibilities.

The moving essay by Jeanne Hersch, inspired by a deep concern with modern man, appears to me ambiguous, therefore. It engages in a type of rational thinking which sees in the course of events only ruin, and which even in what today is affirmed as good and true sees only the beginning of the end. The essay is nevertheless borne by confidence, which does not, however, manage to break through to overcome the annihilating perspective which mere intellectual understanding would like to extort.

It is as if Jeanne Hersch were dissolving striking observations and deep thoughts into a rationality against which she herself is struggling even while she performs it in an annihilating fashion. Not by the intellect alone can these thoughts be refuted, although it [certainly] is important to use intellectual understanding in order to show it its own not-knowing *in concreto*. In Jeanne Hersch anxiety, the love of man makes use of the intellect in order to express her terror. How could one want to oppose such anxiety, wherever it is effective in helping others as well as one's self — even onto illuminating answers to children's questions, which she reports! How contradictory, however, would be her endeavor, if anxiety were to be lost in desolation. As over against that there remains the way of Job: in the very face of the deity to implore the deity by pointing at the injustice, and yet, in the end, to trust the deity, — and the way of Abraham: without doubting it, to speak to the unjust deity in behalf of men, of the just ones in Sodom and Gomorrha!

5. THE RELATION OF PHILOSOPHICAL THINKING TO RELIGION

The intent of my philosophizing, in the succession of philosophy which has lasted for thousands of years, is the affirmation of the independent origin of philosophical faith. Several critics have put my attitude towards religion in question. They are striking at a central point. If it is by-passed, philosophizing remains in the dark. The decisiveness with which I carry out the self-assertion of philosophical origins by distancing it from religion is by no means peculiar merely to my own philosophical attempt: philosophy stands in polarity to religion, not merely in animosity to it, but rather over against it and at the same time bound to it.

My philosophizing does not, therefore, fit into the scheme which opposes faith and intellect, religion and science, Christianity and nihilism, in such fashion as to think that these alternatives are exhausting the problem. My thinking proceeds from a third, which does not occur in those alternatives and which is rejected by both sides as something impossible or as a compromise or as a blunting of the edges.

In the tradition of Plato, Bruno, Spinoza, Kant, Lessing, and Goethe, I would like once again to emphasize the eternal independent origin of all philosophizing, the philosophical faith which communicates itself in the thinking of reason. This faith is neither confessional theology nor science, neither a church-creed nor unbelief. It recognizes itself again in the great ancestors, even in those of India and China.

I agree in a certain sense with Holm, therefore, when he asserts that the philosophy of religion is not a separate subject in my thinking, but permeates my entire philosophy. My philosophy, he insists, *is* itself philosophy of religion, it does not *have* a philosophy of religion.

Throughout, theologians do not pay much attention to such a philosophy; and, if they do, then mostly in such a fashion that they see it within the scheme of the type of philosophy with which they are familiar: as science or as unbelief. They fail to find here the usual opponent, against whom they are used to turn victoriously with the old weapons; they fail to find here the type of intellect which claims everything for itself, they do not find ostentatious disbelief, not the enemy of religion, nor that of the churches, not nihilism.

Perhaps such a way of philosophizing is either invisible or uncomfortable to them. In it they meet the more substantial opponent or actually the ally. We are opponents in questions concerning origin and authority, but allies in the struggle against the forces of waste and of destruction, against the spectres of rationalism and nihilism.

My critics in this volume do not participate in that fruitless struggle, in which the opponents do not even catch sight of each other. Rather, they discuss questions of great seriousness on the same ground on which my own thinking is going on. They point at dangers which all original philosophizing should always keep in mind. I shall make an effort to listen to them with an open mind, as if the questions were my own.

When Ricoeur feels that I am inclined to see the tension between philosophy and religion in terms of their mutual exclusiveness instead of their polarity, I would agree with him only where, in any of my writings, that kind of a position should have intervened against my own tendencies. I defend myself rather against every kind of claim to exclusiveness on the part both of any ecclesiastical creedal truth and of any philosophical truth.

The misunderstanding arises out of the fact that the concept of religion is not unambiguous. Philosophy itself has been called religion, "philosophical religion" (Schelling). By religion, in that case, is meant the relation of man to Transcendence, meditation to the very border of prayer, speculative thinking (all of this belongs to philosophy as well). Beyond this, however, by religion is meant revelation as an event in the world by which God speaks directly and thereby bestows upon texts and institutions (churches) absolute authority through holiness, which demands obedience

even where understanding is wanting. This religion is implied
in the cult, in the actuality of something specifically holy in
places, objects, acts. Finally, religion is belief in the connections
of the mediation of grace by means of the authoritarian faith
itself. The biggest example is the knowledge, gained by grace, of
one's own completed unabrogatable sinfulness, together with
grace's offer of salvation by faith in the substitutionary sacrifice of
God: the faith in justification by such faith. For the clarity of our
philosophical position a separation seems to me necessary between
the universal concept of religion — which also includes philosophical religion — on the one hand, and the concept of a specific
religion, the inexhaustibly rich world of which has been only
superficially indicated by the few sentences above. Now it is true
of any specific religion that philosophy need in no sense be its
opponent, that philosophy in fact can neither comprehend nor
produce it nor be a substitute for it. For this reason, religion
remains for philosophy always a polar other, with which it is
concerned, from which it receives stimuli, and to which it in turn
returns stimuli. Religion is for philosophizing "like a pole which
constantly concerns it, or like a weight which it cannot lift, or
like an opposition which is insuperable and whose conquest,
once it seems accomplished, instead of leading to the satisfaction
in the now fully achieved one truth, produces rather something
like terror over the suddenly noticeable emptiness." (From my
essay dealing with Bultmann's de-mythologizing).

Ricoeur differentiates convincingly between religion in its
estranged form *(pretension)* and in its true nature *(intention)*.
I would make the same distinction in philosophizing. Whenever
I have made remarks concerning institutional religion in general,
which strike at such deviations, these remarks are justifiably
rejected by the faithful, inasmuch as they do not get at the essence
(a few of Hennig's remarks I could, in this sense, accept as corrections). It is no different with the deviations in philosophy.
They must not be mistaken for philosophy. We shall do well
constantly to keep in mind the dangers which threaten us in the
process of philosophizing. It is in this that I see the significance
of the essay by Ricoeur.

According to Ricoeur, the essence of religion consists in the
mystical relationship of immediacy to God. This is no intellectual
experience, it cannot be speculatively forced, but as the outermost
limit it is possible in philosophizing itself, and belongs to that
religion which can be common both to philosophizing and to a
specific religion. It is to be found in Plotinus, Spinoza, and Bruno.

It is an element in the philosophizing of Cusanus. I do not think (although Ricoeur seems to want to reproach me with it) that in such experience man's freedom is annulled or the world betrayed.

The problem of freedom — namely, that it does not have its being in itself, but rather that the more decisively freedom actually becomes conscious of itself the more it knows itself as granted to itself, and that freedom can fail to appear to itself and therefore points to Transcendence as its origin — is discussed in almost all of my philosophical writings. I consider it as the unavoidable element of truth in the philosophical illumination of *Existenz*, which, without St. Paul, St. Augustine, and Luther, would perhaps not have come so clearly into our consciousness. My philosophizing looks totally different, however, when the problem of guilt arises. There is no such thing in philosophizing as liberation from freedom by the grace of a divine act which cancels guilt, an act mediated by faith in the death of Jesus on the cross as substitutionary atonement in such fashion that faith in it justifies, whereas without this faith one is lost. More than that, philosophy rejects such assertions of belief outright. Only by transforming its meaning can philosophy find any possible truth acceptable which may lie hidden therein.

I cannot agree with Ricoeur, therefore, when he places the problem of guilt in the center. Even though, in harmony with the entire philosophical tradition, I, too, connect guilt with man's finite nature, I have not the slightest inclination to veil it as unavoidable and therefore as innocent necessity. The difference begins only where forgiveness of guilt is sought and found in the religious relation to the thou of the godhead. I do not deny the possibility of this cipher, could even talk about it; but I can only say that to myself it does not speak in any essential fashion. This implies no diminution of guilt on my part. Nobody forgives guilt. I have to answer for it. This is by no means the last word; but it is one which does intrude when I hear of redemption of guilt, of which redemption men, in their faith, are certain — and go on sinning courageously because of this faith (in the terrible *pecca fortiter* of Luther) .

Ricoeur sees dangers in my philosophizing: the danger of a vanity of subjectivity which is unable to see through itself, which effects a philosophical *gnosis* aesthetically, without obligation; — the danger of the transformation of Transcendence into the dark depths of subjectivity; — the danger of a cancellation of the unconditioned nature of the '*existential*' relation to Transcendence by the universality and manifoldness of the ciphers; — the danger of the transformation of the genuine transcendental relationship into a troubled philosophical lyricism.

These dangers conjured up by Ricoeur are the same ones against which I am battling in my philosophizing. If — falsely, I believe — my philosophizing gives the impression that these dangers had already overcome me, I can only give two answers. In the first place, no man in the final analysis knows about himself, even though he stands in the quietude of a faith, since in time this quietude can at any moment be overthrown. Secondly: it could be a misunderstanding due to the inescapable form of philosophizing for which I have striven hard. *'Existential'* reality cannot be anticipated. In philosophizing which finds expression in writings the suspension of possibilities must remain, in order that the genuine character of original *Existenz* may not bind itself absolutely to the objectivity of the assertion of another. The tentative character of communication is the necessary form of unconditional seriousness. A philosophy which does justice to its task must offer an appearance of adhering to the non-obligatory character of the manifold, which latter the author rejects absolutely both in his reader as well as in himself. But this rejection can be carried out, not by a declared confession, but always only by the historical acts of one's own *Existenz* which gives an account of itself to Transcendence.

Holm emphasizes quite rightly that I turn against every materialization, against every embodiment of Transcendence. He reports that I deny demons and devils. But he asks whether the concept of Transcendence (or of God) in my philosophy is an expression of that reality out of which all things come as do the waves out of the ocean, or whether this Being is not real but only meant. In other words, whether it is only the written cipher which is real, but God himself only a fiction; whether God really exists or is only an idea. He finds it difficult to distinguish reality from symbolism in my philosophy. A decisive Either-Or between the two, between Transcendence and cipher-script, would seem impossible. The undifferentiation of the dialectical tension is said to be impenetrable. Beyond this, Holm asks whether the being of God in my thinking bears the character of reality or only that of value, whether, therefore, it is to be understood ontologically or only axiologically. He finally concludes all these questions with the statement that, not only had I not put these issues sharply, but presumably I would reject these alternatives.

With this last sentence Holm has understood me excellently. I do indeed see in all such rationally fixed alternatives the disposition towards the radical mistake to want to talk about the non-objective, the Encompassing, in a rationally determined and therefore objectively decisive and knowing manner. All of those concepts occur in the marvelous wealth of movement possible in transcending thinking. These concepts themselves cannot be questioned about their content of knowledge, but only about the expressive power of their movements of thought, their power to conjure up the reality of Transcendence.

This type of thinking is devoted to the inescapable objectivities in the fullness of their possibilities which, rationally considered, contradict and exclude each other and therefore logically cause themselves to vanish. Nevertheless it performs again and again the basic operation: in the process of thinking to find one's way out of what is being thought into the Encompassing. In this process materialisation and rationalisation are overcome, although, in the foreground of consciousness, they remain at the same time insuperable.

That reality speaks in the cipher, even though it itself is not the cipher, that the symbol is not Being itself, this is too little for man whenever he wants Transcendence corporeally, just like the objects which he grasps as existence. On the other hand, it always suffices and in certain moments is even effusive whenever man becomes certain of himself as *him*-self, as potential *Existenz*.

Now, on the one hand, one finds in my philosophizing an openness for myths, the claim to bring mythical contents again into our present consciousness — and immediately I am being re-proached for the aesthetic non-obligatoriness of the many ciphers. On the other hand, one finds an unpictured deity — and imme-diately reproaches me for having extinguished all the fulness and grandeur of Being in the emptiness of this dimensionless point *(Punktuelle)*, in Nothingness. This is the antinomy, which runs through thousands of years of Occidental thinking, in which I am participating.

Whenever I turn to myths in all their forms I am anxious to read the ciphers and to hear that language which ultimately refers to or derives from the One, which itself is not present in any cipher nor in any myth. When I speak of de-mythification, I do not mean the translation of mythical content into something like a purer truth nor its interpretation in terms of some un-mythical truth-content. I mean rather a passing beyond all myths, — the picturesque foregrounds of the infinite manifold, — to an unpictured godhead, which appears neither as picture to the eye nor as thought to thinking, but which is the reality beyond all myths and beyond all possibilities of thinking, a reality, which is experienced and touched by us only in myths and in thoughts.

As over against this, there is the demand of theological thinking to save the reality of God as a knowable object. The attempts in this direction are manifold. I hear from critics *(Thyssen)* that cipher is too little, that analogy opens access. To this I reply: Transcending thinking in analogies, too, has been a substantial procedure from antiquity to Kant and even to the present. It is to be adopted in its own way. But it remains in the realm of ciphers.

If it is asserted that, in this kind of philosophizing, God turns into nothing, it is to be replied: this objection is valid only if the mode of knowing by consciousness-as-such (the intellect) is taken as the only and universally valid form in which reality is present. Philosophizing stands opposed to this: true, for it consciousness-as-such is the medium of all thinking, even of the transcending and speculative kind. But in this medium the appropriate and proper implementation occurs by way of the knowable reality of the being of the world. Making use of its forms, this medium is being surpassed wherever transcendent reality becomes present. The way this happens is that the objective, because of (inherent) contradictions, circles, and tautologies, becomes void as itself and thereby becomes the springboard from which the leap takes place. Whatever in this process was historically present as object in the world, becomes then the medium of a quite different proximity. The object, in its fulness before our very eyes, is no longer merely object. The subject-object division, unbridgeable in consciousness-as-such, is then surpassed.

I am grateful to Lichtigfeld that, over against the objections of the theologians, in agreement with me he recognizes in my philosophizing the movement towards the Biblical idea of an unpictured God, toward the carrying out of the commandment: "Thou shalt not make unto thee an image or likeness."

But the objections made till now do not yet strike at the center of philosophizing. The real objection runs: this God who cannot be grasped by knowledge, this God for whom everything which is can become cipher, is not God. In this kind of thinking, God himself, who manifests himself, is missing; the God who is real, because he reveals himself, is missing.

Among the critics in this volume, Pfeiffer has expressed this objection most beautifully. He asks whether it is not an encroachment of metaphysical speculation to speak of God at all. Of God one could speak only if he himself makes himself perceptible in an event which dawns upon us as divine revelation through a "demonstration of the spirit and of power."

In reply it must be said: To speak of God in a philosophizing manner is not merely "metaphysical speculation," but is, in the philosophical tradition since Xenophanes and Plato, the language of a fundamental philosophical experience of faith or of a basic *'existential'* act in such fashion that God does not speak at some privileged place in space or time but rather, in so far as possible, everywhere, yet always indirectly and ambiguously. For, God is hidden and every certainty about him is fraught with danger.

The direct revelation of God, his unequivocal pronouncements, God himself in his objective form and his claim as such, — all these are experienced by the faithful and as experience asserted and attested. But such revelation cannot be grasped, not be affirmed or negated, neither proved nor disputed by philosophy. However, everything that men who give such witness say, do, and are, and themselves claim to believe, can be object of examination, according to the principle: by their fruits ye shall know them.

Pfeiffer demands the honest acknowledgment that no thinking reason could decide whether, in any information handed down by men, God himself is actually speaking, or whether it is a case of presumptuous absolutizing. In both instances this God remains withdrawn from metaphysical speculation, whether we leave that question undecided in pious awe, or whether we learn that here an immemorial and therefore unavailable certainty is given to us. To this one may agree, provided that this certitude does not result in making claims upon others, nor in force or intolerance.

Pfeiffer's description of the condition that follows from such faith in revelation is, to be sure, identical with that of the philosophical condition, which is not based on revelation: Emptied of our worldly character to the very ground of our being, we would gain the power to open ourselves towards whatever at any specific moment approaches us with an unpredictable claim.

Holm has another objection against the circumvention of revelation by philosophy. He interprets revelation as a leap in history. New thoughts come into the world. They were formerly not present. Having come of themselves, by way of some individuals, such new thoughts are now a spiritual reality, although causally inconceivable in their derivation. We feel ourselves historically dependent upon those ideas, which have reached us by way of tradition, as well as responsible towards them. "The simplest solution is to ascribe them to revelation." To see the great secret everywhere in history, to see those leaps, this ever new originality,

this underivable and unpredictable, in all of this I am in unreserved agreement with Holm. But to attempt to identify the
revelation of God: — that he himself makes a singular appearance
in time and speaks at a definite place — with that universal secret
of history, this would, after all, be all too harmless a liberation
from the seriousness of the assertion and attestation of the believers in revelation.

6. THE PROBLEM OF COMMUNICATION

Fritz Kaufmann wants to give to communication a broad, yes
all-encompassing meaning. He distinguishes three types of communication: impersonal communication among objects; personal
communication among men; and super-personal communication,
the language in which Transcendence speaks to us. Whereas in
my thinking communication, in its proper sense, means communication among men only, Kaufmann wants to broaden and deepen
the content of communication to such an extent that communication becomes the *syndesmos* in Being itself, a covenant of Being.
He wants to take coexistence, community, and communication in
the universal sense to which poets and artists seem to confess, in
that they bestow a voice to things, to nature, and to what used to
be dumb, which voice gives them access to us. This voice, on the
other hand, is realized by those men who open up their innermost
(in prayer) before God as a personal instance to which they are
accountable. He wants to formulize communication as fundamental concept in such a way that it becomes absolutely universal.
But, at the same time, he would thereby like to fill it with the
most positive content out of the reality of Being itself.

I follow Kaufmann in his fine analyses: concerning the harmony
between man and nature, which can already be shown psychologically in sensation and awareness and which is realized by the
artist on a higher plane as articulation in the transparency of
things. Psychology and aesthetics supply him with confirmation.
I consider this true under one condition: namely, that it does
not lose its sense as the language of symbols in distinction from
communication proper. This latter obtains only from man to
man in mutual reciprocity. Only between men does the process
obtain in which the self properly becomes itself only in its relation
with the other self. Without a real reply by the other, communication, being one-sided, is not the vital kind from self to self. It is
only an invention of the *vis-a-vis*, a mute communication. The

language of nature, poetry, and art can have reality for me only by way of analogy to communication proper. For there is lacking in all of this the confirmation by the other. Real communication serves only as simile for those factually one-sided relationships to nature and to Transcendence. These latter are infinitely essential, but they lack the reality of the other personal self. I follow Kaufmann's speculation concerning the being of deity; but I limit its meaning to the character of a cipher. The consequences of this difference between Kaufmann and myself are perhaps only those of emphasis; but they could also lie much deeper. I would like to single them out quite clearly:

Kaufmann speaks of his faith in communication. This is a word which I use also. But this faith means something different. In Kaufmann it means anticipating agreement with and confidence in the ground of all things which for him stop to be mute; whereas, in their articulation in poetry and art, measured on actual communication, they still remain mute, simply because no self is present to answer. In my thinking, faith in communication means confidence in the possibility of that mode of being oneself which is capable of infinite revelation in the present, which becomes itself *only* in loving struggle with the other and here surrenders its reserve; a reserve in which — to use Kierkegaard's words — it is not transparent to itself, wants desperately to be itself and desperately wants not to be itself. This is a completely different meaning of faith in communication. But the one meaning does not exclude the other. Kaufmann's emphasis upon an ontological meaning of communication — which, as simile, occurs in my writings also and was noticed there by Kaufmann — can not, however, be accepted by me as an expansion of what I mean.

Kaufmann's interpretation entails that he does not occupy himself in detail with the steps and movements of communication which I have developed (especially in a chapter of the second volume of my *Philosophie*).[2] The big question concerning the misuse of the language of nature, of poetry, of art, of the speculative penetration into Transcendence as pseudo-communication, in virtue of which a single person or a collective frees itself from the genuine, real communication among men; this question Kaufmann touches only incidentally. To me this question was a theme of my writings; but such that nowhere do I deny the great truth which becomes distorted only by misuse. This truth remains

---

2 Kaufmann's treatment thus differs in method from, for example, Latzel's treatment of my chapter dealing with ultimate situations.

pure only if its manifestations in language are placed under the condition of communicative truth among men as individuals in the concrete realization of their relation to each other.

From this emphasis of mine arises Kaufmann's charge that I am inclined to exist, if not unworldly *(weltlos)*, then at least somewhat unnaturally *(naturlos)*. This reproach I cannot accept. I do not deny either the glory or the terror of nature, of things, or of the language of art and poetry by placing the experience of all of these under the conditions of *'existential'* reality. But I insist that I find in none of those facts that unconditional which lies in the claims of communication. I believe I can see a grave danger in the realization of the kind of language which becomes sufficient unto itself, the danger, that is to say, that men run away from the claims of communication; and, by doing so, really also run away from themselves and thus must find themselves cheated in spite of all the glory.

Kaufmann's reproach is further that, in place of the loving communication of a personal God with his creatures, I put the incommunicable, impersonal Transcendence. He compares Transcendence as I think of it with the unmoved mover of Aristotle and with the deity of Spinoza, both of whom are being loved, but themselves do not love in return. Kaufmann discusses what is discussed in my writings: even the communication with God contains within itself a tendency to break off or to degrade the communication with man (like Luther in the sentence: they can pray with each other, but not speak to each other) ; — and the other possibility that communication between men first becomes the place where Transcendence let its voice trustworthily be heard. That the deity approaches man as a person, in this powerful cipher for *Existenz* in historical situations, makes God by no means himself a person — except in the corporeal embodiment into realities of the world for such as believe in it. This corporeally embodied self, being spatially far removed and temporally past, indeed does not reply. Because real communication takes place only between men and rests in the final analysis upon faith (a faith which some deny), any other communication can be asserted only as a simile, inasmuch as it is carried out by us one-sidedly.

Referring back to Thomistic epistemology, Kaufmann sees in intercourse with any and all reality a form of communication. He describes in impressive and, it seems to me, true fashion that to make sense is at the same time to discover sense. The hiddenness of things is removed in the discovery by our soul, and the things themselves are, so to speak, liberated in this communication. The penetration into appearances is just as much an opening of our spirit for them; thinking and thanking belong to each other. Receptivity, he says, is present even in concept and productivity even in awareness (which Kant already pointed out). Consciousness *(conscientia)*, he says, is being solicitous about *coexistentia*, is already communication in both giving and taking, a *connubium* between man and things. The latent meaning of things is brought to awakening by our consciousness. Things have in themselves the possibility of communicable forms. Their meaning is their manifest essence which gets into the meaning of the words. This is why man may have confidence in the economy of the universe and in his human task, fulfilling instead of destroying it.

I do not dispute the metaphysical truth of such statements. But I hesitate to strain the symbol of communication for such relation to things to the point that the symbol suddenly stands for reality. In that case the meaning of communication itself, which goes from self to self and is an historical event in constantly possible reciprocity, is missed at its very roots.

What Kaufmann illuminates under the simile of communication is the subject-object relationship in the Encompassing. Through the Encompassing subject and object are indissolubly related to each other, as long as they signify truth. In the subject-object relation the nature of the recipient determines what is being received and *vice versa*.

Not the subject and a self, but subject and object stand here in relation. This relation can be conceived under the picture of communication and then also under the picture of quite definite types of communication; for example: the natural scientist forces nature to reply by submitting quite specific questions in the experiment; he examines the realities like witnesses in a court trial; he surrenders himself in love, in order, by dwelling on something, to bring to complete actuality what is immediately present; he breaks through communication by force; he breaks off.

If the picture of communication becomes the objective picture of all being in the chain from God to everything in the universe and to man in it, the question necessarily arises: what does this picture mean and to what can it lead?

It manages to hold fast to the sense of the Encompassing, it can prevent that subject or object, by isolating themselves from each other, fall away entirely. It manages to deepen the confidence that in the world one meets in everything some of that reason which the thinking person seeks and realizes in himself.

By doing this, however, something usually happens which limits and makes untrue the experience of being: reality's rupture of reason and meaning becomes veiled. Seeing of reason becomes dependence upon reason. Then we neglect to view the two threats which we must constantly struggle against and which we never conquer:

In the first place, a uniform picture of the totality of the world produces an illusion. It seduces us to abandon the only path which is possible for us: namely, to carry out, in the situation of our existence, the never completed illumination of the Encompassing, and to avail ourselves of the task of realizing our potential *Existenz*. Monstrous irrationality as well as distortions of reason are no longer taken seriously. To be on the road to the One and miss it by prematurely seizing the One as a will-of-the-wisp (even if it be in the most grandiose, Luciferic forms), this is to let oneself be blinded by a pretense to clarity.

In the second place, the knowledge of the total harmony in the communication of all being acually deflects from proper communication, from its genuine task and possible realization. The contentment found in a comprehensive glory displaces true communication — from one self to another — from the center of our real *Existenz* and makes it appear as a mere result and as something incidental and second-rate. It offers the opportunity to run away to God or to nature from man, from the neighbor, from the pressing task of communication. Within the realm of real communication from man to man those ciphers of nature, of the world, and of the language of Transcendence disclose themselves much less deceptively. They give to this communication its content in wealth and breadth of consciousness.

7. The idea of the Encompassing

The questions which Fritz Kaufmann has raised under the theme of communication reach way beyond it. Their answer is connected with the basic conception which, in the process of philosophizing, we have of the nature of objective being, whether we envisage it as object of thought, of art, of poetry, or as nature, life, landscape, thing, as man in his potential *Existenz* or as Transcendence. That I regard the personal God, the meaning of works of art, the content of the experience of nature, as ciphers, this appears to Kaufmann as too little. It looks as if, by the concept of the cipher, I am robbing the intended of its reality. Kaufmann pleads for objectivity as over against my apparent tendencies towards subjectivizing. In order to answer Kaufmann in his thoroughgoing effort I must begin farther back. What is at stake here is a central point of my philosophical attempts, to which I can refer only briefly.

I am urging to go beyond the division between subject and object, between the I and the object, and with it beyond the alternatives, which are erected between subjectivity and objectivity, where the one is constantly played against the other. My thesis is: Reality is neither the object nor the subject, but that which encompasses both, the Encompassing which is illuminated in the division between subject and object. In this division, however, both have their changing forms which belong to each other. Thus, in factual existence the sensory objectivity of the environment belongs to the corporeal-vital subjectivity of the living being. Thus, in consciousness-as-such the universal and everywhere identical "I think" of the subject belongs to the objectivity of the correctly thought-of object. Thus, in *Existenz*, Transcendence, which permits it [*Existenz*] to come to itself in its freedom, belongs to the freedom of the subject and of his responsibility. I shall not continue these mere enumerations. For our purpose the main point is that there are basically different modes of object-being, different for a subject according to the specific aspect of the Encompassing. These various modes must be kept distinct, if confusion is to be avoided. The Transcendence of the deity exists for potential *Existenz* and for it only, not for consciousness-as-such nor for existence. Inasmuch, however, as our consciousness lets everything which we encompass come together into one, the objectivity of Transcendence speaks to *Existenz* only through the medium of the thinking of consciousness-as-such and through that of the sensoriness of existence without, in the process, becoming these themselves.

Here is the epistemologically decisive point which is in question. Scientific knowledge is objective knowledge, which aims at the object itself. Philosophizing is a process which transcends the objective in, always objective, thinking.

If the aim of cognition is to understand everything properly, as object, such cognition loses philosophy proper. In order to preserve our philosophical consciousness — the content of thousands of years of philosophizing, the right to carry through the kind of philosophical thinking which sustains our life — I have tried to understand which methods of thinking have actually been used in philosophy since time immemorial. They all think in objects in such a fashion that they find themselves thereby directed to something non-objective, whereas the ultimate concern of the sciences is with objects as such.

It is the philosophical thought-operation *par excellence,* therefore, to lift us out of the subject-object division, in which we live in unquestioned self-evidence, to that which is before and encompasses it, which becomes clear to itself in the division, but in an incompletable fashion. Out of the Encompassing come the impulses and fulfilments which, in the subject-object division, give to the objective — along with the subjective which belongs to it — their meaning.

When, in my youth, I studied Kant's doctrine of Ideas (in the Appendix to my *Psychologie der Weltanschauungen,* offprint of a seminar-paper I had written as a student), Kant's procedure became clear to me: He thinks of the Idea in its objective meaning, as subjective impulse, as the methodical source of systematic investigation. The Idea in this triple sense shifts its meaning according to the relationship of the discussions, but in such fashion that a whole develops in which the Idea undergoes this necessary change of meaning.

What I understood at this point as a single instance, became clear to me in principle and in its encompassing consequences only after I had completed work on my *Philosophie.* The Encompassing, which is prior to all subject-object division, finds its illumination in the division and remains the ground, the goal, the nourishing and the moving in all division in which it never exhausts itself. The Encompassing is present in the object, in the subject, and in their mutual relations. In speech this encompassing is touched upon in varied ways, mostly in subjectivising idioms, but also in objectivising: "my intuition tells me this," — one speaks of "state," "mood," "inner disposition," — there is such a thing as "feeling one with nature" — one speaks of *Pneuma,* the spirit which moves us, of inspiration.

Everything which became thus psychologically subjectivised and with it became, as something accidental and passing, merely incidental; or everything which became metaphysically objectivised and therewith was addressed as a super-sensory force; all of this was meant to be caught by the concept of the Encompassing in its entire compass. I have attempted to circumscribe its meaning. We do not wish to content ourselves with "feeling" in any form, but to illumine it by an expansion at once in the objective and in the subjective, each bound to the other. Only thus can we gain the way to ourselves by becoming communicable, by communication and renewed recognition. After that, one must learn, however, that the Encompassing is present in many ways — in existence, in conciousness-as-such, in *Existenz,* in the spirit, in the world —, and that all these ways finally point to one, the Encompassing of everything Encompassing, which nowhere is definitively understood or possessed, and which yet leads everywhere where our path reaches its essential possibility. This is why I tried to illuminate the Encompassing in its manifoldness as well as in its unity. In analogy to Kantian transcendental thinking, it was to be ascertained as the condition of all possibility. The concept together with its elaboration was meant to serve as encouragement by virtue of the reality concentrated in it, which reality accounts for everything we are and that is. It was meant to be a claim with the demand to listen to it. What incalculably speaks from there shall not be passed over indifferently nor left on one side. The development of this concept was meant to teach us to ascertain all the content of our existence, our knowledge, our *existing.* It was supposed to bar us from either cultivating a mere subjectivity or losing ourselves into a mere objectivity. It was meant to bring to consciousness the fact that everything which we are and which is for us has weight and content only through the Encompassing, and that it loses this content by sliding off into mere subjectivity or into mere objectivity. It was meant to educate philosophically in such fashion as to go beyond the division in the division, from thence to gain strength and peace, and yet constantly to push back into the division, which latter, after all, only makes possible every kind of realization, expansion, and clarity.

But the Encompassing itself is no object. In fact, is it at all possible to think it and to speak of it? If it is possible, then in any case only indirectly. Inasmuch as our thinking is in each moment bound to objects, it is possible to speak of this non-objective (Encompassing) only in terms of objective thought. This again became clear to me first in Kant's method, as he factually uses it (without mentioning it as such). In his famous transcendental deduction of the possibility of all objectivity and of all knowing, he proceeds as follows. By the guiding thread of psychological, methodological, and metaphysical objectifications he thinks that which itself is none of these objectifications, although being the necessary condition of all of them, that which itself is neither subject nor object. This is the reason why Kant's texts are so very difficult to understand precisely at the points where they touch upon these questions — according to his own

assertion the very heart of his philosophy. Many a reader is at a
loss in this perplexity. The interpretations are inclined to mistake one of the guiding lines for the matter itself, and then critically to eliminate the others as aberrations of thought not conquered by Kant; as, for example, the psychological interpretation
(Fries), the logical one (Lask), the methodological one (Cassirer), and the metaphysical one (Paulsen). It seemed to me that
Kant's transcendental thinking can be understood only if one
rejects these interpretations, which lead onto unequivocal, objective tracks, and throws oneself instead with Kant into the language
of symbols, guided by multifarious threads, any one of which
may contradict any other one, so long as one takes the guiding
lines themselves as direct assertions. One only begins to understand, if, with Kant, one ascertains that which, touched by all
guiding lines although struck by none, in the totality of this
only seemingly perplexing procedure becomes beautifully clear.
But, whether or not, in this interpretation, I have correctly
understood Kant, both historically and factually, (I have not yet
published my Kant-interpretation, although I have been teaching
it for thirty years), that which through all this I began to see
clearly for the first time was the method of thinking the Encompassing.

The basic question came to be this: shall we be satisfied with
knowledge of tangible objects — and reject all thinking which
goes beyond this as "empty chatter," as "romantic fancy," as
"metaphysics"? — in other words: shall we practice science only
and not philosophy? and use the noble name of philosophy
superfluously for something which actually is science and which
retains nothing of the character of more than a thousand years
of philosophy? As something new it would be better if it would
name itself after its new content: logistics, phenomenology,
anthropology, under all of whose names scientific knowledge is
indeed gained, even though in most cases mixed with no longer
scientific, philosophical impulses, hidden from themselves.

This same basic question sounds different, if we ask: shall we
give up the basic operation just because we are not immediately
successful?, and, by doing so, remain under the spell of the
objects which are taken for absolute reality or of the propositions
which claim absolute validity?

The answer is already anticipated in the way in which this
question has been put. To this we must add: such resignation
and renunciation are not possible even for one who is willing. For,
whoever rejects philosophizing, unavoidably practices philosophy

after all; although he doesn't know it, he practices an unnoticed, bad philosophy. It develops — even though it cannot be implemented here — that, in absolutizing science, there either occur unnoticed presuppositions of precisely that kind of bad philosophic character, or that the truly strict and ceaseless analysis of unfounded presuppositions leads to bottomlessness, since nothing is any longer certain in any absolute sense, but only in the relative: if . . . then.

But if philosophy itself is chosen, then it demands today what it has always demanded: a turn-about or conversion or rebirth in thinking. This is a matter which must be treated in a philosophical work. The part of thinking in this transformation may be formulated something like this: to carry out the basic philosophical operation, to think about objects in non-objective terms, to jump over one's own shadow in thinking, to think in methods which in using the intellect go beyond the intellect. But it is again all too easy to misunderstand the nature of this transformation. If we say: going beyond the intellect, we must add at once: without losing one's head. In the breadth of philosophizing this means: the sciences do remain presuppositions of philosophizing, not as if philosophical truth were grounded in them, nor as a court of higher appeal upon which philosophy would depend, but because they are unavoidable and inviolable. Today the historically new phenomenon of modern science gives to all philosophizing a different degree of methodical clarity and a different breadth of objective orientation than ever existed before. As a result, philosophy today has a new, great opportunity, which until now she has by no means convincingly grasped to any degree commensurate with her high, original descent. Philosophy has the sciences as presupposition, without itself being a science and without itself making any of the claims of science. But philosophy comes forward with the higher claims which arise out of the Encompassing.

Against this basic attitude of philosophizing within the Encompassing, which expresses itself in the design of specific philosophic methods, the methods of transcending, and then in a sharp distinction between science and philosophy, objections have been raised. They occur again, in a new and impressive form, among some of the contributors to this volume:

1. I am being charged with absolutizing the finiteness of man and the finiteness of our thinking. To this I reply: to bring this finiteness to clarity in our consciousness in very definite outlines

is the condition, first of all, of our veracity, secondly, of the meaningfulness of the task we set ourselves, and, thirdly, of the true basic constitution of the consciousness of freedom as concerns our potential *Existenz*. But in each move of these ascertainments finiteness touches the infinite. In the consciousness of the limit finiteness is being transcended. In the consciousness of being granted to oneself in freedom there is also given the certainty of the infinite potentiality and the infinite meaning of *Existenz*.

2. The attempt to reach the non-objective — even though by means of the guiding thread of objects — is said to constitute an impossibility. This attempt would abolish the ability to think at all, would demand the doing of something absurd, namely to think without thinking. One simply can not jump across one's own shadow.

Against this stands our philosophical thesis, which we are trying to confirm in factual philosophical thinking in areas of metaphysical speculation, as it has been carried out by the greatest philosophers. It runs: Although no thinking is without object, the non-objective becomes noticeable as soon as the question concerning the function of the objective is raised. Or: the non-objective Encompassing itself is being conceived in the objective; directly, in the contents of the thought of living practice where subject is matched with object; indirectly, in philosophizing which would like to bring the Encompassing to consciousness. This philosophizing is a transcending of the objective. Its methods are multiple, they arrange philosophizing in itself, and they produce the sublime fabric of philosophy in the first instance as a matter for the few. But this matter concerns man as such. It brings to clarity merely what, without reflection, is being done or can be done by every human being in his '*existential*' reality.

The ascent to the niveau of philosophical thought by way of reflection is opposed today by the presupposition that truth is accessible to common sense without ado. That it lies on the same plane of thinking with any kind of knowledge whatsoever. Of aid against this presupposition and a plea for the ascent, however, is the age-old Asiatic as well as Occidental philosophic insight that by knowledge we do not merely increase the range of our information, but we can rise by steps in the ways of thinking itself. If this succeeds, we do not merely add to the endless information about things, but, by our ability to engage in a new type of thinking, increase our insight into the whole, and gain thereby a new consciousness of being. From the higher level it is possible to see through the lower one, but not vice versa. The lower levels remain after the higher ones have been reached. They are surpassed only insofar as it is assumed that the Absolute, truth itself, has been seized on them; but they are not destroyed; for they fulfill a function for later thinking which may make use of them.

An example: All our knowing is in space and time. Reality is existence in space and time. What does not possess this existence is unreal. The soul is immortal, says faith. This is impossible, says our temporal knowledge based on experience. For the soul is bound to the body and to its functions. Dreamless sleep already brings unconsciousness without memory and without awareness of the present. In death this not-being of the soul becomes absolute, for now even the possibility of awakening, which even in deep sleep is still possible because of the continuing life of the body, is extinguished. Philosophizing, however, arrives at the insight that space and time are the forms of perception in the world of appearance, in which we live, think, and know, not the in-itself of Being proper. This insight is common both to the classical Occidental as well as to Asiatic philosophy, which, though they differ in method and aim, are in formal agreement in principle. This insight implies something which leads to paradoxical assertions, but assertions which are paradoxical only in the world of appearance, not in their proper sense: what is eternal is decided in time, — immortality is our eternal presence (we are conscious of it in high moments which efface time), — with what we essentially are, we are secure in eternity. Such sentences say nothing so long as we remain in our thinking in the world of appearance. They look fraudulent here, if they seem to want to explain away mortality in time. Rather, such statements are ways of expression arising out of a type of thinking which can be achieved, not in the form of expanded knowing information, but as a transformation of basic consciousness. How this is to be achieved, this is the task of philosophy. Thinking within the world of appearance leads to limits. When these latter become clear on the intellectual level, there remain two possibilities: the not-knowing which remains indifferent and does not take the unknowable into consideration; and, the possible jump to another level of thought which, however, is reached only simultaneously with one's own essential transformation.

If this succeeds, with one stroke all the great myths, symbols, and dogmas from the history of our faith — after their apparent annihilation by a type of enlightenment which was bad because it could not see through itself but absolutized itself — gain new meaning. On the lower level of thought they are the forms of knowing about the eternal in a materialistic form. The symbols, myths and dogmas are seemingly identified with the realities of the world of appearance, even though the — still unclear — honesty of pious faith practically bars such identification. On the higher level they become the language of reality proper, which speaks into the world of appearance and is addressed by us human beings. Within these languages, within their manifoldness, then, the struggle for genuine reality takes place; but now on a level where this struggle is meaningful. It takes place without materializing what is thought, but rather by virtue of the realization of potential *Existenzen,* which latter hear therein their language in an historically manifold, by us nowhere surveyable, fashion.

3. These difficulties of thinking, these claims which seem impossible of fulfillment, would all disappear if one objection were correct, which says: Objective knowing reaches farther than the positions which are now called "phenomenalistic" would like to admit as true; it is possible even to think the deity; objective intention does not imprison our consciousness in the mere appearance of existence, but is capable to light up the very foundation of things.

Collins, indeed, finds my differentiation between science and philosophy interesting, but he annuls it in essence because he recognizes only two levels of the one knowledge of being which is always objective. He compares my differentiation with Maritain's between empiriological and ontological knowledge. The former is appropriate to sensory objects insofar as they are observable and measurable; the latter applies to the world as a whole, to the self and to God. Both are knowledge in the sense of knowledge of something.

Thyssen turns against my "epistemology" in the very same way. Not only appearance but also being-in-itself can be perceived as object. Concerning my radically different way of thinking he opines that in it an enmity against objective knowledge finds expression. This basically irrationalistic character is said to be a part of existentialist philosophy as such. Against this charge I must protest. I philosophize neither irrationalistically nor rationalistically, but I feel that I find each unique form and figure of thinking in its own particular place. Enmity against objective knowing is so foreign to me that, on the contrary, I manifest in my writings not merely an unconditional interest in science and have myself participated in scientific research, but have also attested at every opportunity that no philosophy can succeed without science. My elaboration of the forms of thinking the non-objective has its motivation in my desire for the maximum of objectivity. Only on its guiding thread is the non-objective accessible. For, we always gain satisfaction only in objective thinking and reject the kind of abstraction to which the unphilosophical intellect tends to lean.

In regard to the specific area of the philosophical illumination of *Existenz,* which cannot become an object of investigative psychology, Earle raises the same objection. I agree with Earle that in my writings the concepts "object" and "objectivity" are employed in a wider and in a narrower sense and are, therefore, not unequivocal. I admit that it is a separate problem whether and to what extent spatial intuition becomes the prototype of all objectivity (time is intuited by me as a line which I draw, — non-Euclidean geometry is indirectly intuited in a projection onto Euclidean geometry, — V-1 as a sign on paper constitutes the remnant of spatial intuition, from the guiding thread of which I cannot absolutely free myself in thinking, — in these examples the intent of the relation of the spatial to what is meant in thought is different every time). I admit that here the vast problem of the objectivity of universals is touched upon.

What I cannot grant to Earle is that this affects or refutes what I mean by the sentence: *Existenz* cannot become an object. The form of my expression may, in some specific sentences, not have been too happy and this fact may justify the critic in his demand that I should speak more precisely. What really is at stake is this: I cannot think without objectivity. What I think and what I know moves necessarily into some form of objectivity. This latter is either the matter at hand or else refers to it. If it refers only, that which is meant is something else and is insofar — even though not adequately objective — nevertheless an intended objective as something which is not I. But, whenever objectivity refers to what I am, or can be, myself, there whatever stands inadequately over against me in the objective, whatever is indirectly hit upon in thinking is, at the same time, what I am myself and, therefore, what I can fulfill in thinking in a way radically different from any other inadequate objective thought: by means of my inner activity, by means of what I am, of what I can be (as Earle, indeed, reports quite correctly in the beginning of his critique).

The question is: by what methods do I ascertain a type of thinking in which I am able to come to myself while thinking in objectivities, at the same time transcending them, meaning something which is not something else, but which I am myself? This is the age-old secret of self-consciousness, so easily spoken and, in its depth, so difficult to actualize in the present. My entire "illumination of *Existenz*" is meant to serve its enlightenment.

Here the discussion might proceed. I do not assert that I have achieved complete clarity; but I do claim that I am conscious of the problem (especially in my book, *Philosophie)* in a fashion which, insofar as I can see, is not refuted by Earle's arguments. The problem is present both in carrying out the illumination of *Existenz* as well as in thinking about it.

The objections of Collins, Thyssen, and Earle indicate a basic difference, a so far irreconcilable opposition which today expresses itself above all in Kantianism and Thomism. Whatever becomes object to and knowable by us is in some sense appearance, not Being itself (Kant) — our knowledge is able to grasp Being itself as thought object (St. Thomas). What motives confront each other in this opposition, what entangled multiplicity is at work in them on both sides, I can not even intimate here. The ways of testing, the methods of thought to be employed in arriving at a decision on this question, this is one of the great areas of modern philosophizing, where there is no poverty of ideas. In any case, what is at stake here is not knowledge of something specific, but rather the knowledge of knowledge: this is why this thinking moves in a circle, so that only the content and the capacity of the circle differ from each other. It is not yet the question about specific methods of research, but rather in which sense it is possible to speak of knowledge beyond research as well as in research itself. My own thinking moves within the Kantian position, as the critics have correctly pointed out.

I call attention to some of the consequences which ensue from turning to the one or to the other side.

1. In the Thomistic position I am constantly led to the things, from the sensory object of awareness all the way to the deity; in the Kantian I am led to a point where the basic operation of my thinking lifts this thinking itself to another level and only thus brings about the presupposition of philosophizing.

2. In the Thomistic position all questioning is dissolved in non-contradictory answers; in the Kantian one arrives at paradoxical assertions concerning the Encompassing. In the Thomistic position the being of finite, sensory being is as good as any other

being even as the being of God; in the Kantian there is a radical difference between appearance and the thing-in-itself. In the Thomistic position particular and total knowledge are differentiated, but both are recognized as knowledge; in the Kantian all knowledge is particular and belongs to the world of appearance; total knowledge is impossible; its place is taken by philosophizing in its soaring to totality as a kind of truth which differs in principle.

3. In the Thomistic position the following consequences have appeared without perhaps being altogether necessary: the hidden materialisation of Transcendence, the satisfaction of "common sense," which — no matter what is under discussion — gets its fingers on it, so to speak. Inasmuch as it is claimed that all processes of thinking are of a cognitive character, the universal validity of such cognition is demanded. This is joined with the orthodoxy of faith, so that it is not considered absurd to confess that one believes to know by means of an universally valid proof (namely, the existence of God as in the oath of Catholic Modernism). Against the objections of factual knowledge, however, the content of the knowing orthodoxy of faith becomes defenseless. Where it is a matter of materialisation, in the sense of assertions about realities in the world, this position can not maintain itself (a corpse cannot come alive, lift the cover of the casket and leave the grave). Where proof for the intellect is not possible (for the actuality of God, for immortality as continued life after death), there this thesis must be given up, at least insofar as it wanted to base itself on proof. The content of faith itself becomes thereby discredited. In the Kantian position, on the other hand, the world of the contents of faith and the forms in which they are thought becomes free precisely in virtue of the critical waiver of unfounded and false knowledge.

In the Thomistic position there is the assertion of mysteries which are revealed. They are super-rational and cannot be understood. They are to be accepted obediently by virtue of the authority of a last resort in the world, which claims to hand down this revelation by virtue of its plenary power. In the Kantian position this claim is denied, without rejecting it for anyone who believes to perceive it, so long as such a person does not want to force or exact the demand of others to accept the content of what is perceived in obedience to authority.—

Knauss made my concept of the Encompassing the object of an interpreting exposition and critique in his beautiful essay, which reached me only at the conclusion of my Reply. He sees the basic idea in its relation to the history of philosophy, draws a few basic lines in terms of his own emphases and transformations, and finally offers a few critical observations. The latter are levelled, not against my basic thought, but against my systematic exposition. He says: The seven modes of the Encompassing do not possess clear connections nor order. Consciousness-as-such enjoys pre-eminence as the all-inclusive structure of ourselves as thinking beings; at the same time, however, it is still only one mode alongside of others. The number of the modes of the Encompassing seems accidental. The derivation is missing. They appear to be an arbitrarily set down list. The manifoldness of the modes includes obviously heterogeneous appearances. Thus there is but one Transcendence, one world, one consciousness-as-such, but many existences and many *Existenzen*.

This criticism makes correct observations, but does not interpret them in my sense. I have expressly declared myself against any derivation. It is not a systematic viewpoint which yields the seven modes, but the conscious perception of each mode of the Encompassing in the process of transcending the subject-object division. Not arbitrariness, but the acceptance of having had the experience is the basis for the unfolding. Some of the modes, Knauss seems to think, could be dispensed with, and others might be added. Perhaps, I reply; let them try, I am eager to hear. For, I feel by no means certain to have found in my enumeration the definitive answer which corresponds to the ground of Being, precisely because there is lacking the derivation from a principle. That derivation is impossible, unless we could find that principle of Being from which everything that is or can be would have to be derived. That was the fruitless dream of the great speculative German idealists (Fichte, Hegel, Schelling) . The being alongside of each other of the modes of the Encompassing and then the pre-eminence of some of these is correctly observed by Knauss. I have discussed this in detail (cf. *Von der Wahrheit*, 123-150, 162-169, 217-222) . Each type gains pre-eminence in a certain sense, includes everything within itself, and then is one type alongside of others. As such, however, it retains the heterogeneity of its origin. The Encompassing can [therefore] not be a generic concept, whose kinds are the seven modes of the Encompassing. We must not let this unavoidable way of speaking deceive us.

My conception is not based on derivation nor is it arbitrary or based on the "togetherness" [of the types; it arose] out of being receptive to the way in which I find myself in the world, [coupled] with the will to neglect nothing which occurs in my experience. The basic constitution in which we find ourselves, the ideas which occupy us, the impulses which motivate us are by no means unequivocal and not at all unitary. By way of similes we can circumscribe it with many sentences: We have thrown ourselves into it (Plotinus), or, we are thrown into it (St. Augustine), we are over-powered, we float freely in the bottomless, we expand, we narrow ourselves, we lose ourselves and get into the rising tide, a world is building itself in us, the world disappears like a dream confronted by an absolute Transcendence. With many other similes there is circumscribed what, thus brought to our attention, is always different. The One, the same fails to appear.

In this basic situation of our being human we ascertain for ourselves what it is possible basically for us to know. I have tried not to get hooked by one of the similes, by any single experience, or by one thought-construction. The greatest possible inclusiveness was my aim. But this enterprise is bound to get stuck in the paradox of wanting thoughtfully to assign to every type of experience, to every possibility its "place," without knowing the country as a whole in which the "places" lie; or thus: to assign to everyone his room, without knowing the building in which the rooms are. The consequence is a basic knowledge of the Encompassing, which is suspended, which cannot be brought to a common denominator, cannot be derived from any principle, and yet is somehow expanding.

Dissatisfaction is bound to remain whenever such knowledge is measured by the absolute total-knowledge which has so often been deceptively attempted. This dissatisfaction finds two philosophically legitimate ways which are necessarily trod. The one way is that which finds fulfillment not in the philosophical thought-structure, but in each specific historical realization, for which philosophizing is preparation and remembrance. Philosophy must not become sufficient unto itself, since it possesses the open flank towards reality, which it completes. Only taken together with reality is philosophy true. The other way is to find the better, the more profound and the purer in the philosophical thought-realm itself. This is the direction in which Knauss' criticism points, and rightly so. But, how can one proceed further?

Knauss proposes two possibilities. The first of these, as over against my development of the modes of the Encompassing, asks for the presuppositions. "What this ground is on which Jaspers finds himself in the first place, when he asks concerning the nature of Being, remains yet to be examined." After the first transformation of the question concerning Being (as I have carried it through and described) a second transformation would have to be demanded: as what must Being be pre-understood in order that it may be re-recognized in such modes of appearance? Knauss' radical position takes its formal justification from a general philosophical principle: to inquire constantly into the unnoticed presuppositions of our thoughts. But this principle makes sense only in factual performance, i.e., in the substantial demonstration of such presuppositions, from which there follows restriction as well as establishment of the ideas which refer to that presupposition. The principle is, on the other hand, unproductive so long as it is abstractly expressed. For in this case it leads into an empty infinity, into that agonizing progression which finds rest only in the circle of a closedness of the endless.

It is the big problem of the beginning in philosophy as well as in thinking. The beginning is a presupposition, something previously given, a pre-conscious, something that was before; cognate things return in analogous forms: if I awaken, it is out of preceding sleep; if as a child I become conscious, it is out of a world which produced me; if history starts, it is out of prehistoric conditions. With each beginning a prior is presupposed. In thinking the procedure follows from presuppositions which are not grounded in thought-movements, i.e., from thinking which is simply an accepting. The accepted may, of course, be questioned. One may begin with other, contradictory, presuppositions. Where a philosophical system is desired, it demands a principle: whence comes this principle? The system presupposes itself. When the question concerns the totality of Being, it runs: whence does it come?; if the reply is: by God's creation, the question becomes: whence is God?, which, in philosophical abstraction, amounts to: why is anything at all, why is there not nothing? (Schelling)

We always begin, so to speak, in the middle, whence we proceed backward and forward, outward and inward. In this we are driven ahead by the challenge to ask for the presuppositions, the pre-givens, the pre-conscious. But in order to be able to ask, we must first of all jump into the midst and begin factually to see where and how we are. Knauss' challenge to ask for the presuppositions may be allowed, but under the condition to show what in any specific instance becomes visible thereby. The abstract assertion that we proceed from the pre-given is always correct, but as such is still unfruitful.

The second way which Knauss proposes in connection with the

first is the attempt at maximum formalisation. He makes the demand for an encompassing, no longer contentual, logic, whereas my sketch of the Encompassing is said to be bound by content.

My reply is: Try and see what will happen! I do not know what the result will be. Form and content are categories, which on their part can not claim absolute validity which precedes everything else. In their meaning and ramifications they are shown up in a system of categories and are thereby at the same time being delimited. They are a pair of categories among other equally essential ones which are appropriate for making ideas thinkable. In the conception of my sketch of the modes of the Encompassing I would not ascribe any decisive significance to this pair (of categories). They themselves are a simile when it comes to the unfolding of basic knowledge.

Knauss himself has already tried himself out on the road to formalisations, in his excellent treatise (*Gegenstand und Umgreifendes,* Basel, 1953). Insofar as these formalisations work in mathematics and logistics I presume that they have extraordinary philosophical significance, without, however, seeing a clear possession as yet. It would be the sketch of an encompassing logic which as logic fails and thereby offers in thinking a pointer by means of thinking.

Philosophically it would be of extraordinary significance to be able to demonstrate the failure of thinking by way of formalisations (something of this spirit seems to impress one rather strangely in the works of Wittgenstein). The failure of thinking at limits recognized by thinking itself and compellingly performed, would thereby open up indeterminable realms. The involuntary and philosophically ancient equation of thought and Being, of Logos and world, would be radically abolished by this insight, [and this] not merely for experiencing, emotion, and irrational experience.

But such an encompassing logic would not be the formalisation of the sketch of the Encompassing, in which content and form are indivisible. What Knauss means here by formalisation I shall only know after he has carried it out. His buoyancy indicates that he is being led by something which must have substance.

8. About Psychology

I began as a psychopathologist, psychology was the subject of the work of my youth, and to this very day I am attached to it.

From the very beginning I was conscious of the limits of psychology. In order to save the sick person from a pseudo-knowledge of the physician, I spoke at that time of the infinity and inexhaustibleness of each mentally ill patient. The title of my inaugural lecture of 1913 was: "Concerning the Limits of Psychology."

Working out the methods of psychological research, of its meaning and its limits (in my *Allgemeine Psychopathologie*) had a double significance, therefore: the furtherance of the purity, productivity, and determination of psychological research, on the one hand, and, on the other, keeping open the space at the limits of knowledge, its protection against veiling and confusing pseudo-knowledge.

It was a joy for me to see my work in this field highly valued in this volume by experts in psychology and psychiatry (Kolle, Lefebre). All the greater is my interest in hearing their criticism. To these must be added as essential the critiques which on principle put in question my delimitation of scientific psychology from philosophy (Earle, Kunz).

a) Kolle's basic conceptions are in such wide agreement with my own that I find little to say by way of reply. Nevertheless, his critical remarks, since they grow out of common soil, are by no means incidental.

Kolle's objection that I am not doing justice to the realities of the physician's every-day experience is probably analogous to the reproach, raised elsewhere, against the aristocratic tone of my philosophy. He seems to think that I demand too much. In the first place, of the physician himself: I might possibly be right in my assumption that there are rare individuals who can do without training analysis, because they could illuminate themselves. For most people, however, direction by an expert would be the desirable aid in training analysis in order for them to take a few steps on the road to their true self. The masses in the modern world need many good psychiatrists, who, themselves belonging to the mass, could not be those rare select individuals, but who themselves would need training analysis in order to arrive at the attitude which would make them equal to their great task. Next, Kolle thinks, I am expecting and demanding too much of the patient. I over-estimate, he says, the person of the good average, I idealize him in an unpermissible fashion. The great mass needs the little remedies, among which he also counts psychotherapy.

These conceptions of Kolle's, prejudicious to man in the mass, whether for physicians or for patients, seem to be contradicted by his sentences which he formulates as the advocate of both: "However, in our unpretentious activity we physicians do not wish to stand there as expellees, who have nothing to offer to men except communication in the garment of questionable truth." And of the patients he says: ordinary men often are animated by the divine spark and in that spark are to be addressed in proper fashion.

In reply to these difficulties Kolle cites an oral expression of mine: the psychotherapist must be tolerant in action, the philosopher intolerant in thinking. Should I have said this, the sentence is ambiguous. What I mean is this: In the illumination of principles our standards should be as high as possible, we should discuss the meaning of unconditional decisions without reservation. Here there can be no compromise. In practice, however, we all experience our insufficiency. In the area which is illumined by those philosophical movements of thought, we do, out of historical responsibility, whatever is possible in view of the situations. Thereby it turns out that those self-contradictory sentences of Kolle do not at all contradict each other. For, in the situation which immediately requires action the physician is forced to apply "little remedies," even ineffectual ones; he must do the best possible for the patient, without full acknowledgment of the truth as the wiser one not tell everything. Yet, the same physician sees in the very same patient, whom, for the moment, he leads because of the patient's spiritual and *existential* helplessness, the "divine spark" and does whatever he can in order to further the conditions by which this spark can be kindled into a flame.

The truth is, there is no solution of this problem except by the reality of the physician in each singular situation. In the discussions about what is to be done and to be demanded in general — for example, about training analysis, or the application of Freudian psychoanalysis as such — one can give both reasons and also raise objections. But, eventually a point is reached where the practice, training and education of the physician depend on *existential* decisions of each specific individual. These must not be anticipated or violated by any coercion in the form of a prescribed education or by the demands of examinations.

Hereby it could become apparent that in today's spiritual world-situation errors have crept into psychotherapy, which can be scientifically perceived and philosophically illumined.

If I assert that training analysis, as rule and prescription, actually disturbs or even hinders the genuine illumination of life, this is no aristocratic opinion out of contempt for the masses.

Rather, what is at stake is insight into the essence of such illumination by inner action, as it has taken place in the entire philosophical tradition. Stimulated by the texts and by association with those who have become wise, each individual can be brought on the road to himself only by himself. For the self-illumination in inner activity (in contrast to mere psychological observation of inner phenomena) there can be no self-observation under the control of others. Such "controlled self-observation" is a deceptive euphemism. It is precisely by this that a deviation from one's own real self to an imaginary self occurs, a deviation from genuine freedom to pseudo-freedom, from the openness of one's nature to delight in spiritual violence.

But what happens if training analysis belongs to the education of masses of physicians in order to supply the masses of men with a sufficient number of "good psychotherapists"? Shall the "experts" who direct the training analysis themselves belong to the "select group" or to the "masses"? In the latter case, does not the training analysis become a technique of "non-selected" ones for the "non-selected," whereby self-illumination loses its essence? For, such training analysis, if it were to be realized, would endlessly slide into the non-essential, it would be guided by alternating dogmatic theories even to the accidental pleasure in some customary jargon. Real direction on this road is in principle impossible. For, direction takes place not by way of scientific information (except for particular purposes) but by faith. True faith has its origin in historical greatness and tradition, and understands itself in an objectivity of an entirely different character from that of scientific knowledge. Throughout modern psychoanalytic therapy many types of faith are present in confusion. But there remains the lack of clarity concerning the type of faith and its direction which makes so many deceptions possible. Objective ascertainment of faith by symbols, speculative ideas, and philosophical transcending is replaced by supposedly scientific information and its application by a theoretically oriented and "practically experienced" psychotherapist. But this practical experience also is a questionable basis if the experiences are not clearly communicable.

The difference between modern, altogether faithless psychoanalysis (whose pseudo-faith as concerns its type of thinking I formerly compared with the type of faith of Marxism and of Racism), on the one hand; and that of illuminating and life-directing exercises which mold the mind and which take place under genuine direction of faith, on the other, is shown when one casts a look upon the exercises of the Jesuits or upon the meditation exercises of the Buddhists. That would lead us too far here. My fervor, objected to by my critic, in the struggle against these modern movements of faith rests not merely upon the will to scientific clarity in knowing, but also upon the philosophical faith which turns against forms of pseudo-faith that are mistaken, unable to see through themselves, uncritical and contentually so very meager.

With this I have reached Kolle's objection to my critique of Freud, in which I am said to be going "too far." In the specificities of my criticism Kolle agrees with me all along the line. Only at one point, where actually we are also in agreement, does he raise an objection: in consequence of a misunderstanding. The neurosis, he says, is not merely characterised by a conversion of emotional difficulties into bodily events, but manifests itself also in the mental phenomena themselves. Now this has been set forth by me many times. At the place cited by Kolle it is merely passed over. But, the essential point is this: These mental conversions are, as neurotic ones, conditioned by meaningless, extra-conscious "mechanisms," which we do not know, but which are the specific causes of these phenomena. What really matters is the truth that, in the first place, meaningful connections or freedom are neither healthy nor sick, and that, secondly, the acts of evading, repressing, forgetting, and circumventing necessary decisions do not as such by any means cause illness or neuroticism, but only occur with the added, and to us till now unknown, conditions, which are by no means peculiar to all men, but merely to a small minority, namely to the neurotics.

The questions that arise at this point refer in the final analysis to the struggle for true forms of faith, which may be many, and against faithless substitutes which threaten to overpower humanity today.

As concerns the specific question of training analysis I remain, therefore, true to my philosophical insight: the demand for the training analysis to be carried out on oneself by another as condition for admission to psychotherapeutic practice is an act of spiritual violence. Training analysis is open to anyone, but may not be demanded of anyone. Kolle, it seems to me, has, in his tolerance as a physician, in his "psychiatric gentleness" — a spiritual attitude which I share with him — erroneously made a concession to his fellow-psychotherapists, the consequence of which may very well be far greater than he thinks.

An entirely different point of Kolle's critique is the reproach that I am said to reject every kind of eugenic action too radically.

He points to the increase of the inferior, to the danger of suppression, elimination and disappearance of valuable minorities, a danger which, with the increase of the world's population, has grown enormously. I do not hide from myself the threatening picture of a future dominated by ever less valuable masses of men as far as the facts have been established. I can not offhand reject Kolle's critique of my position, briefly expressed in my psychopathology. For further discussion I would like to call attention only to a few points of view:

The entire question does not lie merely in the area of knowledge, but also concerns the Ethos for which the respective individual is determined to live. Eugenic intervention, on the basis of knowledge, with the purpose to better our race or, at any rate, not to permit it to deteriorate, leads, from my point of view, finally to wars of extermination of races against each other or else to acts of murder on entire groups of men. The harmless beginning, which appears so rational, accomplishes practically nothing. In some specific instance, the prevention of reproduction seems, within our knowledge, well justified. But in intervening by force, an attitude has been arrived at where man thinks he can and may dispose of man in general on the basis of his knowledge. The question is one concerning the limit of human planning. The concrete answer is so complicated that it cannot even be begun here. However, the simple last question always remains: who disposes of whom? Not a knowing God of men, but here men with their limited knowledge and even without knowledge dispose of men by virtue of their power. Selection among men, in order to rob the selected ones unilaterally of their freedom, is an act which in history has been carried out again and again, and which today is supposed to be carried out on the basis of genetic biology. I resist this as a border-transgression on the part of man at a point where, for want of sufficient knowledge, he has to leave the course of events in the hands of what is unknown to him, if he wants to preserve human freedom. The relatively small number of cases, which, on the basis of definitive knowledge, reasonably should not reproduce themselves, are to be handled by persuasion. When persuasion proves unsuccessful, accepting the irresponsible might actually be better here than the abolition of freedom by force. In many supposedly certain instances current opinion often is not even correct. The reproduction of schizophrenics, for example, occurs in the majority of instances before the outbreak of the illness; the illness appears too late to serve in preventing reproduction. The probability of the occurrence of mental illness among the descendants of schizophrenics is, although greater than in the case of healthy persons, still only quite limited, barely going beyond ten per-cent. This knowledge is entirely fluid, exceedingly interesting, but very difficult to achieve.

Whether perhaps a general limitation of reproduction of mankind could and should take place by means of mutuality of contract, I do not here consider. Where there is contract, there is freedom. Not a selected number is being restricted by others, but all are being restricted in mutuality. This would no longer be eugenics, which — as is shown by unbiased critical examination of the facts, — is very well possible for types of animals desirable to man, but not for human beings, which transcends merely racial being.

b) Lefebre has briefly paraphrased the principles of my methodological foundation of the entire realm of psychological research. In doing so he has designated my enterprise as a change of locale of psychology. I consider this characteristic, introduced by Lefebre, excellent. He recognizes that the totality of psychological methods presupposes the psychologist who uses them. This "introducing of the psychologist into psychology," as he calls it, means that the meaning of the totality of these methods and knowledge crumbles and loses its validity, if the psychologist does not direct it in each concrete situation. But he is this psychologist only insofar as he illumines himself philosophically.

The opposite of this would be a psychologist who himself would be a mere point of knowledge, exchangeable for any other who can learn the same knowledge, and who would be willing to let himself be led in practice by the content of psychological knowledge. The genuine psychologist applies the possibilities of scientific knowledge out of an enveloping consciousness, which latter unites him with the man and patient who confronts him. The spurious psychologist thinks he can transfer extant knowledge technically into actual application in such fashion that he himself becomes a mere function of this knowledge.

Lefebre follows his precise presentation with a critique, in which, out of his own earnest experience, he thinks he recognizes a deficiency in my founding and ordering of psychological knowledge. He sees this in my reservations and partial rejection of the attempts to make a conception of man, based on Heidegger's *Daseinsanalytik* (analysis of existence, cf. *Sein und Zeit),* the foundation of its total view. Lefebre develops his critique on the basis of this *Daseinsanalytik.* His critique makes three points:

first, he claims that I hold fast to the subject-object division, and therefore, secondly, I do not sufficiently nor in principle distinguish between syncretic and linear thinking, nor, in the third place, between experience and behavior.

The principle of all these deficiencies is said to be that I am "too much committed to the subject-object division." He quotes Binswanger as saying that for experiencing, as it appears to the experiencing subject, there is no such thing as a division between subject and object. To experience and to experience the world are identical. The investigation of the nature of such worlds, of world-designs, is to be placed in the center of psychological consideration. Then the subject-object division — that "cancer of all psychology up till now" (Binswanger) — would be overcome. This study of the "worlds," Lefebre opines, would be the natural completion of Jaspers' psychology.

However, this completion has, obviously, two sides, which I do not find considered either by Lefebre nor by the *Daseins*-analysts: the demands for the extension of the object of psychological research, and the demand for the self-illumination of the psychologist. We must, therefore, turn our attention first to the patient and then to the psychotherapist.

First the patient: Lefebre thinks that I probably know those three points of his listed criticism and also make the distinctions which are demanded in those points. The deficiency is said to consist in the fact that I do not assign to those points the central position which is their due. What follows from the polarity and the overcoming of the subject-object division, I should have used as continuous principle of order throughout alongside of my order according to methods.

I answer Lefebre that the subject-object division remains the indispensable medium of every searching knowledge, of every science. Of whatever I speak in psychology, by doing so it becomes an object. The distinction between the subject of the investigator and the object of what has been investigated is irrevocable in scientific research. To hold fast to this distinction is a condition of any scientific research and of barring their becoming confused with philosophically transcending thought-movements. Such confusion results in the blurring of both.

Something altogether different is the Encompassing, wherein as psychologist I live and think, and wherein man, whom I am psychologically investigating, moves on his part. When I represent this as that which the subject-object division has not yet reached or is again overcoming, I either make it into an object and de-nature it, or else I philosophize and enable it thereby to display itself more brightly.

It is this de-naturing objectification which the psychologist carries out because he attempts every possible type of objectification. In my *Psychopathologie* I have done this under the title *"Weltpsychologie"* and delimited it critically. Because I can only speak of something by making it an object, objectification wins its place, but only as *verstehende* description of conditions, of sick constitutions in a world, such as the *Daseins*analysts have carried out. They did this in continuing former attempts, such as, for example, the depicting of schizophrenic worlds by Bleuler. Thereby they increased not merely our descriptive psychological language but also the knowledge of the objectified appearance of such conditions.

Kolle, too, touches upon these discussions by Lefebre. Kolle thinks that I am going too far in my criticism of psychiatric *Daseins*analysis. To this I reply that, insofar as it has any descriptive meaning, I have actually taken it into my psychopathology. What I resist is the notion as if there were something like a falling ill of meaningful existence as a whole, or, otherwise expressed: that an illness, conceived as a transformation of existence, in essence has its own meaning by virtue of a new and basic way of being-in-the-world. Psychiatric *Daseins*analysis denudes illness of its character as alien to meaning. To this I reply: what is thus grasped would no longer be illness. What is thus seen appears to me as a phantom. Psychiatric *Daseins*analysis as a means of describing mental conditions is to be examined with a view to the power it has to recognize definite, again-recognizable conditions of sick persons. For this it has, on occasion, proved useful, for example in regard to epileptic conditions. But most of what has been published under this heading, insofar as it came to my attention, is just talk, not knowledge. What I oppose here is that the concept of sickness is made unclear in principle.

Secondly, the psychologist and psychotherapist: The completion demanded by Lefebre would, according to him, fill the gap which I am supposed to have left by omitting the analysis of the living experience of the psychologist, thereby omitting what is precisely the foundation of all his methods. *Verstehen* and explanation, which I am said to be merely distinguishing, would, so he thinks, have to be referred to realms of experience. Only then would the instruments become clear which implement *Verstehen* and explanation. Then, too, the thinking which is already directed, towards objects would be differentiated from the syncretic experience of the psychologist himself, and the relationship of precisely this syncretic experience to its *Verstehen* would become clear.

I answer Lefebre that his noble desire, which is quite suited to him as a psychotherapist and which he realizes by his humane efforts, simply cannot be fulfilled in psychological knowledge. What he is aiming at may very well be the profoundest truth of the *'existential'* psychotherapist, but it is no object of psychological knowledge. That truth disappears the moment I try to investigate it psychologically.

It is, of course, true that the "instrument" of the *verstehenden* psychologist is his own essence. "Each one sees what he carries in his heart." One may very well call the presence of the Encompassing in the psychologist a "syncretic experience." But what this experience is I do not grasp by directing my investigating gaze upon it (the possibility of illuminating philosophical and finally objectless thought-movements is something else again), but it shows itself in what it understands and makes communicable. This, however, is valid also: I understand not merely because I myself am what is understood and what I perform, but also because I understand what I can be, without being it, and perhaps, up to an indeterminate limit, even what I neither am nor can be.

The great attraction of psychiatric *Daseins*analysis lies in the fact that one means to light upon the deepest reality in the psychological object, in man as a patient, a reality which is identical with the reality in the observer, viz., in the psychologist and psychotherapist. The satisfaction derived from this process is not accidental. In fact, in the absence of a critical consciousness of methods it appears to me almost as a necessary deception. Psychiatric *Daseins*analysis, which started out as a modest method of description, quite conscious of its own limitations, turns into a ruinous inroad of philosophy into the object of research. But the truth-content of philosophy can never be an object of psychology. Philosophy in the psychologist should be rather the clarity of his accomplished knowledge of himself, from which follows the attitude of methodical self-limitation in research. This philosophical clarity furthers the veracity of knowledge as well as the integrity of one's own being. Through that confusion, however, a new substitute for faith becomes possible under the appearance of scientific knowledge.

Scientific psychology is methodologically manifold, ruptures the unity of man, and breaks up research into endless mutiplicity.

What Lefebre demands for the completion of this only possible psychology seems to me, in his own train of thought, very curious indeed. The gap which he wants filled up is precisely what he recognizes as my accomplishment, namely, the "bringing of the psychologist into psychology." It is as if he wanted to transform the philosophically self-illuminating psychologist — without whom psychological research and knowledge remains leaderless — himself now into an object of psychological research. Such introduction of the psychologist into psychology, however, would result in levelling the inquiring psychologist, who illumines himself philosophically, into an object of psychology alongside of others. Its presupposition would be the claim of a psychology which becomes a universal science, supersedes philosophy and becomes, so to speak, totalitarian.

The great verity that all of psychology is unable to lead the way, but in its practical application requires something which itself is no longer psychology, namely the *Existenz* of the psychologist, — this verity misleads to the deception that this *Existenz* itself could again become an object of psychology. Thereby psychological knowledge becomes sovereign. The consequences which can be observed — not in Lefebre but elsewhere — are: The psychification of all being, of man and of the world; the transformation into a psychical object of every *Existenz* which is able to come to itself in all types of the Encompassing. The earnestness, which finds its genuine direction in the objectivities of the content of faith and in the medium of philosophical thought-movements, is being replaced by the applicability of what has become known through scientifically achieved knowledge as the final court of appeal. There arises an awful methodological and '*existential*' confusion. This happening is a part of that universal modern trend of the transformation of religion, of philosophy, and of education into psychology and its application. But psychology as research and teachable knowledge can always extend only to methodically and critically perceivable particularities. Insofar as it claims to be the locus which sets the goal it leads to an emptying of life and to an absence of earnestness. When the betrayed modern man, having lost himself in business, sensations, and pleasures, feels himself unhappy, he goes to the psychologist. Both no longer know what happiness is and together put on a dance which, for a while at least, manages to deceive about the growing emptiness. This transformation of everything into an object of psychology is one instance of the phenomenon of the loss of faith, which manages to veil itself in the rush after remedies which only increase the loss.

True enough, these events constitute a threat to being-human, but they do not at all imply a fateful total process to which everyone would have to adapt himself. Nietzsche's "God is dead," — with him the expression of terror and of a nihilistic will, together with the impulse to get beyond both —, as an expression of knowledge in the philosophy of history, taken over from him, is simply false. In that case it is merely an epigonal negative acknowledgment of the emptiness in virtue of not taking one's own practice of life seriously.

Lefebre did not turn his attention to these relationships because they do not concern him at all. He would, therefore, rightfully reject these discussions as a critique of his position. Nevertheless, it may perhaps be permitted, even against his claim, to call attention to what dare not be confused; not the physician with the priest, not the psychotherapist with the bringer of salvation, not psychological counselling with philosophical communication in loving struggle. True, both may combine with each other. But in that case one should honestly know what one is doing, what claim one is making, to what accomplishment one knows himself qualified. And in no case is it possible to integrate bringer of salvation, priest and philosopher into the psychological profession where performance is paid for in money, without their losing their essential character. Profession and performance happen on a level where something entirely different may enter anywhere like a gift from above: that free human activity arising from a higher authority, incalculable, unlearnable, unbelievable. But it does not belong to psychology.

I return to Lefebre's objection. He calls it paradox — and justifiably so — that at the end of a psychology like the one advocated by myself, which consistently carries through the distinction between subject and object (viz., in the attitude of psychological research), there is supposed to stand the annulment of this distinction. If, in spite of this, he holds this to be the natural completion of my psychology, he seems to me not to take cognizance of the following:

The endeavor to overcome the subject-object division, which he demands, is the fundamental concern of all my philosophizing. The ways of such overcoming, the performances of thinking in becoming conscious of the Encompassing, I have carried out in my philosophical, not in my psychological writings. The demanded completion does in fact exist, but as what it is: as the completion of psychology, of the sciences as such, by philosophy.

Where I make the psychological attempt to describe the states of the presence of the Encompassing as psychological states, I know that, despite all the inner perceptiveness of such description, the essential element escapes.

In philosophizing itself already lies the great temptation, in the very process of objectifying talk — which is the guide of that genuine philosophical assurance in the appeal, in awakening, in conjuring — to treat these objectifications as objects of knowledge. This is to slide from the seriousness of philosophy into the informality of knowledge, but in such a way that the satisfaction of knowing that man "is so" becomes at the same time a peculiar kind of dogmatism. It is that which gives to the pseudo-scientific efforts of some writings in *Daseins*analysis, it seems to me, that appearance of faith, which, despite the efforts in behalf of the convention of scientific language, even in its mood already has an unscientific effect.

Beyond his critique, Lefebre shows again an astonishingly close understanding for the basic attitude which realizes itself in my psychology and philosophy. It seems to me to be his own attitude. In expressing it, he says about me: that I attempt to take into consideration, both in theory and in practice, the being-alive of the real, existing man — who, in essence is potentiality — up to every single psychological action. That I am aiming to make man, whom as psychologist I make an object, as a philosopher free in his subjectivity. That I participate in the maximal and manifold objectification of man, without forgetting that man himself is in essence subject. That what Lefebre characterizes as the "change of locale in psychology," which he says has been undertaken in my work, is the way to remind the psychologist constantly that the objectivity, by which the psychologist thinks man, is never identical with the object of this thinking. For man is free, which is something that does not enter into any psychological objectification. Over against the psychology of any replaceable and entirely determined individual, i.e., against the psychology of manipulation, there stands my psychology of freedom. For this reason, he insists, a decision is necessary on the part of every psychologist, either for or against the psychology of freedom. I agree with this, with the exception of the paradoxical formulation "psychology of freedom." For the decisive element is precisely that this psychology leaves freedom untouched, cannot at all reach freedom. Man is more than he can know of himself psycho-

logically. In conclusion, Lefebre cites a few of my formulations
on this topic.

On the whole, therefore, my answer to him is as follows:
Lefebre is right in his demand for the completion of psychology
by philosophy on the part of the psychologist, who, *qua* psychologist, can never become in practice the last court of appeal. But
I must contradict him when it looks as if this completion could
be pulled into psychology itself by a sort of total psychology, which
latter would be neither accurate psychological knowledge nor
genuine philosophy.

c) Although by a different route and from other motives, it yet
seems to me that the critique of Earle is concerned with the same
problem. As object of his discussion he chooses not my psychological works, but my philosophical illumination of *Existenz*. Concerning it he attempts to show that, although it has made essential
contributions to the study of man, I had not correctly grasped
its factual meaning in the method of my procedure. For, I acknowledged that illumination neither as science, in the sense of
psychological knowledge, nor as a form of rational, scientific
philosophy. Actually, however, Earle thinks, it is science and it
is rational. My discovery, he thinks, stands up, but my conception
of it he thinks wrong.

Earle performs his simple and clear critique in the following
way. What I assert of the character of the illumination of *Existenz*,
he claims, is valid for all knowledge: indirect knowledge *about*
something instead of direct knowledge *of* something — the inex-
haustibility of the individual — the method of antithesis, and
their dialectic and synthesis. Consciousness of one's self, he claims,
is as objective as any knowledge.

Earle sets forth the following theses: Either something is known
in an objective way or else it is not known at all. If something
is not known at all, either directly or indirectly, our words become meaningless. Either there is no such thing at all as objective
knowledge, or the illumination of *Existenz* is a mode of such
knowledge.

When I say of the illumination of *Existenz* that it is not de-
scribable but only a matter for appeal, Earle does not wish to
object to the hortative way of speaking; but even the hortative
would be useful only if what is said has an objective character,
is communication of knowledge. To say what cannot be said
would make no sense hortatively either, since it would merely
be an ununderstandable summons.

If, concerning the illumination of *Existenz* I say that it is supposed to bring the thinker to himself, then this could make sense only if I say about myself what is true for all selves. If the reader understands my words, he must have what I am saying before his inner eye, and that is he himself insofar as he is like me. My reader then compares what I am saying concerning the self with what he knows, and thereby comes either to agreement or rejection. This, he claims, is the same concept of truth and falsity as in any other assertion.

On the basis of such criticism, Earle says how disappointing it is to learn, after reading a "brilliant" chapter, that none of this is to be understood as objective knowledge, but as an appeal to the reader to become himself. Earle affirms large parts of my illumination of *Existenz*, but insists that what this illumination produces is factually communicable knowledge of a difficult and subtle kind.

If Earle is thus able to accept the content of my illumination of *Existenz* as phenomenological description (as anthropology), it might seem that I should be satisfied. For, what really is at stake is the truth of the content, not the opinion concerning the form or sense in which the truth is uttered. By affirming the specific and only negating me from the point of view of the totality of the conception of science, Earle agrees with me in essence. However, this agreement seems to me to include much more than a mere acknowledgment of phenomenological descriptions. What are the grounds of such agreement? To me they appear as follows: they proceed from Earle's going along in terms of his own *'existential'* potentialities and realities, towards which many men seem to be blind or at any rate resistful. If the description were compelling for everyone, the surprise and concern over the fact that universal agreement is wanting would have to be great, indeed. In that case it could appear as if what is involved were only subjective arbitrariness and this would apply to such descriptions also. If what is involved, however, is truth, then it must obviously be truth of a character which is not accessible through mere description of a state, but only through a co-operative inner performance out of one's own readiness. We can think of this readiness as universally human because we live out of it unconditionally. But we must face up to the fact that this is something which is by no means universally accessible, conceivable or acknowledged as is scientific knowledge. By letting go of the claim to scientific validity I wanted to secure the sense of the unconditional truth of potential *Existenz* against the danger of seeing such philosophizing destroyed by declaring it to be unscientific.

It is an indubitable fact that, in the illumination of *Existenz,* I am constantly making use of conceptual schemes, which, as such, make assertions about structures, and which, as such, are to be culled out as systematic insights into such structures of being human, insights which can be found in great number in the history of philosophy. It is essential and notable, however, that I do not recite these structures outright nor as the main point. True enough, they play a rôle in the disposition of and offer guidance for changing formulations, but they are not the motors of the movement of thought. Furthermore, they are without claim to absolute validity. There are several schemes. They are tools of communication, not objects of knowledge. The freedom of my philosophizing, which appeals to freedom, has to make use of those tools and of the historically existing schemes demoted to tools, but it must not permit them to become the masters of thought. This would happen, however, if the matter itself would be thought to be known in them.

Actually there exists a radical difference between the phenomenology of consciousness and the illumination of *Existenz.* This difference would be badly designated if one were to call it a return from consciousness to what lies before consciousness and supports it; it is described more correctly as the leap from observing to philosophizing, that is, from knowing something to inner action through thinking.

Only in experiencing *Existenz*-illuminating thinking in a movement which leads to inner action can the ascertainment concerning the great difference take place: whether I know objects or guided by the objective meet the non-objective (be this accomplished in one's own *Existenz* or by touching Transcendence) — whether I acquire a generally valid point of view or become myself, — whether I confront the inexhaustible of an individual, examining it endlessly, or produce, as well as become filled with, an infinitely illuminable in the movement of thought.

Then the difference between scientific knowledge and philosophy, too, will become convincing, a difference which I have characterized as follows: in science the object itself is appropriately communicated; for comprehension it demands only the point of the universal intellect common to us all, called consciousness-as-such; — in philosophizing two wings have to flap in order to gain height; one is what is universally communicable in the philosophic texts; and the other is the, in each instance singular, irreplaceable *Existenz* which, in its historical completion in becoming itself, does precisely that which gives to the universal meanings of those texts their authentic sense.

One may ask whether, in such formulations, I do not over-reach myself, so that the content becomes absurd, because I seem to take what is senseless as something sensible. I confess that for me the decision between the being and not-being of philosophy lies precisely at this point. I suggest that the reader compare what was said concerning the objective in the section on the Encompassing (as well as the essay by Latzel).

d) Despite all the differences among themselves, three critics (Lefebre, Earle, and Kunz) meet at the same point, they aim to give to scientific psychology more room, more comprehensive possibilities, than, after methodical reflection, I am willing to grant to psychological knowledge. And they are inclined, so to speak, to annex performances of thinking, which I introduce as philosophical, as psychologically admissible knowledge. Lefebre demands a completion of my psychology in this sense. Earle takes my *Existenz*-illuminating presentations to be a phenomenology of inner structures, which — according to him — I misunderstand in their methodical sense. Kunz interprets a number of transcending philosophical thoughts from my writings as a *Verstehen* of psychological reality, which he on his part wishes to make accessible by conceiving of a pre-conscious basic occurrence of the soul. My conception of scientific psychology is too narrow for all three. They accuse me of rejecting what, in their opinion, is actually possible in psychology and what I had even in part contributed to it myself. I now turn to Kunz's essay, who, by way of a psychological theory, wishes to transform into psychology what occurs in my statements as Transcendence.

Kunz refers to the "fact" of an original certainty of death, which we are said to possess in distinction to the certainty of our own future death, a certainty which comes to us only from the outside by the experience of the death of others. From this "fact," — which he also calls "circumstance" — he reaches the conjecture that the pure act of thinking is already the mode of being presented with the loss of being. In contradistinction to the death which factually comes to every living being, "potential death" is said to be a constituent element of the essence of man. In contradistinction to mere thinking of death the "potential death," — also called possible or immanent death — is said to be that which precedes thinking, precedes thinking of death and precedes the approaching actual death as a basis of being human. The decisive step of this conjecture — which he also calls "hypothesis," — is said to be "to move back objectively known factual death, as potential death, into the non-objective dimension which is the source of the act of knowing." Only out of this, he thinks it possible "to understand the exceptional certainty of precisely this particular objective knowledge" (namely of death) ; for this knowledge "attains its elusive object from the objectification of its own origin." There the "happening in the foundation of being human" takes place. This potential death holds open an "inconceivable unfathomableness." From it there follow or become possible thought itself, then the conception of Transcendence, further the transformation of existence into *Existenz*, in fact there follows everything which makes man into man.

This psychological hypothesis — which, with its abstract ideas, can be understood only with some effort — appears to me to be a new example of those psychological theories whose sense, limitations, and errors I have discussed, for scientific and philosophical reasons, for decades (cf., for example, the chapter on "Theories" in my *Psychopathologie*). Often they can neither be proved nor disproved. Nothing results from them except an intellectual game. They become a torment in which, at one moment, knowledge is being feigned which then proves to be nothing. All these theories proceed from matters of fact and then interpret events by the construction of illustrations given in images. I now attempt a critique of the theory sketched by Kunz.

In the first place, the "fact" of the original certainty of death, which is said not to arise from the external experience of the dying of others, is questionable. There is also the contradictory fact: I do not believe in my death, even though I know by experience that it will occur; I am so penetrated by being alive as something inextinguishable that inwardly I do not realize death, even though I acknowledge it intellectually and must admit its reality for myself. Goethe expressed it thus: "If I work without rest to my end, then nature is obligated to assign another form of existence to me." It is the original certainty of "entelechy." True enough, "we are not equally immortal." In order to manifest one's self in the future as a great entelechy, "one must first be one." With that Goethe pointed to the possible difference of the consciousness of life and death. For some life has become forfeited to death; they live in the consciousness of their constant dying (of "potential death"). For others death is consumed in life. For them death seems to have no reality. The sole fact, which

Kunz claims, does not exist. If we objectifyingly describe such facts as "psychological states," then the question concerning the empirical connections out of which they have arisen is more essential for psychological research than the question concerning the content of such states. They depend, perhaps, upon a periodic change, upon conditions of illness and upon constitutions, which also have other empirical characteristics which occur together. By way of *verstehende* psychology one may further ask psychologically in what intelligible connection an apparently original consciousness of death — this pitch of a life's mood — might, perhaps, stand with abysmal disappointments, with radical failure, with a factual emptiness of life. To which ever observations and descriptions these questions may lead, it is certain that there exists no unambiguous circumstance, no fact which is common to all men.

But suppose, for the sake of argument, one were to grant that the universal fact of the original certainty of death is not to be doubted, then the second step Kunz takes must be examined: the step to the assumption of a fundamental happening which is supposed to constitute the being-human. This is the mode of cognition which invents a foundation hypothetically in order to deduce from this never directly accessible the factual appearances and to make them comprehensible. We call this procedure building theories. Kunz speaks, therefore, of a mere probability of his thought: the presence of potential death in the origin of thought is the hidden foundation of being human, but cannot be immediately comprehended.

Such theories make sense to the degree to which they lead to the clear formulation of questions, which are then to be unambiguously affirmed or rejected by carrying out the necessary observations. Or they make sense if they lead to observations, to knowledge and perceptions, which are not gained without them and which are not self-evident. Kunz's hypothesis does not achieve this. It is not at all put forth as a psychological research instrument. Rather, it achieves something else, an "interpretation." By his hypothesis about the origin of being-human in "potential death," Kunz wants now to re-interpret what appears in philosophical thinking as such and in my philosophizing. A few examples:

According to Kunz, thought has its origin in potential death. To this origin there is supposed to correspond the boundlessness of being able to think. The presence in man of the negativity of thinking is supposed to document this origin. The dialectic of

Being and nothingness, a very ancient philosophical problem, newly developed by Hegel, and picked up by myself, transforms itself for Kunz "into a basic process pervading man's being: the constant breaking through of potential death within man as the source of the idea of Being." Negativity, the universality of thinking, the continuous loss and disappearance in existence, immanent death — all of these are supposed to be consequences of that hypothetical secret of man's becoming man out of "potential death."

The interpretation proceeds: Kunz wants to understand the specific potential character of being human out of the reference to potential death. From it are supposed to come all of man's *'existential'* possibilities, which, possessed by no other living existence, are given to man only. He alone has the capacity to proceed from radical insufficiency to a searching quest for Transcendence. To him alone the leap is open from mere existence to *Existenz*. Everything which, in broad development, is demonstrated by my illumination of *Existenz* has no need of any Transcendence. It is immanent death which, out of the basic process of man's being, produces Transcendence as psychologically compresensible.

With this idea of derivation, on which I am unable to perform any evidence, Kunz connects a question which appears meaningful to me: what kind of possibility would be intended when one speaks of potential *Existenz,* of the possibilities of freedom. Here it can not be a matter of logical nor of real possibility (as it occurs in the traditional doctrine of the modal categories), but it must be something quite different, which is to become clear. Indeed, Kunz demands quite rightly the, until now quite insufficient, answer concerning the categorial meaning of possibility. In the unfolding of the categories of freedom this answer would have to be given. Kunz himself does not, however, attempt it. He asserts merely the origin of *'existential'* possibility in immanent death. Of this notion he says that its content could "not be shown as an indubitable fact," but constitutes on its part "only a possibility." The question concerning the categorial meaning of possibility, where *'existential"* possibilities are under discussion, still remains.

Kunz's interpretation proceeds: he explains my formula of being granted to one's self in freedom. Kunz sees the necessity of an accommodation on the part of the occurrence — inaccessible to intentional production — in the ground of being human, i.e., on the part of immanent death. That at this point I should refer to Transcendence, should speak of being granted to one's self by Transcendence, this, Kunz thinks, is like a last, abstract and purified offshoot of the ancient, self-alienated demonological interpretation of human nature. For, this Transcendence, he claims, is nothing else but immanent death. This is also supposedly demonstrated by the fact that immanent death is non-objective and could not be thought of as an object. For, this non-objectivity is said to correspond to the non-objectivity of Transcendence as which this immanent death had been falsely interpreted. When I speak of the non-objectivity of *Existenz* and of Transcendence, Kunz replies: this is the non-objectivity of potential death and nothing else.

Let me note one last interpretation by Kunz: When I speak in my philosophizing about foundering, in which Transcendence is able to show itself; and about the infinite calm, which, in the leap from foundering, becomes possible, Kunz replies: this idea must be radicalized, death must take the place of Transcendence. The proposition of certainty in foundering: it is sufficient that God remains (in the sense of Jeremiah), is to be replaced by the true proposition: immanent death is the only thing whose certainty is itself absolutely timeless. Eternity is the timelessness of death. The calm in foundering is nothing else than the momentary extension of immanent death in silence. This is however supposed to be — as Kunz constantly repeats — only a supposition, a probable hypothesis.

Enough of the examples of this interpretation. They are directed in principle against my way of philosophizing. They interpret hypothetically out of a basic occurrence where I think in terms of an appeal to possibilities, They offer a doctrine in theses where I would like to generate something in the thinker by way of movements of thought. They omit and reject what for me is the very meaning of philosophizing.

Methodologically I think I can understand the difference. Kunz's attempt does not seem to me scientifically maintainable, and it seems, as if blind, to pass by a philosophical possibility. This I shall try to clarify a bit more.

From the very start he does not sharply distinguish between matter of fact and hypothesis. For, his procedure is *ab initio* not an unambiguous observing but interpretation of meaning which, in the nature of the case, is ambiguous. The content of such interpretation of meaning is already falsely taken by him to be matter of fact and the fact of the case; falsely, because the "matter of fact" carries force of conviction only for a specific, by no means for every, basic mood of the soul. This specific basic mood (the certainty of death as immanent death) takes itself as the universal human mood. This may also be expressed as follows: Insofar as a state of mind, which is psychologically to be observed and to be described, serves as the ground of a conviction, the conviction is not free. There is to be demanded, first of all, the psychological determination of the peculiarity and the question concerning its derivation, and, secondly, the insight into the double character of even such descriptions:

In the understanding of "meaning" we have to distinguish two ways; the way of psychological observation and of empirical knowledge, which establishes something; and the other way of appealing and conjuring designs of possibilities of meaning, a way which appeals to freedom. This I take to be one of my basic philosophic-methodological insights. It may perhaps aid the purification of a scientific psychology. Kunz denies this insight. His proposal, in which he constructs the constitution of human nature out of the immanent death, is an example which shows where this non-differentiation leads.

Because Kunz ignores that distinction, he proceeds on the premise that with his theory he is aiming at the same facts which I had in mind in my *Existenz*-illuminating movements of thought towards Transcendence. He merely interprets it differently. He wants, therefore, to approach these supposedly identical facts merely from another aspect, and thereby uncover in them something different. He thinks that with a view to the facts we coincide, and that we differ merely in the interpretation. Unfortunately the difference goes deeper. For, my *Existenz*-illuminating thoughts are not at all concerned with matters of fact, but with freedom and its possible contents.

Kunz indeed denies freedom or understands by the word something different; perhaps something not unrelated to the linguistic usage of some psychotherapists, who wish to help their patients to freedom and who think they possess scientific knowledge of freedom, gained by research. Kunz expresses this denial by his apparently so evident thesis: The freedom of potential *Existenz* and the behaving and experiencing man (who is said to be the object of psychological research) are, from the standpoint of being, not two separate realms, but only one single reality, namely that of concrete man who lives in determinate situations.

This unity as factuality is, according to Kunz, the 'having to be' of this whole. It includes not merely the body and its functions, but also being free, that is to say that which we have to do and, within limits, can do. Hereditary, according to him, are not merely determinate objective capacities, but also human nature as a whole. Against this it must be said that speaking of heredity is meaningful only with reference to specific marks which either are there or not there. Talking about heredity in general remains empty and produces that false consciousness of a biological total knowledge. If, nontheless, Kunz says at one point that freedom is not recognizable, one might, in view of his other explanations, suppose that he fails to understand his own uttered sentence.

The unity of human nature is for him an object of psychology. He demands the explication of the nature of the being of man as a creature who acts, experiences, and understands himself. Quite right; only every such illumination is itself a design that remains in suspense. We cannot help thinking such structures of human nature. That, however, they are not applicable, we can make harmless only by trying ourselves out in several and in numerous ones. But in that case these designs are not theories of the basic occurrence or of the basic constitution in behalf of psychological research, but philosophical conjurings as impulses toward freedom.

Proceeding from his claim to achieve the totality of human nature as the object of psychological research, Kunz reproaches me: I should not be satisfied to use objective knowledge in the form of *verstehender* psychology merely as medium for the illumination of *Existenz*, viz., for an appeal to *Existenz* which, in its type of being, remains unquestioned and is left in the dark. Against this I may remark that, quite consciously, I have done both. How *verstehende* psychology works as means of psychological research I have enlarged upon in my *Psychopathologie* (5th ed., especially pp. 250-374). How *verstehende* psychology serves as means of the illumination of *Existenz* I have developed in my *Philosophie*. I have discussed the difference between the two ways: the way to the knowledge of spiritual reality, and the way to the kindling of the impulse to freedom. I consider this distinction important not merely for the clarity of scientific research, but also for the honesty of psychotherapeutic practice. That this latter is to a large extent disastrous is due to the confusion of psychology with philosophy, to the non-differentiation of the methods of knowledge. The unity of man's being insisted upon by Kunz is not an object but an idea. The distinctions within the objective are not concerned with different ontological realms, but with different methods together with the specific objectivities which belong to those methods. In all of my psychological and philosophical work I stand opposed to the rationalistic levelling of everything thinkable into research, objectivity, and theory.

That, in his hypothesis, Kunz has disregarded the philosophical side of his *verstehenden* movements of thought shows itself in his report of what I designate as the ultimate situation of death. Whereas my thoughts have meaning only in motion and themselves disappear in the fixation of assertions which are picked out, Kunz, in his report makes a theory out of it, which he treats argumentatively pro and con, like a scientific position. Whereas my thoughts remind of or prepare for an experience as the performance of freedom; in this performance offer no knowledge, but only incite to realization, whereby all arguing and asserting is merely a means on the way and carries no independent weight; Kunz lets this motion drop and retains in his hand only dead partial ideas as positions which I supposedly represent. In Latzel's essay on ultimate situations the movement in my sense is strikingly understood.

I shall attempt now to examine Kunz's undertaking as a whole. Kunz offers a new example of the psychological theories concerning the basic ongoings of the soul. What is to be said of such theories in general applies to his also: It is a design without genuine verifiability. It concerns itself with whether it is more or less plausible that the foundation [of man] — in itself inaccessible — is thus and so. It does not further the scientific research of psychology, to which latter it does not give any point of approach for empirical investigations. Nothing factual is gained by it.

If, however, from the point of view of psychology I take Kunz's suggestion as an example of the futility of this type of psychological hypothesizing, the factual interest which Kunz has developed is by no means exhausted thereby. Indeed, this interest has at the same time a philosophical character which must be taken into consideration. The question is, what in his proposal expresses the will of the author, or otherwise: what becomes *Existenz*-illuminating to him, or again: how the cipher of the basic design of his being impels him toward self-realization.

To this question Kunz gives an answer; in the thought of the radical transitoriness he finds the impulse to experience "the irreplaceable preciousness of every action and of all being," and the demand "for a while to be the guardian of eluding Being and therewith of humaneness."

Therein lies the philosophical energy of this circumspect scholar and hidden philosopher, to which I raise no opposition. My opposition is directed against the attempt to ground this energy on the proposal of "immanent death."

By way of summary: I find a theory, difficult to execute in thought and agonizing in construction, which seems to me to fall like a blight upon the content of my *Existenz*-illuminating attempts. They disappear in the re-interpretations of Kunz. As psychological theory the proposal moves along the road of psychologizing the world and therewith on that of a reduction of the contents to the paltriness of the mental. As cipher the proposal appears to me as effective as the wretched cipher of the Naught. Nevertheless one still hears the sound of the ancient philosophic thoughts, which never entirely disappear even in such a reduction.

9. Concerning My Basic Philosophical Attitude

A few critics come to speak about the basic attitude of my entire philosophizing. Penetratingly, carefully, and many-sidedly it is discussed by Fritz Kaufmann. The ultimate experiences from which this philosophizing arises, Kaufman thinks, are the raggedness of Being and the loneliness of the self. For this reason, although the self refers in this type of thinking to the One and actually exists in view of its faith in the One, it will never enjoy itself in a perfect union with the One and never grasp absolute unity. And the self even with the other self would never get rid of its loneliness, into which it falls back of necessity.

This aspect of my thinking is not false insofar as such movements too are carried out in it. But I see in it by no means the basic attitude of my philosophizing, the attitude, so to say, of an eternal starveling. I surmise that Fritz Kaufmann himself perceives the basic attitude of my entire work differently. True enough, my attitude is not that of the joy of life, not that of the fulness of the meditation on divinity, not that of being continuously carried away into the richness of divine nature. On the other hand, I do not at all deny the harmony of the soul in the high moment of communication and in the quiet confidence of the common daily mood which maintains itself on the basis of such moments. Nor do I at all deny that fulfilment in joy and meditation. So far from declaring it to be untrue, my philosophizing is the road there and thence. What, however, is inexorably articulated in my philosophizing is the fact that there is no remaining on that height insofar as we live in time. True enough,

we become more real in the repetition. But there is for us no
such thing as knowing Transcendence forever, no point of rest
in time, which would remain as such, but only eternity by way
of the moment. It is not a universal validity of Being which
would permit it to be possessed by knowledge, but in time the
order always is: move on. We lose ourselves and win ourselves
again. I philosophize on the road, I get anxious about false anticipations, but all of this in order thereby to make possible and
to recall the more purely the true, absolutely historical fulfilments
which are incommunicable beyond the community of individuals.
Philosophy, for its realization, has its open sides. For itself it is not
already fulfilment. It is one of my worries that philosophy, wherever it is such fulfilment in general thought, can at the same time
involuntarily be used as a means to withdraw from the communication of self with self, by losing oneself in this fulfilment. I do
not even deny the pictures of the completed totality as ciphers.
They are not fictions, but may be the language of reality, even
if not as its unambiguous revelation. I see their danger: premature
calming, inversion, and evasion into a supposed possession of
Being itself. I do not deny the truth of art, but I see its perception
as anticipation in the play of what thereby is not yet reality in time.
This play liberates, points to, and makes possible *Existenz;* but
such contemplation and witnessing is not yet *'existential'* reality
itself.

Fritz Kaufmann remarks that, in the succession of Kierkegaard
and Nietzsche, there is valid for my philosophizing the demand
upon the reader: "Do not follow me, follow yourself! Self-being
arouses self-being, but it does not force itself upon one." He adds:
that, although I do not offer a system of thinking as the only true
one, I nevertheless work in behalf of my own ideas. Nor are these
[ideas] in any sense presuppositionless, they do not leave everything in suspense. There lies at bottom a decision. What I do is
to invite to an analogous decision, namely for the same kind of
self-evidence, to come to one's self as *Existenz.*

This seems to me to hit the point. I only fear even such alternative formulations. They would be true, if the entire content of
the concept "self" could be present and unambiguous. This it
is not. Language makes the word [self] substantival, as if with it
one had a definite meaning in hand; whereas words actually have
their meaning only in connected thoughts. This meaning of the
self varies in a manifold articulation, without being able to arrive
at a concluding survey about it. This is why the movements of
such a meaning have to be carried out in a philosophizing fashion,

as, for example, the concept of the "I" in the second chapter of
the second volume of my *Philosophie*. And yet Fritz Kaufmann's
hint remains correct. It is an original power, or a will, or a decision, which has its echo in the individual historical decisions of
one's own existence. It also lies at the base of the entire philosophizing of an individual. One may call it the presupposition. To
formulate it, however, succeeds only apparently. When we try it,
we find ourselves as force among forces, belonging to one, necessarily in conflict, terrified by the abysses which seem to divide.
We cannot survey the total realm of those forces but, in our work,
carry on a spiritual battle within it and, in doing so, we are
really in search of precise fronts. It is this presupposition which
produces seriousness in philosophizing. Without it philosophy
would be an intellectual game in the garment of scientific behavior, as if one were establishing facts on the basis of universal
validity. If one then tries to express one's own *'existentially'*
effective basic will in words, this may easily lead astray. Mere
waving of the flag and thoughtless talking becomes then what
originally was philosophizing motion. A whole string of such
formulations I have used in my philosophizing, and yet I hesitate
to prefer one as the appropriate one. But once again: Fritz Kaufmann is right. And the battle of the basic attitudes or of the
forces in philosophizing should, in so far as it can at all succeed,
be brought to consciousness again. On the lowest step, entirely
misleading — since they do not affect origins, but rational constructions — lie the many isms as the pretended presuppositions
of types.

Again, Fritz Kaufmann has named the question of communication at one and the same time the cornerstone and the stumbling-block of my philosophizing. When he addresses it as one of
the necessary, and at the same time inescapable and insoluble
problems, I agree with him. But it is no theoretical problem,
which could be stated unambiguously and solved by a cogent
insight. Here lies one basis for the force from which one may
philosophize as I am doing it. This basis is a faith, which dares to
live and realize itself out of itself, and, by doing so, illumines
itself. Never is knowledge achieved here. There remain the other
forces, which in practice and in part also in theory, deny genuine
communication. —

Hennig characterizes my basic attitude in a different way. With
me, he declares, the emphasis lies more on striving than on possession, more on form than on content, more upon potentiality
than on stability, more on freedom than on obedience, more on

the future than on the past. This does not touch me as strange; for it does not deny entirely what, in these polarities, I am supposed to have let fall in the shade. For my writings it is perhaps correct.

It sounds different when Hennig asserts that, by the standards of a philosophy like mine, one would not dare to measure, for example, Ezekiel's conception of the law of God, Thomas Aquinas' conception of truth, Descartes' conception of objectivity, Goethe's conception of fidelity. This I am as yet unable to understand entirely. For, I am not at all conscious of such fixed standards as measuring-rods. From my point of view, I have analyzed an aspect in the prophet Ezekiel, with reservation, but not without cause. Whoever wants to see Ezekiel should, it seems to me, not ignore the facts I have emphasized. Descartes I have critically analyzed as a force in the modern world, which, at decisive points, I consider untrue and disastrous: his grounding upon the bottomlessness of the "I think" (in contradistinction to the fulness of the only seemingly analogous Augustinian thought), the conscious demolition of history, his lack of understanding for genuine natural science (as, for example, Galileo's), his design of a pseudo-science which lacks every cogent objectivity. The idea of truth in St. Thomas I have never treated. I confront him with the greatest of respect, even though, for myself, at the decisive points I must reject him. Goethe's fidelity is for me a reverential reality, Goethe himself one of the for me authoritative philosophers and steady companion of my life. —

Thyssen comes to terms with my philosophy of foundering. This is a characteristic feature of my thinking. Briefly it asserts approximately the following:

In temporal existence death is given with life. Nothing that is can remain. Duration is limited in every case. As such it is a possible symbol of eternity, but is never, as unending duration, eternity itself. The instant which, as mere moment of endless time disappears, can be eternity as fulfilment of *Existenz*. In the disappearing temporal existence what is comes to itself, but not as temporal existence but as that which fulfills itself in the brightness of the present.

In front of what genuinely is — and wherein I participate as potential *Existenz* — veiling it and causing it to be forgotten, steps time, in which I falsely take stability and duration as the ultimate goal. I become real as potential *Existenz* only by entry into the reality of the transitory, into life and death, into the way of freedom, which dares and lets itself be granted to itself. It is the secret of sacrifice, reality in devotion to the very point of giving life itself.

In order to ward off unauthentic because unnecessary foundering, for the construction of duration as a symbol of eternity, a philosophy of the intellect has at all times been justified and uplifting for the foreground of the institution of existence. It carries out such construction, it plans and appraises as to usefulness and purpose, it keeps to facts as the realities identically accessible to everyone, it understands, out of the realm of the finite, and it pushes towards the sciences. But this philosophy of the intellect becomes un-philosophy when it covers up reality itself, i.e., eternity in time, when it loses any sense for the great venture at the limits, when it loses openness for Being itself, for the truth in foundering, and thereby cancels the possibility of living high-spiritedly in disaster.

False optimism is blind to eternity, talks death away, lives as if there were neither dying nor foundering, puts its trust in the intellect: everything will turn out all right. It enjoys a happy courage, forgetful of self and being. True optimism — which, however, is essentially neither optimism nor pessimism — looks into the abysses of reality, experiences foundering. It gets its high — not blind — courage from an unfoundable confidence, on the foundation of a life of *Existenz* that enters completely into its historicity.

Thyssen does not deny the possibility of such experiences. He occupies himself with these thoughts from a religious interest. He sees in them the intent of an "undogmatic religion by means of philosophy." His critical question is: Does Transcendence actually appear in these experiences? He does not deny the leap from anguish into calm, "but is therein Transcendence, the Divine, truly touched?" If Transcendence really is said to be experienced there, then he puts the further question: Is with *Existenz*, then, not experienced an authentic Not-I, an Other which stands over against me? Or, do both I and Not-I here, too, belong to the world of appearances?

To this it must be replied: That, concerning which the illumination of *Existenz* in foundering speaks of as Transcendence can precisely not be pulled down to the level of objective knowledge, even though talk about it must take place in the medium of objectivities. This talk does, indeed, belong to the world of appearance; but that which is circumscribed in it does not. But we are barred from an objective wanting to know, from an objective guarantee. The form to know of God as of an object, to carry out, so to say, a faith-knowledge, remains true only if the realism and materialism of wanting to have the Godhead as something Other is avoided. But just as untrue is the psychologism of a mere knowledge of subjective, immanent appearances. To philosophize means to achieve the ascent to a mode of thought which does not push away the substructure of objective thinking (which, in the temporal existence of our finite nature, would lead to the Naught), but steps beyond it; it is a mode of thought which happens through all millenia of the great cultures in polarity to the revelation of mysteries. —

Baumgarten asserts that my philosophy circles about a hidden, fixed center. Yes, I hope so; but not around a formulated, or formulatable single thought, not around something which is posited or could be posited as object; but around something which, as center, is guidance. Thence thought receives its impulses for understanding in greatest possible breadth, for being just to everything that shows itself; here, too, arise the impulses of everyday life. Thence come the well founded decisions, the either-or of concrete conduct which cannot be dissolved in abstract formulas. For this reason my philosophizing contains both: the purpose of complete tolerance and at the same time the mood of unconditional determination in face of the incalculable claim. For decades, therefore, I have heard both reproaches: that of relativizing, which is said to lead to nihilism, — and that of intolerant illiberality, which mercilessly makes itself the judge and condemns. Both reproaches mean to see something in me against which I have, in fact, consciously fought all my life. But, the dangers remain. —

Insofar as the style of my writings corresponds with my basic attitude, a style which at the same time expresses the method, Fritz Kaufmann has characterized both its "strength and its weakness." Because, as potential being-myself, I would like to turn to potential self-being, he thinks, I am paying the price of avoiding exciting effects. Because I display possibilities to the reader, I get into a mosaic of observations among which the forest sometimes becomes invisible for the trees. Because I would like to bring the reader to come to himself I evade any dramatic aggressive verve as well as the artistic *mise en scene*.

Insofar as my deficient talents also are here, in friendly fashion, understood out of a deep sense of such philosophizing, I may be satisfied. Only one thing I would like to see understood differently. It is correct that, from the desire not to buttonhole the reader in definite positions, a mosaic actually pushes to the fore in my writings; or, stated in other words, that, instead of a movement of thought which builds up into a picture, there remains an order of sketched possibilities whose manifoldness, like the realm of the living, has no limits. But my purpose was otherwise. In the *Psychologie der Weltanschauungen* there is most of that mosaic, in the *Philosophie* least. Here the mosaic has been surpassed, the positions are not built side by side, but in succession so that the thought-movement of one chapter — if a reader keeps at and comprehends it as a whole — is linked with the next and in the end makes it possible to have all of it present in a comprehensive survey. To follow this my intent is difficult even where I have, perhaps, succeeded (as I think I have above all in chapters of my *Philosophie* and of my *Nietzsche* and in a few parts of the book *Von der Wahrheit*). —

With my basic attitude and my work there is something connected to which several critics refer incidentally as deplorable, to which they object or which some even deem an advantage of my philosophizing and which is called its "small penetrating effect."

Already in 1913 my *Psychopathologie* was praised by Bumke, one of the prominent German psychiatrists, as extraordinary and unique, but with the addition that the most ultimate and difficult problems were treated therein. For this reason the book would hardly be appropriate for students. And today the complaint is voiced that the actual effect of the book does not correspond to its breadth of psychiatric thinking, nor to the significance of its insights.

Golo Mann, whose agreement with my thinking concerning freedom made me happy, and who evaluates the entirety of my work positively, opines that this philosophy is not suitable for political propaganda purposes. He finds it difficult of access, prohibiting romantic theses of penetrating effect, forbidding easy reference. Golo Mann turns all of this into advantages.

Jeanne Hersch reports a conversation, in which I am supposed to have said: I am air, I am nothing. She fears that, on my path, despite the fact that she herself considers it as the only true one today, there is no going for others.

I meet these well intended complaints also — not in the essays of this volume, but elsewhere — as deprecative dicta of an attitude that negates me: with my thinking I had betaken myself into isolation — I might, perhaps occupy the worthy place of a professor who is being mentioned but not read, — as the philosopher of communication I am today the loneliest among all philosophers — I am the never-foundering philosopher of foundering, —

as world-alien spider I am spinning the net of my constructions —
and more of the same.

It is not simple to find one's way in the collocation of motives
and realities which have managed somehow to get together in
the phrase "wanting effective penetration." There is a truth in
the whole, but which?

The reply would be only external and would miss the heart
of the matter, if I were to point out that, on the basis of the
number of sold copies of my printed works, I find myself among
the favored philosophical authors. Other literary works achieve,
of course, incomparably larger distribution-numbers.

The problem is not a personal, but a matter-of-fact one. It has
a perhaps peculiarly analogous form in the discussion of the
spiritual chances of the free as over against the totalitarian world.
One hears for instance: against a faith only faith has power,
because of its faithlessness the free world is powerless against the
totalitarian faith; — one cannot fight for freedom, if one does not
know what freedom is good for; as slogan in battle it is empty,
if its content is not clearly held in view. In 1930 I heard liberal
German politicians talk: we must seek ideas, slogans, which will
strengthen us against the growing national-socialist faith. Similarly
today: freedom is supposed to become a faith-front, what is desired
are the methods and mood of aggression. One becomes discouraged in the face of the fact of the totalitarian slogans, thought-
forms and undiscussed basic attitudes. We see in the intellectual
world how the demagogic energy of gifted theologians, philosophers, and politicians is able to silence the listeners who listen
in secret reverence to what they meet there as something supposedly extraordinary, as something which goes beyond the ability
of the intellect to grasp, as something before which, in dreadful
anticipation, one bows thoughtlessly.

This despondency of freedom is, however, present only where
man does not genuinely wish to be free, does not assume his own
responsibility, desires submission to something mysterious which
is supposedly coming. In philosophizing on freedom — as, indeed,
in all free thought — the presupposition for the ascertainment
of the true is that each individual man should perform it with
his own essence which comes to itself in so doing. Where philosophizing wants freedom, this philosophizing offers the conditions
and the occasions, not the fulfilling historical reality of *Existenz*
itself.

That turn in the conversation with Jeanne Hersch: "I am nothing, I am air, just as is reason," if it took place, is true in the

sense of what I have just said, but is certainly easily misunderstood. What was being discussed was not I (I do not know what I am and need not talk about myself), but my philosophizing. However, in that instance, not philosophy as a whole, but the reason in it is meant. True reason can be compared with pure air, in which one can breathe and thereby come to all assurances. But one can not live on it.

The philosophical intent in my writings, therefore, is: I would like to co-operate in producing the purity of the spiritual air we breathe when, thoughtfully, we come to what concerns us, to decision, to our selves. I would not like obedient or oppositionless repeating of propositions, but I would like to incite the thought-acts which teach one to see and to converse with one's self. I offer no substance, which each individual, open to the contents of being, must find in himself. In spoken philosophizing these contents remain mere possibilities. No one shall be seduced to evade his own freedom, in which he has his own non-shirkable responsibility. Every thought, every manner which seduces one to free himself from his own freedom is untrue, even if this evasion ensues into something known, believed, or aesthetically enjoyed. "I am nothing," this could only mean: not something to which others can cling when they abandon themselves. The man who becomes free has only one support, namely Transcendence; and this does not speak unambiguously through any medium in the world, through none exclusively, through no revelation for everyone and always, but only through freedom itself and through whatever shows itself to freedom.

Now it would be a sad misunderstanding to take the pure air of reason for life itself. What, in the form of reason, can be awakened as potential *Existenz* by thought processes is not itself given in thought. For it is dependent upon the self which does not come to the one with whom it communicates in thought, but to itself.

Against this there is the objection which wants to make the freedom of philosophizing, as indeed any freedom, hopeless: This pure air of reason exists only for rare, for a few free, men, who can breathe it and who contribute the substance out of their own ground. But the masses of men remain abandoned to themselves, surrendered to the Naught. This objection would be true only if no chain of communication led from the highest peaks of philosophical freedom to every man as man. Those peaks themselves are, at best, only low hills under the infinite heavens. In every human heart lies the possibility to raise itself. Only one philosophy could justifiably be exposed to the above objection: one which, mistaking its own narrowness, would lose the inner communion with men, and which, in the richness of a pseudo-aristocratic education, would find selfish satisfaction.

We have the choice of: either together in truth, mutually illuminating each other at every step, to reach the community which is only there possible, without any man's deceptively being made into more than a man can be; or else to get into the devil's circle of automatic servitude under despotic forces which let the despots themselves become serfs. Philosophy as such is political. For it encourages freedom, lives only in freedom and works for freedom.

The "want of effective penetration" is perhaps, the stillness of the penetrating power of human freedom. In everyone who feels a spark of this freedom within himself this power will assert itself against all the forms of magic, of unfreedom, powers which, for the moment, are penetratingly effective, because they are luciferic powers aiming at unfreedom and originating in unfreedom.

It is something else again that such philosophy, too, has its basic ideas, its basic knowledge, it propositions and formulas, although they are not a guaranteed possession. But one has them, so to speak, at hand as a guide, in order by them to remember what is in it and again to re-present what was present in them. We may reach for them in moments of emptiness, in need, in perplexity. They stem from the works of philosophy, from poetry, from the Bible. It is as if we had in hand a note which our good demon had written us. But what is written on it is no slogan, no flag.

In the gentle force of freedom may lie unswervability. It makes daring possible in those basic situations which, in virtue of the blind violence of human nature, keep returning: situations which necessitate the choice either to risk life in battle or to prefer servitude to saving one's life.

Inasmuch as this battle ultimately becomes the battle of the nations and of political principles, the question arises what men *en masse* can do. What are they able to comprehend and believe in order to set the venture of their life against the forces which would destroy freedom? That there have been genuine fighters for freedom at all, who knew what it was all about, may give us encouragement. There is no such thing as certainty concerning the future by trusting in what is humanly possible. But the individual can know for what he wants to think and work.

Philosophy as such wants freedom. It must waive "effective

penetration" in order to achieve that calm in man where the will to freedom confirms itself in listening to the other. For this reason, whoever philosophizes, teaches, and writes will wish to be effective because he knows for what he thinks. But he must not think in terms of a planned effectiveness, he does not play a cunning political game of indirect influence, but he speaks quite openly at all times. What becomes of the thought of freedom does not depend upon him alone. To begin with he must be satisfied with the fact that such thinking is present in the world, and that he prove himself, as a tiny link, in the chain of free thought. He must renounce prognosis which, in virtue of the guarantees of a supposed scientific knowledge or of a revelation, triumphantly claims the future for its own thinking and believing. For him the consciousness of the truth of freedom in the illumination of all possibilities is sufficient. Sufficient for him also is a basic confidence in the "must"of his own way, a confidence which he cannot justify by anything else. This is why there is in philosophizing at one and the same time a great modesty as well as an unobtrusive self-certainty.—

None of my critics disputes the unity of my basic position throughout the sequence of my writings over four decades. A few, nevertheless, although observing no break, seem to note an essential shifting of accent.

In his careful study of my writings, Fritz Kaufmann has noticed that the concept of reason is expressly stressed by me only after 1933 and brought into the center of my thinking. This is correct. When, however, Kaufmann sees something like a conversion in this, that is too much. The matter is present in all of my earlier writings and has always been their genuine vital power. It is true, none the less, that I was instigated to work these out by the realities of National Socialism in Germany. I have become conscious of this fact only now through Kaufmann. This elaboration, yes, the glorification of reason in some of my later writings, the perhaps new, version of reason on the foundation of Kantian thought, meant for me, at the same time, the clear separation from philosophical movements which could be brought into relationship with my own attempts and from which I had not, until then, distanced myself.

Kunz notes a shift of accent in so far as he claims that Transcendence had won a more positive content and greater certainty since the publication of my *Philosophie* (1931). Faith, in opposition to nihilism, had moved into the foreground, "although, as philosophical faith, it had always constituted a supporting element." Golo Mann expresses himself similarly: "In his more mature age Jaspers seems no longer to believe that philosophy is able to give us a positive content. It has increasingly become a mere guidepost for him, the gateway to religion. What he calls philosophical faith is, in substance if not in form or dogma, the Christian faith."

It is correct that, after the long interruption since my school-years, I only read the Bible in the years of National Socialism, aided in my reading by commentaries and by the historical works of O. T. and N. T. scholars. But it is also a fact that, afterwards as before, I told the student, who in conversation with me asked more of philosophy than it is able to give: the arms of the churches are wide open, there you will find what you are looking for. I comprehended historically, and at that time carried it out more consciously, that our Occidental philosophizing rests also on Biblical ground, even in Spinoza and in Marx. But at no time, also not today, have I looked upon philosophy as the gateway to ecclesiastical religion (even though someone at one time said that I was a good one to drive people to the churches), but the polar opposite to it. The insufficient element in the philosophical work of philosophy as it exists in books and doctrine lies in the fact that philosophy wants to be the gateway to that philosophizing which can be carried out only by each individual in his own reality. That the work does not "give," but only induces, is precisely its own strength. For, philosophy is philosophy of freedom.

Whether I have, according to the conventional notion of aging, become more believing, more mystical, more religious in my age, I consider doubtful. One could just as well say: more sober, less mysterious, more experienced. Kunz, it seems to me, hit the nail on the head with his sentence that faith had always been the supporting element in my thinking. That in the end I have expressly lifted it out as "philosophical faith," implies the self-affirmation of one's own philosophical origin, which, in its association with the philosophical tradition (of which the Bible is a part, which we read as we do other texts), finds its way to itself.

10. CONCERNING THE POSSIBILITIES AND LIMITS OF CRITICISM

Schilpp's undertaking in these volumes of the LIBRARY OF LIVING PHILOSOPHERS to let an author be addressed and criticized by a number of his contemporaries and to give the author himself the opportunity to reply to his critics, aims not merely at bringing philosophy into a dramatic position of public discussion. It rests on the fundamental idea that philosophical criticism is both possible and fruitful. This undertaking itself invites reflection on the possibilities of criticism, so many examples of which, in address as well as in reply, are at hand. —

By following a scheme the possibilities of criticism may be ordered in stages. To begin with, there is the possibility of a criticism analogous to scientific criticism, insofar as assertions of scientific character are concerned which become material for philosophical movements. At this level it is possible to arrive at universally valid decisions between right and false. Next, there is the possibility of the logical illumination of the form and rational consistency of philosophical structures.

Their presuppositions may be adduced, alternatives are set forth between positions, the lines of the structure are rationally drawn in purer form. Although the presuppositions are shown up, since these are not definitely definable, the contents of these presuppositions must be circumscribed as perceptions and experiences. They do not possess the character of being producable or identically repeatable, yet they are something wherein those who think with each other are able to recognize each other again. Finally, there takes place contact with the forces which set all philosophical thinking in motion, give it meaning and direction, effect its self-assertion and its struggle with other forces. —

One basic difficulty, found already in each criticism and then also in my reply, arises from the nature of philosophizing itself: how can one speak of something which is meant not as object, but which in the objective means something else? By what can criticism be guided, if the formulated and formulable standards of measurement and principles are not, indeed, the final ones? How can one reply so long as one is unable genuinely to visualize this guidance, insofar as it is another one in the critic from one's own? Does the discussion not take place in a sham-illumination, in which the essential is not lighted up, but which rather makes reciprocally visible only the garments and the gestures?

Here the reasons must be sought why the results of a philosophy cannot genuinely be reported, not even by the author himself. One must go along with its ideas in order to experience what thereby happens to one in the dawning of insights. These do not exist as learnable content, but as the performance of the thought processes themselves which effect an inner attitude. In it there becomes illuminated for us how we find ourselves in the world, in what aspects everything shows itself to us, and then in which directions we transcend to the Encompassing.

And yet, reporting is indispensable. It is already justified by the fact that it shows, so to speak, the skeleton of comprehensibility, yet unavoidably in such fashion that, as in the osteology of the anatomists, it becomes an apparatus of dead bones. In spite of the usefulness of such reporting as information and as facilitating one's own reading of the original texts, a wrong impression is bound to arise. In all historically existing philosophy the frightening question is: what becomes of it if it receives its public character not from its source, but from what can be reported about it? If the report does not become the way to the source, then, even in calling attention to this philosophy, it will at the same time veil it. The meritorious aspects of reporting in the essays of this volume I may be allowed to pass over without examining them as to accuracy or inaccuracy.

It is something else again when the critic, in discussing the philosophizing on which he reports, himself goes along philosophizing in the spirit of what he has understood. In that case, he gives a present to his author, lends him his own thinking, and brings the reader into the same specific realm in which the author philosophizes. This latter is deeply stirred by the originality of the other, in which he discovers his own efforts all over again. Where I in this sense agree, where I feel the critic to be on the same road with myself, I may be permitted to remain silent in my reply (with few exceptions). —

Every critique, on its own part, makes conscious or involuntary presuppositions, as for example, concerning what it expects from a philosophical work in general, that is to say, what philosophy itself is and which philosophy it stands ready to recognize as such; then of the standards it applies; and, finally, of a surveying, comparing standpoint, which provides for the critic a deceptive sovereignty from the outside.

Consequently, in an anti-critique the moving questions are: whether the critique attends to the real intention of the one being criticized or makes improper demands; which are the standards it really applies; whether it has an inner connection within itself or is more a conglomeration of accidental observations and remarks from greatly varying points of view; whether these latter can be lifted out or are lost in the conglomeration; what, conceivably, might be the unconsciously claimed standpoint outside.

Above all, however, the criticized philosopher is in each case helpfully called upon by the criticism to examine whether, in his writings, he has done justice to his idea, where he has failed, and where he has expressed it inadequately. He sees where his writings occupy a place in a common realm of comprehensibility; but also where they seem to stand outside and therefore remain incomprehensible; where it might be possible to increase the comprehensibility and by what means. In every case he experiences the critique as a moving sting. It becomes fruitful if it increases comprehensibility on its part or forces it to be increased. It remains only an exciting impulse, if it seems to obstruct this comprehensibility on its part by leading the reader of the one being criticized upon inappropriate ways of reading and of understanding. —

A number of my critics have touched upon such questions concerning the meaning and possibility of criticism.

Latzel follows my philosophical thoughts carefully and with inner participation, with the result that he does not wish to accept these thoughts as a recognized truth, but wants to transpose them into his own philosophical reality. For, the intent is not to follow me, but to come to himself with this kind of thinking; not to live out of alien but out of one's own origin. "It is perhaps the decisive test of the inner truth of this kind of thinking, whether the *Existenz*-illuminating thinking succeeds in educating the reader to be able to get critical distance even as over against this kind of thinking itself." With this I agree without reservation.

Latzel develops the methods of such critical understanding out of authentic participation. In doing so he calls attention to the following essential point. A representation and critique of my philosophizing, he claims, would miss the point if it partly gathered up all discussions of the same object without paying attention to the respective function of the specific discussion in its peculiar connections. This is excellently said, but may be complemented by pointing out that it is always useful to report even on a skeleton of concepts, as I discussed above, which constitute, so to speak, the apparatus of this kind of thinking. True, the thus repeated concepts are dead; it is nevertheless useful to know even these, so that one can adopt the thought movement all the more clearly. What, at varying points, has a disparate and in the external possibilities of definition contradictory meaning, shows an orderly connection in this variety of deviations. The manifoldness of the meaning shows itself as a necessity, and the contradictions resolve themselves. Or else ultimate, insoluble contradictions turn up, producing the new question concerning the meaning of these contradictions which point into darkness. Are they themselves only a deficiency which leads to the breakdown of the work? Or are they the telling expression of a truth which has not yet come to light? —

Hennig testifies to his going along with essential aspects of my work; he expresses this with a gratitude which deeply stirs me. Then, with the ardour which unites us, he turns the content of this thought-movement against ideas which, for the historical decisions of life, are illuminating and essential to me. I confront the touching riddle of a coincidence which expresses itself in the most complete difference. Is this a factual possibility (in Latzel's meaning of the word), or only a personal community, or both?

Cautiously Fritz Kaufmann goes the same way, with me to think against me. Only he remains closer to me, is perhaps not separated from me at all, at least not in what can be said. Hennig carries out a radical distance which objectifies itself at the very beginning. Fritz Kaufmann remains in what can be objectified in such a way that he is able to accept my thoughts, [and] I his, without touching the "forces." True enough, Kaufmann wants to shed light into the origins of my thinking; for he can see fruitful criticism only by such procedure. He wants to reorganize a few lines in my thinking. But he does not contradict in principle; he only shifts the emphases. He does not want to refute, but to supplement. He talks with me in the thought-possibilities, out of a hidden tension, affirming my path. In his sense he performs a *"dialogo d'amore."* For this reason, even where he contradicts [me], he often already brings the corrections from my own writings, corrections which cancel again the contradiction as insurmountable. —

In my writings I have critically represented a few great figures of history. In part the critics turn on my critique of Descartes, Nietzsche, Goethe.

Hennig thinks that a total antagonism on my part hinders my understanding of Descartes. I assume the opposite: out of a definite antagonism the sensitivity to weaknesses becomes clearer. What is then seen is historically accessible to demonstration and disproof; but not by means of general assertions, but by research in the texts and by delivering proofs. Perhaps there is in me a fundamental antagonism against Descartes' essence. Yet it is possible to enter into relationships with men above and beyond every antagonism. Something else again is a quite definite, relevant antagonism — not against his essence but — against Descartes' notion of science and its consequences in the last centuries. Here is effective not merely an alien, dark force, but a clearly demonstrable error. Here it is cogently recognizable that Descartes did not know either the method or the basic attitude of modern natural science. This can be discussed only under the guidance of the specific matters of fact, as I did in my Descartes-book. Hennig's judgment of my Descartes-critique seems to me unjust. His judgment does not rest on a thorough examination of the matter. The proof of my not understanding Descartes would be very important to me. This is apart from the few factually not necessary pages of my book about him, where I attempt to characterize the total phenomenon.

Baumgarten has criticized my Goethe-critique. He thinks that I am choosing Kant as over against Goethe. What I have done, however, is to insist upon the philosophical truth of Kant's doctrine concerning the radical evil, as over against Goethe's rejection of this doctrine. In doing so I aim, in the first place, only at these particular remarks of Goethe and not at Goethe as such; and, secondly, I do not reject what the truth may be for Goethe, but only refuse my participation therein. Elsewhere I have pointed out certain of Goethe's limitations (as for example, the well known ones in his comprehension of Newton). But never have I chosen Kant against Goethe or vice-versa. How should I dream of such folly with reference to two such great figures, both of whom are irreplaceable companions of my life!

Then again Baumgarten charges me with the intent of making Kant, Kierkegaard and Nietzsche into a single truth. What a strange intent! As if philosophical truth came into being by stirring together historically immeasurably impressive, insurmountable figures as into a stew! Each such figure is infinite for us, knowledge of them never complete, their interpretation never to be concluded. It would never enter my head to do anything of the kind. But it does make sense to me to show, on pregnantly demonstrated essential thoughts — which have not been taken out of their context — how thoughts (not personalities) harmonize with one another. Or, to express it in other words: to illumine the work of the great figures without thereby wanting to comprehend it; but to carry out this illumination methodically, in a distinct and in each case definite way, and not by the preparation of mixtures.

Baumgarten offers still another reproach. That, in my interpretation of Nietzsche, I let "the results of Nietzsche's philosophizing for practical conduct, in its annihilating for (nihilism), founder and sink in their specific content." By illuminating them in their foundering, I manage, according to Baumgarten, at the same time to silence them. This method of mine, of managing to silence what I do not like (Walter Kaufmann makes a similar reproach), is said to show itself in the way in which I bring Nietzsche and Kierkegaard together. I make the contrast disappear between "the Christian enchantment of suffering in Kierkegaard's personal conduct" and the "disenchantment of suffering and of Christianity in the conduct of Nietzsche."

In each case the meaning of my interpretation seems to me to be misunderstood in the critic's assigning significance precisely to what I consciously (and not without express reference to the fact) leave aside. Consequently what I am actually doing and what, it seems to me, I am doing methodically and have proved at each step, is not at all seen as such, but is rejected *in toto*.

The other emphasis I carry out, it is true, is not arbitrary, but neither does it rest on a rationally comprehensible basis. It testifies to what both the interpreter and the critic of the interpreter want in their existence, to what they hold to be true, to the sources of their lives. At this point the "forces" touch each other, but so do the forms of confusion.

As concerns my critical interpretations of historical figures in philosophy I maintain the following against my critics: I do not judge any of the figures in totality. I penetrate, but I do not survey the whole. I see the effects of masses of thought, but I am unable to evaluate the extent or the force of their significance. I see aspects which circle around the center, but I do not reach the center. If one expects of my interpretations what they do not achieve nor want, one overlooks what actually is achieved in them. By expecting everything, one lets the particular insight drop. By substituting what was not claimed, one refutes what was never asserted. —

The question concerning the "forces" — never answerable, but to be discussed — is readily put on the surface level of isms. Collins compares my thinking with naturalism and Thomism and takes mine to be Kantianism. He treats the three as positions which, as partners — and therefore of similar nature — can and should meet on one level in order to learn from each other and to achieve unity. He, therefore, makes proposals and offers advice as to where, as a Kantian, I could learn from the others, and they from me.

But the question is: Are the three actually similar forces? Are not positions, which are to be determined rationally, surfaces on their part, which must be questioned as to what works through them? May not apparently identical positions stand in the service of entirely different forces?

In that case: Does the discussion really take place in a common medium? What is that medium? Does not the decisive [factor] remain unsaid in the background? Is this decisive [factor] clear perhaps only in Thomism so that it does not stand at all on the same level as the other two, which are not at all an unambiguous expression of forces?

Furthermore: Is the kind of conviction, the strength of evidence, the not-doubting in the three cases at all of identical nature? Or do the expressed logical positions in each instance rest upon presuppositions which, in their very nature, cannot be comprehended definitionally or positionally, tendencies [arising] out of the Encompassing, which conflict with each other on a deeper stratum than that of logically argumentative decision? Is it not the philosophical task to probe this depth and to become clear, if not concerning the ultimate origin — which is impossible —, at least concerning this depth itself?

This same question may be put differently: Whence do questions and problems get their weight? Through what do they become essential or indifferent? There is such a thing as a difference in the questioning itself. Questions are rejected as meaningless. There cannot be logical presuppositions of such questioning.

Finally: To turn attention in this direction is not an incidental matter. One recognizes by what philosophy becomes serious business and not merely a superfluous play at leisure. The harmlessness of common argumentation on common principles is actually broken through. Peaceful discussion in scholastic or scientific fashion either falls by the wayside or reveals only now its deeper origins. The forces themselves become language in their ethical and factual consequences. Only then do the ultimate reserves and points of orientation come to light. Suspended is the false appearance that anything could be decided by common logical argumentation. At the end of these situations acts of violence turn up, at least on the part of some forces, acts of physical or intellectual violence in the world, and then the question at issue is no longer what is true, but who survives.

The questions about the "self-evidences" of the speaker, which are not common to all men, show their true nature only if one looks in this direction. There lies the blunt granite, which for the most part does not even let itself be touched, nor struck by any question, which simply is there and remains there, which does not enter into communication and which yet, with all the talk, silently asserts itself in the midst of all the floods which break against it. The great question becomes, whether this type of granite can yet become open to discussion in the clarity of the light of reason. Out of its particular nature *(Sosein)* it will open up in illumination, if it is human. Or else it remains the brutal, indeterminable other. In that case, no communication can succeed; there remains only the choice whether to shun it, to dominate it, or to be slain by it.

Throughout my life I have known myself in the spiritual struggle with the other forces, did I want to become clear about the force which guides and motivates me. Philosophically I aimed, in objectifying thinking, to overcome all rational alternatives in favor of the genuine historical decisions in each singular situation of life — in favor also of the genuine alternatives which, in scientific thinking, force one to an either-or, where the decision rests upon the insight of consciousness-as-such. But there remained a few final alternatives, which could not be decided in philosophically objectifying thinking itself, but in which basic decisions of a conscious life-disposition could again recognize themselves.

In our time I have thought against the totalitarianisms of thinking in Marxism, psychoanalysis and the theories of race (all considered false). There has been surprise about my severity and also about the kind of critique I have exercised on these; especially in view of the fact that in my writings there predominates an irenic basic attitude, the inclination to understand truth even in the untrue. And, indeed, I know myself at this point in a struggle, not against positions, theses, or theories, but against forces which I sense behind the veils and which I see beforehand in what they effect. I do not mean formulations, but tendencies which I recognize as perversions of philosophy, as *Ersatzphilosophie,* as something which does not openly show itself as philosophy.

There has been surprise over the urgency with which I am pointing to the purity of scientific knowledge, this great possibility and reality of modern times. I do, indeed, strive here for that purity which is decisive for the truth of scientific knowledge, and which today is the condition of truth in philosophical consciousness itself. This explains, too, my demand that psychology shall become scientific and free itself from pseudo-philosophical twaddle.

My philosophical struggle is for the maintenance of the independent origin of philosophy in philosophical faith. The potentialities of man are not exhausted in the alternative between ecclesiastical religion and nihilism. There is this third, philosophy, which, from both sides, sees itself threatened with annihilation.

When I survey the critics in this volume and my Reply as a whole I feel as if we were moving in a common realm. The friendliness of the disposition, even in the severity of the criticisms, could not be missed. Although immensely important questions have been touched upon in this common realm and not rarely the principles of philosophizing themselves were at stake, I am, nevertheless, clear in my own mind that, even with all that, we have not yet entered the realm where the "forces" meet, where, so to speak, God and Lucifer themselves stand in the background, and take part in our own as well as in the opponent's conversation; where the ultimate is at stake. This great battle of the spirit for its ultimate origins and standards cannot systematically be sought or undertaken. Nor are these Schilpp-volumes the place for it. But, let us not deceive ourselves but recognize that — despite the friendly encounter, despite our participation, and despite the great interest aroused — we have not yet stepped on the threshold, where, confronted by the abyss of incommunicability, the battle in behalf of communication takes place with a view to the possibility of that ultimate battle. Just a few remarks concerning that battle.

The question concerning the possibilities of philosophical criticism is an extraordinary problem, one of the most stirring in a philosophy which seeks communication. It is the question concerning meaningful discussion in philosophizing, a question which even today has, perhaps, not been sufficiently clarified, let alone been answered by action and insight. I'm going to circumscribe the problem with a few propositions.

1. The question is whether essential criticism and polemics are at all possible in authentic philosophy, or whether there remains here only a silent acceptance. This would be like the attitude towards a poem, which may well be analyzed aesthetically, measured critically by aesthetic norms, interpretatively brought closer, but which allows of no real discussion, except, perhaps, a substantival one by the standard whether it be true — because it helps man to rise —, or false — because it lets him sink. In that case questions addressed to philosophy such as the following would be valid: Does philosophy arouse potential *Existenz* for entrance into reality? Is philosophy seduction to evade reality? Does philosophy demonstrate truth which becomes binding? Is philosophy a type of thinking which remains *'existentially'* nil?

Philosophy is not already itself knowledge of something, is not engaged in producing a work of art in thought; rather, [philosophical] thinking is itself an act of the essence of the thinking person, an essence which produces itself by touching an Other, viz., Transcendence.

2. In this essential type of thinking or inner action, as the origin of the communication of philosophizing, forces are, so to speak, effective. Such forces which, in philosophy, gain expression, recognize themselves again therein, attract and repulse each other, let themselves be misknown and seduced. We would, of course, like to see these directly. But this is not possible. For, with each step of our thinking, we stand within them, not outside. We are ourselves in the service of such forces, without being able to survey a world of forces. The "world of forces," this is only a symbol pointing to what is genuinely at stake in the authentic criticism of philosophical reality.

If we turn our gaze upon the forces themselves, we are no longer looking at a possible object. The invitation to such a view rather means only to look beyond the objects to the origin in the forces, of their being-thought and their being-real. Then, too, it is an all too abbreviated procedure if one thought to comprehend the forces themselves in the form of communicated insights. The insights remain, after all, always only foreground. If I take these insights — which, as something directly expressible are the last — as the truly ultimate, I shall only veil the essential from myself. What really matters is, in the expressed insights, to catch sight of what is precisely not visible. How, then, is criticism and how is agreement to be achieved when, what is at stake are not objectively comprehensible matters and matters of fact, but philosophy itself as the language of those forces?

3. In talking with each other we make the silent but deceptive assumption of a common theme, of, so to speak, the issue of philosophizing, of an objective philosophical world of truth, in which each one of us, whoever he may be and whatever he might be thinking, co-operates. Then we turn to matters of fact, attack sentences and series of thoughts in the form of a scientific discussion. This does, indeed, make sense, which, however, is limited to rational objectivity. Inasmuch as objectivity is the indispensable medium of all speaking, such criticism, even though based on the foreground, is yet correct as concerns the medium by which the deeper forces make themselves known. How, then, is it pos-

sible to exhibit and question those forces, not merely argumentatively, not just in the discussion of something, not only in agreement with the forms of scientific discussion? How is it possible to show the consequences not merely of the thought, but of the inner disposition, the results for those who affirmatively follow along on this path? How can it be made clear in which way the thoughts are the preparation for something else?

The discussion in the foreground can become an unnoticed hoax. One lets himself be drawn unto the level of scientific discussion on the assumption of a common scientific philosophy. Thereby one gets only to incidentals. Diverted from what really matters, one has unknowingly already recognized the substance of the opponent as true.

And yet this discussion in the foregrounds is inevitable. But it becomes philosophically impressive only if it is taken up into that deeper discussion of the forces, as their language.

Now the picture of public philosophical discussion is curious. In many instances a critic obviously is tied to his opponent — the more so, if the latter is a creative philosopher —, by the fact that unnoticed he has permitted himself to be hitched to the thought-trains of the one attacked. This has often been the case in the critique of Hegel on the part both of Hegelians and anti-Hegelians. However interesting such criticism may be in cultural history, as criticism it is quite non-essential, because it has no genuine opponent but walks the same path with the pseudo-opponent, laid in chains by him, caught in his way of thinking, unwillingly and unconsciously in bonds. Moreover, in a pseudo-discussion, even after the severest rejection, the essential discussion has not at all begun yet. This prisoner wants to free himself from the fetters, but in vain.

4. This deeper element, the genuinely philosophical force, this something which one feels or does not feel and which cannot be forced on any intellectual knowledge, this which is the genuinely effective aspect of spiritual endowment and speaks to it as such, — the question regarding 'this' is, in the first place: does it exist at all or does it not? That is to say, is it something or is it magic? The second question, then, is this: what kind of force or forces push toward validity there? To answer this will never succeed definitively. One may perhaps characterize a force, touching it either by warding off or appropriating it. But the real task is to get at it, so to speak, face to face, not to subsume it under the concept of a genus or type.

A discussion of this type makes sense only if its questions penetrate to the very roots and if it seeks the appropriate thoughts for the motives which originally come thence. In this case the exhibition of the matters of fact thought by the opponent will teach us to see something which, having no meaning in itself, is significant as sign, as symptom, as symbol of a philosophical will to essence.

To perform this as universally valid knowledge is impossible. However one may circle around or express what is thought, what is thus thought critically is itself always again a tendency which arises in one's own origin. This tendency comes to be known in its critical types of thinking, but on its own part is subject again to reflection and questioning.

In the philosophically thinking life a struggle of the forces shows itself. But it must not be forgotten that no one completely sees this world, the organism, so to say, of the original forces of truth battling each other. Nor does anyone in a definitive universal knowledge recognize the difference in all of these from those forces of untruth and of evil which destroy existence, potential *Existenz,* reason, and reality itself. Totality is a symbol for that in which we stand and which we cannot possibly step out of, in order to survey it truly from the outside.

5. If the gaze is turned upon the original forces, then the question concerns something which is incarnate as much in the conduct of the thinker as in the contents of his thoughts. This kind of questioning seeks something general in the most personal.

That is why, in philosophizing, the living person himself in his factuality is included in every criticism. This is inevitable, since the time when it became impossible to treat the content of philosophy as scientifically discoverable, recognized knowledge, expanding through the ages on the basis of discoveries and demonstrations. Together with this, however, the limit and the degree of criticism must strictly be impressed upon one's mind and must decisively be held to: Just as little as any man is capable of being surveyed as a whole or known as such, just so little is it possible to know the philosophical thinker with his work. One can penetrate, but not survey. One can question, but not draw up something like a balance-sheet.

Philosophical criticism, aiming to penetrate into the origins, where such criticism seems to reach the boundary of the almost cogently convincing (which nevertheless it can never reach), confronts a possible objection which annuls the entire critical attempt with one fell swoop. Actually it is valid only as regards contemporaries, only potentially as regards the dead. The objection runs like this: It is said to be impossible to demand of the opponent that he should deny his own essence, to expect an insight of him which would have to paralyze his own authentic productivity. Goethe said that whatever goes against the conditions of one's own existence, he could not permit to enter.

Against such objection it is to be maintained: It is the very glory of philosophizing that here — and only here — such an objection is invalid. For, he who philosophizes desires every possible insight, otherwise he would not be philosophizing. For him spirit and its productivity is only an instrument, not an end in itself. He experiences that this instrument works the better the more decisively he succumbs to the impetus of truth. This is why he who philosophizes seeks the utmost in criticism. He wants nothing concealed, wants to close off nothing, wants to become visible in unreserved openness, would like, in the fire of criticism, so to speak, melt down in order to rise again as himself. Or is this saying too much? In any case, a philosophical critic, if he practices criticism at all, desires not to destroy a spiritual person but to remind that person of its origin. True criticism remains communication, and communication is not deadly. To dig at the roots is possible in loving readiness for communication, where to question oneself is not forgotten. It occurs in the perplexity in face of the true hidden in my origin. Where this is lacking, Nietzsche's word is valid: Where you can not love, you must pass by.

11. Remarks

If I look upon the entirety of the essays in this volume, I become conscious of the fact that it was even impossible to do justice to the majority of the statements. Taking all points of view into consideration, in my discussion, would require a book of like or of greater extent than that of the essays themselves. I could reply only to a few questions. Many deserve, in truth, a much more thorough discussion. In part, answers may be found in my writings, not always at citable places in which one could inform himself, but also in trains of thought in which one has to train himself.

I have replied most fully where I have been criticized most sharply and where, at the same time, a fundamental point seemed to me attacked. Where, however, thought penetrated, and carried further, my own ideas, I have, for the most part, kept still. In addition, there has been no reference to what, among the themes selected in the above, could find no place. I would like, therefore, to add at least a few scattered remarks.

a. Kurt Hoffman has given a desirable, brief exposition of the basic concepts of my philosophical writings. To this end it was necessary for him consciously to fixate, not to enter into the movements of thought. He sees the tensions of my thinking: to integrate what came into the world through Kierkegaard and Nietzsche, and what, in the nature of the case, is unsystematic; — to arrest in concepts what becomes real in the movement of thinking. He sees the philosophical task as that of becoming open to all forms of being true. For this purpose, he thinks, I have created for myself the ideal instrument in the flexible doctrine of the Encompassing, which evades any definition.

Thus he characterizes both my strength and my weakness. True, he opines, I have reached the highest self-reflection of philosophy, produced a philosophy of philosophy; but the consequence is: inasmuch as I see all philosophy as cipher, I would necessarily have to see my own as such also. He asks whether it is possible to view one's own philosophical thinking as one metaphor among others. An excellent question this: Hoffman asks it out of comprehension for this kind of philosophizing. He recognizes its position of positionlessness as well as its "new objectivity." I approve his closing sentence concerning the meaning of the foundering of philosophy. It is as if he saw my philosophy as the opposite pole to Hegel's "Courage of Truth," to which everything opens itself to the very depth of the godhead.

b. Latzel reports my philosophy of ultimate situations. But he does not merely report, he analyzes. He calls the reader's attention to structures, which are not readily seen in my own exposition. From Latzel's numerous philosophical observations I cite a single one:

The question remains, nevertheless, whether the anticipated insight into the necessity of foundering does not necessarily impair the originality of my active struggle against foundering; and the danger in appropriating Jaspers' philosophy is that thereby the philosophizing on the ultimate situations could, entirely contrary to its intentions, be perverted into a kind of 'shell,' to a kind of covering the rear, by which a truly genuine, original foundering could actually be prevented.

This is quite accurately seen. Where an author has such clear and telling insight into the lines of my philosophizing as Latzel, the paradoxical result is that there is least talk of him in my Reply. This paltriness is the form of highest esteem.

c. Two authors have written on the spiritual extraction of my philosophizing, namely E. M. Manasse on my relations to Max Weber, and Julius Löwenstein concerning the Biblical foundation.

With loving thoroughness Manasse sought and found in my writings whatever refers or could refer to Max Weber. The picture he thus gained he has described clearly, simply and beautifully, schooled by his steady association with the Greek world. He lets the facts simply speak for themselves; he ponders cautiously; he interprets courageously, yes, wantonly out of the depth of his own philosophizing, well grounded in Plato. The picture is amazing. In my relation to Max Weber he sees a repetition of the relation of Plato to Socrates. When something so tiny is compared with something so great, it can mean only that prototypes of human potentialities are mirrored at all stages, just as the sun in the ocean and in the dewdrop.

I approve Manasse's exposition, myself deeply stirred by the reminiscences which his quotations, from writings I had almost forgotten, have called back, as well as by the truth of his basic thought.

It is marvellous for a young man to meet a man whom he can lovingly revere without deifying him and without pushing himself on him. At quiet distance he circles about him, asking him, listening to him. The great man arouses the degree of claim which the one who looks up to him makes upon himself. Anew I am becoming conscious of that strange good fortune which came to me in my youth, a fortune which could neither be expected nor produced. At that time, when it happened, I did not objectify it all. It was neither increased nor falsified in any way by even the slightest suggestion of a look at the historical prototype conjured up by Manasse. It was a self-evident, unreflective, original attitude.

Philosophizing grows hardly out of the Naught of a single individual. Plato in his relation to Socrates is, indeed, the singularly great, never achievable and unsurpassable model, which, nevertheless, may perhaps be valid for all human philosophy. It is as if one only dared to philosophize in looking at the other. On the twisted roads life forces one to take, Max Weber became, for my wife and myself, ever and again the road to an irreplaceable assurance. Thinking of him, even in dark hours, this was always still a guarantee. In him we could know what a man is capable of, what trustworthiness and depth of the spirit is, what German can be. The question, what would Max Weber say, became the claim to envisage the essential. The content of his being, once taken up in youth, became a lasting source, out of which throughout a lifetime, ever new things are capable of growing.

Just as cautiously as upon the analogy does Manasse look upon the differences in the "Repetition." They are so vast that the comparison — which, in the depth of the younger one's coming to himself by means of the older, is true, because it strikes the familiar chord of an eternal phenomenon of human nature — no longer fits when applied to specific appearances. In our age Max Weber was the man of most comprehensive scientific capacity, specialist as a scholar, and, at the same time, at home in all sciences. He himself is present in an immortal scientific work. But perhaps here, too, Manasse's analogy to Socrates may still be applicable: in this scientific world Max Weber showed by deed and insight, the limits of the greatest possible knowledge, the splendor as well as the foundering of knowledge; he realized a new form of not-knowing.

How completely different in significance the relationship to a great man can be by the way in which the latter becomes authority, come to light in a comparison with the disciples of the poet Stefan George. On one occasion Gundolf said to me: "Had I not been a disciple of George, I would have become one of Weber." To which I replied: "That's just it, to become a Weberian is impossible." Everyone who would be so stupid as to want to become his disciple, did not comprehend him. Max Weber met everyone on principle *al pari;* he referred any young man, who had the impulse of wanting to become a disciple, back to himself and to his own freedom. Discipleship is disastrous and cannot be carried through in truthfulness. Gundolf experienced and suffered it with magnificent integrity, and drew the consequences. —

Julius Löwenstein has carefully laid bare the ground of my philosophizing in Biblical thought. He sees that this philosophizing is equally far from ecclesiastical Christianity as from orthodox Judaism, and yet is rooted in Biblical thinking. He notes in my writings the basic characteristics of the Bible: the question concerning Being is originally tied in with the question about Transcendence, and this latter with the question about God. When the answers mutually interpret each other, they still achieve no knowledge. The ontological and metaphysical answers are rejected, insofar as they want to be knowledge, not rejected as possible ciphers. Himself Biblically grounded, Löwenstein recog-

nizes my sense for the religious, for Pascal and Kierkegaard; yet
I do not make the religious a philosophical "cornerstone" nor
demand it either as confession or perform it myself. As a decisive
counterthrust against a large trend permeating the Bible, he mentions my rejection of the claim to exclusiveness on the part of the
supposedly single truth with its horrible consequences for humaneness and truthfulness. This explains, he thinks, my inclination for the universal, my interest in India and China. The weakness of my philosophizing, therefore, [he says] lies in its inability
to grant faith; its strength, in the fact that through this kind of
thinking the freedom of man in its immense potentialities is
being preserved, and in the fact that what is really seriously important depends upon one's own thinking and conduct in its
inevitable responsibility.

I agree with Löwenstein and am glad for his own so truthful
analysis, which, at the same time, inclines toward my own thinking. He emphasizes one point which, in the discussion of the
extraction of my thinking, may not be treated incidentally. How
much tradition I owe to my Jewish wife, not in the multiplicity
of contents but in the experience of original Biblical impulses
and of the piety each day pervading in her parental home, this
is difficult for me to estimate. I have known many Jews and have,
occasionally, employed the paradoxical remark, authentic Christians (in the sense of the New Testament) I had encountered
today only among Jews — very rarely. Over against that is the
other trend of Biblical religion common to both accentuatedly
believing Jews and Christians, those dedicated to the Law and
those committed to dogma; but the philosophizing man is repelled
by this.

Several contributors to this volume have justly called attention
to the derivation of my philosophizing out of Kant. There has,
however, been no detailed discussion of this. I have always owned
up to Kant. Apropos of a few remarks I may briefly say to this:
Thyssen understands me out of Kant. Although, taken by itself,
this is correct, it is no real help to the reader. For, what really
matters is *how* Kant is understood. This method of understanding
from derivation is appropriate only insofar as a common understanding of the sources, and not some familiar scheme of Kant-
interpretation from the history of philosophy (as in the fashion
of the so-called Neo-Kantianism), exerts conscious and express
guidance. As a "Kantian" I stand in opposition to Neo-Kantianism.

Walter Kaufmann, too, points out how inexpressibly much I

owe to Kant. However, when he thinks that I stand above all on the ground of the *Critique of Practical Reason,* this is hardly correct. I know this work, of course; but I have repeatedly and thoroughly studied, and again and again thought through, only the other two *Critiques.*

d) Surprising to me were two contributions which treat the significance of my philosophizing for the comprehension of poetry and art.

Helmut Rehder took the trouble to bring together, out of my writings, what can be thought of as contributions to the science of literature. He made this effort the occasion to reflect upon the philosophical presuppositions of literary research. I have read this with great interest and often with agreement.

Johannes Pfeiffer supplies more than merely a clear and beautiful report concerning the three temporal stages in which I speak, in my writings, of art and poetry, viz., in the *Psychologie der Weltanschauungen,* in *Philosophie,* and in the *Philosophische Logik.* On my own part I am conscious of having appropriated what I have said on this subject throughout from the great tradition and of having brought it, in each case, into my own respective connection. The total conception and description by Pfeiffer I take to be quite appropriate. In the objectively simple and sovereign way, which he has demonstrated so often, he has expanded and deepened my statements by tracing them in the manner peculiar to him. His critique concerning the limitation of philosophical language constitutes a gentle reproach. God means something else to him than everything He could ever mean in philosophizing. I have nothing to say to this, but must simply accept it.

e) The essay by Walter Kaufmann, which completely falls outside the tone of the other essays, demands a few separate remarks. The theme is Nietzsche. Both of us, Kaufmann and I, have written a book on Nietzsche. Kaufmann thinks that I reject his Nietzsche, and he mine. The second part of that statement is obviously correct, the first not. I appreciate the explanations of Kaufmann in his book on Nietzsche, which call special attention to aspects rarely noted (as, for example, the problem of sublimation).

"Everyone is entitled to his own Nietzsche," he continues. But, he adds, that my method is indefensible. This judgment seems astounding to me. If Kaufmann had said that this is not the correct key to an understanding of the essential Nietzsche, then I could hold this as possibly correct — although it did become the key for myself. When, however, he rejects it absolutely — as he does —, he is rejecting one of the possibilities which, it seems to me, by my rather careful performance teach something which is indispensable in Nietzsche. That Kaufmann has not accepted this, limits, in my opinion, his view of Nietzsche, but does not prevent his showing something, by way of his own observations, which is worth while.

A decisive point is the conception of Nietzsche's self-contradictoriness. To show this self-contradiction is easy. It is to be found in all philosophers, but in Nietzsche it seems to occur in a total fashion: it can be said that he takes no position without it being possible to find the opposite one in him also. The essential question is, whether these contradictions are so rich in their fulfillment that they can, in each instance, be reproduced in one thought-operation as a movement with a steady demonstration by quotations. Such an operation puts in place of a confusion — into which so many readers of Nietzsche get in reading him —, an ordered whirl which is to be executed in such fashion as to make the contradictions themselves meaningful. The co-performance of this whirl is no comfortable matter. One needs to have wind enough for at least one chapter in order to hold out as far as remembering, penetrating and mastering the whole are concerned. If one undertakes this effort, — which can succeed only through the realization of one's own total essence, assisted by intellectual operations — then this practice procures a freedom of thinking, which, without getting stuck in the false alternatives of the foreground implies not helplessness, not arbitrariness, but the systematically conscious domination of one's own thinking. Of the three Parts of my Nietzsche-volume the middle and most comprehensive Part contains this material and sets the task for the movements of thought. Of all this Kaufmann has noticed nothing. He only attacks the externality of my turns of self-contradictoriness and ambiguity. Since he himself wants to demonstrate what he takes to be a positive Nietzsche — in the doctrine of the superman and his process of sublimation, and in the doctrine of the eternal return — he conceals the quotations I have cited, in which Nietzsche himself questions these positions, although he often treats them in his texts as definitive, and, in his associations with his friends, occasionally even treats them as horrible secrets. Nietzsche's entire diction as well as his momentary behavior is such that he constantly seems to say the definitive, the absolute, and the unshakable. This stands in contrast to his innermost trend and is understandable only from the perspective of the violent passion of his thinking at the respective moment.

This is why, out of the truth of his encompassing nature, he said that it was unbearable for him to read his writings. Now, the method of my work was not at all to demonstrate the contradictoriness and oscillation as such, but to carry out the task of letting the continuous connections in the contradictions, the inner dialectic of Nietzsche's thinking, stand out.

Kaufmann reproaches me for neglecting the epochs of Nietzsche's development. But in my book (1st ed., pp. 31-46) I have expressly pointed this out and justified the sense in which the totality of that development is a unity, both in Nietzsche's own sense as well as for the interpreter. He further reproaches me with having so grossly intermingled the posthumous notes with the valid sayings of the publications that they cancel each other. Yet it was I who called attention to the posthumous notes and also to the criterion to be used in eliminating [from these notes] the merely momentary, the accidental and the deviating (this, however, also in Nietzsche's own later publications). Not by taking advantage of slips, but out of the content itself, again by proof delivered in terms of Nietzsche's own sentences, I am demonstrating the factual movement of Nietzsche's thinking as a room-making, illuminating, dialectically daring, never fixating kind of thinking.

The exposition of my Nietzsche-book, is, in all its steps, verified by Nietzsche himself. It is not easy, in the whirl of this kind of thinking, to make the factually magnificent structure and the truly disciplined and orderly thought-energy one's own. It is much easier to lift out of Nietzsche a supposedly essential positive element as the center of the whole. Bäumler did this when he drew up an alleged Nietzsche-system (of the effectiveness of quantities of power as the reality of the world), in analogy to Leibniz. This, too, is what Löwith did, although much more cautiously and emphasizing an important line of thought (with emphasis on the eternal return). And this is what Kaufmann is now doing, when he expounds the healthy content [of Nietzsche] as the doctrine of the superman, who conquers the greatest force of his passions by still greater self-control and therefore is creative. I am unable to approve this conception of Nietzsche, which minimizes him into something positive, which, after all, is always only one trend among others.

Every form of singling out is arbitrary. It is also possible, as was done by National Socialism, to ground the theory of race and the glorification of the German with its Nazi consequences, down to every detail, upon Nietzsche; just as one can see the exactly opposite position represented by Nietzsche with equal vehemence.

Kaufmann's tendency, therefore, as far as its form is concerned, is one which has been current for a long time; he simply realizes it with a new content in his Nietzsche book. Over and again one has been wanting to get positions from Nietzsche, either in order to make them one's own or else in order to fight them. In each instance this was possible only by leaving many, very essential aspects unnoticed. In this process the immense spiritual energy of Nietzsche's thinking had to disappear from sight in favor of such positions. From that point of view my method of Nietzsche-interpretation, by which all positions without exception are denuded of their absoluteness, will have to be rejected as a procedure which — as a critic says and Kaufmann thinks — silences Nietzsche.

By reference to my book, which demonstrates the movement of the questions in detail, I must deny that I interpret Nietzsche's thetic results away or that I am making a flighty romantic out of him. My entire book shows Nietzsche as an event manifesting modernity by his own sacrifice, an event the magnificence of which is lost by singling out any isolated positions.

Kaufmann, who rejects my Nietzsche-book globally by finally judging my exposition of Nietzsche as self-interpretation of my own philosophizing, i.e., as an introduction to Jaspers not to Nietzsche, deduces my attempt equally as globally from its origins. My philosophy, he claims, is an appropriation of Kantian philosophy (this is true) ; this is why I expound Nietzsche's philosophy in such a fashion that the theoretical reason is led therein to its limits without outlets (this is but one emphasis among many others in my exposition and as such is correct). This method, [based on] a reawakening of Kant, implies leading Nietzsche's thinking to Kant's backdoor-philosophy. For Nietzsche this would be an absurd irony. To me it appears equally absurd to conceive of Kant in this fashion (something which Nietzsche occasionally does in deviating misunderstandings: he read Kant very little and knew him essentially through F. A. Lange) as it is absurd to impute to me such a conception of Kant and such an application to Nietzsche.

Reaching beyond Kaufmann's propositions, I want to make a general remark. As concerns Nietzsche, there is a position in which opponents of my Nietzsche-exposition, who differ widely among themselves, agree. It has been said that Nietzsche is a last radical tear in the history of philosophy. The entire previous

philosophy is said to be negated by him. His famous sayings:
"God is dead," — "Nothing is true, everything is allowed," — "the
rise of nihilism," and many others of this kind are said to be the
signs of a complete rupture. There is said to remain only the
choice of standing either against or with him, either to continue
in the old great tradition of philosophy or else, by following
Nietzsche, to throw it over board. This is said to be the sharpness
of his position. This should not be permitted to be made harmless. But to make Nietzsche harmless is said to be precisely my
way of thinking. I am supposed not to have recognized that
sharpness. I am supposed to want the impossible, to take Nietzsche
together with the ancient great philosophy. It is supposed to be
my inclination to interpret away all these ultimate positions.

Against this conception — in which traditional Nietzsche-en-
emies and despairingly triumphant nihilists, who consider themselves entirely up-to-date and modern, are one — I have turned in
my book, not by way of mere assertions, but by a carefully executed labor of thinking, which to carry out after me will cost
some effort. I have not the slightest intention of wishing to unite
Nietzsche with the ancients — the form of expression of historically operating philosophy — nor do I wish the opposite. All such
intentions I consider senseless. Whoever has them narrows himself into a form of interpretation which has been used against
former philosophers as well: to take great philosophers as combinations and syntheses. Rather, my tendency is the natural one:
to philosophize today as is possible in the spiritual situation of
our age, on the basis of a knowledge of past events. This means
that one can not get at former philosophy honestly without being
moved and taught by what has happened afterwards. An option
against Nietzsche in favor of ancient philosophy seems to me just
as impossible as an option for Nietzsche against ancient philosophy. Such an option, if ensuing against Nietzsche, would mean
to neglect the originality in the appropriation of the great old
philosophy which is possible today. On these problems I find
nothing in Kaufmann. He has lifted out one complex of Nietzsche's thought and asserted its positivity as Nietzsche's doctrine.
This, it appears to me, is a naive behavior, which is justified
neither by Nietzsche nor by the ancient great philosophy. Yet
even this can be useful, since Kaufmann, after all, works out
thought-complexes which do occur in Nietzsche and makes these
clear. Something like that does occur in Nietzsche, but is not
on that account the philosophy of Nietzsche.

As concerns me Walter Kaufmann seems to stand on precisely

the opposite side from Latzel. To answer Kaufmann, therefore, becomes difficult for me for exactly the opposite reason: my thinking is, it seems to me, so alien to him that I find it difficult to find the point of departure from which to say anything to him.

In his brisk style, interspersed with friendlinesses and sarcasms, provocative and interesting, he shows without reservation his aversion to philosophical speculation. He likes Kant's earlier writings better than the obscurity of Kant's great works (which yet, according to one view, which also is my own, mark in philosophy an epoch in world history). True enough, stylistically speaking, obscurity is bad, as lack of clarity it is presumptuous; but on the road which leads into the depth of illuminated philosophy it is indispensable. This is why Goethe, after reading the late and perhaps most thoughtful work of Kant, the *Critique of Judgment*, wrote that, in reading Kant, he felt as if he had stepped into a bright room. One may perhaps say against Kaufmann that the surface quality of an easily understandable style actually obscures. Philosophy, which to begin with is always difficult, first goes beyond the so-called common sense in order finally to bring to its consciousness in the simplest possible form what it genuinely thinks and wills. Difficulty at this point — rarely it is true, but certainly in Kant — is the sign of a philosophical break-through into new illuminations. To reach this stage one must himself philosophize. Literary information, manifold orientation, and rational quick understanding are not sufficient.

Amazing to me are a few misjudgments of Walter Kaufmann's concerning the extraction of my thinking. He discovers an influence of the George-circle upon my thinking and proves it by a few quotations from Bertram's *Nietzsche*. However, in order to recognize Nietzsche's eternal return as a deceptive idea it is not necessary to read Bertram. I have read only through a few pages of Bertram's Nietzsche-book, because one recognizes immediately the type of spirit from which one gets no nourishment. From my youth on I have kept clear of the George-circle, recognizing by the symptoms that things were going on there which are alien to me, perhaps even hostile. For this reason I have not penetrated there at all, know neither George's poetry (except for a few individual poems) nor the works of his circle, with the exception of objectively so eminent works as Kantorowicz's *Friedrich II* or Gundolf's *Shakespeare* (which he wrote when he had already been repudiated by George). It must appear odd to me to see myself brought into contact with this spiritual world.

Amazing, too, are some of Kaufmann's evaluations, as for example when, following a contemporary aberration, he assigns equal rank to Freud and Nietzsche. Both, according to Kaufmann, have the distinction of being good Europeans, whereas I remain caught in the German tradition: this latter I hear gladly, but it does not exclude the former. Both stood in the great world of the enlightenment, I not: I hope to be allowed to contradict this radically for my person.

f) The not easily surveyable essay by Eduard Baumgarten provokes a separate reply. From among his numerous disclosures of my not understanding Max Weber, Goethe, Kant, I single out a particularly surprising one. He reproaches me with a radical deviation from Max Weber. First of all in method. For, according to Baumgarten, I do not, in my discussions of evil "in fully carried through value discussion," arrive at the clear view of opposite possibilities between which the decision is to be made. Yet, to demand and to do this is said to be the philosophy of Max Weber. Although speaking methodologically at this point, Baumgarten does not enter upon the multiplicity of methods which are at one's disposal in talking about evil. Rather, he considers the thinking which chooses alternatives as the essential and philosophical one.

Max Weber, however, considered precisely this procedure as not philosophical. At one point in his famous sketch of the directions and stages of religious world-rejection he says:

The constructed scheme has of course only the purpose of being an ideal typical medium of orientation, not of teaching a philosophy of its own. Its intellectually constructed types of conflicts of the 'orders of life' signify merely: at these points inner conflicts are possible and 'adequate,' — but by no means: there is no standpoint from which they could be considered 'cancelled.'

Not possibilities for choice of action, therefore, but a scheme for orientation did Max Weber have in mind. With that he finds in the inexhaustible and self-contradictory reality of human life a few lines of meaningful consequences, which, insofar as they are realized, make reality comprehensible.

Baumgarten, however, will reply that he did not mean this. Rather, Max Weber says somewhere else that we can note what we genuinely want only by confronting concrete problems, that is to say, only in real situations and by our reactions to those situations. We never get there by abstract, that is to say, theoretical, situation-less reflections about possibilities. Now Baumgarten seems to interpret this to mean that real choice is the decision between general possibilities which speak genuinely, with the force of reality, only now, possibilities which otherwise are only distantly seen. It is as if concrete action followed only from a general, formulatable principle, from a final, expressable position. If one knows the ultimately possible theoretical positions, one could, so to say, figure out from them what must be done. The ideal is said to be to follow the consequence of the ideal type to which one belongs. This, however, is the disastrous confusion between the orientation of research on ideal types constructed by the standard of consequences, and the *'existential'* reality of living, responsible man (such confusion can not claim to follow Max Weber). The concrete situation, which Max Weber pictures so impressively as revelatory, does not culminate in knowledge, the schematic character of which for the purpose of orientation in contrast to philosophy Max Weber so expressly emphasizes.

In the progress of his discussions Baumgarten confuses the concreteness of the situation calling for decision with the concreteness of the empirically given and with the concreteness of a philosophical problem. But, if all of this is called concreteness, then the first is of *'existential,'* the second of theoretical, and the third of speculative significance. According to Baumgarten, Max Weber's testing of one's own position by one's attitude towards the sharply pointed, entirely concrete problems should take place in my philosophizing with reference to the concrete problem of radical evil. Here is, first of all, the concreteness of a decisive situation confused with the concreteness of a philosophical problem. Then Baumgarten thinks erroneously that I have selectively sacrificed Goethe's position to that of Kant.

Now, for the discussion of evil it is quite correct to point to the concrete situation in which the discussion takes place. How do things lie here? I have discussed the content of Kant's essay on the radical evil in lecture-courses in Heidelberg and in a lecture in Zürich in 1935. This [essay] clarified for me the situation under the domination of the National Socialists, a domination which was illegally achieved but affirmed by the majority of the German people. In the situation of complete helplessness one could not speak directly on the matter, but indirectly. What was involved were my colleagues in Heidelberg and my occasional discussions there. Not evil as deviltry (a conception which Baumgarten falsely ascribes to Kant), but as the self-deceiving inversion of the conditional relationship between the will to happiness and moral claim: this was the basic appearance of the co-operation on the part of so many otherwise quite decent men. They wanted to be a part of it, justify it, because they received and increased their happiness, as they understood it, from participation in the regime, under the self-deceiving proviso of opposition in special cases. It was in this that I saw Kant's radical evil and explained my own conduct; I did precisely not see the deviltry which Kant denied completely and which now may perhaps still have been a reality in several individual national-socialist leaders and their accomplices. Yet not this deviltry, but the ones who submitted were the problem. Whoever at that time listened and understood, and who today reads these apparently so abstract statements, comprehends them as behavior-understanding in a situation in harmony with Max Weber's meaning. Baumgarten discusses my expositions as taking a position in philosophy, afar from the world. I make my choice *in concreto* of my own doings, not in the judgment concerning positions which are formulated theoretically. But such formulations in their movement are of the greatest significance for the choice; not in order to have at one's disposal a means to figure out the correct choice, but to illuminate the realm in which such a choice takes place.

Max Weber's thoughts which — aside from their significance for objective knowledge — lead to the seriousness of the historical decision but do not anticipate that decision; which, above all, do not pretend to be a survey of ultimate possibilities into which, as definitively known, every decision is squeezed; [these thoughts] are falsely conceived by Baumgarten as philosophy. This would, however, in practice lead to an endlessly arguing, tapeworm-like continuous discussion, whereby one either withdraws from the decision — because in the meantime one has only reflected on it so that it overwhelms him as if from the outside — or else whereby one is in a position to justify and to reject all and everything. The confusion between the means of scientific orientation and philosophy leads to the loss of thoroughness in research as well as to the loss of the seriousness of decision, in favor of just talk.

In consequence of this misunderstanding Baumgarten speaks of my "decision" against Goethe's critique of Kant's radical evil. There is no such thing. In this reflection on evil there is neither action nor decision. Nor is it a value discussion concerning the possibilities of behavior, but immersion into the possibilities of speculation. One may call this speculation abstract because no situation in it presses to a choice. What is abstract here can, however, in another sense have an extremely concrete character, and it has such character wherever genuine philosophizing is going on. It is a thinking, not in a specific situation, but in the situation of man as such. Whether and how I assure myself in it, this arises out of definite individual situations and reacts back upon them.

True enough, Max Weber's value-discussion — a discussion which orients, compares and thinks out consequences — too, is a means to illumination. It helps to make the hidden effects transparent. It can help to notice the difference between psychological passions and the seriousness of eternal decisions, in which one's own affects expire in favor of the calm, unswervable decision of the essence. But it does not yet lead into the meaning of the historical decisions themselves. It is able to think rational objectifications of thinkable meaning as an echo of that reality. To confuse it with reality itself leads to complete entanglement. Ultimate positions, which are rationally formulated, are never the sufficient expression for the historical struggles and differences.

According to Baumgarten, objectively I leave Max Wexer by holding the practical consequence of philosophizing, in his opinion, as insignificant; whereas Max Weber was interested precisely in these in all his investigations of the forms of belief. Here the types of practical consequences are being confused by Baumgarten. If, with Kant, I see the depth of the categorical imperative in its formal character and in the fact that its significance is so comprehensive that its concrete historical application can not already support itself on firm, definite, specific prescriptions, but must first find itself with its [i.e., the categorical imperative's] help by means of "practical judgment;" I have not, by so doing, deemed the practical consequences as trivial. On the contrary, all philosophy has its concrete meaning in these consequences. But these consequences cannot already be found by rational deduction, whereby life would be transformed into an arithmetical problem. Rather, the practical philosophical consequences tend to be real in the calm of unswervable, illuminated self-evidence. In it men are united; whereas mere philosophical propositions, by dint of their rational multiplicity, seduce to substancelessness. This saves itself by thinking in the firmly held distance from reality, but remains thereby a saved naught of the arbitrarily movable point of being able to think thusly, a place of opinions.

Baumgarten's misunderstanding, of taking Weber's magnificent orientations for the purpose of historical research themselves for philosophy, leads in his critical discussions — or so it seems to me — into a procedure which looks like a political transaction among the Great Powers. One acts as if there existed definite, firm substances, which meet each other, discuss, lay down their differences, make compromises. Such political negotiations, which Baumgarten elsewhere has so excellently and impressively depicted as American procedure, belong and are truthful on their own level, for purposes of existence, on the presupposition of a mutual, already uniting confidence. But this confidence already has its root on a higher plane, on which there can be no compromises. Here there is only suspended communication from out of the origin of the Unconditional and the One. That only is philosophy. No one can claim possession of the One for himself, even though he stakes everything on achieving relation with It. When he philosophizes he speaks out of a perhaps erroneous contact with It.

Communicability takes place only in the objectivity of identifiable knowledge, which, alternatively, leads to a result in objective discussion. This form is improper in philosophizing. Baumgarten treats sentences that occur in the philosophical movement of thought like positions, opinions, and then these as on a par with each other, which now argumentatively discuss with each other as equals. In philosophizing this appears to me to be a strange and unproductive procedure. It is carried over to philosophy from scientific discussion and from political action. Only in so far as those other two forms of communication are a basis also for philosophizing do they apply, but then precisely only in their own purity, not in a mixture.

Amazing substantial errors (not mere inaccuracies) slip into Baumgarten's angry and cheerful game of argumentation, with which he grasps dramatic points. In the exposition of the contrast between Goethe and Kant as concerns the concept of the radical evil, he thinks Kant asserts malice as the radical evil, whereas Kant expressly denies malicious reason to man because man is not a devilish being. The depth of Kant's thought is entirely lost in such a dualistic, Manichaic conception. Baumgarten returns repeatedly to this thesis of the malevolence of man, which Kant rejected, as supposedly Kantian.

Another, less weighty, example: Baumgarten cites that, before the abyss of disaster, I spoke of "what caused us to lay down all books, even Aeschylus, Shakespeare and the Bible, in frightened terror." My sentence read: "we have come to know situations in which we no longer had any inclination to read Goethe, in which we reached for Shakespeare, the Bible, Aeschylus, if we were still able to read at all."

A third example of his wrong quoting. He has me saying: "Everything good, all love stems from its opposite movement, which the sting of the radical evil unchains — this hardly to be surpassed claim to the inwardness of man." My sentence, which he has disfigured by pulling in words which occur in other connections, reads: "The genuine lighting up of things, every light by which existence is illuminated, every origin of love in which men and world first become visible as themselves — all of this grows up into trustworthy truth only by bringing the continuous tendency for perversion of the radical evil again into correct order by constantly renewed decision." That was said in view of the comfortable self-satisfaction, in which even love itself becomes questionable. In no way do I speak of a counter movement, nor do I intend anywhere at all to derive the formation of the most positive from the negative.

If I wish to answer Baumgarten I become helpless, and that for a methodically essential reason. In the underbrush of endlessly changing oppositions one feels himself without a path. The clear question and the clear advance of thought are replaced by always new, always other turns, sometimes perceptibly applicable, sometimes abstractly formal, which, on the whole, remain aimless or else are motivated by the aim to find surprising possibilities of opposition. Thus he builds windmills, which he declares to be my positions, in order, like Don Quixote, to fight them. I cannot deny that I follow such a game with a certain sad enjoyment. It is as if an excellent race-driver led his horses outside the track and, playfully changing, let them race now against this and then against the other handicap, at the one already forgetting the other. In manner and talent it is a brilliant symbol for that with which all of us constantly have to do in our own spiritual life, for the necessity of conquering the unendingnesses into which intellect and idea lure us, to go astray in immense sidepaths, pieces of news, possibilities which have run away from the leading guidance of the idea. Baumgarten's bubbling argumentation entices, it seems to me, by paradoxes, by disclosures which dupe for the moment, and it disappoints by its non-committal character (Unverbindlichkeit). All of this, however, takes place in friendly community, like a social game, so that one does not wish to become cross.

Only to one sentence I must still say a word. Baumgarten desires that I should answer his attack by my showing "why and how far he [Jaspers], in the progress of his philosophizing, had found it necessary to deviate from Max Weber's positions, to gain distance against them or decisively to criticize, to overcome them." My reply: I was not compelled to do anything of the kind, for possible developments of Max Weber's demand for the "value freedom of the sciences" are no pertinent corrections of his intention. Max Weber did not at all expressly philosophize. His great philosophic act is his will to science in its total extent, the constitution of the purity of scientific research in sociology and history — with few followers until now —, and therewith his knowledge of the methods and limitations of science. In the self-illumination of modern science his work is epochal. What sort of incidentals Baumgarten has in his head, when in view of the greatness of this work, he thinks of over-taking it, I do not know. The Nietzsche-quotation, which he marshals, I take to be one of the boyish assertions, which slipped into Nietzsche in consequence of his mental illness. My conception of the work and of the philosophical personality of Max Weber can be ascertained in two of my writings (1920 and 1932). My conception has not changed.

* * * * *

In concluding this reply I repeat my thanks. May the two last authors, whose style of lively attack I tried to answer in similar fashion, pardon me. They, too, have shown me friendliness and stand in the circle of all these men and women to whom I am so greatly obligated. My gratitude belongs not last to those authors of whom least has been said precisely because they followed my works with penetrating and at the same time approving understanding. All, however, without exception, I thank that I have heard important things from them, that I have learned and got ahead, that I was encouraged to re-examine my thinking. I am glad that I was able to reply to at least some of their objections.

Karl Jaspers

BIBLIOGRAPHY OF THE WRITINGS OF KARL JASPERS TO 1957

Compiled by
KURT ROSSMANN

Revised and continued from 1958 to 1973 by GISELA GEFKEN

NOTE TO THE BIBLIOGRAPHY

THE BIBLIOGRAPHY appears in chronological order. Because of the unusual length of this volume, it has not been possible to include the tables of contents of any volumes with the exception of books such as RECHENSCHAFT UND AUSBLICK, which is a collection of addresses and essays. Reprints of essays and tracts in daily papers or in nontechnical journals have been omitted. The critical reports in the fields of neurology, psychiatry and psychology from 1910 to 1921 are cited without titles, only by dates.

KURT ROSSMANN

HEIDELBERG, GERMANY
JULY 11, 1957

WRITINGS OF KARL JASPERS THROUGH 1972

NOTE: Items marked with an asterisk are books.

1909

*1. HEIMWEH UND VERBRECHEN. – Inaugural Dissertation, Heidelberg. – Leipzig (F. C. W. Vogel), 116 pp. – Reprinted in: Gross' *Arch. f. Krim.-Anthropol.,* Vol. 35, Nr. 1, 1909.

1910

2. EIFERSUCHTSWAHN. Ein Beitrag zur Frage: 'Entwicklung einer Persönlichkeit' oder 'Prozess'? – In: *Zs. f. d. ges. Neurologie & Psychiatrie,* Berlin & Leipzig (J. Springer/J. A. Barth), Originalien, Vol. 1, pp. 567-637.
3. DIE METHODEN DER INTELLIGENZPRÜFUNG UND DER BEGRIFF DER DEMENZ. Critical report. – In: *Zs. f. d. ges. Neurologie & Psychiatrie,* Referate & Ergebnisse, Vol. 1, pp. 402-452.
4. Critical Reports on work in the fields of neurology, psychiatry & psychology. – In: *Zs. f. d. ges. Neurol. & Psych.,* Referate & Ergebnisse, Vol. 1, pp. 194-196; 335; 394-396.

1911

5. ZUR ANALYSE DER TRUGWAHRNEHMUNGEN (LEIBHAFTIGKEIT UND REALITÄTSURTEIL). – In: *Zs. f. d. ges. Neurol. & Psych.,* Originalien, Vol. 6, pp. 460-535.
6. Critical Reports on work in the fields of neurology, psychiatry & psychology. – In: *Zs. f. d. ges. Neurol. & Psych.,* Referate & Ergebnisse, Vol. 2, pp. 98; 149f; 160.

1912

7. DIE TRUGWAHRNEHMUNGEN. – In: *Zs. f. d. ges. Neurol. & Psych.,* Referate & Ergebnisse, Vol. 4, pp. 289-354.
8. DIE PHÄNOMENOLOGISCHE FORSCHUNGSRICHTUNG IN DER PSYCHOPATHOLOGIE. – In: *Zs. f. d. ges. Neurol. & Psych.,* Originalien, Vol. 9, pp. 391-408.
Translation: Into *English:* THE PHENOMENOLOGICAL APPROACH IN PSYCHOPATHOLOGY, in: *British Journal of Psychiatry,* London, T. 114, Nr. 516, 1968, pp. 1313-1323.

9. Critical Reports on work in the fields of neurology, psychiatry & psychology. — In: *Zs. f. d. ges. Neurol. & Psych.*, Referate & Ergebnisse, Vol. 4, pp. 375-380; 382f; 886f; 887f; 888; 934f; 948f. Same Vol. also pp. 159f; 160f; 163; 164.

1913

*10. ALLGEMEINE PSYCHOPATHOLOGIE. EIN LEITFADEN FÜR STUDIERENDE, ÄRZTE UND PSYCHOLOGEN. — Berlin (J. Springer), xv + 338 pp. 2nd ed'n, revised, 1920, xiv + 416 pp. — 3rd revised ed'n, 1922, xv + 458 pp. — 4th entirely revised ed'n, 1946, xvi + 748 pp. — 5th (unchanged) ed'n, 1948. — 6th (unchanged) ed'n, 1953. — 7th (unchanged) ed'n, 1959. — 8th (unchanged) ed'n, 1965. — 9th (unchanged) ed'n, 1973.
Translations: Of 3rd ed'n into *French:* PSYCHOPATHOLOGIE GÉNÉRALE by A. Kastler & J. Mendousse, Paris (Alcan), 1928; 2nd ed'n, 1934. — Of 4th ed'n into *Spanish:* PSICOPATOLOGÍA GENERAL by R. O. Saubidet & D. A. Santillán, Buenos Aires (Editorial Beta), 1950/51; 2nd ed'n, 1955; 3rd ed'n, 1960. — Of 4th ed'n into *Japanese:* SEISHIN BY ORIGAKU SORON by Y. Uchimura *et al.*, Tokyo (Iwanami-Shoten), 1953/56. — Of 7th ed'n into *English:* GENERAL PSYCHOPATHOLOGY by J. Hoenig & Marian W. Hamilton (with Foreword by E. W. Anderson), Manchester (Manchester Univ. Pr.), 1963. — Of 7th ed'n into *Italian:* PSICOPATOLOGIA GENERALE by Romolo Priori, Roma (Il Pensiero Scientifico), 1964. Partial Reprint: WESEN UND KRITIK DER PSYCHOTHERAPIE. — München (R. Piper), 1954; 63 pp. — 2nd ed'n, 1958.
Translations: Into *French:* DE LA PSYCHOTHÉRAPIE by Hélène Naef, Paris (Presses Univ. de France), 1956. — Into *Spanish:* ESENCIA Y CRÍTICA DE LA PSICOTERAPIA, by Roberto Podestá, Buenos Aires (Comp. Gen. Fabril Ed.), 1959. — Into *English:* THE NATURE OF PSYCHOTHERAPY, (Partial Reprint from: GENERAL PSYCHOPATHOLOGY), Manchester (Manchester Univ. Pr.), 1964. — Into *Japanese:* SEISHIN RYOHO by Akaji Fujita, Tokyo (Risôsha), 1966.

11. KAUSALE UND 'VERSTÄNDLICHE' ZUSAMMENHÄNGE ZWISHEN SCHICKSAL UND PSYCHOSE BEI DER DEMENTIA PRAECOX (SCHIZOPHRENIE). — In: *Zs. f. d. ges. Neurol. & Psych.*, Originalien, Vol. 14, pp. 158-263.

12. ÜBER LEIBHAFTIGE BEWUSSTHEITEN (BEWUSSTHEITSTÄUSCHUNGEN). EIN PSYCHOPATHOLOGISCHES ELEMENTARSYMPTOM. — In: *Zs. f. Pathopsychologie*, Leipzig, Vol. 2, pp. 151-161.

13. Critical Reports on work in the fields of neurology, psychiatry & psychology. — In: *Zs. f. d. ges. Neurol. & Psych.*, Referate & Ergebnisse, Vol. 6, pp. 247f; 248f; 504f; 548ff; 583; 583f; 584f; 700; 885; 885f; 886f; 887; 899; 970f; 1141f; 1144f; 1145; 1145f; 1146; 1146f; 1151; 1173; 1290. Vol. 7, pp. 33f; 89ff; 268; 270f; 271; 403; 403f; 477f; 800ff; 1088.

1914

14. Critical Reports on work in the fields of neurology, psychiatry & psychology. — In: *Zs. f. d. ges. Neurol. & Psych.*, Referate & Ergebnisse,

Vol. 8, pp. 22f; 461f; 464; 582f; 584. Vol. 9, pp. 191; 194f; 195; 417f; 474.

1915

15. Critical Reports on work in the fields of neurology, psychiatry & psychology. — In: *Zs. f. d. ges. Neurol. & Psych.,* Referate & Ergebnisse, Vol. 11, pp. 37f; 38f; 39f; 40; 168f; 169; 170; 170f; 171; 172f; 173; 182f; 183; 186; 221f; 224; 234; 436; 436f; 437f; 438; 438f; 633f.

1916

16. Critical Reports on work in the fields of neurology, psychiatry & psychology. — In: *Zs. f. d. ges. Neurol. & Psych.,* Referate & Ergebnisse, Vol. 12, pp. 124; 125; 126; 218; 219; 219f; 220; 220f; 221; 313; 454f; 455f; 456; 456f; 457; 457f; 458.

1917

17. Critical Reports on work in the fields of neurology, psychiatry & psychology. — In: *Zs. f. d. ges. Neurol. & Psych.,* Referate & Ergebnisse, Vol. 13, pp. 116; 117f; 162ff; 394; 394f; 396; 397; 397f; 403f; 447f; 543f; 549f; 550; 550f; 582; 611; 612; 613. Vol. 14, pp. 9; 9ff; 11; 11f; 12; 123.

1919

*18. PSYCHOLOGIE DER WELTANSCHAUUNGEN. — Berlin (J. Springer), xii + 428 pp.
    2nd rev. ed'n., 1920, xiii + 486 pp. — 3rd (unchanged) ed'n, 1925. — 4th ed'n (with a new Preface, pp. viii-xii), 1954. 5th (unchanged) ed'n, 1960. — 6th (unchanged) ed'n, 1971.
    Translations: Into *Italian:* PSICOLOGIA DELLE VISIONI DEL MONDO by Vincenzo Loriga, Rome (Astrolabio), 1950. (From the 3rd ed'n.) — Into *Spanish:* PSICOLOGÍA DE LAS CONCEPCIONES DEL MUNDO by Mariano Marin Casero, Madrid (Ed. Gredos), 1967. (From the 4th ed'n.) — Into *Japanese:* SEKAIKAN NO SHINRIGAKU by Tadao Uemura and Toshio Maeda, Tokyo (Risôsha), 1971.

19. Critical Reports on work in the fields of neurology, psychiatry & psychology. — In: *Zs. f. d. ges. Neurol. & Psych.,* Referate & Ergebnisse, Vol. 18, pp. 113f; 114; 123f.

1920

20. Critical Reports on work in the fields of neurology, psychiatry & psy-

chology.— In: *Zs. f. d. ges. Neurol. & Psych.*, Referate & Ergebnisse, Vol. 21, pp. 6; 7; 10; 10f; 11; 12; 12f; 13f; 14f; 15; 15f; 16; 22; 96f; 99; 99f; 100f; 101f; 102; 113; 113f.

1921

*21. MAX WEBER. Address at the Memorial Service arranged by the students of the University of Heidelberg on July 17, 1920.— Tübingen (C. B. J. Mohr), 27 pp. (Not identical with #28.) 2nd ed'n, 1926.
Translation: Into *Japanese:* MAX WEBER by T. Kanba, Tokyo (Sôgensha), 1950; 2nd ed'n, Tokyo (Risôsha), 1966.
 22. Critical Reports on work in the fields of neurology, psychiatry & psychology.— In: *Zs. f. d. ges. Neurol. & Psych.*, Referate & Ergebnisse, Vol. 23, pp. 133f; 302f; 303; 324. Vol. 25, pp. 111f.

1922

*23. STRINDBERG UND VAN GOGH. (Attempt at a pathological analysis, drawing also on Swedenborg and Hölderlin for additional comparison.) — Essay in cooperative volume: ARBEITEN ZUR ANGEWANDTEN PSYCHIATRIE, Bern (Bircher), 125 pp.
2nd rev'd ed'n, Berlin (Springer), 1926, 151 pp.; 3rd (unchanged) ed'n, Bremen (Johs. Storm), 1949 & 1951, 131 pp.; 4th (unchanged) ed'n, München (Piper), 1957.
Translations: Into *Japanese:* STRINDBERG TO VAN GOGH by Masashi Murakami, Kyoto (Yamaguchi-Shoten), 1946; 2nd ed'n, Tokyo (Sôgensha), 1952; 3rd ed'n, Tokyo (Misuzushobô), 1959.— Into *French:* STRINDBERG ET VAN GOGH, SWEDENBORG, HOELDERLIN by Hélène Naef (with a Foreword by Maurice Blanchot), Paris (Les Éditions de Minuit), 1953; 2nd ed'n, 1970.— Into *Spanish:* GENIO Y LOCURA by A. C. Robredo, Madrid (Aguilar), 1955; 2nd ed'n, 1956; 3rd ed'n, 1961; 4th ed'n, 1968.
 24. ENTGEGNUNG.— Reply to: Birnbaum, K., "Von der Geistigkeit der Geisteskranken und ihrer psychiatrischen Erfassung." Open letter to Professor Jaspers.— In: *Zs. f. d. ges. Neurol. & Psych.*, Originalien, Vol. 77, pp. 515-518.

1923

*25. DIE IDEE DER UNIVERSITÄT.— Berlin (J. Springer), vi + 81 pp. (Not identical with #40.)

1931

*26. DIE GEISTIGE SITUATION DER ZEIT.— Berlin (W. de Gruyter & Co.), Volume 1,000 of Sammlung Göschen, 191 pp.

2nd, 3rd, & 4th (unchanged) ed'ns, 1931, 1932, 1932; 5th, partially revised ed'n, 1933. New printings of 5th ed'n, 1947, 1949, 1955, 1960, 1965, 1971.
Translations: (all from the 5th ed'n) Into *English:* MAN IN THE MODERN AGE by E. and C. Paul, London (Routledge), 1st ed'n, 1933; 2nd ed'n, 1951; 3rd ed'n 1959. — Into *Spanish:* AMBIENTE ESPIRITUAL DE NUESTRO TIEMPO by R. de la Serna, Barcelona, Buenos Aires (Editorial Labor), 1933; 2nd (unchanged) ed'n, 1955. — Into *Japanese:* GENDAI NO TETSUGAKUTEKI KOSATSU by I. Tokunaga and M. Tomioka, Tokyo (Mikasashobô), 1936. — Into *French:* LA SITUATION SPIRITUELLE DE NOTRE ÉPOQUE by J. Ladrière and W. Biemel, Paris (Desclée de Brouwer) and Louvain (Nauwelaerts), 1951; 2nd and 3rd (unchanged) ed'n, 1952; 4th ed'n (with Postface by X. Tilliette), 1966. — Into *Japanese:* GENDAI NO SEISHINTEKI JOKYO by M. Iijima, Tokyo (Kawadeshobô), 1954; 2nd ed'n, 1955; 3rd ed'n, 1971. Into *Korean:* HYONDAE UI CHONGSINJOK WIGI by Yun Myŏng-no *et al.,* Seoul (Ilsinsa), 1959. Into *Korean:* SIDAE UI CHONGSINJÔK SANGHWANG by Chi Song, Seoul (Yangjisa), 1965. — Into *Portuguese:* A SITUAÇÃO ESPIRITUAL DO NOSSO TEMPO by J. Modesto, Lisboa, São Paulo (Moraes Editores), 1968. Partial reprint of the German text (Introduction) with linguistic and contentual annotations for use in public schools, Tokyo (Daigakusyorin), 1950.

1932

*27. PHILOSOPHIE. — 3 vols. — Berlin (J. Springer).
Vol. I: Philosophische Weltorientierung; xiv + 340 pp. Vol. II: Existenzerhellung; 441 pp. Vol. III: Metaphysik; 237 pp.; 2nd (unchanged) ed'n in *one* vol., 1948, xix + 913 pp.; 3rd (unchanged) ed'n (with an added postscript) in 3 vols. (I: LV + 340 pp.; II: XI + 440 pp.; III: VIII + 276 pp.), 1956. 4th (unchanged) ed'n, 1973.
Translations: Into *Japanese:* TETSUGAKU by M. Mutô, Tokyo (Sôgensha). 1953. Into *Japanese:* TETSUGAKU by M. Mutô, S. Shida and S. Suzuki, Tokyo (Sôbunsha), 1964/69. — Into *Spanish:* FILOSOFÍA by F. Vela, Madrid (Revista de Occidente), 1958/59. — Into *English:* PHILOSOPHY by E. B. Ashton, Chicago and London (Univ. of Chicago Press), 1969/71.
*28. MAX WEBER. Deutsches Wesen im politischen Denken, im Forschen und Philosophieren. — Oldenburg i. O. (G. Stalling), 79 pp.; 2nd (unchanged) ed'n, Bremen (J. Storm), 1946; 3rd ed'n, Bremen (Storm), 1948; 4th ed'n, München (Piper), 1958 (with a new Foreword).
Translations: Into *Japanese:* MAX WEBER by T. Kanba, Tokyo (Sôgensha), 1950. (Not identical with #21.) 2nd ed'n, Tokyo (Risôsha), 1966. — Into *English:* MAX WEBER AS POLITICIAN, SCIENTIST, PHILOSOPHER by R. Manheim, in: Jaspers: *Three Essays,* New York (Harcourt, Brace & World), 1964, pp. 187-274; also in: Jaspers: *Leonardo, Descartes, Max Weber,* London (Routledge & Kegan Paul), 1965, pp. 187-274. — Into *Italian:* MAX WEBER POLITICO, SCIENZIATO, FILOSOFO by E. Pocar, Napoli (Morano), 1969.

1935

*29. VERNUNFT UND EXISTENZ. – Five lectures given at the University of Groningen (Netherlands), Groningen (J. W. Wolters), 115 pp.; 2nd (unchanged) ed'n, Bremen (J. Storm), 1947, 124 pp.; 3rd ed'n, 1949; 4th (unchanged) ed'n, München (Piper), 1960, 155 pp.; 5th (unchanged) ed'n, 1973, 126 pp.
Translations: Into *Italian:* RAGIONE ED ESISTENZA by Enzo Paci, Milano (Bocca), 1942. Into *Japanese:* RISEI TO JITSUZON by Masao Kusanagi, Tokyo (Sôgensha), 1949. 2nd ed'n, 1951. 3rd ed'n, Tokyo (Shinchôsha), 1955. 4th ed'n, 1966. – Into *English:* REASON AND EXISTENZ by William Earle, New York (Noonday Press), 1955. 2nd ed'n, 1959. – Into *Spanish:* RAZÓN Y EXISTENCIA by Haraldo Kahnemann, Buenos Aires (Nova), 1959. – Into *Korean:* ISONG KWA SILCHON by Hwang Mun-su, Seoul (Hwimun ch'ulp'ansa), 1972, pp. 351-464.

1936

*30. NIETZSCHE. Einführung in das Verständnis seines Philosophierens. – Berlin (W. de Gruyter & Co.), 487 pp.; 2nd and 3rd (unchanged) ed'ns, 1947 & 1950.
Translations: Into *French:* NIETZSCHE by H. Niel (with a prefatory letter from Jean Wahl), Paris (Gallimard), 1950. Into *Japanese:* NIETZSCHE by M. Kusanagi, Tokyo (Sôgensha), 1949/50. 2nd ed'n, Tokyo (Shinchôsha), 1954/55. 3rd ed'n, Tokyo (Risôsha), 1966/67. – Into *Spanish:* NIETZSCHE by Emilio Estiú, Buenos Aires (Editorial Sudamericana), 1963. – Into *English:* NIETZSCHE by Charles F. Wallraff and Frederick J. Schmitz, Tucson (Univ. of Arizona Press), 1965.

1937

*31. LA PENSÉE DE DESCARTES ET LA PHILOSOPHIE. – Special 'DESCARTES' Supplement to *Revue philosophique,* Paris (Alcan), Vol. 62, Nos. 5/6 & 7/8, pp. 40-148, 1937, and as a separate volume, 1938, 112 pp. (translated into French by H. Pollnow).
Translations: Into *German:* DESCARTES UND DIE PHILOSOPHIE, Berlin (W. de Gruyter & Co.), 1937, 104 pp.; 2nd (unchanged) ed'n, 1948; 3rd ed'n, 1956; 4th ed'n, 1966. – Into *Spanish:* DESCARTES Y LA FILOSOFÍA by Oswald Bayer, Buenos Aires (Leviatán), 1958. Into *Japanese:* DEKARUTO TO TETSUGAKU by Eisei Shigeta, Tokyo (Risôsha), 1961; 2nd ed'n, 1965. – Into *English:* DESCARTES AND PHILOSOPHY by Ralph Manheim, in: Jaspers: *Three Essays,* New York (Harcourt, Brace & World), 1964, pp. 59-185; also in: Jaspers: *Leonardo, Descartes, Max Weber,* London (Routledge & Kegan Paul), 1965, pp. 59-185.
32. SUBJECTIVITÉ ET TRANSCENDANCE. – Correspondence with the Société française de philosophie, meeting of December 4. – In: *Bulletin de la Société française de philosophie,* Paris.

1938

*33. EXISTENZPHILOSOPHIE. Three lectures given at the Freie Hochstift in Frankfurt a/Main, in Sept. 1937. — Berlin & Leipzig (W. de Gruyter & Co.), 86 pp.; 2nd enlarged ed'n (with postscript), 1956, vi + 90 pp.; 3rd ed'n, 1964.
Translations: Into *Greek:* HYPOSTATIKE PHILOSOPHIA by P. Kanellopoulos, in: *Archeion Philosophias,* Vol. IX, Nr. 1, pp. 117-145; Nr. 3, pp. 257-289; Nr. 4, pp. 361-394, Athens, 1938. Into *Italian:* LA FILOSOFIA DELL' ESISTENZA by O. Abate (together with a preface by A. Banfi and a translation of the 5th lecture from REASON AND EXISTENZ), Milan (Bompiani), 1940. 2nd ed'n, 1943; 3rd ed'n, 1964; 4th ed'n, 1967. — Into *Japanese:* JITSUZON TETSUGAKU by S. Suzuki, Tokyo (Mikasa), 1940; 2nd ed'n (Risôsha), 1950; 3rd ed'n, 1961; 4th ed'n, 1964. — Into *Spanish:* FILOSOFÍA DE LA EXISTENCIA by Luis Rodríguez Aranda, Madrid (Aguilar), 1958; 2nd ed'n, 1961; 3rd ed'n, 1968. — Into *Serbo-Croatian:* FILOSOFIJA EGZISTENCIJE by Miodrag Cekić, in: Jaspers: *Filozofija egzistencije/Uvod u filozofiju,* Beograd (Prosveta), 1967, pp. 33-120. — Into *English:* PHILOSOPHY OF EXISTENCE by Richard F. Grabeu, Philadelphia (Univ. of Pennsylvania Press), 1971. — Into *Korean:* SILCHON CH'ORHAK by Yi Sang-ch'ŏl, Seoul (Hwimun ch'ulp'ansa), 1972, pp. 270-350.
34. WESEN UND WERT DER WISSENSCHAFT. — In: *Eltheto,* Vol. 92, Nr. 4, Groningen.
Translation: Into *French:* ESSENCE ET VALEUR DE LA SCIENCE, in: *Revue philosophique,* Vol. 64, Jan.-June 1939, Paris (Alcan), pp. 5-13.

1939

35. ANTICIPATION SUR L'AVENIR DE LA CIVILISATION. — In: *Civilisation,* Paris, Vol. I, Nr. 4 (translated into French by D. Halévy).

1941

36. LA FILOSOFIA DELL' ESISTENZA NEL MIO SVILUPPO SPIRITUALE (with remarks for university-education by Prof. Aliotta). — In: *Rivista Internazionale di Filosofia 'Logos,'* Gubbio (Oderisi), Fasc. III, pp. 1-36.

1945

37. GELEITWORT FÜR DIE MONATSSCHRIFT *DIE WANDLUNG.* — In: *Die Wandlung,* Heidelberg (Schneider), Vol. I, Nr. 1, pp. 3-6.
38. ERNEUERUNG DER UNIVERSITÄT. Address at the reopening of the Medical Faculty of the University of Heidelberg in 1945. — In: *Die Wandlung,* Heidelberg (L. Schneider), Vol. I, Nr. 1, pp. 66-74; also in: *Vom neuen Geist der Universität,* Berlin/Heidelberg, 1947, pp. 18-26; *Reprint* of the German text with annotations for use in public schools, Tokyo (Ikubundo), 1963.

Translations: Into *French:* RETOUR A L'UNITÉ DE LA SCIENCE, in: *Université,* Paris, 1946, Vol. IX, pp. 24-31.—Into *English:* THE RE-DEDICATION OF GERMAN SCHOLARSHIP, by Marianne Zuckerkandl, in: *The American Scholar,* New York, Vol. XV, No. 2, pp. 180-188.—Into *French:* RENOUVEAU DE L' UNIVERSITÉ, in: *Documents,* Paris, Köln, 1947, Nr. 6, pp. 340-345.

1946

*39. DIE SCHULDFRAGE.—Heidelberg (L. Schneider), 106 pp.; and Zürich (Artemis), 96 pp.; 2nd, 3rd, 4th ed'n, Zürich, 1947.
Translations: Into *English:* THE QUESTION OF GERMAN GUILT by E. B. Ashton, New York (The Dial Press), 1947. 2nd ed'n, New York (Putnam), 1961.—Into *Italian:* LA COLPA DELLA GERMANIA (with an introduction by Renato de Rosa) by Renato de Rosa, Naples (Edizioni Scientifici Italiane), 1947.—Into *Swedish:* DEN TYSKA SKULDFRAGAN (with a preface by A. Ahlberg) by A. Ahlberg, Stockholm (Natur och Kultur), 1947.—Into *Spanish:* ¿ES CULPABLE ALEMANIA? by R. Fechter, Madrid (Nueva Epoca), 1948.—Into *French:* LA CULPABILITÉ ALLE-MANDE by Jeanne Hersch, Paris (Les Éditions de Minuit), 1948.—Into *Japanese:* SENSO NO SEKIZAI by F. Hashimoto, Tokyo (Sakurai-Shoten), 1950; another ed'n: SENSO NO TSUMI by F. Hashomoto, Tokyo (Sôgensha), 1952; another ed'n: SEKIZAIRON by F. Hashimoto, Tokyo (Risôsha), 1965.—Into *Greek:* TO PROBLEMA TES GERMANIKES EUTHYNES by D. L. Kyriazis-Gouvelis, Athens, 1959.—Into *Czech:* OTAZKA VINY by Jiři Navrátil, Praha (Nakladat. Mladá fronta), 1969.
*40. DIE IDEE DER UNIVERSITÄT.—Berlin & Heidelberg (Springer), 123 pp. Berlin ed'n has 132 pp. (Not identical with #25, although both carry the same title.)
Translations: Into *Japanese:* DAIGAKU NO RINEN by Akira Mori, Tokyo (Risôsha), 1955; 2nd ed'n, 1964.—Into *Spanish:* LA IDEA DE LA UNIVERSIDAD by Agustina Schröder de Castelli, in: *La idea de la universidad en Alemania,* Buenos Aires (Editorial Sudamericana), 1959, pp. 391-524.—Into *English:* THE IDEA OF THE UNIVERSITY, by H. A. T. Reiche and H. F. Vanderschmidt (with preface by Robert Ulich), Boston (Beacon Press), 1959; another ed'n (with preface by Oliver L. Zangwill), London (Owen), 1960; 2nd ed'n, London 1965. Partial Reprint of the English text (with notes by Mine Okachi), Tokyo (Bunshudo), 1962.
41. VOM LEBENDIGEN GEIST DER UNIVERSITÄT.—In *Vom lebendigen Geist und vom Studieren!* Two lectures by Karl Jaspers and Fritz Ernst. Schriften der 'Wandlung,' Vol. I, Heidelberg (L. Schneider), pp. 7-40; also in: *Vom neuen Geist der Universität,* Berlin, Heidelberg, 1947, pp. 113-132.
*42. L'ESPRIT EUROPÉEN.—Lecture delivered at the Rencontres Inter-nationales de Genève. In: *L'Esprit Européen, Recontres internationales de Genève,* Paris (La presse française et étrangère, O. Zeluck), pp. 291-323 (translated into French by Jeanne Hersch).
German: VOM EUROPÄISCHEN GEIST, München (R. Piper), 1947, 31 pp. Under the title: EUROPA DER GEGENWART, Wien (Amadeus-Edition), 1947.

Translations: Into *English:* THE EUROPEAN SPIRIT by R. G. Smith (with introduction by the same), London (SCM Press), 1948 and New York (Macmillan), 1949.—Into *Dutch:* VERANTWOORDELIJKHEID EN OPDRACHT, in: *Rekenschap van Europa,* Amsterdam (Uitgev. "Vrij Nederland"), 1947, pp. 199-227.—Into *Italian:* SPIRITO EUROPEO by Paolo Santarcangeli, in: *Spirito europeo,* Milano (Edizioni di Comunità), 1950, pp. 304-345.—Into *Spanish:* ¿QUÉ ES EUROPA? by M. Riaza, in: *El espíritu europeo,* Madrid (Ediciones Guadarrama), 1957, pp. 283-330. —Into *Portuguese:* CONFERENCIA by J. Bénard Da Costa, in: *O espirito europeu.* Lisboa (Publicações Europa-América), 1962, pp. 299-330.

Partial Reprint in *French:* L'HOMME ET SON DESTIN, in: *La Nef* (Paris Editions Albin Michel), 1946, Vol. III, No. 24, pp. 53-61, 90-91, 97.

*43. NIETZSCHE UND DAS CHRISTENTUM. Basis of a lecture which was delivered on the invitation of the scientific union of clergymen in Hannover, May 12, 1938.—Hameln (Seifert), 87 pp. Unchanged new printing: München (Piper), 1952, 71 pp.; 2nd ed'n, München, 1963.

Translations: Into *French:* NIETZSCHE ET LE CHRISTIANISME by Jeanne Hersch, Paris (Les Éditions de Minuit), 1949.—Into *Japanese:* NIETZSCHE TO KIRISUTO-KYO by F. Hashimoto, Tokyo (Sakurai-Shoten), 1951; 2nd ed'n, Tokyo (Risôsha), 1965.—Into *Spanish:* NIETZSCHE Y EL CRISTIANISMO by Daniel Cruz Machado, Buenos Aires (Deucalión), 1955.—Into *Korean:* NIICH'E WA KIDOKKYO by Sŏ Yunt'aek, Taegu (Hyŏngsŏl ch'ulp-ansa), 1959.—Into *English:* NIETZSCHE AND CHRISTIANITY by E. B. Ashton, Chicago (Regnery), 1961. Into *Dutch:* NIETZSCHE EN HET CHRISTENDOM by D. L. Couprie, in: Jaspers: *Leonardo en Nietzsche,* Utrecht, Antwerpen (Het Spectrum), 1966, pp. 77-154.

*44. LA MIA FILOSOFIA. A cura die Renato de Rosa.—Turin (G. Einaudi), xii + 279 pp. Being translations into Italian of selected writings by Karl Jaspers, with a preface by N. Bobbio.

45. VON DER BIBLISCHEN RELIGION. A discussion: Open letter to Professor Alfred Weber and reply by Karl Jaspers.—In: *Die Wandlung,* Heidelberg (L. Schneider), Vol. I, Nr. 1, pp. 406-415. Laid before the Congresso Internazionale di Filosofia in Rome in November 1946.

46. THESEN ÜBER POLITISCHE FREIHEIT.—In: *Die Wandlung,* Heidelberg (L. Schneider), Nr. 6, pp. 460-465.

47. DAS UNBEDINGTE DES GUTEN UND DAS BÖSE.—In: *Die Wandlung,* Heidelberg (L. Schneider), Nr. 8, pp. 672-683.

48. SCIENZA E FILOSOFIA (translated into Italian and annotated by Renato de Rosa).—In: *Archivio di Filosofia,* Milan (Bocca), Vol. I/II, pp. 1-23.

49. GEGEN FALSCHE HEROSIERUNG.—In: *Rhein-Neckar-Zeitung,* Heidelberg, 2nd year, No. 8 (Jan. 25, 1946).

1947

*50. VON DER WAHRHEIT. (Der PHILOSOPHISCHEN LOGIK erster Band.)—München (R. Piper), xxiii + 1,103 pp.; 2nd ed'n, 1958. Partial Reprint: ÜBER DAS TRAGISCHE (pp. 915-961 of VON DER WAHRHEIT), München (Piper), 1952 (Piper-Bücherei Nr. 49), 63 pp.; 2nd ed'n, 1954; 3rd ed'n, 1958; 4th ed'n, 1961.

Reprint translated into *English:* TRAGEDY IS NOT ENOUGH by H. A. T.
Reiche, H. T. Moore and K. W. Deutsch, Boston (Beacon Press), 1952
and London (Gollancz), 1953, 123 pp. Reprint (unchanged), Hamden,
Conn. (Archon Books), 1969. — Into *Japanese:* HIGEKIRON by Fumio
Hashimoto, Tokyo (Risôsha), 1955; 2nd ed'n, 1965. — Into *Italian:* DEL
TRAGICO by Italo A. Chiusano, Milano (Il Saggiatore), 1959. — Into
Spanish: ESENCIA Y FORMAS DE LO TRÁGICO by N. Silvetti Paz, Buenos
Aires (Editorial Sur), 1960. — Into *Korean:* PIGUK NON by Sin Il-ch'ŏl,
Seoul (Sinjo munhwasa), 1962, pp. 21-126; 2nd ed'n, 1968. — Partial
Reprint translated into *English:* TRUTH AND SYMBOL FROM 'VON DER
WAHRHEIT' (pp. 1022-1054 of VON DER WAHRHEIT), by Jean T. Wilde,
William Kluback, and William Kimmel, New York (Twayne), 1959
and London (Vision Press), 1959; Reprint: New Haven, Conn. (College
and Univ. Press), 1962, 79 pp. — Partial Reprint: DIE SPRACHE (pp.
395-449 of VON DER WAHRHEIT), München (Piper), 1964 (Piper-
Bücherei Nr. 203), 96 pp. — Partial Reprint translated into *Italian:*
SULLA VERITA by Umberto Galimberti, Brescia (Editrice La Scuola),
1970, lxxxvi +295 pp.

51. ANTWORT AN SIGRID UNDSET MIT BEITRÄGEN UBER DIE WISSEN-
SCHAFT IM HITLERSTAAT UND DEN NEUEN GEIST DER UNIVERSITÄT.
Konstanz (Südverlag), 31 pp.
Reprint of DIE WISSENSCHAFT IM HITLERSTAAT in: *Schweizerische
Rundschau,* Zürich (Leemann & Co.), Nr. 9, pp. 7-12.

*52. UNSERE ZUKUNFT UND GOETHE. Address delivered in Frankfurt
a/Main August 28, 1947, in connection with receiving of the Goethe-
Prize. — In: *Die Wandlung,* Heidelberg (L. Schneider), Vol. II, No. 7,
pp. 559-578. Also in: *Goethe-Schriften in Artemisverlag,* Zürich
(Artemis), Nr. 3. — New printing: Bremen (J. Storm), 1949.
Translations: Into *English:* GOETHE AND OUR FUTURE, in: *World
Review,* London, 1949, New Series No. 4-6. — Into *Japanese:* WARE-
WARE NO MIRAI TO GOETHE by Kusuo Seki, in: Sekaibungaku taikei,
Tokyo, Vol. 19, 1960, pp. 445-458.

53. DER PROPHET EZECHIEL. A pathographic study. — In: *Arbeiten zur
Psychiatrie, Neurologie und ihren Grenzgebieten.* Festschrift for Kurt
Schneider on his 60th birthday. — Heidelberg (Scherer), pp. 1-9.

54. VOLK UND UNIVERSITÄT. — In: *Die Wandlung,* Heidelberg (L. Schnei-
der), Vol. II, No. 1, pp. 54-64.
Translated: Into *Spanish:* PUEBLO Y UNIVERSIDAD by Mario de La
Cueva, in: *Medio Siglo,* México, T. 2, 1953, Nr. 3, pp. 51-66.

1948

*55. DER PHILOSOPHISCHE GLAUBE. Guest lectures delivered on the invita-
tion of the free academic foundation and of the historic-philosophical
faculty of the University of Basel in July 1947. — Zürich (Artemis), 106
pp. Also: München (Piper), 136 pp. 2nd, 3rd, 4th, 5th ed'n, 1948, 1951,
1954, 1963; also: Frankfurt a/Main, Hamburg (Fischer Bücherei), 1958;
2nd ed'n, 1960.
Translations: Into *English:* THE PERENNIAL SCOPE OF PHILOSOPHY,
by R. Manheim, New York (Philosophical Library), 1949; also: London

(Routledge & Kegan Paul), 1950; also: Hamden, Conn. (Archon Books), 1968. — Into *Dutch:* WIJSGERIG GELOOF (with a preface by Philipp Kohnstamm) by J. C. van Dijk, Haarlem (Willink & Zoon), 1950; 2nd ed'n, 1957; 3rd ed'n, 1962. — Into *French:* LA FOI PHILOSOPHIQUE by J. Hersch and H. Naef, Paris (Plon), 1953. — Into Spanish: LA FE FILOSÓFICA by J. R. Armengol, Buenos Aires (Losada), 1953; 2nd ed'n, 1968.

*56. PHILOSOPHIE UND WISSENSCHAFT. Inaugural lecture at the University of Basel. — In: *Die Wandlung,* Heidelberg (L. Schneider), Vol. 3, No. 8, pp. 721-733. New printing as separate tract: Zürich (Artemis), 1949, 16 pp.; German text with annotations by Fumio Hashimoto, Tokyo (Daigakusyorin), 1950, 38 pp.
Translations: Into *English:* PHILOSOPHY AND SCIENCE by R. Manheim, in *Partisan Review,* New York, Vol. XVI, No. 9. Also in: *World Review,* N.S., London, T. 13, 1950, March, pp. 7-17. — Into *Dutch:* PHILOSOFIE EN WETENSCHAP by John Vandenbergh, in: *Perspectieven,* Wilgenhof, 's-Graveland, T. 17, 1950, Nr. 5, pp. 1-10; Nr. 6, pp. 10-16. — Into *Italian:* FILOSOFIA E SCIENZA by Norberto Bobbio, in: *Rivista di Filosofia,* Torino, T. 41, 1950, pp. 245-259. — Into *Spanish:* FILOSOFÍA Y CIENCIA, in: *Cuadernos de Filosofía,* Buenos Aires, 1953, Nr. 39, pp. 255-268.

57. UNIVERSITIES IN DANGER. THE COHERENCE OF KNOWLEDGE. — In: *The (London) Times,* Educational Supplement, London, Feb. 7, 1948. 1/2 pp.

58. SOLON. — In: *Synopsis.* Festgabe for Alfred Weber (July 30, 1868-July 30, 1948). Heidelberg (L. Schneider), pp. 179-190. Also in: *Die Neue Rundschau,* Frankfurt a/Main, 1949, Nr. 16, pp. 447-456.

59. VORWORT to: "Descartes und die Freiheit" by Jean Paul Sartre in: *René Descartes, Discours de la Méthode,* Mainz, pp. 5-7.

60. VORBEMERKUNG to: "HEILUNG" DURCH DEN SCHOCK? Zwei Briefe und eine Antwort. In: *Die Wandlung,* Heidelberg, T. 3, 1948, p. 57.

1949

*61. VOM URSPRUNG UND ZIEL DER GESCHICHTE. — Zürich (Artemis), 360 pp.; and München (Piper), 1949, 349 pp.; 2nd-6th ed'n, München, 1950, 1952, 1963, 1963, 1966; also: Frankfurt a/Main, Hamburg (Fischer Bücherei), 1955; 2nd-5th ed'n, Frankfurt, Hamburg, 1956, 1957, 1957, 1959.
Translations: Into *Spanish:* ORIGEN Y META DE LA HISTORIA by Fernando Vela, Madrid (Revista de Occidente), 1950; 2nd-4th ed'n, 1953, 1965, 1968. — Into *English:* THE ORIGIN AND GOAL OF HISTORY by Michael Bullock, New Haven (Yale Univ. Press), 1953; and London (Routledge & Kegan Paul), 1953; Reprint: New Haven, 1959. — Into *French:* ORIGINE ET SENS DE L'HISTOIRE by Hélène Naef (and W. Achterberg), Paris (Plon), 1954. — Into *Japanese:* REKISHI NO KIGEN TO MOKUHYO by Eisei Shigeta, Tokyo (Risôsha), 1964. — Into *Italian:* ORIGINE E SENSO DELLA STORIA by Amerigo Guadagnin, Milano (Edizioni di Comunità), 1965; 2nd ed'n, 1972.
Partial Reprint of the German text: DIE GEGENWÄRTIGE SITUATION

DER WELT (from VOM URSPRUNG UND ZIEL DER GESCHICHTE, München, 1949, pp. 162-179), with annotations of Makio Takiuchi, Tokyo (Dôgakusha), 1970, 30 pp.

62. CONDITIONS ET POSSIBILITÉS D'UN NOUVEL HUMANISME. — Lecture delivered at the Rencontres Internationales de Genève. — In: *Pour un nouvel Humanisme*, Paris (Éditions de la Baconnière) (tr. into French by Jeanne Hersch), pp. 181-209. In *German:* ÜBER BEDINGUNGEN UND MÖGLICHKEITEN EINES NEUEN HUMANISMUS, in: *Die Wandlung,* Heidelberg (L. Schneider), Vol. 4, No. 8, pp. 710-734. German text with annotations of Fumio Hashimoto, Tokyo (Ikubundo), 1951, 58 pp. *Translations:* Into *Japanese:* ARATANA HUMANISM NO JOKEN TO KANOSEI NI TSUITE by Fumio Hashimoto, in: *Riso,* Tokyo, T. 209, 1950, Sept., pp. 1-25. — Into *Spanish:* CONDICIONES Y POSIBILIDADES DE UN NUEVO HUMANISMO by E. Caballero Calderón, in: *Hacia un nuevo humanismo,* Madrid, Bogotá (Ediciones Guadarrama), 1957, pp. 353-385. — Into *Portuguese:* CONDICÕES E POSSIBILIDADES DE UM NOVO HUMANISMO by J. Bénard Da Costa, in: *Para um novo humanismo,* Lisboa (Publicações Europa-America), 1964, pp. 179-207.

63. GOETHES MENSCHLICHKEIT. — In: *Basler Universitätsreden,* Basel (Helbing & Lichtenhahn), No. 26, pp. 11-33; also in: *Der Monat,* München, Bd 1, 1948/49, Nr. 11, pp. 3-12.

64. VOM STUDIUM DER PHILOSOPHIE. — In *Zofingue,* Feuille centrale, Genève, Vol. 89, Feb-Mar., pp. 231-235.

65. HOCHSCHULREFORM? DAS GUTACHTEN DES HAMBURGER STUDIENAUSSCHUSSES FÜR HOCHSCHULREFORM. — In: *Die Wandlung,* Heidelberg (L. Schneider), Vol. 4, No. 4, pp. 340-348.

66. DER ÜBERNATIONALE SINN DER ABENDLÄNDISCHEN UNIVERSITÄT. — In: *Quaestiones Academicae Hodiernae,* Groningen (J. B. Wolter), pp. 9-12.

67. VOM CHARAKTER DER MODERNEN WISSENSCHAFT. — In: *Der Monat,* Berlin, Vol. I, No. 12, pp. 12-17. *Translation* into *English:* IS SCIENCE EVIL? by Irving Kristol, in: *Commentary,* New York, T. 9, 1950, pp. 229-233.

68. DIE SITUATION DER PHILOSOPHIE HEUTE. — In. *Actas del primer congreso nacional de filosofía,* Mendoza/Argentina (Universidad Nacional de Cuyo), Vols. 1-3 (German text on pp. 922-926; Spanish translation on pp. 927-930.)

1950

*69. EINFÜHRUNG IN DIE PHILOSOPHIE. Twelve radio-lectures. — Zürich (Artemis), 159 pp.; and München (Piper), 1953, 163 pp.; 2nd-6th ed'n, Zürich, 1952-1973; 2nd-14th ed'n, München, 1953-1972; also: Darmstadt (Moderner Buchclub), 1959, 169 pp. *Translations:* Into *English:* WAY TO WISDOM by Ralph Manheim, London (Gollancz), 1951; and New Haven (Yale Univ. Press), 1951; 2nd ed'n, New Haven, 1954; 3rd ed'n, 1959; 4th ed'n, 1960; 5th ed'n, 1962. — Into *French:* INTRODUCTON À LA PHILOSOPHIE by Jean Hersch, Paris (Plon), 1951; 2nd ed'n, 1965. — Into *Dutch:* INLEIDING TOT DE PHILOSOPHIE by H. F. Torringa, Assen (Born), 1951; 2nd ed'n,

1952; 3rd ed'n, 1954; 4th ed'n, 1962.—Into *Japanese:* TETSUGAKU JUNI-KO by Masao Kusanagi, Tokyo (Sôgensha), 1951; 2nd ed'n, 1952; revised ed'n under the title: TETSUGAKU NYUMON, Tokyo (Shinchôsha), 1954; 2nd ed'n, 1966.—Into *Danish:* FILOSOFIENS GRUNDBEGREBER by Merete Engel and Helge Hultberg, København (Haase), 1953; 2nd ed'n under the title: HVAD ER FILOSOFI?, 1965.—Into *Spanish:* LA FILOSOFÍA DESDE EL PUNTO DE VISTA DE LA EXISTENCIA by José Gaos, Mexico, Buenos Aires (Fondo de Cultura Económica), 1953; 2nd ed'n, 1957; 3rd ed'n, 1962; 4th ed'n, 1965; 5th ed'n, 1968; 6th ed'n, 1970.— Into *Korean:* CH'ORHAK SIBI KANG by Yi Chong-hu, Seoul (Pŏmjosa), 1957; another ed'n under the title: SILCHON CH'ORHAK IMMUN by Yun Sŏng-bŏm, Seoul (Sinyangsa), 1958.—Into *Italian:* INTRODUZIONE ALLA FILOSOFIA by Pietro Chiodi, Milano (Longanesi), 1959.—Into *Vietnamese:* TRIÊT-HỌC NHÂP MÔN by Lê-Tôn-Nghiệm, Huế (Đại-học), 1960. — Into *Portuguese:* INIÇIÃCÁO FILOSOFICA by Manuela Pinto dos Santos, Lisboa (Guimarães), 1961; 2nd ed'n, 1967.—Into *Swedish:* INTRODUKTION TILL FILOSOFIN by Anders Byttner (with a preface by Ulla Åhgren-Langes), Stockholm (Bonnier), 1963.—Into *Norwegian:* INNFØRING I FILOSOFIEN by Tore Lindholm, Oslo (Tanum), 1965.— Into *Arabic:* MADKHAL ILÃ AL-FALSAFAH by Muhammed Fathī al-Shineitī, Al-Qāhirah (Maktabat al-Qāhirah al-hadītah), 1967.—Into *Serbo-Croatian:* UVOD U FILOZOFIJU by Ivan Ivanji, in: Jaspers: *Filozofija egzistencije/Uvod u filozofiju,* Beograd (Prosveta), 1967, pp. 121-270.—Into *Vietnamese:* TRIÊT-HỌC NHÂP MÔN by Tê-Xuyên, Saigon (Eds. Khai Trí), 1967.—Into *Greek:* EISAGOGE STE PHILOSOPHIA by Christos Malevitsis, Athens (Bibliopoleion "Dodone"), 1968.—Into *Finnish:* JOHDATUS FILOSOFIAAN by Sinikka Kallio, Helsingissä (Otava), 1970.—Partial Reprint: DIE GESCHICHTE DER MENSCHHEIT, in: *Universitas,* Stuttgart, T. 7, 1952, Nr. 12, pp. 1165-1273.

*70. VERNUNFT UND WIDERVERNUNFT IN UNSERER ZEIT. Three guest lectures delivered at the University of Heidelberg on the invitation of Asta.— München (Piper), 71 pp. 2nd ed'n, 1952.
Translations: Into *English:* REASON AND ANTI-REASON IN OUR TIME by Stanley Godman, London (SCM Press), 1952, and New Haven (Yale Univ. Press), 1952; Reprint: Hamden, Conn. (Archon Books), 1971. (This English ed'n contains some remarks on the historio-scientific significance of Freud, which are not contained in the German text.)— Into *Danish:* FORNUFT OG ANTI-FORNUFT I VOR TID by H. Hultberg, Kopenhagen (Steen Hasselbach), 1952.—Into *Norwegian:* FORNUFT OG ANTI-FORNUFT I VAR TID by L. Holmboe, Oslo (J. W. Cappelen), 1952.—Into *Spanish:* LA RAZÓN Y SUS ENEMIGOS EN NUESTRO TIEMPO by L. P. Prebisch, Buenos Aires (Editorial Sudamericana, Biblioteca de filosofía), 1953; 2nd ed'n, 1958; 3rd ed'n, 1967.—Into *French:* RAISON ET DÉRAISON À NOTRE ÉPOQUE by H. Naef (and M. L. Solms), Paris (Desclée de Brouwer), 1953.—Into *Portuguese:* RAZÃO E ANTI-RAZÃO EM NOSSO TEMPO by Fernando Gil, Rio de Janeiro (Ministério da Educação e Cultura, Inst. Sup. de Estudos Brasileiros), 1958; also under the title: RAZÃO E CONTRA RAZÃO NO NOSSO TEMPO by Fernando Gil (with preface by Delfim Santos), Lisboa (Minotauro), 1961.—Into *Italian:* RAGIONE E ANTIRAGIONE NEL NOSTRO TEMPO by Giulio Saccomano (with preface by Pietro Chiodi), Firenze (Sansoni), 1970.

Partial translations: Into *Japanese:* MARXISMUS-HIHAN by Fumio Hashimoto, in: *Kaizo,* Tokyo, T. 32, 1951, Nr. 6, pp. 32-37. — Into *Japanese:* RISEI NI TSUITE by Fumio Hashimoto, in: *Jitsuzon,* Tokyo, T. 1, 1951, Nr. 1, pp. 3-10. — Into *Spanish:* CARÁCTER DE LA ACTITUD CIENTÍFICA, in: *La Torre,* Puerto Rico, T. 1, 1953, Nr. 3, pp. 23-42.

71. ZUR KRITIK DER PSYCHOANALYSE. In honor of Hans W. Gruhle on his 70th birthday. — In: *Der Nervenarzt,* Berlin-Göttingen-Heidelberg (Springer), Vol. 21, No. 11, pp. 465-468.
    Translations: Into *Japanese:* SEISHINBUNSEKIGAKU NO HIHAN by Shōzō Shida, in: *Shiso,* Tokyo, 1952, pp. 110 ff. — Into *Italian:* CONTRIBUTO ALLA CRITICA DELLA PSICOANALISI by Renato de Rosa, in: *Archivio di Filosofia,* Milano, 1952, Nr. 'Filosofia e psicopatologia', pp. 37-46.

72. GEFAHREN UND CHANCEN DER FREIHEIT. — In: *Der Monat,* Berlin, Vol. 2, No. 22/23, pp. 396-406.

73. ZU NIETZSCHES BEDEUTUNG IN DER GESCHICHTE DER PHILOSOPHIE. In: *Die Neue Rundschau,* Frankfurt a/Main (S. Fischer), Vol. 61, pp. 346-358.
    Translations: Into *English:* under the title, THE IMPORTANCE OF NIETZSCHE, in: *The Hibbert Journal,* London, Vol. 49, April 1951; and under the title, NIETZSCHE AND THE PRESENT, in: the *Partisan Review,* New York, Jan-Feb., 1952.

74. NIETZSCHES NACHTLIED. — In: *Pro Regno Pro Sanctuario,* Festschrift for the 60th birthday of Prof. v. d. Leeuw, Nijerk (G. F. Callenbach), 1950.

75. GELEITWORT to Ernst Mayer's *Dialektik des Nichtwissens,* Basel (Verlag für Recht und Gesellschaft), 1950, p. v.

76. DAS GEWISSEN VOR DER BEDROHUNG DURCH DIE ATOMBOMBE. — In: *Comprende,* Milan (Società Europea di Cultura).
    Translation: Into *Dutch:* DE ATOOMBOM EN HET GEWETEN by H. Methorst, in: *Perspectieven,* Wilgenhof, -s'Graveland, T. 18, 1951, Nr. 11/12, pp. 8-15.

                    1951

*77. RECHENSCHAFT UND AUSBLICK. REDEN UND AUFSÄTZE. — München (Piper), 368 pp.; 19 essays and addresses here collected in one volume, only two of which have not appeared in print before, viz., DAS RADIKAL BÖSE BEI KANT and MEIN WEG ZUR PHILOSOPHIE. 2nd ed'n, 1958.
    Translations: Into *Spanish:* BALANCE Y PERSPECTIVA. DISCURSOS Y ENSAYOS by. F. Vela, Madrid (Revista de Occidente), 1953. — Into *Japanese* (in three volumes): 1. JITSUZONTEKI NINGEN by Toshio Kanba *et al.* 2. DAIGAKU NO HONSHITSU by T. Kuwaki *et al.* 3. GENDAI NO SEISHINTEKI KADAI by M. Kusanagi *et al.* Tokyo (Shinchôsha), 1954/55. — Into *French:* BILAN ET PERSPECTIVES by Hélène Naef et Jeanne Hersch, Paris (Desclée de Brouwer), 1956. Of "Das radikal Böse bei Kant" into *French:* LE MAL RADICAL CHEZ KANT by Jeanne Hersch in: *Deucalion,* Paris, Oct. 1952. Of three essays, viz., "Solon", "Unsere Zukunft und Goethe", and "Bedingungen und Möglichkeiten eines neuen Humanismus", into *English:* EXISTENTIALISM AND HUMANISM by H. E. Fischer, New York (Russell F. Moore Co.), 1952.

78. KIERKEGAARD—LEBEN UND WERK. Lecture in Basel's Pen-Club in Feb. 1951.—In: *Basler Nachrichten*, Vol. 45, Sonntagsblatt of March 18, 1951, pp. 41-44; also in: *Universitas*, Stuttgart, Vol. 6, No. 10, 1951; and also in: *Der Monat*, München, Vol. 3, 1950/51, Nr. 33, pp. 227-236. *Translations:* Into *English:* THE IMPORTANCE OF KIERKEGAARD in: *Cross Currents*, Vol. 2, No. 3, Spring 1952.—Into *Japanese:* KIERKE-GAARD by Eiichi Kito, in: *Jitsuzon*, Tokyo, 1952, Nr. 3, pp. 5-18.

79. FREITHEIT UND AUTORITÄT.—In: Protokoll der Konferenz Schweizerischer Gymnasial-Rektoren in Basel 1951 (38th Konferenz), Basel (privately printed), 1951, 21 pp.; also in: *Schweizerische Theologische Umschau*, Bern, Vol. 22, No. 1, 1952; and also in: *Arqué*, Cordoba, T. 2, 1953, pp. 31-52 [German text]. Also in: *Diogenes* [German ed'n], Köln, Berlin, T. 1, 1953/54, pp. 9-26. Also in: *Universitas*, Stuttgart, T. 17, 1962, pp. 345-361. Also in: *Der Architekt*, Essen, T. 11, 1962, pp. 197-202.
Translations: Into *French:* LIBERTÉ ET AUTORITÉ in: *Diogène*, Paris, 1952, Nr. 1, pp. 9-29.—Into *Spanish:* LIBERTAD Y AUTORIDAD by J. Rovira Armengol, in: *Diogenes* [Spanish ed'n], Buenos Aires, T. 1, 1952/53, Nr. 1, pp. 15-36.—Into *English:* FREEDOM AND AUTHORITY in: *Diogenes* [English ed'n], New York, 1952/53, Nr. 1, pp. 25-42.—Into *Spanish:* LIBERTAD Y AUTORIDAD by Walter Brüning, in: *Arqué*, Cordoba, T. 2, 1953, pp. 379-390. Into *Arabic:* AL-HURIYA WA AL-SULTAH by Muhammed Fathī al-Shineitī, in: *Jāsbarz, Kārl / Gīms, Willim: Muskilāt falsafīja, Al-Qāhira* (Maktabat al-Qāhira al hadītah), 1957, pp. 49-82.—Into *English:* FREEDOM AND AUTHORITY by Marguerite Wolff, in: *Universitas* [English edition], Stuttgart, T. 5, 1962, pp. 121-137.—Into *Spanish:* LIBERTAD Y AUTORIDAD in: *Universitas* [Spanish ed'n], Stuttgart, T. 1, 1963, Nr. 3, pp. 225-242.—Into *Spanish:* LIBERTAD Y AUTORIDAD in: *Folia humanistica*, Barcelona, T. 4, 1966, pp. 769-788.—Into *Japanese:* JIYU TO KEN'I by Takeo Saitô, in: Jaspers: *Shinri, jiyû, heiwa*, Tokyo (Risôsha), 1966, pp. 33-69.

80. GELEITWORT to Gerhard Kloos' *Die Konstitutionslehre von Carl Gustav Carus mit besonderer Berücksichtigung seiner Physiognomik*, Basel, New York (Karger), 1951, p. 3.

1952

81. VON DEN GRENZEN PÄDAGOGISCHEN PLANENS.—In: *Basler Schulblatt*, Vol. 13, No. 4, pp. 72-77, Basel. Also in: *Wuppertaler Buch fur Schule und Lehrerbildung*. Wuppertal (Born), 1958, pp. 38-43. Also in: *Bildungsphilosophie*, Frankfurt a/Main (Akadem. Verlags-Gesellschaft), Vol. 2, 1968, pp. 217-223.

82. DER WELTSCHÖPFUNGSGEDANKE.—In: *Merkur*, Vol. 4, No. 5, pp. 401-407, Stuttgart.
Translations: Into *Spanish:* LA IDEA DE LA CREACIÓN DEL MUNDO by F. P. Navarro in: *Theoria*, Madrid, 1952.—Into *French:* IDÉE SUR L'ORIGINE DU MONDE in: *La revue de culture européenne*, Vol. III, No. 8, Paris, 1953.—Into *Norwegian:* TANKEN OM VERDENS SKAPELSE by John Baardsgaard, in: *Minervas Kvartalsskrift*, Oslo, T. 4, 1960, pp. 141-146.

83. NATURE AND ETHICS. — In: *Moral Principles of Action* ("Science of Culture Series"), ed. by Ruth Anshen, New York and London (Harper's), 1952.

84. MARX UND FREUD. MARXISMUS UND PSYCHOANALYSE ALS MODERNE GLAUBENSSURROGATE. — In: *Universitas*, Nos. 3 & 4, pp. 226-232 and 337-344, Tübingen, 1952.

85. A BALE, CHEZ KARL JASPERS. — In: *Les Nouvelles Littéraires*, Paris, T. 31, Nr. 1272, 17.1.1952, pp. 1 and 4. (Interview with Jean Rounault.)

86. NIPPON NO TOMO NI YOSERU NENTO NO JI. — In: *Jitsuzon*, Tokyo, 1952, Nr. 3, pp. 1-4. [A New Year address to Japanese friends, translated into Japanese by Fumio Hashimoto.]

1953

*87. LIONARDO ALS PHILOSOPH. Bern (Francke Verlag), 77 pp.
Translations: Into *Spanish:* LEONARDO COMO FILÓSOFO by Jorge Oscar Pickenhayn, Buenos Aires (Editorial Sur), 1956. — Into *Japanese:* RIONARUDO DA VINCI by Akaji Fujita, Tokyo (Risôsha), 1958; 2nd ed'n, 1963. — Into *Italian:* LEONARDO FILOSOFO by Ferruccio Masini, Firenze (Philosophia), 1960. — Into *English:* LEONARDO AS PHILOSOPHER by Ralph Manheim, in: Jaspers: *Three Essays*, New York (Harcourt, Brace & World), 1964, pp. 1-58; also in: Jaspers: *Leonardo, Descartes, Max Weber*, London (Routledge & Kegan Paul), 1965, pp. 1-58. — Into *Dutch:* LEONARDO ALS FILOSOOF by D. L. Couprie, in: Jaspers: *Leonardo en Nietzsche*, Utrecht, Antwerpen (Het Spectrum), 1966, pp. 9-73.

88. WAHRHEIT UND UNHEIL DER BULTMANNSCHEN ENTYMYTHOLOGISIE-RUNG. — In: *Schweizerische Theologische Umschau*, Vol. 23, No. 3/4, pp. 74-108, Bern, 1953; and in: *Merkur*, Vol. 7, No. 11 & 12, pp. 1001-1022 and 1107-1126, Stuttgart, 1953. Also in: *Kerygma and Mythos*, Vol. 3, Hamburg-Volksdorf (Reich), 1954, pp. 9-46.
Translation: Into *French:* CE QU'IL Y A DE VRAI ET DE FACHEUX DANS LA DEMYTHISATION BULTMANIENNE by P. Barthel, in: *Etudes théologiques et religieuses*, Montpellier, T. 29, 1954, Nr. 1, pp. 21-75.

89. DIE IDEE DES ARZTES. Address delivered on the festival occasion of the Swiss Medical Convention on June 6, 1953 in Basel. — In: *Schweizerische Ärztezeitung*, Vol. 27, No. 3-7, Bern, 1953; also in: *Ärztliche Mitteilungen*, Köln, Vol. 38, 1953, Nr. 18, pp. 476-479; also under the title, DIE IDEE DES ARZTES UND IHRE ERNEUERUNG in: *Universitas*, Vol. 8, No. 11, pp. 1121-1131, Tübingen, 1953; also under the title, DIE IDEE DES ARZTES UND IHRE ERNEUERUNG in: *Umstrittene Probleme der Medizin*, Stuttgart, Zürich (Medica Verlag), 1954, pp. 151-163; also in: *Hippokrates: Der wahre Arzt*. Zürich, Stuttgart (Artemis), 1959, pp. 69-80; 2nd ed'n, 1963; German text with annotations by Jirô Okuyama, Tokyo (Daisanshobô), 1962, 26 pp.

90. ARZT UND PATIENT. — In: *Studium Generale*, Berlin-Göttingen-Heidelberg (Springer), Vol. 6, No. 8, pp. 435-443.
Translation: Into *Dutch:* ARTS EN PATIËNT by R. F. Beerling, in: *Wijsgerig Perspectief op Maatschappij en Wetenschap*, Amsterdam, T. 5, 1964, Nr. 2, pp. 103-122.

91. Vorwort to C. Miłosz' *Verführtes Denken* (German by A. Loepfe),
Köln-Berlin (Kiepenheuer & Witsch), pp. 7-9. 2nd ed'n, 1954; 3rd ed'n,
1955; 4th ed'n, 1959.
Translations: Into *French:* Preface by Jeanne Hersch, in: C. Miłosz:
La pensée captive, Paris (Gallimard), 1953, pp. 9-13.—Into *Spanish:*
Prefacio by E. Revol, in: C. Miłosz: *El pensamiento cautivo,* Rio
Piedras (Ediciones de La Toore), 1954, pp. 11-14; 2nd ed'n, 1957.

92. Die Auffassung der Persönlichkeit Jesu.—In: Council for the
Protection of the Rights and Interests of Jews from Germany (Fest-
schrift in honor of the 80th birthday of Rabbi Dr. Leo Baeck), London
(Fairfax Mansions).
Also in: *Essays presented to Leo Baeck on the occasion of his 80th
birthday,* London (East & West Library), 1954, pp. 36-49.

93. Der Brief des Baseler Philosophen an die "Ehemaligen".—In:
Die alte Schulglocke, Jever, 1953, Nr. 6, pp. 1-2; also under the title:
Professor Karl Jaspers und Jever in: *Der Oldenburgische Haus-
kalender,* Oldenburg, T. 128, 1954, pp. 28-29; also under the title:
Karl Jaspers und Jever in: Karl Fissen: *Das alte Jever,* Jever
(Mettcker), 1965, pp. 11-13.

1954

*94. Die Frage der Entmythologisierung. (By Karl Jaspers and
Rudolf Bultmann).—München (Piper), 118 pp.; 2nd ed'n, 1954.
Translations: Into *English:* Myth and Christianity by Norbert
Guterman, New York (Noonday Press), 1958.—Into *Japanese:* Seisho
no Hishinwaka-hihan by Kôzô Nishida, Tokyo (Risôsha), 1962.—
Into *Spanish:* La Desmitologizacion del Nuevo Testamento by
Ansgar Klein, Buenos Aires (Sur), 1968, pp. 153-251.
Partial translation: Into *French:* Fragment de La Lettre . . . by
Hélène Naef, in: *La Table Ronde,* Paris, 1956, Nr. 107, pp. 143-155
(with preface by Jeanne Hersch: *La Polémique de Jaspers et de Bult-
mann sur la Démythisation).*

95. Schellings Grösse und Sein Verhängnis.—In: *Studia Philoso-
phica,* Annual of the Swiss Philosophische Gesellschaft, Vol. XIV
(Proceedings of the Schelling-anniversary at Bad Ragaz, Sept. 22-25,
1954), Basel (Verlag für Recht und Gesellschaft), 1954, pp. 12-38 and
contribution to the discussion on pp. 42-49.—Reprinted in: *Merkur,*
Vol. 9, No. 1, pp. 11-34, Stuttgart, 1955.

96. Die Aufgabe der Philosophie in der Gegenwart.—In: *Nach 50
Jahren,* Almanach, München (Piper), 1954, pp. 153-163; also in:
Stifterverband für die deutsche Wissenschaft, Jahrbuch, Essen-Brede-
ney, 1954, pp. 15-20; also under the title Welche Aufgabe Hat die
Philosophie Heute? in: *Wissenschaft und Weltbild,* Wien, T. 9, 1956,
pp. 82-87; also under the title: Die Aufgaben der Philosophie in
Unserer Zeit, in: *Ruperto Carola,* Heidelberg, T. 9, 1957, Nr. 22,
pp. 55-59.
Translations: Into *Japanese:* Gendai ni Okeru Tetsugaku no Kadai
by Masao Kusanagi, in: *Jitsuzon,* Tokyo, 1955, Nr. 8, pp. 1-8.—Into
English: The Task of Philosophy in Our Day by Edith A. Daechsler

and Annie Taffs, in: *This Is My Philosophy,* New York (Harper), 1957, and London (Allen & Unwin), 1958, pp. 190-198. — Into *Italian:* IL FILOSOFO NELLA SOCIETA CONTEMPORANEA by F. Bianco, in: *Il Veltro,* Roma, T. 7, 1963, Febraio, pp. 9-18.

97. IMMANUEL KANT. ZU SEINEM 150. TODESTAG. In: *Der Monat,* Vol. VI, No. 65 (Feb.), pp. 451-455. Berlin.
Translation: Into *Spanish:* MANUEL KANT. EN EL ANIVERSARIO DE SU MUERTE. In: *Cuadernos de filosofia,* No. 7 (July-Aug.), Buenos Aires.

98. THE FIGHT AGAINST TOTALITARIANISM. In: *Confluence,* Cambridge (Mass.), Vol. 3, No. 3 (Sept.) Also in: *The Dilemma of Organizational Society,* New York (Dutton), 1963, pp. 3-19, viz. #123.
Translations: Into *Italian:* LA BATTAGLIA CONTRO IL TOTALITARISMO by Glauco Cambon and Aldo Canonici, in: *Totalitarismo e Cultura,* Milano (Edizioni di "Comunità"), 1957, pp. 305-325. — Into *Japanese:* ZENTAISHUGI TONO TOSO NI OITE by Takeo Saitô, in: Jaspers: *Shinri, jiyû, heiwa,* Tokyo (Risôsha), 1966, pp. 89-121.

99. THE POLITICAL VACUUM IN GERMANY. — In: *Foreign Affairs* (American Quarterly Review), New York, 1954, Vol. 32, No. 4.
Translation: Into *Danish:* DET POLITISKE VAKUUM I TYSKLAND in: *Fremtiden,* København, T. 9, 1954, Nr. 7, pp. 7-14.

100. DIE NICHTCHRISTLICHEN RELIGIONEN UND DAS ABENDLAND. In: *Die grossen nichtchristlichen Religionen unserer Zeit,* Stuttgart (A. Kröner), pp. 117-126.

101. PLAN DER AKADEMIE. Ein offener Brief. — In: *Neue Schweizer Rundschau,* N.F., Zürich, T. 22, 1954/55, pp. 465-470.

102. GELEITWORT to Adolph Lichtigfeld' *Jaspers' Metaphysics,* London (Colibri Press), 1954, p. 8 (with English translation, p. 9).

1955

*103. SCHELLING. GRÖSSE UND VERHÄNGNIS. — München (Piper), 346 pp.

104. KIERKEGAARD. — In: *Die Gegenwart,* Frankfurt a/Main, Vol. 10, No. 24 (Nov. 19, 1955), pp. 759-762.
Translation: Into *French:* ACTUALITÉ DE KIERKEGAARD in: *La Table Ronde,* Paris (Plon), No. 95, pp. 53-65.

105. GELEITWORT to Hannah Arendt's *Elemente und Ursprünge totaler Herrschaft,* Frankfurt a/Main (Europäische Verlagsanstalt), pp. vii-ix; 2nd ed'n, 1958.

106. DOKTOR DER PHILOSOPHIE. — In: *Theodor Haubach zum Gedächtnis,* Frankfurt a/Main (Europäische Verlagsanstalt), 1955, pp. 14-17; 2nd ed'n, 1955.

107. KÜNDER UNSERER ZEIT. Nachruf auf Thomas Mann. — In: *Aufbau,* New York, Vol. 21, Nr. 33, 19.8. 1955, p. 1.

1956

108. DAS KOLLEKTIV UND DER EINZELNE. — In: *Mensch und Menschlichkeit,* Stuttgart (A. Kröner), pp. 65-76. Also under the title: DAS COLLEK-

TIV UND DER EINZELNE in: *Deutsche Universitätszeitung,* Göttingen, T. 11, 1956, Nr. 9, pp. 8-10. Also in: *Universitas,* Stuttgart, T. 12, 1957, pp. 113-120. Also in: *Der Architekt,* Essen, T. 8, 1959, pp. 175-177.

Translations: Into *Spanish:* COLECTIVIDAD E INDIVIDUO by Oswald Bayer, in: *Aletheia,* Buenos Aires, T. 1, 1956, Nr. 3, pp. 4-12.—Into *English:* THE INDIVIDUAL AND THE COLLECTIVITY by Norbert Guterman, in: *Noonday,* New York, 1958, Nr. 1, pp. 54-62.—Into *English:* THE INDIVIDUAL AND MASS SOCIETY by Harold O. J. Brown, in: *Religion and Culture,* New York (Harper), 1959, pp. 37-43.—Into *Japanese:* SHUDAN TO KOJIN by Takeo Saitô, in Jaspers: *Shinri, jiyû, heiwa,* Tokyo (Risôsha), 1966, pp. 71-88.—Into *Spanish:* LA COLECTIVIDAD Y EL INDIVIDUO, in: *Humboldt,* Hamburgo, T. 8, 1967, Nr. 30, pp. 2-4.

109. VOM RECHTEN GEIST DER UNIVERSITÄT.—In: *Die Gegenwart,* Frankfurt a/Main, Vol. 11, No. 13 (June 30, 1956), pp. 405-406.

110. GELEITWORT to Jeanne Hersch's *Die Illusion: Der Weg der Philosophie,* Bern (Francke A. G.), pp. 5-8. *Translation:* Into *French:* PREFACE by J. Hersch, in: J. Hersch: *L'Illusion Philosophique,* 2nd ed'n, Paris (Plon), 1964, pp. 9-18.

111. DIE ATOMBOMBE UND DIE ZUKUNFT DES MENSCHEN. A radio address. In: *Die Gegenwart,* Frankfurt a/Main, T. 11, 1956, Nr. 21, pp. 665-670. Also in: *Technische Rundschau,* Bern, T. 48, 1956, Nr. 51, pp. 1-3. Also published in booklet form: München (Piper), 1957, 26 pp.; also published in booklet form: Zürich (Janus-Presse), 1957. German text with annotations by Jiro Tanaka, Tokyo (Sansyusya), 1966, 49 pp.

Translations: Into *Dutch:* DE ATOOMBOM EN DE TOEKOMST VAN DE MENS by I. R. Schuurman, Amsterdam (van Ditmar), 1957.—Into *English:* THE ATOM BOMB AND THE FUTURE OF MAN by Norbert Guterman, in: *Evergreen Review,* New York, T. 2, 1958, Nr. 5, pp. 37-57.—Into *French:* LA BOMBE ATOMIQUE ET L'AVENIR DE L'HOMME by Ré Soupault, Paris (Plon), 1958.—Into *Japanese:* GENBAKU TO JINRUI NO SHORAI in: *Sekai,* Tokyo, 1958, Nr. 149, pp. 17-35.—Into *Portuguese:* A BOMBA ATOMICA E O FUTURO DO HOMEM by Marco Aurélio Matos and Ronaldo Vertis, Rio de Janeiro (Agir), 1958.—Into *Portuguese:* A BOMBA ATOMICA E O FUTURO DO HOMEM by L. Pacheco, Régua (Contraponto), 1958.—Into *Spanish:* LA BOMBA ATÓMICA Y EL FUTURO DEL HOMBRE by L. Castro, Madrid (Taurus Ediciones), 1958; 2nd ed'n, 1966.

112. ANTWORT VON PROF. KARL JASPERS.—In: *Freies Volk,* Bern, Nr. 3, 20.1.1956, p. 3. Also under the title: DER STANDPUNKT DES PSYCHIATERS, in: *Gibt es Geister?* Bern (Viktoria-Verlag), 1956, pp. 139-144.

1957

*113. DIE GROSSEN PHILOSOPHEN. Vol. I.—München (Piper), 968 pp. 2nd ed'n, 1959.

Translations: Into *English:* THE GREAT PHILOSOPHERS by Ralph Manheim, Vol. 1. 2. New York (Harcourt, Brace & World), 1962/66; also: London (Hart-Davis), 1962/66.—Into *French:* LES GRANDS PHILO-

SOPHES by R. Bouvier, G. Floquet, H. de Gandillac, J. Hersch, J.-P. Leyvraz, H. Naef, X. Tilliette, Paris (Plon), 1963. — Into *Spanish:* Los Grandes Filosofos by Pablo Simon, Vol. 1. 2. Buenos Aires (Sur), 1966/68. [Vol. 3 not yet published.] — Into *Italian:* I Grandi Filosofi by Filippo Costa, Milano (Longanesi), 1973.
Partial Reprints: I. Die Massgeben den Menschen. *Sokrates, Buddha, Konfuzius, Jesus,* München (Piper), 1964, 210 pp; 2nd ed'n, 1965; 3rd ed'n, 1967, 4th ed'n, 1971.
Translations: Into *Dutch:* Socrates, Boeddha, Confucius, Jezus by J. Sperna Weiland, Utrecht (Bijleveld), 1960. — Into *English:* Socrates, Buddha, Confucius, Jesus by Ralph Manheim, New York (Harcourt, Brace & World), 1962. — Into *French:* Les Grands Philosophes, Vol. 1. By G. Floquet, J. Hersch, H. Naef, X. Tilliette, Paris (Union Générale d'Editions), 1966; 2nd ed'n, 1970.
II. Plato, Augustin, Kant. *Drei Gründer des Philosophierens.* München (Piper), 1961, 397 pp.; 2nd ed'n, 1962; 3rd ed'n, 1962; 4th ed'n, 1963; 5th ed'n, 1964; 6th ed'n, 1965; 7th ed'n, 1966; 8th ed'n, 1967.
Translations: Into *English:* Vol. 1: Plato and Augustine. Vol. 2: Kant. By Ralph Manheim, New York (Harcourt, Brace & World), 1962. Into *French:* Les Grands Philosophes, Vol. 2. 3. By G. Floquet, J. Hersch, and H. Naef, Paris (Union Générale d'Editions), 1967; 2nd ed'n, 1970.
III. Aus dem Ursprung Denkende Metaphysiker. *Anaximander, Heraklit, Parmenides, Plotin, Anselm, Spinoza, Laotse, Nagarjuna.* München (Piper), 1966, 350 pp.
Translation: Into *French:* Les Grands Philosophes, Vol. 4. By J. Hersch, J. P. Leyvraz, M. de Gandillac, X. Tilliette, and R. Bouvier, Paris (Union Générale d'Editions), 1972.
Translations of particular parts of the book: Into *Dutch:* Platoon by W. van Zoeterwoude, Brugge (Desclée de Brouwer), 1958. Kant by M. Mok, Utrecht, Antwerpen (Het Spectrum), 1967. — Into *Japanese:* Butsuda to Ryuju by Hideo Minejima, Tokyo (Risôsha), 1960; 2nd ed'n, 1964. Kant by Eisei Shigeta, Tokyo (Risôsha), 1962; Jesu to Augustinus by Shinji Hayashida, Tokyo (Risôsha), 1965; Socrates to Platon by Tomosaburô Yamanouchi, Tokyo (Risôsha), 1966. Koshi to Roshi by Hajime Tanaka, Tokyo (Risôsha), 1967; Spinoza by Kisaku Kudô, Tokyo (Risôsha), 1967.

114. Philosophical Autobiography. — In: *The Philosophy of Karl Jaspers* (ed. by Paul Arthur Schilpp, as Vol. IX of his "Library of Living Philosophers"), New York (Tudor Publishing Co.), now published by Open Court, being Part I of the present volume.
Translations: In *German:* Philosophische Autobiographie in *Karl Jaspers' Philosophie,* Stuttgart (Kohlhammer Verlag), 1956. Also in: Karl Jaspers: Werk und Wirkung. München (Piper), 1963, pp. 19-129. — Into *French:* Autobiographie Philosophique by Pierre Boudot, Paris (Aubier), 1963. — Into *Spanish:* Autobiografía Filosófica by Pablo Simon, Buenos Aires (Editorial Sur), 1964. — Into *Japanese:* Tetsugakuteki Jiden by Eisei Shigeta, Tokyo (Risôsha), 1965. — Into *Italian:* Autobiografia Filosofica by Ervino Pocar, Napoli (Morano), 1969.

115. REPLY TO MY CRITICS.—In: *The Philosophy of Karl Jaspers* (Paul A. Schilpp, ed.), being Part III of the present volume. The original German in *Karl Jaspers' Philosophie*.

116. UNSTERBLICHKEIT. Address in the series on 'Immortality' by Radio Basel.—In: *Unsterblichkeit*, Basel (Friedrich Reinhardt AG), pp. 31-41. *Translations:* Into *Danish:* UDØDELIGHED, in: *Vindrosen*, København, T. 5, 1958, pp. 233-238.—Into *French:* IMMORTALITÉ by Hélène Naef, in: *Immortalité*, Neuchâtel, Paris (Delachaux & Niestlé), 1958, pp. 41-55.—Into *Italian:* IMMORTALITA by Gino Conte, in: *Immortalità*, Torino (Ed. Claudiana), 1961, pp. 29-37.—Into *Spanish:* EL HOMBRE Y LA INMORTALIDAD by Jorge L. Carcia Venturini, in: *El Hombre y la Inmortalidad*, Buenos Aires (Troquel), 1964, pp. 41-54.

117. KANTS "ZUM EWIGEN FRIEDEN".—In: *Wesen und Wirklichkeit des Menschen. Festschrift für Helmuth Plessner*. Göttingen (Vandenhoeck & Ruprecht), 1957, pp. 131-152. [Not identical with #118.] *Translation:* Into *Spanish:* LA PAZ PERPETUA DE KANT, in: *Folia Humanistica*, Barcelona, T. 4, 1966, Nr. 42, pp. 481-510.

118. ZUM EWIGEN FRIEDEN.—In: *Gehört gelesen*, München, T. 4, 1957, November, pp. 961-967. [A radio address.] Also in: *Aachener Prisma*, Aachen, T. 6, Januar 1958, Nr. 2, pp. 10-11. Also under the title: KANTS SCHRIFT "ZUM EWIGEN FRIEDEN", in: *Universitas*, Stuttgart, T. 13, 1958, Nr. 7, pp. 711-719. Also under the title: KANTS SCHRIFT "ZUM EWIGEN FRIEDEN", in: Immanuel Kant: *Zum ewigen Frieden*, Essen-Bredeney (Stifter-Verband für die Deutsche Wissenschaft), 1958, pp. 3-8.

119. A NOTE ON EXISTENZPHILOSOPHIE AND EXISTENTIALISM. Translated by Edith A. Daechsler and Annie Taffs, in: *This Is My Philosophy*, New York (Harper), 1957, and London (Allen & Unwin), 1958, pp. 198-199.

120. THE TASK OF PHILOSOPHY TODAY.—In: *Universitas*, Stuttgart, Vol. I, No. 3, pp. 233-238.

1958

*121. DIE ATOMBOMBE UND DIE ZUKUNFT DES MENSCHEN. *Politisches Bewußtsein in unserer Zeit*. München (Piper), 1958, 506 pp.; 2nd ed'n, 1958; 3rd ed'n, 1958; 4th ed'n, 1960; 5th ed'n, 1962; abridged ed'n, München (Deutscher Taschenbuch-Verlag), 1961, 368 pp.; 2nd ed'n, 1964. *Translations:* Into *Italian:* LA BOMBA ATOMICA E IL DESTINO DELL' UOMO by Luigi Quattrocchi, (with preface by Remo Cantoni). Milano (Il Saggiatore), 1960—Into *English:* THE FUTURE OF MANKIND by E. B. Ashton, Chicago and London (Univ. of Chicago Press), 1961; 2nd ed'n, 1962; 3rd ed'n, 1963; 4th ed'n, 1967; 5th ed'n, 1968.—Into *Spanish:* LA BOMBA ATÓMICA Y EL FUTURO DE LA HUMANIDAD by Irene Garfeldt-Klever de Leal, Buenos Aires (Comp. General Fabril), 1961. —Into *French:* LA BOMBE ATOMIQUE ET L'AVENIR DE L'HOMME by Edmond Saget, Paris (Buchet & Chastel), 1963.—Into *Korean:* WONJAT'AN KWA ILLYU ÛI MIRAE by Kim Chong-ho and Ch'oe Tong-hŭi, Vol. 1.2. Seoul (Sasanggyesa), 1963.—Into *Greek:* HE ATOMIKE BOMBA

KAI TO MELLON TOU ANTHROPOU POLITIKE SYNEIDESIS TES SYN-
CHRONOU EPOCHES by K. A. Anagnostopoulos. Tome A. B. Athenai
1965/66. – Into *Japanese:* GENDAI NO SEIJI ISHIKI by Munetaka
Iijima and Noboru Hosoo. T. 1. Tokyo (Risôsha), 1966.

122. WAHRHEIT, FREIHEIT UND FRIEDE. – In: *Börsenblatt für den deutschen
Buchhandel,* Frankfurt a/Main, T. 14, 1958, Nr. 79, pp. 1318-1322.
Also in: Jaspers: *Wahrheit, Freiheit und Friede* / Hannah Arendt: *Karl
Jaspers. Reden zur Verleihung des Friedenspreises des Deutschen
Buchhandels 1958,* München (Piper), 1958, pp. 9-26; 2nd ed'n, 1958;
3rd ed'n, 1958. Also in: Karl Jaspers: *4 Ansprachen anläßlich der
Verleihung des Friedenspreises des Deutschen Buchhandels,* Frank-
furt a. M. (Börsenverein des Dt. Buchhandels), 1958, pp. 29-45. Also
in: *Ruperto Carola,* Heidelberg, T. 10, 1958, Nr. 24, pp. 20-26. Also
in: *Duitse Kroniek,* Den Haag, 1959, Nr. 1, pp. 12-22 (German text).
Also in: *Friedenspreis des Deutschen Buchhandels. Reden und Würdi-
gungen 1951-1960.* Frankfurt a. M. (Börsenverein), 1961, pp. 171-185.
Translations: Into *Danish:* SANDHED, FRIHED, FRED by Christl von
Kohl, in: *Perspektiv,* København, T. 6, 1958, Nr. 5, pp. 33-40. – Into
French: VERITE, PAIX ET LIBERTE, in: *Documents,* Paris, Köln, T. 13,
1958, Nr. 6, pp. 718-730. – Into *Swedish:* SANNING, FRIHET OCH
FRED, in: *Samtid och Framtid,* Stockholm, T. 15, 1958, pp. 196-202.
– Into *Spanish:* VERDAD, LIBERTAD Y PAZ, in: *La Torre,* Puerto Rico,
1959, Nr. 26, pp. 55-70. – Into *Japanese:* SHINRI, JIYŪ, HEIWA by
Takeo Saito, in: Jaspers: *Shinri, jiyū, heiwa,* Tokyo (Risōsha), 1966,
pp. 5-31.

123. PHILOSOPHIE UND WELT. *Reden und Aufsätze.* München (Piper), 1958,
403 pp. [14 essays, Nr. 6: IM KAMPF MIT DEM TOTALITARISMUS first
publication in German]; 2nd ed'n, 1963.
Translations: Into *English* (without Nr. 13): PHILOSOPHY AND THE
WORLD by E. B. Ashton, Chicago (Regnery), 1963. – Into *Japanese*
(without Nr. 4, 5, 6, 13 and 14): TETSUGAKU TO SEKAI by Masao
Kusanagi *et al.,* Tokyo (Risôsha), 1968.

124. DER ARZT IM TECHNISCHEN ZEITALTER. – In: *Klinische Wochenschrift,*
Berlin, München, T. 36, 1958, pp. 1037-1043. Also in: *Wege der
Heilung,* Stuttgart (Kröner), 1959, pp. 167-192. Also in: *Universitas,*
Stuttgart, T. 14, 1959, pp. 337-354. Also in: *Schweizerische Ärztezeitung,* Bern, T. 40, 1959, pp. 625-628 and 642-644 and 654-656. Also
under the title: DIE SCHICKSALSFRAGE IM TECHNISCHEN ZEITALTER:
DEN TECHNISCHEN FORTSCHRITT ZUM GUTEN WENDEN, in: *Der Architekt,* Essen, T. 9, 1960, pp. 131-136. Also in: *Nederlands Tijdschrift
voor medische Studenten,* Amsterdam, T. 6, 1960, Nr. 1, pp. 16-22 and
27-34 (German text). Also in: *Ruperto Carola,* Heidelberg, T. 15, 1963,
Nr. 33, pp. 23-31. Also in: *Technische Rundschau,* Bern, Vol. 56, Nr.
21, 15.5.1964, pp. 1-5.

125. PROFESSOR KARL JASPERS – In: *Strix. Schülerzeitung des Alten Gym-
nasiums Oldenburg.* Oldenburg i. O., 1958, Nr. 1, pp. 4-7. [Letter to
the pupils; theme: "Schülermitverwaltung".]

126. VORWORT to Melvin J. Lasky's *Die ungarische Revolution,* Berlin
(Colloquium-Verlag), 1958, pp. 11-13.

127. ISRAEL UND DAS ABENDLAND. – In: *Aufbau. Reconstruction.* New
York, 25.7.1958, pp. 10 and 38. Also in: *Aufbau. Reconstruction.*

Dokumente einer Kultur im Exil. New York (Overlook Press) and Köln (Kiepenheuer & Witsch), 1972, pp. 294-297.

1959

*128. VERNUNFT UND FREIHEIT. *Ausgewählte Schriften.* Stuttgart, Zürich, Salzburg (Europäischer Buchklub), 1959, 564 pp. (With a postface by Kurt Rossmann.) [11 essays.]
129. THE UN IS UNDEPENDABLE. — In: *The New Republic,* New York, 18.5.1959, pp. 12-13, Solution for Berlin, II.

1960

130. NUR DIE FREIHEIT — ALLEIN DARAUF KOMMT ES AN. *Das Gespräch mit Prof. Karl Jaspers im Fernsehen des Norddeutschen Rundfunks.* — In: *Frankfurter Allgemeine Zeitung,* Frankfurt a. M., Nr. 191, 17.8. 1960, p. 9. [Conversation with Thilo Koch, 10.8.1960.] Also in: W. Wentholt: *Neo-Nazisme of Vrijheid en Waarheid?* Amsterdam (Wentholt), 1960, Bijlage 1, pp. 17-22. [German text.]
131. FREIHEIT UND WIEDERVEREINIGUNG. — [5 articles.] In: *Die Zeit,* Wochenzeitung, Hamburg, T. 15, 1960, Nr. 35, 26.8.1960, p. 3; Nr. 36, 2.9.1960, p. 3; Nr. 37, 9.9.1960, p. 3; Nr. 38, 16.9.1960, p. 3; Nr. 39, 23.9.1960, p. 3.
Partial translations: Into *French:* LIBERTÉ ET RÉUNIFICATION by Jeanne Hersch, in: *Preuves,* Paris, 1960/61, Nr. 118, pp. 3-12; Nr. 119, pp. 26-37. — Into *Spanish:* LA LIBERTAD Y LA UNIDAD DE ALEMANIA, in: *Cuadernos,* Paris, 1961, Nr. 46, pp. 9-18.
*132. FREIHEIT UND WIEDERVEREINIGUNG. *Über Aufgaben deutscher Politik.* München (Piper), 1960, 123 pp. [The 5 articles from *Die Zeit,* together with 3 new articles and the Interview with Thilo Koch, 1960.]
Translations: Into *Italian:* LA GERMANIA TRA LIBERTA E RIUNIFICA-ZIONE by Altiero Spinelli, Milano (Edizioni di Comunità), 1961. — Into *French:* LIBERTÉ ET RÉUNIFICATION by Hélène Naef et Jeanne Hersch, Paris (Gallimard), 1962.
133. WO STEHEN WIR HEUTE? — In: *Wo stehen wir heute?* Gütersloh (Bertelsmann), 1960, pp. 33-46. Also in: *Universitas,* Stuttgart, T. 15, 1960, pp. 473-486. Also in: *Neue deutsche Hefte,* Gütersloh, T. 7, 1960/61, pp. 481-491. Also as booklet: Olten (Rentsch), 1961, 40 pp.
Translations: Into *Italian:* A CHE PUNTO SIAMO OGGI? by Gemma Felice, in: *Il Baretti,* Napoli, T. 2, 1961, pp. 16-30. — Into *Spanish:* ¿DÓNDE ESTAMOS HOY? by Adela Grego de Jiménez, in: *Humboldt,* Hamburgo, T. 2, 1961, Nr. 5, pp. 4, 5, 8-10. — Into *English:* WHERE DO WE STAND TODAY? by Margaret D. Senft-Howie, in: *Man and Modern Time,* München (Hueber), 1962, pp. 9-13. — Into *Spanish:* ¿DÓNDE ESTAMOS HOY? by Germán Bleiberg, in: *¿Dónde estamos hoy?* Madrid (Revista de Occidente), 1962, pp. 59-80.
134. WAHRHEIT UND WISSENSCHAFT. — In: *National-Zeitung,* Basel, Nr. 302, 3.7.1960, Sonntagsbeilage. Also in: Jaspers: *Wahrheit und Wissenschaft/* Adolf Portmann: *Naturforschung und Humanismus.* Reden, Basel

(Helbing & Lichtenhahn), 1960, pp. 3-29; 2nd ed'n, 1960; and München (Piper), 1960, pp. 5-25. Also in: *Deutsche Universitäts-Zeitung,* Göttingen, T. 15, 1960, Nr. 9, pp. 3-9. Also in: *Universitas,* Stuttgart, T. 16, 1961, pp. 913-929.
Translations: Into *English:* OF LIGHT DIVINER THAN THE COMMON SUN. Truth and science. By Don Travis, Jr., in: *Graduate Journal,* Austin, Texas, T. 5, 1962, Nr. 1, Spring, pp. 24-42. Also: TRUTH AND SCIENCE by Robert E. Wood, in: *Philosophy Today,* Indiana, T. 6, 1962, pp. 200-211. — Into *Spanish:* LA VERDAD Y LA CIENCIA by Adela Grego de Jiménez, in: *Humboldt,* Hamburgo, T. 3, 1962, Nr. 11, pp. 4, 5, 7, 8, 10, 11.

135. DAS DOPPELGESICHT DER UNIVERSITÄTSREFORM. — In: *Deutsche Universitäts-Zeitung,* Göttingen, T. 15, 1960, Nr. 3, pp. 3-8. Also in: *Universität und moderne Welt.* Berlin (de Gruyter), 1962, pp. 36-51. *Translation:* Into *Spanish:* LOS DOS ASPECTOS DE LA REFORMA DE LA UNIVERSIDAD by Antonio Millán Puelles, in: *Atlantida,* Madrid, T. 1, 1963, Nr. 4, pp. 409-421.

136. DER PHILOSOPHISCHE GLAUBE ANGESICHTS DER CHRISTLICHEN OFFEN-BARUNG. — In: *Philosophie und christliche Existenz.* Basel, Stuttgart (Helbing & Lichtenhahn), 1960, pp. 1-92.

137. WILHELM DILTHEY, 1833-1911. — In: *Professoren der Universität Basel aus 5 Jahrhunderten.* Basel (Reinhardt), 1960, p. 184.

138. PHILOSOPHIE. — In: *Lehre und Forschung an der Universität Basel zur Zeit der Feier ihres 500 jährigen Bestehens.* Basel (Birkhäuser), 1960, pp. 268-272.

139. EPIKUR. — In: *Weltbewohner und Weimaraner.* Zürich, Stuttgart (Artemis-Verlag), 1960, pp. 111-133.

1961

*140. DIE IDEE DER UNIVERSITÄT. Für die gegenwärtige Situation entworfen von Karl Jaspers und Kurt Rossmann. Berlin, Göttingen, Heidelberg (Springer), 1961, VIII, 250 pp. — Chapter II of the German text with annotations of Taizen Seo and Atsushi Yamamoto, Tokyo (Sansyusya), 1968, 43 pp.

141. ERKENNTNIS UND WILLE IN DER POLITIK HEUTE. — In: *Der Monat,* München, T. 13, 1960/61, Nr. 150, pp. 7-20.

142. KARL JASPERS ZUM EICHMANN-PROZESS. Ein Gespräch mit François Bondy. — In: *Der Monat,* München, T. 13, 1960/61, Nr. 152, pp. 15-19. *Translations:* Into *French:* AU-DELA DU PROCÈS EICHMANN, in: *Préuves,* Paris, 1961, Nr. 123, Mai, pp. 3-6. — Into *Japanese:* JASPERS EICHMANN SAIBAN O KATARU by Masami Yoshida, in: Jiyu, Tokyo, 1961, Nr. 22, pp. 90-95.

143. KEIN SCHÖNER MYTHOS. — In: *Magnum,* Köln, 1961, Nr. 35, April, pp. 38-39.

144. CHIFFERN DER TRANSCENDENZ. Die Basler Abschiedsvorlesung von Prof. Karl Jaspers. — In: *National-Zeitung,* Basel, Nr. 323, 16.7.1961, Sonntagsbeilage. Also in: *Der Glaube der Gemeinde und die mündige Welt,* München (Kaiser), 1969, pp. 141-151. Also in: *Jaspers: Chiffren der Transzendenz,* München (Piper), 1970, pp. 97-109; 2nd ed'n, 1972.

145. WISSENSCHAFT, LEHRFREIHEIT UND POLITIK.—In: *Deutsche Universitäts-Zeitung*, Göttingen, T. 16, 1961, Nr. 12, pp. 34-39.
146. HEIDELBERGER ERINNERUNGEN.—In: *Heidelberger Jahrbücher*, Heidelberg, T. 5, 1961, pp. 1-10.

1962

*147. DER PHILOSOPHISCHE GLAUBE ANGESICHTS DER OFFENBARUNG. München (Piper), 1962, 539 pp. 2nd ed'n, 1963.
Translations: Into *English:* PHILOSOPHICAL FAITH AND REVELATION by E. B. Ashton, New York (Harper & Row) and London (Collins), 1967.—Into *Spanish:* LA FE FILOSÓFICA ANTE LA REVELACIÓN by Gonzalo Diaz y Diaz, Madrid (Editorial Gredos), 1968.—Into *Italian:* LA FEDE FILOSOFICA DI FRONTE ALLA RIVELAZIONE by Filippo Costa, Milano (Longanesi), 1970.
*148. ÜBER BEDINGUNGEN UND MÖGLICHKEITEN EINES NEUEN HUMANISMUS. Drei Vorträge. (With postface by Kurt Rossmann.) Stuttgart (Reclam), 1962, 93 pp.; reprint 1965.
149. BEMERKUNGEN ZU MAX WEBERS POLITISCHEM DENKEN.—In: *Antidoron*, Tübingen (Mohr), 1962, pp. 200-214.
Translation: Into *Japanese:* MAX WEBER NO SEIJITEKI SHISO by Yukiyoshi Ogura, in: *Jitsuzonshugi*, Tokyo, 1962, Nr. 26, pp. 2-11.
150. WERDEN WIR RICHTIG INFORMIERT?—In: *Gehört gelesen*, München, T. 9, 1962, Nr. 6, pp. 609-619. Also in: *Universitas*, Stuttgart, T. 18, 1963, pp. 1-14. Also in: *Werden wir richtig informiert?* München (Ehrenwirth), 1964, pp. 9-28. Also in: *Information oder herrschen die Souffleure?* Reinbek bei Hamburg (Rowohlt), 1964, pp. 22-34.
Translations: Into *Spanish:* ¿SE NOS INFORMA CORRECTAMENTE? in: *Folia Humanistica*, Barcelona, T. 1, 1963, Nr. 4, pp. 289-301.—Into *Dutch:* WORDEN WIJ WEL JUIST VOORGELICHT? By Johan Winkler, in: *Worden wij wel juist voorgelicht?* Rotterdam (Univ. Pers Rotterdam), 1965, pp. 1-20.
151. FREIHEIT UND SCHICKSAL IN DER WIRTSCHAFT.—In: *Basler Nachrichten*, Basel, Nr. 424, 8.10.1962, pp. 13-14. Also in: *Ruperto Carola*, Heidelberg, T. 14, 1962, Nr. 32, pp. 6-12. Also in: Jaspers: *Freiheit und Schicksal in der Wirtschaft*/Sieber, Hugo: *Wirtschaftsüberlegenheit und Wirtschaftswettlauf*. Zwei Vorträge. Wabern-Bern (Schweizerischer Aufklärungsdienst), 1963, pp. 3-21.
Translation: Into *Spanish:* LA LIBERTAD Y EL DESTINO EN EL TERRENO DE LA ECONOMÍA, in: *Folia Humanistica*, Barcelona, T. 1, 1963, Nr. 3, pp. 193-205.
152. HIOB.—In: *Einsichten*. Frankfurt a.M. (Klostermann), 1962, pp. 86-106.
153. NINGEN NO JIYU NO MIRAI NO TAMENI [on the future of human liberty].—In: *Jiyu*, Tokyo, 1962, Januar, Nr. 26, pp. 2-18. [Conversation with Mitsurô Mutô, translated by Masami Yoshida.]
154. HEIWA TO JIYU [on peace and liberty].—In: *Sekai*, Tokyo, 1962, Nr. 194, pp. 25-30. [Translated answer to an international symposium.]

1963

*155. GESAMMELTE SCHRIFTEN ZUR PSYCHOPATHOLOGIE. Berlin, Göttingen, Heidelberg (Springer), 1963, viii, 421 pp. [8 essays collected in one vol.]
Translation: Into *Japanese:* SEISHIN BYORIGAKU KENKYU. Vol. I. II. By Fujimori Hideyuki, Tokyo (Misuzushobô), 1969/71.

*156. LEBENSFRAGEN DER DEUTSCHEN POLITIK. München (Deutscher Taschenbuch-Verlag), 1963, 314 pp. [12 essays, here first published Nr. 12: BRIEFWECHSEL MIT GENERAL A. HEUSINGER.]

*157. PHILOSOPHIE UND OFFENBARUNGSGLAUBE. *Ein Zwiegespräch.* Hamburg (Furche-Verlag), 1963, 102 pp.
Translation: Into *Japanese:* TETSUGAKU TO KEIJI SHINKO by Shigeo Arai, Tokyo (Risôsha), 1966.

158. DIE KRAFT DER HOFFNUNG. – In: *Merkur,* Stuttgart, T. 17, 1963, pp. 213-222. Also in: *Die Hoffnungen unserer Zeit.* München (Piper), 1963, pp. 9-23. Also in: *Libro Jubilar de Victor Andres Belaunde en su 80. Aniversario,* Lima, 1963, pp. 269-279 (German text).
Translations: Into *Dutch:* DE KRACHT VAN HET HOPEN by Hans Wagemans, in: Jaspers: *De kracht van het hopen*/Oppenheimer, J. Robert: *Nieuwe Perspectieven in Kunst en Wetenschap,* Hilversum, Antwerpen (Brand), 1964, pp. 4-16. – Into *Spanish:* LA FUERZA DE LA ESPERANZA by Ramon de Haro, in: *Humboldt,* Hamburgo, T. 7, 1966, Nr. 28, pp. 4, 6-7, 9.

159. WIE WIRD MAN PHILOSOPH? *Karl Jaspers.* In Basel interviewte François Bondy den achtzigjährigen Philosophen. – In: *Die Zeit,* Wochenzeitung, Hamburg, T. 18, Nr. 9, 1.3.1963, p. 8.

160. DER PHILOSOPH IN DER POLITIK. Aus einem Gespräch mit François Bondy. – In: *Der Monat,* München, T. 15, 1963, Nr. 175, pp. 22-29.

161. INFORMATION, GEHEIMHALTUNG UND "SPIEGEL"-AFFÄRE. – In: *Rheinische Post,* Düsseldorf, T. 18, Nr. 196, 24.8.1963, p. 21. Also under the title: WERDEN WIR RICHTIG INFORMIERT? in: *Der Spiegel,* Hamburg, T. 17, 1963, Nr. 42, pp. 60, 62-63. Also in: *Information oder herrschen die Souffleure?* Reinbek bei Hamburg (Rowohlt), 1964, pp. 103-107.

162. DIE KRAFT ZU LEBEN. – In: *Die Kraft zu leben. Bekenntnisse unserer Zeit.* Gütersloh (Bertelsmann), 1963, pp. 102-114. Also under the title: AUS WELCHEN KRÄFTEN LEBEN WIR? in: *Universitas.* Stuttgart, T. 19, 1964, pp. 113-123.
Translations: Into *Spanish:* ¿GRACIAS A QUÉ FUERZAS VIVIMOS? In: *Universitas,* Revista alemana de letras, ciencias y arte, Stuttgart, T. 2, 1964, Nr. 2, pp. 113-123. – Into *English:* WHENCE SPRING OUR VITAL POWERS? In: *Universitas,* A German review of the arts and sciences, Stuttgart, T. 7, 1965, Nr. 3, pp. 253-264.

163. DIE VERFASSUNG IST DER EINZIGE FESTE PUNKT, AUF DEN MAN SICH VERLASSEN KANN. Gespräch mit dem Baseler Philosophen Karl Jaspers [by Karl-Heinz Briam]. In: *Die Welt der Arbeit,* Köln, T. 14, Nr. 51/52, 20.12.1963, pp. 9-11.

164. L'HUMANITÉ A LA MERCI D'UN FOU . . . In: *Le Monde,* Paris, 1. 11. 1963, p. 11. [Partial publication of an interview with Jean-Pierre Alkabbache in RTF, Paris.]

1964

*165. NIKOLAUS CUSANUS. München (Piper), 1964, 270 pp. Also: München (Deutscher Taschenbuch-Verlag), 1968, 256 pp.
Translations: Into English: NICHOLAS OF CUSA by Ralph Manheim, in: Jaspers: The Great Philosophers, Vol. 2: The Original Thinkers, New York (Harcourt, Brace & World) and London (Hart-Davis), 1966. pp. 116-272. — Into Japanese: NIKORAUSU KUZANUSU by Tan Sonoda, Tokyo (Risôsha), 1970. — Into Italian: CUSANO by Filippo Costa, in: Jaspers: I grandi filosofi, Milano (Longanesi), 1973, pp. 845-1036.
166. UMGANG MIT DEM MYTHOS. — In: Merkur, Stuttgart, T. 18, 1964, pp. 1-13.
167. ZUR AUFFÜHRUNG VON HOCHHUTHS "STELLVERTRETER". — In: Basler Stadtbuch 1965, Basel, 1964, pp. 212-216.
168. THE HISTORY OF MANKIND AS SEEN BY THE PHILOSOPHER. — In: Universitas, A German review of the arts and sciences, Stuttgart, T. 6, 1964, pp. 211-220.

1965

*169. KLEINE SCHULE DES PHILOSOPHISCHEN DENKENS. Vorlesungen, gehalten im 1. Trimester des Studienprogramms des Bayerischen Fernsehens Herbst 1964. München (Piper), 1965, 174 pp.; 2nd ed'n, 1965; 3rd ed'n, 1967; 4th ed'n, 1971.
Translations: Into Japanese: TETSUGAKU NO GAKKO by Shinzaburô Matsunami, Tokyo (Kawade Shobô), 1966. — Into French: INITIATION A LA MÉTHODE PHILOSOPHIQUE by Laurent Jospin, Paris (Payot), 1966. — Into English: PHILOSOPHY IS FOR EVERYMAN by R. F. C. Hull and Grete Wels, New York (Harcourt, Brace & World), 1967 and London (Hutchinson), 1969. — Into Norwegian: LITEN SKOLE I FILOSOFISK TENKNING by Finn Jor, Oslo (Aschehoug), 1967. — Into Italian: PICCOLA SCUOLA DEL PENSIERO FILOSOFICO, by Carlo Mainoldi, Milano (Edizioni di comunita), 1968. — Into Portuguese: INTRODUÇÃO AC PENSAMENTO FILOSOFICO by Leônidas Hegenberg and Octanny Silveira da Mota, São Paulo (Editôra Cultrix), 1971.
*170. WAHRHEIT UND LEBEN. Ausgewählte Schriften. Stuttgart, Zürich, Salzburg (Europäischer Buchklub), 1965, 541 pp. (With postface by Kurt Rossmann.) [19 essays collected in one vol.]
*171. HOFFNUNG UND SORGE. Schriften zur deutschen Politik 1945-1965. München (Piper), 1965, 370 pp. [14 essays collected in one vol., two of which have not appeared in print before: Nr. 13: WAS IST DEUTSCH? and Nr. 14: POLITISCHE SCHRIFTSTELLER UND POLITISCHES HANDELN.]
172. PROF. KARL JASPERS ZUR ÜBERBELASTUNG FÜHRENDER PERSÖNLICHKEITEN. — In: Die Tat, Zürich, T. 30, Nr. 36, 12.2.1965, pp. 3, 12. [Conversation with "Jeremias", i.e. Alfred a. Häsler.] Also under the title: IST DIE ÜBERBELASTUNG EIN FAKTUM? in: Alfred A. Häsler: Überfordertes Kader? Prominente antworten. Zürich (Buchclub Ex Libris), 1965, pp. 67-77.
173. FÜR VÖLKERMORD GIBT ES KEINE VERJÄHRUNG. Spiegel-Gespräch mit dem Philosophen Karl Jaspers [by Rudolf Augstein]. — In: Der Spiegel, Hamburg, T. 19, 1965, Nr. 11, pp. 49-71.

Translation: Into *English:* NO STATUTE OF LIMITATIONS FOR GENO-CIDE by Harry Zohn, in: *Midstream,* New York, T. 12, 1966, Nr. 2, pp. 3-18.

174. DEUTSCHLAND LIEGT MIR WARM AM HERZEN.—In: *Kontraste,* Freiburg i. Br., 1965, Nr. 20, p. 33.

175. DIE UNZUVERLÄSSIGKEIT DER MENSCHENRECHTE.—In: *Euros,* Köln, Wien, Sommer 1965, Nr. 2, pp. 83-90.
Translations: Into *Dutch:* DE ONBETROUWBAARHEID VAN DE RECHTEN VAN DE MENS, in: *Euros,* Hilversum, Antwerpen, Winter 1964/65, Nr. 2, pp. 84-91.—Into *English:* THE INADEQUACY OF HUMAN RIGHTS, in: *Euros,* London, Spring 1965, Nr. 2, pp. 73-79.

176. MYTHOS UND PHILOSOPHIE.—In: *Die Wirklichkeit des Mythos,* München, Zürich (Knaur), 1965, pp. 53-65.

177. SOMMES-NOUS SURS QUE LA GUERRE SOIT IMPOSSIBLE? Un entretien avec le Socrate de notre temps par Guy Valaire.—In: *Réalités,* Paris, Septembre 1965, Nr. 236, pp. 70-72.
Translation: Into *English:* THE BALANCE OF TERROR WON'T PROTECT US FROM THE BOMB, in: *Réalités,* Paris, London, New York, 1965, Nr. 181, pp. 27-29.

178. GELEITWORT to: Gerhard Schmidt's *Selektion in der Heilanstalt.* Stuttgart (Evangelisches Verlagswerk), 1965, pp. 9-12.

1966

*179. WOHIN TREIBT DIE BUNDESREPUBLIK? *Tatsachen, Gefahren, Chancen.* München (Piper), 1966, 280 pp.; 2nd-6th ed'n, 1966; 7th and 8th ed'n, 1967.
Translations: Into *Spanish:* ¿DÓNDE VA ALEMANIA? by Javier Martinez Pantoja, Madrid (Ediciones Cid), 1967.—Into *Italian:* GERMANIA D'OGGI by Maria Carla Beretta, Milano (Mursia), 1969.
Partial translations: Into *English:* THE FUTURE OF GERMANY by E. B. Ashton, Chicago, London (Univ. of Chicago Press), 1967. Into *Serbo-Croatian:* KUDA IDE SR NEMACKA? by Svetislav Ristić, Beograd (Sedma sila), 1967.—Into *Japanese:* DOITSU NO SHORAI by Shinzaburô Matsunami, Tokyo (Taimu Raifu Bukkusu), 1969.—Into *Russian:* KUDA DVIZETSJA FEDERATIVNAJA RESPUBLIKA GERMANII? by A. Guterman and V. Ivanov, Moskva (Izdatel'stvo "Meždunarodnye Otnošenija"), 1969. Partial German reprint: ASPEKTE DER BUNDESREPUBLIK. (With postface by Hans Saner.) München (Piper), 1972, 159 pp.

180. EINE CHANCE WIRD VERTAN.—In: *Welt am Sonntag,* Hamburg, Essen, Frankfurt, Berlin, Nr. 19, 8.5.1966, p. 4.

181. DIE ANTWORT KARL JASPERS' AN ULBRICHT.—In: *Basler Nachrichten,* Basel. T. 122, Nr. 242, 11./12.6.1966, p. 1.

182. FRAGEN AN KARL JASPERS. Von Armin Eichholz.—In: *Münchener Merkur,* München, 16./17.6.1966, pp. 17-19. Also under the title: INTERVIEW MIT KARL JASPERS in: *Konkret,* Hamburg, 1966, Nr. 7, pp. 22-25, 37.

183. SE GLI STATI SBAGLIANO SONO CORREI DELLA ROVINA DI TUTTI.—In: *La Nazione,* Firenze, T. 108, Nr. 144, 24.6.1966, pp. 13-14. [Interview with Luigi Forni.]

184. KEIN DEUTSCHER DIALOG. *Der Redneraustausch—eine Chance, die*

dahin ist. — In: *Die Zeit,* Wochenzeitung, Hamburg, T. 21, Nr. 27, 1.7.1966, p. 3.

185. GRUßBOTSCHAFT. — In: *Deutsche und Juden, ein unlösbares Problem.* Düsseldorf (Verlag Kontakte), 1966, pp. 59-70. Also in: *Deutsche und Juden,* Frankfurt a.M. (Suhrkamp), 1967, pp. 109-120.

186. DIE GROßE WARNUNG AUS BASEL. *Wenn Rußland und Amerika einig gegen China sind* . . . Gespräch mit Prof. Karl Jaspers. — In: *Schweizer Illustrierte,* Zürich, T. 55, Nr. 31, 1.8.1966, pp. 12-14.

187. KIERKEGAARD VIVANT. — By Jeanne Hersch. In: *Kierkegaard vivant,* Paris (Gallimard), 1966, pp. 81-93.
Translation: Into *Spanish:* KIERKEGAARD HOY by Andrés-Pedro Sánchez Pascual, in: *Sartre, Heidegger, Jaspers y otros: Kierkegaard vivo,* Madrid (Alianza Editorial), 1968, pp. 63-72.

1967

*188. ANTWORT. *Zur Kritik meiner Schrift "Wohin treibt die Bundesrepublik?"* München (Piper), 1967, 234 pp.
Partial translations: Into *English:* THE FUTURE OF GERMANY by E. B. Ashton, Chicago, London (Univ. of Chicago Press), 1967. — Into *Japanese:* DOITSU NO SHORAI by Shinzaburô Matsunami, Tokyo (Taimu Raifu Bukkusu), 1969. — Into Russian: KUDA DVIZETSJA FEDERATIVNAJA RESPUBLIKA GERMANII? by A. Guterman and V. Ivanov, Moskva (Izdatel'stvo "Meždunarodnye Otnošenija"), 1969.

*189. PHILOSOPHISCHE AUFSÄTZE. Frankfurt a.M., Hamburg (Fischer-Bücherei), 1967, 249 pp. [14 essays.]
Translation: Into *French:* ESSAIS PHILOSOPHIQUES by L. Jospin, Paris (Payot), 1970. [Nr. 3 and 13 are not translated.]

*190. SCHICKSAL UND WILLE. Autobiographische Schriften. München (Piper), 1967, 185 pp. [5 essays. Nr. 2, 3, and 4 here published for the first time.]
Translation: Into *Japanese:* UMMEI TO ISHI by Shinji Hayashida, Tokyo (Ibunsha), 1972.

191. KARL JASPERS — EIN SELBSTPORTRAIT. — In: *Das Selbstportrait. Große Künstler und Denker unserer Zeit erzählen von ihrem Leben und ihrem Werk.* Hamburg (Wegner), 1967, pp. 77-108. Also under the title: O MÄCHTIGER GEIST IN DEUTSCHLAND in: *Der Spiegel,* Hamburg, T. 21, Nr. 50, 4.12.1967, pp. 84-100. Also under the title: EIN SELBSTPORTRÄT, with annotations by Z. Takemura, Tokyo (Geirin-Shobo), 1969.

192. ERFAHRUNG DES AUSGESTOSSENSEINS. Karl Jaspers über seinen Weggang aus Deutschland. — In: *Der Spiegel,* Hamburg, T. 21, Nr. 41, 20.10.1967, pp. 40-54.

193. DAS LETZTE PORTRÄT. — In: Fritz Eschen: *Das letzte Porträt,* Berlin (Haude & Spener), 1967, pp. 7-11.

194. GRÜSSWORT AN JOHANNES PFEIFFER, Basel, im Juni 1967. — In: *Gestalt, Gedanke, Geheimnis.* Festschrift für J. Pfeiffer zu seinem 65. Geburtstag. Berlin (Dorbrandt), 1967, pp. 17-18.

195. GRÜSSADRESSE VON PROF. KARL JASPERS AN DAS KURATORIUM. — In: *Notstand der Demokratie,* Frankfurt a/Main (Europäische Verlags-Anstalt), 1967, p. 24.

196. MESSAGE DU PROFESSEUR KARL JASPERS. — In: *Prix littéraire de la paix,*

10. anniversaire, prix litt. internat. de la paix 1965. Liège, 1967, pp. 52-54, French translation pp. 55-58.

1968

*197. ANEIGNUNG UND POLEMIK. Gesammelte Reden und Aufsätze zur Geschichte der Philosophie. München (Piper), 1968, 517 pp. (With postface by Hans Saner.) [27 essays, Nr. 1, 4, 6, 16, 17, here published for the first time; Nr. 20 first German publication.]
Translation: Into *Spanish* (without Nr. 2, 3, 8, 9, 13, 15, 16 and 17): CONFERENCIAS Y ENSAYOS SOBRE HISTORIA DE LA FILOSOFÍA by Rufino Jimeno Peña, Madrid (Editorial Gredos), 1972.

*198. MITVERANTWORTLICH. Ein philosophisch-politisches Lesebuch. Gütersloh (Mohn); Stuttgart (Europäischer Buch- und Phonoklub); Wien (Buchgemeinschaft Donauland), 1968, 635 pp. [13 essays.]

199. VORLESUNG UND SCRIPTEN. — In: *Kolibri,* Riehen, Nr. 149 "Vorlesung und Scripten. 35 Professoren schreiben für das kolibri", Februar 1968, p. 11.

200. DIE ODER-NEISSE-GRENZE MÜSSTE BEDINGUNGSLOS VON BONN ANERKANNT WERDEN. Der Philosoph sieht pessimistisch in die Zukunft deutscher Politik. — In: *Kölner Stadt-Anzeiger,* Köln, Nr. 45, 22.2.1968, pp. 3-4. (Interview with Gerhard Fauth.)

201. GEDANKEN AM 85. GEBURTSTAG. — In: *Stern,* Hamburg, Nr. 10, 10.3.1968, pp. 177-180. (Interview with Erich Kuby.)

202. JULIUS LEBER. — In: *Gedächtnisschrift für Gustav Radbruch,* Göttingen (Vandenhoeck & Ruprecht), 1968, pp. 207-220.

203. GANDHI ON HIS 100TH BIRTHDAY. — [English translation] in: *Mahatma Gandhi 100 years,* New Delhi (Gandhi Peace Foundation), 1968, pp. 167-170. Also under the title: ONE OF KARL JASPERS' LAST COMMENTARIES: GANDHIJI, in: *Le Courrier,* Mensuel publié par l'UNESCO, Organisation des Nations Unies pour l'Education, la Science et la Culture, Paris, English and American edition, T. 22, 1969, October, pp. 26-27. German text: GANDHIS BOTSCHAFT, in: *Le Courrier,* German edition, T. 10, 1969, Nr. 10, pp. 26 27.
"Le Courrier" with the translation of Jaspers' article has also appeared in the following 10 languages:
French: L'UNE DES DERNIÈRES REFLEXIONS DE KARL JASPERS: GANDHI, T. 22, 1969, Octobre, pp. 26-27. — *Italian:* DIMOSTRO CHE L'AZIONE POLITICA DEVE ESSERE RELIGIOSA E MORALE, T. 7, 1969, Nr. 10, pp. 26-27. — *Spanish:* REFLEXIONES SOBRE GANDHI, T. 22, 1969, Oct., pp. 26-27. — *Russian:* FILOSOF OB UROKACH GANDI, 1969, Nr. 154, Okt., pp. 26-27. — *Arabic:* MIN TA'AMULLAT KARL JASPERS AL-AHIRAH: GANDHI, 1969, November, pp. 26-27. — *Hebrew:* BSORATO SHEL GANDHI MITOCH RESHIMOTAV HA'ACHARONOT SHEL KARL YASPERS, T. 2, 1969, Nr. 3, pp. 24-25. — *Persian:* NEVECHTEH KARLE JESPERS: GANDHI by Iradj Nik Ain, T. 1, 1969, November, pp. 26-27. — *Hindi:* KARL JASPERS KI ANTIM VYAKHYAO ME SE EK: GANDIJI, T. 3, 1969, November, pp. 26-27. — *Tamil:* KARL JASPERCHIN ERRUTHIK KURUTHUR AIKALLIL UNRRU: GANDHIYADIKAL, 1969, November, pp. 26-27. — *Japanese:* KARU YASUPASU NO SAIGO NO HYORON NO HITOTSU — GANJI, T. 9, 1969, Nr. 12, pp. 26-27.

1969

*204. PROVOKATIONEN. *Gespräche und Interviews.* München (Piper), 1969, 223 pp. (With preface by Hans Saner.) [13 interviews, six of them having not appeared in print before: Nr. 1: IST DIE PHILOSOPHIE AM ENDE? Ein Gespräch mit Willy Hochkeppel; Nr. 2: PHILOSOPHIE UND WELT. Ein Gespräch mit François Bondy; Nr. 3: OFFENER HORIZONT. Ein Gespräch mit Thilo Koch; Nr. 7: EICHMANN IN JERUSALEM. Ein Gespräch mit Peter Wyss; Nr. 9: WIE ERINNERUNG AN DAS ERLEBTE ZUR AUFFASSUNG DER GEGENWART FÜHRT. Ein Gespräch mit Klaus Harpprecht; Nr. 12: WOHIN TREIBT DIE BUNDESREPUBLIK? Ein Gespräch mit Fritz René Allemann.
Translation: Into *Japanese:* KONGENTEKI NI TOU by Mitsurô Mutô and Tatsuo Akabane, Tokyo (Yomiuri Shimbunsha), 1970.

205. ZUR GENERELLEN STRAFBARKEIT DER HOMOSEXUALITÄT. – In: *Weder Krankheit noch Verbrechen,* Hamburg (Gala Verlag), 1969, pp. 24-27.

206. NEKROLOG VON KARL JASPERS SELBST VERFASST. – In: *Gedenkfeier für Karl Jaspers am 4. März 1969 in der Martinskirche,* Basel (Helbing & Lichtenhahn), 1969, pp. 3-4.

1970

*207. CHIFFREN DER TRANSZENDENZ. München (Piper), 1970, 111 pp. (with postface by Hans Saner); 2nd ed'n, 1972.
[The last lecture of these eight lectures was previously published as 1961, #144.]

1972

208. ALLE PHILOSOPHEN SIND AUCH POLITISCH. – In: François Bondy: *Gespräche,* Wien, München, Zürich (Europa-Verlag), 1972, pp. 85-108.

CHRONOLOGICAL LIST OF PRINCIPAL BOOKS

1909 HEIMWEH UND VERBRECHEN
1913 ALLGEMEINE PSYCHOPATHOLOGIE (6th ed'n, 1953)
1919 PSYCHOLOGIE DER WELTANSCHAUUNGEN
1921 MAX WEBER
1922 STRINDBERG UND VAN GOGH
1923 DIE IDEE DER UNIVERSITÄT
1931 DIE GEISTIGE SITUATION DER ZEIT
1932 PHILOSOPHIE (3 vols.)
     MAX WEBER: DEUTSCHES WESEN IM POLITISCHEN DENKEN, IM
        FORSCHEN UND IM PHILOSOPHIEREN
1935 REASON AND EXISTENZ
1936 NIETZSCHE: EINFÜHRUNG IN DAS VERSTÄNDNIS SEINES
        PHILOSOPHIERENS
1937 LA PENSÉE DE DESCARTES ET LA PHILOSOPHIE
1938 EXISTENZPHILOSOPHIE
1946 LA MIA FILOSOFIA
     DIE SCHULDFRAGE
     DIE IDEE DER UNIVERSITÄT (new interpretation)
     NIETZSCHE UND DAS CHRISTENTUM
     THE EUROPEAN SPIRIT
1947 VON DER WAHRHEIT (the PHILOSOPHISCHEN LOGIK first volume)
     UNSERE ZUKUNFT UND GOETHE
1948 THE PERENNIAL SCOPE OF PHILOSOPHY
     PHILOSOPHY AND SCIENCE
1949 THE ORIGIN AND GOAL OF HISTORY
1950 THE WAY TO WISDOM
     REASON AND ANTI-REASON IN OUR TIME
1951 RECHENSCHAFT UND AUSBLICK (addresses and essays)
1953 LIONARDO ALS PHILOSOPH
1954 DIE FRAGE DER ENTMYTHOLOGISIERUNG (together with R.
        Bultmann)
1955 SCHELLING. GRÖSSE UND VERHÄNGNIS
1957 DIE GROSSEN PHILOSOPHEN, Vol. I.
1958 DIE ATOMBOMBE UND DIE ZUKUNFT DES MENSCHEN
     PHILOSOPHIE UND WELT
1959 VERNUNFT UND FREIHEIT
1960 FREIHEIT UND WIEDERVEREINIGUNG
1961 DIE IDEE DER UNIVERSITÄT
1962 DER PHILOSOPHISCHE GLAUBE ANGESICHTS DER
        OFFENBARUNG
     ÜBER BEDINGUNGEN UND MÖGLICHKEITEN EINES NEUEN
        HUMANISMUS
1963 GESAMMELTE SCHRIFTEN ZUR PSYCHOPATHOLOGIE
     LEBENSFRAGEN DER DEUTSCHEN POLITIK
     PHILOSOPHIE UND OFFENBARUNGSGLAUBE

INDEX

(Arranged by ROBERT P. SYLVESTER)

905

of psychology, 815; human spirit, 701
Freedom, 29, 100ff, 108, 130f, 134ff; academic, in University, 51; actuality of, and proof, 503f; an existing center of, 134; and accidental being, 758; and being, through-myself, 507f; and commitment of *Existenz*, 64; and consciousness of its truth, 838; and contract, 810; and eugenic intervention, 809; and *Existenz*, 501; and Kant, 497; and my being, 300; and nature, antithesis, 322; and necessity, 637; and object of science, 563; and objective redemption, 504; and objectivity, 553; and one who philosophizes, 837f; and our heritage, 776; and philosophical faith, 553; and political propaganda, 834; and potential *Existenz*, 325f; a psychic fact, 690; and psychology, 496; and rebellion, 595; and responsibility, 554; and scientific psychology, 825; and selfhood, 227; and spirit, knowledge of, 671; and status of being, 300; and the future, 368; and tradition, 594; and "ultimate situation," 156; and uncertainty, 135; annihilates itself in Wholly-Other, 637; antinomy of, 322; as a cipher, 638; as a faith front, 835; as absolute energy, 607; as experienced, 671; as never complete, 634; as 'petrified' by religion, 613; as philosophical problem, 120; as temporal possibilities, 163; as the choice of my Self, 635; as transcendentally granted, 508; aspire to transcendence, 322; authentic, and choice, 637; authentic, and comic relief, 745; being granted one's self, 823; burden of, and the cult, 617; category of, 100; complete, 53; concept of, 551; criterion of, aspects of religion, 616; Descartes' respect for, 121; despondency of, and *Existenz*, 835; doctrine of, and empiricism, 690; "existential," 101, 108; existential, its limitations, 101; experience of, and *Existenz*, 318; form of, and potential *Existenz*, 776; gentle force of, 837; Golo Mann on, 755; "grace" and "election," 638; ground for, 99; human, 124; human, its power, 837; human, socialism, 557f; human, struggle for, 752; in history, 163; inner, 273; inner reality of, 131; intellectual freedom of University, 49; loss of, 590; notion of, Transcendence as a "wall", 304f, of a substance, 608; of being human, *Psychopathologie*, 458;

of being one's self, 90; of decision, 248; of *Existenz*, 306; of *Existenz*, through communication, 218; of man, 69; of personal life, 56; of the professor, 53; of Socratic doubt, 642; of students, 46; of study, 47; of the will, 101; political idea of, 756; problem of, points to transcendence, 780; psychology of, 496; real, and paradoxical, 672; salvation of, and question of appearance to Being, 631; source of, and death, 518; ultimate, and choice, 636; will to, as *Existenz*, 737; *passim*
Free-self, authentic, and tragic, 714
French, army, 39; occupation by, 57; philosophy, and Jaspers, 434; and psychiatry, 440; Revolution, 374
Freud('s), Sigmund, 18, 25, 124f; and conceptions of the self, 538; and degenerated universal science, 552f; and Nietzsche, 863; and training analysis, 462; and Wernicke, theories of, 19; as a medical man, 460; as a theorist, 460; as heir of Nietzsche, 429f; central intentions, 431; critique of, 808; radical individualism, 429; Sex Theory of, fanaticism, 464; influence limited to small circles in 1910, 15f; *Introduction to Psychoanalysis*, 430; Jaspers' judgment of, 442f; total knowledge of man, 460, 806
Friedrich, Carl Joachim, 549n
Fries, Jakob F., and Kant, 793

Galileo, 616; and science, 831; controversy with the church, 641
Ganzwerdenwollen, 193
Gartenlaube, 32
Gaupp, Robert E., 440
Gebsattel, V. E. von, 457, 493n
Gehlen, A., 590n
Geistige Situation der Zeit (Man in the Modern Age), (Jaspers), 39, 60, 558, 757
General Psychopathology, (Jaspers), 441, 446f, 451, 458, 462, 466, *passim*
Genesis I, 246; myth of creation, 544
Geneva, 79
George, Stefan, 730, 855; and Nietzsche, 416, 418, 423; Circle, the, and Jaspers, 418, 423, 431
German (s), 61, 68; academic life, traditions of, at Heidelberg, 14; being-German, 63f; culture, 58; guilt, the question of, 655; language, 101, 228, 231; meaning of the word, 65; military reestablishment, 50; people and Swiss

the 'monadizing' of the world, 286
Lenin, man of action, 336
Leonardo, and superman, 422
Leonidas, and testimony of Simonides, 588
Leopardi, Conte G., 360
Lessing, G., 87, 272, 625, 725; and history, 762; and nationalism, 427; philosophical faith and reason, 777; *Nathan the Wise*, 215
Lewin, Kurt, 494
Liberty of the Christian Man, The (Luther), 274
Lichtigfeld, A., essay by, 693-701; reply to, 783
Life, 87, 123, 275; communicative, on various levels, 215; evaluating development of, 138; genuine illumination of, 806; meaning of, 87f; moral, ultimate goals, 133; and of the nothing, 776; -realization, 79; spiritual dignity of, 260
"Limit," beyond consciousness in existence, 188
Limiting concept, 104
Limits of thought, 314
Linguistic-artistic discipline, 713; difficulties, historical philosophy, 365
Lippmann, Walter, 281; and neo-liberals, 557
Lipps, Theodor, 9, 253
Literary critics, and fundamental mood in Jaspers, 745; and philosophical faith, 738f; and *Psychologie der Weltanschauungen*, 724
Literary criticism, 719-746; and 'existential' philosophy, 728, 742; existentialist, and consciousness of human existence, 741; its philosophical purpose, 741; modern, and aesthetic evaluation, 729; premises of, and philosophical implications, 723; problems of, 725
Locke, John, 212; and concept of the self, 538
Löwenstein, Julius, essay by, 643-666; reply to, 854-857
Logic, 36, 72, 96; and possibilities, 165; an encompassing, a demand for, 804; as the universal science, 165; fundamental operation is disjunction, 165; its laws, 98; its scope, 552; of the Encompassing, 170; of the sciences, 137; philosophical, 71f, 74, 83
Logical object, and the Encompassing, 166
Logik, Philosophische, 857; *passim*

Logos, 30, 230, 243; and the world, 804; movement of, 222
Lotz, B., challenges Jaspers, 694; criticism of God concept, 695ff; principle of analogy, 696
Lotze, Hermann, 120
Love, 29, 269; and determination, 574; in communication, 275; power of, self-assertion, 771; subject and object, 574; unconditional guidance of (and reason), 87; what it is not, 651
Loye, Fritz zur, 10
Luciferic existences, 238
Ludendorff, Erich von, 56, 59
Luther, Martin, 81, 274, 261, 661, 669; and communication with God, 787; and inwardness, 347; *De Servo Arbitrio*, 670; on the commandments, 425
Lutheran, 620

Magdeburg, Mechthild von, 72
Maier, Heinrich, vacates chair of philosophy, 33
Man ('s), 104, 485; and causal determinism, 496; and freedom, 553; and knowledge, 524; and outbreak of freedom, 524f; as believer and non-believer, 658; as authentic being, 524; as *Existenz* and individual, 525; as conceptual object, 470; as *faciendum*, 163; as man, 86; as a moment of his age, 87; as object, 525; as object of knowledge, 479f; as object of research, 482f; as potentially incarnate, 496; authenticity of, 282; being and Transcendence, 504; being alive, 495f; cannot be known, 471; concept of, and planning, 557; chaotic and demonic, 415; definition of, 523; essence of, its self-consciousness, 84; existence and philosophy, 132; free, and Transcendence, 836; future and science, 553; history, construction of, 377f; idea of, 163; inner factor in, 494; interest in, 28; knowledge of, 21; language of, 109; malevolence of, and Kant, 867; modes of contemplating, and psychology, 485; nature of, 151; nature of, and factual death, 511f; nature of, determined, 501; nature of, and loss of Transcendence, 519; object of investigation, 20; the one, and demonology, 682f; potentialities of, 525; power of passionate, 434; purity of, 349; religious, as an individualist, 680; situation of, 29; temporal condition of, 103;

DATE DUE